Christian Writers'
Market Guide
2009

The **Essential**
Reference Tool
for the
Christian Writer

Sally E. Stuart

WATERBROOK
PRESS

Christian Writers' Market Guide 2009
PUBLISHED BY WATERBROOK PRESS
12265 Oracle Boulevard, Suite 200
Colorado Springs, Colorado 80921

ISSN 1080-3955

ISBN 978-0-30744-643-5

Printed in the United States of America
2009—First edition

10 9 8 7 6 5 4 3 2 1

CONTENTS

INTRODUCTION

The Christian publishing industry continues to change. As I worked on this year's guide, I began to see the book and periodical markets like a large sphere. In the center are the larger publishers and better-paying markets. Those are shrinking down to become a solid core that is often difficult to penetrate. The core of book publishers is made up of houses that require you to have an agent. The core of periodicals is made up of publications that tend to make assignments and pay higher rates. That doesn't need to be discouraging for the freelance writer—it is simply an indication that the industry is becoming more market savvy and professional. If you polish your craft and become the best writer you can be, it's still possible to penetrate that core.

Around that center core is a ring of paying markets that are open to both new and experienced freelance writers who are willing to work hard at their craft, study the needs of the market, and produce what the publisher wants. It is those publishers and publications you will most often be targeting with your freelance submissions because they are open to what you have to offer.

However, this sphere has one more outer ring: subsidy publishers and periodicals that don't pay. Initially, it is more important to get published than to get paid. Working for nonpaying markets gives you the opportunity to develop a reputation as someone who can write in certain topic areas. A subsidy or print-on-demand company might also be a good option for you if you have a book with a limited market, or if you cannot get the attention of a royalty publisher. As you perfect your writing, you can move from the outer ring into the core of the Christian writing sphere.

It is also more apparent to me every year that e-mail and Web sites have taken over communication. More and more publishers are dropping their fax number, phone number, and even addresses from their listings because they prefer e-mail contact and submissions. A few more publishers have blogs, but that doesn't seem to be catching on too quickly.

The topical listings for book publishers this year have a new addition: publishers that require an agent are now marked with an (a). That will help you eliminate those publishers from your list if you don't have an agent. (Since you now have the guide on CD, you can print out a list of only the publishers that do not require an agent.)

This edition has 416 book publishers (including 33 new), and 654 periodicals (including 52 new). As usual, a few new topics appear in the book and periodical lists. This year I have also added listings of African American and Hispanic publishers—two markets that are growing rapidly. I'm sure I will be adding more to these lists in the future. More listings indicate what formats the book publishers produce—such as hard cover, trade paperbacks, mass market paperbacks, and coffee table books—and more of them indicate that they are open to photographs or art work.

The "Resources for Writers" section, which is now exclusively on the CD-ROM, includes over 100 new entries and two new subsections: "Writers' Helps" and "Writing Communities." I encourage you to spend some time in that section, identifying those listings that will help you do your job better and more easily. You will also find the Glossary of Terms only on the CD.

This year I want to remind you again not to rely entirely on the topical listings for potential markets. Many good markets never fill out their list of topics, so you are likely to miss opportunities if you look only at that list.

Since a number of periodical publishers are now making assignments only, it is even more important that you establish a reputation in your areas of interest and expertise. Once you have acquired a number of credits in a given field, write to some of those assignment-only editors, giving your credits, and ask for an assignment. In general, you will be better off striving to get some of those assignments rather than hoping to fill one of the few slots left for unsolicited material.

Although agents always come and go, this year the list has dropped to fewer than 100 again—which is a reflection of tightening up my qualifications for appropriate agents. It is still crucial that you carefully check out agents before signing a contract or committing to work with them. See the introduction to the agent section for some tips on how to do that. Because contacting agents has become more important in a writer's quest for publication, I indicate which conferences have agents, as well as editors, on staff. Attending conferences is becoming one of the best way to make contact with agents as well as publishers.

If you are new to the guide or only want to find specific markets for your work, you'll want to discover the supplementary lists throughout the book. Read through the glossary and spend a few minutes learning terms you are not familiar with. Review the lists of writers' groups and conferences and mark those you might be interested in pursuing. The denominational listing and corporate-family listing will help you start connecting periodicals and book publishers with their different denominations or publishing groups. With so many publishers being bought out or merging, this will help keep you up to date with the new members of these growing families.

Also be sure to study the "How to Use This Book" section. It will save you time in trying to understand the meaning of the notations in the primary listings, and it's full of helpful hints. Remember to send for a catalog and guidelines or sample copies for any of the publishers or periodicals you are not familiar with. Study those carefully before submitting anything to that publisher or periodical. Also remember that publishers who make their guidelines available on their Website often include a great deal more information online than you get in the usual guidelines sheet.

One of the biggest complaints I've gotten from publishers over the years is that the material they receive is often not appropriate for their needs. Editors tell me repeatedly that they are looking for writers who understand their periodical or publishing house and their unique approach to the marketplace. With a little time and effort, you can meet an editor's expectations, distinguish yourself as a professional, and sell what you write.

I also want to let you know that I have started a marketing blog (see below) where you can find all kinds of information about the industry and keep your market guide up to date during the year. I make entries almost every day.

Finally, my special thanks for to Donna Schlachter for producing the "Resources for Writers" section this year—always a daunting project. I also want to thank her husband, Patrick, for developing and overseeing the database I use to produce the guide each year. I couldn't do it without his professional help.

As always, I wish you well as you travel this exciting road to publication, whether for the first time or as a longtime veteran. And as I remind you every year, each of you has been given a specific mission in the field of writing. You and I often feel inadequate to the task, but I learned a long time ago that the writing assignments God has given me cannot be written quite as well by anyone else.

Sally E. Stuart
1647 S.W. Pheasant Dr.
Aloha, OR 97006
(503)642-9844 (Please call after 9 a.m. Pacific time.)
Fax (503)848-3658
E-mail: stuartcwmg@aol.com
Website: www.stuartmarket.com
Blog: www.stuartmarket.blogspot.com

Please contact me for information on how to receive the market guide automatically every year and freeze the price at $34.99, plus postage, for future editions, or for information on getting the guide at a discounted group rate or getting books on consignment for your next seminar or conference.

HOW TO USE THIS BOOK

The purpose of this market guide is to make your marketing job easier and more targeted. It will only serve you well, however, if you use it as a springboard for becoming an expert on those publishers best suited to your writing topics and style. Keeping the following explanations and guidelines in mind will help you become an expert on marketing yourself:

1.   Spend time getting acquainted with the setup of this resource book. You cannot make the best use of it until you know exactly what it has to offer. Study the contents pages, where you will find listings of all the periodical and book topics.

2.   When looking at the topical section, be sure to check topics related to your primary subject. Some cross-referencing may be helpful. For example, if you have a novel that deals with doctor-assisted suicide, you might look at the list for adult novels and the list for controversial issues and see which publishers are on both lists. Those would be good potential markets. In the topical sections you will find a letter R following both book and periodical publishers that accept reprints (pieces that have been printed in other publishers/publications but for which you retain the rights). You will find a dollar sign ($) in front of the periodicals that ate paying markets. That will help you pick those out quickly when getting paid is your primary goal for a particular piece. New this year, you will find an (a) in front of book publishers that require the use of an agent.

3.   In each book publisher listing you will find the following information (as available) in this format:

a)   Name of publisher

b)   Address, phone and fax numbers, e-mail address, Website

c)   Denomination or affiliation

d)   Name of editor—This may include the senior editor's name, followed by the name of another editor to whom submissions should be sent. In a few cases, several editors are named with the type of books each is responsible for. Address to appropriate editor.

e)   A statement of purpose

f)   A list of imprint names

g)   Number of inspirational/religious titles published per year, followed by formats of books published (hardcover, trade paperbacks, mass-market paperbacks, coffee-table books). Note that coffee-table books have a listing in the "Topical Listings of Book Publishers."

h)   Number of submissions received annually

i)   Percentage of books from first-time authors

j)   Most listings indicate whether they accept, prefer, require, or don't accept manuscripts through agents.

k)   The percentage of books from freelance authors they subsidy publish (if any). This does not refer to percentage paid by author. If percentage of subsidy is over 50%, the publisher will be listed in a separate section under "Subsidy Publishers."

l)   Whether they reprint out-of-print books from other publishers

m)   Preferred manuscript length in words or pages; pages refers to double-spaced manuscript pages.

n)   Average amount of royalty, if provided. If royalty is a percentage of wholesale or net, it is based on price paid by bookstores or distributors. If it is on retail price, it is based on cover price of the book.

o)   Average amount paid for advances. Whether a publisher pays an advance or not is noted in the listing; if they did not answer the question, there is no mention of it.

p)   Whether they pay flat fees (in these cases the author receives no royalties)

q)   Average first printing (number of books usually printed for a first-time author)

r) Average length of time between acceptance of a manuscript and publication of the work

s) Whether they consider simultaneous submissions. This means you can send a query or complete manuscript simultaneously to more than one publisher, as long as you advise everyone involved that you are doing so.

t) Length of time it should take them to respond to a query/proposal or to a complete manuscript (when two lengths of time are given, the first refers to a query and the latter to a complete manuscript). Give them a one-month grace period beyond that and then send a polite follow-up letter if you haven't heard from them.

u) Whether a publisher "accepts," "prefers," or "requires" the submission of an accepted manuscript on disk. (Do not send your unsolicited manuscripts/submissions on disk). Most publishers now do accept or require that books be sent on a computer disk (usually along with a hard copy) or by e-mail, but since each publisher's needs are different, that information will be supplied to you by the individual publisher when the time comes. This section also indicates if they accept submissions by e-mail and whether they want it sent as an attachment or copied into the message.

v) If they have a preference, it will indicate what Bible version they prefer.

w) It will also indicate if they do print-on-demand publishing.

x) Availability and cost for writer's guidelines and book catalogs. If the listing says "guidelines," it means guidelines are available for a #10 (business size) SASE with a first-class stamp. The cost of the catalog (if any), the size of envelope, and amount of postage are given, if specified (affix stamps to envelope; don't send loose). Tip: If postage required is more than $2.13, I suggest you put $2.13 in postage on the envelope and clearly mark it "Media Mail." (That is enough for up to 1 pound.) If the listing says "free catalog," it means you need only request it; they do not ask for payment or SASE. Note: If sending for both guidelines and catalog, it is not necessary to send two envelopes; guidelines will be sent with catalog. If guidelines are available by e-mail or Website, that will be indicated.

y) Nonfiction and Fiction Sections—Preference for query letter, book proposal, or complete manuscript, and if they accept phone, fax, or e-queries (if it does not say they accept them, assume they do not; this reference applies to fiction as well as nonfiction). If they want a query letter, send just a letter describing your project. If they want a query letter/proposal, you can add a chapter-by-chapter synopsis and sample chapters. If not specified, send from one to three chapters. This data is often followed by a quote from them about their needs or what they don't want to see.

z) Special Needs—If a publisher has specific needs, especially those that are not included in the subject listings, they are indicated here.

aa) Ethnic Books—Usually specifies which ethnic groups they target

bb) Also Does—Indicates which publishers also publish booklets, pamphlets, tracts, or e-books

cc) Photos/Artwork—Indicates if they accept freelance photos for book covers. If interested, contact them for details or photography guidelines. This year I have also added information on whether a publisher will accept queries about artwork from freelancers.

dd) Tips—Specific tips provided by the editor/publisher

Note: At the end of some listings you will find an indication that the publisher receives mailings of book proposals from The Writer's Edge (see Editorial Services/Illinois for an explanation of that service) and/or ChristianManuscriptSubmissions.com (see Website or index).

4. In each periodical listing you will find the following information (as available) in this format:

a) Name of periodical

b) Address, phone, fax, e-mail address, Website

c) Denomination or affiliation

d) Name of editor and editor to submit to (if different)

e) Theme of publication

f) Format of publication, frequency of publication, number of pages and size of circulation—Tells whether magazine, newsletter, journal, tabloid, newspaper, or take-home paper. Frequency of publication indicates quantity of material needed. Number of pages usually indicates how much material they can use. Circulation indicates the amount of exposure your material will receive and often indicates how well they might pay or the probability that they will stay in business.

g) Subscription rate—Amount given is for a one-year subscription in the country of origin. I suggest you subscribe to at least one of your primary markets every year to become better acquainted with its specific focus.

h) Date established—Included only if 2004 or later

i) Openness to freelance; percentage freelance written. This year, this information has been expanded to indicate the percentage of unsolicited freelance and the percentage of assigned articles. Since not all publishers have responded to this question, some will still give the two percentages combined or indicate only the unsolicited number. If they buy only a small percentage, it often means they are open but receive little material that is appropriate. When you have a choice, choose those with the higher percentage of freelance written, but only if you have done your homework and know they are an appropriate market for your material.

j) Preference for query or complete manuscript also tells if they want a cover letter with complete manuscripts and whether they will accept phone, fax, or e-mail queries. (If it does not mention cover letters or phone, fax, or e-mail queries, assume they do not accept them.)

k) Payment schedule, payment on acceptance (they pay when the piece is accepted) or publication (they pay when it is published), and rights purchased. (See glossary for definitions of different rights.)

l) If a publication does not pay, or pays in copies or subscription, that is indicated in bold capital letters.

m) If a publication is not copyrighted, you should ask for your copyright notice to appear on your published piece so your rights will be protected.

n) Preferred word lengths and average number of manuscripts purchased per year (in parentheses)

o) Response time—The time they usually take to respond to your query or manuscript submission (add at least two weeks for delays for mailing)

p) Seasonal material (also refers to holiday)—Holiday or seasonal material should reach them at least the specified length of time in advance.

q) Acceptance of simultaneous submissions and reprints—If they accept simultaneous submissions, it means they will look at submissions (usually timely topic or holiday material) sent simultaneously to several publishers. Best to send to nonoverlapping markets (such as denominational), and be sure to indicate that it is a simultaneous submission. Reprints are pieces you have sold previously, but to which you hold the rights (which means you sold only first or one-time rights to the original publisher and the rights reverted to you as soon as they were published).

r) If they accept, prefer, or require submissions on disk or by e-mail. Many now prefer an e-mail submission, rather than on disk. Most will want a query or hard copy first. If it does not say they prefer or require disks, you should wait and see if they ask for them. If they accept an e-mail submission, it will indicate whether they want it as an attached file or copied into the message. If it says they accept e-mail submissions, but doesn't indicate a preference, it usually means they will take it either way.

s) Average amount of kill fee, if they pay one (see glossary for definition)

t) Whether or not they use sidebars (see glossary for definition), and whether they use them regularly or sometimes

u) Their preferred Bible version is indicated. The most popular version is the NIV (New International Version). If no version is indicated, they usually have no preference. See glossary for Bible Versions list.

v) Whether they accept submissions from children or teens. Young writers will find a list of the publishers open to submissions from them in the topical listings under "Young Writer Markets."

w) Availability and cost for writer's guidelines, theme list, and sample copies—If the listing says "Guidelines," it means they are available for a #10 SASE (business size) with a first-class stamp. Many more now have guidelines available by e-mail or Website, and the listing will indicate that. The cost for a sample copy, the size of envelope, and number of stamps required are given, if specified (affix stamps to envelope; don't send loose). Tip: If postage required is more than $2.13, I suggest you put $2.13 in postage on the envelope and clearly mark it "Media Mail." (That is enough for up to one pound.) If the listing says "free sample copy," it means you need only to request them; they do not ask for payment or SASE. Note: If sending for both guidelines and sample copy, it is not necessary to send two envelopes; guidelines will be sent with sample copy. If a listing doesn't mention guidelines or sample copy, they probably don't have them.

x) "Not in topical listings" means the publisher has not supplied a list of topics they are interested in. Send for their guidelines or study sample copies to determine topics used.

y) Poetry—Name of poetry editor (if different). Average number of poems bought each year. Types of poetry; number of lines. Payment rate. Maximum number of poems you may submit at one time.

z) Fillers—Name of fillers editor (if different). Types of fillers accepted; word length. Payment rate.

aa) Columns/Departments—Name of column editor. Names of columns in the periodical (information in parentheses gives focus of column); word length requirements. Payment rate. Be sure to see sample before sending ms or query. Most columns require a query.

bb) Special Issues or Needs—Indicates topics of special issues they have planned for the year or unique topics not included in regular subject listings

cc) Ethnic—Any involvement they have in the ethnic market

dd) Contest—Information on contests they sponsor or how to obtain that information. See Contest section at back of book for full list of contests.

ee) Tips—Tips from the editor on how to break into this market or how to be successful as an author

ff) At the end of some listings you will find a notation as to where that particular periodical placed in the Top 50+ Christian Periodical list in 2007, and/or their place in previous years. This list is compiled annually to indicate the most writer-friendly publications. To receive a complete listing, plus a prepared analysis sheet and writer's guidelines for the top 50 of those markets, send $25 (includes postage) to: Sally Stuart, 1647 S.W. Pheasant Dr., Aloha, OR 97006, or order from www.stuartmarket.com.

gg) Some listings also include EPA winners. These awards are made annually by the Evangelical Press Association (a trade organization for Christian periodicals). This section also indicates the top ten best-selling magazines in Christian retail stores.

5. It is important that you adhere closely to the guidelines set out in these listings. If a publisher asks for a query only, do not send a complete manuscript. Following these guidelines will mark you as a professional.

6. If your manuscript is completed, select the proper topical listing and target audience, and make up a list of possible publishers. Check first to see which ones will accept a complete manuscript (if you want to send it to those that require a query, you will have to write a query letter

or book proposal to send first). Please do not assume that your manuscript will be appropriate for all those on the list. Read the primary listing for each, and if you are not familiar with a publisher, read their writer's guidelines and study one or more sample copies or book catalog. (The primary listings tell how to get these.) Be sure the slant of your manuscript fits the slant of the publisher.

7. If you have an idea for an article, short story, or book but you have not written it yet, a reading of the appropriate topical listing will help you decide on a possible slant or approach. Select some publishers to whom you might send a query about your idea. If your idea is for an article, do not overlook the possibility of writing on the same topic for a number of different periodicals listed under that topic, either with the same target audience or another from the list. For example, you could write on money management for a general adult magazine, a teen magazine, a women's publication, or a magazine for pastors. Each would require a different slant, but you would get a lot more mileage from that idea.

8. If you do not have an idea, simply start reading through the topical listings or the primary listings. They are sure to trigger any number of book or magazine article ideas you could go to work on.

9. If you run into words or terms you are not familiar with, check the glossary on the CD-ROM for definitions.

10. If you need someone to look at your material to evaluate it or to give it a thorough editing, look up the section "Editorial Services" and find someone to send it to for such help. That often will make the difference between success or failure in publishing.

11. If you are a published author with other books to your credit, you may be interested in finding an agent. Some agents will consider unpublished authors (their listing will indicate that), but many require an author to have a completed manuscript before being considered (see agent list). Christian agents are at a premium, so it can be hard to find an agent unless you have had some success in book writing. The agent list also includes secular agents who handle religious/inspirational material.

12. Check the "Writers' Clubs/Groups" section to find a group to join in your area. Go to the "Writers' Conferences" section to find a conference you might attend this year. Attending a conference every year or two is almost essential to your success as a writer, especially when you get into book writing.

13. Send an SASE with every query or manuscript. If you do not want your manuscript returned, indicate that in your cover letter and send a #10 SASE for their acceptance or rejection

14. Do not rely solely on the information provided in this guide! It is just that—a guide—and is not intended to be complete by itself. It is important to your success as a freelance writer that you learn how to use writer's guidelines and study book catalogs or sample copies before submitting to any publisher.

TOPICAL LISTINGS OF BOOK PUBLISHERS

One of the most difficult aspects of marketing yourself is determining which publishers might be interested in your book. This topical listing was designed to help you do just that.

First, look up your topic of interest in the following lists. If you don't find the specific topic, check the list of topics in the table of contents and pursue any related topics. Once you have discovered which publishers are interested in a particular topic, the next step is to secure writer's guidelines and book catalogs from those publishers. Just because a particular publisher is listed under your topic, don't assume that it would automatically be interested in your book. It is your job to determine whether your approach to the subject will fit within the unique scope of that publisher's catalog. It is also helpful to visit a Christian bookstore to see some of the books produced by each publisher you are interested in pursuing.

Note, too, that the primary listings for each publisher indicate what the publisher prefers to see in the initial contact—a query, book proposal, or complete manuscript.

R—Indicates which publishers reprint out-of-print books from other publishers.

An asterisk (*) following a topic indicates it is a new topic this year.

An (s) before a listing indicates it is a publisher listed in the "Subsidy Publishers" section and does at least 50% subsidy publishing or print-on-demand. Please note that some of these publishers do some royalty publishing as well (check their listings), so if you aren't interested in a subsidy deal, you can contact them indicating you are interested only in a royalty contract.

An (a) before a listing indicates they accept submissions through agents only.

AFRICAN AMERICAN MARKETS*

Lift Every Voice—R
National Black Theatre
One World/Ballantine
Third World Press—R
Torch Legacy Public.
Walk Worthy Press—R

APOLOGETICS

Aadeon Publishing—R
Aaron Book—R
Abingdon Press
(s)-ACW Press—R
Ambassador-Emerald—R
(s)-American Binding—R
AMG Publishers
(s)-Baal Hamon—R
(a)-B & H Publishing
Baylor Univ. Press
Bethany House
(s)-Black Forest/Tennessee—R
Blue Dolphin
BMH Books—R
(s)-Booklocker.com—R
Bridge-Logos—R
(s)-Brown Books
Cambridge Scholars Pub.
Chalice Press
Chapter Two—R
Christian Family—R
Christian Heritage—R

College Press—R
Continuum Intl.—R
(s)-Creation House—R
CSS Publishing
Discovery House—R
Earthen Vessel—R
Eerdmans Pub., Wm. B.—R
(s)-Elderberry Press
(s)-Essence—R
Evangelical Press
Fair Havens—R
(s)-Fairway Press—R
(a)-FaithWords
Father's Press—R
Forward Movement
Green Key Books
GRQ—R
Guardian Angel
(a)-Harvest House
Hendrickson—R
Hensley Publishing
Hidden Brook Press—R
(s)-Holy Fire Publishing—R
Hope Publishing—R
Howard Books
(s)-IMD Press—R
(s)-Insight Publishing—R
InterVarsity Press—R
(a)-Kregel—R
Lighthouse Publishing—R
Lighthouse Trails—R
Lion and Lamb
Magnus Press—R

Master Books
Messianic Jewish—R
Millennium III—R
Monarch Books
NavPress Student—R
(a)-Nelson, Thomas
New Leaf
New Seeds—R
(s)-One World Press—R
Our Sunday Visitor—R
P & R Publishing—R
Parson Place—R
Pauline Books—R
(s)-Pleasant Word—R
Power Publishing—R
(s)-Providence Pub.—R
Randall House
Reformation Trust
(a)-Regal
Rose Publishing
Salt Works—R
Samaritan Press
Scepter Publishers—R
St. Anthony Mess. Press—R
(s)-Star Bible Public.
Strang Book Group—R
(s)-Tate Publishing—R
(s)-Trafford Publishing—R
VBC Publishing
Whitaker House
(s)-WinePress—R
(s)-Word Alive

ARCHAEOLOGY

Aaron Book—R
Abingdon Press
(s)-ACW Press—R
(s)-American Binding—R
Baker Academic
(a)-Baker Books
Baker Trittin
Baker's Plays—R
(s)-Black Forest/Tennessee—R
Blue Dolphin
(s)-Booklocker.com—R
Boyds Mills Press—R
(s)-Brentwood—R
(s)-Brown Books
Cambridge Scholars Pub.
Chapter Two—R
Christian Writer's Ebook—R
Comfort Publishing—R
Conciliar Press—R
(a)-Doubleday Relig.—R
Dover Publications—R
Eerdmans Pub., Wm. B.—R
(s)-Elderberry Press
(s)-Essence—R
Facts on File
(s)-Fairway Press—R
FaithWalk
Fordham Univ. Press—R
Gollehon Press
Green Key Books
(a)-HarperOne
Hendrickson—R
Hidden Brook Press—R
(s)-Holy Fire Publishing—R
(s)-Insight Publishing—R
InterVarsity Press—R
Johns Hopkins—R
(a)-Kregel—R
Lighthouse Publishing—R
Lion and Lamb
Lutterworth Press—R
Master Books
Monarch Books
New Leaf
New Seeds—R
(s)-One World Press—R
Pacific Press
(s)-Pleasant Word—R
Power Publishing—R
(s)-Providence Pub.—R
Rose Publishing
T & T Clark—R
(s)-Tate Publishing—R
(s)-TEACH Services—R
Third World Press—R
(s)-Trafford Publishing—R
Univ. Press of America—R
VBC Publishing

(s)-WinePress—R
(s)-Word Alive
Yale Univ. Press—R

ART—FREELANCE

Aadeon Publishing—R
Anglicans United—R
(s)-Baal Hamon—R
BelleBooks—R
BJU/Journey Forth—R
(s)-Black Forest/Tennessee—R
(s)-Booklocker.com—R
Cambridge Scholars Pub.
Carson-Dellosa
Chelsea House—R
Christian Ed. Pub.
Comfort Publishing—R
Dove Inspirational—R
Earthen Vessel—R
Eerdmans/Yg. Readers
Fair Havens—R
FamilyLife (books)—R
Fifth Estate—R
(a)-Focus on the Family—R
Guardian Angel
Halo Publishing
(s)-Holy Fire Publishing—R
(s)-IMD Press—R
Jebaire Publishing
Judson Press—R
Knight George Pub.
Lighthouse Publishing—R
Lighthouse Trails—R
Lion and Lamb
Liturgy Training—R
Messianic Jewish—R
Mission City Press
Monarch Books
Mt. Olive College Press
Parson Place—R
Parsons Publishing—R
Pauline Books—R
Pauline Kids
Pelican Publishing—R
Players Press—R
(s)-Pleasant Word—R
Power Publishing—R
(s)-Providence Pub.—R
Quintessential Books—R
Randall House
Ravenhawk Books—R
Rose Publishing
Salt Works—R
Samaritan Press
Sheed & Ward—R
(s)-TEACH Services—R
VBC Publishing
White Stone Books—R
Wilshire Book—R
(s)-WinePress—R

AUTOBIOGRAPHY

Aaron Book—R
(s)-ACW Press—R
Ambassador-Emerald—R
(s)-American Binding—R
(s)-Baal Hamon—R
(a)-Baker Books
Believe Books
(s)-Black Forest/Tennessee—R
(s)-Booklocker.com—R
(s)-Book Publishers—R
Boyds Mills Press—R
(s)-Brentwood—R
Bridge-Logos—R
(s)-Brown Books
Carey Library, Wm.—R
Chapter Two—R
Christian Heritage—R
Christian Writer's Ebook—R
Comfort Publishing—R
Continuum Intl.—R
(s)-Creation House—R
(s)-Dean Press, Robbie—R
(a)-Doubleday Relig.—R
(s)-Elderberry Press
(s)-Essence—R
Evergreen Press
(s)-Fairway Press—R
(a)-FaithWords
Father's Press—R
Georgetown Univ. Press
Greenwood/Praeger
(a)-HarperOne
Hidden Brook Press—R
His Work Christian Pub.
(s)-Holy Fire Publishing—R
(s)-IMD Press—R
(s)-Insight Publishing—R
Kirk House
KNB Publications
Life Changing Media
(s)-LifeVest Publishing
Lighthouse Publishing—R
Lighthouse Trails—R
Lion and Lamb
Lutterworth Press—R
(s)-McDougal Publishing—R
Monarch Books
(a)-Nelson, Thomas
New Seeds—R
(s)-One World Press—R
Pacific Press
Parson Place—R
Parsons Publishing—R
(s)-Path Pub. in Christ—R
(s)-Pleasant Word—R
Power Publishing—R
(s)-Providence Pub.—R
(a)-Regal
(a)-Regnery

Revival Nation
(s)-Selah Publishing—R
(s)-So. Baptist Press—R
Still Waters Revival—R
Strang Book Group—R
(s)-Tate Publishing—R
(s)-TEACH Services—R
(s)-Trafford Publishing—R
Univ. Press of America—R
(s)-VMI Publishers
(a)-WaterBrook Press—R
(s)-WinePress—R
(s)-Word Alive
(s)-Zoe Life Publishing

BIBLE/BIBLICAL STUDIES
Aadeon Publishing—R
Aaron Book—R
Abingdon Press
ACTA Publications
(s)-ACW Press—R
Ambassador Books
Ambassador-Emerald—R
(s)-American Binding—R
AMG Publishers
Anglicans United—R
(s)-Baal Hamon—R
Baker Academic
(a)-Baker Books
Baker Trittin
Baylor Univ. Press
Bethany House
BJU/Journey Forth—R
BMH Books—R
(s)-Booklocker.com—R
(s)-Brentwood—R
Bridge-Logos—R
(s)-Brown Books
Cambridge Scholars Pub.
Canticle Books—R
Carey Library, Wm.—R
Catholic Answers—R
Chalice Press
Chapter Two—R
Christian Ed. Pub.
Christian Family—R
Christian Focus—R
Christian Liberty Press
Christian Writer's Ebook—R
Clarke & Co., James—R
College Press—R
Conciliar Press—R
Congregational Life
Contemporary Drama
Continuum Intl.—R
CSS Publishing
(s)-DCTS Publishing
(s)-Dean Press, Robbie—R
Deo Volente
Discovery House—R
(a)-Doubleday Relig.—R
Editorial Portavoz

Eerdmans Pub., Wm. B.—R
(s)-Elderberry Press
(a)-Emmaus Road—R
(s)-Essence—R
Evangelical Press
Evergreen Press
Fair Havens—R
(s)-Fairway Press—R
Faith Alive
FaithWalk
Father's Press—R
Fifth Estate—R
First Fruits of Zion
Fortress Press
Foursquare Media
Good Book—R
Gospel Publishing
Greenwood/Praeger
Group Publishing
Grupo Nelson
Hannibal Books
Harcourt Religion
Harrison House
(a)-Harvest House
Hensley Publishing
Hidden Brook Press—R
(s)-Holy Fire Publishing—R
(s)-IMD Press—R
Inkling Books—R
(s)-Insight Publishing—R
InterVarsity Press—R
Jubilant Press—R
Judson Press—R
(s)-Kindred Books—R
(a)-Kregel—R
Libros Liguori
Lift Every Voice—R
Lighthouse Publishing—R
Lighthouse Trails—R
Lion and Lamb
Lutheran Univ. Press
Lutterworth Press—R
Magnus Press—R
(s)-McDougal Publishing—R
Mercer Univ. Press—R
Messianic Jewish—R
Monarch Books
NavPress
NavPress Student—R
New Hope—R
New Leaf
New York Univ. Press
(s)-One World Press—R
Our Sunday Visitor—R
P & R Publishing—R
Pacific Press
Paradise Research—R
Parson Place—R
Parsons Publishing—R
(s)-Path Pub. in Christ—R
Pauline Books—R
Pauline Kids

Paulist Press
Pflaum Publishing
Pilgrim Press—R
(s)-Pleasant Word—R
Power Publishing—R
Presbyterian Pub.
(s)-Providence Pub.—R
Randall House Digital
(a)-Regal
Rose Publishing
Salt Works—R
Samaritan Press
Sheed & Ward—R
Smyth & Helwys
(s)-So. Baptist Press—R
St. Anthony Mess. Press—R
St. Pauls/Alba House—R
(s)-Star Bible Public.
T & T Clark—R
(s)-Tate Publishing—R
(s)-TEACH Services—R
(s)-Trafford Publishing—R
UMI Publishing—R
Univ. Press of America—R
VBC Publishing
(s)-VMI Publishers
Walk Worthy—R
(a)-WaterBrook Press—R
Wesleyan Publishing
Westminster John Knox
Whitaker House
(s)-WinePress—R
Woodland Gospel
(s)-Word Alive
Yale Univ. Press—R
Youth Specialties
(s)-Zoe Life Publishing
Zondervan

BIBLE COMMENTARY
Aaron Book—R
Abingdon Press
(s)-ACW Press—R
Ambassador Books
Ambassador-Emerald—R
(s)-American Binding—R
AMG Publishers
Anglicans United—R
(s)-Baal Hamon—R
(a)-Baker Books
BJU/Journey Forth—R
(s)-Black Forest/Tennessee—R
BMH Books—R
(s)-Booklocker.com—R
(s)-Brown Books
Cambridge Scholars Pub.
Carey Library, Wm.—R
Catholic Answers—R
Chalice Press
Chapter Two—R
Christian Family—R

Christian Focus—R
Christian Writer's Ebook—R
Clarke & Co., James—R
College Press—R
Conciliar Press—R
Continuum Intl.—R
(a)-Cook, David C.
CSS Publishing
Discovery House—R
(a)-Doubleday Relig.—R
Editorial Portavoz
Eerdmans Pub., Wm. B.—R
(s)-Elderberry Press
(a)-Emmaus Road—R
(s)-Essence—R
Evangelical Press
(s)-Fairway Press—R
Father's Press—R
Fifth Estate—R
Greenwood/Praeger
Grupo Nelson
Harrison House
Hendrickson—R
Hidden Brook Press—R
(s)-Holy Fire Publishing—R
(s)-IMD Press—R
Inkling Books—R
(s)-Insight Publishing—R
InterVarsity Press—R
Intl. Awakening—R
(a)-Kregel—R
Libros Liguori
Lighthouse Publishing—R
Lutheran Univ. Press
Lutterworth Press—R
Messianic Jewish—R
Monarch Books
New Canaan—R
New Leaf
New Seeds—R
(s)-One World Press—R
Our Sunday Visitor—R
P & R Publishing—R
Pauline Books—R
Paulist Press
(s)-Pleasant Word—R
Power Publishing—R
(s)-Providence Pub.—R
Reformation Trust
Rose Publishing
Scepter Publishers—R
Sheed & Ward—R
St. Anthony Mess. Press—R
St. Pauls/Alba House—R
(s)-Star Bible Public.
(s)-Synergy Publishers—R
(s)-Tate Publishing—R
(s)-TEACH Services—R
(s)-Trafford Publishing—R
(a)-Tyndale House—R
UMI Publishing—R
VBC Publishing

Wesleyan Publishing
Westminster John Knox
(s)-WinePress—R
Wipf and Stock
(s)-Word Alive
Yale Univ. Press—R
(s)-Zoe Life Publishing
Zondervan

BIOGRAPHY

Aaron Book—R
(s)-ACW Press—R
Ambassador-Emerald—R
(s)-American Binding—R
(s)-Baal Hamon—R
(a)-Baker Books
Baker Trittin
Baker's Plays—R
(a)-Ballantine
Believe Books
(s)-Black Forest/Tennessee—R
(s)-Booklocker.com—R
(s)-Book Publishers—R
Boyds Mills Press—R
Branden Publishing—R
(s)-Brentwood—R
Bridge-Logos—R
(s)-Brown Books
Carey Library, Wm.—R
Catholic Answers—R
Chalice Press
Chapter Two—R
CharismaKids
Christian Family—R
Christian Focus—R
Christian Heritage—R
Christian Liberty Press
Christian Writer's Ebook—R
Cistercian—R
Clarke & Co., James—R
College Press—R
Comfort Publishing—R
Conciliar Press—R
Continuum Intl.—R
(s)-Creation House—R
(s)-Dean Press, Robbie—R
Discovery House—R
(a)-Doubleday Relig.—R
Dove Inspirational—R
Earthen Vessel—R
Eerdmans Pub., Wm. B.—R
(s)-Elderberry Press
(a)-Emmaus Road—R
(s)-Essence—R
Evangelical Press
Facts on File
Fair Havens—R
(s)-Fairway Press—R
FaithWalk
Fordham Univ. Press—R
Friends United Press
Georgetown Univ. Press

Greenwood/Praeger
GuidepostsBooks
Hannibal Books
(a)-HarperOne
Hidden Brook Press—R
His Work Christian Pub.
(s)-Holy Fire Publishing—R
Hope Publishing—R
Inkling Books—R
(s)-Insight Publishing—R
Jossey-Bass
Kaleidoscope Press—R
Kirk House
KNB Publications
(s)-LifeVest Publishing
Lighthouse Publishing—R
Lighthouse Trails—R
Lion and Lamb
Lutterworth Press—R
Magnus Press—R
(s)-McDougal Publishing—R
Mercer Univ. Press—R
Mission City Press
Monarch Books
(a)-Nelson, Thomas
New Leaf
New Seeds—R
(s)-One World Press—R
(a)-One World/Ballantine
P & R Publishing—R
Pacific Press
Parson Place—R
Parsons Publishing—R
(s)-Path Publishing—R
Pauline Books—R
Pauline Kids
Pelican Publishing—R
(s)-Pleasant Word—R
Power Publishing—R
(s)-Providence Pub.—R
Quintessential Books—R
Ravenhawk Books—R
(a)-Regnery
Revival Nation
Scepter Publishers—R
(s)-Selah Publishing—R
Sheed & Ward—R
(s)-So. Baptist Press—R
Still Waters Revival—R
Strang Book Group—R
(s)-Tate Publishing—R
(s)-TEACH Services—R
(s)-Trafford Publishing—R
Univ. of AR Press—R
Univ. Press of America—R
(s)-VMI Publishers
(a)-WaterBrook Press—R
Whitaker House
(s)-WinePress—R
Woodland Gospel
(s)-Word Alive
W Publishing

Yale Univ. Press—R
(s)-Zoe Life Publishing

BOOKLETS

Aaron Book—R
(s)-American Binding—R
(s)-Baal Hamon—R
Catholic Answers—R
Chapter Two—R
Christian Writer's Ebook—R
Concordia
(s)-Dean Press, Robbie—R
(s)-Essence—R
Evergreen Press
Fair Havens—R
FamilyLife (books)—R
Forward Movement
(s)-FruitBearer Pub.
Good Book—R
(a)-Harvest House
(s)-Insight Publishing—R
InterVarsity Press—R
Intl. Awakening—R
Judson Press—R
Libros Liguori
Life Cycle Books—R
Lighthouse Trails—R
Liguori Public.—R
Liturgy Training—R
(s)-One World Press—R
Our Sunday Visitor—R
P & R Publishing—R
Pacific Press
Paulist Press
Power Publishing—R
(s)-Providence Pub.—R
Randall House
Rose Publishing
Salt Works—R
Strang Book Group—R
(s)-Tate Publishing—R
Trinity Foundation—R
(s)-WinePress—R
(s)-Word Alive
(s)-Xulon Press—R

CANADIAN/FOREIGN

Ambassador-Emerald—R
Canadian Inst. for Law—R
Chapter Two—R
Christian Focus—R
Clarke & Co., James—R
(s)-Essence—R
Guernica Editions—R
Hidden Brook Press—R
(s)-Kindred Books—R
Kingsley, Jessica Pub.—R
Lighthouse Publishing—R
Monarch Books
(s)-One World Press—R
Ponder Publishing
Skysong Press

Still Waters Revival—R
(s)-Trafford Publishing—R
(s)-Word Alive

CELEBRITY PROFILES

Aaron Book—R
(s)-ACW Press—R
Ambassador-Emerald—R
(s)-American Binding—R
(a)-Baker Books
(s)-Booklocker.com—R
Branden Publishing—R
(s)-Brown Books
Christian Writer's Ebook—R
Comfort Publishing—R
(s)-Elderberry Press
(s)-Essence—R
(s)-Fairway Press—R
FaithWalk
(a)-FaithWords
Greenwood/Praeger
(a)-Hay House
Hidden Brook Press—R
(s)-Holy Fire Publishing—R
Howard Books
(s)-Insight Publishing—R
Life Changing Media
Lighthouse Publishing—R
Monarch Books
(a)-Nelson, Thomas
(s)-One World Press—R
(s)-Pleasant Word—R
Power Publishing—R
(s)-Providence Pub.—R
Ravenhawk Books—R
Salt Works—R
(s)-Selah Publishing—R
Strang Book Group—R
(s)-Tate Publishing—R
(s)-Trafford Publishing—R
(s)-VMI Publishers
Whitaker House
(s)-WinePress—R
Woodland Gospel
(s)-Word Alive

CHARISMATIC

Aaron Book—R
(s)-ACW Press—R
(s)-American Binding—R
Anglicans United—R
(s)-Baal Hamon—R
(s)-Black Forest/Tennessee—R
Blue Dolphin
(s)-Booklocker.com—R
Bridge-Logos—R
(s)-Brown Books
Canticle Books—R
Comfort Publishing—R
(s)-Creation House—R
CSS Publishing

Destiny Image (books)—R
Eerdmans Pub., Wm. B.—R
(s)-Elderberry Press
(a)-Emmaus Road—R
(s)-Essence—R
(s)-Fairway Press—R
Hidden Brook Press—R
(s)-Holy Fire Publishing—R
(s)-IMD Press—R
Life Changing Media
Lighthouse Publishing—R
Lutheran Univ. Press
Magnus Press—R
Monarch Books
Nelson Ignite
(a)-Nelson, Thomas
(s)-One World Press—R
Parsons Publishing—R
Pauline Books—R
(s)-Pleasant Word—R
Power Publishing—R
(s)-Providence Pub.—R
(a)-Regal
Revival Nation
(s)-Salvation Publisher—R
Strang Book Group—R
(s)-Synergy Publishers—R
(s)-Tate Publishing—R
(s)-Trafford Publishing—R
Whitaker House
(s)-WinePress—R
(s)-Word Alive
(s)-Zoe Life Publishing

CHILDREN'S BOARD BOOKS

Big Idea
Candy Cane Press
Eerdmans/Yg. Readers
(s)-Elderberry Press
Ideals Publications
Knight George Pub.
(a)-Kregel—R
(a)-Kregel Kidzone
Messianic Jewish—R
New Leaf
(s)-One World Press—R
Pauline Books—R
Pauline Kids
(s)-Tate Publishing—R
(s)-Trafford Publishing—R
(s)-WinePress—R
(s)-Word Alive

CHILDREN'S EASY READERS

Aaron Book—R
Ambassador Books
Atheneum/Yg. Readers
(a)-Baker Books
Big Idea
(s)-Booklocker.com—R

Branden Publishing—R
(s)-Brown Books
Carson-Dellosa
CharismaKids
Conciliar Press—R
(a)-Cook, David C.
(s)-Creation House—R
(s)-Dean Press, Robbie—R
E-Digital Books
(s)-Elderberry Press
(s)-Essence—R
Evergreen Press
(s)-Fairway Press—R
Father's Press—R
Guardian Angel
Harvest Day
Hidden Brook Press—R
His Work Christian Pub.
(s)-Holy Fire Publishing—R
Ideals Publications
(s)-IMD Press—R
Inkling Books—R
Journey Stone—R
Legacy Press—R
Lift Every Voice—R
Lighthouse Publishing—R
Lion and Lamb
Master Books
McRuffy Press
New Leaf
(s)-One World Press—R
Our Sunday Visitor—R
Pacific Press
Pauline Books—R
Pauline Kids
(s)-Providence Pub.—R
Reformation Trust
Salt Works—R
Salty's Books
Samaritan Press
Standard Publishing
Strang Book Group—R
(s)-Tate Publishing—R
(s)-Trafford Publishing—R
(a)-Tyndale House—R
VBC Publishing
(s)-VMI Publishers
(s)-Word Alive
(s)-Zoe Life Publishing

CHILDREN'S PICTURE BOOKS

Aaron Book—R
Abingdon Press
Ambassador Books
Atheneum/Yg. Readers
(a)-Baker Books
Big Idea
(s)-Black Forest/Tennessee—R
(s)-Book Publishers—R
Boyds Mills Press—R
Bridge-Logos—R

(s)-Brown Books
Candy Cane Press
Christian Focus—R
Conciliar Press—R
(a)-Cook, David C.
(s)-Creation House—R
E-Digital Books
Editorial Portavoz
Eerdmans Pub., Wm. B.—R
Eerdmans/Yg. Readers
(s)-Elderberry Press
(s)-Essence—R
Evergreen Press
Extreme Diva
Faith Communications
Father's Press—R
Grupo Nelson
Guardian Angel
Halo Publishing
Harvest Day
(s)-Holy Fire Publishing—R
Ideals Publications
(s)-IMD Press—R
Journey Stone—R
Judson Press—R
Kaleidoscope Press—R
(a)-Kregel—R
(a)-Kregel Kidzone
(s)-LifeVest Publishing
Lighthouse Publishing—R
Lighthouse Trails—R
Lion and Lamb
Master Books
Messianic Jewish—R
Monarch Books
New Leaf
(s)-One World Press—R
Pauline Books—R
Pauline Kids
(s)-Pleasant Word—R
(s)-Providence Pub.—R
Putnam/Young Readers
Salt Works—R
Salty's Books
Samaritan Press
(s)-Selah Publishing—R
(s)-Tate Publishing—R
(s)-TEACH Services—R
Third World Press—R
(s)-Trafford Publishing—R
(a)-Tyndale House—R
(a)-WaterBrook Press—R
White Stone Books—R
(s)-WinePress—R
(s)-Zoe Life Publishing

CHRIST

Aaron Book—R
(s)-ACW Press—R
Ambassador-Emerald—R
(s)-American Binding—R
Atheneum/Yg. Readers

(s)-Baal Hamon—R
Baker Trittin
Baker's Plays—R
(a)-B & H Publishing
Barbour
Bethany House
(s)-Black Forest/Tennessee—R
Blue Dolphin
(s)-Booklocker.com—R
(s)-Brown Books
Canticle Books—R
Catholic Answers—R
CharismaKids
Christian Family—R
Christian Focus—R
Christian Heritage—R
Christian Writer's Ebook—R
Continuum Intl.—R
(a)-Cook, David C.
(s)-Creation House—R
CSS Publishing
Discovery House—R
(a)-Doubleday Relig.—R
Eerdmans Pub., Wm. B.—R
(s)-Elderberry Press
Eldridge Plays
(a)-Emmaus Road—R
(s)-Essence—R
Evangelical Press
(s)-Fairway Press—R
Father's Press—R
Fifth Estate—R
Gollehon Press
GRQ—R
Guardian Angel
GuidepostsBooks
Hendrickson—R
Hidden Brook Press—R
(s)-Holy Fire Publishing—R
Howard Books
(s)-IMD Press—R
(s)-Insight Publishing—R
InterVarsity Press—R
Jebaire Publishing
Judson Press—R
Lift Every Voice—R
Lighthouse Publishing—R
Lillenas
Lion and Lamb
Lutheran Univ. Press
Magnus Press—R
Monarch Books
NavPress Student—R
(a)-Nelson, Thomas
New Leaf
New Seeds—R
(s)-One World Press—R
Our Sunday Visitor—R
P & R Publishing—R
Paradise Research—R
Parson Place—R
Pauline Books—R

Pilgrim Press—R
(s)-Pleasant Word—R
Power Publishing—R
Presbyterian Pub.
(s)-Providence Pub.—R
Quintessential Books—R
Reformation Trust
Rose Publishing
Salt Works—R
St. Anthony Mess. Press—R
(s)-Star Bible Public.
Strang Book Group—R
(s)-Synergy Publishers—R
(s)-Tate Publishing—R
(s)-TEACH Services—R
Torch Legacy
(s)-Trafford Publishing—R
VBC Publishing
(s)-VMI Publishers
(s)-WinePress—R
(s)-Word Alive
Yale Univ. Press—R
(s)-Zoe Life Publishing

CHRISTIAN BUSINESS

Aaron Book—R
(s)-ACW Press—R
Ambassador-Emerald—R
(s)-American Binding—R
Anglicans United—R
(s)-Baal Hamon—R
(a)-B & H Publishing
BJU/Journey Forth—R
(s)-Black Forest/Tennessee—R
BMH Books—R
(s)-Booklocker.com—R
(s)-Brown Books
Chalice Press
Christian Family—R
Christian Writer's Ebook—R
Comfort Publishing—R
(a)-Cook, David C.
(s)-Creation House—R
CSS Publishing
Dabbling Mum Press
Deo Volente
(a)-Doubleday Relig.—R
Eerdmans Pub., Wm. B.—R
(s)-Elderberry Press
(s)-Essence—R
Evergreen Press
(s)-Fairway Press—R
Father's Press—R
Forward Movement
Green Key Books
Grupo Nelson
Hannibal Books
Hidden Brook Press—R
(s)-Holy Fire Publishing—R
Hourglass Books—R
Howard Books

(s)-IMD Press—R
(s)-Insight Publishing—R
InterVarsity Press—R
Jubilant Press—R
Judson Press—R
Kirk House
Lift Every Voice—R
Lighthouse Publishing—R
Lion and Lamb
Lutheran Univ. Press
Millennium III—R
Monarch Books
(a)-Nelson, Thomas
New Leaf
(s)-One World Press—R
(s)-Path Pub. in Christ—R
Pilgrim Press—R
(s)-Pleasant Word—R
Power Publishing—R
PREP Publishing—R
(s)-Providence Pub.—R
Quintessential Books—R
Ravenhawk Books—R
(a)-Regal
(s)-Salvation Publisher—R
St. Anthony Mess. Press—R
(s)-Star Bible Public.
Strang Book Group—R
(s)-Synergy Publishers—R
(s)-Tate Publishing—R
(s)-TEACH Services—R
(s)-Trafford Publishing—R
Trinity Foundation—R
VBC Publishing
(s)-VMI Publishers
(a)-WaterBrook Press—R
Westminster John Knox
Whitaker House
(s)-WinePress—R
(s)-Word Alive
(s)-Zoe Life Publishing

CHRISTIAN EDUCATION

Aaron Book—R
(s)-ACW Press—R
Ambassador-Emerald—R
(s)-American Binding—R
(s)-Baal Hamon—R
Baker Academic
(a)-Baker Books
Baker Trittin
Big Idea
(s)-Booklocker.com—R
(s)-Brentwood—R
(s)-Brown Books
Carson-Dellosa
Chalice Press
Christian Ed. Pub.
Christian Family—R
Christian Heritage—R
Christian Liberty Press

Christian Writer's Ebook—R
Church Growth Inst.
College Press—R
Congregational Life
Contemporary Drama
(a)-Cook, David C.
CSS Publishing
(s)-DCTS Publishing
(s)-Dean Press, Robbie—R
Deo Volente
(a)-Doubleday Relig.—R
Eerdmans Pub., Wm. B.—R
(s)-Elderberry Press
Eldridge Plays
(s)-Essence—R
ETC Publications
Evangelical Press
(s)-Fairway Press—R
Faith Alive
Father's Press—R
Fifth Estate—R
Gospel Publishing
Group Publishing
Harcourt Religion
Harvest Day
Hensley Publishing
Hidden Brook Press—R
(s)-Holy Fire Publishing—R
(s)-IMD Press—R
(s)-Insight Publishing—R
Judson Press—R
Kingsley, Jessica Pub.—R
Kirk House
Knight George Pub.
(a)-Kregel—R
Lift Every Voice—R
Lighthouse Publishing—R
Lion and Lamb
Liturgical Press
Lutheran Univ. Press
Lutterworth Press—R
Master Books
Millennium III—R
Monarch Books
New Canaan—R
New Leaf
Northwestern
(s)-One World Press—R
Our Sunday Visitor—R
Pacific Press
(s)-Path Pub. in Christ—R
Pauline Books—R
Pilgrim Press—R
(s)-Pleasant Word—R
Power Publishing—R
(s)-Providence Pub.—R
Quintessential Books—R
Rainbow Publishers—R
Randall House
Reference Service
Rose Publishing
(s)-Salvation Publisher—R

Samaritan Press
Smyth & Helwys
(s)-So. Baptist Press—R
Standard Publishing
(s)-Star Bible Public.
Starik Publishing
Still Waters Revival—R
(s)-Tate Publishing—R
(s)-TEACH Services—R
Torch Legacy
(s)-Trafford Publishing—R
Trinity Foundation—R
UMI Publishing—R
Univ. Press of America—R
VBC Publishing
(s)-WinePress—R
(s)-Word Alive
(s)-Zoe Life Publishing

CHRISTIAN HOMESCHOOLING

Aaron Book—R
(s)-ACW Press—R
Ambassador-Emerald—R
(s)-American Binding—R
(a)-Baker Books
Big Idea
(s)-Booklocker.com—R
(s)-Brentwood—R
(s)-Brown Books
Carson-Dellosa
Chalice Press
Christian Family—R
Christian Focus—R
Christian Writer's Ebook—R
(s)-CrossHouse—R
CSS Publishing
(s)-Dean Press, Robbie—R
Eerdmans Pub., Wm. B.—R
(s)-Elderberry Press
(a)-Emmaus Road—R
(s)-Essence—R
ETC Publications
Evangelical Press
(s)-Fairway Press—R
Father's Press—R
Hannibal Books
Harcourt Religion
(a)-Harvest House
Hidden Brook Press—R
(s)-Holy Fire Publishing—R
(s)-IMD Press—R
Inkling Books—R
(s)-Insight Publishing—R
Jubilant Press—R
Judson Press—R
Kaleidoscope Press—R
Lift Every Voice—R
Lighthouse Publishing—R
Lion and Lamb
Little Lauren Books
Master Books

Mission City Press
Monarch Books
New Leaf
(s)-One World Press—R
P & R Publishing—R
Pacific Press
Parsons Publishing—R
(s)-Path Pub. in Christ—R
Pauline Books—R
(s)-Pleasant Word—R
Power Publishing—R
(s)-Providence Pub.—R
Rose Publishing
Standard Publishing
(s)-Star Bible Public.
Starik Publishing
Still Waters Revival—R
(s)-Tate Publishing—R
(s)-TEACH Services—R
Virginia Pines Press
(s)-WinePress—R
(s)-Word Alive
(s)-Zoe Life Publishing

CHRISTIAN LIVING

Aadeon Publishing—R
Aaron Book—R
Abingdon Press
ACTA Publications
(s)-ACW Press—R
Ambassador Books
Ambassador-Emerald—R
(s)-American Binding—R
(s)-Baal Hamon—R
(a)-Baker Books
Baker Trittin
(a)-B & H Publishing
Barbour
Beacon Hill Press—R
Bethany House
BJU/Journey Forth—R
(s)-Black Forest/Tennessee—R
BMH Books—R
(s)-Booklocker.com—R
(s)-Brentwood—R
(s)-Brown Books
Canticle Books—R
Chalice Press
Christian Family—R
Christian Focus—R
Christian Writer's Ebook—R
Cladach Publishing
Comfort Publishing—R
(a)-Cook, David C.
(s)-Creation House—R
CSS Publishing
(s)-DCTS Publishing
Destiny Image (books)—R
Dimensions for Living
Discovery House—R
(a)-Doubleday Relig.—R

Editorial Portavoz
Eerdmans Pub., Wm. B.—R
(s)-Elderberry Press
Elijah Press
(s)-Essence—R
Evangelical Press
Evergreen Press
Fair Havens—R
(s)-Fairway Press—R
FaithWalk
(a)-FaithWords
Father's Press—R
Forward Movement
Friends United Press
(s)-FruitBearer Pub.
Good News Pub.
Green Key Books
Greenwood/Praeger
GRQ—R
GuidepostsBooks
(a)-HarperOne
Harrison House
(a)-Harvest House
HeartSpring Pub.—R
Hendrickson—R
Hidden Brook Press—R
His Work Christian Pub.
(s)-Holy Fire Publishing—R
Hope Publishing—R
Howard Books
(s)-IMD Press—R
(s)-Impact Christian—R
(s)-Insight Publishing—R
InterVarsity Press—R
Jebaire Publishing
Jireh Publishing
Judson Press—R
(s)-Kindred Books—R
Kingsley, Jessica Pub.—R
(a)- Kregel—R
Life Changing Media
Life Cycle Books—R
Lift Every Voice—R
Lighthouse Publishing—R
Lillenas
Lion and Lamb
Liturgical Press
Lutheran Univ. Press
Lutterworth Press—R
Magnus Press—R
(s)-McDougal Publishing—R
Monarch Books
(a)-Moody Publishers
(a)-Multnomah
NavPress
NavPress Student—R
Nelson Ignite
(a)-Nelson, Thomas
New Hope—R
(s)-One World Press—R
Our Sunday Visitor—R
P & R Publishing—R

Parsons Publishing—R
(s)-Path Pub. in Christ—R
Pauline Books—R
Pilgrim Press—R
(s)-Pleasant Word—R
Power Publishing—R
Presbyterian Pub.
(s)-Providence Pub.—R
Quintessential Books—R
Ragged Edge—R
Randall House
Reformation Trust
(a)-Regal
Revell
Revival Nation
Rose Publishing
(s)-Salvation Publisher—R
Samaritan Press
(s)-Selah Publishing—R
Smyth & Helwys
St. Anthony Mess. Press—R
Standard Publishing
(s)-Star Bible Public.
Starik Publishing
Still Waters Revival—R
Strang Book Group—R
(s)-Synergy Publishers—R
(s)-Tate Publishing—R
Tau-Publishing—R
(s)-TEACH Services—R
Torch Legacy
(s)-Trafford Publishing—R
(a)-Tyndale House—R
UMI Publishing—R
Univ. Press of America—R
VBC Publishing
(s)-VMI Publishers
(a)-WaterBrook Press—R
Wesleyan Publishing
Westminster John Knox
White Stone Books—R
(s)-WinePress—R
Woodland Gospel
(s)-Word Alive
W Publishing
(s)-Zoe Life Publishing

CHRISTIAN SCHOOL BOOKS

Aaron Book—R
(s)-ACW Press—R
(s)-American Binding—R
(a)-Baker Books
Baker Trittin
Big Idea
(s)-Booklocker.com—R
(s)-Brown Books
Carson-Dellosa
Christian Liberty Press
Christian Writer's Ebook—R
CSS Publishing

(s)-Dean Press, Robbie—R
Eerdmans Pub., Wm. B.—R
(s)-Elderberry Press
(s)-Essence—R
ETC Publications
(s)-Fairway Press—R
Father's Press—R
Hidden Brook Press—R
(s)-Holy Fire Publishing—R
(s)-IMD Press—R
Inkling Books—R
(s)-Insight Publishing—R
Kaleidoscope Press—R
Kingsley, Jessica Pub.—R
Knight George Pub.
Lighthouse Publishing—R
Lion and Lamb
Master Books
Monarch Books
New Canaan—R
New Leaf
(s)-One World Press—R
Our Sunday Visitor—R
Pacific Press
(s)-Pleasant Word—R
Power Publishing—R
(s)-Providence Pub.—R
Rose Publishing
(s)-So. Baptist Press—R
(s)-Star Bible Public.
(s)-Tate Publishing—R
(s)-Trafford Publishing—R
Trinity Foundation—R
(s)-WinePress—R
(s)-Word Alive
(s)-Zoe Life Publishing

CHURCH HISTORY

Aaron Book—R
Abingdon Press
ACTA Publications
(s)-ACW Press—R
Ambassador-Emerald—R
(s)-American Binding—R
Anglicans United—R
(s)-Baal Hamon—R
(a)-Baker Books
Baker Trittin
Baker's Plays—R
(a)-B & H Publishing
Baylor Univ. Press
(s)-Black Forest/Tennessee—R
BMH Books—R
(s)-Booklocker.com—R
Boyds Mills Press—R
(s)-Brown Books
Carey Library, Wm.—R
Catholic Answers—R
Chalice Press
Chapter Two—R
Christian Family—R

Christian Focus—R
Christian Heritage—R
Christian Writer's Ebook—R
Cistercian—R
Clarke & Co., James—R
College Press—R
Continuum Intl.—R
(s)-Creation House—R
(s)-CrossHouse—R
CSS Publishing
Deo Volente
(a)-Doubleday Relig.—R
Editorial Portavoz
Eerdmans Pub., Wm. B.—R
(s)-Elderberry Press
Elijah Press
(a)-Emmaus Road—R
(s)-Essence—R
Evangelical Press
(s)-Fairway Press—R
FaithWalk
Father's Press—R
Fortress Press
Forward Movement
Founders Press
Gollehon Press
Greenwood/Praeger
Hannibal Books
(a)-HarperOne
Hendrickson—R
Hidden Brook Press—R
(s)-Holy Fire Publishing—R
(s)-IMD Press—R
(s)-Insight Publishing—R
InterVarsity Press—R
Intl. Awakening—R
Johns Hopkins—R
Judson Press—R
Kirk House
(a)-Kregel—R
Libros Liguori
Lighthouse Publishing—R
Lion and Lamb
Loyola Press
Lutheran Univ. Press
Lutterworth Press—R
Messianic Jewish—R
Millennium III—R
Monarch Books
NavPress Student—R
New Canaan—R
New Leaf
New Seeds—R
New York Univ. Press
(s)-One World Press—R
Our Sunday Visitor—R
P & R Publishing—R
Pacific Press
(s)-Path Pub. in Christ—R
Pauline Books—R
Paulist Press

(s)-Pleasant Word—R
Power Publishing—R
Presbyterian Pub.
(s)-Providence Pub.—R
Quintessential Books—R
Randall House
Reformation Trust
Revival Nation
Rose Publishing
Scepter Publishers—R
(s)-Selah Publishing—R
Sheed & Ward—R
Smyth & Helwys
St. Anthony Mess. Press—R
St. Bede's Publications
(s)-Star Bible Public.
(s)-Tate Publishing—R
(s)-Trafford Publishing—R
Trinity Foundation—R
Univ. of AR Press—R
Univ. Press of America—R
VBC Publishing
Westminster John Knox
(s)-WinePress—R
Wipf and Stock
(s)-Word Alive
Yale Univ. Press—R
(s)-Zoe Life Publishing
Zondervan

CHURCH LIFE

Aaron Book—R
Abingdon Press
(s)-ACW Press—R
(s)-American Binding—R
(s)-Baal Hamon—R
(a)-Baker Books
Baker's Plays—R
(a)-B & H Publishing
Bethany House
(s)-Black Forest/Tennessee—R
BMH Books—R
(s)-Booklocker.com—R
(s)-Brentwood—R
(s)-Brown Books
Chalice Press
Chapter Two—R
CharismaKids
Christian Writer's Ebook—R
Clarke & Co., James—R
Continuum Intl.—R
(s)-Creation House—R
CSS Publishing
(s)-DCTS Publishing
Destiny Image—R
Discovery House—R
(a)-Doubleday Relig.—R
Eerdmans Pub., Wm. B.—R
(s)-Elderberry Press
(a)-Emmaus Road—R
(s)-Essence—R

Evangelical Press
(s)-Fairway Press—R
FaithWalk
Father's Press—R
Forward Movement
Greenwood/Praeger
Hannibal Books
(a)-HarperOne
Harrison House
Hidden Brook Press—R
(s)-Holy Fire Publishing—R
Hope Publishing—R
(s)-IMD Press—R
(s)-Impact Christian—R
(s)-Insight Publishing—R
InterVarsity Press—R
Jubilant Press—R
Judson Press—R
Kirk House
(a)-Kregel—R
Libros Liguori
Lift Every Voice—R
Lighthouse Publishing—R
Lillenas
Lion and Lamb
Lutheran Univ. Press
Lutterworth Press—R
Monarch Books
NavPress
NavPress Student—R
(a)-Nelson, Thomas
New Leaf
(s)-One World Press—R
P & R Publishing—R
Pacific Press
(s)-Path Pub. in Christ—R
Pauline Books—R
Pilgrim Press—R
(s)-Pleasant Word—R
Power Publishing—R
Presbyterian Pub.
(s)-Providence Pub.—R
Quintessential Books—R
Randall House
Reformation Trust
Revival Nation
(s)-Selah Publishing—R
Smyth & Helwys
St. Anthony Mess. Press—R
(s)-Star Bible Public.
Strang Book Group—R
(s)-Tate Publishing—R
(s)-TEACH Services—R
Torch Legacy
Touch Publications—R
(s)-Trafford Publishing—R
VBC Publishing
(s)-VMI Publishers
Wesleyan Publishing
Westminster John Knox
(s)-WinePress—R

Woodland Gospel
(s)-Word Alive
W Publishing
Youth Specialties
(s)-Zoe Life Publishing

CHURCH MANAGEMENT

Aaron Book—R
Abingdon Press
(s)-ACW Press—R
(s)-American Binding—R
(s)-Baal Hamon—R
(a)-B & H Publishing
BJU/Journey Forth—R
(s)-Black Forest/Tennessee—R
BMH Books—R
(s)-Booklocker.com—R
(s)-Brown Books
Chalice Press
Christian Heritage—R
(s)-Creation House—R
CSS Publishing
(a)-Doubleday Relig.—R
Eerdmans Pub., Wm. B.—R
(s)-Elderberry Press
(s)-Essence—R
Evangelical Press
(s)-Fairway Press—R
Father's Press—R
Hannibal Books
Hidden Brook Press—R
(s)-Holy Fire Publishing—R
Hope Publishing—R
(s)-IMD Press—R
(s)-Insight Publishing—R
InterVarsity Press—R
Judson Press—R
Kirk House
Lighthouse Publishing—R
Lion and Lamb
Lutheran Univ. Press
Monarch Books
New Leaf
(s)-One World Press—R
Our Sunday Visitor—R
(s)-Pleasant Word—R
Power Publishing—R
Presbyterian Pub.
(s)-Providence Pub.—R
(a)-Regal
St. Anthony Mess. Press—R
(s)-Star Bible Public.
Strang Book Group—R
(s)-Tate Publishing—R
(s)-TEACH Services—R
(s)-Trafford Publishing—R
VBC Publishing
Wesleyan Publishing
(s)-WinePress—R
(s)-Word Alive

CHURCH RENEWAL

Aaron Book—R
Abingdon Press
(s)-ACW Press—R
Ambassador-Emerald—R
(s)-American Binding—R
(s)-Baal Hamon—R
(a)-Baker Books
(a)-B & H Publishing
(s)-Booklocker.com—R
(s)-Brentwood—R
(s)-Brown Books
Canticle Books—R
Carey Library, Wm.—R
Chalice Press
CharismaKids
Christian Focus—R
Christian Writer's Ebook—R
(s)-Creation House—R
CSS Publishing
Destiny Image—R
Destiny Image (books)—R
(a)-Doubleday Relig.—R
Eerdmans Pub., Wm. B.—R
(s)-Elderberry Press
(a)-Emmaus Road—R
(s)-Essence—R
Evangelical Press
(s)-Fairway Press—R
FaithWalk
Father's Press—R
Forward Movement
Greenwood/Praeger
Hannibal Books
(a)-HarperOne
Hidden Brook Press—R
(s)-Holy Fire Publishing—R
Hope Publishing—R
(s)-IMD Press—R
(s)-Impact Christian—R
(s)-Insight Publishing—R
InterVarsity Press—R
Intl. Awakening—R
Judson Press—R
(a)-Kregel—R
Libros Liguori
Lighthouse Publishing—R
Lillenas
Lion and Lamb
Lutheran Univ. Press
Magnus Press—R
(s)-McDougal Publishing—R
Monarch Books
NavPress Student—R
(s)-One World Press—R
Pacific Press
Parson Place—R
(s)-Path Pub. in Christ—R
Pauline Books—R
Pilgrim Press—R

(s)-Pleasant Word—R
Power Publishing—R
Presbyterian Pub.
(s)-Providence Pub.—R
Quintessential Books—R
(a)-Regal
Revival Nation
(s)-Salvation Publisher—R
(s)-Selah Publishing—R
(s)-Sermon Select Press
Smyth & Helwys
(s)-So. Baptist Press—R
St. Anthony Mess. Press—R
(s)-Star Bible Public.
(s)-Tate Publishing—R
(s)-TEACH Services—R
(s)-Trafford Publishing—R
(s)-VMI Publishers
Wesleyan Publishing
Westminster John Knox
(s)-WinePress—R
(s)-Word Alive

CHURCH TRADITIONS

Aaron Book—R
Abingdon Press
(s)-ACW Press—R
(s)-American Binding—R
Anglicans United—R
Atheneum/Yg. Readers
(s)-Baal Hamon—R
(a)-Baker Books
Baker's Plays—R
(a)-B & H Publishing
(s)-Black Forest/Tennessee—R
(s)-Booklocker.com—R
Boyds Mills Press—R
(s)-Brown Books
Carey Library, Wm.—R
Catholic Answers—R
Chalice Press
Christian Family—R
Christian Heritage—R
Christian Writer's Ebook—R
Cistercian—R
Clarke & Co., James—R
Conciliar Press—R
Continuum Intl.—R
(s)-Creation House—R
Crossroad Publishing—R
CSS Publishing
(a)-Doubleday Relig.—R
Eerdmans Pub., Wm. B.—R
(s)-Elderberry Press
(a)-Emmaus Road—R
(s)-Essence—R
(s)-Fairway Press—R
FaithWalk
Father's Press—R
Forward Movement
Founders Press

Greenwood/Praeger
Hendrickson—R
Hidden Brook Press—R
(s)-Holy Fire Publishing—R
(s)-IMD Press—R
Inkling Books—R
(s)-Insight Publishing—R
InterVarsity Press—R
Libros Liguori
Lighthouse Publishing—R
Lion and Lamb
Lutheran Univ. Press
Monarch Books
NavPress Student—R
(a)-Nelson, Thomas
New York Univ. Press
(s)-One World Press—R
Our Sunday Visitor—R
Pacific Press
(s)-Path Pub. in Christ—R
Pauline Books—R
(s)-Pleasant Word—R
Power Publishing—R
Presbyterian Pub.
(s)-Providence Pub.—R
Randall House
(a)-Regal
Rose Publishing
St. Anthony Mess. Press—R
St. Pauls/Alba House—R
(s)-Star Bible Public.
(s)-Tate Publishing—R
(s)-Trafford Publishing—R
(s)-VMI Publishers
(s)-WinePress—R
(s)-Word Alive

COFFEE-TABLE BOOKS

Aaron Book—R
ACTA Publications
(s)-ACW Press—R
(s)-Black Forest/Tennessee—R
(s)-Brown Books
Cistercian—R
(s)-Creation House—R
Father's Press—R
GRQ—R
(a)-Harvest House
Hidden Brook Press—R
(s)-IMD Press—R
Kirk House
Liturgy Training—R
Lutheran Univ. Press
Monarch Books
New Leaf
Players Press—R
(s)-Pleasant Word—R
(s)-Providence Pub.—R
Salt Works—R
(s)-Synergy Publishers—R
(s)-Trafford Publishing—R

(s)-VMI Publishers
(s)-WinePress—R
(s)-Zoe Life Publishing

COMPILATIONS

Aaron Book—R
(s)-ACW Press—R
(s)-American Binding—R
(s)-Baal Hamon—R
Baker's Plays—R
Barbour
(s)-Black Forest/Tennessee—R
(s)-Booklocker.com—R
(s)-Brentwood—R
(s)-Brown Books
Christian Heritage—R
Christian Writer's Ebook—R
(s)-Creation House—R
(a)-Doubleday Relig.—R
Eerdmans Pub., Wm. B.—R
(s)-Elderberry Press
(s)-Essence—R
(s)-Fairway Press—R
Father's Press—R
GRQ—R
Hidden Brook Press—R
(s)-Holy Fire Publishing—R
Howard Books
Judson Press—R
Lighthouse Publishing—R
Monarch Books
(s)-One World Press—R
P & R Publishing—R
(s)-Pleasant Word—R
(s)-Providence Pub.—R
Reformation Trust
Salt Works—R
Strang Book Group—R
(s)-Tate Publishing—R
(s)-Trafford Publishing—R
Univ. Press of America—R
(s)-VMI Publishers
(a)-WaterBrook Press—R
(s)-WinePress—R
Woodland Gospel
(s)-Word Alive

CONTROVERSIAL ISSUES

Aadeon Publishing—R
Aaron Book—R
(s)-ACW Press—R
Ambassador-Emerald—R
(s)-American Binding—R
AMG Publishers
Atheneum/Yg. Readers
(s)-Baal Hamon—R
(a)-Baker Books
Baker's Plays—R
(s)-Black Forest/Tennessee—R
Blue Dolphin
(s)-Booklocker.com—R

Branden Publishing—R
(s)-Brentwood—R
(s)-Brown Books
Canadian Inst. for Law—R
Canticle Books—R
Catholic Answers—R
Chalice Press
Chapter Two—R
Christian Family—R
Christian Writer's Ebook—R
Conciliar Press—R
Continuum Intl.—R
(s)-Creation House—R
(s)-Dean Press, Robbie—R
Destiny Image—R
Destiny Image (books)—R
(a)-Doubleday Relig.—R
Eerdmans Pub., Wm. B.—R
(s)-Elderberry Press
(s)-Essence—R
Evangelical Press
(s)-Fairway Press—R
FaithWalk
(a)-FaithWords
Father's Press—R
Fifth Estate—R
Gollehon Press
Green Key Books
Greenwood/Praeger
Hannibal Books
(a)-HarperOne
(a)-Hay House
Hidden Brook Press—R
(s)-Holy Fire Publishing—R
Hope Publishing—R
Howard Books
Inkling Books—R
(s)-Insight Publishing—R
Jireh Publishing
Jossey-Bass
Judson Press—R
Kingsley, Jessica Pub.—R
(a)-Kregel—R
Lighthouse Publishing—R
Lighthouse Trails—R
Little Lauren Books
Lutterworth Press—R
Magnus Press—R
Monarch Books
MountainView
NavPress Student—R
New Leaf
(s)-One World Press—R
Pilgrim Press—R
(s)-Pleasant Word—R
Power Publishing—R
(s)-Providence Pub.—R
Ravenhawk Books—R
(a)-Regal
(a)-Regnery
Revival Nation

Rose Publishing
Salt Works—R
(s)-Selah Publishing—R
Still Waters Revival—R
Strang Book Group—R
(s)-Tate Publishing—R
(s)-Trafford Publishing—R
Virginia Pines Press
(s)-VMI Publishers
(s)-WinePress—R
(s)-Word Alive
(s)-Zoe Life Publishing

COOKBOOKS

Aaron Book—R
Adams Media
(s)-American Binding—R
(a)-Ballantine
Barbour
(s)-Black Forest/Tennessee—R
(s)-Booklocker.com—R
(s)-Book Publishers—R
(s)-Brentwood—R
Bridge-Logos—R
(s)-Brown Books
Christian Writer's Ebook—R
Countryman, J.
(s)-CrossHouse—R
Dabbling Mum Press
DiskUs Publishing
Dover Publications—R
(s)-Elderberry Press
(s)-Essence—R
Evergreen Press
Extreme Diva
(s)-Fairway Press—R
Guardian Angel
Hannibal Books
Hidden Brook Press—R
His Work Christian Pub.
(s)-Holy Fire Publishing—R
(s)-IMD Press—R
Journey Stone—R
(s)-LifeVest Publishing
Monarch Books
(a)-Nelson, Thomas
(s)-One World Press—R
(a)-One World/Ballantine
Pacific Press
Pelican Publishing—R
(s)-Pleasant Word—R
Power Publishing—R
(s)-Providence Pub.—R
Salt Works—R
Siloam
(s)-So. Baptist Press—R
Strang Book Group—R
(s)-Tate Publishing—R
(s)-TEACH Services—R
(s)-Trafford Publishing—R
(s)-WinePress—R

(s)-Word Alive
Xyzzy Press
(s)-Zoe Life Publishing

COUNSELING AIDS

Aaron Book—R
(s)-ACW Press—R
(s)-American Binding—R
(s)-Baal Hamon—R
(a)-Baker Books
(s)-Black Forest/Tennessee—R
Blue Dolphin
BMH Books—R
(s)-Booklocker.com—R
(s)-Brentwood—R
Bridge-Logos—R
(s)-Brown Books
CarePoint Publishing—R
Chalice Press
Christian Family—R
Christian Writer's Ebook—R
CSS Publishing
(s)-Dean Press, Robbie—R
Editorial Portavoz
Eerdmans Pub., Wm. B.—R
(s)-Elderberry Press
(s)-Essence—R
Evangelical Press
Evergreen Press
Fair Havens—R
(s)-Fairway Press—R
FaithWalk
Father's Press—R
Fifth Estate—R
Good Book—R
Harcourt Religion
Harrison House
Hidden Brook Press—R
(s)-Holy Fire Publishing—R
Howard Books
(s)-Insight Publishing—R
InterVarsity Press—R
Judson Press—R
Kaleidoscope Press—R
Kingsley, Jessica Pub.—R
(a)-Kregel—R
Langmarc
Life Cycle Books—R
Lighthouse Publishing—R
Lion and Lamb
(s)-McDougal Publishing—R
Monarch Books
(a)-Nelson, Thomas
(s)-One World Press—R
P & R Publishing—R
Paradise Research—R
Pauline Books—R
Pilgrim Press—R
(s)-Pleasant Word—R
Power Publishing—R
(s)-Providence Pub.—R
Quintessential Books—R

Randall House
Reference Service
(s)-Sermon Select Press
(s)-So. Baptist Press—R
(s)-Star Bible Public.
Strang Book Group—R
(s)-Tate Publishing—R
(s)-Trafford Publishing—R
(s)-VMI Publishers
(s)-WinePress—R
(s)-Word Alive
Youth Specialties

CREATION SCIENCE

Aaron Book—R
(s)-ACW Press—R
Ambassador-Emerald—R
(s)-American Binding—R
(s)-Baal Hamon—R
(s)-Black Forest/Tennessee—R
Blue Dolphin
BMH Books—R
(s)-Booklocker.com—R
Bridge-Logos—R
(s)-Brown Books
Cambridge Scholars Pub.
Chapter Two—R
Christian Family—R
Christian Writer's Ebook—R
Editorial Portavoz
Eerdmans Pub., Wm. B.—R
(s)-Elderberry Press
(s)-Essence—R
Evangelical Press
Fair Havens—R
(s)-Fairway Press—R
Hidden Brook Press—R
(s)-Holy Fire Publishing—R
Hope Publishing—R
Howard Books
Inkling Books—R
(s)-Insight Publishing—R
Kaleidoscope Press—R
Lighthouse Publishing—R
Master Books
Monarch Books
NavPress Student—R
New Leaf
(s)-One World Press—R
P & R Publishing—R
Pacific Press
Parson Place—R
(s)-Path Pub. in Christ—R
(s)-Pleasant Word—R
Power Publishing—R
(s)-Providence Pub.—R
Salt Works—R
(s)-Star Bible Public.
Strang Book Group—R
(s)-Tate Publishing—R
(s)-TEACH Services—R
(s)-Trafford Publishing—R

Whitaker House
(s)-WinePress—R
(s)-Word Alive
(s)-Zoe Life Publishing

CULTS/OCCULT

Aaron Book—R
(s)-ACW Press—R
Ambassador-Emerald—R
(s)-American Binding—R
(a)-Baker Books
Baker Trittin
Baker's Plays—R
(s)-Black Forest/Tennessee—R
(s)-Booklocker.com—R
(s)-Brown Books
Catholic Answers—R
Chapter Two—R
Christian Writer's Ebook—R
Comfort Publishing—R
Conciliar Press—R
Editorial Portavoz
Eerdmans Pub., Wm. B.—R
(s)-Elderberry Press
(s)-Essence—R
Evangelical Press
(s)-Fairway Press—R
Greenwood/Praeger
(a)-HarperOne
Harrison House
Hidden Brook Press—R
(s)-Holy Fire Publishing—R
(s)-Impact Christian—R
(s)-Insight Publishing—R
(a)-Kregel—R
Lighthouse Publishing—R
Monarch Books
New York Univ. Press
(s)-One World Press—R
P & R Publishing—R
(s)-Pleasant Word—R
Power Publishing—R
(s)-Providence Pub.—R
Ravenhawk Books—R
Revival Nation
Rose Publishing
(s)-Selah Publishing—R
(s)-Star Bible Public.
(s)-Synergy Publishers—R
(s)-Tate Publishing—R
(s)-Trafford Publishing—R
Whitaker House
(s)-WinePress—R
(s)-Word Alive

CURRENT/SOCIAL ISSUES

Aadeon Publishing—R
Aaron Book—R
(s)-ACW Press—R
Ambassador-Emerald—R
(s)-American Binding—R

AMG Publishers
Atheneum/Yg. Readers
Baker Academic
(a)-Baker Books
Baker Trittin
Baker's Plays—R
(a)-B & H Publishing
Beacon Hill Press—R
BJU/Journey Forth—R
(s)-Black Forest/Tennessee—R
Blue Dolphin
(s)-Booklocker.com—R
Boyds Mills Press—R
Branden Publishing—R
(s)-Brentwood—R
Bridge-Logos—R
(s)-Brown Books
Canadian Inst. for Law—R
Catholic Answers—R
Chalice Press
Christian Family—R
Christian Writer's Ebook—R
Comfort Publishing—R
Conari Press
(s)-Creation House—R
Crossroad Publishing—R
(s)-DCTS Publishing
Destiny Image—R
(a)-Doubleday Relig.—R
Editorial Portavoz
Eerdmans Pub., Wm. B.—R
(s)-Elderberry Press
Eldridge Plays
(s)-Essence—R
Evangelical Press
(s)-Fairway Press—R
FaithWalk
(a)-FaithWords
Father's Press—R
Forward Movement
Georgetown Univ. Press
Gollehon Press
Greenwood/Praeger
Hannibal Books
(a)-HarperOne
Harrison House
Hendrickson—R
Hidden Brook Press—R
(s)-Holy Fire Publishing—R
Howard Books
Inkling Books—R
(s)-Insight Publishing—R
InterVarsity Press—R
Judson Press—R
Kingsley, Jessica Pub.—R
(a)-Kregel—R
Life Cycle Books—R
Lighthouse Publishing—R
Lighthouse Trails—R
Lillenas
Loyola Press
Lutheran Univ. Press

Monarch Books
NavPress Student—R
(a)-Nelson, Thomas
New Canaan—R
New Hope—R
New York Univ. Press
(s)-One World Press—R
P & R Publishing—R
Pilgrim Press—R
(s)-Pleasant Word—R
Power Publishing—R
(s)-Providence Pub.—R
Putnam/Young Readers
Ravenhawk Books—R
(a)-Regal
(a)-Regnery
Revival Nation
Rose Publishing
Salt Works—R
(s)-Selah Publishing—R
Sheed & Ward—R
Smyth & Helwys
(s)-Star Bible Public.
Still Waters Revival—R
Strang Book Group—R
(s)-Synergy Publishers—R
(s)-Tate Publishing—R
(s)-Trafford Publishing—R
(a)-Tyndale House—R
VBC Publishing
(s)-VMI Publishers
Whitaker House
(s)-WinePress—R
(s)-Word Alive
W Publishing
Yale Univ. Press—R
(s)-Zoe Life Publishing

CURRICULUM

Aaron Book—R
Baker Trittin
Big Idea
(s)-Brown Books
CarePoint Publishing—R
Christian Ed. Pub.
Christian Liberty Press
College Press—R
Concordia
Congregational Life
(a)-Cook, David C.
Eerdmans Pub., Wm. B.—R
(s)-Elderberry Press
(s)-Fairway Press—R
Faith Alive
Friends United Press
Gospel Light
Gospel Publishing
Hannibal Books
Harcourt Religion
Hidden Brook Press—R
(s)-Holy Fire Publishing—R
(s)-IMD Press—R

Knight George Pub.
Lighthouse Publishing—R
Lighthouse Trails—R
Lion and Lamb
Messianic Jewish—R
Monarch Books
New Leaf
Northwestern
(s)-One World Press—R
Power Publishing—R
(s)-Providence Pub.—R
Randall House Digital
Smyth & Helwys
Standard Publishing
(s)-Tate Publishing—R
(s)-Trafford Publishing—R
UMI Publishing—R
Univ. Press of America—R
(s)-WinePress—R
(s)-Word Alive
W Publishing
Youth Specialties
(s)-Zoe Life Publishing

DATING/SEX

Aaron Book—R
(s)-ACW Press—R
Ambassador-Emerald—R
(s)-American Binding—R
(s)-Baal Hamon—R
Baker's Plays—R
(a)-Ballantine
Barbour
Bethany House
Blue Dolphin
(s)-Booklocker.com—R
Bridge-Logos—R
(s)-Brown Books
Catholic Answers—R
Chapter Two—R
Christian Writer's Ebook—R
Comfort Publishing—R
(a)-Cook, David C.
Destiny Image (books)—R
(a)-Doubleday Relig.—R
Eerdmans Pub., Wm. B.—R
(s)-Elderberry Press
(a)-Emmaus Road—R
(s)-Essence—R
Evangelical Press
Evergreen Press
(s)-Fairway Press—R
FaithWalk
(a)-FaithWords
FamilyLife (books)—R
Fell, Frederick—R
Fifth Estate—R
Forward Movement
Greenwood/Praeger
GRQ—R
(a)-HarperOne
Harrison House

(a)-Harvest House
Hidden Brook Press—R
(s)-Holy Fire Publishing—R
Howard Books
(s)-Insight Publishing—R
InterVarsity Press—R
Judson Press—R
(a)-Kregel—R
Lift Every Voice—R
Lighthouse Publishing—R
Lillenas
Little Lauren Books
Monarch Books
NavPress Student—R
(a)-Nelson, Thomas
(s)-One World Press—R
Pauline Books—R
(s)-Pleasant Word—R
Power Publishing—R
(s)-Providence Pub.—R
Randall House
(a)-Regal
Resource Public.
Rose Publishing
Siloam
St. Anthony Mess. Press—R
(s)-Star Bible Public.
Strang Book Group—R
(s)-Tate Publishing—R
(s)-Trafford Publishing—R
(s)-VMI Publishers
Walk Worthy—R
(a)-WaterBrook Press—R
Whitaker House
(s)-WinePress—R
(s)-Word Alive
Youth Specialties
(s)-Zoe Life Publishing

DEATH/DYING

Aaron Book—R
Abingdon Press
ACTA Publications
(s)-ACW Press—R
Ambassador-Emerald—R
(s)-American Binding—R
(s)-Baal Hamon—R
(a)-Baker Books
Baker's Plays—R
(s)-Black Forest/Tennessee—R
Blue Dolphin
BMH Books—R
(s)-Booklocker.com—R
(s)-Book Publishers—R
Bridge-Logos—R
(s)-Brown Books
Chalice Press
Christian Family—R
Christian Writer's Ebook—R
Comfort Publishing—R
(a)-Cook, David C.
(s)-Creation House—R

CSS Publishing
Discovery House—R
(a)-Doubleday Relig.—R
Editorial Portavoz
Eerdmans Pub., Wm. B.—R
(s)-Elderberry Press
(a)-Emmaus Road—R
(s)-Essence—R
Evangelical Press
Evergreen Press
(s)-Fairway Press—R
FaithWalk
Father's Press—R
Fifth Estate—R
Forward Movement
Greenwood/Praeger
Guardian Angel
(a)-HarperOne
Harrison House
(a)-Harvest House
Hidden Brook Press—R
(s)-Holy Fire Publishing—R
Hope Publishing—R
(s)-Insight Publishing—R
Judson Press—R
Kingsley, Jessica Pub.—R
(a)-Kregel—R
Life Cycle Books—R
Lift Every Voice—R
Lighthouse Publishing—R
Lillenas
Lion and Lamb
Loyola Press
Lutheran Univ. Press
Lutterworth Press—R
Monarch Books
(a)-Nelson, Thomas
New Seeds—R
(s)-One World Press—R
Pacific Press
Pauline Books—R
Paulist Press
Pilgrim Press—R
(s)-Pleasant Word—R
Power Publishing—R
(s)-Providence Pub.—R
Randall House
Resource Public.
Rose Publishing
Sheed & Ward—R
Siloam
Smyth & Helwys
St. Anthony Mess. Press—R
(s)-Star Bible Public.
Strang Book Group—R
(s)-Tate Publishing—R
(s)-TEACH Services—R
(s)-Trafford Publishing—R
(s)-VMI Publishers
(a)-WaterBrook Press—R
Whitaker House
(s)-WinePress—R

(s)-Word Alive
(s)-Zoe Life Publishing

DEVOTIONAL BOOKS

Aaron Book—R
Abingdon Press
(s)-ACW Press—R
Ambassador Books
Ambassador-Emerald—R
(s)-American Binding—R
(s)-Baal Hamon—R
(a)-Baker Books
Baker Trittin
(a)-B & H Publishing
Barbour
Bethany House
(s)-Black Forest/Tennessee—R
(s)-Booklocker.com—R
(s)-Brentwood—R
(s)-Brown Books
Canticle Books—R
Chapter Two—R
Christian Family—R
Christian Focus—R
Christian Heritage—R
Christian Writer's Ebook—R
Comfort Publishing—R
Congregational Life
Contemporary Drama
Continuum Intl.—R
(a)-Cook, David C.
Countryman, J.
(s)-Creation House—R
CSS Publishing
Dimensions for Living
Discovery House—R
(a)-Doubleday Relig.—R
Editorial Portavoz
Eerdmans Pub., Wm. B.—R
(s)-Elderberry Press
(a)-Emmaus Road—R
(s)-Essence—R
Evangelical Press
Evergreen Press
Extreme Diva
Fair Havens—R
(s)-Fairway Press—R
FaithWalk
(a)-FaithWords
Forward Movement
Founders Press
(s)-FruitBearer Pub.
Gollehon Press
Green Key Books
Greenwood/Praeger
GRQ—R
Hannibal Books
(a)-HarperOne
Harrison House
Harvest Day
(a)-Harvest House

HeartSpring Pub.—R
Hidden Brook Press—R
(s)-Holy Fire Publishing—R
Howard Books
(s)-IMD Press—R
(s)-Impact Christian—R
Inkling Books—R
(s)-Insight Publishing—R
Jireh Publishing
Judson Press—R
KNB Publications
(a)-Kregel—R
Legacy Press—R
Libros Liguori
Lift Every Voice—R
Lighthouse Publishing—R
Liguori Public.—R
Lion and Lamb
Lutterworth Press—R
Magnus Press—R
(s)-McDougal Publishing—R
Messianic Jewish—R
Mission City Press
Monarch Books
MOPS Intl.
Mt. Olive College Press
(a)-Nelson, Thomas
New Hope—R
New Seeds—R
(s)-One World Press—R
P & R Publishing—R
Parson Place—R
Parsons Publishing—R
(s)-Path Pub. in Christ—R
Pauline Books—R
Pilgrim Press—R
(s)-Pleasant Word—R
Power Publishing—R
(s)-Providence Pub.—R
Ragged Edge—R
Randall House
(a)-Regal
Revival Nation
Rose Publishing
(s)-Salvation Publisher—R
Samaritan Press
(s)-Selah Publishing—R
Smyth & Helwys
St. Anthony Mess. Press—R
Standard Publishing
(s)-Star Bible Public.
Strang Book Group—R
(s)-Synergy Publishers—R
(s)-Tate Publishing—R
(s)-Trafford Publishing—R
Tsaba House
(a)-Tyndale House—R
VBC Publishing
(s)-VMI Publishers
(a)-WaterBrook Press—R
Wesleyan Publishing
White Stone Books—R

(s)-WinePress—R
(s)-Word Alive
W Publishing
Youth Specialties
(s)-Zoe Life Publishing

DISCIPLESHIP

Aadeon Publishing—R
Aaron Book—R
Abingdon Press
(s)-ACW Press—R
Ambassador-Emerald—R
(s)-American Binding—R
Anglicans United—R
(s)-Baal Hamon—R
(a)-Baker Books
Baker Trittin
Baker's Plays—R
(a)-B & H Publishing
Barbour
Beacon Hill Press—R
Bethany House
BJU/Journey Forth—R
(s)-Black Forest/Tennessee—R
BMH Books—R
(s)-Booklocker.com—R
(s)-Brentwood—R
Bridge-Logos—R
(s)-Brown Books
Carey Library, Wm.—R
Chalice Press
Chapter Two—R
CharismaKids
Christian Family—R
Christian Focus—R
Christian Heritage—R
Christian Writer's Ebook—R
College Press—R
Comfort Publishing—R
Continuum Intl.—R
(a)-Cook, David C.
(s)-Creation House—R
CSS Publishing
(s)-DCTS Publishing
Deo Volente
Destiny Image (books)—R
Discovery House—R
(a)-Doubleday Relig.—R
Editorial Portavoz
Eerdmans Pub., Wm. B.—R
(s)-Elderberry Press
(s)-Essence—R
Evangelical Press
Evergreen Press
Fair Havens—R
(s)-Fairway Press—R
FaithWalk
Father's Press—R
Forward Movement
Founders Press
Foursquare Media
Gospel Publishing

Green Key Books
(a)-HarperOne
Harrison House
Hendrickson—R
Hensley Publishing
Hidden Brook Press—R
(s)-Holy Fire Publishing—R
Howard Books
(s)-IMD Press—R
Inkling Books—R
(s)-Insight Publishing—R
InterVarsity Press—R
Jebaire Publishing
Judson Press—R
(a)-Kregel—R
Lift Every Voice—R
Lighthouse Publishing—R
Lillenas
Lion and Lamb
Lutheran Univ. Press
(s)-McDougal Publishing—R
Messianic Jewish—R
Mission City Press
Monarch Books
(a)-Moody Publishers
NavPress
NavPress Student—R
(a)-Nelson, Thomas
New Hope—R
(s)-One World Press—R
P & R Publishing—R
Pacific Press
Parson Place—R
Pauline Books—R
Pilgrim Press—R
(s)-Pleasant Word—R
Power Publishing—R
(s)-Providence Pub.—R
Quintessential Books—R
Randall House
Reformation Trust
(a)-Regal
Revival Nation
Rose Publishing
(s)-Salvation Publisher—R
Samaritan Press
Smyth & Helwys
(s)-So. Baptist Press—R
St. Anthony Mess. Press—R
Standard Publishing
(s)-Star Bible Public.
Strang Book Group—R
(s)-Synergy Publishers—R
(s)-Tate Publishing—R
(s)-TEACH Services—R
Touch Publications—R
(s)-Trafford Publishing—R
VBC Publishing
(s)-VMI Publishers
(a)-WaterBrook Press—R
Wesleyan Publishing
Whitaker House

(s)-WinePress—R
(s)-Word Alive
W Publishing
Youth Specialties
(s)-Zoe Life Publishing

DIVORCE

Aaron Book—R
ACTA Publications
(s)-ACW Press—R
Ambassador Books
Ambassador-Emerald—R
(s)-American Binding—R
(s)-Baal Hamon—R
(a)-Baker Books
Baker's Plays—R
Bethany House
(s)-Black Forest/Tennessee—R
Blue Dolphin
(s)-Booklocker.com—R
(s)-Brentwood—R
Bridge-Logos—R
(s)-Brown Books
Chalice Press
Christian Writer's Ebook—R
Comfort Publishing—R
(a)-Cook, David C.
(s)-Creation House—R
CSS Publishing
Dabbling Mum Press
(s)-Dean Press, Robbie—R
Editorial Portavoz
Eerdmans Pub., Wm. B.—R
(s)-Elderberry Press
(s)-Essence—R
Evangelical Press
Fair Havens—R
(s)-Fairway Press—R
FaithWalk
Forward Movement
Greenwood/Praeger
GuidepostsBooks
(a)-Harvest House
Hidden Brook Press—R
(s)-Holy Fire Publishing—R
(s)-IMD Press—R
(s)-Insight Publishing—R
(a)-Kregel—R
Lighthouse Publishing—R
Lillenas
Lion and Lamb
Messianic Jewish—R
Monarch Books
(a)-Nelson, Thomas
(s)-One World Press—R
Pacific Press
(s)-Pleasant Word—R
Power Publishing—R
(s)-Providence Pub.—R
Randall House
(a)-Regal
(a)-Regnery

Rose Publishing
Samaritan Press
(s)-So. Baptist Press—R
St. Anthony Mess. Press—R
(s)-Star Bible Public.
Strang Book Group—R
(s)-Synergy Publishers—R
(s)-Tate Publishing—R
(s)-Trafford Publishing—R
(s)-VMI Publishers
(a)-WaterBrook Press—R
(s)-WinePress—R
(s)-Word Alive
(s)-Zoe Life Publishing

DOCTRINAL

Aaron Book—R
(s)-ACW Press—R
(s)-American Binding—R
(s)-Baal Hamon—R
(a)-Baker Books
Baker's Plays—R
(a)-B & H Publishing
Beacon Hill Press—R
Bethany House
(s)-Black Forest/Tennessee—R
BMH Books—R
(s)-Booklocker.com—R
(s)-Brentwood—R
(s)-Brown Books
Canticle Books—R
Catholic Answers—R
Chalice Press
Chapter Two—R
Christian Family—R
Christian Focus—R
Christian Heritage—R
Christian Writer's Ebook—R
Cistercian—R
Clarke & Co., James—R
College Press—R
Concordia
Continuum Intl.—R
(s)-Creation House—R
(s)-DCTS Publishing
(a)-Doubleday Relig.—R
Editorial Portavoz
Eerdmans Pub., Wm. B.—R
(s)-Elderberry Press
(s)-Essence—R
Evangelical Press
Fair Havens—R
(s)-Fairway Press—R
Forward Movement
Harrison House
Hidden Brook Press—R
(s)-Holy Fire Publishing—R
(s)-IMD Press—R
(s)-Impact Christian—R
(s)-Insight Publishing—R
InterVarsity Press—R
Intl. Awakening—R

(a)-Kregel—R
Libros Liguori
Lighthouse Publishing—R
Lighthouse Trails—R
Liturgical Press
Lutheran Univ. Press
Magnus Press—R
Messianic Jewish—R
Monarch Books
(s)-One World Press—R
P & R Publishing—R
Pacific Press
Pauline Books—R
(s)-Pleasant Word—R
Power Publishing—R
(s)-Providence Pub.—R
Reformation Trust
Revival Nation
Rose Publishing
Scepter Publishers—R
(s)-So. Baptist Press—R
St. Anthony Mess. Press—R
(s)-Star Bible Public.
Still Waters Revival—R
(s)-Tate Publishing—R
(s)-Trafford Publishing—R
Trinity Foundation—R
(a)-Tyndale House—R
UMI Publishing—R
VBC Publishing
(s)-WinePress—R
(s)-Word Alive
(s)-Zoe Life Publishing

DRAMA

Aaron Book—R
(s)-American Binding—R
Baker Trittin
Baker's Plays—R
Big Idea
(s)-Black Forest/Tennessee—R
(s)-Brentwood—R
(s)-Brown Books
Contemporary Drama
(s)-Elderberry Press
Eldridge Plays
(s)-Fairway Press—R
Guardian Angel
Guernica Editions—R
Hidden Brook Press—R
(s)-Holy Fire Publishing—R
Judson Press—R
Lighthouse Publishing—R
Lillenas
Lion and Lamb
Meriwether
Monarch Books
(s)-One World Press—R
Players Press—R
(s)-Pleasant Word—R
Power Publishing—R
(s)-Providence Pub.—R

Randall House
Ravenhawk Books—R
Salt Works—R
Samaritan Press
(s)-So. Baptist Press—R
(s)-Tate Publishing—R
(s)-Trafford Publishing—R
(s)-WinePress—R
(s)-Word Alive
Youth Specialties
(s)-Zoe Life Publishing

E-BOOKS

Blue Dolphin
(s)-Booklocker.com—R
(s)-Booklocker Jr.
Christian Writer's Ebook—R
College Press—R
Comfort Publishing—R
Company B Pub.
Dabbling Mum Press
(s)-Dean Press, Robbie—R
DiskUs Publishing
E-Digital Books
Evangelical Press
Fair Havens—R
Fifth Estate—R
Guardian Angel
InterVarsity Press—R
Jireh Publishing
Jubilant Press—R
Life Changing Media
Lighthouse Publishing—R
MoreThanNovellas
(s)-One World Press—R
Paradise Research—R
(s)-Path Pub. in Christ—R
Power Publishing—R
Randall House Digital
Resource Public.
Samaritan Press
(s)-Selah Publishing—R
Smyth & Helwys
Sweetheart Romances
(s)-Trafford Publishing—R
(a)-Tyndale House—R
White Rose—R
White Stone Books—R
(s)-Word Alive
(s)-Xulon Press—R

ECONOMICS

Aaron Book—R
(s)-ACW Press—R
(s)-American Binding—R
(a)-Baker Books
Baylor Univ. Press
(s)-Booklocker.com—R
(s)-Brentwood—R
(s)-Brown Books
Canadian Inst. for Law—R
Christian Writer's Ebook—R

Comfort Publishing—R
(s)-Creation House—R
Eerdmans Pub., Wm. B.—R
(s)-Elderberry Press
(s)-Essence—R
(s)-Fairway Press—R
FaithWalk
Father's Press—R
(a)-Harvest House
Hidden Brook Press—R
(s)-Holy Fire Publishing—R
(s)-Insight Publishing—R
InterVarsity Press—R
Lighthouse Publishing—R
Monarch Books
New Hope—R
(s)-One World Press—R
Pilgrim Press—R
(s)-Pleasant Word—R
Power Publishing—R
(s)-Providence Pub.—R
Quintessential Books—R
(a)-Regnery
(s)-Salvation Publisher—R
Sheed & Ward—R
(s)-Star Bible Public.
(s)-Tate Publishing—R
(s)-TEACH Services—R
(s)-Trafford Publishing—R
Trinity Foundation—R
Univ. Press of America—R
(s)-VMI Publishers
(s)-WinePress—R
(s)-Word Alive
(s)-Zoe Life Publishing

ENCOURAGEMENT

Aaron Book—R
(s)-ACW Press—R
Ambassador-Emerald—R
(s)-American Binding—R
Baker's Plays—R
Barbour
(s)-Black Forest/Tennessee—R
BMH Books—R
(s)-Booklocker.com—R
(s)-Brown Books
CarePoint Publishing—R
Christian Family—R
Christian Focus—R
Comfort Publishing—R
(s)-Creation House—R
CSS Publishing
Discovery House—R
(a)-Doubleday Relig.—R
Eerdmans Pub., Wm. B.—R
(s)-Elderberry Press
(a)-Emmaus Road—R
(s)-Essence—R
Evangelical Press
Fair Havens—R
(s)-Fairway Press—R

Father's Press—R
Guardian Angel
(a)-Harvest House
Hidden Brook Press—R
(s)-Holy Fire Publishing—R
Howard Books
(s)-IMD Press—R
(s)-Insight Publishing—R
Jebaire Publishing
Judson Press—R
(a)-Kregel—R
Life Changing Media
Lift Every Voice—R
Lighthouse Publishing—R
Lion and Lamb
Messianic Jewish—R
Monarch Books
NavPress Student—R
New Hope—R
(s)-One World Press—R
Parson Place—R
Pauline Books—R
(s)-Pleasant Word—R
Power Publishing—R
(s)-Providence Pub.—R
Quintessential Books—R
Randall House
(s)-Salvation Publisher—R
Samaritan Press
(s)-Star Bible Public.
Strang Book Group—R
(s)-Synergy Publishers—R
(s)-Tate Publishing—R
(s)-Trafford Publishing—R
VBC Publishing
(a)-WaterBrook Press—R
White Stone Books—R
(s)-WinePress—R
(s)-Word Alive
(s)-Zoe Life Publishing

ENVIRONMENTAL ISSUES

Aaron Book—R
ACTA Publications
(s)-ACW Press—R
(s)-American Binding—R
(a)-Baker Books
Baker's Plays—R
(s)-Black Forest/Tennessee—R
Blue Dolphin
(s)-Booklocker.com—R
Boyds Mills Press—R
(s)-Brown Books
Christian Writer's Ebook—R
Comfort Publishing—R
Dawn Publications
(a)-Doubleday Relig.—R
Eerdmans Pub., Wm. B.—R
(s)-Elderberry Press
(s)-Essence—R
Evangelical Press
Facts on File

(s)-Fairway Press—R
FaithWalk
Forward Movement
Georgetown Univ. Press
Grupo Nelson
Hendrickson—R
Hidden Brook Press—R
(s)-Holy Fire Publishing—R
(s)-Insight Publishing—R
InterVarsity Press—R
Johns Hopkins—R
Judson Press—R
Lighthouse Publishing—R
Lutterworth Press—R
Monarch Books
New Leaf
(s)-One World Press—R
Pilgrim Press—R
(s)-Pleasant Word—R
Power Publishing—R
(s)-Providence Pub.—R
Quintessential Books—R
Ravenhawk Books—R
Sheed & Ward—R
(s)-So. Baptist Press—R
Tarcher, Jeremy P.—R
(s)-Tate Publishing—R
(s)-Trafford Publishing—R
Univ. Press of America—R
(s)-VMI Publishers
(s)-WinePress—R
(s)-Word Alive

ESCHATOLOGY

Aaron Book—R
(s)-ACW Press—R
(s)-American Binding—R
Anglicans United—R
(a)-Baker Books
(s)-Black Forest/Tennessee—R
Blue Dolphin
BMH Books—R
(s)-Booklocker.com—R
Bridge-Logos—R
(s)-Brown Books
Chalice Press
Chapter Two—R
Christian Family—R
Christian Heritage—R
Christian Writer's Ebook—R
College Press—R
Comfort Publishing—R
Continuum Intl.—R
(s)-Creation House—R
CSS Publishing
(s)-DCTS Publishing
Eerdmans Pub., Wm. B.—R
(s)-Elderberry Press
(a)-Emmaus Road—R
(s)-Essence—R
Evangelical Press

(s)-Fairway Press—R
Grupo Nelson
Hendrickson—R
Hidden Brook Press—R
(s)-Holy Fire Publishing—R
(s)-IMD Press—R
(s)-Insight Publishing—R
Kirk House
(a)-Kregel—R
Lighthouse Publishing—R
Lighthouse Trails—R
Lutheran Univ. Press
Messianic Jewish—R
Millennium III—R
Monarch Books
(a)-Nelson, Thomas
New Leaf
New Seeds—R
(s)-One World Press—R
Pacific Press
Parson Place—R
Pauline Books—R
(s)-Pleasant Word—R
Power Publishing—R
(s)-Providence Pub.—R
Rose Publishing
(s)-Selah Publishing—R
St. Pauls/Alba House—R
(s)-Star Bible Public.
Strang Book Group—R
(s)-Strong Tower—R
(s)-Tate Publishing—R
(s)-TEACH Services—R
(s)-Trafford Publishing—R
VBC Publishing
(s)-WinePress—R
(s)-Word Alive
(s)-Zoe Life Publishing

ETHICS

Aadeon Publishing—R
Aaron Book—R
(s)-ACW Press—R
(s)-American Binding—R
(a)-Baker Books
Baker's Plays—R
(s)-Black Forest/Tennessee—R
Blue Dolphin
BMH Books—R
(s)-Booklocker.com—R
(s)-Brentwood—R
(s)-Brown Books
Cambridge Scholars Pub.
Catholic Answers—R
Chalice Press
Christian Heritage—R
Christian Writer's Ebook—R
Clarke & Co., James—R
Conciliar Press—R
Continuum Intl.—R
(s)-Creation House—R

Dover Publications—R
Eerdmans Pub., Wm. B.—R
(s)-Elderberry Press
(a)-Emmaus Road—R
(s)-Essence—R
Evangelical Press
(s)-Fairway Press—R
FaithWalk
Father's Press—R
Fortress Press
Forward Movement
Georgetown Univ. Press
Greenwood/Praeger
Guardian Angel
Hannibal Books
Hendrickson—R
Hidden Brook Press—R
(s)-Holy Fire Publishing—R
Howard Books
(s)-IMD Press—R
Inkling Books—R
(s)-Insight Publishing—R
InterVarsity Press—R
Judson Press—R
Kingsley, Jessica Pub.—R
Kirk House
(a)-Kregel—R
Libros Liguori
Life Cycle Books—R
Lift Every Voice—R
Lighthouse Publishing—R
Lion and Lamb
Lutheran Univ. Press
Lutterworth Press—R
Messianic Jewish—R
Monarch Books
NavPress Student—R
(s)-One World Press—R
Our Sunday Visitor—R
P & R Publishing—R
Pacific Press
Paragon House—R
Paulist Press
Pilgrim Press—R
(s)-Pleasant Word—R
Power Publishing—R
Presbyterian Pub.
(s)-Providence Pub.—R
Quintessential Books—R
Ravenhawk Books—R
(a)-Regnery
Resource Public.
Salt Works—R
Sheed & Ward—R
Smyth & Helwys
St. Anthony Mess. Press—R
St. Pauls/Alba House—R
(s)-Star Bible Public.
Still Waters Revival—R
(s)-Synergy Publishers—R
T & T Clark—R

(s)-Tate Publishing—R
(s)-TEACH Services—R
(s)-Trafford Publishing—R
Trinity Foundation—R
Univ. Press of America—R
(s)-VMI Publishers
Walk Worthy—R
Westminster John Knox
Whitaker House
(s)-WinePress—R
(s)-Word Alive
Yale Univ. Press—R

ETHNIC/CULTURAL

Aaron Book—R
(s)-ACW Press—R
(s)-Ali Literary, Alfred—R
(s)-American Binding—R
(s)-Baal Hamon—R
(a)-Baker Books
Baker Trittin
Baker's Plays—R
(s)-Black Forest/Tennessee—R
Blue Dolphin
(s)-Booklocker.com—R
Boyds Mills Press—R
Branden Publishing—R
(s)-Brown Books
Cambridge Scholars Pub.
Carey Library, Wm.—R
Chalice Press
Christian Writer's Ebook—R
College Press—R
Comfort Publishing—R
Concordia
(s)-Creation House—R
(s)-Dean Press, Robbie—R
(a)-Doubleday Relig.—R
E-Digital Books
Eerdmans Pub., Wm. B.—R
(s)-Elderberry Press
(s)-Essence—R
Evangelical Press
Facts on File
(s)-Fairway Press—R
FaithWalk
Fortress Press
Forward Movement
Georgetown Univ. Press
Greenwood/Praeger
Grupo Nelson
Guardian Angel
Guernica Editions—R
(a)-HarperOne
Hendrickson—R
Hidden Brook Press—R
(s)-Holy Fire Publishing—R
Howard Books
(s)-IMD Press—R
(s)-Insight Publishing—R
InterVarsity Press—R

Jossey-Bass
Judson Press—R
Kaleidoscope Press—R
Kirk House
Libros Liguori
Lighthouse Publishing—R
Liguori Public.—R
Lutheran Univ. Press
Millennium III—R
Monarch Books
(a)-Moody Publishers
NavPress Student—R
New Hope—R
New Seeds—R
New York Univ. Press
(s)-One World Press—R
(a)-One World/Ballantine
Oregon Catholic
P & R Publishing—R
Pacific Press
Paulist Press
Pilgrim Press—R
(s)-Pleasant Word—R
Power Publishing—R
(s)-Providence Pub.—R
Salt Works—R
St. Anthony Mess. Press—R
Standard Publishing
(s)-Tate Publishing—R
Third World Press—R
Torch Legacy
(s)-Trafford Publishing—R
UMI Publishing—R
Univ. of AR Press—R
Univ. Press of America—R
(s)-VMI Publishers
Walk Worthy—R
Whitaker House
(s)-WinePress—R
(s)-Word Alive
Yale Univ. Press—R
(s)-Zoe Life Publishing

EVANGELISM/WITNESSING

Aaron Book—R
(s)-ACW Press—R
Ambassador-Emerald—R
(s)-American Binding—R
Anglicans United—R
(s)-Baal Hamon—R
(a)-Baker Books
Baker Trittin
(a)-B & H Publishing
BJU/Journey Forth—R
(s)-Black Forest/Tennessee—R
BMH Books—R
(s)-Booklocker.com—R
(s)-Brentwood—R
Bridge-Logos—R
(s)-Brown Books
Carey Library, Wm.—R

Chapter Two—R
Christian Family—R
Christian Focus—R
Christian Heritage—R
Christian Writer's Ebook—R
Church Growth Inst.
Comfort Publishing—R
(a)-Cook, David C.
(s)-Creation House—R
(s)-CrossHouse—R
CSS Publishing
(s)-DCTS Publishing
Deo Volente
Discovery House—R
Earthen Vessel—R
Editorial Portavoz
Eerdmans Pub., Wm. B.—R
(s)-Elderberry Press
(a)-Emmaus Road—R
(s)-Essence—R
Evangelical Press
Evergreen Press
Fair Havens—R
(s)-Fairway Press—R
Faith Alive
FaithWalk
Father's Press—R
Founders Press
Gollehon Press
Good Book—R
Good News Pub.
Group Publishing
Harrison House
Harvest Day
(a)-Harvest House
Hidden Brook Press—R
(s)-Holy Fire Publishing—R
(s)-IMD Press—R
(s)-Impact Christian—R
(s)-Insight Publishing—R
InterVarsity Press—R
Jebaire Publishing
Judson Press—R
(a)-Kregel—R
Lift Every Voice—R
Lighthouse Publishing—R
Lillenas
Lion and Lamb
Lutheran Univ. Press
(s)-McDougal Publishing—R
Messianic Jewish—R
Monarch Books
(a)-Moody Publishers
NavPress Student—R
Nelson Ignite
(a)-Nelson, Thomas
New Hope—R
(s)-One World Press—R
Pacific Press
Paradise Research—R
Parson Place—R

Pilgrim Press—R
(s)-Pleasant Word—R
Power Publishing—R
(s)-Providence Pub.—R
Randall House
Revival Nation
Rose Publishing
Salt Works—R
Samaritan Press
(s)-Selah Publishing—R
(s)-So. Baptist Press—R
St. Anthony Mess. Press—R
(s)-Star Bible Public.
Still Waters Revival—R
Strang Book Group—R
(s)-Tate Publishing—R
(s)-TEACH Services—R
(s)-Testimony Press
(s)-Trafford Publishing—R
(a)-Tyndale House—R
VBC Publishing
(s)-VMI Publishers
Wesleyan Publishing
(s)-WinePress—R
Woodland Gospel
(s)-Word Alive
W Publishing
Yale Univ. Press—R
(s)-Zoe Life Publishing

EXEGESIS

Aaron Book—R
Abingdon Press
(s)-ACW Press—R
(s)-American Binding—R
(a)-Baker Books
(s)-Black Forest/Tennessee—R
BMH Books—R
(s)-Booklocker.com—R
(s)-Brown Books
Catholic Answers—R
Chapter Two—R
Christian Family—R
Christian Focus—R
Christian Writer's Ebook—R
Cistercian—R
College Press—R
Continuum Intl.—R
CSS Publishing
(a)-Doubleday Relig.—R
Eerdmans Pub., Wm. B.—R
(s)-Elderberry Press
(s)-Essence—R
Evangelical Press
(s)-Fairway Press—R
Greenwood/Praeger
Hendrickson—R
Hidden Brook Press—R
(s)-Holy Fire Publishing—R
(s)-IMD Press—R
(s)-Insight Publishing—R

InterVarsity Press—R
Johns Hopkins—R
(a)-Kregel—R
Lighthouse Publishing—R
(s)-McDougal Publishing—R
Monarch Books
New Leaf
(s)-One World Press—R
P & R Publishing—R
Paradise Research—R
Pauline Books—R
Paulist Press
(s)-Pleasant Word—R
Power Publishing—R
(s)-Providence Pub.—R
Reformation Trust
Rose Publishing
St. Anthony Mess. Press—R
(s)-Star Bible Public.
(s)-Tate Publishing—R
(s)-Trafford Publishing—R
VBC Publishing
(s)-VMI Publishers
Westminster John Knox
(s)-WinePress—R
(s)-Word Alive
Yale Univ. Press—R
(s)-Zoe Life Publishing

EXPOSÉS

Aaron Book—R
(s)-ACW Press—R
(s)-American Binding—R
(a)-Baker Books
(s)-Booklocker.com—R
(s)-Brentwood—R
(s)-Brown Books
Chapter Two—R
Christian Writer's Ebook—R
Eerdmans Pub., Wm. B.—R
(s)-Elderberry Press
(s)-Fairway Press—R
Greenwood/Praeger
Hidden Brook Press—R
(s)-Holy Fire Publishing—R
(s)-Insight Publishing—R
Lighthouse Publishing—R
(s)-One World Press—R
Power Publishing—R
(s)-Providence Pub.—R
Ravenhawk Books—R
(s)-So. Baptist Press—R
(s)-Star Bible Public.
(s)-Trafford Publishing—R
(s)-WinePress—R
(s)-Word Alive
(s)-Zoe Life Publishing

FAITH

Aadeon Publishing—R
Aaron Book—R

Abingdon Press
ACTA Publications
(s)-ACW Press—R
Ambassador Books
Ambassador-Emerald—R
(s)-American Binding—R
(s)-Baal Hamon—R
(a)-Baker Books
Baker Trittin
Baker's Plays—R
(a)-B & H Publishing
Barbour
Bethany House
(s)-Black Forest/Tennessee—R
BMH Books—R
(s)-Booklocker.com—R
Bridge-Logos—R
(s)-Brown Books
Chalice Press
Chapter Two—R
Christian Family—R
Christian Focus—R
Christian Heritage—R
Christian Writer's Ebook—R
Comfort Publishing—R
Continuum Intl.—R
(s)-Creation House—R
(s)-DCTS Publishing
Destiny Image—R
Destiny Image (books)—R
Discovery House—R
(a)-Doubleday Relig.—R
Eerdmans Pub., Wm. B.—R
(s)-Elderberry Press
Eldridge Plays
(a)-Emmaus Road—R
(s)-Essence—R
Evangelical Press
Evergreen Press
(s)-Fairway Press—R
Faith Communications
FaithWalk
(a)-FaithWords
Father's Press—R
Forward Movement
(s)-FruitBearer Pub.
Gollehon Press
Good Book—R
Green Key Books
Greenwood/Praeger
GRQ—R
Grupo Nelson
Guardian Angel
GuidepostsBooks
Halo Publishing
(a)-HarperOne
Harrison House
(a)-Harvest House
Hensley Publishing
Hidden Brook Press—R
(s)-Holy Fire Publishing—R

Howard Books
(s)-IMD Press—R
(s)-Insight Publishing—R
Jebaire Publishing
Jireh Publishing
Judson Press—R
(a)-Kregel—R
Legacy Publishers
Life Changing Media
Lift Every Voice—R
Lighthouse Publishing—R
Lillenas
Lion and Lamb
Loyola Press
Lutheran Univ. Press
Lutterworth Press—R
(s)-McDougal Publishing—R
Mission City Press
Monarch Books
NavPress Student—R
(a)-Nelson, Thomas
New Hope—R
New Seeds—R
(s)-One World Press—R
P & R Publishing—R
Pacific Press
Paradise Research—R
Parson Place—R
Parsons Publishing—R
(s)-Path Pub. in Christ—R
Pauline Books—R
Pflaum Publishing
Pilgrim Press—R
(s)-Pleasant Word—R
Power Publishing—R
(s)-Providence Pub.—R
Quintessential Books—R
Randall House
(a)-Regal
Revival Nation
Rose Publishing
Salt Works—R
(s)-Salvation Publisher—R
Samaritan Press
Scepter Publishers—R
(s)-Selah Publishing—R
St. Anthony Mess. Press—R
St. Pauls/Alba House—R
(s)-Star Bible Public.
Strang Book Group—R
(s)-Synergy Publishers—R
(s)-Tate Publishing—R
(s)-TEACH Services—R
(s)-Testimony Press
(s)-Trafford Publishing—R
(a)-Tyndale House—R
UMI Publishing—R
VBC Publishing
Virginia Pines Press
(s)-VMI Publishers
(a)-WaterBrook Press—R

Wesleyan Publishing
Whitaker House
White Stone Books—R
(s)-WinePress—R
(s)-Word Alive
W Publishing
Youth Specialties
(s)-Zoe Life Publishing

FAMILY LIFE
Aaron Book—R
Abingdon Press
ACTA Publications
(s)-ACW Press—R
Ambassador Books
Ambassador-Emerald—R
(s)-American Binding—R
(s)-Baal Hamon—R
(a)-Baker Books
Baker Trittin
Baker's Plays—R
Barbour
Beacon Hill Press—R
BelleBooks—R
Bethany House
Big Idea
BJU/Journey Forth—R
(s)-Black Forest/Tennessee—R
BMH Books—R
(s)-Booklocker.com—R
Boyds Mills Press—R
(s)-Brentwood—R
Bridge-Logos—R
(s)-Brown Books
CarePoint Publishing—R
Chalice Press
Chapter Two—R
Christian Family—R
Christian Focus—R
Christian Writer's Ebook—R
Cladach Publishing
College Press—R
Comfort Publishing—R
Conari Press
Concordia
(a)-Cook, David C.
(s)-Creation House—R
Dabbling Mum Press
(s)-DCTS Publishing
Destiny Image—R
Destiny Image (books)—R
Dimensions for Living
Discovery House—R
E-Digital Books
Editorial Portavoz
Eerdmans Pub., Wm. B.—R
(s)-Elderberry Press
Eldridge Plays
(a)-Emmaus Road—R
(s)-Essence—R
Evangelical Press

Evergreen Press
Extreme Diva
Fair Havens—R
(s)-Fairway Press—R
Faith Communications
FaithWalk
(a)-FaithWords
FamilyLife (books)—R
Father's Press—R
(a)-Focus on the Family—R
Forward Movement
(s)-FruitBearer Pub.
Greenwood/Praeger
Group Publishing
Grupo Nelson
Guardian Angel
GuidepostsBooks
Halo Publishing
Hannibal Books
(a)-HarperOne
Harrison House
(a)-Harvest House
Health Commun.
Hensley Publishing
Hidden Brook Press—R
(s)-Holy Fire Publishing—R
Hope Publishing—R
Howard Books
Ideals/Children
(s)-IMD Press—R
(s)-Insight Publishing—R
Jebaire Publishing
Jireh Publishing
Judson Press—R
(a)-Kregel—R
Langmarc
(s)-Leading Lady
Legacy Press—R
Life Changing Media
Life Cycle Books—R
Lift Every Voice—R
Lighthouse Publishing—R
Liguori Public.—R
Lillenas
Lion and Lamb
Loyola Press
Lutterworth Press—R
(s)-McDougal Publishing—R
Millennium III—R
Monarch Books
MOPS Intl.
MountainView
Nelson Ignite
(a)-Nelson, Thomas
New Hope—R
(s)-One World Press—R
Our Sunday Visitor—R
P & R Publishing—R
Pacific Press
(s)-Path Pub. in Christ—R
Pauline Books—R

Pilgrim Press—R
(s)-Pleasant Word—R
Power Publishing—R
(s)-Providence Pub.—R
(s)-Quiet Waters
Quintessential Books—R
Randall House
(s)-Recovery Commun.
(a)-Regal
(s)-Salvation Publisher—R
Samaritan Press
(s)-Selah Publishing—R
Sheed & Ward—R
(s)-So. Baptist Press—R
St. Anthony Mess. Press—R
(s)-Star Bible Public.
Starik Publishing
Still Waters Revival—R
Strang Book Group—R
(s)-Synergy Publishers—R
(s)-Tate Publishing—R
(s)-TEACH Services—R
(s)-Testimony Press
Torch Legacy
(s)-Trafford Publishing—R
(a)-Tyndale House—R
VBC Publishing
(s)-VMI Publishers
(a)-WaterBrook Press—R
Whitaker House
White Stone Books—R
(s)-WinePress—R
Woodland Gospel
(s)-Word Alive
W Publishing
(s)-Zoe Life Publishing

FICTION: ADULT/GENERAL

Aaron Book—R
Ambassador-Emerald—R
(s)-American Binding—R
(a)-Ballantine
(a)-B & H Publishing
Blue Dolphin
(s)-Book Publishers—R
(s)-Brown Books
Cladach Publishing
Comfort Publishing—R
(s)-Creation House—R
(s)-Essence—R
Fair Havens—R
(a)-FaithWords
Father's Press—R
Fell, Frederick—R
Friends United Press
Guernica Editions—R
(s)-Holy Fire Publishing—R
Howard Books
Invisible College Press
(a)-Kregel—R
Lifesong Publishers
(s)-LifeVest Publishing

Lighthouse Publishing—R
MountainView
(a)-Multnomah
(a)-Nelson, Fiction, Thomas
(a)-One World/Ballantine
P & R Publishing—R
Parson Place—R
(s)-Providence Pub.—R
Quintessential Books—R
Ravenhawk Books—R
Salt Works—R
Samaritan Press
Steeple Hill/Single Title
Strang Book Group—R
Sweetheart Romances
(s)-Trafford Publishing—R
Treble Heart Books—R
Virtual Tales
Whitaker House
White Stone Books—R
Xyzzy Press

FICTION: ADULT/RELIGIOUS

Aaron Book—R
Abingdon Press
(s)-ACW Press—R
Adams Media
Ambassador Books
Ambassador-Emerald—R
(s)-American Binding—R
(s)-Baal Hamon—R
(a)-Baker Books
Baker's Plays—R
(a)-Ballantine
(a)-B & H Publishing
Barbour
BelleBooks—R
Bethany House
(s)-Black Forest/Tennessee—R
(s)-Booklocker.com—R
(s)-Book Publishers—R
Branden Publishing—R
Bridge-Logos—R
(s)-Brown Books
Capstone Fiction—R
Christian Focus—R
Christian Liberty Press
Christian Writer's Ebook—R
Cladach Publishing
Comfort Publishing—R
(s)-Creation House—R
(s)-CrossHouse—R
Destiny Image—R
Destiny Image (books)—R
DiskUs Publishing
(a)-Doubleday Relig.—R
E-Digital Books
Eerdmans Pub., Wm. B.—R
(s)-Elderberry Press
Elijah Press
Emerald Pointe

(s)-Essence—R
Evergreen Press
(s)-Fairway Press—R
FaithWalk
(a)-FaithWords
Father's Press—R
(a)-Focus on the Family—R
GuidepostsBooks
Hannibal Books
(a)-HarperOne
(a)-HeartQuest
Heartsong Presents
HeartSpring Pub.—R
Hidden Brook Press—R
His Work Christian Pub.
(s)-Holy Fire Publishing—R
Howard Books
(s)-IMD Press—R
(s)-Insight Publishing—R
Invisible College Press
Jireh Publishing
KNB Publications
(a)-Kregel—R
(s)-LifeVest Publishing
Lift Every Voice—R
Lighthouse Publishing—R
Lighthouse Trails—R
Lillenas
Lion and Lamb
Love Inspired
Love Inspired Historical
(s)-McDougal Publishing—R
Messianic Jewish—R
(a)-Moody Publishers
MountainView
Mt. Olive College Press
(a)-Multnomah
NavPress
(a)-Nelson, Fiction, Thomas
New Seeds—R
(s)-One World Press—R
(a)-One World/Ballantine
P & R Publishing—R
Pacific Press
Parson Place—R
Parsons Publishing—R
(s)-Path Pub. in Christ—R
(s)-Path Publishing—R
(s)-Pleasant Word—R
Power Publishing—R
PREP Publishing—R
(s)-Providence Pub.—R
Quintessential Books—R
Randall House
Revell
Salt Works—R
Samaritan Press
Scepter Publishers—R
(s)-Selah Publishing—R
(s)-Self Publish Press—R
(s)-Star Bible Public.
Starik Publishing

Steeple Hill/Single Title
Strang Book Group—R
Sweetheart Romances
(s)-Tate Publishing—R
(s)-Testimony Press
(s)-Trafford Publishing—R
Treble Heart Books—R
Tsaba House
Vintage Romance
Virginia Pines Press
Virtual Tales
Vision Forum
(s)-VMI Publishers
Walk Worthy—R
(a)-WaterBrook Press—R
Whitaker House
White Rose—R
White Stone Books—R
(s)-WinePress—R
(s)-Word Alive
(s)-Xulon Press—R
Xyzzy Press

FICTION: ADVENTURE

Aaron Book—R
(s)-ACW Press—R
Ambassador Books
Ambassador-Emerald—R
(s)-American Binding—R
Atheneum/Yg. Readers
(a)-Baker Books
Baker Trittin
Baker's Plays—R
Barbour
BJU/Journey Forth—R
(s)-Black Forest/Tennessee—R
(s)-Booklocker.com—R
(s)-Book Publishers—R
Boyds Mills Press—R
(s)-Brentwood—R
Bridge-Logos—R
(s)-Brown Books
Christian Ed. Pub.
Christian Family—R
Christian Writer's Ebook—R
(s)-Creation House—R
DiskUs Publishing
E-Digital Books
Eerdmans/Yg. Readers
(s)-Elderberry Press
(s)-Essence—R
Evergreen Press
Fair Havens—R
(s)-Fairway Press—R
FaithWalk
Father's Press—R
(a)-Harvest House
Hidden Brook Press—R
(s)-Holy Fire Publishing—R
Howard Books
Ideals Publications

(s)-Insight Publishing—R
Kaleidoscope Press—R
Knight George Pub.
(s)-LifeVest Publishing
Lift Every Voice—R
Lighthouse Publishing—R
Lion and Lamb
Messianic Jewish—R
Mission City Press
MountainView
(a)-Multnomah
(a)-Nelson, Fiction, Thomas
(s)-One World Press—R
(a)-One World/Ballantine
Parson Place—R
Parsons Publishing—R
(s)-Path Publishing—R
Pauline Kids
(s)-Pleasant Word—R
PREP Publishing—R
Quintessential Books—R
Randall House
Ravenhawk Books—R
Salt Works—R
Samaritan Press
(s)-Selah Publishing—R
(s)-Self Publish Press—R
(s)-So. Baptist Press—R
Starik Publishing
Strang Book Group—R
(s)-Tate Publishing—R
(s)-Testimony Press
(s)-Trafford Publishing—R
Treble Heart Books—R
Virginia Pines Press
(s)-VMI Publishers
(a)-WaterBrook Press—R
White Stone Books—R
(s)-WinePress—R

FICTION: ALLEGORY

Aaron Book—R
(s)-ACW Press—R
Ambassador-Emerald—R
(s)-American Binding—R
Atheneum/Yg. Readers
(a)-Baker Books
Baker Trittin
Baker's Plays—R
Barbour
(s)-Black Forest/Tennessee—R
(s)-Booklocker.com—R
Bridge-Logos—R
(s)-Brown Books
Capstone Fiction—R
Christian Family—R
Christian Writer's Ebook—R
(s)-Creation House—R
Destiny Image (books)—R
(s)-Elderberry Press
(s)-Essence—R
Evergreen Press

(s)-Fairway Press—R
Hidden Brook Press—R
(s)-Holy Fire Publishing—R
(s)-Insight Publishing—R
(s)-LifeVest Publishing
Lighthouse Publishing—R
Lion and Lamb
(a)-Multnomah
New Seeds—R
(s)-One World Press—R
P & R Publishing—R
(s)-Pleasant Word—R
Randall House
Realms
Reformation Trust
Salt Works—R
Samaritan Press
(s)-Selah Publishing—R
Strang Book Group—R
(s)-Tate Publishing—R
(s)-TEACH Services—R
(s)-Trafford Publishing—R
(s)-VMI Publishers
White Stone Books—R
Wilshire Book—R
(s)-WinePress—R

FICTION: BIBLICAL

Aaron Book—R
Abingdon Press
(s)-ACW Press—R
Ambassador-Emerald—R
(s)-American Binding—R
Atheneum/Yg. Readers
(a)-Baker Books
Baker Trittin
Baker's Plays—R
(s)-Black Forest/Tennessee—R
(s)-Booklocker.com—R
(s)-Brentwood—R
Bridge-Logos—R
(s)-Brown Books
Capstone Fiction—R
CharismaKids
Christian Family—R
Christian Writer's Ebook—R
Cladach Publishing
College Press—R
Comfort Publishing—R
(s)-Creation House—R
Destiny Image—R
Destiny Image (books)—R
Eerdmans Pub., Wm. B.—R
Eerdmans/Yg. Readers
(s)-Elderberry Press
(s)-Essence—R
Evergreen Press
Fair Havens—R
(s)-Fairway Press—R
Father's Press—R
Friends United Press
GuidepostsBooks

Hannibal Books
Hidden Brook Press—R
(s)-Holy Fire Publishing—R
Howard Books
(s)-IMD Press—R
(s)-Insight Publishing—R
(s)-Kindred Books—R
Lifesong Publishers
(s)-LifeVest Publishing
Lift Every Voice—R
Lighthouse Publishing—R
Lillenas
Lion and Lamb
Love Inspired Historical
Messianic Jewish—R
Mission City Press
(a)-Moody Publishers
(a)-Multnomah
NavPress
NavPress Student—R
New Seeds—R
(s)-One World Press—R
Pacific Press
Parsons Publishing—R
Pauline Kids
(s)-Pleasant Word—R
Power Publishing—R
(s)-Providence Pub.—R
Quintessential Books—R
Randall House
Realms
Reformation Trust
Salt Works—R
Samaritan Press
(s)-Self Publish Press—R
(s)-So. Baptist Press—R
Steeple Hill/Single Title
Strang Book Group—R
(s)-Tate Publishing—R
(s)-Trafford Publishing—R
(s)-VMI Publishers
Walk Worthy—R
(a)-WaterBrook Press—R
White Stone Books—R
(s)-WinePress—R

FICTION: CHICK LIT

Aaron Book—R
(s)-ACW Press—R
Ambassador Books
Atheneum/Yg. Readers
Baker's Plays—R
BelleBooks—R
(s)-Black Forest/Tennessee—R
(s)-Booklocker.com—R
(s)-Brown Books
By Grace Publications
Christian Writer's Ebook—R
(s)-Creation House—R
(s)-Elderberry Press
(s)-Essence—R

(a)-HeartQuest
Hidden Brook Press—R
(s)-Holy Fire Publishing—R
(s)-Insight Publishing—R
(s)-LifeVest Publishing
Lighthouse Publishing—R
Lion and Lamb
Little Lauren Books
Love Inspired Suspense
(a)-Multnomah
NavPress Student—R
(a)-Nelson, Fiction, Thomas
(s)-One World Press—R
(s)-Pleasant Word—R
Randall House
Ravenhawk Books—R
Steeple Hill/Single Title
Strang Book Group—R
(s)-Trafford Publishing—R
(s)-VMI Publishers
(a)-WaterBrook Press—R
Whitaker House
White Stone Books—R
(s)-WinePress—R

FICTION: CHILDREN'S PICTURE BOOKS

Aaron Book—R
Atheneum/Yg. Readers
(s)-Black Forest/Tennessee—R
(s)-Booklocker.com—R
(s)-Book Publishers—R
Boyds Mills Press—R
(s)-Brown Books
(s)-CrossHouse—R
Eerdmans/Yg. Readers
(s)-Essence—R
Father's Press—R
Guardian Angel
Halo Publishing
His Work Christian Pub.
(s)-Holy Fire Publishing—R
Ideals Publications
Illumination Arts
(s)-IMD Press—R
Knight George Pub.
(a)-Kregel—R
(a)-Kregel Kidzone
Legacy Press—R
(s)-LifeVest Publishing
Lighthouse Publishing—R
Messianic Jewish—R
P & R Publishing—R
Pauline Books—R
Pauline Kids
Pelican Publishing—R
(s)-Providence Pub.—R
Putnam/Young Readers
Salt Works—R
Salty's Books
Samaritan Press
White Stone Books—R

(s)-WinePress—R

FICTION: CONTEMPORARY

Aaron Book—R
(s)-ACW Press—R
Ambassador Books
(s)-American Binding—R
Atheneum/Yg. Readers
(a)-Avon Inspire
(a)-Baker Books
Baker Trittin
Baker's Plays—R
(a)-Ballantine
(a)-B & H Publishing
Barbour
BelleBooks—R
Bethany House
BJU/Journey Forth—R
(s)-Black Forest/Tennessee—R
(s)-Booklocker.com—R
Branden Publishing—R
(s)-Brentwood—R
(s)-Brown Books
Capstone Fiction—R
CharismaKids
Christian Ed. Pub.
Christian Writer's Ebook—R
Cladach Publishing
Comfort Publishing—R
(s)-Creation House—R
Destiny Image—R
Destiny Image (books)—R
DiskUs Publishing
E-Digital Books
Eerdmans/Yg. Readers
(s)-Elderberry Press
Emerald Pointe
(s)-Essence—R
(s)-Fairway Press—R
FaithWalk
(a)-FaithWords
Fell, Frederick—R
(a)-Focus on the Family—R
(a)-Harvest House
(a)-HeartQuest
Heartsong Presents
Hidden Brook Press—R
(s)-Holy Fire Publishing—R
Howard Books
(s)-Insight Publishing—R
Invisible College Press
Jireh Publishing
(a)-Kregel—R
(s)-LifeVest Publishing
Lift Every Voice—R
Lighthouse Publishing—R
Lillenas
Lion and Lamb
Love Inspired
(s)-McDougal Publishing—R
Mission City Press

(a)-Moody Publishers
MountainView
(a)-Multnomah
NavPress
NavPress Student—R
(a)-Nelson, Fiction, Thomas
(s)-One World Press—R
(a)-One World/Ballantine
P & R Publishing—R
(s)-Pleasant Word—R
Putnam/Young Readers
Randall House
Ravenhawk Books—R
Revell
Salt Works—R
Samaritan Press
(s)-Self Publish Press—R
(s)-So. Baptist Press—R
Steeple Hill/Single Title
Strang Book Group—R
(s)-Tate Publishing—R
(s)-Testimony Press
Third World Press—R
(s)-Trafford Publishing—R
Treble Heart Books—R
(a)-Tyndale House—R
(s)-VMI Publishers
Walk Worthy—R
(a)-WaterBrook Press—R
Whitaker House
White Stone Books—R
(s)-WinePress—R

FICTION: COZY MYSTERIES*

Aaron Book—R
(s)-ACW Press—R
(s)-Black Forest/Tennessee—R
(s)-Brown Books
(s)-Essence—R
Heartsong/Mysteries
(s)-Holy Fire Publishing—R
(s)-Insight Publishing—R
(a)-Kregel—R
Lighthouse Publishing—R
MountainView
(s)-Pleasant Word—R
Strang Book Group—R
(s)-Trafford Publishing—R
Treble Heart Books—R
(s)-WinePress—R

FICTION: ETHNIC

Aaron Book—R
(s)-ACW Press—R
(s)-American Binding—R
Atheneum/Yg. Readers
(a)-Baker Books
Baker Trittin
Baker's Plays—R
(a)-Ballantine
(s)-Black Forest/Tennessee—R

(s)-Booklocker.com—R
Boyds Mills Press—R
Branden Publishing—R
(s)-Brown Books
Christian Writer's Ebook—R
Comfort Publishing—R
Destiny Image—R
DiskUs Publishing
E-Digital Books
(s)-Elderberry Press
(s)-Essence—R
Evergreen Press
(s)-Fairway Press—R
(a)-Focus on the Family—R
Guernica Editions—R
Hidden Brook Press—R
(s)-Holy Fire Publishing—R
Howard Books
(s)-IMD Press—R
(s)-Insight Publishing—R
Kaleidoscope Press—R
(s)-LifeVest Publishing
Lift Every Voice—R
Lighthouse Publishing—R
(a)-Multnomah
(s)-One World Press—R
(a)-One World/Ballantine
(s)-Pleasant Word—R
Putnam/Young Readers
Salt Works—R
Samaritan Press
Strang Book Group—R
(s)-Tate Publishing—R
(s)-Testimony Press
Third World Press—R
(s)-Trafford Publishing—R
(s)-VMI Publishers
Walk Worthy—R
White Stone Books—R
(s)-WinePress—R

FICTION: FABLES/PARABLES

Aaron Book—R
(s)-ACW Press—R
(s)-American Binding—R
Baker's Plays—R
(s)-Black Forest/Tennessee—R
Blue Dolphin
(s)-Booklocker.com—R
(s)-Brown Books
(s)-Elderberry Press
(s)-Essence—R
(a)-HarperOne
Hidden Brook Press—R
(s)-Holy Fire Publishing—R
(s)-Insight Publishing—R
(s)-LifeVest Publishing
Lighthouse Publishing—R
(s)-One World Press—R
(s)-Pleasant Word—R
Quintessential Books—R

Randall House
Resource Public.
Salt Works—R
Samaritan Press
(s)-Tate Publishing—R
(s)-Trafford Publishing—R
(s)-VMI Publishers
(s)-WinePress—R

FICTION: FANTASY

Aaron Book—R
(s)-ACW Press—R
(s)-American Binding—R
AMG Publishers
Atheneum/Yg. Readers
Baker Trittin
Baker's Plays—R
(a)-Ballantine
Barbour
BelleBooks—R
Big Idea
BJU/Journey Forth—R
(s)-Black Forest/Tennessee—R
(s)-Booklocker.com—R
(s)-Brown Books
Capstone Fiction—R
Christian Writer's Ebook—R
Comfort Publishing—R
(s)-Creation House—R
Destiny Image—R
Destiny Image (books)—R
DiskUs Publishing
Dover Publications—R
E-Digital Books
Eerdmans Pub., Wm. B.—R
(s)-Elderberry Press
(s)-Essence—R
Evergreen Press
(s)-Fairway Press—R
(a)-Harvest House
Hidden Brook Press—R
(s)-Holy Fire Publishing—R
(s)-Insight Publishing—R
Invisible College Press
(s)-LifeVest Publishing
Lighthouse Publishing—R
Mission City Press
MountainView
(a)-Multnomah
NavPress Student—R
(a)-Nelson, Fiction, Thomas
(s)-One World Press—R
P & R Publishing—R
Parsons Publishing—R
(s)-Pleasant Word—R
Putnam/Young Readers
Ravenhawk Books—R
Realms
Samaritan Press
Starik Publishing
Strang Book Group—R
(s)-Tate Publishing—R

(s)-Trafford Publishing—R
Treble Heart Books—R
(s)-VMI Publishers
(a)-WaterBrook Press—R
Whitaker House
(s)-WinePress—R

FICTION: FRONTIER

Aaron Book—R
(s)-ACW Press—R
(s)-American Binding—R
Atheneum/Yg. Readers
(a)-Baker Books
Baker Trittin
Baker's Plays—R
Bethany House
BJU/Journey Forth—R
(s)-Black Forest/Tennessee—R
(s)-Booklocker.com—R
(s)-Brentwood—R
(s)-Brown Books
Christian Writer's Ebook—R
Cladach Publishing
Comfort Publishing—R
(s)-Elderberry Press
(s)-Essence—R
(s)-Fairway Press—R
Father's Press—R
Guardian Angel
(a)-Harvest House
Hidden Brook Press—R
(s)-Holy Fire Publishing—R
(s)-Insight Publishing—R
Kaleidoscope Press—R
(s)-LifeVest Publishing
Lighthouse Publishing—R
Lion and Lamb
Mission City Press
MountainView
(a)-Multnomah
(s)-One World Press—R
P & R Publishing—R
Parson Place—R
(s)-Pleasant Word—R
Randall House
Ravenhawk Books—R
Samaritan Press
(s)-Self Publish Press—R
(s)-So. Baptist Press—R
Strang Book Group—R
(s)-Tate Publishing—R
(s)-Trafford Publishing—R
Treble Heart Books—R
(s)-VMI Publishers
Whitaker House
(s)-WinePress—R

FICTION: FRONTIER/ ROMANCE

Aaron Book—R
(s)-ACW Press—R

(s)-American Binding—R
(a)-Baker Books
Baker's Plays—R
Barbour
Bethany House
(s)-Black Forest/Tennessee—R
(s)-Booklocker.com—R
(s)-Brentwood—R
(s)-Brown Books
Christian Writer's Ebook—R
Comfort Publishing—R
(s)-Elderberry Press
(s)-Essence—R
(s)-Fairway Press—R
Father's Press—R
(a)-Harvest House
Heartsong Presents
Hidden Brook Press—R
(s)-Holy Fire Publishing—R
(s)-Insight Publishing—R
(s)-LifeVest Publishing
Lighthouse Publishing—R
Love Inspired Historical
MoreThanNovellas
MountainView
(a)-Multnomah
(s)-One World Press—R
Parson Place—R
(s)-Pleasant Word—R
Randall House
Ravenhawk Books—R
Samaritan Press
(s)-Self Publish Press—R
(s)-So. Baptist Press—R
Steeple Hill/Single Title
Strang Book Group—R
Sweetheart Romances
(s)-Tate Publishing—R
(s)-Trafford Publishing—R
Treble Heart Books—R
Vintage Romance
(s)-VMI Publishers
Whitaker House
White Rose—R
White Stone Books—R
(s)-WinePress—R

FICTION: HISTORICAL

Aaron Book—R
Abingdon Press
(s)-ACW Press—R
Ambassador Books
Ambassador-Emerald—R
(s)-American Binding—R
Atheneum/Yg. Readers
(a)-Avon Inspire
(a)-Baker Books
Baker Trittin
Baker's Plays—R
(a)-Ballantine
Bethany House

BJU/Journey Forth—R
(s)-Black Forest/Tennessee—R
Blue Dolphin
(s)-Booklocker.com—R
(s)-Book Publishers—R
Boyds Mills Press—R
Branden Publishing—R
(s)-Brentwood—R
Bridge-Logos—R
(s)-Brown Books
Capstone Fiction—R
CharismaKids
Christian Family—R
Christian Liberty Press
Christian Writer's Ebook—R
Comfort Publishing—R
DiskUs Publishing
Dove Inspirational—R
E-Digital Books
Eerdmans Pub., Wm. B.—R
Eerdmans/Yg. Readers
(s)-Elderberry Press
Emerald Pointe
(s)-Essence—R
Fair Havens—R
(s)-Fairway Press—R
(a)-FaithWords
Father's Press—R
(a)-Focus on the Family—R
Hannibal Books
(a)-Harvest House
(a)-HeartQuest
Hidden Brook Press—R
(s)-Holy Fire Publishing—R
Howard Books
(s)-Insight Publishing—R
(a)-Kregel—R
(s)-LifeVest Publishing
Lift Every Voice—R
Lighthouse Publishing—R
Mission City Press
(a)-Moody Publishers
MountainView
(a)-Multnomah
NavPress
(a)-Nelson, Fiction, Thomas
New Canaan—R
(s)-One World Press—R
(a)-One World/Ballantine
P & R Publishing—R
Parson Place—R
Parsons Publishing—R
Pauline Kids
(s)-Pleasant Word—R
(s)-Providence Pub.—R
Putnam/Young Readers
Quintessential Books—R
Randall House
Ravenhawk Books—R
Realms
Reformation Trust

Revell
Samaritan Press
(s)-Self Publish Press—R
(s)-So. Baptist Press—R
Strang Book Group—R
(s)-Tate Publishing—R
(s)-TEACH Services—R
(s)-Testimony Press
Third World Press—R
(s)-Trafford Publishing—R
Treble Heart Books—R
Vintage Romance
Vision Forum
(s)-VMI Publishers
(a)-WaterBrook Press—R
Whitaker House
White Stone Books—R
(s)-WinePress—R

FICTION: HISTORICAL/ ROMANCE

Aaron Book—R
Abingdon Press
(s)-ACW Press—R
Ambassador-Emerald—R
(s)-American Binding—R
(a)-Baker Books
Baker's Plays—R
(a)-B & H Publishing
Barbour
Bethany House
(s)-Black Forest/Tennessee—R
(s)-Booklocker.com—R
(s)-Brentwood—R
(s)-Brown Books
Christian Writer's Ebook—R
Comfort Publishing—R
(s)-Elderberry Press
Emerald Pointe
(s)-Essence—R
(s)-Fairway Press—R
Father's Press—R
Hannibal Books
(a)-Harvest House
Heartsong Presents
Hidden Brook Press—R
(s)-Holy Fire Publishing—R
(s)-Insight Publishing—R
(a)-Kregel—R
(s)-LifeVest Publishing
Lift Every Voice—R
Lighthouse Publishing—R
Love Inspired Historical
MoreThanNovellas
MountainView
(a)-Multnomah
(a)-Nelson, Fiction, Thomas
(s)-One World Press—R
Parson Place—R
(s)-Pleasant Word—R
PREP Publishing—R

Randall House
Ravenhawk Books—R
(s)-Self Publish Press—R
(s)-So. Baptist Press—R
Steeple Hill/Single Title
Strang Book Group—R
Sweetheart Romances
(s)-Tate Publishing—R
(s)-Trafford Publishing—R
Treble Heart Books—R
(a)-Tyndale House—R
Vintage Romance
(s)-VMI Publishers
(a)-WaterBrook Press—R
Whitaker House
White Rose—R
White Stone Books—R
(s)-WinePress—R

FICTION: HUMOR

Aaron Book—R
(s)-ACW Press—R
Ambassador Books
(s)-American Binding—R
Atheneum/Yg. Readers
(a)-Baker Books
Baker Trittin
Baker's Plays—R
(a)-Ballantine
BelleBooks—R
Big Idea
BJU/Journey Forth—R
(s)-Black Forest/Tennessee—R
(s)-Booklocker.com—R
Boyds Mills Press—R
(s)-Brown Books
Christian Focus—R
Christian Writer's Ebook—R
(s)-Creation House—R
DiskUs Publishing
E-Digital Books
Eerdmans/Yg. Readers
(s)-Elderberry Press
(s)-Essence—R
Evergreen Press
(s)-Fairway Press—R
(a)-FaithWords
Hidden Brook Press—R
His Work Christian Pub.
(s)-Holy Fire Publishing—R
(s)-Insight Publishing—R
Kaleidoscope Press—R
(a)-Kregel—R
(s)-LifeVest Publishing
Lighthouse Publishing—R
Lillenas
Lion and Lamb
MountainView
(a)-Multnomah
NavPress Student—R
(s)-One World Press—R

(a)-One World/Ballantine
P & R Publishing—R
Parson Place—R
Parsons Publishing—R
(s)-Pleasant Word—R
PREP Publishing—R
Putnam/Young Readers
Quintessential Books—R
Randall House
Ravenhawk Books—R
Salt Works—R
Samaritan Press
(s)-Selah Publishing—R
Strang Book Group—R
(s)-Tate Publishing—R
(s)-Trafford Publishing—R
Treble Heart Books—R
(s)-VMI Publishers
White Stone Books—R
(s)-WinePress—R

FICTION: JUVENILE (Ages 8-12)

Aaron Book—R
(s)-ACW Press—R
Ambassador Books
(s)-American Binding—R
Atheneum/Yg. Readers
(a)-Avon Inspire
(s)-Baal Hamon—R
(a)-Baker Books
Baker Trittin
Barbour
BelleBooks—R
Big Idea
BJU/Journey Forth—R
(s)-Black Forest/Tennessee—R
Blue Dolphin
(s)-Booklocker.com—R
(s)-Book Publishers—R
Boyds Mills Press—R
Branden Publishing—R
(s)-Brown Books
Carson-Dellosa
Christian Focus—R
Comfort Publishing—R
(s)-Creation House—R
(s)-CrossHouse—R
(s)-Dean Press, Robbie—R
DiskUs Publishing
Dover Publications—R
E-Digital Books
Eerdmans Pub., Wm. B.—R
Eerdmans/Yg. Readers
(s)-Elderberry Press
(s)-Essence—R
Evergreen Press
Fair Havens—R
(s)-Fairway Press—R
Guardian Angel
Halo Publishing

Hidden Brook Press—R
His Work Christian Pub.
(s)-Holy Fire Publishing—R
Ideals Publications
(s)-Insight Publishing—R
Kaleidoscope Press—R
(s)-Kindred Books—R
(a)-Kregel—R
(a)-Kregel Kidzone
Lifesong Publishers
(s)-LifeVest Publishing
Lift Every Voice—R
Lighthouse Publishing—R
Lion and Lamb
Mission City Press
(a)-Moody Publishers
New Canaan—R
(s)-One World Press—R
P & R Publishing—R
Pacific Press
Parson Place—R
Pauline Books—R
Pauline Kids
Pelican Publishing—R
(s)-Pleasant Word—R
Power Publishing—R
(s)-Providence Pub.—R
Putnam/Young Readers
Reformation Trust
Salt Works—R
Salty's Books
Samaritan Press
(s)-Selah Publishing—R
(s)-Self Publish Press—R
Standard Publishing
Strang Book Group—R
(s)-Tate Publishing—R
(s)-TEACH Services—R
(s)-Testimony Press
Third World Press—R
(s)-Trafford Publishing—R
(a)-Tyndale House—R
Vintage Romance
(s)-VMI Publishers
Walk Worthy—R
White Stone Books—R
(s)-WinePress—R
(s)-Word Alive

FICTION: LITERARY

Aaron Book—R
(s)-ACW Press—R
Ambassador Books
(s)-American Binding—R
Atheneum/Yg. Readers
(a)-Baker Books
Baker's Plays—R
(a)-Ballantine
Bethany House
(s)-Black Forest/Tennessee—R
(s)-Booklocker.com—R

Boyds Mills Press—R
Branden Publishing—R
(s)-Brown Books
Christian Writer's Ebook—R
Cladach Publishing
DiskUs Publishing
Dover Publications—R
E-Digital Books
Eerdmans Pub., Wm. B.—R
Eerdmans/Yg. Readers
(s)-Elderberry Press
(s)-Essence—R
(s)-Fairway Press—R
FaithWalk
(a)-FaithWords
(a)-Focus on the Family—R
Guernica Editions—R
(a)-HarperOne
Hidden Brook Press—R
(s)-Holy Fire Publishing—R
(s)-Insight Publishing—R
Invisible College Press
(s)-LifeVest Publishing
Lighthouse Publishing—R
(a)-Moody Publishers
(a)-Multnomah
NavPress
(a)-Nelson, Fiction, Thomas
(s)-One World Press—R
(a)-One World/Ballantine
P & R Publishing—R
Pauline Books—R
(s)-Pleasant Word—R
(s)-Providence Pub.—R
Putnam/Young Readers
Quintessential Books—R
Ravenhawk Books—R
Salt Works—R
(s)-Self Publish Press—R
Skysong Press
Strang Book Group—R
(s)-Tate Publishing—R
(s)-Testimony Press
Third World Press—R
(s)-Trafford Publishing—R
Virginia Pines Press
(s)-VMI Publishers
Walk Worthy—R
(a)-WaterBrook Press—R
White Stone Books—R
(s)-WinePress—R

FICTION: MYSTERY/ ROMANCE

Aaron Book—R
(s)-ACW Press—R
Ambassador-Emerald—R
(s)-American Binding—R
(a)-Baker Books
Baker's Plays—R
(a)-Ballantine

(a)-B & H Publishing
Barbour
Bethany House
(s)-Black Forest/Tennessee—R
(s)-Booklocker.com—R
(s)-Brentwood—R
(s)-Brown Books
Christian Writer's Ebook—R
Comfort Publishing—R
Destiny Image—R
(s)-Elderberry Press
(s)-Essence—R
(s)-Fairway Press—R
Father's Press—R
GuidepostsBooks
Heartsong/Mysteries
Hidden Brook Press—R
(s)-Holy Fire Publishing—R
Howard Books
(s)-Insight Publishing—R
(a)-Kregel—R
(s)-LifeVest Publishing
Lift Every Voice—R
Lighthouse Publishing—R
Little Lauren Books
Love Inspired Suspense
MoreThanNovellas
MountainView
(a)-Multnomah
(a)-Nelson, Fiction, Thomas
(s)-One World Press—R
Parson Place—R
(s)-Pleasant Word—R
PREP Publishing—R
Randall House
(s)-Selah Publishing—R
(s)-Self Publish Press—R
(s)-So. Baptist Press—R
Starik Publishing
Steeple Hill/Single Title
Strang Book Group—R
Sweetheart Romances
(s)-Tate Publishing—R
(s)-Trafford Publishing—R
Treble Heart Books—R
Vintage Romance
(s)-VMI Publishers
White Rose—R
White Stone Books—R
(s)-WinePress—R

FICTION: MYSTERY/ SUSPENSE

Aaron Book—R
(s)-ACW Press—R
Ambassador Books
Ambassador-Emerald—R
(s)-American Binding—R
(a)-Avon Inspire
(a)-Baker Books
Baker's Plays—R

(a)-Ballantine
(a)-B & H Publishing
Bethany House
(s)-Black Forest/Tennessee—R
Blue Dolphin
(s)-Booklocker.com—R
(s)-Brown Books
Capstone Fiction—R
Christian Ed. Pub.
Christian Focus—R
Christian Writer's Ebook—R
Comfort Publishing—R
(s)-Creation House—R
DiskUs Publishing
E-Digital Books
Eerdmans/Yg. Readers
(s)-Elderberry Press
(s)-Essence—R
(s)-Fairway Press—R
Father's Press—R
(a)-Focus on the Family—R
GuidepostsBooks
(a)-HeartQuest
Heartsong/Mysteries
Hidden Brook Press—R
His Work Christian Pub.
(s)-Holy Fire Publishing—R
Howard Books
(s)-Insight Publishing—R
Invisible College Press
Jireh Publishing
(a)-Kregel—R
(s)-LifeVest Publishing
Lift Every Voice—R
Lighthouse Publishing—R
Love Inspired Suspense
Mission City Press
(a)-Moody Publishers
MountainView
(a)-Multnomah
(a)-Nelson, Fiction, Thomas
(s)-One World Press—R
(a)-One World/Ballantine
Parson Place—R
Parsons Publishing—R
(s)-Pleasant Word—R
PREP Publishing—R
(s)-Providence Pub.—R
Putnam/Young Readers
Quintessential Books—R
Ravenhawk Books—R
Revell
Salt Works—R
(s)-Selah Publishing—R
(s)-Self Publish Press—R
Starik Publishing
Steeple Hill/Single Title
Strang Book Group—R
(s)-Tate Publishing—R
(s)-Trafford Publishing—R
Treble Heart Books—R

(a)-Tyndale House—R
(s)-VMI Publishers
(s)-WinePress—R

FICTION: NOVELLAS

Aaron Book—R
(s)-ACW Press—R
(s)-American Binding—R
Atheneum/Yg. Readers
(a)-Baker Books
Barbour
(s)-Black Forest/Tennessee—R
(s)-Booklocker.com—R
(s)-Brown Books
Christian Writer's Ebook—R
Comfort Publishing—R
(s)-Elderberry Press
(s)-Essence—R
(s)-Fairway Press—R
Guernica Editions—R
Hidden Brook Press—R
(s)-Holy Fire Publishing—R
Howard Books
(s)-Insight Publishing—R
Lighthouse Publishing—R
Little Lauren Books
Mission City Press
MoreThanNovellas
MountainView
(s)-One World Press—R
(s)-Path Pub. in Christ—R
(s)-Pleasant Word—R
Quintessential Books—R
Salt Works—R
Samaritan Press
(s)-Trafford Publishing—R
Treble Heart Books—R
Virtual Tales
White Stone Books—R
(s)-WinePress—R

FICTION: PLAYS

(s)-American Binding—R
Baker's Plays—R
(s)-Brentwood—R
(s)-Brown Books
CSS Publishing
Dover Publications—R
Eldridge Plays
Encore Performance
(s)-Essence—R
(s)-Fairway Press—R
Guardian Angel
Guernica Editions—R
(s)-Holy Fire Publishing—R
(s)-IMD Press—R
Lighthouse Publishing—R
Lillenas
Meriwether
Mission City Press
(s)-One World Press—R

(s)-Path Pub. in Christ—R
(s)-Path Publishing—R
Players Press—R
(s)-Pleasant Word—R
Salt Works—R
(s)-So. Baptist Press—R
Third World Press—R

FICTION: ROMANCE

Aaron Book—R
(s)-ACW Press—R
Ambassador-Emerald—R
(s)-American Binding—R
(a)-Baker Books
Baker's Plays—R
(a)-Ballantine
Barbour
Bethany House
(s)-Black Forest/Tennessee—R
(s)-Booklocker.com—R
(s)-Brown Books
By Grace Publications
Capstone Fiction—R
Christian Writer's Ebook—R
Comfort Publishing—R
(s)-Creation House—R
DiskUs Publishing
E-Digital Books
(s)-Elderberry Press
(s)-Essence—R
(s)-Fairway Press—R
Hannibal Books
Heartsong Presents
Hidden Brook Press—R
(s)-Holy Fire Publishing—R
(s)-Insight Publishing—R
Jireh Publishing
(s)-LifeVest Publishing
Lift Every Voice—R
Lighthouse Publishing—R
Little Lauren Books
Love Inspired
Love Inspired Suspense
MoreThanNovellas
MountainView
(a)-Multnomah
(a)-Nelson, Fiction, Thomas
(s)-One World Press—R
(a)-One World/Ballantine
Parson Place—R
(s)-Pleasant Word—R
Randall House
(s)-Selah Publishing—R
Steeple Hill/Single Title
Strang Book Group—R
Sweetheart Romances
(s)-Tate Publishing—R
(s)-Trafford Publishing—R
Treble Heart Books—R
(a)-Tyndale House—R
Vintage Romance

(s)-VMI Publishers
(a)-WaterBrook Press—R
Whitaker House
White Rose—R
White Stone Books—R
(s)-WinePress—R

FICTION: SCIENCE FICTION

Aaron Book—R
(s)-ACW Press—R
(s)-American Binding—R
Atheneum/Yg. Readers
Baker's Plays—R
(s)-Black Forest/Tennessee—R
(s)-Booklocker.com—R
(s)-Brown Books
Capstone Fiction—R
Christian Focus—R
Christian Writer's Ebook—R
Comfort Publishing—R
(s)-Creation House—R
Destiny Image—R
DiskUs Publishing
Dover Publications—R
(s)-Elderberry Press
(s)-Essence—R
Evergreen Press
(s)-Fairway Press—R
Hidden Brook Press—R
(s)-Holy Fire Publishing—R
(s)-Insight Publishing—R
Invisible College Press
(s)-LifeVest Publishing
Lighthouse Publishing—R
MountainView
(s)-One World Press—R
P & R Publishing—R
(s)-Pleasant Word—R
PREP Publishing—R
Putnam/Young Readers
Quintessential Books—R
Realms
Skysong Press
Strang Book Group—R
(s)-Tate Publishing—R
(s)-Trafford Publishing—R
Treble Heart Books—R
(s)-VMI Publishers
(a)-WaterBrook Press—R
(s)-WinePress—R

FICTION: SHORT STORY COLLECTION

Aaron Book—R
(s)-ACW Press—R
Ambassador-Emerald—R
(s)-American Binding—R
Atheneum/Yg. Readers
(a)-Baker Books
Baker Trittin
(a)-Ballantine

BelleBooks—R
(s)-Black Forest/Tennessee—R
(s)-Booklocker.com—R
Branden Publishing—R
(s)-Brown Books
Christian Writer's Ebook—R
Comfort Publishing—R
DiskUs Publishing
E-Digital Books
Eerdmans Pub., Wm. B.—R
(s)-Elderberry Press
(s)-Essence—R
(s)-Fairway Press—R
Hidden Brook Press—R
His Work Christian Pub.
(s)-Holy Fire Publishing—R
(s)-IMD Press—R
(s)-Insight Publishing—R
Kaleidoscope Press—R
Knight George Pub.
Lighthouse Publishing—R
MountainView
Mt. Olive College Press
(s)-One World Press—R
(s)-Pleasant Word—R
(s)-Providence Pub.—R
Quintessential Books—R
Randall House
Salt Works—R
Samaritan Press
(s)-Tate Publishing—R
Third World Press—R
(s)-Trafford Publishing—R
Treble Heart Books—R
(s)-VMI Publishers
Walk Worthy—R
(s)-WinePress—R

FICTION: SPECULATIVE

Aaron Book—R
(s)-ACW Press—R
(s)-American Binding—R
(a)-Baker Books
Baker's Plays—R
(s)-Black Forest/Tennessee—R
(s)-Booklocker.com—R
(s)-Brown Books
Capstone Fiction—R
Christian Writer's Ebook—R
(s)-Elderberry Press
(s)-Essence—R
Hidden Brook Press—R
(s)-Holy Fire Publishing—R
(s)-Insight Publishing—R
(s)-LifeVest Publishing
Lighthouse Publishing—R
MountainView
(a)-Multnomah
(s)-One World Press—R
(s)-Pleasant Word—R
Realms
Strang Book Group—R

(s)-Tate Publishing—R
(s)-Trafford Publishing—R
(s)-VMI Publishers
(s)-WinePress—R

FICTION: TEEN/YOUNG ADULT

Aaron Book—R
(s)-ACW Press—R
Ambassador Books
(s)-American Binding—R
AMG Publishers
Atheneum/Yg. Readers
(s)-Baal Hamon—R
(a)-Baker Books
Baker Trittin
Barbour
BelleBooks—R
Big Idea
BJU/Journey Forth—R
(s)-Black Forest/Tennessee—R
Blue Dolphin
(s)-Booklocker.com—R
(s)-Book Publishers—R
Boyds Mills Press—R
(s)-Brown Books
Christian Focus—R
Christian Writer's Ebook—R
Comfort Publishing—R
(s)-Creation House—R
DiskUs Publishing
E-Digital Books
Eerdmans Pub., Wm. B.—R
Eerdmans/Yg. Readers
(s)-Elderberry Press
(s)-Essence—R
Evergreen Press
(s)-Fairway Press—R
Faith Communications
(a)-FaithWords
Hidden Brook Press—R
His Work Christian Pub.
(s)-Holy Fire Publishing—R
(s)-Insight Publishing—R
(a)-Kregel—R
Legacy Press—R
(s)-LifeVest Publishing
Lift Every Voice—R
Lighthouse Publishing—R
Lion and Lamb
Little Lauren Books
Mission City Press
(a)-Moody Publishers
MountainView
(a)-Multnomah
NavPress
NavPress Student—R
(a)-Nelson, Fiction, Thomas
New Canaan—R
(s)-One World Press—R
Parson Place—R
Parsons Publishing—R

Pauline Books—R
(s)-Pleasant Word—R
Power Publishing—R
Putnam/Young Readers
Randall House
Ravenhawk Books—R
Samaritan Press
(s)-Selah Publishing—R
Starik Publishing
Strang Book Group—R
(s)-Tate Publishing—R
(s)-TEACH Services—R
Third World Press—R
(s)-Trafford Publishing—R
Treble Heart Books—R
Vintage Romance
Virginia Pines Press
(s)-VMI Publishers
Walk Worthy—R
(a)-WaterBrook Press—R
(s)-WinePress—R
(s)-Word Alive

FICTION: WESTERNS

Aaron Book—R
(s)-ACW Press—R
Ambassador-Emerald—R
(s)-American Binding—R
(a)-Baker Books
Baker Trittin
Baker's Plays—R
BJU/Journey Forth—R
(s)-Black Forest/Tennessee—R
(s)-Booklocker.com—R
(s)-Brown Books
Christian Writer's Ebook—R
DiskUs Publishing
E-Digital Books
(s)-Elderberry Press
(s)-Essence—R
(s)-Fairway Press—R
Father's Press—R
Hidden Brook Press—R
(s)-Holy Fire Publishing—R
(s)-Insight Publishing—R
(s)-LifeVest Publishing
Lighthouse Publishing—R
MountainView
(a)-Multnomah
(s)-One World Press—R
P & R Publishing—R
Parson Place—R
(s)-Pleasant Word—R
Quintessential Books—R
Randall House
Ravenhawk Books—R
Strang Book Group—R
(s)-Tate Publishing—R
(s)-Trafford Publishing—R
Treble Heart Books—R
Vintage Romance
(s)-VMI Publishers

Whitaker House
White Stone Books—R
(s)-WinePress—R

FORGIVENESS

Aaron Book—R
Abingdon Press
(s)-ACW Press—R
Ambassador-Emerald—R
(s)-American Binding—R
(s)-Baal Hamon—R
Baker Trittin
Baker's Plays—R
(a)-B & H Publishing
Barbour
(s)-Black Forest/Tennessee—R
BMH Books—R
(s)-Booklocker.com—R
Bridge-Logos—R
(s)-Brown Books
CarePoint Publishing—R
Chalice Press
Chapter Two—R
Christian Family—R
Christian Focus—R
Christian Writer's Ebook—R
Comfort Publishing—R
(s)-Creation House—R
CSS Publishing
(s)-DCTS Publishing
Destiny Image (books)—R
Discovery House—R
(a)-Doubleday Relig.—R
Editorial Portavoz
Eerdmans Pub., Wm. B.—R
(s)-Elderberry Press
Eldridge Plays
(s)-Essence—R
Evangelical Press
Evergreen Press
(s)-Fairway Press—R
FaithWalk
(a)-FaithWords
Father's Press—R
Forward Movement
Green Key Books
Greenwood/Praeger
Guardian Angel
(a)-HarperOne
Harrison House
(a)-Harvest House
Hensley Publishing
Hidden Brook Press—R
(s)-Holy Fire Publishing—R
Howard Books
(s)-IMD Press—R
(s)-Insight Publishing—R
Jossey-Bass
Judson Press—R
(a)-Kregel—R
Lift Every Voice—R
Lighthouse Publishing—R

Lillenas
Lion and Lamb
Lutheran Univ. Press
Monarch Books
NavPress
NavPress Student—R
(a)-Nelson, Thomas
New Hope—R
(s)-One World Press—R
P & R Publishing—R
Pacific Press
Parson Place—R
Parsons Publishing—R
(s)-Path Pub. in Christ—R
Pilgrim Press—R
(s)-Pleasant Word—R
Power Publishing—R
PREP Publishing—R
(s)-Providence Pub.—R
Randall House
(a)-Regal
Revival Nation
Rose Publishing
Salt Works—R
(s)-Salvation Publisher—R
Samaritan Press
St. Anthony Mess. Press—R
St. Pauls/Alba House—R
(s)-Star Bible Public.
Strang Book Group—R
(s)-Synergy Publishers—R
(s)-Tate Publishing—R
(s)-TEACH Services—R
Torch Legacy
(s)-Trafford Publishing—R
VBC Publishing
(s)-VMI Publishers
Wesleyan Publishing
White Stone Books—R
(s)-WinePress—R
(s)-Word Alive
(s)-Zoe Life Publishing

GAMES/CRAFTS

(a)-Baker Books
Big Idea
(s)-Booklocker.com—R
(s)-Brown Books
Contemporary Drama
(s)-Elderberry Press
(s)-Essence—R
(s)-Fairway Press—R
Group Publishing
Guardian Angel
Harcourt Religion
Hidden Brook Press—R
(s)-Holy Fire Publishing—R
Jubilant Press—R
Kaleidoscope Press—R
Knight George Pub.
Legacy Press—R
Lighthouse Publishing—R

Lion and Lamb
Mission City Press
Monarch Books
(s)-One World Press—R
Players Press—R
Rainbow Publishers—R
Salt Works—R
Samaritan Press
Standard Publishing
(s)-Tate Publishing—R
(s)-Trafford Publishing—R
(s)-Zoe Life Publishing

GIFT BOOKS

Aaron Book—R
ACTA Publications
(s)-Black Forest/Tennessee—R
(s)-Book Publishers—R
Bridge-Logos—R
(s)-Brown Books
Comfort Publishing—R
(s)-Creation House—R
Eerdmans Pub., Wm. B.—R
(s)-Essence—R
Evangelical Press
GRQ—R
(a)-Harvest House
(s)-Holy Fire Publishing—R
Lion and Lamb
(s)-Pleasant Word—R
Power Publishing—R
Ravenhawk Books—R
Strang Book Group—R
(s)-Trafford Publishing—R
(s)-WinePress—R

GRIEF

Aaron Book—R
Abingdon Press
ACTA Publications
(s)-ACW Press—R
(s)-American Binding—R
Anglicans United—R
(a)-B & H Publishing
Bethany House
(s)-Black Forest/Tennessee—R
BMH Books—R
(s)-Booklocker.com—R
Bridge-Logos—R
(s)-Brown Books
Cambridge Scholars Pub.
CarePoint Publishing—R
Chalice Press
(s)-Creation House—R
Dabbling Mum Press
Discovery House—R
Eerdmans Pub., Wm. B.—R
(s)-Elderberry Press
(s)-Essence—R
Evangelical Press
Father's Press—R
GRQ—R

Halo Publishing
Hendrickson—R
(s)-Holy Fire Publishing—R
(s)-IMD Press—R
(s)-Insight Publishing—R
Judson Press—R
Kingsley, Jessica Pub.—R
(a)-Kregel—R
Lighthouse Publishing—R
Lillenas
Lion and Lamb
Lutterworth Press—R
Monarch Books
(a)-Nelson, Thomas
New Hope—R
Parson Place—R
Pauline Books—R
(s)-Pleasant Word—R
Power Publishing—R
(s)-Providence Pub.—R
Randall House
Resource Public.
Rose Publishing
(s)-Salvation Publisher—R
(s)-Star Bible Public.
(s)-TEACH Services—R
(s)-Trafford Publishing—R
VBC Publishing
Whitaker House
(s)-WinePress—R

GROUP STUDY BOOKS

Aaron Book—R
Abingdon Press
(s)-ACW Press—R
(s)-American Binding—R
AMG Publishers
(a)-Baker Books
Baker Trittin
BMH Books—R
(s)-Booklocker.com—R
(s)-Brentwood—R
Bridge-Logos—R
(s)-Brown Books
CarePoint Publishing—R
Carey Library, Wm.—R
Chalice Press
Christian Writer's Ebook—R
(s)-CrossHouse—R
CSS Publishing
Eerdmans Pub., Wm. B.—R
(a)-Emmaus Road—R
(s)-Essence—R
Evangelical Press
Evergreen Press
Fair Havens—R
(s)-Fairway Press—R
Founders Press
Good Book—R
Gospel Publishing
Hannibal Books
(a)-Harvest House

Hensley Publishing
Hidden Brook Press—R
(s)-Holy Fire Publishing—R
(s)-IMD Press—R
Jubilant Press—R
Judson Press—R
(a)-Kregel—R
Lighthouse Publishing—R
Lion and Lamb
Mission City Press
Monarch Books
NavPress Student—R
New Hope—R
(s)-One World Press—R
P & R Publishing—R
Pacific Press
Paradise Research—R
Parson Place—R
(s)-Path Pub. in Christ—R
Pilgrim Press—R
(s)-Pleasant Word—R
Power Publishing—R
(s)-Providence Pub.—R
Randall House
Rose Publishing
Smyth & Helwys
(s)-So. Baptist Press—R
St. Anthony Mess. Press—R
(s)-Star Bible Public.
(s)-Tate Publishing—R
(s)-Trafford Publishing—R
UMI Publishing—R
(s)-VMI Publishers
Wesleyan Publishing
(s)-WinePress—R
(s)-Word Alive
(s)-Zoe Life Publishing

HEALING

Aaron Book—R
ACTA Publications
(s)-ACW Press—R
(s)-American Binding—R
(s)-Baal Hamon—R
(a)-Baker Books
Baker's Plays—R
(a)-B & H Publishing
(s)-Black Forest/Tennessee—R
Blue Dolphin
(s)-Booklocker.com—R
(s)-Book Publishers—R
(s)-Brentwood—R
Bridge-Logos—R
(s)-Brown Books
Cambridge Scholars Pub.
Canticle Books—R
CarePoint Publishing—R
Chalice Press
Christian Heritage—R
Christian Writer's Ebook—R
Comfort Publishing—R
(a)-Cook, David C.

(s)-Creation House—R
CSS Publishing
Destiny Image—R
Destiny Image (books)—R
Eerdmans Pub., Wm. B.—R
(s)-Elderberry Press
(s)-Essence—R
(s)-Fairway Press—R
FaithWalk
(a)-FaithWords
Father's Press—R
Forward Movement
Good Book—R
Greenwood/Praeger
Harrison House
(a)-Harvest House
(a)-Hay House
Hidden Brook Press—R
(s)-Holy Fire Publishing—R
Hope Publishing—R
(s)-Impact Christian—R
(s)-Insight Publishing—R
Jireh Publishing
Kingsley, Jessica Pub.—R
Life Changing Media
Lighthouse Publishing—R
Lillenas
Lion and Lamb
Loyola Press
Lutheran Univ. Press
Lutterworth Press—R
Magnus Press—R
(s)-McDougal Publishing—R
Monarch Books
(a)-Nelson, Thomas
(s)-One World Press—R
Pacific Press
Paradise Research—R
Parson Place—R
Parsons Publishing—R
(s)-Path Pub. in Christ—R
Pauline Books—R
Pilgrim Press—R
(s)-Pleasant Word—R
Power Publishing—R
(s)-Providence Pub.—R
(s)-Recovery Commun.
Revival Nation
(s)-Salvation Publisher—R
(s)-Selah Publishing—R
Siloam
(s)-So. Baptist Press—R
(s)-Star Bible Public.
Strang Book Group—R
(s)-Synergy Publishers—R
(s)-Tate Publishing—R
(s)-TEACH Services—R
(s)-Trafford Publishing—R
(s)-VMI Publishers
Wesleyan Publishing
Whitaker House
(s)-WinePress—R

(s)-Word Alive
(s)-Zoe Life Publishing

HEALTH

Aaron Book—R
(s)-ACW Press—R
Ambassador Books
(s)-American Binding—R
(s)-Baal Hamon—R
(a)-Baker Books
Baker's Plays—R
(a)-Ballantine
Blue Dolphin
(s)-Booklocker.com—R
(s)-Book Publishers—R
Branden Publishing—R
(s)-Brentwood—R
(s)-Brown Books
Cambridge Scholars Pub.
Chalice Press
Christian Writer's Ebook—R
Cladach Publishing
Comfort Publishing—R
(s)-Creation House—R
Destiny Image (books)—R
Eerdmans Pub., Wm. B.—R
(s)-Elderberry Press
(s)-Essence—R
Evangelical Press
Evergreen Press
Facts on File
Fair Havens—R
(s)-Fairway Press—R
(a)-FaithWords
Forward Movement
Good Book—R
Greenwood/Praeger
Grupo Nelson
Guardian Angel
Harrison House
(a)-Harvest House
(a)-Hay House
Health Commun.
Hidden Brook Press—R
His Work Christian Pub.
(s)-Holy Fire Publishing—R
Hope Publishing—R
(s)-IMD Press—R
(s)-Insight Publishing—R
Judson Press—R
Kaleidoscope Press—R
Kingsley, Jessica Pub.—R
Langmarc
Legacy Publishers
Life Changing Media
Life Cycle Books—R
Lighthouse Publishing—R
Lion and Lamb
Loyola Press
Messianic Jewish—R
Monarch Books
MountainView

(a)-Nelson, Thomas
New Hope—R
(s)-One World Press—R
Pacific Press
Paradise Research—R
Parsons Publishing—R
(s)-Path Pub. in Christ—R
(s)-Pleasant Word—R
Power Publishing—R
(s)-Providence Pub.—R
Quintessential Books—R
(s)-Recovery Commun.
(a)-Regal
(a)-Regnery
(s)-Salvation Publisher—R
Siloam
(s)-So. Baptist Press—R
(s)-Star Bible Public.
Strang Book Group—R
Tarcher, Jeremy P.—R
(s)-Tate Publishing—R
(s)-TEACH Services—R
Third World Press—R
(s)-Trafford Publishing—R
Treble Heart Books—R
VBC Publishing
(s)-VMI Publishers
(s)-WinePress—R
(s)-Word Alive
Xyzzy Press
(s)-Zoe Life Publishing

HISPANIC MARKETS*

Editorial Portavoz
Editorial Unilit
Grupo Nelson
Libros Liguori
Strang/Casa Creacion
Tyndale Espanol

HISTORICAL

Aadeon Publishing—R
Aaron Book—R
(s)-ACW Press—R
Ambassador Books
(s)-American Binding—R
Atheneum/Yg. Readers
Baker Academic
(a)-Baker Books
Baker's Plays—R
(s)-Black Forest/Tennessee—R
Blue Dolphin
(s)-Booklocker.com—R
Boyds Mills Press—R
Branden Publishing—R
(s)-Brentwood—R
Bridge-Logos—R
(s)-Brown Books
Cambridge Scholars Pub.
Canadian Inst. for Law—R
Carey Library, Wm.—R
Catholic Answers—R

Chalice Press
Chapter Two—R
Christian Family—R
Christian Heritage—R
Christian Writer's Ebook—R
Cistercian—R
Clarke & Co., James—R
College Press—R
Comfort Publishing—R
Conciliar Press—R
Continuum Intl.—R
(s)-Creation House—R
Custom Communications
(a)-Doubleday Relig.—R
E-Digital Books
Eerdmans Pub., Wm. B.—R
(s)-Elderberry Press
(s)-Essence—R
ETC Publications
Evangelical Press
Facts on File
(s)-Fairway Press—R
FaithWalk
Fordham Univ. Press—R
Founders Press
Foursquare Media
Greenwood/Praeger
(a)-HarperOne
Harvest Day
Hidden Brook Press—R
His Work Christian Pub.
(s)-Holy Fire Publishing—R
(s)-IMD Press—R
(s)-Impact Christian—R
Inkling Books—R
(s)-Insight Publishing—R
Johns Hopkins—R
Jossey-Bass
Kirk House
(a)-Kregel—R
(s)-LifeVest Publishing
Lift Every Voice—R
Lighthouse Publishing—R
Lion and Lamb
Loyola Press
Lutheran Univ. Press
Lutterworth Press—R
Mercer Univ. Press—R
Messianic Jewish—R
Monarch Books
(a)-Nelson, Thomas
New Seeds—R
New York Univ. Press
(s)-One World Press—R
(a)-One World/Ballantine
P & R Publishing—R
Paradise Research—R
(s)-Path Pub. in Christ—R
Pauline Books—R
(s)-Pleasant Word—R
Power Publishing—R

(s)-Providence Pub.—R
Quintessential Books—R
Ragged Edge—R
(a)-Regnery
Scepter Publishers—R
(s)-So. Baptist Press—R
St. Augustine's Press—R
(s)-Star Bible Public.
Still Waters Revival—R
(s)-Tate Publishing—R
(s)-TEACH Services—R
Third World Press—R
(s)-Trafford Publishing—R
Trinity Foundation—R
Univ. of AR Press—R
Univ. Press of America—R
Virginia Pines Press
(s)-WinePress—R
(s)-Word Alive
Yale Univ. Press—R

HOLIDAY/SEASONAL

Aaron Book—R
Abingdon Press
(s)-ACW Press—R
Ambassador Books
(s)-American Binding—R
Baker Trittin
Baker's Plays—R
Barbour
(s)-Booklocker.com—R
(s)-Brown Books
Chalice Press
Christian Writer's Ebook—R
Comfort Publishing—R
(a)-Cook, David C.
CSS Publishing
Discovery House—R
(s)-Elderberry Press
Eldridge Plays
(s)-Essence—R
Evangelical Press
Evergreen Press
(s)-Fairway Press—R
(a)-FaithWords
FamilyLife (books)—R
Forward Movement
Greenwood/Praeger
Group Publishing
Guardian Angel
GuidepostsBooks
(a)-HarperOne
(a)-Harvest House
Hidden Brook Press—R
(s)-Holy Fire Publishing—R
(s)-IMD Press—R
(s)-Insight Publishing—R
Judson Press—R
Lighthouse Publishing—R
Lion and Lamb
Meriwether

Messianic Jewish—R
Monarch Books
New Hope—R
(s)-One World Press—R
Pelican Publishing—R
Pflaum Publishing
(s)-Pleasant Word—R
Power Publishing—R
(s)-Providence Pub.—R
Putnam/Young Readers
Randall House
Ravenhawk Books—R
Salt Works—R
St. Anthony Mess. Press—R
Standard Publishing
Strang Book Group—R
(s)-Tate Publishing—R
(s)-Trafford Publishing—R
(s)-VMI Publishers
White Stone Books—R
(s)-WinePress—R
(s)-Word Alive

HOLINESS

Aaron Book—R
(s)-ACW Press—R
Ambassador-Emerald—R
(s)-American Binding—R
(s)-Baal Hamon—R
(a)-B & H Publishing
Bethany House
(s)-Black Forest/Tennessee—R
(s)-Booklocker.com—R
Bridge-Logos—R
(s)-Brown Books
Chalice Press
Chapter Two—R
Christian Family—R
Christian Focus—R
Christian Heritage—R
Comfort Publishing—R
(s)-Creation House—R
Deo Volente
Eerdmans Pub., Wm. B.—R
(s)-Elderberry Press
(a)-Emmaus Road—R
(s)-Essence—R
Evangelical Press
Father's Press—R
Forward Movement
GRQ—R
Hidden Brook Press—R
(s)-Holy Fire Publishing—R
(s)-IMD Press—R
(s)-Insight Publishing—R
Lighthouse Publishing—R
Lillenas
Monarch Books
NavPress Student—R
Parson Place—R
Parsons Publishing—R

Pauline Books—R
(s)-Pleasant Word—R
Power Publishing—R
(s)-Providence Pub.—R
Revival Nation
(s)-Salvation Publisher—R
St. Anthony Mess. Press—R
St. Pauls/Alba House—R
(s)-Star Bible Public.
Strang Book Group—R
(s)-Synergy Publishers—R
(s)-Tate Publishing—R
(s)-TEACH Services—R
(s)-Trafford Publishing—R
Wesleyan Publishing
(s)-WinePress—R
(s)-Zoe Life Publishing

HOLY SPIRIT

Aaron Book—R
(s)-ACW Press—R
Ambassador-Emerald—R
(s)-American Binding—R
(s)-Baal Hamon—R
Baker Trittin
Baker's Plays—R
(a)-B & H Publishing
Baylor Univ. Press
(s)-Black Forest/Tennessee—R
(s)-Booklocker.com—R
Bridge-Logos—R
(s)-Brown Books
Canticle Books—R
Chapter Two—R
Christian Family—R
Christian Focus—R
Christian Heritage—R
Christian Writer's Ebook—R
Comfort Publishing—R
(s)-Creation House—R
CSS Publishing
Destiny Image—R
Destiny Image (books)—R
Eerdmans Pub., Wm. B.—R
(s)-Elderberry Press
(a)-Emmaus Road—R
(s)-Essence—R
Evangelical Press
(s)-Fairway Press—R
Father's Press—R
Forward Movement
(s)-FruitBearer Pub.
Gospel Publishing
Greenwood/Praeger
Halo Publishing
Harrison House
Hidden Brook Press—R
(s)-Holy Fire Publishing—R
(s)-IMD Press—R
(s)-Insight Publishing—R
Judson Press—R

(a)-Kregel—R
Lift Every Voice—R
Lighthouse Publishing—R
Lillenas
Lion and Lamb
Lutheran Univ. Press
Magnus Press—R
Monarch Books
NavPress Student—R
(a)-Nelson, Thomas
(s)-One World Press—R
P & R Publishing—R
Pacific Press
Parson Place—R
Parsons Publishing—R
(s)-Path Pub. in Christ—R
Pauline Books—R
Pilgrim Press—R
(s)-Pleasant Word—R
Power Publishing—R
(s)-Providence Pub.—R
(a)-Regal
Revival Nation
Rose Publishing
(s)-Salvation Publisher—R
St. Anthony Mess. Press—R
St. Pauls/Alba House—R
(s)-Star Bible Public.
Strang Book Group—R
(s)-Synergy Publishers—R
(s)-Tate Publishing—R
(s)-TEACH Services—R
(s)-Trafford Publishing—R
VBC Publishing
(s)-VMI Publishers
Wesleyan Publishing
Westminster John Knox
Whitaker House
(s)-WinePress—R
(s)-Word Alive
(s)-Zoe Life Publishing

HOMESCHOOLING RESOURCES

Aaron Book—R
(s)-ACW Press—R
(s)-American Binding—R
(a)-Baker Books
Big Idea
(s)-Booklocker.com—R
(s)-Book Publishers—R
(s)-Brentwood—R
(s)-Brown Books
Chapter Two—R
Christian Focus—R
Christian Writer's Ebook—R
(s)-CrossHouse—R
Eerdmans Pub., Wm. B.—R
(s)-Elderberry Press
Eldridge Plays
(a)-Emmaus Road—R

(s)-Essence—R
Evangelical Press
Fair Havens—R
(s)-Fairway Press—R
Guardian Angel
Hannibal Books
Heart of Wisdom
Hidden Brook Press—R
(s)-Holy Fire Publishing—R
(s)-IMD Press—R
Judson Press—R
Lighthouse Publishing—R
Lighthouse Trails—R
Lion and Lamb
Little Lauren Books
Master Books
McRuffy Press
Mission City Press
Monarch Books
New Canaan—R
New Leaf
(s)-One World Press—R
P & R Publishing—R
(s)-Path Pub. in Christ—R
(s)-Pleasant Word—R
Power Publishing—R
(s)-Providence Pub.—R
Rose Publishing
Samaritan Press
Starik Publishing
(s)-Tate Publishing—R
(s)-Testimony Press
(s)-Trafford Publishing—R
Virginia Pines Press
(s)-WinePress—R
(s)-Word Alive
(s)-Zoe Life Publishing

HOMILETICS

Aaron Book—R
Abingdon Press
(s)-ACW Press—R
(s)-American Binding—R
(a)-Baker Books
(s)-Black Forest/Tennessee—R
BMH Books—R
(s)-Booklocker.com—R
(s)-Brown Books
Chalice Press
Christian Family—R
Christian Focus—R
Christian Writer's Ebook—R
CSS Publishing
(s)-DCTS Publishing
Earthen Vessel—R
Eerdmans Pub., Wm. B.—R
(s)-Elderberry Press
(a)-Emmaus Road—R
(s)-Essence—R
Evangelical Press
(s)-Fairway Press—R

Hendrickson—R
Hidden Brook Press—R
(s)-Holy Fire Publishing—R
(s)-IMD Press—R
(s)-Insight Publishing—R
InterVarsity Press—R
Judson Press—R
(a)-Kregel—R
Lighthouse Publishing—R
Lutheran Univ. Press
Monarch Books
(s)-One World Press—R
P & R Publishing—R
Pauline Books—R
(s)-Pleasant Word—R
Power Publishing—R
Presbyterian Pub.
(s)-Providence Pub.—R
Resource Public.
Rose Publishing
St. Anthony Mess. Press—R
St. Pauls/Alba House—R
(s)-Star Bible Public.
(s)-Tate Publishing—R
(s)-Trafford Publishing—R
VBC Publishing
(s)-VMI Publishers
Wesleyan Publishing
Westminster John Knox
(s)-WinePress—R
(s)-Word Alive
(s)-Zoe Life Publishing

HOW-TO

Aaron Book—R
(s)-ACW Press—R
Adams Media
(s)-American Binding—R
(a)-Baker Books
(a)-Ballantine
(s)-Black Forest/Tennessee—R
Blue Dolphin
(s)-Booklocker.com—R
(s)-Brentwood—R
Bridge-Logos—R
(s)-Brown Books
Christian Writer's Ebook—R
Church Growth Inst.
Dabbling Mum Press
Destiny Image—R
DiskUs Publishing
(s)-Elderberry Press
(s)-Essence—R
Evangelical Press
Evergreen Press
Fair Havens—R
(s)-Fairway Press—R
FaithWalk
Fell, Frederick—R
Gospel Light
Greenwood/Praeger

GRQ—R
Guardian Angel
Harcourt Religion
Hidden Brook Press—R
His Work Christian Pub.
(s)-Holy Fire Publishing—R
(s)-IMD Press—R
Inkling Books—R
(s)-Insight Publishing—R
Judson Press—R
Kaleidoscope Press—R
Kirk House
(s)-LifeVest Publishing
Lighthouse Publishing—R
Lion and Lamb
Meriwether
Monarch Books
MountainView
(a)-Nelson, Thomas
(s)-One World Press—R
(a)-One World/Ballantine
Our Sunday Visitor—R
Pacific Press
Parson Place—R
(s)-Path Pub. in Christ—R
(s)-Path Publishing—R
Perigee Books
Players Press—R
(s)-Pleasant Word—R
Power Publishing—R
PREP Publishing—R
(s)-Providence Pub.—R
Quintessential Books—R
(s)-Recovery Commun.
Revell
Salt Works—R
(s)-Salvation Publisher—R
(s)-So. Baptist Press—R
Standard Publishing
Still Waters Revival—R
Tarcher, Jeremy P.—R
(s)-Tate Publishing—R
(s)-Trafford Publishing—R
Treble Heart Books—R
VBC Publishing
Vintage Romance
(s)-VMI Publishers
Walk Worthy—R
Wilshire Book—R
(s)-WinePress—R
(s)-Word Alive
(s)-Zoe Life Publishing

HUMOR

Aaron Book—R
(s)-ACW Press—R
Ambassador Books
(s)-American Binding—R
(a)-Baker Books
Baker's Plays—R
(a)-Ballantine

Barbour
BelleBooks—R
(s)-Black Forest/Tennessee—R
Blue Dolphin
(s)-Booklocker.com—R
Boyds Mills Press—R
(s)-Brentwood—R
Bridge-Logos—R
(s)-Brown Books
Christian Writer's Ebook—R
(a)-Cook, David C.
Countryman, J.
(s)-Creation House—R
Crossroad Publishing—R
(s)-Elderberry Press
Eldridge Plays
(s)-Essence—R
Evergreen Press
(s)-Fairway Press—R
(a)-FaithWords
Forward Movement
GuidepostsBooks
(a)-Harvest House
Hidden Brook Press—R
(s)-Holy Fire Publishing—R
Ideals/Children
(s)-Insight Publishing—R
Kaleidoscope Press—R
Kirk House
Lighthouse Publishing—R
Lillenas
Lion and Lamb
Loyola Press
Meriwether
Monarch Books
MOPS Intl.
NavPress Student—R
(a)-Nelson, Thomas
(s)-One World Press—R
(a)-One World/Ballantine
Pacific Press
Parson Place—R
(s)-Path Pub. in Christ—R
(s)-Path Publishing—R
(s)-Pleasant Word—R
Power Publishing—R
(s)-Providence Pub.—R
Putnam/Young Readers
Quintessential Books—R
(a)-Regal
(s)-Salvation Publisher—R
Samaritan Press
(s)-Selah Publishing—R
(s)-So. Baptist Press—R
(s)-Tate Publishing—R
(s)-Trafford Publishing—R
Treble Heart Books—R
(s)-VMI Publishers
Walk Worthy—R
White Stone Books—R
(s)-WinePress—R

(s)-Word Alive
Xyzzy Press
(s)-Zoe Life Publishing

INSPIRATIONAL
Aadeon Publishing—R
Aaron Book—R
Abingdon Press
(s)-ACW Press—R
Adams Media
(s)-Ali Literary, Alfred—R
Ambassador Books
(s)-American Binding—R
(s)-Baal Hamon—R
(a)-Baker Books
Baker Trittin
Baker's Plays—R
(a)-B & H Publishing
Barbour
Beacon Hill Press—R
Bethany House
(s)-Black Forest/Tennessee—R
Blue Dolphin
(s)-Booklocker.com—R
(s)-Brentwood—R
Bridge-Logos—R
(s)-Brown Books
Canticle Books—R
Catholic Book
Chapter Two—R
CharismaKids
Christian Family—R
Christian Focus—R
Christian Writer's Ebook—R
Comfort Publishing—R
Concordia
Continuum Intl.—R
Countryman, J.
(s)-Creation House—R
(s)-CrossHouse—R
Crossroad Publishing—R
CSS Publishing
(s)-DCTS Publishing
Deo Volente
Destiny Image—R
Destiny Image (books)—R
Dimensions for Living
Discovery House—R
(a)-Doubleday Relig.—R
Dove Inspirational—R
(s)-Elderberry Press
Eldridge Plays
(s)-Essence—R
Evangelical Press
Evergreen Press
(s)-Fairway Press—R
Faith Communications
FaithWalk
(a)-FaithWords
Forward Movement
Gollehon Press

Green Key Books
GRQ—R
Grupo Nelson
Guardian Angel
Harrison House
(a)-Harvest House
(a)-Hay House
Health Commun.
HeartSpring Pub.—R
Hidden Brook Press—R
(s)-Holy Fire Publishing—R
Hope Publishing—R
Howard Books
Ideals/Children
Illumination Arts
(s)-IMD Press—R
(s)-Impact Christian—R
(s)-Insight Publishing—R
Jebaire Publishing
Journey Stone—R
Judson Press—R
Kaleidoscope Press—R
Kirk House
(a)-Kregel—R
Langmarc
Life Changing Media
(s)-LifeVest Publishing
Lighthouse Publishing—R
Lillenas
Lion and Lamb
Loyola Press
Magnus Press—R
(s)-McDougal Publishing—R
Monarch Books
MountainView
NavPress Student—R
(a)-Nelson, Thomas
New Seeds—R
(s)-One World Press—R
Pacific Press
Paradise Research—R
Parson Place—R
Parsons Publishing—R
(s)-Path Pub. in Christ—R
(s)-Path Publishing—R
Pauline Books—R
Paulist Press
Pelican Publishing—R
Perigee Books
Pilgrim Press—R
(s)-Pleasant Word—R
Power Publishing—R
(s)-Providence Pub.—R
Quintessential Books—R
Ragged Edge—R
Ravenhawk Books—R
(a)-Regal
Revival Nation
(s)-Salvation Publisher—R
Samaritan Press
(s)-Selah Publishing—R

Smyth & Helwys
(s)-So. Baptist Press—R
St. Anthony Mess. Press—R
St. Pauls/Alba House—R
(s)-Star Bible Public.
Strang Book Group—R
(s)-Synergy Publishers—R
(s)-Tate Publishing—R
Tau-Publishing—R
(s)-TEACH Services—R
(s)-Testimony Press
Torch Legacy
(s)-Trafford Publishing—R
(a)-Tyndale House—R
VBC Publishing
Vintage Romance
(s)-VMI Publishers
(a)-WaterBrook Press—R
Wesleyan Publishing
Whitaker House
White Stone Books—R
(s)-WinePress—R
Woodland Gospel
(s)-Word Alive
W Publishing
(s)-Zoe Life Publishing

LAY COUNSELING*
Aaron Book—R
(s)-ACW Press—R
(s)-American Binding—R
(a)-B & H Publishing
(s)-Brown Books
Eerdmans Pub., Wm. B.—R
(s)-Essence—R
Evangelical Press
(s)-Holy Fire Publishing—R
(s)-Insight Publishing—R
Kingsley, Jessica Pub.—R
Lighthouse Publishing—R
Lion and Lamb
Paradise Research—R
Parsons Publishing—R
(s)-Pleasant Word—R
Power Publishing—R
(s)-Providence Pub.—R
Samaritan Press
(s)-Trafford Publishing—R
(s)-WinePress—R

LEADERSHIP
Aaron Book—R
Abingdon Press
(s)-ACW Press—R
(s)-American Binding—R
(s)-Baal Hamon—R
(a)-Baker Books
Baker's Plays—R
(a)-B & H Publishing
Beacon Hill Press—R
Bethany House

BJU/Journey Forth—R
(s)-Black Forest/Tennessee—R
BMH Books—R
(s)-Booklocker.com—R
Bridge-Logos—R
(s)-Brown Books
Chalice Press
Christian Family—R
Christian Focus—R
Christian Writer's Ebook—R
Church Growth Inst.
College Press—R
Comfort Publishing—R
(a)-Cook, David C.
(s)-Creation House—R
Crossroad Publishing—R
CSS Publishing
(s)-DCTS Publishing
Deo Volente
Destiny Image—R
Editorial Portavoz
Eerdmans Pub., Wm. B.—R
(s)-Elderberry Press
(s)-Essence—R
Evangelical Press
Evergreen Press
(s)-Fairway Press—R
Faith Alive
FaithWalk
Gospel Publishing
Greenwood/Praeger
Group Publishing
Grupo Nelson
Guardian Angel
(a)-Harvest House
Hidden Brook Press—R
(s)-Holy Fire Publishing—R
(s)-IMD Press—R
(s)-Insight Publishing—R
InterVarsity Press—R
Jossey-Bass
Jubilant Press—R
Judson Press—R
Kirk House
(a)-Kregel—R
Lift Every Voice—R
Lighthouse Publishing—R
Lillenas
Lion and Lamb
(s)-McDougal Publishing—R
Monarch Books
NavPress
NavPress Student—R
Neibauer Press—R
(a)-Nelson, Thomas
New Hope—R
(s)-One World Press—R
Parsons Publishing—R
Pilgrim Press—R
(s)-Pleasant Word—R

Ponder Publishing
Power Publishing—R
(s)-Providence Pub.—R
Quintessential Books—R
Randall House
Ravenhawk Books—R
(a)-Regal
Revival Nation
(s)-Salvation Publisher—R
(s)-Selah Publishing—R
Standard Publishing
(s)-Star Bible Public.
Strang Book Group—R
(s)-Synergy Publishers—R
(s)-Tate Publishing—R
(s)-Trafford Publishing—R
UMI Publishing—R
Univ. Press of America—R
VBC Publishing
(s)-VMI Publishers
(a)-WaterBrook Press—R
Whitaker House
White Stone Books—R
(s)-WinePress—R
(s)-Word Alive
(s)-Zoe Life Publishing

LIFESTYLE

Aaron Book—R
(s)-ACW Press—R
(s)-American Binding—R
Bethany House
BMH Books—R
(s)-Booklocker.com—R
(s)-Brown Books
Chalice Press
Comfort Publishing—R
(s)-Creation House—R
Dabbling Mum Press
Discovery House—R
Eerdmans Pub., Wm. B.—R
(s)-Elderberry Press
(s)-Essence—R
Evangelical Press
Fair Havens—R
GRQ—R
(a)-Harvest House
(s)-Holy Fire Publishing—R
Howard Books
(s)-Insight Publishing—R
Judson Press—R
Lift Every Voice—R
Lighthouse Publishing—R
Messianic Jewish—R
Monarch Books
NavPress
NavPress Student—R
Pauline Books—R
(s)-Pleasant Word—R
Power Publishing—R
(s)-Providence Pub.—R

Ravenhawk Books—R
(a)-Regal
Revival Nation
(s)-Salvation Publisher—R
Samaritan Press
(s)-Star Bible Public.
Strang Book Group—R
(s)-TEACH Services—R
(s)-Trafford Publishing—R
(s)-WinePress—R
Xyzzy Press

LITURGICAL STUDIES

Aaron Book—R
(s)-ACW Press—R
(s)-American Binding—R
American Cath. Press—R
(a)-Baker Books
Baker's Plays—R
(s)-Booklocker.com—R
(s)-Brentwood—R
(s)-Brown Books
Catholic Answers—R
Catholic Book
Chalice Press
Christian Heritage—R
Christian Writer's Ebook—R
Cistercian—R
Clarke & Co., James—R
Conciliar Press—R
Continuum Intl.—R
CSS Publishing
(a)-Doubleday Relig.—R
Eerdmans Pub., Wm. B.—R
(s)-Elderberry Press
(s)-Fairway Press—R
Greenwood/Praeger
Hidden Brook Press—R
(s)-Holy Fire Publishing—R
(s)-Insight Publishing—R
Johns Hopkins—R
Lighthouse Publishing—R
Liturgy Training—R
Lutheran Univ. Press
Lutterworth Press—R
Messianic Jewish—R
Monarch Books
New Seeds—R
(s)-One World Press—R
Oregon Catholic
Parson Place—R
Pauline Books—R
Pilgrim Press—R
(s)-Pleasant Word—R
Power Publishing—R
(s)-Providence Pub.—R
Ravenhawk Books—R
Resource Public.
(s)-So. Baptist Press—R
St. Anthony Mess. Press—R
(s)-Tate Publishing—R

(s)-Trafford Publishing—R
Univ. Press of America—R
(s)-WinePress—R
(s)-Word Alive

MARRIAGE

Aaron Book—R
ACTA Publications
(s)-ACW Press—R
Ambassador Books
Ambassador-Emerald—R
(s)-American Binding—R
Anglicans United—R
(s)-Baal Hamon—R
(a)-Baker Books
Baker's Plays—R
(a)-B & H Publishing
Barbour
Beacon Hill Press—R
BelleBooks—R
Bethany House
BJU/Journey Forth—R
(s)-Black Forest/Tennessee—R
Blue Dolphin
(s)-Booklocker.com—R
(s)-Brentwood—R
(s)-Brown Books
Catholic Answers—R
Chapter Two—R
Christian Family—R
Christian Writer's Ebook—R
College Press—R
Comfort Publishing—R
(a)-Cook, David C.
(s)-Creation House—R
(s)-CrossHouse—R
CSS Publishing
Dabbling Mum Press
(s)-Dean Press, Robbie—R
Destiny Image—R
Destiny Image (books)—R
Dimensions for Living
Discovery House—R
(a)-Doubleday Relig.—R
Editorial Portavoz
Eerdmans Pub., Wm. B.—R
(s)-Elderberry Press
(a)-Emmaus Road—R
(s)-Essence—R
Evangelical Press
Evergreen Press
Fair Havens—R
(s)-Fairway Press—R
FaithWalk
(a)-FaithWords
FamilyLife (books)—R
(a)-Focus on the Family—R
Forward Movement
Greenwood/Praeger
GRQ—R
GuidepostsBooks

(a)-HarperOne
Harrison House
(a)-Harvest House
Hensley Publishing
Hidden Brook Press—R
(s)-Holy Fire Publishing—R
Hope Publishing—R
Howard Books
(s)-IMD Press—R
(s)-Insight Publishing—R
Judson Press—R
(a)-Kregel—R
Legacy Publishers
Life Changing Media
Lift Every Voice—R
Lighthouse Publishing—R
Lillenas
Lion and Lamb
Loyola Press
(s)-McDougal Publishing—R
Messianic Jewish—R
Millennium III—R
Monarch Books
MOPS Intl.
Nelson Ignite
(a)-Nelson, Thomas
New Hope—R
(s)-One World Press—R
P & R Publishing—R
Pacific Press
Parson Place—R
Parsons Publishing—R
Pauline Books—R
Paulist Press
Pilgrim Press—R
(s)-Pleasant Word—R
Power Publishing—R
(s)-Providence Pub.—R
(s)-Quiet Waters
Quintessential Books—R
Randall House
(a)-Regal
Revell
Samaritan Press
Scepter Publishers—R
(s)-Selah Publishing—R
(s)-So. Baptist Press—R
St. Anthony Mess. Press—R
Standard Publishing
(s)-Star Bible Public.
Still Waters Revival—R
Strang Book Group—R
(s)-Synergy Publishers—R
(s)-Tate Publishing—R
(s)-TEACH Services—R
(s)-Trafford Publishing—R
(a)-Tyndale House—R
VBC Publishing
(s)-VMI Publishers
(a)-WaterBrook Press—R
Whitaker House

(s)-WinePress—R
(s)-Word Alive
W Publishing
(s)-Zoe Life Publishing

MEMOIRS

Aaron Book—R
(s)-ACW Press—R
Ambassador-Emerald—R
(s)-American Binding—R
(s)-Baal Hamon—R
(a)-Baker Books
Baker's Plays—R
(a)-Ballantine
BelleBooks—R
(s)-Black Forest/Tennessee—R
(s)-Booklocker.com—R
(s)-Book Publishers—R
(s)-Brown Books
Christian Heritage—R
Christian Writer's Ebook—R
Cistercian—R
Cladach Publishing
Comfort Publishing—R
(s)-Creation House—R
(a)-Doubleday Relig.—R
(s)-Elderberry Press
(s)-Essence—R
(s)-Fairway Press—R
FaithWalk
(a)-FaithWords
Forward Movement
(s)-FruitBearer Pub.
Greenwood/Praeger
GuidepostsBooks
(a)-HarperOne
Hidden Brook Press—R
His Work Christian Pub.
(s)-Holy Fire Publishing—R
Ideals/Children
(s)-Insight Publishing—R
(s)-Leading Lady
(s)-LifeVest Publishing
Lighthouse Publishing—R
Lighthouse Trails—R
Lutterworth Press—R
Monarch Books
NavPress Student—R
(a)-Nelson, Thomas
(s)-One World Press—R
(a)-One World/Ballantine
Pacific Press
(s)-Pleasant Word—R
Power Publishing—R
(s)-Providence Pub.—R
Quintessential Books—R
Randall House
(a)-Regal
(s)-Salvation Publisher—R
Samaritan Press
(s)-Tate Publishing—R

(s)-TEACH Services—R
(s)-Trafford Publishing—R
Univ. Press of America—R
(s)-VMI Publishers
(s)-WinePress—R
(s)-Word Alive
(s)-Zoe Life Publishing

MEN'S BOOKS

Aaron Book—R
(s)-ACW Press—R
Ambassador Books
Ambassador-Emerald—R
(s)-American Binding—R
AMG Publishers
(s)-Baal Hamon—R
(a)-Baker Books
(a)-B & H Publishing
Barbour
Beacon Hill Press—R
Bethany House
(s)-Black Forest/Tennessee—R
Blue Dolphin
(s)-Booklocker.com—R
Bridge-Logos—R
(s)-Brown Books
Christian Writer's Ebook—R
College Press—R
Comfort Publishing—R
(s)-Creation House—R
Dimensions for Living
(a)-Doubleday Relig.—R
Editorial Portavoz
Eerdmans Pub., Wm. B.—R
(s)-Elderberry Press
(a)-Emmaus Road—R
(s)-Essence—R
Evangelical Press
Evergreen Press
Fair Havens—R
(s)-Fairway Press—R
Faith Communications
FaithWalk
Green Key Books
GRQ—R
(a)-Harvest House
Hensley Publishing
Hidden Brook Press—R
(s)-Holy Fire Publishing—R
(s)-IMD Press—R
Inkling Books—R
(s)-Insight Publishing—R
Judson Press—R
(a)-Kregel—R
Lift Every Voice—R
Lighthouse Publishing—R
Loyola Press
(s)-McDougal Publishing—R
Messianic Jewish—R
Monarch Books
NavPress Student—R

(a)-Nelson, Thomas
(s)-One World Press—R
Pacific Press
Parson Place—R
Pilgrim Press—R
(s)-Pleasant Word—R
Power Publishing—R
(s)-Providence Pub.—R
Quintessential Books—R
Randall House
Ravenhawk Books—R
Samaritan Press
(s)-Selah Publishing—R
(s)-Star Bible Public.
Strang Book Group—R
(s)-Synergy Publishers—R
(s)-Tate Publishing—R
(s)-Trafford Publishing—R
VBC Publishing
(s)-VMI Publishers
(a)-WaterBrook Press—R
Whitaker House
White Stone Books—R
(s)-WinePress—R
(s)-Word Alive
W Publishing
(s)-Zoe Life Publishing

MINIBOOKS

(s)-American Binding—R
(s)-Baal Hamon—R
(s)-Black Forest/Tennessee—R
GRQ—R
(s)-Holy Fire Publishing—R
(s)-IMD Press—R
Legacy Press—R
Lighthouse Publishing—R
Little Lauren Books
Monarch Books
(s)-One World Press—R
(s)-Path Pub. in Christ—R
Rose Publishing
Strang Book Group—R
(s)-Tate Publishing—R
(s)-Trafford Publishing—R

MIRACLES

Aaron Book—R
(s)-ACW Press—R
(s)-American Binding—R
(a)-Baker Books
Baker's Plays—R
(s)-Black Forest/Tennessee—R
Blue Dolphin
(s)-Booklocker.com—R
(s)-Brentwood—R
(s)-Brown Books
Christian Heritage—R
Christian Writer's Ebook—R
Comfort Publishing—R
(s)-Creation House—R

CSS Publishing
Destiny Image (books)—R
(s)-Elderberry Press
(s)-Essence—R
Evangelical Press
Evergreen Press
(s)-Fairway Press—R
Gollehon Press
Greenwood/Praeger
GuidepostsBooks
(a)-HarperOne
Harrison House
(a)-Harvest House
Hidden Brook Press—R
(s)-Holy Fire Publishing—R
(s)-IMD Press—R
(s)-Impact Christian—R
(s)-Insight Publishing—R
Lighthouse Publishing—R
Lillenas
Lion and Lamb
Loyola Press
(s)-McDougal Publishing—R
Monarch Books
(s)-One World Press—R
Pacific Press
Paradise Research—R
Parson Place—R
Parsons Publishing—R
(s)-Path Pub. in Christ—R
Pauline Books—R
(s)-Pleasant Word—R
Power Publishing—R
(s)-Providence Pub.—R
Revival Nation
(s)-Salvation Publisher—R
Samaritan Press
(s)-Selah Publishing—R
(s)-So. Baptist Press—R
St. Anthony Mess. Press—R
(s)-Star Bible Public.
Strang Book Group—R
(s)-Tate Publishing—R
(s)-TEACH Services—R
(s)-Testimony Press
(s)-Trafford Publishing—R
(s)-VMI Publishers
Whitaker House
(s)-WinePress—R
(s)-Word Alive
(s)-Zoe Life Publishing

MISSIONARY

Aaron Book—R
(s)-ACW Press—R
Ambassador-Emerald—R
(s)-American Binding—R
(s)-Ampelos Press
(a)-Baker Books
Baker's Plays—R
(a)-B & H Publishing

(s)-Black Forest/Tennessee—R
(s)-Booklocker.com—R
(s)-Brentwood—R
(s)-Brown Books
Carey Library, Wm.—R
Chapter Two—R
Christian Focus—R
Christian Heritage—R
Christian Writer's Ebook—R
Comfort Publishing—R
(s)-Creation House—R
(s)-CrossHouse—R
CSS Publishing
Discovery House—R
Eerdmans Pub., Wm. B.—R
(s)-Elderberry Press
(s)-Essence—R
Evangelical Press
Evergreen Press
Fair Havens—R
(s)-Fairway Press—R
FaithWalk
Father's Press—R
Forward Movement
Friends United Press
Greenwood/Praeger
Hannibal Books
Harrison House
Harvest Day
Hidden Brook Press—R
(s)-Holy Fire Publishing—R
Hope Publishing—R
(s)-IMD Press—R
(s)-Insight Publishing—R
Lift Every Voice—R
Lighthouse Publishing—R
Lighthouse Trails—R
Lillenas
Lion and Lamb
Lutterworth Press—R
(s)-McDougal Publishing—R
Monarch Books
(s)-One World Press—R
Pacific Press
Parson Place—R
Parsons Publishing—R
(s)-Path Pub. in Christ—R
Pauline Books—R
(s)-Pleasant Word—R
Power Publishing—R
(s)-Providence Pub.—R
(s)-Quiet Waters
Randall House
Rose Publishing
Salt Works—R
(s)-So. Baptist Press—R
St. Anthony Mess. Press—R
(s)-Star Bible Public.
Strang Book Group—R
(s)-Tate Publishing—R
(s)-TEACH Services—R

(s)-Testimony Press
(s)-Trafford Publishing—R
VBC Publishing
(s)-VMI Publishers
(s)-WinePress—R
(s)-Word Alive
Yale Univ. Press—R
(s)-Zoe Life Publishing

MONEY MANAGEMENT

Aaron Book—R
(s)-ACW Press—R
(s)-American Binding—R
(a)-Baker Books
Barbour
Blue Dolphin
BMH Books—R
(s)-Booklocker.com—R
(s)-Brentwood—R
(s)-Brown Books
Christian Writer's Ebook—R
Comfort Publishing—R
(a)-Cook, David C.
(s)-Creation House—R
Dabbling Mum Press
Editorial Portavoz
Eerdmans Pub., Wm. B.—R
(s)-Elderberry Press
(s)-Essence—R
Evangelical Press
Evergreen Press
(s)-Fairway Press—R
FaithWalk
(a)-FaithWords
Forward Movement
Greenwood/Praeger
Grupo Nelson
Hannibal Books
Harrison House
(a)-Harvest House
Hensley Publishing
Hidden Brook Press—R
His Work Christian Pub.
(s)-Holy Fire Publishing—R
(s)-IMD Press—R
(s)-Insight Publishing—R
Judson Press—R
(s)-Leading Lady
Legacy Publishers
Lift Every Voice—R
Lighthouse Publishing—R
Lion and Lamb
Millennium III—R
(a)-Moody Publishers
MountainView
(a)-Nelson, Thomas
New Hope—R
(s)-One World Press—R
Pacific Press
Parson Place—R
(s)-Pleasant Word—R

Power Publishing—R
(s)-Providence Pub.—R
Quintessential Books—R
Ravenhawk Books—R
Reference Service
(a)-Regnery
(s)-Salvation Publisher—R
Samaritan Press
(s)-So. Baptist Press—R
(s)-Star Bible Public.
Starik Publishing
Strang Book Group—R
(s)-Synergy Publishers—R
(s)-Tate Publishing—R
(s)-TEACH Services—R
(s)-Trafford Publishing—R
VBC Publishing
(s)-VMI Publishers
Walk Worthy—R
(a)-WaterBrook Press—R
(s)-WinePress—R
(s)-Word Alive
Xyzzy Press
(s)-Zoe Life Publishing

MUSIC-RELATED BOOKS

Aaron Book—R
American Cath. Press—R
(a)-Baker Books
Blue Dolphin
BMH Books—R
(s)-Booklocker.com—R
(s)-Brown Books
Cambridge Scholars Pub.
Christian Writer's Ebook—R
Contemporary Drama
Countryman, J.
Destiny Image (books)—R
Eerdmans Pub., Wm. B.—R
(s)-Essence—R
Evangelical Press
(s)-Fairway Press—R
FaithWalk
Guardian Angel
Hidden Brook Press—R
His Work Christian Pub.
(s)-Holy Fire Publishing—R
(s)-Insight Publishing—R
Lighthouse Publishing—R
Lion and Lamb
Lutheran Univ. Press
Monarch Books
(s)-One World Press—R
(s)-Pleasant Word—R
Power Publishing—R
(s)-Providence Pub.—R
(a)-Regal
Samaritan Press
Standard Publishing
(s)-Star Bible Public.
T & T Clark—R

(s)-Tate Publishing—R
(s)-Trafford Publishing—R
(s)-VMI Publishers
(s)-WinePress—R
(s)-Word Alive

NOVELTY BOOKS FOR KIDS

Atheneum/Yg. Readers
(a)-Baker Books
Baker Trittin
Big Idea
(s)-Elderberry Press
(s)-Fairway Press—R
Guardian Angel
(s)-IMD Press—R
Journey Stone—R
(a)-Kregel Kidzone
Legacy Press—R
Lift Every Voice—R
Lion and Lamb
Monarch Books
(s)-One World Press—R
Salt Works—R
Samaritan Press
Standard Publishing
(s)-Tate Publishing—R
(s)-Trafford Publishing—R
White Stone Books—R
(s)-Word Alive

PAMPHLETS

Chalice Press
Chapter Two—R
Christian Writer's Ebook—R
Concordia
(s)-Essence—R
Evangelical Press
Forward Movement
Founders Press
(s)-FruitBearer Pub.
Good Book—R
(a)-Harvest House
(s)-IMD Press—R
InterVarsity Press—R
Intl. Awakening—R
Libros Liguori
Liguori Public.—R
Liturgy Training—R
Neibauer Press—R
(s)-One World Press—R
Our Sunday Visitor—R
Paradise Research—R
Paulist Press
Rose Publishing
Salt Works—R
Trinity Foundation—R

PARENTING

Aaron Book—R
ACTA Publications
(s)-ACW Press—R

Adams Media
Ambassador Books
(s)-American Binding—R
AMG Publishers
(a)-Baker Books
Baker Trittin
Baker's Plays—R
(a)-Ballantine
(a)-B & H Publishing
Barbour
Beacon Hill Press—R
Bethany House
BJU/Journey Forth—R
(s)-Black Forest/Tennessee—R
Blue Dolphin
(s)-Booklocker.com—R
(s)-Book Publishers—R
(s)-Brentwood—R
(s)-Brown Books
Christian Family—R
Christian Writer's Ebook—R
College Press—R
Conari Press
Conciliar Press—R
Concordia
(a)-Cook, David C.
(s)-Creation House—R
Dabbling Mum Press
(s)-Dean Press, Robbie—R
Destiny Image (books)—R
Dimensions for Living
Discovery House—R
Editorial Portavoz
Eerdmans Pub., Wm. B.—R
(s)-Elderberry Press
(s)-Essence—R
Evangelical Press
Evergreen Press
(s)-Fairway Press—R
(a)-FaithWords
(a)-Focus on the Family—R
Forward Movement
(s)-FruitBearer Pub.
Greenwood/Praeger
Grupo Nelson
Halo Publishing
Harrison House
(a)-Harvest House
Health Commun.
Hensley Publishing
Hidden Brook Press—R
His Work Christian Pub.
(s)-Holy Fire Publishing—R
Howard Books
(s)-IMD Press—R
(s)-Insight Publishing—R
Judson Press—R
Kaleidoscope Press—R
Kingsley, Jessica Pub.—R
Langmarc
(s)-Leading Lady
Life Changing Media

Lift Every Voice—R
Lighthouse Publishing—R
Liguori Public.—R
Lillenas
Lion and Lamb
(s)-McDougal Publishing—R
Messianic Jewish—R
Millennium III—R
Mission City Press
Monarch Books
MOPS Intl.
(a)-Nelson, Thomas
New Hope—R
(s)-One World Press—R
Our Sunday Visitor—R
P & R Publishing—R
Pacific Press
Parsons Publishing—R
Pauline Books—R
(s)-Pleasant Word—R
Power Publishing—R
(s)-Providence Pub.—R
Quintessential Books—R
Randall House
(a)-Regal
Revell
Rose Publishing
Scepter Publishers—R
(s)-Selah Publishing—R
St. Anthony Mess. Press—R
Standard Publishing
(s)-Star Bible Public.
Starik Publishing
Still Waters Revival—R
Strang Book Group—R
Tarcher, Jeremy P.—R
(s)-Tate Publishing—R
(s)-TEACH Services—R
(s)-Testimony Press
Torch Legacy
(s)-Trafford Publishing—R
(a)-Tyndale House—R
VBC Publishing
(s)-VMI Publishers
Walk Worthy—R
(a)-WaterBrook Press—R
Whitaker House
(s)-WinePress—R
(s)-Word Alive
W Publishing
(s)-Zoe Life Publishing

PASTORS' HELPS

Aaron Book—R
(s)-ACW Press—R
(s)-American Binding—R
(s)-Baal Hamon—R
Baker Academic
(a)-Baker Books
(a)-B & H Publishing
Beacon Hill Press—R
BJU/Journey Forth—R

BMH Books—R
(s)-Booklocker.com—R
(s)-Brentwood—R
Bridge-Logos—R
(s)-Brown Books
Chalice Press
Christian Focus—R
Christian Writer's Ebook—R
Church Growth Inst.
(s)-Creation House—R
CSS Publishing
(s)-DCTS Publishing
Earthen Vessel—R
Editorial Portavoz
Eerdmans Pub., Wm. B.—R
(s)-Elderberry Press
(s)-Essence—R
Evangelical Press
(s)-Fairway Press—R
Fortress Press
Gospel Publishing
Greenwood/Praeger
Group Publishing
Harcourt Religion
Harrison House
Hendrickson—R
Hidden Brook Press—R
(s)-Holy Fire Publishing—R
(s)-IMD Press—R
(s)-Insight Publishing—R
Judson Press—R
(s)-Kindred Books—R
Kingsley, Jessica Pub.—R
(a)-Kregel—R
Lighthouse Publishing—R
Lion and Lamb
Liturgy Training—R
Lutheran Univ. Press
Monarch Books
Neibauer Press—R
(s)-One World Press—R
P & R Publishing—R
Pilgrim Press—R
(s)-Pleasant Word—R
Power Publishing—R
(s)-Providence Pub.—R
Randall House
(a)-Regal
(s)-Sermon Select Press
(s)-So. Baptist Press—R
St. Anthony Mess. Press—R
Standard Publishing
(s)-Star Bible Public.
(s)-Tate Publishing—R
(s)-TEACH Services—R
Torch Legacy
(s)-Trafford Publishing—R
VBC Publishing
(s)-VMI Publishers
Wesleyan Publishing
(s)-WinePress—R
(s)-Word Alive

(s)-Zoe Life Publishing
Zondervan

PERSONAL EXPERIENCE
Aaron Book—R
(s)-ACW Press—R
(s)-American Binding—R
(s)-Baal Hamon—R
(a)-Baker Books
Baker's Plays—R
(s)-Black Forest/Tennessee—R
Blue Dolphin
(s)-Booklocker.com—R
(s)-Brentwood—R
Bridge-Logos—R
(s)-Brown Books
CarePoint Publishing—R
Chicken Soup
Christian Family—R
Christian Writer's Ebook—R
Comfort Publishing—R
(s)-Creation House—R
(s)-DCTS Publishing
Destiny Image—R
(s)-Elderberry Press
(s)-Essence—R
Evangelical Press
(s)-Fairway Press—R
FaithWalk
(s)-FruitBearer Pub.
Greenwood/Praeger
GRQ—R
Hannibal Books
(a)-HarperOne
(a)-Harvest House
Hidden Brook Press—R
(s)-Holy Fire Publishing—R
(s)-IMD Press—R
(s)-Insight Publishing—R
Life Changing Media
Lighthouse Publishing—R
Lighthouse Trails—R
Lion and Lamb
(s)-McDougal Publishing—R
Monarch Books
NavPress Student—R
(a)-Nelson, Thomas
(s)-One World Press—R
Pacific Press
(s)-Path Pub. in Christ—R
(s)-Pleasant Word—R
Power Publishing—R
(s)-Providence Pub.—R
Randall House
Ravenhawk Books—R
(a)-Regal
Revival Nation
(s)-Salvation Publisher—R
Samaritan Press
(s)-So. Baptist Press—R
(s)-Star Bible Public.
Strang Book Group—R

(s)-Tate Publishing—R
(s)-TEACH Services—R
(s)-Testimony Press
(s)-Trafford Publishing—R
(s)-VMI Publishers
(s)-WinePress—R
(s)-Word Alive
W Publishing
(s)-Zoe Life Publishing

PERSONAL GROWTH
Aadeon Publishing—R
Aaron Book—R
(s)-ACW Press—R
(s)-Ali Literary, Alfred—R
Ambassador Books
Ambassador-Emerald—R
(s)-American Binding—R
(s)-Baal Hamon—R
(a)-Baker Books
Baker's Plays—R
Barbour
Bethany House
BJU/Journey Forth—R
(s)-Black Forest/Tennessee—R
Blue Dolphin
BMH Books—R
(s)-Booklocker.com—R
(s)-Book Publishers—R
Bridge-Logos—R
(s)-Brown Books
Canticle Books—R
CarePoint Publishing—R
CharismaKids
Christian Family—R
Christian Writer's Ebook—R
Comfort Publishing—R
Conari Press
(s)-Creation House—R
Dabbling Mum Press
(s)-DCTS Publishing
Deo Volente
Destiny Image—R
Destiny Image (books)—R
Discovery House—R
(s)-Elderberry Press
(s)-Essence—R
Evangelical Press
Evergreen Press
(s)-Fairway Press—R
FaithWalk
(a)-FaithWords
Forward Movement
(s)-FruitBearer Pub.
Greenwood/Praeger
GRQ—R
GuidepostsBooks
Hannibal Books
(a)-HarperOne
(a)-Hay House
Hendrickson—R
Hensley Publishing

Hidden Brook Press—R
(s)-Holy Fire Publishing—R
(s)-IMD Press—R
(s)-Insight Publishing—R
Jebaire Publishing
Judson Press—R
(s)-Kindred Books—R
(a)-Kregel—R
Life Changing Media
Lift Every Voice—R
Lighthouse Publishing—R
Lillenas
Lion and Lamb
Magnus Press—R
(s)-McDougal Publishing—R
Monarch Books
NavPress
NavPress Student—R
(a)-Nelson, Thomas
New Hope—R
New Seeds—R
(s)-One World Press—R
P & R Publishing—R
Pacific Press
Parson Place—R
Parsons Publishing—R
(s)-Path Pub. in Christ—R
(s)-Path Publishing—R
Pilgrim Press—R
(s)-Pleasant Word—R
Power Publishing—R
(s)-Providence Pub.—R
Quintessential Books—R
Randall House
Ravenhawk Books—R
(a)-Regal
Revival Nation
Samaritan Press
(s)-Star Bible Public.
Strang Book Group—R
(s)-Synergy Publishers—R
(s)-Tate Publishing—R
(s)-TEACH Services—R
(s)-Trafford Publishing—R
(a)-Tyndale House—R
(s)-VMI Publishers
(a)-WaterBrook Press—R
White Stone Books—R
(s)-WinePress—R
(s)-Word Alive
W Publishing
Xyzzy Press
(s)-Zoe Life Publishing

PERSONAL RENEWAL

Aaron Book—R
(s)-ACW Press—R
(s)-Ali Literary, Alfred—R
(s)-American Binding—R
(s)-Baal Hamon—R
(a)-Baker Books

Baker's Plays—R
Barbour
(s)-Black Forest/Tennessee—R
(s)-Booklocker.com—R
Bridge-Logos—R
(s)-Brown Books
CharismaKids
Christian Writer's Ebook—R
Comfort Publishing—R
Conari Press
(s)-Creation House—R
(s)-DCTS Publishing
Destiny Image—R
Destiny Image (books)—R
(s)-Elderberry Press
(s)-Essence—R
Evangelical Press
Evergreen Press
(s)-Fairway Press—R
FaithWalk
Forward Movement
(s)-FruitBearer Pub.
Greenwood/Praeger
GRQ—R
Hannibal Books
(a)-HarperOne
Hendrickson—R
Hensley Publishing
Hidden Brook Press—R
(s)-Holy Fire Publishing—R
(s)-IMD Press—R
(s)-Impact Christian—R
(s)-Insight Publishing—R
Intl. Awakening—R
Jebaire Publishing
Judson Press—R
Kirk House
Life Changing Media
Lift Every Voice—R
Lighthouse Publishing—R
Lillenas
Lion and Lamb
(s)-McDougal Publishing—R
Monarch Books
NavPress
NavPress Student—R
New Hope—R
New Seeds—R
(s)-One World Press—R
P & R Publishing—R
Pacific Press
(s)-Path Pub. in Christ—R
(s)-Path Publishing—R
Pilgrim Press—R
(s)-Pleasant Word—R
Power Publishing—R
(s)-Providence Pub.—R
Randall House
Ravenhawk Books—R
(a)-Regal
Revival Nation

(s)-Star Bible Public.
Strang Book Group—R
(s)-Synergy Publishers—R
(s)-Tate Publishing—R
(s)-TEACH Services—R
(s)-Trafford Publishing—R
(a)-Tyndale House—R
(s)-VMI Publishers
Wesleyan Publishing
(s)-WinePress—R
(s)-Word Alive
(s)-Zoe Life Publishing

PHILOSOPHY

Aaron Book—R
(s)-ACW Press—R
(s)-American Binding—R
(s)-Baal Hamon—R
(a)-Baker Books
Baker's Plays—R
Baylor Univ. Press
(s)-Black Forest/Tennessee—R
Blue Dolphin
(s)-Booklocker.com—R
(s)-Brentwood—R
(s)-Brown Books
Cambridge Scholars Pub.
Cambridge Univ. Press
Christian Writer's Ebook—R
Clarke & Co., James—R
Continuum Intl.—R
(s)-Creation House—R
(a)-Doubleday Relig.—R
Dover Publications—R
Eerdmans Pub., Wm. B.—R
(s)-Elderberry Press
(s)-Essence—R
Evangelical Press
(s)-Fairway Press—R
FaithWalk
Fifth Estate—R
Fordham Univ. Press—R
Greenwood/Praeger
(a)-HarperOne
Hidden Brook Press—R
(s)-Holy Fire Publishing—R
(s)-IMD Press—R
Inkling Books—R
(s)-Insight Publishing—R
InterVarsity Press—R
Larson Publications—R
Lighthouse Publishing—R
Lutheran Univ. Press
Lutterworth Press—R
Mercer Univ. Press—R
Monarch Books
New Seeds—R
(s)-One World Press—R
(a)-One World/Ballantine
P & R Publishing—R
Paragon House—R

Pauline Books—R
(s)-Pleasant Word—R
Power Publishing—R
(s)-Providence Pub.—R
Quintessential Books—R
(a)-Regnery
Salt Works—R
St. Augustine's Press—R
St. Bede's Publications
St. Pauls/Alba House—R
(s)-Star Bible Public.
Still Waters Revival—R
Tarcher, Jeremy P.—R
(s)-Tate Publishing—R
(s)-TEACH Services—R
Third World Press—R
(s)-Trafford Publishing—R
Trinity Foundation—R
Univ. Press of America—R
(s)-VMI Publishers
(s)-WinePress—R
Wipf and Stock
(s)-Word Alive
Xyzzy Press

PHOTOGRAPHS (FOR COVERS)

Abingdon Press
(s)-Ali Literary, Alfred—R
Ambassador Books
(s)-American Binding—R
(s)-Baal Hamon—R
(s)-Black Forest/Tennessee—R
(s)-Booklocker.com—R
(s)-Book Publishers—R
(s)-Brentwood—R
Bridge-Logos—R
Cambridge Scholars Pub.
Canadian Inst. for Law—R
CarePoint Publishing—R
Carey Library, Wm.—R
Catholic Answers—R
Catholic Univ. of Amer. Press
Christian Focus—R
Church Growth Inst.
Cistercian—R
Comfort Publishing—R
Conciliar Press—R
Continuum Intl.—R
(s)-Creation House—R
(s)-CrossHouse—R
(s)-Dean Press, Robbie—R
Dove Inspirational—R
(s)-Essence—R
ETC Publications
Fair Havens—R
FaithWalk
FamilyLife (books)—R
Father's Press—R
Fifth Estate—R
(s)-FruitBearer Pub.

Georgetown Univ. Press
Guardian Angel
Guernica Editions—R
Harcourt Religion
(s)-IMD Press—R
Intl. Awakening—R
Jebaire Publishing
Jireh Publishing
Journey Stone—R
Jubilant Press—R
Kingsley, Jessica Pub.—R
Knight George Pub.
Life Changing Media
Lift Every Voice—R
Lighthouse Publishing—R
Lion and Lamb
Liturgy Training—R
Lutheran Univ. Press
Monarch Books
MountainView
Neibauer Press—R
New Canaan—R
New Hope—R
New Leaf
(s)-One World Press—R
Oregon Catholic
Our Sunday Visitor—R
Parson Place—R
(s)-Path Pub. in Christ—R
Paulist Press
Pelican Publishing—R
Pilgrim Press—R
Players Press—R
(s)-Pleasant Word—R
Power Publishing—R
Quintessential Books—R
Ravenhawk Books—R
Samaritan Press
(s)-Selah Publishing—R
Sheed & Ward—R
St. Anthony Mess. Press—R
(s)-Star Bible Public.
Strang Book Group—R
(s)-Synergy Publishers—R
T & T Clark—R
(s)-Tate Publishing—R
Tau-Publishing—R
(s)-TEACH Services—R
Touch Publications—R
Trinity Foundation—R
Troitsa Books
United Methodist
Univ. of AR Press—R
Virginia Pines Press
Wilshire Book—R
(s)-WinePress—R
(s)-Xulon Press—R
(s)-Zoe Life Publishing

POETRY

Aaron Book—R

(s)-ACW Press—R
(s)-American Binding—R
Atheneum/Yg. Readers
(s)-Baal Hamon—R
Baker's Plays—R
(s)-Black Forest/Tennessee—R
Blue Dolphin
(s)-Booklocker.com—R
Boyds Mills Press—R
(s)-Brentwood—R
(s)-Brown Books
Christian Writer's Ebook—R
Comfort Publishing—R
(s)-Creation House—R
(s)-Dean Press, Robbie—R
DiskUs Publishing
E-Digital Books
Eerdmans Pub., Wm. B.—R
(s)-Elderberry Press
(s)-Essence—R
(s)-Fairway Press—R
(s)-FruitBearer Pub.
Guernica Editions—R
Halo Publishing
Harvest Day
Hidden Brook Press—R
(s)-Holy Fire Publishing—R
(s)-Insight Publishing—R
(s)-Leading Lady
(s)-LifeVest Publishing
Lighthouse Publishing—R
MoreThanNovellas
Mt. Olive College Press
New Seeds—R
(s)-One World Press—R
(s)-Path Pub. in Christ—R
(s)-Path Publishing—R
(s)-Pleasant Word—R
(s)-Poems By Me—R
(s)-Poet's Cove Press
Power Publishing—R
(s)-Providence Pub.—R
(s)-Selah Publishing—R
(s)-So. Baptist Press—R
(s)-Tate Publishing—R
(s)-Trafford Publishing—R
(s)-WinePress—R
(s)-Word Alive
Xyzzy Press
(s)-Zoe Life Publishing

POLITICAL

Aadeon Publishing—R
Aaron Book—R
(s)-ACW Press—R
(s)-American Binding—R
AMG Publishers
(a)-Baker Books
Baker's Plays—R
Baylor Univ. Press
(s)-Black Forest/Tennessee—R

(s)-Booklocker.com—R
Branden Publishing—R
(s)-Brentwood—R
(s)-Brown Books
Cambridge Scholars Pub.
Canadian Inst. for Law—R
Christian Writer's Ebook—R
Comfort Publishing—R
(s)-Creation House—R
(a)-Doubleday Relig.—R
Eerdmans Pub., Wm. B.—R
(s)-Elderberry Press
(s)-Essence—R
(s)-Fairway Press—R
Fordham Univ. Press—R
Georgetown Univ. Press
Gollehon Press
Greenwood/Praeger
(a)-HarperOne
Hidden Brook Press—R
(s)-Holy Fire Publishing—R
Inkling Books—R
(s)-Insight Publishing—R
InterVarsity Press—R
Invisible College Press
Lighthouse Publishing—R
Mercer Univ. Press—R
(a)-Nelson, Thomas
New Canaan—R
(s)-One World Press—R
(a)-One World/Ballantine
(s)-Path Publishing—R
Pilgrim Press—R
(s)-Pleasant Word—R
Power Publishing—R
(s)-Providence Pub.—R
Ravenhawk Books—R
(a)-Regnery
Still Waters Revival—R
Strang Book Group—R
(s)-Synergy Publishers—R
(s)-Tate Publishing—R
Third World Press—R
(s)-Trafford Publishing—R
Trinity Foundation—R
Univ. Press of America—R
(s)-VMI Publishers
(s)-WinePress—R
(s)-Word Alive
Yale Univ. Press—R

POPULAR CULTURE*

Aaron Book—R
(s)-ACW Press—R
Ambassador-Emerald—R
(s)-American Binding—R
Bethany House
(s)-Brown Books
(s)-Creation House—R
Eerdmans Pub., Wm. B.—R
Eldridge Plays

(s)-Essence—R
(a)-FaithWords
GRQ—R
Hendrickson—R
(s)-Holy Fire Publishing—R
Howard Books
(s)-Insight Publishing—R
Jossey-Bass
(a)-Kregel—R
Lift Every Voice—R
Lighthouse Publishing—R
Lillenas
Lutterworth Press—R
Millennium III—R
(s)-Pleasant Word—R
Power Publishing—R
(s)-Providence Pub.—R
Ravenhawk Books—R
(s)-Trafford Publishing—R
(s)-WinePress—R
Yale Univ. Press—R

POSTMODERNISM

Aaron Book—R
(s)-ACW Press—R
(s)-American Binding—R
(s)-Booklocker.com—R
(s)-Brown Books
Cambridge Scholars Pub.
Chalice Press
(s)-Creation House—R
Eerdmans Pub., Wm. B.—R
(s)-Elderberry Press
(s)-Essence—R
Evangelical Press
Fair Havens—R
Hendrickson—R
(s)-Holy Fire Publishing—R
Howard Books
(s)-Insight Publishing—R
InterVarsity Press—R
Jossey-Bass
(a)-Kregel—R
Lighthouse Publishing—R
Monarch Books
(a)-Nelson, Thomas
P & R Publishing—R
Paragon House—R
(s)-Pleasant Word—R
Power Publishing—R
(s)-Providence Pub.—R
Resource Public.
Salt Works—R
(s)-Star Bible Public.
Strang Book Group—R
(s)-Trafford Publishing—R
(s)-WinePress—R

PRAYER

Aaron Book—R
Abingdon Press

ACTA Publications
(s)-ACW Press—R
Ambassador Books
Ambassador-Emerald—R
(s)-American Binding—R
American Cath. Press—R
Anglicans United—R
(s)-Baal Hamon—R
(a)-Baker Books
Baker Trittin
Baker's Plays—R
(a)-B & H Publishing
Barbour
Beacon Hill Press—R
Bethany House
(s)-Black Forest/Tennessee—R
BMH Books—R
(s)-Booklocker.com—R
(s)-Brentwood—R
Bridge-Logos—R
(s)-Brown Books
Catholic Book
CharismaKids
Christian Family—R
Christian Focus—R
Christian Heritage—R
Christian Writer's Ebook—R
Cistercian—R
College Press—R
Comfort Publishing—R
Continuum Intl.—R
(a)-Cook, David C.
(s)-Creation House—R
(s)-CrossHouse—R
Crossroad Publishing—R
CSS Publishing
(s)-DCTS Publishing
Deo Volente
Destiny Image—R
Destiny Image (books)—R
Discovery House—R
(a)-Doubleday Relig.—R
Eerdmans Pub., Wm. B.—R
(s)-Elderberry Press
(a)-Emmaus Road—R
(s)-Essence—R
Evangelical Press
Evergreen Press
Fair Havens—R
(s)-Fairway Press—R
Faith Alive
FaithWalk
(a)-FaithWords
Father's Press—R
Forward Movement
(s)-FruitBearer Pub.
Good Book—R
Gospel Publishing
Greenwood/Praeger
GRQ—R
GuidepostsBooks

Harcourt Religion
(a)-HarperOne
Harrison House
(a)-Harvest House
Hendrickson—R
Hensley Publishing
Hidden Brook Press—R
(s)-Holy Fire Publishing—R
Hope Publishing—R
Howard Books
(s)-IMD Press—R
(s)-Impact Christian—R
(s)-Insight Publishing—R
InterVarsity Press—R
Intl. Awakening—R
Jireh Publishing
Judson Press—R
(a)-Kregel—R
Legacy Press—R
Libros Liguori
Lift Every Voice—R
Lighthouse Publishing—R
Liguori Public.—R
Lillenas
Lion and Lamb
Liturgy Training—R
Loyola Press
Lutterworth Press—R
(s)-McDougal Publishing—R
Messianic Jewish—R
Monarch Books
(a)-Moody Publishers
Morehouse—R
NavPress Student—R
(a)-Nelson, Thomas
New Seeds—R
(s)-One World Press—R
Our Sunday Visitor—R
P & R Publishing—R
Pacific Press
Paradise Research—R
(s)-Path Pub. in Christ—R
Pauline Books—R
Pauline Kids
Paulist Press
Pflaum Publishing
Pilgrim Press—R
(s)-Pleasant Word—R
Power Publishing—R
(s)-Providence Pub.—R
Quintessential Books—R
Randall House
(a)-Regal
Revival Nation
Rose Publishing
(s)-Salvation Publisher—R
Samaritan Press
Scepter Publishers—R
(s)-Selah Publishing—R
Smyth & Helwys
(s)-So. Baptist Press—R

St. Anthony Mess. Press—R
St. Bede's Publications
St. Pauls/Alba House—R
Standard Publishing
(s)-Star Bible Public.
Still Waters Revival—R
Strang Book Group—R
(s)-Synergy Publishers—R
(s)-Tate Publishing—R
(s)-TEACH Services—R
(s)-Testimony Press
(s)-Trafford Publishing—R
(a)-Tyndale House—R
VBC Publishing
(s)-VMI Publishers
Walk Worthy—R
(a)-WaterBrook Press—R
Wesleyan Publishing
Westminster John Knox
Whitaker House
White Stone Books—R
(s)-WinePress—R
Woodland Gospel
(s)-Word Alive
W Publishing
(s)-Zoe Life Publishing

PRINT-ON-DEMAND

Aadeon Publishing—R
Aaron Book—R
(s)-ACW Press—R
(s)-American Binding—R
(s)-Baal Hamon—R
(s)-Black Forest/Tennessee—R
Blue Dolphin
(s)-Booklocker.com—R
(s)-Booklocker Jr.
(s)-Brentwood—R
Bridge-Logos—R
Capstone Fiction—R
Christian Writer's Ebook—R
Comfort Publishing—R
Continuum Intl.—R
Crossroad Publishing—R
CSS Publishing
(s)-Dean Press, Robbie—R
Editorial Portavoz
(s)-Elderberry Press
Evangelical Press
Evergreen Press
Fifth Estate—R
Georgetown Univ. Press
Hannibal Books
Hidden Brook Press—R
(s)-Holy Fire Publishing—R
(s)-Infinity Publishing
Inkling Books—R
(s)-Insight Publishing—R
(s)-Kindred Books—R
Lighthouse Publishing—R
Lion and Lamb

Little Lauren Books
Lutterworth Press—R
(s)-One World Press—R
Players Press—R
(s)-Pleasant Word—R
(s)-Poems By Me—R
Power Publishing—R
Randall House Digital
Ravenhawk Books—R
(s)-Salvation Publisher—R
(s)-Self Publish Press—R
Sheed & Ward—R
(s)-Strong Tower—R
(s)-Synergy Publishers—R
(s)-Trafford Publishing—R
Univ. Press of America—R
VBC Publishing
(s)-Word Alive
(s)-Xulon Press—R

PROGRAM RESOURCES*

Aaron Book—R
Abingdon Press
(s)-Brown Books
Eerdmans Pub., Wm. B.—R
Eldridge Plays
(s)-Essence—R
Evangelical Press
Good Book—R
Gospel Publishing
Group Publishing
(s)-Holy Fire Publishing—R
Lillenas
Lion and Lamb
Paradise Research—R
Power Publishing—R
(s)-Trafford Publishing—R
(s)-WinePress—R

PROPHECY

Aaron Book—R
(s)-ACW Press—R
(s)-American Binding—R
(s)-Baal Hamon—R
(a)-Baker Books
Baker's Plays—R
(s)-Black Forest/Tennessee—R
BMH Books—R
(s)-Booklocker.com—R
(s)-Brentwood—R
Bridge-Logos—R
(s)-Brown Books
Chapter Two—R
CharismaKids
Christian Writer's Ebook—R
Comfort Publishing—R
(s)-Creation House—R
CSS Publishing
Destiny Image (books)—R
Eerdmans Pub., Wm. B.—R
(s)-Elderberry Press

(s)-Essence—R
Evangelical Press
Fair Havens—R
(s)-Fairway Press—R
FaithWalk
Father's Press—R
(s)-FruitBearer Pub.
Greenwood/Praeger
Harrison House
(a)-Harvest House
Hidden Brook Press—R
(s)-Holy Fire Publishing—R
(s)-IMD Press—R
(s)-Insight Publishing—R
(a)-Kregel—R
Lighthouse Publishing—R
Lutterworth Press—R
(s)-McDougal Publishing—R
Monarch Books
New Leaf
(s)-One World Press—R
P & R Publishing—R
Pacific Press
Parson Place—R
Parsons Publishing—R
(s)-Path Pub. in Christ—R
(s)-Pleasant Word—R
Power Publishing—R
(s)-Providence Pub.—R
Randall House
Ravenhawk Books—R
Revival Nation
(s)-Salvation Publisher—R
Samaritan Press
(s)-Selah Publishing—R
(s)-So. Baptist Press—R
(s)-Star Bible Public.
Still Waters Revival—R
Strang Book Group—R
(s)-Synergy Publishers—R
(s)-Tate Publishing—R
(s)-TEACH Services—R
(s)-Trafford Publishing—R
(s)-VMI Publishers
(s)-WinePress—R
(s)-Word Alive
W Publishing
(s)-Zoe Life Publishing

PSYCHOLOGY

Aaron Book—R
(s)-ACW Press—R
Adams Media
(s)-American Binding—R
Baker Academic
Baker's Plays—R
Blue Dolphin
BMH Books—R
(s)-Booklocker.com—R
(s)-Book Publishers—R
(s)-Brentwood—R
(s)-Brown Books

Cambridge Scholars Pub.
CarePoint Publishing—R
Christian Writer's Ebook—R
Comfort Publishing—R
(s)-Creation House—R
Eerdmans Pub., Wm. B.—R
(s)-Elderberry Press
(s)-Essence—R
Evangelical Press
Evergreen Press
(s)-Fairway Press—R
FaithWalk
Fifth Estate—R
Greenwood/Praeger
GRQ—R
(a)-Harvest House
Health Commun.
Hidden Brook Press—R
(s)-Holy Fire Publishing—R
Hope Publishing—R
(s)-IMD Press—R
(s)-Insight Publishing—R
InterVarsity Press—R
Jossey-Bass
Larson Publications—R
Life Changing Media
Lighthouse Publishing—R
Lion and Lamb
Lutterworth Press—R
Monarch Books
MountainView
(s)-One World Press—R
(a)-One World/Ballantine
Paragon House—R
(s)-Pleasant Word—R
Power Publishing—R
(s)-Providence Pub.—R
Quintessential Books—R
(s)-Recovery Commun.
Samaritan Press
Siloam
(s)-So. Baptist Press—R
(s)-Star Bible Public.
Tarcher, Jeremy P.—R
(s)-Tate Publishing—R
(s)-TEACH Services—R
Third World Press—R
(s)-Trafford Publishing—R
Treble Heart Books—R
(a)-Tyndale House—R
Univ. Press of America—R
(s)-VMI Publishers
Wilshire Book—R
(s)-WinePress—R
(s)-Word Alive

RACISM

Aaron Book—R
(s)-ACW Press—R
(s)-Ali Literary, Alfred—R
(s)-American Binding—R
Atheneum/Yg. Readers

(a)-Baker Books
Baker's Plays—R
(s)-Black Forest/Tennessee—R
Blue Dolphin
(s)-Booklocker.com—R
(s)-Book Publishers—R
(s)-Brown Books
Cambridge Scholars Pub.
Chalice Press
Christian Writer's Ebook—R
Comfort Publishing—R
(s)-DCTS Publishing
Destiny Image—R
Eerdmans Pub., Wm. B.—R
(s)-Elderberry Press
(s)-Essence—R
Evangelical Press
(s)-Fairway Press—R
FaithWalk
Forward Movement
Greenwood/Praeger
Guernica Editions—R
Hidden Brook Press—R
(s)-Holy Fire Publishing—R
Howard Books
(s)-Insight Publishing—R
InterVarsity Press—R
Judson Press—R
Kirk House
Lift Every Voice—R
Lighthouse Publishing—R
Monarch Books
New Hope—R
(s)-One World Press—R
Pilgrim Press—R
(s)-Pleasant Word—R
Power Publishing—R
(s)-Providence Pub.—R
Salt Works—R
(s)-Star Bible Public.
Strang Book Group—R
(s)-Tate Publishing—R
(s)-Trafford Publishing—R
Univ. Press of America—R
(s)-VMI Publishers
(s)-WinePress—R
(s)-Word Alive

RECOVERY BOOKS

Aaron Book—R
(s)-ACW Press—R
Ambassador Books
Ambassador-Emerald—R
(s)-American Binding—R
(a)-Baker Books
(s)-Black Forest/Tennessee—R
Blue Dolphin
(s)-Booklocker.com—R
(s)-Book Publishers—R
(s)-Brown Books
CarePoint Publishing—R
Chalice Press

Christian Writer's Ebook—R
Comfort Publishing—R
(s)-Creation House—R
Crossroad Publishing—R
CSS Publishing
Eerdmans Pub., Wm. B.—R
(s)-Elderberry Press
(s)-Essence—R
Evangelical Press
Evergreen Press
(s)-Fairway Press—R
Faith Communications
FaithWalk
Good Book—R
Greenwood/Praeger
GRQ—R
Hannibal Books
(a)-HarperOne
(a)-Harvest House
Health Commun.
Hidden Brook Press—R
(s)-Holy Fire Publishing—R
Hope Publishing—R
(s)-IMD Press—R
(s)-Insight Publishing—R
Judson Press—R
Langmarc
Lighthouse Publishing—R
Lion and Lamb
(s)-McDougal Publishing—R
Monarch Books
(s)-One World Press—R
Paradise Research—R
Parsons Publishing—R
Pauline Books—R
(s)-Pleasant Word—R
Power Publishing—R
Randall House
(s)-Recovery Commun.
Siloam
(s)-Star Bible Public.
Strang Book Group—R
(s)-Tate Publishing—R
(s)-Testimony Press
(s)-Trafford Publishing—R
(a)-Tyndale House—R
VBC Publishing
(s)-VMI Publishers
(a)-WaterBrook Press—R
Wilshire Book—R
(s)-WinePress—R
(s)-Word Alive
(s)-Zoe Life Publishing

REFERENCE BOOKS

Aaron Book—R
Abingdon Press
(s)-ACW Synergy—R
Ambassador-Emerald—R
(s)-American Binding—R
Baker Academic
(a)-Baker Books

Barbour
Bethany House
BMH Books—R
(s)-Booklocker.com—R
Branden Publishing—R
(s)-Brentwood—R
Bridge-Logos—R
(s)-Brown Books
Cambridge Scholars Pub.
Christian Heritage—R
Christian Writer's Ebook—R
Clarke & Co., James—R
(a)-Cook, David C.
(s)-Creation House—R
(a)-Doubleday Relig.—R
Dover Publications—R
Eerdmans Pub., Wm. B.—R
(s)-Elderberry Press
(s)-Essence—R
Evangelical Press
Facts on File
(s)-Fairway Press—R
FaithWalk
GRQ—R
Grupo Nelson
Guardian Angel
(a)-HarperOne
Hidden Brook Press—R
(s)-Holy Fire Publishing—R
(s)-IMD Press—R
(s)-Impact Christian—R
InterVarsity Press—R
Intl. Awakening—R
Invisible College Press
Johns Hopkins—R
Kaleidoscope Press—R
(a)-Kregel—R
Life Cycle Books—R
Lighthouse Publishing—R
Lion and Lamb
Lutterworth Press—R
Millennium III—R
Monarch Books
New Leaf
(s)-One World Press—R
Our Sunday Visitor—R
Power Publishing—R
(s)-Providence Pub.—R
Randall House
Reference Service
Rose Publishing
Sheed & Ward—R
(s)-So. Baptist Press—R
(s)-Star Bible Public.
Starik Publishing
Still Waters Revival—R
(s)-Synergy Publishers—R
(s)-Tate Publishing—R
(s)-TEACH Services—R
Third World Press—R
(s)-Trafford Publishing—R

(a)-Tyndale House—R
Univ. Press of America—R
VBC Publishing
(s)-WinePress—R
(s)-Word Alive
Zondervan

RELATIONSHIPS

Aaron Book—R
(s)-ACW Press—R
Adams Media
Ambassador Books
Ambassador-Emerald—R
(s)-American Binding—R
(s)-Baal Hamon—R
Barbour
Bethany House
(s)-Black Forest/Tennessee—R
(s)-Booklocker.com—R
Bridge-Logos—R
(s)-Brown Books
CarePoint Publishing—R
Christian Focus—R
Church Growth Inst.
Cladach Publishing
Comfort Publishing—R
(s)-Creation House—R
(s)-CrossHouse—R
Crossroad Publishing—R
Discovery House—R
Eerdmans Pub., Wm. B.—R
(s)-Elderberry Press
(s)-Essence—R
Evangelical Press
Extreme Diva
(a)-FaithWords
FamilyLife (books)—R
Forward Movement
Hannibal Books
(a)-Harvest House
Health Commun.
Hensley Publishing
Hidden Brook Press—R
(s)-Holy Fire Publishing—R
Howard Books
(s)-IMD Press—R
(s)-Insight Publishing—R
Judson Press—R
(a)-Kregel—R
Life Changing Media
Lift Every Voice—R
Lighthouse Publishing—R
Lillenas
Lion and Lamb
Little Lauren Books
Lutterworth Press—R
Monarch Books
MOPS Intl.
NavPress
NavPress Student—R
(a)-Nelson, Thomas
New Hope—R

Pauline Books—R
Power Publishing—R
(s)-Providence Pub.—R
Quintessential Books—R
Ravenhawk Books—R
(a)-Regal
Samaritan Press
St. Anthony Mess. Press—R
(s)-Star Bible Public.
Starik Publishing
Strang Book Group—R
(s)-Tate Publishing—R
(s)-TEACH Services—R
Torch Legacy
(s)-Trafford Publishing—R
VBC Publishing
Whitaker House
(s)-WinePress—R
(s)-Zoe Life Publishing

RELIGION

Aaron Book—R
Abingdon Press
ACTA Publications
(s)-ACW Press—R
(s)-Ali Literary, Alfred—R
Ambassador Books
(s)-American Binding—R
Atheneum/Yg. Readers
(s)-Baal Hamon—R
Baker Academic
(a)-Baker Books
Baker Trittin
Baker's Plays—R
(a)-Ballantine
(a)-B & H Publishing
Baylor Univ. Press
(s)-Black Forest/Tennessee—R
Blue Dolphin
(s)-Booklocker.com—R
Boyds Mills Press—R
(s)-Brentwood—R
(s)-Brown Books
Cambridge Scholars Pub.
Cambridge Univ. Press
Catholic Answers—R
Catholic Univ. of Amer. Press
Chalice Press
Chapter Two—R
Chelsea House—R
Christian Family—R
Christian Heritage—R
Christian Writer's Ebook—R
Church Growth Inst.
Clarke & Co., James—R
Comfort Publishing—R
Concordia
Continuum Intl.—R
(s)-Creation House—R
Crossroad Publishing—R
CSS Publishing
(a)-Doubleday Relig.—R

E-Digital Books
Eerdmans Pub., Wm. B.—R
(s)-Elderberry Press
(a)-Emmaus Road—R
(s)-Essence—R
Evangelical Press
Facts on File
(s)-Fairway Press—R
FaithWalk
(a)-FaithWords
Father's Press—R
Fifth Estate—R
Fordham Univ. Press—R
Fortress Press
Forward Movement
Georgetown Univ. Press
Greenwood/Praeger
GRQ—R
Halo Publishing
(a)-HarperOne
(a)-Harvest House
Hidden Brook Press—R
His Work Christian Pub.
(s)-Holy Fire Publishing—R
Howard Books
(s)-Impact Christian—R
(s)-Insight Publishing—R
Invisible College Press
Johns Hopkins—R
Jossey-Bass
Kirk House
(a)-Kregel—R
Larson Publications—R
Libros Liguori
Life Changing Media
Life Cycle Books—R
Lighthouse Publishing—R
Lillenas
Lion and Lamb
Liturgy Training—R
Loyola Press
Lutheran Univ. Press
Lutterworth Press—R
(s)-McDougal Publishing—R
Mercer Univ. Press—R
Monarch Books
Morehouse—R
Mountain Church Books
NavPress Student—R
(a)-Nelson, Thomas
New Seeds—R
New York Univ. Press
(s)-One World Press—R
Oregon Catholic
Our Sunday Visitor—R
Pacific Press
Paradise Research—R
Parsons Publishing—R
(s)-Path Pub. in Christ—R
Pauline Books—R
Paulist Press
Pflaum Publishing

Pilgrim Press—R
(s)-Pleasant Word—R
Power Publishing—R
Presbyterian Pub.
(s)-Providence Pub.—R
Quintessential Books—R
Ragged Edge—R
(a)-Regnery
Revell
Rose Publishing
Sheed & Ward—R
Smyth & Helwys
(s)-So. Baptist Press—R
St. Anthony Mess. Press—R
St. Bede's Publications
St. Pauls/Alba House—R
(s)-Star Bible Public.
Still Waters Revival—R
Strang Book Group—R
(s)-Synergy Publishers—R
T & T Clark—R
Tarcher, Jeremy P.—R
(s)-Tate Publishing—R
Tau-Publishing—R
(s)-TEACH Services—R
Third World Press—R
Torch Legacy
(s)-Trafford Publishing—R
Treble Heart Books—R
Trinity Foundation—R
(a)-Tyndale House—R
Univ. of AR Press—R
Univ. Press of America—R
(s)-VMI Publishers
(a)-WaterBrook Press—R
Westminster John Knox
Whitaker House
(s)-WinePress—R
(s)-Word Alive
W Publishing
Xyzzy Press
Yale Univ. Press—R
(s)-Zoe Life Publishing

RELIGIOUS TOLERANCE

Aaron Book—R
ACTA Publications
(s)-ACW Press—R
(s)-American Binding—R
(s)-Baal Hamon—R
(a)-Baker Books
Baker's Plays—R
Baylor Univ. Press
(s)-Black Forest/Tennessee—R
Blue Dolphin
(s)-Booklocker.com—R
Boyds Mills Press—R
(s)-Brown Books
Cambridge Scholars Pub.
Chalice Press
Christian Writer's Ebook—R
Comfort Publishing—R

(s)-Creation House—R
Crossroad Publishing—R
Eerdmans Pub., Wm. B.—R
(s)-Elderberry Press
(s)-Essence—R
Evangelical Press
(s)-Fairway Press—R
FaithWalk
(a)-FaithWords
Forward Movement
Greenwood/Praeger
Hidden Brook Press—R
(s)-Holy Fire Publishing—R
Howard Books
(s)-Insight Publishing—R
Johns Hopkins—R
Judson Press—R
Lighthouse Publishing—R
Lillenas
Lion and Lamb
Lutterworth Press—R
Monarch Books
New Canaan—R
New Seeds—R
(s)-One World Press—R
Paragon House—R
(s)-Pleasant Word—R
Power Publishing—R
(s)-Providence Pub.—R
Resource Public.
Salt Works—R
St. Anthony Mess. Press—R
(s)-Star Bible Public.
Strang Book Group—R
(s)-Tate Publishing—R
(s)-TEACH Services—R
(s)-Trafford Publishing—R
(s)-VMI Publishers
Westminster John Knox
(s)-WinePress—R
(s)-Word Alive
Yale Univ. Press—R

RETIREMENT

Aaron Book—R
ACTA Publications
(s)-ACW Press—R
(s)-American Binding—R
(a)-Baker Books
Baker's Plays—R
(s)-Black Forest/Tennessee—R
Blue Dolphin
BMH Books—R
(s)-Booklocker.com—R
(s)-Brown Books
Christian Writer's Ebook—R
College Press—R
Comfort Publishing—R
Eerdmans Pub., Wm. B.—R
(s)-Elderberry Press
(s)-Essence—R
Evangelical Press

(s)-Fairway Press—R
Forward Movement
Greenwood/Praeger
Hidden Brook Press—R
(s)-Holy Fire Publishing—R
(s)-Insight Publishing—R
Judson Press—R
Kirk House
Lighthouse Publishing—R
Lillenas
Lion and Lamb
Monarch Books
(s)-One World Press—R
(s)-Pleasant Word—R
Power Publishing—R
(s)-Providence Pub.—R
(a)-Regnery
(s)-So. Baptist Press—R
(s)-Star Bible Public.
Strang Book Group—R
(s)-Tate Publishing—R
(s)-TEACH Services—R
(s)-Trafford Publishing—R
(s)-WinePress—R
(s)-Word Alive
(s)-Zoe Life Publishing

SCHOLARLY

Aaron Book—R
Abingdon Press
(s)-ACW Press—R
(s)-American Binding—R
American Cath. Press—R
(s)-Baal Hamon—R
Baker Academic
(a)-Baker Books
Baker's Plays—R
Baylor Univ. Press
BJU/Journey Forth—R
Blue Dolphin
(s)-Booklocker.com—R
(s)-Brown Books
Cambridge Scholars Pub.
Chalice Press
Christian Heritage—R
Christian Writer's Ebook—R
Cistercian—R
Clarke & Co., James—R
Continuum Intl.—R
(a)-Cook, David C.
(a)-Doubleday Relig.—R
Eerdmans Pub., Wm. B.—R
(s)-Elderberry Press
(s)-Essence—R
Evangelical Press
(s)-Fairway Press—R
Fifth Estate—R
Fordham Univ. Press—R
Fortress Press
Georgetown Univ. Press
Gollehon Press
Greenwood/Praeger

Guardian Angel
Hidden Brook Press—R
(s)-Holy Fire Publishing—R
(s)-IMD Press—R
(s)-Impact Christian—R
Inkling Books—R
(s)-Insight Publishing—R
InterVarsity Press—R
Intl. Awakening—R
(a)-Kregel—R
Life Cycle Books—R
Lighthouse Publishing—R
Lion and Lamb
Liturgy Training—R
Lutheran Univ. Press
Master Books
Mercer Univ. Press—R
Mt. Olive College Press
New Leaf
New York Univ. Press
(s)-One World Press—R
P & R Publishing—R
Paragon House—R
Pilgrim Press—R
(s)-Pleasant Word—R
Power Publishing—R
(s)-Providence Pub.—R
(s)-Quiet Waters
Quintessential Books—R
Smyth & Helwys
St. Augustine's Press—R
(s)-Star Bible Public.
T & T Clark—R
(s)-Tate Publishing—R
(s)-Trafford Publishing—R
Trinity Foundation—R
Univ. of AR Press—R
Univ. Press of America—R
VBC Publishing
(s)-VMI Publishers
Westminster John Knox
(s)-WinePress—R
Wipf and Stock
(s)-Word Alive
Yale Univ. Press—R
Youth Specialties
(s)-Zoe Life Publishing
Zondervan

SCIENCE

Aaron Book—R
(s)-ACW Press—R
(s)-American Binding—R
(s)-Baal Hamon—R
(a)-Baker Books
Baker's Plays—R
(s)-Black Forest/Tennessee—R
Blue Dolphin
(s)-Booklocker.com—R
Boyds Mills Press—R
(s)-Brown Books
Cambridge Scholars Pub.

Christian Family—R
Christian Writer's Ebook—R
(a)-Doubleday Relig.—R
Eerdmans Pub., Wm. B.—R
(s)-Elderberry Press
(s)-Essence—R
Evangelical Press
Facts on File
(s)-Fairway Press—R
Fifth Estate—R
Fordham Univ. Press—R
Forward Movement
Greenwood/Praeger
Guardian Angel
Hidden Brook Press—R
(s)-Holy Fire Publishing—R
Inkling Books—R
(s)-Insight Publishing—R
InterVarsity Press—R
Jossey-Bass
Kaleidoscope Press—R
Knight George Pub.
Lighthouse Publishing—R
Lion and Lamb
Lutterworth Press—R
Master Books
Monarch Books
New Leaf
(s)-One World Press—R
Parsons Publishing—R
(s)-Pleasant Word—R
Power Publishing—R
Quintessential Books—R
(a)-Regnery
(s)-Star Bible Public.
T & T Clark—R
(s)-Tate Publishing—R
(s)-TEACH Services—R
(s)-Trafford Publishing—R
Trinity Foundation—R
Troitsa Books
(s)-WinePress—R
(s)-Word Alive

SELF-HELP

Aaron Book—R
(s)-ACW Press—R
Adams Media
(s)-Ali Literary, Alfred—R
Ambassador Books
(s)-American Binding—R
(s)-Baal Hamon—R
(a)-Baker Books
(a)-Ballantine
(s)-Black Forest/Tennessee—R
Blue Dolphin
BMH Books—R
(s)-Booklocker.com—R
(s)-Book Publishers—R
Bridge-Logos—R
(s)-Brown Books

CarePoint Publishing—R
Christian Writer's Ebook—R
Comfort Publishing—R
(s)-Creation House—R
(s)-DCTS Publishing
(s)-Dean Press, Robbie—R
Destiny Image—R
Dimensions for Living
(s)-Elderberry Press
(s)-Essence—R
Evangelical Press
Evergreen Press
Extreme Diva
Fair Havens—R
(s)-Fairway Press—R
FaithWalk
Fell, Frederick—R
Fifth Estate—R
(s)-FruitBearer Pub.
Gollehon Press
Good Book—R
GRQ—R
Grupo Nelson
GuidepostsBooks
Halo Publishing
(a)-HarperOne
(a)-Harvest House
(a)-Hay House
Health Commun.
Hidden Brook Press—R
His Work Christian Pub.
(s)-Holy Fire Publishing—R
Howard Books
(s)-IMD Press—R
(s)-Insight Publishing—R
Judson Press—R
Langmarc
(s)-Leading Lady
Life Changing Media
Lighthouse Publishing—R
Lutterworth Press—R
Monarch Books
MountainView
(a)-Nelson, Thomas
(s)-One World Press—R
(a)-One World/Ballantine
Paradise Research—R
(s)-Path Pub. in Christ—R
(s)-Path Publishing—R
Pauline Books—R
Perigee Books
Pilgrim Press—R
(s)-Pleasant Word—R
Power Publishing—R
PREP Publishing—R
(s)-Providence Pub.—R
Quintessential Books—R
Ragged Edge—R
Revell
(s)-Salvation Publisher—R
(s)-Selah Publishing—R

(s)-Star Bible Public.
Starik Publishing
Strang Book Group—R
(s)-Synergy Publishers—R
Tarcher, Jeremy P.—R
(s)-Tate Publishing—R
Third World Press—R
Torch Legacy
(s)-Trafford Publishing—R
Treble Heart Books—R
Tsaba House
(a)-Tyndale House—R
VBC Publishing
(s)-VMI Publishers
Walk Worthy—R
(a)-WaterBrook Press—R
Wilshire Book—R
(s)-WinePress—R
(s)-Word Alive

SENIOR ADULT CONCERNS

Aaron Book—R
(s)-ACW Press—R
(s)-American Binding—R
(a)-Baker Books
Baker's Plays—R
(s)-Black Forest/Tennessee—R
Blue Dolphin
(s)-Booklocker.com—R
(s)-Brown Books
Chalice Press
Christian Writer's Ebook—R
(a)-Cook, David C.
Discovery House—R
Eerdmans Pub., Wm. B.—R
(s)-Elderberry Press
(s)-Essence—R
Evangelical Press
Evergreen Press
Fair Havens—R
(s)-Fairway Press—R
(a)-Focus on the Family—R
Gollehon Press
Hidden Brook Press—R
(s)-Holy Fire Publishing—R
(s)-IMD Press—R
(s)-Insight Publishing—R
Judson Press—R
Langmarc
Lighthouse Publishing—R
Lillenas
Lion and Lamb
Monarch Books
Morehouse—R
New Hope—R
(s)-One World Press—R
(s)-Path Pub. in Christ—R
Pauline Books—R
(s)-Pleasant Word—R
Power Publishing—R
(s)-Providence Pub.—R

Samaritan Press
(s)-So. Baptist Press—R
(s)-Star Bible Public.
Strang Book Group—R
(s)-Synergy Publishers—R
(s)-Tate Publishing—R
(s)-Trafford Publishing—R
VBC Publishing
(s)-VMI Publishers
(s)-WinePress—R
(s)-Word Alive
(s)-Zoe Life Publishing

SERMONS

Aaron Book—R
Abingdon Press
(s)-ACW Press—R
(s)-American Binding—R
American Cath. Press—R
(s)-Baal Hamon—R
(a)-Baker Books
(a)-B & H Publishing
(s)-Black Forest/Tennessee—R
(s)-Booklocker.com—R
(s)-Brentwood—R
(s)-Brown Books
Chalice Press
Chapter Two—R
Christian Family—R
Christian Focus—R
Christian Writer's Ebook—R
Church Growth Inst.
Continuum Intl.—R
CSS Publishing
(s)-DCTS Publishing
Editorial Portavoz
Eerdmans Pub., Wm. B.—R
(s)-Elderberry Press
(s)-Essence—R
Evangelical Press
(s)-Fairway Press—R
Hidden Brook Press—R
(s)-Holy Fire Publishing—R
(s)-IMD Press—R
(s)-Insight Publishing—R
Judson Press—R
(a)-Kregel—R
Lighthouse Publishing—R
Lion and Lamb
Liturgical Press
Lutterworth Press—R
(s)-McDougal Publishing—R
Monarch Books
Morehouse—R
MountainView
Mt. Olive College Press
(s)-One World Press—R
P & R Publishing—R
Pacific Press
(s)-Pleasant Word—R
Power Publishing—R

(s)-Providence Pub.—R
(s)-Salvation Publisher—R
Samaritan Press
(s)-Sermon Select Press
(s)-So. Baptist Press—R
St. Pauls/Alba House—R
(s)-Star Bible Public.
Still Waters Revival—R
(s)-Tate Publishing—R
(s)-TEACH Services—R
Torch Legacy
(s)-Trafford Publishing—R
(s)-VMI Publishers
(s)-WinePress—R
(s)-Word Alive
(s)-Zoe Life Publishing

SINGLES ISSUES

Aaron Book—R
(s)-ACW Press—R
Ambassador Books
(s)-American Binding—R
(a)-Baker Books
Baker's Plays—R
Barbour
Bethany House
(s)-Black Forest/Tennessee—R
(s)-Booklocker.com—R
(s)-Brentwood—R
(s)-Brown Books
Christian Focus—R
Christian Writer's Ebook—R
(a)-Cook, David C.
(s)-Creation House—R
(s)-Dean Press, Robbie—R
Destiny Image—R
Eerdmans Pub., Wm. B.—R
(s)-Elderberry Press
(s)-Essence—R
Evangelical Press
Evergreen Press
Fair Havens—R
(s)-Fairway Press—R
FaithWalk
(a)-FaithWords
Green Key Books
Greenwood/Praeger
Harrison House
(a)-Harvest House
Hensley Publishing
Hidden Brook Press—R
(s)-Holy Fire Publishing—R
Howard Books
(s)-IMD Press—R
(s)-Insight Publishing—R
Judson Press—R
Lift Every Voice—R
Lighthouse Publishing—R
Lillenas
Lion and Lamb
Little Lauren Books

(s)-McDougal Publishing—R
Messianic Jewish—R
Monarch Books
NavPress Student—R
New Hope—R
(s)-One World Press—R
Pacific Press
Parsons Publishing—R
Pauline Books—R
Perigee Books
(s)-Pleasant Word—R
Power Publishing—R
(s)-Providence Pub.—R
Quintessential Books—R
Samaritan Press
(s)-Star Bible Public.
Strang Book Group—R
(s)-Synergy Publishers—R
(s)-Tate Publishing—R
(s)-Trafford Publishing—R
VBC Publishing
(s)-VMI Publishers
Walk Worthy—R
Whitaker House
(s)-WinePress—R
(s)-Word Alive
(s)-Zoe Life Publishing

SOCIAL JUSTICE ISSUES

Aaron Book—R
(s)-ACW Press—R
(s)-American Binding—R
Atheneum/Yg. Readers
(a)-Baker Books
Baker's Plays—R
(s)-Black Forest/Tennessee—R
(s)-Booklocker.com—R
(s)-Brentwood—R
(s)-Brown Books
Canadian Inst. for Law—R
Chalice Press
Christian Writer's Ebook—R
Comfort Publishing—R
(s)-DCTS Publishing
Destiny Image—R
Destiny Image (books)—R
Eerdmans Pub., Wm. B.—R
(s)-Elderberry Press
(s)-Essence—R
Evangelical Press
(s)-Fairway Press—R
(a)-FaithWords
Forward Movement
Georgetown Univ. Press
Greenwood/Praeger
(a)-HarperOne
Hendrickson—R
Hidden Brook Press—R
(s)-Holy Fire Publishing—R
Hope Publishing—R
Howard Books

Inkling Books—R
(s)-Insight Publishing—R
InterVarsity Press—R
Jossey-Bass
Judson Press—R
Kingsley, Jessica Pub.—R
Libros Liguori
Life Cycle Books—R
Lift Every Voice—R
Lighthouse Publishing—R
Monarch Books
NavPress
NavPress Student—R
(a)-Nelson, Thomas
New Hope—R
(s)-One World Press—R
Our Sunday Visitor—R
Paulist Press
Pilgrim Press—R
(s)-Pleasant Word—R
Power Publishing—R
(s)-Providence Pub.—R
Quintessential Books—R
Ravenhawk Books—R
(a)-Regnery
Sheed & Ward—R
St. Anthony Mess. Press—R
(s)-Star Bible Public.
Still Waters Revival—R
Strang Book Group—R
(s)-Synergy Publishers—R
(s)-Tate Publishing—R
(s)-Trafford Publishing—R
(s)-VMI Publishers
(s)-WinePress—R
(s)-Word Alive
Yale Univ. Press—R
Youth Specialties

SOCIOLOGY

Aaron Book—R
(s)-ACW Press—R
(s)-American Binding—R
(a)-Baker Books
Baker's Plays—R
(s)-Black Forest/Tennessee—R
Blue Dolphin
(s)-Booklocker.com—R
Branden Publishing—R
(s)-Brentwood—R
(s)-Brown Books
Cambridge Scholars Pub.
Carey Library, Wm.—R
Christian Writer's Ebook—R
Comfort Publishing—R
Eerdmans Pub., Wm. B.—R
(s)-Elderberry Press
(s)-Essence—R
Evangelical Press
(s)-Fairway Press—R
FaithWalk
Fordham Univ. Press—R

Greenwood/Praeger
Hendrickson—R
Hidden Brook Press—R
(s)-Holy Fire Publishing—R
(s)-IMD Press—R
(s)-Insight Publishing—R
InterVarsity Press—R
Life Cycle Books—R
Lighthouse Publishing—R
Lion and Lamb
(s)-McDougal Publishing—R
Monarch Books
New York Univ. Press
(s)-One World Press—R
(s)-Pleasant Word—R
Power Publishing—R
(s)-Providence Pub.—R
(s)-Star Bible Public.
Still Waters Revival—R
Strang Book Group—R
(s)-Tate Publishing—R
Third World Press—R
(s)-Trafford Publishing—R
Univ. Press of America—R
(s)-VMI Publishers
(s)-WinePress—R
(s)-Word Alive

SPIRITUAL GIFTS

Aaron Book—R
(s)-ACW Press—R
Ambassador Books
(s)-American Binding—R
(s)-Baal Hamon—R
(a)-Baker Books
Baker's Plays—R
(a)-B & H Publishing
(s)-Black Forest/Tennessee—R
Blue Dolphin
(s)-Booklocker.com—R
Bridge-Logos—R
(s)-Brown Books
Canticle Books—R
Chapter Two—R
Christian Writer's Ebook—R
Comfort Publishing—R
(s)-Creation House—R
(s)-CrossHouse—R
CSS Publishing
(s)-Dean Press, Robbie—R
Destiny Image—R
Destiny Image (books)—R
Eerdmans Pub., Wm. B.—R
(s)-Elderberry Press
(s)-Essence—R
Evangelical Press
(s)-Fairway Press—R
FaithWalk
Father's Press—R
Forward Movement
Friends United Press
Gospel Publishing

Greenwood/Praeger
Grupo Nelson
Guardian Angel
Harrison House
Hensley Publishing
Hidden Brook Press—R
(s)-Holy Fire Publishing—R
Howard Books
(s)-IMD Press—R
(s)-Insight Publishing—R
Jebaire Publishing
(a)-Kregel—R
Lift Every Voice—R
Lighthouse Publishing—R
Lillenas
Lion and Lamb
Magnus Press—R
Monarch Books
(a)-Nelson, Thomas
New Hope—R
(s)-One World Press—R
Pacific Press
Parson Place—R
Parsons Publishing—R
(s)-Path Pub. in Christ—R
Pauline Books—R
(s)-Pleasant Word—R
Power Publishing—R
(s)-Providence Pub.—R
(a)-Regal
Revival Nation
Rose Publishing
(s)-Salvation Publisher—R
(s)-Selah Publishing—R
St. Anthony Mess. Press—R
(s)-Star Bible Public.
Strang Book Group—R
(s)-Synergy Publishers—R
(s)-Tate Publishing—R
Tau-Publishing—R
(s)-TEACH Services—R
(s)-Trafford Publishing—R
(s)-VMI Publishers
Wesleyan Publishing
Whitaker House
(s)-WinePress—R
(s)-Word Alive
W Publishing
(s)-Zoe Life Publishing

SPIRITUALITY

Aaron Book—R
Abingdon Press
ACTA Publications
(s)-ACW Press—R
(s)-Ali Literary, Alfred—R
Ambassador Books
(s)-American Binding—R
(s)-Baal Hamon—R
(a)-Baker Books
Baker's Plays—R
(a)-Ballantine

(a)-B & H Publishing
Bethany House
(s)-Black Forest/Tennessee—R
Blue Dolphin
(s)-Booklocker.com—R
(s)-Book Publishers—R
(s)-Brentwood—R
Bridge-Logos—R
(s)-Brown Books
Cambridge Scholars Pub.
Canticle Books—R
Chapter Two—R
Christian Heritage—R
Christian Writer's Ebook—R
Cistercian—R
Clarke & Co., James—R
Comfort Publishing—R
Conari Press
Continuum Intl.—R
(s)-Creation House—R
Crossroad Publishing—R
CSS Publishing
Destiny Image—R
Destiny Image (books)—R
Discovery House—R
(a)-Doubleday Relig.—R
E-Digital Books
Eerdmans Pub., Wm. B.—R
(s)-Elderberry Press
Elijah Press
(a)-Emmaus Road—R
(s)-Essence—R
Evangelical Press
Evergreen Press
Fair Havens—R
(s)-Fairway Press—R
Faith Communications
FaithWalk
(a)-FaithWords
Fell, Frederick—R
Fifth Estate—R
Forward Movement
Friends United Press
Good Book—R
Greenwood/Praeger
GRQ—R
Guardian Angel
Halo Publishing
(a)-HarperOne
(a)-Hay House
Health Commun.
Hendrickson—R
Hidden Brook Press—R
(s)-Holy Fire Publishing—R
Howard Books
(s)-IMD Press—R
(s)-Impact Christian—R
(s)-Insight Publishing—R
InterVarsity Press—R
Invisible College Press
Johns Hopkins—R
Jossey-Bass

Judson Press—R
Kingsley, Jessica Pub.—R
Kirk House
(a)-Kregel—R
Larson Publications—R
Libros Liguori
Lighthouse Publishing—R
Liguori Public.—R
Lillenas
Lion and Lamb
Loyola Press
Lutheran Univ. Press
Lutterworth Press—R
Magnus Press—R
Monarch Books
Morehouse—R
NavPress Student—R
(a)-Nelson, Thomas
New Hope—R
New Seeds—R
(s)-One World Press—R
P & R Publishing—R
Pacific Press
Paradise Research—R
Paragon House—R
Parsons Publishing—R
(s)-Path Pub. in Christ—R
Pauline Books—R
Paulist Press
Perigee Books
Pilgrim Press—R
(s)-Pleasant Word—R
Power Publishing—R
(s)-Providence Pub.—R
Quintessential Books—R
Ragged Edge—R
Ravenhawk Books—R
(a)-Regal
(a)-Regnery
Resource Public.
Revival Nation
(s)-Selah Publishing—R
Sheed & Ward—R
Smyth & Helwys
(s)-So. Baptist Press—R
St. Anthony Mess. Press—R
St. Bede's Publications
St. Pauls/Alba House—R
(s)-Star Bible Public.
Strang Book Group—R
(s)-Synergy Publishers—R
(s)-Tate Publishing—R
Tau-Publishing—R
(s)-TEACH Services—R
(s)-Trafford Publishing—R
Treble Heart Books—R
(a)-Tyndale House—R
(s)-VMI Publishers
(a)-WaterBrook Press—R
Wesleyan Publishing
(s)-WinePress—R
(s)-Word Alive

W Publishing
(s)-Zoe Life Publishing

SPIRITUAL LIFE

Aadeon Publishing—R
Aaron Book—R
Abingdon Press
(s)-ACW Press—R
Ambassador Books
Ambassador-Emerald—R
(s)-American Binding—R
Anglicans United—R
(s)-Baal Hamon—R
Baker Trittin
Baker's Plays—R
(a)-B & H Publishing
Barbour
Bethany House
(s)-Black Forest/Tennessee—R
(s)-Booklocker.com—R
Bridge-Logos—R
(s)-Brown Books
Chapter Two—R
Christian Family—R
Christian Focus—R
Christian Writer's Ebook—R
Church Growth Inst.
Comfort Publishing—R
Continuum Intl.—R
(s)-Creation House—R
(s)-CrossHouse—R
Crossroad Publishing—R
CSS Publishing
Destiny Image (books)—R
Eerdmans Pub., Wm. B.—R
(s)-Elderberry Press
Eldridge Plays
(s)-Essence—R
Evangelical Press
Evergreen Press
(s)-Fairway Press—R
FaithWalk
(a)-FaithWords
Father's Press—R
Forward Movement
GRQ—R
Guardian Angel
(a)-HarperOne
Harrison House
Hendrickson—R
Hidden Brook Press—R
(s)-Holy Fire Publishing—R
Howard Books
(s)-IMD Press—R
(s)-Insight Publishing—R
InterVarsity Press—R
Jossey-Bass
Judson Press—R
(a)-Kregel—R
Legacy Publishers
Life Changing Media
(s)-LifeVest Publishing

Lift Every Voice—R
Lighthouse Publishing—R
Lillenas
Lion and Lamb
Lutterworth Press—R
Monarch Books
Morehouse—R
NavPress
NavPress Student—R
(a)-Nelson, Thomas
New Hope—R
New Seeds—R
(s)-One World Press—R
P & R Publishing—R
Parsons Publishing—R
(s)-Path Pub. in Christ—R
Pauline Books—R
Paulist Press
Pilgrim Press—R
(s)-Pleasant Word—R
Power Publishing—R
(s)-Providence Pub.—R
Quintessential Books—R
Randall House
Reformation Trust
(a)-Regal
Revival Nation
Rose Publishing
(s)-Salvation Publisher—R
Samaritan Press
St. Anthony Mess. Press—R
(s)-Star Bible Public.
Strang Book Group—R
(s)-Synergy Publishers—R
(s)-Tate Publishing—R
(s)-TEACH Services—R
(s)-Testimony Press
(s)-Trafford Publishing—R
(s)-VMI Publishers
(a)-WaterBrook Press—R
Wesleyan Publishing
Whitaker House
(s)-WinePress—R
(s)-Word Alive
(s)-Zoe Life Publishing

SPIRITUAL WARFARE

Aadeon Publishing—R
Aaron Book—R
(s)-ACW Press—R
(s)-American Binding—R
Anglicans United—R
(s)-Baal Hamon—R
(a)-Baker Books
Baker's Plays—R
(a)-B & H Publishing
(s)-Black Forest/Tennessee—R
BMH Books—R
(s)-Booklocker.com—R
Bridge-Logos—R

(s)-Brown Books
Carey Library, Wm.—R
Chapter Two—R
Christian Family—R
Christian Focus—R
Christian Writer's Ebook—R
Comfort Publishing—R
(s)-Creation House—R
Deo Volente
Destiny Image—R
Destiny Image (books)—R
Editorial Portavoz
Eerdmans Pub., Wm. B.—R
(s)-Elderberry Press
(s)-Essence—R
Evangelical Press
Evergreen Press
(s)-Fairway Press—R
FaithWalk
Father's Press—R
Greenwood/Praeger
Grupo Nelson
Harrison House
(a)-Harvest House
Hensley Publishing
Hidden Brook Press—R
(s)-Holy Fire Publishing—R
(s)-IMD Press—R
(s)-Impact Christian—R
(s)-Insight Publishing—R
Jireh Publishing
Judson Press—R
Legacy Publishers
Lighthouse Publishing—R
Lion and Lamb
(s)-McDougal Publishing—R
Messianic Jewish—R
Monarch Books
NavPress Student—R
(a)-Nelson, Thomas
New Hope—R
(s)-One World Press—R
P & R Publishing—R
Parson Place—R
Parsons Publishing—R
(s)-Pleasant Word—R
Power Publishing—R
(s)-Providence Pub.—R
(a)-Regal
Revival Nation
(s)-Salvation Publisher—R
Samaritan Press
(s)-Selah Publishing—R
St. Anthony Mess. Press—R
(s)-Star Bible Public.
Strang Book Group—R
(s)-Synergy Publishers—R
(s)-Tate Publishing—R
(s)-TEACH Services—R
(s)-Testimony Press
(s)-Trafford Publishing—R

VBC Publishing
Virginia Pines Press
Whitaker House
(s)-WinePress—R
(s)-Word Alive
W Publishing
(s)-Zoe Life Publishing

SPORTS/RECREATION

Aaron Book—R
ACTA Publications
(s)-ACW Press—R
Ambassador Books
(s)-American Binding—R
(a)-Baker Books
Baker's Plays—R
(a)-Ballantine
(s)-Booklocker.com—R
Boyds Mills Press—R
(s)-Brown Books
Christian Writer's Ebook—R
Comfort Publishing—R
(s)-Elderberry Press
(s)-Essence—R
Evangelical Press
Evergreen Press
Facts on File
(s)-Fairway Press—R
Greenwood/Praeger
Guardian Angel
(a)-Harvest House
Hidden Brook Press—R
His Work Christian Pub.
(s)-Holy Fire Publishing—R
(s)-Insight Publishing—R
Lighthouse Publishing—R
Lion and Lamb
Lutterworth Press—R
Monarch Books
(s)-One World Press—R
(a)-One World/Ballantine
(s)-Pleasant Word—R
Power Publishing—R
(s)-Providence Pub.—R
Ravenhawk Books—R
(a)-Regal
Strang Book Group—R
(s)-Tate Publishing—R
(s)-Trafford Publishing—R
(s)-VMI Publishers
(s)-WinePress—R
(s)-Word Alive
Xyzzy Press
(s)-Zoe Life Publishing

STEWARDSHIP

Aaron Book—R
(s)-ACW Press—R
(s)-American Binding—R
(a)-Baker Books
(a)-B & H Publishing

Bethany House
(s)-Black Forest/Tennessee—R
BMH Books—R
(s)-Booklocker.com—R
(s)-Brown Books
Christian Focus—R
Christian Writer's Ebook—R
College Press—R
Comfort Publishing—R
(s)-Creation House—R
CSS Publishing
Eerdmans Pub., Wm. B.—R
(s)-Elderberry Press
(s)-Essence—R
Evangelical Press
Evergreen Press
(s)-Fairway Press—R
FaithWalk
Father's Press—R
Forward Movement
Harrison House
Hendrickson—R
Hensley Publishing
Hidden Brook Press—R
(s)-Holy Fire Publishing—R
Hope Publishing—R
(s)-IMD Press—R
(s)-Insight Publishing—R
Judson Press—R
Kirk House
(a)-Kregel—R
Lift Every Voice—R
Lighthouse Publishing—R
Lillenas
Lion and Lamb
Lutheran Univ. Press
(s)-McDougal Publishing—R
Monarch Books
Morehouse—R
Neibauer Press—R
New Hope—R
(s)-One World Press—R
Our Sunday Visitor—R
Pacific Press
Parson Place—R
Parsons Publishing—R
Pilgrim Press—R
(s)-Pleasant Word—R
Power Publishing—R
Presbyterian Pub.
(s)-Providence Pub.—R
Rose Publishing
(s)-Salvation Publisher—R
St. Anthony Mess. Press—R
(s)-Star Bible Public.
(s)-Synergy Publishers—R
(s)-Tate Publishing—R
(s)-TEACH Services—R
(s)-Trafford Publishing—R
VBC Publishing
(s)-VMI Publishers

Wesleyan Publishing
Westminster John Knox
(s)-WinePress—R
(s)-Word Alive
(s)-Zoe Life Publishing

THEOLOGY

Aaron Book—R
Abingdon Press
(s)-ACW Press—R
(s)-American Binding—R
American Cath. Press—R
(s)-Baal Hamon—R
(a)-Baker Books
Baker's Plays—R
(a)-B & H Publishing
Bethany House
Blue Dolphin
BMH Books—R
(s)-Booklocker.com—R
(s)-Brentwood—R
(s)-Brown Books
Canticle Books—R
Catholic Answers—R
Catholic Univ. of Amer. Press
Chalice Press
Chapter Two—R
Christian Family—R
Christian Focus—R
Christian Heritage—R
Christian Writer's Ebook—R
Clarke & Co., James—R
College Press—R
Conciliar Press—R
Concordia
Continuum Intl.—R
(a)-Cook, David C.
(s)-Creation House—R
Crossroad Publishing—R
CSS Publishing
Deo Volente
(a)-Doubleday Relig.—R
Earthen Vessel—R
Eerdmans Pub., Wm. B.—R
(s)-Elderberry Press
(a)-Emmaus Road—R
(s)-Essence—R
Evangelical Press
(s)-Fairway Press—R
FaithWalk
Father's Press—R
Fifth Estate—R
First Fruits of Zion
Fortress Press
Forward Movement
Founders Press
Georgetown Univ. Press
Gollehon Press
(a)-HarperOne
Hendrickson—R
Hidden Brook Press—R

(s)-Holy Fire Publishing—R
(s)-IMD Press—R
(s)-Impact Christian—R
Inkling Books—R
(s)-Insight Publishing—R
InterVarsity Press—R
Intl. Awakening—R
Judson Press—R
Kingsley, Jessica Pub.—R
Kirk House
(a)-Kregel—R
Lift Every Voice—R
Lighthouse Publishing—R
Lighthouse Trails—R
Lion and Lamb
Liturgical Press
Lutheran Univ. Press
Lutterworth Press—R
Magnus Press—R
Mercer Univ. Press—R
Monarch Books
Morehouse—R
(a)-Multnomah
NavPress Student—R
(a)-Nelson, Thomas
(s)-One World Press—R
P & R Publishing—R
Pacific Press
Pauline Books—R
Paulist Press
Pflaum Publishing
Pilgrim Press—R
(s)-Pleasant Word—R
Power Publishing—R
Presbyterian Pub.
(s)-Providence Pub.—R
Randall House
Ravenhawk Books—R
Reformation Trust
Resource Public.
Revival Nation
Rose Publishing
Sheed & Ward—R
Smyth & Helwys
(s)-So. Baptist Press—R
St. Anthony Mess. Press—R
St. Augustine's Press—R
St. Bede's Publications
St. Pauls/Alba House—R
(s)-Star Bible Public.
Still Waters Revival—R
(s)-Synergy Publishers—R
T & T Clark—R
(s)-Tate Publishing—R
(s)-TEACH Services—R
(s)-Trafford Publishing—R
Trinity Foundation—R
(a)-Tyndale House—R
UMI Publishing—R
Univ. Press of America—R
VBC Publishing

(s)-VMI Publishers
Westminster John Knox
(s)-WinePress—R
Wipf and Stock
(s)-Word Alive
Yale Univ. Press—R
(s)-Zoe Life Publishing
Zondervan

TIME MANAGEMENT

Aaron Book—R
(s)-ACW Press—R
(s)-American Binding—R
(a)-Baker Books
Barbour
(s)-Black Forest/Tennessee—R
(s)-Booklocker.com—R
(s)-Brown Books
Christian Writer's Ebook—R
Comfort Publishing—R
(a)-Cook, David C.
(s)-CrossHouse—R
(s)-DCTS Publishing
(s)-Elderberry Press
(s)-Essence—R
Evangelical Press
Evergreen Press
(s)-Fairway Press—R
Forward Movement
GRQ—R
Hensley Publishing
Hidden Brook Press—R
(s)-Holy Fire Publishing—R
(s)-IMD Press—R
(s)-Insight Publishing—R
Judson Press—R
Kirk House
Lighthouse Publishing—R
Lillenas
Lion and Lamb
Monarch Books
(a)-Nelson, Thomas
New Hope—R
(s)-One World Press—R
Pauline Books—R
(s)-Pleasant Word—R
Power Publishing—R
(s)-Providence Pub.—R
(s)-Salvation Publisher—R
(s)-Star Bible Public.
Starik Publishing
Strang Book Group—R
(s)-Tate Publishing—R
(s)-Trafford Publishing—R
VBC Publishing
(s)-VMI Publishers
Walk Worthy—R
(s)-WinePress—R
(s)-Word Alive
(s)-Zoe Life Publishing

TRACTS

Chapter Two—R
Christian Writer's Ebook—R
Crossway Books
(s)-Essence—R
Evangelical Press
Forward Movement
(s)-FruitBearer Pub.
Good News Pub.
(s)-Holy Fire Publishing—R
(s)-IMD Press—R
Intl. Awakening—R
Libros Liguori
Liguori Public.—R
Neibauer Press—R
(s)-One World Press—R
(s)-Path Pub. in Christ—R
Randall House
Tract League
Trinity Foundation—R
(s)-Word Alive

TRAVEL

Aaron Book—R
(s)-ACW Press—R
(s)-American Binding—R
(a)-Baker Books
Baker's Plays—R
(a)-Ballantine
(s)-Booklocker.com—R
(s)-Book Publishers—R
(s)-Brentwood—R
(s)-Brown Books
Cambridge Scholars Pub.
Chapter Two—R
Christian Heritage—R
Christian Writer's Ebook—R
Comfort Publishing—R
E-Digital Books
(s)-Elderberry Press
(s)-Essence—R
(s)-Fairway Press—R
FaithWalk
Greenwood/Praeger
Hidden Brook Press—R
(s)-Holy Fire Publishing—R
Hope Publishing—R
Ideals/Children
(s)-IMD Press—R
(s)-Insight Publishing—R
(s)-LifeVest Publishing
Lighthouse Publishing—R
Liguori Public.—R
Lion and Lamb
Lutterworth Press—R
Monarch Books
(s)-One World Press—R
(a)-One World/Ballantine
(s)-Pleasant Word—R
Power Publishing—R

(s)-Providence Pub.—R
(s)-Tate Publishing—R
(s)-Trafford Publishing—R
(s)-WinePress—R
(s)-Word Alive
Xyzzy Press

TWEEN BOOKS

Aaron Book—R
(s)-ACW Press—R
Ambassador Books
(s)-American Binding—R
Atheneum/Yg. Readers
Baker Trittin
Barbour
(s)-Black Forest/Tennessee—R
(s)-Booklocker.com—R
(s)-Brown Books
Eerdmans Pub., Wm. B.—R
(s)-Elderberry Press
(s)-Essence—R
Hidden Brook Press—R
(s)-Holy Fire Publishing—R
(s)-Insight Publishing—R
Journey Stone—R
(s)-Kindred Books—R
(a)-Kregel—R
Legacy Press—R
Lighthouse Publishing—R
Lion and Lamb
Little Lauren Books
Messianic Jewish—R
Mission City Press
New Leaf
Parsons Publishing—R
Pauline Books—R
Power Publishing—R
Putnam/Young Readers
(s)-Tate Publishing—R
(s)-Trafford Publishing—R
White Stone Books—R
(s)-WinePress—R
(s)-Zoe Life Publishing

WOMEN'S ISSUES

Aaron Book—R
ACTA Publications
(s)-ACW Press—R
Adams Media
Ambassador Books
Ambassador-Emerald—R
(s)-American Binding—R
AMG Publishers
Baker Academic
(a)-Baker Books
Baker's Plays—R
(a)-Ballantine
(a)-B & H Publishing
Barbour
Beacon Hill Press—R

BelleBooks—R
Bethany House
BJU/Journey Forth—R
(s)-Black Forest/Tennessee—R
Blue Dolphin
BMH Books—R
(s)-Booklocker.com—R
(s)-Book Publishers—R
Bridge-Logos—R
(s)-Brown Books
Chalice Press
Christian Writer's Ebook—R
College Press—R
Comfort Publishing—R
(a)-Cook, David C.
(s)-Creation House—R
(s)-CrossHouse—R
Crossroad Publishing—R
(s)-Dean Press, Robbie—R
Deo Volente
Destiny Image—R
Discovery House—R
(a)-Doubleday Relig.—R
Eerdmans Pub., Wm. B.—R
(s)-Elderberry Press
Eldridge Plays
(a)-Emmaus Road—R
(s)-Essence—R
Evangelical Press
Evergreen Press
Facts on File
Fair Havens—R
(s)-Fairway Press—R
Faith Communications
FaithWalk
(a)-FaithWords
FamilyLife (books)—R
(a)-Focus on the Family—R
Fortress Press
Green Key Books
Greenwood/Praeger
GRQ—R
Guernica Editions—R
(a)-HarperOne
Harrison House
(a)-Harvest House
Health Commun.
Hendrickson—R
Hensley Publishing
Hidden Brook Press—R
(s)-Holy Fire Publishing—R
Hope Publishing—R
(s)-IMD Press—R
Inkling Books—R
(s)-Insight Publishing—R
Johns Hopkins—R
Jubilant Press—R
Judson Press—R
Kirk House
(a)-Kregel—R
Langmarc

Legacy Publishers
Life Cycle Books—R
Lift Every Voice—R
Lighthouse Publishing—R
Lion and Lamb
Little Lauren Books
Loyola Press
(s)-McDougal Publishing—R
Messianic Jewish—R
Monarch Books
(a)-Moody Publishers
Morehouse—R
NavPress
NavPress Student—R
(a)-Nelson, Thomas
New Hope—R
New York Univ. Press
(s)-One World Press—R
(a)-One World/Ballantine
Parson Place—R
Pauline Books—R
Perigee Books
Pilgrim Press—R
(s)-Pleasant Word—R
Power Publishing—R
(s)-Providence Pub.—R
Randall House
Ravenhawk Books—R
(a)-Regal
Resource Public.
Samaritan Press
(s)-Selah Publishing—R
Sheed & Ward—R
(s)-So. Baptist Press—R
St. Anthony Mess. Press—R
(s)-Star Bible Public.
Starik Publishing
Still Waters Revival—R
Strang Book Group—R
(s)-Synergy Publishers—R
Tarcher, Jeremy P.—R
(s)-Tate Publishing—R
(s)-TEACH Services—R
Third World Press—R
(s)-Trafford Publishing—R
Treble Heart Books—R
Univ. of AR Press—R
VBC Publishing
(s)-VMI Publishers
Whitaker House
White Stone Books—R
(s)-WinePress—R
(s)-Word Alive
W Publishing
(s)-Zoe Life Publishing

WORLD ISSUES

Aadeon Publishing—R
Aaron Book—R
(s)-ACW Press—R
Ambassador-Emerald—R

(s)-American Binding—R
AMG Publishers
(a)-Baker Books
Baker's Plays—R
(s)-Black Forest/Tennessee—R
Blue Dolphin
(s)-Booklocker.com—R
Boyds Mills Press—R
Bridge-Logos—R
(s)-Brown Books
Carey Library, Wm.—R
Chalice Press
Christian Writer's Ebook—R
Comfort Publishing—R
(s)-Creation House—R
(a)-Doubleday Relig.—R
Eerdmans Pub., Wm. B.—R
(s)-Elderberry Press
(s)-Essence—R
Evangelical Press
(s)-Fairway Press—R
FaithWalk
Fifth Estate—R
Georgetown Univ. Press
Greenwood/Praeger
(a)-HarperOne
Harrison House
Hidden Brook Press—R
(s)-Holy Fire Publishing—R
(s)-Insight Publishing—R
InterVarsity Press—R
Kirk House
(a)-Kregel—R
Lift Every Voice—R
Lighthouse Publishing—R
Lillenas
Lion and Lamb
Monarch Books
NavPress
NavPress Student—R
New Hope—R
(s)-One World Press—R
Pilgrim Press—R
(s)-Pleasant Word—R
Power Publishing—R
(s)-Providence Pub.—R
Quintessential Books—R
Ravenhawk Books—R
(a)-Regnery
(s)-Selah Publishing—R
(s)-Star Bible Public.
Still Waters Revival—R
Strang Book Group—R
(s)-Synergy Publishers—R
(s)-Tate Publishing—R
(s)-Trafford Publishing—R
(a)-Tyndale House—R
VBC Publishing
(s)-VMI Publishers
(s)-WinePress—R
(s)-Word Alive

Yale Univ. Press—R
(s)-Zoe Life Publishing

WORSHIP

Aaron Book—R
Abingdon Press
(s)-ACW Press—R
Ambassador-Emerald—R
(s)-American Binding—R
American Cath. Press—R
(s)-Baal Hamon—R
Baker's Plays—R
(a)-B & H Publishing
Barbour
Bethany House
(s)-Black Forest/Tennessee—R
BMH Books—R
(s)-Booklocker.com—R
Bridge-Logos—R
(s)-Brown Books
Chalice Press
Chapter Two—R
CharismaKids
Christian Focus—R
Christian Heritage—R
Christian Writer's Ebook—R
Clarke & Co., James—R
College Press—R
Comfort Publishing—R
Continuum Intl.—R
(a)-Cook, David C.
(s)-Creation House—R
CSS Publishing
Deo Volente
Destiny Image—R
Eerdmans Pub., Wm. B.—R
(s)-Elderberry Press
Eldridge Plays
(s)-Essence—R
Evangelical Press
(s)-Fairway Press—R
Faith Alive
FaithWalk
Father's Press—R
Forward Movement
Founders Press
Greenwood/Praeger
GRQ—R
Harrison House
Harvest Day
(a)-Harvest House
Hidden Brook Press—R
(s)-Holy Fire Publishing—R
(s)-IMD Press—R
(s)-Insight Publishing—R
InterVarsity Press—R
Judson Press—R
(a)-Kregel—R
Lift Every Voice—R
Lighthouse Publishing—R
Lillenas
Lion and Lamb

Liturgy Training—R
Lutheran Univ. Press
Lutterworth Press—R
Messianic Jewish—R
Monarch Books
Morehouse—R
NavPress Student—R
(a)-Nelson, Thomas
New Hope—R
(s)-One World Press—R
Oregon Catholic
P & R Publishing—R
Pacific Press
Parsons Publishing—R
(s)-Path Pub. in Christ—R
Pauline Books—R
Pilgrim Press—R
(s)-Pleasant Word—R
Power Publishing—R
(s)-Providence Pub.—R
Randall House
Reformation Trust
(a)-Regal
Resource Public.
Rose Publishing
Salt Works—R
Samaritan Press
(s)-Selah Publishing—R
St. Anthony Mess. Press—R
(s)-Star Bible Public.
Strang Book Group—R
(s)-Synergy Publishers—R
(s)-Tate Publishing—R
(s)-TEACH Services—R
(s)-Testimony Press
(s)-Trafford Publishing—R
VBC Publishing
(s)-VMI Publishers
Wesleyan Publishing
Westminster John Knox
(s)-WinePress—R
(s)-Word Alive
W Publishing

WORSHIP RESOURCES

Aaron Book—R
Abingdon Press
(s)-ACW Press—R
(s)-American Binding—R
(s)-Baal Hamon—R
(a)-Baker Books
(a)-B & H Publishing
(s)-Black Forest/Tennessee—R
(s)-Booklocker.com—R
(s)-Brown Books
Catholic Book
Chalice Press
Christian Writer's Ebook—R
CSS Publishing
(s)-DCTS Publishing
Eerdmans Pub., Wm. B.—R
(s)-Elderberry Press

Eldridge Plays
(s)-Essence—R
Evangelical Press
(s)-Fairway Press—R
Faith Alive
FaithWalk
Forward Movement
Founders Press
Greenwood/Praeger
Harvest Day
Hidden Brook Press—R
(s)-Holy Fire Publishing—R
(s)-IMD Press—R
(s)-Insight Publishing—R
InterVarsity Press—R
Judson Press—R
(a)-Kregel—R
Lighthouse Publishing—R
Lillenas
Lion and Lamb
Liturgical Press
Liturgy Training—R
Lutheran Univ. Press
Monarch Books
(s)-One World Press—R
Our Sunday Visitor—R
Parsons Publishing—R
(s)-Path Pub. in Christ—R
Pilgrim Press—R
(s)-Pleasant Word—R
Power Publishing—R
Presbyterian Pub.
(s)-Providence Pub.—R
Randall House
Resource Public.
Salt Works—R
Smyth & Helwys
Standard Publishing
(s)-Tate Publishing—R
(s)-TEACH Services—R
(s)-Trafford Publishing—R
(s)-VMI Publishers
Wesleyan Publishing
Westminster John Knox
(s)-WinePress—R
(s)-Word Alive
(s)-Zoe Life Publishing

WRITING HOW-TO

Aaron Book—R
(s)-American Binding—R
(s)-Booklocker.com—R
(s)-Brown Books
Christian Writer's Ebook—R
Dabbling Mum Press
(s)-Elderberry Press
(s)-Essence—R
Evergreen Press
Fair Havens—R
(s)-Fairway Press—R
FaithWalk
Hidden Brook Press—R

(s)-Holy Fire Publishing—R
Lighthouse Publishing—R
Lion and Lamb
Little Lauren Books
Mission City Press
(s)-One World Press—R
Parson Place—R
(s)-Path Pub. in Christ—R
(s)-Pleasant Word—R
Power Publishing—R
(s)-Providence Pub.—R
(s)-Selah Publishing—R
(s)-Tate Publishing—R
(s)-Trafford Publishing—R
(s)-VMI Publishers
(s)-WinePress—R
(s)-Word Alive
Write Now—R

YOUTH BOOKS (Nonfiction)

Note: Listing denotes books for 8- to 12-year-olds, junior highs, or senior highs. If all three, it will say "all." If no age group is listed, they did not specify.

Aaron Book—R (8-12/Jr. High)
(s)-ACW Press—R (All)
Ambassador Books (All)
(s)-American Binding—R (Jr./Sr. High)
Anglicans United—R (8-12/Jr. High)
Atheneum/Yg. Readers (All)
(a)-Baker Books
Baker Trittin (All)
Barbour (8-12/Jr. High)
Big Idea (8-12/Jr. High)
(s)-Black Forest/Tennessee—R (All)
(s)-Booklocker.com—R (All)
(s)-Book Publishers—R (All)
Boyds Mills Press—R (All)
(s)-Brown Books (All)
Carson-Dellosa (8-12)
CharismaKids (8-12/Jr. High)
Christian Ed. Pub.
Christian Focus—R (All)
Christian Writer's Ebook—R (All)
Conciliar Press—R (8-12)
Concordia (All)
Contemporary Drama

(s)-Creation House—R (All)
(s)-CrossHouse—R (All)
Dawn Publications (Jr. High)
Eerdmans Pub., Wm. B.—R (All)
(s)-Elderberry Press (All)
(a)-Emmaus Road—R (Jr./Sr. High)
(s)-Essence—R (All)
Evergreen Press
Facts on File
Father's Press—R (All)
(a)-Focus on the Family—R (Sr. High)
Grupo Nelson (Jr. High)
Guardian Angel (8-12)
Halo Publishing (8-12)
Harcourt Religion (Sr. High)
Harrison House (All)
Health Commun.
Hidden Brook Press—R (All)
(s)-Holy Fire Publishing—R (All)
Illumination Arts (8-12)
(s)-IMD Press—R (All)
(s)-Insight Publishing—R (All)
Journey Stone—R (8-12/Jr. High)
(s)-Kindred Books—R (All)
Knight George Pub. (All)
(a)-Kregel—R (All)
Legacy Press—R (8-12)
Life Cycle Books—R (8-12)
Lift Every Voice—R (All)
Lighthouse Publishing—R (All)
Lighthouse Trails—R (All)
Lion and Lamb (All)
Little Lauren Books (Jr./Sr. High)
Master Books (All)
McRuffy Press (8-12)
Meriwether (Jr./Sr. High)
Mission City Press (8-12)
Monarch Books (All)
(a)-Moody Publishers
NavPress (Sr. High)
NavPress Student—R (Sr. High)
New Canaan—R (All)
New Leaf (All)
(s)-One World Press—R (All)
P & R Publishing—R (All)
Pacific Press
Pauline Books—R (All)
Pauline Kids (8-12)
(s)-Pleasant Word—R (All)

Power Publishing—R (All)
Randall House (All)
Ravenhawk Books—R (Jr./Sr. High)
(a)-Regal (Sr. High)
Salt Works—R (All)
Starik Publishing (Sr. High)
(s)-Tate Publishing—R (All)
(s)-Trafford Publishing—R (All)
(s)-VMI Publishers (All)
(a)-WaterBrook Press—R (All)
White Stone Books—R (All)
(s)-WinePress—R (All)
(s)-Word Alive (All)
Youth Specialties (Jr./Sr. High)
(s)-Zoe Life Publishing

YOUTH PROGRAMS

(s)-ACW Press—R
(s)-American Binding—R
(a)-Baker Books
(a)-B & H Publishing
(s)-Brown Books
Carson-Dellosa
Christian Writer's Ebook—R
Church Growth Inst.
Contemporary Drama
Eldridge Plays
(s)-Fairway Press—R
Faith Alive
Gospel Publishing
Harcourt Religion
(s)-Holy Fire Publishing—R
(s)-IMD Press—R
(s)-Insight Publishing—R
Judson Press—R
Lillenas
Lion and Lamb
Mission City Press
Monarch Books
NavPress Student—R
(s)-One World Press—R
Pilgrim Press—R
Ponder Publishing
Power Publishing—R
(s)-Providence Pub.—R
Randall House Digital
Salt Works—R
Standard Publishing
(s)-Tate Publishing—R

ALPHABETICAL LISTINGS OF BOOK PUBLISHERS

If you do not find the publisher you are looking for, check the General Index. See the introduction to that index for the codes used to identify the current status of each unlisted publisher. If you do not understand all the terms or abbreviations used in these listings, read the "How to Use This Book" section. Remember to check out any publisher thoroughly before signing a contract. (See the Resources section on the CD-ROM for ideas on how to do this.)

(+) A plus sign before a listing indicates it is a new listing this year and was not included last year.

AADEON PUBLISHING COMPANY, PO Box 223, Hartford CT 06141. Fax (206)666-5132. E-mail: submissions@aadeon.com. Website: www.aadeon.com. Submit to The Editor. Addresses spiritual, social, and cultural issues related to the United States of America; must be insightful, historically and biblically accurate, and focused toward a Christian readership. Publishes 1 title/yr.; trade paperback. Will accept mss through agents. Does print-on-demand. Reprints books. Requires 160,000 wds. or more. Royalty 8% on net; no advance. Average first printing 100-5,000. Publication within 1 yr. Considers simultaneous submissions. Requires accepted ms on disk in Microsoft Word. Responds in 1-4 mos. Requires NKJV. Guidelines on Website; no catalog.
> **Nonfiction:** Proposal/3 chapters or complete ms; no phone/fax/e-query.
> **Artwork:** Open to queries from freelance artists.
> **Tips:** "We are particularly interested in manuscripts that challenge average people to confront and overcome the negative influences of an increasingly secular and godless society. Manuscripts must be well organized, professionally edited, easy to understand, biblically based, and scripturally supported (frequent quotations from the Bible—chapter and verse—to support writings). Manuscripts must clearly speak to both a Christian and non-Christian audience."

+AARON BOOK PUBLISHING, 1093 Bristol Caverns Hwy., Bristol TN 37620. (423)212-1208. E-mail: info@aaronbookpublishing.com. Website: www.AaronBookPublishing.com. Imprint of Black Forest Press. Tim Rouse, ed. Honesty, uniqueness, service. Publishes hardcover, mass-market, coffee-table books. Some subsidy; does print-on-demand. Reprints books. Any length. Royalty on retail. Considers simultaneous submissions. Prefers mss by e-mail. Prefers KJV. Guidelines; catalog for 9x12 SAE/5 stamps.
> **Nonfiction:** Query first; proposal/2-3 chapters; phone/e-query OK.
> **Fiction:** Query first; proposal/2-3 chapters; phone/e-query OK.
> **Special Needs:** Books of good content. Strong characters and a great storyline.
> **Artwork:** Open to queries from freelance artists.
> **Contest:** Sponsors contests occasionally.
> **Tips:** Open to almost any topic.

+ABC BOOK PUBLISHING, LLC., 20609 N.E. Lakeside Dr., Fairview OR 97024. Website: www.ABCBookPublishing.com. Rich Brett, pub. Publishes 20 titles/yr.; trade paperbacks. Does print-on-demand. Royalty 10% on net; no advance. Publication within 6 mos. Wants accepted mss by e-mail. Guidelines by e-mail; catalog online.
> **Nonfiction:** E-query.
> **Tips:** "We are a new publisher intent on providing a vehicle for worldwide distribution of nonfiction works."

ABINGDON PRESS, 201—8th Ave. S., PO Box 801, Nashville TN 37202. (615)749-6000. Fax (615)749-6512. E-mail: (first initial and last name) @umpublishing.org. Website: www

.abingdonpress.com. United Methodist Publishing House. Editors: Mary C. Dean, ed-in-chief; Ron Kidd, gen. interest bks.; Robert Ratcliff, professional and academic bks.; John Kutsko, dir. of acq.; Joseph A. Crowe, gen. interest bks.; Judith Pierson, children's bks. Books and church supplies directed primarily to a mainline religious market. Publishes 120 titles/yr.; hardcover, trade paperbacks. Receives 3,000 submissions annually. Less than 5% of books from first-time authors. Will accept mss through agents. No reprints. Prefers 144 pgs. Royalty 5-10% on retail; advance. Average first printing 3,500-4,000. Publication within 18 mos. No simultaneous submissions. Requires requested ms on disk. Responds in 8-12 wks. Prefers NRSV or a variety of which NRSV is one. Guidelines on Website; free catalog.

Nonfiction: Proposal/2 chapters; no phone/fax/e-query.

Fiction: Solicited or agented material only.

Ethnic Books: African American, Hispanic, Native American, Korean.

Photos: Accepts freelance photos for book covers.

Tips: "We develop and produce materials to help more people in more places come to know and love God through Jesus Christ and to choose to serve God and neighbor."

**Note: This publisher serviced by ChristianManuscriptSubmissions.com.

ACTA PUBLICATIONS, 5559 W. Howard St., Skokie IL 60077-2621. Toll-free (800)397-2282. (847)676-2282. Fax (800)397-0079. (847)676-2287. E-mail: acta@actapublications.com. Website: www.actapublications.com. Catholic. Gregory F. Augustine Pierce, pres. & co-pub. Wants books that successfully integrate daily life and spirituality. Publishes 10 titles/yr.; hardcover, trade paperbacks, coffee-table books. Receives 100 submissions annually. 50% of books from first-time authors. Prefers 150-200 pgs. Royalty 10-12% of net; no advance. Average first printing 3,000. Publication within 1 yr. Responds in 2 mos. Prefers NRSV. Guidelines; catalog for 9x12 SAE/2 stamps.

Nonfiction: Query or proposal/1 chapter; no phone/fax/e-query.

Tips: "Most open to books that are useful to a large number of average Christians. Read our catalog and one of our books first."

ADAMS MEDIA CORP., 57 Littlefield St., Avon MA 02322. (508)427-7100. Fax (800)872-5628. E-mail through Website: www.adamsmedia.com. Division of F + W Publications. Jill Alexander, sr. ed. Publishes 230 titles/yr. Receives 5,000 submissions annually. 40% of books from first-time authors. Will accept mss through agents. Royalty; variable advance; or outright purchase. Publication within 12-18 mos. Considers simultaneous submissions. Responds in 3 mos. to queries. No mss accepted by e-mail. Guidelines on Website; catalog for 9x12 SAE/5 stamps.

Nonfiction: Query first; no phone/fax/e-query.

Tips: General publisher that does some inspirational books.

ALBA HOUSE/ST. PAULS, 2187 Victory Blvd., Staten Island NY 10314-6603. (718)761-0047. Fax (718)761-0057. E-mail: Edmund_Lane@juno.com. Website: www.stpauls.us. Catholic/Society of St. Paul. Edmund C. Lane, SSP, ed-in-chief; Frank Sadowski, SSP, ed. Imprint: St. Pauls. Publishes 24 titles/yr.; trade paperbacks. Receives 450 submissions annually. 20% of books from first-time authors. No mss through agents. Reprints books. Prefers 124 pgs. Royalty 7-10% on retail; no advance. Average first printing 3,500. Publication within 9 mos. Prefers requested ms on disk. Responds in 1-2 mos. Free guidelines/catalog.

Nonfiction: Query.

Special Needs: Spirituality in the Roman Catholic tradition; lives of the saints.

AMBASSADOR BOOKS INC., 91 Prescott St., Worcester MA 01605-1702. (508)756-2893. Fax (508)757-7055. E-mail: info@ambassadorbooks.com, or through Website: www.ambassadorbooks.com. Catholic. Mr. Chris Driscoll, acq. ed. Books of intellectual and spiritual excellence. Publishes 9 titles/yr.; hardcover, trade paperbacks. Receives 2,100 submissions annually. 50% of books from first-time authors. Will accept mss through agents.

No reprints. Royalty 8-10% of retail; no advance. Publication within 1 yr. Considers simultaneous submissions. Responds in 3-4 mos. Prefers NAB. Guidelines (also by e-mail/Website); free catalog (or on Website).

Nonfiction: Query; no phone/fax/e-query.

Fiction: Query. Juvenile, young adult, adult; picture books & board books.

Photos: Accepts freelance photos for book covers.

Tips: "Most open to books that will have a positive impact on readers' lives. Must be well written and fit with our mission."

AMBASSADOR-EMERALD, INTL., 427 Wade Hampton Blvd., Greenville SC 29609. (864)235-2434. Fax (864)235-2491. E-mail: publisher@emeraldhouse.com. Website: www.emerald house.com. European office: Ambassador Productions, Providence House, Ardenlee, Belfast BT6 8QJ, N. Ireland. Phone 028 90450010. Fax 028 90739659. E-mail: info@ambassador-productions.com. Emerald House Group Inc. Sam Lowry, ed. Dedicated to spreading the gospel of Christ and empowering Christians through the written word. Publishes 55 titles/yr.; hardcover, trade paperbacks, mass-market paperbacks, coffee-table books. Receives 400 submissions annually. 15% of books from first-time authors. Will accept mss through agents. SUBSIDY PUBLISHES 20%. Reprints books. Prefers 150-200 pgs. Royalty 5-15% of net; advance. Average first printing 5,000. Publication within 1 yr. Considers simultaneous submissions. Prefers requested ms on disk or by e-mail. Responds in 3 mos. Prefers KJV. Guidelines (also by e-mail); free catalog.

Nonfiction: Query only; fax/e-query OK.

Fiction: Query only; fax/e-query OK. All ages.

Tips: "We're most open to nonfiction writing for women."

AMERICAN CATHOLIC PRESS, 16565 State St., South Holland IL 60473-2025. (708)331-5485. Fax (708)331-5484. E-mail: acp@acpress.org. Website: www.acpress.org, or www.leaflet missal.com. Catholic worship resources. Father Michael Gilligan, ed. dir. Publishes 4 titles/yr.; hardcover. Receives 10 submissions annually. Reprints books. Pays $25-100 for outright purchases only. Average first printing 3,000. Publication within 1 yr. No simultaneous submissions. Responds in 2 mos. Prefers NAS. No guidelines; catalog for SASE.

Nonfiction: Query first; no phone/fax/e-query.

Tips: "We publish only materials on the Roman Catholic liturgy. Especially interested in new music for church services. No poetry or fiction."

AMG PUBLISHERS/LIVING INK BOOKS, 6815 Shallowford Rd. (37421), PO Box 22000, Chattanooga TN 37422. Toll-free (800)266-4977. (423)894-6060. Toll-free fax (800)265-6690. (423)894-9511. E-mail: danp@amginternational.org. Website: www.amgpublishers.com. AMG International. Dan Penwell, dir. of product development/acquisitions; Dr. Warren Baker, sr. ed.; Richard Steele, assoc. ed. To provide biblically oriented books for reference, learning, and personal growth. Imprint: Living Ink Books. Publishes 25-30 titles/yr.; hardcover, trade paperbacks, and oversized Bible studies. Receives 2,500 submissions annually. 30% of books from first-time authors. Will accept mss through agents. Prefers 40,000-60,000 wds. Royalty 10-16% of net; advance $1,500 and up. Average first printing 3,000. Publication within 15 mos. Accepts simultaneous submissions. Prefers accepted ms by mail. Responds in 1-4 mos. Prefers KJV, NASB, NIV, NKJV, NLT. Guidelines (also by e-mail/ Website); catalog for 9x12 SAE/5 stamps.

Nonfiction: Query letter first; e-query preferred. "Looking for well-written nonfiction. We have a broad interest in biblically oriented books."

Fiction: Teen fantasy (no other fiction at this time other than fantasy).

Special Needs: Women's issues, men's issues, and other current issues—including Christian-political action books.

Also Does: Bible software, Bible audio cassettes, CD-ROMs.

Tips: "Most open to a book that is well thought out, clearly written, and finely edited. A professional proposal, following our specific guidelines, has the best chance of acceptance. Spend extra time in developing a good proposal. AMG is always looking for something new and different—with a niche. Write, and rewrite, and rewrite, and rewrite again."
Note: This publisher serviced by The Writer's Edge and ChristianManuscriptSubmissions .com.

ANGLICANS UNITED/LATIMER PRESS, PO Box 763217, Dallas TX 75376. (972)293-7443. Fax (972)293-7559. E-mail: anglicansunited@sbcglobal.net. Website: www.anglicansunited .com; www.latimerpress.com. Episcopal Church USA. Cheryl M. Wetzel, ed. Provides educational materials for biblically orthodox Anglicans and Episcopalians. Publishes 4 titles/yr.; trade paperbacks, mass-market paperbacks. Receives 20 submissions annually. 90% of books from first-time authors. Will accept mss through agents. SOME SUBSIDY. Reprints books. Prefers up to 225 pgs. Outright purchase for $100-500. Average first printing 1,500-2,000. Publication within 6 mos. Considers simultaneous submissions. Prefers ms by disk or e-mail. Responds in 1 mo. Prefers NIV. Guidelines; catalog for #10 SAE/1 stamp.

Nonfiction: Query letter only first; no phone query; fax/e-query OK. "Looking for Anglican history and practice; adult education."
Ethnic Books: Beginning to translate classical Anglican books into Spanish for Latin American market.
Also Does: Booklets; videos/DVDs.
Artwork: Open to queries from freelance artists.
Tips: "Most open to (1) a book (60-110 pages total), used in Christian education classes for adults and teens; (2) a book (60 pages) on baptism, marriage, grief, confirmation, or stewardship."
Note: This publisher serviced by The Writer's Edge.

ATHENEUM BOOKS FOR YOUNG READERS, 1230 Avenue of the Americas, New York NY 10020. (212)698-2715. Fax (212)698-2796. Website: www.simonsayskids.com. Imprint of Simon & Schuster. Submit to The Editor. Publishes books for preschool through high school. Publishes in hardcover. Prefers mss through agents. Royalty; advance. Considers simultaneous submissions. Guidelines.

Nonfiction: Query only; no phone/fax/e-query. For children/young adult readers only.
Fiction: Query only. For children and teens.
Tips: "Most open to well-written, fast-paced, unique books for middle-grade readers. Subjects include religion."

AVON INSPIRE, HarperCollins, 10 E. 53rd St., New York NY 10022. (212)207-7000. E-mail: AvonInspire@HarperCollins.com. Website: www.avoninspire.com. Published in partnership with HarperOne. Cynthia DiTiberio, ed. Inspirational women's fiction. Publishes 6-10 titles/yr. Agented submissions only. Royalty and advance negotiable.

Fiction: Historical & contemporary for now; also planning suspense and children's novels.

BAKER ACADEMIC, PO Box 6287, Grand Rapids MI 49516-6287. (616)676-9185. Fax (616)676-2315. E-mail: submissions@bakeracademic.com. Website: www.bakeracademic .com. Imprint of Baker Publishing Group. Jim Kinney, ed. dir. Publishes religious academic books and professional books for students and church leaders. Publishes 50 titles/yr.; hardcover, trade paperbacks. 10% of books from first-time authors. Will accept mss through agents. Royalty; advance. Publication within 1 yr. Guidelines on Website; catalog for 10x13 SAE/3 stamps.

Nonfiction: No unsolicited queries.

BAKER BOOKS, Box 6287, Grand Rapids MI 49516-6287. (616)676-9185. Fax (616)676-9573. Website: www.bakerbooks.com. Imprint of Baker Publishing Group. Submit to Book Editor. Ministry titles for the church. No unsolicited proposals. Guidelines; catalog for

10x13 SAE/3 stamps. Submit only through an agent, Writer's Edge, or ChristianManuscript Submissions.com.

BAKER'S PLAYS INC., 45 W. 25th St., New York NY 10010-2035. West coast: 7623 W. Sunset Blvd., Los Angeles CA 90046-2714. (212)206-8990. E-mail: publications@bakers plays.com. Website: www.bakersplays.com. Samuel French, Inc. Roxane Heinze-Bradshaw, mng. ed. Publishes 2-5 titles/yr. Receives 800 submissions annually. 60% of plays from first-time authors. Will accept mss through agents. Reprints plays. Book royalty 10% on retail; amateur performance royalty 70%; professional performance royalty 80%; no advance. Average first printing 1,000. Publication within 6 mos. Considers simultaneous submissions. Accepts requested ms by e-mail. Responds in 6-8 mos. Guidelines on Website; separate section in their general catalog, $4.

Plays: E-query. "Most open to plays that deal with modern Christian life."

Tips: "We currently publish full-length plays, one-act plays for young audiences, theater texts and musicals, plays written by high schoolers, with a separate division which publishes religious plays. We consider plays year round." If your play has been produced, send copies of press clippings. If sending music, you must include a CD, or sheet music.

BAKER TRITTIN PRESS, PO Box 277, Winona Lake IN 46590. (574)269-6100. Fax (574)269-6130. E-mail: info@btconcepts.com. Website: www.bakertrittinpress.com. Marvin G. Baker, ed-in-chief. Books for tweens and young adults 8- to 18-year-olds. Publishes 6-8 fiction titles/yr. 50% of books from first-time authors. No mss through agents. No reprints. Prefers 20,000-40,000 wds. Royalty 7-10% on retail; no advance. Average first printing 2,500. Publication within 18 mos. No simultaneous submissions. Responds in 3 mos. Accepts mss on disk or by e-mail. Prefers NIV.

Nonfiction: Proposal/3 chapters; no phone query; fax/e-query OK.

Fiction: Proposal/3 chapters; no phone query; fax/e-query OK.

BALLANTINE PUBLISHING GROUP, 1745 Broadway, 18th Fl., New York NY 10019. (212)782-9000. Website: www.randomhouse.com/BB. A Division of Random House. Dan Smetanka, religion ed. General publisher that does a few religious books. Mss from agents only. No e-query. Royalty 8-15%; variable advances. Nonfiction & fiction. Guidelines on Website; no catalog.

B & H PUBLISHING GROUP, 127—9th Ave. N., Nashville TN 37234-0115. (615)251-2438. Fax (615)251-3752. E-mail: pat.carter@bhpublishinggroup.com, or through Website: www.bh publishinggroup.com. Book and Bible division of LifeWay Christian Resources. David Shepherd, pub.; Thomas Walters, sr. acq. ed. (nonfiction); David Webb, sr. acq. ed. (fiction); Ray Clenden, sr. acq. ed. (academic). Imprints: B & H Books, B & H Academic, Holman Bible Publishers, Holman Reference, Broadman Supplies, B & H Espanol. Publishes books in the conservative, evangelical tradition by and for the larger Christian world. Publishes 90-100 titles/yr.; hardcover, trade paperback. Receives 3,000 submissions annually. 10% of books from first-time authors. Requires submissions through agents. Royalty on net; advance. Publication within 18 mos. Considers simultaneous submissions. Responds in 9-12 mos. Prefers HCSB, NIV, NASB. Guidelines (also on Website); free catalog.

Nonfiction: Query first; no phone/fax query.

Fiction: Query first; no phone/fax query. Adult.

Ethnic: Spanish translations.

Also Does: Licensing, Kindle Reader, some audio.

Blog: www.holmantv.com. A series of weekly video episodes for high school and college students.

Tips: "Follow guidelines when submitting. Be informed that the market in general is very crowded with the book you might want to write. Do the research before submitting."

Note: This publisher serviced by The Writer's Edge and ChristianManuscriptSubmissions .com.

BANTAM BOOKS—See Doubleday Religious.

BARBOUR PUBLISHING INC., 1810 Barbour Dr., PO Box 719, Uhrichsville OH 44683. (740) 922-6045. Fax (740)922-5948. E-mail: editors@barbourbooks.com. Website: www .barbourbooks.com. Paul Muckley (pmuckley@barbourbooks.com), sr. ed./nonfiction; Rebecca Germany (rgermany@barbourbooks.com), sr. ed./romance and women's fiction (novels & novellas); Kelly Williams (kwilliams@barbourbooks.com), mng. ed. and youth/ children/gift acquisitions. To publish and distribute inspirational products offering exceptional value and biblical encouragement to the masses. Imprints: Barbour Books (fiction and nonfiction) and Heartsong Presents (romance: see separate listing). Publishes 200 titles/yr.; hardcover, trade paperbacks, mass-market paperbacks. Receives 1,500 submissions annually. 40% of books from first-time authors. Will accept mss through agents. No subsidy. Prefers 50,000 wds. (nonfiction), or 80,000-100,000 wds. (fiction). Royalty 8-12% of net; outright purchases $500-5,000; advance $500-5,000. Average first printing 15,000-20,000. Publication within 24 mos. Considers simultaneous submissions. Responds in 1 mo. to queries. Prefers NIV, KJV. Guidelines (also on Website); catalog for 9x12 SAE/2 stamps.

Nonfiction: Proposal/3 chapters; no phone/fax query; e-query OK. E-mail: submissions@ barbourbooks.com.

Fiction: Proposal/3 chapters to Rebecca Germany, fiction ed. Novellas 20,000 wds. For all ages. "We are interested in a mystery/romance series." E-mail: fictionsubmit@ barbourbooks.com. See separate listing for Heartsong Presents & Heartsong Presents— Mysteries.

Tips: "We seek solid, evangelical books with the greatest mass appeal. A good title on practical Christian living will go much farther with Barbour than will a commentary on Jude. Do your homework before sending us a manuscript; send material that will work well within our publishing philosophy."

Note: This publisher serviced by The Writer's Edge and ChristianManuscriptSubmissions .com.

BARCLAY PRESS, 211 N. Meridian St., Ste. 101, Newberg OR 97132. (503)538-9775. Fax (503) 554-8597. E-mail: info@barclaypress.com. Website: www.barclaypress.com. Friends/ Quaker. Dan McCracken, gen. mngr. No unsolicited manuscripts.

Note: This publisher serviced by The Writer's Edge.

BAYLOR UNIVERSITY PRESS, One Bear Pl., #97363, Waco TX 76798-7308. (254)710-3164. Fax (254)710-3440. Website: www.baylorpress.com. Baptist. Dr. Carey C. Newman, dir., (254)710-3522, carey_newman@baylor.edu; Casey Blaine, acq. ed., (254)710-2846), casey_blaine@baylor.edu. Imprint: Markham Press Fund. Academic press producing scholarly books on religion and social sciences; church-state studies. Publishes 30 academic titles/yr.; hardcover, trade paperback. Receives 100+ submissions annually. 10% of books from first-time authors. Will accept mss through agents. No subsidy publishing. No reprints. Royalty 10% on net; no advance. Average first printing 1,000. Publication within 12 mos. Accepts simultaneous submissions. Responds in 2 mos. Guidelines on Website; free catalog.

Nonfiction: Query only first; no phone/fax query, e-query OK. "Looking for academic books; religion and public life."

BEACON HILL PRESS OF KANSAS CITY, PO Box 419527, Kansas City MO 64141. (816)931-1900. Fax (816)753-4071. E-mail: jap@bhillkc.com. Website: www.bhillkc.com. Nazarene Publishing House/Church of the Nazarene. Bonnie Perry, pub. dir.; Richard Buckner, ministry line ed.; Judi Perry, consumer ed. A Christ-centered publisher that provides authentically

Christian resources that are faithful to God's Word and relevant to life. Imprint: Beacon Hill Books. Publishes 30 titles/yr.; hardcover, trade paperbacks. Will accept mss through agents. Reprints books. Prefers 30,000-60,000 wds. or 250 pgs. Royalty 12-14% of net; advance; some outright purchases. Average first printing 5,000. Publication within 2 yrs. Considers simultaneous submissions. Responds in 3 mos. or longer. Free guidelines/catalog.

Nonfiction: Proposal/2 chapters; no phone/fax query. "Looking for practical Christian living, felt needs, Christian care, spiritual growth, and ministry resources."

Tips: "Nearly all our titles come through acquisitions, and the number of freelance submissions has declined dramatically. If you wish to submit, follow guidelines above. You are always welcome to submit after sending for guidelines."

**Note: This publisher serviced by The Writer's Edge.

BELIEVE BOOKS, 450 Massachusetts Ave. N.W., Ste. 1223, Washington DC 20001. Phone/fax (202)787-1532. E-mail: BelieveBooks@gmail.com. Website: www.BelieveBooks.com. Elizabeth Stalcup, ed. Publishes inspirational life stories of people from around the world. E-query.

BELLEBOOKS, PO Box 67, Smyrna GA 30081. Phone/fax (770)384-1348. E-mail: bellebooks@bellebooks.com. Website: www.bellebooks.com. Deborah Smith, ed. Publishes Southern, wholesome, feel-good fiction and nonfiction. Publishes 1 title/yr. Receives 25-40 submissions annually. 0% of books from first-time authors. Will accept mss through agents. Reprints books. Prefers 75,000 wds. or 300 pgs. Royalty; advance. Average first printing 3,000. Publication within 12 mos. Considers simultaneous submissions. Responds in 3 mos. No guidelines or catalog.

Nonfiction: Query by e-mail only; no unsolicited mss. "Looking for nondenominational books with an emphasis on general spirituality."

Fiction: Query by e-mail only "We only publish books with Southern (S.E. USA) settings."

Artwork: Open to queries from freelance artists.

Tips: "We publish humorous, nondenominational, general inspiration suitable for mainstream as well as Christian readers."

BETHANY HOUSE PUBLISHERS, 11400 Hampshire Ave. S., Bloomington MN 55438. (952)829-2500. Fax (952)829-2768. Website: www.bethanyhouse.com. Baker Publishing Group. To help Christians apply biblical truth in all areas of life—whether through a well-told story, a challenging devotional, or the message of an illustrated children's book. Publishes 90-120 titles/yr.; hardcover, trade paperbacks. 2% of books from first-time authors. Will accept mss through agents. No reprints. Negotiable royalty on net; negotiable advance. Publication within 1 yr. Considers simultaneous submissions. Responds in 3 mos. Guidelines for fiction/nonfiction/juvenile on Website; catalog for 9x12 SAE/5 stamps.

Nonfiction: "Seeking well-planned and developed books in the following categories: personal growth, deeper-life spirituality, contemporary issues, women's issues, reference, applied theology, and inspirational."

Fiction: See Website for current acquisitions needs.

Tips: "We do not accept unsolicited queries or proposals via telephone, regular mail, fax, or e-mail."

**Note: This publisher serviced by The Writer's Edge and ChristianManuscriptSubmissions .com.

BIG IDEA INC., 230 Franklin Rd., Bldg. 2-A, Franklin TN 37064. Toll-free (800)295-0557. (615)224-2200. E-mail: customerservice@bigidea.com. Website: www.bigidea.com. Classic Media. Cindy Kenney, sr. mng. ed. To creatively impact the lives of children, ages 2 through 12, with stories that teach biblical values. Publishes 20 titles/yr.; hardcover. Receives 2,500 submissions annually. 5% of books from first-time authors. Will accept mss through agents. No reprints. Prefers 1,500-2,000 wds. Negotiable outright purchase (no royalties); no advance. Average first printing 10,000-20,000. Publication within 20 mos. Considers simultaneous submissions. Responds in 3-6 mos. Prefers NIV. No catalog (see online).

Nonfiction: Query first; complete ms for picture or board books; no phone/fax query; e-query OK.

Fiction: Query first; complete ms for picture books; no phone/fax query; e-query OK.

Tips: Not accepting unsolicited manuscripts for now.

BJU PRESS/JOURNEYFORTH, 1700 Wade Hampton Blvd., Greenville SC 29614. (864)370-1800, ext. 4350. Fax (864)298-0268, ext. 4324. E-mail: jb@bju.edu. Website: www.bjupress .com. Bob Jones University Press. Nancy Lohr, youth ed.; Suzette Jordan, adult ed. Our goal is to publish excellent, trustworthy books for children and Christian living titles for adults. Publishes 8-10 titles/yr.; hardcover, trade paperbacks. Receives 800 submissions annually (200 Christian living/600 youth novels). 10% of books from first-time authors. Will accept mss through agents. Reprints youth books only. Royalty. Average first printing 5,000. Publication within 12-18 mos. Considers simultaneous submissions. No submissions by disk or e-mail. Responds in 8-12 wks. Requires KJV. Guidelines (also by e-mail/Website); free catalog.

Nonfiction: Proposal/3-5 chapters; e-query OK.

Fiction: Proposal/5 chapters or complete ms. For children & teens. "We prefer overtly Christian or Christian world-view."

Artwork: Open to queries from freelance artists.

Tips: "Any of the topics indicated have a good chance, provided the writing is clear and compelling. Mediocre writing is not going to get past the first reader. The precollege, homeschool market welcomes print-rich, well-written novels. No picture books, please, but compelling novels for early readers are always good for us. Biographies on the lives of Christian heroes and statesmen are also a good fit. We focus on conservative biblical books for all ages that will help to develop skill with the written word as well as discernment as a believer; we complement the educational goals of BJU Press, or K-12 textbook division."

**Note: This publisher serviced by The Writer's Edge.

BLUE DOLPHIN PUBLISHING INC., PO Box 8, Nevada City CA 95959. (530)477-1503. Fax (530)477-8342. E-mail: Bdolphin@bluedolphinpublishing.com. Website: www.bluedolphin publishing.com. Paul M. Clemens, pub. Imprint: Pelican Pond (fiction & poetry), Papillon Publishing (juvenile), and Symposium Publishing (nonfiction). Books that help people grow in their social and spiritual awareness. Publishes 20-24 titles/yr. (includes 10-12 print-on-demand). Receives 4,800 submissions annually. 90% of books from first-time authors. Prefers about 60,000 wds. or 200-300 pgs. Royalty 10-15% of net; no advance. Average first printing 300, then on demand. Publication within 10 mos. Considers simultaneous submissions. Requires requested ms on disk. Responds in 3-6 mos. Guidelines (also on Website); catalog for 6x9 SAE/2 stamps.

Nonfiction: Query or proposal/1 chapter; no phone/e-query. "Looking for books that will increase people's spiritual and social awareness. We will consider all topics."

Fiction: Query/2-pg. synopsis. Pelican Pond Imprint. For teens and adults; no children's board books or picture books.

Artwork: Open to queries from freelance artists.

Tips: "Looking for mature writers whose focus is to help people lead better lives. Our authors are generally professionals who write for others—not just for themselves. We look for topics that would appeal to the general market, are interesting, different, and will aid in the growth and development of humanity. See Website before submitting."

Note: This publisher also publishes books on a range of topics, including cross-cultural spirituality. They also may offer a co-publishing arrangement, not necessarily a royalty deal.

BMH BOOKS, PO Box 544, Winona Lake IN 46590. (574)268-1122. Fax (574)268-5384. E-mail: tdwhite@bmhbooks.com. Website: www.BMHbooks.com. Blog: www.fgbc-world .blogspot.com. Fellowship of Grace Brethren Churches. Terry White, ed./pub. Long-lasting material of conservative theology. Publishes 15-18 titles/yr.; hardcover, trade paperbacks. Receives 30 submissions annually. 50% of books from first-time authors. Will accept mss through agents. No subsidy or print-on-demand. Seldom reprints books. Prefers 50,000-75,000 wds., or 128-256 pgs. Royalty 8-10% on retail; rarely pays an advance. Average first printing 4,000. Publication within 1 yr. Prefers not to consider simultaneous submissions. Responds in 3 mos. Prefers KJV or NIV. Requires accepted mss by e-mail. Guidelines by e-mail; free catalog.

Nonfiction: Proposal/2 chapters; no phone/fax query; e-query OK.

Tips: "Most open to biblically based, timeless, discipleship material."

BOYDS MILLS PRESS, 815 Church St., Honesdale PA 18431. Website: www.boydsmills press.com. General publisher. Submit to Manuscript Submissions. Publishes a wide range of literary children's titles, for preschool through young adult; very few religious. Publishes 80 titles/yr.; hardcover, trade paperbacks. Receives 15,000 submissions annually. 40% of books from first-time authors. Reprints books. Royalty 4-12% on retail; advances vary. Considers simultaneous submissions. Guidelines.

Nonfiction: Query/proposal package, outline, 3 sample chapters (expert review of manuscript recommended).

Fiction: Outline/synopsis/first 3 chapters for novels; complete ms for picture books. "We are always interested in multicultural settings."

Tips: "We look for a broad range of books with fresh voices for children and young adults. We publish very few specifically religious books that are not multicultural or otherwise of broad appeal. Please consult our Website for the types of books we publish before submitting your manuscript."

BRANDEN PUBLISHING CO., PO Box 812094, Wellesley MA 02482. (781)235-3634. Fax (781)790-1056. E-mail through Website: www.branden.com. Adolph Caso, ed. Books by or about women, children, military, Italian American or African American themes; religious fiction. Publishes 15 titles/yr.; hardcover, trade paperbacks. 80% of books from first-time authors. Receives 1,000 submissions annually. 80% of books from first-time authors. Will accept mss through agents. Reprints books. Royalty 5-10% of net; advance $1,000 max. Publication within 10 mos. Responds in 1 mo.

Nonfiction: Paragraph query only with author's vita & SASE; no phone/fax/e-query.

Fiction: Paragraph query only with author's vita & SASE. Ethnic, religious fiction.

BRIDGE-LOGOS, 17750 N.W. 115th Ave., Bldg. 200, Ste. 220, Alachua FL 32615. (386)462-2525. Fax (586)462-2535. E-mail: editorial@bridgelogos.com, or phildebrand@bridge-logos .com. Website: www.bridgelogos.com. Peggy Hildebrand, acq. ed. Publishers classics, books by spirit-filled authors, and inspirational books that appeal to the general evangelical market. Imprint: Unity. Publishes 40 titles/yr.; hardcover, trade paperbacks, mass-market paperbacks. Receives 200+ submissions annually. 30% of books from first-time authors. Will accept mss through agents. SUBSIDY PUBLISHES TO 5%; does very little print-on-demand. Reprints books. Prefers 250 pgs. Royalty 10-15% on net; rarely pays $500 advance. Average first printing 4,000-5,000. Publication within 3-6 mos. Considers simultaneous submissions. Responds in 6 wks. Prefers accepted mss by e-mail. Guidelines on Website; free catalog.

Nonfiction: Proposal/3-5 chapters; no phone/fax query; e-query OK. "Most open to evangelism, spiritual growth, self-help, and education." Charges a $50 manuscript submission/evaluation fee.

Fiction: Proposal/3-5 chapters; no phone/fax query; e-query OK.

Special Needs: Reference, biography, current issues, controversial issues, church renewal, women's issues, and Bible commentary.

Photos: Accepts freelance photos for book covers.

Tips: "Looking for well-written timely books that are aimed at the needs of people, and that glorify God. Have a great message, a well-written manuscript, and a specific plan and willingness to market your book. Looking for previously published authors with an active ministry who are experts on their subject."

**Note: This publisher serviced by ChristianManuscriptSubmissions.com.

BY GRACE PUBLICATIONS, PO Box 83, Monroe AR 72108-0083. E-mail: bygracepublishing@ yahoo.com. Website: www.bygracepublishing.com. Blog: http://ue_authors.bravejournal .com. Division of Unique Enterprises. Sheila Holloway, sr. ed. Inspirational Romance, Tender Romance, and Chick-Lit—all in three different lengths: 30,000-40,000 wds., 45,000-55,000 wds., or 60,000-65,000 wds.; plus a few Special Releases (3/yr.) of 70,000-85,000 wds. Royalty 50% of net; no advance. Guidelines on Website.

Fiction: Proposal/1st 3 chapters by e-mail (uniqueenterprisessubmit@yahoo.com). Attach RTF files only.

+CAMBRIDGE SCHOLARS PUBLISHING, Unit 12 Chillingham Industrial Est., Book Chapman St., Newcastle Upon Tyne NE6 2XX, United Kingdom. Fax (+44) 0191 2652056. E-mail: admin@c-s-p.org. Website: www.c-s-p.org. Dr. A. Nereessian, ed. Publishes 15 titles/yr. Receives 100 submissions annually. 70% of books from first-time authors. No mss through agents. No reprints. No subsidy or print-on-demand. Prefers 100-500 pgs. Royalty 15%; no advance. Average first printing 500. Publication within 3 mos. Considers simultaneous submissions. Responds in 3 mos. Prefers accepted ms on disk. Guidelines on Website; free catalog.

Nonfiction: Proposal/1 chapter; e-query OK.

Ethnic Books: Black, Hispanic, and others.

Photos/Artwork: Accepts freelance photos for book covers; open to queries from freelance artists.

Tips: "We will consider very specialized books which others are likely to reject on the grounds of an absence of market. Our titles are mostly of interest to scholars and university academic staff."

CAMBRIDGE UNIVERSITY PRESS, 32 Avenue of the Americas, New York NY 10013-2473. Toll-free (800)872-7423. (212)924-3900 or (212)337-5941. Fax (212)691-3239. E-mail: information@cup.org. Website: www.cup.org. University of Cambridge. Andrew Beck, religion ed. (abeck@cambridge.org). Editors for other topics listed on Website.

Nonfiction: Proposal; no complete mss. Scholarly nonfiction.

CANADIAN INSTITUTE FOR LAW, THEOLOGY & PUBLIC POLICY INC., 89 Douglasview Rise S.E., Calgary AB T2Z 2P5, Canada. (403)720-8714. Fax (403)720-4746. E-mail: ciltpp@ cs.com. Website: www.ciltpp.com. Will Moore, pres. Integrating Christianity with the study of law and political science. Publishes 2-4 titles/yr.; trade paperbacks. Receives 4-5 submissions annually. 1% of books from first-time authors. Will accept mss through agents. Reprints books. Royalty 7% on retail; no advance. Average first printing 1,000. Publication within 12-24 mos. No simultaneous submissions. Responds in 6-12 mos. Prefers NIV. Guidelines (also by e-mail); free catalog.

Nonfiction: Proposal/1 chapter. "Looking for books integrating Christianity with law and political science."

Photos/Artwork: Accepts freelance photos for book covers.

CANDY CANE PRESS—See Ideals Publications.

CANTICLE BOOKS, PO Box 2666, Carlsbad CA 92018. (760)806-3743. Fax (760)806-3689. E-mail: magnuspres@aol.com. Website: www.magnuspress.com. Imprint of Magnus Press. Warren Angel, ed. dir. To publish biblical studies by Catholic authors which are written for the average person and which minister life to Christ's Church. Publishes 2 titles/yr.; trade paperbacks. Receives 60 submissions annually. 50% of books from first-time authors. Will accept mss through agents. Reprints books. Prefers 105-300 pgs. Royalty 6-12% on retail; no advance. Average first printing 2,500. Publication within 1 yr. Considers simultaneous submissions. Accepts requested ms on disk. Responds in 1 mo. Guidelines (also by e-mail); free catalog.

Nonfiction: Query or proposal/2-3 chapters; fax query OK. "Looking for spirituality, thematic biblical studies, unique inspirational/devotional books."

Tips: "Our writers need solid knowledge of the Bible and a mature spirituality that reflects a profound relationship with Jesus Christ. Most open to well-researched, popularly written biblical studies geared to Catholics, or personal experience books that share/emphasize a person's relationship with Christ."

CAPSTONE FICTION GROUP, LLC, PO Box 8, Waterford VA 20197. (540)882-9062. Fax (540)882-3719. E-mail: inquiries@capstonefiction.com, or rtucker@capstonefiction.com. Website: www.capstonefiction.com. Jeff Nesbitt, mng. dir.; Ramona Tucker, ed. dir. To create opportunities for new, talented Christian writers, and to promote leading-edge fiction by established Christian authors; inspirational fiction only. Estab. 2006. Does print-on-demand. Reprints books. Royalty; no advance. Guidelines on Website.

Fiction: Submit by e-mail (attached file) in one Word file. For all ages.

CAREPOINT PUBLISHING, PO Box 870490, Stone Mountain GA 30087. Toll-free (800)378-9584. (404)625-9217. E-mail: info@carepointministry.com. Website: www.christian carepoint.org. Independent Christian publisher. Dr. Scott Philip Stewart, ed. Publishes Christian care books and software to help 21st-century Christians and seekers and those who minister to them. Publishes 12 titles/yr.; trade paperbacks. Receives 100+ submissions annually. 75% of books from first-time authors. Will accept mss through agents. Reprints books. Royalty 10-15% of net; no advance. Publication within 6 mos. Considers simultaneous submissions, if notified. Accepts requested manuscript on disk or by e-mail. Responds in 4 wks. Guidelines on Website.

Nonfiction: Proposal/2-3 chapters; prefers e-mail query. "Looking for support-group resources."

Photos/Artwork: Accepts freelance photos for book covers.

Special Needs: Self-help, personal growth, counseling aids, resources for peer and professional Christian caregivers and counselors.

Also Does: Interactive multimedia; book/CD sets.

Tips: "Most open to practical, grace-full support group resources that minister our Lord's healing love, grace, and mercy to the wounded among us. Encourage one another!"

WILLIAM CAREY LIBRARY PUBLISHERS & DISTRIBUTORS, 1605 E. Elizabeth St., Pasadena CA 91104. (626)720-8210. E-mail through Website: www.missionbooks.org. A ministry of the U.S. Center for World Mission (www.uscwm.org). Naomi Bradley, editorial mngr. (626-720-8202). Purpose is to publish the latest insights on frontier Christian missions. Publishes 10-15 titles/yr.; trade paperbacks. Reprints books. Variable lengths. Royalty 10% on net; no advance. Publication time varies. Guidelines on Website; free catalog.

Nonfiction: Query only; e-query OK. No unsolicited mss. "We are a specialized publisher focusing on books and studies of church growth, missions, world issues, and ethnic/cultural issues."

Special Needs: Anthropology and cross-cultural.

Photos: Accepts freelance photos for book covers.

Tips: "We mostly publish books on missions, evangelization, and unreached people groups. We welcome books that missionaries and mission-minded people would find useful and encouraging. For more information, please click on 'Publishing' on our Website."

CARSON-DELLOSA CHRISTIAN EDUCATION, 7027 Albert Pick Rd., PO Box 35665, Greensboro NC 27425. (336)632-0084. Fax (336)808-3249. E-mail: clayton@carsondellosa.com. Website: www.carsondellosa.com. Carson-Dellosa Publishing Inc. Carol Layton, ed. dir. Creates high quality children's products (interactive activities) that teach the Word of God, share His love and goodness, assist in faith development, and glorify His Son, Jesus Christ. Publishes 12 titles/yr.; soft-cover, reproducible, 8 1/2 x 11, teacher resource books. Receives 50 submissions annually. 25% of books from first-time authors. No reprints. Prefers 64 pgs. Royalty & advance confidential. Publication within 18 mos. Considers simultaneous submissions. Responds in 12 wks. Prefers NIV. Guidelines on Website; free catalog.

Nonfiction: Proposal/2 chapters; hard copy only. "Looking for books that teach the Word of God to children in an engaging and fun way, particularly in a classroom setting."

Fiction: Proposal/2 chapters. "Fiction must be suited for classroom use."

Artwork: Accepts queries from freelance artists.

Also Does: Board games, teaching beach balls.

Tips: "Understand the type of books we publish and submit an engaging, well-written proposal. Most open to lesson and activity books that are fun for students and teachers."

**Note: This publisher serviced by ChristianManuscriptSubmissions.com.

CASCADIA PUBLISHING HOUSE LLC., 126 Klingerman Rd., Telford PA 18969. (215)723-9125. E-mail: editor@cascadiapublishinghouse.com. Website: www.cascadiapublishing house.com. Mennonite. Michael A. King, ed. Imprint: DreamSeeker Books. Open to freelance; uses little unsolicited. Some books are subsidized by interested institutions. Guidelines/catalog on Website. Not included in topical listings.

Nonfiction: Query only/vita; e-query OK.

CATHOLIC ANSWERS, 2020 Gillespie Way, El Cajon CA 92020. (619)387-7200. Fax (619)387-0042. E-mail through Website: www.catholic.com. Karl Keating, pres.; Mary Jane O'Brien, submissions ed. Publishes 10 titles/yr. Receives 10-15 submissions annually. 1% of books from first-time authors. No mss through agents. No subsidy. Reprints books. Prefers 40,000 wds. Royalty on retail; negotiable advance. Average first printing 5,000. Publication within 12 mos. Accepts simultaneous submissions. Responds in 1-3 mos. Prefers RSV-Catholic edition. Guidelines by e-mail; free catalog.

Nonfiction: Query first; no phone/fax/e-query.

Photos: Accepts freelance photos for book covers.

Tips: "Most open to Catholic apologetics and evangelization."

CATHOLIC BOOK PUBLISHING CO., 77 West End Rd., Totowa NJ 07512. (973)890-2400. Fax (973)890-2410. E-mail: info@catholicbookpublishing.com. Website: www.catholicbook publishing.com. Catholic. Anthony Buono, mng. ed. Inspirational books for Catholic Christians. Publishes 15-20 titles/yr. Receives 75 submissions annually. 30% of books from first-time authors. No mss through agents. Variable royalty or outright purchases; no advance. Average first printing 3,000. Publication within 12-15 mos. No simultaneous submissions. Responds in 2-3 mos. Catalog for 9x12 SAE/5 stamps.

Nonfiction: Query letter only; no phone/fax query.

Tips: "We publish mainly liturgical books, Bibles, Missals, and prayer books. Most of the books are composed in-house or by direct commission with particular guidelines. We strongly prefer query letters in place of full manuscripts."

+CATHOLIC UNIVERSITY OF AMERICA PRESS, 620 Michigan Ave. N.E., Washington DC 20064. (202)319-5052. Fax (202)319-4985. E-mail: cua-press@cua.edu. Website: http://cuapress.cua.edu. David J. McGonagle, editor; submit to James Kruggel. Works of original scholarship and works intended for the college/university classroom in various fields, including theology and religious studies. Publishes 10 titles/yr.; hardcover & trade paperback. Receives 230 submissions annually. 25% of books from first-time authors. No mss through agents. No reprints. Prefers 200-300 pgs. Royalty 10% on net; no advance. Average first printing 750. Publication within 6 mos. Considers simultaneous submissions. Responds as soon as possible. Guidelines (also by e-mail/Website); free catalog.

Nonfiction: Query first; no phone/fax/e-query.

Special Needs: Works of original scholarship and works intended for the college and university classroom in theology.

Photos: Accepts freelance photos for book covers.

CHALICE PRESS, 1221 Locust St., Ste. 670, St. Louis MO 63103. (314)231-8500. Fax (314) 231-8524. E-mail: submissions@cbp21.com. Website: www.cbp21.com. Christian Church (Disciples of Christ)/Christian Board of Publication. Trent Butler, ed. (tbutler@cbp21 .com). Books for a thinking, caring church; in Bible, theology, ethics, homiletics, pastoral care, Christian education, Christian living, and spiritual growth. Publishes 35 titles/yr.; hardcover, trade paperbacks, mass-market paperbacks. Receives 550 submissions annually. 15% of books from first-time authors. No mss through agents. Prefers 144-160 pgs. for general books, 160-300 pgs. for academic books. Royalty 14% of net. Average first printing 2,500-3,000. Publication within 1 yr. Accepts simultaneous submissions. Requires requested proposal and ms by e-mail. Responds in 1-3 mos. Guidelines on Website; catalog for 9x12 SAE/2 stamps.

Nonfiction: Proposal/1 chapter; e-proposal preferred. "Looking for books on evangelism, leadership, and spiritual growth."

Also Does: Pamphlets.

CHAPTER TWO, Fountain House, Conduit Mews, London SE18 7AP, United Kingdom. Phone ++44 (0) 20 8316 5389. Fax ++44 (0) 20 8854 5963. E-mail: chapter2uk@aol.com. Website: www.chaptertwobooks.org.uk. Plymouth Brethren. Mr. E. Cross, ed. Publishing Plymouth Brethren titles and evangelistic materials to promote New Testament faith and practice. Publishes 20-30 titles/yr.; hardcover, trade paperbacks. No mss through agents. Reprints books. Royalty 0-10% on retail (most of their authors donate their work). Average first printing 3,000. Publication within 12 mos. No simultaneous submissions. Prefers KJV, NKJV. No guidelines; free catalog.

Nonfiction: Query first; phone/e-query OK.

Special Needs: Plymouth Brethren commentaries.

Ethnic Books: Hispanic.

Tips: "Writer must be in a Plymouth Brethren assembly and have orthodox Christian doctrine."

CHARIOT BOOKS—See David C. Cook.

CHARIOT VICTOR PUBLISHING—See David C. Cook.

CHARISMA KIDS, 600 Rinehart Rd., Lake Mary FL 32746. (407)333-0600. Fax (407)333-7100. E-mail: Custsvc@strang.com. Website: www.charismakids.com. Strang Book Group. Submit to The Editor. Books to help children experience God's presence, find His purpose for their lives, and receive the power of the Holy Spirit. Publishes 12 titles/yr. Receives hundreds of submissions annually. 10% of books from first-time authors. Prefers mss through agents. No reprints. Prefers 2,400 wds. or 32 pgs. Royalty on net; advance. Average first printing 10,000. Publication within 1 yr. Considers simultaneous submissions. Responds in 6 mos. Guidelines & catalog on Website.

Nonfiction: Proposal/1 chapter; fax/e-query OK.

Fiction: Proposal/1 chapter. Charismatic children's books; for children 4-8 years. Does not publish 24-32 page picture books.

Ethnic Books: Black, Charismatic.

Tips: "Most open to books with a Charismatic world-view for children."

**Note: This publisher serviced by ChristianManuscriptSubmissions.com.

THE CHARLES PRESS, PUBLISHERS, 133 N. 21st St., Ste. 2, Philadelphia PA 19103. (212) 561-2786. Fax (215)561-0191. E-mail: mailbox@charlespresspub.com. Website: www .charlespresspub.com. Lauren Metzler, pub. (lauren@charlespresspub.com). Responds in 4-16 wks. Guidelines on Website; catalog.

Nonfiction: Proposal (to 10 pgs.); no fax submissions.

CHELSEA HOUSE PUBLISHERS, 132 W. 31st St., Fl. 17, New York NY 10001. Toll-free (800)322-8755. (212)896-4211. Toll-free fax (800)678-3633. E-mail: editorial@facts onfile.com. Website: www.chelseahouse.com. Imprint of Infobase Publishing Group. Submit to Editorial Director. Publishes curriculum-based nonfiction books for middle school and high school students, including on religion. Publishes in hardcover. Reprints books. Considers simultaneous submissions. Guidelines and catalog on Website.

Nonfiction: Query or proposal/ 2-3 chapters.

Artwork: Open to queries from freelance artists; send photocopies.

CHICKEN SOUP FOR THE SOUL BOOKS—See listing in Periodical section.

CHOSEN BOOKS, Division of Baker Publishing Group, 3985 Bradwater St., Fairfax VA 22031-3702. (703)764-8250. (703)764-3995. E-mail: chosenbooks@cox.net. Website: www .chosenbooks.com. Jane Campbell, editorial dir. Charismatic; Spirit-filled life titles. No unsolicited mss, but will respond to e-mails. Submit through Writer's Edge or Christian ManuscriptSubmissions.com.

CHRISTIAN ED. PUBLISHERS, Box 26639, San Diego CA 92196. (858)578-4700. Fax (858)578-2431 (for queries only). E-mail: Editor@cehouse.com. Website: www.ChristianEdWarehouse .com. Janet Ackelson, asst. ed. An evangelical publisher of Bible Club materials for ages two through high school, church special-event programs, and online Bible lessons. Publishes 80 curriculum titles/yr. Receives 150 submissions annually. 10% of books from first-time authors. No mss through agents. Outright purchases for .03/wd.; no advance. Publication within 1 yr. Accepts requested ms on disk or by e-mail. Responds in 3-5 mos. No simultaneous submissions or reprints. Prefers NIV, KJV. Guidelines (also by e-mail); catalog for 9x12 SAE/4 stamps.

Nonfiction: Query only; phone/fax/e-query OK. Children's Bible studies, curriculum, and take-home papers.

Fiction: On assignment only."

Artwork: Open to freelance illustrators. Send files in Adobe Illustrator.

Tips: "All writing done on assignment. Request our guidelines, then complete a writer application before submitting. Need Bible-teaching ideas for preschool through sixth grade. Also publishes Bible stories for preschool and primary take-home papers, 200 words." Using freelance writers mostly for Bible stories, rather than fiction.

CHRISTIAN FAMILY PUBLICATIONS, 1854 Makarios Dr., St. Augustine FL 32080. (904)471-4307. E-mail: christianfamily@mail.com. Website: www.christianfamilybooks.com. Gene Fedele, ed./pub. Imprints: Christian Family Library, Great Christian Biographies. Publishes 1-3 titles/yr.; hardcover, trade paperbacks. Receives 20-30 submissions annually. 50% of books from first-time authors. No mss through agents. Reprints books. Prefers KJV or NKJV. Accepted mss on disk or by e-mail. Free catalog.

Tips: "Most open to books from a Reformed theological position."

CHRISTIAN FOCUS PUBLICATIONS, LTD., Geanies House, Fearn, Tain, Ross-shire IV20 1TW, Scotland, UK. Phone 01862 871011. Fax 01862 871699. E-mail: info@christianfocus.com.

Website: www.christianfocus.com. Willie MacKenzie, adult editorial mngr.; Catherine MacKenzie, children's ed. Focuses on having strong biblical content. Imprints: Mentor, Christian Heritage, Christian Focus, Christian Focus 4 Kids. Publishes 90 titles/yr.; hardcover, trade paperbacks, mass-market paperbacks. Receives 300+ submissions annually. 10% of books from first-time authors. Will accept mss through agents. Reprints books. Royalty on net or outright purchase. Publication within 24 mos. Considers simultaneous submissions. Accepts requested ms on disk. Responds typically in 4 mos. Guidelines on Website; free catalog.

Nonfiction: Proposal/2 chapters; fax/e-query OK.

Fiction: Complete ms. For children and teens only. See guidelines for descriptions of children's fiction lines.

Photos: Accepts freelance photos for book covers.

Tips: "We are 'reformed,' though we don't insist all our authors would consider themselves reformed." Most open to issues-based popular books, and children's fiction and biography. A prize-winning British publisher with good worldwide coverage.

CHRISTIAN HERITAGE SOCIETY, Box 519, Baldwin Place NY 10505. Phone/fax (914)962-3287. E-mail: gtkurian@aol.com. Website: www.encyclopediasocierty.com. George Kurian, ed. Publishes 6 titles/yr.; hardcover, trade paperbacks. Receives 100 submissions annually. 50% of books from first-time authors. Prefers mss through agents. No subsidy. Reprints books. Prefers 120,000 wds. Royalty 10-15% on net; no advance. Average first printing 10,000. Publication within 1 yr. Considers simultaneous submissions. Responds in 3 mos. Guidelines; free catalog.

Nonfiction: Query; e-query OK. "Looking for Christian history, reference books, memoirs, devotionals, and evangelism."

CHRISTIAN LIBERTY PRESS, 502 W. Euclid Ave., Arlington Heights IL 60004. (847)259-4444. Fax (847)259-2941. E-mail: acquisitions@christianlibertypress.com, or larsj@christian libertypress.com. Website: www.christianlibertypress.com. Publishing arm of Christian Liberty Academy and Christian Liberty Academy School System (CLASS). Lars Johnson, admin. dir. Dedicated to publishing works that are consistent with the Word of God. Curriculum for kindergarten through high school.

Nonfiction: Proposal/2 chapters. A variety of enrichment and support books, including biographies, education resources, and Bible study materials.

Fiction: Proposal/2 chapters. Christian and historical.

CHRISTIAN WRITER'S EBOOK NET, PO Box 446, Ft. Duchesne UT 84026. (435)772-3429. E-mail: editor@writersebook.com. Website: www.writersebook.com. Nondenominational/Evangelical Christian. Linda Kay Stewart Whitsitt, ed-in-chief; Terry Gordon Whitsitt, asst. ed. Gives first-time authors the opportunity to bring their God-given writing talent to the Christian market. Publishes 15 titles/yr. Receives 100 submissions annually. 95% of books from first-time authors. Will accept mss through agents. SUBSIDY PUBLISHES 25%. Reprints books. Prefers 60+ pgs. Royalty 35-50%; no advance. E-Books only. Publication within 6 mos. Considers simultaneous submissions. Electronic queries and submissions only; mss need to be in electronic form (MS Word, WordPerfect, ASCII, etc.) to be published; send by e-mail (preferred). No mail submissions accepted without contact by e-mail first. Responds in 1-2 mos. Guidelines on Website.

Nonfiction: E-query only. Any topic.

Fiction: E-query only. Any genre.

Also Does: Booklets, pamphlets, tracts.

Tips: "Make sure your work is polished and ready for print. The books we publish are sold in our online store. If you are not sure what an e-book is, check out our Website's FAQ page."

CHURCH & SYNAGOGUE LIBRARY ASSN. INC., 2920 S.W. Dolph Ct., Ste. 3A, Portland OR 97219. (503)244-6919. Fax (503)977-3734. E-mail: csla@worldaccessnet.com. Website: www.cslainfo.org. Mark Olson, ed. An interfaith group established to help librarians set up and organize/reorganize their religious libraries. Publishes 6 titles/yr.; trade paperbacks. No mss through agents. No reprints. No royalty. Average first printing 750. Catalog.

CHURCH GROWTH INSTITUTE, PO Box 7, Elkton MD 21922-0007. (434)525-0022. Fax (434)525-0608. E-mail: cgimail@churchgrowth.org. Website: www.churchgrowth.org. Ephesians Four Ministries. Cindy G. Spear, resource development dir. Providing practical tools for leadership, evangelism, and church growth. Publishes 3 titles/yr.; trade paperbacks. Receives 40 submissions annually. 7% of books from first-time authors. No mss through agents. Prefers 64-160 pgs. Royalty 6% on retail or outright purchase; no advance. Average first printing 100. Publication within 1 yr. Considers simultaneous submissions. Responds in 3 mos. Requires requested ms on disk. Guidelines sent after query/outline is received; catalog for 9x12 SAE/4 stamps, or on Website.

Nonfiction: Query; no phone/fax query; e-query OK. "We prefer our writers to be experienced in what they write about, to be experts in the field."

Special Needs: Topics that help churches grow spiritually and numerically; leadership training; attendance and stewardship programs; new or unique ministries (how-to). Self-discovery and evaluation tools, such as our Spiritual Gifts Inventory and Spiritual Growth Survey.

Photos: Accepts freelance photos for book covers.

Tips: "Most open to a practical manual or audio album (CDs/audiotapes and workbooks) for the pastor or other church leaders—something unique with a special niche. Must be practical and different from anything else on the same subject—or must be a topic/slant few others have published. Also very interested in evaluation tools as mentioned above. Please no devotionals, life testimonies, commentaries, or studies on books of the Bible."

CISTERCIAN PUBLICATIONS INC., PO Box 7500, Collegeville MN 56321-7500. E-mail: sales@litpress.org. Website: www.cistercianpublications.org. H. Christoffersen, ed. Works of monastic tradition and studies that foster renewal, spirituality, and ongoing formation of monastics. Publishes 8-14 titles/yr.; hardcover, trade paperbacks, some coffee-table books. Receives 30 submissions annually. 50% of books from first-time authors. No mss through agents. Reprints books. Prefers 204-286 pgs. Royalty on net; no advance. Average first printing 1,500. Publication within 2-10 yrs. Requires requested ms on disk. Guidelines on Website; free style sheet/catalog.

Nonfiction: Query only; no phone query; fax query OK. History, spirituality, and theology.

Photos: Accepts freelance photos for book covers.

Tips: "We publish only on the Christian Monastic Tradition. Most open to a translation of a monastic text, or study of a monastic movement, author, or subject."

CLADACH PUBLISHING, PO Box 336144, Greeley CO 80633. (970)371-9530. Fax (970)351-8240. E-mail: staff@cladach.com. Website: www.cladach.com. Independent Christian publisher. Catherine Lawton, pub. (cathyl@cladach.com); Hannah Lawton, ed. Seeks to influence those inside and outside the body of Christ by giving a voice to talented writers with a clear, articulate, and Christ-honoring vision. Publishes 2-3 titles/yr. Receives 200 submissions annually. 70% of books from first-time authors. Will accept proposals through agents. No reprints. Prefers 160-256 pgs. Royalty 7-10% on net; no advance. Average first printing 1,500. Publication within 1 yr. Considers simultaneous submissions. Accepted mss by e-mail. Responds in 3-6 mos. Guidelines on Website; free catalog.

Nonfiction: Query letter only first; phone/e-query OK. "Looking for nonfiction that helps people in their relationship with God."

Fiction: Query letter only first (1-2 pgs.); phone/e-query OK (copied into message). For adults. "Prefers gripping stories depicting inner struggles and real-life issues; well crafted. Would like to see Christian world-view, literary fiction."

Tips: "We want writing that shows God active in our world and that helps readers experience His presence and power in their lives."

JAMES CLARKE & CO. LTD., PO Box 60, Cambridge CB1 2NT, England. Phone +44 (0)1223 350865. Fax +44 (0)1223 366951. E-mail: publishing@jamesclarke.co.uk. Website: www.jamesclarke.co.uk. Adrian Brink, ed. Publishes academic and reference books, particularly, but not exclusively, books on church history and systematic theology. Imprints: The Lutterworth Press (general books). Publishes 25 titles/yr. (15 reprints, 10 new); hardcover & trade paperbacks. Receives 100 submissions annually. 90% of books from first-time authors. Will accept mss through agents. Does print on demand. Reprints books. SUBSIDY PUBLISHES 2%. Royalty on retail; advance. Publication within 18 mos. No simultaneous submissions. Responds in 3 mos. Requested ms by mail. Guidelines on Website; free catalog.

Nonfiction: Proposal/2 chapters; e-query OK.

Tips: "For full author guidelines, visit our Website."

COLLEGE PRESS PUBLISHING CO. INC., 223 W. Third St. (64801), PO Box 1132, Joplin MO 64802. Toll-free (800)289-3300. (417)623-6280. Fax (417)623-8250. E-mail through Website: www.collegepress.com. Christian Church/Church of Christ. Submit to Acquisitions Ed. Christian materials that will help fulfill the Great Commission and promote unity on the basis of biblical truth and intent. Imprint: HeartSpring Publishing (see separate listing). Publishes 15-20 titles/yr.; hardcover, trade paperbacks. Receives 700 submissions annually. 25% of books from first-time authors. Will accept mss through agents. Reprints books. Prefers 250-300 pgs. (paperback) or 300-600 pgs. (hardback). Royalty 5-15% of net; no advance. Average first printing 3,000. Publication within 6 mos. Considers simultaneous submissions. Requires requested ms on disk; no e-mail submissions. Responds in 2-3 mos. Prefers NIV, NASB, NAS. Guidelines on Website; catalog for 9x12 SAE/5 stamps.

Nonfiction: Query only first, then proposal/2-3 chapters; no phone/fax query. "Looking for Bible study, reference, divorced leaders, blended families, and leadership." Expanding search for new authors, especially in women's ministry.

Ethnic Books: Reprints their own books in Spanish.

Also Does: E-books.

Tips: "We develop and supply Christian resources for use by individuals, churches, colleges/universities/seminaries, and small groups. We are interested in biblical studies and resources that come from an 'Arminian' view and/or 'amillennial' slant."

**Note: This publisher serviced by ChristianManuscriptSubmissions.com.

+COMFORT PUBLISHING, 9450 Plantation Ave. N.W., Concord NC 28027. (704)782-2353. Fax (704)782-2393. E-mail: acquisitions@comfortpublishing.com. Website: www.comfort publishing.com. Also has a blog. Comfort Publishing Services, LLC. Pamilla S. Tolen, Sr. VP.; Kristy Huddle & James Warder, acq. eds. Caters to unrecognized authors, but operates as a traditional publisher assuming the financial risks of publishing a book. Publishes 500 titles/yr.; hardcovers, trade paperbacks, mass-market paperbacks, coffee-table books. Receives 2,000 submissions annually. 75% of books from first-time authors. Will accept mss through agents. Does print on demand. Reprints books. Prefers 150-300 pgs. Royalty 8-15% on retail; advances for established authors only. Average first printing 500-2,000. Publication within 3 mos. Considers simultaneous submissions. Responds in 3-4 wks. Accepts requested mss on disk or by e-mail. Guidelines & catalog on Website.

Nonfiction: Book proposal/4 chapters or complete ms; phone/fax/e-query OK.

Fiction: Book proposal/4 chapters or complete ms; phone/fax/e-query OK. For all ages. "Must contain a relevant message for Christians today."

Photos/Artwork: Accepts freelance photos for book covers; open to queries from freelance artists.

Tips: "Most open to any well-written book with a message relevant to modern-day Christians."

**Note: This publisher serviced by The Writer's Edge.

+COMPANY B PUBLISHING, E-mail: submissions@companybpublishing.com. Website: www .companybpublishing.com. Submit to Editor. Estab: 2005. POD publisher that does not charge for production of book. Agent not necessary. Royalty 8% of retail; no advance. Responds in 4-6 wks. Guidelines on Website. Open to most topics.

Nonfiction: Use online submission form.

Fiction: Use online submission form.

Also Does: All books also available as e-books.

Tips: "Author retains all subsidiary rights. Marketing is up to the author."

CONARI PRESS, 500 Third St., Ste. 230, San Francisco CA 94107. E-mail: info@redwheel weiser.com. Website: www.conari.com or www.redwheelweiser.com. An imprint of Red Wheel/Weiser, LLC. Ms. Pat Bryce, acq. ed. Books on spirituality, personal growth, parenting, and social issues. Publishes 30 titles/yr. Responds in up to 3 mos. Guidelines and catalog on Website. Incomplete topical listings.

CONCILIAR PRESS, PO Box 76, Ben Lomand CA 95005-0076. Toll-free (800)967-7377. (831)336-5118. Fax (831)336-8882. E-mail: Service@conciliarpress.com. Website: www .conciliarpress.com. Antiochian Orthodox Christian Archdiocese of N.A. Father Thomas Zell, ed.; submit to Katherine Hyde (katherineh@cruzio.com). Publishes 5-10 titles/yr. Receives 50 submissions annually. 20% of books from first-time authors. Will accept mss through agents. SUBSIDY PUBLISHES 10%. Reprints books. Royalty; no advance. Average first printing 3,000. Prefers e-mail submission. Responds in 3 mos. Prefers NKJV. Guidelines on Website; catalog for 9x12 SAE/5 stamps.

Nonfiction: E-query/proposal with up to 50-60 pgs. of the manuscript (including first chapter); phone query OK.

Photos: Accepts freelance photos for book covers.

Children's Books: Send hard copy to Jane G. Meyer, children's book project mngr., Conciliar Press Ministries, 3112 Calle Rosales, Santa Barbara CA 93105.

CONCORDIA ACADEMIC PRESS, 3558 S. Jefferson Ave., St. Louis MO 63118-3968. (314)268-1098. Fax (314)268-1329. E-mail: editorial.concordia@cph.org. Website: www.concordia academicpress.org. Lutheran Church/Missouri Synod. Imprint of Concordia Publishing House. Mark E. Sell, ed. Scholarly and professional books in biblical studies, 16th-century studies, historical theology, and theology and culture. Publication within 2 yrs. Responds in 8-12 wks. Guidelines on Website.

Nonfiction: Proposal/sample chapters.

Tips: "Freelance submissions are welcome. Prospective authors should consult the guidelines on the Website for an author prospectus and submissions guidelines."

CONCORDIA PUBLISHING HOUSE, 3558 S. Jefferson Ave., St. Louis MO 63118-3968. (314)268-1187. Fax (314)268-1329. Website: www.cph.org. Lutheran Church/Missouri Synod. Rev. Paul T. McCain, pub. (paul.mccain@cph.org); Peggy Kuethe: children's resources, children's and family devotions, teaching resources, adult nonfiction, and devotionals; Mark Sell: academic books; Fred Bauer: pastoral and congregational resources. Publishes 50 titles/yr.; hardcover, trade paperbacks. Receives 3,000 submissions annually. 10% of books from first-time authors. Royalty 2-12% on retail; some outright purchases; some advances $500-1,500. Average first printing 6,000-8,000. Publication within 2 yrs. Considers simultaneous submissions. Responds in 6 mos. Prefers accepted submissions on disk. Prefers NIV. Guidelines on Website; catalog for 9x12 SAE/4 stamps.

Nonfiction: Proposal/2 chapters; no phone/fax query. No poetry, personal experience, or biography.

Ethnic Books: Hispanic; Asian American.

Also Does: Pamphlets, booklets.

Tips: "Publishes Christ-centered resources for The Lutheran Church—Missouri Synod. Most open to family, devotional, and teaching resources. Any proposal should be Christ-centered, Bible-based, and life-directed. It must be creative in its presentation of solid scriptural truths. Call for current needs."

**Note: This publisher serviced by The Writer's Edge and ChristianManuscriptSubmissions .com.

CONGREGATIONAL LIFE AND LEARNING, Augsburg Fortress Canada, 500 Trillium Dr., Box 9940, Kitchener ON N2G 4Y4, Canada. E-mail: cllsub@augsburgfortress.org. Website: www.afcanada.com. Evangelical Lutheran Church in Canada. Submit using online form. Works to provide congregations with materials and resources for group and individual use that nurture faith, foster learning, and promote spiritual renewal among children, youth, and adults. All material is work-for-hire. Responds in 16 wks. Guidelines at www.afcanada .com/company/submitcongregational.jsp.

Nonfiction: Query first; e-query OK. "Looking for Sunday school materials, Bible study materials, and devotionals."

CONTEMPORARY DRAMA SERVICE, Meriwether Publishing Co., 885 Elkton Dr., Colorado Springs CO 80907. E-mail: merPCDS@aol.com. Website: www.meriwetherpublishing.com. Publishes Christian plays for mainline churches. Also supplemental textbooks on theatrical subjects. Prefers comedy, but does publish some serious works. Accepts full-length or one-act plays—comedy or musical. General and Christian. Publishes 30 plays/yr. See the Meriwether Publishing listing for additional details.

CONTINUUM INTERNATIONAL PUBLISHING, 80 Maiden Lane, Rm. 704, New York NY 10038-4814. Toll-free (800)561-7704. (212)953-5858. Fax (212)953-5944. E-mail: info@ continuumbooks.com. Website: www.continuumbooks.com. Thomas Kraft, assoc. pub. Imprints: T and T Clark (see separate listing); Burns & Oates. Publishes 60 titles/yr.; hardcover, trade paperbacks. Receives 500 submissions annually. 10% of books from first-time authors. Will accept mss through agents. SUBSIDY PUBLISHES 5%. Does print-on-demand. Reprints books. Royalty to 15%; advance. Prefers 60,000-120,000 wds. Publication within 9 mos. No simultaneous submissions. Responds in 1 mo. Guidelines by e-mail/Website; free catalog.

Nonfiction: Query, proposal/1 chapter, or complete ms; phone/fax/e-query OK.

Photos: Accepts freelance photos for book covers.

Contest: Trinity Prize.

DAVID C. COOK, 4050 Lee Vance View, Colorado Springs CO 80918. (719)536-0100. Fax (719)536-3269. Website: www.cookministries.com. Dan Rich, Sr. VP & pub.; Ingrid Beck, mng. ed. Discipleship is foundational; everything we publish needs to move the reader one step closer to maturity in Christ. Brands: David C. Cook (for teachers or program leaders who want Bible-based discipleship resources; Bible and study resources for serious Bible students; books for Christian families seeking biblical answers to life problems; books to equip kids—birth to age 12—for life); and fiction (inspiring fiction for mature believers). Publishes 85 titles/yr.; hardcover, trade paperbacks. 10% of books from first-time authors. Requires mss through agents. Publication within 1-2 yrs. Considers simultaneous submissions. Responds in 3-6 mos. Prefers requested ms by e-mail. Prefers NIV. Guidelines (also by e-mail/Website).

Nonfiction: Not currently accepting any unsolicited or unagented submissions.

Fiction: Not currently accepting any unsolicited or unagented submissions.

Note: Cook has eliminated all brands/imprints except David C. Cook—including Nex-Gen, Victor, Life Journey, and FaithKidz.

**Note: This publisher serviced by The Writer's Edge and ChristianManuscriptSubmissions .com.

J. COUNTRYMAN, PO Box 141000, Nashville TN 37214-1000. (615)902-3134. Fax (615)902-3200. Website: www.jcountryman.com. Thomas Nelson Inc. Gift-book imprint. No longer accepting unsolicited manuscripts or proposals.

**Note: This publisher serviced by The Writer's Edge.

THE CROSSROAD PUBLISHING CO., 16 Penn Plaza, Ste. 1550, New York NY 10001. (212)868-1801. Fax (212)868-2171. E-mail: editor@crossroadpublishing.com. Website: www.cpcbooks.com. Dr. John Jones, ed. dir.; Nancy Neal, acq. ed. Books on religion, spirituality, and personal growth that speak to the diversity of backgrounds and beliefs; hopeful books that inform, enlighten, and heal; particular strengths in Catholic and Anglican titles as well as Christian spirituality and leadership. Imprints: see below. Publishes 45 titles/yr.; hardcover, trade paperbacks. Receives 1,200 submissions annually. 10% of books from first-time authors. Will accept mss through agents. Does print-on-demand. Reprints books. Prefers 50,000-60,000 wds. or 160-176 pgs. Royalty 6-14% of net; small advance (more for established authors). Average first printing 4,000. Publication within 14 mos. Considers simultaneous submissions. Responds in 6 wks. Accepts requested ms on disk. Guidelines on Website; free catalog.

Nonfiction: Query letter only first; e-query required. Books that explore and celebrate the Christian life.

Tips: "Most authors need some combination of (1) exceptional writing ability, (2) expertise or authority in a field, (3) an existing platform for sales (speaking engagements, etc.)."

Herder & Herder: 200 years of international publishing in the service of theology and church. Monographs, reference works, theological, and philosophical discourse. Special focus on younger and emerging theologians as well as the Christian spiritual disciplines.

CROSS TRAINING PUBLISHING, PO Box 1874, Kearney NE 68848. Toll-free (800)430-8588. Fax (308)338-2058. E-mail: gordon@crosstrainingpublishing.com. Website: www.cross trainingpublishing.com. Gordon Thiessen, pub. Sports books for children and adults.

CROSSWAY BOOKS AND BIBLES, 1300 Crescent St., Wheaton IL 60187. (630)682-4300. Fax (630)682-4785. E-mail: editorial@gnpcb.org. Website: www.crossway.org. A publishing ministry of Good News Publishers. Allan Fisher, VP editorial; submit to Jill Carter, editorial administrator. Publishes books that combine the Truth of God's Word with a passion to live it out, with unique and compelling Christian content. Publishes 70 titles/yr.; hardcover, trade paperbacks. Receives 1,000 submissions annually. 1% of books from first-time authors. Will accept mss through agents. No reprints. Prefers 25,000 wds. & up. Royalty 10-21% of net; advance varies. Average first printing 5,000-10,000. Publication within 18 mos. Considers simultaneous submissions. Responds in 6-8 wks. Prefers ESV. Guidelines (also on Website); free catalog.

Nonfiction: Currently not accepting unsolicited submissions.

Also Does: Tracts. See Good News Publishers.

**Note: This publisher serviced by The Writer's Edge and ChristianManuscriptSubmissions .com.

**Recipient of five 2006 Silver Angel Awards from Excellence in Media.

CSS PUBLISHING GROUP INC., 517 S. Main St., Lima OH 45804. (419)227-1818. Fax (419) 228-9184. E-mail: editor@csspub.com, or through Website: www.csspub.com. Rebecca Allen, mng. ed. Serves the needs of pastors, worship leaders, and parish program planners in the broad Christian mainline of the American church. Imprints: Fairway Press (subsidy—

see separate listing); Academic Renewal Press (reprints textbooks for professors and colleges); B.O.D. (Books On Demand); FaithWalk Books. Publishes 60-70 titles/yr. Receives 1,200-1,500 submissions annually. 50% of books from first-time authors. SUBSIDY PUBLISHES 40% through Fairway Press. Prefers 100-125 pgs. No royalty or advance. Average first printing 1,000. Publication within 6-10 mos. Considers simultaneous submissions. Responds in 3 wks. to 3 mos.; final decision within 12 mos. Requires requested ms on disk and in hard copy. Prefers NRSV. Guidelines (also on Website); free catalog.

Nonfiction: Query or proposal/3 chapters; no e-mail submissions; complete ms for short works. "Looking for pastoral resources for ministry. Our material is practical in nature."

Fiction: Complete ms. Easy-to-perform dramas and pageants for all age groups. "Our drama interest primarily includes Advent, Christmas, Epiphany, Lent, and Easter. We do not publish long plays."

Tips: "We're looking for authors who will help with the marketing of their books."

CUSTOM COMMUNICATIONS SERVICES INC./SHEPHERD PRESS/CUSTOM BOOK, 77 Main St., Tappan NY 10983. Toll-free (800)631-1362. (845)365-0414. Fax (845)365-0864. E-mail: customusa@aol.com. Website: www.customstudios.com. Norman Shaifer, pres. Publishes 50-75 titles/yr. 50% of books from first-time authors. No mss through agents. Royalty on net; some outright purchases for specific assignments. Publication within 6 mos. Responds in 1 mo. Guidelines.

Nonfiction: Query/proposal/chapters. "Histories of individual congregations, denominations, or districts."

Tips: "Find stories of larger congregations (750 or more households) who have played a role in the historic growth and development of the community or region."

THE DABBLING MUM PRESS, 508 W. Main St., Beresford SD 57004. Toll-free (866)548-9327. E-mail: dm@thedabblingmum.com. Website: www.thedabblingmum.com. Alyice Edrich, ed./pub. E-book publisher. Publishes 12-24 titles/yr. Receives 6 submissions annually. 90% of books from first-time authors. No mss through agents. No subsidy publishing. No reprints. Prefers 150-300 pgs. Royalty 50% on retail; no advance. Offers a nonexclusive contract; author can sell e-book on other sites. Publication within 5 mos. No simultaneous submissions. Responds monthly. Prefers NIV. Guidelines on Website; no catalog.

Nonfiction: Proposal/1 chapter; no phone/fax query; e-query OK. "Any book that fits: parenting, recipes, home, small business, writing. Well researched, professionally edited, and with a hands-on approach."

Tips: "We like to focus on niches. Books that can't or won't be published by traditional publishers; books that need updating on a regular basis."

DAWN PUBLICATIONS, 12402 Bitney Springs Rd., Nevada City CA 95959. (530)274-7775. Fax (530)274-7778. E-mail: submission@dawnpub.com. Website: www.dawnpub.com. Glenn Hovemann, acq. ed. Dedicated to inspiring in children a sense of appreciation for all of life on earth. Publishes 6 titles/yr.; hardcover, trade paperbacks. Receives 3,050 submissions annually. 15% of books from first-time authors. Will accept mss through agents. No reprints. Royalty on net; advance. Publication within 1-2 yrs. Considers simultaneous submissions. Responds in 2 mos. Guidelines & catalog on Website.

Nonfiction: Complete manuscript by mail or e-mail.

Artwork: Open to queries from freelance artists (send sample c/o Muffy Weaver).

Tips: "Most open to creative nonfiction. We look for nature awareness and appreciation titles that promote a relationship with the natural world and specific habitats, usually through inspiring treatment and nonfiction."

+DEEPER REVELATION BOOKS, PO Box 4260, Cleveland TN 37320-4260. (423)478-2843. Fax (423)479-2980. E-mail: MikeShreve@aol.com, or through Website: www.deeperrevelation books.org. Mike Shreve, pub. Publishes nonfiction. Not included in topical listings.

+DEO VOLENTE PUBLISHING, 1970 Gadsden Todd Levee Rd., Humboldt TN 38343. (731)824-2919. Fax (731)824-2526. E-mail: books@delvolente.net. Website: www.deo volente.net. Larry Byars, owner. Books that are consistent with reformed theology and promote and assist the Christian walk. Publishes 2-3 titles/yr.; trade paperbacks. Receives 10-20 submissions annually. Will accept mss through agents. Royalty 8-10% on retail; no advance. Considers simultaneous submissions. Send accepted mss by disk or e-mail. Guidelines (also on Website); no catalog.

    Nonfiction: Query first; fax/e-query OK.

DESTINY IMAGE PUBLISHERS, PO Box 310, Shippensburg PA 17257. (717)532-3040. Fax (717)532-9291. E-mail: dlm@destinyimage.com, or through Website: www.destinyimage .com. Don Milam, ed. mngr. To help people grow deeper in their relationship with God and others. Imprints: Destiny Image Fiction, Destiny Image Dark Matter. Publishes 36 titles/yr. Receives 1,500 submissions annually. 10% of books from first-time authors. Will accept mss through agents. SUBSIDY PUBLISHES 1-2%. Reprints books. Prefers 128-190 pgs. Royalty 10-15% on net; no advance. Average first printing 10,000. Publication within 9 mos. Considers simultaneous submissions. Send unsolicited mss via their online Manuscript Submission Form. Responds in up to 6 mos. Guidelines on Website; free catalog.

    Nonfiction: Query or proposal/chapters; no e-query. Charges a $25 fee for unsolicited manuscripts (enclose with submission).

    Fiction: Proposal/1-2 chapters. Adult.

    Tips: "Most open to books on the deeper life, charismatic interest."

DIMENSIONS FOR LIVING, 201—8th Ave. S., Nashville TN 37203. Fax (615)749-6512. E-mail: sbriese@umpublishing.org. Website: www.abingdonpress.com. United Methodist Publishing House. Joseph A. Crowe, ed.; submit to Manuscript Submissions (by mail only). Books for the general Christian reader. Publishes 120 titles/yr. Receives 2,000 submissions annually. Less than 1% of books from first-time authors. No reprints. Prefers 144 pgs. Royalty 7.5% on retail; some outright purchases; no advance. Average first printing 3,000. Publication within 2 yrs. Requires requested ms on disk. Responds in 8 wks. Guidelines on Website; free catalog.

    Nonfiction: Proposal/2 chapters; no phone query. Open to inspiration/devotion, self-help, home/family, special occasion gift books.

DISCOVERY HOUSE PUBLISHERS, PO Box 3566, Grand Rapids MI 49501. Toll-free (800)653-8333. (616)942-9218. Fax (616)974-2224. E-mail: dhptc@dhp.org. Website: www.dhp.org. RBC Ministries. Carol Holquist, pub.; submit to Manuscript Review Editor. Publishes books that foster Christian growth and godliness. Publishes 12-18 titles/yr.; hardcover, trade paperbacks, mass-market paperbacks. Will accept mss through agents. Reprints books. Royalty 10-14% on net; no advance. Publication within 12-18 mos. Considers simultaneous submissions. Requires accepted mss on disk or by e-mail. Responds in 4-6 wks. Guidelines (also by e-mail/Website); free catalog.

    Nonfiction: Query letter only. If by e-mail, "Attn: Ms Review Editor" in subject line.

    **Note: This publisher serviced by The Writer's Edge and ChristianManuscriptSubmissions .com.

DISKUS PUBLISHING, PO Box 43, Albany IN 47320. E-mail: editor@diskuspublishing.com. Submissions to: editor@diskuspublishing.com, or submissions@diskuspublishing.com. Website: www.diskuspublishing.com. Marilyn Nesbitt, ed-in-chief; Joyce McLaughlin, inspirational ed. E-book & print publisher. Publishes 50 titles/yr. Royalty 40%. Publication within 6-8 mos. Considers simultaneous submissions if noted. Prefers manuscripts by e-mail. Guidelines (also on Website); catalog online.

    Nonfiction: Complete ms or query by mail or e-mail.

    Fiction: Complete ms by e-mail. Includes religious fiction.

    Tips: "Follow very specific guidelines on Website."

DOUBLEDAY RELIGIOUS PUBLISHING, 1745 Broadway, New York NY 10019. (212)782-9000. Fax (212)782-8338. E-mail: tmurphy@randomhouse.com. Website: www.random house.com. Imprint of Random House Inc. Trace Murphy, editorial dir. Imprints: Image, Galilee, New Jerusalem Bible, Three Leaves Press, Anchor Bible Commentaries, Anchor Bible Reference Library. Publishes 45-50 titles/yr.; hardcover, trade paperbacks. Receives 1,500 submissions annually. 10% of books from first-time authors. Requires mss through agents. Reprints books. Royalty 7.5-15% on retail; advance. Average first printing varies. Publication within 8 mos. Considers simultaneous submissions. Responds in 4 mos. No disk. No guidelines; catalog for 9x12 SAE/3 stamps.

　　Nonfiction: Agented submissions only. Proposal/3 chapters; no phone query.

　　Fiction: Religious fiction. Agented submissions only.

　　Ethnic Books: African American; Hispanic.

　　Tips: "Most open to a book that has a big and well-defined audience. Have a clear proposal, lucid thesis, and specified audience."

　　**Note: This publisher serviced by ChristianManuscriptSubmissions.com.

DOVE INSPIRATIONAL PRESS, 1000 Burmaster St., Gretna LA 70053. (504)368-1175. Fax (504)368-1195. E-mail: editorial@pelicanpub.com. Website: www.pelicanpub.com. Nina Kooij, ed-in-chief. To publish books of quality and permanence that enrich the lives of those who read them. Imprint of Pelican Publishing. Publishes 1 title/yr.; hardcover, trade paperbacks. Receives 250 submissions annually. No books from first-time authors. Will accept mss through agents. Reprints books. Prefers 200+ pgs. Royalty; some advances. Publication within 9-18 mos. No simultaneous submissions. Responds in 1 mo. on queries. Requires accepted ms on disk. Prefers KJV. Guidelines (also on Website); catalog for 9x12 SAE/6 stamps.

　　Nonfiction/Fiction: Proposal/2 chapters; no phone/fax/e-query.

　　Photos/Artwork: Accepts freelance photos for book covers; open to queries from freelance artists.

DOVER PUBLICATIONS INC., 31 E. 2nd St., Mineola NY 11501-3852. (516)294-7000, ext. 173. Fax (516)873-1401 or (516)742-6953. E-mail: mwaldrep@doverpublications.com. Website: www.doverpublications.com. Attn: Editorial Dept. Publishes some religious titles, reprints only. Makes outright purchases. Does not return submissions. Guidelines & free catalog on Website.

　　Nonfiction: Proposal/synopsis, contents & 1 chapter; no submissions by e-mail. Religion topics.

EARTHEN VESSEL PUBLISHING, 289 Miller Ave., Mill Valley CA 94941. Phone/fax (415)381-6020. E-mail: kentphilpott@comcast.net. Website: www.earthenvessel.net. Reformed Baptist. Kent Philpott, ed. Publishes 2 titles/yr. Receives 1-3 submissions annually. 50% of books from first-time authors. No mss through agents. Reprints books. Outright purchases. Average first printing varies. Publication time varies. Considers simultaneous submissions. Responds soon. No guidelines or catalog.

　　Nonfiction: Accepts phone query.

　　Artwork: Open to queries from freelance artists.

E-DIGITAL BOOKS, LLC, 1155 S. Havana St., #11-364, Aurora CO 80012. E-mail: submissions@edigitalbooks.com. Website: www.edigitalbooks.com. T. R. Allen, ed-in-chief. Publishes 10-15 titles/yr. Receives 10 submissions annually. 50% of books from first-time authors. No mss through agents. Royalty 30-60% on retail. Publication within 6 mos. Considers simultaneous submissions. Responds in 6 mos. by e-mail. Guidelines/catalog by e-mail.

　　Nonfiction: Query by e-mail only. (Put "Nonfiction Query" in subject line.)

　　Fiction: Query by e-mail.

Tips: "Interested in Christian religious poetry with uplifting, positive, and inspirational themes. We have a family-oriented Christian audience." Also see: www.E-digitalCatholic.com.

EDITORIAL PORTAVOZ, PO Box 2607, Grand Rapids MI 49501-2607. Toll-free (800)733-2607. (616)451-4775. Fax (616)451-9330. E-mail: editor@portavoz.com, or portavoz@portavoz.com. Website: www.portavoz.com. Spanish Division of Kregel Publishing. Submit to The Editor. To provide trusted, biblically based resources that challenge and encourage Spanish-speaking individuals in their Christian lives and service. Publishes 40+ titles/yr. 2-5% of books from first-time authors. Will accept mss through agents. Does print-on-demand. No reprints. Negotiable royalty on net; negotiable advance. Average first printing 5,000. Publication within 13 mos. Considers simultaneous submissions. Responds in 2-4 mos. Guidelines on Website.

Nonfiction: Send proposal by e-mail or CD-ROM, with 2-3 chapters. "Looking for original Spanish reference works."

Artwork: Purchases artwork outright.

EDITORIAL UNILIT, 1360 N.W. 88th Ave., Miami FL 33172-3093. Toll-free (800)767-7726. (305)592-6136. Fax (305)592-0087. E-mail: info@editorialunilit.com. Website: www.editorialunilit.com. Spanish House. Submit to The Editor. To glorify God by providing the church and Spanish-speaking people with the tools to communicate clearly the gospel of Jesus Christ and help them grow in their relationship with Him and His church.

EERDMANS BOOKS FOR YOUNG READERS, 2140 Oak Industrial Dr. N.E., Grand Rapids MI 49505. Toll-free (800)253-7521. (616)459-4591. Fax (616)459-6540. E-mail: youngreaders@eerdmans.com, or info@eerdmans.com. Website: www.eerdmans.com/youngreaders. Wm. B. Eerdmans Publishing. Submit to Acquisitions Editor. Produces books for general trade, school, and library markets. Publishes 6-7 titles/yr.; hardcover, trade paperbacks. Receives 5,000 submissions annually. 3% of books from first-time authors. Prefers mss through agents. Age-appropriate length. Royalty & advance vary. Average first printing varies. Publication within 36 mos. No simultaneous submissions (mark "Exclusive" on envelope). Responds in 3 mos. Guidelines (also by e-mail/Website); catalog for 9x12 SAE/4 stamps.

Fiction: Proposal/3 chapters for book length; complete ms for picture books. For children and teens. No e-mail or fax submissions.

Artwork: Please do not send illustrations with picture book manuscripts unless you are a professional illustrator. When submitting artwork, send color copies, not originals. Send illustrations sample to Gayle Brown, art dir.

Tips: "Most open to thoughtful submissions that address needs in children's literature. We are not looking for retold Bible stories or Christmas stories at this time."

WM. B. EERDMANS PUBLISHING CO., 2140 Oak Industrial Dr. N.E., Grand Rapids MI 49505. Toll-free (800)253-7521. (616)459-4591. Fax (616)459-6540. E-mail: info@eerdmans.com. Website: www.eerdmans.com. Protestant/Academic/Theological. Jon Pott, ed-in-chief. Imprint: Eerdmans Books for Young Readers (see separate listing). Publishes 120-130 titles/yr.; hardcover, trade paperbacks. Receives 3,000-4,000 submissions annually. 10% of books from first-time authors. Will accept mss through agents. Reprints books. Royalty; occasional advance. Average first printing 4,000. Publication within 1 yr. Considers simultaneous submissions. Responds in 4 wks. to query; several months for mss. Guidelines on Website (www.eerdmans.com/submit.htm); free catalog.

Nonfiction: Proposal/2-3 chapters; no fax/e-query. "Looking for religious approaches to contemporary issues, spiritual growth, scholarly works."

Fiction: Proposal/chapter; no fax/e-query. For all ages. "We are looking for adult novels with high literary merit."

Tips: "Most open to material with general appeal, but well-researched, cutting-edge material that bridges the gap between evangelical and mainline worlds."

**Note: This publisher serviced by The Writer's Edge.

ELDRIDGE CHRISTIAN PLAYS & MUSICALS, PO Box 14367, Tallahassee FL 32317. (850)385-2463. Fax (850)385-2463. E-mail: info@histage.com. Website: www.95church.com. Independent Christian drama publisher. Susan Shore, new plays ed. To provide superior religious drama to enhance preaching and teaching, whatever your Christian denomination. Publishes 15 plays and 2 musicals/yr. Receives 350-400 plays annually. 75% of plays from first-time authors. One-act to full-length plays. Outright purchases of $100-1,000 on publication; no advance. Publication within 1 yr. Considers simultaneous submissions. Responds in 2 mos. Requires requested ms on disk or by e-mail. Free guidelines (also by e-mail or Website)/catalog.

Plays: Complete ms; e-query OK. For children, teens, and adults. Send by e-mail to New Works@histage.com, or by mail to editor and address above.

Special Needs: Always looking for high quality Christmas and Easter plays but open to other holiday and "anytime" Christian plays too. Can be biblical or contemporary, for performance by all ages, children through adult.

Tips: "Have play produced at your church and others prior to submission, to get out the bugs. At least try a stage reading."

ELIJAH PRESS, Meadow House Communications Inc., PO Box 317628, Cincinnati OH 45231-7628. (513)521-7362. Fax (513)521-7364. Website: www.elijahpress.com. Publishes quality religious/spiritual fiction and nonfiction books and tapes on and related to Christian living, church history, and spiritual reflection. S. R. Davis, ed. Publishes 3-5 titles/yr. Prefers 50,000-100,000 wds. Responds in 1 mo. Guidelines on Website. Incomplete topical listings.

Nonfiction: One-page query; must have completed ms; no phone/e-query.

Fiction: Accepts fiction.

EMERALD POINTE BOOKS, Box 35035, Tulsa OK 74153. Toll-free (800)888-4126. (918)523-5400. E-mail: customerservice@harrisonhouse.com. Website: www.harrisonhouse.com. Evangelical/charismatic. Submit to Fiction Editor. Fiction imprint of Harrison House. No mss through agents. No reprints. Royalty on net or retail; no advance. Average first printing 5,000. Publication within 12-24 mos. Responds in 6 mos. Accepts requested ms by e-mail. No guidelines or catalog.

Fiction: Query. Adult. Contemporary and historical.

EMMAUS ROAD PUBLISHING, 827 N. Fourth St., Steubenville OH 43952. Toll-free (800)398-5470. (740)283-2880. Fax (740)283-4011. E-mail: questions@emmausroad.org. Website: www.emmausroad.org. Catholics United for the Faith. Shannon Minch-Hughes, V.P. Operations. To produce solid Catholic resources. Publishes 8 titles/yr.; hardcover, trade paperbacks. Receives 60 submissions annually. 20% of books from first-time authors. Requires mss through agents. Reprints books. Prefers 200 pgs. Royalty; advance. Average first printing 5,000. Publication within 18 mos. Considers simultaneous submissions. No guidelines; free catalog.

Nonfiction: Proposal/2 chapters.

Special Needs: Bible studies.

Ethnic Books: Hispanic.

$+ENCORE PERFORMANCE PUBLISHING. E-mail: editor@encoreplay.com. Website: www.encoreplay.com. Meredith Edwards, mng. dir.

ETC PUBLICATIONS, 1456 Rodeo Rd., Palm Springs CA 92262. Toll-free (866)514-9969. (760)316-9695. Fax (760)316-9681. Website: www.etcpublications.com. Education Technology Communications. Dr. Richard W. Hostrop, pub.; Lee Ona S. Hostrop, ed. dir. Publishes textbooks for the Christian and general markets at all levels of education. Publishes 6-12 titles/yr.; hardcover, trade paperbacks. Receives 50 submissions annually. 75% of books from first-time authors. Will accept mss through agents. No reprints. Prefers 128-256 pgs. Royalty 5-15% on net or retail; no advance. Average first printing 1,500-2,500. Publication within 9 mos. No simultaneous submissions. Responds in 10 days. No guidelines (use *Chicago Manual of Style*); catalog for #10 SAE/1 stamp.

Nonfiction: Complete ms; e-query OK. "We are interested only in Christian-oriented, state history textbooks to be used in Christian schools and by homeschoolers."

Photos: Accepts freelance photos for book covers.

Tips: "Open only to state histories that are required at a specific grade level and are Christian oriented, with illustrations."

+EVANGELICAL PRESS, PO Box 825, Webster NY 14580. Toll free phone/fax (866)588-6778. E-mail: usa.sales@evangelicalpress.org. Website: www.evangelicalpress.org. Evangelical Press and Services Ltd. Submit to Book Editor. Committed to the dissemination of biblical Christianity throughout the world in numerous languages; and to support local Christians in local churches to live lives that glorify God. Publishes 24 titles/yr.; hardcover, trade paperbacks, mass-market paperbacks. Receives 300+ submissions annually. 80% of books from first-time authors. No mss through agents. Does print-on-demand. No reprints. Royalty on net; no advance. Average first printing 3,000. Publication within 12-18 mos. No simultaneous submissions. Accepts requested mss by e-mail. Responds within 3 mos. Prefers NIV/ESV/NKJV/AV. Guidelines by e-mail or Website; free catalog.

Nonfiction: Query, proposal/2 chapter/complete ms; phone/e-query OK.

Tips: "Understand what our publishing company stands for."

EVERGREEN PRESS, 6140 Rangeline Rd. #A, Theodore AL 36582-5201. (251)973-0680. Fax (251)973-0682. E-mail: Brian@evergreenpress.com. Website: www.evergreenpress.com. Genesis Communications. Brian Banashak, pub.; Kathy Banashak, ed-in-chief. Publishes books that empower people for breakthrough living by being practical, biblical, and engaging. Imprints: Evergreen Press, Gazelle Press, Axiom Press (print-on-demand). Publishes 30 titles/yr. Receives 250 submissions annually. 40% of books from first-time authors. Will accept mss through agents. SUBSIDY PUBLISHES 35%. Does print-on-demand. No reprints. Prefers 96-160 pgs. Royalty on net; no advance. Average first printing 4,000. Publication within 6 mos. Considers simultaneous submissions. Requires requested ms on disk or by e-mail. Responds in 4-6 wks. Guidelines on Website; free catalog.

Nonfiction: Complete ms; fax/e-query OK. Submission form on Website.

Fiction: For all ages. Complete ms; phone/fax/e-query OK. Submission form on Website.

Special Needs: Business, finance, personal growth, women's issues, family/parenting, relationships, prayer, humor, and angels.

Also Does: Booklets.

Tips: "Most open to books with a specific market (targeted, not general) that the author is qualified to write for and that is relevant to today's believers and seekers. Author must also be open to editorial direction."

EXTREME DIVA MEDIA INC. E-mail: query@extremedivamedia.com. Website: www.extreme divamedia.com. Jean Ann Duckworth, ed./pub. Publishes books in 4 areas: reducing stress, increasing joy, simplifying life, and enhancing relationships. Guidelines on Website.

Nonfiction: E-query only. Full manuscripts will be discarded unless requested.

Special Needs: Devotions to Go (30-day devotionals); Self Improvement; Cookbooks/Entertainment Guides. New series, Girlfriends On..., to be introduced in 2009. Now accepting submissions. Guidelines on Website.

Tips: "We create books to help women live better lives. Show us how your book contributes to this mission."

FACTS ON FILE INC., 132 W. 31st St., 17th Fl., New York NY 10001. Toll-free (800)322-8755. (212)967-8800. Fax (212)967-9196. E-mail: llikoff@factsonfile.com, or editorial@facts onfile.com. Website: www.factsonfile.com. Laurie Likoff, ed. dir. School and library reference and trade books (for middle- to high-school students) tied to curriculum and areas of cross-cultural studies, including religion. Imprint: Checkmark Books. Publishes 3-5 religious titles/yr. Receives 10-20 submissions annually. 2% of books from first-time authors. Will accept mss through agents. No reprints. Prefers 224-480 pgs. Royalty 10% on retail; outright purchases of $2,000-10,000; advance $5,000-10,000. Some work-for-hire. Average first printing 2,500. Publication within 9-12 mos. Considers simultaneous submissions. Responds in 2 mos. Requires requested ms on disk. Guidelines (also on Website)/free catalog.

Nonfiction: Query or proposal/1 chapter; fax/e-query OK.

Tips: "Most open to reference books tied to curriculum subjects or disciplines."

FAIR HAVENS PUBLICATIONS, PO Box 1238, Gainesville TX 76241-1238. Toll-free (800)771-4861. (940)668-6044. Fax (940)668-6984. E-mail: fairhavens@fairhavenspub.com, or through Website: www.fairhavenspub.com. Submit to Acquisitions Department. Produces quality books, teaching and evangelistic literature, audiotapes and videotapes, CD-ROMs, dramas, and artworks that inspire faith and courage. Publishes 1-2 titles/yr.; hardcover, trade paperbacks. Receives 100 submissions annually. No first-time authors. Will accept mss through agents. SUBSIDY PUBLISHES 25%; does print-on-demand. Reprints books. Prefers 250-300 pgs. Royalty 10-18% on net; no advance (negotiable for published authors). Average first printing 3,000-12,000. Publication within 8 mos. Considers simultaneous submissions. Responds in 12 or more wks. Requires requested ms on disk. Prefers NKJV. Guidelines on Website; no catalog.

Nonfiction: Proposal/3 chapters; no phone/fax/e-query. "We are interested in books based on original research based on compiled data, case studies, etc."

Special Needs: Nonfiction; personal experience; how-to books packed with practical information relating to a felt need.

Also Does: Booklets, audio & videotapes, CD-ROMs, dramas.

Photos/Artwork: Accepts freelance photos for book covers; open to queries from freelance artists.

Tips: "We are flexible and work closely with our authors. We will help authors to self-publish if we do not elect to publish their manuscripts."

FAITH ALIVE CHRISTIAN RESOURCES, 2850 Kalamazoo Ave. S.E., Grand Rapids MI 49560. Toll-free (800)333-8300. (616)224-0819. E-mail: editors@faithaliveresources.org. Website: www.faithaliveresources.org. CRC Publications/Christian Reformed Church. Ruth Vanderhart, mng. ed. Guidelines on Website.

Artwork: Open to queries from freelance artists; contact Dean Heetderks, art dir.

FAITH COMMUNICATIONS, 3201 S.W. 15th St., Deerfield Beach FL 33442. (954)360-0909. Fax (954)360-0034. Website: www.hcibooks.com. Christian imprint of Health Communications Inc. Submit to Editorial Committee. Dedicated to publishing exceptional products that cultivate the desire to pursue Christ, grow in faith, and share his love with others. No phone/e-queries. Guidelines on Website. Incomplete topical listings.

Nonfiction/Fiction: Proposal/2 chapters.

Tips: "Books should have a very clear Christian focus—fiction or nonfiction."

+FAITHFUL LIFE PUBLISHERS. E-mail: editor@flpublishers.com. Website: www.FLPublishers .com. James A. Wendorf, ed.

FAITHGIRLZ/ZONDERKIDZ, 5300 Patterson S.E., Grand Rapids MI 49530-0002. (616)698-6900. Fax (616)698-3578. E-mail: zpub@zondervan.com. Website: www.zonderkidz.com. Zondervan/HarperCollins. Not currently accepting submissions for this line.

FAITHWALK PUBLISHING, 517 S. Main St., Lima OH 45804. Toll-free (800)241-4056. (419)227-1818. Fax (419)228-9184. E-mail: submissions@faithwalkpub.com. Website: www.faithwalkpub.com. Imprint of CSS Publishing. Dirk Wierenga, ed. (Send submission c/o Dirk Wierenga, 14140 Payne Forest, Grand Haven MI 49417 or e-query to dirk@

faithwalkpub.com). Called to publish books which appeal to seekers and believers who might otherwise never purchase a religious book. Publishes 10 titles/yr. Receives 500+ submissions annually. 10% of books from first-time authors. Will accept mss through agents. No reprints. Prefers 160-356 pgs. Royalty 6-10% of retail; no advance. Average first printing 2,000-5,000. Publication within 12-18 mos. Considers simultaneous submissions (if indicated). Does not respond to submissions unless interested (no SASE needed). Prefers NIV, NRSV. Guidelines (also by e-mail/Website); catalog.

Nonfiction: Proposal/1-2 chapters; no fax submissions; e-query OK. No children's or gift books.

Fiction: Proposal/1-2 chapters; e-query OK. Adult; adventure, contemporary, and literary.

Photos: Accepts freelance photos for book covers.

FAITHWORDS, 10 Cadillac Dr., Ste. 220, Brentwood TN 37027. (615)221-0996. Fax (615)221-0962. Website: www.faithwords.com. Hachette Book Group USA. Anne Horch, ed. Imprint: Center Street. Publishes 40 titles/yr.; hardcover, trade paperbacks, mass-market paperbacks. Few books from first-time authors. Requires mss through agents. Prefers 50,000-90,000 wds. Royalty on retail; advance. Publication within 12 mos. Considers simultaneous submissions. Prefers accepted ms by e-mail.

Nonfiction: Proposal/table of contents & 3 chapters. No phone/fax query; e-query OK.

Fiction: For teens and adults. Proposal/3 chapters.

**Note: This publisher serviced by ChristianManuscriptSubmissions.com.

FAMILYLIFE PUBLISHING, PO Box 7111, Little Rock AR 72223. Toll-free (800)358-6329. E-mail through Website: www.familylife.com. Campus Crusade for Christ. Margie Clark, product development mngr. Our uniqueness is creating/publishing connecting resources: marrying together truth, relationship, and experience. Publishes 10 titles/yr.; hardcover, trade paperbacks. Receives 100 submissions annually. 10% of books from first-time authors. Will accept mss through agents. Reprints books. Royalty 2-18% of net or outright purchase; advance. Average first printing 10,000. Publication within 12 mos. Considers simultaneous submissions. Requires submissions on disk or by e-mail. Responds in 6 mos. Prefers NASB, ESV, NIV. Guidelines (also by e-mail/Website); catalog on Website or for 9x12 SAE/4 stamps.

Nonfiction: Proposal/2 chapters; e-query OK. "Looking for books on marriage: intimacy, communication."

Also Does: Booklets; multipiece activity packs.

Photos/Artwork: Accepts freelance photos for book covers; open to queries from freelance artists.

Tips: "Most open to multipiece, interactive products. The query and proposal should be professional. Before you submit to us, be sure to read our writer's guidelines and The Family Manifesto (both on Website). If you don't know who we are or what we do, please send your material elsewhere."

**Note: This publisher serviced by ChristianManuscriptSubmissions.com.

+FATHER'S PRESS, 2424 S.E. 6th St., Lee's Summit MO 64063. Phone/fax (816)600-6288. E-mail: fatherspress@yahoo.com. Website: www.fatherspress.com. Mike Smitley, owner (mike smitley2@yahoo.com). Publishes controversial and risky books that present the biblical truth about issues facing Christians and nonbelievers today. Publishes 4-5 titles/yr.; hardcover, trade paperbacks, mass-market paperbacks, coffee-table books. Receives 300 submissions annually. 50% of books from first-time authors. No mss through agents. Reprints books. Prefers up to 500 pgs. Royalty 10% on net; no advance. Average first printing 500. Publication within 3 mos. Considers simultaneous submissions. Accepted mss by disk or e-mail. Responds in 7 days. Prefers KJV. Guidelines (also by e-mail/Website); no catalog.

Nonfiction: Query first; phone/fax/e-query OK.

Fiction: For all ages. Query first; phone/fax/e-query OK.

Special Needs: Books that deal with issues that contribute to the decline of our economy and culture.

Photos: Accepts freelance photos for book covers.

Tips: "We prefer books with strong social, economic, and religious relevance. We like writers with a clear marketing strategy with strong sales leads and endorsements."

FREDERICK FELL PUBLISHERS INC., 2131 Hollywood Blvd., Ste. 305, Hollywood FL 33020. (954)925-5242. Fax (954)925-5244. E-mail: fellpub@aol.com, info@fellpub.com, or through Website: www.fellpub.com. Barbara Newman, sr. ed. General publisher that publishes 2-4 religious titles/yr.; hardcover, trade paperbacks. Receives 4,000 submissions annually. 95% of books from first-time authors. Reprints books. Prefers 60,000 wds. or 200-300 pgs. Royalty 6-15% on retail; advance $500-10,000. Average first printing 7,500. Publication within 1 yr. Considers simultaneous submissions. Responds in 5-13 wks. Requires submissions by e-mail. Guidelines on Website.

Nonfiction: Proposal/2 chapters; no phone/fax/e-query. Looking for self-help and how-to books. Include a clear marketing and promotional strategy.

Fiction: Complete ms; no phone/fax/e-query. For adults; adventure and historical. "Looking for great story lines, with potential movie prospects."

Tips: "Spirituality, optimism, and a positive attitude have international appeal. Steer clear of doom and gloom; less sadness and more gladness benefits all." Also publishes New Age books. SASE required.

FIFTH ESTATE PUBLISHERS, PO Box 116, Blountsville AL 35031. Toll-free (888)734-2476. E-mail: admin@fifth-estate.net. Website: www.fifth-estate.net. Joseph Lumpkin, exec. ed. Publishes 10 titles/yr.; hardcover, trade paperbacks, mass-market paperbacks. Receives 100+ submissions annually. 50% of books from first-time authors. Prefers mss through agents. Does print-on-demand. Reprints books. Prefers 104-730 pgs. Royalty on net; no advance. Publication within 6 mos. Considers simultaneous submissions. Responds in 1 mo. Requires accepted ms on disk or by e-mail. Guidelines (also by e-mail or Website); free catalog for SASE.

Nonfiction: Query only first; mail/phone/e-query OK. "Looking for spiritual and children's books."

Fiction: No fiction or poetry accepted at this time.

Photos/Artwork: Accepts freelance photos for book covers; open to queries from freelance artists.

Tips: "When an author tells me their book is different, I usually find it is not. Find what is in demand; write about it; and write it well."

FIRST FRUITS OF ZION, PO Box 649, Marshfield MO 65706-0649. Toll-free (800)775-4807. (417)468-2741. Fax (417)468-2745. E-mail through Website: www.FFOZ.org. Hope Egan, ed. A nonprofit ministry devoted to strengthening the love and appreciation of the Body of Messiah for the land, people, and Scripture of Israel. Publishes 2-6 titles/yr.; trade paperbacks. No mss through agents. Royalty; no advance. Publication within 6 mos. Considers simultaneous submissions. Responds in 1 mo. Prefers NASB.

Nonfiction: Query first; no phone/fax/e-query.

Special Needs: Books on Jewish or Hebraic roots only.

Tips: "Be very familiar with our material before submitting to us."

FOCUS ON THE FAMILY BOOK PUBLISHING AND RESOURCE DEVELOPMENT, 8605 Explorer Dr., Colorado Springs CO 80920-1051. (719)531-3400. Fax (719)531-3448. E-mail through Website: www.focusonthefamily.com. Exists to support the family; all our products are about topics pertaining to families. Publishes 30-40 titles/yr.; hardcover, trade paperbacks, mass-market paperbacks (rarely). 12% of books from first-time authors. Rarely reprints books. Length depends on genre. Royalty or work-for-hire; advance varies. Average first printing varies. Publication within 18 mos. No longer considers unsolicited submissions. Responds in 1-3 mos. Prefers NIV (but accepts 10 others). Guidelines by e-mail/Website; no catalog. **Nonfiction:** Query letter only through an agent or writer's conference contact with a Focus editor. "Most open to family advice topics. We look for excellent writing and topics that haven't been done to death—or that have a unique angle."

Fiction: Query letter only through an agent or writer's conference contact with a Focus editor. Stories must incorporate traditional family values or family issues; from 1900 to present day. Also does Mom Lit.

Artwork: Open to queries from freelance artists (but not for specific projects).

**Note: This publisher serviced by The Writer's Edge and ChristianManuscriptSubmissions .com.

FORDHAM UNIVERSITY PRESS, 2546 Belmont Ave., University Box L, Bronx NY 10458. (718) 817-4795. Fax (718)817-4785. E-mail: tartar@fordham.edu. Website: www.fordhampress.com. Helen Tartar, ed. dir. Publishes for both an academic and general audience; includes religion. Publishes hardcover & trade paperbacks. Reprints books. Guidelines on Website; catalog.

Nonfiction: Query; no e-query.

FORTRESS PRESS, Box 1209, Minneapolis MN 55440-1209. (612)330-3300. Fax (612)330-3215. E-mail: booksub@augsburgfortress.org. Website: www.fortresspress.com. J. Michael West, ed-in-chief. Publishes religious academic books. Publishes 60 titles/yr.; hardcover, trade paperbacks. Receives 1,000 submissions annually. 10% of books from first-time authors. Will accept mss through agents. No reprints. Royalty on net. Considers simultaneous submissions. Responds in 3 mos. Guidelines on Website; free catalog (call 1-800-328-4648).

Nonfiction: Query/sample pages. "Please study guidelines before submitting."

Ethnic Books: African American studies.

FORWARD MOVEMENT, 300 W. 4th St., Cincinnati OH 45202-2666. Toll-free (800)543-1813. (513)721-6659. Fax (513)721-0729. E-mail: rschmidt@forwarddaybyday.com. Website: www .forwardmovement.org. Episcopal. Submit to The Editor. Provides resources to support persons in their lives of prayer and faith. Publishes 2-3 books/yr., and 25 tracts & booklets. Receives 1,000 submissions annually. 50% of books from first-time authors. No mss through agents. No reprints. Prefers up to 200 pgs. One-time honorarium; no advance. Average first printing 5,000. Publication within 9 mos. Considers simultaneous submissions. Prefers requested ms on disk as an RTF file. Responds in 1-2 mos. Prefers NRSV. Guidelines; free catalog.

Nonfiction: Query for book, complete ms if short; no phone/fax/e-query. "Looking for books on prayer and spirituality, devotionals, Christian living, and spiritual life."

Ethnic Books: Black & Hispanic pamphlets.

Also Does: Booklets, 4-32 pgs.; pamphlets 4-8 pgs.; tracts.

Tips: "We sell primarily to a mainline Protestant audience. Most open to books that deal with the central doctrines of the Christian faith. Spirituality and Christian living."

FOUNDERS PRESS, PO Box 150931, Cape Coral FL 33915. (239)772-1400. Fax (239)772-1140. E-mail through Website: www.founders.org. Founders Ministries/Southern Baptist. Kenneth Puls, ed. Committed to producing and distributing books, pamphlets, and other materials that are consistent with the doctrines of grace and that speak from a historic Southern Baptist perspective. Responds in 4 mos. (or contact them). Guidelines on Website. Incomplete topical listings.

Nonfiction: Proposal, plus completed author information sheet (available on the Website).

Also Does: Pamphlets.

FOURSQUARE MEDIA, 1910 W. Sunset Blvd., Ste. 200, Los Angeles CA 90026-0176. (213)989-4494. E-mail: media@foursquare.org. Website: www.foursquare.org/landing_pages/ 83,3.html. The Foursquare Church; in partnership with Creation House (Strang Communications). Rick Wulfestieg, dir.; Larry Libby, sr. ed. To capture Foursquare history, vision, and values; for cell study groups, church ministry institutes, and pastoral-led congregational studies. Estab. 2006. Publishes 4+ titles/yr.

Nonfiction: E-query.

Also Does: Will host writers' conferences in the future to encourage ministry leaders in developing writing and publishing skills.

FRIENDS UNITED PRESS, 101 Quaker Hill Dr., Richmond IN 47374. (765)962-7573. Fax (765)966-1293. E-mail: friendspress@fum.org. Website: www.fum.org/shop. Friends United Meeting (Quaker). Katie Terrell, ed. To gather persons into a fellowship where Jesus Christ is known as Lord and Teacher. Publishes 3 titles/yr. Receives 25 submissions annually. 50% of books from first-time authors. No mss through agents. Does print-on-demand. Prefers 150-200 pgs. Royalty 7.5% of net; no advance. Publication within 1 yr. Considers simultaneous submissions; e-mail submissions preferred. Responds in 3 mos. Prefers requested ms by e-mail. Guidelines (also by e-mail/Website); free catalog.

Nonfiction: Proposal/2 chapters; e-query preferred.

Fiction: Proposal/2 chapters; e-query preferred.

Ethnic Books: Howard Thurman Books (African American), Underground Railroad.

Tips: "Primarily open to Quaker authors. Looking for Quaker-related spirituality, or current faith issues/practice addressed from a Christian Quaker experience or practice."

GEORGETOWN UNIVERSITY PRESS, 3240 Prospect St. N.W., Washington DC 20007. (202)687-5889. Fax (202)687-6340. E-mail: reb7@georgetown.edu or gupress@george town.edu. Website: www.press.georgetown.edu. Georgetown University. Richard Brown, dir. Scholarly books in religion, theology, ethics, and other fields, with an emphasis on cross-disciplinary and cross-cultural studies. Publishes 10 titles/yr. Receives 100 submissions annually. 10% of books from first-time authors. Will accept mss through agents. No reprints. Prefers 80,000 wds. Royalty 8-12% on net; negotiable advance. Average first printing 2,000-3,000. Publication within 9-10 mos. Considers simultaneous submissions. Requires requested ms on disk. Responds in 6-8 wks. Prefers NRSV. Does print-on-demand. Guidelines on Website; free catalog.

Nonfiction: Guidelines for submitting a proposal are posted on Website. "Should be thoroughly researched and original."

Special Needs: Work relations, theology, ethics—with scholarly bent.

Ethnic Books: Hispanic.

Also Does: CD-ROMs.

Photos: Accepts freelance photos for book covers.

GOLLEHON PRESS INC., 6157—28th St. S.E., Grand Rapids MI 49546. (616)949-3515. Fax (616)949-8674. E-mail: john@gollehonbooks.com. Website: www.gollehonbooks.com. Becky Anderson, ed. Small press willing to work with first-time writers, especially if un-agented. Publishes 3-4 titles/yr.; hardcover, trade paperbacks. Receives 50-100 submissions annually. 90% of books from first-time authors. Will accept mss through agents. No subsidy publishing. No reprints. Prefers 50,000-80,000 wds., or 200-250 pgs. Royalty 6-8% on retail; advance to $1,000. Average first printing 5,000-10,000. Publication within 8-10 mos. Encourages simultaneous submissions. Responds in 1-2 mos., if interested. Prefers KJV. Guidelines pending; no catalog.

Nonfiction: Brief book proposal; if interested will request full ms. Do not send unsolicited mss. Unable to respond to all queries.

Tips: "Most open to inspirational, miracles, and from the heart. Also more scholarly books, such as the first century church. Will help writers understand publishing, what to expect, and what is expected of them to promote their work. We offer a working relationship that is unusual today." Note that although their Website highlights their gaming books, they are now actively seeking manuscripts on Christian themes.

GOOD BOOK PUBLISHING COMPANY, PO Box 837, Kihei HI 96753-0837. Phone/fax (808)874-4876. E-mail: dickb@dickb.com. Website: www.dickb.com/index.shtml. Christian/ Protestant/Bible Fellowship. Ken Burns, pres. Researches and publishes books on the biblical/Christian roots of Alcoholics Anonymous. Publishes 1 title/yr.; publishes trade paperbacks, mass-market paperbacks. Receives 8 submissions annually. 80% of books from first-time authors. No mss through agents. Reprints books. Prefers 250 pgs. Royalty 10%; no advance. Average first printing 3,000. Publication within 2 mos. Considers simultaneous submissions. Responds in 1 wk. No disk. Prefers KJV. No guidelines; free catalog.

Nonfiction: Proposal; no phone/fax/e-query. Books on the spiritual history and success of AA; 12-step spiritual roots; Bible study.

Also Does: Pamphlets, booklets.

GOOD NEWS PUBLISHERS, 1300 Crescent St., Wheaton IL 60187. (630)682-4300. Fax (630) 682-4785. E-mail: tracts@gnpcb.org. Website: www.goodnewspublishers.org. Kate Felinski, dir. of Literature Ministries. Tracts only; committed to producing solid, biblically sound gospel tracts, with excellent design, and relevant to today's culture. Publishes 30 tracts/yr. Receives 500 submissions annually. 2% of tracts from first-time authors. Prefers 650-800 wds. Pays about $150 or a quantity of tracts. Average first printing 100,000. Publication within 16 mos. Considers simultaneous submissions. Responds in 12 wks. Prefers ESV. Guidelines; free tract catalog.

Tracts: Complete ms.

Also Does: Pamphlets.

Tips: "Most open to seasonal tracts—Easter, Halloween, or Christmas. Be concise, clear, and careful with Christian terms."

**Note: This publisher serviced by ChristianManuscriptSubmissions.com.

GOSPEL LIGHT, 1957 Eastman Ave., Ventura CA 93003. Toll-free (800)4-GOSPEL. (805)-644-9721, ext. 1223. Website: www.gospellight.com. Anita Griggs, ed. Accepts proposals for Sunday school and Vacation Bible School curriculum and related resources for children from birth through the preteen years; also teacher resources. Guidelines on Website.

Also Does: Sometimes has openings for readers of new curriculum projects. See Website for how to apply.

Tips: "All our curriculum is written and field-tested by experienced teachers; most of our writers are on staff."

**Note: This publisher serviced by ChristianManuscriptSubmissions.com.

GOSPEL PUBLISHING HOUSE, 1445 N. Boonville Ave., Springfield MO 65802. Toll-free (800)641-4310. (417)831-8000. E-mail: newproducts@gph.org. Website: www.gospelpublishing.com. Assemblies of God. Julie Horner, ed. The majority of titles specifically address Pentecostal audiences in a variety of ministries in the local church. Publishes 5-10 titles/yr. Receives 250 submissions annually. 5% of books from first-time authors. Will accept mss through agents. No reprints. Royalty 5-10% of retail; no advance. Average first printing 2,000. Publication within 1 yr. Considers simultaneous submissions. Responds in 4 mos. Requires accepted mss on disk or by e-mail. Guidelines on Website; free catalog.

Nonfiction: Proposal/1 chapter; no phone query, e-query OK. "Looking for Holy Spirit; Pentecostal focus for pastors, local church lay leaders, and individuals; children's ministry programs and resources; small group resources."

Tips: "Most open to a new program or resource for small groups, children's ministry, compassion ministry, or evangelistic outreach, written by someone who is actively leading it at the local church."

GREEN KEY BOOKS, 2514 Aloha Pl., Holiday FL 34691. Toll-free (888)900-0197. (727)934-0927. Fax (727)934-4241. E-mail through Website: www.greenkeybooks.com. Christian publisher. Krissi Castor, mng. ed./acquisitions. Publishes 10-12 titles/yr.; hardcover, trade paperbacks. Receives 200-400 submissions annually. 10% of books from first-time authors. Will accept mss through agents. No reprints. Royalty; no advance. Average first printing 5,000. Publication within 9-12 mos. No simultaneous submissions. Accepts mss by e-mail. Responds in 16 wks. Guidelines on Website; free catalog.

Nonfiction: Query first; e-query OK. Query can include a synopsis or brief project outline. "Looking for men's devotionals, niche topics, books for military families."

Fiction: Not currently considering fiction or children's books.

Tips: "Most open to a book that is editorially tight (specifically grammar and punctuation) in adherence to the *Chicago Manual of Style*."

**Note: This publisher serviced by The Writer's Edge and ChristianManuscriptSubmissions .com.

GREENWOOD PUBLISHING GROUP/PRAEGER PUBLISHERS, 88 Post Road W., Westport CT 06881. (203)226-3571. Fax (203)222-1502. E-mail: suzanne.staszak-silva@greenwood .com. Website: www.Greenwood.com. Reed Elsevier Co. (USA). Suzanne Staszak-Silva, ed. List of editors by subject on Website. Imprints: Greenwood, Praeger, PSI. Publishes 5-30 titles/yr.; hardcover. Receives 40-60 submissions annually. No reprints. Prefers up to 100,000 wds. Variable royalty on net; some advances. Average first printing 1,500. Publication within 8-10 mos. Considers simultaneous submissions. Responds in 1-3 mos. Guidelines & catalog on Website.

Nonfiction: Book proposal/1-2 chapters or all chapters available; e-query preferred.

Special Needs: Religious studies (general interest); criminology (general interest); literary studies, science.

Ethnic Books: Black studies (general interest); Islamic studies; Jewish studies; Native American studies; Hispanic/Latino studies.

Tips: "Most open to general interest books."

GROUP PUBLISHING INC., 1515 Cascade Ave., Loveland CO 80539-0481. Toll-free (800)447-1070. (970)292-4243. Fax (970)622-4370. E-mail: kloesche@group.com. Website: www .group.com. Nondenominational. Kerri Loesche, contract & copyright administrator. Imprint: Group Books. To equip churches to help children, youth, and adults grow in their relationship with Jesus, with resources that are R.E.A.L. (relational, experiential, applicable, learner based). Publishes 40 titles/yr.; trade paperbacks. Receives 1,000+ submissions annually. 5% of books from first-time authors. Will accept mss through agents. SOME SUBSIDY. No reprints. Prefers 128-250 pgs. Outright purchases of $25-3,000 or royalty of 8-10% of net; advance $3,000. Average first printing 5,000. Publication within 12-18 mos. Considers simultaneous submissions. Responds in 6 mos. Requires requested ms on disk or by e-mail. Prefers NLT. Guidelines on Website; catalog.

Nonfiction: Query or proposal/2 chapters/intro/cover letter/SASE; no phone/fax/ e-query. "Looking for practical ministry tools for youth workers, C. E. directors, and teachers with an emphasis on active learning."

Tips: "Most open to a practical resource that will help church leaders change lives. Tell our readers something they don't already know, in a way that they've not seen before."

**Note: This publisher serviced by The Writer's Edge and ChristianManuscriptSubmissions .com.

GRQ INC., PO Box 1067, Brentwood TN 37204. (615)776-3275. Fax (615)507-1709. E-mail: rzaloba@comcast.net. Robert Zaloba, pres. A book packager. Publishes 40-50 titles/yr.; hardcover, trade paperbacks, coffee-table books. Receives 200-300 submissions annually. 70% of books from first-time authors. Will accept mss through agents. SUBSIDY PUBLISHES 5%. Reprints books. Does mostly work-for-hire; rates depend on project; ranges from $1,500-$20,000; advance. Average first printing varies, 10,000-50,000. Publication within

10 mos. Considers simultaneous submissions. Response time varies. Requires accepted ms on disk. No guidelines or catalog.

Nonfiction: Query only first; no phone/fax query; e-query OK.

Tips: "We are a book packager who produces books that speak to the Christian market at large. Our books are found outside of the traditional CBA market. They are uniquely formatted and targeted for an 'average' reader. Most open to practical, unique self-help; unique devotions."

GRUPO NELSON, PO Box 141000, Nashville TN 37214. Toll-free (800)322-7423. (615)902-2372/2375. Fax (615)883-9376. E-mail: storres@thomasnelson.com. Website: www.grupo nelson.com. Thomas Nelson has reformed its Spanish division into Grupo Nelson, with five Spanish-language imprints listed below. Larry Downs, VP/Publisher. Targets the needs and wants of the Hispanic community. Publishes 65-80 titles/yr. Receives 50 submissions annually. 90% of books from first-time authors. No mss through agents. Prefers 192 pgs. Royalty on net; advance $500. Average first printing 4,000. Publication within 15 mos. Accepts e-mail submissions. No guidelines; free catalog.

Nonfiction: Query letter only; no phone/fax/e-query.

Ethnic Books: Hispanic imprints.

Also Does: Computer games.

Tips: "Most open to Christian books based on the Bible."

Editorial Diez Puntos: Specializes in parenting & family, personal finance, health and fitness, self-help, and popular culture.

Leader Latino: Business & leadership.

Editorial Caribe: Bibles, Bible reference, and electronic products.

Editorial Betania: Inspirational, popular religious, and children's.

Editorial Catolica: Catholic books and Bibles.

GUARDIAN ANGEL PUBLISHING INC., 12430 Teeson Ferry Rd., #186, St. Louis MO 63128. (314)276-8482. Fax (314)843-8517. E-mail: publisher@guardianangelpublishing.com. Website: www.guardianangelpublishing.com. Lynda S. Burch, pub. Goal is to inspire children to learn and grow and develop character skills to instill a Christian and healthy attitude of learning, caring, and sharing. Imprints: Wings of Faith, Angel to Angel, Angelic Harmony, Littlest Angels, Academic Wings, Guardian Angel Pets, Guardian Angel Health & Hygiene. Publishes 24-36 titles/yr.; trade paperbacks, coffee-table books. Receives 300-600 submissions annually. 75% of books from first-time authors. No subsidy; does print-on-demand. Prefers 100-5,000 wds. or 32 pgs. Royalty 30-50% on download; no advance. Average first printing 50-100. Print books are wholesaled and distributed; e-books are sold through many distribution networks. Publication within 6-12 mos. No simultaneous submissions. Responds in 1 wk.-1 mo. Accepted mss by e-mail. Guidelines on Website; catalog as e-book PDF.

Nonfiction: Complete ms; no phone/fax query; e-query OK. "Looking for all kinds of kids' books."

Fiction: Complete ms; no phone/fax query; e-query OK.

Photos/Artwork: Accepts freelance photos for book covers; open to queries from freelance artists.

Contest: Sponsors children's writing contest for schools.

Tips: "Most open to books that teach children to read and love books; to learn or grow from books."

GUERNICA EDITIONS, 11 Mount Royal Ave., Toronto ON M6H 2S2, Canada. (416)658-9888. Fax (416)657-8885. E-mail: guernicaeditions@cs.com. Website: www.guernicaeditions .com. Antonio D'Alfonso, ed. Deals with cultural bridging; interested in the next generation of writers. Publishes 1 religious title/yr.; trade paperbacks, mass-market paperbacks. Receives 100 submissions annually. 5% of books from first-time authors. No mss through agents. Reprints books. Prefers 100 pgs. Royalty 8-10% of retail; some outright purchases of $200-5,000; advance $200-2,000. Average first printing 1,500. Publication within 10 mos. Responds in 1-6 mos. Requires requested ms on disk; no e-mail. No guidelines (read one of our books to see what we like); catalog online.

Nonfiction: Query only first; no phone/fax/e-query. "Looking for books on world issues."

Fiction: Query only first. "Looking for short and profound literary works."

Ethnic Books: Concentration on other cultures. "We are involved in translations and ethnic issues."

Photos: Accepts freelance photos for book covers.

Tips: "Know what we publish. We're interested in books that bridge time and space; works that fit our editorial literary policies." Responds only if you include International Reply Coupons.

GUIDEPOSTSBOOKS, 16 E. 34th St., 12th Fl., New York NY 10016-4397. (212)251-8143. Website: www.guidepostsbooks.com. Guideposts Inc. Linda Raglan Cunningham, VP/ed-in-chief; Andrew Attaway, sr. acq. ed. Focuses on inspirational fiction, memoirs, story collections, devotionals, and faith-based true stories. Publishes 20 titles/yr.

**Note: This publisher serviced by ChristianManuscriptSubmissions.com.

+HALO PUBLISHING INTL., 10000 N.W. 25th St., #1M, Doral FL 33172-2204. E-mail: lisa@halopublishing.com. Website: www.halopublishing.com. Lisa M. Umina, ed. Publishes books that change and influence a child at an early age. Imprints: Olly Publishing, Hickory Tree Nut Publishing. Publishes 15-20 titles/yr.; hardcover. Receives 50-100 submissions annually. 100% of books from first-time authors. Prefers mss through agents. Prefers 32 pgs. Royalty 60-70% of retail. Average first printing 2,000. Publication within 6 mos. Considers simultaneous submissions. Responds in 4-6 wks. Accepts mss by e-mail. Guidelines on Website; free catalog.

Nonfiction: Complete ms; phone query OK.

Fiction: Complete ms; phone query OK.

Special Needs: Inspirational books and books dealing with life values.

Artwork: Open to queries from freelance artists.

HANNIBAL BOOKS, PO Box 461592, Garland TX 75046-1592. Toll-free (800)747-0738. Toll-free fax (888)252-3022. E-mail: hannibalbooks@earthlink.net. Website: www.hannibal books.com. KLMK Communications Inc. Louis Moore, pub. Evangelical Christian publisher specializing in missions, marriage and family, critical issues, and Bible-study curriculum. Publishes 8-10 titles/yr.; trade paperbacks, mass-market paperbacks. Receives 300 submissions annually. 80% of books from first-time authors. Will accept mss through agents. Some print-on-demand. Prefers 50,000-60,000 wds. Royalty on net or outright purchase; no advance. Average first printing 2,000-10,000. Publication within 3 mos. No simultaneous submissions. Responds in 3 mos. Prefers NIV. Guidelines; free catalog.

Nonfiction: Book Proposal/1-3 chapters; no phone/fax/e-query. "Looking for missionary, marriage restoration, homeschooling, and devotionals."

Fiction: Book Proposal/1-3 chapters; no phone/fax/e-query.

Tips: "We are looking for go-get-'em new authors with a passion to be published. Most open to missionary life and Bible studies. Obtain our guidelines and answer each question thoroughly."

HARCOURT RELIGION PUBLISHERS, 6277 Sea Harbor Dr., Orlando FL 32887. Toll-free (800) 922-7696. (407)345-3800. Fax (407)345-3798. E-mail: hrpwebmaster@harcourt.com. Website: www.harcourtreligion.com. Catholic. Craig O'Neil, sr. ed. Catholic educational market; high school curriculum. Publishes 50-100 titles/yr. Receives 100-300 submissions annually. Variable

royalty or outright purchase; rarely pays advance. Average first printing 1,000-3,000. Publication within 1 yr. Considers simultaneous submissions. Responds in 6 mos. Free catalog.
Nonfiction: Complete ms. "Looking primarily for school and parish textbooks."
Photos: Accepts freelance photos for book covers. Submit to Lynn Molony, prod. mngr.
HARPERONE, 353 Sacramento St., #500, San Francisco CA 94111-3653. (415)477-4400. Fax (415)477-4444. E-mail: hcsanfrancisco@harpercollins.com. Website: www.harpercollins .com. Religious division of HarperCollins. Michael G. Maudlin, ed. dir. Strives to be the preeminent publisher of the most important books across the full spectrum of religion and spiritual literature, adding to the wealth of the world's wisdom by respecting all traditions and favoring none; emphasis on quality Christian spirituality and literary fiction. Publishes 75 titles/yr.; hardcover, trade paperbacks. Receives 10,000 submissions annually. 5% of books from first-time authors. Prefers mss through agents. No reprints. Prefers 160-256 ms pgs. Royalty 7.5-15% on retail; advance $20,000-100,000. Average first printing 10,000. Publication within 18 mos. Considers simultaneous submissions. Responds in 3 mos. Requires requested ms on disk. No guidelines/catalog.
Nonfiction: Proposal/1 chapter; fax query OK.
Fiction: Complete ms; contemporary adult fiction, literary, fables & parables, spiritual.
Tips: "Agented proposals only."
HARRISON HOUSE PUBLISHERS, Box 35035, Tulsa OK 74153. Toll-free (800)888-4126. (918)523-5400. E-mail: customerservice@harrisonhouse.com. Website: www.harrisonhouse.com. Evangelical/charismatic. Julie Lechlider, mng. ed. To challenge Christians to live victoriously, grow spiritually, and know God intimately. Fiction imprint: Emerald Pointe Books (see separate listing). Publishes 20 titles/yr.; hardcover, trade paperbacks, mass-market paperbacks. 5% of books from first-time authors. No mss through agents. No reprints. Royalty on net or retail; no advance. Average first printing 5,000. Publication within 12-24 mos. Responds in 6 mos. Accepts requested ms by e-mail. No guidelines or catalog. Not currently accepting proposals or manuscripts.
Nonfiction: Query first; then proposal/table of contents/1 chapter; no phone/fax query; e-query OK.
**Note: This publisher serviced by ChristianManuscriptSubmissions.com.
HARVEST DAY BOOKS, 10300 E. Leelanau Ct., Traverse City MI 49684. (231)929-1999. Fax (231)929-1993. E-mail: Info@bookmarketingsolutions.com. Website: www.BookMarketing Solutions.com. Imprint of Book Marketing Solutions LLC. Tom White, pres. (tom@Book MarketingSolutions.com). Publishes works of the Christian faith. Guidelines on Website.
Nonfiction: Submission form on Website.
Poetry: Also accepting submissions for a 5-book poetry series called "Of the Heart." Although not exclusively Christian, they are hoping for an excellent Christian representation. For details, see Website or contact Tom White.
HARVEST HOUSE PUBLISHERS, 990 Owen Loop N., Eugene OR 97402. (541)343-0123. E-mail: admin@harvesthousepublishers.com. Website: www.harvesthousepublishers.com. Evangelical. Books and products that affirm biblical values and help people grow spiritually strong. Publishes 170 titles/yr.; hardcover, trade paperbacks, mass-market paperbacks, coffee-table books. No longer accepting unsolicited submissions, proposals, queries, etc.
Nonfiction: Self-help; Christian living.
Fiction: Interesting women's fiction.
Tips: "Find a good agent."
**Note: This publisher serviced by The Writer's Edge and ChristianManuscriptSubmissions .com.
HAY HOUSE INC., PO Box 5100, Carlsbad CA 92018-5100. (760)431-7695. Fax (760)431-6948. E-mail: editorial@hayhouse.com. Website: www.hayhouse.com. Jill Kramer, ed. dir.;

Jessica Kelley, submissions ed. Books to help heal the planet. Publishes 1 religious title/yr.; hardcover, trade paperbacks. Receives 200 religious submissions annually. 5% of books from first-time authors. Agented submissions only. Prefers 70,000 wds. or 250 pgs. Royalty. Average first printing 5,000. Publication within 12-15 mos. Considers simultaneous submissions. Responds in 1-2 mos. Guidelines (also by e-mail); free catalog for SASE.

Nonfiction: Proposal/3 chapters; hard copy only. "Looking for self-help/spiritual with a unique ecumenical angle."

Also Does: Some gift books.

Tips: "We are looking for books with a unique slant, ecumenical, but not overly religious. We want an open-minded approach." Includes a broad range of religious titles, including New Age.

HEALTH COMMUNICATIONS INC., 3201 S.W. 15th St., Deerfield Beach FL 33442. Toll-free (800)441-5569. (954)360-0909 (no phone calls). Fax (954)360-0034. E-mail: editorial@hcibooks.com. Website: www.hci-online.com, or www.hcibooks.com. Amy Hughes, religion ed.; submit to Editorial Committee. Nonfiction that emphasizes self-improvement, personal motivation, psychological health, and overall wellness; recovery/addiction, self-help/psychology, soul/spirituality, inspiration, women's issues, relationships, and family. Imprint: HCI Teens. Publishes 50 titles/yr.; hardcover, trade paperbacks. 20% of books from first-time authors. Will accept mss through agents. Prefers 250 pgs. Royalty 15% of net. Publication within 9 mos. Considers simultaneous submissions. Responds in 3 mos. Follow guidelines for submission. Guidelines on Website; catalog for 9x12 SASE.

Nonfiction: Query/outline and 2 chapters; no phone/fax/e-query. Needs books for Christian teens.

HEART OF WISDOM PUBLISHERS, 200 Coble Rd., Shelbyville TN 37160-6353. E-mail: info@heartofwisdom.com. Website: www.heartofwisdom.com. Publishes a variety of academic materials to help Christian families bring up children with a heart's desire for and knowledge of the Lord. Robin Sampson, ed. Query only. Guidelines on Website.

Special Needs: Currently accepting queries for high-quality history, science, and life skills unit studies for grades 4-12. Not accepting any other titles.

Tips: "We market to home educators and Christian schools."

HEARTQUEST/TYNDALE HOUSE PUBLISHERS, PO Box 80, Wheaton IL 60189-0080. (630)668-8310. Fax (630)668-3245. Website: www.heartquest.com. Anne Goldsmith, sr. ed. To encourage and challenge readers in their faith journey and Christian walk. Accepts mss through agents or by request only. Prefers fiction 75,000-90,000 wds. (contemporary), and 100,000+ wds. (historical). Responds in 3 mos. Royalty on net; advance. Guidelines (also by e-mail).

HEARTSONG PRESENTS, Imprint of Barbour Publishing Inc., PO Box 721, 1810 Barbour Dr., Uhrichsville, OH 44683. E-mail: fictionsubmit@barbourbooks.com. Website: www.heartsongpresents.com. JoAnne Simmons, ed. Produces affordable, wholesome entertainment through a book club that also helps to enhance and spread the gospel. Publishes 52 titles/yr.; mass-market paperbacks. Receives 1,000 submissions annually. 10% of books from first-time authors. Will accept mss through agents. Prefers 45,000-50,000 wds. Royalty 8% of net; advance $2,200. Average first printing 20,000. Publication within 1 yr. Considers simultaneous submissions. Responds in 6-12 mos. Requires electronic submissions; no proposals via regular mail. Prefers KJV for historicals; NIV for contemporary. Guidelines (also by e-mail); no catalog.

Fiction: Proposal/3 chapters; electronic submissions only (fictionsubmit@barbourbooks.com). Adult. "We publish 2 contemporary and 2 historical romances every 4 weeks. We cover all topics and settings. Specific guidelines available."

Tips: "Romance only, with a strong conservative-Christian theme. Read our books and study our style before submitting."

**Note: This publisher serviced by The Writer's Edge.

HEARTSONG PRESENTS/MYSTERIES, Imprint of Barbour Publishing Inc., PO Box 719, 1810 Barbour Dr., Uhrichsville, OH 44683. (740)922-6045. Fax (740)922-5948. E-mail: acqui sitions@barbourbooks.com. Website: www.barbourbooks.com. Editor's blog: www.editcafe .blogspot.com. Susan Downs, ed. Produces affordable, wholesome entertainment through a book club that also helps to enhance and spread the gospel. Publishes 32 titles/yr.; mass-market paperbacks. 25% of books from first-time authors. Will accept mss through agents. No subsidy. Prefers 63,000 wds. Royalty or outright purchase; advance. Average first printing 15,000-20,000. Publication within 9-12 mos. Considers simultaneous submissions. Responds in 3-6 mos. Accepts mss by e-mail. Guidelines (also by e-mail/Website).

Fiction: Proposal/3 chapters; no phone/fax query; e-query OK. Accepts only cozy mysteries with a romance plot thread.

Tips: "Cozy mysteries should feature an amateur sleuth in a setting that has a small-town 'feel.' The inciting crime should occur in the first chapter or two so the majority of the plot focuses on solving the 'whodunit' of the mystery. Study our specific guidelines thoroughly prior to proposal submission."

**Note: This publisher serviced by The Writer's Edge.

HEARTSPRING PUBLISHING, 223 W. Third St. (64801), PO Box 1132, Joplin MO 64802. Toll-free (800)289-3300. (417)623-6280. Fax (417)623-8250. E-mail: jmcclarnon@collegepress.com, or through Website: www.collegepress.com. Christian Church/Church of Christ. Submit to Acquisitions Editor. Nonacademic imprint of College Press Publishing Co. Publishes 15-20 titles/yr.; trade paperbacks. Receives 700 submissions annually. 25% of books from first-time authors. Will accept mss through agents. Reprints books. Prefers 250-300 pgs. Royalty 5-15% of net; no advance. Average first printing 3,000. Publication within 6 mos. Considers simultaneous submissions. Requires requested ms on disk; no e-mail submissions. Responds in 2-3 mos. Prefers NIV, NASB, NAS. Guidelines on Website; catalog for 9x12 SAE/5 stamps.

Nonfiction: Query only, then proposal/2-3 chapters; no phone/fax query.

Fiction: Christian fiction.

HENDRICKSON PUBLISHERS, 140 Summit St., PO Box 3473, Peabody MA 01961. (978)532-6546. Fax (978)573-8276. E-mail: editorial@hendrickson.com. Website: www.hendrickson .com. Submit to: Editorial Dept./Book Proposals. To provide biblically oriented books for reference, learning, and personal growth, and resources for pastors. Publishes 25-35 titles/yr.; hardcover, trade paperbacks. Receives 500-600 submissions annually. 10% of books from first-time authors. Will accept mss through agents. Reprints books. Prefers 150-500 pgs. Royalty; some advances. Average first printing 2,000. Publication within 12-18 mos. No simultaneous submissions. Responds in 4-6 mos. Prefers accepted ms by e-mail; will accept on disk. Follow *Chicago Manual of Style.* Prefers NIV. Guidelines (also by e-mail/Website); catalog for 9x12 SAE/$2.23 postage (mark "Media Mail").

Nonfiction: Query only first; fax, e-query OK. "Looking for popular reference material." Also publishes academic books through their Academic Book Division. No fiction, devotionals, children's books, or poetry.

Tips: "Best chance: Scholarly/academic or biblical studies. High standards for trade books."

**Note: This publisher serviced by The Writer's Edge and ChristianManuscriptSubmissions .com.

HENSLEY PUBLISHING, 6116 E. 32nd St., Tulsa OK 74135. (918)664-8520. Fax (918)664-8562. E-mail: editorial@hensleypublishing.com. Website: www.hensleypublishing.com. Terri

Kalfas, dir. of publishing. Goal is to get people studying the Bible instead of just reading books about the Bible; Bible study only. Publishes 5-10 titles/yr.; trade paperbacks. Receives 800 submissions annually. 50% of books from first-time authors. No mss through agents. No reprints. Royalty on net; some outright purchases; no advance. Average first printing 2,500. Publication within 12-18 mos. Considers simultaneous submissions. Requires requested ms in MAC format. Responds in 2 mos. Guidelines & catalog on Website.

Nonfiction: Query first, then proposal/first 3 chapters; no phone/fax query. "Looking for Bible studies of varying length for use by small or large groups, or individuals."

Special Needs: Bible study workbooks for small or large groups, or individuals.

**Note: This publisher serviced by The Writer's Edge.

HIDDEN BROOK PRESS, 109 Bayshore Rd., RR#4, Brighton ON K0K 1H0, Canada. (613)475-2368. E-mail: writers@hiddenbrookpress.com. Website: www.hiddenbrookpress.com. Richard M. Grove, ed./pub. Imprints: Hidden Brook Press, Arc Communications. Does hardcover, trade paperbacks, coffee-table books. Receives 1,000 submissions annually. 98% of books from first-time authors. Accepts mss through agents and authors directly. Does subsidy and print-on-demand, as well as royalty contracts. Reprints books. Royalty on retail or net; no advance. Average first printing 50-5,000. Accepts simultaneous submissions. Guidelines by e-mail.

Nonfiction: E-query or e-submissions. All topics.

Fiction: E-query or e-submissions. All genres.

+HIS WORK CHRISTIAN PUBLISHING, PO Box 5732, Ketchikan AK 99901. Fax (614)388-0664. E-mail: hiswork@hisworkpub.com. Website: www.hisworkpub.com. Angela J. Perez, acq. ed. (editor@hisworkpub.com). Books suitable for a Christian audience only. Estab. 2005. Publishes 3-5 titles/yr.; hardcover, trade paperbacks, electronic. Receives 40 submissions annually. 100% of books from first-time authors. No mss through agents. Reprints books. Royalty 10-20% on net. Publication within 1 yr. Considers simultaneous submissions. Responds in 1-3 mos. Guidelines/catalog on Website.

Nonfiction: Proposal/3 chapters or complete ms.

Fiction: Religious fiction. Proposal/3 chapters or complete ms.

HOPE PUBLISHING HOUSE, PO Box 60008, Pasadena CA 91106. (626)792-6123. Fax (626)792-2121. E-mail: hopepublishinghouse@gmail.com. Website: www.hope-pub.com. Southern California Ecumenical Council. Faith A. Sand, pub. Produces thinking books that challenge the faith community to be serious about their pilgrimage of faith. Imprint: New Paradigm Books. Publishes 6 titles/yr. Receives 40 submissions annually. 30% of books from first-time authors. No mss through agents. Reprints books. Prefers 200 pgs. Royalty 10% on net; no advance. Average first printing 3,000. Publication within 6 mos. No simultaneous submissions. Accepts mss by disk or e-mail. Responds in 3 mos. Prefers NRSV. No guidelines; catalog for 7x10 SAE/4 stamps.

Nonfiction: Query only first; no phone/fax query; e-query OK.

Tips: "Most open to a well-written manuscript, with correct grammar, that is provocative, original, challenging, and informative."

HOURGLASS BOOKS, 387 Northgate Rd., Lindenhurst IL 60046. E-mail: editor@hourglass books.org. Website: www.hourglassbooks.org/submissions.html. Gina Frangello and Molly McQuade, eds. Publishes anthologies of short stories assembled around a common theme. Accepts simultaneous submissions & reprints. Shared royalties for contributors to the anthologies. Guidelines on Website.

Fiction: Submit by e-mail (copied into message). Literary fiction only. Currently working on Occupational Hazards: Stories from the World of Work. No word limits, or fixed closing dates.

HOWARD BOOKS, 3117 N. 7th St., West Monroe LA 71291. (318)396-3122. Fax (318)397-1882. E-mail: denny.boultinghouse@simonandschuster.com. Website: www.howard

publishing.com. John Howard, pres.; Denny Boultinghouse, exec. ed.; submit to Manuscript Review Committee. A division of Simon & Schuster Inc. Imprint: Howard Kids/LSI. Publishes 65 titles/yr.; hardcover, trade paperbacks. Receives 1,000 submissions annually. 5% of books from first-time authors. Prefers 200-250 pgs. Negotiable royalty & advance. Average first printing 10,000. Publication within 16 mos. Considers simultaneous submissions. Accepted ms by e-mail. Responds in 6-8 mos. No disk. Prefers NIV. No guidelines/catalog.

Nonfiction: Accepting queries only, by e-mail; no phone queries.

Fiction: Accepting queries only, by e-mail. Adult; mystery suspense.

Tips: "Our authors must first be Christ-centered in their lives and writing, then qualified to write on the subject of choice. Public name recognition is a plus. Authors who are also public speakers usually have a ready-made audience."

**Note: This publisher serviced by The Writer's Edge and ChristianManuscriptSubmissions .com.

IDEALS CHILDREN'S BOOKS—See Ideals Publications.

IDEALS PUBLICATIONS, 2636 Elm Hill Pike, Ste. 120, Nashville TN 37214. E-mail: pjay@ guideposts.org. Website: www.idealsbooks.com. A Guideposts company. Peggy Schaefer, pub.; submit to Candy Cane Press Submissions, or Ideals Children's Book Submissions. No longer does adult Christian books. Publishes 25-30 children's titles/yr. Variable payment structure. Publication within 24-36 mos. Considers simultaneous submissions. Responds in 3 mos. Accepts manuscripts by mail only. Guidelines (also on Website); no catalog.

ILLUMINATION ARTS PUBLISHING INC., PO Box 1865, Bellevue WA 98009. (425)644-7185. Fax (425)644-9274. E-mail: JThompson@Illumin.com. Website: www.Illumin.com. Blog: www.illumin.com/blog. John M. Thompson, pres.; Ruth Thompson, ed. dir. Publishes high quality, enlightening children's picture books with enduring, inspirational, and spiritual values (inspirational, not religious). Publishes 1-4 titles/yr.; hardcover. Receives 2,000 submissions annually. 80% of books from first-time authors. Prefers 500-1,500 wds. Royalty on net; advance for artists. Responds in 3 mos. Considers simultaneous submissions. Guidelines (also on Website); catalog for 9x12 SASE.

Nonfiction: Complete ms/cover letter; no phone/fax/e-query. No accepted mss on disk or by e-mail.

Fiction: Complete ms/cover letter. Picture books under 1,000 wds. (preferred); 1,500 wds. max. No chapter books.

Special Needs: Picture books only.

Tips: "Our current preference is books for the youngest readers—4 to 6 years. Include a description of what makes your book special or different from others currently on the market."

INKLING BOOKS, 6528 Phinney Ave. N., Seattle WA 98103. (206)365-1624. E-mail: editor@ inklingbooks.com. Website: www.InklingBooks.com. Michael W. Perry, pub. Publishes 6 titles/yr.; hardcover, trade paperbacks. No mss through agents. Reprints books. Prefers 150-400 pgs. No advance. Print-on-demand. Publication within 2 mos. No guidelines or catalog. Not currently accepting submissions.

INTERNATIONAL AWAKENING PRESS, 139 N. Washington, PO Box 232, Wheaton IL 60187. Phone/fax (630)653-8616. E-mail: internationalawakening@juno.com. Website: www .intl-awaken.com. Intl. Awakening Ministries Inc. Richard Owen Roberts, ed./pres. Scholarly books on religious awakenings or revivals. Publishes 4 titles/yr. Receives 12 submissions annually. Reprints books. Royalty negotiated; no advance. Average first printing 3,000. Publication within 6 mos. Responds in 3 mos. Prefers requested ms on disk. Any translation; no paraphrases. No guidelines; free catalog.

Nonfiction: Query only; no phone/fax/e-query. "Looking for scholarly theology, especially Bible commentaries, church history, and revival-related material."

Also Does: Booklets, pamphlets, tracts.

Photos: Accepts freelance photos for book covers.

Tips: "Most open to scholarly books."

INTERVARSITY PRESS, Box 1400, Downers Grove IL 60515-1426. Receptionist: (630)734-4000 or 4036. Fax (630)734-4200. E-mail: email@ivpress.com. Website: www.ivpress.com. InterVarsity Christian Fellowship. Andrew T. LePeau, ed. dir.; submit to General Book Editor or Academic Editor. IVP books are characterized by a thoughtful, biblical approach to the Christian life that transforms the hearts, souls, and minds of readers in the university, church, and the world, on topics ranging from spiritual disciplines to apologetics, to current issues, to theology. Imprints: IVP Academic (Gary Deddo, ed.), IVP Connect (Cindy Bunch, ed.), IVP General (Al Hsu, ed.). Publishes 80-90 titles/yr.; hardcover, trade paperbacks, mass-market paperbacks. Receives 2,500 submissions annually. 15% of books from first-time authors. Will accept mss through agents. Reprints books. Prefers 50,000 wds. or 200 pgs. Negotiable royalty on retail or outright purchase; negotiable advance. Average first printing 5,000. Publication within 12 mos. Considers simultaneous submissions. Responds in 3 mos. Prefers NIV, NRSV. Accepts e-mail submissions after acceptance. Guidelines on Website; catalog for 9x12 SAE/5 stamps.

Nonfiction: Query only first, with detailed letter according to submissions guidelines, then proposal with 2 chapters: no phone/fax/e-query.

Ethnic Books: Especially looking for ethnic writers (black, Hispanic, Asian American).

Also Does: Booklets, 5,000 wds.; pamphlets; e-books.

Blogs: www.ivpress.com/blogs/behindthebooks; www.ivpress.com/blogs/andyunedited; www.ivpress.com/blogs/addenda-errata.

Tips: "Most open to books written by pastors (though not collections of sermons) or other church staff, by professors, by leaders in Christian organizations. Authors need to bring resources for publicizing and selling their own books, such as a Website, an organization they are part of that will promote their books, speaking engagements, well-known people they know personally who will endorse and promote their book, writing articles for national publication, etc."

**Note: This publisher serviced by The Writer's Edge and ChristianManuscriptSubmissions .com.

INVISIBLE COLLEGE PRESS, PO Box 209, Woodbridge VA 22194-0209. (703)590-4005. E-mail: submissions@invispress.com. Website: www.invispress.com. Dr. Phillip Reynolds, nonfiction ed.; Paul Mossinger, fiction ed. This publisher majors on the paranormal, science fiction, spiritual, religious, etc. Publishes 12 titles/yr.; trade paperbacks. Receives 150 submissions annually. 75% of books from first-time authors. Will accept mss through agents. No reprints. Prefers 70,000 wds. or more. Royalty 10-25% on net; $100 advance. Publication within 4 mos. Considers simultaneous submissions. Responds in 1-3 mos. Guidelines & catalog on Website.

Nonfiction: E-query preferred (copied into message), or query/SASE/proposal package/1 chapter. Reference, religion, spirituality.

Fiction: E-query preferred, or query/synopsis & 1 chapter.

JEBAIRE PUBLISHING, PO Box 843, Snellville GA 30078. (770)823-9017. E-mail: info@jebairepublishing.com. Website: www.jebairepublishing.com. Shannon Clark, acq. ed. Our mission is "to give gifted writers a voice and hungry souls a full meal." Publishes 2-4 titles/yr.; trade paperbacks. 50% of books from first-time authors. No mss through agents. No subsidy, print-on-demand, or reprints. Prefers 125-250 pgs. Royalty 12-15% on net; no advance. Average first printing 1,000. Publication within 12 mos. Considers simultaneous submissions. Responds in 4-6 weeks (to proposals). Requires accepted mss on disk. Guidelines (also by e-mail); no catalog.

Nonfiction: Proposal/2-3 chapters; no phone/fax query; e-query OK. "Looking for women's devotionals, Christian living, personal growth, and faith."

Photos/Artwork: Accepts freelance photos for book covers; open to queries from freelance artists.

Contest: Sponsors an annual contest for youth, ages 9-16. Essays 700-1,200 words on specific topics. Submit between April 1 and June 15. Guidelines available. Submissions must be mailed to above address. Twenty winners will have their work published in a nonfiction anthology and receive a copy of the book.

Tips: "We look for writers who have an 'approachable' writing style. We want our readers to feel uplifted and encouraged rather than 'talked down to' or discouraged."

JIREH PUBLISHING CO., PO Box 1911, Suisun City CA 94585-1911. (425)645-0423. E-mail: jaholman@jirehpublishing.com. E-mail inquires first to: jireh_subms@jirehpublishing .com, or through Website: www.jirehpublishing.com. Janice Holman, ed. To spread the gospel and teach the Word of God throughout the world. Publishes 2-5 titles/yr. Receives 100 submissions annually. 95% of books from first-time authors. Will accept mss through agents. No reprints. Prefers 96+ pgs. Royalty 10-12% of net; no advance. Average first printing 500-1,000. Publication within 9-12 mos. Considers simultaneous submissions. Responds in 2-8 days. Guidelines/catalog on Website.

Nonfiction: Proposal/3 chapters; fax/e-query OK (copied into message). "Looking for manuscript which helps teach believers how to walk by faith and receive all the blessings that God has for them." Likes to see first and last chapter.

Fiction: Proposal/3 chapters. Adult only in romance/suspense and mystery. Looking for Christian Sci-fi, thriller, and fantasy writers for e-books. Contact them at jaholman@ jirehpublishing.com.

Also Does: E-books.

Photos: Accepts freelance photos for book covers.

Tips: "We are looking for authors who would like to work with us to create e-books (initially fiction titles)." Responds only to accepted manuscripts.

JOHNS HOPKINS UNIVERSITY PRESS, 2715 N. Charles St., Baltimore MD 21218-4363. (410)516-6900. Fax (410)516-6968. E-mail: tcl@press.jhu.edu. Website: www.press.jhu .edu. Nondenominational. Trevor Lipscombe, ed-in-chief. Publishes 4-6 religious titles/yr.; hardcover, trade paperbacks. Receives 50-75 submissions annually. 10-25% of books from first-time authors. Will accept mss through agents. Reprints books. Prefers 100,000 wds. Royalty. Publication within 1 yr. Considers simultaneous submissions only on proposals. Guidelines/catalog on Website.

Nonfiction: Query only; no phone/fax/e-query.

JOSSEY-BASS, a Wiley Imprint, 989 Market St., 5th Fl., San Francisco CA 94103-1741. (415) 782-3145. Fax (415)433-0499. E-mail: Sfullert@jbp.com. Website: www.jossey-bass.com. John Wiley & Sons Inc. Sheryl Fullerton, exec. ed. Because of a nondenominational focus on Christian spirituality and general corporate ownership, they are able to reach the broadest range of markets and readership. Imprint: Religion and Spirituality. Publishes 40 titles/yr.; hardcover, trade paperbacks. Receives hundreds of submissions annually. Up to 10% of books from first-time authors. Will accept mss through agents. No reprints. Prefers 60,000 wds. or 250 pgs. Royalty negotiable on net; advance. Average first printing 10,000. Publication within 1 yr. Considers simultaneous submissions. Responds in 1 mo. Prefers NRSV, NIV. Guidelines (also by e-mail); free catalog.

Nonfiction: Proposal/2 chapters; e-query OK. "Looking for fresh, vital resources to deepen faith and Christian identity."

Tips: "Our mission is to provide innovative, thoughtful, and useful resources for people on their faith journeys. Authors with compelling ideas and an established audience (and/or track record) from which to promote and market themselves, as well as clearly relevant credentials and expertise will be enthusiastically received. We are not interested in books that would be considered 'more of the same,' nor in books that are narrow or marginal in their perspective. We are particularly interested in books for the emerging church and those that encourage a generous orthodoxy. Create an excellent proposal that clearly presents your idea in a way that is viable for its market and fully describes your platform."

JOURNEY STONE CREATIONS, 3533 Danbury Rd., Fairfield OH 45014. (513)860-5616. Fax (513)860-0176. E-mail: pat@jscbooks.com. Website: www.jscbooks.com. Not currently accepting submissions.

JUBILANT PRESS: An Electronic & Print Publisher, PO Box 6421, Longmont CO 80501. E-mail: jubilantpress@aol.com. Website: www.JubilantPress.com. Supports Right to the Heart Ministries. Linda Shepherd, & Rebekah Montgomery, pubs. Publishes downloadable e-books with instant information to change your life. Publishes 10 e-titles/yr., plus 1 print bk. Acquires print & e-books by invitation only. 0% of books from first-time authors. Will accept mss through agents. Reprints books. Prefers 20-100 pgs. Pays for the right to publish, plus a percentage of author's online sales (author must have an active Web page); variable advance. Publication within 6 mos. Prefers NIV. Guidelines provided for specific projects.

Nonfiction: Brief e-mail query only; no phone/fax query.

Special Needs: Women's ministry helps, banquet-planning helps, speaking and writing helps.

Photos: Accepts freelance photos for book covers.

Tips: "Submissions accepted by invitation only. Best to send a brief e-mail with description of your idea. Please see our Web page to best understand our publishing program. Most open to a how-to, informational book with a need-to-know marketability."

JUDSON PRESS, PO Box 851, Valley Forge PA 19482-0851. Toll-free (800)4-JUDSON. Fax (610) 768-2441. E-mail: jpacquisitions@abc-usa.org. Website: www.judsonpress.com. American Baptist Churches USA/National Ministries. Rebecca Irwin-Diehl, ed. Publishes Christ-centered leadership resources for the transformation of persons, congregations, communities, and cultures. Publishes 12-15 titles/yr.; hardcover, trade paperbacks. Receives 800 submissions annually. 20% of books from first-time authors. Will accept mss through agents. No subsidy; print-on-demand rarely. Rarely reprints books. Prefers 100-200 pgs., or 30,000-75,000 wds. Royalty 10-15% on net; some work-for-hire agreements or outright purchases; occasional advance $300. Average first printing 4,500. Publication within 1 yr. Considers simultaneous submissions. Requires accepted submissions on disk or by e-mail. Responds in 4-6 mos. Prefers NRSV. Guidelines on Website; catalog for 9x12 SAE/4 stamps.

Nonfiction: Query or proposal/2-3 chapters; fax/e-query OK.

Ethnic Books: African American & Hispanic.

Artwork: Open to queries from freelance artists. Attn: Wendy Ronga, creative dir.

Tips: "Most open to books that are unique, compelling, and practical. Theologically and socially we are a moderate publisher. And we like to see a detailed marketing plan from an author committed to partnering with us."

**Note: This publisher serviced by The Writer's Edge.

+JESSICA KINGSLEY PUBLISHERS, 116 Pentonville Rd., London N1 9JB, United Kingdom. Phone: (+44)20 7833 2307. Fax (+44)20 7837 2917. E-mail: Post@JKP.com. Website: www.JKP.com. Jessica Kingsley, CEO; submit to: New Book Proposals at JKP. Publishes books that create social change. Imprint: Singing Dragon. Publishes 45+ titles/yr.; hardcover, trade paperback. Receives 300+ submissions annually. 60% of books from first-time authors. Will accept mss through agents. Print on demand for older books. Reprints books. Any length. Royalty 5-10% on net; no advance. Average first printing 1,500. Publication within 6 mos.

No simultaneous submissions. Responds in up to 6 mos. Requires accepted mss on disk or by e-mail. Prefers NIV. Guidelines (also by e-mail); free catalog.

Nonfiction: Proposal/2 chapters; no phone/fax query; e-query OK.

Special Needs: Practical theology.

Photos: Accepts freelance photos for book covers.

Tips: "Most open to books that combine theory with practice; books for practitioners."

KIRK HOUSE PUBLISHERS, PO Box 390759, Minneapolis MN 55439. Toll-free (888)696-1828. (952)835-1828. Fax (952)835-2613. E-mail: publisher@kirkhouse.com. Website: www.kirkhouse.com. Leonard Flachman, pub. Imprints: Lutheran University Press, Quill House Publishers. Publishes 6-8 titles/yr.; hardcover, trade paperbacks, coffee-table books. Receives hundreds of submissions annually. 95% of books from first-time authors. No mss through agents. No reprints. Royalty 10-15% on net; no advance. Average first printing 500-3,000. Publication within 6 mos. No simultaneous submissions. Requires disk or e-mail submission. Responds in 2-3 wks. No guidelines; free catalog.

Nonfiction: Proposal/1-2 chapters.

+KNB PUBLICATIONS, PO Box 831648, Stone Mountain GA 30083. (404)294-1457. Fax (404)294-9732. E-mail: info@knb-publications.com. Website: www.knbpublications.com. Kendra Norman-Bellamy, pub. Guidelines on Website. Incomplete topical listings.

Nonfiction: Query by mail or e-mail; no complete mss without permission.

Fiction: Query by mail or e-mail; no complete mss without permission.

KNIGHT GEORGE PUBLISHING HOUSE, LLC, 24 Leslie Ln., #307, Waterford MI 48328 (moving, check Website for current address before submitting). (586)481-0466. E-mail: authors@knightgeorge.com. Website: www.KnightGeorge.com. Matt Jones, pres. A privately owned, independent provider of innovative Christian educational materials to Lutherans. New publisher; hardcover, trade paperbacks. 16% of books from first-time authors. No mss through agents. No subsidy or print-on-demand. Royalty 2-15% of net; no advance. Considers simultaneous submissions. Responds in 3 mos. Accepted mss on disk. Guidelines (also by e-mail); no catalog.

Nonfiction: Proposal/2 chapters; no phone/fax query; e-query OK.

Fiction: Query only first. Children's stories and classroom reading books. We seek to compete with Golden Books.

Special Needs: Classroom materials: textbooks, workbooks, hands-on learning aids. Innovative teaching methods and newest technology is preferred.

Also Does: Board games, computer games, all hands-on learning methods.

Photos/Artwork: Accepts freelance photos for book covers; open to queries from freelance artists.

Tips: "We prefer books be submitted complete with original artwork. Most open to textbooks (teacher's editions should contain full student's edition within them), workbooks (as applicable), and projects, preferably as a package. Find new and creative ways to teach. We are a publishing house, but will consider any other products (within pricing limits) that educate. Of course, God should be at least implicit, but don't force biblical examples in your work."

KREGEL KIDZONE, PO Box 2607, Grand Rapids MI 49501-2607. (616)451-4775. Fax (616)451-9330. E-mail: kregelbooks@kregel.com. Website: www.kregelpublications.com. Publishes books and collateral materials that target both the spiritual and educational development of children. Royalty; some outright purchases. Publication within 16 mos. Responds in 4 mos. Catalog for 9x12 SAE/3 stamps. No longer reviewing unsolicited queries, proposals, or manuscripts, except through agents, Writer's Edge or ChristianManuscriptSubmissions.com.

KREGEL PUBLICATIONS, PO Box 2607, Grand Rapids MI 49501-2607. (616)451-4775. Fax (616)451-9330. E-mail: kregelbooks@kregel.com. Website: www.kregelpublications.com.

Blog: www.kregelpublications.blogspot.com. Evangelical/Conservative. Dennis R. Hillman, pub.; Jim Weaver, academic & professional books ed.; submissions policy on Website. To provide tools for ministry and Christian growth from a conservative, evangelical perspective. Imprints: Kregel Kidzone (see separate listing), Kregel Academic and Professional, Kregel Classics. Publishes 75 titles/yr.; hardcover, trade paperbacks. 20% of books from first-time authors. Prefers mss through agents. Reprints books. Royalty 8-16% of net; some outright purchases; advance $200-2,000. Average first printing 5,000. Publication within 12 mos. Considers simultaneous submissions. Responds in 4 mos. Guidelines by e-mail; catalog for 9x12 SAE/3 stamps. No longer reviewing unsolicited queries, proposals, or manuscripts, except through agents, Writer's Edge, or ChristianManuscriptSubmissions.com.

Nonfiction: "Most open to contemporary issues or academic works."

Fiction: For all ages. "Looking for high-quality contemporary fiction with strong Christian themes and characters."

Tips: "We are adding more fiction, but again, we are very selective. Strong story lines with an evident spiritual emphasis are required."

**Note: This publisher serviced by The Writer's Edge and ChristianManuscriptSubmissions.com.

LANGMARC PUBLISHING, PO Box 90488, Austin TX 78709-0488. (512)394-0989. Fax (512) 394-0829. E-mail: langmarc@booksails.com. Website: www.langmarc.com. Lutheran. Lois Qualben, pub. Focuses on spiritual growth of readers. Publishes 3-5 titles/yr.; hardcover, trade paperbacks. Receives 230 submissions annually. 60% of books from first-time authors. Will accept mss through agents. No reprints. Prefers 150-300 pgs. Royalty 10-14% on net; no advance. Average first printing varies. Publication usually within 18 mos. Considers simultaneous submissions. Responds in 3 mos. Requires requested ms on disk. Prefers NIV. Guidelines on Website); free catalog.

Nonfiction: Proposal/3 chapters; no phone query. "Most open to inspirational books."

LARSON PUBLICATIONS/PBPF, 4936 NYS Rte. 414, Burdett NY 14818-9729. (607)546-9342. Fax (607)546-9344. E-mail: larson@lightlink.com. Website: www.larsonpublications.org. Paul Cash, dir. Books cover philosophy, psychology, religion, and spirituality. Publishes 4-5 titles/yr.; hardcover, trade paperbacks. Receives 1,000 submissions annually. 5% of books from first-time authors. Some reprints. Variable royalty; rarely gives an advance. Publication within 1-2 yrs. Considers simultaneous submissions. Requires accepted mss on disk. Responds in 4-6 mos. Prefers NIV. No guidelines/catalog.

Nonfiction: Query by mail/outline & SASE; no phone/fax/e-query.

LEGACY PRESS, PO Box 261129, San Diego CA 92196. Toll-free (800)638-4428. Toll-free fax (800)331-0297. E-mail: editor@rainbowpublishers.com. Website: www.rainbowpublishers.com. Rainbow Publishers. Submit to The Editor. Publishes nondenominational nonfiction and fiction for children in the evangelical Christian market. Publishes 15 titles/yr. Receives 250 submissions annually. 50% of books from first-time authors. Reprints books. Prefers 150 pgs. & up. Royalty 8% & up on net; advance $500+. Average first printing 5,000. Publication within 2 yrs. Considers simultaneous submissions. Prefers requested ms on disk. Responds in 3 mos. Prefers NIV. Guidelines (also on Website); catalog for 9x12 SAE/2 stamps.

Nonfiction: Proposal/3-5 chapters; no e-queries. "Looking for nonfiction for girls and boys ages 2-12."

Fiction: Proposal/3 chapters. For ages 2-12 only. Must include an additional component beyond fiction (e.g., devotional, Bible activities, etc.)

Special Needs: Nonfiction for ages 10-12, particularly Christian twists on current favorites, such as cooking, jewelry making, games, etc.

Tips: "All books must offer solid Bible teaching in a fun, meaningful way that appeals to kids. Research popular nonfiction for kids in the general market, then figure out how to present those fun ideas in ways that teach the Bible. As a smaller publisher, we seek to publish unique niche books that stand out in the market."

LEGACY PUBLISHERS INTERNATIONAL, 1301 S. Clinton St., Denver CO 80247. (303)283-7480. Fax (303)283-7536. E-mail: dmiller@hccweb.org, or through Website: www.legacy publishersinternational.com. Michele Leonard, acq. ed. To pass the Gospel of Jesus Christ on to future generations through the written word. Accepts some freelance. Catalog. Incomplete topical listings.

LIBROS LIGUORI, 1 Liguori Dr., Liguori MO 63057-9999. (636)464-2500. Fax (636)464-8449. E-mail: amedina@liguori.org. Website: www.liguori.org. Spanish division of Liguori Publications. Jose Antonio Medina (636-223-1471), ed. To spread the gospel in the Hispanic community by means of low-cost publications. Publishes 5 titles/yr. Receives 6-8 submissions annually. 5% of books from first-time authors. Prefers up to 30,000 wds. Royalty 8-10% of net or outright purchases of $450 (book and booklet authors get royalties; pamphlet authors get $400 on acceptance); advance. Average first printing 3,500-5,000. Publication within 18 mos. No simultaneous submissions. Requires accepted mss on electronic file. Responds in 4-8 wks. Free guidelines/catalog.

Nonfiction: Proposal/2 chapters; fax/e-query OK. "Looking for issues families face today—substance abuse, unwanted pregnancies, etc.; family relations; religion's role in immigrants' experiences, pastoral Catholic faith."

Ethnic Books: Focuses on Spanish-language products.

Also Does: Pamphlets, booklets, tracts, PC software, clip art.

Tips: "Contact us before writing. It's much easier to work together from the beginning of a project. We need books on the Hispanic experience in the U.S. Keep it concise, avoid academic/theological jargon, and stick to the tenets of the Catholic faith. Avoid abstract arguments."

LIFE CHANGING MEDIA, 10777 W. Sample Rd., Unit 302, Coral Springs FL 33065-3768. (954)554-1921. E-mail: submissions@lifechangingmedia.net, or through Website: www .lifechangingmedia.net. Life Changing Publications. Paul Gundotra, pres.; Sindhu Roy, chief ed. Mass-market paperbacks. Royalty on retail; no advance. Average first print run varies. Publication within 3 mos. Considers simultaneous submissions (if indicated). Prefers accepted mss by e-mail. Responds in 30-60 days. Guidelines by e-mail/Website; no catalog.

Nonfiction: Query first; e-query OK. "Please include a description of the book project, brief bio including publishing history. Let us know if you have the ability for public speaking."

Photos: Accepts freelance photos for book covers.

Tips: "Looking for books that entertain, inform, but most of all that are life changing."

LIFE CYCLE BOOKS, PO Box 1008, Niagara Falls NY 14304-1008. Toll-free (800)214-5849. (416)690-5860. Toll-free fax (888)690-8532. (416)690-8532. E-mail: paulb@lifecycle books.com. Website: www.lifecyclebooks.com. Paul Broughton, gen. mngr.; submit to The Editor. Specializes in pro-life material. Publishes 6 titles/yr.; trade paperbacks. Receives 100 submissions annually. No mss through agents. 50% of books from first-time authors. Reprints books. Royalty 8-10% of net; outright purchase of brochure material, $250+; advance $250-1,000. SUBSIDY PUBLISHES 10%. Publication within 1 yr. No simultaneous submissions. Responds in 1 mo. Catalog on Website.

Nonfiction: Query or complete ms. "Our emphasis is on pro-life and pro-family titles."

Tips: "We are most involved in publishing leaflets of about 1,500 words, and we welcome submissions of manuscripts of this length."

LIFESONG PUBLISHERS, PO Box 183, Somis CA 93066. (805)655-5644. Fax (614)455-5030. E-mail: mailbox@lifesongpublishers.com. Website: www.lifesongpublishers.com. Laurie Donahue, pub. Provides Christian families with tools that will aid in spiritual development of family members. Publishes 1-4 titles/yr.; trade paperbacks. No mss through agents. No reprints. WOULD CONSIDER SUBSIDY. Royalty 10% on net; small advance. Publication within 12 mos. Considers simultaneous submissions. Responds in 2-4 wks. No guidelines; catalog for 9x12 SAE/2 stamps. Not included in topical listings.

Nonfiction: Proposal/3 chapters; e-query OK. "Looking for an author with an existing ministry."

LIFT EVERY VOICE, 820 N. LaSalle Blvd., Chicago IL 60610. (312)329-2140. Fax (312)329-4157. E-mail: lifteveryvoice@moody.edu. Website: www.lifteveryvoicebooks.com. African American imprint of Moody Publishers. Moody Bible Institute and Institute for Black Family Development. Cynthia Ballenger, acq. ed.; Nora Darby, asst. coord. To advance the cause of Christ through publishing African American Christians who educate, edify, and disciple Christians. Publishes 15 titles/yr. Receives 50-60 submissions annually. 98% of books from first-time authors. Will accept mss through agents. No subsidy. Reprints books. Prefers 40,000 wds., or 250 pgs. Royalty on retail; advance. Average first printing 5,000. Publication within 12 mos. Considers simultaneous submissions. Responds biannually. Accepts requested ms by e-mail. Prefers KJV. Guidelines; free catalog.

Nonfiction: Proposal/4 chapters; e-query OK.

Fiction: Proposal/4 chapters; e-query OK. For all ages. Send for fiction writers' guidelines.

Special Needs: Children's fiction, especially for boys; nonfiction books for teen girls.

Ethnic Books: This is an African American imprint.

Contest: Essay contest; August 31 deadline. See Website for details.

Photos: Accepts freelance photos for book covers.

Tips: "Looking for quality fiction and nonfiction. good, strong, and focused writing is what LEV is looking for, but mostly writing that is Christ-centered and speaks to the African American community."

**Note: This publisher serviced by ChristianManuscriptSubmissions.com.

LIGHTHOUSE PUBLISHING, 5531 Dufferin Dr., Savage MN 55378. (952)447-8604. E-mail: Andy Overett@lighthousechristianpublishing.com. Website: www.lighthousechristianpublishing.com. Nondenominational. Andy Overett, ed.; submit to Chris Wright, sr. ed. To distribute a wide variety of Christian media to vast parts of the globe so people can hear about the gospel for free or very inexpensively (e-books, comics, movies, and online radio). Imprints: Lighthouse Publishing, Lighthouse Music Publishing. Publishes 20-30 titles/yr.; hardcover, trade paperbacks, mass-market paperbacks. Receives 100-150 submissions annually. 60% of books from first-time authors. Will accept mss through agents. SUBSIDY PUBLISHES 15-20%. Does print-on-demand. Reprints books. Any length. Royalty on net; no advance. Average first printing 300-400. Publication within 6 mos. Considers simultaneous submissions. Prefers submissions by e-mail. Responds in 6-8 wks. Prefers NAS. Guidelines by e-mail; catalog $10.

Nonfiction: Complete ms by e-mail (info@lighthousechristianpublishing.com). Any topic. "Looking for children's books, Intelligent Design, and science."

Fiction: Complete ms by e-mail. Any genre, for all ages.

Ethnic Books: Publishes books for almost all foreign language markets.

Also Does: Comics, animation on CD, music CDs, plans to do Christian computer games in the future.

Photos/Artwork: Accepts freelance photos for book covers; open to queries from freelance artists.

Tips: "Most open to children's books, comics, and graphic novels; scientific and academic works with a Christian perspective."

LIGHTHOUSE TRAILS PUBLISHING, PO Box 958, Silverton OR 97381. (503)873-9092. Fax (503)873-3879. E-mail: editors@lighthousetrails.com. Website: www.lighthousetrails.com. Blog: www.lighthousetrailsresearch.com/blog. David Dombrowski, acq. ed. Books that bring clarity and light to areas of spiritual darkness or deception, and to preserving the integrity of God's Word in all our books. Imprint: Falling Sparrow Series. Publishes 4 titles/yr. Receives 100-150 submissions annually. 35% of books from first-time authors. Will accept mss through agents. No subsidy or print-on-demand. Reprints books. Prefers 160-300 pgs. Royalty 12-17% of net, or 20% of retail; advance $1,000. Average first printing 2,500. Publication within 6-9 mos. Considers simultaneous submissions. Requires accepted ms on disk or by e-mail. Responds in 8 wks. Prefers KJV, NKJV, NAS. Guidelines on Website; free catalog.

Nonfiction: Proposal/2 chapters; no phone/fax query; e-query OK.

Fiction: Proposal/2-3 chapters. For teens and adults. "We are looking for a fiction or fiction series that would include elements from our books exposing the emerging church and mystical spirituality; bible prophecy/eschatological."

Special Needs: Will look at autobiographies or biographies about people who have courageously endured through overwhelming circumstances (Holocaust survivors, child-abuse survivors, etc.) with a definite emphasis on the Lord's grace and faithfulness.

Artwork: Open to queries from freelance artists.

Tips: "No poetry at this time. Any book we consider will not only challenge the more scholarly reader, but also be able to reach those who may have less experience and comprehension. Our books will include human interest and personal experience scenarios as a means of getting the point across. Read a couple of our books to better understand the style of writing we are looking for. Also check our research Website for an in-depth look at who we are (www.lighthousetrailsresearch.com)."

LIGUORI PUBLICATIONS, 1 Liguori Dr., Liguori MO 63057-9999. Toll-free (800)325-9521. (636)464-2500. Fax (636)464-8449. Website: www.liguori.org. Catholic/Redemptorists. Submit to manuscriptsubmission@liguori.org. Spreading the good news of the gospel by means of low-cost publications. Imprints: Libros Liguori (Spanish language), Liguori Books. Publishes 50 titles/yr.; trade paperbacks. Receives 20-30 submissions annually. 5% of books from first-time authors. Reprints books. Prefers up to 30,000 wds. for books; 40-100 pgs. for booklets; pamphlets 16-18 pgs. Book & booklet authors get royalties; pamphlet authors receive a flat fee on acceptance; advance varies. No simultaneous submissions. Requires requested ms by e-mail attachment. Responds in 4-8 wks. Requires NRSV. Guidelines on Website; free catalog.

Nonfiction: Proposal/2 chapters; fax/e-query OK. "Looking for issues families face today—substance abuse, unwanted pregnancies, etc.; family relations; pastoral Catholic faith."

Ethnic Books: Publishes books in Spanish. See separate listing for Libros Liguori.

Also Does: Booklets, pamphlets, tracts; books on Catholic faith.

Tips: "Keep it concise, avoid academic/theological jargon, and stick to the tenets of the Catholic faith. Avoid abstract arguments. Manuscripts accepted by us must have strong, middle-of-the-road, practical spirituality."

LILLENAS PUBLISHING CO., Program Builder Series and Other Drama Resources, Box 419527, Kansas City MO 64141-6527. (816)931-1900. Fax (816)412-8390. E-mail: drama@lillenas .com. Website: www.lillenasdrama.com. Kimberly R. Messer, product line mngr. Imprint: Lillenas Drama Resources. Publishes 12+ titles/yr.; mass-market paperbacks or electronic versions. Will accept mss through agents. Royalty 10% of retail for drama resources; outright purchase of program builder material; no advance. No simultaneous submissions. Responds in 3-4 mos. Guidelines on Website; catalog.

Drama Resources: Query or complete ms; phone/fax/e-query OK. Accepts readings, one-act and full-length plays, program and service features, monologues, and sketch collections. Religion & life issues.

Special Needs: Sketch collections and plays; full-length and one-act plays for adults. Seasonal; children's or youth 5-minute sketches.

Tips: "We are focused on providing ministry tools to churches—both large and small. Most open to biblically based sketches and plays that have small- to medium-size casts and are easy to stage; short sketches—4 to 8 minutes."

+LION AND LAMB PUBLICATIONS, 8 Three Coins Ct., Fountain Inn SC 29644. (864)409-0015. E-mail: info@LionandLambPublications.com. Website: www.LionandLambPublications.com. Andriea Chenot, ed.; submit to: submissions@LionandLambPublications.com. To win souls, equip saints, and strengthen faith through the power of God's Word; and be a part of God opening doors for new authors. Publishes 25 titles/yr.; hardcover. Receives 300 submissions annually. 80% of books from first-time authors. Will accept mss through agents. Does some print-on-demand. No reprints. Royalty 10-15% on retail; variable advance. Average first printing 5,000. Publication within 6-12 mos. Considers simultaneous submissions. Responds in 2-4 wks. Accepted mss on disk or by e-mail. Prefers NIV or Good News Bible. Guidelines on Website.

Nonfiction: Proposal/6 chapters; e-query OK.

Fiction: Complete ms. For all ages.

Special Needs: Ministry resources primarily for children and youth ministries; Sunday school curriculum; Christian homeschool curriculum.

Also Does: Computer games and other specialty products

Photos/Artists: Accepts freelance photos for book covers; open to queries from freelance artists.

Tips: "We are most open to ministry resources; and most concerned with books that help win souls, equip saints, and strengthen faith."

LION PUBLISHING, 4050 Lee Vance View, Colorado Springs CO 80918-7102. (719)536-3271. David C. Cook. Accepts no freelance submissions.

+LITTLE LAUREN BOOKS, PO Box 145, Summit Point WV 25446. (304)886-4272. Website: www.LittleLauren.com. Lauren's Grace Inc. Jessica Adriel, pub. Books for teens. Publishes 2-3 titles/yr.; trade paperbacks. Receives 150 submissions annually. 90% of books from first-time authors. Prefers mss through agents. No reprints. Does print on demand. Prefers 60,000-75,000 wds. Royalty on net; no advance. Average first printing up to 1,000 or POD. Publication within 9-15 mos. Responds in 3 wks. Guidelines on Website; no catalog.

Nonfiction: Proposal/2-3 chapters; no phone/fax query; e-query preferred.

Fiction: Proposal/2-3 chapters; no phone/fax query; e-query preferred. For all ages. "Looking for YA fiction from new authors with a fresh style."

Special Needs: Teen-centered titles.

Also Does: T-shirts; novelty items.

Tips: "We are looking for a solid message geared for secular teens or used by Christian teens to be given to a friend as a tool for salvation."

**Note: This publisher serviced by The Writer's Edge.

LITTLE SIMON INSPIRATIONS, 1230 Avenue of the Americas, New York NY 10020. Website: www.simonsayskids.com. Faith-based imprint of Simon & Schuster Children's Publishing Division. No unsolicited manuscripts.

THE LITURGICAL PRESS, PO Box 7500, St. John's Abbey, Collegeville MN 56321-7500. Toll-free (800)858-5450, ext. 2218. (320)363-2213. Toll-free fax (800)445-5899. (320)363-3299. E-mail: Sales@litpress.org. Website: www.litpress.org. St. John's Abbey (a Benedictine group). Imprints: Liturgical Press Books, Michael Glazier Books, Pueblo Books. Peter Dwyer, dir.; submit to Hans Christoffersen, ed. dir. (hchristoffe@csbsju.edu). Publishes 75 titles/yr. Prefers 100-300 pgs. Royalty 10% of net; some outright purchases; no advance. No simultaneous submissions. Responds in 3 mos. Guidelines (also on Website); free catalog.

Nonfiction: Query/proposal. Adult only.

Tips: "We publish liturgical, scriptural, theological, pastoral, and monastic wisdom resources."

LITURGY TRAINING PUBLICATIONS, Archdiocese of Chicago, 1800 N. Hermitage Ave., Chicago IL 60622-1101. Toll-free (800)933-1800. (773)486-8970. Fax (773)486-7094. E-mail: editorialmanager@ltp.org. Website: www.LTP.org. Catholic/Archdiocese of Chicago. Donna M. Crilly, mng. ed. Resources for liturgy in Christian life. Imprint: Hillenbrand Books (Kevin Thornton, ed.). Publishes 25 titles/yr.; hardcover, trade paperbacks, coffee-table books. Receives 150 submissions annually. 25% of books from first-time authors. Will accept mss through agents. No subsidy or print-on-demand. Reprints books. Variable royalty on net or work-for-hire; advance. Average first printing 2,000-5,000. Publication within 18 mos. Considers simultaneous submissions. Accepts full mss by e-mail. Responds in 3 mos. Prefers RNAB, NRSV Catholic edition. Guidelines (also by e-mail/Website); free catalog.

Nonfiction: Proposal/1 chapter; no phone/fax/e-query.

Ethnic Books: Hispanic.

Photos/Artwork: Accepts freelance photos for book covers; open to queries from freelance artists.

Tips: "Our focus is on providing materials to aid in participation in Catholic worship."

LIVING THE GOOD NEWS, 600 Grant St., Ste. 400, Denver CO 80203. Fax (303)832-4971. Division of the Morehouse Group. Not currently accepting submissions.

LOYOLA PRESS, 3441 N. Ashland Ave., Chicago IL 60657. Toll-free (800)621-1008. (773)281-1818. Fax (773)281-0152. E-mail: editorial@loyolapress.com. Website: www.loyolapress .org. Catholic. Joseph Durepos, acq. ed. (durepos@loyolapress.com). Publishes in the Jesuit and Ignatian Spirituality tradition. Publishes 20-30 titles/yr.; hardcover, trade paperbacks. Receives 500 submissions annually. Will accept mss through agents. Prefers 25,000-75,000 wds. or 150-300 pgs. Standard royalty; reasonable advance. Average first printing 7,500-10,000. Considers simultaneous submissions and first-time authors without agents. Responds in 10-12 wks. Prefers NRSV (Catholic Edition). Guidelines & catalog on Website.

Nonfiction: Query first; proposal/sample chapters; no phone query; e-query OK.

Tips: "Looking for books and authors that help make Catholic faith relevant and offer practical tools for the well-lived spiritual life."

LUTHERAN UNIVERSITY PRESS, PO Box 390759, Minneapolis MN 55439. Toll-free (888) 696-1828. (952)835-1828. Fax (952)835-2613. E-mail: publisher@lutheranupress.org. Website: www.lutheranupress.org. Leonard Flachman, pub.; Karen Walhof, ed. Publishes 8-10 titles/yr.; hardcover, trade paperbacks, coffee-table books. Receives dozens of submissions annually. SUBSIDY PUBLISHES 25%. No print-on-demand or reprints. Royalty 10-15% of net; no advance. Average first printing 500-2,000. Publication within 6 mos. No simultaneous submissions. Responds in 3 wks. Guidelines on Website; free catalog.

Nonfiction: Proposal/sample chapters in electronic format.

Photos: Accepts freelance photos for book covers.

Tips: "We accept manuscripts only from faculty of Lutheran colleges, universities, seminaries, and Lutheran faculty from other institutions."

LUTHERAN VOICES, Book Submissions, Augsburg Fortress, PO Box 1209, Minneapolis MN 55440-1209. E-mail: lutheranvoices@augsburgfortress.org. Website: www.augsburg fortress.org. Evangelical Lutheran Church in America. Develops quality, accessible books written primarily by ELCA authors that inform, teach, inspire, and renew. Series of books; 96 pgs. ea. Royalty. Responds in 8-12 wks. Guidelines on Website.

Nonfiction: Proposal.

Tips: "We are seeking prophets and preachers, politicians and pastors; educators and scientists; caregivers and counselors; professors and students; scholars and homemakers—people who have a story to tell, topics to illumine, and ideas to explore. It is expected that authors will write out of a foundational understanding of Lutheran theology and practice, though topics may be of interest to a wider Christian audience."

LUTTERWORTH PRESS, PO Box 60, Cambridge CB1 2NT, England. Phone +44 (0)1223 350865. Fax +44 (0)1223 366951. E-mail: publishing@lutterworth.com. Website: www.lutterworth.com. Adrian Brink, ed. Publishes academic and reference books, particularly, but not exclusively, books on church history and systematic theology. Imprints: The Lutterworth Press (general books). Publishes 25 titles/yr. (15 reprints, 10 new); hardcover & trade paperbacks. Receives 100 submissions annually. 90% of books from first-time authors. Will accept mss through agents. SUBSIDY PUBLISHES 2%. Does print on demand. Royalty on retail; advance. Publication within 18 mos. No simultaneous submissions. Responds in 3 mos. Requested ms by mail. Guidelines on Website; free catalog.

Nonfiction: Proposal/2 chapters; e-query OK.

Tips: "For full author guidelines, visit our Website."

MACALESTER PARK PUBLISHING, 24558—546th Ave., Austin MN 55912. Toll-free fax (800) 407-9078. (507)396-0135. E-mail: Macalesterpark@macalesterpark.com, or through Website: www.macalesterpark.com. Focuses on reprinting books. Sue Franklin, owner.

MAGNUS PRESS, PO Box 2666, Carlsbad CA 92018. (760)806-3743. Fax (760)806-3689. E-mail: magnuspres@aol.com. Website: www.magnuspress.com. Warren Angel, ed. dir. All books must reflect a strong belief in Christ, solid biblical understanding, and the author's ability to relate to the average person. Imprint: Canticle Books. Publishes 3 titles/yr.; trade paperbacks. Receives 60 submissions annually. 50% of books from first-time authors. Will accept mss through agents. Reprints books. Prefers 105-300 pgs. Graduated royalty on retail; no advance. Average first printing 2,500. Publication within 1 yr. Considers simultaneous submissions. Accepts requested ms on disk. Responds in 1 mo. Guidelines (also by e-mail); free catalog.

Nonfiction: Query or proposal/2-3 chapters; fax query OK. "Looking for spirituality, thematic biblical studies, unique inspirational/devotional books, e.g., *Adventures of an Alaskan Preacher.*"

Tips: "Our writers need solid knowledge of the Bible and a mature spirituality that reflects a profound relationship with Jesus Christ. Most open to a popularly written biblical study that addresses a real concern/issue in the church at large today; or a unique inspirational book. Study the market; know what we do and don't publish."

**Note: This publisher serviced by The Writer's Edge.

+MARCHER LORD PRESS. E-mail: jeffgerke@earthlink.net. Website: www.marcherlordpress.com. Jeff Gerke, ed/pub. Specializes in speculative fiction.

MASTER BOOKS, PO Box 726, Green Forest AR 72638. (870)438-5288. Fax (870)438-5120. E-mail: submissions@newleafpress.net, or through Website: www.masterbooks.net. Imprint of New Leaf Press. Amanda Price, ed. Publisher of creation science books; all books are completely evolution free. Publishes 15-20 titles/yr.; hardcover, trade paperbacks. Receives 1,200 submissions annually. 10% of books from first-time authors. Will accept mss through agents. No subsidy, print-on-demand, or reprints. Prefers 140-240 pgs. Variable royalty; rarely gives an advance. Average first printing 5,000. Publication within 12 mos. Considers simultaneous submissions. Responds in 3 mos. Guidelines (also by e-mail/Website); catalog for 9x12 SAE/5 stamps.

Nonfiction: Proposal/no chapters; no phone/fax query; e-query OK; submission form on Website. "Looking for biblical creationism, biblical science, creation/evolution debate material."

Special Needs: Creation science books, and books for the Christian Education/homeschool markets.

Tips: "Most open to books for education with lots of hands-on activities."

**Note: This publisher serviced by The Writers' Edge.

MCDOUGAL PUBLISHING, PO Box 3595, Hagerstown MD 21742. (301)797-6637. Fax (301) 733-2767. E-mail: publishing@mcdougal.org. Website: www.mcdougalpublishing.com. Evangelical. Diane McDougal, pres. Publishes books for the body of Christ. Imprints: McDougal Publishing, Fairmont Books, Parable Publishing, and Serenity Books. Publishes 10-15 titles/yr. Receives 150 submissions annually. 70% of books from first-time authors. Will accept mss through agents. SUBSIDY PUBLISHES 20%. Does print on demand (author charged for print set up). Reprints books. Prefers 80-192 pgs. Royalty 10-15% of net; no advance. Requires authors to buy minimum of 2,000 copies of their book. Average first printing 3,000-5,000. Publication within 6 mos. Considers simultaneous submissions. Responds in 2 mos. Guidelines (also on Website); free catalog.

> **Nonfiction:** Proposal/1-2 chapters (preferred); phone/fax/e-query OK. "Looking for titles on all topics relevant to the Christian life."

> **Fiction:** Complete ms. "Now considering adult fiction from authors with an established market; no romance."

> **Tips:** "Know who your audience is, and write to that audience. Also, keep focused on one central theme."

MCRUFFY PRESS, PO Box 212, Raymore MO 64083. Toll-free (888)967-1200. Toll-free fax (888)967-1300. E-mail: brian@mcruffy.com. Website: www.mcruffy.com. Brian Davis, ed. Christian publisher of children's trade books, children's audio, and homeschool materials. Open to freelance. Requires e-query. Incomplete topical listings.

> **Tips:** "Most open to seeing elementary educational materials, any subject area. Not currently accepting picture book manuscripts."

MERCER UNIVERSITY PRESS, 1400 Coleman Ave., Macon GA 31207-0003. (478)301-2880. Fax (478)301-2264. E-mail: jolley_ma@mercer.edu. Website: www.mupress.org. Baptist. Submit to Editor-in-Chief. Publishes 35 titles/yr. Receives 300 submissions annually. 40% of books from first-time authors. Accepts some mss through agents. Some reprints. Royalty on net; no advance. Average first printing 800-1,200. Publication within 24 mos. Prefers requested ms in hard copy; no disk or e-mail submissions. Responds in 3-4 mos.

> **Nonfiction:** Proposal/2 chapters; fax/e-query OK. "We are looking for books on history, philosophy, theology, literary studies, and religion, including history of religion, philosophy of religion, Bible studies, and ethics."

> **Fiction:** No religious fiction, only Southern literary. Author information form on Website.

MERIWETHER PUBLISHING LTD./CONTEMPORARY DRAMA SERVICE, 885 Elkton Dr., Colorado Springs CO 80907. (719)594-4422. Fax (719)594-9916. E-mail: MerPCDS@aol.com, or editor@meriwether.com. Website: www.meriwetherpublishing.com. Nondenominational. Arthur L. Zapel, exec. ed.; submit to Rhonda Wray, Christian ed. Publishes 30-45 plays & books/yr. Primarily a publisher of plays for Christian and general markets; must be acceptable for use in a wide variety of Christian denominations. Imprint: Contemporary Drama Service (see separate listing). Publishes 3 bks./25 plays/yr. Receives 1,200 submissions annually (mostly plays). 75% of submissions from first-time authors. Will accept mss through agents. No reprints. Prefers 225 pgs. Royalty 10% of net or retail; no advance. Average first printing of books 1,500-2,500, plays 500. Publication within 6 mos. Considers simultaneous submissions. No e-mail submissions. Responds in up to 2 mos. Any Bible version. Guidelines (also by e-mail); catalog for 9x12 SASE.

> **Nonfiction:** Table of contents/1 chapter; fax/e-query OK. "Looking for creative worship

books, i.e., drama, using the arts in worship, how-to books with ideas for Christian education." Submit books to Meriwether.

Fiction: Complete ms for plays. Plays only, for all ages. Always looking for Christmas and Easter plays (1 hr. maximum). Submit plays to Contemporary Drama.

Special Needs: Religious drama—or religious plays—mainstream theology. We prefer plays that can be staged during a worship service.

Tips: "Our books are on drama or any creative, artistic area that can be a part of worship. Writers should familiarize themselves with our catalog before submitting to ensure that their manuscript fits with the list we've already published." Contemporary Drama Service wants easy-to-stage comedies, skits, one-act plays, large-cast musicals, and full-length comedies for schools (junior high through college), and churches (including chancel dramas for Christmas and Easter). Most open to anything drama related. "Study our catalog so you'll know what we publish and what would fit our list."

MESSIANIC JEWISH PUBLISHERS, 6120 Day Long Ln., Clarksville MD 21029. (410)531-6644. Fax (410)531-9440. E-mail: guidelines@messianicjewish.net. Website: www .MessianicJewish.net. Lederer/Messianic Jewish Communications. Submit to The Editor. Books that build up the Messianic Jewish community, witness to unbelieving Jewish people, or help Christians understand their Jewish roots. Imprints: Lederer Books. Publishes 6-12 titles/yr.; hardcover, trade paperbacks. Receives 100+ submissions annually. 50% of books from first-time authors. No mss through agents. Reprints books. Prefers 50,000-88,000 wds. Royalty 7-15% on net. Average first printing 5,000. Publication within 12-24 mos. No simultaneous submissions. Responds in 3-6 mos. Requires requested ms on disk. Prefers Complete Jewish Bible. Guidelines by e-mail; free catalog.

Nonfiction: Write or call for submission guidelines first; then query. Messianic Judaism, Jewish evangelism, or Jewish roots of Christian faith. "Must have Messianic Jewish theme and demonstrate familiarity with Jewish culture and thought."

Fiction: Write or call for submission guidelines first. For adults. Jewish themes only.

Special Needs: Messianic Jewish commentaries.

Ethnic Books: Jewish; Messianic Jewish.

Artwork: Open to queries from freelance artists.

Tips: "Must request guidelines before submitting book proposal; all submissions must meet our requirements. Looking for Messianic Jewish commentaries. Books must address one of the following: Jewish evangelism, Jewish roots of Christianity, or Messianic Judaism."

MILLENNIUM III PUBLISHERS, 174 N. Moore Rd., Simpsonville SC 29680. E-mail: will .ramsey@millenniatech.info. Willard A. Ramsey, sr. ed. To define the cause of the moral and spiritual decline, and to help restore Christian influence, in our national culture. Publishes 4-5 titles/yr. Receives 100+ submissions annually. 50% of books from first-time authors. Will accept mss through agents. Reprints books. Prefers 200-300 pgs. Royalty 10-15% on net; some advances. Publication within 10-12 mos. Considers simultaneous submissions. Responds in 6-8 wks. Prefers NKJV. Guidelines.

Nonfiction: Query; no e-query.

Tips: "Most open to nonfiction books applying Christian solutions to contemporary cultural problems."

MISSION CITY PRESS, 202—2nd Ave. S., Franklin TN 37064-2650. (615)591-1007. Fax (615)591-1006. E-mail: info@missioncitypress.com. Website: www.missioncitypress.com, or www.alifeoffaith.com. Wendy Witherow, ed. coordinator. Provides nondenominational Christian print, gift, and toy products that help young people develop a strong foundation of faith in God. Imprints: A Life of Faith; Faith & Friends. Publishes 5 titles/yr.; hardcover, trade paperbacks. 50% of books from first-time authors. Prefers mss through agents. No subsidy publishing or reprints. Prefers 50,000 wds./224 pgs.; or 25,000 wds./112 pgs. Outright purchases. Publication within 6 months. Free catalog.

Nonfiction: Query only first. All topics indicated are for children and youth only.

Fiction: Proposal/2 chapters. A Life of Faith uses life stories of fictional girls living in the 19th and early 20th centuries to help today's 8-14-year-old girls learn to live a lifestyle of faith.

Also Does: Board games, dolls, and accessories.

Artwork: Open to queries from freelance artists.

Contest: Sponsors a contest (see Website).

Tips: "Spend a lot of time on our Website first and only pitch us things that fit our brand."

**Note: This publisher serviced by ChristianManuscriptSubmissions.com.

MONARCH BOOKS, Wilkinson House, Jordan Hill Rd, Oxford OX2 8DR, England. Phone (01144)(0)1865 302750. Fax (01144)(0)1865 302757. E-mail: enquiries@lionhudson .com, or info@lionhudson.com. Website: www.lionhudson.com. Lion Hudson PLC. Tony Collins, editorial dir. The largest independent British publisher of books inspired by the Christian faith. Imprints: Monarch, Candle, Lion, Lion Children's. Publishes 160 titles/yr.; hardcover, trade paperbacks, mass-market paperbacks, coffee-table books. Receives 750 submissions annually. 20% of books from first-time authors. Will accept mss through agents. No subsidy, print-on-demand, or reprints. Prefers 30,000 wds. & up. Royalty 12.5-15% on net; advance. Average first printing 6,000. Publication within 9 mos. Considers simultaneous submissions. Prefers accepted mss by e-mail. Responds in 4-6 wks. Any Bible version. Guidelines by e-mail; free catalog (don't send U.S. stamps).

Nonfiction: Proposal/2 chapters; phone/fax/e-query OK.

Fiction: Only Lion Hudson imprint printing any fiction.

Special Needs: Original, saleable books with integrity and Christian core.

Photos/Artwork: Accepts freelance photos for book covers; open to queries from freelance artists.

Tips: "Most open to original, energetic, Spirit-filled books."

MOODY PUBLISHERS, 820 N. LaSalle Blvd., Chicago IL 60610. Fax (312)329-2144. E-mail: pressinfo@moody.edu. Website: www.moodypublishers.org. Imprints: Northfield Publishing, Lift Every Voice (African American/see separate listing). Moody Bible Institute. Paul Santhouse, dir. of acquisitions; Jennifer Lyell, women's acq. ed.; Elizabeth Cody Newenhuyse, acq. ed. for family, lifestyle, and relationships; submit to Acquisitions Coordinator. To provide books that evangelize, edify the believer, and educate concerning the Christian life. Publishes 65-70 titles/yr.; hardcover, trade paperbacks, mass-market paperbacks. Receives 3,500 submissions annually. 1% of books from first-time authors. Will accept mss through agents. Royalty on net; advance $500-50,000. Average first printing 10,000. Publication within 1 yr. No simultaneous submissions. Requires requested ms on disk. Responds in 2-3 mos. Prefers NAS, NLT, NIV. Guidelines; catalog for 9x12 SASE/$2.23 postage (mark "Media Mail").

Nonfiction: Considers agented proposals only; no phone/fax/e-query. "For nonfiction, we review only those proposals that come from professional literary agents." Closed to all other unsolicited mss.

Fiction: Proposal/3-5 chapters; for all ages. "We are looking for stories that glorify God both in content and style. We believe that God gives some of his children the talents to write beautiful works of fiction, and we will seek out those artists and the stories they create. We wish to direct people toward God through beauty and truth." No picture books or romance genre fiction.

Ethnic Books: African American.

Tips: "Most open to books where the writer is a recognized expert and already has a platform to promote the book."

Note: This publisher serviced by The Writer's Edge and ChristianManuscriptSubmissions .com.

MOPS INTERNATIONAL, 2370 S. Trenton Way, Denver CO 80231-3822. (303)733-5353. Fax (303)733-5770. E-mail: jblackmer@MOPS.org. Website: www.MOPS.org. Jean Blackmer, pub. mngr.; Carla Foote, dir. of media. Publishes books dealing with the needs and interests of mothers with young children, who may or may not be Christians. Publishes 4-5 titles/yr. Catalog on Website.

Nonfiction: Query or proposal/3 chapters; by mail, fax, or e-mail.

Tips: "Review existing titles on our Website to avoid duplication."

MOREHOUSE PUBLISHING CO., 4775 Linglestown Rd., Harrisburg PA 17112. (212)592-1800. E-mail: morehouse@morehousegroup.com. Website: www.morehousepublishing .org. Episcopal/Church Publishing Inc. Nancy Fitzgerald, exec. ed. Publishes 35 titles/yr.; hardcover, trade paperbacks. Receives 750 submissions annually. 60% of books from first-time authors. Will accept mss through agents. No print-on-demand. Reprints books. Prefers 100-200 pgs. Royalty 10% of net; advance $1,000. Average first printing 3,000. Publication within 12 mos. Considers simultaneous submissions. Responds in 12 wks. Guidelines; for free catalog visit www.churchpublishing.org.

Nonfiction: Proposal/1 chapter; no phone/fax/e-query.

Special Needs: Spirituality, Episcopal oriented.

Tips: "We primarily accept books in our stated categories that are written by Episcopalians and written from an Anglican perspective. Not currently accepting children's book manuscripts."

MORE THAN NOVELLAS.COM. E-mail: lizdelayne@hotmail.com. Website: www.MoreThan Novellas.com. Liz DeLayne, ed. To promote and build a library of family-friendly fiction— with values that exemplify the teachings and walk of Christ—for people to read on the Web. Novellas online. No payment. Guidelines on Website.

Nonfiction: Some romantic poetry.

Fiction: Complete ms by e-mail (attached or copied into the message).

WILLIAM MORROW, 10 E. 53rd St., New York NY 10022. (212)207-7000. Fax (212)207-7145. Website: www.harpercollins.com. Imprint of HarperCollins Publishers. General trade imprint; religious titles published by HarperOne. Submit to Acquisitions Editor. Royalty on retail; advance. Agented submissions only.

+MOUNTAIN CHURCH BOOKS, an imprint of Alexander Books, 65 Macedonia Rd., Alexander NC 28701. (828)252-9515. Fax (828)255-8719. E-mail: pat@abooks.com. Website: www.abooks.com. Submit to Editor. Christian books from a mainly Protestant viewpoint. Publishes hardcover & trade paperbacks. Reprints books. Royalty on net. Guidelines/catalog on Website. Incomplete topical listings.

Nonfiction: Query or proposal/3 sample chapters first; no phone/fax/e-query.

MOUNTAINVIEW PUBLISHING, 1284 Overlook Dr., Sierra Vista AZ 85635-5512. (520)458-5602. Fax (520)459-0162. E-mail: leeemory@earthlink.net. Website: www.trebleheart books.com. Christian division of Treble Heart Books. Ms. Lee Emory, ed./pub. Online Christian publisher; books never have to go out of print as long as they're being marketing and are selling. Imprints: Treble Heart (see separate listing), Sundowners, Whoodo Mysteries. Publishes 6-9 titles/yr; trade paperbacks. Receives 75 submissions annually. 30% of books from first-time authors. Agent not necessary. No reprints. No word-length preference. Royalty 35% of net on most sales; no advance. Books are published electronically; average first printing 30-500. Publication usually within 1 yr. No simultaneous submissions (a 90-day exclusive is required on all submissions). Responds in 3-4 mos. to submissions, 1-2 wks. to queries. Guidelines on Website.

Nonfiction: Complete ms (by e-mail only) to: 1thbsubmissions2@earthlink.net. Submissions are now open between the 1st and 14th of each month. Excellent nonfiction, inspirational books are highly desired here.

Fiction: Complete ms (by e-mail only). Genres: Historical romances; contemporary romances; novellas; mainstream and traditional inspirations in most categories; also Christian mysteries, Christian horror, and Christian westerns.

Photos: Accepts high quality freelance photos for book covers.

Tips: "All inspirational fiction should contain faith elements. Challenge the reader to think, to look at things through different eyes. Avoid point of view head-hopping and clichés; avoid heavy-handed preaching. No dark angel stories, hardcore science fiction/fantasy, though will consider futuristic Christian works. Send consecutive chapters, not random. A well-developed marketing plan must accompany all submissions, and no submissions will be accepted for consideration unless guidelines are followed. Actively seeking more nonfiction at this time."

MOUNT OLIVE COLLEGE PRESS, 634 Henderson St., Mount Olive NC 28365. (919)658-2502. Fax (919)658-7180. Dr. Pepper Worthington, ed. Publishes 5 titles/yr. Receives 2,500 submissions annually. 75% of books from first-time authors. Prefers 220 pgs. Negotiated royalty. Average first printing 500. Publication within 1-3 yrs. No simultaneous submissions. Responds in 6-12 mos. No disk. Free guidelines/catalog.

Tips: Accepting no freelance for now.

MULTNOMAH BOOKS, 12265 Oracle Blvd., Ste. 200, Colorado Springs CO 80921. (719)590-4999. Fax (719)590-8977. E-mail: info@waterbrookpress.com. Websites: www.mpbooks .com. Part of WaterBrook Multnomah, a division of Random House Inc. Ken Petersen, VP/pub. dir. Imprint information listed below. Publishes 75 titles/yr.; hardcover, trade paperbacks. Royalty on net; advance. Publication within 2 yrs. Multnomah is currently not accepting unsolicited manuscripts, proposals, or queries; no proposals for biographies, poetry, or children's books. Queries will be accepted through literary agents and at writers' conferences at which a Multnomah representative is present.

Multnomah Books: Christian living and popular theology books.

Multnomah Fiction: Well-crafted fiction that uses truth to change lives.

**Note: This publisher serviced by The Writer's Edge and ChristianManuscriptSubmissions .com.

NATIONAL BLACK THEATRE INC., 2031-33 National Black Theatre Way, Fifth Ave. (between 126th & 127th sts.), Harlem NY 10035. (212)722-3800. Fax (212)860-8004. E-mail: nbitca@aol.com, or info@nationalblacktheatre.org. Website: www.nationalblacktheatre .org. Does drama, musicals, and children's plays. Scripts need to reflect an African or African American lifestyle. Especially open to historical or inspirational forms. Also holds workshops and readings.

NATIONAL DRAMA SERVICE, LifeWay Christian Resources, One Lifeway Plaza, Nashville TN 37234. E-mail: terry@lifeway.com. Website: www.lifeway.com. Publishes dramatic material for use in Christian ministry: drama in worship, puppet & clown scripts, Christian comedy, mime/movement scripts, readers theater, creative worship services, monologues. Open to scripts 2-10 minutes long. E-mail for specific submissions guidelines.

NAVPRESS, Box 35001, Colorado Springs CO 80935. Website: www.navpress.com. To advance the calling of the Navigators by publishing life-transforming products that are biblically rooted, culturally relevant, and which glorify the Gospel of Jesus Christ and His Kingdom. Publishes 60-65 titles/yr. Is not considering unsolicited proposals at this time.

**Note: This publisher serviced by The Writer's Edge and ChristianManuscriptSubmissions .com.

NAVPRESS STUDENT RESOURCES (formerly NavPress Th1nk), 3820 N. 30th St., Colorado Springs CO 80904. Fax (719)260-7223. E-mail: rebekah.guzman@navpress.com. Website: www.navpress.com. NavPress Publishing. Rebekah Guzman, sr. ed. Books for the teen/YA market. Receives 100-250 submissions annually. 40% of books from first-time authors. Will accept mss through agents. Reprints books. Average first printing varies. Publication within 12 mos. Considers simultaneous submissions. Responds in 8-12 wks. Prefers The Message (Bible version). Guidelines by e-mail/Website.

> **Nonfiction:** Proposal/2 chapters; no phone/fax query; e-query OK. Prefers accepted mss by e-mail.

> **Fiction:** Proposal/2 chapters; no phone/fax query; e-query OK. Prefers accepted mss by e-mail. "Must be suitable for teen/YA audience."

NAZARENE PUBLISHING HOUSE—See Beacon Hill Press of Kansas City.

NEIBAUER PRESS, 20 Industrial Dr., Warminster PA 18974. (215)322-6200, ext. 255. Fax (215)322-2495. E-mail: Nathan@Neibauer.com. Website: www.Neibauer.com. Nathan Neibauer, ed. For Evangelical/Protestant clergy and church leaders. Publishes 8 titles/yr. Receives 100 submissions annually. 5% of books from first-time authors. No mss through agents. Reprints books. Prefers 200 pgs. Royalty on net; some outright purchases; no advance. Average first printing 1,500. Publication within 6 mos. Considers simultaneous submissions. Responds in 4 wks. Prefers e-mail submissions. Prefers NIV. No guidelines/catalog.

> **Nonfiction:** Query or proposal/2 chapters; fax query OK.

> **Also Does:** Pamphlets, tracts.

> **Photos:** Accepts freelance photos for book covers.

> **Tips:** "Publishes only religious books on stewardship and church enrollment, stewardship and tithing, and church enrollment tracts."

TOMMY NELSON—See Thomas Nelson Publishers.

NELSON BOOKS—See Thomas Nelson Publishers.

THOMAS NELSON, FICTION, PO Box 141000, Nashville TN 37215. (615)889-9000. Website: www.ThomasNelson.com. Thomas Nelson Inc. Ami McConnell, sr. acq. ed.; Amanda Bostic, assoc. acq. ed. Fiction from a Christian world-view. Publishes less than 30 titles/yr.; hardcover, trade paperbacks, mass-market paperbacks. Requires mss through agents; does not accept unsolicited manuscripts. Prefers 80,000-100,000 wds. Royalty on net; advance. Publication within 12 mos. Accepts simultaneous submissions. Responds in about 60 days. Guidelines on Website; free catalog.

> **Fiction:** Proposal/3 chapters. For teens and adults. All unsolicited manuscripts returned unopened.

> **Special Needs:** Southern fiction.

NELSON IGNITE—See Thomas Nelson Publishers.

NELSON/NAKED INK—See Thomas Nelson Publishers.

THOMAS NELSON PUBLISHERS, PO Box 141000, Nashville TN 37214-1000. (615)889-9000. Fax (615)902-2745. Website: www.thomasnelson.com. Does not accept or review any unsolicited queries, proposals, or manuscripts.

> ****Note:** This publisher serviced by The Writer's Edge and ChristianManuscriptSubmissions.com.

NEW CANAAN PUBLISHING CO. INC., PO Box 752, New Canaan CT 06840. (203)966-3408. Fax (203)548-9072. E-mail: info@newcanaanpublishing.com. Website: www.newcanaanpublishing.com. Kathy Mittelstadt, ed. Children's books with strong educational and moral content, for grades 1-9 (ages 5-16); also aggressively building its Christian titles list. Publishes 3-4 titles/yr.; hardcover, trade paperbacks. Receives 120 submissions annually. 50% of books from first-time authors. Will accept mss through agents. Reprints books. Prefers

20,000-50,000 wds. or 120-250 pgs. Royalty 8-10% of net; occasional advance. Average first printing 500-5,000. Publication within 1 yr. No simultaneous submissions. Responds in 3-4 mos. Requires requested ms on disk; no e-mail submissions. Guidelines and catalog on Website, or for #10 SASE.

Nonfiction: Proposal/2 chapters or complete ms; no e-query. Does not return submissions.

Fiction: Proposal/2 chapters or complete ms; no e-query. For children and teens, 6-14 yrs. "We want children's books with strong educational and moral content; 10,000-20,000 wds." Now accepts picture books.

Special Needs: Middle-school-level educational books.

Photos: Accepts freelance photos for book covers.

Tips: "Looking for teen/youth fiction and religious instructional materials for teens/ youth."

NEW HOPE PUBLISHERS, Box 12065, Birmingham AL 35202-2065. (205)991-8100. Fax (205)991-4015. E-mail: new_hope@wmu.org. Website: www.newhopepublishers.com. Division of WMU. Submit to Acquisitions Editor. Publishes Christian nonfiction for women and families, and books with a missional focus. Imprints: New Hope Impact (missional community, social, personal-commitment, church-growth, and leadership issues); New Hope Arise (inspiring women, changing lives); New Hope Grow (Bible-study & teaching resources). Publishes 20-28 titles/yr.; hardcover, trade paperbacks. Receives 350 submissions annually. 25% of books from first-time authors. Will accept mss through agents. Reprints books. Royalty on net. Average first printing 5,000-10,000. Publication within 2 yrs. Considers simultaneous submissions. Responds in 3-6 mos. Requires requested ms by e-mail. Guidelines; free catalog.

Nonfiction: Proposal/2 chapters; no phone/fax/e-query. "We look for authors whose messages have a missional emphasis."

Ethnic Books: Black & Hispanic.

Photos: Accepts freelance photos for book covers.

**Note: This publisher serviced by The Writer's Edge and ChristianManuscriptSubmissions .com.

NEW LEAF PUBLISHING GROUP, PO Box 726, Green Forest AR 72638-0726. (870)438-5288. Fax (870)438-5120. E-mail: submissions@newleafpress.net. Website: www.nlpg.com. Amanda Price, acq. ed. Endeavors to bring the lost to Christ and understanding to the body of Christ. Imprints: New Leaf Press, Master Books, Balfour Books, Attic Books. Publishes 35-40 titles/yr.; hardcover, trade paperbacks, coffee-table books. Receives 1,200 submissions annually. 15% of books from first-time authors. Will accept mss through agents. No subsidy, print-on-demand, or reprints. No length preference. Variable royalty on net; advance. Average first printing varies. Publication within 8 mos. Considers simultaneous submissions. Responds within 90 days. Requires accepted ms on disk. Responds in 3 mos. Prefers KJV. Guidelines (also by e-mail/Website); free catalog.

Nonfiction: Query letter only; no phone query; fax/e-query OK. "Looking for books for the homeschool market, especially grades 1-8."

Special Needs: Stewardship of the earth; ancient man technology, inventions, etc.; educational products for grades K-6.

Tips: "The best way to submit to us is to fill out the Author's Proposal form available by e-mail or on our Website."

**Note: This publisher serviced by The Writers' Edge.

NEW SEEDS BOOKS, 300 Massachusetts Ave., Boston MA 02115. (617)424-0030. Fax (617)236-1563. E-mail: editor@newseeds-books.com. Website: www.newseeds-books .com. Shambhala Publications Inc. David O'Neal, sr. ed.; Katie Keach, asst. ed. (kkeach@ shambhala.com). A new imprint devoted to publishing works of the Christian contemplative traditions, cross-traditionally; also new and readable translations of classic texts. Publishes 10 titles/yr.; hardcover & trade paperbacks. Will accept mss through agents. Reprints books. Length open. Royalty 7.5-15% on retail; advance. Average first printing 10,000-30,000. Publication within 1 yr. Considers simultaneous submissions. Responds in 3 mos. Prefers accepted ms on disk or by e-mail. Guidelines by e-mail; free catalog.

Nonfiction: Query, proposal/2 chapters, or complete ms; e-query OK.

NEW YORK UNIVERSITY PRESS, 838 Broadway, 3rd Fl., New York NY 10003-4812. (212)998-2575. Fax (212)995-3833. E-mail: information@nyupress.org. Website: www.nyupress.org. Jennifer Hammer, religion ed. Embraces ideological diversity. Publishes 100 titles/yr.; hardback, trade paperbacks. Receives 800-1,000 submissions annually. 30% of books from first-time authors. Few mss through agents. Royalty on net. Publication within 10-12 mos. Considers simultaneous submissions. Initial response usually within 1 mo. (peer reviewed). Guidelines on Website.

Nonfiction: Query or proposal/1 chapter.

Tips: "As a university press, we primarily publish works with a scholarly foundation written by PhDs affiliated with a university department. Our focus within religious studies is on religion in American history, culture, and politics. We do not publish liturgical studies, pastoral care, spiritual guides, or exegesis. If you are not a university or seminary-affiliated scholar (or a professional journalist) it is unlikely that your work will be appropriate for our list."

NORTHFIELD PUBLISHING CO., 820 N. LaSalle Blvd., Chicago IL 60610. Fax (312)329-2019. Website: www.moodypublishers.org. Imprint of Moody Publishers. Submit to Acquisitions Coordinator. Books for non-Christians or those exploring the faith. Publishes 3-5 titles/yr.; hardcover, trade paperbacks, mass-market paperbacks. 1% of books from first-time authors. Royalty on net; advance $500-50,000. Publication within 1 yr. No simultaneous submissions. Responds in 2-3 mos. Guidelines (also on Website); catalog for 9x12 SAE/2 stamps. Incomplete topical listings.

Nonfiction: Proposal/2-3 chapters. "We decline all unsolicited proposals."

Fiction: For all ages.

NORTHWESTERN PUBLISHING HOUSE, 1250 N. 113th St., Milwaukee WI 53226-3284. Toll-free (800)662-6022. Fax (414)475-7684. E-mail: braunj@nph.wels.net. Website: www.nph.net. Lutheran. Rev. John A. Braun, VP of publishing services. Open to freelance. Responds in 2-3 mos. Guidelines on Website (www.nph.net/cgi-bin/site.pl?aboutUs Manuscript). Incomplete topical listings.

Nonfiction: Complete ms/cover letter; or query letter/outline.

ONE WORLD/BALLANTINE BOOKS, 1745 Broadway, New York NY 10036. (212)782-9000. Fax (212)572-4949. Website: www.randomhouse.com. Submit to Senior Editor. Imprint of Ballantine Books. Novels that are written by and focus on African Americans, but from an American perspective. Publishes 24 titles/yr.; hardcover, trade paperbacks, mass-market paperbacks. Receives 850 submissions annually. 50% of books from first-time authors. Submissions from agents only. No reprints. Prefers 80,000 wds. Royalty 7.5-15% on retail; advance $40,000-200,000. Average first printing 10,000. Publication within 18 mos. Considers simultaneous submissions. Responds in 2 mos. No disk or e-mail. No guidelines/catalog. Note: No unsolicited submissions, proposals, manuscripts, or queries at this time.

Fiction: Proposal/3 chapters; no phone/fax/e-query. "Contemporary/ethnic novels only; for African American women."

Ethnic Books: All are ethnic books.

Tips: "You must understand African American culture and avoid time-worn stereotypes."

OREGON CATHOLIC PRESS, PO Box 18030, Portland OR 97218-0030. Toll-free (800)548-8749. (503)281-1191. Toll-free fax (800)462-7329. E-mail: submissions@ocp.org. Website: www.ocp.org. Bari Colombari, sr. ed. To enhance the worship in the Catholic Church in the United States. Imprint: Pastoral Press. Publishes 8 titles/yr. Receives 80 submissions annually. 5% of books from first-time authors. No mss through agents. No reprints. Prefers 192 pgs. Royalty 5-12% of net; no advance. Average first printing 500. Publication within 12 mos. Considers simultaneous submissions. Prefers requested ms on disk; no e-mail submissions. Responds in 3 mos. Prefers NAB. Guidelines on Website; free catalog.

    Nonfiction: Proposal/1 chapter; no phone/fax/e-query. "Looking for liturgical ministries."

    Ethnic Books: Hispanic/Spanish language.

    Photos: Accepts freelance photos for book covers.

    Tips: "Most open to Catholic liturgical works."

OUR SUNDAY VISITOR INC., 200 Noll Plaza, Huntington IN 46750-4303. Toll-free (800)348-2440. (260)356-8400. Fax (260)356-8472. E-mail: booksed@osv.com, or oursunvis@osv.com. Website: www.osv.com. Catholic. Submit to Acquisitions Editor. To assist Catholics to be more aware and secure in their faith and capable of relating their faith to others. Publishes 30-40 titles/yr.; hardcover, trade paperbacks. Receives 500+ submissions annually. 10% of books from first-time authors. Prefers not to work through agents. Reprints books. Royalty 10-12% of net; advance $1,500 average. Average first printing 5,000. Publication within 1-2 yrs. No simultaneous submissions. Responds in 3 mos. Requires requested ms on disk. Guidelines on Website; catalog for 9x12 SASE.

    Nonfiction: Proposal/2 chapters; e-query OK. "Most open to devotional books (not first person), church history, heritage and saints, the parish, prayer, and family."

    Also Does: Pamphlets, booklets.

    Photos: Occasionally accepts freelance photos for book covers.

    Tips: "All books published must relate to the Catholic Church; unique books aimed at our audience. Give as much background information as possible on author qualification, why the topic was chosen, and unique aspects of the project. Follow our guidelines. We are expanding our religious education product line and programs."

PACIFIC PRESS PUBLISHING ASSN., Box 5353, Nampa ID 83653-5353. (208)465-2500. Fax (208)465-2531. E-mail: booksubmissions@pacificpress.com. Website: www.pacificpress .com. Seventh-day Adventist. David Jarnes, book ed.; submit to Acquisitions Editor. Books of interest and importance to Seventh-day Adventists and other Christians of all ages. Publishes 45 titles/yr. Receives 500 submissions annually. 5% of books from first-time authors. Will accept mss through agents. Prefers 50,000-130,000 wds. or 160-400 pgs. Royalty 12-15% of net; advance $1,500. Average first printing 5,000. Publication within 12-24 mos. Considers simultaneous submissions. Responds in 3 mos. Requires requested ms on disk or by e-mail. Guidelines at www.pacificpress.com/index/php?pgName=newsBookSub; free catalog.

    Nonfiction: Query only; e-query OK.

    Fiction: Query only; almost none accepted; mainly biblical. Children's books: "Must be on a uniquely Seventh-day Adventist topic. No talking animals or fantasy."

    Ethnic Books: Occasionally publishes for ethnic market.

    Also Does: Booklets.

    Tips: "Most open to spirituality, inspirational, and Christian living. Our Website has the most up-to-date information, including samples of recent publications. For more information, see www.adventistbookcenter.com. Do not send full manuscript unless we request it after reviewing your proposal."

P & R PUBLISHING CO., PO Box 817, Phillipsburg NJ 08865. (908)454-0505. Fax (908)454-0859. E-mail: editorial@prpbooks.com. Website: www.prpbooks.com. Marvin Padgett, ed. dir.; Melissa Craig, acq. ed. Devoted to stating, defending, and furthering the gospel in the modern world. Publishes 40 titles/yr.; hardcover, and trade paperbacks. Receives 400 submissions annually. 5% of books from first-time authors; electronic submissions only. Will accept mss through agents. Reprints books. Prefers 140-240 pgs. Royalty 10-14% of net; advance. Average first printing 4,000. Publication within 10-12 mos. Considers simultaneous submissions. Responds in 1-4 mos. Guidelines on Website (Potential Authors section); free catalog.

> **Nonfiction:** E-query only.
> **Fiction:** Query only. For children or teens.
> **Also Does:** Booklets.
> **Tips:** "Direct biblical/reformed content. Clear, engaging, and insightful applications of reformed theology to life. Offer us fully developed proposals and polished sample chapters. All books must be consistent with the Westminster Confession of Faith."
> ****Note:** This publisher serviced by The Writer's Edge and ChristianManuscriptSubmissions .com.

PARADISE RESEARCH PUBLICATIONS INC., PO Box 837, Kihei HI 96753-0837. Phone/fax (808)874-4876. E-mail: dickb@dickb.com. Website: www.dickb.com/index.shtml. Ken Burns, VP. Imprint: Tincture of Time Press. Publishes 5 titles/yr.; trade paperbacks. Receives 8 submissions annually. 80% of books from first-time authors. No mss through agents. Reprints books. Prefers 250 pgs. Royalty 10% of retail; no advance. Average first printing 5,000. Publication within 2 mos. Considers simultaneous submission. Responds in 1 wk. No disk. Prefers KJV. No guidelines; free catalog.

> **Nonfiction:** Query only; no phone/fax/e-query. Books on the biblical/Christian history of early Alcoholics Anonymous.
> **Also Does:** Pamphlets, booklets, e-books.
> **Tips:** "Most open to the history of early AA Christian Fellowship Program; healing of alcoholism/addiction by power of God."

PARAGON HOUSE, 1925 Oakcrest Ave., Ste. 7, St. Paul MN 55113-2619. (651)644-3087. Fax (651)644-0997. E-mail: paragon@paragonhouse.com. Website: www.paragonhouse.com. Rosemary Yokoi, acq. ed. Serious nonfiction and texts with an emphasis on religion, philosophy, and society. Imprints: Omega, Vision of... Publishes 12-15 titles/yr.; hardcover, trade paperbacks. Receives 1,200 submissions annually. 20% of books from first-time authors. Will accept mss through agents or author. Reprints books. Prefers average 250 pgs. Royalty 7-10% of net; advance $1,000. Average first printing 1,500-3,000. Publication within 12-18 mos. Considers few simultaneous submissions. Prefers requested ms as hard copy; accepts e-mail submissions. Responds in 2-3 mos. Guidelines on Website; catalog available online.

> **Nonfiction:** Query; proposal/2-3 chapters, or complete ms; no phone/fax query. "Looking for scholarly overviews of topics in religion and society; textbooks in philosophy; ecumenical subjects; and reference books."

PARSON PLACE PRESS LLC, PO Box 8277, Mobile AL 36689-0277. E-mail: info@parson placepress.com. Website: www.parsonplacepress.com. Michael L. White, mng. ed. Devoted to giving both Christian authors and Christian readers a fair deal. Publishes 3-5 titles/yr.; hardcover, trade paperbacks. Receives 50 submissions annually. 75% of books from first-time authors. Will accept mss through agents. SUBSIDY PUBLISHES 10-20%; does print-on-demand. Reprints books. Prefers 104-200 pgs. Royalty 50% of net; no advance. Average first printing 4 (because of print-on-demand capabilities). Publication within 3 mos. No simultaneous submissions. Responds in 4-6 wks. Requested mss by e-mail (attached file). Prefers NASB. Guidelines on Website; no catalog.

Nonfiction: Proposal/2 chapters; e-query OK. Christian topic/content only.

Fiction: Proposal/2 chapters; e-query OK. For all ages.

Special Needs: In nonfiction, discipleship, encouragement, personal growth, pastoral ministry, church growth, development, leadership. In fiction, mystery, suspense, romance, serials.

Contests: Sponsors a poetry contest; guidelines on Website.

Photos/Artwork: Accepts freelance photos for book covers; open to queries from freelance artists.

Tips: "Most open to conservative, biblically based content that ministers to Christians. Write intelligently, clearly, sincerely, and engagingly."

PARSONS PUBLISHING HOUSE, 33 Carlsbad Dr., Stafford VA 22554. (850)867-3061. Fax (540)659-9043. E-mail: info@parsonspublishinghouse.com. Website: www.parsonspublishinghouse.com. Nondenominational. Diane Parsons, chief ed. Exists to partner with authors to release their voice into their world. Publishes 10 titles/yr.; hardcover, trade paperbacks. Receives 40 submissions annually. 85% of books from first-time authors. Will accept mss through agents. Reprints books. Prefers 120-160 pgs. Royalty 10% on net; no advance. Average first printing 300. Publication within 6 mos. Considers simultaneous submissions. Responds in 60 days. Prefers accepted mss by e-mail. Guidelines by e-mail; no catalog.

Nonfiction: Query; e-query OK.

Fiction: Query; proposal/3 chapters; e-query OK. For teens & adults.

Ethnic Books: Hispanic.

Artwork: Open to queries from freelance artists.

Tips: "Most open to Christian living and worship."

PATH PUBLISHING IN CHRIST, 4302 W. 51st, #121, Amarillo TX 79109-6159. Phone/fax (806)322-7007. E-mail: path2@pathpublishing.com. Website: www.pathpublishing.com. Path Publishing Inc. John Schmidt, ed./pub. Spiritual creations for an aspiring world. Publishing 1-2 titles; trade paperbacks. Receives 60 submissions annually. 95% of books from first-time authors. Will accept mss through agents. Would reprint books. SUBSIDY 0-50%; exploring print-on-demand. Prefers 80-102 pgs. Royalty 8-15% on net; no advance. Average first printing 200. Considers simultaneous submissions. Prefers accepted submissions on disk or by e-mail. Responds in 1 wk. Prefers KJV. Guidelines (also by e-mail/Website); book fliers for #10 SASE; no catalog.

Nonfiction: Query letter ONLY first; e-query preferred.

Fiction: Does little; maybe a short novella.

Special Needs: Looking for self-help books: original point of view, insightful, and aware of future trends; also devotionals.

Also Does: Christian music, CDs, chapbooks (72 pgs.), and CD-ROM books.

Photos: Accepts freelance photos for book covers.

Tips: "We are also a printing broker, and may become a literary agency ."

PAULINE BOOKS & MEDIA, Daughters of St. Paul, 50 Saint Pauls Ave., Jamaica Plain MA 02130-3491. (617)522-8911. Fax (617)524-9805. E-mail: editorial@paulinemedia.com. Website: www.pauline.org. Catholic. Sr. Maria Grace Dateno, FSP, ed.; Submit to Tiffany Fox, ed. assoc. Responds to the hopes and needs of their readers with the Word of God and in the spirit of St. Paul, utilizing all available forms of media so others can find and develop faith in Jesus within the current culture. Imprint: Pauline Kids (see separate listing). Publishes 20 titles/yr.; trade paperbacks. Receives 350-400 submissions annually. 10% of books from first-time authors. No ms through agents. No subsidy or print-on-demand. Reprints books. Prefers 10,000-60,000 wds. Royalty 8-12% on net; advance. Average first printing 4,000-10,000. Publication within 24 mos. Considers simultaneous submissions. Responds in 2 mos. Accepts requested ms by e-mail. Prefers NRSV. Guidelines (also by e-mail/Website); free catalog.

Nonfiction: Written query only/synopsis/2 chapters; e-query OK.

Special Needs: "Spirituality (prayer/holiness of life/seasonal titles), faith formation (religious instruction/catechesis), family life (marriage/parenting issues), biographies of the saints, prayer books. Of particular interest is our faith and culture line, which includes titles that show how Christ is present and may be more fully embraced and proclaimed within our media culture."

Tips: "Submissions are evaluated on adherence to Gospel values, harmony with the Catholic tradition, relevance of topic, and quality of writing."

+PAULINE KIDS, 50 St. Pauls Ave., Jamaica Plain MA 02130. (617)522-8911. Fax (617)524-9805. E-mail: editorial@paulinemedia.com. Website: www.pauline.org. Pauline Books & Media/Catholic. Christina M. Wegendt FSP, children's ed.; Diana Lynch, assoc. children's ed.; submit to Tiffany Fox, ed. asst. Seeks to provide wholesome and entertaining reading that can help children develop strong Christian values. Publishes 20-25 titles/yr.; hardcover, trade paperbacks. Receives 300-350 submissions annually. 10% of books from first-time authors. No mss through agents. Royalty 5-12%; advance. Average first printing 4,000-10,000. Publication within 24 mos. Considers simultaneous submissions. Responds in 1-3 mos. Prefers NRSV. Guidelines (also by e-mail/Website); no catalog.

Nonfiction: Proposal/2 chapters for easy-to-read & middle-grade readers; complete ms for board and picture books; e-query OK.

Fiction: Proposal/2 chapters for easy-to-read & middle-grade readers; complete ms for board and picture books; e-query OK.

Special Needs: Biographies on the lives of Saints. Easy-to-read and middle-reader chapter fiction.

Photos/Artwork: Accepts freelance photos for book covers; open to queries from freelance artists.

PAULIST PRESS, 997 Macarthur Blvd., Mahwah NJ 07430. (201)825-7300. Fax (201)825-8345. E-mail: info@paulistpress.com. Website: www.paulistpress.com. Catholic. Lawrence Boadt, ed. dir. To bring Catholic values and beliefs into dialogue with the North American culture. Imprints: Newman Press, HiddenSpring, Stimulus. Publishes 80 titles/yr. Receives 1,000 submissions annually. 15% of books from first-time authors. Will accept mss through agents. Prefers 150-250 pgs. Royalty 7-10% of net; advance $500-1,000. Average first printing 2,000-2,500. Publication within 18-24 mos. Considers simultaneous submissions (prefers 1st option). Requires requested ms on disk. Responds in 2 mos. Prefers NRSV. Guidelines (also by e-mail/Website); free catalog.

Nonfiction: Proposal/2 chapters or complete ms; e-query OK. "Looking for theology (Catholic and ecumenical Christian), popular spirituality, liturgy, and religious education texts." Children's books for 2-5, 5-8, 8-12, 9-14 years, as per guidelines; complete ms.

Ethnic Books: A few Hispanic.

Also Does: Booklets, pamphlets.

Photos: Accepts freelance photos for book covers.

Tips: "Most open to good spirituality books that have solid input and a clear sense of tradition behind them. Demonstrate grounded convictions. Stay well read. Pay attention to contemporary social needs."

PELICAN PUBLISHING CO. INC., 1000 Burmaster St., Gretna LA 70053. (504)368-1175. Fax (504)368-1195. E-mail: editorial@pelicanpub.com. Website: www.pelicanpub.com. Nina Kooij, ed-in-chief. To publish books of quality and permanence that enrich the lives of those who read them. Imprints: Firebird Press, Jackson Square Press, Dove Inspirational Press (see separate listing). Publishes 3 titles/yr.; hardcover, trade paperbacks. Receives 250 submissions annually. No books from first-time authors. Will accept mss through agents. Reprints books. Prefers 200+ pgs. Royalty; some advances. Publication within 9-18 mos. No simultaneous submissions. Responds in 1 mo. on queries. Requires accepted ms on disk. Prefers KJV. Guidelines (also on Website); catalog for 9x12 SAE/6 stamps.

Nonfiction: Proposal/2 chapters; no phone/fax/e-query. Children's picture books to 1,100 wds. (send complete ms); middle readers about Louisiana (ages 8 & up) at least 25,000 wds.; cookbooks at least 200 recipes.

Fiction: Complete ms. Children's picture books. For ages 5-8 only.

Photos/Artwork: Accepts freelance photos for book covers; open to queries from freelance artists.

Tips: "On inspirational titles we need a high-profile author who already has an established speaking circuit so books can be sold at these appearances."

PENGUIN PRAISE, 375 Hudson St., New York NY 10014. (212)366-2000. Website: www .penguin.com. Joel Fotinos, pub.; Denise Silvestro, exec. ed. Christian publishing imprint of Penguin Group (USA). Will publish books by top-tier Christian authors. Distribution handled by Strang Communications and Noble sales group.

PERIGEE BOOKS, 375 Hudson St., New York NY 10014. (212)366-2000. Fax (212)366-2365. Website: www.penguingroup.com. Penguin Group (USA) Inc. John Duff, pub.; Sheila Curry Oakes, exec. ed.; Michelle Howry, ed. (spirituality). Publishes 3-5 spirituality titles out of 55-60 titles/yr. Receives 300 submissions annually. 30% of books from first-time authors. Strongly prefers mss through agents (but accepts freelance). Prefers 60,000-80,000 wds. Royalty 6-7.5%; advance $5,000-150,000. Average first printing varies. Publication within 18 mos. Considers simultaneous submissions. Responds in 2 mos. Guidelines available with contract; free catalog.

Nonfiction: Query only; no phone/e-query; fax query OK. "Looking for spiritual, prescriptive, self-help, and women's issues; no memoirs or personal histories."

PFLAUM PUBLISHING GROUP, 2621 Dryden Rd., Ste. 300, Dayton OH 45439. (935)293-1415. Fax (937)293-1310. E-mail: kcannizzo@pflaum.com, or jeanlarkin@pflaum.com. Website: www.pflaum.com. Peter Li Education Group/Catholic. Karen Cannizzo, ed. dir., or Jean Larkin, ed. dir. Weekly lectionary-based magazines for pre-K through 8; sacramental preparation programs for primary, junior high, and high school; catechetical resources for pre-K through 12, and religious educators. Publishes 20 titles/yr.; trade paperbacks. Receives 25 submissions annually. 10% of books from first-time authors. No reprints. Royalty on net or outright purchase; advance depends on author arrangement. Average first printing 2,000. Publication within 9 mos. No simultaneous submissions. Requires accepted ms on disk or by e-mail. Responds as soon as possible. Prefers NRSV. Free guidelines/catalog.

Nonfiction: Proposal with at least 1 chapter; e-query OK. "We like user-friendly resources."

Tips: "We are looking for user-friendly, field-tested resources, particularly related to sacramental preparation and lectionary-based catechesis. We specialize in consumable resources—one book per user—that need to be replaced every year, for example, for Lent and Advent."

THE PILGRIM PRESS, 700 Prospect Ave. E., Cleveland OH 44115-1100. (216)736-3755. Fax (216)736-2207. E-mail: ksadler@thepilgrimpress.com, or tstaveteig@thepilgrimpress.com.

Website: www.thepilgrimpress.com. United Church of Christ. Timothy G. Staveteig, pub.; Kim Sadler, ed. dir. Church and educational resources. Publishes 55 titles/yr. Receives 500 submissions annually. 60% of books from first-time authors. Prefers mss through agents. Reprints books. Royalty 10% of net; or work-for-hire, one-time fee; negotiable advance. Average first printing 2,000. Publication within 18 mos. No simultaneous submissions. Responds in 13 wks. Accepts submissions on disk or by e-mail. Guidelines/catalog on Website.

Nonfiction: Query first. Proposal/2 chapters; e-query through Website.

Special Needs: Children's sermons, worship resources, youth materials, and religious materials for ethnic groups.

Ethnic Books: African American, Native American, Asian American, Pacific Islanders, and Hispanic.

Photos: Accepts freelance photos for book covers.

Tips: "Most open to well-written manuscripts that address mainline Protestant-Christian needs and that use inclusive language and follow the *Chicago Manual of Style*."

PLAYERS PRESS INC., PO Box 1132, Studio City CA 91614-0132. (818)789-4980. E-mail: players press@att.net. Players Press International. Robert W. Gordon, ed. To create is to live life's purpose. Publishes only dramatic works; prides themselves on high quality titles. Imprint: Phantom Publications. Publishes 1-6 religious titles/yr.; hardcover, trade paperbacks, coffee-table books. Receives 50-80 religious submissions annually. 90% of books from first-time authors. Will accept mss through agents. No subsidy publishing. Does print-on-demand with older titles. Rarely reprints books. Variable length. Royalty on net; advance. Average first printing 1,000-10,000. Publication within 12 mos. No simultaneous submissions. No submissions by disk or e-mail. Responds in 1-3 wks. on query; 3-12 mos. on ms. Guidelines; catalog for 9x12 SAE/7 stamps or $2.

Nonfiction/Plays: Query only; no phone/fax/e-query. "Always looking for plays and musicals, books on theatre, film and/or television. For all ages."

Photos/Artwork: Accepts freelance photos for book covers; open to queries from freelance artists.

Tips: "Most open to plays, musicals, books on theatre, film, television, and supporting areas: cameras, lighting, costumes, etc."

PONDER PUBLISHING, 15128 27B Ave., Surrey BC V4P 1P2, Canada. E-mail: connect@ponder publishing.ca. Website: www.PonderPublishing.ca. Darian Kovacs, pub. Focuses on Canadian writers primarily, writing material for youth and youth workers.

POWER PUBLISHING, 5641 W. 73rd St., Indianapolis IN 46278. (317)347-1051. Fax (317)347-1068. E-mail: info@powerpublishinginc.com. Website: www.powerpublishing inc.com. Janet Schwind, ed.; submit by mail or through Website. Our innovative culture is author-focused, assuming great care and consideration with each manuscript and offering a unique line of publishing programs to meet the needs of nearly every author. Publishes hardcover, trade paperbacks, mass-market paperbacks. Receives 7,200 submissions annually. 50% of books from first-time authors. Will accept mss through agents. SUBSIDY/CO-OP PUBLISHES 10%; PRINT ON DEMAND UP TO 10%. Reprints books. Prefers 150+ pgs. Royalty on net. Publication within 6 mos. Considers simultaneous submissions. Responds in 2 wks. to initial review; 60-90 days for second review. Prefers accepted mss by e-mail. Prefers NIV. Guidelines (also by e-mail/Website); no catalog.

Nonfiction: Proposal/3-6 chapters; complete ms; phone/fax/e-query OK.

Fiction: Proposal/3-6 chapters; complete ms; phone/fax/e-query OK. For all ages.

Special Needs: Christian leadership, emergent church, church/pastor resources, and general Christian living.

Photos/Artwork: Accepts freelance photos for book covers; open to queries from freelance artists.

Tips: "Most open to nonfiction—inspiring and written to appeal to a mass market, as well as spiritual-growth related, or church resources. We require all authors to complete and submit a New Author form with each manuscript submission. Form available by e-mail: info@powerpublishing.com, or on the Website."

PRAY! BOOKS, PO Box 35004, Colorado Springs CO 80932. (719)531-3555. This imprint has been folded into NavPress.

PREP PUBLISHING, 1110 1/2 Hay St., Fayetteville NC 28305. (910)483-2336. Fax (910)483-2439. E-mail: preppub@aol.com. Website: www.prep-pub.com. PREP Inc. Anne McKinney, mng. ed. (mckinney@prep-pub.com); submit to Frances Sweeney (sweeney@prep-pub.com). Books to enrich people's lives and help them find joy in the human experience. Publishes 10 titles/yr.; hardcover, trade paperbacks. Receives 1,500+ submissions annually. 85% of books from first-time authors. Reprints books. Prefers 250 pgs. Royalty 6-10% of retail; advance. Average first printing 3,000-5,000. Publication within 18 mos. Considers simultaneous submissions. Responds in 1 mo. Guidelines (also on Website) & catalog for #10 SAE/2 stamps.

Nonfiction: Query only; no phone query. Charges a $350 nonrefundable reading fee.

Fiction: Query only (cover letter and up to 3-page synopsis). All ages. "We are attempting to grow our Judeo-Christian fiction imprint."

Tips: "Rewrite, rewrite, rewrite with your reader clearly in focus."

PRESBYTERIAN PUBLISHING CORP., 100 Witherspoon St., Louisville KY 40202-1396. Toll-free (800)523-1631. (502)569-5052. E-mail: customer_service@wjkbooks.com. Website: www.presbypub.com. Submit to The Editor. Addresses the needs of the Christian community by fostering religious and cultural dialog by contributing to the intellectual, moral, and spiritual nurture of the church and the broader human family. Imprints: Geneva Press, Westminster John Knox Press. Publishes 80 titles/yr.; hardcover, trade paperbacks. Receives 2,000 submissions annually. Less than 10% of books from first-time authors. Will accept mss through agents. No subsidy. No reprints. Royalty; no advance. Average first printing 2,000. Publication within 24 mos. Reluctantly considers simultaneous submissions. Responds in 8-12 wks. Prefers NRSV. Guidelines (also by e-mail/Website); catalog for 9x12 SASE.

Nonfiction: Proposal/1-2 chapters; no phone/fax/e-query. Mailed submissions preferred.

G. P. PUTNAM'S SONS BOOKS FOR YOUNG READERS, 345 Hudson St., 14th Fl., New York NY 10014. (212)414-3610. Website: www.penguingroup.com. Submit to Children's Manuscript Editor. Imprint: Penguin Group USA. Publishes 45 titles/yr.; hardcover. Will accept mss through agents. No reprints. Variable royalty on retail; negotiable advance. Considers simultaneous submissions. No disk or e-mail submissions. Responds in 6 mos. Guidelines for SASE.

Nonfiction: Proposal/1-2 chapters. "We publish some religious/inspirational books and books for ages 2-18."

Fiction: For children or teens. Complete ms for picture books; proposal/3 chapters for novels. Primarily picture books or middle-grade novels.

QUINTESSENTIAL BOOKS, PO Box 8755, Kansas City MO 64114-0755. (816)561-1555. E-mail: support@quintessentialbooks.com. Website: www.quintessentialbooks.com. Laura C. Joyce, ed. dir. Books that will challenge people to think deeply and live passionately in accordance with sound principles. Publishes 5-10 titles/yr.; hardcover, trade paperbacks, mass-market paperbacks. Receives 150 submissions annually. 25% of books from first-time authors. Prefers mss through agents. Reprints books. Prefers 60,000-70,000 wds. or 224 pgs. Royalty on net; negotiable advance. Average first printing varies. Publication within 18 mos. Considers simultaneous submissions. Responds in 3-4 mos. Requires requested ms by e-mail. Prefers NIV or NLT. Guidelines (also on Website).

Nonfiction: Query only; no phone/fax/e-query. "Nonfiction books must address significant topics in a fresh way, must speak boldly on controversial issues, and must be clear and accurate. Manuscripts on medicine, mental health, and nutrition will only be accepted from credentialed health professionals."

Fiction: Query only; no phone/fax/e-query. For adults. "Fiction must exhibit an understanding of human hearts and relationships, must create a complete and credible world for the reader, and must have multifaceted characters and aesthetic depth."

Photos/Artwork: Accepts freelance photos for book covers; open to queries from freelance artists.

Tips: "We are interested in reaching an intelligent, widely read audience. Avoid submitting simplistic material."

**Note: This publisher serviced by The Writer's Edge.

RAGGED EDGE PRESS, 73 W. Burd St., PO Box 708, Shippenburg PA 17257. (717)532-2237. Fax (717)532-6110. E-mail: marketing@whitemane.com, or editorial@whitemane.com. Website: www.whitemane.com. White Mane Publishing Co. Inc. Harold E. Collier, acq. ed. Christian, social science, and self-help books that make a difference in people's lives. Publishes 10-15 titles/yr. Receives 50-75 submissions annually. 50% of books from first-time authors. SUBSIDY PUBLISHES 20%. Reprints books. Prefers 200 pgs. Variable royalty on net; no advance. Average first printing 3,000. Publication within 12-18 mos. Considers simultaneous submissions. Responds in 30-90 days. Guidelines (also by e-mail); catalog online.

Nonfiction: Query only; fax/e-query OK.

Tips: "Most open to a Protestant book in the middle of the spectrum."

RAINBOW PUBLISHERS, PO Box 261129, San Diego CA 92196. Toll-free (800)323-7337. Toll-free fax (800)331-0297. E-mail: editor@rainbowpublishers.com. Website: www.rainbow publishers.com. Submit to The Editor. Publishes Bible-teaching, reproducible books for children's teachers. Publishes 20 titles/yr. Receives 250 submissions annually. 50% of books from first-time authors. Reprints books. Prefers 96 pgs. Outright purchases $640 & up. Average first printing 2,500. Publication within 2 yrs. Considers simultaneous submissions. Responds in 3 mos. No disk or e-mail submissions. Prefers NIV. Guidelines (also on Website); catalog for 9x12 SAE/2 stamps.

Nonfiction: Proposal/2-5 chapters; no phone/e-query. "Looking for fun and easy ways to teach Bible concepts to kids, ages 2-12."

Special Needs: Creative puzzles and unique games.

Tips: "Request a catalog or visit your Christian bookstore to see what we have already published. We have over 100 titles and do not like to repeat topics, so a proposal needs to be unique for us but not necessarily unique in the market. Most open to writing that appeals to teachers who work with kids and Bible activities that have been tried and tested on today's kids. No preachy, old-fashioned methods."

RANDALL HOUSE DIGITAL, 114 Bush RD.; PO Box 17306, Nashville TN 37217. Toll-free (800)877-7030. (615)361-1221. Fax (615)367-0535. E-mail through Website: www .randallhouse.com. National Assn. of Free Will Baptists. Keith Fletcher, dir. Estab. 2006. Produces curriculum-on-demand via the Internet, and electronic resources to supplement existing printed curriculum. Guidelines by e-mail.

Nonfiction: Query first; e-query OK.

Special Needs: Teacher-training material (personal or group), elective Bible studies for adults, children's curriculum (other than Sunday school), and elective materials for teens.

Tips: "We are looking for writers with vision for worldwide ministry who would like to see their works help a greater section of the Body of Christ than served by the conventionally printed products."

RANDALL HOUSE PUBLICATIONS, 114 Bush Rd., Nashville TN 37217. Toll-free (800)877-7030. (615)361-1221. Fax (615)367-0535. E-mail: michelle.orr@randallhouse.com. Website: www.randallhouse.com. Free Will Baptist. Michelle Orr, acq. ed. Publishes Sunday school and Christian education materials to make Christ known, from a conservative perspective. Publishes 5-10 titles/yr.; hardcover, trade paperbacks, mass-market paperbacks. Receives 100-150 submissions annually. 50% of books from first-time authors. Will accept mss through agents. No reprints. Length flexible. Royalty 10-15% on net; rarely gives an advance. Average first printing 2,000-5,000. Publication within 12-14 mos. Considers simultaneous submissions. Accepts requested mss by e-mail. Responds in 10-12 wks. Guidelines (also by e-mail/Website); free catalog.

Nonfiction: Query; e-query OK; proposal/4 chapters. Must fill out book proposal form they provide.

Fiction: For teens & adults. Query first; e-query OK; proposal/6 chapters. Must fill out book proposal form they provide.

Artwork: Open to queries from freelance artists (andrea.young@randallhouse.com).

Tips: "We are expanding our book division with a conservative perspective. We have a very conservative view as a publisher."

**Note: This publisher serviced by ChristianManuscriptSubmissions.com.

RAVENHAWK BOOKS, 7739 E. Broadway Blvd., #95, Tucson AZ 85710. E-mail: ravenhawk 6dof@yahoo.com. Website: www.6dofsolutions.com. Blog: see Website. The 6DOF Group. Hans B. Shepherd or Carl Lasky, eds.; Shelly Geraci, submissions ed. Publishes variable number of titles/yr.; hardcover, trade paperbacks. Receives 20-30 submissions annually. 70% of books from first-time authors. Print-on-demand. Reprints books. Royalty 40-50% on gross profits; no advance. Average first printing 2,500. Publication in up to 18 mos. Considers simultaneous submissions. Responds in 6 wks. Catalog on Website.

Nonfiction: Query first; e-query OK. "Looking for profitable books from talented writers."

Fiction: Query first. For all ages. Unsolicited full mss returned unopened.

Special Needs: Looking for books from young authors, 16-22 years old.

Photos/Artwork: Accepts freelance photos for book covers; open to queries from freelance artists.

Tips: "Most open to crisp, creative, entertaining writing that also informs and educates. Writing, as any creative art, is a gift from God. Not everyone has the innate talent to do it well. We are author-oriented. We don't play games with the numbers."

REALMS—Fiction for all ages. See Strang Book Group.

REFERENCE SERVICE PRESS, 5000 Windplay Dr., Ste. 4, El Dorado Hills CA 95762. (916)939-9620. Fax (916)939-9626. E-mail: info@rspfunding.com. Website: www.rspfunding.com. Stuart Hauser, ed. Books related to financial aid and Christian higher education. Publishes 1 title/yr.; hardcover, trade paperbacks. Receives 3-5 submissions annually. Most books from first-time authors. No reprints. Royalty 10% of net; usually no advance. Publication within 5 mos. May consider simultaneous submissions. No guidelines; free catalog for 2 stamps.

Nonfiction: Proposal/several chapters.

Special Needs: Financial aid directories for Christian college students.

REFORMATION TRUST PUBLISHING, Editorial Dept., 400 Technology Park, Lake Mary FL 32746. Toll-free (800)435-4343. (407)333-4244. Fax (407)333-4233. E-mail: gbailey@ligonier.org.

Website: www.ligonier.org/publishing_reformationtrust.php. Imprint of Ligonier Ministries. Greg Bailey, dir. of publications. Exists to publish books true to the historic Christian faith from the best of today's pastors and scholars. Publishes 8-10 titles/yr.; hard cover, trade paperbacks. Receives 100 submissions annually. Open to first-time authors. Will accept mss through agents. No subsidy or reprints. Prefers 40,000-80,000 wds. Royalty on net; no advance. Average first printing 5,000. Publication within 10 mos. Considers simultaneous submissions. Responds in 3 mos. Prefers ESV. Guidelines on Website; free catalog.

Nonfiction: Proposal/2 chapters; no complete mss. Accepted ms by disk or e-mail.

Fiction: Proposal/2 chapters. Children's fiction only. "As in all our titles, we want our children's books to touch the deep truths of the Christian faith."

Tips: "We are looking for books that teach the historic Christian faith in layman's language. Our books are not academic, but good scholarship is important. Above all, our books must be based on scripture. Our theological stance is Reformed/Calvinist."

**Note: This publisher serviced by ChristianManuscriptSubmissions.com.

REGAL BOOKS, 1957 Eastman Ave., Ventura CA 93003. (805)644-9721. Fax (805)644-9728. E-mail: editors@gospellight.com. Website: www.regalbooks.com. Gospel Light. Submit to The Editor. To know Christ and to make Him known; publishing resources to create meaningful dialogue. Publishes 75 titles/yr.; hardcover, trade paperbacks. Receives 1,000 submissions annually. 20% of books from first-time authors. Requires mss through agents. No subsidy, print-on-demand, or reprints. Royalty. Publication within 18 mos. Considers simultaneous submissions. Prefers NIV. No guidelines or catalog.

Nonfiction: All unsolicited mss returned unopened, if SASE provided.

Tips: "Most open to books that are well-written; unique in some way. Work through an agent."

**Note: This publisher serviced by The Writer's Edge.

REGNERY PUBLISHING, One Massachusetts Ave. N.W., Washington DC 20001. Toll-free (888)219-4747. (202)216-0600. Fax (202)216-0612. E-mail: submissions@regnery.com. Website: www.regnery.com. Eagle Publishing. Trade publisher that does conservative political and cultural books. Requires mss through agents. Prefers 250-500 pgs. Royalty 8-15% on retail; advances to $50,000. Average first printing 5,000. Publication within 1 yr. Responds in 3 mos.

Nonfiction: Accepts manuscripts through agents only. Proposal/1-3 chapters or query; no fax/e-query.

Tips: "Books should relate to politics, current affairs, biography, and public policy. Most open to a book that deals with a topical issue from a conservative point of view."

RESOURCE PUBLICATIONS INC., 160 E. Virginia St., Ste. 290, San Jose CA 95112-5876. (408)286-8505. Fax (408)287-8748. E-mail: info@rpinet.com. Website: www.rpinet.com. William Burns, pub. Publishes 10 titles/yr.; trade paperbacks. Receives 450 submissions annually. 30% of books from first-time authors. Prefers 50,000 wds. Royalty 8% of net; rare advance. Average first printing 3,000. Publication within 1 yr. Responds in 10 wks. Prefers requested ms on disk. Guidelines/catalog on Website.

Nonfiction: Proposal/1 chapter; phone/fax/e-query OK.

Fiction: Proposal/2-3 chapters. Adult. Only read-aloud stories for storytellers; fables and parables. "Must be useful in ministerial, counseling, or educational settings."

Also Does: Computer programs; aids to ministry or education. E-books.

Tips: "Know our market. We cater to ministers in Catholic and mainstream Protestant settings. We are not an evangelical house or general interest publisher. Looking for nonfiction ideas that save people time, save money, or help people do their jobs better. Most open to a book that will help a practicing minister understand and deal with a pressing problem he or she faces."

REVELL BOOKS, Fleming H. Revell, Box 6287, Grand Rapids MI 49516. Toll-free (800)877-2665. (616)676-9185. Toll-free fax (800)398-3111. (616)676-2315. Website: www.revell books.com. Imprint of Baker Publishing Group. Publishes inspirational fiction and nonfiction for the broadest Christian market. Guidelines & catalog on Website. No unsolicited mss. Submit through Writer's Edge or ChristianManuscriptSubmissions.com.

REVIEW AND HERALD PUBLISHING ASSN., 55 W. Oak Ridge Dr., Hagerstown MD 21740-7390. (301)393-3000. Fax (301)393-4055. E-mail: editorial@rhpa.org. Website: www.rhpa.org. Seventh-day Adventist. Richard Coffen, VP/editorial; Jeannette Johnson, acq. ed. No freelance.

REVIVAL NATION PUBLISHING, PO Box 30001, Sarnia ON N7T 0A7, Canada. (519)330-6346. E-mail: publishing@revivalnation.com. Website: www.revivalnation.com. Revival Nation Evangelistic Ministries. Greg Holmes, pres. A not-for-profit publisher; all publishing revenue goes back to building God's Kingdom. Publishes 15-20 titles/yr.; trade paperbacks. 90% of books from first-time authors. Will accept mss through agents. No reprints. Prefers 200-300 pgs. Royalty 15-20% on wholesale; no advance. Average first printing 1,000. Publication within 6 mos. Accepts simultaneous submissions. Responds in 4-6 wks. Prefers e-mail submissions (attached file in Word). Prefers NIV. Guidelines by e-mail/Website; no catalog.

> **Nonfiction:** Complete ms; e-query OK. "We look for passion in the writing—something the author would die for."

> **Special Needs:** Looking for revival, renewal, holiness, Holy Spirit, prayer, and Charismatic.

> **Contest:** Spirit Word Writing Contest. Nonfiction. October 31 deadline. Entry fee: $25. Prize: Publication with a $1,000 advance. Details on Website.

> **Tips:** Gives preference to Canadian authors but open to all.

> ****Note:** This publisher serviced by The Writer's Edge.

ROSE PUBLISHING, 4733 Torrance Blvd., #259, Torrance CA 90503. Toll-free (800)532-4278. (310)353-2100. Fax (310)353-2116. E-mail: rosepubl@aol.com. Website: www.rose-publishing.com. Nondenominational. Lynnette Pennings, acq./mng. ed. Publishes primarily Bible studies, apologetics; Sunday school wall charts and visual aids. Publishes 30-40 titles/yr. 2% of projects from first-time authors. No mss through agents. No reprints. Outright purchases. Publication within 18 mos. Considers simultaneous submissions. Requires accepted mss by disk or e-mail. Responds in 2-3 mos. Catalog for 9x12 SAE/4 stamps.

> **Nonfiction:** Query or proposal. No books, mainly booklets/pamphlets, wall charts/posters, or PowerPoints.

> **Special Needs:** Query with sketch of proposed chart or poster (nonreturnable); fax query OK; e-query OK if less than 100 wds. (copied into message). Open to material that makes difficult Bible topics or theological topics easier; wall charts, study guides and worksheets on sharing your faith and salvation with skeptics. Typical subjects include: cults, books of the Bible, church history, world religions, discipleship, angels, prayer, teens, hot topics.

> **Also Does:** PowerPoint presentations for biblical subjects.

> **Artwork:** Open to queries from freelance artists.

> **Tips:** "Now accepting more freelance submissions. No fiction." Publishes a unique format that makes difficult Bible topics easy to understand.

> ****Note:** This publisher serviced by ChristianManuscriptSubmissions.com.

+SAINT CATHERINE OF SIENA PRESS, 4812 N. Park Ave., Indianapolis IN 46205. Toll-free (888)544-8674. E-mail: service@saintcatherineofsienapress.com. Website: www.saint catherineofsienapress.com. Catholic. Jean Zander, ed. dir. Established to promote "excellence in catechesis…in faithfulness to Rome." Responds in up to 2 mos. Guidelines/catalog on Website.

> **Nonfiction:** Proposal/2 chapters.

THE SALT WORKS, 1655 Booth Rd, Roseville CA 95747. (916)784-0500. Fax (916)773-7421. E-mail: books@publishersdesign.com. Website: www.publishersdesign.com. Division of Publishers Design Group Inc. Robert Brekke, pub. Seeks to demonstrate through books that God is sovereign, just, and merciful in all He does. Imprint: Salty's Books (children's—see separate listing). Publishes 2-5 titles/yr.; hard cover, trade paperbacks, coffee-table books. Receives 20-35 submissions annually. 70% of books from first-time authors. No mss through agents. SUBSIDY PUBLISHES 35%; no print-on-demand. Reprints few books. Prefers 85,000-120,000 wds. Royalty 5-12% on net/advance; co-publishing and subsidy publishing by agreement. Average first printing 7,500 for CBA (10,000 for ABA). Publication within 18 mos. Considers simultaneous submissions. Responds in 30-45 days. Prefers ESV/NASB/NKJV/NIV (in that order). Guidelines by mail (after initial phone interview); free catalog.

Nonfiction: E-query only; followed by proposal. Unsolicited mss returned unopened. "Looking for titles that communicate a biblical Christian world-view without promoting overly simplistic, idealistic, or theoretical solutions to life's questions; books that honestly show no timidity in addressing our humanness, and yet, do not sensationalize a subject."

Fiction: E-query only; followed by proposal. Unsolicited mss returned unopened. For adults and children. "Looking for titles that help believers in exploring and facing common issues surrounding God's sovereignty, His grace and forgiveness, their own sin and idolatry, and the areas where pop-culture has influenced the church. Characters are blatantly human."

Also Does: Board games and other specialty products: fitness products, art projects and products, interactive projects for children.

Artwork: Open to queries from freelance artists.

Tips: "Most open to books that look at the Christian experience through a realistic biblical and reformed perspective. Books that address the Christian's real problems as a 'heart' problem—not a theological problem, not from a victim mindset, not a mental or logical one, not from a perspective of merely needing another program, pep-talk, or the latest rehash of formulas for victorious living. Books that show the author understands that unless God changes the heart and brings a person to repentance, there are no real and lasting answers."

**Note: This publisher serviced by The Writer's Edge and ChristianManuscriptSubmissions .com.

SALTY'S BOOKS, 1655 Booth Rd., Roseville CA 95747. (916)784-0500. Fax (916)773-7421. E-mail: books@publishersdesign.com. Website: www.publishersdesign.com. Division of Publishers Design Group Inc. Robert Brekke, pub. Imprint for children's Christian books.

+SAMARITAN PRESS, PO Box 14451, Knoxville TN 37914. (865)335-0072. Fax (865)249-7206. Website: www.samaritanpress.com. R. Michael Henegar, ed.; submit to Kristy Lynn. Believes that every person has a story to tell and readers to enjoy that story. Publishes 15-20 titles/yr.; hardcover, mass-market paperbacks, coffee-table books. Receives 300 submissions annually. 70% of books from first-time authors. Will accept mss through agents. SUBSIDY PUBLISHES 10%; does print on demand. Reprints books. Prefers 80+ pgs. Royalty 10-15% on retail; no advance. Average first printing 5,000. Publication within 12 mos. No simultaneous submissions. Responds in 3 mos. Wants accepted mss on disk. Prefers NKJV. Guidelines on Website; no catalog.

Nonfiction: Query first or complete ms; e-query OK.

Fiction: Query first or complete ms; e-query OK. For all ages.

Special Needs: All genres of fiction, Christian living, Bible study, and personal experience.

Photos/Artwork: Accepts freelance photos for book covers; open to queries from freelance artists.

Tips: "All types of fiction are considered and we enjoy regular people submitting regular stories that can become great lessons of faith and devotion to Jesus Christ."

SCEPTER PUBLISHERS INC., PO Box 211, New York NY 10018. Toll-free (800)322-8773. (212)354-0670. Fax (212)354-0736. E-mail: info@scepterpublishers.org. Website: www.scepterpublishers.org. Catholic. John Powers, ed. Books on how to struggle to live faith and virtue in one's daily life. Publishes 20 titles/yr. 0-2% of books from first-time authors. Will accept mss through agents. Reprints books. Prefers 200-250 pgs. Royalty on net; advance $2,000-10,000. Average first printing 2,000. Publication within 24 mos. No simultaneous submissions. Responds after 12 mos. Free catalog.

Nonfiction: Query only first with a 1-2 pg. synopsis; no phone/fax/e-query. Does not return material.

Fiction: Query only first; no phone/fax/e-query.

Tips: "Looking for books that help readers struggle better to live Christian virtues and practice seriously their faith."

SCRIPTURE PRESS—See David C. Cook.

SHEED & WARD, 4501 Forbes Blvd., Ste. 200, Lanham MD 20706. Toll-free (800)462-6420. (301)459-3366. Fax (301)429-5747. Website: www.sheedandward.com. Imprint of Rowman & Littlefield Publishers Inc. Jon Sisk, pub. (jsisk@rowmanlittlefield.com); Ross Miller (rmiller@rowman.com) & John Loudon (jloudon@rowman.com), eds. Submit to Sarah Johnson. Publishes books of contemporary impact and enduring merit in Catholic-Christian thought and action. Publishes 25-30 titles/yr.; hardcover, trade paperbacks. Receives 2,000 submissions annually. 25% of books from first-time authors. Does print-on-demand. Reprints books. Prefers 35,000-65,000 wds. Royalty 6-12% on retail; $500-2,000 advance. Average first printing 3,000. Publication within 8 mos. No simultaneous submissions. Responds in 1-2 mos. Requires requested ms on disk. Prefers NAB, NRSV (Catholic editions). Guidelines/catalog on Website.

Nonfiction: Proposal/1-2 chapters; phone/fax/e-query OK. "Looking for parish ministry (health care, spirituality, leadership, general trade books for mass audiences, sacraments, small group, or priestless parish facilitating books)."

Photos/Artwork: Considers photos/artwork as part of book package.

Tips: "Looking for general trade titles and academic titles (oriented toward the classroom) in areas of spirituality, parish ministry, leadership, sacraments, prayer, faith formation, church history, and Scripture."

SHORELINE, 23 Ste-Anne, Ste-Anne-de-Bellevue QC H9X 1L1, Canada. Phone/fax (514)457-5733. E-mail: shoreline@sympatico.ca. Website: www.shorelinepress.ca. Judith Isherwood, ed. Not accepting freelance submissions at this time.

SILOAM—See Strang Book Group.

SKYSONG PRESS, 35 Peter St. S., Orillia ON L3V 5A8, Canada. E-mail: skysong@bconnex.net. Website: www.bconnex.net/~skysong. Steve Stanton, ed. Imprint: Dreams & Visions. Publishes 2 titles/yr. Guidelines on Website.

Fiction: Publishers of Christian or "spiritual" short stories under the imprint Dreams & Visions.

SMYTH & HELWYS PUBLISHING INC., 6316 Peake Rd., Macon GA 31210-3960. Toll-free (800)747-3016. (478)757-0564. Fax (478)757-1305. E-mail: Proposals@helwys.com. Website: www.helwys.com. Submit to Book Editor. Quality resources for the church, the academy, and individual Christians who are nurtured by faith and informed by scholarship. Publishes 25-30 titles/yr. Receives 600 submissions annually. 40% of books from first-time authors. Prefers 144 pgs. Royalty 7%. Considers simultaneous submissions. Responds in 3 mos. Free guidelines (also by e-mail/Website); free catalog.

Nonfiction: Query only; fax/e-query OK. "Manuscripts requested for topics appropriate for mainline church and seminary/university textbook market."
Also Does: E-books. Copies of print books and original books. Go to: www.next sunday.com.
Tips: "Most open to books with a strong secondary or special market. Niche titles and short-run options available for specialty subjects."

STANDARD PUBLISHING, 8805 Governor's Hill Dr., Ste. 400, Cincinnati OH 45249. (513)931-4050. Fax (513)931-0950. Website: www.standardpub.com. An evangelical Christian publisher of church resources for all ages. See guidelines on Website for details.
Tips: "We provide true-to-the-Bible resources that inspire, educate, and motivate Christians to a growing relationship with Jesus Christ."
**Note: This publisher serviced by The Writer's Edge and ChristianManuscriptSubmissions .com.

ST. ANTHONY MESSENGER PRESS and FRANCISCAN COMMUNICATIONS, 28 W. Liberty St., Cincinnati OH 45202. Toll-free (800)488-0488. (513)241-5615. Fax (513)241-0399. E-mail: StAnthony@AmericanCatholic.org. Websites: www.AmericanCatholic.org; www .sampbooks.org; www.servantbooks.org. Catholic. Lisa Biedenbach, ed. dir. (lisab@ AmericanCatholic.org); Katie Carroll, mng. ed.; Mary Hackett, book ed.; Cynthia Cavnar, acq. ed. (cynthiac@americancatholic.org). Seeks to publish affordable resources for living a Catholic-Christian lifestyle. Imprints: Servant Books, Franciscan Communications, Fischer Productions, Ikonographics (videos). S.A.M.P. publishes 25-30 titles/yr.; Servant publishes 18 titles/yr.; trade paperbacks (mostly). Receives 450 submissions annually. 5% of books from first-time authors. Will accept mss through agents. Reprints books (seldom). Prefers 25,000-50,000 wds. or 100-300 pgs. Royalty 10-14% on net; advance $1,000-3,000. Average first printing 5,000. Publication within 18 mos. No simultaneous submissions. Requires accepted ms on disk; e-mail OK. Responds in 5-9 wks. Prefers NRSV. Guidelines on Website; catalog for 9x12 SAE/4 stamps.
Nonfiction: Query only/500-wd. summary; fax/e-query OK. "Looking for family-based catechetical programs; living the Catholic-Christian life at home and in workplace; and Franciscan topics."
Special Needs: Catholic identity, spirituality, resources for new and inactive Catholics, young adult Catholics.
Ethnic Books: Hispanic, occasionally.
Tips: "Most open to books with sound Catholic doctrine that include personal experiences or anecdotes applicable to today's culture. Our books are decidedly Catholic."

STARIK PUBLISHING, PO Box 307, Slaton TX 79364. E-mail: submissions@starikpublishing .com. Website: www.starikpublishing.com. Blog: www.starikpublishing.com/wordpress. Stacie Craig, exec. ed. A family-oriented publishing house seeking to improve families through literature. Publishes 1-3 titles/yr.; trade paperbacks. Receives 75 submissions annually. 30% of books from first-time authors. No mss through agents. No subsidy or reprints. Prefers 100-400 pgs. Royalty; no advance. Average first print run 2,000. Considers simultaneous submissions. Responds in 6-8 wks. Guidelines (also by e-mail/Website); no catalog.
Nonfiction: Proposal/3 chapters & short author bio; e-query OK. Accepts disk or e-mail submissions.
Fiction: Proposal/3 chapters & short author bio; e-query OK. Teen/young adult & adult Christian fiction.
Artwork: Open to queries from freelance artists.

ST. AUGUSTINE'S PRESS, PO Box 2285, South Bend IN 46680. (574)291-3500. Fax (574)291-3700. E-mail: bruce@staugustine.net. Website: www.staugustine.net. A conservative, nondenominational (although mostly Catholic) scholarly publisher of academic titles, mainly in academic philosophy, theology, and cultural history. Bruce Fingerhut, pres. Publishes 20-40 titles/yr.; hardcover, trade paperbacks. Receives 100+ submissions annually. 5% of books from first-time authors. Will accept mss through agents. Reprints books. Royalty 6-15% of net; advance $1,000. Average first printing 1,000. Publication within 1 yr. Considers simultaneous submissions. Responds in 3 mos. No guidelines; free catalog.

Nonfiction: Query or proposal/chapters. "Most of our titles are philosophy." Cultural history.

Tips: "Most open to books on subjects or by authors similar to what/who we already publish."

+ST. BEDE'S PUBLICATIONS, St. Scholastica Priory, PO Box 545, Petersham MA 01366-0545. (978)724-3213. Fax (978)724-3216. Catholic/St. Scholastica Priory. Submit to Acquisitions Editor. Publishes 3-4 titles/yr.; hardcover & trade paperbacks. 30-40% of books from first-time authors. Will accept mss through agents. Reprints books. Royalty 5-10% of net or retail. Publication within 2 yrs. Considers simultaneous submissions. Responds in 2 mos. Prefers NIV. Guidelines; catalog for 9x12 SAE/2 stamps.

Nonfiction: Query or outline/sample chapters.

STEEPLE HILL (Single Title), 233 Broadway, Ste. 1001, New York NY 10279-0001. (212)553-4200. Fax (212)277-8969. E-mail: Emily_Rodmell@harlequin.ca. Website: www.Steeple Hill.com. Harlequin Enterprises. Submit to any of the following: Joan Marlow Golan, exec. ed.; Melissa Endlich, ed.; Krista Stroever, sr. ed.; Emily Rodmell, asst. ed.; Sarah McDaniel, ed. asst. (sarah_mcdaniel@harlequin.ca). Single title, trade paperback Christian women's fiction that will help women guide themselves and their families toward purposeful, faith-driven lives. Lines: Love Inspired (mass-market category romances), see separate listing; Love Inspired Suspense; Love Inspired Historical, see separate listing; Steeple Hill Café (women's fiction). Publishes 96-108 titles/yr.; trade paperbacks, mass-market paperbacks. Receives 500-1,000 submissions annually. 15% of books from first-time authors. Will accept mss through agents. No reprints. Prefers 80,000-125,000 wds. or 350-500 pgs. Royalty on retail; competitive advance. Publication within 12-24 mos. Considers simultaneous submissions for trade books, not for mass market. Requires accepted ms on disk/hard copy. Responds in 3 mos. Prefers KJV. Guidelines (also on Website): no catalog.

Fiction: Query letter for single titles or complete ms for series; no phone/fax/e-query.

Tips: "We want quality inspirational novels that focus on the more complex and thoughtfully developed stories, with many characters, subplots, and so on. They are mostly character-driven, depicting sympathetic protagonists as they learn important lessons about the power of faith. Subgenres include relationship novels, contemporary and historical romances, family dramas, Christian chick lit, romantic suspense, mysteries, and thrillers."

**Note: This publisher serviced by ChristianManuscriptSubmissions.com.

STEEPLE HILL/LOVE INSPIRED, 233 Broadway, Ste. 1001, New York NY 10279-0001. (212) 553-4200. Fax (212)277-8969. E-mail: Sarah_McDaniel@harlequin.ca. Website: www .SteepleHill.com. Harlequin Enterprises. Submit to any of the following: Joan Marlow Golan, exec. ed.; Krista Stroever, sr. ed.; Melissa Endlich, ed.; Emily Rodmell, asst. ed.; Sarah McDaniel, ed. asst. Mass-market Christian romance novels. Publishes 48 titles/yr.; mass-market paperbacks. Receives 500-1,000 submissions annually. 15% of books from first-time authors. Will accept mss through agents. No reprints. Prefers 55,000-60,000 wds. Royalty on retail; competitive advance. Publication within 12-24 mos. Requires ms on disk/hard copy. Responds in 3 mos. Prefers KJV. Guidelines (also on Website); no catalog.

Fiction: Query letter or 3 chapters and up to 5-page synopsis; no phone/fax/e-query.

Tips: "We want character-driven romance with an author voice that inspires."

**Note: This publisher serviced by ChristianManuscriptSubmissions.com.

STEEPLE HILL/LOVE INSPIRED HISTORICAL, 233 Broadway, Ste. 1001, New York NY 10279-0001. (212)553-4200. Fax (212)227-8969. E-mail: Emily_Rodmell@harlequin.ca. Website: www.SteepleHill.com. Harlequin Enterprises. Submit to any of the following: Melissa Endlich, ed.; Diane Dietz, asst. ed.; Emily Rodmell, ed. asst. Mass-market Christian historical romance novels. Publishes 24 titles/yr.; mass-market paperbacks. Receives 500-1,000 submissions annually. 15% of books from first-time authors. Will accept mss through agents. No subsidy; no reprints. Prefers 70,000-75,000 wds. Royalty on retail; competitive advance. Publication within 12-24 mos. No simultaneous submissions. Responds in 3 mos. Prefers KJV. Guidelines by e-mail/Website; no catalog.

Fiction: Proposal/3 chapters. Biblical, frontier romance, or historical romance.

Tips: "We are looking for complex stories rich in historical detail, featuring Christian characters facing challenges of life and love."

**Note: This publisher serviced by ChristianManuscriptSubmissions.com.

STEEPLE HILL/LOVE INSPIRED SUSPENSE, 233 Broadway, Ste. 1001, New York NY 10279-0001. (212)553-4200. Fax (212)277-8969. E-mail: Sarah_McDaniel@harlequin.ca. Website: www.SteepleHill.com. Harlequin Enterprises. Submit to any of the following: Joan Marlow Golan, exec. ed.; Krista Stroever, sr. ed.; Melissa Endlich, ed.; Emily Rodmell, asst. ed.; Elizabeth Mazer, ed. asst. Mass-market Christian romantic suspense novels. Publishes 48 titles/yr.; mass-market paperbacks. Receives 500-1,000 submissions annually. 15% of books from first-time authors. Will accept mss through agents. No reprints. Prefers 55,000-60,000 wds. Royalty on retail; competitive advance. Publication within 12-24 mos. Requires accepted ms on disk/hard copy. Responds in 3 mos. Prefers KJV. Guidelines (also on Website); no catalog.

Fiction: Query letter or 3 chapters and up to 5-page synopsis; no phone/fax/e-query.

Special Needs: "We are looking for edge-of-the-seat, contemporary romantic suspense tales of intrigue and romance featuring Christian characters facing challenges to their faith—and to their lives. Each story should have a compelling mystery or a suspenseful situation threatening the hero and the heroine, combined with an emotional, satisfying, and mature romance. An element of faith must be present in the books, and should be well integrated into the plot."

Tips: "We want character-driven fiction with an author voice that inspires."

**Note: This publisher serviced by ChristianManuscriptSubmissions.com.

STILL WATERS REVIVAL BOOKS, 4710—37A Ave., Edmonton AB T6L 3T5, Canada. (708)450-3730. Fax (708)468-1096. E-mail: swrb@swrb.com. Website: www.swrb.com. Covenanter Church. Reg Barrow, pres. Publishes 100 titles/yr. Receives few submissions. Very few books from first-time authors. Reprints books. Prefers 128-160 pgs. Negotiated royalty or outright purchase. Considers simultaneous submissions. Catalog for 9x12 SAE/2 stamps.

Nonfiction: Proposal/2 chapters.

Tips: "Only open to books defending the Covenanted Reformation, nothing else."

ST. MICHAEL'S ABBEY PRESS, Farnborough, Hampshire, England GU14 7NQ. Phone 44(0)1252 546105. Fax 44(0)1252 372822. E-mail: abbeypress@farnboroughabbey.org or info@farnboroughabbey.org. Website: www.farnboroughabbey.org/press/index.php. Open to freelance submissions. Details on Website.

STRANG BOOK GROUP, 600 Rinehart Rd., Lake Mary FL 32746. (407)333-0600. Fax (407)333-7100. E-mail: creationhouse@strang.com. Website: www.strang.com. Strang Communications. Submit to Acquisitions Assistant for specific imprint. To inspire and equip people to live a Spirit-led life and walk in the divine purpose for which they were called. This house has 8 imprints, which are listed below with descriptions/details. Publishes 150 titles/yr.; hardcovers, trade paperbacks, mass-market paperbacks. Receives 1,500 submissions annually. 65% of books from first-time authors. Prefers mss through agents. Reprints books.

Prefers 55,000 wds. Royalty on net or outright purchase; advance. Average first printing 7,500. Publication within 9 mos. Considers simultaneous submissions. Accepts requested ms on disk or on Website. Responds in 6-10 wks. Guidelines (also by e-mail); free catalog.

Nonfiction: Proposal or complete ms; by mail or e-query OK; no phone query. Book proposal application on Website. "Open to any books that are well written and glorify Jesus Christ."

Fiction: Proposal or complete ms; by mail or e-query OK; no phone query. Book proposal application on Website. "For all ages. Fiction must have a biblical world-view and point the reader to Christ."

Photos: Accepts freelance photos for book covers.

Charisma House: Books on Christian living, mainly from a Charismatic/Pentecostal perspective. Topics: Christian living, work of the Holy Spirit, prophecy, prayer, Scripture, adventures in evangelism and missions, popular theology.

Siloam: Books about living in good health—body, mind, and spirit. Topics: alternative medicine; diet and nutrition; and physical, emotional, and psychological wellness. We prefer manuscripts from certified doctors, nutritionists, trainers, and other medical professionals. Proof of credentials may be required.

FrontLine: Books on contemporary political and social issues from a Christian perspective.

Creation House: Co-publishing imprint for a wide variety of Christian books. Author is required to buy a quantity of books from the first press run. This is not self-publishing or print-on-demand.

Realms: Christian fiction in the supernatural, speculative genre. Full-length adult novels, 80,000-120,000 wds. Will also consider historical or biblical fiction if supernatural element is substantial.

+Excel: Publishes books that are targeted toward success in the workplace and businesses.

Charisma Kids (see separate listing): Children's books. No 24- to 32-page picture books.

Casa Creacion: Publishes and translates books into Spanish. (800)987-8432. E-mail: casacreacion@strang.com. Website: www.casacreacion.com.

Publicaciones Casa: Publishes the same as Creation House and is for people who like to co-publish in Spanish. Contact info same as Casa Creacion.

**Note: This publisher serviced by ChristianManuscriptSubmissions.com.

SWEETHEART ROMANCES CO, PO Box 870, Oregon City OR 97045. (360)589-5004. E-mail: bearingup@juno.com. Website: www.sweetheartromances.com. Melanie Emry, ed. A Sweetheart Romance will leave its readers feeling good when they finish the novel. E-book publisher. Prefers 40,000-75,000 wds. Royalty 25% of earnings from downloads (paid every other month); no advance. Responds in 3 mos. Guidelines on Website; no catalog.

Fiction: Proposal/chapter-by-chapter synopsis & 3 chapters (incl. 1st & last chapters).

Tips: "Can you tell a powerful love story without resorting to anatomy texts and clinical descriptions of love making? Can you avoid obscene language? Can you write a story that will leave readers a little better than they were? If you answered Yes to these questions, we invite you to try."

TAN BOOKS AND PUBLISHERS INC., PO Box 424, Rockford IL 61105-0424. Toll-free (800) 437-5876, ext. 205. (815)226-7777. Fax (815)226-7770. E-mail: taneditor@tanbooks .com. Website: www.TanBooks.com. Catholic. Thomas A. Nelson, ed. Not included in topical listings.

T & T CLARK INTERNATIONAL, PO Box 1321, Harrisburg PA 17108. (717)541-8130. Fax (717)541-8128. E-mail: tkraft@continuumbooks.com. Website: www.tandtclarkinter national.com. Continuum Publishing. Thomas Kraft, assoc. pub. A nondenominational, academic religious publisher. Imprints: Trinity Press International; Continuum. Publishes 50-60 titles/yr.; trade paperbacks. Receives 150-200 submissions annually. 3% of books from first-time authors. Will accept mss through agents. Reprints books. Royalty 10% of net; advance $500 & up. Average first printing 1,000. Publication within 9 mos. Considers simultaneous submissions. Responds in 4-6 wks. Prefers NRSV. Guidelines (also by e-mail); free catalog.

Nonfiction: Proposal/1 chapter, or complete ms; fax/e-query OK. "Looking for biblical studies, theology, religion, and music." No dissertations or essays.

Special Needs: Religion and film; American religious history; and religion and science.

Photos: Accepts freelance photos for book covers.

Tips: "Most open to a book that is academic, to be used in undergraduate biblical studies, theology, or religious studies programs."

JEREMY P. TARCHER, 375 Hudson St., New York NY 10014. (212)366-2000. Fax (212)366-2670. Website: www.penguinputnam.com. Imprint of Penguin Group. Mitch Horowitz, exec. ed.; Sara Carder, sr. ed. Publishes ideas and works about human consciousness that are large enough to include matters of spirit and religion. Publishes 40-50 titles/yr.; hardcover, trade paperbacks. Receives 2,000 submissions annually. 20% of books from first-time authors. Will accept mss through agents. Reprints books. Royalty 5-8% of retail; advance. Considers simultaneous submissions. Free catalog.

Nonfiction: Query. Religion.

TAU-PUBLISHING, 1422 E. Edgemont Ave., Phoenix AZ 85006. (602)264-4828. Fax (602)248-9656. E-mail: phoenixartist@msn.com, or through Website: www.tau-publishing.org. Catholic. Jeffrey Campbell, pub. Imprint: Aleph-First. Publishes 3-4 titles/yr. Receives 25 submissions annually. 50% of books from first-time authors. Prefers mss through agents. SOME SUBSIDY. Reprints books. Prefers 25,000-50,000 wds. or 100-200 pgs. Royalty on net; no advance. Average first printing 3,000. Publication within 8 mos. Considers simultaneous submissions. Responds in 4-6 mos. Guidelines on Website; no catalog.

Nonfiction: Query; fax/e-query OK. "Looking for Catholic inspirational material; reflections and meditations."

Photos: Accepts freelance photos for book covers.

THIRD WORLD PRESS, PO Box 19730, 7822 S. Dobson Ave., Chicago IL 60619. (773)651-0700. Fax (773)651-7286. E-mail: GwenMTWP@aol.com, or TWPress3@aol.com. Website: www.ThirdWorldPressInc.com. Submit to Asst. to the Publisher. African American publisher. Publishes 20 titles/yr.; hard cover, trade paperbacks. Receives 400-500 submissions annually. 20% of books from first-time authors. Will accept mss through agents. Reprints books. Royalty on retail; advance varies. Publication within 18 mos. Considers simultaneous submissions. Responds in 5-6 mos. Guidelines on Website; free catalog. Note: this company is open to submissions in July only. Submissions are not returned.

Nonfiction/Fiction: Query by mail, or proposal/5 chapters.

Ethnic Books: African American.

Tips: "Submit complete manuscript for poetry; must be African American centered."

TORCH LEGACY PUBLICATIONS, PO Box 165046, Irving TX 75016. (877)TORCHLP. Fax (817)887-3089. E-mail: info@torchlegacy.com. Website: www.torchlegacy.com. Daniel Whyte III, pres. Dedicated to publishing Bible-based books of all genres by and for African Americans and whosoever will. Publishes 7+ titles/yr. 80% of books from first-time authors. Royalty 10% of net; no advance. Average first printing 5,000. Publication within 12 mos. No simultaneous submissions. Responds in 2 mos.

Nonfiction: Query first; e-query preferred. "We are especially interested in Christian self-help books for the African American community for all age groups. Outright submissions in all categories are welcome."

Ethnic Books: African American.

Also Does: "We also handle the production and publishing of sermon books by local pastors for local churches, and we transcribe sermons for pastors under our imprint, St. Paul Press."

Tips: "We are looking for books that are Bible-based but at the same time are exciting and life changing. Our mission is to 'turn many from darkness to light' in the Black community in America through presenting a clear, understandable presentation of the Gospel of Jesus Christ."

TOUCH PUBLICATIONS, 509 Garden Oaks Blvd., Houston TX 77018. Toll-free (800)735-5865. (713)884-8893. Fax (713)742-5998. E-mail: randall@touchusa.org, or from Website: www.touchusa.org. Touch Outreach Ministries. Randall Neighbour, dir. of publishing. To empower pastors, group leaders, and members to transform their lives, churches, and the world through basic Christian communities called cells. Publishes 8 titles/yr. Receives 25 submissions annually. 40% of books from first-time authors. Reprints books. Prefers 75-200 pgs. Royalty 10-15% of net; no advance. Average first printing 2,000. Guidelines (also by e-mail). Not in topical listings.

Nonfiction: Query only. "Must relate to cell church life."

Photos: Accepts freelance photos for book covers.

Tips: "Our market is extremely focused. We publish books, resources, and discipleship tools for churches, using a cell group strategy."

THE TRACT LEAGUE, 2627 Elmridge Dr., Grand Rapids MI 49534-1329. (616)453-7695. Fax (616)453-2460. E-mail: info@tractleague.com. Website: www.tractleague.com. Publishes very few tracts from outside writers, but willing to look at ideas. Submit to General Manager.

TREBLE HEART BOOKS, 1284 Overlook Dr., Sierra Vista AZ 85635. (520)458-5602. Fax (520)459-0162. E-mail: leeemory@earthlink.net. Website: www.trebleheartbooks.com. Ms. Lee Emory, ed./pub. Online publisher offers four divisions: Romance, Christian, Westerns, Mystery/Suspense. Imprint: MountainView (Christian division—see separate listing). Receives 100 submissions annually. 20% of books from first-time authors. No word length preference. Reprints few books. Royalty 35% of net on most sales. Publication within 12 mos. Books are published electronically in trade-size print. No simultaneous submissions (a 90-day exclusive is required on all submissions and a viable marketing plan must accompany every submission). Responds in 3-4 mos. to complete mss; 1-2 wks. on queries. Guidelines on Website.

Nonfiction: Submit by e-mail only to: 1thbsubmissions2@earthlink.net. Submissions open the 1st-14th of each month. Excellent nonfiction books are highly desired here.

Fiction: E-mail submissions only. Welcomes most genres for their imprints, but no poetry, alternative life style, porno/erotica, or small children's books. We accept outstanding young adult material.

Photos: Accepts high-quality freelance photos for book covers.

Tips: "All fiction should be fresh and intriguing. Challenge the reader to think, to look at things through different eyes. Avoid point-of-view head-hopping and clichés. Send consecutive chapters, not random. A well-developed marketing plan must accompany all submissions. You must follow our guidelines."

THE TRINITY FOUNDATION, PO Box 68, Unicoi TN 37692. (423)743-0199. Fax (423)743-2005. E-mail: jrob1517@aol.com. Website: www.trinityfoundation.org. John W. Robbins, pres. To promote the logical system of truth found in the Bible. Publishes 5 titles/yr.; hardcover, trade paperbacks. Receives 3 submissions annually. No books from first-time authors. No mss through agents. Reprints books. Prefers 200 pgs. Outright purchases up to $1,500; free books; no advance. Average first printing 2,000. Publication within 9 mos. No simultaneous submissions. Requires requested ms on disk. Responds in 2-3 mos. No guidelines; catalog on Website.

Nonfiction: Query letter only. Open to Calvinist/Clarkian books, Christian philosophy, economics, and politics.

Also Does: Pamphlets, booklets, tracts.

Photos: Accepts freelance photos for book covers.

Tips: "Most open to doctrinal books that conform to the Westminster Confession of Faith; nonfiction, biblical, and well-reasoned books, theologically sound, clearly written, and well organized."

TROITSA BOOKS, 400 Oser Ave., Ste. 1600, Hauppauge NY 11788-3619. (631)231-7269. Fax (631)231-8175. E-mail: Novaeditorial@earthlink.net, or through Website: www.nova publishers.com. Religious imprint of Nova Science Publishers Inc. Submit to Editor-in-Chief. Publishes 5-20 titles/yr. Receives 50-100 submissions annually. No mss through agents. Various lengths. Royalty; no advance. Publication within 6-18 mos. Considers simultaneous submissions. Accepts requested ms on disk or by e-mail (prefers e-mail for all submissions and correspondence). Responds in 1 mo. Guidelines on Website; free catalog.

Nonfiction: Proposal/2 chapters by e-mail. Send to above e-mail with a copy to novascil@ aol.com.

Fiction: Proposal/2 chapters by e-mail. For adults.

Photos: Accepts freelance photos for book covers.

TSABA HOUSE, 2252—12th St., Reedley CA 93654. (559)643-8575. E-mail: info@tsaba house.com. Website: www.tsabahouse.com. Jodie Nazaroff, VP & sr. ed. Christian publishing company currently publishing fiction, nonfiction, self-help, teaching, and devotionals; no children's books or poetry. Will accept mss through agents. Royalty. Guidelines on Website.

Nonfiction/Fiction: Proposal/cover letter, chapter-by-chapter synopsis, 1 chapter, and word count; no e-query. Accepts during the month of January ONLY.

Tips: "Your manuscript must be completed. We offer contracts to authors with a 3 book option only. You must commit to publish one book at least every two years—annually is preferable."

TYNDALE ESPANOL, 351 Executive Dr., Carol Stream IL 60188. (630)784-5272. Fax (630)344-0943. E-mail: andresschwartz@tyndale.com. Website: www.tyndale.com. Andres Schwartz, dir. Spanish division of Tyndale House Publishers.

TYNDALE HOUSE PUBLISHERS, 351 Executive Dr., Carol Stream IL 60188. Toll-free (800)323-9400. (630)668-8300. Toll-free fax (800)684-0247. Website: www.tyndale.com. Submit to Manuscript Review Committee. Practical Christian books for home and family. Imprints: HeartQuest (see separate listing); Tyndale Espanol (Spanish imprint); Picket Fence Press (resources for women juggling multiple priorities in and outside the home). Publishes 225-250 titles/yr.; hardcover, trade paperbacks, mass-market paperbacks (reprints). 5% of books from first-time authors. Requires mss through agents. Reprints books. Royalty negotiable; outright purchase of some children's books; advance negotiable. Average first printing 5,000-10,000. Publication within 9 mos. Considers simultaneous submissions. Responds in 3-6 mos. Prefers NLT. No unsolicited mss. Guidelines/catalog on Website.

Nonfiction: Query from agents or published authors only; no phone/fax query. No unsolicited mss (they will not be acknowledged or returned).

Fiction: "We accept queries only from agents, Tyndale authors, authors known to us from other publishers, or other people in the publishing industry. Novellas, 25,000-30,000 wds.; novels 75,000-100,000 wds. All must have an evangelical Christian message."

Also Does: E-books.

**Note: This publisher serviced by The Writer's Edge and ChristianManuscriptSubmissions .com.

UMI PUBLISHING, 1551 Regency Court, Calumet IL 60409. Toll-free (800)860-8642. (708)868-7100. Fax (708)868-6759. E-mail: customerservice@urbanministries.com. Website: www.urbanministries.com. Urban Ministries Inc. Not currently accepting unsolicited manuscripts.

UNITED METHODIST PUBLISHING HOUSE—See Abingdon Press or Dimensions for Living.

UNIVERSITY OF ARKANSAS PRESS, McIlroy House, 105 N. McIlroy Ave., Fayetteville AR 72701. Toll-free (800)626-0090. (479)575-3246. Fax (479)575-6044. E-mail: uapress@uark.edu. Website: www.uapress.com. Lawrence Malley, ed. (lmalley@uark.edu). Academic publisher. Publishes 30 titles/yr.; hardcover, trade paperbacks. Receives 1,000 submissions annually. 30% of books from first-time authors. Will accept mss through agents. Reprints books. Prefers 300 pgs. Royalty on net; no advance. Average first printing 1,000-2,000. Publication within 1 yr. Reluctantly considers simultaneous submissions. Responds in 3 mos. Requires accepted ms on disk. Guidelines on Website; free catalog.

Nonfiction: Query. "All our books are scholarly." Looking for regional books.

Photos: Accepts freelance photos for book covers.

UNIVERSITY PRESS OF AMERICA, 4501 Forbes Blvd., Ste. 200, Lanham MD 20706. (301)459-3366. Fax (301)429-5748. E-mail: submitupa@univpress.com. Website: www.univpress.com. Rowman & Littlefield Publishing Group/Academic. Patti Belcher, acq. ed. (pbelcher@univpress.com). Publishes scholarly works in the social sciences and humanities; established by academics for academics. Imprint: Hamilton Books (biographies & memoirs). Publishes 75 religion titles/yr. Receives 700 submissions annually. 75% of books from first-time authors. Will accept mss through agents. SOME SUBSIDY. Does Digital Printing. Reprints books. Prefers 90-300 pgs. Royalty up to 12% of net; no advance. Average first printing 200-300. Publication within 4-6 mos. Considers simultaneous submissions. Accepts e-mail submissions. Responds in 2 wks. Accepts requested ms on disk or by e-mail. Guidelines on Website; free catalog.

Nonfiction: Proposal/3 chapters or complete ms; phone/fax/e-query OK. "Looking for scholarly manuscripts."

Ethnic Books: African studies; black studies.

Tips: "Most open to timely, thoroughly researched, and well-documented books. Moderately controversial topics. We publish academic and scholarly books only. Authors are typically affiliated with a college, university, or seminary."

+VBC PUBLISHING, PO Box 9101, Vallejo CA 94591. (707)315-1219. Fax (707)648-2169. E-mail: kevin@astroaire.com. Website: www.www.geocities.com/vallejobiblecollege. Vallejo Bible College. Kevin Gordon, pres. To glorify the Lord through Christian literature; to provide the Christian community with material to aid them in their personal studies and to help in their life and ministry. New publisher; plans 1-5 titles/yr.; hardcover, trade paperbacks. Plans to publish 50% of books from first-time authors. Will accept mss through agents. Print-on-demand publisher. No reprints. Prefers 100+ pgs. Royalty 8-12% on net; no advance. Publication within 8 mos. Considers simultaneous submissions. Responds in 2-6 wks. Accepted mss on disk. Prefers KJV, NKJV, NASB, NIV. Guidelines (also on Website); no catalog.

Nonfiction: Proposal/2 chapters or complete ms; phone query OK; no fax/e-query.

Special Needs: Biblical theology, Bible study, and Christian living.

Artwork: Open to queries from freelance artists.

Tips: "Most open to doctrinally sound and relevant manuscripts. Have a well-written manuscript and a plan to market your book. Follow guidelines when submitting and trust in the Lord!"

VINTAGE ROMANCE PUBLISHING LLC, PO Box 1165, Ladson SC 29456-1165. (843)225-9735. E-mail: editor@vrpublishing.com. Website: www.vrpublishing.com. Dawn Carrington, ed-in-chief. Old-fashioned romance fiction set anytime before the 1960s. Publishes 12+

titles/yr. Currently closed to submissions except by author referral or invitation by publisher, but actively seeking strong inspirational romances. Will accept mss through agents. No subsidy. Prefers 75,000 wds. Royalty 6% on retail; no advance. Average first printing 100+. Publication within 18 mos. Guidelines on Website.

Fiction: E-query only; no attachments; no phone/fax query. "Please include previous publication information. Authors should be familiar with marketing and promotions and be willing to submit a detailed marketing plan."

Tips: "We do not accept formulaic romances, nor do we accept inspirational romances which preach or teach readers about a certain type of religion. All our inspirational romances should weave faith into the story line seamlessly. Also seeking inspirational nonfiction that motivates, inspires, and encourages. No self-help books. Author must have a nonfiction background and be familiar with (more than general knowledge) the subject about which he/she is writing. We prefer to see a nonfiction proposal with chapter outlines, author credentials, and author platform information. Especially looking for books on promoting and marketing inspirational novels and inspirational romances."

VIRGINIA PINES PRESS, 7092 Jewell-North, Kinsman OH 44428. (330)876-3504. Fax (209) 882-5803. Website: www.virginiapines.com. Helen C. Caplan, pub. Publishes fiction with a Christian viewpoint and creative nonfiction that helps document 21st-century America. Publishes 3-5 titles/yr. Receives 40-50 submissions annually. 90% of books from first-time authors. Will accept mss through agents. No reprints. Prefers 80,000-100,000 wds. Royalty 6-8% on net; some outright purchases; no advance. Average first printing 1,000. Publication within 8 mos. Considers simultaneous submissions. Prefers requested ms on disk. Responds in 1-10 mos. Prefers NKJV. Guidelines on Website; free catalog.

Nonfiction: Query, proposal, or complete ms; phone/fax/e-query OK. "We are always on the lookout for third-person, full-length, creative nonfiction works, to which we give top priority."

Fiction: Query, proposal, or complete ms; phone/fax/e-query OK. "Looking for excellent, full-length spiritual warfare works that teach by example of the characters within the story how to identify spiritual warfare in daily life and how to become victorious over these types of attacks on family, finances, business, and peace of mind."

Photos: Accepts freelance photos for book covers.

Contest: Sponsors several cover design contests each year. See Website for details of current contest.

+VIRTUAL TALES, E-mail through Website: www.virtualtales.com. P. June Diel, ed. dir; Jake George, acq. ed. Estab. 2006. Produces eBook and paperback novels and novellas. Requires e-mail submissions. Guidelines on Website. Incomplete topical listings.

THE VISION FORUM, 4719 Blanco Rd., San Antonio TX 78212. (210)340-5250. Fax (210)340-8577. Website: www.visionforum.com. Douglas W. Phillips, pres. Dedicated to the restoration of the biblical family. Historical fiction.

WALK WORTHY PRESS, (248)737-1747. Fax (248)737-1766. E-mail: manuscriptcoordinator@walkworthypress.net, or editor@walkworthypress.net. Website: www.walkworthypress.net. Denise Stinson, pub. Primarily fiction for the African American Christian. Publishes 10 titles/yr. Receives 200 submissions annually. 95% of books from first-time authors. Will accept mss through agents. Reprints books. Prefers 75,000-100,000 wds., or 300 pgs. Royalty 10-15% on retail; variable advance. Average first printing varies. Publication within 9 mos. Considers simultaneous submissions (if informed). No disk or e-mail submissions. Responds in 2-8 wks. Prefers KJV, NKJV, NIV, Amplified. Guidelines on Website; free catalog.

Nonfiction: Proposal/2 chapters by e-mail (see Website). "We do primarily fiction. Our nonfiction is generally from authors who have a high profile."

Fiction: Submission guidelines on Website. Seasoned fiction author may send proposal/3 chapters. For all ages. Contemporary, ethnic, fantasy, juvenile, literary, short-story collection. Big commercial fiction.

Ethnic Books: African American.

Tips: "Present a good package. Read our books first. Do a story synopsis, not book-jacket copy. We like manuscripts that explore little-explored areas of life in Christian books."

WATERBROOK PRESS, 12265 Oracle Blvd., Ste. 200, Colorado Springs CO 80921. Toll-free (800)603-7051. (719)590-4999. Fax (719)590-8977. Website: www.waterbrookpress .com. WaterBrook Multnomah Publishing Group/Random House Inc. Imprint: Shaw (Fisherman Bible Studyguides). Jeanette Thomason, ed. dir. Publishes 70 titles/yr. Receives 1,000 submissions annually. 15% of books from first-time authors. Requires mss through agents. Reprints books. Royalty; advance. Publication in approximately 12 mos. Considers simultaneous submissions. Responds in 1-2 mos. No guidelines; catalog on Website.

Nonfiction/Fiction: Agented submissions only.

**Note: This publisher serviced by ChristianManuscriptSubmissions.com.

WESLEYAN PUBLISHING HOUSE, PO Box 50434, Indianapolis IN 46250-0434. (317)774-7900. E-mail: wph@wesleyan.org. Website: www.wesleyan.org/wph. The Wesleyan Church. Lawrence Wilson, ed. dir. Explain spiritual concepts simply and show readers how to make practical life change. Publishes 15 titles/yr.; hardcover, trade paperbacks. Receives 150 submissions annually. 20% of books from first-time authors. Will accept mss through agents. No reprints. Prefers 25,000-40,000 wds. Royalty and advance. Average first printing 4,000. Publication within 9-12 mos. Considers simultaneous submissions. Prefers requested ms by e-mail. Responds within 2 mos. Prefers NIV. Guidelines (also by e-mail/Website); free catalog.

Nonfiction: Proposal/3-5 chapters; no phone/fax/e-query. "Looking for books that help Christians understand the faith and apply it to their lives."

**Note: This publisher serviced by ChristianManuscriptSubmissions.com.

WESTBOW PRESS—See Thomas Nelson, Fiction.

WESTMINSTER JOHN KNOX PRESS—See Presbyterian Publishing Corporation.

WHITAKER HOUSE, 1030 Hunt Valley Cir., New Kensington PA 15068. (724)334-7000. (724)334-1200. E-mail: publisher@whitakerhouse.com. Website: www.whitakerhouse .com. Whitaker Corp. Tom Cox, sr. ed. To advance God's Kingdom by providing biblically based products that proclaim the power of the Gospel and minister to the spiritual needs of people around the world. Publishes 30-40 titles/yr.; hardcover, trade paperbacks, massmarket paperbacks. Receives 500 submissions annually. 25% of books from first-time authors. Will accept mss through agents. No subsidy, print-on-demand, or reprints. Prefers 50,000 wds. Royalty 6-15% on net; some variable advances. Average first printing 5,000. Publication within 10 mos. Considers simultaneous submissions. Prefers accepted ms by e-mail. Responds in 4 mos. Prefers NIV. Guidelines on Website; no catalog.

Nonfiction: Query only first; no phone/fax query; e-query OK.

Fiction: Query only first; no phone/fax query; e-query OK.

Special Needs: Charismatic & spiritual warfare.

Ethnic Books: Hispanic translations of current English titles.

Tips: "Looking for quality fiction and previously published authors with a national marketing platform. Most open to high-quality, well-thought-out, compelling pieces of work. Do the research and work required by our guidelines."

**Note: This publisher serviced by The Writer's Edge.

WHITE ROSE /THE WILD ROSE PRESS, PO Box 706, Adams Basin NY 14410. (585)752-8770. E-mail: rpenders@thewildrosepress.com. Website: www.thewildrosepress.com. Rhonda Penders, ed. To give writers a background and forum to perfect their craft; the "garden" is truly a place for new authors to grow and "bloom" along with giving experienced writers a place to gain some flexibility. White Rose imprint is devoted specifically to inspirational, Christian romances. Publishes about 12 titles/yr; trade paperbacks. Receives 1,000 submissions annually. 60% of books from first-time authors. Will accept mss through agents. Does e-publishing for anything under 55,000 wds.; over that is print & e-publishing. Does print-on-demand. Reprints books. Prefers up to 100,000 wds. Royalty 30% on download; 7% on POD. No advance. Publication in up to 12 mos. Considers simultaneous submissions reluctantly. Responds quarterly. Prefers NIV. Guidelines by e-mail; no catalog.

Fiction: Query first; romance only. "We accept all romance but are actively pursuing inspirational romance." Accepts short stories as well as full-length manuscripts.

Tips: "We don't do form rejection slips. We are prompt and believe in communication."

WHITE STONE BOOKS, PO Box 2835, Lakeland FL 33806. Toll-free (866)253-8622. E-mail: info@whitestonebooks.com. Website: www.whitestonebooks.com. Christian books. Amanda Pilgrim, ed. Publishes 25 titles/yr.; hardcover, trade paperbacks, mass-market paperbacks. 30% of books from first-time authors. Will accept mss through agents. SUBSIDY PUBLISHES OCCASIONALLY. Reprints books. Publication within 18 mos. Considers simultaneous submissions. Guidelines (also by e-mail); free catalog.

Nonfiction: Proposal/1 chapter.

Fiction: Proposal/1 chapter. For all ages. "We prefer scripts with several connecting layers, with story lines that are compelling and thought provoking."

Special Needs: Adult & teen novels; seasonally appropriate for gift giving, especially for Mother's Day and Christmas.

Artwork: Open to queries from freelance artists.

Tips: "Most open to books that are seasonally appropriate, but not seasonally specific: Mothers/Mother's Day; Fathers/Father's Day."

**Note: This publisher serviced by The Writers Edge and ChristianManuscriptSubmissions .com.

WILSHIRE BOOK COMPANY, 9731 Variel Ave., Chatsworth CA 91311-4315. (818)700-1522. Fax (818)700-1527. E-mail: mpowers@mpowers.com. Website: www.mpowers.com. A general publisher of motivational books. Melvin Powers, pres.; Marcia Powers, ed. Books that help you become who you choose to be tomorrow. Publishes 6 titles/yr. 80% of books from first-time authors. Will accept mss through agents. Reprints books. Prefers 30,000 wds. or 128-160 pgs. Royalty 5% on retail; variable advance. Average first printing 5,000. Publication within 6 mos. Considers simultaneous submissions. No disk or e-mail submissions. Responds in 2 mos. Guidelines on Website.

Nonfiction: Query or proposal/3 chapters; phone/e-query OK.

Fiction: Allegory for adults that teaches principles of psychological/spiritual growth.

Photos/Artwork: Accepts freelance photos for book covers; open to queries from freelance artists.

Tips: "We are looking for adult allegories such as *Illusions* by Richard Bach, *The Little Prince* by Antoine de Saint-Exupéry, and *The Greatest Salesman in the World* by Og Mandino. Analyze each one to discover what elements make it a winner. Duplicate those elements in your own style, using a creative, new approach and fresh material. We need 30,000-60,000 words."

+WIPF AND STOCK PUBLISHERS, 199 W. 8th Ave., Ste. 3. Eugene OR 97401-2960. (541)344-1528. Fax (541)344-1506. E-mail: info@wipfandstock.com. Website: www.wipfandstock .com. K.C. Hanson, ed-in-chief (KCHanson@wipfandstock.com); Charlie Collier & Chris Spinks, eds. Specializes in new and reprinted academic books. Imprints: Cascade Books, Pickwick Publications, and Resource Publications. Guidelines/catalog on Website. Incomplete topical listings.

WOODLAND GOSPEL PUBLISHING HOUSE, 118 Woodland Dr., Ste. 1101, Chapmanville WV 25508. (304)752-7500. Fax (304)752-9002. E-mail: info@woodlandpress.com, or from Website: www.woodlandpress.com. Woodland Press LLC. Cheryl Davis, ed; submit to Mike Collins. Publishes 7 titles/yr. Receives 150 submissions annually. 90% of books from first-time authors. Will accept mss through agents. No reprints. Prefers 60,000 wds. or 230 pgs. Royalty on net; no advance. Average first printing 2,000. Publication within 1 yr. No simultaneous submissions. Responds in 2 mos. No mss by disk or e-mail. No guidelines or catalog.

    Nonfiction: Proposal/3 chapters; no phone/fax/e-query.

W PUBLISHING GROUP, PO Box 141000, Nashville TN 37214. (615)889-9000. Fax (615)902-2112. Website: www.Wpublishinggroup.com. Thomas Nelson Inc. David Moberg, pub.; Greg Daniel, assoc. pub. Publishes 75 titles/yr. Less than 3% of books from first-time authors. Prefers mss through agents. No reprints. Does not accept unsolicited manuscripts. Prefers 65,000-95,000 wds. Royalty. No guidelines.

    Nonfiction: Query letter only first; no unsolicited ms. "Nonfiction dealing with the relationship and/or application of biblical principles to everyday life; 65,000-95,000 words."

    **Note: This publisher serviced by The Writer's Edge & ManuscriptSubmissions.com.

WRITE NOW PUBLICATIONS, PO Box 110390, Nashville TN 37222. Toll-free (800)21-WRITE. E-mail: RegAForder@aol.com. Website: www.writenowpublications.com. Reg A. Forder, exec. ed. To train and develop quality Christian writers; books on writing and speaking for writers and speakers. Royalty division of ACW Press. Publishes 1-2 titles/yr.; trade paperbacks. Receives 6 submissions annually. 0% from first-time authors. Will accept mss through agents. Reprints books. Royalty 10% of net. Average first printing 2,000. Publication within 12 mos. Considers simultaneous submissions. Requires requested ms on disk. No guidelines/catalog.

    Nonfiction: Writing how-to only. Query letter only; e-query OK.

+XYZZY PRESS. E-mail: acquisitions@xyzzypress.com. Website: www.xyzzypress.com. Responds in several wks. Guidelines on Website.

    Nonfiction: Proposal/several chapters by e-mail.

    Fiction: Proposal/several chapters by e-mail.

YALE UNIVERSITY PRESS, PO Box 209040, New Haven CT 06518-9040. (203)432-6807. Fax (203)436-1064. No e-mail submissions. Website: www.yalepress.yale.edu. Jennifer Banks, ed. Publishes scholarly and general-interest books, including religion. Publishes 10 religious titles/yr.; hardcover, trade paperbacks. Receives 200 submissions annually. 15% of books from first-time authors. Will accept mss through agents. Reprints books. Prefers up to 100,000 wds. or 400 pgs. Royalty from 0% to standard trade royalties; advance $0-100,000. Average first printing varies by field. Publication within 1 yr. Considers simultaneous submissions. Requires requested ms on disk; no e-mail submissions. Responds in 2 mos. Guidelines & catalog on Website (www.yalebooks.com).

    Nonfiction: Query or proposal/sample chapters; fax query OK; no e-query. "Excellent and salable scholarly books."

    Contest: Yale Series of Younger Poets competition. Open to poets under 40 who have not had a book of poetry published. Submit manuscripts of 48-64 pages by November 15. Entry fee $15. Send SASE for guidelines (also on Website). Send complete manuscript.

YOUTH SPECIALTIES, 300 S. Pierce St., El Cajon CA 92020. Toll-free (888)346-4179. (619)440-2333. Fax (619)440-8542. E-mail: jay@youthspecialties.com. Website: www.youth specialties.com. Zondervan. Jay Howver, pub. Books for youth workers and teenagers. Imprint: Invert Books. Publishes 30 titles/yr. Will accept mss through agents. No reprints. Prefers 35,000 wds. Royalty on net or outright purchase of $3,000-8,000; advance. Publication within 18 mos. Considers simultaneous submissions. Responds in 4-6 wks. Prefers NIV. Guidelines by e-mail/Website; free catalog

Nonfiction: Proposal/2 chapters.

Tips: "We prefer books from youth workers who are in the trenches working with students."

ZONDERKIDZ, 5300 Patterson S.E., Grand Rapids MI 49530-0002. (616)698-6900. Fax (616)698-3578. E-mail: zpub@zondervan.com. Website: www.zonderkidz.com. Zondervan/ HarperCollins. Barbara Scott, children's ed. Children's book line of Zondervan; ages 12 & under. Not currently accepting proposals.

**Note: This publisher serviced by ChristianManuscriptSubmissions.com.

ZONDERVAN, General Trade Books; Academic and Professional Books, 5300 Patterson S.E., Grand Rapids MI 49530-0002. (616)698-6900. Manuscript submission line: (616)698-3447. Website: www.zondervan.com. HarperCollins Publishers. Mission is to be the leading Christian communications company meeting the needs of people with resources that glorify Jesus Christ and promote biblical principles. Publishes 120 trade titles/yr.; hardcover, trade paperbacks, mass-market paperbacks. Few books from first-time authors. Will accept mss through agents. No subsidy or reprints. Royalty 12-14% of net; variable advance. Publication within 12-18 mos. Considers simultaneous submissions. Requires requested ms by e-mail. Prefers NIV. Guidelines on Website.

Nonfiction: Submissions only by e-mail and only certain types of mss. See Website for e-mail address and submission guidelines.

Fiction: No fiction at this time; refer to Website for updates.

Children's Lines: ZonderKidz and Faithgirlz (not currently accepting new products).

Ethnic Books: Vida Publishers division: Spanish and Portuguese.

Tips: "Almost no unsolicited manuscripts are published. Book proposals should be single-spaced with one-inch margins on all sides."

**Note: This publisher serviced by ChristianManuscriptSubmissions.com.

SUBSIDY PUBLISHERS

In this section you will find any publishers who do 50 percent or more subsidy publishing. For our purposes, I am defining a subsidy publisher as any publisher that requires the author to pay for any part of the publishing costs. They may call themselves by a variety of names, such as a book packager, a cooperative publisher, a self-publisher, or simply someone who helps authors get their books published. Print-on-demand businesses (also known as POD) publish books one at a time and usually much faster than typical publishers. A new designation in the listing this year is custom publisher, which refers to a publisher that develops new authors to eventually work with royalty publishers.

To my knowledge the following publishers are legitimate subsidy publishers (as opposed to companies simply out to take your money without offering knowledge of the industry), but I cannot guarantee that. It is important that you understand that any time you are asked to pay for any part of the production of your book, you are entering into a nontraditional relationship with a publisher. Note that some subsidy publishers do at least some royalty publishing, so you could approach them as a royalty publisher. You just need to realize that they are likely to offer you a subsidy deal, so if you are interested only in a royalty arrangement, indicate that in your cover letter.

Some subsidy publishers will publish any book, as long as the author is willing to pay for it. Others are as selective about what they publish as a royalty publisher would be. As subsidy publishers become more selective, the professional quality of subsidy books is improving overall. Many will do only nonfiction—no novels or children's books. These distinctions will be important as you seek the right publisher.

Subsidy publishing can be confusing, and many authors go into agreements with these publishers having little or no knowledge of what to expect. As a result, many writers come away unhappy or disillusioned; I frequently get complaints from authors who feel they have been cheated or taken advantage of. Each complaint brings with it an expectation that I should drop that publisher from this book. Although I am sensitive to these complaints, I also realize that I am not in a position to pass judgment on which publishers should be dropped. It has been my experience that for every complaint I get about a publisher, I find several other authors who sing the praises of the same publisher. For that reason, I feel I can serve the needs of authors better by giving a brief overview of what to expect from a subsidy publisher and what kinds of terms should send up a red flag.

First, unless you know your book has a limited audience or you have your own method of distribution (such as being a speaker who can sell your own books when you speak), I recommend that you try all the appropriate royalty publishers before looking at a subsidy house.

If you are unsuccessful with the royalty publishers but feel strongly about seeing your book published, a subsidy publisher may be able to help you. A subsidy publisher has the contacts, know-how, and resources to make printing your book easier and often less expensive than doing it yourself.

It is always good to get more than one bid to determine whether the terms you are being offered are competitive with other such publishers. A legitimate subsidy publisher will be happy to provide you with a list of former clients as references. Don't just ask for that list; follow through and contact more than one of those references. Get a catalog of the publisher's books or a list of books they have published and then review a few of the books yourself to check the quality of their work, the bindings, etc. See if their books are available through Amazon.com or similar online services. Get answers to all your questions before you commit yourself to anything. Also have someone review your contract before signing it. I do such reviews, as do a number of others listed in the Editorial Services section of this book. Be sure that any terms agreed upon are *in writing*. The listings below include printers who could help you complete the printing process yourself, so you will want to check out those as well.

Keep in mind that the more copies of a book printed, the lower the cost per copy, but never let a publisher talk you into publishing more copies than you think is reasonable for your situation. Also, find out up front, and have included in the contract, how much promotion, if any, the publisher is going to do. Some will do as much as a royalty publisher; others do none at all. If the publisher is not doing promotion, and you don't have any means of distribution yourself, it may not be a good idea to pursue subsidy publication. You don't want to end up with a garage full of books you can't sell.

Following this section I include the names and addresses of Christian book distributors. I have asked them if they will consider distributing a subsidy-published book, and some have responded positively. You may want to contact some of them to find out their interest before you sign a contract with a subsidy publisher. For more help on self-publishing, go to: www.book market.com/index.html.

(+) A plus sign before a listing indicates it is a new listing this year or was not included last year.

ACW PRESS, American Christian Writers, PO Box 110390, Nashville TN 37222. Toll-free (800)21-WRITE. E-mail: Jim@JamesWatkins.com. Website: www.acwpress.com. Reg A. Forder, owner; Jim Watkins, editorial advisor. A self-publishing book packager. Imprint: Write Now Publications (see separate listing). Publishes 40 titles/yr.; hardcover, trade paperbacks, mass-market paperbacks, coffee-table books. Reprints books. SUBSIDY PUBLISHES 95%; does print-on-demand. Average first printing 2,500. Publication within 4-6 mos. Responds in 48-72 hrs. Request for Estimate form available on Website. Not in topical listings; will consider any nonfiction or fiction topic. Guidelines by e-mail/Website.

> **Nonfiction/Fiction:** All types considered.
>
> **Tips:** "We offer a high quality publishing alternative to help Christian authors get their material into print. High standards, high quality. If authors have a built-in audience, they have the best chance to make self-publishing a success." Has a marketing program available to authors.
>
> ****Note:** This publisher serviced by The Writer's Edge and ChristianManuscriptSubmissions .com.

ALFRED ALI LITERARY WORKS INC., PO Box 582, Southfield MI 48076. (248)356-5111. Fax (248)356-1367. E-mail: AALiterary@aol.com. Website: www.AlfredAli.com. San Serif, ed. Spreading the word on how the Word of God can change and improve lives. Publishes 1 title/yr. Receives 5 submissions annually. 80% of books from first-time authors. Accepts mss through agents. Reprints books. SUBSIDY PUBLISHES 70%. Prefers 210 pgs. Royalty 25% of retail; no advance. Average first printing 1,000-5,000. Publication within 9 mos. Accepts e-mail submissions. No guidelines; catalog $3.

> **Nonfiction:** Query only; fax query OK.
>
> **Ethnic Books:** Publishes for the African American market.
>
> **Photos:** Accepts freelance photos for book covers.
>
> **Tips:** "Most open to books that are based on inspiration that leads to self-awareness."

AMERICAN BINDING & PUBLISHING CO., PO Box 60049, Corpus Christi TX 78466-0049. Toll-free (800)863-3708. (361)658-4221. E-mail: rmagner@grandecom.net. Website: www .americanbindingpublishing.com. Rose Magner, pub. Publishes 60 titles/yr. Receives 200 submissions annually. 95% of books from first-time authors. No mss through agents. Reprints books. SUBSIDY PUBLISHES 100%; does print-on-demand. Prefers 200 pgs. Royalty 15% on retail; no advance. Publication within 2 wks. Considers simultaneous submissions. Requires requested ms on disk (Microsoft Word format). Responds in 2 wks. Any Bible version. Guidelines (also by e-mail); free catalog.

> **Nonfiction:** Complete ms; phone/e-query OK. Will consider any topic.

Fiction: Complete ms; phone/e-query OK. For all ages; all genres.

Ethnic Books: Black and Hispanic.

Photos: Accepts freelance photos for book covers.

Tips: "We are print-on-demand; authors are responsible for their own marketing. We will consider any topic—nonfiction or fiction, but most open to fiction."

AMPELOS PRESS, 316 Blanchard Rd., Drexel Hill PA 19026. Phone/fax (610)626-6833. E-mail: mbagnull@aol.com. Website: www.writehisanswer.com. Marlene Bagnull, LittD, pub./ed. Services (depending on what is needed) include critiquing, editing, proofreading, typesetting, and cover design. Publishes 1-3 titles/yr. SUBSIDY PUBLISHES 100%. Query only. Not included in topical listings (see Tips).

Special Needs: Books about missions both at home and abroad.

Tips: "Our vision statement reads: 'Strongly, unashamedly, uncompromisingly Christ-centered. Exalting the name of Jesus Christ. Seeking to teach His ways through holding up the Word of God as the Standard.' (Ampelos is the Greek word for 'vine' in John 15:5.)"

+ANOMALOS PUBLISHING, PO Box 5, Crane MO 65633. (417)723-0610. E-mail: info@ Anomalospublishing.com. Website: www.anomalospublishing.com. Tom Horn, pub.; Michelle Warner, mng. ed. CO-OP PUBLISHER; AUTHOR BUYS 1,000 OR MORE BOOKS. Guidelines & details on Website. Not included in topical listings.

BAAL HAMON PUBLISHER, Ste. T219, 244 Fifth Ave., New York NY 10001. Phone: + 646 213 1019. E-mail: publishers@baalhamon.com. Website: www.baalhamon.com. Joy and Truth Christian Ministry. Submit to Acquisitions Editor (submissions@baalhamon.com). Company is named for the biblical town in which Solomon had a vineyard that was kept for him by a husbandman; company motto is "the vineyard of life-changing words." Estab. 2006. Publishes 30-40 titles/yr.; hardcover, trade paperbacks. Receives 600 submissions annually. 75% of books from first-time authors. Accepts mss through agents. SUBSIDY PUBLISHES 6-8%; does print-on-demand; REQUIRES PURCHASE OF PROMOTION PACKAGE. Reprints books. Prefers 40,000-60,000 wds., or 160-240 pgs. Royalty 10-20% on retail; seldom gives $2,000 advance. Average first printing 2,500. Publication within 3-6 mos. Considers simultaneous submissions. Responds in 1-3 wks. Prefers accepted mss by e-mail. Prefers NIV/GNB. Guidelines by e-mail.

Nonfiction: Proposal/1 chapter; unsolicited mss returned unopened; e-query OK.

Fiction: Proposal/1-2 chapters; unsolicited mss returned unopened; e-query OK. For all ages.

Ethnic Books: Black.

Photos/Artwork: Accepts freelance photos for book covers; open to queries from freelance artists.

Contest: Short Story Contest. Guidelines by e-mail (info@baalhamon.com).

Tips: "Writers should aim at an international, multicultural audience."

BETHANY PRESS—CUSTOM SOLUTIONS, 6820 W. 115th St., Bloomington MN 55438. Toll-free (888)717-7400. (952)914-7436. Fax (952)914-7410. E-mail: customsolutions@ bethanypress.com. Website: www.bethanypress.com. Bethany International. Submit to Book Editor by e-mail. Exclusive-to-Christian-author SELF-PUBLISHING SERVICE whose company profits go entirely to a Christian missionary-sending agency, Bethany International. Offers services including typesetting, cover design, and printing. Details on Website. Not included in topical listings; open to any fiction or nonfiction that is not in conflict with their statement of faith.

**Note: This publisher serviced by ChristianManuscriptSubmissions.com.

BLACK FOREST PRESS/TENNESSEE PUBLISHING HOUSE, Belle Arden Run Estate, 488 Mountain View Dr., Mosheim TN 37818-3524. Phone/fax (423)422-4711 (call ahead for fax). E-mail: dahkknox@embarqmail.com. Pentecostal Holiness. Dr. Dahk Knox, pub.;

Dr. Jan Knox, CFO. Provides truthful information about an author's book; whether you publish with them or not, you get free help and advice. Imprints: Tennessee Publishing House, World Truth Publishing House, Abenteure Books, Kinder Books, Sonnerschein Books, Dichter Books, Segen Books. Publishes up to 35 titles/yr.; hardcover, trade paperbacks, coffee-table books. Receives 100 submissions annually. 70% of books from first-time authors. Accepts mss through agents. SUBSIDY PUBLISHES 50%; does print-on-demand. Reprints books (with permission). Prefers 120-325 pgs. Royalty on net (100% of sales, minus $1/bk., unless other arrangements made), or outright purchase; no advance. Average first printing 2,000, or 250 POD. Publication within 2 mos. Considers simultaneous submissions. Requires accepted ms by e-mail (attached). Responds in 2 wks. Prefers NIV/NKJV. Guidelines by e-mail/Website; no catalog.

Nonfiction: Complete ms by e-mail (attached); phone/e-query OK.

Fiction: Complete ms. All genres for all ages.

Special Needs: Historical fiction, nonfiction biographies, religious books of any kind.

Photos/Artwork: Accepts freelance photos for book covers; open to queries from freelance artists.

Tips: "Most open to well-written nonfiction or historical novels. Our imprint, Tennessee Publishing House, provides tax-exemption write-offs with certain religious book offerings."

BOOKLOCKER.COM INC., PO Box 2399, Bangor ME 04402-2399. (207)262-9696. Fax (207) 262-5544. E-mail: angela@booklocker.com. Website: www.booklocker.com. Angela Hoy, pub. We seek unique, eclectic, and different manuscripts. Publishes 40-50 titles/yr.; hard cover, trade paperbacks, e-books. 90% of books from first-time authors. No mss through agents. SUBSIDY PUBLISHES 100%; does print-on-demand. Reprints books. Prefers 48-740 pgs. Royalty 35% on retail (15% on wholesale orders; 35% on booklocker.com orders; 50-70% for e-books); no advance. Publication within 4-6 wks. Considers simultaneous submissions. Responds in less than a week. Bible version is author's choice. Guidelines on Website; no catalog.

Nonfiction: Complete ms; e-query OK. "We're open to all ideas."

Fiction: Complete ms; e-query OK. All genres for all ages.

Ethnic Books: Publishes for all ethnic groups.

Photos/Artwork: Accepts freelance photos for book covers; open to queries from freelance artists.

Contest: The WritersWeekly.com 24-Hour Short Story Contest is held quarterly.

BOOKLOCKER JR, PO Box 2399, Bangor ME 04402-2399. Fax (207)262-5544. E-mail from Website: www.booklocker.com/getpublished/published.html. E-books or print-on-demand. Seeking submissions from young authors, under 18 years. Royalty varies according to product/price. Prices, terms, guidelines, and contract on Website.

BOOK PUBLISHERS NETWORK, PO Box 2256, Bothell WA 98041. (425)483-3040. Fax (425)483-3098. E-mail: sherynhara@bookpublishersnetwork.com. Website: www.book publishersnetwork.com. Sheryn Hara, ed. Publishes 5-8 titles/yr.; hardcover, trade paperbacks. Receives 20 submissions annually. 100% of books from first-time authors. Accepts mss through agents. 100% SUBSIDY. Reprints books. No preference on length. No royalty/advance. Publication within 3 mos. Considers simultaneous submissions. Responds in 1 mo. Guidelines on Website; no catalog.

Nonfiction: Proposal or complete ms; phone/fax/e-query OK.

Fiction: Proposal or complete ms; phone/fax/e-query OK. For all ages.

Photos: Accepts freelance photos for book covers.

Tips: "We take good care of our authors. We work hand-in-hand with them to produce a quality product."

+BOOKS JUST BOOKS.COM, 51 E. 42nd St., Ste. 1202, New York NY 10017. Toll-free (800)621-2556. Fax (212)681-8002. E-mail: ron@rjcom.com. Website: www.booksjust

books.com. R J Communications. Ron Pramschufer, pub. 100% SUBSIDY. Guidelines on Website. Not included in topical listings.

+BOOKSTAND PUBLISHING/EBOOKSTAND.COM, 7790 Eigleberry St., Ste. B, Gilroy CA 95020. (408)852-1832. E-mail: support@bookstandpublishing.com. Website: www.book standpublishing.com. Kari Baldwin, ed. 100% PRINT ON DEMAND. Guidelines (by e-mail/ Website). Not included in topical listings.

BRENTWOOD CHRISTIAN PRESS, 4000 Beallwood Ave., Columbus GA 31904. Toll-free (800)334-8861. (706)576-5787. Fax (706)317-5808. E-mail: Brentwood@aol.com. Website: www.BrentwoodBooks.com. Mainline. U. D. Roberts, exec. ed. Publishes 267 titles/yr. Receives 2,000 submissions annually. Reprints books. SUBSIDY PUBLISHES 95%. Offers InstaBooks and Just in Time publishing (print-on-demand). Average first printing 500. Publication within 1 mo. Considers simultaneous submissions. Responds in 2 days. Guidelines.

> **Nonfiction:** Complete ms. "Collection of sermons on family topics, poetry, relation of Bible to current day."
>
> **Fiction:** Complete ms. "Stories that show how faith helps overcome small, day-to-day problems."
>
> **Photos:** Accepts freelance photos for book covers.
>
> **Tips:** "Keep it short; support facts with reference." This publisher specializes in small print runs of 300-1,000. Can best serve the writer who has a completed manuscript.

BROWN BOOKS PUBLISHING GROUP, 16200 N. Dallas Pkwy., Ste. 170, Dallas TX 75248. (972)381-0009. Fax (972)248-4336. E-mail: kgrant@brownbooks.com. Website: www.brownbooks.com. Milli A. Brown, pub.; submit to Kathryn Grant, sr. ed. Publishes books in the areas of self-help, religion/inspirational, relationships, business, mind/ body/spirit, and women's issues; we build relationships with our authors. Imprints: Personal Profiles, The P3 Press. Publishes 10-30 titles/yr.; hardcover, trade paperbacks, coffee-table books. Receives 2,000 submissions annually. 80% of books from first-time authors. No mss through agents. SUBSIDY PUBLISHES 100% through Personal Profiles & P3 imprints. No reprints. Royalty 100% of retail; no advance. Authors retain rights to their work. Average first printing 3,000-5,000. Publication in 6 mos. Accepts simultaneous submissions. Responds in 2 wks. Requires mss on disk or by e-mail. Responds in 2 wks. Guidelines on Website.

> **Nonfiction:** Complete ms; phone/e-query OK.
>
> **Fiction:** Complete ms; phone/e-query OK. For all ages.
>
> **Tips:** "We accept any type of manuscript."

CHRISTIAN SERVICES NETWORK, 1975 Janich Ranch Ct., El Cajon CA 92019-1150. Toll-free (866)484-6184. Fax (619)579-0685. Website: www.csnbooks.com. Michael Wourms, ed. SELF-PUBLISHING COMPANY. Details on Website.

CREATION HOUSE, 600 Rinehart Rd., Lake Mary FL 32746-4872. (407)333-0600. Fax (407) 333-7100. E-mail: creationhouse@strang.com. Website: www.creationhouse.com. Strang Communications Co. Submit to Acquisitions Editor. To inspire and equip people to live a Spirit-led life and to walk in the divine purpose for which they were created. Publishes 125 titles/yr.; hardcover, trade paperbacks, mass-market paperbacks, coffee-table books. Receives 1,500 submissions annually. 80% of books from first-time authors. Accepts mss through agents. No subsidy or print-on-demand. Reprints books. Prefers 25,000+ wds. or 100-200 pgs. Royalty 12-15% of net; no advance. Average first printing 6,000. Publication within 5 mos. Considers simultaneous submissions. Responds in 10-12 wks. Open to submissions on disk or by e-mail. Guidelines (also by e-mail); free catalog.

> **Nonfiction:** Proposal/3 chapters or complete ms; no phone/fax query; e-query OK. "Open to any books that are well written and glorify Jesus Christ."
>
> **Fiction:** Proposal/3 chapters or complete ms; no phone/fax query; e-query OK. For all ages. "Fiction must have a biblical world-view and point the reader to Christ."

Photos: Accepts freelance photos for book covers.

Tips: "We use the term 'co-publishing' to describe a hybrid between conventional royalty publishing and self or subsidy publishing, utilizing the best of both worlds. We produce a high quality book for our own inventory, market it, distribute it, and pay the author a royalty on every copy sold. In return, the author agrees to buy, at a deep discount, a portion of the first print run."

+CREDO HOUSE PUBLISHERS, 3148 Plainfield Ave. NE, Ste. 111, Grand Rapids MI 49525-3285. (616)363-2686. E-mail: connect@credocommunications.net. Website: www.credocommunications.net. Timothy J. Beals, pres. Estab. 2006. Custom publisher; see Website for details. Responds in 48 hrs. Guidelines on Website. Not included in topical listings.

Nonfiction: Send description of project.

Fiction: Send description of project.

CROSSHOUSE PUBLISHING, PO Box 461592, Garland TX 75046. Toll-free (877)212-0933. Toll-free fax (888)252-3022. E-mail: crosshousepublishing@earthlink.net. Website: www.crosshousepublishing.org. Self-publishing branch of KLMK Communications. Katie Welch, pub. To achieve excellence in Christian self-publishing without sacrificing personal interest and care for customers. Publishes hardcover, trade paperbacks. No mss through agents. SUBSIDY PUBLISHER. Royalty 25% on net; no advance. Publication within 3 mos. Guidelines by e-mail.

Nonfiction: Accepts.

Fiction: Accepts. For all ages.

Photos: Accepts freelance photos for book covers.

Tips: "We provide authors the opportunity to have their books distributed through a wide array of Christian and general bookstores. We aspire to offer the marketplace superior Christian literature that will impact reader's lives."

DCTS PUBLISHING, PO Box 40216, Santa Barbara CA 93140. Toll-free (800)965-8150. Fax (805)653-6522. E-mail: dennis@dctspub.com. Website: www.dctspub.com. Dennis Stephen Hamilton, ed. Books are designed to enrich the mind, encourage the heart, and empower the spirit. Publishes 5 titles/yr. Receives 25 submissions annually. 35% of books from first-time authors. No mss through agents. SUBSIDY PUBLISHES 70%. No reprints. Prefers 100-300 pgs. Royalty 17% of retail; no advance. Average first printing 3,500. Publication within 6-8 mos. No simultaneous submissions. Prefers KJV. Guidelines; free catalog & brochure.

Nonfiction: Query or proposal/2-3 chapters; e-query OK.

ROBBIE DEAN PRESS, 2910 E. Eisenhower Parkway, Ann Arbor MI 48108. (734)973-9511. Fax (734)973-9475. E-mail: Fairyha@aol.com. Website: www.RobbieDeanPress.com. Interested in works that are multiculturally appealing and that approach a topic in a unique manner. Dr. Fairy C. Hayes-Scott, owner. Publishes 1 title/yr. Receives 20 submissions annually. 100% of books from first-time authors. Accepts mss through agents. SUBSIDY PUBLISHES 75%; does print-on-demand. Reprints books. Length flexible. Royalty 10-20%; no advance. Average first printing 250. Publication within 6 mos. Considers simultaneous submissions. Responds in 2-6 wks. Guidelines by e-mail; free catalog.

Nonfiction: Query first. "We're open to new ideas."

Fiction: "We seldom do fiction." For children only.

Ethnic Books: Multicultural.

Also Does: Booklets; e-books; computer games.

Photos: Accepts freelance photos for book covers.

Tips: "Most open to self-help, reference, senior adult topics, and parenting."

ELDERBERRY PRESS INC., 1393 Old Homestead Rd., 2nd Fl., Oakland OR 97462. (541)459-6043. Toll-free fax (888)259-5484. E-mail: editor@elderberrypress.com. Website: www.elderberrypress.com. David W. St. John, exec. ed. Publishes 15 titles/yr. Receives 150-250 submissions annually. 90% of books from first-time authors. No mss through agents.

SUBSIDY PUBLISHES 50%; does print-on-demand. Royalty 10-25%; no advance. Publication within 3 mos. Considers simultaneous submissions. Accepts disk or e-mail submissions. Responds in 1 mo. Guidelines on Website; free catalog.

Nonfiction: Complete ms; phone/fax/e-query OK. "We consider all topics."

Fiction: Complete ms; phone/fax/e-query OK. All genres for all ages.

ESSENCE PUBLISHING CO. INC., 20 Hanna Ct., Belleville ON K8P 5J2, Canada. (613)962-0234. Toll-free (800)238-6376. Fax (613)962-3055. E-mail: info@essence-publishing.com. Website: www.essence-publishing.com. Essence Communications Group. David Visser, mng. ed.; Sherrill Brunton, acq. mgr. Provides affordable, short-run book publishing to the Christian community; dedicated to furthering the work of Christ through the written word. Imprints: Guardian Books, Epic Press. Publishes 100-150+ titles/yr. Receives 250+ submissions annually. 75% of books from first-time authors. SUBSIDY PUBLISHES 90%. Reprints books. Any length. Average first printing 500-1,000. Publication within 3-5 mos. Considers simultaneous submissions. Responds in 3-4 wks. Prefers requested ms on disk or by e-mail. Guidelines (also by e-mail/Website); catalog online (www.essencebookstore.com).

Nonfiction: Complete ms; phone/fax/e-query OK. Accepts all topics.

Fiction: Complete ms. All genres for all ages. Also picture books.

Also Does: Pamphlets, booklets, tracts.

Photos: Accepts freelance photos for book covers.

FAIRWAY PRESS, subsidy division for CSS Publishing Company, 517 S. Main St., Box 4503, Lima OH 45802-4503. Toll-free (800)241-4056. (419)227-1818. Fax (419)228-9184. E-mail: editor@csspub.com. Website: www.fairwaypress.com. David Runk, ed. (david@csspub .com). Imprint: Express Press. Publishes 100 titles/yr. Receives 200-300 submissions annually. 80% of books from first-time authors. Reprints books. SUBSIDY PUBLISHES 100%. Royalty to 50%; no advance. Average first printing 500-1,000. Publication within 6-9 mos. Considers simultaneous submissions. Responds in up to 1 mo. Prefers requested ms on disk; no e-mail submissions. Prefers NRSV. Guidelines on Website/catalog for 9x12 SAE.

Nonfiction: Complete ms; phone/fax/e-query OK. All types. "Looking for manuscripts with a Christian theme, and seasonal material."

Fiction: Complete ms. For adults, teens, or children; all types. No longer producing anything in full color or with four-color illustrations.

FRUITBEARER PUBLISHING, PO Box 777, Georgetown DE 19947. (302)856-6649. Fax (302) 856-7742. E-mail: candy.abbott@verizon.net. Website: www.fruitbearer.com. Branch of Candy's Creations. Candy Abbott, pres. Offers editing services and advice for self-publishers. Publishes 5-10 titles/yr. Receives 10-20 submissions annually. 90% of books from first-time authors. SUBSIDY PUBLISHES 100%. No reprints. Average first printing 30-5,000. Publication within 1-6 mos. Responds in 3 mos. Brochure for #10 SAE/1 stamp.

Nonfiction: Proposal/2 chapters; phone/fax/e-query OK.

Also Does: Pamphlets, booklets, tracts.

Photos: Accepts freelance photos for book covers.

Tips: "Accepting limited submissions."

GESHER—See Winer Foundation.

HOLY FIRE PUBLISHING, 1525 Old Trolley Rd., #116, Summerville SC 29485-8928. (843)628-0319. E-mail: publisher@christianpublish.com. Website: www.christianpublish.com. Venessa Hensel, VP. Important that everything we publish be clean and honoring to Christ and be inline with core Christian beliefs. Publishes 100 titles/yr.; hardcover, trade paperbacks. Receives 2,000+ submissions annually. 50% of books from first-time authors. Accepts mss through agents. Only does print-on-demand. Reprints books. Prefers 48-750 pgs. Royalty 50-100% on net; no advance. Publication within 2 mos. Prefers submissions on disk or by e-mail. Guidelines on Website; no catalog.

Nonfiction: Proposal/1 chapter; phone/fax/e-query OK. "Looking for Christian Living or Christian poetry." All topics.

Fiction: Proposal/1 chapter; phone/fax/e-query OK. For all ages. All genres.

Artwork: Open to queries from freelance artists.

IMD PRESS, 7140 Hooker St., Westminster CO 80030-5459. (303)482-1426. Fax (303)232-5009. E-mail: JimH@IMDPress.com. Website: www.IMDPress.com. IMD International. Phil Largent, exec. dir. Jim Hawley, IMD Press project manager. A nonprofit self-publishing ministry whose profits support IMD International church planting and Christian leadership development. Publishes 10 titles/yr.; hardcover and mostly trade paperbacks. Receives 10-15 submissions annually. 75% of books from first-time authors. Editing experience in nonfiction discipleship, training, and curriculum resources. Custom cover/interior design. Accepts mss through agents. 100% SUBSIDY; reprints books (with permission). Prints 100-5000+. Average first printing 1,000. Publication within 3 mos. Considers simultaneous submissions. Responds in 48 hrs. Guidelines and bookstore on Website.

Nonfiction: Complete ms; phone/e-query OK. Generally adult; curriculum all ages.

Fiction: Complete ms; phone/e-query OK. Generally adult.

Ethnic Books: Translation services for worldwide languages, esp. from India, Africa, and SE Asia.

Photos/Artwork: Accepts freelance photos for book covers; open to queries from freelance artists.

Tips: "Fifteen years editing and 25 years design experience gives you publishing with integrity and excellence."

IMPACT CHRISTIAN BOOKS INC., 332 Leffingwell Ave., Ste. 101, Kirkwood MO 63122. (314) 822-3309. Fax (314)822-3325. E-mail: info@impactchristianbooks.com. Website: www .impactchristianbooks.com. William D. Banks, pres. Books of healing, miraculous deliverance, and spiritual warfare, drawing individuals into a deeper walk with God. Publishes 20+ titles/yr. Receives 20-50 submissions annually. 50-70% of books from first-time authors. No mss through agents. SUBSIDY PUBLISHES 50-70%. Reprints books. Average first printing 5,000. Publication within 2 mos. Considers simultaneous submissions. Responds by prior arrangement in 30 days. Requires requested ms on disk. Guidelines; catalog for 9x12 SAE/5 stamps. Not in topical listings.

Nonfiction: Query only; phone/fax query OK. Outstanding personal testimonies and Christ-centered books.

INFINITY PUBLISHING, 1094 New Dehaven St., Ste. 100, West Conshohocken PA 19428-2713. Toll-free (877)BUY-BOOK. (610)941-9999. Fax (610)941-9959. E-mail: info@infinity publishing.com. Website: www.infinitypublishing.com. 100% PRINT-ON-DEMAND. Charges $400 up-front fee. First order of books is at 50% discount; additional orders 40% discount. Royalty 10%.

INSIGHT PUBLISHING GROUP, 8810 S. Yale, Ste. 410, Tulsa OK 74137. (918)493-1718. Fax (918)493-2219. E-mail: mail@freshword.com. Website: www.freshword.com. Christian Publisher. John Mason, ed. Owned by a best-selling author who established the company to serve authors. Publishes 50 titles/yr.; hardcover, trade paperbacks, mass-market paperbacks. Receives 50 submissions annually. 50% of books from first-time authors. Accepts mss through agents. 60% PRINT-ON-DEMAND; 40% SUBSIDY. Reprints books. Prefers 160 pgs. Royalty 15-17% on net; no advance. Average first printing 5,000. Publication within 6 mos. Considers simultaneous submissions. Requires disk or e-mail submission. Responds in 2 mos. Guidelines by e-mail/Website; no catalog. Will consider most fiction and nonfiction topics.

Nonfiction: Complete ms; phone/fax/e-query OK.

Fiction: Complete ms; phone/fax/e-query OK. Nondenominational Christian. For all ages.

Also Does: Booklets.

Tips: "We help people self-publish. To those authors we can offer a variety of services including distribution and small print runs. Most open to books that are unique, authentic, and relevant."

+IUNIVERSE (iUniverse), 1663 Liberty Dr., Ste. 300, Bloomington IN 47403. Toll-free (800)288-4677. Intl. (402)323-7800. Fax (812)355-4085. E-mail through Website: www.iuniverse.com. 100% self-publishing. Bought out by Author Solutions, Inc. (formerly AuthorHouse). Not included in topical listings. Guidelines on Website.

J AND J PUBLISHING CO., PO Box 291205, Columbia SC 29229. (803)968-5196. Fax (803) 234-4071. E-mail: jjpublisher@yahoo.com. Website: www.jandjpublishingonline.com. Stephanie McKenny, ed. A self-publishing company that will assist the author throughout the lifetime of the book. Publishes 5 titles/yr.; trade paperbacks. 90% of books from first-time authors. No mss through agents. 100% SELF-PUBLISHING. No reprints. Prefers 40 pgs. and up. Royalty 55-70%; no advance. Publication within 3-6 mos. Considers simultaneous submissions. Responds in 3-6 wks. Prefers KJV or AB. Guidelines by mail/e-mail; no catalog.

    Nonfiction: Proposal/5 chapters.

    Fiction: Proposal/5 chapters. For all ages. "No erotica or explicit language."

    Special Needs: Christian novels, inspirational, women's issues, relationships, self-help.

    Photos: Accepts freelance photos for book covers.

KINDRED BOOKS, 1310 Taylor Ave., Winnipeg MB R3M 3Z6, Canada. Toll-free (800)545-7322. (204)669-6575. Fax (204)654-1865. E-mail: kindred@mbconf.ca. Website: www.kindredproductions.com. Mennonite Brethren/Imprint of Kindred Productions. Submit to: Attn. Manager. Publisher for the Mennonite Brethren Church in North America. Publishes 3-4 titles/yr.; hardcover, trade paperbacks. Receives 20 submissions annually. 95% of books from first-time authors. No mss through agents. SUBSIDY PUBLISHES 100%; does print-on-demand. Reprints books. Prefers 60,000 wds. or 200 pgs. Average first printing 1,000-2,000. Publication within 18 mos. Considers simultaneous submissions. Responds in 4 mos. Accepts requested ms by e-mail. Prefers NIV. Guidelines (by e-mail/Website); free catalog.

    Nonfiction: Proposal/2-3 chapters; no phone query, fax/e-query OK. "Looking for Christian living and inspirational books."

    Fiction: Proposal/2-3 chapters. For children & teens.

    Tips: "Most open to Christian living or inspirational books that help everyday people grow in their relationship with Jesus. Books that help meet basic church needs. Material submitted should be in line with the Christian/evangelical faith."

LEADING LADY PUBLICATIONS, PO Box 35, Worton MD 21678. Toll-free (800)597-9428. E-mail: leadingladyenterprises@yahoo.com. Website: www.leadingladypublications.com, or www.publishyourchristianbook.com. Anointed Word Media Group. Tamika Johnson, CEO & pub. Committed to publishing and promoting Christian works that equip, educate, and empower women to overcome their struggles in life and step into their destiny. SUBSIDY PUBLISHER. Details of their publishing program on their Website.

    Nonfiction: Query first.

    Fiction: Query first.

LIFEVEST PUBLISHING INC., 4901 E. Dry Creek Rd., #170, Centennial CO 80122. Toll-free (877)843-1007. (303)221-1007. Website: www.lifevestpublishing.com. Ric Simmons, CEO. Specializes in children's books, educational literature, inspirational works, family/personal histories, and poetry. 100% SUBSIDY. Submission form on Website.

+LULU.COM. Website: www.lulu.com. Bob Young, pub. 100% SUBSIDY; PRINT ON DEMAND. Guidelines/details on Website. Not included in topical listings; will consider any topic.

MARKETING NEW AUTHORS.COM, 2910 E. Eisenhower Pkwy., Ann Arbor MI 48108. Toll-free (800)431-1579. (734)975-0028. Fax (734)973-9475. E-mail: info@marketingnewauthors.com, or MarketingNewAuth@aol.com. Website: www.MarketingNewAuthors.com. Imprint of Robbie Dean Press. To primarily serve authors who wish to self-publish. Dr. Fairy C. Hayes-Scott, owner. 100% of books from first-time authors. Accepts mss through agents. SUBSIDY PUBLISHES 100%. Reprints books. Length flexible. Publication within 6 mos. Considers simultaneous submissions. Responds in 2-6 wks. Guidelines by e-mail/Website. Offers 7 different marketing plans; see Website.

MEN OF STANDARD PUBLICATIONS, PO Box 35, Worton MD 21678. Toll-free (800)597-9428. E-mail: manuscripts@publishyourchristianbook.com. Website: www.publishyour christianbook.com. Anointed Word Media Group. Tamika Johnson, CEO & pub. Committed to publishing and promoting works by Christian men. SUBSIDY PUBLISHER. Details of their publishing program on their Website. No questionnaire returned.

    Nonfiction: Query first.

    Fiction: Query first.

MILESTONES INTERNATIONAL PUBLISHERS, 140 Danika Dr. N.W., Huntsville AL 35806-2274. (256)830-0362. Fax (256)830-9206. E-mail: jimrill@milestoneintl.com, or mile stoneintl@bellsouth.net. Website: www.milestonesintl.com. Jim Rill, pres. Bringing significance to life's journey. Author is asked to buy 3,000 books at $6/ea.

ONE WORLD PRESS, 1042 Willow Creek Rd., Prescott AZ 86301. Toll-free (800)250-8171. (928)445-2081. Fax (928)717-1779. E-mail: dasya@oneworldpress.com. Website: www .oneworldpress.com. Joe Zuccarello, operations mngr. Publishes many titles/yr. Receives 25-50 submissions annually. 50% of books from first-time authors. Accepts mss through agents. SUBSIDY PUBLISHES 100%; does print-on-demand. Reprints books. Average first printing up to author. Publication within 2 mos. Considers simultaneous submissions. Responds in 2-4 wks. No guidelines or catalog.

    Nonfiction: Complete manuscript. All ages. "We publish about anything within decency and reason."

    Also Does: Booklets, e-books, pamphlets, tracts.

PATH PUBLISHING INC., 4302 W. 51st, #121, Amarillo TX 79109-6159. Phone/fax (806)322-7007 (call first for fax). E-mail: path2@pathpublishing.com. Website: www.pathpublishing .com. John Schmidt, ed. This imprint focuses on self-help and children's books. Has published 15 titles to date. Receives 60 submissions annually. 95% of books from first-time authors. Accepts mss through agents. Would reprint books. Prefers 80-120 pgs. SUBSIDY PUBLISHES 80%. Considers simultaneous submissions. Responds in days. Guidelines (also by e-mail/Website); flyer for #10 SASE, no catalog.

    Nonfiction: Query letter only first; e-query preferred.

    Also Does: Expanding into e-books, Christian music sales, Website design, and more.

    Artwork: Open to queries from freelance artists.

    Contest: Periodically sponsors contests.

    Tips: "We also do lots of poetry books. Check our Website for 'Tips for Writers' and more."

PLEASANT WORD, 1730 Railroad St., PO Box 428, Enumclaw WA 98022. Toll-free (800)326-4674. (360)802-9758. Fax (360)802-9992. E-mail: acquisitions@pleasantword.com. Website: www.pleasantword.com. WinePress Publishing. Submit via Website or call acquisitions dept. In an industry where print-on-demand publishers will print almost anything, Pleasant Word has high standards for both design and content of POD books. Publishes 300 titles/yr.; hardcover, trade paperbacks, coffee-table books. Receives 700+ submissions annually between WinePress and Pleasant Word. 70% of books from first-time authors. Accepts mss through agents. 100% SUBSIDY; print-on-demand division. Reprints books. Prefers 10,000-150,000 wds. or 48-740 pgs. Royalties explained on Website; discounts for author purchases. Average first printing 150. Publication within 4-9 mos., depending on editing level. Considers simultaneous submissions. Responds in 48 hrs. Accepted mss on disk. No Bible version preference. Guidelines (also by e-mail); free catalog.

Nonfiction: Complete ms; e-query OK. Publishes all family-friendly, biblically oriented topics.

Fiction: Complete ms; e-query OK. Publishes all family-friendly, biblically oriented material and genres.

Also Does: Audio books, eBooks, multimedia, Website design & hosting, Weblogs, DVD production, CD/book packages, manuals, genuine leather Bibles, full-color children's books, board books, publicity and marketing materials.

Photos/Artwork: Accepts copyright-free photos and artwork.

Tips: "Since 1991, WinePress has been an innovator in the Christian custom printing market. We partner with authors through a wide range of services provided by our in-house departments: including production, design, video, multimedia, Internet, publicity, promotions, warehousing fulfillment, and distribution departments. To ensure the highest quality, everything is coordinated by our unique online Co-C.A.P.T.A.I.N. software and friendly staff. We do not accept all manuscripts for publication and advise potential authors to first review our doctrinal standards on our Website."

**Note: This publisher serviced by The Writer's Edge and ChristianManuscriptSubmissions .com.

POEMS BY ME, 4000 Beallwood Ave., Columbus GA 31904. Toll-free (800)334-8861. E-mail: Brentwood@aol.com. Website: www.PoemsByMe.com. Brentwood Christian Press. Joyce Warren, ed. Poetry that is spiritual, personal, emotional. Receives 80 submissions annually. 75% of books from first-time authors. Accepts mss through agents. 100% SUBSIDY; does print-on-demand. Reprints books. Need at least 40 poems for a book. Same-week response.

POET'S COVE PRESS, 4000 Beallwood Ave., Columbus GA 31904. Toll-free (800)334-8861. (706) 576-5787. E-mail: Brentwood@aol.com. Website: www.BrentwoodBooks.com. Subsidiary of Brentwood Publishers Group. U. D. Roberts, exec. dir. Publishes 75 titles/yr. SUBSIDY OR CUSTOM PUBLISHES 100%. Specializes in self-publishing books of religious or inspirational poetry, in small press runs of under 500 copies. Publication in 45 days. Same-day response.

 Tips: "Type one poem per page; include short bio and photo with first submission."

PROVIDENCE HOUSE PUBLISHERS, 238 Seaboard Ln., Franklin TN 37174. Toll-free (800)321-5692. (615)771-2020. Fax (615)771-2002. E-mail: books@providencehouse .com. Website: www.providencehouse.com. Submit to Kelly Bainbridge, acq. ed. Produces books which honor God and reflect the knowledge, commitment, and accomplishments of His people. Publishes 20+ religious titles/yr.; hardcover, trade paperbacks, coffee-table books. Receives 100+ submissions annually. 90% of books from first-time authors. No mss through agents. SUBSIDY PUBLISHES 90%; no print-on-demand. Reprints books. Prefers 96-512 pgs. Author receives 100% income from sales. Average first printing 3,000. Publication within 9-10 mos. Considers simultaneous submissions. Responds in up to 6 mos. Prefers accepted ms on disk. Prefers NIV, NKJV. Guidelines; no catalog (see Website).

 Nonfiction: Proposal/2 chapters or complete ms.; phone/fax/e-query OK. Accepts requested ms by e-mail.

 Fiction: Proposal/2 chapters or complete ms. For all ages. "Looking for Christian suspense."

 Special Needs: Biography, church histories, ministry histories, missionary memoirs.

 Artwork: Open to queries from freelance artists.

 Tips: "Most open to biblically based books; history or memoir; those with a speaking ministry tend to receive more attention. Well-written texts only."

QUIET WATERS PUBLICATIONS, PO Box 34, Bolivar MO 65613-0034. (417)326-5001. Fax (617)249-0256. E-mail: QWP@usa.net. Website: www.QuietWatersPub.com. Stephen Trobisch, ed. SUBSIDY PUBLISHER. Books on marriage, family, and missions.

RECOVERY COMMUNICATIONS INC., PO Box 19910, Baltimore MD 21211. (410)243-8352. Fax (410)243-8558. E-mail: tdrews3879@aol.com. Website: www.GettingThemSober.com.

Toby R. Drews, ed. Publishes 4-6 titles/yr. No mss through agents. SUBSIDY PUBLISHER. Prefers 110 pgs. Co-op projects; no royalty or advance. Average first printing 5,000. Publication within 9 mos. Excellent nationwide distribution and marketing in bookstores. Send for their free information packet.

Nonfiction: Query only.

Tips: "Although technically we are a subsidy publisher, we are more of a hybrid publisher in that we give the author enough free books to sell in the back of the room to totally recoup all the money they have paid; plus we share 50/50 on net sales at bookstores. Over half of our authors have gotten their money back and made a great profit. We are also aggressive in our pursuit of catalog sales and foreign rights sales (we recently sold to a German publisher). We also individually coach all our authors, at no cost to them, to help them successfully obtain speaking engagements."

SALVATION PUBLISHER AND MARKETING GROUP, PO Box 40860, Santa Barbara CA 93140. (805)682-0316. Fax (call first). E-mail: opalmaedailey@aol.com. Wisdom Today Ministries. Opal Mae Dailey, ed-in-chief. We encourage, inspire, and educate; author has the choice to be involved as much or little as desired—which gives the opportunity to control income; personal coaching and collective marketing available. Publishes 5-7 titles/yr.; hardcover, trade paperbacks, mass-market paperbacks. 60% of books from first-time authors. No mss through agents. SUBSIDY PUBLISHES 80%; does print-on-demand. Reprints books. Prefers 96-224 pgs. Average first printing 1,000. Publication within 3-4 mos. No simultaneous submissions. Accepts requested ms on disk or by e-mail (not attachments). Responds in 1 mo. Prefers KJV. Guidelines (also by e-mail).

Nonfiction: Query only first; phone/fax/e-query OK.

Tips: "Turning taped messages into book form for pastors is a specialty of ours. We do not accept any manuscript that we would be ashamed to put our name on."

SELAH PUBLISHING GROUP, LLC., 300 Hickory Rd., Bristol TN 37620-6033. Toll-free (877)616-6451. E-mail: garlen@selahbooks.com. Website: www.selahbooks.com. Garlen Jackson, pub. A publisher that does not water down the author's message. Publishes 45 titles/yr. Receives 20 submissions annually. 75% of books from first-time authors. Prefers mss through agents. Reprints books. Prefers 40,000 wds. or 144 pgs. SUBSIDY PUBLISHER/BOOK PACKAGER. Royalty 12-18% of net; no advance. Average first printing 2,500. Publication within 6 mos. No simultaneous submissions. Prefers requested ms on disk. Responds in 2 mos. Prefers ASV. Guidelines by e-mail; free catalog.

Nonfiction: Complete ms; no phone/fax/e-query.

Fiction: Complete ms; no phone/fax/e-query. For all ages.

Also Does: E-books.

Photos: Accepts freelance photos for book covers.

Tips: "Most open to time-sensitive, current events, and controversial books. Writers should spend more time selling who they are in regard to character and integrity."

**Note: This publisher serviced by ChristianManuscriptSubmissions.com.

SELF PUBLISH PRESS, 4000 Beallwood Ave., Columbus GA 31904. Toll-free (800)334-8861. (706)576-5787. Fax (706)317-5808. E-mail: Brentwood@aol.com. Website: www.Publish MyBook.com. Brentwood Publishing Group. U. D. Roberts, exec. ed.; submit to Marie Warren, ed. All books must be family suitable. Receives 100 submissions annually. 98% of books from first-time authors. Accepts mss through agents. SUBSIDY PUBLISHES 98%; does print-on-demand. Offers InstaBooks and Just in Time publishing (print-on-demand). Reprints books. Prefers 64-300 pgs. Publication within 1 mo. Considers simultaneous submissions. Responds in 3 days. Guidelines on Website; no catalog.

Nonfiction: Complete ms/disk; no phone/fax/e-query. All religious—for family or youth.

Fiction: Complete ms/disk; no phone/fax/e-query. For all ages.

SERMON SELECT PRESS, 4000 Beallwood Ave., Columbus GA 31904. Toll-free (800)334-8861. (706)576-5787. Fax (706)317-5808. E-mail: Brentwood@aol.com. Website: www .BrentwoodBooks.com. Subsidiary of Brentwood Publishers Group. U. D. Roberts, exec. dir. SUBSIDY OR CUSTOM PUBLISHES 100%. Focus is on sermon notes, outlines, illustrations, plus news that pastors would find interesting. Publishes 100 copies. Cost of about $3-4/ book. Publication in 45 days. Same-day response.

SOUTHERN BAPTIST PRESS, 4000 Beallwood, Columbus GA 31904. Toll-free (800)334-8861. (706)576-5787. E-mail: Brentwood@aol.com. Website: www.SouthernBaptistPress.com. U. D. Roberts, exec. ed. Publishes 25 books/yr. Receives 600 submissions annually. Reprints books. SUBSIDY OR CUSTOM PUBLISHES 95%. Average first printing 500. Publication within 2 mos. Considers simultaneous submissions. Responds in 1 week. Guidelines.

Nonfiction: Complete ms. "Collections of sermons on family topics; poetry; relation of Bible to current day."

Fiction: Complete ms. "Stories that show how faith helps overcome small, day-to-day problems."

Tips: "Keep it short; support facts with reference."

STAR BIBLE PUBLICATIONS, 1105 S. Airport Cir., Ste. C, Euless TX 76040. Toll-free (800)433-7507. (817)354-6004. Fax (817)354-6006. E-mail: publishing@starbible.com. Website: www.starbible.com. Church of Christ. Books that will be in harmony with New Testament principles and useful among general audience markets and among Churches of Christ. Publishes 10-15 titles/yr.; mass-market paperbacks. Receives 20-25 submissions annually. 50% of books from first-time authors. No mss through agents. SUBSIDY PUBLISHES 80%. No reprints. Prefers 110 pgs. Royalty on retail; no advance. Average first printing 1,000-1,500. Publication within 2 mos. No simultaneous submissions. Responds in 1 mo. Accepts mss on disk or by e-mail. Prefers ASV, KJV, NIV. Guidelines (also by e-mail/Website); catalog on Website.

Nonfiction: Complete ms; phone/fax/e-query OK.

Fiction: Complete ms. For adults.

Photos: Accepts freelance photos for book covers.

Tips: "We are looking for general audience books that focus on the gospel and encourage readers to read the Bible, books that encourage people in their Christian walk, books on doctrine, studies on the Bible or specific books of the Bible, and topical studies."

STRONG TOWER PUBLISHING, PO Box 973, Milesburg PA 16853. E-mail: strongtower pubs@aol.com. Website: www.strongtowerpublishing.com. Heidi L. Nigro, pub. Specializes in eschatology and books that challenge the reader to think more deeply about their faith and scriptural truths; must be biblically responsible, doctrinally defensible, and consistent with their statement of faith. Publishes 1-2 titles/yr.; trade paperbacks. 50% of books from first-time authors. No mss through agents. Reprints books. PRINT-ON-DEMAND 100%. Royalty 25% of net; no advance. Average first printing 50. Publication within 3-4 mos. Guidelines, information, and prices on Website.

Nonfiction: Query. Eschatology.

Tips: "We recommend that all first-time authors have their manuscript professionally edited. We will consider putting first-time authors into print, but by invitation only. That invitation comes only after the manuscript has been thoroughly evaluated and we have discussed the pros and cons of our unique on-demand publishing model with the author."

SYNERGY PUBLISHERS, 17750 N.W. 115th Ave., Bldg. 200, Ste. 220, Alachua FL 32615. Toll free (800)631-5802. (386)462-2525. Fax (386)462-2535. E-mail: manuscript@bridgelogos .com. Website: www.bridgelogos.com. Submit to Editor. Imprint of Bridge-Logos. Pays for cost of production and royalties, but author is required to buy a certain number of books up-front. Publishes 5 titles/yr.; hardcover, trade paperbacks, mass-market paperbacks, coffee-table books. Receives 200 submissions annually. 90% of books from first-time authors.

Accepts mss through agents. SUBSIDY PUBLISHES 1%; does print-on-demand. Reprints books. Prefers 200 pgs. Average first printing 4,000. Publication within 12 mos. Considers simultaneous submissions. Responds in 12 mos. No disk; prefers accepted ms by e-mail. Guidelines on Website; free catalog.

Nonfiction: Proposal/5 chapters; no phone/fax/e-query.

Special Needs: Reference, biography, current issues, controversial issues, church renewal, women's issues, and Bible commentary.

Photos: Accepts freelance photos for book covers.

Tips: "Have a great message, a well-written manuscript, and a specific plan and willingness to market your book. Looking for previously published authors with an active ministry who are experts on their subject."

Note: This publisher serviced by The Writer's Edge.

TATE PUBLISHING & ENTERPRISES, LLC., Tate Publishing Bldg., 127 E. Trade Center Ter., Mustang OK 73064-4421. Toll free (888)361-9473. Fax (405)376-4401. E-mail: publish@tatepublishing.com. Website: www.tatepublishing.com. Curtis Winkle, sr. ed.; Trinity Tate, dir. of acquisitions. Owns and operates its own, state-of-the-art printing plant facility; pays to produce audio book. Publishes 120 titles/yr.; hardcover, trade paperbacks, mass-market paperbacks. Receives 60,000-75,000 contacts annually. 60% of books from first-time authors. Requires mss through agents. SUBSIDY LIKELY (most authors asked to contribute $3,985.50 toward promotion—refunded if book does well). No print-on-demand. Accepts reprints. Prefers 115,000 wds. Royalty 15-40% of net; negotiable advance. Average first printing 5,000. Publication within 4-6 mos. Considers simultaneous submissions. Responds in 3-6 wks. Accepts submissions by disk or e-mail. Any Bible version. Guidelines (also by e-mail/Website); free catalog.

Nonfiction: Proposal with synopsis & any number of chapters, or complete ms; phone/fax/e-query OK. Any topic. "Looking for books that sell."

Fiction: Proposal with synopsis & any number of chapters or complete ms; phone/fax/e-query OK. For all ages. Any genre.

Ethnic Books: For all ethnic markets.

Contest: For those in author pool.

Artwork: Has 31 full-time artists on staff; open to queries from freelance artists.

Tips: "We invest resources in every work we accept, and accept first-time authors."

Note: This publisher serviced by The Writer's Edge.

TEACH SERVICES INC., 254 Donovan Rd., Brushton NY 12916. (518)358-3494. Fax (518)358-3028. E-mail: publishing@TEACHservices.com. Website: www.teachservices.com. Timothy Hullquist, pres.; submit to Jennifer Aiken, acq. ed. To publish uplifting books for the lowest price. Publishes 48 titles/yr.; hardcover, trade paperbacks, coffee-table books. Receives 100+ submissions annually. 35% of books from first-time authors. No mss through agents. SUBSIDY PUBLISHES 75% (author has to pay for first printing, then publisher keeps it in print); limited print on demand. Reprints books. Prefers 40,000 wds. or 96 pgs. Royalty 10% of retail; no advance. Average first printing 2,000. Publication within 6 mos. Considers simultaneous submissions. Responds in 3 wks. Prefers accepted mss by e-mail. Prefers KJV. Guidelines (also by e-mail/Website); catalog on Website.

Nonfiction: Complete ms; no phone/fax query.

Fiction: Complete ms; allegory and historical. For all ages.

Photos/Artwork: Accepts freelance photos for book covers; open to queries from freelance artists.

+TESTIMONY PRESS, 5427 N. Wall St., Spokane WA. (509)244-8745. E-mail: cellic@prodigy.net. Website: www.testimonypress.com. Cheryl Ellicott, ed. Guidelines by e-mail/Website.

Nonfiction: Query; e-query OK.

Fiction: Query; e-query OK.

Ethnic: Eskimo-Yupik.

Also Does: Gospel tracts; gospel comics.

TRAFFORD PUBLISHING, 2657 Wilfert Rd., Victoria BC V9B 5Z3, Canada. Toll-free (888)232-4444. (250)383-6864. Fax (250)383-6804. E-mail: info@trafford.com. Website: www.trafford.com. Trafford Holdings. Gord Hooker, pres. Your book, your way. Publishes 100-200 titles/yr.; hardcover, trade paperbacks, mass-market paperbacks, coffee-table books. Receives thousands of submissions annually. 85% of books from first-time authors. No mss through agents. 100% PRINT-ON-DEMAND. Reprints books. Prefers less than 700 pgs. Royalty 60%. Average first printing 40. Publication within 3 mos. Considers simultaneous submissions. Responds immediately. Prefers accepted mss on disk. Guidelines (also by e-mail); no catalog.

Tips: "Authors choose the retail price for their books and their royalty is 60% of the gross margin."

VMI PUBLISHERS, 26306 Metolius Meadows Dr., Camp Sherman OR 97730. E-mail: bill@vmipublishers.com, nancie@vmipublishers.com. Website: www.vmipublishers.com. Virtue Ministries Inc. Bill and Nancie Carmichael, pubs. Partnering with new authors. Publishes 8-12 titles/yr.; hardback, trade paperbacks, coffee-table books. Receives dozens of submissions annually. 95% of books from first-time authors. Accepts mss through agents. No reprints. Prefers 65,000+ wds., or 192-400 pgs. Royalty 12-18% of net; no advance. CUSTOM PUBLISHER; SEE WEBSITE FOR DETAILS. Average first printing 2,500+. Publication within 6-12 mos. Considers simultaneous submissions. Requires accepted ms on disk or by e-mail. Responds in 2 mos. Guidelines on Website.

Nonfiction: Query first by e-mail only.

Fiction: Query first by e-mail only. For all ages. "Anything Christian or inspirational that is well written, especially from new authors."

Tips: "Go to our Website first, and read how we partner with new authors. Then, if you feel VMI would be a good fit for you, e-mail your proposal."

**Note: This publisher serviced by ChristianManuscriptSubmissions.com.

WINEPRESS PUBLISHING, PO Box 428, 1730 Railroad St., Enumclaw WA 98022. Toll-free (800)326-4674. (360)802-9758. Fax (360)802-9992. E-mail: acquisitions@winepress group.com. Website: www.winepresspub.com. The WinePress Group. Submit via Website, or call acquisitions department. To ensure the highest quality and service, WP uses custom on-line software that allows you to track your book project from beginning to end. Imprints: WinePress Publishing, WinePress Kids (children's books), Annotation Press (general market, family friendly), UpWrite Books (writers resources), Pleasant Word (print on demand—see separate listing). Publishes 75 titles/yr.; hardcover, trade paperbacks, mass-market paperbacks, coffee-table books. Receives 700+ submissions annually. 70% of books from first-time authors. Accepts mss through agents. BOOK PACKAGERS 100%. Reprints books. Lengths range from 10,000-150,000 wds. or 48-1,300 pgs. Author pays production costs, keeps all profit from sales. Average first printing 3,000 (2,500 min.). Publication in 6-9 mos. Considers simultaneous submissions. Responds in 48 hrs. Accepts requested mss on disk. No Bible version preference. Guidelines (also by e-mail)/free catalog.

Nonfiction: Complete ms; e-query OK. Publishes all family-friendly, biblically oriented topics.

Fiction: Complete ms. Publishes all family-friendly, biblically oriented material and genres.

Also Does: Audio books, eBooks, multimedia, Website design & hosting, Weblogs, DVD production, CD/book packages, manuals, genuine leather Bibles, full-color children's books, board books, publicity and marketing materials.

Photos/Artwork: Accepts copyright-free photos and artwork.

Tips: "Since 1991, WinePress has been an innovator in the Christian custom printing market. We partner with authors through a wide range of services provided by our in-house departments: including production, design, video, multimedia, Internet, publicity, promotions, warehousing fulfillment, and distribution departments. To ensure the highest quality, everything is coordinated by our unique online Co-C.A.P.T.A.I.N. software and friendly staff. We do not accept all manuscripts for publication and advise potential authors to first review our doctrinal standards on our Website."

**Note: This publisher serviced by The Writer's Edge and ChristianManuscriptSubmissions .com.

WORD ALIVE PRESS, 131 Cordite Rd., Winnipeg MB R3W 1S1, Canada. Toll-free (866) 967-3782. (204)777-7100. Toll-free fax (800)352-9272. (204)669-0947. E-mail: Cschmidt@wordalive.ca. Website: www.wordalive.ca. C. Schmidt, ed. At least 6,000 wds. or 50 pgs. 100% PRINT-ON-DEMAND. Guidelines and price list available. Request their Free Guide to Publishing brochure.

   Nonfiction: "Looking for books on family, marriage, and character."

   Fiction: For all ages.

XLIBRIS, International Plz., Ste. 340, Philadelphia PA 19113-1513. Toll-Free (888)795-4274, ext. 278. (610)915-5214. Fax (610)915-0294. E-mail: info@xlibris.com or submissions@ xlibris.com. Website: www.xlibris.com. Random House. Mercedes Bournias, publishing consultant. 100% SUBSIDY. Can produce novels to 700 pgs. and picture books to 24 pgs. Basic Package is $499; up to Executive Package at $5,999. Open to any topic.

XULON PRESS INC., 2180 W. State Rd. 434, Ste. 2140, Longwood FL 32779. Toll-free (866)381-2665. Fax (407)339-9898. E-mail: acquisitions@xulonpress.com. Website: www.xulonpress.com. Blog: www.xulonpress.com/blog. Division of Salem Communications. Tom Freiling, VP & gen. mngr. Uses digital and print-on-demand technologies to help Christian authors get published. Imprints: Townhall Press. Publishes 1,500 titles/yr.; hardcover, trade paperbacks. Receives 1,500 submissions annually. 80% of books from first-time authors. Accepts mss through agents. Reprints books. 100% PRINT-ON-DEMAND. Royalty 100% of net; no advance. Average first printing 1,000. Publication within 30 days. Considers simultaneous submissions. Responds in 1 mo. Not in topical listings; will consider all appropriate Christian topics. Guidelines on Website or by phone; free catalog.

   Nonfiction/Fiction: Phone/fax/e-query OK.

   Photos: Accepts freelance photos for book covers.

   Tips: "We offer on-demand publishing, bookstore distribution, and publicity and promotional services. We also exhibit at the annual International Christian Retail Show (ICRS), BookExpo America (BEA), and Evangelical Christian Publishers Assn. (ECPA). Please refer to the Website for information about how we promote and publicize books."

   **Note: This publisher (royalty division) serviced by The Writer's Edge and Christian ManuscriptSubmissions.com.

ZOE LIFE PUBLISHING, PO Box 871066, Canton MI 48187. (734)547-7801. Fax (734)547-7805. E-mail: submissions@zoelifepub.com. Website: www.zoelifepub.com. Zoe Life Industries LLC. Sabrina Adams, ed. Imprints: Pen of a Ready Writer, Titus, Business Builders. Publishes 40 titles/yr.; hardcover, trade paperbacks, mass-market paperbacks, coffee-table books. 50+% of books from first-time authors. Prefers mss through agents. SUBSIDY PUBLISHES 50%; no print-on-demand or reprints. Length open. Royalty 5-25%; usually no advance. Average first printing 3,000. Publication within 6-12 mos. Responds in 21 days. Open on Bible version. Guidelines by e-mail/Website; free catalog.

   Photos: Accepts freelance photos for book covers.

DISTRIBUTORS

LISTING OF CHRISTIAN BOOK/MUSIC/GIFT DISTRIBUTORS

ALLIANCE—MUSIC, 4250 Coral Ridge Dr., Coral Springs FL 33065-7615. Toll-free (800)329-7664. (954)255-4600. Fax (954)255-4825. E-mail: custsvc@aent.com. Website: www.aent.com. Alliance Entertainment Corp. Music.

AMAZON ADVANTAGE PROGRAM. Go to Amazon.com, scroll down to "Features & Services" and click on "Advantage Program" in left-hand column. This is the site to contact if you want Amazon to distribute your book.

ANCHOR-WHITAKER DISTRIBUTORS, 1030 Hunt Valley Cir., New Kensington PA 15068. Toll-free (800)444-4484. (724)334-7000. Toll-free fax (800)765-1960. (724)334-1200. E-mail: purchasing@anchordistributors.com, or marketing@anchordistributors.com. Website: www.anchordistributors.com. Donna Bonarati, intl. sales mngr. (800)444-4484, ext. 246. Christian books, Bibles, music, and gifts. Distributes self-published books on a contract distribution basis. Mail a copy of the book and all pertinent information to John Whitaker.

B. BROUGHTON CO., LTD., 322 Consumers Rd., North York ON M2J 1P8, Canada. Toll-free (800)268-4449 (Canada only). (416)690-4777. Fax (416)690-5357. E-mail: brian@bbroughton.com. Website: www.bbroughton.com. Brian Broughton, owner. Canadian distributor. Distributes books, DVDs, gifts, greeting cards. Does not distribute self-published books.

CAMPUS CRUSADE FOR CHRIST/NEW LIFE RESOURCES, 375 Hwy. 74 S., Ste. A, Peachtree City GA 30269. Toll-free (800)827-2788. Fax (770)631-9916. E-mail: pat.pearce@campuscrusade.org. Website: www.campuscrusade.org. Contact: Pat Pearce. Resources for evangelism, discipleship, and spiritual multiplication; books, tracts, Bible studies, and training resources. Does not handle self-published books.

CBA MAILING LISTS OF CHRISTIAN BOOKSTORES, PO Box 62000, Colorado Springs CO 80962-2000. (719)265-9895. Fax (719)272-3510. E-mail: cbender@cbaonline.org. Website: www.cbaonline.org. Available for rental. Three different lists available, including non-member stores, 4,600 addresses ($249); member stores, 1,275 addresses ($599); or a combined list of all stores, 5,875 addresses ($699). Prices subject to change. Call toll-free (800)252-1950 for full details.

CENTRAL SOUTH DISTRIBUTION, 3730 Vulcan Dr., Nashville TN 37211. Toll-free (800)251-3052. (615)833-5960. Fax (615)331-2501. E-mail through Website: www.centralsouthdistribution.com. Contact: Chuck Adams (cadams@csouth.com). Distributes Black music and devotionals.

CHRISTIAN BOOK DISTRIBUTORS, PO Box 7000, Peabody MA 01961-7000. Toll-free (800)247-4784. (978)977-5080. Fax (978)977-5010. E-mail: customer.service@christianbooks.com, or through Website: www.christianbooks.com.

CONSORTIUM BOOK SALES & DISTRIBUTION INC., 34 13th Ave. N.E., Ste. 101, Minneapolis MN 55413. (612)746-2600. Fax (612)746-2606. E-mail: info@cbsd.com. Website: www.cbsd.com. Distributes a small number of religion titles—more ecumenical in nature, than Christian. Does not distribute self-published books.

CORNERSTONE FULFILLMENT SERVICE, LL, PO Box 44, Bondville VT 05340. (802)297-3771. Fax (802)297-3326. E-mail: ContactUs@cornerstonefulfillmentservice.com. Website: www.CornerstoneFulFillmentService.com. Sue Leonard, owner. Distributes books, videos, DVDs, CDs, journals, consumer literature. Specializes in self-published books, videos, DVDs, CDs. Distributes self-published books. Contact by phone/fax/e-mail.

CROWN DISTRIBUTION, Toll-free (800)661-9467. (780)471-1417. Distributes Christian film & video in U.S., Canada, and around the world.

DDMDIRECT.COM, PO Box 1984, Buffalo NY 14240-1984. Toll-free (800)597-5605. (716)893-8671. Fax (877)632-9657. Website: www.ddmdirect.com. Distributes books, children's books.

DICKSONS, PO Box 368, Seymour IN 47274. (812)522-1308. Fax (812)522-1319. E-mail: marketing@dicksonsgifts.com. Website: www.dicksonsgifts.com. Distributes gift products only. Open to outside submissions for its product line. Website includes a list of additional distributors.

EFULFILLMENT SERVICE INC., 6893 Sullivan Rd., Grawn MI 49637. (231)276-5057, ext. 100. Fax (231)276-5074. E-mail: alc@efulfillmentservice.com, or info@efulfillmentservice.com, or through Website: www.efulfillmentservice.com. Jordan Lindberg, pres. Services include storage and order fulfillment.

FOUNDATION DISTRIBUTING INC., 9 Cobbledick St., PO Box 98, Orono ON L0B 1M0, Canada. Toll-free (877)368-3600. (905)983-1188. Fax (905)983-1190. E-mail: info@fdi.ca, or WebHelp@fdi.ca. Website: www.fdi.ca. Canadian distributor.

GENESIS MARKETING, 850 Wade Hampton Blvd., Bldg. A, Ste. 100, Greenville SC 29609. Toll-free (800)627-2651. (864)233-2651. Toll-free fax (800)849-4363. E-mail: Customer Relations@genesislink.com. Website: www.genesislink.com.

GL SERVICES, 1957 Eastman Ave., Ventura CA 93003. (805)677-6815. Fax (805)644-4729. E-mail: JeffMesinoff@GLServices.com, or through Website: www.GLServices.com. Contact: Jeff Mesinoff. A division of Gospel Light. Does not distribute books for individual authors.

INGRAM BOOK GROUP/DISTRIBUTION, One Ingram Blvd., La Vergne TN 37086-1986. Toll-free (800)937-8000. (615)793-5000. Website: www.ingrambookgroup.com. The best way to have your book/product distributed by this company is to go through one of their trading partners. For a list of distributing partners and more information, visit their Website.

KEY MARKETING GROUP, 2448 E. 81st St., Ste. 4802, Jenks OK 74137. Toll-free (877)727-0697. (918)298-0232. Fax (918)299-5912. E-mail: info@keymgc.com. Website: www.key mgc.com. Bryan Norris, owner (bryan@keymgc.com).

LIGHTNING SOURCE INC., 1246 Heil Quaker Blvd., La Vergne TN 37086. (615)213-5815. Fax (615)213-4725. E-mail: inquiry@lightningsource.com. Website: www.lightningsource.com.

MALACO CHRISTIAN DISTRIBUTION, 3023 W. Northside Dr., Jackson MS 39213. Toll-free (877)462-3623. (601)982-4522. Fax (601)982-4528. E-mail: tgoodwin@malaco.com, or malaco@malaco.com. Website: www.malaco.com. Tony Goodwin, mng. dir. of sales. Music distributor.

MCBETH CORP, Fulfillment and Distribution Headquarters, PO Box 400, Chambersburg PA 17201. Toll-free (800)876-5112. (717)263-5600. Fax (717)263-5909. E-mail: mcbeth corp@supernet.com. Gary McBeth, owner. Distributes Christian gift products.

R. G. MITCHELL FAMILY BOOKS INC., 565 Gordon Baker Rd., Willowdale ON M2H 2W2, Canada. Toll-free (800)268-3445. (416)499-4615. Toll-free fax (800)268-5696. Fax (416)499-6340. E-mail: info@rgm.ca. Website: www.rgm.ca. Steve Atkinson, mngr. (satkinson@rgm.ca).

NEW DAY CHRISTIAN DISTRIBUTORS, 126 Shivel Dr., Hendersonville TN 37075. Toll-free (800)251-3633. (615)822-3633. Toll-free fax (800)251-3633. E-mail: service@new daychristian.com. Website: www.newdaychristian.com. Contact: Jeff Stangenberg (jstangen berg@newdaychristian.com). Music (primarily), books, Bibles, gift items. Distributes self-published books. Contact by e-mail.

NOAH'S ARK DISTRIBUTION, 28545 Felix Valdez Ave., Ste. B4, Temecula CA 92590-1859. Toll-free (800)562-8093. (760)723-3101. Fax (951)693-2747. E-mail: slvanyo@msn.com. Website: www.christianbooksanddvds.com. Contact: Scott Vanyo, mngr.

THE PARABLE GROUP, 3563 Empleo St., San Luis Obispo CA 93401. Toll-free (800)366-6031, ext. 525. (805)549-2500. Toll-free fax (800)543-2136. E-mail: info@parable.com, or through Website: www.parable.com. A marketing program for Christian bookstores. Chris Scotti, member services and sales director.

PUBLISHERS GROUP WEST, National Headquarters: 1700 Fourth St., Berkeley CA 94710. (510)809-3700. Fax (510)809-3777. E-mail: info@pgw.com. Website: www.pgw.com. Submissions inquiries to: rose.anderson@pgw.com.

PUBLISHERS MARKETING ASSN., 627 Aviation Way, Manhattan Beach CA 90266-7107. (310) 372-2732. Fax (310)374-3342. E-mail: info@pma-online.org. Website: www.pma-online .org. Trade association of independent publishers. Provides cooperative marketing programs for books, e-books, and audio books. Jan Nathan, exec. dir. (jan@pma-online.org).

QUALITY BOOKS, 1003 W. Pines Rd., Oregon IL 61061. Toll-free (800)323-4241. (815)732-4450. Fax (815)732-4499. E-mail: info@quality-books.com Website: www.quality-books.com. Tiffani Griffin, mngr. of product & database management (tiffani.griffin@quality-books.com). Distributes small press books, videos, audios, DVDs, and CD-ROMs to public libraries. Distributes self-published books; asks for 1 copy of your book.

RANDOLF PRODUCTIONS INC., 18005 Sky Park Cir., Ste. K, Irvine CA 92614-6514. Toll-free (800)266-7741. (949)794-9109. Fax (949)794-9117. E-mail: sales@go2rpi.com. Website: www.go2rpi.com, and www.goccc.com. Distributor of Christian DVDs, books, and music. A subsidiary of Campus Crusade for Christ. Contact: Randy Ray, pres. (randy@go2rpi.com).

SPRING ARBOR DISTRIBUTORS, PO Box 3006, One Ingram Blvd., Mailstop 671, La Vergne TN 37086. Toll-free (800)395-4340. Toll-free fax (800)876-0186. (615)213-5192. E-mail: custserv@springarbor.com, or through Website: www.springarbor.com. Contact: Mary Lou Alexander (800)395-4340, ext. 33319; e-mail: marylou.alexander@springarbor.com. Books, music, Bibles; no gift items or church supplies.

STL DISTRIBUTION, NORTH AMERICA, 522 Princeton Rd., Johnson City TN 37601. Toll-free (800)289-2772. Fax (800)759-2779. E-mail: david.dykhouse@stl-distribution.com. Website: www.STL-Distribution.com. David Dykhouse, VP of marketing. Distributes books, Bibles, CDs, audio books, DVDs, homeschool, gifts, church supplies, marketing materials and services, including the homeschool market and Catholic products. Distributes self-published books. Submit to the attention of Darren Henry.

TRIUMPH MARKETING, LLC., 2450 Atlanta Hwy., Ste. 1803, Cumming GA 30040. Toll-free (877)494-0525. (678)947-5615. Fax (678)947-1490. Website: www.triumphmarketing llc.com. Stephen McGonigle, pres. (steve@triumphmarketingllc.com); Gary Costello, dir. of sales, marketing, and acquisitions (gary@triumphmarketingllc.com). Submit books/products for consideration.

WINDFLOWER COMMUNICATIONS, 67 Flett Ave., Winnipeg MB R2K 3N3, Canada. Toll-free (800)465-6564. (204)668-7475. Fax (204)661-8530. E-mail: windflower@brandt family.com. Website: www.brandtfamily.com. Brandt Family Enterprises. Gilbert Brandt, pres. Book & music distributor.

WORD ALIVE INC., 131 Cordite Rd., Winnipeg MB R3W 1S1, Canada. Toll-free (800)665-1468. (204)667-1400. Toll-free fax (800)352-9272. (204)669-0947. E-mail: orderdesk@wordalive.ca. Website: www.wordalive.ca. Distributes Christian books. Contact: Caroline Schmidt. Distributes self-published books. Contact by mail.

MARKET ANALYSIS

PUBLISHERS IN ORDER OF MOST BOOKS PUBLISHED PER YEAR

Comfort Publishing 500
Adams Media 230
Tyndale House 225-250
Barbour Publishing 200
Harvest House 170
Monarch Books 160
Strang Book Group 150
Eerdmans, Wm. B. 120-130
Abingdon Press 120
Dimensions for Living 120
Zondervan 120
New York Univ. Press 100
Still Waters Revival 100
Steeple Hill/single title 96-108
Bethany House 90-120
B & H Publishing 90-100
Christian Focus 90
David C. Cook 85
InterVarsity Press 80-90
Boyds Mills Press 80
Christian Ed. Publishers 80
Paulist Press 80
Presbyterian Publishing 80
HarperOne 75
Kregel 75
Liturgical Press 75
Multnomah Books 75
Regal Books 75
Univ. Press/America 75
W Publishing Group 75
Crossway 70
WaterBrook Press 70
Grupo Nelson 65-80
Moody Publishers 65-70
Howard Books 65
CSS Publishing 60-70
NavPress 60-65
Continuum Intl. 60
Fortress Press 60
Ambassador-Emerald 55
Pilgrim Press 55
Heartsong Presents 52
Harcourt Religion 50-100
Custom Commun. 50-75
T & T Clark. 50-60
Baker Academic 50
Concordia 50
DiskUs Publishing 50
Health Communications 50
Liguori Publications 50
Love Inspired 48
Love Inspired Suspense 48
Doubleday Religious 45-50
Jessica Kingsley Publishers 45+
Crossroad Publishing 45
Pacific Press 45

G. P. Putnam/Yg. Readers 45
GRQ 40-50
Jeremy P. Tarcher 40-50
Editorial Portavoz 40+
Bridge-Logos 40
FaithWords 40
Group Publishing 40
Jossey-Bass 40
P & R Publishing 40
Destiny Image 36
New Leaf Press 35-40
Chalice Press 35
Mercer Univ. Press 35
Morehouse Publishing 35
Heartsong Presents/Mysteries 32
Meriwether Publishing 30-45
Focus on the Family 30-40
Our Sunday Visitor 30-40
Rose Publishing 30-40
Whitaker House 30-40
Baylor Univ. Press 30
Beacon Hill Press 30
Conari Press 30
Contemporary Drama 30 (plays)
Evergreen Press 30
Good News Publishers (tracts) 30
Thomas Nelson, Fiction 30
Univ. of AR Press 30
Youth Specialties 30
Hendrickson 25-35
AMG Publishers 25-30
Ideals Publications 25-30
Sheed & Ward 25-30
Smyth & Helwys 25-30
St. Anthony Mess. Press 25-30
James Clarke 25
Lion and Lamb 25
Liturgy Training 25
Lutterworth Press 25
Meriwether (plays) 25
White Stone Books 25
Guardian Angel Pub. 24-36
Alba House 24
Evangelical Press 24
Love Inspired Historical 24
One World 24
St. Augustine's Press 20-40
Chapter Two 20-30
Lighthouse Publishing 20-30
Loyola Press 20-30
New Hope 20-28
Pauline Kids 20-25
Blue Dolphin 20-24
ABC Book Publishing 20
Big Idea 20
GuidepostsBooks 20

Harrison House 20
Pauline Books 20
Pflaum Publishing 20
Rainbow Publishers 20
Scepter Publishers 20
Third World Press 20
Eldridge (plays) 17
Catholic Book Publishing 15-20
College Press 15-20
Halo Publishing 15-20
HeartSpring Publishing 15-20
Master Books 15-20
Revival Nation 15-20
Samaritan Press 15-20
BMH Books 15-18
Branden Publishing 15
Cambridge Scholars Pub. 15
Christian Writers Ebook 15
Legacy Press 15
Lift Every Voice 15
Wesleyan Publishing House 15
Dabbling Mum Press 12-24
Discovery House 12-18
Judson Press 12-15
Paragon House 12-15
Lillenas 12+
Vintage Romance 12+
CarePoint 12
Carson-Dellosa Christian 12
Charisma Kids 12
Invisible College Press 12
White Rose 12
Wm. Carey Library 10-15
E-Digital 10-15
McDougal Publishing 10-15
Ragged Edge 10-15
Green Key 10-12
ACTA Publications 10
Catholic Answers 10
Catholic Univ./America Press 10
FaithWalk Publishing 10
FamilyLife Publishing 10
Fifth Estate Publishers 10
Georgetown University Press 10
Jubilant Press 10 (e-books)
New Seeds 10
Parsons Publishing 10
PREP Publishing 10
Resource Publications 10
Walk Worthy Press 10
Yale Univ. Press 10
Ambassador Books 9
Cistercian Publications 8-14
BJU Press 8-10
Hannibal Books 8-10
Lutheran University Press 8-10

Reformation Trust 8-10
Emmaus Road 8
Neibauer Press 8
Oregon Catholic Press 8
Touch Publications 8
Torch Legacy 7+
Woodland Gospel 7
ETC Publications 6-12
Messianic Jewish 6-12
Avon Inspire 6-10
Mountainview Pub. 6-9
Baker Trittin 6-8
Kirk House Publishers 6-8
Eerdmans/Young Readers 6-7
Christian Heritage 6
Church & Synagogue Libraries 6
Dawn Publications 6
Hope Publishing 6
Inkling Books 6
Life Cycle Books 6
Wilshire Book Co. 6
Greenwood Publishing 5-30
Troitsa Books 5-20
Conciliar Press 5-10
Gospel Publishing House 5-10
Hensley Publishing 5-10
Quintessential Books 5-10
Randall House 5-10
Libros Liguori 5
Mission City Press 5
Mt. Olive College Press 5
Paradise Research 5
Trinity Foundation 5
Johns Hopkins Univ. 4-6
Father's Press 4-5
Larson Publications 4-5
Millennium III 4-5
MOPS Intl. 4-5
Foursquare Media 4+
American Catholic Press 4
Anglicans United 4
Intl. Awakening Press 4
Lighthouse Trails 4
Elijah Press 3-5

Facts on File 3-5
His Work 3-5
Langmarc Publishing 3-5
Northfield Publishing 3-5
Parson Place Press 3-5
Perigee Books 3-5
Virginia Pines Press 3-5
Gollehon Press 3-4
New Canaan 3-4
St. Bede's 3-4
Tau-Publishing 3-4
Church Growth Institute 3
Friends United Press 3
Magnus Press 3
Pelican Publishing 3
First Fruits of Zion 2-6
Baker's Plays 2-5
Jireh Publishing 2-5
Salt Works 2-5
Canadian Institute for Law 2-4
Frederick Fell 2-4
Jebaire Publishing 2-4
Cladach Publishing 2-3
Deo Volente 2-3
Forward Movement 2-3
Little Lauren Books 2-3
Canticle Books 2
Earthen Vessel 2
Players Press 1-6
VBC Publishing 1-5
Illumination Arts 1-4
LifeSong Publishers 1-4
Christian Family 1-3
Starik Publishing 1-3
Fair Havens Publications 1-2
Path Publishing in Christ 1-2
Write Now 1-2
Aadeon Publishing 1
BelleBooks 1
Dove Inspirational 1
Good Book 1
Guernica Editions 1
Hay House 1
Reference Service 1

SUBSIDY PUBLISHERS

Xulon Press 1,500
Pleasant Word 300
Brentwood 267
Creation House 125
Tate Publishing 120
Trafford Publishing 100-200
Essence Publishing 100-150+
Fairway Press 100
Holy Fire 100
Poet's Cove Press 75
WinePress 75
American Binding 60
Insight Publishing 50
TEACH Services 48
Selah Publishing 45
Booklocker.com 40-50
ACW Press 40
Zoe Life 40
Black Forest Press 35
Baal Hamon 30-40
Southern Baptist Press 25
Bookstand Publishing 20+
Impact Christian Books 20+
Providence House 20+
Elderberry Press 15
Brown Books 10-30
Star Bible 10-15
VMI Publishers 8-12
Fruitbearer Publishing 5-10
IMD Press 5-10
Book Publishers 5-8
Salvation Publisher 5-7
DCTS Publishing 5
J and J Publishing 5
Synergy Publishers 5
Recovery Communications 4-6
Kindred Books 3-4
Ampelos Press 1-3
Strong Tower Publishing 1-2
Alfred Ali 1
Robbie Dean Press 1

BOOK TOPICS MOST POPULAR WITH PUBLISHERS

The numbers following the topics below indicate how many publishers said they were interested in seeing a book on that topic. To find the list of publishers interested in each topic, go to the Topical Listings for books (see Contents).

MISCELLANEOUS TALLIES

Art-Freelance 52
Booklets 45
Canadian/Foreign 21
Coffee-table books 28
E-books 37
Minibooks 11
Photographs for covers 89
Print-on-demand 53
Tracts 19

TOPICS BY POPULARITY

1. Inspirational 149
2. Family Life 147
3. Prayer 146
4. Christian Living 145
5. Religion 142
6. Bible/Biblical Studies 139
7. Spirituality 135
8. Devotional Books 127
9. Women's Issues 127
10. Faith 126
11. Discipleship 124
12. Marriage 121
13. Theology 120
14. Fiction: Adult/Religious 118
15. Parenting 114
16. Biography 109
17. Church History 106
18. Self-help 106
19. Historical 105
20. Personal Growth 102
21. Evangelism/Witnessing 100
22. Spiritual Life 100
23. Current/Social Issues 99
24. Leadership 99
25. Church Life 98
26. Christian Education 95
27. Ethics 95
28. Ethnic/Cultural 93
29. Fiction: Contemporary 90
30. Forgiveness 90
31. How-to 89
32. Worship 88
33. Youth Books (nonfiction) 88
34. Fiction: Historical 87
35. Death/Dying 86
36. Personal Renewal 85
37. Bible Commentary 84
38. Church Renewal 84
39. Controversial Issues 84
40. Christ 83
41. Healing 83
42. Scholarly 82

43. Health 81
44. Doctrinal 80
45. Fiction: Juvenile (ages 8-12) 80
46. Christian Business 79
47. Spiritual Gifts 77
48. Apologetics 76
49. Spiritual Warfare 75
50. Men's Books 74
51. Fiction: Biblical 73
52. Fiction: Adventure 72
53. Humor 72
54. Pastors' Helps 72
55. Church Traditions 71
56. Fiction: Mystery/Suspense 71
57. Reference Books 71
58. Fiction: Teen/Young Adult 70
59. Social Justice Issues 70
60. Dating/Sex 69
61. Counseling Aids 68
62. Gift Books 68
63. Group Study Books 68
64. Holy Spirit 68
65. Psychology 67
66. Autobiography 66
67. Divorce 66
68. Missionary 66
69. Money Management 66
70. Philosophy 66
71. Stewardship 66
72. Fiction: Literary 65
73. Encouragement 64
74. Holiday/Seasonal 64
75. Personal Experience 63
76. Singles Issues 63
77. Children's Picture Books 62
78. Prophecy 62
79. Recovery Books 61
80. Fiction: Humor 60
81. Memoirs 60
82. World Issues 60
83. Eschatology 59
84. Fiction: Fantasy 59
85. Miracles 59
86. Sermons 59
87. Worship Resources 59
88. Christian Homeschooling 58
89. Exegesis 57
90. Fiction: Romance 57
91. Political 57
92. Archaeology 56
93. Relationships 55
94. Fiction: Mystery/Romance 54
95. Senior Adult Concerns 54
96. Time Management 54

97. Children's Easy Readers 53
98. Homiletics 53
99. Fiction: Ethnic 51
100. Fiction: Historical/Romance 50
101. Poetry 50
102. Science 50
103. Liturgical Studies 48
104. Church Management 47
105. Fiction: Allegory 47
106. Religious Tolerance 47
107. Christian School Books 46
108. Environmental Issues 46
109. Cookbooks 45
110. Fiction: Science Fiction 45
111. Charismatic 44
112. Cults/Occult 44
113. Fiction: Short Story Collection 44
114. Racism 44
115. Creation Science 43
116. Holiness 43
117. Sociology 43
118. Curriculum 42
119. Homeschooling Resources 42
120. Fiction: Frontier/Romance 41
121. Compilations 40
122. Economics 40
123. Retirement 40
124. Fiction: Frontier 39
125. Sports/Recreation 39
126. Fiction: Chick Lit 38
127. Drama 37
128. Fiction: Westerns 37
129. Travel 37
130. Celebrity Profiles 34
131. Grief 32
132. Music-related Books 32
133. Youth Programs 32
134. Fiction: Speculative 30
135. Games/Crafts 30
136. Pamphlets 29
137. Writing How-to 29
138. Fiction: Fables/Parables 28
139. Fiction: Adult/General 27
140. Fiction: Children's Picture Books 27
141. Fiction: Novellas 25
142. Fiction: Plays 25
143. Tween Books 25
144. Lifestyle 23
145. Novelty Books For Kids 22
146. Post Modernism 22
147. Exposés 21
148. Children's Board Books 13
150. Commentaries 7

BOOK PUBLISHERS WITH THE MOST BOOKS ON THE BESTSELLER LIST FOR THE LAST YEAR

This tally is based on actual sales in Christian bookstores reported from July 2007 to June 2008. Numbers behind the names indicate the number of titles each publisher had on that particular bestseller list during the year. Note that the division of categories was changed this year (combined into fewer categories), so numbers could be slightly off—but still representative of which publishers excelled in each category.

BIBLICAL STUDIES/ THEOLOGY/MINISTRY
1. Thomas Nelson 9
2. InterVarsity 5
3. NavPress 4
4. Zondervan 4
5. B & H Publishing 3
6. Standard 3
7. Tyndale 3
8. WaterBrook 3
9. AMG Publishers 1
10. Baker 1
11. Barbour 1
12. Bridge Logos 1
13. David C. Cook 1
14. Crossway 1
15. Lifeway 1

CHILDREN'S BOOKS
1. ZonderKidz 17
2. Tommy Nelson 13
3. Standard 12
4. Abingdon Press 3
5. B & H Publishing 2
6. Barbour 2
7. Standard 2
8. Zondervan 2
9. Concordia 1
10. David C. Cook 1
11. Golden Books 1
12. Tyndale Kids 1

CHRISTIAN LIVING
1. Thomas Nelson 23
2. Zondervan 23
3. Harvest House 7
4. Faithwords 4
5. Multnomah 4
6. B & H Publishing 3
7. Tyndale House 3
8. WaterBrook 3
9. Charisma (Strang) 2
10. Moody 2
11. Simon & Schuster 2
12. Abingdon Press 1
13. Augsburg 1
14. Baker 1
15. Crossway 1
16. David C. Cook 1
17. Gospel Light 1
18. Harrison House 1

19. Howard 1
20. Regal 1
21. Revell 1
22. Siloam (Strang) 1

FICTION
1. Tyndale 15
2. Thomas Nelson 14
3. Bethany House 13
4. Zondervan 10
5. Barbour 7
6. Harvest House 6
7. Crossway 2
8. Multnomah 2
9. Putnam Adult (Penguin) 2
10. WaterBrook 2
11. Center Street (Hachette) 1
12. FaithWords 1
13. Revell (Baker) 1
14. Windblown Media 1

INSPIRATIONAL/ GENERAL INTEREST
1. Thomas Nelson 19
2. Barbour 16
3. Zondervan 15
4. Tyndale 4
5. American Tract Society 3
6. B & H Publishing 3
7. Charisma (Strang) 3
8. Regal (Gospel Light) 3
9. Whitaker House 3
10. Abingdon Press 2
11. Faithwords (Hachette) 2
12. Chosen (Baker) 1
13. Concordia 1
14. Discovery House 1
15. Frontline (Strang) 1
16. Ideals 1
17. Kregel 1
18. Moody 1
19. NavPress 1
20. Penguin Group USA 1
21. Regal 1
22. Revell (Baker) 1
23. Simon & Schuster 1
24. Upper Room Books 1
25. WaterBrook 1

YOUNG ADULT BOOKS
1. Thomas Nelson 6
2. Harvest House 5
3. Tyndale 4

4. Zondervan 4
5. Revell (Baker) 3
6. WaterBrook 3
7. Barbour 2
8. Bethany House 2
9. Multnomah 2
10. NavPress 2
11. B & H Publishing 1
12. FaithWords (Hachette) 1
13. Howard 1
14. Living Ink (AMG) 1
15. Moody 1
16. ZonderKids 1

COMBINED BESTSELLER LISTS
1. Thomas Nelson 71
2. Zondervan 58
3. Tyndale 29
4. Barbour 28
5. Harvest House 18
6. ZonderKids 18
7. Standard 17
8. Bethany House 15
9. Tommy Nelson 13
10. B & H Publishing 12
11. WaterBrook 12
12. FaithWords 8
13. Multnomah 8
14. NavPress 7
15. Abingdon Press 6
16. Revell 6
17. Charisma 5
18. InterVarsity 5
19. Crossway 4
20. Moody 4
21. Regal 4
22. American Tract 3
23. David C. Cook 3
24. Simon & Schuster 3
25. Whitaker House 3
26. Baker 2
27. Concordia 2
28. Howard 2
29. Putnam Adult 2
30. AMG 1
31. Augsburg 1
32. Bridge Logos 1
33. Center Street 1
34. Chosen 1
35. Discovery House 1
36. Frontline 1

37. Golden Books 1
38. Gospel Light 1
39. Harrison House 1
40. Ideals 1

41. Kregel 1
42. Lifeway 1
43. Living Link (AMG) 1
44. Penguin 1

45. Siloam 1
46. Tyndale Kids 1
47. Upper Room 1
48. Windblown 1

Top-50 Book Publishers

This year the list is based on which publishers had the most books on the list of the Top 50 books each month. It varies from the previous list in that it tracks the top 50 sellers regardless of genre (those listed previously are in specific genres). It is interesting to note that there were only 34 publishers with books on this list during the last year (one more than last year)—and the field is dominated by the top two.

1. Zondervan 50
2. Thomas Nelson 45
3. Barbour 15
4. Tyndale House 13
5. Harvest House 10
6. B & H Publishing Group 7
7. WaterBrook 7
8. Charisma (Strang) 6
9. FaithWords (Hachette) 6
10. Bethany House (Baker) 5
11. Crossway 3
12. Moody Publishing 3

13. Multnomah (WaterBrook) 3
14. Revell (Baker) 3
15. Simon & Schuster 3
16. Standard 3
17. David C. Cook 2
18. Ideals 2
19. Upper Room Books 2
20. ZonderKidz 2
21. Abingdon Press 1
22. Baker 1
23. Center Street (Hachette) 1
24. Family Life 1

25. Gospel Light 1
26. Group Publishing 1
27. Harrison House 1
28. Howard Publishing 1
29. Northfield (Moody) 1
30. Penguin Group USA 1
31. Putnam Adult (Penguin) 1
32. Siloam (Strang) 1
33. Teach All Nations 1
34. Windblown Media 1

TOPICAL LISTINGS OF PERIODICALS

As soon as you have an article or story idea, look up that topic in the following topical listings (see table of contents for a full list of topics). Study the appropriate periodicals in the primary/alphabetical listings (as well as their writers' guidelines and sample copies) and select those that are most likely targets for the piece you are writing.

Note that most ideas can be written for more than one periodical if you slant them to the needs of different audiences, for example, current events for teens, or pastors, or women. Have a target periodical and audience in mind before you start writing. Each topic is divided by age group/audience, so you can pick appropriate markets for your particular slant.

If the magazine prefers or requires a query letter, be sure to write that letter first and then follow any suggestions they make if they give you a go-ahead to write the article.

R—Takes reprints
(*)—Indicates new topic this year
$—Indicates a paying market
($)—Indicates a market pays sometimes or pays with books or merchandise

AFRICAN AMERICAN MARKETS*

ADULT/GENERAL
Chocolate Pages
$-Direction
$-Message
$-Precepts for Living
Purpose Magazine—R
3V Magazine
$-Upscale

CHILDREN
$-Juniorway
$Preschool Playhouse
$-Primary Street

PASTORS/LEADERS
$-African American Pulpit
$-Torch Legacy Leader

TEEN/YOUNG ADULT
$-InTeen—R
$-J.A.M.
$-Young Adult Today

WOMEN
$-Written
$-Heart & Soul
Precious Times—R
Today's Leading Ladies—R

APOLOGETICS

ADULT/GENERAL
$-Arkansas Catholic—R
$-Aujourd'hui Credo—R
$-Bible Advocate—R
Bread of Life—R
$-Catholic Insight
CBN.com—R
$-Celebrate Life—R

Christian C. L. RECORD—R
Christian Online
Christian Ranchman
$-Christian Research
$-Christian Standard—R
$-Christianity Today—R
Church of England News
$-City Light News—R
Desert Call—R
Desert Voice—R
E-Channels—R
($)-E-Quality
Encompass
Evangelical Advocate—R
$-Focus on the Family
$-Horizons (adult)—R
($)-Impact—R
$-In His Presence—R
Koinonia
$-Light & Life
$-Live—R
$-Lookout
$-Manna—R
MovieGuide
$-National Catholic
$-On Mission
$-Our Sunday Visitor—R
Perspectives—R
Perspectives/Science
PrayerWorks—R
Priscilla Papers
SCP Journal
$-Seek—R
$-Social Justice—R
Sword and Trumpet
Sword of the Lord—R
$-Today's Christian—R
$-Way of St. Francis—R
Wisconsin Christian

CHILDREN
$-SHINEbrightly—R

CHRISTIAN EDUCATION/ LIBRARY
Teach Kids Essentials—R

DAILY DEVOTIONALS
$-Brink Magazine—R
Penned from the Heart—R

PASTORS/LEADERS
$-Catholic Servant
$-Christian Century—R
$-Enrichment—R
$-Lutheran Partners—R
$-Outreach—R
Pulpit Helps—R
Theological Digest—R
$-This Rock

TEEN/YOUNG ADULT
$-Boundless Webzine—R
$-Breakaway
$-Brio—R
$-CLEAR Direction
$-CLEAR Horizon
$-Ignite Your Faith
$-True Girl
$-Young Salvationist—R

WOMEN
$-Canticle
Right to the Heart—R
Woman of Worth—R

BIBLE STUDIES

ADULT/GENERAL
$-Advance
($)-AGAIN—R

$-Alive Now—R
$-Annals of St. Anne
$-Arlington Catholic
$-Aujourd'hui Credo—R
Bread of Life—R
Breakthrough Intercessor—R
$-Catholic Peace Voice—R
$-Catholic Yearbook—R
CBN.com—R
Christian C. L. RECORD—R
Christian Computing—R
$-Christian Journal—R
Christian Motorsports
Christian Online
Christian Ranchman
$-Christian Research
$-Christian Standard—R
Church Herald & Holiness—R
$-City Light News—R
Connecting Point—R
Creation Care—R
$-Culture Wars—R
Desert Call—R
$-DreamSeeker—R
Eternal Ink—R
FaithWebbin—R
$-Gem—R
Heartlight—R
($)-HopeKeepers—R
$-In His Presence—R
$-In Touch
$-Light & Life
LiteraryTNT.com—R
$-Lutheran Journal—R
$-Mature Years—R
Methodist History
$-New Wineskins—R
$-Our Sunday Visitor—R
Perspectives—R
$-Positive Thinking—R
PrayerWorks—R
$-Precepts for Living
Priscilla Papers
Quaker Life—R
Reverent Submissions—R
$-Seek—R
$-Social Justice—R
$-Spiritual Life
$-St. Anthony Messenger
Sword and Trumpet
Sword of the Lord—R
Trumpeter—R
Victory Herald—R
$-War Cry—R
$-Way of St. Francis—R
Wisconsin Christian

CHILDREN
$-Archaeology
$-Primary Street
$-SHINEbrightly—R

CHRISTIAN EDUCATION/
LIBRARY
Catholic Library
$-Children's Ministry
Congregational Libraries
$-Group
$-Preschool Playhouse (CE)
$-RTJ—R

DAILY DEVOTIONALS
$-Brink Magazine—R

MISSIONS
MissionsMagizinet
Railroad Evangelist—R
Women of the Harvest

PASTORS/LEADERS
$-African American Pulpit
$-Catholic Servant
$-Let's Worship
Pulpit Helps—R
Sewanee Theo. Review
Sharing the Practice—R
$-Small Groups.com—R
Theological Digest—R
$-This Rock
$-Word & World

TEEN/YOUNG ADULT
$-Breakaway
Clarity Publishers
$-CLEAR Direction
$-Sharing the VICTORY—R
TeensForJC—R

WOMEN
($)-Beyond the Bend—R
CelebrateMoms—R
Precious Times—R
Proverbs 31 Sisters
Right to the Heart—R
($)-Simply Blessed—R
Virtuous Woman—R
Woman of Worth—R
Women's Ministry

BOOK EXCERPTS
ADULT/GENERAL
($)-AGAIN—R
$-Alive Now—R
$-Associated Content—R
$-BGC World—R
Books & Culture
$-Catholic Digest—R
CBN.com—R
$-Charisma
$-Chicken Soup Books—R
Christian C. L. RECORD—R
Christian Observer
$-Christian Renewal—R
$-Christian Retailing
$-Christianity Today—R

Church of England News
$-Covenant Companion—R
Creation Care—R
$-Culture Wars—R
E-Channels—R
($)-E-Quality
$-Home Times—R
($)-HopeKeepers—R
$-Indian Life—R
$-Interim—R
Island Catholic—R
LiteraryTNT.com—R
New Heart—R
$-New Wineskins—R
$-Power for Living—R
Priscilla Papers
$-Prism
Prison Living—R
Quaker Life—R
Regent Global—R
Rock & Sling
Sacred Journey—R
SingleAgain.com—R
Spirituality for Today
$-STEPS
$-Today's Christian—R
Trumpeter—R
$-United Church Observer—R
$-Upscale
Urban Kingdom—R
Wisconsin Christian
$-Wittenburg Door—R
$-Written

CHRISTIAN EDUCATION/
LIBRARY
Christian Early Ed.—R
$-Journal/Adventist Ed.—R
Teach Kids Essentials—R

MISSIONS
East-West Church
Intl. Jour./Frontier—R

PASTORS/LEADERS
$-African American Pulpit
$-Christian Century—R
Jour./Amer. Soc./Chur. Growth—R
$-Ministry Today
$-Outreach—R
Rick Warren's Ministry—R
$-Small Groups.com—R

TEEN/YOUNG ADULT
$-Boundless Webzine—R
$-Breakaway
$-J.A.M.
TeensForJC—R

WOMEN
($)-Beyond the Bend—R
CelebrateMoms—R
Elegance—R
$-Heart & Soul

$-Link & Visitor—R
Proverbs 31 Sisters
Share
$-SpiritLed Woman
Today's Leading Ladies—R
Virtuous Woman—R
Woman of Worth—R

WRITERS
$-Freelance Writer's Report—R
Money the Write Way—R
$-Writer

BOOK REVIEWS
ADULT/GENERAL
$-Abilities
$-Advance
African Voices—R
($)-AGAIN—R
$-America
$-Anglican Journal
$-Arkansas Catholic—R
$-Arlington Catholic
$-Associated Content—R
$-Atlantic Catholic
$-Aujourd'hui Credo—R
Books & Culture
Bread of Life—R
Breakthrough Intercessor—R
byFaith
$-Cathedral Age
$-Catholic Insight
$-Catholic Peace Voice—R
CBN.com—R
$-Charisma
Charlotte World
Chocolate Pages
Christian C. L. RECORD—R
Christian Computing—R
$-Christian Courier/Cdn.—R
$-Christian Herald—R
$-Christian Journal—R
Christian Media—R
Christian Observer
Christian Ranchman
$-Christian Renewal—R
$-Christian Research
$-Christian Retailing
$-Christianity Today—R
Chronicle - IN Edition
$-Citizen USA
$-City Light News—R
Creation Care—R
$-Cresset
CrossHome.com
$-Culture Wars—R
Desert Voice—R
Diamond Dust
$-DisciplesWorld
Divine Ascent
$-Dovetail—R
E-Channels—R

($)-E-Quality
$-Episcopal Life—R
Eternal Ink—R
$-Eureka Street
Evangelical Advocate—R
$-Faith & Family
$-Faith & Friends—R
$-Faith Today
Founders Journal
Good News Journal—R
Good News Today
Good News!
$-Good News/S. Florida
$-Haruah—R
Heartland Gatekeeper—R
($)-HopeKeepers—R
$-Image/WA
$-Imagine
($)-Impact—R
$-Indian Life—R
Infuze
$-Interim—R
Island Catholic—R
Koinonia
$-Liguorian
LiteraryTNT.com—R
($)-Mennonite Historian—R
Methodist History
Michiana Christian
$-MindFlights—R
$-Minnesota Christian—R
MovieGuide
($)-Mutuality—R
New Frontier
$-New Wineskins—R
$-Our Sunday Visitor—R
Ozarks Christian
Penwood Review
Perspectives/Science
$-Prairie Messenger—R
Presbyterian Outlook
Priscilla Papers
$-Prism
Prison Living—R
$-Pure Inspiration—R
Purpose Magazine—R
Quaker Life—R
Radix
Regent Global—R
Reverent Submissions—R
Rock & Sling
Sacred Journey—R
$-Science & Spirit
$-Significant Living—R
Silver Wings—R
SingleAgain.com—R
$-Social Justice—R
$-Spiritual Life
Studio—R
$-Testimony—R
Time of Singing—R

Trumpeter—R
$-Upscale
Urban Kingdom—R
Victory Herald—R
$-Way of St. Francis—R
$-Weavings—R
Wisconsin Christian
$-World & I—R
$-Written
Xavier Review

CHILDREN
$-New Moon—R
$-SHINEbrightly—R
$-Sparkle—R

CHRISTIAN EDUCATION/ LIBRARY
Catholic Library
Christian Early Ed.—R
Christian Librarian—R
Christian School Ed.—R
$-Church Libraries—R
Congregational Libraries
$-Group
Jour. of Christian Ed.
Jour. of Christianity—R
Jour./Ed. & Christian Belief—R
Jour./Research on Christian Ed.
$-Journal/Adventist Ed.—R
$-Momentum
$-Teachers of Vision—R

DAILY DEVOTIONALS
$-Brink Magazine—R

MISSIONS
East-West Church
$-Evangelical Missions—R
$-Glad Tidings (Canada)—R
Intl. Jour./Frontier—R
Missiology
OpRev Equipper—R
Women of the Harvest

MUSIC
$-Creator—R
Hymn

PASTORS/LEADERS
$-African American Pulpit
$-Catechumenate
$-Christian Century—R
Cross Currents
$-Diocesan Dialogue—R
$-Emmanuel
$-Enrichment—R
$-Interpreter
Jour./Amer. Soc./Chur. Growth—R
Jour./Pastoral Care
$-Leadership—R
$-Let's Worship
$-Lutheran Partners—R
$-Ministry

Ministry in Motion—R
$-Ministry Today
Pulpit Helps—R
$-Reformed Worship—R
Sharing the Practice—R
$-Small Groups.com—R
Theological Digest—R
$-Willow—R
$-Word & World
$-Worship Leader
$-Your Church—R

TEEN/YOUNG ADULT
$-Boundless Webzine—R
$-CLEAR Direction
$-CLEAR Horizon
$-Devo'Zine—R
G4T Ink—R
$-J.A.M.
TeensForJC—R
$-True Girl

WOMEN
($)-Beyond the Bend—R
$-Esprit
$-Heart & Soul
$-Herizons
Hope for Women
$-Horizons (women)—R
$-inSpirit—R
$-Pauses…
Precious Times—R
Proverbs 31 Sisters
Right to the Heart—R
Share
($)-Simply Blessed—R
Today's Leading Ladies—R
Virtuous Woman—R
Woman of Worth—R
Women's Ministry
WT Online—R

WRITERS
$-Adv. Christian Writer—R
Areopagus
$-Christian Communicator—R
$-Cross & Quill—R
Esdras' Scroll—R
$-Fellowscript—R
Money the Write Way—R
NW Christian Author—R
Opinari—R
$-Spirit-Led Writer—R
$-Tickled by Thunder
$-WIN-Informer
Write Connection
$-Writer
$-Writers' Journal

CANADIAN/FOREIGN MARKETS
ADULT/GENERAL
$-Abilities

$-Anglican Journal
$-Annals of St. Anne
$-Atlantic Catholic
$-Aujourd'hui Credo—R
$-Australian Catholics—R
$-B.C. Catholic—R
Bread of Life—R
$-Canada Lutheran—R
Canadian Lutheran
$-Canadian Mennonite—R
CanadianChristianity
$-Catholic Insight
Catholic Register
Challenge Weekly
$-Christian Courier/Cdn.—R
Christian Courier/WI—R
$-Christian Herald—R
Christian Outlook
$-Christian Renewal—R
$-ChristianWeek—R
Church of England News
$-City Light News—R
$-Common Ground—R
Creation
$-Dreams & Visions—R
E-Channels—R
$-Eureka Street
Evangelical Times
$-Faith & Friends—R
$-Faith Today
Fellowship
($)-Impact—R
$-Indian Life—R
$-Interim—R
Island Catholic—R
LifeSite News
$-Living Light—R
($)-Mennonite Historian—R
$-Messenger, The
$-Messenger/Sacred Heart
$-Messenger/St. Anthony
Mosaic—R
$-Prairie Messenger—R
Rhubarb
Studio—R
$-Testimony—R
$-United Church Observer—R

CHRISTIAN EDUCATION/ LIBRARY
$-Christian Educators—R
Jour. of Christian Ed.
Jour./Ed. & Christian Belief—R

DAILY DEVOTIONALS
$-Rejoice!

MISSIONS
$-Glad Tidings (Canada)—R
Koinonia

MUSIC
Church Music

PASTORS/LEADERS
$-Evangelical Baptist
Technologies for Worship—R
Theological Digest—R

WOMEN
Christian Women Today—R
$-Esprit
$-Herizons
Life Tools for Women
$-Link & Visitor—R
Making Waves
Women Today—R
WT Online—R

WRITERS
Areopagus
$-Canadian Writer's Jour.—R
$-Fellowscript—R
$-Tickled by Thunder
Writers Manual

CELEBRITY PIECES
ADULT/GENERAL
American Tract—R
$-Angels on Earth
$-Annals of St. Anne
$-Arlington Catholic
$-Associated Content—R
$-Australian Catholics—R
Breakthrough
$-Catholic Digest—R
CBN.com—R
$-Celebrate Life—R
$-Christian Herald—R
$-Christian Journal—R
Christian Motorsports
Christian Online
Christian Ranchman
$-Christianity Today Movies—R
$-Chronicle Christian/KS
Church of England News
$-City Light News—R
($)-Community Spirit—R
$-DisciplesWorld
$-Episcopal Life—R
$-Focus on the Family
$-Focus on Your Child
Good News Journal—R
$-Good News, Etc.—R
$-Guideposts—R
Heartland Gatekeeper—R
Heartlight—R
$-Home Times—R
($)-HopeKeepers—R
($)-Impact—R
$-In Touch
$-Indian Life—R
$-Light & Life
$-Living Light—R
$-Minnesota Christian—R

MovieGuide
($)-Mutuality—R
$-New Wineskins—R
$-Our Sunday Visitor—R
$-Positive Thinking—R
$-Power for Living—R
$-Priority!—R
$-Prism
Prison Living—R
$-Pure Inspiration—R
Sacred Journey—R
$-Significant Living—R
Spirituality for Today
$-St. Anthony Messenger
$-Today's Christian—R
Tri-State Voice
Trumpeter—R
Urban Kingdom—R
$-Vibrant Life—R
$-War Cry—R
Wisconsin Christian
$-Wittenburg Door—R

CHILDREN
$-American Girl—R
$-Cadet Quest—R
$-SHINEbrightly—R
$-Sparkle—R
$-Winner—R

DAILY DEVOTIONALS
$-Brink Magazine—R

MUSIC
$-Christian Music Today—R
Christian Music Weekly—R

PASTORS/LEADERS
$-Catholic Servant
$-Ministry Today

TEEN/YOUNG ADULT
$-Brio—R
$-Essential Connection
G4T Ink—R
$-J.A.M.
$-Listen—R
$-Sharing the VICTORY—R
$-Steelroots
$-TC Magazine
TeensForJC—R
$-Young Salvationist—R

WOMEN
($)-Beyond the Bend—R
$-Canticle
$-Heart & Soul
$-Journey
More to Life
Precious Times—R
Today's Leading Ladies—R
Virtuous Woman—R
Woman of Worth—R

WRITERS
$-Cross & Quill—R

CHRISTIAN BUSINESS
ADULT/GENERAL
$-Angels on Earth
$-CBA Retailers
CBN.com—R
Christian Business
$-Christian Courier/Cdn.—R
$-Christian Journal—R
Christian Motorsports
Christian Online
Christian Ranchman
$-Christian Retailing
$-ChristianWeek—R
$-Chronicle Christian/KS
$-Citizen USA
$-City Light News—R
($)-Community Spirit—R
Creation Care—R
Desert Call—R
Desert Voice—R
Disciple's Journal—R
Evangel/OR—R
$-Faith Today
$-Gem—R
Good News Journal—R
$-Gospel Today—R
$-Guideposts—R
Heartland Gatekeeper—R
Heartlight—R
Highway News—R
$-Home Times—R
$-In Touch
$-Light & Life
Light of the World
LiteraryTNT.com—R
$-Living—R
$-Lookout
$-Manna—R
Marketplace
$-Minnesota Christian—R
MissionWares
Nostalgia—R
($)-NRB Magazine—R
$-Our Sunday Visitor—R
($)-P.O.W.E.R.
$-Power for Living—R
$-Prism
Prison Living—R
Purpose Magazine—R
Regent Global—R
$-Science & Spirit
SingleAgain.com—R
Spirituality for Today
$-St. Anthony Messenger
$-Today's Christian—R
$-Together—R
Trumpeter—R
Urban Kingdom—R

Victory Herald—R
$-War Cry—R
Wisconsin Christian

CHRISTIAN EDUCATION/
LIBRARY
Christian School Ed.—R
Teach Kids Essentials—R

DAILY DEVOTIONALS
$-Brink Magazine—R

MISSIONS
$-Evangelical Missions—R

MUSIC
Gospel Synergy

PASTORS/LEADERS
$-African American Pulpit
$-Catholic Servant
$-Clergy Journal—R
$-InSite—R
$-Interpreter
Ministry in Motion—R
Rick Warren's Ministry—R
Technologies for Worship—R
$-Today's Parish
$-Willow—R
$-Your Church—R

TEEN/YOUNG ADULT
$-Boundless Webzine—R
$-Brio—R
$-CLEAR Direction
$-J.A.M.

WOMEN
($)-Beyond the Bend—R
Christian Women Today—R
$-Dabbling Mum—R
Elegance—R
$-Heart & Soul
Precious Times—R
($)-Simply Blessed—R
Today's Leading Ladies—R
Virtuous Woman—R
Women Today—R

WRITERS
Money the Write Way—R
Writing Corner—R

CHRISTIAN EDUCATION
ADULT/GENERAL
$-Advance
African Voices—R
$-America
$-Anglican Journal
$-Animal Trails—R
$-Annals of St. Anne
$-Arlington Catholic
$-Atlantic Catholic
$-Aujourd'hui Credo—R
$-B.C. Catholic—R

$-Canada Lutheran—R
$-Catholic Peace Voice—R
$-Celebrate Life—R
Christian C. L. RECORD—R
$-Christian Courier/Cdn.—R
$-Christian Examiner
$-Christian Home & School
$-Christian Journal—R
Christian Observer
Christian Online
Christian Ranchman
$-Christian Renewal—R
$-Christian Retailing
$-Christian Standard—R
$-Christianity Today—R
$-ChristianWeek—R
$-Chronicle Christian/KS
Church Herald & Holiness—R
$-Citizen USA
$-City Light News—R
$-Columbia—R
($)-Community Spirit—R
$-Company—R
Creation Care—R
$-Cresset
$-Culture Wars—R
Desert Call—R
Desert Voice—R
$-Direction
$-DisciplesWorld
E-Channels—R
Encompass
Eternal Ink—R
Evangelical Advocate—R
$-Faith & Family
$-Faith Today
Family Journal—R
$-Gem—R
Good News Journal—R
$-Good News, Etc.—R
$-Gospel Today—R
Heartlight—R
Highway News—R
$-Home Times—R
$-Homeschooling Today—R
$-In His Presence—R
$-In Touch
Koinonia
$-Light & Life
Light of the World
LiteraryTNT.com—R
$-Living Church
$-Lookout
$-Manna—R
$-Messenger/Sacred Heart
Methodist History
$-Minnesota Christian—R
Mosaic—R
MovieGuide
$-National Catholic
$-New Wineskins—R

Nostalgia—R
$-Our Sunday Visitor—R
Penned from the Heart—R
Perspectives—R
PrayerWorks—R
$-Precepts for Living
Presbyterian Outlook
$-Presbyterians Today—R
$-Prism
Prison Living—R
$-Purpose—R
Quaker Life—R
Reverent Submissions—R
$-Seek—R
SingleAgain.com—R
Spirituality for Today
$-St. Anthony Messenger
Sword and Trumpet
Sword of the Lord—R
$-Testimony—R
$-Together—R
Trumpeter—R
Urban Kingdom—R
Victory Herald—R
$-War Cry—R
$-Way of St. Francis—R
Wisconsin Christian

CHILDREN
$-Archaeology
$-Guide—R
$-JuniorWay
$-Kid Zone
$-Primary Street
$-Sparkle—R

CHRISTIAN EDUCATION/ LIBRARY
$-Catechist
$-Children's Ministry
Christian Early Ed.—R
$-Christian Educators—R
Christian Librarian—R
Christian School Ed.—R
$-Group
Ideas Unlimited—R
Jour. of Christian Ed.
Jour. of Christianity—R
Jour./Ed. & Christian Belief—R
Jour./Research on Christian Ed.
$-Journal/Adventist Ed.—R
$-Kids' Ministry Ideas
$-Momentum
$-Preschool Playhouse (CE)
$-RTJ—R
Teach Kids Essentials—R
$-Teachers of Vision—R
$-Today's Catholic Teacher—R
$-Youth & CE Leadership

MISSIONS
$-Evangelical Missions—R
$-Glad Tidings (Canada)—R

PASTORS/LEADERS
$-African American Pulpit
$-Catechumenate
$-Catholic Servant
$-Christian Century—R
Christian Ed. Jour. (CA)—R
$-Clergy Journal—R
Cross Currents
$-Enrichment—R
$-Interpreter
$-Lutheran Partners—R
$-Ministry Today
Pulpit Helps—R
$-RevWriter Resource
Rick Warren's Ministry—R
$-Small Groups.com—R
Technologies for Worship—R
$-This Rock
$-Today's Parish
$-Word & World
$-Youthworker

TEEN/YOUNG ADULT
$-Boundless Webzine—R
$-CLEAR Direction
$-CLEAR Horizon
G4T Ink—R
$-Insight—R
$-J.A.M.
TeensForJC—R
$-True Girl
$-Young Adult Today
$-Young Christian—R

WOMEN
CelebrateMoms—R
Christian Woman's Page—R
Crowned with Silver
Hearts at Home—R
$-Horizons (women)—R
$-inSpirit—R
Just Between Us—R
Precious Times—R
Right to the Heart—R
Share
Today's Leading Ladies—R
Woman of Worth—R
WT Online—R

CHRISTIAN LIVING
ADULT/GENERAL
3V Magazine
$-Advance
($)-AGAIN—R
$-Alive Now—R
$-America
American Tract—R
$-Angels on Earth
$-Annals of St. Anne
$-Arkansas Catholic—R
$-Arlington Catholic
$-Atlantic Catholic

$-Aujourd'hui Credo—R
$-Australian Catholics—R
$-B.C. Catholic—R
$-BGC World—R
$-Bible Advocate—R
Bread of Life—R
Breakthrough Intercessor—R
$-Bridal Guides—R
$-Canada Lutheran—R
$-Cathedral Age
$-Catholic Digest—R
$-Catholic Forester—R
$-Catholic New York
$-Catholic Yearbook—R
CBN.com—R
$-Celebrate Life—R
Central FL Episcopalian
$-CGA World—R
$-Charisma
$-Chicken Soup Books—R
$-Christian Courier/Cdn.—R
Christian Courier/WI—R
$-Christian Examiner
$-Christian Home & School
$-Christian Journal—R
Christian Observer
Christian Online
Christian Ranchman
$-Christian Research
$-Christian Standard—R
$-Christianity Today—R
$-ChristianWeek—R
$-Chronicle Christian/KS
Church Herald & Holiness—R
Church of England News
$-Citizen USA
$-City Light News—R
$-Columbia—R
($)-Community Spirit—R
Connecting Point—R
$-Covenant Companion—R
Creation Care—R
$-Culture Wars—R
Desert Call—R
Desert Voice—R
$-Discipleship Journal—R
$-DisciplesWorld
Divine Ascent
$-DreamSeeker—R
DuPage Christian
E-Channels—R
($)-E-Quality
$-EFCA Today—R
Encompass
$-Enfoque a La Familia
Eternal Ink—R
$-Evangel/IN—R
Evangel/OR—R
Evangelical Advocate—R
$-Faith & Family
$-Faith & Friends—R

$-Faith Today
FaithWebbin—R
$-Family Digest—R
Family Journal—R
FGBC World
Florida Baptist Witness
$-Focus on the Family
$-Gem—R
$-Gems of Truth—R
$-Good News—R
Good News Journal—R
$-Good News, Etc.—R
$-Gospel Today—R
$-Guideposts—R
Halo Magazine
$-Haruah—R
Heartlight—R
Highway News—R
$-Home Times—R
$-Homeschooling Today—R
($)-HopeKeepers—R
$-Horizons (adult)—R
($)-Impact—R
$-In His Presence—R
$-In Touch
$-Indian Life—R
IPHC Experience
Island Catholic—R
Keys to Living—R
Koinonia
Leaves—R
$-Light & Life
Light of the World
$-Liguorian
LiteraryTNT.com—R
$-Live—R
$-Living—R
$-Living Church
$-Lookout
$-Lutheran Digest—R
$-Lutheran Journal—R
Lutheran Witness
$-Majellan—R
$-Manna—R
$-Marian Helper
$-Mature Living
$-Mature Years—R
$-Men of Integrity—R
Men of the Cross
$-Men.AG.org—R
Mensajero ala Blanca
MESSAGE/Open Bible—R
$-Messenger/Sacred Heart
Methodist History
Michiana Christian
$-Minnesota Christian—R
$-Montgomery's Journey
Mosaic—R
($)-Mutuality—R
New Heart—R
$-New Wineskins—R

Nostalgia—R
$-Our Sunday Visitor—R
$-Over the Back Fence—R
$-Ozarks Senior Living—R
Penned from the Heart—R
Perspectives—R
$-Positive Thinking—R
$-Power for Living—R
PrayerWorks—R
$-Presbyterians Today—R
Prison Living—R
$-Psychology for Living—R
$-Pure Inspiration—R
$-Purpose—R
Quaker Life—R
Regent Global—R
Reverent Submissions—R
Saved Magazine
$-Science & Spirit
$-Seek—R
Sharing—R
Silver Wings—R
SingleAgain.com—R
$-Spiritual Life
Spirituality for Today
$-St. Anthony Messenger
$-Standard—R
$-Storyteller—R
SW Kansas Faith
Sword and Trumpet
Sword of the Lord—R
$-Testimony—R
$-Today's Christian—R
$-Today's Pentecostal—R
$-Together—R
Trumpeter—R
$-U.S. Catholic
$-United Church Observer—R
Urban Kingdom—R
$-Vibrant Life—R
Victory Herald—R
$-Victory in Grace—R
$-Vision—R
$-Vista
$-War Cry—R
$-Way of St. Francis—R
$-Wesleyan Life—R
Wisconsin Christian

CHILDREN
$-Archaeology
$-BREAD/God's Children—R
$-Cadet Quest—R
$-Focus/Clubhouse Jr.
$-Guide—R
$-JuniorWay
$-Kid Zone
$-Partners—R
$-Passport—R
$-Pockets—R
$-Primary Street

CHRISTIAN EDUCATION/ LIBRARY
Congregational Libraries
$-Group
Teach Kids Essentials—R
$-Teachers of Vision—R
$-Youth & CE Leadership

DAILY DEVOTIONALS
$-Brink Magazine—R
Penned from the Heart—R

MISSIONS
$-Evangelical Missions—R
$-Glad Tidings (Canada)—R
Women of the Harvest

PASTORS/LEADERS
$-African American Pulpit
$-Barefoot—R
$-Catechumenate
$-Catholic Servant
$-Christian Century—R
$-Interpreter
$-Net Results
$-Preaching Well—R
$-Proclaim—R
Pulpit Helps—R
$-Review for Religious
$-RevWriter Resource
Rick Warren's Ministry—R
Technologies for Worship—R
$-Word & World

TEEN/YOUNG ADULT
$-Boundless Webzine—R
$-Breakaway
$-Brio—R
$-CLEAR Direction
$-CLEAR Horizon
$-Credo—R
$-Devo'Zine—R
$-Essential Connection
G4T Ink—R
$-Ignite Your Faith
$-Insight—R
$-J.A.M.
$-Real Faith in Life—R
$-Sharing the VICTORY—R
$-TC Magazine
TeensForJC—R
$-True Girl
$-Young Salvationist—R

WOMEN
$-At the Center—R
($)-Beyond the Bend—R
$-Canticle
CelebrateMoms—R
Christian Woman's Page—R
$-Come to the Fire—R
Crowned with Silver
$-Dabbling Mum—R

Elegance—R
First Lady
Handmaidens
Hearts at Home—R
Hope for Women
$-Horizons (women)—R
Inspired Women
$-inSpirit—R
$-Journey
Just Between Us—R
$-Link & Visitor—R
Lutheran Woman's Quar.
$-MomSense—R
P31 Woman—R
$-Pauses…
Precious Times—R
Proverbs 31 Sisters
Right to the Heart—R
Share
($)-Simply Blessed—R
$-SpiritLed Woman
$-Today's Christian Woman—R
Today's Leading Ladies—R
Together with God—R
Virtuous Woman—R
Woman of Worth—R
Women of the Cross
Women Today—R
Women's Ministry
WT Online—R

CHURCH GROWTH
ADULT/GENERAL
($)-AGAIN—R
$-America
$-Annals of St. Anne
$-Atlantic Catholic
Bread of Life—R
Breakthrough Intercessor—R
$-Catholic Peace Voice—R
$-Christian Examiner
$-Christian Journal—R
Christian News NW—R
Christian Online
$-Christian Standard—R
$-ChristianWeek—R
Church of England News
$-City Light News—R
($)-Community Spirit—R
$-Culture Wars—R
Desert Call—R
$-DisciplesWorld
E-Channels—R
Encompass
$-Evangel/IN—R
Evangelical Advocate—R
$-Faith & Family
$-Faith Today
$-Gem—R
$-Good News—R
$-Good News, Etc.—R

$-Home Times—R
$-In His Presence—R
Koinonia
$-Light & Life
$-Liguorian
LiteraryTNT.com—R
$-Living Church
$-Lookout
$-Men.AG.org—R
MESSAGE/Open Bible—R
$-Messenger/Sacred Heart
Mosaic—R
$-National Catholic
$-New Wineskins—R
$-Our Sunday Visitor—R
Penned from the Heart—R
Presbyterian Outlook
$-Presbyterians Today—R
Prison Living—R
$-Purpose—R
Quaker Life—R
$-Seek—R
Spirituality for Today
$-St. Anthony Messenger
Sword and Trumpet
Sword of the Lord—R
$-Testimony—R
Trumpeter—R
$-U.S. Catholic
Urban Kingdom—R
$-Victory in Grace—R
$-Way of St. Francis—R
$-Wesleyan Life—R
Wisconsin Christian

CHILDREN
$-Archaeology

CHRISTIAN EDUCATION/ LIBRARY
$-Children's Ministry
Congregational Libraries
$-Group
$-Youth & CE Leadership

MISSIONS
$-Evangelical Missions—R
$-Glad Tidings (Canada)—R
Missiology
$-PIME World—R

MUSIC
$-Creator—R

PASTORS/LEADERS
$-African American Pulpit
$-Catechumenate
$-Catholic Servant
$-Christian Century—R
Christian Ed. Jour. (CA)—R
$-Clergy Journal—R
$-Enrichment—R
$-Growth Points—R
$-Interpreter

Jour./Amer. Soc./Chur. Growth—R
$-Leadership—R
$-Let's Worship
$-Lutheran Partners—R
Ministry in Motion—R
$-Ministry Today
$-Net Results
$-Outreach—R
Pulpit Helps—R
$-RevWriter Resource
Rick Warren's Ministry—R
Sharing the Practice—R
Technologies for Worship—R
Theological Digest—R
$-This Rock
$-Willow—R
$-Worship Leader
$-Your Church—R

TEEN/YOUNG ADULT
$-CLEAR Direction
$-CLEAR Horizon
G4T Ink—R
$-J.A.M.
TeensForJC—R

WOMEN
($)-Beyond the Bend—R
Elegance—R
Hope for Women
$-inSpirit—R
Just Between Us—R
Right to the Heart—R
Share

CHURCH HISTORY

ADULT/GENERAL
African Voices—R
$-America
$-Annals of St. Anne
$-Atlantic Catholic
$-Aujourd'hui Credo—R
Bread of Life—R
Breakthrough Intercessor—R
$-Catholic Digest—R
$-Catholic Insight
$-Catholic Peace Voice—R
$-Catholic Sentinel
$-Catholic Yearbook—R
CBN.com—R
$-Christian History—R
Christian Online
$-Christian Renewal—R
$-Christian Standard—R
Church Herald & Holiness—R
Church of England News
$-City Light News—R
$-Columbia—R
$-Company—R
Creation Care—R
$-Cresset

Desert Call—R
Desert Voice—R
Divine Ascent
E-Channels—R
($)-E-Quality
Encompass
Evangelical Advocate—R
$-Family Digest—R
Founders Journal
Friends Journal—R
$-Home Times—R
$-Horizons (adult)—R
$-In Touch
Island Catholic—R
Jour. of Church & State
Koinonia
$-Leben—R
$-Light & Life
$-Liguorian
$-Lookout
$-Lutheran Journal—R
$-Majellan—R
($)-Mennonite Historian—R
$-Messiah
Methodist History
Mosaic—R
MovieGuide
$-National Catholic
$-New Wineskins—R
$-Our Sunday Visitor—R
PrayerWorks—R
Presbyterian Outlook
$-Presbyterians Today—R
Priscilla Papers
Prison Living—R
$-Purpose—R
$-Science & Spirit
$-Social Justice—R
Spirituality for Today
$-St. Anthony Messenger
Sword and Trumpet
Sword of the Lord—R
Trumpeter—R
$-U.S. Catholic
Urban Kingdom—R
Victory Herald—R
$-Way of St. Francis—R
$-Wesleyan Life—R
Wisconsin Christian

CHILDREN
$-Archaeology
$-BREAD/God's Children—R
$-Guide—R

CHRISTIAN EDUCATION/LIBRARY
Catholic Library
$-Group

DAILY DEVOTIONALS
Penned from the Heart—R

MISSIONS
$-Evangelical Missions—R
$-Glad Tidings (Canada)—R
Missiology
OpRev Equipper—R
Railroad Evangelist—R

PASTORS/LEADERS
$-African American Pulpit
$-Catechumenate
$-Christian Century—R
$-Clergy Journal—R
Cross Currents
$-Enrichment—R
$-Leadership—R
Lutheran Forum
$-Ministry & Liturgy—R
Pulpit Helps—R
Sharing the Practice—R
Theological Digest—R
$-This Rock

TEEN/YOUNG ADULT
$-Boundless Webzine—R
$-Breakaway
$-CLEAR Direction
$-CLEAR Horizon
$-Essential Connection
$-J.A.M.
$-Living My Faith
$-Real Faith in Life—R
TeensForJC—R

WOMEN
($)-Beyond the Bend—R
($)-History's Women—R
$-Horizons (women)—R
$-Link & Visitor—R
Share

CHURCH LIFE

ADULT/GENERAL
($)-AGAIN—R
$-America
$-Annals of St. Anne
$-Arkansas Catholic—R
$-Atlantic Catholic
$-Aujourd'hui Credo—R
$-Australian Catholics—R
Bread of Life—R
Breakthrough Intercessor—R
$-Bridal Guides—R
$-Cathedral Age
$-Catholic Digest—R
$-Catholic Insight
$-Catholic Sentinel
$-Catholic Yearbook—R
CBN.com—R
$-Christian Home & School
$-Christian Journal—R
Christian News NW—R
Christian Online

$-Christian Standard—R
$-Christianity Today—R
$-ChristianWeek—R
Church Herald & Holiness—R
Church of England News
$-City Light News—R
$-Columbia—R
($)-Community Spirit—R
$-Company—R
$-Covenant Companion—R
Creation Care—R
Desert Call—R
Desert Voice—R
$-DisciplesWorld
$-DreamSeeker—R
E-Channels—R
($)-E-Quality
Encompass
Eternal Ink—R
$-Evangel/IN—R
Evangel/OR—R
Evangelical Advocate—R
$-Faith & Family
$-Faith Today
$-Family Digest—R
$-Gem—R
$-Good News—R
$-Good News, Etc.—R
$-Home Times—R
$-Horizons (adult)—R
$-In His Presence—R
$-In Touch
Island Catholic—R
Koinonia
Leaves—R
$-Light & Life
$-Liguorian
$-Live—R
$-Living Church
$-Lookout
$-Lutheran Journal—R
$-Men.AG.org—R
($)-Mennonite Historian—R
MESSAGE/Open Bible—R
$-Messenger/St. Anthony
$-Minnesota Christian—R
Mosaic—R
($)-Mutuality—R
$-National Catholic
$-New Wineskins—R
Nostalgia—R
$-Our Sunday Visitor—R
Penned from the Heart—R
$-Precepts for Living
Presbyterian Outlook
$-Presbyterians Today—R
Priscilla Papers
Prison Living—R
$-Purpose—R
Quaker Life—R
Reverent Submissions—R

$-Seek—R
Silver Wings—R
Spirituality for Today
$-St. Anthony Messenger
Sword of the Lord—R
$-Testimony—R
$-Today's Christian—R
$-Today's Pentecostal—R
Trumpeter—R
$-U.S. Catholic
Urban Kingdom—R
Victory Herald—R
$-Way of St. Francis—R
$-Wesleyan Life—R
Wisconsin Christian

CHILDREN
$-Archaeology
$-Primary Street

CHRISTIAN EDUCATION/ LIBRARY
$-Children's Ministry
$-Group
Teach Kids Essentials—R
$-Youth & CE Leadership

DAILY DEVOTIONALS
Penned from the Heart—R

MISSIONS
$-Evangelical Missions—R
$-Glad Tidings (Canada)—R

PASTORS/LEADERS
$-African American Pulpit
$-Catholic Servant
$-Christian Century—R
$-Enrichment—R
$-Interpreter
$-Leadership—R
$-Ministry
Ministry in Motion—R
$-Ministry Today
$-Net Results
$-Priest
$-RevWriter Resource
Rick Warren's Ministry—R
Sharing the Practice—R
Technologies for Worship—R
$-Willow—R
$-Worship Leader
$-Youthworker

TEEN/YOUNG ADULT
$-Boundless Webzine—R
$-Brio—R
$-CLEAR Direction
$-CLEAR Horizon
$-J.A.M.

WOMEN
($)-Beyond the Bend—R
$-Canticle
Christian Woman's Page—R

Handmaiden—R
Hope for Women
$-Horizons (women)—R
$-inSpirit—R
$-Pauses...
Right to the Heart—R
Share
$-Today's Christian Woman—R

CHURCH MANAGEMENT
ADULT/GENERAL
$-America
$-Atlantic Catholic
$-Bridal Guides—R
Christian Computing—R
Christian News NW—R
Christian Online
$-Christian Standard—R
$-ChristianWeek—R
Church of England News
$-City Light News—R
($)-Community Spirit—R
$-Covenant Companion—R
Creation Care—R
$-Culture Wars—R
Disciple's Journal—R
E-Channels—R
Encompass
Evangelical Advocate—R
$-Faith Today
$-Gem—R
$-Gospel Today—R
Koinonia
$-Living Church
$-Lookout
Mosaic—R
$-Our Sunday Visitor—R
Presbyterian Outlook
Priscilla Papers
Prison Living—R
Regent Global—R
$-St. Anthony Messenger
Sword of the Lord—R
Trumpeter—R
$-U.S. Catholic
Wisconsin Christian

CHILDREN
$-Archaeology

CHRISTIAN EDUCATION/ LIBRARY
$-Children's Ministry
$-Group
$-Youth & CE Leadership

DAILY DEVOTIONALS
Penned from the Heart—R

MISSIONS
$-Evangelical Missions—R

PASTORS/LEADERS
$-African American Pulpit

$-Catholic Servant
Christian Ed. Jour. (CA)—R
Christian Management—R
$-Clergy Journal—R
$-Enrichment—R
$-Growth Points—R
$-Interpreter
Jour./Amer. Soc./Chur. Growth—R
$-Leadership—R
$-Lutheran Partners—R
$-Ministry
Ministry in Motion—R
$-Ministry Today
$-Net Results
Pulpit Helps—R
$-RevWriter Resource
Rick Warren's Ministry—R
Sharing the Practice—R
Technologies for Worship—R
$-Word & World
$-Worship Leader
$-Your Church—R

TEEN/YOUNG ADULT
$-CLEAR Direction
$-CLEAR Horizon

WOMEN
Just Between Us—R
Right to the Heart—R
Share
Women's Ministry

CHURCH OUTREACH
ADULT/GENERAL
($)-AGAIN—R
$-America
$-Annals of St. Anne
$-Atlantic Catholic
$-BGC World—R
$-Bible Advocate—R
Bread of Life—R
Breakthrough Intercessor—R
$-Bridal Guides—R
$-Catholic Sentinel
CBN.com—R
$-Christian Home & School
$-Christian Journal—R
Christian News NW—R
Christian Online
$-Christian Research
$-Christian Standard—R
$-ChristianWeek—R
Church Herald & Holiness—R
Church of England News
$-City Light News—R
$-Columbia—R
($)-Community Spirit—R
$-Company—R
$-Covenant Companion—R
Creation Care—R
$-Culture Wars—R

Desert Call—R
Desert Voice—R
$-DisciplesWorld
E-Channels—R
Encompass
$-Episcopal Life—R
Eternal Ink—R
$-Evangel/IN—R
Evangel/OR—R
Evangelical Advocate—R
$-Faith & Friends—R
$-Faith Today
$-Gem—R
$-Good News—R
$-Good News, Etc.—R
Heartland Gatekeeper—R
$-Home Times—R
($)-HopeKeepers—R
$-In His Presence—R
Koinonia
$-Light & Life
$-Live—R
$-Living Church
$-Lookout
$-Men.AG.org—R
MESSAGE/Open Bible—R
$-Montana Catholic
Mosaic—R
$-National Catholic
Network
$-New Wineskins—R
$-On Mission
$-Our Sunday Visitor—R
$-Precepts for Living
Presbyterian Outlook
$-Presbyterians Today—R
$-Priority!—R
Priscilla Papers
$-Prism
Prison Living—R
$-Purpose—R
Quaker Life—R
$-Science & Spirit
$-Seek—R
Spirituality for Today
$-St. Anthony Messenger
Sword of the Lord—R
$-Testimony—R
$-Today's Christian—R
Trumpeter—R
$-U.S. Catholic
Urban Kingdom—R
Victory Herald—R
$-Wesleyan Life—R
Wisconsin Christian

CHILDREN
$-Primary Street

CHRISTIAN EDUCATION/ LIBRARY
$-Children's Ministry

$-Group
$-Journal/Adventist Ed.—R
$-Kids' Ministry Ideas
$-Momentum
Teach Kids Essentials—R
$-Youth & CE Leadership

MISSIONS
East-West Church
$-Evangelical Missions—R
$-Glad Tidings (Canada)—R
Missiology
$-PIME World—R
Railroad Evangelist—R

PASTORS/LEADERS
$-African American Pulpit
$-Catholic Servant
$-Christian Century—R
$-Clergy Journal—R
$-Cornerstone Youth—R
$-Enrichment—R
$-Growth Points—R
$-Interpreter
Jour./Amer. Soc./Chur. Growth—R
$-Leadership—R
$-Let's Worship
$-Lutheran Partners—R
$-Ministry
Ministry in Motion—R
$-Ministry Today
$-Net Results
$-Outreach—R
$-Rev. Magazine
$-RevWriter Resource
Rick Warren's Ministry—R
Sharing the Practice—R
Technologies for Worship—R
$-This Rock
$-Today's Parish
$-Willow—R
$-Word & World
$-Worship Leader
$-Youthworker

TEEN/YOUNG ADULT
$-CLEAR Direction
$-CLEAR Horizon
$-Credo—R
$-Insight—R
TeensForJC—R
$-True Girl

WOMEN
Christian Woman's Page—R
Hope for Women
$-inSpirit—R
Just Between Us—R
$-Pauses…
Proverbs 31 Sisters
Right to the Heart—R
Share
Women's Ministry

CHURCH TRADITIONS
ADULT/GENERAL
($)-AGAIN—R
$-America
$-Annals of St. Anne
$-Arkansas Catholic—R
$-Atlantic Catholic
$-Aujourd'hui Credo—R
$-Bridal Guides—R
$-Canada Lutheran—R
$-Catholic Digest—R
$-Catholic Yearbook—R
CBN.com—R
$-Celebrate Life—R
$-CGA World—R
$-Christian Examiner
$-Christian History—R
Christian Online
$-Christian Research
$-Christian Standard—R
Church of England News
$-City Light News—R
$-Columbia—R
$-Cresset
Desert Call—R
$-DisciplesWorld
E-Channels—R
($)-E-Quality
Encompass
Eternal Ink—R
Evangelical Advocate—R
$-Faith & Family
$-Faith Today
$-Gem—R
$-Gospel Today—R
Koinonia
$-Light & Life
$-Liguorian
$-Living Church
$-Lutheran Journal—R
($)-Mennonite Historian—R
Mosaic—R
$-National Catholic
$-New Wineskins—R
Nostalgia—R
$-Our Sunday Visitor—R
Perspectives—R
$-Presbyterians Today—R
Priscilla Papers
Prison Living—R
$-Science & Spirit
$-St. Anthony Messenger
$-Testimony—R
$-Together—R
Trumpeter—R
$-U.S. Catholic
$-Way of St. Francis—R
Wisconsin Christian

CHILDREN
$-Archaeology

CHRISTIAN EDUCATION/
LIBRARY
$-Children's Ministry
$-Group
$-RTJ—R

DAILY DEVOTIONALS
Penned from the Heart—R

MISSIONS
$-Glad Tidings (Canada)—R

PASTORS/LEADERS
$-African American Pulpit
$-Barefoot—R
$-Catechumenate
$-Christian Century—R
$-Clergy Journal—R
$-Interpreter
$-Leadership—R
Lutheran Forum
$-Ministry & Liturgy—R
$-Ministry Today
Pulpit Helps—R
Rick Warren's Ministry—R
Sharing the Practice—R
Theological Digest—R
$-This Rock

TEEN/YOUNG ADULT
$-CLEAR Direction
$-CLEAR Horizon
$-J.A.M.
TeensForJC—R
$-True Girl

WOMEN
$-Canticle
Handmaiden—R
$-Horizons (women)—R
$-Pauses...
Share

CONTROVERSIAL ISSUES
ADULT/GENERAL
3V Magazine
($)-AGAIN—R
$-America
American Tract—R
$-Animal Trails—R
$-Associated Content—R
$-Aujourd'hui Credo—R
$-Bible Advocate—R
Biblical Recorder
CanadianChristianity
$-Catholic Insight
$-Catholic Peace Voice—R
CBN.com—R
$-Celebrate Life—R
Challenge Weekly
Christian C. L. RECORD—R
$-Christian Courier/Cdn.—R
$-Christian Examiner

$-Christian Home & School
Christian Media—R
Christian Online
$-Christian Renewal—R
$-Christian Response—R
$-Christian Standard—R
$-Christianity Today—R
$-Christianity Today Movies—R
$-ChristianWeek—R
$-Chronicle Christian/KS
Church of England News
$-City Light News—R
($)-Community Spirit—R
Creation Care—R
$-Creative Nonfiction
$-Culture Wars—R
Desert Christian
Desert Voice—R
$-DisciplesWorld
$-Dovetail—R
$-DreamSeeker—R
E-Channels—R
($)-E-Quality
Encompass
$-Enfoque a La Familia
Eternal Ink—R
$-Eureka Street
Evangelical Advocate—R
Evangelical Times
$-Faith Today
$-Good News—R
Good News Today
Good News!
$-Good News, Etc.—R
$-Good News/S. Florida
$-Gospel Today—R
Heartland Gatekeeper—R
$-Home Times—R
$-Homeschooling Today—R
($)-Impact—R
$-Indian Life—R
$-Interim—R
$-LarkNews.com
$-Light & Life
$-Living Church
$-Lookout
$-Majellan—R
$-Manna—R
$-Minnesota Christian—R
MovieGuide
($)-Mutuality—R
$-National Catholic
$-New Wineskins—R
$-Now What?—R
$-Our Sunday Visitor—R
Perspectives—R
$-Prairie Messenger—R
Priscilla Papers
$-Prism
$-Psychology for Living—R
$-Purpose—R

Rock & Sling
Sacred Journey—R
$-Science & Spirit
SingleAgain.com—R
$-Social Justice—R
$-St. Anthony Messenger
Sword of the Lord—R
$-Today's Christian—R
Tri-State Voice
Trumpeter—R
$-U.S. Catholic
Urban Kingdom—R
$-War Cry—R
$-Way of St. Francis—R
Wisconsin Christian
$-Wittenburg Door—R
$-World & I—R
Xavier Review

CHILDREN
$-Archaeology
$-New Moon—R
Skipping Stones

CHRISTIAN EDUCATION/ LIBRARY
Catholic Library
$-Group
$-Teachers of Vision—R
$-Today's Catholic Teacher—R

DAILY DEVOTIONALS
$-Brink Magazine—R

MISSIONS
$-Evangelical Missions—R
Intl. Jour./Frontier—R
OpRev Equipper—R

MUSIC
$-Christian Music Today—R
Hymn

PASTORS/LEADERS
$-African American Pulpit
Alpha News
$-Christian Century—R
$-Clergy Journal—R
Cross Currents
$-Enrichment—R
$-InSite—R
$-Interpreter
Jour./Pastoral Care
$-Let's Worship
$-Ministry & Liturgy—R
$-Ministry Today
$-Outreach—R
Pulpit Helps—R
$-This Rock
$-Word & World
$-Worship Leader

TEEN/YOUNG ADULT
$-Boundless Webzine—R

$-Brio—R
$-CLEAR Direction
$-CLEAR Horizon
Focus/Dare 2 Dig Deeper
G4T Ink—R
$-Ignite Your Faith
$-J.A.M.
$-Sharing the VICTORY—R
$-TC Magazine
TeensForJC—R
$-True Girl
$-Young Salvationist—R

WOMEN
($)-Beyond the Bend—R
$-Canticle
$-Esprit
$-Heart & Soul
$-Herizons
Hope for Women
$-inSpirit—R
Precious Times—R
Right to the Heart—R
$-Today's Christian Woman—R
WT Online—R

WRITERS
Areopagus

CRAFTS
ADULT/GENERAL
$-Associated Content—R
$-Atlantic Catholic
$-CGA World—R
Christian Online
($)-Community Spirit—R
Diamond Dust
$-Faith & Family
Family Journal—R
$-Imagine
$-Indian Life—R
LiteraryTNT.com—R
$-Living—R
$-Mature Living
$-ParentLife
Prison Living—R
Sword of the Lord—R
Urban Kingdom—R
Victory Herald—R
$-World & I—R

CHILDREN
$-Adventures
$-American Girl—R
$-BREAD/God's Children—R
$-Cadet Quest—R
$-Celebrate
$-Focus/Clubhouse
$-Focus/Clubhouse Jr.
$-Junior Companion—R
$-JuniorWay
$-Kid Zone

$-Passport—R
$-Pockets—R
$-Preschool Playhouse (child)
$-SHINEbrightly—R
$-Sparkle—R
$-Story Mates—R

CHRISTIAN EDUCATION/ LIBRARY
$-Catechist
$-Children's Ministry
$-RTJ—R
Teach Kids Essentials—R
$-Youth & CE Leadership

MISSIONS
$-Glad Tidings (Canada)—R

PASTORS/LEADERS
$-Interpreter

TEEN/YOUNG ADULT
$-Brio—R
$-J.A.M.
TeensForJC—R
$-True Girl

WOMEN
CelebrateMoms—R
Christian Woman's Page—R
$-MomSense—R
P31 Woman—R
Proverbs 31 Sisters
Right to the Heart—R
Virtuous Woman—R
Woman of Worth—R
Women's Ministry

CREATION SCIENCE
ADULT/GENERAL
Answers
CBN.com—R
$-Christian Courier/Cdn.—R
$-Christian Examiner
Christian Observer
$-Christian Renewal—R
$-Christian Research
Church Herald & Holiness—R
$-City Light News—R
Desert Voice—R
$-Faith Today
$-Haruah—R
$-Home Times—R
$-Homeschooling Today—R
$-Horizons (adult)—R
$-Indian Life—R
$-Living—R
$-Lookout
Perspectives/Science
$-Salvo
$-St. Anthony Messenger
Sword and Trumpet
Sword of the Lord—R

Trumpeter—R
$-War Cry—R
$-Way of St. Francis—R
Wisconsin Christian

CHILDREN
$-BREAD/God's Children—R
$-Guide—R
$-Nature Friend—R
$-Sparkle—R

CHRISTIAN EDUCATION/ LIBRARY
$-Journal/Adventist Ed.—R
Teach Kids Essentials—R

PASTORS/LEADERS
Cross Currents
Pulpit Helps—R
$-This Rock

TEEN/YOUNG ADULT
$-Boundless Webzine—R
$-Breakaway
$-J.A.M.
$-Real Faith in Life—R
$-Young Salvationist—R

CULTS/OCCULT
ADULT/GENERAL
American Tract—R
$-Annals of St. Anne
$-Bible Advocate—R
CBN.com—R
Christian C. L. RECORD—R
$-Christian Examiner
$-Christian Renewal—R
$-Christian Research
$-Citizen USA
$-City Light News—R
$-Creative Nonfiction
$-Culture Wars—R
Desert Voice—R
$-Faith Today
$-In His Presence—R
$-Lookout
New Heart—R
$-Now What?—R
SCP Journal
Sword of the Lord—R
Trumpeter—R
Wisconsin Christian

DAILY DEVOTIONALS
$-Brink Magazine—R

MISSIONS
Intl. Jour./Frontier—R

PASTORS/LEADERS
$-Ministry Today
$-Word & World

TEEN/YOUNG ADULT
$-Boundless Webzine—R

$-Real Faith in Life—R
$-TC Magazine
TeensForJC—R
$-Young Salvationist—R

WOMEN
$-Journey

CURRENT/SOCIAL ISSUES
ADULT/GENERAL
3V Magazine
$-Advance
American Tract—R
$-Anglican Journal
$-Apocalypse Chronicles—R
$-Arlington Catholic
$-Associated Content—R
$-Aujourd'hui Credo—R
$-B.C. Catholic—R
$-BGC World—R
$-Bible Advocate—R
Biblical Recorder
Breakthrough Intercessor—R
CanadianChristianity
$-Catholic Insight
$-Catholic New York
$-Catholic Peace Voice—R
CBN.com—R
Challenge Weekly
Christian C. L. RECORD—R
$-Christian Courier/Cdn.—R
Christian Courier/WI—R
$-Christian Examiner
$-Christian Home & School
Christian Observer
Christian Online
Christian Outlook
Christian Ranchman
$-Christian Renewal—R
$-Christian Research
$-Christian Standard—R
$-Christianity Today—R
$-Christianity Today Movies—R
$-ChristianWeek—R
$-Chronicle Christian/KS
Church of England News
$-Citizen USA
$-City Light News—R
$-Columbia—R
($)-Community Spirit—R
($)-Covenant Companion—R
Creation Care—R
$-Creative Nonfiction
$-Cresset
$-Culture Wars—R
Desert Call—R
Desert Christian
$-Disaster News
$-Discipleship Journal—R
$-DisciplesWorld
$-Dovetail—R
$-DreamSeeker—R

E-Channels—R
($)-E-Quality
Encompass
$-Enfoque a La Familia
$-Eureka Street
Evangel/OR—R
Evangelical Advocate—R
Evangelical Times
$-Faith Today
$-Focus on the Family
Friends Journal—R
$-Gem—R
$-Good News—R
Good News Connection
Good News Journal—R
Good News Today
$-Good News, Etc.—R
$-Good News/S. Florida
Heartland Gatekeeper—R
Heartlight—R
$-Homeschooling Today—R
$-In Touch
$-Indian Life—R
Island Catholic—R
Jour. of Church & State
$-LarkNews.com
$-Liberty
LifeSite News
$-Light & Life
$-Liguorian
LiteraryTNT.com—R
$-Living—R
$-Lookout
$-Majellan—R
$-Manna—R
$-Marian Helper
$-Mature Living
$-Men of Integrity—R
$-Men.AG.org—R
$-MESSAGE
MESSAGE/Open Bible—R
$-Messenger/St. Anthony
$-Minnesota Christian—R
Mosaic—R
MovieGuide
($)-Mutuality—R
$-National Catholic
New Heart—R
$-New Wineskins—R
$-Now What?—R
$-Our Sunday Visitor—R
$-Ozarks Senior Living—R
$-ParentLife
Perspectives—R
$-Prairie Messenger—R
PrayerWorks—R
$-Priority!—R
Priscilla Papers
$-Prism
Prison Living—R
$-Psychology for Living—R

$-Purpose—R
Sacred Journey—R
SCP Journal
$-Seek—R
Silver Wings—R
SingleAgain.com—R
$-Social Justice—R
Society/Prevention of Cruelty
$-Special Living—R
$-St. Anthony Messenger
$-Storyteller—R
Sword of the Lord—R
$-Today's Christian—R
$-Together—R
Tri-State Voice
Trumpeter—R
$-U.S. Catholic
Urban Kingdom—R
$-War Cry—R
$-Way of St. Francis—R
West Wind Review
Wisconsin Christian
$-Wittenburg Door—R
$-World & I—R
$-Written

CHILDREN
$-Archaeology
$-JuniorWay
$-New Moon—R
$-SHINEbrightly—R
Skipping Stones
$-Sparkle—R

CHRISTIAN EDUCATION/ LIBRARY
Catholic Library
$-Children's Ministry
Teach Kids Essentials—R

DAILY DEVOTIONALS
$-Brink Magazine—R
Penned from the Heart—R

MISSIONS
$-Glad Tidings (Canada)—R
$-New World Outlook
$-One
OpRev Equipper—R
$-PIME World—R
Women of the Harvest

MUSIC
$-Christian Music Today—R

PASTORS/LEADERS
$-African American Pulpit
Alpha News
$-Barefoot—R
$-Catholic Servant
$-Christian Century—R
$-Enrichment—R
$-InSite—R
$-Interpreter

$-Leadership—R
Lutheran Forum
$-Lutheran Partners—R
$-Ministry Today
$-Outreach—R
Pulpit Helps—R
$-This Rock
$-Willow—R
$-Word & World

TEEN/YOUNG ADULT
$-Boundless Webzine—R
$-Breakaway
$-CLEAR Direction
$-CLEAR Horizon
$-Credo—R
$-Devo'Zine—R
Exodus Magazine
Focus/Dare 2 Dig Deeper
$-Ignite Your Faith
$-Insight—R
$-J.A.M.
$-Listen—R
$-Risen
$-Sharing the VICTORY—R
$-TC Magazine
TeensForJC—R
$-True Girl
$-Young Adult Today
$-Young Christian—R
$-Young Salvationist—R

WOMEN
($)-Beyond the Bend—R
Comfort Café
$-Esprit
$-Fullfill
Handmaiden—R
$-Heart & Soul
$-Herizons
Hope for Women
$-Horizons (women)—R
$-inSpirit—R
$-Link & Visitor—R
Making Waves
$-Pauses...
$-SpiritLed Woman
$-Today's Christian Woman—R
Today's Leading Ladies—R
Virtuous Woman—R
Women Today—R
WT Online—R

WRITERS
Areopagus

DEATH/DYING
ADULT/GENERAL
($)-AGAIN—R
$-America
American Tract—R
$-Arlington Catholic

$-Associated Content—R
$-Atlantic Catholic
$-Aujourd'hui Credo—R
$-BGC World—R
$-Bible Advocate—R
Bread of Life—R
Breakthrough Intercessor—R
CBN.com—R
$-Celebrate Life—R
$-Chicken Soup Books—R
$-Christian Journal—R
Christian Online
Christian Ranchman
$-Christianity Today—R
$-ChristianWeek—R
$-Chronicle Christian/KS
$-City Light News—R
($)-Community Spirit—R
$-Creative Nonfiction
Desert Call—R
$-Discipleship Journal—R
$-Dovetail—R
E-Channels—R
Evangelical Advocate—R
$-Faith Today
$-Family Digest—R
$-Focus on the Family
$-Gem—R
$-Good News, Etc.—R
$-Guideposts—R
Heartlight—R
$-Homeschooling Today—R
($)-HopeKeepers—R
$-Horizons (adult)—R
$-In His Presence—R
$-In Touch
$-Indian Life—R
Island Catholic—R
$-Liguorian
$-Live—R
$-Lookout
$-Majellan—R
$-Mature Living
$-Men of Integrity—R
$-Messenger/Sacred Heart
$-Montgomery's Journey
$-National Catholic
New Heart—R
$-New Wineskins—R
$-Now What?—R
$-Our Sunday Visitor—R
$-ParentLife
Perspectives/Science
$-Positive Thinking—R
$-Prairie Messenger—R
PrayerWorks—R
Presbyterian Outlook
$-Presbyterians Today—R
Prison Living—R
$-Psychology for Living—R
Sacred Journey—R

$-Seek—R
$-Significant Living—R
Silver Wings—R
SingleAgain.com—R
$-Social Justice—R
Spirituality for Today
$-St. Anthony Messenger
Sword of the Lord—R
$-Testimony—R
$-Today's Christian—R
Trumpeter—R
$-U.S. Catholic
Urban Kingdom—R
$-War Cry—R
$-Way of St. Francis—R
Wisconsin Christian

CHILDREN
$-New Moon—R
Skipping Stones
$-Sparkle—R

CHRISTIAN EDUCATION/ LIBRARY
Teach Kids Essentials—R

DAILY DEVOTIONALS
Penned from the Heart—R

MISSIONS
$-Glad Tidings (Canada)—R

PASTORS/LEADERS
$-Catholic Servant
$-Christian Century—R
$-Clergy Journal—R
$-Enrichment—R
$-InSite—R
$-Interpreter
Jour./Pastoral Care
$-Leadership—R
$-Lutheran Partners—R
$-RevWriter Resource
Sharing the Practice—R

TEEN/YOUNG ADULT
$-Boundless Webzine—R
$-Brio—R
$-CLEAR Direction
$-J.A.M.
TeensForJC—R
$-True Girl

WOMEN
($)-Beyond the Bend—R
$-Canticle
Comfort Café
Hope for Women
$-inSpirit—R
$-Pauses…
Precious Times—R
Virtuous Woman—R
Woman of Worth—R
Women Today—R
WT Online—R

DEVOTIONALS/ MEDITATIONS

ADULT/GENERAL
$-Advance
$-Alive Now—R
$-America
$-Annals of St. Anne
$-Arlington Catholic
$-Aujourd'hui Credo—R
$-Australian Catholics—R
$-Bible Advocate—R
Bread of Life—R
Breakthrough Intercessor—R
$-Bridal Guides—R
$-Catholic Peace Voice—R
CBN.com—R
$-Chicken Soup Books—R
$-Christian Home & School
$-Christian Journal—R
Christian Online
Christian Ranchman
Church Herald & Holiness—R
$-City Light News—R
$-Covenant Companion—R
Creation Care—R
CrossHome.com
Desert Call—R
Diamond Dust
Divine Ascent
($)-E-Quality
Esdras' Scroll
Eternal Ink—R
$-Evangel/IN—R
Evangelical Advocate—R
Evangelical Times
$-Faith & Family
$-Faith & Friends—R
FaithWebbin—R
$-Family Digest—R
Founders Journal
$-Gem—R
$-Good News—R
Good News Journal—R
$-Haruah—R
Heartlight—R
($)-HopeKeepers—R
$-In His Presence—R
Keys to Living—R
Koinonia
Leaves—R
LifeTimes Catholic
$-Liguorian
LiteraryTNT.com—R
$-Living Church
$-Lutheran Digest—R
$-Mature Living
$-Messenger/Sacred Heart
$-Messenger/St. Anthony
Mosaic—R
($)-Mutuality—R

$-National Catholic
New Heart—R
$-New Wineskins—R
Penned from the Heart—R
Perspectives—R
$-Positive Thinking—R
PrayerWorks—R
Prison Living—R
$-Pure Inspiration—R
Quaker Life—R
Radix
Reverent Submissions—R
Silver Wings—R
$-Sports Spectrum
$-St. Anthony Messenger
Sword of the Lord—R
$-Today's Christian—R
$-Today's Pentecostal—R
Trumpeter—R
$-U.S. Catholic
Urban Kingdom—R
Victory Herald—R
$-Victory in Grace—R
$-Vision—R
$-War Cry—R
$-Way of St. Francis—R
$-Weavings—R
$-Wesleyan Life—R
$-Written

CHILDREN
$-Archaeology
$-Keys for Kids—R
$-Passport—R
$-Pockets—R
$-Sparkle—R

CHRISTIAN EDUCATION/ LIBRARY
Congregational Libraries
$-Group

DAILY DEVOTIONALS
Anchor Devotional
$-Brink Magazine—R
CLEAR Living
Daily Dev. for Deaf
$-Devotions
$-Forward Day by Day
Fruit of the Vine
$-Light from the Word
$-My Daily Visitor
Our Daily Journey
Penned from the Heart—R
$-Quiet Hour
$-Rejoice!
$-Secret Place
$-These Days
$-Upper Room
$-Word in Season

MISSIONS
$-Glad Tidings (Canada)—R

$-One
Women of the Harvest

PASTORS/LEADERS
$-Catholic Servant
$-Emmanuel
$-Ministry Today
$-RevWriter Resource

TEEN/YOUNG ADULT
$-CLEAR Direction
$-CLEAR Horizon
$-Devo'Zine—R
G4T Ink—R
$-J.A.M.
$-Real Faith in Life—R
$-Take Five Plus
TeensForJC—R
$-True Girl
$-Young Adult Today
$-Young Christian—R

WOMEN
($)-Beyond the Bend—R
$-Canticle
CelebrateMoms—R
Christian Woman's Page—R
Comfort Café
Elegance—R
Handmaidens
Hearts at Home—R
$-Horizons (women)—R
$-InspiredMoms—R
$-Journey
$-MD Women of Worship
$-Melody of the Heart
Precious Times—R
Proverbs 31 Sisters
Right to the Heart—R
($)-Simply Blessed—R
$-SpiritLed Woman
Today's Leading Ladies—R
Together with God—R
Virtuous Woman—R
Woman of Worth—R
WT Online—R

WRITERS
ChristianWriters
$-Cross & Quill—R
$-Fellowscript—R
$-Shades of Romance—R
$-Spirit-Led Writer—R

DISCIPLESHIP
ADULT/GENERAL
$-Alive Now—R
$-Arlington Catholic
$-Aujourd'hui Credo—R
$-Bible Advocate—R
Bread of Life—R
Breakthrough Intercessor—R
$-Canada Lutheran—R

CBN.com—R
Christian C. L. RECORD—R
$-Christian Journal—R
Christian Motorsports
Christian News NW—R
Christian Online
Christian Ranchman
$-Christian Research
$-Christian Standard—R
$-ChristianWeek—R
$-Chronicle Christian/KS
Church Herald & Holiness—R
Church of England News
$-City Light News—R
($)-Community Spirit—R
$-Covenant Companion—R
$-Decision
Desert Call—R
$-Discipleship Journal—R
$-DisciplesWorld
Eternal Ink—R
$-Evangel/IN—R
Evangelical Advocate—R
$-Faith & Family
$-Faith & Friends—R
$-Faith Today
$-Family Digest—R
$-Gem—R
$-Good News—R
Heartlight—R
Highway News—R
$-Homeschooling Today—R
$-Horizons (adult)—R
$-In His Presence—R
$-In Touch
$-Light & Life
$-Liguorian
LiteraryTNT.com—R
$-Live—R
$-Lookout
$-Manna—R
$-Men of Integrity—R
Men of the Cross
$-Men.AG.org—R
MESSAGE/Open Bible—R
MissionWares
Mosaic—R
MovieGuide
$-National Catholic
$-New Wineskins—R
($)-NRB Magazine—R
Penned from the Heart—R
Perspectives—R
$-Precepts for Living
Prison Living—R
$-Purpose—R
Quaker Life—R
Regent Global—R
Reverent Submissions—R
$-Seek—R
$-St. Anthony Messenger

$-Standard—R
$-Stewardship—R
Sword of the Lord—R
$-Today's Christian—R
Trumpeter—R
$-U.S. Catholic
Urban Kingdom—R
Victory Herald—R
$-War Cry—R
$-Way of St. Francis—R
$-Wesleyan Life—R
Wisconsin Christian

CHILDREN
$-Primary Street
$-SHINEbrightly—R
$-Sparkle—R

CHRISTIAN EDUCATION/
LIBRARY
$-Group
Teach Kids Essentials—R
$-Youth & CE Leadership

DAILY DEVOTIONALS
$-Brink Magazine—R
Penned from the Heart—R

MISSIONS
$-Glad Tidings (Canada)—R
$-PIME World—R

PASTORS/LEADERS
$-African American Pulpit
$-Barefoot—R
$-Catholic Servant
$-Christian Century—R
Christian Ed. Jour. (CA)—R
$-Enrichment—R
$-Growth Points—R
$-InSite—R
$-Interpreter
Jour./Amer. Soc./Chur. Growth—R
$-Leadership—R
$-Lutheran Partners—R
$-Net Results
$-Proclaim—R
Pulpit Helps—R
$-Rev. Magazine
$-RevWriter Resource
$-Small Groups.com—R
Theological Digest—R
$-This Rock
$-Word & World

TEEN/YOUNG ADULT
$-Boundless Webzine—R
$-Breakaway
$-Brio—R
$-CLEAR Direction
$-CLEAR Horizon
$-Credo—R
$-Devo'Zine—R
$-Insight—R

$-J.A.M.
$-Real Faith in Life—R
$-TC Magazine
TeensForJC—R
$-Young Salvationist—R

WOMEN
($)-Beyond the Bend—R
CelebrateMoms—R
Christian Woman's Page—R
Christian Women Today—R
Elegance—R
$-Horizons (women)—R
$-inSpirit—R
$-Journey
Just Between Us—R
$-Link & Visitor—R
P31 Woman—R
Precious Times—R
Proverbs 31 Sisters
Right to the Heart—R
Today's Leading Ladies—R
Virtuous Woman—R
Woman of Worth—R
Women of the Cross
WT Online—R

DIVORCE
ADULT/GENERAL
American Tract—R
$-Angels on Earth
$-Arlington Catholic
$-Associated Content—R
$-Aujourd'hui Credo—R
$-Bridal Guides—R
$-Catholic Digest—R
CBN.com—R
$-Christian Examiner
$-Christian Journal—R
Christian Motorsports
Christian Online
Christian Ranchman
$-ChristianWeek—R
$-Chronicle Christian/KS
Church of England News
$-City Light News—R
($)-Community Spirit—R
$-Culture Wars—R
$-Dovetail—R
Evangelical Advocate—R
$-Faith Today
$-Family Smart e-Tips—R
$-Focus on the Family
$-Gem—R
$-Good News, Etc.—R
$-Guideposts—R
$-Home Times—R
$-Homeschooling Today—R
($)-HopeKeepers—R
$-In His Presence—R
$-In Touch
Island Catholic—R

$-Living—R
$-Living Church
$-Lookout
$-Majellan—R
$-Manna—R
$-Minnesota Christian—R
$-Montgomery's Journey
$-National Catholic
New Heart—R
$-New Wineskins—R
$-Our Sunday Visitor—R
$-ParentLife
Perspectives—R
$-Positive Thinking—R
Priscilla Papers
Prison Living—R
$-Psychology for Living—R
$-Seek—R
SingleAgain.com—R
$-St. Anthony Messenger
$-Storyteller—R
$-Today's Christian—R
Trumpeter—R
Urban Kingdom—R
$-War Cry—R
Wisconsin Christian
$-World & I—R

CHILDREN
$-Winner—R

MISSIONS
$-Glad Tidings (Canada)—R

PASTORS/LEADERS
$-Christian Century—R
$-Interpreter
$-Lutheran Partners—R
$-Word & World

TEEN/YOUNG ADULT
$-Brio—R
$-J.A.M.
$-Young Salvationist—R

WOMEN
($)-Beyond the Bend—R
CelebrateMoms—R
Comfort Café
Hope for Women
$-InspiredMoms—R
$-inSpirit—R
$-Journey
Precious Times—R
$-Today's Christian Woman—R
Women Today—R
WT Online—R

DOCTRINAL
ADULT/GENERAL
($)-AGAIN—R
$-Anglican Journal
$-Atlantic Catholic
$-Aujourd'hui Credo—R

$-B.C. Catholic—R
$-Bible Advocate—R
$-Catholic Insight
CBN.com—R
Christian Media—R
Christian Online
$-Christian Research
$-Christian Standard—R
Church Herald & Holiness—R
$-City Light News—R
($)-Community Spirit—R
Creation Care—R
$-Culture Wars—R
E-Channels—R
Evangelical Advocate—R
Evangelical Times
$-Faith & Family
$-Faith Today
Founders Journal
$-Homeschooling Today—R
$-Horizons (adult)—R
($)-Impact—R
Koinonia
$-Light & Life
$-Majellan—R
MESSAGE/Open Bible—R
MovieGuide
$-National Catholic
$-New Wineskins—R
$-Our Sunday Visitor—R
Perspectives—R
Priscilla Papers
$-Social Justice—R
$-St. Anthony Messenger
Sword and Trumpet
Sword of the Lord—R
Trumpeter—R
$-U.S. Catholic
Urban Kingdom—R
$-Way of St. Francis—R
$-Wesleyan Life—R
Wisconsin Christian

CHRISTIAN EDUCATION/ LIBRARY
Catholic Library

MISSIONS
Intl. Jour./Frontier—R
Missiology

PASTORS/LEADERS
$-Catholic Servant
$-Interpreter
Lutheran Forum
$-Lutheran Partners—R
Sewanee Theo. Review
Sharing the Practice—R
Theological Digest—R
$-This Rock
$-Word & World
$-Worship Leader

TEEN/YOUNG ADULT
$-CLEAR Horizon
$-Essential Connection
$-J.A.M.
$-Real Faith in Life—R

WOMEN
WT Online—R

WRITERS
Opinari—R

DVD REVIEWS*
ADULT/GENERAL
Breakthrough Intercessor—R
$-Citizen USA
$-City Light News—R
Creation Care—R
$-Eureka Street
Island Catholic—R
LiteraryTNT.com—R
$-Our Sunday Visitor—R
Quaker Life—R

DAILY DEVOTIONALS
$-Brink Magazine—R

MISSIONS
$-Glad Tidings (Canada)—R

TEEN/YOUNG ADULT
$-Breakaway
Exodus Magazine
$-Ignite Your Faith

ECONOMICS
ADULT/GENERAL
$-America
$-Associated Content—R
$-Aujourd'hui Credo—R
$-Catholic Peace Voice—R
$-CBA Retailers
CBN.com—R
Christian Business
Christian Media—R
Christian Motorsports
Christian Online
Christian Ranchman
$-Christian Renewal—R
$-Christian Retailing
$-ChristianWeek—R
$-City Light News—R
($)-Community Spirit—R
$-Creative Nonfiction
$-Culture Wars—R
Evangelical Advocate—R
$-Faith Today
Good News Journal—R
$-Home Times—R
$-Homeschooling Today—R
$-In Touch
Island Catholic—R
$-Light & Life

$-Live—R
$-Living—R
$-Men.AG.org—R
MovieGuide
$-National Catholic
($)-NRB Magazine—R
$-Our Sunday Visitor—R
Perspectives—R
$-Positive Thinking—R
Prison Living—R
Regent Global—R
$-Social Justice—R
$-St. Anthony Messenger
Trumpeter—R
Urban Kingdom—R
Wisconsin Christian
$-World & I—R

PASTORS/LEADERS
$-Today's Parish
$-Word & World

TEEN/YOUNG ADULT
$-Boundless Webzine—R
$-J.A.M.
TeensForJC—R

WOMEN
Today's Leading Ladies—R

ENCOURAGEMENT
ADULT/GENERAL
Ambassador
$-BGC World—R
$-Bible Advocate—R
Bread of Life—R
Breakthrough Intercessor—R
$-Bridal Guides—R
$-Catholic Digest—R
$-Catholic Forester—R
CBN.com—R
Central FL Episcopalian
$-Christian Home & School
$-Christian Journal—R
Christian Online
Christian Ranchman
$-Christian Standard—R
$-Chronicle Christian/KS
Church Herald & Holiness—R
$-City Light News—R
($)-Community Spirit—R
Connections Leadership/MOPS
$-Discipleship Journal—R
E-Channels—R
$-EFCA Today—R
$-Evangel/IN—R
Evangelical Advocate—R
$-Faith & Family
$-Faith & Friends—R
$-Faith Today
$-Family Digest—R
$-Focus on the Family

$-Gems of Truth—R
Halo Magazine
$-Home Times—R
$-Homeschooling Today—R
($)-HopeKeepers—R
$-Horizons (adult)—R
$-In His Presence—R
$-In Touch
$-Indian Life—R
Keys to Living—R
Leaves—R
$-Lifeglow—R
$-Light & Life
$-Liguorian
LiteraryTNT.com—R
$-Live—R
$-Lookout
$-Lutheran Digest—R
$-Majellan—R
$-Manna—R
$-Mature Living
Men of the Cross
$-Minnesota Christian—R
MissionWares
$-Montgomery's Journey
Mosaic—R
($)-Mutuality—R
New Heart—R
$-New Wineskins—R
Nostalgia—R
$-Ozarks Senior Living—R
$-ParentLife
Penned from the Heart—R
PrayerWorks—R
Prison Living—R
$-Pure Inspiration—R
Regent Global—R
Reverent Submissions—R
Sacred Journey—R
$-Seek—R
$-Significant Living—R
Silver Wings—R
$-Storyteller—R
Sword of the Lord—R
$-Today's Christian—R
$-Together—R
Urban Kingdom—R
Victory Herald—R
$-Victory in Grace—R
$-Vista
$-Way of St. Francis—R
$-Wesleyan Life—R

CHILDREN
$-Archaeology
$-BREAD/God's Children—R
$-Cadet Quest—R
$-SHINEbrightly—R
Skipping Stones
$-Sparkle—R

CHRISTIAN EDUCATION/ LIBRARY
Teach Kids Essentials—R
$-Youth & CE Leadership

DAILY DEVOTIONALS
$-Brink Magazine—R
Penned from the Heart—R

MISSIONS
$-Glad Tidings (Canada)—R

PASTORS/LEADERS
Pulpit Helps—R
$-RevWriter Resource

TEEN/YOUNG ADULT
$-Boundless Webzine—R
$-Breakaway
$-Brio—R
$-CLEAR Direction
G4T Ink—R
$-Insight—R
$-J.A.M.
$-Young Christian—R
$-Young Salvationist—R

WOMEN
$-Canticle
CelebrateMoms—R
$-Come to the Fire—R
Crowned with Silver
Elegance—R
First Lady
Hearts at Home—R
Hope for Women
$-inSpirit—R
$-Journey
L.I.V.E.
P31 Woman—R
$-Pauses…
Precious Times—R
Right to the Heart—R
($)-Simply Blessed—R
$-Today's Christian Woman—R
Today's Leading Ladies—R
Together with God—R
Virtuous Woman—R
Woman of Worth—R
Women of the Cross
WT Online—R

WRITERS
$-Christian Communicator—R
$-Cross & Quill—R
$-Fellowscript—R
Opinari—R

ENVIRONMENTAL ISSUES
ADULT/GENERAL
$-America
$-Anglican Journal
$-Animal Trails—R
$-Associated Content—R

$-Aujourd'hui Credo—R
$-Cathedral Age
$-Catholic Peace Voice—R
$-Christian Courier/Cdn.—R
Christian Online
Christian Outlook
$-ChristianWeek—R
$-Chronicle Christian/KS
$-City Light News—R
$-Common Ground—R
($)-Community Spirit—R
$-Covenant Companion—R
Creation Care—R
$-Creation Illustrated—R
$-Creative Nonfiction
Desert Call—R
$-Disaster News
Evangelical Advocate—R
$-Faith Today
($)-HopeKeepers—R
$-In Touch
$-LarkNews.com
$-Light & Life
$-Liguorian
$-Living—R
$-Living Church
$-Lookout
$-Minnesota Christian—R
$-National Catholic
$-New Wineskins—R
$-Our Sunday Visitor—R
Pegasus Review—R
Perspectives—R
Perspectives/Science
$-Prairie Messenger—R
Presbyterian Outlook
$-Prism
Prison Living—R
Quaker Life—R
Ruminate
Sacred Journey—R
$-Science & Spirit
$-Seek—R
$-St. Anthony Messenger
Trumpeter—R
Urban Kingdom—R
$-War Cry—R
$-Way of St. Francis—R
Wisconsin Christian
$-World & I—R

CHILDREN
$-Archaeology
$-New Moon—R
$-Pockets—R
$-SHINEbrightly—R
Skipping Stones
$-Sparkle—R

CHRISTIAN EDUCATION/ LIBRARY
Jour./Research on Christian Ed.

DAILY DEVOTIONALS
$-Brink Magazine—R

MISSIONS
$-Glad Tidings (Canada)—R

PASTORS/LEADERS
$-Christian Century—R
$-InSite—R
$-Interpreter
$-Word & World

TEEN/YOUNG ADULT
$-Boundless Webzine—R
$-Brio—R
$-Devo'Zine—R
$-J.A.M.
$-TC Magazine
TeensForJC—R
$-Young Salvationist—R

WOMEN
$-Esprit
$-Herizons
$-Horizons (women)—R
$-inSpirit—R
Share
$-Today's Christian Woman—R
Today's Leading Ladies—R

ESSAYS
ADULT/GENERAL
African Voices—R
$-America
$-Annals of St. Anne
$-Arlington Catholic
$-Associated Content—R
Books & Culture
$-Cathedral Age
$-Catholic Digest—R
$-Catholic Peace Voice—R
$-Chicken Soup Books—R
Christian C. L. RECORD—R
$-Christian Courier/Cdn.—R
Christian Online
$-Christian Renewal—R
$-Christianity Today—R
$-Company—R
$-Covenant Companion—R
Creation Care—R
$-Creative Nonfiction
$-Culture Wars—R
$-DisciplesWorld
$-Dovetail—R
($)-E-Quality
$-Faith Today
$-Gem—R
Heartland Gatekeeper—R
$-Home Times—R
($)-HopeKeepers—R
$-Imagine
($)-Impact—R
$-In Touch

Island Catholic—R
Koinonia
$-Lifeglow—R
$-Liguorian
LiteraryTNT.com—R
$-Lutheran Digest—R
$-MindFlights—R
($)-Mutuality—R
$-National Catholic
$-New Wineskins—R
$-Our Sunday Visitor—R
$-Ozarks Senior Living—R
Pegasus Review—R
Penwood Review
$-Prism
Prison Living—R
$-Pure Inspiration—R
Quaker Life—R
Reverent Submissions—R
Rock & Sling
$-Rose & Thorn
Ruminate
Sacred Journey—R
$-Science & Spirit
$-Seek—R
$-Significant Living—R
$-Spiritual Life
Spirituality for Today
$-St. Anthony Messenger
$-STEPS
$-Storyteller—R
$-This I Believe
Tiferet—R
Tri-State Voice
Trumpeter—R
$-U.S. Catholic
Urban Kingdom—R
$-War Cry—R
$-Way of St. Francis—R
$-Wittenburg Door—R
$-World & I—R
$-Written
Xavier Review

CHILDREN
$-Nature Friend—R
$-New Moon—R
Skipping Stones

CHRISTIAN EDUCATION/ LIBRARY
Catholic Library
$-Journal/Adventist Ed.—R

MISSIONS
$-Evangelical Missions—R
$-Glad Tidings (Canada)—R
$-PFI Global—R
$-PIME World—R
Railroad Evangelist—R

MUSIC
$-Creator—R

PASTORS/LEADERS
$-African American Pulpit
$-Catholic Servant
$-Christian Century—R
Cross Currents
Jour./Pastoral Care
Lutheran Forum
$-Priest
Theological Digest—R
$-Torch Legacy Leader
$-Word & World
$-Youthworker

TEEN/YOUNG ADULT
$-CLEAR Direction
$-InsideOut—R
$-TC Magazine
TeensForJC—R

WOMEN
Christian Woman's Page—R
Handmaidens
Hearts at Home—R
$-Herizons
$-Horizons (women)—R
$-Today's Christian Woman—R
Today's Leading Ladies—R

WRITERS
$-Adv. Christian Writer—R
$-Christian Communicator—R
Money the Write Way—R
Once Upon a Time—R
Opinari—R
$-Spirit-Led Writer—R
$-Writer
$-Writer's Digest

ETHICS
ADULT/GENERAL
($)-AGAIN—R
$-America
$-Angels on Earth
$-Associated Content—R
$-Aujourd'hui Credo—R
$-Canada Lutheran—R
$-Cathedral Age
$-Catholic Digest—R
$-Catholic Insight
$-Catholic Peace Voice—R
CBN.com—R
$-Celebrate Life—R
Christian C. L. RECORD—R
$-Christian Courier/Cdn.—R
$-Christian Examiner
Christian Media—R
Christian Observer
Christian Online
Christian Ranchman
$-Christian Renewal—R
$-Christian Research
$-Christian Standard—R

$-ChristianWeek—R
$-Chronicle Christian/KS
Church of England News
$-City Light News—R
($)-Community Spirit—R
Creation Care—R
$-Creative Nonfiction
$-Cresset
$-Culture Wars—R
Desert Call—R
Desert Voice—R
$-DisciplesWorld
$-Dovetail—R
E-Channels—R
($)-E-Quality
$-Eureka Street
Evangelical Advocate—R
$-Faith Today
$-Focus on the Family
Good News Journal—R
$-Good News, Etc.—R
$-Home Times—R
$-Homeschooling Today—R
$-Horizons (adult)—R
$-In His Presence—R
$-Interim—R
Island Catholic—R
Koinonia
$-Light & Life
$-Liguorian
$-Live—R
$-Living Church
$-Lookout
$-Manna—R
$-Men of Integrity—R
$-Men.AG.org—R
$-Minnesota Christian—R
MissionWares
MovieGuide
$-National Catholic
New Heart—R
$-New Wineskins—R
($)-NRB Magazine—R
$-Our Sunday Visitor—R
Pegasus Review—R
Perspectives—R
Perspectives/Science
$-Positive Thinking—R
$-Prairie Messenger—R
Presbyterian Outlook
Priscilla Papers
$-Prism
Prison Living—R
$-Pure Inspiration—R
Quaker Life—R
Regent Global—R
Sacred Journey—R
$-Science & Spirit
$-Seek—R
Silver Wings—R
$-Social Justice—R

$-St. Anthony Messenger
Trumpeter—R
$-U.S. Catholic
Urban Kingdom—R
$-War Cry—R
$-Way of St. Francis—R
$-World & I—R

CHILDREN
$-New Moon—R
Skipping Stones

CHRISTIAN EDUCATION/
LIBRARY
Christian Librarian—R
Jour./Research on Christian Ed.

DAILY DEVOTIONALS
$-Brink Magazine—R
Penned from the Heart—R

MISSIONS
$-Glad Tidings (Canada)—R

PASTORS/LEADERS
$-Christian Century—R
$-Clergy Journal—R
Cross Currents
$-Enrichment—R
$-Interpreter
Jour./Pastoral Care
Lutheran Forum
$-Lutheran Partners—R
$-Ministry Today
Sewanee Theo. Review
Sharing the Practice—R
Theological Digest—R
$-This Rock
$-Word & World

TEEN/YOUNG ADULT
$-Boundless Webzine—R
$-Brio—R
$-CLEAR Direction
$-CLEAR Horizon
$-Devo'Zine—R
$-Real Faith in Life—R
$-Risen
TeensForJC—R
$-Young Salvationist—R

WOMEN
$-Esprit
Handmaiden—R
Today's Leading Ladies—R
Women Today—R

ETHNIC/CULTURAL
PIECES
ADULT/GENERAL
$-Advance
African Voices—R
($)-AGAIN—R
$-America
$-Arlington Catholic

$-Associated Content—R
$-Aujourd'hui Credo—R
Breakthrough Intercessor—R
$-Catholic Digest—R
$-Catholic Peace Voice—R
$-CBA Retailers
CBN.com—R
$-Celebrate Life—R
Chocolate Pages
$-Christian Courier/Cdn.—R
$-Christian Home & School
Christian News NW—R
Christian Online
$-ChristianWeek—R
$-Chronicle Christian/KS
$-City Light News—R
$-Columbia—R
$-Commonweal
($)-Community Spirit—R
$-Creative Nonfiction
Desert Call—R
Desert Voice—R
$-Dovetail—R
E-Channels—R
($)-E-Quality
$-Enfoque a La Familia
$-Episcopal Life—R
$-Eureka Street
Evangel/OR—R
Evangelical Advocate—R
$-Faith Today
$-Gem—R
$-Good News—R
Good News!
$-Good News, Etc.—R
$-Gospel Today—R
$-Haruah—R
$-Home Times—R
$-Homeschooling Today—R
($)-Impact—R
$-Indian Life—R
Koinonia
$-Light & Life
$-Live—R
$-Lookout
$-Manna—R
$-Men of Integrity—R
Mensajero ala Blanca
$-MESSAGE
MESSAGE/Open Bible—R
$-Minnesota Christian—R
MovieGuide
($)-Mutuality—R
$-National Catholic
$-New Wineskins—R
$-Our Sunday Visitor—R
Penned from the Heart—R
$-Prairie Messenger—R
Priscilla Papers
$-Prism
Prison Living—R
Purpose Magazine—R

Quaker Life—R
Sacred Journey—R
$-Salvo
Saved Magazine
$-Science & Spirit
SCP Journal
$-Seek—R
Society/Prevention of Cruelty
Spirituality for Today
$-St. Anthony Messenger
$-Today's Christian—R
$-Together—R
Trumpeter—R
$-U.S. Catholic
$-Upscale
Urban Kingdom—R
$-War Cry—R
$-Way of St. Francis—R
$-Wesleyan Life—R
West Wind Review
$-World & I—R
$-Written
Xavier Review

CHILDREN
$-Archaeology
$-Faces
$-New Moon—R
Skipping Stones
$-Sparkle—R

CHRISTIAN EDUCATION/
LIBRARY
$-Momentum
Teach Kids Essentials—R

DAILY DEVOTIONALS
$-Brink Magazine—R
Penned from the Heart—R

MISSIONS
$-Evangelical Missions—R
$-Glad Tidings (Canada)—R
Missiology
OpRev Equipper—R
$-PIME World—R
Women of the Harvest

PASTORS/LEADERS
$-African American Pulpit
$-Barefoot—R
$-Christian Century—R
$-Enrichment—R
$-Interpreter
Jour./Pastoral Care
$-Lutheran Partners—R
$-Ministry Today
$-Net Results
Pulpit Helps—R
$-This Rock
$-Torch Legacy Leader
$-Worship Leader

TEEN/YOUNG ADULT
$-Boundless Webzine—R

$-Brio—R
$-CLEAR Horizon
$-Credo—R
$-Devo'Zine—R
$-Essential Connection
$-Real Faith in Life—R
TeensForJC—R
$-Young Christian—R
$-Young Salvationist—R

WOMEN
$-Esprit
$-Heart & Soul
$-Herizons
$-Horizons (women)—R
$-inSpirit—R
L.I.V.E.
$-Link & Visitor—R
Precious Times—R
$-SpiritLed Woman
$-Today's Christian Woman—R
Today's Leading Ladies—R

EVANGELISM/ WITNESSING
ADULT/GENERAL
Ambassador
$-America
American Tract—R
$-Anglican Journal
$-Animal Trails—R
$-Annals of St. Anne
$-Aujourd'hui Credo—R
$-BGC World—R
$-Bible Advocate—R
Bread of Life—R
Breakthrough Intercessor—R
$-Canada Lutheran—R
$-Catholic Telegraph
$-Catholic Yearbook—R
CBN.com—R
Central FL Episcopalian
Christian Courier/WI—R
$-Christian Home & School
Christian Online
Christian Ranchman
$-Christian Research
$-Christian Standard—R
$-Christianity Today—R
$-Chronicle Christian/KS
Church Herald & Holiness—R
Church of England News
$-City Light News—R
($)-Community Spirit—R
$-Decision
$-Discipleship Journal—R
E-Channels—R
Encompass
$-Episcopal Life—R
$-Evangel/IN—R
Evangel/OR—R
Evangelical Advocate—R

$-Faith & Family
$-Faith Today
Florida Baptist Witness
$-Gem—R
$-Good News—R
Good News Today
$-Good News, Etc.—R
Halo Magazine
Heartbeat/CMA
$-Horizons (adult)—R
$-In His Presence—R
$-In Touch
IPHC Experience
Koinonia
Leaves—R
$-Light & Life
LiteraryTNT.com—R
$-Live—R
$-Living Church
$-Lookout
$-Lutheran Journal—R
Lutheran Witness
$-Manna—R
$-Mature Living
$-Men of Integrity—R
$-Men.AG.org—R
MESSAGE/Open Bible—R
$-Minnesota Christian—R
Mosaic—R
New Heart—R
$-New Wineskins—R
$-On Mission
$-Our Sunday Visitor—R
$-ParentLife
Penned from the Heart—R
$-Power for Living—R
PrayerWorks—R
$-Priority!—R
Prison Living—R
$-Purpose—R
Quaker Life—R
Regent Global—R
Reverent Submissions—R
$-Seek—R
Sharing—R
Spirituality for Today
$-St. Anthony Messenger
Sword of the Lord—R
$-Testimony—R
$-Today's Christian—R
Trumpeter—R
Urban Kingdom—R
Victory Herald—R
$-War Cry—R
$-Way of St. Francis—R
$-Wesleyan Life—R
Wisconsin Christian

CHILDREN
$-Archaeology
$-BREAD/God's Children—R
$-Focus/Clubhouse Jr.

$-Guide—R
$-JuniorWay
$-Sparkle—R

CHRISTIAN EDUCATION/ LIBRARY
Catholic Library
$-Group
$-Kids' Ministry Ideas
$-RTJ—R
Teach Kids Essentials—R
$-Youth & CE Leadership

DAILY DEVOTIONALS
$-Brink Magazine—R
Penned from the Heart—R

MISSIONS
East-West Church
$-Evangelical Missions—R
$-Glad Tidings (Canada)—R
Intl. Jour./Frontier—R
Lausanne World Pulse
$-Leaders for Today
Missiology
OpRev Equipper—R

MUSIC
Christian Music Weekly—R

PASTORS/LEADERS
$-Catholic Servant
Cook Intl.
$-Enrichment—R
$-Growth Points—R
$-Interpreter
Jour./Amer. Soc./Chur. Growth—R
$-Leadership—R
$-Let's Worship
$-Lutheran Partners—R
$-Ministry Today
$-Outreach—R
Pulpit Helps—R
$-RevWriter Resource
Rick Warren's Ministry—R
$-This Rock
$-Willow—R

TEEN/YOUNG ADULT
$-Boundless Webzine—R
$-Breakaway
$-Brio—R
$-CLEAR Direction
$-CLEAR Horizon
$-Credo—R
$-Devo'Zine—R
$-Essential Connection
$-Insight—R
$-J.A.M.
$-Real Faith in Life—R
$-TC Magazine
TeensForJC—R
$-True Girl
$-Young Christian—R
$-Young Salvationist—R

WOMEN
$-At the Center—R
$-Canticle
$-Come to the Fire—R
$-inSpirit—R
$-Journey
Just Between Us—R
$-Link & Visitor—R
P31 Woman—R
Precious Times—R
Proverbs 31 Sisters
Share
$-SpiritLed Woman
$-Today's Christian Woman—R
Today's Leading Ladies—R
WT Online—R

EXEGESIS
ADULT/GENERAL
$-Alive Now—R
$-Aujourd'hui Credo—R
$-Catholic Insight
CBN.com—R
Christian Ranchman
$-Christian Standard—R
Church Herald & Holiness—R
E-Channels—R
($)-E-Quality
Evangelical Advocate—R
$-Light & Life
$-Living Church
$-National Catholic
$-Our Sunday Visitor—R
Perspectives—R
Priscilla Papers
Regent Global—R
Reverent Submissions—R
$-Social Justice—R
$-St. Anthony Messenger
Sword and Trumpet
Sword of the Lord—R
Trumpeter—R
$-Way of St. Francis—R
$-Wesleyan Life—R
Wisconsin Christian

MISSIONS
$-Glad Tidings (Canada)—R

PASTORS/LEADERS
$-Enrichment—R
Lutheran Forum
Pulpit Helps—R
Theological Digest—R
$-This Rock

TEEN/YOUNG ADULT
$-Boundless Webzine—R
$-Brio—R
$-Young Adult Today

WRITERS
Opinari—R

FAITH
ADULT/GENERAL
African Voices—R
$-America
$-Animal Trails—R
$-Arkansas Catholic—R
$-Aujourd'hui Credo—R
($)-Believer's Bay
$-BGC World—R
$-Bible Advocate—R
Bread of Life—R
Breakthrough Intercessor—R
$-Bridal Guides—R
byFaith
$-Canada Lutheran—R
$-Catholic Digest—R
$-Catholic Insight
$-Catholic Peace Voice—R
$-Catholic Yearbook—R
CBN.com—R
Christian C. L. RECORD—R
$-Christian Courier/Cdn.—R
$-Christian Home & School
$-Christian Journal—R
Christian Online
$-Christian Research
$-Christian Retailing
$-Christian Standard—R
$-Christianity Today—R
$-ChristianWeek—R
$-Chronicle Christian/KS
Church Herald & Holiness—R
Church of England News
$-City Light News—R
$-Columbia—R
($)-Community Spirit—R
$-Covenant Companion—R
Desert Call—R
Desert Voice—R
Disciple's Journal—R
$-Discipleship Journal—R
$-Dovetail—R
E-Channels—R
Encompass
Eternal Ink—R
Evangel/OR—R
Evangelical Advocate—R
$-Faith & Family
$-Faith & Friends—R
$-Faith Today
$-Family Digest—R
Family Journal—R
$-Focus on the Family
$-Gem—R
Good News Journal—R
$-Haruah—R
Highway News—R
$-Home Times—R
($)-HopeKeepers—R
$-In His Presence—R

$-In Touch
$-Indian Life—R
Koinonia
LifeTimes Catholic
$-Light & Life
$-Liguorian
LiteraryTNT.com—R
$-Live—R
$-Lookout
$-Lutheran Digest—R
$-Lutheran Journal—R
$-Majellan—R
$-Manna—R
$-Mature Living
$-Men of Integrity—R
$-Men.AG.org—R
$-MindFlights—R
$-Minnesota Christian—R
$-Montgomery's Journey
Mosaic—R
$-National Catholic
New Heart—R
$-New Wineskins—R
Nostalgia—R
$-Now What?—R
$-Our Sunday Visitor—R
$-ParentLife
Pegasus Review—R
Penned from the Heart—R
$-Positive Thinking—R
$-Prairie Messenger—R
PrayerWorks—R
$-Precepts for Living
Priscilla Papers
$-Psychology for Living—R
$-Pure Inspiration—R
Quaker Life—R
Reverent Submissions—R
Sacred Journey—R
$-Seek—R
$-Significant Living—R
$-Social Justice—R
Spirituality for Today
$-St. Anthony Messenger
$-Standard—R
SW Kansas Faith
Sword and Trumpet
Sword of the Lord—R
$-Testimony—R
$-Today's Christian—R
$-Together—R
Trumpeter—R
$-U.S. Catholic
$-United Church Observer—R
Urban Kingdom—R
$-Victory in Grace—R
$-Vista
$-Way of St. Francis—R
$-Weavings—R
$-Wesleyan Life—R
$-World & I—R

CHILDREN

$-Archaeology
$-BREAD/God's Children—R
$-Focus/Clubhouse Jr.
$-JuniorWay
$-Kid Zone
$-Our Little Friend—R
$-Primary Street
$-Primary Treasure—R
$-SHINEbrightly—R
$-Sparkle—R

CHRISTIAN EDUCATION/ LIBRARY

Catholic Library
$-Children's Ministry
Christian Librarian—R
$-Group
$-Momentum
$-Teachers of Vision—R
$-Youth & CE Leadership

DAILY DEVOTIONALS

$-Brink Magazine—R
Penned from the Heart—R

MISSIONS

$-Glad Tidings (Canada)—R
$-PIME World—R

MUSIC

Christian Music Weekly—R

PASTORS/LEADERS

$-African American Pulpit
$-Interpreter
$-Ministry Today
Plugged In
$-Proclaim—R
$-RevWriter Resource
$-Worship Leader

TEEN/YOUNG ADULT

$-Boundless Webzine—R
$-Breakaway
$-Brio—R
$-CLEAR Direction
$-CLEAR Horizon
$-Credo—R
$-Devo'Zine—R
Exodus Magazine
$-Ignite Your Faith
$-Insight—R
$-J.A.M.
$-Risen
$-TC Magazine
TeensForJC—R
$-True Girl
$-Young Adult Today
$-Young Salvationist—R

WOMEN

($)-Beyond the Bend—R
$-Canticle

CelebrateMoms—R
Christian Woman's Page—R
Comfort Café
Elegance—R
$-Esprit
Hearts at Home—R
Hope for Women
$-Horizons (women)—R
$-inSpirit—R
$-Journey
Just Between Us—R
Life Tools for Women
P31 Woman—R
$-Pauses...
Proverbs 31 Sisters
Right to the Heart—R
$-SpiritLed Woman
$-Today's Christian Woman—R
Today's Leading Ladies—R
Virtuous Woman—R
Woman of Worth—R
Women of the Cross
Women Today—R
WT Online—R

WRITERS

Areopagus
Opinari—R

FAMILY LIFE

ADULT/GENERAL

3V Magazine
$-Abilities
$-Advance
African Voices—R
($)-AGAIN—R
$-America
$-Angels on Earth
$-Animal Trails—R
$-Annals of St. Anne
Anointed Pages
Arizona Family
$-Arkansas Catholic—R
$-Arlington Catholic
$-Associated Content—R
$-Atlantic Catholic
$-Aujourd'hui Credo—R
$-Australian Catholics—R
$-B.C. Catholic—R
($)-Believer's Bay
$-BGC World—R
Bread of Life—R
Breakthrough Intercessor—R
$-Bridal Guides—R
byFaith
$-Canada Lutheran—R
$-Catholic Digest—R
$-Catholic Forester—R
$-Catholic Insight
CBN.com—R
$-Chicken Soup Books—R

Christian C. L. RECORD—R
$-Christian Courier/Cdn.—R
Christian Courier/WI—R
$-Christian Home & School
$-Christian Journal—R
Christian Online
Christian Ranchman
$-Christian Renewal—R
$-ChristianWeek—R
$-Chronicle Christian/KS
Church Herald & Holiness—R
$-City Light News—R
$-Columbia—R
($)-Community Spirit—R
Connecting Point—R
$-Covenant Companion—R
Creation Care—R
$-Creative Nonfiction
$-Culture Wars—R
Desert Call—R
Desert Voice—R
Disciple's Journal—R
$-Dovetail—R
E-Channels—R
$-EFCA Today—R
Eternal Ink—R
Evangelical Advocate—R
$-Faith & Family
$-Faith & Friends—R
$-Faith Today
FaithWebbin—R
$-Family Digest—R
Family Journal—R
$-Family Smart e-Tips—R
$-Focus on the Family
$-Focus on Your Child
$-Gem—R
Godly Places
Gold Country Families—R
Good News Journal—R
$-Good News, Etc.—R
$-Grand
$-Guideposts—R
Heartlight—R
Highway News—R
$-Home Times—R
$-Homeschooling Today—R
$-Horizons (adult)—R
$-Ideals—R
$-In His Presence—R
$-In Touch
$-Indian Life—R
Keys to Living—R
Koinonia
LifeSite News
LifeTimes Catholic
$-Light & Life
$-Liguorian
LiteraryTNT.com—R
$-Live—R
$-Living—R

$-Living Church
$-Living Light—R
$-Lookout
$-Lutheran Digest—R
$-Majellan—R
$-Manna—R
$-Mature Living
$-Mature Years—R
$-Men of Integrity—R
Men of the Cross
$-Men.AG.org—R
($)-Mennonite Historian—R
$-Messenger/St. Anthony
$-Minnesota Christian—R
$-Montgomery's Journey
($)-Mutuality—R
$-New Wineskins—R
Nostalgia—R
$-Now What?—R
$-Our Sunday Visitor—R
$-Over the Back Fence—R
$-ParentLife
Pegasus Review—R
Penned from the Heart—R
$-Positive Thinking—R
$-Power for Living—R
$-Prairie Messenger—R
PrayerWorks—R
Priscilla Papers
Prison Living—R
$-Psychology for Living—R
$-Purpose—R
Quaker Life—R
Reverent Submissions—R
Sacred Journey—R
$-Science & Spirit
$-Seek—R
$-Significant Living—R
SingleAgain.com—R
$-Social Justice—R
$-Special Living—R
Spirituality for Today
$-St. Anthony Messenger
$-Standard—R
$-STEPS
$-Storyteller—R
SW Kansas Faith
Sword and Trumpet
Sword of the Lord—R
$-Testimony—R
$-Today's Christian—R
$-Today's Pentecostal—R
$-Together—R
Trumpeter—R
$-U.S. Catholic
$-United Church Observer—R
Urban Kingdom—R
$-Vibrant Life—R
$-Victory in Grace—R
$-War Cry—R
$-Way of St. Francis—R

$-Wesleyan Life—R
West Wind Review
Wisconsin Christian
$-World & I—R

CHILDREN
$-Archaeology
$-BREAD/God's Children—R
$-Focus/Clubhouse
$-Focus/Clubhouse Jr.
$-Guide—R
$-JuniorWay
$-Kid Zone
$-New Moon—R
$-Pockets—R
$-Sparkle—R

CHRISTIAN EDUCATION/ LIBRARY
$-Children's Ministry
$-Group
$-Youth & CE Leadership

DAILY DEVOTIONALS
Penned from the Heart—R

MISSIONS
$-Glad Tidings (Canada)—R
Women of the Harvest

PASTORS/LEADERS
$-African American Pulpit
$-Catholic Servant
$-Enrichment—R
$-InSite—R
$-Interpreter
Jour./Pastoral Care
$-Ministry Today
$-Preaching Well—R
$-Rev. Magazine
$-Today's Parish
$-Word & World

TEEN/YOUNG ADULT
$-Breakaway
$-Brio—R
$-CLEAR Direction
$-Credo—R
Exodus Magazine
$-Insight—R
$-J.A.M.
$-Real Faith in Life—R
$-TC Magazine
TeensForJC—R
$-Young Adult Today
$-Young Salvationist—R

WOMEN
$-Canticle
CelebrateMoms—R
Christian Woman's Page—R
$-Come to the Fire—R
Comfort Café
Crowned with Silver
$-Dabbling Mum—R

Elegance—R
$-Esprit
$-Girlfriend 2 Girlfriend
Handmaiden—R
Hearts at Home—R
Hope for Women
$-Horizons (women)—R
$-InspiredMoms—R
$-inSpirit—R
$-Journey
Just Between Us—R
Ladies First
Life Tools for Women
$-Link & Visitor—R
Lutheran Woman's Quar.
$-MomSense—R
P31 Woman—R
$-Pauses...
Precious Times—R
Proverbs 31 Sisters
Share
($)-Simply Blessed—R
$-SpiritLed Woman
$-Today's Christian Woman—R
Today's Leading Ladies—R
Together with God—R
Virtuous Woman—R
Woman of Worth—R
Women of the Cross
Women Today—R
WT Online—R

FEATURE ARTICLES*
ADULT/GENERAL
$-Angels on Earth
$-Animal Trails—R
$-Bible Advocate—R
Breakthrough Intercessor—R
$-Bridal Guides—R
$-Cappers
$-Catholic Digest—R
$-Covenant Companion—R
Creation Care—R
Desert Christian
($)-E-Quality
Eternal Ink—R
Evangel/OR—R
Evangelical Advocate—R
$-Faith & Family
$-Faith Today
$-Good News, Etc.—R
Heartland Gatekeeper—R
$-Homeschooling Today—R
$-In His Presence—R
Jour. of Church & State
LiteraryTNT.com—R
$-Lookout
$-Manna—R
$-Marian Helper
$-Mature Living
$-Minnesota Christian—R

$-Montana Catholic
$-Montgomery's Journey
$-Our Sunday Visitor—R
$-ParentLife
$-Prairie Messenger—R
Prison Living—R
Quaker Life—R
Regent Global—R
$-Relevant
Trumpeter—R
$-Vibrant Life—R

CHILDREN
$-Archaeology

MISSIONS
$-Glad Tidings (Canada)—R
MissionsMagizinet

PASTORS/LEADERS
$-InSite—R
$-Outreach—R
Preaching
Relevant Leader

TEEN/YOUNG ADULT
$-Breakaway
$-Brio—R
$-Devo'zine—R

WOMEN
Christian Women Today—R
Elegance—R
$-Today's Christian Woman—R
Today's Leading Ladies—R
Virtuous Woman—R
Woman of Worth—R

WRITERS
$-Writer

FILLERS: ANECDOTES
ADULT/GENERAL
$-Advance
$-Angels on Earth
$-Animal Trails—R
Breakthrough Intercessor—R
$-Bridal Guides—R
$-Catholic Digest—R
$-Catholic Yearbook—R
$-Chicken Soup Books—R
Christian Courier/WI—R
$-Christian Journal—R
Christian Motorsports
Christian Ranchman
$-Christian Response—R
$-Chronicle Christian/KS
Church Herald & Holiness—R
$-City Light News—R
Desert Call—R
Disciple's Journal—R
E-Channels—R
Eternal Ink—R
$-Faith & Family

$-Family Digest—R
$-Gem—R
Good News Journal—R
Heartlight—R
Highway News—R
$-Home Times—R
($)-Impact—R
$-In His Presence—R
LiteraryTNT.com—R
$-Living—R
$-Lutheran Digest—R
$-Lutheran Journal—R
$-Manna—R
MovieGuide
New Heart—R
$-Now What?—R
Prison Living—R
$-Purpose—R
Reverent Submissions—R
$-Significant Living—R
SingleAgain.com—R
Spirituality for Today
$-St. Anthony Messenger
$-STEPS
$-Today's Pentecostal—R
Urban Kingdom—R
Victory Herald—R
$-Vista
$-War Cry—R

CHILDREN
Skipping Stones

CHRISTIAN EDUCATION/ LIBRARY
Christian Librarian—R
$-RTJ—R

MISSIONS
Railroad Evangelist—R

MUSIC
$-Creator—R

PASTORS/LEADERS
$-Barefoot—R
$-Enrichment—R
$-Leadership—R
$-Preaching Well—R
$-PreachingToday.com
Pulpit Helps—R
Sharing the Practice—R
$-Sunday Sermons—R

TEEN/YOUNG ADULT
$-InsideOut—R
$-Young Christian—R
$-Young Salvationist—R

WOMEN
($)-Beyond the Bend—R
CelebrateMoms—R
Christian Woman's Page—R
Hearts at Home—R

Just Between Us—R
Proverbs 31 Sisters
Right to the Heart—R
$-Today's Christian Woman—R
Today's Leading Ladies—R
Virtuous Woman—R
WT Online—R

WRITERS
$-ByLine
$-Canadian Writer's Jour.—R
$-Cross & Quill—R
$-Fellowscript—R
Money the Write Way—R
$-New Writer's Mag.
NW Christian Author—R
Once Upon a Time—R
$-Tickled by Thunder
Write Connection
$-Writers' Journal

FILLERS: CARTOONS
ADULT/GENERAL
$-Advance
African Voices—R
American Tract—R
$-Angels on Earth
$-Animal Trails—R
Breakthrough Intercessor—R
$-Bridal Guides—R
$-Catholic Digest—R
$-Chicken Soup Books—R
Christian Computing—R
$-Christian Herald—R
$-Christian Journal—R
Christian Motorsports
Christian Ranchman
$-Chronicle Christian/KS
$-Citizen USA
$-City Light News—R
Connecting Point—R
$-Culture Wars—R
Disciple's Journal—R
E-Channels—R
$-Eureka Street
$-Evangel/IN—R
Evangel/OR—R
$-Faith & Family
$-Faith & Friends—R
$-Gem—R
Good News Journal—R
$-Gospel Today—R
Heartlight—R
Highway News—R
$-Home Times—R
($)-Impact—R
$-In His Presence—R
$-Interchange
$-Interim—R
Light of the World
$-Liguorian

$-Lutheran Digest—R
$-Mature Years—R
MovieGuide
New Heart—R
Pegasus Review—R
$-Power for Living—R
$-Presbyterians Today—R
Prison Living—R
$-Purpose—R
$-Significant Living—R
$-Special Living—R
$-St. Anthony Messenger
$-STEPS
$-Storyteller—R
Trumpeter—R
$-United Church Observer—R
Urban Kingdom—R
$-Vista
$-Wittenburg Door—R

CHILDREN
$-American Girl—R
$-Passport—R
$-SHINEbrightly—R
Skipping Stones

CHRISTIAN EDUCATION/ LIBRARY
$-Children's Ministry
Christian Librarian—R
$-Group
$-Journal/Adventist Ed.—R
$-Teachers of Vision—R
$-Today's Catholic Teacher—R
$-Youth & CE Leadership

MISSIONS
$-Glad Tidings (Canada)—R
Mission Frontiers
Railroad Evangelist—R

MUSIC
Christian Music Weekly—R
$-Creator—R
Tradition

PASTORS/LEADERS
$-Barefoot—R
$-Catholic Servant
$-Christian Century—R
Christian Management—R
$-Diocesan Dialogue—R
$-Enrichment—R
$-Leadership—R
$-Lutheran Partners—R
$-Priest
Pulpit Helps—R
$-Rev. Magazine
Sharing the Practice—R
$-Small Groups.com—R
$-Your Church—R

TEEN/YOUNG ADULT
G4T Ink—R

$-InsideOut—R
$-Listen—R
TeensForJC—R
$-Young Christian—R
$-Young Salvationist—R

WOMEN
Hearts at Home—R
Just Between Us—R
Proverbs 31 Sisters
($)-Simply Blessed—R

WRITERS
$-Canadian Writer's Jour.—R
$-Cross & Quill—R
$-Fellowscript—R
$-New Writer's Mag.
Once Upon a Time—R
$-Writer
$-Writers' Journal

FILLERS: FACTS
ADULT/GENERAL
$-Animal Trails—R
Bread of Life—R
Breakthrough Intercessor—R
$-Bridal Guides—R
$-Catholic Digest—R
$-Catholic Yearbook—R
$-Chicken Soup Books—R
Christian Courier/WI—R
$-Christian Herald—R
Christian Motorsports
Christian Ranchman
$-Christian Response—R
$-Chronicle Christian/KS
$-City Light News—R
Desert Call—R
Diamond Dust
Disciple's Journal—R
$-Gem—R
Good News Journal—R
Highway News—R
$-Home Times—R
$-Interchange
LiteraryTNT.com—R
$-Lutheran Digest—R
$-Lutheran Journal—R
MESSAGE/Open Bible—R
MovieGuide
$-Now What?—R
PrayerWorks—R
Prison Living—R
$-Significant Living—R
SingleAgain.com—R
$-St. Anthony Messenger
Sword and Trumpet
Sword of the Lord—R
$-Today's Pentecostal—R
Urban Kingdom—R
$-Vista
$-Written

CHILDREN
$-Kid Zone
$-Nature Friend—R

CHRISTIAN EDUCATION/ LIBRARY
$-RTJ—R
$-Teachers of Vision—R
$-Today's Catholic Teacher—R

PASTORS/LEADERS
$-Enrichment—R
$-Interpreter

TEEN/YOUNG ADULT
$-Real Faith in Life—R
TeensForJC—R
$-True Girl
$-Young Christian—R
$-Young Salvationist—R

WOMEN
($)-Beyond the Bend—R
CelebrateMoms—R
Christian Woman's Page—R
Hearts at Home—R
Proverbs 31 Sisters
($)-Simply Blessed—R
Today's Leading Ladies—R
Virtuous Woman—R
Woman of Worth—R

WRITERS
Areopagus
$-Fellowscript—R
Money the Write Way—R
$-New Writer's Mag.
Write Connection
$-Writers' Journal

FILLERS: GAMES
ADULT/GENERAL
$-Catholic Yearbook—R
$-CGA World—R
$-Christian Herald—R
Christian Motorsports
Christian Ranchman
$-Chronicle Christian/KS
$-Citizen USA
Connecting Point—R
$-Creation Illustrated—R
Diamond Dust
Disciple's Journal—R
$-Faith & Friends—R
$-Family Smart e-Tips—R
$-Gem—R
Good News Journal—R
Heartlight—R
LiteraryTNT.com—R
$-Lutheran Journal—R
MovieGuide
Prison Living—R
Victory Herald—R
$-Vista

CHILDREN
$-American Girl—R
$-Guide—R
$-Pockets—R
$-SHINEbrightly—R
$-Sparkle—R

CHRISTIAN EDUCATION/ LIBRARY
Catholic Library
$-Group
$-RTJ—R

MISSIONS
$-Glad Tidings (Canada)—R

PASTORS/LEADERS
$-Barefoot—R

TEEN/YOUNG ADULT
$-Listen—R
TeensForJC—R
$-Young Salvationist—R

WOMEN
CelebrateMoms—R
Proverbs 31 Sisters

FILLERS: IDEAS
ADULT/GENERAL
$-Animal Trails—R
Breakthrough Intercessor—R
$-Bridal Guides—R
$-CGA World—R
$-Christian Home & School
Christian Motorsports
Christian Ranchman
$-Chronicle Christian/KS
($)-Community Spirit—R
Diamond Dust
Disciple's Journal—R
Evangel/OR—R
$-Family Smart e-Tips—R
$-Gem—R
Good News Journal—R
Heartlight—R
Highway News—R
$-Home Times—R
LiteraryTNT.com—R
$-Manna—R
MovieGuide
Reverent Submissions—R
$-Seek—R
SingleAgain.com—R
Urban Kingdom—R
$-Vista

CHRISTIAN EDUCATION/ LIBRARY
$-Children's Ministry
Christian Librarian—R
Congregational Libraries
$-Group
$-Preschool Playhouse (CE)

$-RTJ—R
$-Youth & CE Leadership

MISSIONS
$-Evangelical Missions—R

MUSIC
$-Creator—R

PASTORS/LEADERS
$-Barefoot—R
$-Interpreter
$-Lutheran Partners—R
$-Pray!—R
$-Preaching Well—R
$-Rev. Magazine
$-RevWriter Resource
$-Small Groups.com—R

TEEN/YOUNG ADULT
$-Real Faith in Life—R
$-Young Christian—R

WOMEN
($)-Beyond the Bend—R
CelebrateMoms—R
Christian Woman's Page—R
Hearts at Home—R
Just Between Us—R
P31 Woman—R
Proverbs 31 Sisters
Right to the Heart—R
Today's Leading Ladies—R
Virtuous Woman—R
WT Online—R

WRITERS
Areopagus
$-Canadian Writer's Jour.—R
Money the Write Way—R
Once Upon a Time—R
$-Tickled by Thunder
Write Connection
$-Writers' Journal

FILLERS: JOKES
ADULT/GENERAL
$-Catholic Digest—R
$-Christian Journal—R
Christian Motorsports
Christian Ranchman
$-City Light News—R
Desert Voice—R
Disciple's Journal—R
Eternal Ink—R
$-Faith & Friends—R
$-Gem—R
Good News Journal—R
Heartlight—R
$-Home Times—R
($)-Impact—R
$-In His Presence—R
$-Interchange
Light of the World

$-Liguorian
LiteraryTNT.com—R
$-Lutheran Digest—R
$-Mature Years—R
Miracles, Healings
MovieGuide
New Heart—R
PrayerWorks—R
Prison Living—R
Reverent Submissions—R
$-Significant Living—R
SingleAgain.com—R
$-St. Anthony Messenger
$-Vista

MUSIC
$-Creator—R

PASTORS/LEADERS
Churchlife Inspiration
$-Preaching Well—R
Pulpit Helps—R
Sharing the Practice—R

TEEN/YOUNG ADULT
G4T Ink—R
TeensForJC—R

WOMEN
Proverbs 31 Sisters
Virtuous Woman—R

WRITERS
Write Connection
$-Writers' Journal

FILLERS: KID QUOTES
ADULT/GENERAL
$-Animal Trails—R
Breakthrough Intercessor—R
$-Bridal Guides—R
$-Chicken Soup Books—R
$-Christian Journal—R
$-Chronicle Christian/KS
$-City Light News—R
Desert Voice—R
Eternal Ink—R
Highway News—R
$-Home Times—R
$-Indian Life—R
LiteraryTNT.com—R
MovieGuide
Prison Living—R
Reverent Submissions—R
SingleAgain.com—R
$-Today's Christian—R
$-Upscale
Victory Herald—R

CHRISTIAN EDUCATION/ LIBRARY
$-Children's Ministry

MISSIONS
$-Glad Tidings (Canada)—R

WOMEN
CelebrateMoms—R
Proverbs 31 Sisters

FILLERS: NEWSBREAKS
ADULT/GENERAL
$-Anglican Journal
$-Arkansas Catholic—R
$-B.C. Catholic—R
$-Canada Lutheran—R
$-Catholic Telegraph
Christian Courier/WI—R
$-Christian Journal—R
Christian Motorsports
Christian Ranchman
$-Christian Renewal—R
$-Chronicle Christian/KS
$-City Light News—R
Disciple's Journal—R
Evangel/OR—R
Friends Journal—R
$-Gem—R
Good News Journal—R
Heartlight—R
Highway News—R
$-Home Times—R
MovieGuide
($)-NRB Magazine—R
$-STEPS
Sword and Trumpet
Sword of the Lord—R
Urban Kingdom—R
$-Vista

CHRISTIAN EDUCATION/
LIBRARY
Christian Librarian—R

MISSIONS
OpRev Equipper—R

PASTORS/LEADERS
$-Preaching Well—R

TEEN/YOUNG ADULT
$-Real Faith in Life—R

WOMEN
Hope for Women

WRITERS
Areopagus
$-New Writer's Mag.
$-Writers' Journal

FILLERS: PARTY IDEAS
ADULT/GENERAL
$-Animal Trails—R
$-Bridal Guides—R
Christian Ranchman
$-Chronicle Christian/KS
Disciple's Journal—R
Good News Journal—R
Highway News—R

LiteraryTNT.com—R
$-Manna—R
MovieGuide
Urban Kingdom—R
Victory Herald—R

CHILDREN
$-Sparkle—R

CHRISTIAN EDUCATION/
LIBRARY
$-Youth & CE Leadership

MUSIC
$-Creator—R

PASTORS/LEADERS
$-Barefoot—R

TEEN/YOUNG ADULT
TeensForJC—R
$-Young Christian—R

WOMEN
CelebrateMoms—R
Hearts at Home—R
Hope for Women
P31 Woman—R
Proverbs 31 Sisters
Right to the Heart—R
Today's Leading Ladies—R
Virtuous Woman—R

FILLERS: PRAYERS
ADULT/GENERAL
$-Angels on Earth
$-Animal Trails—R
Breakthrough Intercessor—R
$-Bridal Guides—R
$-Catholic Yearbook—R
$-CGA World—R
$-Christian Herald—R
$-Christian Journal—R
Christian Motorsports
Christian Online
Christian Ranchman
$-Chronicle Christian/KS
Desert Call—R
Diamond Dust
Disciple's Journal—R
E-Channels—R
Eternal Ink—R
$-Family Digest—R
$-Gem—R
Good News Journal—R
Heartlight—R
Highway News—R
$-Home Times—R
LifeTimes Catholic
LiteraryTNT.com—R
$-Mature Years—R
MovieGuide
PrayerWorks—R
Prison Living—R

Reverent Submissions—R
SingleAgain.com—R
Spirituality for Today
Urban Kingdom—R
Victory Herald—R
$-Vista

CHILDREN
$-SHINEbrightly—R
$-Sparkle—R

CHRISTIAN EDUCATION/
LIBRARY
$-RTJ—R

DAILY DEVOTIONALS
$-Word in Season

MISSIONS
$-Glad Tidings (Canada)—R

TEEN/YOUNG ADULT
G4T Ink—R
TeensForJC—R
$-True Girl
$-Young Christian—R
$-Young Salvationist—R

WOMEN
CelebrateMoms—R
Just Between Us—R
Proverbs 31 Sisters
Right to the Heart—R
($)-Simply Blessed—R
Today's Leading Ladies—R
Virtuous Woman—R

WRITERS
$-Cross & Quill—R
Write Connection
$-Writers' Journal

FILLERS: PROSE
ADULT/GENERAL
$-Animal Trails—R
$-Bible Advocate—R
Bread of Life—R
Breakthrough Intercessor—R
$-Bridal Guides—R
Christian Motorsports
Christian Online
Christian Ranchman
$-Chronicle Christian/KS
$-Decision
Desert Call—R
Diamond Dust
Disciple's Journal—R
Esdras' Scroll
Eternal Ink—R
Evangel/OR—R
$-Faith & Family
$-Gem—R
Good News Journal—R
Heartlight—R
Highway News—R

$-Home Times—R
LiteraryTNT.com—R
MovieGuide
$-Now What?—R
Pegasus Review—R
Reverent Submissions—R
SingleAgain.com—R
Sword and Trumpet
Sword of the Lord—R
$-Today's Pentecostal—R
Urban Kingdom—R
Victory Herald—R
$-Vista

CHILDREN
$-Partners—R

PASTORS/LEADERS
$-Preaching Well—R

TEEN/YOUNG ADULT
$-Brio—R
$-Listen—R
$-Real Faith in Life—R
TeensForJC—R
$-Young Christian—R

WOMEN
CelebrateMoms—R
$-Melody of the Heart

WRITERS
Areopagus
$-Freelance Writer's Report—R
Write Connection
$-Writer
$-Writers' Journal

FILLERS: QUIZZES
ADULT/GENERAL
$-Animal Trails—R
$-Bridal Guides—R
$-Catholic Yearbook—R
Christian Motorsports
Christian Online
Christian Ranchman
$-Chronicle Christian/KS
Church Herald & Holiness—R
Diamond Dust
Disciple's Journal—R
$-Faith & Friends—R
$-Gem—R
Good News Journal—R
$-Home Times—R
($)-Impact—R
Light of the World
LiteraryTNT.com—R
$-Lutheran Journal—R
MovieGuide
Urban Kingdom—R
$-Wittenburg Door—R

CHILDREN
$-Cadet Quest—R

$-Focus/Clubhouse
$-Guide—R
$-Nature Friend—R
$-Partners—R
$-SHINEbrightly—R
Skipping Stones
$-Sparkle—R
$-Story Mates—R

TEEN/YOUNG ADULT
G4T Ink—R
$-Listen—R
$-Real Faith in Life—R
TeensForJC—R
$-True Girl
$-Young Christian—R
$-Young Salvationist—R

WOMEN
CelebrateMoms—R
$-Melody of the Heart
Proverbs 31 Sisters
Virtuous Woman—R

WRITERS
Once Upon a Time—R
$-Writers' Journal

FILLERS: QUOTES
ADULT/GENERAL
$-Animal Trails—R
Bread of Life—R
Breakthrough Intercessor—R
$-Bridal Guides—R
$-Catholic Digest—R
$-Catholic Yearbook—R
$-Chicken Soup Books—R
$-Christian Herald—R
$-Christian Journal—R
Christian Motorsports
Christian Ranchman
$-Christian Response—R
$-Chronicle Christian/KS
$-Culture Wars—R
Desert Call—R
Desert Voice—R
Disciple's Journal—R
$-Faith & Friends—R
$-Family Smart e-Tips—R
$-Gem—R
Good News Journal—R
Heartlight—R
$-Home Times—R
$-Indian Life—R
$-Lutheran Journal—R
MESSAGE/Open Bible—R
MovieGuide
$-Now What?—R
Pegasus Review—R
PrayerWorks—R
Prison Living—R
Reverent Submissions—R

$-Seek—R
Spirituality for Today
$-St. Anthony Messenger
$-Storyteller—R
Urban Kingdom—R
$-Vista
$-Written

CHILDREN
$-Partners—R
Skipping Stones

MISSIONS
Railroad Evangelist—R

PASTORS/LEADERS
Pulpit Helps—R
$-Rev. Magazine

TEEN/YOUNG ADULT
$-True Girl
$-Young Christian—R

WOMEN
($)-Beyond the Bend—R
CelebrateMoms—R
Just Between Us—R
Proverbs 31 Sisters
Right to the Heart—R
Today's Leading Ladies—R

WRITERS
$-Canadian Writer's Jour.—R
Money the Write Way—R
Write Connection
$-Writers' Journal

FILLERS: SERMON ILLUSTRATIONS
ADULT/GENERAL
Urban Kingdom—R

PASTORS/LEADERS
Churchlife Inspiration
$-Preaching Well—R
$-PreachingToday.com
Pulpit Helps—R
$-RevWriter Resource
$-Sunday Sermons—R

WOMEN
($)-Beyond the Bend—R
Proverbs 31 Sisters

FILLERS: SHORT HUMOR
ADULT/GENERAL
$-Angels on Earth
$-Animal Trails—R
Breakthrough Intercessor—R
$-Bridal Guides—R
$-Chicken Soup Books—R
$-Christian Journal—R
Christian Motorsports
Christian Online
Christian Ranchman

$-Chronicle Christian/KS
$-Citizen USA
$-City Light News—R
Diamond Dust
Disciple's Journal—R
Eternal Ink—R
$-Family Digest—R
Friends Journal—R
$-Gem—R
Good News Journal—R
Heartlight—R
Highway News—R
$-Home Times—R
($)-Impact—R
$-In His Presence—R
$-Indian Life—R
$-Leben—R
LiteraryTNT.com—R
$-Living—R
$-Lutheran Digest—R
$-Manna—R
MESSAGE/Open Bible—R
MovieGuide
New Heart—R
PrayerWorks—R
$-Presbyterians Today—R
Prison Living—R
$-Purpose—R
Reverent Submissions—R
$-Rose & Thorn
$-Seek—R
$-Significant Living—R
SingleAgain.com—R
$-STEPS
Urban Kingdom—R
Victory Herald—R
$-Vista
$-Wittenburg Door—R

CHILDREN
$-SHINEbrightly—R
$-Sparkle—R

CHRISTIAN EDUCATION/ LIBRARY
Christian Librarian—R

MISSIONS
$-Glad Tidings (Canada)—R

MUSIC
Christian Music Weekly—R
$-Creator—R

PASTORS/LEADERS
$-Barefoot—R
$-Catholic Servant
Churchlife Inspiration
$-Enrichment—R
$-Interpreter
$-Leadership—R
$-Preaching Well—R
Pulpit Helps—R
Sharing the Practice—R

TEEN/YOUNG ADULT
G4T Ink—R
$-InsideOut—R
$-Real Faith in Life—R
TeensForJC—R
$-Young Christian—R
$-Young Salvationist—R

WOMEN
($)-Beyond the Bend—R
CelebrateMoms—R
Christian Woman's Page—R
Hearts at Home—R
Just Between Us—R
$-Melody of the Heart
Proverbs 31 Sisters
Woman of Worth—R

WRITERS
Areopagus
$-Christian Communicator—R
$-New Writer's Mag.
Once Upon a Time—R
$-Tickled by Thunder
Write Connection
$-Writers' Journal

FILLERS: TIPS
ADULT/GENERAL
$-Animal Trails—R
$-Bridal Guides—R
Christian Ranchman
$-Chronicle Christian/KS
Diamond Dust
Highway News—R
$-Home Times—R
$-Manna—R
MovieGuide
Prison Living—R
Reverent Submissions—R
SingleAgain.com—R
$-Special Living—R
$-Storyteller—R
Urban Kingdom—R
Victory Herald—R
$-Vista
$-Written

CHILDREN
$-Cadet Quest—R

CHRISTIAN EDUCATION/ LIBRARY
$-Youth & CE Leadership

PASTORS/LEADERS
$-Barefoot—R
$-Enrichment—R
$-Your Church—R

TEEN/YOUNG ADULT
TeensForJC—R
$-Young Christian—R

WOMEN
($)-Beyond the Bend—R
CelebrateMoms—R
Christian Woman's Page—R
Hope for Women
$-MomSense—R
Proverbs 31 Sisters
($)-Simply Blessed—R
Today's Leading Ladies—R
Virtuous Woman—R
Woman of Worth—R
Women's Ministry

WRITERS
$-Fellowscript—R
$-Freelance Writer's Report—R
Money the Write Way—R
NW Christian Author—R
Once Upon a Time—R
Write Connection
$-Writers' Journal

FILLERS: WORD PUZZLES
ADULT/GENERAL
$-Animal Trails—R
$-Bridal Guides—R
$-Catholic Yearbook—R
$-CGA World—R
$-Christian Herald—R
$-Christian Journal—R
Christian Ranchman
$-Chronicle Christian/KS
$-Citizen USA
Connecting Point—R
Desert Voice—R
Diamond Dust
Disciple's Journal—R
$-Evangel/IN—R
$-Faith & Friends—R
Friends Journal—R
$-Gem—R
Good News Journal—R
$-Gospel Today—R
Heartlight—R
$-Home Times—R
$-Horizons (adult)—R
($)-Impact—R
Light of the World
LiteraryTNT.com—R
$-Mature Years—R
MovieGuide
$-Power for Living—R
Prison Living—R
$-Significant Living—R
$-Standard—R
$-Vista

CHILDREN
$-Adventures
$-American Girl—R
$-Cadet Quest—R
$-Faces

$-Focus/Clubhouse
$-Guide—R
$-Kid Zone
$-Nature Friend—R
$-Our Little Friend—R
$-Partners—R
$-Passport—R
$-Pockets—R
$-SHINEbrightly—R
Skipping Stones
$-Story Mates—R

CHRISTIAN EDUCATION/LIBRARY
$-RTJ—R
$-Youth & CE Leadership

MISSIONS
$-Glad Tidings (Canada)—R

TEEN/YOUNG ADULT
G4T Ink—R
$-Real Faith in Life—R
TeensForJC—R
$-True Girl
$-Young Christian—R
$-Young Salvationist—R

WOMEN
CelebrateMoms—R
$-Melody of the Heart

WRITERS
$-Writers' Journal

FOOD/RECIPES
ADULT/GENERAL
$-Animal Trails—R
$-Associated Content—R
$-Bridal Guides—R
CBN.com—R
Christian Online
Diamond Dust
$-Dovetail—R
$-Faith & Family
$-Home Times—R
($)-HopeKeepers—R
($)-Impact—R
$-In His Presence—R
$-Indian Life—R
LiteraryTNT.com—R
$-Mature Living
$-ParentLife
Prison Living—R
$-Significant Living—R
$-St. Anthony Messenger
Urban Kingdom—R
Victory Herald—R
$-World & I—R
$-Written

CHILDREN
$-Adventures
$-American Girl—R

$-Archaeology
$-Cadet Quest—R
$-Celebrate
$-Faces
$-Focus/Clubhouse
$-Focus/Clubhouse Jr.
$-Pockets—R
$-SHINEbrightly—R
$-Sparkle—R

MISSIONS
$-Glad Tidings (Canada)—R
Women of the Harvest

TEEN/YOUNG ADULT
$-Boundless Webzine—R
$-Brio—R
$-J.A.M.
TeensForJC—R

WOMEN
($)-Beyond the Bend—R
CelebrateMoms—R
Christian Women Today—R
Crowned with Silver
$-Dabbling Mum—R
Elegance—R
First Lady
$-Girlfriend 2 Girlfriend
Hearts at Home—R
Hope for Women
$-Melody of the Heart
Precious Times—R
Proverbs 31 Sisters
Today's Leading Ladies—R
Virtuous Woman—R
Woman of Worth—R
Women Today—R
WT Online—R

GRANDPARENTING
ADULT/GENERAL
$-CGA World—R
$-Christian Home & School
$-City Light News—R
$-Family Digest—R
Family Journal—R
$-Focus on the Family
Gold Country Families—R
$-Grand
$-Home Times—R
$-Ideals—R
$-In His Presence—R
$-In Touch
$-Indian Life—R
Island Catholic—R
$-Liguorian
LiteraryTNT.com—R
$-Live—R
$-Lutheran Digest—R
$-Majellan—R
$-Our Sunday Visitor—R

$-ParentLife
PrayerWorks—R
Prison Living—R
$-Seek—R
$-Significant Living—R
$-Today's Pentecostal—R
Wisconsin Christian

MISSIONS
$-Glad Tidings (Canada)—R

WOMEN
Crowned with Silver
Elegance—R
Hearts at Home—R
$-Pauses...
Today's Leading Ladies—R
Virtuous Woman—R

HEALING
ADULT/GENERAL
$-Advance
$-America
$-Angels on Earth
Anointed Pages
$-Associated Content—R
Bread of Life—R
Breakthrough Intercessor—R
$-Canada Lutheran—R
CBN.com—R
$-Celebrate Life—R
$-Christian Home & School
$-Christian Journal—R
Christian Motorsports
Christian Online
Christian Ranchman
$-ChristianWeek—R
$-Chronicle Christian/KS
$-City Light News—R
($)-Community Spirit—R
Connecting Point—R
E-Channels—R
Evangelical Advocate—R
$-Faith Today
$-Gem—R
$-Good News—R
$-Guideposts—R
$-Home Times—R
($)-HopeKeepers—R
Island Catholic—R
$-Light & Life
LiteraryTNT.com—R
$-Live—R
$-Majellan—R
Miracles, Healings
$-National Catholic
New Heart—R
Nostalgia—R
$-Our Sunday Visitor—R
Perspectives—R
$-Positive Thinking—R
Prayer Closet

Prison Living—R
$-Pure Inspiration—R
Quaker Life—R
Sacred Journey—R
$-Seek—R
Sharing—R
$-Significant Living—R
SingleAgain.com—R
$-Sound Body—R
$-Spiritual Life
$-St. Anthony Messenger
$-Storyteller—R
$-Testimony—R
$-Today's Christian—R
Trumpeter—R
$-United Church Observer—R
Urban Kingdom—R
$-Way of St. Francis—R
$-World & I—R

CHILDREN
$-BREAD/God's Children—R
Skipping Stones

DAILY DEVOTIONALS
Penned from the Heart—R

MISSIONS
$-Glad Tidings (Canada)—R

PASTORS/LEADERS
$-Word & World

TEEN/YOUNG ADULT
$-Boundless Webzine—R
$-J.A.M.

WOMEN
$-Canticle
Christian Woman's Page—R
Hearts at Home—R
Hope for Women
Precious Times—R
Share
$-SpiritLed Woman
$-Today's Christian Woman—R
Today's Leading Ladies—R
Virtuous Woman—R
Woman of Worth—R
WT Online—R

WRITERS
Areopagus

HEALTH
ADULT/GENERAL
$-Abilities
$-Angels on Earth
$-Anglican Journal
Anointed Pages
$-Apocalypse Chronicles—R
$-Associated Content—R
$-Aujourd'hui Credo—R
$-B.C. Catholic—R

Breakthrough Intercessor—R
$-Canada Lutheran—R
$-Catholic Forester—R
CBN.com—R
$-Celebrate Life—R
$-CGA World—R
$-Christian Courier/Cdn.—R
Christian Courier/WI—R
Christian Health Care
$-Christian Home & School
$-Christian Journal—R
Christian Online
Christian Ranchman
$-ChristianWeek—R
$-Chronicle Christian/KS
$-City Light News—R
$-Common Ground—R
($)-Community Spirit—R
$-Creative Nonfiction
Disciple's Journal—R
E-Channels—R
Evangelical Advocate—R
$-Faith Today
Family Journal—R
$-Gospel Today—R
$-Guideposts—R
$-Home Times—R
($)-HopeKeepers—R
$-In His Presence—R
Island Catholic—R
$-Lifeglow—R
$-Light & Life
LiteraryTNT.com—R
$-Lookout
$-Majellan—R
$-Mature Living
$-Mature Years—R
$-MESSAGE
New Heart—R
Nostalgia—R
$-Our Sunday Visitor—R
$-Ozarks Senior Living—R
$-ParentLife
Penned from the Heart—R
Perspectives/Science
($)-Portrait of Achievement
$-Positive Thinking—R
($)-P.O.W.E.R.
Prison Living—R
$-Pure Inspiration—R
Purpose Magazine—R
Quaker Life—R
Sacred Journey—R
$-Significant Living—R
SingleAgain.com—R
$-Sound Body—R
$-Special Living—R
$-St. Anthony Messenger
$-Testimony—R
$-Today's Christian—R
$-Today's Pentecostal—R

Trumpeter—R
$-Upscale
Urban Kingdom—R
$-Vibrant Life—R
$-War Cry—R
Wisconsin Christian
$-World & I—R
$-Written

CHILDREN
$-American Girl—R
$-BREAD/God's Children—R
$-Guide—R
$-New Moon—R
Skipping Stones
$-Sparkle—R

CHRISTIAN EDUCATION/ LIBRARY
$-Teachers of Vision—R

DAILY DEVOTIONALS
Penned from the Heart—R

MISSIONS
$-Glad Tidings (Canada)—R

PASTORS/LEADERS
$-Christian Century—R
$-InSite—R
$-Interpreter
$-Word & World

TEEN/YOUNG ADULT
$-Boundless Webzine—R
$-Brio—R
$-Devo'Zine—R
G4T Ink—R
$-J.A.M.
$-Listen—R
TeensForJC—R
$-True Girl

WOMEN
$-At the Center—R
Christian Woman's Page—R
Christian Women Today—R
Comfort Café
Elegance—R
$-Esprit
$-Heart & Soul
Hearts at Home—R
$-Herizons
$-Horizons (women)—R
$-InspiredMoms—R
$-inSpirit—R
$-Journey
Life Tools for Women
Lutheran Woman's Quar.
Precious Times—R
Share
($)-Simply Blessed—R
$-SpiritLed Woman
$-Today's Christian Woman—R

Today's Leading Ladies—R
Virtuous Woman—R
Woman of Worth—R
Women Today—R
WT Online—R

HISTORICAL

ADULT/GENERAL
($)-AGAIN—R
$-Angels on Earth
$-Arlington Catholic
$-Associated Content—R
Breakthrough Intercessor—R
$-Cappers
$-Catholic Peace Voice—R
CBN.com—R
$-Celebrate Life—R
$-Christian Courier/Cdn.—R
$-Christian History—R
Christian Motorsports
Christian Observer
Christian Online
$-Christian Renewal—R
$-Chronicle Christian/KS
$-City Light News—R
$-Company—R
Creation Care—R
$-Dovetail—R
E-Channels—R
$-Eureka Street
Evangelical Advocate—R
Evangelical Times
$-Faith Today
Family Journal—R
$-Haruah—R
$-Home Times—R
$-In His Presence—R
$-Indian Life—R
Island Catholic—R
$-Leben—R
$-Lifeglow—R
$-Light & Life
$-Lutheran Digest—R
$-Mature Living
($)-Mennonite Historian—R
$-Messiah
Messianic Times
Methodist History
$-National Catholic
$-New Wineskins—R
Nostalgia—R
$-Our Sunday Visitor—R
Perspectives—R
Perspectives/Science
$-Power for Living—R
PrayerWorks—R
Presbyterian Outlook
Priscilla Papers
Prison Living—R
Sharing—R
$-Social Justice—R

$-St. Anthony Messenger
$-Storyteller—R
Sword of the Lord—R
Trumpeter—R
$-U.S. Catholic
$-Upscale
Urban Kingdom—R
$-Way of St. Francis—R
$-Wesleyan Life—R
Wisconsin Christian
$-World & I—R

CHILDREN
$-Archaeology
$-Faces
$-Focus/Clubhouse Jr.
$-Guide—R
$-New Moon—R
$-Sparkle—R

CHRISTIAN EDUCATION/ LIBRARY
Catholic Library
Teach Kids Essentials—R
$-Teachers of Vision—R

MISSIONS
$-Glad Tidings (Canada)—R
$-One
Women of the Harvest

MUSIC
$-Creator—R
Hymn

PASTORS/LEADERS
$-Leadership—R
Lutheran Forum
$-Ministry Today
$-Priest
Pulpit Helps—R
Sewanee Theo. Review
Theological Digest—R
$-This Rock
$-Today's Parish
$-Word & World

TEEN/YOUNG ADULT
$-Boundless Webzine—R
$-Breakaway
$-InsideOut—R
$-J.A.M.
$-Real Faith in Life—R
TeensForJC—R
$-Young Adult Today

WOMEN
($)-History's Women—R
Just Between Us—R
$-SpiritLed Woman

WRITERS
Areopagus
$-Tickled by Thunder

HOLIDAY/SEASONAL

ADULT/GENERAL
$-Advance
$-Alive Now—R
American Tract—R
$-Angels on Earth
$-Animal Trails—R
$-Annals of St. Anne
$-Arlington Catholic
$-BGC World—R
Breakthrough Intercessor—R
$-Bridal Guides—R
$-Canada Lutheran—R
$-Cappers
$-Cathedral Age
$-Catholic Digest—R
$-Catholic New York
CBN.com—R
$-CGA World—R
$-Chicken Soup Books—R
$-Christian Courier/Cdn.—R
Christian Courier/WI—R
$-Christian Home & School
$-Christian Journal—R
Christian Online
$-Christian Renewal—R
$-Christian Retailing
$-ChristianWeek—R
$-Chronicle Christian/KS
$-City Light News—R
($)-Community Spirit—R
Connecting Point—R
$-Covenant Companion—R
Desert Call—R
Diamond Dust
$-Dovetail—R
E-Channels—R
Eternal Ink—R
Evangelical Advocate—R
$-Faith & Family
$-Faith Today
$-Family Digest—R
$-Family Smart e-Tips—R
$-Focus on the Family
$-Gem—R
$-Gems of Truth—R
Good News Journal—R
$-Good News, Etc.—R
$-Guideposts—R
Heartlight—R
$-Home Times—R
($)-HopeKeepers—R
$-Horizons (adult)—R
$-Ideals—R
$-In His Presence—R
$-In Touch
$-Lifeglow—R
$-Light & Life
$-Liguorian
LiteraryTNT.com—R

$-Live—R
$-Living—R
$-Living Church
$-Living Light—R
$-Lookout
$-Manna—R
$-Mature Living
$-Mature Years—R
MESSAGE/Open Bible—R
$-Minnesota Christian—R
$-Miraculous Medal
$-Montana Catholic
$-Montgomery's Journey
$-National Catholic
$-On Mission
$-Our Sunday Visitor—R
$-ParentLife
Pegasus Review—R
Penned from the Heart—R
$-Positive Thinking—R
$-Power for Living—R
$-Prairie Messenger—R
PrayerWorks—R
Prison Living—R
$-Psychology for Living—R
$-Pure Inspiration—R
$-Purpose—R
Reverent Submissions—R
Sacred Journey—R
$-Seek—R
Sharing—R
$-Significant Living—R
$-Special Living—R
$-St. Anthony Messenger
$-Storyteller—R
Sword of the Lord—R
$-Today's Christian—R
$-Together—R
Trumpeter—R
$-U.S. Catholic
$-United Church Observer—R
Urban Kingdom—R
$-Vibrant Life—R
Victory Herald—R
$-Victory in Grace—R
$-War Cry—R
$-Way of St. Francis—R
$-Wesleyan Life—R
$-World & I—R

CHILDREN
$-Archaeology
$-Focus/Clubhouse
$-Focus/Clubhouse Jr.
$-Guide—R
$-Junior Companion—R
$-JuniorWay
$-Nature Friend—R
$-Pockets—R
$-Primary Street
$-SHINEbrightly—R
Skipping Stones

$-Sparkle—R

CHRISTIAN EDUCATION/ LIBRARY
$-Group
Ideas Unlimited—R
Teach Kids Essentials—R
$-Teachers of Vision—R
$-Today's Catholic Teacher—R
$-Youth & CE Leadership

DAILY DEVOTIONALS
$-Brink Magazine—R
Penned from the Heart—R
$-These Days

MISSIONS
$-Glad Tidings (Canada)—R
Railroad Evangelist—R
Women of the Harvest

MUSIC
$-Creator—R

PASTORS/LEADERS
$-Catholic Servant
$-Interpreter
$-Preaching Well—R
Pulpit Helps—R
$-Sunday Sermons—R

TEEN/YOUNG ADULT
$-Boundless Webzine—R
$-Breakaway
$-Brio—R
$-Credo—R
$-Essential Connection
$-Ignite Your Faith
$-J.A.M.
$-Real Faith in Life—R
TeensForJC—R
$-True Girl
$-Young Salvationist—R

WOMEN
($)-Beyond the Bend—R
$-Canticle
CelebrateMoms—R
Christian Women Today—R
Elegance—R
$-Esprit
Handmaiden—R
Hearts at Home—R
($)-History's Women—R
Hope for Women
$-InspiredMoms—R
$-inSpirit—R
$-Journey
Lutheran Woman's Quar.
P31 Woman—R
$-Pauses…
Precious Times—R
$-Today's Christian Woman—R
Today's Leading Ladies—R
Together with God—R

Virtuous Woman—R
WT Online—R

WRITERS
Areopagus
$-Cross & Quill—R

HOLY SPIRIT
ADULT/GENERAL
Bread of Life—R
Breakthrough Intercessor—R
Christian C. L. RECORD—R
$-Christian Home & School
$-Christian Journal—R
Christian Ranchman
Church Herald & Holiness—R
$-City Light News—R
$-Discipleship Journal—R
Esdras' Scroll
Eternal Ink—R
$-Home Times—R
LiteraryTNT.com—R
$-Live—R
$-Majellan—R
$-Our Sunday Visitor—R
PrayerWorks—R
Prison Living—R
$-Pure Inspiration—R
Quaker Life—R
Reverent Submissions—R
Saved Magazine
$-Seek—R
Spirituality for Today
Urban Kingdom—R
Victory Herald—R
$-Way of St. Francis—R
Wisconsin Christian

CHILDREN
$-BREAD/God's Children—R

MISSIONS
$-Glad Tidings (Canada)—R

PASTORS/LEADERS
$-Enrichment—R
$-Lutheran Partners—R
$-Ministry Today
$-RevWriter Resource

TEEN/YOUNG ADULT
$-Boundless Webzine—R
$-Breakaway
$-Brio—R
$-CLEAR Direction

WOMEN
$-Come to the Fire—R
Elegance—R
Hearts at Home—R
$-Pauses…
Today's Leading Ladies—R
Woman of Worth—R

HOMESCHOOLING

ADULT/GENERAL

$-Animal Trails—R
Breakthrough Intercessor—R
$-City Light News—R
Desert Voice—R
Family Journal—R
$-Good News, Etc.—R
$-In His Presence—R
LiteraryTNT.com—R
$-Our Sunday Visitor—R
$-ParentLife
Prison Living—R
Wisconsin Christian

CHILDREN

$-Archaeology
$-BREAD/God's Children—R
$-New Moon—R
Skipping Stones

CHRISTIAN EDUCATION/ LIBRARY

Jour./Ed. & Christian Belief—R

MISSIONS

$-Glad Tidings (Canada)—R
Women of the Harvest

TEEN/YOUNG ADULT

$-Boundless Webzine—R
$-Brio—R
$-Insight—R
$-J.A.M.
$-True Girl

WOMEN

$-Canticle
CelebrateMoms—R
Christian Woman's Page—R
Crowned with Silver
Hearts at Home—R
Hope for Women
$-InspiredMoms—R
$-inSpirit—R
$-Journey
$-Today's Christian Woman—R
Virtuous Woman—R
Woman of Worth—R
WT Online—R

HOMILETICS

ADULT/GENERAL

CBN.com—R
Christian Ranchman
$-City Light News—R
E-Channels—R
Evangelical Advocate—R
$-New Wineskins—R
Perspectives—R
Priscilla Papers
$-Social Justice—R
$-St. Anthony Messenger

$-Stewardship—R
$-Testimony—R
Trumpeter—R
$-Wesleyan Life—R

MISSIONS

$-Glad Tidings (Canada)—R

PASTORS/LEADERS

$-African American Pulpit
$-Christian Century—R
$-Clergy Journal—R
$-Enrichment—R
$-Lutheran Partners—R
$-Ministry & Liturgy—R
Preaching
$-Preaching Well—R
$-Priest
$-Proclaim—R
$-Rev. Magazine
Sewanee Theo. Review

WOMEN

$-SpiritLed Woman

HOW-TO

ADULT/GENERAL

$-Animal Trails—R
$-Associated Content—R
$-CBA Retailers
CBN.com—R
$-Celebrate Life—R
$-CGA World—R
$-Christian Journal—R
Christian Motorsports
Christian Observer
Christian Online
$-Christian Retailing
$-City Light News—R
Connecting Point—R
Diamond Dust
$-Direction
$-Dovetail—R
E-Channels—R
$-Faith & Family
$-Faith Today
$-Family Digest—R
Family Journal—R
$-Family Smart e-Tips—R
$-Focus on the Family
Good News Journal—R
$-Good News, Etc.—R
$-Home Times—R
($)-HopeKeepers—R
$-Imagine
$-Light & Life
LiteraryTNT.com—R
$-Live—R
$-Living—R
$-Living Church
$-Majellan—R
$-Mature Living
$-MESSAGE

$-Montgomery's Journey
($)-Mutuality—R
$-On Mission
($)-Portrait of Achievement
$-Positive Thinking—R
PrayerWorks—R
$-Presbyterians Today—R
Prison Living—R
Quaker Life—R
Regent Global—R
$-St. Anthony Messenger
$-Testimony—R
$-Today's Christian—R
Trumpeter—R
$-U.S. Catholic
Urban Kingdom—R
$-Vibrant Life—R
Victory Herald—R
$-Village Note Cards—R
$-Vista
$-World & I—R
$-Written

CHILDREN

$-Archaeology
$-Sparkle—R

CHRISTIAN EDUCATION/ LIBRARY

$-Catechist
Catholic Library
$-Christian Educators—R
Christian Librarian—R
$-Church Libraries—R
Congregational Libraries
$-Group
Ideas Unlimited—R
$-Journal/Adventist Ed.—R
$-Kids' Ministry Ideas
$-Preschool Playhouse (CE)
$-RTJ—R
$-Teachers of Vision—R
$-Today's Catholic Teacher—R
$-Youth & CE Leadership

DAILY DEVOTIONALS

$-Brink Magazine—R

MISSIONS

$-Glad Tidings (Canada)—R
$-PFI Global—R

PASTORS/LEADERS

$-African American Pulpit
$-Cornerstone Youth—R
$-Lead—R
$-Lutheran Partners—R
$-Ministry
$-Ministry Today
$-Net Results
$-Newsletter Newsletter
$-Outreach—R
$-RevWriter Resource
$-Willow—R

$-Worship Leader
$-Your Church—R

TEEN/YOUNG ADULT
$-Listen—R
$-Real Faith in Life—R
TeensForJC—R
$-True Girl
$-Young Christian—R

WOMEN
($)-Beyond the Bend—R
CelebrateMoms—R
Christian Woman's Page—R
Christian Women Today—R
$-Dabbling Mum—R
Elegance—R
Hearts at Home—R
Hope for Women
Just Between Us—R
$-Melody of the Heart
Precious Times—R
Proverbs 31 Sisters
$-Today's Christian Woman—R
Today's Leading Ladies—R
Virtuous Woman—R
Woman of Worth—R

WRITERS
Author-Me
$-Christian Communicator—R
$-Cross & Quill—R
Esdras' Scroll—R
$-Fellowscript—R
$-Freelance Writer's Report—R
Money the Write Way—R
Once Upon a Time—R
$-Poets & Writers
$-Spirit-Led Writer—R
$-Writer's Digest

HOW-TO ACTIVITIES (JUV.)
ADULT/GENERAL
$-Animal Trails—R
$-Associated Content—R
$-Bridal Guides—R
$-Christian Home & School
Christian Online
$-City Light News—R
($)-Community Spirit—R
$-Dovetail—R
E-Channels—R
$-Faith & Family
$-Family Digest—R
Family Journal—R
$-Family Smart e-Tips—R
Good News Journal—R
$-Homeschooling Today—R
Keys to Living—R
$-Light & Life
LiteraryTNT.com—R
$-Montgomery's Journey

$-On Mission
Quaker Life—R
$-St. Anthony Messenger
$-World & I—R

CHILDREN
$-Adventures
$-American Girl—R
$-Archaeology
$-BREAD/God's Children—R
$-Cadet Quest—R
$-Celebrate
$-Faces
$-Focus/Clubhouse
$-Focus/Clubhouse Jr.
$-Guide—R
$-Junior Companion—R
$-JuniorWay
$-Kid Zone
$-Nature Friend—R
$-Pockets—R
$-Preschool Playhouse (CE)
$-Preschool Playhouse (child)
$-Seeds
$-SHINEbrightly—R
$-Sparkle—R
$-Winner—R

CHRISTIAN EDUCATION/ LIBRARY
$-Children's Ministry
Christian Early Ed.—R
$-Group
$-Kids' Ministry Ideas
$-Preschool Playhouse (CE)
$-RTJ—R
Teach Kids Essentials—R
$-Teachers of Vision—R

MISSIONS
$-Glad Tidings (Canada)—R

PASTORS/LEADERS
$-Interpreter

TEEN/YOUNG ADULT
$-Brio—R
$-Listen—R
$-True Girl

WOMEN
Elegance—R
Hearts at Home—R
Just Between Us—R
Today's Leading Ladies—R

HUMOR
ADULT/GENERAL
$-Abilities
American Tract—R
$-Angels on Earth
$-Animal Trails—R
$-Associated Content—R
Breakthrough Intercessor—R

$-Catholic Digest—R
$-Catholic Forester—R
$-Catholic Peace Voice—R
CBN.com—R
$-CGA World—R
$-Chicken Soup Books—R
Christian Computing—R
$-Christian Courier/Cdn.—R
$-Christian Home & School
$-Christian Journal—R
Christian Online
Christian Ranchman
$-Christianity Today—R
$-Chronicle Christian/KS
$-City Light News—R
($)-Community Spirit—R
Connecting Point—R
Creation Care—R
$-Creative Nonfiction
Desert Voice—R
Disciple's Journal—R
$-Dovetail—R
E-Channels—R
Eternal Ink—R
$-Faith & Family
$-Faith Today
$-Family Digest—R
Family Journal—R
$-Family Smart e-Tips—R
$-Focus on the Family
$-Focus on Your Child
$-Gem—R
Good News Journal—R
$-Good News, Etc.—R
$-Haruah—R
Highway News—R
$-Home Times—R
$-Homeschooling Today—R
($)-HopeKeepers—R
$-Horizons (adult)—R
$-Imagine
$-In His Presence—R
$-In Touch
$-Indian Life—R
Island Catholic—R
$-Lifeglow—R
$-Light & Life
$-Liguorian
LiteraryTNT.com—R
$-Living—R
$-Living Church
$-Living Light—R
$-Lookout
$-Majellan—R
$-Manna—R
$-Mature Living
$-Men.AG.org—R
Miracles, Healings
$-National Catholic
New Heart—R
$-New Wineskins—R

Nostalgia—R
$-Our Sunday Visitor—R
$-Over the Back Fence—R
$-Ozarks Senior Living—R
$-ParentLife
Pegasus Review—R
Penned from the Heart—R
$-Positive Thinking—R
PrayerWorks—R
Prison Living—R
$-Psychology for Living—R
Reverent Submissions—R
$-Rose & Thorn
Ruminate
Sacred Journey—R
$-Seek—R
$-Significant Living—R
Silver Wings—R
$-St. Anthony Messenger
$-Storyteller—R
$-Testimony—R
$-Today's Christian—R
$-Together—R
Trumpeter—R
$-U.S. Catholic
Urban Kingdom—R
Victory Herald—R
$-Victory in Grace—R
$-Vista
$-War Cry—R
$-Way of St. Francis—R
$-Weavings—R
$-Wildwood Reader—R
$-Wittenburg Door—R
$-World & I—R
Xavier Review

CHILDREN
$-Faces
$-Focus/Clubhouse Jr.
$-SHINEbrightly—R
$-Sparkle—R

CHRISTIAN EDUCATION/ LIBRARY
$-Children's Ministry
Teach Kids Essentials—R
$-Teachers of Vision—R

DAILY DEVOTIONALS
Penned from the Heart—R

MISSIONS
$-Glad Tidings (Canada)—R
Women of the Harvest

MUSIC
Christian Music Weekly—R
$-Creator—R

PASTORS/LEADERS
$-Catholic Servant
Churchlife Inspiration
$-Enrichment—R

$-Leadership—R
$-Lutheran Partners—R
$-Preaching Well—R
$-Priest
$-Today's Parish
$-Willow—R

TEEN/YOUNG ADULT
$-Boundless Webzine—R
$-Breakaway
$-Brio—R
$-CLEAR Direction
$-Essential Connection
$-Ignite Your Faith
$-Real Faith in Life—R
$-TC Magazine
TeensForJC—R
$-Young Salvationist—R

WOMEN
($)-Beyond the Bend—R
CelebrateMoms—R
Crowned with Silver
Elegance—R
$-Esprit
Hearts at Home—R
Hope for Women
$-Horizons (women)—R
$-Journey
Just Between Us—R
Lutheran Woman's Quar.
$-MD Women of Worship
$-Melody of the Heart
$-MomSense—R
($)-Simply Blessed—R
$-SpiritLed Woman
$-Today's Christian Woman—R
WT Online—R

WRITERS
Areopagus
$-ByLine
$-Christian Communicator—R
$-New Writer's Mag.
Once Upon a Time—R

INNER LIFE
ADULT/GENERAL
Breakthrough Intercessor—R
$-Bridal Guides—R
$-Catholic Digest—R
CBN.com—R
$-Christian Journal—R
Christian Ranchman
$-ChristianWeek—R
$-Chronicle Christian/KS
$-City Light News—R
($)-Community Spirit—R
$-Discipleship Journal—R
Divine Ascent
E-Channels—R
$-Faith & Family

$-Faith Today
$-Focus on the Family
Halo Magazine
$-Home Times—R
$-In Touch
Island Catholic—R
LifeTimes Catholic
$-Light & Life
LiteraryTNT.com—R
$-Live—R
$-Living—R
$-Majellan—R
$-Mature Years—R
$-Men of Integrity—R
$-MindFlights—R
$-Minnesota Christian—R
Mosaic—R
$-National Catholic
$-New Wineskins—R
$-Now What?—R
$-Our Sunday Visitor—R
Penned from the Heart—R
$-Positive Thinking—R
($)-P.O.W.E.R.
$-Presbyterians Today—R
Prison Living—R
$-Pure Inspiration—R
Quaker Life—R
Regent Global—R
Reverent Submissions—R
Rock & Sling
Sacred Journey—R
$-Seek—R
$-Significant Living—R
Silver Wings—R
Spirituality for Today
$-Testimony—R
$-Together—R
Urban Kingdom—R
Victory Herald—R
$-Way of St. Francis—R
$-Weavings—R
$-Wildwood Reader—R
$-World & I—R

CHRISTIAN EDUCATION/ LIBRARY
$-Teachers of Vision—R

MISSIONS
$-Glad Tidings (Canada)—R

PASTORS/LEADERS
$-Interpreter
Jour./Pastoral Care
$-Lutheran Partners—R

TEEN/YOUNG ADULT
$-Boundless Webzine—R
$-Breakaway
$-Brio—R
$-CLEAR Direction
Exodus Magazine

$-TC Magazine
TeensForJC—R
$-Young Salvationist—R

WOMEN
$-Canticle
Christian Woman's Page—R
$-Come to the Fire—R
Crowned with Silver
$-Fullfill
$-Journey
L.I.V.E.
$-Today's Christian Woman—R
Today's Leading Ladies—R
Women Today—R
WT Online—R

INSPIRATIONAL
ADULT/GENERAL
$-Advance
African Voices—R
$-Alive Now—R
$-Angels on Earth
$-Animal Trails—R
$-Annals of St. Anne
$-Arlington Catholic
$-Associated Content—R
$-Aujourd'hui Credo—R
Bread of Life—R
Breakthrough Intercessor—R
$-Bridal Guides—R
$-Canada Lutheran—R
$-Cappers
$-Catholic Forester—R
$-Catholic Peace Voice—R
CBN.com—R
$-Celebrate Life—R
$-CGA World—R
$-Chicken Soup Books—R
$-Christian Home & School
$-Christian Journal—R
Christian Motorsports
Christian Online
Christian Ranchman
$-Chronicle Christian/KS
$-City Light News—R
($)-Community Spirit—R
Connecting Point—R
$-Covenant Companion—R
$-Decision
Diamond Dust
$-Discipleship Journal—R
$-DisciplesWorld
Divine Ascent
$-DreamSeeker—R
E-Channels—R
Eternal Ink—R
$-Evangel/IN—R
Evangelical Advocate—R
$-Faith & Family
$-Faith Today
$-Family Digest—R

Family Journal—R
$-Focus on the Family
$-Gem—R
$-Good News—R
Good News Journal—R
$-Gospel Today—R
$-Guideposts—R
Halo Magazine
Heartlight—R
Highway News—R
$-Home Times—R
($)-HopeKeepers—R
$-In His Presence—R
$-In Touch
$-Indian Life—R
Keys to Living—R
Koinonia
Leaves—R
$-Lifeglow—R
$-Light & Life
$-Liguorian
LiteraryTNT.com—R
$-Live—R
$-Living—R
$-Living Church
$-Lookout
$-Lutheran Digest—R
$-Majellan—R
$-Marian Helper
$-Mature Living
($)-Mennonite Historian—R
$-MESSAGE
MESSAGE/Open Bible—R
$-Messenger/Sacred Heart
$-MindFlights—R
$-Minnesota Christian—R
Mosaic—R
($)-Mutuality—R
$-National Catholic
New Heart—R
$-Now What?—R
$-ParentLife
Pegasus Review—R
Penned from the Heart—R
$-Positive Thinking—R
$-Power for Living—R
$-Prairie Messenger—R
PrayerWorks—R
$-Precepts for Living
$-Presbyterians Today—R
$-Priority!—R
Prison Living—R
$-Psychology for Living—R
$-Pure Inspiration—R
Quaker Life—R
Reverent Submissions—R
Sacred Journey—R
$-Seek—R
$-Significant Living—R
Silver Wings—R
SingleAgain.com—R
Spirituality for Today

$-St. Anthony Messenger
$-Stewardship—R
$-Storyteller—R
SW Kansas Faith
Sword and Trumpet
Sword of the Lord—R
$-Testimony—R
$-Today's Christian—R
$-Together—R
Trumpeter—R
$-U.S. Catholic
$-United Church Observer—R
$-Upscale
Urban Kingdom—R
Victory Herald—R
$-Victory in Grace—R
$-Vision—R
$-Vista
$-War Cry—R
$-Way of St. Francis—R
$-Wesleyan Life—R
$-Wildwood Reader—R
$-World & I—R

CHILDREN
$-Archaeology
$-BREAD/God's Children—R
$-Cadet Quest—R
$-Partners—R
$-Passport—R
$-Primary Street
$-SHINEbrightly—R
$-Sparkle—R

CHRISTIAN EDUCATION/ LIBRARY
Catholic Library
$-Children's Ministry
Congregational Libraries
$-Journal/Adventist Ed.—R
$-Teachers of Vision—R
$-Youth & CE Leadership

DAILY DEVOTIONALS
$-Brink Magazine—R
CLEAR Living
Penned from the Heart—R
$-Rejoice!

MISSIONS
$-Glad Tidings (Canada)—R
Women of the Harvest

MUSIC
$-Creator—R

PASTORS/LEADERS
$-African American Pulpit
$-Catholic Servant
Churchlife Inspiration
$-Interpreter
$-Let's Worship
$-Ministry Today
$-Preaching Well—R
$-Priest

Technologies for Worship—R

TEEN/YOUNG ADULT

$-Boundless Webzine—R
$-Breakaway
$-Brio—R
$-CLEAR Direction
$-CLEAR Horizon
$-Devo'Zine—R
Exodus Magazine
G4T Ink—R
$-InsideOut—R
$-Insight—R
$-J.A.M.
TeensForJC—R
$-True Girl
$-Young Christian—R
$-Young Salvationist—R

WOMEN

($)-Beyond the Bend—R
CelebrateMoms—R
Christian Women Today—R
$-Come to the Fire—R
Elegance—R
$-Esprit
$-Fullfill
Handmaiden—R
Hearts at Home—R
Hope for Women
$-Horizons (women)—R
$-InspiredMoms—R
$-inSpirit—R
$-Journey
Just Between Us—R
L.I.V.E.
$-Link & Visitor—R
Lutheran Woman's Quar.
$-MomSense—R
P31 Woman—R
$-Pauses...
Precious Times—R
Proverbs 31 Sisters
Share
($)-Simply Blessed—R
$-SpiritLed Woman
$-Today's Christian Woman—R
Today's Leading Ladies—R
Virtuous Woman—R
Woman of Worth—R
WT Online—R

WRITERS

Areopagus
NW Christian Author—R
Once Upon a Time—R
Opinari—R
$-Writer's Digest

INTERVIEWS/PROFILES

ADULT/GENERAL

$-Abilities
($)-AGAIN—R

American Tract—R
$-Anglican Journal
Anointed Pages
$-Arkansas Catholic—R
$-Arlington Catholic
$-Associated Content—R
$-Australian Catholics—R
Baptist Standard
Beacon
Biblical Recorder
Books & Culture
Breakthrough Intercessor—R
CanadianChristianity
$-Cathedral Age
$-Catholic New York
$-Catholic Peace Voice—R
CBN.com—R
$-Celebrate Life—R
Challenge Weekly
$-Charisma
Charlotte World
Christian Business
Christian Chronicle
Christian Courier/WI—R
$-Christian Herald—R
Christian Motorsports
Christian News NW—R
Christian Observer
Christian Online
Christian Ranchman
$-Christianity Today—R
$-Christianity Today Movies—R
$-ChristianWeek—R
$-Chronicle Christian/KS
Church of England News
$-City Light News—R
$-Columbia—R
($)-Community Spirit—R
Creation Care—R
$-Culture Wars—R
Desert Call—R
Desert Christian
$-DisciplesWorld
Divine Ascent
$-Dovetail—R
E-Channels—R
$-EFCA Today—R
Encompass
$-Episcopal Life—R
Esdras' Scroll
Eternal Ink—R
$-Faith Today
$-Focus on the Family
$-Gem—R
$-Good News—R
Good News Connection
Good News Today
$-Good News, Etc.—R
$-Good News/S. Florida
$-Gospel Today—R
$-Guideposts—R
Heartland Gatekeeper—R

Heartlight—R
$-Home Times—R
($)-HopeKeepers—R
$-In His Presence—R
$-In Touch
$-Indian Life—R
$-Interim—R
$-Kindred Spirit—R
$-Lifeglow—R
LifeSite News
$-Light & Life
$-Liguorian
$-Living Church
$-Lookout
$-Majellan—R
$-Manna—R
$-Mature Living
$-MESSAGE
$-MindFlights—R
$-Minnesota Christian—R
($)-Mutuality—R
$-National Catholic
New Heart—R
$-On Mission
$-Our Sunday Visitor—R
$-Ozarks Senior Living—R
$-ParentLife
$-Positive Thinking—R
$-Power for Living—R
PrayerWorks—R
$-Precepts for Living
Presbyterian Outlook
$-Priority!—R
$-Prism
Prison Living—R
$-Pure Inspiration—R
Quaker Life—R
Regent Global—R
Rock & Sling
Sacred Journey—R
$-Science & Spirit
$-Significant Living—R
$-St. Anthony Messenger
$-Stewardship—R
$-Testimony—R
$-Today's Christian—R
Tri-State Voice
Trumpeter—R
$-United Church Observer—R
$-Upscale
Urban Kingdom—R
$-Vibrant Life—R
$-War Cry—R
$-Way of St. Francis—R
$-Weavings—R
Wisconsin Christian
$-Wittenburg Door—R
$-World & I—R

CHILDREN

$-American Girl—R
$-Cadet Quest—R

$-Faces
$-New Moon—R
$-Pockets—R
$-Primary Street
$-SHINEbrightly—R
Skipping Stones
$-Sparkle—R
$-Winner—R

CHRISTIAN EDUCATION/ LIBRARY
$-Children's Ministry
Christian Librarian—R
$-Church Libraries—R
$-Teachers of Vision—R
$-Youth & CE Leadership

DAILY DEVOTIONALS
$-Brink Magazine—R

MISSIONS
$-Evangelical Missions—R
$-Glad Tidings (Canada)—R
$-Leaders for Today
OpRev Equipper—R
$-PFI Global—R

MUSIC
$-Christian Music Today—R

PASTORS/LEADERS
$-African American Pulpit
Alpha News
$-Catholic Servant
$-Christian Century—R
$-Enrichment—R
$-InSite—R
Ministry in Motion—R
$-Ministry Today
$-Outreach—R
$-Priest

TEEN/YOUNG ADULT
$-Boundless Webzine—R
$-Breakaway
$-Brio—R
$-CLEAR Horizon
$-Credo—R
$-Essential Connection
Exodus Magazine
$-Ignite Your Faith
$-J.A.M.
$-Listen—R
$-Risen
$-Spirit
$-TC Magazine
TeensForJC—R
$-True Girl
$-Young Salvationist—R
$-YouthWalk

WOMEN
CelebrateMoms—R
Elegance—R
$-Esprit

$-Herizons
$-Horizons (women)—R
$-Journey
$-Link & Visitor—R
More to Life
$-Pauses…
Precious Times—R
Proverbs 31 Sisters
Today's Leading Ladies—R
Virtuous Woman—R
Woman of Worth—R
WT Online—R

WRITERS
$-Adv. Christian Writer—R
Areopagus
$-Christian Communicator—R
$-Cross & Quill—R
$-Fellowscript—R
Money the Write Way—R
$-New Writer's Mag.
Once Upon a Time—R
$-Poets & Writers
Write Connection
$-Writer
$-Writer's Digest
Writers Manual

LEADERSHIP
ADULT/GENERAL
$-Advance
African Voices—R
$-Angels on Earth
Bread of Life—R
Breakthrough Intercessor—R
CBN.com—R
Christian Business
Christian C. L. RECORD—R
$-Christian Courier/Cdn.—R
$-Christian Home & School
Christian Motorsports
Christian News NW—R
$-Christian Retailing
$-Christian Standard—R
$-ChristianWeek—R
$-Chronicle Christian/KS
$-City Light News—R
($)-Community Spirit—R
Connections Leadership/MOPS
$-Culture Wars—R
Desert Voice—R
Disciple's Journal—R
E-Channels—R
($)-E-Quality
$-EFCA Today—R
Evangelical Advocate—R
$-Faith Today
$-Gem—R
$-Good News—R
$-Good News, Etc.—R
Heartlight—R
$-Home Times—R

($)-HopeKeepers—R
$-In Touch
$-Light & Life
LiteraryTNT.com—R
$-Living Church
$-Lookout
$-Manna—R
$-Men of Integrity—R
Men of the Cross
$-Men.AG.org—R
$-Minnesota Christian—R
MissionWares
Mosaic—R
($)-Mutuality—R
$-National Catholic
$-New Wineskins—R
($)-NRB Magazine—R
$-Our Sunday Visitor—R
Presbyterian Outlook
Priscilla Papers
Prison Living—R
Quaker Life—R
Regent Global—R
Reverent Submissions—R
Sacred Journey—R
$-St. Anthony Messenger
$-Stewardship—R
$-Testimony—R
Trumpeter—R
$-United Church Observer—R
Urban Kingdom—R
Victory Herald—R
$-Way of St. Francis—R
Wisconsin Christian
$-World & I—R

CHILDREN
$-BREAD/God's Children—R

CHRISTIAN EDUCATION/ LIBRARY
Catholic Library
$-Children's Ministry
Christian Early Ed.—R
Christian School Ed.—R
$-Group
Ideas Unlimited—R
Jour./Research on Christian Ed.
$-Momentum
Teach Kids Essentials—R
$-Today's Catholic Teacher—R
$-Youth & CE Leadership

MISSIONS
$-Glad Tidings (Canada)—R
$-Leaders for Today
Mission Connection

PASTORS/LEADERS
$-African American Pulpit
$-Catholic Servant
$-Christian Century—R
Christian Ed. Jour. (CA)—R

Christian Management—R
$-Clergy Journal—R
$-Enrichment—R
$-Growth Points—R
$-InSite—R
$-Interpreter
Jour./Amer. Soc./Chur. Growth—R
$-Lead—R
$-Leadership—R
$-Lutheran Partners—R
$-Ministry
Ministry in Motion—R
$-Ministry Today
$-Net Results
$-Outreach—R
Plugged In
Pulpit Helps—R
Relevant Leader
$-Rev. Magazine
$-RevWriter Resource
Rick Warren's Ministry—R
$-Small Groups.com—R
Theological Digest—R
$-Willow—R
$-Word & World
$-Worship Leader
$-Your Church—R

TEEN/YOUNG ADULT
$-Boundless Webzine—R
$-Breakaway
$-Brio—R
$-CLEAR Horizon
TeensForJC—R

WOMEN
($)-Beyond the Bend—R
Elegance—R
$-Esprit
$-Horizons (women)—R
Just Between Us—R
Precious Times—R
Proverbs 31 Sisters
Right to the Heart—R
Share
$-SpiritLed Woman
$-Today's Christian Woman—R
Today's Leading Ladies—R
Women of the Cross
Women Today—R
WT Online—R

LIFESTYLE ARTICLES
ADULT/GENERAL
3V Magazine
Anointed Pages
Breakthrough
Breakthrough Intercessor—R
byFaith
$-Catholic Insight
CBN.com—R
$-Christian Journal—R

Christian Ranchman
$-ChristianWeek—R
$-Chronicle Christian/KS
$-Citizen USA
$-City Light News—R
($)-Community Spirit—R
Connections Leadership/MOPS
Creation Care—R
Evangel/OR—R
Family Journal—R
$-Focus on the Family
$-Good News, Etc.—R
$-Home Times—R
$-In His Presence—R
$-In Touch
IPHC Experience
Island Catholic—R
$-Liguorian
LiteraryTNT.com—R
$-Live—R
$-Lookout
$-Majellan—R
$-Manna—R
$-Mature Living
$-Men.AG.org—R
$-Montgomery's Journey
Nostalgia—R
$-Our Sunday Visitor—R
Ozarks Christian
$-ParentLife
$-Priority!—R
Prison Living—R
$-Pure Inspiration—R
Saved Magazine
$-Seek—R
$-Significant Living—R
Urban Kingdom—R
$-Vibrant Life—R
Victory Herald—R
$-Way of St. Francis—R

CHILDREN
$-BREAD/God's Children—R

DAILY DEVOTIONALS
$-Brink Magazine—R

MISSIONS
$-Glad Tidings (Canada)—R

TEEN/YOUNG ADULT
$-Boundless Webzine—R
$-Breakaway
$-Brio—R
$-CLEAR Direction
$-CLEAR Horizon
Exodus Magazine
$-Ignite Your Faith
$-Insight—R
$-TC Magazine

WOMEN
($)-Beyond the Bend—R

Christian Woman's Page—R
Crowned with Silver
Elegance—R
$-Fullfill
Hope for Women
$-Today's Christian Woman—R
Today's Leading Ladies—R
Women Today—R
WT Online—R

LITURGICAL
ADULT/GENERAL
($)-AGAIN—R
$-Alive Now—R
$-Arlington Catholic
$-Aujourd'hui Credo—R
$-Cathedral Age
$-Catholic Yearbook—R
$-City Light News—R
$-Culture Wars—R
Divine Ascent
$-Dovetail—R
E-Channels—R
$-Episcopal Life—R
Island Catholic—R
$-Living Church
$-Lutheran Journal—R
$-Majellan—R
$-Messenger/Sacred Heart
$-National Catholic
$-New Wineskins—R
$-Our Sunday Visitor—R
Perspectives—R
$-Prairie Messenger—R
Silver Wings—R
$-Social Justice—R
$-St. Anthony Messenger
$-Testimony—R
Urban Kingdom—R
$-Way of St. Francis—R

CHRISTIAN EDUCATION/ LIBRARY
$-Momentum

MISSIONS
$-Glad Tidings (Canada)—R

PASTORS/LEADERS
$-African American Pulpit
$-Barefoot—R
$-Catholic Servant
$-Christian Century—R
$-Clergy Journal—R
Cross Currents
$-Diocesan Dialogue—R
Lutheran Forum
$-Lutheran Partners—R
$-Ministry & Liturgy—R
$-Parish Liturgy—R
$-Preaching Well—R
$-Reformed Worship—R

$-RevWriter Resource
Rick Warren's Ministry—R
Sewanee Theo. Review
$-This Rock
$-Today's Parish
$-Word & World

WOMEN

$-Horizons (women)—R
Today's Leading Ladies—R

MARRIAGE

ADULT/GENERAL

3V Magazine
$-Advance
$-Angels on Earth
Anointed Pages
$-Arlington Catholic
$-Associated Content—R
$-Atlantic Catholic
$-BGC World—R
$-Bible Advocate—R
Bread of Life—R
Breakthrough Intercessor—R
$-Bridal Guides—R
$-Canada Lutheran—R
$-Catholic Digest—R
CBN.com—R
$-Celebrate Life—R
Christian C. L. RECORD—R
$-Christian Courier/Cdn.—R
$-Christian Examiner
$-Christian Home & School
$-Christian Journal—R
Christian Motorsports
Christian Online
Christian Ranchman
$-Christian Research
$-Christian Standard—R
$-ChristianWeek—R
$-Chronicle Christian/KS
$-City Light News—R
$-Columbia—R
($)-Community Spirit—R
$-Culture Wars—R
$-Decision
Desert Voice—R
Disciple's Journal—R
$-Discipleship Journal—R
$-Dovetail—R
E-Channels—R
($)-E-Quality
$-EFCA Today—R
$-Evangel/IN—R
Evangelical Advocate—R
$-Faith & Family
$-Faith Today
FaithWebbin—R
$-Family Digest—R
Family Journal—R
$-Family Smart e-Tips—R
$-Focus on the Family

$-Gem—R
Godly Places
Good News Journal—R
$-Good News, Etc.—R
$-Guideposts—R
Heartlight—R
$-Home Times—R
$-Homeschooling Today—R
($)-HopeKeepers—R
$-In His Presence—R
$-In Touch
$-Indian Life—R
Island Catholic—R
$-Lifeglow—R
$-Light & Life
$-Liguorian
LiteraryTNT.com—R
$-Live—R
$-Living—R
$-Living Church
$-Living Light—R
$-Lookout
$-Majellan—R
$-Manna—R
$-Mature Living
$-Men of Integrity—R
Men of the Cross
$-Men.AG.org—R
$-Minnesota Christian—R
$-Montgomery's Journey
Mosaic—R
($)-Mutuality—R
$-New Wineskins—R
$-Our Sunday Visitor—R
$-ParentLife
Pegasus Review—R
Penned from the Heart—R
Perspectives—R
$-Positive Thinking—R
$-Prairie Messenger—R
PrayerWorks—R
Priscilla Papers
Prison Living—R
$-Psychology for Living—R
$-Pure Inspiration—R
$-Purpose—R
$-Seek—R
$-Significant Living—R
SingleAgain.com—R
Spirituality for Today
$-St. Anthony Messenger
$-Testimony—R
$-Today's Christian—R
$-Together—R
Trumpeter—R
$-U.S. Catholic
Urban Kingdom—R
$-Vibrant Life—R
$-War Cry—R
$-Way of St. Francis—R
$-Wesleyan Life—R
$-Wildwood Reader—R

Wisconsin Christian
$-World & I—R

DAILY DEVOTIONALS

Penned from the Heart—R

MISSIONS

$-Glad Tidings (Canada)—R

PASTORS/LEADERS

$-African American Pulpit
$-Catholic Servant
$-Christian Century—R
$-Interpreter
Jour./Pastoral Care
$-Lutheran Partners—R
$-Ministry Today
$-Preaching Well—R
$-Rev. Magazine
Theological Digest—R
$-Today's Parish
$-Word & World

TEEN/YOUNG ADULT

$-Boundless Webzine—R
TeensForJC—R
$-Young Adult Today

WOMEN

CelebrateMoms—R
Christian Woman's Page—R
$-Come to the Fire—R
Comfort Café
Crowned with Silver
Elegance—R
First Lady
$-Girlfriend 2 Girlfriend
$-Heart & Soul
Hearts at Home—R
Hope for Women
$-Horizons (women)—R
$-inSpirit—R
$-Journey
Just Between Us—R
Ladies First
Lutheran Woman's Quar.
$-MomSense—R
P31 Woman—R
$-Pauses...
Precious Times—R
Proverbs 31 Sisters
($)-Simply Blessed—R
$-SpiritLed Woman
$-Today's Christian Woman—R
Today's Leading Ladies—R
Virtuous Woman—R
Woman of Worth—R
Women of the Cross
Women Today—R
WT Online—R

MEN'S ISSUES

ADULT/GENERAL

3V Magazine

$-Advance
$-Annals of St. Anne
$-Arlington Catholic
$-Associated Content—R
$-BGC World—R
Bread of Life—R
CBN.com—R
$-Chicken Soup Books—R
$-Christian Examiner
$-Christian Journal—R
Christian News NW—R
Christian Online
Christian Ranchman
$-ChristianWeek—R
$-Chronicle Christian/KS
$-City Light News—R
$-Columbia—R
($)-Community Spirit—R
$-Creative Nonfiction
Desert Voice—R
Disciple's Journal—R
$-Dovetail—R
E-Channels—R
($)-E-Quality
$-EFCA Today—R
$-Evangel/IN—R
$-Faith Today
Family Journal—R
$-Family Smart e-Tips—R
$-Focus on the Family
$-Gem—R
Godly Places
Good News Journal—R
$-Good News, Etc.—R
Heartlight—R
Highway News—R
$-Home Times—R
$-Homeschooling Today—R
($)-HopeKeepers—R
$-In His Presence—R
$-Indian Life—R
$-Light & Life
$-Live—R
$-Living—R
$-Lookout
$-Majellan—R
$-Manna—R
$-Men of Integrity—R
Men of the Cross
$-Men.AG.org—R
$-Minnesota Christian—R
MissionWares
$-Montgomery's Journey
Mosaic—R
($)-Mutuality—R
$-Our Sunday Visitor—R
Penned from the Heart—R
Perspectives—R
$-Positive Thinking—R
PrayerWorks—R
Presbyterian Outlook
Priscilla Papers

Prison Living—R
$-Psychology for Living—R
$-Purpose—R
Regent Global—R
$-Significant Living—R
SingleAgain.com—R
$-St. Anthony Messenger
$-Testimony—R
$-Today's Christian—R
$-Together—R
Trumpeter—R
$-U.S. Catholic
$-United Church Observer—R
Urban Kingdom—R
$-Vibrant Life—R
$-Wesleyan Life—R
West Wind Review
Wisconsin Christian
$-World & I—R
$-Written

PASTORS/LEADERS
$-African American Pulpit
$-Interpreter
$-Lutheran Partners—R
$-Word & World

TEEN/YOUNG ADULT
$-Boundless Webzine—R
$-Breakaway
TeensForJC—R

WOMEN
$-At the Center—R
Hope for Women

MIRACLES
ADULT/GENERAL
($)-AGAIN—R
$-Angels on Earth
$-Anglican Journal
$-Aujourd'hui Credo—R
$-B.C. Catholic—R
Bread of Life—R
Breakthrough Intercessor—R
$-Bridal Guides—R
$-Catholic Yearbook—R
CBN.com—R
$-CGA World—R
$-Chicken Soup Books—R
$-Christian Home & School
$-Christian Journal—R
Christian Motorsports
Christian Online
Christian Ranchman
$-Christian Standard—R
$-Christianity Today—R
$-ChristianWeek—R
$-Chronicle Christian/KS
$-City Light News—R
($)-Community Spirit—R
Connecting Point—R
$-Culture Wars—R

$-Decision
Diamond Dust
Disciple's Journal—R
Divine Ascent
E-Channels—R
$-Episcopal Life—R
Evangel/OR—R
Evangelical Advocate—R
$-Faith Today
$-Gem—R
Godly Places
$-Good News—R
$-Guideposts—R
$-Home Times—R
($)-HopeKeepers—R
$-Horizons (adult)—R
$-In His Presence—R
$-In Touch
$-Lifeglow—R
$-Light & Life
LiteraryTNT.com—R
$-Live—R
$-Living Church
$-Lookout
$-Lutheran Journal—R
$-Majellan—R
$-Men of Integrity—R
$-Minnesota Christian—R
Miracles, Healings
Mosaic—R
$-National Catholic
New Heart—R
$-New Wineskins—R
Nostalgia—R
$-Our Sunday Visitor—R
Pegasus Review—R
Penned from the Heart—R
Perspectives—R
$-Positive Thinking—R
$-Power for Living—R
PrayerWorks—R
Presbyterian Outlook
$-Priority!—R
Priscilla Papers
$-Pure Inspiration—R
$-Purpose—R
$-Seek—R
$-Significant Living—R
Silver Wings—R
Spirituality for Today
$-St. Anthony Messenger
Sword and Trumpet
Sword of the Lord—R
$-Testimony—R
$-Today's Christian—R
Trumpeter—R
Urban Kingdom—R
Victory Herald—R
Wisconsin Christian

CHILDREN
$-BREAD/God's Children—R

$-Guide—R
$-Sparkle—R

CHRISTIAN EDUCATION/ LIBRARY
Catholic Library
$-Children's Ministry
Christian Librarian—R
$-Youth & CE Leadership

DAILY DEVOTIONALS
Penned from the Heart—R

MISSIONS
$-Evangelical Missions—R
Intl. Jour./Frontier—R
$-Leaders for Today
Missiology
Mission Frontiers
$-New World Outlook
$-One
OpRev Equipper—R
$-PFI Global—R
$-PIME World—R
Railroad Evangelist—R
Women of the Harvest

PASTORS/LEADERS
$-African American Pulpit
$-Clergy Journal—R
$-Interpreter
Jour./Amer. Soc./Chur. Growth—R
$-Lutheran Partners—R
$-Ministry Today
Pulpit Helps—R
Rick Warren's Ministry—R
$-This Rock
$-Word & World

TEEN/YOUNG ADULT
$-Boundless Webzine—R
$-Brio—R
$-Credo—R
$-Devo'Zine—R
G4T Ink—R
$-Insight—R
$-Real Faith in Life—R
$-Young Salvationist—R

WOMEN
$-Come to the Fire—R
Elegance—R
$-Esprit
Hearts at Home—R
Hope for Women
$-Horizons (women)—R
$-Journey
Just Between Us—R
$-Link & Visitor—R
$-SpiritLed Woman
Today's Leading Ladies—R
WT Online—R

WRITERS
Opinari—R

MISSIONS
ADULT/GENERAL
Breakthrough Intercessor—R
$-Christian Home & School
Christian Ranchman
Church Herald & Holiness—R
$-City Light News—R
$-Discipleship Journal—R
$-Good News, Etc.—R
LiteraryTNT.com—R
$-Live—R
$-On Mission
$-Our Sunday Visitor—R
PrayerWorks—R
Quaker Life—R
Spirituality for Today
$-Way of St. Francis—R

CHILDREN
$-BREAD/God's Children—R

CHRISTIAN EDUCATION/ LIBRARY
Teach Kids Essentials—R

DAILY DEVOTIONALS
$-Brink Magazine—R

MISSIONS
East-West Church
$-Glad Tidings (Canada)—R
Intl. Jour./Frontier—R
Lausanne World Pulse
Mission Connection
MissionsMagizinet

PASTORS/LEADERS
$-Enrichment—R

TEEN/YOUNG ADULT
$-Brio—R
$-CLEAR Direction
$-CLEAR Horizon
Exodus Magazine

WOMEN
$-Today's Christian Woman—R
Today's Leading Ladies—R

MONEY MANAGEMENT
ADULT/GENERAL
$-Anglican Journal
$-Associated Content—R
$-Bridal Guides—R
byFaith
$-Catholic Forester—R
$-CBA Retailers
CBN.com—R
$-Christian Journal—R
Christian Motorsports
Christian Online
Christian Ranchman
$-ChristianWeek—R
$-Chronicle Christian/KS

$-City Light News—R
($)-Community Spirit—R
Connecting Point—R
$-Creative Nonfiction
Disciple's Journal—R
$-Discipleship Journal—R
E-Channels—R
Evangelical Advocate—R
$-Faith & Family
$-Faith Today
FaithWebbin—R
$-Family Smart e-Tips—R
$-Focus on the Family
$-Gem—R
Heartlight—R
Highway News—R
$-Home Times—R
$-Homeschooling Today—R
$-In His Presence—R
$-In Touch
$-Lifeglow—R
$-Light & Life
$-Live—R
$-Lookout
$-Manna—R
$-Mature Years—R
$-Men.AG.org—R
$-Montgomery's Journey
($)-NRB Magazine—R
$-Our Sunday Visitor—R
$-ParentLife
Penned from the Heart—R
($)-P.O.W.E.R.
Prison Living—R
$-Significant Living—R
SingleAgain.com—R
$-St. Anthony Messenger
$-Testimony—R
$-Today's Christian—R
$-Together—R
Trumpeter—R
Urban Kingdom—R
$-War Cry—R
Wisconsin Christian
$-World & I—R

CHILDREN
$-Archaeology
$-BREAD/God's Children—R
$-SHINEbrightly—R

DAILY DEVOTIONALS
Penned from the Heart—R

MISSIONS
$-Glad Tidings (Canada)—R

PASTORS/LEADERS
$-African American Pulpit
Christian Management—R
$-Clergy Journal—R
$-Enrichment—R
$-Interpreter

$-Lutheran Partners—R
Rick Warren's Ministry—R
$-Today's Parish
$-Your Church—R

TEEN/YOUNG ADULT
$-Boundless Webzine—R
$-Breakaway
$-Brio—R
$-CLEAR Direction
$-Real Faith in Life—R

WOMEN
CelebrateMoms—R
Christian Women Today—R
Elegance—R
$-Heart & Soul
Hearts at Home—R
Hope for Women
$-Horizons (women)—R
$-InspiredMoms—R
$-Journey
Just Between Us—R
Life Tools for Women
More to Life
Precious Times—R
($)-Simply Blessed—R
$-Today's Christian Woman—R
Today's Leading Ladies—R
Virtuous Woman—R
Woman of Worth—R
Women Today—R
WT Online—R

WRITERS
Money the Write Way—R

MOVIE REVIEWS
ADULT/GENERAL
$-Abilities
$-Associated Content—R
$-Atlantic Catholic
Breakthrough Intercessor—R
byFaith
CBN.com—R
Charlotte World
$-Christian Herald—R
$-Christian Journal—R
$-Christianity Today Movies—R
$-City Light News—R
Creation Care—R
$-Cresset
$-Eureka Street
$-Faith & Friends—R
Good News Today
$-Good News/S. Florida
Heartland Gatekeeper—R
$-Home Times—R
$-Imagine
$-Interim—R
Island Catholic
LiteraryTNT.com—R

MovieGuide
$-Our Sunday Visitor—R
Perspectives—R
$-Prairie Messenger—R
Quaker Life—R
Rock & Sling
Urban Kingdom—R

CHILDREN
$-Sparkle—R

DAILY DEVOTIONALS
$-Brink Magazine—R

MISSIONS
$-Glad Tidings (Canada)—R

MUSIC
Hymn

TEEN/YOUNG ADULT
$-Breakaway
Exodus Magazine
$-Ignite Your Faith
$-Risen
$-TC Magazine

WOMEN
$-Herizons
Hope for Women
Today's Leading Ladies—R
Virtuous Woman—R
Woman of Worth—R
WT Online—R

MUSIC REVIEWS
ADULT/GENERAL
$-Advance
$-Arlington Catholic
$-Associated Content—R
$-Atlantic Catholic
$-Aujourd'hui Credo—R
$-Catholic Peace Voice—R
CBN.com—R
$-Charisma
Charlotte World
$-Christian Herald—R
$-Christian Journal—R
Christian Media—R
$-Christian Renewal—R
$-Christian Retailing
$-Citizen USA
$-City Light News—R
$-Cresset
Desert Voice—R
Diamond Dust
E-Channels—R
$-Eureka Street
$-Faith & Family
$-Faith Today
$-Good News/S. Florida
$-Haruah—R
Heartland Gatekeeper—R
Heartlight—R
$-Imagine

Infuze
$-Interim—R
LiteraryTNT.com—R
$-Minnesota Christian—R
MovieGuide
$-Our Sunday Visitor—R
$-Prairie Messenger—R
$-Presbyterians Today—R
$-Prism
$-Pure Inspiration—R
Quaker Life—R
Rock & Sling
$-Rose & Thorn
$-Testimony—R
Trumpeter—R
Urban Kingdom—R
$-World & I—R

CHILDREN
$-Sparkle—R

CHRISTIAN EDUCATION/ LIBRARY
Catholic Library
$-Church Libraries—R

DAILY DEVOTIONALS
$-Brink Magazine—R

MISSIONS
$-Glad Tidings (Canada)—R
Women of the Harvest

MUSIC
$-Christian Music Today—R
Christian Music Weekly—R
$-Creator—R
Gospel Synergy
Tradition

PASTORS/LEADERS
$-Barefoot—R
$-Christian Century—R
$-Interpreter
$-Ministry Today
$-Reformed Worship—R
Technologies for Worship—R
$-Willow—R
$-Worship Leader

TEEN/YOUNG ADULT
$-Breakaway
$-Credo—R
$-Devo'Zine—R
Exodus Magazine
$-Ignite Your Faith
$-Risen
$-Sharing the VICTORY—R
$-TC Magazine
TeensForJC—R
$-True Girl

WOMEN
$-Herizons
Hope for Women

Precious Times—R
Proverbs 31 Sisters
Today's Leading Ladies—R
Virtuous Woman—R
WT Online—R

NATURE
ADULT/GENERAL
$-Animal Trails—R
$-Associated Content—R
$-Aujourd'hui Credo—R
CBN.com—R
$-Christian Courier/Cdn.—R
$-Christian Renewal—R
$-Chronicle Christian/KS
($)-Community Spirit—R
Creation
Creation Care—R
$-Creation Illustrated—R
$-Creative Nonfiction
$-Gem—R
$-In Touch
Keys to Living—R
$-Lifeglow—R
$-Light & Life
LiteraryTNT.com—R
$-Lutheran Digest—R
$-Our Sunday Visitor—R
$-Over the Back Fence—R
Pegasus Review—R
Penned from the Heart—R
PrayerWorks—R
Prison Living—R
Quaker Life—R
Ruminate
Sacred Journey—R
$-Salvo
$-Science & Spirit
$-Seek—R
$-St. Anthony Messenger
$-Storyteller—R
$-Testimony—R
Trumpeter—R
Urban Kingdom—R
$-Vista
$-Way of St. Francis—R
$-Wildwood Reader—R
Wisconsin Christian
$-World & I—R

CHILDREN
$-Archaeology
$-BREAD/God's Children—R
$-Cadet Quest—R
$-Focus/Clubhouse Jr.
$-Guide—R
$-Nature Friend—R
$-Partners—R
$-SHINEbrightly—R
Skipping Stones
$-Sparkle—R

CHRISTIAN EDUCATION/ LIBRARY
Teach Kids Essentials—R

MISSIONS
$-Glad Tidings (Canada)—R

PASTORS/LEADERS
$-Word & World

TEEN/YOUNG ADULT
$-Boundless Webzine—R
$-Devo'Zine—R

WOMEN
Today's Leading Ladies—R
Virtuous Woman—R
Woman of Worth—R
WT Online—R

NEWS FEATURES
ADULT/GENERAL
Ambassador
Arizona Family
$-Arkansas Catholic—R
$-Associated Content—R
$-Atlantic Catholic
Baptist Standard
Beacon
Biblical Recorder
Breakthrough Intercessor—R
$-Canadian Mennonite—R
CanadianChristianity
$-Cathedral Age
$-Catholic Insight
$-Catholic New York
$-Catholic Peace Voice—R
$-Catholic Sentinel
CBN.com—R
Challenge Weekly
$-Charisma
Charlotte World
Christian C. L. RECORD—R
Christian Chronicle
Christian Courier/WI—R
$-Christian Examiner
Christian News NW—R
Christian Ranchman
$-Christian Renewal—R
$-Christian Research
$-Christian Response—R
$-Christian Retailing
$-Christianity Today Movies—R
$-ChristianWeek—R
Chronicle - IN Edition
$-Chronicle Christian/KS
Church of England News
$-Citizen USA
$-City Light News—R
$-Commonweal
($)-Community Spirit—R
$-Compass Direct
Creation Care—R

Desert Christian
Desert Voice—R
$-Disaster News
$-Dovetail—R
Encompass
$-Eureka Street
Evangel/OR—R
$-Faith Today
Florida Baptist Witness
Founders Journal
Good News Connection
Good News Today
Good News!
$-Good News, Etc.—R
$-Good News/S. Florida
Heartland Gatekeeper—R
$-Home Times—R
($)-HopeKeepers—R
($)-Impact—R
$-Indian Life—R
$-Interchange
Island Catholic—R
$-LarkNews.com
$-Liberty
LifeSite News
$-Light & Life
Louisiana Baptist
$-Manna—R
Messianic Perspectives
Michiana Christian
$-Minnesota Christian—R
$-Montana Catholic
MovieGuide
$-National Catholic
Network
$-Our Sunday Visitor—R
Ozarks Christian
$-Priority!—R
Prison Living—R
Quaker Life—R
$-Science & Spirit
Society/Prevention of Cruelty
$-St. Anthony Messenger
Sword and Trumpet
$-Testimony—R
$-Today's Christian—R
Tri-State Voice
Trumpeter—R
$-Upscale
Urban Kingdom—R
$-War Cry—R
$-World & I—R

CHILDREN
$-Partners—R
$-Pockets—R

CHRISTIAN EDUCATION/ LIBRARY
Teach Kids Essentials—R

DAILY DEVOTIONALS
$-Brink Magazine—R

MISSIONS
$-Glad Tidings (Canada)—R
OpRev Equipper—R

MUSIC
$-Christian Music Today—R

PASTORS/LEADERS
Alpha News
$-Christian Century—R
$-Ministry Today
$-Pray!—R
Pulpit Helps—R
Rick Warren's Ministry—R

TEEN/YOUNG ADULT
$-Breakaway
$-Listen—R

WOMEN
$-Herizons
Hope for Women
Today's Leading Ladies—R
WT Online—R

WRITERS
Money the Write Way—R
$-Poets & Writers

NEWSPAPERS/TABLOIDS
Alpha News
Ambassador
$-Anglican Journal
Arizona Family
$-Arkansas Catholic—R
$-Arlington Catholic
$-Atlantic Catholic
$-B.C. Catholic—R
Baptist Standard
Beacon
Biblical Recorder
CanadianChristianity
$-Catholic New York
Catholic Register
$-Catholic Sentinel
$-Catholic Servant
$-Catholic Telegraph
Challenge Weekly
Charlotte World
Christian Chronicle
$-Christian Courier/Cdn.—R
Christian Courier/WI—R
$-Christian Examiner
$-Christian Herald—R
$-Christian Journal—R
Christian Media—R
Christian News NW—R
Christian Observer
Christian Ranchman
$-Christian Renewal—R
$-ChristianWeek—R
Chronicle - IN Edition
$-Chronicle Christian/KS

Church of England News
$-Citizen USA
$-City Light News—R
$-Common Ground—R
Desert Christian
Desert Voice—R
Disciple's Journal—R
$-Episcopal Life—R
Evangelical Times
Florida Baptist Witness
Good News Connection
Good News Journal—R
Good News Today
Good News!
$-Good News, Etc.—R
$-Good News/S. Florida
Heartland Gatekeeper—R
$-Home Times—R
$-In His Presence—R
$-Indian Life—R
$-Interchange
$-Interim—R
Island Catholic—R
$-Layman
LifeSite News
Light of the World
$-Living—R
$-Living Light—R
Living Stones
Louisiana Baptist
$-Manna—R
Messianic Times
Michiana Christian
$-Minnesota Christian—R
$-Montana Catholic
Mosaic—R
$-National Catholic
Network
New Frontier
$-Our Sunday Visitor—R
Ozarks Christian
$-Ozarks Senior Living—R
$-Prairie Messenger—R
PrayerWorks—R
Pulpit Helps—R
Senior Connection
SW Kansas Faith
Sword of the Lord—R
$-Together—R
Tri-State Voice
Wisconsin Christian

NOSTALGIA
ADULT/GENERAL
$-Associated Content—R
$-Catholic Forester—R
$-Chronicle Christian/KS
$-City Light News—R
($)-Community Spirit—R
Family Journal—R
$-Good News, Etc.—R

$-Home Times—R
$-In Touch
$-Lutheran Digest—R
$-Mature Living
Nostalgia—R
$-Over the Back Fence—R
PrayerWorks—R
Prison Living—R
$-Seek—R
$-Storyteller—R
$-Testimony—R
Urban Kingdom—R
Victory Herald—R
$-Vista

CHILDREN
$-Faces

MISSIONS
$-Glad Tidings (Canada)—R

PASTORS/LEADERS
$-Priest

TEEN/YOUNG ADULT
$-InsideOut—R

WOMEN
Crowned with Silver
$-Journey
WT Online—R

ONLINE PUBLICATIONS
ADULT/GENERAL
$-Advance
$-America
$-Anglican Journal
Answers
$-Apocalypse Chronicles—R
$-Associated Content—R
Behind the Hammer
($)-Believer's Bay
Books & Culture
Breakthrough
Breakthrough Intercessor—R
CanadianChristianity
$-Cathedral Age
$-Catholic Digest—R
CBN.com—R
Challenge Weekly
$-Charisma
Chocolate Pages
Christian C. L. RECORD—R
Christian Chronicle
Christian Computing—R
$-Christian Examiner
$-Christian Journal—R
Christian Media—R
Christian Online
Christian Outlook
$-Christian Single
$-Christian Standard—R

$-Christianity Today—R
$-Christianity Today Movies—R
$-Chronicle Christian/KS
$-Columbia—R
$-Company—R
$-Compass Direct
CrossHome.com
$-Decision
Diamond Dust
$-Disaster News
Disciple's Journal—R
Divine Ascent
$-Drama Ministry—R
$-DreamSeeker—R
($)-E-Quality
Esdras' Scroll
Eternal Ink—R
$-Eureka Street
FaithWebbin—R
Family Journal—R
$-Family Smart e-Tips—R
Godly Places
Gold Country Families—R
Good News Connection
Good News!
$-Good News/S. Florida
Haiku Hippodrome
$-Haruah—R
Heartlight—R
($)-Impact—R
Infuze
$-Interim—R
Koinonia
$-LarkNews.com
$-Layman
$-Leben—R
LifeSite News
LifeTimes Catholic
LiteraryTNT.com—R
$-Lookout
$-Manna—R
$-Marian Helper
Men of the Cross
$-Men.AG.org—R
$-Messenger/St. Anthony
$-MindFlights—R
$-Minnesota Christian—R
MissionWares
$-National Catholic
$-New Wineskins—R
$-Now What?—R
($)-NRB Magazine—R
$-On Mission
Perspectives—R
PrayerWorks—R
$-Priority!—R
Regent Global—R
$-Relevant
$-Rose & Thorn
Sacred Journey—R
SingleAgain.com—R
Society/Prevention of Cruelty

$-Sound Body—R
$-St. Anthony Messenger
$-Testimony—R
$-Today's Christian—R
$-Today's Pentecostal—R
($)-Touched By the Hand
Trumpeter—R
$-U.S. Catholic
Urban Kingdom—R
Victory Herald—R
$-World & I—R

CHILDREN
$-American Girl—R
$-Archaeology
$-Focus/Clubhouse
$-Focus/Clubhouse Jr.
Girls Connection
$-Keys for Kids—R
$-Kids' Ark—R

CHRISTIAN EDUCATION/ LIBRARY
Ideas Unlimited—R

DAILY DEVOTIONALS
$-Forward Day by Day

MISSIONS
Mission Frontiers
OpRev Equipper—R
Women of the Harvest

MUSIC
$-Christian Music Today—R
$-Creator—R

PASTORS/LEADERS
Alpha News
$-Barefoot—R
Churchlife Inspiration
Cook Intl.
$-InSite—R
$-Interpreter
$-Leadership—R
$-Lutheran Partners—R
Ministry in Motion—R
$-Net Results
$-Newsletter Newsletter
Preaching
$-PreachingToday.com
Pulpit Helps—R
$-Reformed Worship—R
Relevant Leader
$-Rev. Magazine
$-RevWriter Resource
Rick Warren's Ministry—R
$-Small Groups.com—R
Technologies for Worship—R
$-Willow—R
$-Youthworker

TEEN/YOUNG ADULT
$-Boundless Webzine—R
Connected

Student Life
TeensForJC—R
$-Young Salvationist—R

WOMEN
$-At the Center—R
Breathe Again
CelebrateMoms—R
Christian Woman's Page—R
Christian Women Today—R
$-Come to the Fire—R
Comfort Café
$-Dabbling Mum—R
Elegance—R
$-Fullfill
$-Girlfriend 2 Girlfriend
Handmaidens
($)-History's Women—R
Hope for Women
Inspired Women
$-InspiredMoms—R
L.I.V.E.
Life Tools for Women
$-Melody of the Heart
Proverbs 31 Sisters
Right to the Heart—R
Today's Leading Ladies—R
Virtuous Woman—R
Women of the Cross
Women Today—R
Women's Ministry
WT Online—R

WRITERS
Author-Me
ChristianWriters
Esdras' Scroll—R
$-Freelance Writer's Report—R
Money the Write Way—R
Opinari—R
$-Shades of Romance—R
$-Spirit-Led Writer—R
WriteToInspire
Writing Corner—R

OPINION PIECES
ADULT/GENERAL
$-Animal Trails—R
$-Annals of St. Anne
$-Arkansas Catholic—R
$-Arlington Catholic
$-Associated Content—R
$-B.C. Catholic—R
Breakthrough Intercessor—R
$-Catholic New York
$-Catholic Peace Voice—R
CBN.com—R
Christian C. L. RECORD—R
$-Christian Courier/Cdn.—R
$-Christian Examiner
$-Christian Renewal—R
$-Christian Research
$-Christianity Today—R

$-Christianity Today Movies—R
$-ChristianWeek—R
$-Chronicle Christian/KS
Church of England News
$-Citizen USA
$-City Light News—R
$-Culture Wars—R
$-DisciplesWorld
($)-E-Quality
$-Episcopal Life—R
$-Eureka Street
$-Faith Today
Good News Journal—R
$-Good News, Etc.—R
$-Home Times—R
($)-HopeKeepers—R
$-Indian Life—R
$-Interim—R
Island Catholic—R
$-Light & Life
$-Living Church
$-Lookout
$-Minnesota Christian—R
Mosaic—R
MovieGuide
$-National Catholic
($)-NRB Magazine—R
$-Our Sunday Visitor—R
Perspectives—R
$-Prairie Messenger—R
Presbyterian Outlook
Prison Living—R
Quaker Life—R
Regent Global—R
$-Salvo
$-Social Justice—R
$-St. Anthony Messenger
$-Testimony—R
Trumpeter—R
$-U.S. Catholic
$-United Church Observer—R
Urban Kingdom—R
$-Wittenburg Door—R
$-World & I—R
$-Written

CHILDREN
$-Archaeology
$-New Moon—R
Skipping Stones

CHRISTIAN EDUCATION/
LIBRARY
Catholic Library
$-Group
Jour. of Christianity—R
$-Teachers of Vision—R

MISSIONS
$-Evangelical Missions—R
$-Glad Tidings (Canada)—R
OpRev Equipper—R

MUSIC
$-Christian Music Today—R

PASTORS/LEADERS
$-Catholic Servant
$-Ministry Today
$-Priest
$-Word & World
$-Worship Leader

TEEN/YOUNG ADULT
TeensForJC—R

WOMEN
($)-Beyond the Bend—R
Crowned with Silver
$-Esprit
Hope for Women
$-Today's Christian Woman—R

WRITERS
$-Adv. Christian Writer—R
Areopagus
Money the Write Way—R
$-New Writer's Mag.
Opinari—R

PARENTING
ADULT/GENERAL
$-Advance
American Tract—R
$-Angels on Earth
$-Annals of St. Anne
$-Arkansas Catholic—R
$-Arlington Catholic
$-Associated Content—R
$-Atlantic Catholic
$-BGC World—R
Bread of Life—R
Breakthrough Intercessor—R
$-Bridal Guides—R
$-Canada Lutheran—R
$-Catholic Digest—R
$-Catholic Yearbook—R
CBN.com—R
$-Celebrate Life—R
$-Chicken Soup Books—R
$-Christian Courier/Cdn.—R
$-Christian Home & School
Christian Motorsports
Christian Observer
Christian Ranchman
$-Christian Renewal—R
$-Christian Research
$-ChristianWeek—R
$-Chronicle Christian/KS
$-City Light News—R
$-Columbia—R
($)-Community Spirit—R
Creation Care—R
$-Culture Wars—R
Disciple's Journal—R
$-Discipleship Journal—R

$-Dovetail—R
Evangelical Advocate—R
$-Faith & Family
$-Faith Today
FaithWebbin—R
$-Family Digest—R
Family Journal—R
$-Family Smart e-Tips—R
$-Focus on the Family
$-Focus on Your Child
$-Gem—R
Gold Country Families—R
Good News Journal—R
$-Good News, Etc.—R
Heartlight—R
Highway News—R
$-Home Times—R
$-Homeschooling Today—R
($)-HopeKeepers—R
$-Ideals—R
$-In His Presence—R
$-Indian Life—R
Koinonia
$-Light & Life
$-Liguorian
LiteraryTNT.com—R
$-Live—R
$-Living—R
$-Living Light—R
$-Lookout
$-Lutheran Journal—R
$-Majellan—R
$-Manna—R
$-Men of Integrity—R
$-Men.AG.org—R
$-Minnesota Christian—R
$-Montgomery's Journey
Mosaic—R
MovieGuide
($)-Mutuality—R
$-New Wineskins—R
$-Our Sunday Visitor—R
$-ParentLife
Pegasus Review—R
Penned from the Heart—R
$-Positive Thinking—R
$-Power for Living—R
$-Prairie Messenger—R
Prison Living—R
$-Psychology for Living—R
$-Seek—R
SingleAgain.com—R
$-Special Living—R
Spirituality for Today
$-St. Anthony Messenger
SW Kansas Faith
$-Testimony—R
$-Today's Christian—R
$-Today's Pentecostal—R
$-Together—R
Trumpeter—R

$-U.S. Catholic
Urban Kingdom—R
$-Vibrant Life—R
Victory Herald—R
$-War Cry—R
$-Wesleyan Life—R
Wisconsin Christian
$-World & I—R

CHILDREN
$-BREAD/God's Children—R

CHRISTIAN EDUCATION/
LIBRARY
$-Children's Ministry

DAILY DEVOTIONALS
Penned from the Heart—R

MISSIONS
$-Glad Tidings (Canada)—R

PASTORS/LEADERS
$-Catholic Servant
$-Interpreter
Plugged In

WOMEN
$-At the Center—R
$-Canticle
CelebrateMoms—R
Christian Woman's Page—R
$-Come to the Fire—R
$-Dabbling Mum—R
Elegance—R
$-Esprit
$-Girlfriend 2 Girlfriend
Handmaiden—R
$-Heart & Soul
Hearts at Home—R
Hope for Women
$-InspiredMoms—R
$-inSpirit—R
$-Journey
Just Between Us—R
$-Link & Visitor—R
Lutheran Woman's Quar.
$-MomSense—R
P31 Woman—R
$-Pauses…
Precious Times—R
Proverbs 31 Sisters
($)-Simply Blessed—R
$-SpiritLed Woman
$-Today's Christian Woman—R
Today's Leading Ladies—R
Virtuous Woman—R
Woman of Worth—R
Women Today—R
WT Online—R

PEACE ISSUES
ADULT/GENERAL
$-Animal Trails—R

$-Associated Content—R
$-Aujourd'hui Credo—R
$-Bible Advocate—R
$-Cathedral Age
CBN.com—R
$-ChristianWeek—R
$-City Light News—R
($)-Community Spirit—R
$-Eureka Street
$-Home Times—R
Island Catholic—R
$-Liguorian
$-Living—R
$-Lookout
($)-Mennonite Historian—R
Mosaic—R
$-National Catholic
$-Our Sunday Visitor—R
Penned from the Heart—R
Perspectives—R
Prison Living—R
$-Pure Inspiration—R
$-Purpose—R
Quaker Life—R
Sacred Journey—R
$-Seek—R
Silver Wings—R
Spirituality for Today
$-Testimony—R
$-Together—R
$-U.S. Catholic
Urban Kingdom—R
$-Way of St. Francis—R

CHILDREN
$-New Moon—R
$-Pockets—R
Skipping Stones

CHRISTIAN EDUCATION/
LIBRARY
Catholic Library

DAILY DEVOTIONALS
$-Brink Magazine—R

MISSIONS
$-Glad Tidings (Canada)—R

PASTORS/LEADERS
$-African American Pulpit
$-Christian Century—R
$-Clergy Journal—R
$-Interpreter
$-Lutheran Partners—R

TEEN/YOUNG ADULT
$-True Girl

WOMEN
$-Esprit
$-Herizons
$-Horizons (women)—R
$-Pauses…

Today's Leading Ladies—R
Women Today—R

PERSONAL EXPERIENCE
ADULT/GENERAL
African Voices—R
($)-AGAIN—R
$-Alive Now—R
$-Angels on Earth
$-Animal Trails—R
$-Annals of St. Anne
$-Associated Content—R
$-Australian Catholics—R
$-B.C. Catholic—R
Behind the Hammer
$-BGC World—R
$-Bible Advocate—R
Bread of Life—R
Breakthrough
Breakthrough Intercessor—R
$-Catholic Digest—R
$-Catholic New York
$-Catholic Peace Voice—R
$-Catholic Yearbook—R
CBN.com—R
$-Celebrate Life—R
$-CGA World—R
$-Chicken Soup Books—R
$-Christian Courier/Cdn.—R
$-Christian Journal—R
Christian Motorsports
Christian Observer
Christian Online
$-Christianity Today—R
$-ChristianWeek—R
$-City Light News—R
$-Commonweal
($)-Community Spirit—R
$-Creative Nonfiction
$-Decision
Diamond Dust
$-DisciplesWorld
$-Dovetail—R
E-Channels—R
($)-E-Quality
$-EFCA Today—R
$-Evangel/IN—R
Evangelical Advocate—R
$-Faith Today
$-Family Digest—R
$-Focus on the Family
$-Gem—R
Gold Country Families—R
Good News Journal—R
$-Good News, Etc.—R
$-Guideposts—R
Halo Magazine
Highway News—R
$-Home Times—R
($)-HopeKeepers—R
$-Horizons (adult)—R

$-Ideals—R
$-In His Presence—R
$-In Touch
Island Catholic—R
Keys to Living—R
Leaves—R
$-Lifeglow—R
$-Light & Life
$-Liguorian
LiteraryTNT.com—R
$-Live—R
$-Living—R
$-Living Church
$-Lookout
$-Lutheran Journal—R
$-Majellan—R
$-Marian Helper
$-Mature Living
$-MESSAGE
$-MindFlights—R
Miracles, Healings
($)-Mutuality—R
New Heart—R
$-New Wineskins—R
Nostalgia—R
$-Now What?—R
$-On Mission
$-Ozarks Senior Living—R
Penned from the Heart—R
$-Positive Thinking—R
$-Power for Living—R
PrayerWorks—R
Prison Living—R
$-Psychology for Living—R
$-Pure Inspiration—R
$-Purpose—R
Quaker Life—R
Reverent Submissions—R
Ruminate
Sacred Journey—R
$-Seek—R
Sharing—R
Silver Wings—R
$-Spiritual Life
$-St. Anthony Messenger
$-Storyteller—R
$-Testimony—R
$-Today's Christian—R
$-Together—R
Trumpeter—R
$-Upscale
Urban Kingdom—R
Victory Herald—R
$-Victory in Grace—R
$-Vision—R
$-Vista
$-War Cry—R
$-Way of St. Francis—R
$-Wesleyan Life—R
$-Wittenburg Door—R
$-World & I—R

CHILDREN

$-Faces
$-Guide—R
$-New Moon—R
$-Partners—R
Skipping Stones
$-Sparkle—R

CHRISTIAN EDUCATION/
LIBRARY

$-Children's Ministry
$-Group
$-Journal/Adventist Ed.—R
Teach Kids Essentials—R
$-Teachers of Vision—R

DAILY DEVOTIONALS

CLEAR Living
Penned from the Heart—R
$-Rejoice!

MISSIONS

$-Evangelical Missions—R
$-Glad Tidings (Canada)—R
$-PIME World—R
Railroad Evangelist—R
Women of the Harvest

PASTORS/LEADERS

$-Catholic Servant
Jour./Pastoral Care
$-Lead—R
$-Lutheran Partners—R
$-Priest
$-Rev. Magazine
$-Today's Parish
$-Worship Leader
$-Youthworker

TEEN/YOUNG ADULT

$-Boundless Webzine—R
$-Breakaway
$-Brio—R
$-CLEAR Direction
$-Devo'Zine—R
Exodus Magazine
$-Ignite Your Faith
$-InsideOut—R
$-Insight—R
$-Real Faith in Life—R
$-Spirit
$-TC Magazine
TeensForJC—R
$-True Girl
$-Young Salvationist—R

WOMEN

CelebrateMoms—R
Christian Woman's Page—R
$-Come to the Fire—R
Comfort Café
$-Dabbling Mum—R
Elegance—R
$-Esprit

Handmaiden—R
Hearts at Home—R
$-Herizons
Hope for Women
Inspired Women
$-Journey
Just Between Us—R
L.I.V.E.
$-Melody of the Heart
$-MomSense—R
$-Pauses…
Precious Times—R
($)-Simply Blessed—R
$-SpiritLed Woman
$-Today's Christian Woman—R
Today's Leading Ladies—R
Virtuous Woman—R
Woman of Worth—R
Women Today—R
WT Online—R

WRITERS

Areopagus
Money the Write Way—R
$-New Writer's Mag.
NW Christian Author—R
Once Upon a Time—R

PERSONAL GROWTH
ADULT/GENERAL

$-Alive Now—R
$-Annals of St. Anne
$-Associated Content—R
$-Bible Advocate—R
Bread of Life—R
Breakthrough Intercessor—R
$-Catholic Digest—R
$-Catholic Forester—R
$-Catholic Peace Voice—R
CBN.com—R
$-Christian Courier/Cdn.—R
$-Christian Journal—R
Christian Online
Christian Ranchman
$-City Light News—R
$-Common Ground—R
($)-Community Spirit—R
Connections Leadership/MOPS
$-Decision
$-Discipleship Journal—R
Divine Ascent
$-Dovetail—R
E-Channels—R
$-Evangel/IN—R
Evangelical Advocate—R
$-Faith & Family
$-Faith & Friends—R
$-Faith Today
$-Family Digest—R
Family Journal—R
$-Focus on the Family

$-Gem—R
Good News Journal—R
$-Good News, Etc.—R
$-Home Times—R
($)-HopeKeepers—R
$-Horizons (adult)—R
$-Ideals—R
$-In His Presence—R
$-In Touch
$-Indian Life—R
IPHC Experience
Island Catholic—R
Keys to Living—R
Leaves—R
$-Light & Life
$-Liguorian
LiteraryTNT.com—R
$-Live—R
$-Living—R
$-Living Church
$-Lookout
$-Lutheran Digest—R
$-Majellan—R
$-Manna—R
$-Mature Living
$-Mature Years—R
$-Men of Integrity—R
$-MindFlights—R
Mosaic—R
($)-Mutuality—R
New Heart—R
$-New Wineskins—R
$-Now What?—R
Penned from the Heart—R
$-Positive Thinking—R
$-Prairie Messenger—R
PrayerWorks—R
Prison Living—R
$-Psychology for Living—R
$-Pure Inspiration—R
$-Purpose—R
Quaker Life—R
Regent Global—R
Reverent Submissions—R
Sacred Journey—R
$-Seek—R
SingleAgain.com—R
$-St. Anthony Messenger
$-Stewardship—R
$-Testimony—R
$-Today's Christian—R
$-Together—R
Trumpeter—R
Urban Kingdom—R
Victory Herald—R
$-Victory in Grace—R
$-War Cry—R
$-Way of St. Francis—R
$-Wildwood Reader—R
$-World & I—R

CHILDREN
$-Archaeology
$-Guide—R
Skipping Stones
$-Sparkle—R
$-Winner—R

CHRISTIAN EDUCATION/ LIBRARY
$-Children's Ministry
Christian Early Ed.—R
Teach Kids Essentials—R
$-Youth & CE Leadership

DAILY DEVOTIONALS
Penned from the Heart—R

MISSIONS
$-Glad Tidings (Canada)—R
Women of the Harvest

PASTORS/LEADERS
Christian Management—R
$-Ministry Today
$-RevWriter Resource

TEEN/YOUNG ADULT
$-Boundless Webzine—R
$-Breakaway
$-Brio—R
$-CLEAR Direction
$-CLEAR Horizon
Exodus Magazine
$-Insight—R
TeensForJC—R
$-True Girl
$-Young Adult Today
$-Young Salvationist—R

WOMEN
CelebrateMoms—R
Christian Woman's Page—R
$-Come to the Fire—R
Elegance—R
$-Esprit
$-Fullfill
Hearts at Home—R
Hope for Women
$-Horizons (women)—R
$-inSpirit—R
$-Journey
Just Between Us—R
L.I.V.E.
$-MomSense—R
P31 Woman—R
Precious Times—R
($)-Simply Blessed—R
$-SpiritLed Woman
$-Today's Christian Woman—R
Today's Leading Ladies—R
Virtuous Woman—R
Women Today—R
WT Online—R

WRITERS
Areopagus
Opinari—R

PHOTO ESSAYS

ADULT/GENERAL
$-Associated Content—R
$-Cathedral Age
Christian Motorsports
Creation Care—R
Desert Voice—R
$-Faith & Family
Family Journal—R
$-Good News, Etc.—R
$-Home Times—R
$-Imagine
$-In Touch
Island Catholic—R
Nostalgia—R
$-Our Sunday Visitor—R
$-Ozarks Senior Living—R
$-Priority!—R
$-Prism
Prison Living—R
Rock & Sling
Sacred Journey—R
$-Salvo
$-St. Anthony Messenger
$-Today's Christian—R
Urban Kingdom—R
$-Wildwood Reader—R
$-World & I—R

CHILDREN
$-Faces
Skipping Stones

CHRISTIAN EDUCATION/ LIBRARY
$-Journal/Adventist Ed.—R

DAILY DEVOTIONALS
$-Brink Magazine—R

MISSIONS
$-Glad Tidings (Canada)—R

PASTORS/LEADERS
$-Ministry & Liturgy—R
$-Outreach—R
$-Priest
$-Youthworker

TEEN/YOUNG ADULT
$-Breakaway
$-Credo—R
TeensForJC—R

WOMEN
Christian Woman's Page—R
$-Horizons (women)—R

PHOTOGRAPHS

Note: "Reprint" indicators (R) have been deleted from this section and "B" for black & white glossy prints or "C" for color transparencies inserted. An asterisk (*) before a listing indicates they buy photos with articles only.

ADULT/GENERAL

Advance
African Voices—B
Alive Now—B/C
American Tract
Ancient Paths—B
Anglican Journal—B/C
*Animal Trails—B/C
*Annals of St. Anne—B/C
*Arkansas Catholic—C
Arlington Catholic—B
Associated Content—C
BGC World—C
Bible Advocate—C
Breakthrough Intercessor—B/C
*Bridal Guides—B/C
Canada Lutheran—B
*Catholic Digest—B/C
Catholic Forester—B/C
*Catholic Insight
Catholic New York—B
Catholic Peace Voice—B/C
Catholic Sentinel—B/C
Catholic Telegraph—B
Catholic Yearbook—C
CBA Retailers—C
*Celebrate Life—C
*Charisma—C
*Christian Courier/Cdn.—B
*Christian Examiner—C
Christian Herald—C
*Christian History—B/C
Christian Home & School—C
*Christian Motorsports—B
*Christian Online
Christian Retailing—C
*Christian Standard—B/C
*Christianity Today—C
ChristianWeek—B/C
Chronicle Christian/KS—B/C
*Church of England News
*Citizen USA—C
City Light News—B/C
*Commonweal—B/C
Connecting Point—B
Covenant Companion—B/C
Culture Wars—B/C
Decision
*Desert Voice
*DisciplesWorld
Divine Ascent—B
Dovetail—B

Episcopal Life—B
Esdras' Scroll
Eureka Street—B/C
*Evangel/IN—B
*Evangel/OR—B/C
Evangelical Advocate—C
Faith & Family—C
*Faith & Friends—C
*Faith Today—C
Focus on the Family—B/C
Gold Country Families
Good News Journal
Gospel Today
*Guideposts—B/C
Highway News—B
Holy House Ministries—B
*Home Times—B/C
Homeschooling Today—B/C
*HopeKeepers—B/C
*Horizons (adult)
Imagine—C
*Impact—C
*In His Presence
*In Touch
Indian Life—B/C
Interchange—B
*Interim—B/C
Island Catholic—B/C
*Layman—B
Leaves—B/C
*Leben—C
Liberty—B/C
*Lifeglow—B/C
Light & Life—B/C
*Liguorian—C
*Live—B/C
Living—B/C
Living Church—B/C
*Living Light—B/C
*Lookout—B/C
*Lutheran Journal—C
*Manna—C
Marian Helper—B/C
*Mature Living
*Mature Years—C
*Minnesota Christian—B/C
*Miracles, Healings
Montana Catholic
Montgomery's Journey
*Mosaic—B/C
Mutuality—B/C
*New Heart—C
New Wineskins—B/C
Nostalgia—B/C
On Mission—B/C
Our Sunday Visitor—B/C
Over the Back Fence—C
*Perspectives—B
($)-P.O.W.E.R.
Power for Living—B
Presbyterian Outlook—B/C

*Presbyterians Today—B/C
*Prism—B/C
Prison Living—B/C
*Psychology for Living—C
*Purpose—B
Quaker Life—B/C
Rhubarb—B
Rock & Sling—B/C
Sacred Journey—B/C
Salvo—C
*Seek—C
*Special Living—B/C
Spiritual Life—B
Sports Spectrum—C
*St. Anthony Messenger—B/C
Standard—B
*Storyteller—B
*Testimony—B/C
Tiferet—B/C
*Today's Christian—B/C
Today's Pentecostal—B/C
*Together—B/C
*United Church Observer—B/C
Upscale
Urban Kingdom—C
*Vibrant Life—C
Vision—B/C
*War Cry—B/C
Way of St. Francis—B/C
West Wind Review—B
*World & I—B/C

CHILDREN

American Girl—C
Cadet Quest—C
Celebrate—C
*Focus/Clubhouse—C
*Focus/Clubhouse Jr.—C
Nature Friend—B/C
*Pockets—C
SHINEbrightly—C
Skipping Stones
*Winner—C

CHRISTIAN EDUCATION/ LIBRARY

*Christian Early Ed.—C
Christian Librarian—B
*Church Libraries—B/C
Journal/Adventist Ed.—B
RTJ—C
*Teachers of Vision—C
*Today's Catholic Teacher—C
*Youth & CE Leadership—C

DAILY DEVOTIONALS

Our Daily Journey—C
Secret Place—B
Upper Room

MISSIONS

Evangelical Missions
*Glad Tidings (Canada)—C

Intl. Jour./Frontier
*New World Outlook—C
*One—C
OpRev Equipper—B/C
PFI Global
*PIME World—B/C

MUSIC
Christian Music Weekly—B
*Creator—B/C

PASTORS/LEADERS
Catechumenate—C
Catholic Servant
Christian Century—B/C
Christian Management—C
*InSite—C
*Leadership—B
*Lutheran Partners—B
Ministry—B
Priest
*Pulpit Helps
Rev. Magazine—C
*This Rock—B/C
Today's Parish—B/C
Willow—C
*Worship Leader—C
*Your Church—C
*Youthworker

TEEN/YOUNG ADULT
Breakaway—C
Brio—C
*CLEAR Direction—B/C
Credo—B/C
Essential Connection—B/C
Exodus Magazine
Ignite Your Faith—C
*InsideOut
Listen—B/C
*Real Faith in Life—B
*Sharing the VICTORY—C
*Spirit
Take Five Plus—B/C
Young Adult Today—B
*Young Christian—B/C

WOMEN
At the Center—C
Beyond the Bend—B/C
*Canticle
*Esprit—B
Handmaidens
Hearts at Home—B/C
Herizons
*Link & Visitor—B
*Precious Times—C
Proverbs 31 Sisters—B/C
Right to the Heart
*Today's Leading Ladies—B/C
Woman of Worth—B/C

WRITERS
Best New Writing—C

*Cross & Quill—B
Esdras' Scroll—B/C
*New Writer's Mag.
*Once Upon a Time
*Poets & Writers
Tickled by Thunder
Write Connection—B
*Writer's Digest—B

POETRY
ADULT/GENERAL
African Voices—R
$-Alive Now—R
$-America
$-Ancient Paths—R
Angel Face—R
$-Associated Content—R
$-Aujourd'hui Credo—R
$-Bible Advocate—R
Bread of Life—R
Breakthrough Intercessor—R
$-Bridal Guides—R
$-Cappers
$-Catholic Forester—R
$-Catholic Peace Voice—R
$-Catholic Yearbook—R
$-Christian Courier/Cdn.—R
$-Christian Journal—R
Christian Motorsports
$-Christian Research
$-Commonweal
Connecting Point—R
Creation Care—R
$-Creation Illustrated—R
$-Cresset
CrossHome.com
$-Culture Wars—R
$-Decision
Desert Call—R
Diamond Dust
$-DisciplesWorld
$-Dovetail—R
E-Channels—R
Esdras' Scroll
Eternal Ink—R
$-Eureka Street
$-Evangel/IN—R
Evangel/OR—R
Friends Journal—R
$-Gem—R
Good News Journal—R
Haiku Hippodrome
Halo Magazine
$-Haruah—R
Highway News—R
$-Home Times—R
$-Image/WA
($)-Impact—R
$-In His Presence—R
$-Indian Life—R
Infuze

Island Catholic—R
Keys to Living—R
Leaves—R
$-Liberty
LifeTimes Catholic
$-Light & Life
Light of the World
LiteraryTNT.com—R
$-Live—R
$-Lutheran Digest—R
$-Lutheran Journal—R
$-Mature Living
$-Mature Years—R
Men of the Cross
$-MindFlights—R
$-Miraculous Medal
New Heart—R
$-New Wineskins—R
Pegasus Review—R
Penned from the Heart—R
Penwood Review
Perspectives—R
$-Poetry Scout
($)-P.O.W.E.R.
$-Prairie Messenger—R
Priscilla Papers
Prison Living—R
$-Pure Inspiration—R
$-Purpose—R
Quaker Life—R
Radix
($)-Relief Journal
Reverent Submissions—R
Rock & Sling
$-Rose & Thorn
Ruminate
Sacred Journey—R
Sharing—R
Silver Wings—R
SingleAgain.com—R
$-St. Anthony Messenger
$-Standard—R
$-Storyteller—R
Studio—R
Sword and Trumpet
Sword of the Lord—R
$-Testimony—R
Tiferet—R
Time of Singing—R
To God Be the Glory!
$-U.S. Catholic
Urban Kingdom—R
Victory Herald—R
$-Vision—R
$-Vista
$-Way of St. Francis—R
$-Weavings—R
West Wind Review
$-Wittenburg Door—R
$-World & I—R
Xavier Review

CHILDREN
$-American Girl—R
$-Faces
$-Focus/Clubhouse Jr.
$-Partners—R
$-Pockets—R
$-SHINEbrightly—R
Skipping Stones
$-Story Mates—R

CHRISTIAN EDUCATION/ LIBRARY
$-Teachers of Vision—R
$-Today's Catholic Teacher—R

DAILY DEVOTIONALS
Penned from the Heart—R
$-Secret Place
$-These Days

MISSIONS
$-Glad Tidings (Canada)—R
Railroad Evangelist—R

PASTORS/LEADERS
$-Catechumenate
$-Christian Century—R
Cross Currents
$-Emmanuel
Jour./Pastoral Care
Lutheran Forum
$-Lutheran Partners—R
$-Preaching Well—R
$-Review for Religious
Sharing the Practice—R

TEEN/YOUNG ADULT
$-Credo—R
$-Devo'Zine—R
$-Essential Connection
Exodus Magazine
G4T Ink—R
$-Ignite Your Faith
$-InsideOut—R
$-Insight—R
$-Take Five Plus
TeensForJC—R
$-Young Christian—R
$-Young Salvationist—R

WOMEN
Christian Woman's Page—R
$-Esprit
Handmaiden—R
Handmaidens
Hearts at Home—R
$-Link & Visitor—R
$-Melody of the Heart
$-MomSense—R
Proverbs 31 Sisters
Today's Leading Ladies—R
Virtuous Woman—R
Woman of Worth—R

WRITERS
Areopagus
$-Best New Writing
$-ByLine
$-Canadian Writer's Jour.—R
$-Christian Communicator—R
ChristianWriters
$-Cross & Quill—R
Esdras' Scroll—R
$-New Writer's Mag.
NW Christian Author—R
Once Upon a Time—R
$-Tickled by Thunder
Write Connection
$-Writer's Digest
$-Writers' Journal

POLITICAL
ADULT/GENERAL
African Voices—R
$-Anglican Journal
$-Arlington Catholic
$-Associated Content—R
$-Cathedral Age
$-Catholic Insight
$-Catholic Peace Voice—R
CBN.com—R
Christian Business
Christian C. L. RECORD—R
$-Christian Courier/Cdn.—R
Christian Courier/WI—R
$-Christian Examiner
Christian Media—R
$-Christian Renewal—R
$-Christianity Today—R
$-ChristianWeek—R
$-Chronicle Christian/KS
Church of England News
$-Citizen USA
$-City Light News—R
$-Commonweal
($)-Community Spirit—R
Creation Care—R
$-Creative Nonfiction
$-Cresset
Desert Voice—R
$-DisciplesWorld
Evangel/OR—R
$-Faith Today
$-Good News, Etc.—R
$-Good News/S. Florida
$-Home Times—R
Island Catholic—R
Jour. of Church & State
$-Light & Life
$-Minnesota Christian—R
MovieGuide
$-National Catholic Network
$-New Wineskins—R
$-Our Sunday Visitor—R

Perspectives—R
Presbyterian Outlook
Prison Living—R
$-Social Justice—R
$-St. Anthony Messenger
$-Testimony—R
Tri-State Voice
Trumpeter—R
Urban Kingdom—R
Wisconsin Christian
$-World & I—R

CHILDREN
$-New Moon—R

DAILY DEVOTIONALS
$-Brink Magazine—R

MISSIONS
$-One

PASTORS/LEADERS
$-Christian Century—R
$-Interpreter
$-Lutheran Partners—R
$-Word & World

TEEN/YOUNG ADULT
$-Boundless Webzine—R
$-InTeen—R

WOMEN
$-Esprit
$-Herizons
$-inSpirit—R
$-Today's Christian Woman—R

PRAYER
ADULT/GENERAL
$-Advance
African Voices—R
($)-AGAIN—R
$-Alive Now—R
$-Angels on Earth
$-Annals of St. Anne
($)-Believer's Bay
$-BGC World—R
$-Bible Advocate—R
Bread of Life—R
Breakthrough Intercessor—R
$-Canada Lutheran—R
$-Cathedral Age
$-Catholic Digest—R
$-Catholic Peace Voice—R
$-Catholic Yearbook—R
CBN.com—R
$-Celebrate Life—R
$-CGA World—R
Christian C. L. RECORD—R
$-Christian Home & School
$-Christian Journal—R
Christian Online
Christian Ranchman
$-Christian Research

$-Christian Standard—R
$-Christianity Today—R
$-ChristianWeek—R
$-Chronicle Christian/KS
Church Herald & Holiness—R
$-City Light News—R
$-Columbia—R
($)-Community Spirit—R
Connecting Point—R
$-Covenant Companion—R
$-Culture Wars—R
$-Decision
Desert Call—R
Desert Voice—R
$-Discipleship Journal—R
Divine Ascent
$-Dovetail—R
$-Episcopal Life—R
$-Evangel/IN—R
Evangelical Advocate—R
$-Faith & Family
$-Faith Today
$-Family Digest—R
$-Gem—R
$-Good News—R
Good News Journal—R
$-Good News, Etc.—R
Heartlight—R
Holy House Ministries—R
$-Home Times—R
($)-HopeKeepers—R
$-Horizons (adult)—R
$-In His Presence—R
$-In Touch
Island Catholic—R
Leaves—R
$-Lifeglow—R
$-Light & Life
$-Liguorian
LiteraryTNT.com—R
$-Live—R
$-Living Church
$-Lookout
$-Lutheran Digest—R
$-Lutheran Journal—R
$-Majellan—R
$-Manna—R
$-Marian Helper
$-Mature Years—R
$-Men of Integrity—R
$-Men.AG.org—R
Miracles, Healings
Mosaic—R
$-National Catholic
$-New Wineskins—R
$-Now What?—R
$-Our Sunday Visitor—R
$-ParentLife
Pegasus Review—R
Penned from the Heart—R
Perspectives—R

$-Positive Thinking—R
Prayer Closet
PrayerWorks—R
$-Precepts for Living
Presbyterian Outlook
$-Presbyterians Today—R
$-Priority!—R
$-Pure Inspiration—R
Quaker Life—R
Reverent Submissions—R
Sacred Journey—R
$-Seek—R
Silver Wings—R
$-Spiritual Life
$-St. Anthony Messenger
$-Standard—R
Sword of the Lord—R
$-Testimony—R
$-Today's Christian—R
$-Today's Pentecostal—R
Trumpeter—R
$-U.S. Catholic
Urban Kingdom—R
Victory Herald—R
$-Vista
$-War Cry—R
$-Way of St. Francis—R
$-Wesleyan Life—R
Wisconsin Christian

CHILDREN
$-BREAD/God's Children—R
$-Guide—R
$-Primary Street
$-Sparkle—R

CHRISTIAN EDUCATION/ LIBRARY
Catholic Library
$-Children's Ministry
$-Group
$-RTJ—R
Teach Kids Essentials—R
$-Teachers of Vision—R
$-Youth & CE Leadership

DAILY DEVOTIONALS
$-Brink Magazine—R
Penned from the Heart—R

MISSIONS
$-Glad Tidings (Canada)—R
Intl. Jour./Frontier—R
$-PFI Global—R
Railroad Evangelist—R

MUSIC
$-Creator—R

PASTORS/LEADERS
$-Catholic Servant
$-Clergy Journal—R
$-Diocesan Dialogue—R
$-Emmanuel

$-Interpreter
$-Leadership—R
$-Lutheran Partners—R
$-Ministry Today
$-Pray!—R
$-Proclaim—R
$-Reformed Worship—R
$-Review for Religious
$-RevWriter Resource
Rick Warren's Ministry—R
Sewanee Theo. Review
Theological Digest—R
$-Today's Parish
$-Word & World
$-Worship Leader

TEEN/YOUNG ADULT
$-Boundless Webzine—R
$-Breakaway
$-Brio—R
$-CLEAR Direction
$-CLEAR Horizon
$-Devo'Zine—R
$-Insight—R
$-InTeen—R
$-J.A.M.
$-Real Faith in Life—R
TeensForJC—R
$-True Girl
$-Young Christian—R
$-Young Salvationist—R

WOMEN
($)-Beyond the Bend—R
$-Canticle
CelebrateMoms—R
Christian Woman's Page—R
$-Come to the Fire—R
Crowned with Silver
Elegance—R
Hope for Women
$-Horizons (women)—R
$-InspiredMoms—R
$-inSpirit—R
$-Journey
Just Between Us—R
Lutheran Woman's Quar.
P31 Woman—R
$-Pauses…
Precious Times—R
Proverbs 31 Sisters
Right to the Heart—R
$-SpiritLed Woman
$-Today's Christian Woman—R
Today's Leading Ladies—R
Virtuous Woman—R
Woman of Worth—R
Women Today—R
WT Online—R

WRITERS
Areopagus
Opinari—R

PROPHECY

ADULT/GENERAL
$-Advance
$-Apocalypse Chronicles—R
($)-Believer's Bay
$-Bible Advocate—R
Bread of Life—R
CBN.com—R
Christian Media—R
Christian Online
$-Christian Research
$-Chronicle Christian/KS
Esdras' Scroll
Evangelical Advocate—R
Godly Places
$-Home Times—R
$-In His Presence—R
LiteraryTNT.com—R
$-Live—R
Midnight Call
$-Our Sunday Visitor—R
SingleAgain.com—R
$-St. Anthony Messenger
Sword of the Lord—R
$-Testimony—R
Trumpeter—R
Urban Kingdom—R

PASTORS/LEADERS
$-Ministry Today
Rick Warren's Ministry—R
$-Word & World

TEEN/YOUNG ADULT
$-InTeen—R
$-Real Faith in Life—R
TeensForJC—R
$-Young Salvationist—R

WOMEN
$-SpiritLed Woman

PSYCHOLOGY

ADULT/GENERAL
$-Animal Trails—R
$-Associated Content—R
$-Aujourd'hui Credo—R
$-Catholic Peace Voice—R
CBN.com—R
$-Christian Courier/Cdn.—R
Christian Online
($)-Community Spirit—R
$-Creative Nonfiction
$-Dovetail—R
Evangelical Advocate—R
$-Gem—R
$-Home Times—R
Island Catholic—R
$-Light & Life
$-Majellan—R
$-Our Sunday Visitor—R
Perspectives/Science

$-Psychology for Living—R
$-Science & Spirit
$-Spiritual Life
$-St. Anthony Messenger
$-Testimony—R
Trumpeter—R
Urban Kingdom—R
$-Vibrant Life—R
$-World & I—R

CHILDREN
$-New Moon—R

MISSIONS
$-Glad Tidings (Canada)—R

PASTORS/LEADERS
Jour./Pastoral Care
$-Word & World

TEEN/YOUNG ADULT
$-Young Christian—R

WOMEN
($)-Beyond the Bend—R
$-Today's Christian Woman—R

PUPPET PLAYS
$-Children's Ministry
Christian Early Ed.—R
$-Imagine
Victory Herald—R

RACISM

ADULT/GENERAL
$-Aujourd'hui Credo—R
$-Catholic Peace Voice—R
CBN.com—R
$-Christianity Today—R
$-ChristianWeek—R
$-Citizen USA
$-City Light News—R
($)-Community Spirit—R
$-Creative Nonfiction
$-Discipleship Journal—R
$-Dovetail—R
($)-E-Quality
$-Eureka Street
$-Faith Today
$-Home Times—R
Island Catholic—R
$-Light & Life
$-Lookout
$-Manna—R
$-Men of Integrity—R
$-Minnesota Christian—R
($)-Mutuality—R
$-New Wineskins—R
$-Our Sunday Visitor—R
Perspectives—R
Priscilla Papers
$-Prism
$-Purpose—R

$-St. Anthony Messenger
$-Testimony—R
$-Today's Christian—R
$-Together—R
Trumpeter—R
$-U.S. Catholic
$-Upscale
Urban Kingdom—R
$-Way of St. Francis—R
$-World & I—R

CHILDREN
$-Guide—R
$-New Moon—R
$-Our Little Friend—R
$-Primary Treasure—R
Skipping Stones
$-Sparkle—R

DAILY DEVOTIONALS
$-Brink Magazine—R

PASTORS/LEADERS
$-Clergy Journal—R
Cross Currents
Jour./Pastoral Care
$-Ministry Today

TEEN/YOUNG ADULT
$-Boundless Webzine—R
$-Ignite Your Faith
TeensForJC—R
$-True Girl
$-Young Salvationist—R

WOMEN
$-Horizons (women)—R
Making Waves
$-SpiritLed Woman
$-Today's Christian Woman—R
WT Online—R

RECOVERY

ADULT/GENERAL
$-Bible Advocate—R
$-Bridal Guides—R
CBN.com—R
$-Christian Journal—R
$-Chronicle Christian/KS
$-City Light News—R
($)-Community Spirit—R
$-Creative Nonfiction
$-Disaster News
Evangelical Advocate—R
$-Focus on the Family
$-Home Times—R
($)-HopeKeepers—R
$-Lookout
$-Majellan—R
$-Manna—R
$-Men of Integrity—R
$-Men.AG.org—R
$-Now What?—R

$-Our Sunday Visitor—R
$-Priority!—R
$-Prism
Prison Living—R
Reverent Submissions—R
Ruminate
$-Seek—R
Urban Kingdom—R
$-Way of St. Francis—R
$-Wildwood Reader—R
Wisconsin Christian
$-Written

MISSIONS
$-Glad Tidings (Canada)—R

PASTORS/LEADERS
Jour./Pastoral Care
$-Ministry Today

TEEN/YOUNG ADULT
$-Boundless Webzine—R

WOMEN
($)-Beyond the Bend—R
Comfort Café
$-inSpirit—R
Right to the Heart—R
$-Today's Christian Woman—R
Today's Leading Ladies—R
Women Today—R
WT Online—R

RELATIONSHIPS
ADULT/GENERAL
3V Magazine
$-Advance
$-Angels on Earth
$-Annals of St. Anne
Anointed Pages
$-Associated Content—R
$-Aujourd'hui Credo—R
$-BGC World—R
Bread of Life—R
Breakthrough Intercessor—R
$-Bridal Guides—R
$-Canada Lutheran—R
$-Canadian Mennonite—R
$-Catholic Digest—R
$-Catholic Forester—R
CBN.com—R
$-Celebrate Life—R
$-Chicken Soup Books—R
$-Christian Home & School
$-Christian Journal—R
Christian Online
Christian Ranchman
$-ChristianWeek—R
$-Chronicle Christian/KS
$-City Light News—R
($)-Community Spirit—R
$-Creative Nonfiction
Desert Call—R
$-Discipleship Journal—R

$-Dovetail—R
E-Channels—R
($)-E-Quality
Eternal Ink—R
$-Evangel/IN—R
Evangel/OR—R
Evangelical Advocate—R
$-Faith Today
Family Journal—R
$-Family Smart e-Tips—R
$-Focus on the Family
$-Gem—R
$-Gems of Truth—R
Good News Journal—R
$-Gospel Today—R
$-Guideposts—R
Heartlight—R
Highway News—R
$-Home Times—R
$-Homeschooling Today—R
($)-HopeKeepers—R
$-Horizons (adult)—R
$-In His Presence—R
$-In Touch
Island Catholic—R
Keys to Living—R
$-Lifeglow—R
$-Light & Life
$-Liguorian
$-Live—R
$-Living—R
$-Lookout
$-Majellan—R
$-Manna—R
$-Mature Living
$-Mature Years—R
$-Men of Integrity—R
Men of the Cross
$-Men.AG.org—R
$-Minnesota Christian—R
$-Montgomery's Journey
($)-Mutuality—R
New Heart—R
$-New Wineskins—R
$-Our Sunday Visitor—R
Ozarks Christian
Pegasus Review—R
Penned from the Heart—R
Perspectives—R
$-Positive Thinking—R
($)-P.O.W.E.R.
PrayerWorks—R
Priscilla Papers
Prison Living—R
$-Pure Inspiration—R
Reverent Submissions—R
Sacred Journey—R
$-Science & Spirit
$-Seek—R
Silver Wings—R
SingleAgain.com—R
$-Special Living—R

Spirituality for Today
$-St. Anthony Messenger
$-Standard—R
$-Storyteller—R
$-Testimony—R
$-Today's Christian—R
$-Today's Pentecostal—R
$-Together—R
Trumpeter—R
$-Upscale
Urban Kingdom—R
$-Vibrant Life—R
$-Vision—R
$-War Cry—R
$-Way of St. Francis—R
$-Wesleyan Life—R
$-Wildwood Reader—R
$-World & I—R

CHILDREN
$-BREAD/God's Children—R
$-Cadet Quest—R
$-Guide—R
$-New Moon—R
$-Passport—R
$-SHINEbrightly—R
Skipping Stones
$-Sparkle—R
$-Winner—R

CHRISTIAN EDUCATION/ LIBRARY
$-Group
$-Teachers of Vision—R
$-Youth & CE Leadership

DAILY DEVOTIONALS
$-Brink Magazine—R

MISSIONS
$-Glad Tidings (Canada)—R

PASTORS/LEADERS
$-Leadership—R
$-Small Groups.com—R
$-Word & World

TEEN/YOUNG ADULT
$-Boundless Webzine—R
$-Breakaway
$-Brio—R
$-CLEAR Direction
$-Credo—R
G4T Ink—R
$-Ignite Your Faith
$-Insight—R
$-Listen—R
$-Real Faith in Life—R
$-TC Magazine
TeensForJC—R
$-True Girl
$-Young Salvationist—R

WOMEN
$-At the Center—R

($)-Beyond the Bend—R
$-Canticle
CelebrateMoms—R
Christian Woman's Page—R
$-Come to the Fire—R
Comfort Café
Crowned with Silver
Elegance—R
First Lady
$-Girlfriend 2 Girlfriend
$-Heart & Soul
Hearts at Home—R
$-Herizons
Hope for Women
$-InspiredMoms—R
$-inSpirit—R
$-Journey
Just Between Us—R
Life Tools for Women
$-Link & Visitor—R
Lutheran Woman's Quar.
$-MomSense—R
P31 Woman—R
$-Pauses…
Precious Times—R
Proverbs 31 Sisters
Right to the Heart—R
($)-Simply Blessed—R
$-SpiritLed Woman
$-Today's Christian Woman—R
Today's Leading Ladies—R
Virtuous Woman—R
Woman of Worth—R
Women Today—R
WT Online—R

RELIGIOUS FREEDOM

ADULT/GENERAL
$-Arlington Catholic
$-Aujourd'hui Credo—R
$-Bridal Guides—R
$-Catholic Peace Voice—R
CBN.com—R
Christian C. L. RECORD—R
Christian Courier/WI—R
$-Christian Examiner
$-Christian Home & School
Christian News NW—R
Christian Observer
Christian Online
Christian Ranchman
$-Christian Response—R
$-Christianity Today—R
$-ChristianWeek—R
$-Chronicle Christian/KS
Church of England News
$-Citizen USA
$-City Light News—R
$-Columbia—R
$-Commonweal
($)-Community Spirit—R

$-Compass Direct
Connecting Point—R
Desert Voice—R
$-Dovetail—R
E-Channels—R
$-Episcopal Life—R
$-Eureka Street
Evangelical Advocate—R
$-Faith Today
$-Gem—R
Good News Today
$-Good News/S. Florida
$-Home Times—R
$-In His Presence—R
$-In Touch
$-Interim—R
Island Catholic—R
Jour. of Church & State
$-Liberty
$-Lifeglow—R
$-Light & Life
$-Live—R
$-Lookout
$-Manna—R
MESSAGE/Open Bible—R
$-Minnesota Christian—R
$-National Catholic
$-New Wineskins—R
$-Our Sunday Visitor—R
Pegasus Review—R
Perspectives—R
$-Prairie Messenger—R
Presbyterian Outlook
$-Prism
Prison Living—R
$-Pure Inspiration—R
$-Salvo
$-Science & Spirit
$-Seek—R
$-Spiritual Life
Spirituality for Today
$-St. Anthony Messenger
$-Standard—R
$-Testimony—R
Trumpeter—R
Urban Kingdom—R
Victory Herald—R
$-Way of St. Francis—R
Wisconsin Christian
$-World & I—R

CHILDREN
$-BREAD/God's Children—R
$-Guide—R
$-New Moon—R
Skipping Stones

CHRISTIAN EDUCATION/ LIBRARY
$-Teachers of Vision—R

DAILY DEVOTIONALS
$-Brink Magazine—R

MISSIONS
East-West Church
$-Evangelical Missions—R
$-Glad Tidings (Canada)—R
OpRev Equipper—R

PASTORS/LEADERS
$-Catholic Servant
$-Christian Century—R
Cross Currents
$-This Rock
$-Word & World

TEEN/YOUNG ADULT
$-Boundless Webzine—R
$-Brio—R
$-CLEAR Direction
$-CLEAR Horizon
$-InTeen—R
TeensForJC—R

WOMEN
$-SpiritLed Woman
Today's Leading Ladies—R
WT Online—R

RELIGIOUS TOLERANCE

ADULT/GENERAL
$-Aujourd'hui Credo—R
Bread of Life—R
$-Bridal Guides—R
$-Catholic Peace Voice—R
CBN.com—R
Christian C. L. RECORD—R
$-Christian Examiner
$-Christian Home & School
Christian Online
$-Christianity Today—R
$-ChristianWeek—R
Church of England News
$-Citizen USA
$-City Light News—R
$-Columbia—R
($)-Community Spirit—R
$-Compass Direct
$-Dovetail—R
E-Channels—R
$-Eureka Street
Evangelical Advocate—R
$-Faith Today
$-Good News, Etc.—R
$-Home Times—R
$-Interim—R
Island Catholic—R
Jour. of Church & State
$-Light & Life
$-Live—R
$-Lookout
$-Manna—R
$-Minnesota Christian—R
$-National Catholic
$-New Wineskins—R
$-Our Sunday Visitor—R

Perspectives—R
$-Prairie Messenger—R
Prison Living—R
$-Pure Inspiration—R
$-Science & Spirit
$-Seek—R
Spirituality for Today
$-St. Anthony Messenger
$-Testimony—R
Trumpeter—R
Urban Kingdom—R
$-Way of St. Francis—R
$-World & I—R

CHILDREN
$-Archaeology
$-New Moon—R
$-Primary Treasure—R
Skipping Stones

DAILY DEVOTIONALS
$-Brink Magazine—R

MISSIONS
$-Glad Tidings (Canada)—R
OpRev Equipper—R

PASTORS/LEADERS
$-Christian Century—R
$-Clergy Journal—R
Cross Currents

TEEN/YOUNG ADULT
$-Boundless Webzine—R
$-Brio—R
$-CLEAR Direction
$-Ignite Your Faith
TeensForJC—R

WOMEN
$-Esprit
Hope for Women
WT Online—R

REVIVAL
ADULT/GENERAL
$-BGC World—R
$-Bible Advocate—R
Breakthrough Intercessor—R
CBN.com—R
$-Christian Home & School
Christian Ranchman
$-Chronicle Christian/KS
$-City Light News—R
($)-Community Spirit—R
Diamond Dust
Evangelical Advocate—R
$-Good News, Etc.—R
$-Home Times—R
$-In His Presence—R
$-Live—R
$-Lookout
$-Manna—R
Prison Living—R
Reverent Submissions—R

Urban Kingdom—R
Victory Herald—R

CHILDREN
$-Archaeology

PASTORS/LEADERS
Jour./Amer. Soc./Chur. Growth—R
$-Ministry Today

TEEN/YOUNG ADULT
$-Boundless Webzine—R
$-Insight—R

WOMEN
$-Come to the Fire—R
Hope for Women
Right to the Heart—R
Today's Leading Ladies—R
WT Online—R

SALVATION TESTIMONIES
ADULT/GENERAL
American Tract—R
($)-Believer's Bay
$-BGC World—R
$-Bible Advocate—R
Bread of Life—R
CBN.com—R
$-Christian Home & School
$-Christian Journal—R
Christian Motorsports
Christian Online
Christian Ranchman
$-Christian Research
$-City Light News—R
($)-Community Spirit—R
Connecting Point—R
$-Decision
E-Channels—R
$-Evangel/IN—R
Evangelical Advocate—R
$-Faith Today
$-Gem—R
$-Good News, Etc.—R
$-Guideposts—R
Heartbeat/CMA
Highway News—R
$-Home Times—R
$-In His Presence—R
Leaves—R
$-Lifeglow—R
$-Light & Life
$-Live—R
$-Men of Integrity—R
$-MESSAGE
New Heart—R
$-Now What?—R
$-On Mission
$-Power for Living—R
PrayerWorks—R
$-Priority!—R
Prison Living—R
Reverent Submissions—R

$-Seek—R
Silver Wings—R
$-St. Anthony Messenger
Sword of the Lord—R
$-Testimony—R
$-Today's Christian—R
$-Together—R
Trumpeter—R
Urban Kingdom—R
Victory Herald—R
$-War Cry—R
$-Wesleyan Life—R
Wisconsin Christian

CHILDREN
$-Guide—R
$-Sparkle—R

CHRISTIAN EDUCATION/LIBRARY
Catholic Library
$-Group

MISSIONS
Railroad Evangelist—R

PASTORS/LEADERS
$-This Rock

TEEN/YOUNG ADULT
$-Boundless Webzine—R
$-CLEAR Direction
$-CLEAR Horizon
Exodus Magazine
$-InTeen—R
TeensForJC—R

WOMEN
CelebrateMoms—R
($)-History's Women—R
Hope for Women
$-Journey
$-MD Women of Worship
Precious Times—R
$-SpiritLed Woman
Today's Leading Ladies—R
Women Today—R
WT Online—R

WRITERS
Areopagus

SCIENCE
ADULT/GENERAL
$-Animal Trails—R
Answers
$-Associated Content—R
$-Aujourd'hui Credo—R
CBN.com—R
$-Christian Courier/Cdn.—R
$-City Light News—R
($)-Community Spirit—R
Creation
Creation Care—R
$-Creation Illustrated—R

$-Creative Nonfiction
$-Eureka Street
$-Faith Today
$-Home Times—R
Island Catholic—R
$-Light & Life
LiteraryTNT.com—R
$-National Catholic
$-Our Sunday Visitor—R
Perspectives—R
Perspectives/Science
Prison Living—R
$-Salvo
$-Science & Spirit
$-St. Anthony Messenger
$-Testimony—R
Trumpeter—R
Urban Kingdom—R
$-World & I—R

CHILDREN
$-Archaeology
$-Nature Friend—R
$-New Moon—R
Skipping Stones
$-Sparkle—R

DAILY DEVOTIONALS
$-Brink Magazine—R

MISSIONS
Intl. Jour./Frontier—R

PASTORS/LEADERS
$-Lutheran Partners—R
$-Word & World

TEEN/YOUNG ADULT
$-InTeen—R
TeensForJC—R

SELF-HELP
ADULT/GENERAL
$-Associated Content—R
$-Catholic Digest—R
CBN.com—R
$-CGA World—R
$-Christian Journal—R
$-Chronicle Christian/KS
$-City Light News—R
($)-Community Spirit—R
Disciple's Journal—R
$-Dovetail—R
Family Journal—R
$-Family Smart e-Tips—R
$-Home Times—R
($)-HopeKeepers—R
$-Lifeglow—R
$-Light & Life
$-Liguorian
$-Lookout
$-Manna—R
Men of the Cross
Prison Living—R

$-Pure Inspiration—R
Reverent Submissions—R
$-Seek—R
$-Significant Living—R
SingleAgain.com—R
$-Special Living—R
$-St. Anthony Messenger
$-Standard—R
$-Testimony—R
Trumpeter—R
Urban Kingdom—R
$-Vibrant Life—R
Victory Herald—R
$-World & I—R

CHILDREN
Skipping Stones
$-Winner—R

MISSIONS
$-Glad Tidings (Canada)—R
Women of the Harvest

PASTORS/LEADERS
$-Interpreter

TEEN/YOUNG ADULT
$-Brio—R
$-Listen—R
TeensForJC—R

WOMEN
CelebrateMoms—R
Christian Woman's Page—R
Elegance—R
$-Fullfill
$-Journey
$-Today's Christian Woman—R
Today's Leading Ladies—R
Women of the Cross
WT Online—R

WRITERS
Money the Write Way—R

SENIOR ADULT ISSUES
ADULT/GENERAL
$-Angels on Earth
$-Anglican Journal
$-Annals of St. Anne
$-Arkansas Catholic—R
$-Associated Content—R
$-B.C. Catholic—R
$-BGC World—R
byFaith
$-Canada Lutheran—R
$-Catholic Forester—R
CBN.com—R
$-CGA World—R
Christian Ranchman
$-Christian Standard—R
$-ChristianWeek—R
$-Chronicle Christian/KS
$-City Light News—R

($)-Community Spirit—R
Desert Voice—R
$-Dovetail—R
$-Evangel/IN—R
Evangel/OR—R
Evangelical Advocate—R
$-Family Smart e-Tips—R
$-Focus on the Family
$-Gem—R
$-Home Times—R
$-Homeschooling Today—R
($)-HopeKeepers—R
$-In His Presence—R
Island Catholic—R
$-Lifeglow—R
$-Light & Life
$-Liguorian
$-Live—R
$-Majellan—R
$-Mature Living
$-Mature Years—R
$-Montgomery's Journey
$-Our Sunday Visitor—R
$-Ozarks Senior Living—R
Penned from the Heart—R
$-Power for Living—R
PrayerWorks—R
Prison Living—R
Reverent Submissions—R
$-Seek—R
Senior Connection
$-Significant Living—R
SingleAgain.com—R
$-St. Anthony Messenger
$-Testimony—R
$-Today's Christian—R
Trumpeter—R
$-U.S. Catholic
$-Vista
$-War Cry—R
$-Way of St. Francis—R
$-Wesleyan Life—R

CHRISTIAN EDUCATION/ LIBRARY
$-Youth & CE Leadership

DAILY DEVOTIONALS
Penned from the Heart—R

MISSIONS
$-Glad Tidings (Canada)—R

PASTORS/LEADERS
$-Diocesan Dialogue—R
$-Interpreter
$-Word & World

WOMEN
$-inSpirit—R
$-Pauses…
($)-Simply Blessed—R
Today's Leading Ladies—R
WT Online—R

SERMONS

ADULT/GENERAL
$-Arlington Catholic
Breakthrough Intercessor—R
$-Catholic Yearbook—R
Church Herald & Holiness—R
($)-Community Spirit—R
Evangelical Advocate—R
$-In His Presence—R
$-Lutheran Journal—R
Pegasus Review—R
$-St. Anthony Messenger
$-Stewardship—R
Sword of the Lord—R
$-Testimony—R
Trumpeter—R
Urban Kingdom—R
Victory Herald—R
$-Weavings—R
Wisconsin Christian

PASTORS/LEADERS
$-African American Pulpit
$-Clergy Journal—R
$-Ministry Today
Preaching
$-Preaching Well—R
$-Proclaim—R
Pulpit Helps—R
Sharing the Practice—R
$-Sunday Sermons—R
$-Today's Parish
$-Torch Legacy Leader

SHORT STORY: ADULT/GENERAL
$-Ancient Paths—R
$-Best New Writing
CBN.com—R
Christian C. L. RECORD—R
Desert Call—R
Desert Voice—R
Diamond Dust
$-DisciplesWorld
$-Esprit
$-Glad Tidings (Canada)—R
Handmaidens
$-Haruah—R
$-Home Times—R
$-Imagine
$-In His Presence—R
$-Liguorian
LiteraryTNT.com—R
$-Ministry & Liturgy—R
$-Miraculous Medal
$-New Writer's Mag.
Perspectives—R
PrayerWorks—R
$-Preaching Well—R
Prison Living—R

($)-Relief Journal
Ruminate
$-Seek—R
Tiferet—R
Urban Kingdom—R
$-Wildwood Reader—R

SHORT STORY: ADULT/RELIGIOUS
$-Advance
African Voices—R
$-Ancient Paths—R
$-Angels on Earth
$-Anglican Journal
$-Annals of St. Anne
Areopagus
$-Associated Content—R
$-Aujourd'hui Credo—R
$-Bridal Guides—R
$-Canadian Writer's Jour.—R
$-Catholic Forester—R
$-Catholic Yearbook—R
CBN.com—R
$-CGA World—R
$-Christian Century—R
$-Christian Courier/Cdn.—R
$-Christian Educators—R
$-Christian Home & School
$-Christian Journal—R
Christian Online
Christian Ranchman
$-Christian Renewal—R
$-Christian Research
Christian Woman's Page—R
$-Come to the Fire—R
Connecting Point—R
$-Covenant Companion—R
Cross Currents
Desert Voice—R
Diamond Dust
$-DisciplesWorld
$-Dreams & Visions—R
Esdras' Scroll—R
$-Esprit
$-Eureka Street
$-Evangel/IN—R
$-Faith & Family
$-Gem—R
$-Gems of Truth—R
$-Glad Tidings (Canada)—R
Good News Journal—R
Handmaidens
$-Haruah—R
Heartlight—R
Hearts at Home—R
$-Home Times—R
$-Horizons (adult)—R
$-Horizons (women)—R
$-Ideals—R
$-Image/WA

$-Imagine
($)-Impact—R
$-In His Presence—R
$-Indian Life—R
Infuze
$-inSpirit—R
Island Catholic—R
Koinonia
$-Liguorian
LiteraryTNT.com—R
$-Live—R
$-Lutheran Journal—R
Lutheran Woman's Quar.
$-Mature Living
$-Mature Years—R
$-Melody of the Heart
$-Messenger/Sacred Heart
$-Messenger/St. Anthony
$-MindFlights—R
$-Miraculous Medal
$-National Catholic
$-New Wineskins—R
$-On Mission
Pegasus Review—R
Perspectives—R
($)-P.O.W.E.R.
PrayerWorks—R
Precious Times—R
Presbyterian Outlook
Prison Living—R
$-Proclaim—R
$-Purpose—R
Railroad Evangelist—R
($)-Relief Journal
Reverent Submissions—R
$-Review for Religious
Rock & Sling
Ruminate
Seeds of Hope
$-Seek—R
$-Shades of Romance—R
$-Sharing the VICTORY—R
($)-Simply Blessed—R
Spirituality for Today
$-St. Anthony Messenger
$-Standard—R
$-Storyteller—R
Studio—R
$-Testimony—R
Tiferet—R
Today's Leading Ladies—R
$-U.S. Catholic
Urban Kingdom—R
Victory Herald—R
$-Vision—R
$-Vista
$-War Cry—R
$-Way of St. Francis—R
$-Wesleyan Life—R
West Wind Review
$-Written

SHORT STORY: ADVENTURE

ADULT
$-Angels on Earth
$-Animal Trails—R
$-Annals of St. Anne
$-Associated Content—R
$-Best New Writing
$-Cappers
CBN.com—R
Desert Voice—R
$-Dreams & Visions—R
Esdras' Scroll—R
Family Journal—R
$-Gem—R
$-Glad Tidings (Canada)—R
$-Haruah—R
Heartlight—R
$-In His Presence—R
$-Indian Life—R
Infuze
$-Liguorian
LiteraryTNT.com—R
PrayerWorks—R
Prison Living—R
$-Rose & Thorn
$-Standard—R
$-Storyteller—R
Studio—R
Today's Leading Ladies—R
Urban Kingdom—R
Victory Herald—R
$-Vision—R
$-Weavings—R

CHILDREN
$-American Girl—R
$-Animal Trails—R
$-Archaeology
$-BREAD/God's Children—R
Connecting Point—R
Eternal Ink—R
$-Focus/Clubhouse Jr.
$-Junior Companion—R
$-Kid Zone
$-Kids' Ark—R
$-New Moon—R
$-Partners—R
$-SHINEbrightly—R
Skipping Stones
$-Sparkle—R
Sword of the Lord—R
$-Young Christian—R

TEEN/YOUNG ADULT
$-Animal Trails—R
$-BREAD/God's Children—R
$-Breakaway
$-Brio—R
$-Cadet Quest—R
$-CLEAR Direction
$-CLEAR Horizon

$-Credo—R
$-InsideOut—R
$-InTeen—R
$-Partners—R
$-SHINEbrightly—R
Sword of the Lord—R
TeensForJC—R
$-Young Adult Today
$-Young Christian—R
$-Young Salvationist—R

SHORT STORY: ALLEGORY

ADULT
$-Animal Trails—R
$-Associated Content—R
CBN.com—R
Christian C. L. RECORD—R
$-Christian Journal—R
Christian Woman's Page—R
$-Covenant Companion—R
$-Dreams & Visions—R
Esdras' Scroll—R
$-Esprit
$-Gem—R
$-Glad Tidings (Canada)—R
Heartlight—R
$-Ideals—R
$-Imagine
$-In His Presence—R
$-Indian Life—R
Infuze
$-Liguorian
$-New Wineskins—R
PrayerWorks—R
Prison Living—R
Railroad Evangelist—R
Reverent Submissions—R
Studio—R
Victory Herald—R
$-Vision—R
$-Way of St. Francis—R

CHILDREN
$-Animal Trails—R
$-Nature Friend—R
Sword of the Lord—R
$-Young Christian—R

TEEN/YOUNG ADULT
$-Animal Trails—R
$-Breakaway
$-Brio—R
$-CLEAR Direction
$-CLEAR Horizon
$-Home Times—R
Sword of the Lord—R
$-Young Salvationist—R

SHORT STORY: BIBLICAL

ADULT
$-Anglican Journal
$-Animal Trails—R

$-Annals of St. Anne
$-Aujourd'hui Credo—R
Bread of Life—R
$-Catholic Yearbook—R
CBN.com—R
$-CGA World—R
Christian C. L. RECORD—R
$-Christian Journal—R
Christian Online
Christian Ranchman
Christian Woman's Page—R
Congregational Libraries
Connecting Point—R
Crowned with Silver
Desert Call—R
Desert Voice—R
$-Dreams & Visions—R
Esdras' Scroll—R
$-Evangel/IN—R
$-Gem—R
$-Glad Tidings (Canada)—R
$-Haruah—R
Heartlight—R
Hearts at Home—R
$-Horizons (women)—R
$-Ideals—R
$-Imagine
$-In His Presence—R
$-Kindred Spirit—R
LiteraryTNT.com—R
$-Lutheran Journal—R
Lutheran Woman's Quar.
$-National Catholic
$-New Wineskins—R
PrayerWorks—R
Prison Living—R
$-Purpose—R
Railroad Evangelist—R
Reverent Submissions—R
$-Seek—R
Studio—R
Urban Kingdom—R
Victory Herald—R
$-Vista
$-War Cry—R
$-Way of St. Francis—R
$-Wesleyan Life—R

CHILDREN
$-Adventures
$-Animal Trails—R
$-Archaeology
$-BREAD/God's Children—R
Christian Ranchman
Eternal Ink—R
$-Focus/Clubhouse
$-Nature Friend—R
$-Pockets—R
$-Sparkle—R
Sword of the Lord—R
Teach Kids Essentials—R

$-Young Christian—R

TEEN/YOUNG ADULT
$-Anglican Journal
$-Animal Trails—R
$-BREAD/God's Children—R
$-Breakaway
$-Brio—R
Christian Ranchman
$-CLEAR Direction
$-CLEAR Horizon
Crowned with Silver
$-Essential Connection
$-Home Times—R
$-InTeen—R
Spirituality for Today
Sword of the Lord—R
TeensForJC—R
$-Young Adult Today
$-Young Christian—R

SHORT STORY: CONTEMPORARY
ADULT
African Voices—R
$-Ancient Paths—R
$-Angels on Earth
$-Animal Trails—R
$-Annals of St. Anne
$-Associated Content—R
$-Aujourd'hui Credo—R
$-ByLine
$-Canada Lutheran—R
CBN.com—R
$-Christian Century—R
$-Christian Courier/Cdn.—R
$-Christian Home & School
$-Christian Renewal—R
Christian Woman's Page—R
Connecting Point—R
$-Covenant Companion—R
Diamond Dust
$-DisciplesWorld
$-Dreams & Visions—R
Esdras' Scroll—R
$-Esprit
$-Eureka Street
$-Evangel/IN—R
$-Gem—R
$-Glad Tidings (Canada)—R
$-Haruah—R
Heartlight—R
$-Horizons (adult)—R
$-Imagine
$-In His Presence—R
$-Indian Life—R
Infuze
$-Liguorian
$-Mature Living
$-National Catholic
$-New Wineskins—R
$-New Writer's Mag.

Perspectives—R
PrayerWorks—R
Precious Times—R
Prison Living—R
Railroad Evangelist—R
($)-Relief Journal
Reverent Submissions—R
Ruminate
$-Seek—R
$-Shades of Romance—R
($)-Simply Blessed—R
$-Standard—R
$-Storyteller—R
Studio—R
Tiferet—R
$-U.S. Catholic
Urban Kingdom—R
$-Vision—R
$-War Cry—R
West Wind Review
$-Wildwood Reader—R
$-Written
Xavier Review

CHILDREN
$-Adventures
$-American Girl—R
$-Animal Trails—R
$-Cadet Quest—R
$-Focus/Clubhouse
$-Focus/Clubhouse Jr.
$-Kids' Ark—R
$-New Moon—R
$-Partners—R
$-Pockets—R
$-SHINEbrightly—R
$-Sparkle—R
$-Story Mates—R
Teach Kids Essentials—R
$-Winner—R
$-Young Christian—R

TEEN/YOUNG ADULT
$-Animal Trails—R
$-Breakaway
$-Brio—R
$-Cadet Quest—R
$-CLEAR Direction
$-CLEAR Horizon
$-Essential Connection
$-Home Times—R
$-Ignite Your Faith
$-InsideOut—R
$-Living My Faith
$-Partners—R
$-Real Faith in Life—R
$-Spirit
TeensForJC—R
$-Young Salvationist—R

SHORT STORY: ETHNIC
ADULT
African Voices—R

$-Animal Trails—R
$-Associated Content—R
$-CGA World—R
$-DisciplesWorld
$-Dreams & Visions—R
Esdras' Scroll—R
$-Eureka Street
$-Gem—R
$-Glad Tidings (Canada)—R
$-Haruah—R
$-Indian Life—R
PrayerWorks—R
$-Purpose—R
$-Seek—R
Spirituality for Today
Studio—R
Today's Leading Ladies—R
$-U.S. Catholic
Urban Kingdom—R
Xavier Review

CHILDREN
$-American Girl—R
$-Animal Trails—R
$-Archaeology
$-Focus/Clubhouse
$-Kids' Ark—R
$-New Moon—R
Skipping Stones
$-Sparkle—R
$-Young Christian—R

TEEN/YOUNG ADULT
$-Animal Trails—R
$-Brio—R
$-InsideOut—R
$-SHINEbrightly—R
TeensForJC—R

SHORT STORY: FANTASY
ADULT
$-Associated Content—R
$-Challenging Destiny—R
Connecting Point—R
$-Dreams & Visions—R
$-Eureka Street
$-Gem—R
$-Glad Tidings (Canada)—R
($)-Impact—R
$-In His Presence—R
Infuze
$-MindFlights—R
Prison Living—R
$-Rose & Thorn
$-Storyteller—R
Studio—R
$-Tickled by Thunder
$-Written

CHILDREN
$-Focus/Clubhouse
$-New Moon—R
$-SHINEbrightly—R

$-Sparkle—R
Sword of the Lord—R

TEEN/YOUNG ADULT
$-Breakaway
$-Brio—R
$-CLEAR Direction
$-CLEAR Horizon
$-Credo—R
$-InTeen—R
$-SHINEbrightly—R
Sword of the Lord—R
TeensForJC—R
$-Young Adult Today

SHORT STORY: FRONTIER
ADULT
$-Animal Trails—R
$-Associated Content—R
$-Cappers
Connecting Point—R
Desert Voice—R
$-Gem—R
$-Glad Tidings (Canada)—R
$-Haruah—R
$-In His Presence—R
$-Indian Life—R
Infuze
PrayerWorks—R
Prison Living—R
$-Storyteller—R
Studio—R

CHILDREN
$-Animal Trails—R
$-Archaeology
Eternal Ink—R
$-Kids' Ark—R
$-New Moon—R
$-SHINEbrightly—R
Sword of the Lord—R
$-Young Christian—R

TEEN/YOUNG ADULT
$-Breakaway
$-CLEAR Direction
$-CLEAR Horizon
$-Credo—R
$-Home Times—R
Sword of the Lord—R

SHORT STORY:
FRONTIER/ROMANCE
$-Archaeology
$-Associated Content—R
$-Bridal Guides—R
$-Cappers
Connecting Point—R
$-Dreams & Visions—R
$-Gem—R
$-Haruah—R
$-Shades of Romance—R
$-Storyteller—R

Studio—R
Urban Kingdom—R

SHORT STORY:
HISTORICAL
ADULT
$-Ancient Paths—R
$-Animal Trails—R
$-Associated Content—R
$-Aujourd'hui Credo—R
$-Cappers
CBN.com—R
$-Christian Renewal—R
Connecting Point—R
Desert Voice—R
$-Gem—R
$-Glad Tidings (Canada)—R
$-Haruah—R
Heartlight—R
$-Home Times—R
$-In His Presence—R
$-Indian Life—R
Infuze
Lutheran Woman's Quar.
$-National Catholic
$-New Writer's Mag.
$-Over the Back Fence—R
Prison Living—R
$-Purpose—R
Railroad Evangelist—R
$-Rose & Thorn
$-Seek—R
Spirituality for Today
$-Storyteller—R
Studio—R
Urban Kingdom—R

CHILDREN
$-American Girl—R
$-Animal Trails—R
$-Archaeology
$-BREAD/God's Children—R
Christian Ranchman
$-Focus/Clubhouse
$-Focus/Clubhouse Jr.
$-Home Times—R
$-Kids' Ark—R
$-Nature Friend—R
$-New Moon—R
$-Partners—R
$-SHINEbrightly—R
Skipping Stones
$-Sparkle—R
Sword of the Lord—R
$-Young Christian—R

TEEN/YOUNG ADULT
$-Animal Trails—R
$-BREAD/God's Children—R
$-Breakaway
$-Brio—R
Christian Ranchman
$-CLEAR Direction

$-CLEAR Horizon
$-Credo—R
$-Home Times—R
$-InsideOut—R
$-InTeen—R
$-Partners—R
$-SHINEbrightly—R
Spirituality for Today
Sword of the Lord—R
$-Young Adult Today

SHORT STORY:
HISTORICAL/ROMANCE
African Voices—R
$-Archaeology
Areopagus
$-Associated Content—R
$-Cappers
CBN.com—R
Connecting Point—R
$-Dreams & Visions—R
Family Journal—R
$-Gem—R
$-Haruah—R
$-Liguorian
$-Shades of Romance—R
$-Storyteller—R
Studio—R
Urban Kingdom—R
$-Written

SHORT STORY: HUMOROUS
ADULT
African Voices—R
$-Ancient Paths—R
$-Animal Trails—R
$-Associated Content—R
$-Canada Lutheran—R
$-Catholic Forester—R
CBN.com—R
$-CGA World—R
$-Christian Courier/Cdn.—R
$-Christian Journal—R
Congregational Libraries
Connecting Point—R
$-Covenant Companion—R
$-Dreams & Visions—R
$-Esprit
$-Eureka Street
Family Journal—R
$-Gem—R
$-Glad Tidings (Canada)—R
$-Haruah—R
Heartlight—R
Hearts at Home—R
$-Home Times—R
$-Horizons (adult)—R
$-Imagine
$-In His Presence—R
Infuze
$-Liguorian
LiteraryTNT.com—R

$-Mature Living
$-Mature Years—R
$-Miraculous Medal
$-National Catholic
$-New Writer's Mag.
$-Over the Back Fence—R
PrayerWorks—R
Presbyterian Outlook
Prison Living—R
Reverent Submissions—R
$-Seek—R
$-Storyteller—R
Studio—R
$-U.S. Catholic
Urban Kingdom—R
Victory Herald—R
$-Vista
West Wind Review

CHILDREN
$-Cadet Quest—R
Christian Ranchman
Congregational Libraries
Eternal Ink—R
$-Focus/Clubhouse
$-Home Times—R
$-New Moon—R
$-SHINEbrightly—R
Skipping Stones
$-Sparkle—R
$-Story Mates—R
Sword of the Lord—R
$-Young Christian—R

TEEN/YOUNG ADULT
$-Animal Trails—R
$-Breakaway
$-Brio—R
$-Cadet Quest—R
Christian Ranchman
$-CLEAR Direction
$-CLEAR Horizon
$-Credo—R
$-Essential Connection
$-Home Times—R
$-Ignite Your Faith
$-InsideOut—R
$-InTeen—R
Sword of the Lord—R
TeensForJC—R
$-Young Adult Today
$-Young Salvationist—R

SHORT STORY: JUVENILE
$-Adventures
$-American Girl—R
$-Animal Trails—R
$-Archaeology
Areopagus
$-Associated Content—R
$-Beginner's Friend—R
$-BREAD/God's Children—R
$-Cadet Quest—R

$-Catholic Forester—R
CBN.com—R
$-Christian Renewal—R
Church Herald & Holiness—R
$-CLEAR Direction
$-CLEAR Horizon
Congregational Libraries
Desert Voice—R
Esdras' Scroll—R
$-Faces
$-Faith & Family
$-Focus/Clubhouse
$-Focus/Clubhouse Jr.
$-In His Presence—R
$-Junior Companion—R
$-Keys for Kids—R
$-Kid Zone
$-Kids' Ark—R
LiteraryTNT.com—R
$-Nature Friend—R
$-New Moon—R
$-Partners—R
$-Pockets—R
$-Primary Pal/KS—R
Prison Living—R
$-Seek—R
$-SHINEbrightly—R
$-Sparkle—R
$-Story Mates—R
TeensForJC—R
$-United Church Observer—R
Victory Herald—R
$-War Cry—R
$-Winner—R

SHORT STORY: LITERARY ADULT
African Voices—R
$-Ancient Paths—R
$-Associated Content—R
$-ByLine
$-Christian Courier/Cdn.—R
$-Covenant Companion—R
$-Dreams & Visions—R
Esdras' Scroll—R
$-Eureka Street
$-Gem—R
$-Glad Tidings (Canada)—R
Handmaidens
$-Haruah—R
$-Horizons (adult)—R
$-Imagine
LiteraryTNT.com—R
$-National Catholic
$-New Wineskins—R
Perspectives—R
Prison Living—R
Reverent Submissions—R
Rock & Sling
$-Rose & Thorn
Ruminate
$-Seek—R

$-Standard—R
$-Storyteller—R
Studio—R
$-Tickled by Thunder
Tiferet—R
$-U.S. Catholic
Urban Kingdom—R
Victory Herald—R
$-War Cry—R
West Wind Review
$-Wildwood Reader—R
$-Written
Xavier Review

CHILDREN
$-New Moon—R

TEEN/YOUNG ADULT
$-CLEAR Direction
$-CLEAR Horizon
$-Home Times—R
Spirituality for Today

SHORT STORY: MYSTERY/ROMANCE
$-Archaeology
$-Associated Content—R
$-ByLine
$-Cappers
Connecting Point—R
$-Dreams & Visions—R
$-Gem—R
$-Haruah—R
Prison Living—R
$-Shades of Romance—R
$-Storyteller—R
Studio—R
TeensForJC—R
Urban Kingdom—R

SHORT STORY: MYSTERY/SUSPENSE ADULT
$-Animal Trails—R
$-Associated Content—R
$-Best New Writing
$-ByLine
$-Cappers
CBN.com—R
Connecting Point—R
Desert Voice—R
$-Dreams & Visions—R
Esdras' Scroll—R
$-Gem—R
$-Glad Tidings (Canada)—R
$-Haruah—R
Heartlight—R
Infuze
Prison Living—R
$-Storyteller—R
Studio—R
$-Tickled by Thunder

CHILDREN

$-American Girl—R
$-Animal Trails—R
$-Archaeology
$-Kids' Ark—R
$-New Moon—R
$-SHINEbrightly—R
$-Sparkle—R
Sword of the Lord—R
$-Young Christian—R

TEEN/YOUNG ADULT

$-Animal Trails—R
$-Breakaway
$-Brio—R
$-Cadet Quest—R
$-CLEAR Horizon
$-Credo—R
$-InTeen—R
$-SHINEbrightly—R
Sword of the Lord—R
TeensForJC—R
$-Young Adult Today

SHORT STORY: PARABLES

ADULT

$-Animal Trails—R
$-Annals of St. Anne
$-Associated Content—R
$-Catholic Yearbook—R
$-Christian Courier/Cdn.—R
$-Christian Journal—R
$-Covenant Companion—R
$-Dreams & Visions—R
Esdras' Scroll—R
$-Esprit
$-Gem—R
$-Glad Tidings (Canada)—R
Heartlight—R
($)-Impact—R
$-In His Presence—R
$-Liguorian
$-Lutheran Journal—R
$-Ministry & Liturgy—R
$-New Wineskins—R
Perspectives—R
$-Preaching Well—R
Prison Living—R
Railroad Evangelist—R
Reverent Submissions—R
$-Seek—R
Studio—R
$-Testimony—R
Urban Kingdom—R
Victory Herald—R
$-Vista
$-Way of St. Francis—R

CHILDREN

$-Animal Trails—R
Eternal Ink—R
$-Faces
$-Focus/Clubhouse Jr.

Skipping Stones
$-Sparkle—R
$-Young Christian—R

TEEN/YOUNG ADULT

$-Animal Trails—R
$-CLEAR Direction
$-CLEAR Horizon
$-Home Times—R
$-InTeen—R
$-SHINEbrightly—R
TeensForJC—R
$-Testimony—R
$-Young Adult Today
$-Young Salvationist—R

SHORT STORY: PLAYS

Areopagus
$-Drama Ministry—R
Esdras' Scroll—R
$-Faces
$-Focus/Clubhouse Jr.
$-Imagine
$-J.A.M.
LiteraryTNT.com—R
$-New Wineskins—R
$-RTJ—R
$-SHINEbrightly—R
Studio—R
TeensForJC—R
Urban Kingdom—R

SHORT STORY: ROMANCE

ADULT

$-Animal Trails—R
$-Associated Content—R
$-Bridal Guides—R
$-Cappers
CBN.com—R
Connecting Point—R
$-Dreams & Visions—R
$-Gem—R
$-Haruah—R
Precious Times—R
$-Rose & Thorn
$-Shades of Romance—R
$-Storyteller—R
Studio—R
Urban Kingdom—R
$-Wildwood Reader—R
$-Written

TEEN/YOUNG ADULT

$-Animal Trails—R
TeensForJC—R

SHORT STORY: SCIENCE FICTION

ADULT

African Voices—R
$-Associated Content—R
$-Challenging Destiny—R
Connecting Point—R

$-Dreams & Visions—R
$-Eureka Street
$-Gem—R
$-Glad Tidings (Canada)—R
Infuze
$-MindFlights—R
Prison Living—R
$-Rose & Thorn
$-Storyteller—R
Studio—R
$-Tickled by Thunder
$-Written

CHILDREN

$-Kids' Ark—R
$-New Moon—R
$-SHINEbrightly—R
$-Sparkle—R
Sword of the Lord—R

TEEN/YOUNG ADULT

$-Breakaway
$-CLEAR Direction
$-CLEAR Horizon
$-Credo—R
$-Home Times—R
$-InTeen—R
$-J.A.M.
$-SHINEbrightly—R
Sword of the Lord—R
$-Young Adult Today

SHORT STORY: SENIOR ADULT FICTION

Desert Voice—R
$-Glad Tidings (Canada)—R
$-In His Presence—R
$-Liguorian
$-Live—R
$-Mature Living
PrayerWorks—R
Reverent Submissions—R
$-Seek—R
$-St. Anthony Messenger
$-Vista

SHORT STORY: SKITS

ADULT

$-Associated Content—R
Crowned with Silver
Desert Voice—R
$-Drama Ministry—R
Esdras' Scroll—R
$-Imagine
LiteraryTNT.com—R
$-New Wineskins—R
Studio—R
Urban Kingdom—R

CHILDREN

$-Focus/Clubhouse Jr.
$-SHINEbrightly—R
Sword of the Lord—R

TEEN/YOUNG ADULT
$-CLEAR Direction
$-CLEAR Horizon
Crowned with Silver
$-J.A.M.
$-SHINEbrightly—R
Sword of the Lord—R
TeensForJC—R

SHORT STORY: SPECULATIVE
ADULT
$-Associated Content—R
Bread of Life—R
$-Dreams & Visions—R
$-Eureka Street
Infuze
$-National Catholic
Prison Living—R
Reverent Submissions—R
Studio—R
$-Tickled by Thunder
Urban Kingdom—R
$-Written

CHILDREN
$-New Moon—R

TEEN/YOUNG ADULT
$-Home Times—R
TeensForJC—R
$-Young Salvationist—R

SHORT STORY: TEEN/YOUNG ADULT
$-Anglican Journal
$-Archaeology
$-Breakaway
$-Brio—R
$-Canada Lutheran—R
$-Catholic Forester—R
CBN.com—R
$-CLEAR Direction
$-CLEAR Horizon
$-Credo—R
Crowned with Silver
Desert Voice—R
Diamond Dust
Esdras' Scroll—R
$-Essential Connection
$-Home Times—R
$-Ignite Your Faith
$-In His Presence—R
$-InsideOut—R
$-InTeen—R
$-J.A.M.
LiteraryTNT.com—R
$-Living My Faith
$-New Moon—R
Precious Times—R
Prison Living—R
$-Real Faith in Life—R
$-Seek—R

$-Sharing the VICTORY—R
Skipping Stones
$-Spirit
Spirituality for Today
TeensForJC—R
$-Testimony—R
Tiferet—R
Urban Kingdom—R
Victory Herald—R
$-War Cry—R
West Wind Review
$-Written
$-Young Adult Today
$-Young Christian—R
$-Young Salvationist—R
$-Youth Compass—R

SHORT STORY: WESTERNS
ADULT
$-Animal Trails—R
$-Associated Content—R
$-Cappers
$-Dreams & Visions—R
Infuze
Prison Living—R
$-Storyteller—R
Studio—R
$-Tickled by Thunder

CHILDREN
$-Animal Trails—R
$-Archaeology
Christian Ranchman
$-Kids' Ark—R
$-Sparkle—R
Sword of the Lord—R
$-Young Christian—R

TEEN/YOUNG ADULT
$-Animal Trails—R
Christian Ranchman
$-CLEAR Direction
$-CLEAR Horizon
$-Credo—R
Sword of the Lord—R

SINGLES ISSUES
ADULT/GENERAL
$-Advance
African Voices—R
$-Annals of St. Anne
Anointed Pages
$-Associated Content—R
$-BGC World—R
$-Bible Advocate—R
Bread of Life—R
CBN.com—R
$-Christian Examiner
$-Christian Journal—R
Christian Online
Christian Ranchman
$-Christian Single
$-ChristianWeek—R

$-Chronicle Christian/KS
$-City Light News—R
($)-Community Spirit—R
Desert Voice—R
Disciple's Journal—R
$-Dovetail—R
E-Channels—R
($)-E-Quality
$-Evangel/IN—R
Evangelical Advocate—R
$-Faith Today
$-Family Smart e-Tips—R
$-Focus on the Family
$-Gem—R
Godly Places
Good News Journal—R
Heartlight—R
$-Home Times—R
$-Homeschooling Today—R
($)-HopeKeepers—R
$-In His Presence—R
$-In Touch
$-Light & Life
$-Live—R
$-Lookout
$-Majellan—R
$-Men.AG.org—R
$-Minnesota Christian—R
$-Montgomery's Journey
($)-Mutuality—R
$-Our Sunday Visitor—R
Penned from the Heart—R
$-Power for Living—R
Priscilla Papers
Prison Living—R
$-Psychology for Living—R
$-Seek—R
SingleAgain.com—R
$-St. Anthony Messenger
$-Testimony—R
$-Today's Christian—R
$-Together—R
Trumpeter—R
$-U.S. Catholic
Urban Kingdom—R
$-Vibrant Life—R
$-War Cry—R
$-Wesleyan Life—R
$-Wildwood Reader—R
Wisconsin Christian
$-World & I—R

CHRISTIAN EDUCATION/ LIBRARY
$-Youth & CE Leadership

DAILY DEVOTIONALS
$-Brink Magazine—R
Penned from the Heart—R

MISSIONS
$-Glad Tidings (Canada)—R
Women of the Harvest

PASTORS/LEADERS
$-Interpreter
$-Ministry Today
$-Word & World

TEEN/YOUNG ADULT
$-Boundless Webzine—R
$-Breakaway
$-Brio—R
$-InsideOut—R
$-InTeen—R
$-TC Magazine
TeensForJC—R
$-Young Salvationist—R

WOMEN
$-At the Center—R
$-Canticle
CelebrateMoms—R
Christian Woman's Page—R
Christian Women Today—R
Elegance—R
Hope for Women
$-inSpirit—R
Ladies First
($)-Simply Blessed—R
$-SpiritLed Woman
$-Today's Christian Woman—R
Today's Leading Ladies—R
Women of the Cross
Women Today—R
WT Online—R

SMALL GROUP HELPS
ADULT/GENERAL
$-Christian Standard—R
$-City Light News—R
$-Discipleship Journal—R
Evangel/OR—R
Prison Living—R
Reverent Submissions—R
$-Seek—R
Urban Kingdom—R
Victory Herald—R

CHILDREN
$-Archaeology

MISSIONS
$-Glad Tidings (Canada)—R

PASTORS/LEADERS
$-Ministry Today
Pulpit Helps—R
$-Small Groups.com—R

TEEN/YOUNG ADULT
$-Boundless Webzine—R
$-Brio—R
$-Young Christian—R

SOCIAL JUSTICE
ADULT/GENERAL
$-Advance

$-Arkansas Catholic—R
$-Arlington Catholic
$-Associated Content—R
$-Aujourd'hui Credo—R
$-Catholic Peace Voice—R
CBN.com—R
$-Christian Courier/Cdn.—R
Christian Online
$-Christian Response—R
$-Christian Standard—R
$-Christianity Today—R
$-ChristianWeek—R
$-Chronicle Christian/KS
$-Citizen USA
$-City Light News—R
$-Commonweal
($)-Community Spirit—R
$-Company—R
$-Covenant Companion—R
Creation Care—R
$-Creative Nonfiction
$-Cresset
$-Culture Wars—R
Desert Call—R
Desert Voice—R
$-Disaster News
$-Discipleship Journal—R
$-Dovetail—R
E-Channels—R
($)-E-Quality
$-Eureka Street
Evangelical Advocate—R
$-Faith & Family
$-Faith Today
$-Gem—R
$-Home Times—R
$-In Touch
$-Indian Life—R
Island Catholic—R
$-Light & Life
$-Liguorian
$-Lookout
$-Majellan—R
$-Men of Integrity—R
$-Minnesota Christian—R
Mosaic—R
($)-Mutuality—R
$-National Catholic
$-New Wineskins—R
$-Our Sunday Visitor—R
Penned from the Heart—R
Perspectives—R
$-Prairie Messenger—R
Priscilla Papers
$-Prism
Prison Living—R
Quaker Life—R
$-Salvo
$-Science & Spirit
$-Seek—R
Silver Wings—R

$-Social Justice—R
Society/Prevention of Cruelty
$-Spiritual Life
Spirituality for Today
$-St. Anthony Messenger
$-Testimony—R
$-Today's Christian—R
$-Together—R
Trumpeter—R
$-U.S. Catholic
$-United Church Observer—R
Urban Kingdom—R
$-Way of St. Francis—R
$-World & I—R

CHILDREN
$-Archaeology
$-Pockets—R
Skipping Stones

CHRISTIAN EDUCATION/
LIBRARY
Catholic Library
$-Journal/Adventist Ed.—R
$-Momentum
$-RTJ—R

DAILY DEVOTIONALS
$-Brink Magazine—R

MISSIONS
$-Glad Tidings (Canada)—R
Missiology

PASTORS/LEADERS
$-African American Pulpit
$-Barefoot—R
$-Christian Century—R
$-Clergy Journal—R
$-Interpreter
Jour./Pastoral Care
Sharing the Practice—R
Theological Digest—R
$-Torch Legacy Leader

TEEN/YOUNG ADULT
$-Boundless Webzine—R
$-Brio—R
$-Devo'Zine—R
$-Spirit
$-TC Magazine
TeensForJC—R
$-True Girl
$-Young Christian—R
$-Young Salvationist—R

WOMEN
$-Esprit
$-Herizons
$-Horizons (women)—R
$-inSpirit—R
Making Waves
$-Pauses...
$-Today's Christian Woman—R

SOCIOLOGY

ADULT/GENERAL
$-Anglican Journal
$-Associated Content—R
$-Catholic Peace Voice—R
$-Christian Courier/Cdn.—R
Christian Online
$-Chronicle Christian/KS
$-Citizen USA
$-City Light News—R
($)-Community Spirit—R
$-Creative Nonfiction
$-Culture Wars—R
$-Dovetail—R
Evangelical Advocate—R
$-Faith Today
$-Gem—R
Island Catholic—R
Jour. of Church & State
$-Light & Life
$-National Catholic
$-Our Sunday Visitor—R
Perspectives—R
Perspectives/Science
Priscilla Papers
Prison Living—R
$-Salvo
$-Science & Spirit
$-Social Justice—R
$-St. Anthony Messenger
$-Testimony—R
Trumpeter—R
Urban Kingdom—R
$-World & I—R

PASTORS/LEADERS
Jour./Amer. Soc./Chur. Growth—R
$-Torch Legacy Leader
$-Word & World

TEEN/YOUNG ADULT
$-Boundless Webzine—R
$-InTeen—R
TeensForJC—R

WOMEN
($)-Beyond the Bend—R
$-Today's Christian Woman—R
Women of the Cross

SPIRITUAL GIFTS

ADULT/GENERAL
African Voices—R
$-Bible Advocate—R
Bread of Life—R
Breakthrough Intercessor—R
CBN.com—R
$-Christian Home & School
$-Christian Journal—R
Christian Motorsports
Christian Online
Christian Ranchman

$-Christian Standard—R
$-Christianity Today—R
$-ChristianWeek—R
$-Chronicle Christian/KS
$-City Light News—R
$-Covenant Companion—R
$-Dovetail—R
E-Channels—R
($)-E-Quality
Evangelical Advocate—R
$-Faith & Family
$-Faith & Friends—R
$-Faith Today
$-Home Times—R
($)-HopeKeepers—R
$-Imagine
Island Catholic—R
$-Light & Life
LiteraryTNT.com—R
$-Live—R
$-Majellan—R
$-Mature Years—R
$-Men of Integrity—R
Mosaic—R
($)-Mutuality—R
$-New Wineskins—R
Penned from the Heart—R
$-Positive Thinking—R
PrayerWorks—R
Priscilla Papers
Prison Living—R
Quaker Life—R
Regent Global—R
Reverent Submissions—R
Sacred Journey—R
$-Seek—R
Silver Wings—R
Spirituality for Today
$-St. Anthony Messenger
$-Stewardship—R
Sword and Trumpet
$-Testimony—R
$-Today's Christian—R
$-Together—R
Trumpeter—R
Urban Kingdom—R
$-Vista
$-Way of St. Francis—R
Wisconsin Christian

CHILDREN
$-Archaeology
$-BREAD/God's Children—R
$-Our Little Friend—R
$-Primary Treasure—R
$-Sparkle—R

CHRISTIAN EDUCATION/ LIBRARY
Teach Kids Essentials—R

DAILY DEVOTIONALS
Penned from the Heart—R

PASTORS/LEADERS
$-Interpreter
Ministry in Motion—R
$-Ministry Today
$-RevWriter Resource
$-Worship Leader

TEEN/YOUNG ADULT
$-Breakaway
$-Brio—R
$-CLEAR Direction
$-CLEAR Horizon
$-TC Magazine
TeensForJC—R

WOMEN
($)-Beyond the Bend—R
Christian Woman's Page—R
Elegance—R
Hope for Women
$-inSpirit—R
$-Journey
Just Between Us—R
P31 Woman—R
Precious Times—R
Proverbs 31 Sisters
$-SpiritLed Woman
$-Today's Christian Woman—R
Today's Leading Ladies—R
Virtuous Woman—R
Woman of Worth—R
Women Today—R
WT Online—R

WRITERS
Opinari—R

SPIRITUALITY

ADULT/GENERAL
African Voices—R
($)-AGAIN—R
$-Alive Now—R
American Tract—R
$-Angels on Earth
$-Annals of St. Anne
Anointed Pages
$-Arkansas Catholic—R
$-Arlington Catholic
$-Associated Content—R
$-Atlantic Catholic
$-Aujourd'hui Credo—R
$-Bible Advocate—R
Bread of Life—R
Breakthrough Intercessor—R
$-Catholic Digest—R
$-Catholic Peace Voice—R
CBN.com—R
$-CGA World—R
Christian C. L. RECORD—R
$-Christian Courier/Cdn.—R
$-Christian Journal—R
Christian Online
$-Christianity Today—R

$-ChristianWeek—R
$-Chronicle Christian/KS
Church of England News
$-City Light News—R
$-Common Ground—R
($)-Community Spirit—R
$-Covenant Companion—R
$-Culture Wars—R
Desert Call—R
$-Discipleship Journal—R
Divine Ascent
$-Dovetail—R
E-Channels—R
$-Episcopal Life—R
$-Eureka Street
Evangelical Advocate—R
$-Faith & Family
$-Faith & Friends—R
$-Faith Today
$-Family Digest—R
$-Gem—R
$-Good News—R
Good News Journal—R
$-Guideposts—R
Heartlight—R
$-Home Times—R
$-Horizons (adult)—R
$-Indian Life—R
Island Catholic—R
Koinonia
Leaves—R
$-Lifeglow—R
LifeTimes Catholic
$-Light & Life
$-Live—R
$-Living Church
$-Lookout
$-Majellan—R
$-Mature Years—R
$-Men of Integrity—R
$-Messenger/Sacred Heart
$-Messenger/St. Anthony
$-Minnesota Christian—R
$-National Catholic
New Heart—R
$-New Wineskins—R
$-Our Sunday Visitor—R
Pegasus Review—R
Penned from the Heart—R
Penwood Review
$-Positive Thinking—R
$-Prairie Messenger—R
Presbyterian Outlook
$-Presbyterians Today—R
Priscilla Papers
$-Pure Inspiration—R
Quaker Life—R
Sacred Journey—R
$-Seek—R
SingleAgain.com—R
$-Spiritual Life
Spirituality for Today

$-St. Anthony Messenger
$-Standard—R
$-Stewardship—R
Sword and Trumpet
$-Testimony—R
$-Today's Christian—R
$-Together—R
Trumpeter—R
$-U.S. Catholic
Urban Kingdom—R
Victory Herald—R
$-Vista
$-War Cry—R
$-Way of St. Francis—R
$-Weavings—R
Wisconsin Christian
$-Wittenburg Door—R
$-World & I—R

CHILDREN
$-Archaeology
$-BREAD/God's Children—R
$-New Moon—R
Skipping Stones

CHRISTIAN EDUCATION/ LIBRARY
Catholic Library
$-Children's Ministry
Jour./Ed. & Christian Belief—R
Jour./Research on Christian Ed.
$-Momentum
$-RTJ—R

DAILY DEVOTIONALS
Penned from the Heart—R

MISSIONS
$-Evangelical Missions—R
$-Glad Tidings (Canada)—R
Missiology

PASTORS/LEADERS
$-Christian Century—R
$-Diocesan Dialogue—R
$-Emmanuel
$-Interpreter
Jour./Pastoral Care
$-Leadership—R
$-Lutheran Partners—R
$-Ministry Today
$-Proclaim—R
$-Review for Religious
$-RevWriter Resource
Rick Warren's Ministry—R
Sharing the Practice—R
Theological Digest—R
$-Today's Parish
$-Word & World
$-Worship Leader

TEEN/YOUNG ADULT
$-Boundless Webzine—R
$-Breakaway
$-Brio—R

$-CLEAR Direction
$-CLEAR Horizon
$-InTeen—R
$-TC Magazine
TeensForJC—R
$-True Girl
$-Young Adult Today

WOMEN
($)-Beyond the Bend—R
$-Canticle
CelebrateMoms—R
Christian Woman's Page—R
Elegance—R
Handmaiden—R
$-Heart & Soul
$-Herizons
Hope for Women
$-Horizons (women)—R
$-inSpirit—R
$-Journey
Just Between Us—R
Lutheran Woman's Quar.
$-Pauses…
Precious Times—R
$-SpiritLed Woman
$-Today's Christian Woman—R
Today's Leading Ladies—R
Women of the Cross
Women Today—R
WT Online—R

WRITERS
Areopagus

SPIRITUAL LIFE
ADULT/GENERAL
$-Arkansas Catholic—R
$-Associated Content—R
$-Atlantic Catholic
$-Aujourd'hui Credo—R
$-Bible Advocate—R
Bread of Life—R
Breakthrough Intercessor—R
$-Cathedral Age
$-Catholic Digest—R
$-Catholic Peace Voice—R
$-Catholic Yearbook—R
CBN.com—R
$-Christian Examiner
$-Christian Home & School
$-Christian Journal—R
Christian Online
Christian Ranchman
$-Christian Research
$-ChristianWeek—R
$-Chronicle Christian/KS
Church Herald & Holiness—R
$-City Light News—R
($)-Community Spirit—R
Connections Leadership/MOPS
$-Covenant Companion—R
$-Discipleship Journal—R

Divine Ascent
E-Channels—R
$-Enfoque a La Familia
Eternal Ink—R
Evangel/OR—R
Evangelical Advocate—R
$-Faith & Family
$-Faith & Friends—R
$-Faith Today
$-Family Digest—R
$-Focus on the Family
$-Home Times—R
$-Homeschooling Today—R
$-Horizons (adult)—R
$-In His Presence—R
$-In Touch
IPHC Experience
Island Catholic—R
Koinonia
$-Light & Life
$-Liguorian
LiteraryTNT.com—R
$-Live—R
$-Lookout
$-Lutheran Journal—R
Lutheran Witness
$-Majellan—R
$-Mature Living
$-Men of Integrity—R
$-Minnesota Christian—R
Mosaic—R
$-National Catholic
New Heart—R
$-New Wineskins—R
$-Our Sunday Visitor—R
$-ParentLife
Penned from the Heart—R
Perspectives—R
($)-P.O.W.E.R.
PrayerWorks—R
$-Presbyterians Today—R
Priscilla Papers
Prison Living—R
$-Pure Inspiration—R
$-Purpose—R
Quaker Life—R
Regent Global—R
Reverent Submissions—R
Ruminate
Sacred Journey—R
$-Science & Spirit
$-Seek—R
$-Significant Living—R
Silver Wings—R
SingleAgain.com—R
Spirituality for Today
$-St. Anthony Messenger
$-Stewardship—R
Sword and Trumpet
$-Testimony—R
$-Today's Christian—R

$-Together—R
$-U.S. Catholic
Urban Kingdom—R
Victory Herald—R
$-Way of St. Francis—R
$-Weavings—R
$-Wildwood Reader—R

CHILDREN
$-Archaeology
$-BREAD/God's Children—R
$-Sparkle—R

CHRISTIAN EDUCATION/ LIBRARY
$-Momentum
$-Youth & CE Leadership

DAILY DEVOTIONALS
$-Brink Magazine—R
Penned from the Heart—R

MISSIONS
$-Glad Tidings (Canada)—R

PASTORS/LEADERS
$-African American Pulpit
$-Barefoot—R
Christian Ed. Jour. (CA)—R
$-Interpreter
Jour./Pastoral Care
$-Leadership—R
$-Ministry
$-Ministry Today
$-Review for Religious
$-RevWriter Resource
$-Willow—R

TEEN/YOUNG ADULT
$-Boundless Webzine—R
$-Breakaway
$-Brio—R
$-CLEAR Horizon
G4T Ink—R
$-InsideOut—R
$-TC Magazine
$-True Girl
$-Young Salvationist—R

WOMEN
$-Canticle
CelebrateMoms—R
Christian Woman's Page—R
Elegance—R
First Lady
$-Fullfill
Hope for Women
$-Horizons (women)—R
$-inSpirit—R
$-Journey
L.I.V.E.
More to Life
P31 Woman—R
$-Pauses…
Precious Times—R

($)-Simply Blessed—R
$-Today's Christian Woman—R
Today's Leading Ladies—R
Women Today—R
WT Online—R

SPIRITUAL RENEWAL ADULT/GENERAL
$-Arkansas Catholic—R
$-Associated Content—R
$-BGC World—R
$-Bible Advocate—R
Bread of Life—R
Breakthrough Intercessor—R
CBN.com—R
$-Christian Home & School
$-Christian Journal—R
Christian Online
Christian Ranchman
$-ChristianWeek—R
$-Chronicle Christian/KS
Church Herald & Holiness—R
$-City Light News—R
($)-Community Spirit—R
$-Discipleship Journal—R
Encompass
Eternal Ink—R
$-Evangel/IN—R
Evangel/OR—R
Evangelical Advocate—R
$-Family Digest—R
$-Good News, Etc.—R
$-Home Times—R
$-In His Presence—R
Island Catholic—R
Koinonia
$-Liguorian
LiteraryTNT.com—R
$-Live—R
$-Lookout
$-Majellan—R
$-Manna—R
$-Men of Integrity—R
Mosaic—R
$-New Wineskins—R
PrayerWorks—R
Prison Living—R
$-Pure Inspiration—R
Quaker Life—R
Reverent Submissions—R
Sacred Journey—R
$-Seek—R
Spirituality for Today
Sword and Trumpet
$-Testimony—R
$-Today's Christian—R
$-Today's Pentecostal—R
Urban Kingdom—R
Victory Herald—R
$-Way of St. Francis—R
$-Wildwood Reader—R

Wisconsin Christian

CHILDREN
$-Archaeology
$-BREAD/God's Children—R
$-Sparkle—R

DAILY DEVOTIONALS
$-Brink Magazine—R

PASTORS/LEADERS
$-African American Pulpit
$-Christian Century—R
Christian Ed. Jour. (CA)—R
$-Interpreter
$-Leadership—R
$-Lutheran Partners—R
$-Ministry Today
$-RevWriter Resource
Theological Digest—R

TEEN/YOUNG ADULT
$-Boundless Webzine—R
$-Breakaway
$-Brio—R
$-CLEAR Direction
$-CLEAR Horizon
$-TC Magazine
$-True Girl
$-Young Salvationist—R

WOMEN
$-Canticle
CelebrateMoms—R
Christian Woman's Page—R
$-Come to the Fire—R
Hearts at Home—R
Hope for Women
$-Horizons (women)—R
$-inSpirit—R
$-Journey
$-Pauses…
Precious Times—R
Proverbs 31 Sisters
$-Today's Christian Woman—R
Today's Leading Ladies—R
Virtuous Woman—R
Women Today—R
WT Online—R

SPIRITUAL
WARFARE
ADULT/GENERAL
($)-AGAIN—R
$-Angels on Earth
$-Associated Content—R
($)-Believer's Bay
$-Bible Advocate—R
Bread of Life—R
Breakthrough Intercessor—R
CBN.com—R
$-Celebrate Life—R
$-CGA World—R
Christian C. L. RECORD—R

$-Christian Home & School
Christian Online
Christian Ranchman
$-Christian Research
$-Christianity Today—R
$-ChristianWeek—R
$-Chronicle Christian/KS
Church Herald & Holiness—R
($)-Community Spirit—R
$-Discipleship Journal—R
E-Channels—R
Evangelical Advocate—R
$-Faith & Friends—R
$-Faith Today
$-Gem—R
$-Good News—R
$-Good News, Etc.—R
Heartlight—R
$-Home Times—R
$-In His Presence—R
Koinonia
Leaves—R
$-Light & Life
LiteraryTNT.com—R
$-Live—R
$-Lookout
$-Manna—R
$-Men of Integrity—R
Mosaic—R
New Heart—R
$-New Wineskins—R
Penned from the Heart—R
Prayer Closet
PrayerWorks—R
$-Purpose—R
Reverent Submissions—R
$-Seek—R
$-St. Anthony Messenger
Sword and Trumpet
Sword of the Lord—R
$-Testimony—R
Trumpeter—R
Urban Kingdom—R
Wisconsin Christian

CHILDREN
$-BREAD/God's Children—R

DAILY DEVOTIONALS
Penned from the Heart—R

MISSIONS
Railroad Evangelist—R

PASTORS/LEADERS
$-Growth Points—R
$-Let's Worship
$-Ministry Today
$-Pray!—R
Rick Warren's Ministry—R

TEEN/YOUNG ADULT
$-Breakaway
$-Brio—R

$-CLEAR Direction
$-CLEAR Horizon
TeensForJC—R
$-Young Salvationist—R

WOMEN
Elegance—R
Handmaiden—R
Hope for Women
$-inSpirit—R
$-Journey
Just Between Us—R
Precious Times—R
($)-Simply Blessed—R
Today's Leading Ladies—R
Women Today—R
WT Online—R

SPORTS/RECREATION
ADULT/GENERAL
$-Abilities
$-Angels on Earth
$-Arlington Catholic
$-Associated Content—R
CBN.com—R
Christian Courier/WI—R
$-Christian Renewal—R
$-Chronicle Christian/KS
$-City Light News—R
($)-Community Spirit—R
Connecting Point—R
Creation Care—R
Diamond Dust
$-Eureka Street
$-Faith Today
Family Journal—R
$-Family Smart e-Tips—R
$-Gem—R
Gold Country Families—R
$-Good News, Etc.—R
$-Gospel Today—R
$-Grand
$-Guideposts—R
Heartbeat/CMA
Heartland Gatekeeper—R
$-Home Times—R
$-In His Presence—R
$-In Touch
$-Lifeglow—R
$-Light & Life
$-Living Light—R
$-Lookout
$-Minnesota Christian—R
$-Our Sunday Visitor—R
Prison Living—R
Reverent Submissions—R
$-Sports Spectrum
$-St. Anthony Messenger
$-Storyteller—R
$-Testimony—R
$-Today's Christian—R
Urban Kingdom—R

$-Vibrant Life—R
Wisconsin Christian
$-World & I—R

CHILDREN
$-American Girl—R
$-Archaeology
$-Cadet Quest—R
$-SHINEbrightly—R
$-Sparkle—R

MISSIONS
$-Glad Tidings (Canada)—R

PASTORS/LEADERS
$-Cornerstone Youth—R

TEEN/YOUNG ADULT
$-Boundless Webzine—R
$-Breakaway
$-Brio—R
$-CLEAR Direction
$-Credo—R
G4T Ink—R
$-InTeen—R
$-Listen—R
$-Real Faith in Life—R
$-Sharing the VICTORY—R
$-Steelroots
$-TC Magazine
TeensForJC—R
$-Young Salvationist—R

WOMEN
Hope for Women
Today's Leading Ladies—R

STEWARDSHIP
ADULT/GENERAL
$-Angels on Earth
$-Bible Advocate—R
Bread of Life—R
$-Catholic Yearbook—R
CBN.com—R
$-Celebrate Life—R
$-Christian Courier/Cdn.—R
Christian Online
Christian Ranchman
$-Christian Standard—R
$-ChristianWeek—R
$-Chronicle Christian/KS
$-City Light News—R
($)-Community Spirit—R
Creation Care—R
$-Discipleship Journal—R
E-Channels—R
$-Evangel/IN—R
Evangelical Advocate—R
$-Faith Today
$-Family Digest—R
$-Focus on the Family
$-Gem—R
Highway News—R
$-In His Presence—R

$-Lifeglow—R
$-Light & Life
$-Liguorian
$-Live—R
$-Living Church
$-Lookout
$-Lutheran Journal—R
$-Majellan—R
$-Manna—R
($)-NRB Magazine—R
$-Our Sunday Visitor—R
Penned from the Heart—R
Perspectives—R
$-Positive Thinking—R
$-Power for Living—R
Presbyterian Outlook
$-Prism
Quaker Life—R
Regent Global—R
$-Seek—R
$-St. Anthony Messenger
$-Stewardship—R
$-Testimony—R
$-Today's Christian—R
Trumpeter—R
$-U.S. Catholic
$-United Church Observer—R
Urban Kingdom—R
$-Way of St. Francis—R
$-Wesleyan Life—R
Wisconsin Christian
$-Written

CHILDREN
$-BREAD/God's Children—R
$-Guide—R
$-SHINEbrightly—R
$-Sparkle—R

CHRISTIAN EDUCATION/LIBRARY
$-Momentum

DAILY DEVOTIONALS
Penned from the Heart—R

MISSIONS
$-Glad Tidings (Canada)—R

PASTORS/LEADERS
Christian Management—R
$-Clergy Journal—R
$-InSite—R
$-Interpreter
$-Let's Worship
Ministry in Motion—R
$-Ministry Today
$-Net Results
$-Preaching Well—R
$-RevWriter Resource
Sharing the Practice—R
$-Your Church—R

TEEN/YOUNG ADULT
$-Boundless Webzine—R

$-Breakaway
$-Brio—R
$-CLEAR Direction
$-CLEAR Horizon
$-TC Magazine
TeensForJC—R
$-Young Salvationist—R

WOMEN
Crowned with Silver
$-Esprit
Hope for Women
$-Horizons (women)—R
$-Journey
Just Between Us—R
P31 Woman—R
Precious Times—R
$-Today's Christian Woman—R
Today's Leading Ladies—R
Woman of Worth—R
WT Online—R

WRITERS
Opinari—R

TAKE-HOME PAPERS
ADULT/GENERAL
$-Evangel/IN—R
$-Gem—R
$-Gems of Truth—R
$-Horizons (adult)—R
$-Live—R
$-Power for Living—R
$-Purpose—R
$-Seek—R
$-Standard—R
$-Vision—R
$-Vista

CHILDREN
$-Adventures
$-Beginner's Friend—R
$-Celebrate
$-Faith Detectives
$-God's Explorers
$-Good News—R
$-Good News (child)
$-Guide—R
$-Junior Companion—R
$-JuniorWay
$-Kid Zone
$-Our Little Friend—R
$-Partners—R
$-Passport—R
$-Preschool Playhouse (child)
$-Primary Pal/KS—R
$-Primary Street
$-Primary Treasure—R
$-Promise
$-Seeds
$-Story Mates—R
$-Venture

TEEN/YOUNG ADULT
$-Insight—R
$-Living My Faith
$-Spirit
$-Visions
$-Youth Compass—R

TEACHER HELPS
ADULT/GENERAL
$-Animal Trails—R
$-City Light News—R
$-Home Times—R
$-Seek—R
Victory Herald—R

CHILDREN
$-Archaeology

CHRISTIAN EDUCATION/ LIBRARY
Christian Early Ed.—R
Christian School Ed.—R
Teach Kids Essentials—R

PASTORS/LEADERS
Christian Ed. Jour. (CA)—R
$-Ministry Today
Pulpit Helps—R

TEEN/YOUNG ADULT
$-Young Christian—R
$-Today's Christian Woman—R

WOMEN
Today's Leading Ladies—R

THEOLOGICAL
ADULT/GENERAL
($)-AGAIN—R
$-Alive Now—R
$-America
$-Anglican Journal
$-Annals of St. Anne
$-Arkansas Catholic—R
$-Arlington Catholic
$-Atlantic Catholic
$-Aujourd'hui Credo—R
$-B.C. Catholic—R
byFaith
$-Cathedral Age
$-Catholic Peace Voice—R
$-Catholic Yearbook—R
CBN.com—R
$-Christian Courier/Cdn.—R
Christian Online
Christian Ranchman
$-Christian Renewal—R
$-Christian Research
$-Christian Standard—R
$-Christianity Today—R
$-Chronicle Christian/KS
Church of England News
$-City Light News—R
($)-Community Spirit—R

Creation Care—R
$-Cresset
$-Culture Wars—R
Divine Ascent
$-Dovetail—R
E-Channels—R
($)-E-Quality
Encompass
$-Episcopal Life—R
$-Eureka Street
Evangelical Advocate—R
Evangelical Times
$-Faith Today
Founders Journal
$-Good News—R
$-Horizons (adult)—R
$-Imagine
$-In His Presence—R
Koinonia
$-Light & Life
$-Living Church
$-Lookout
$-Lutheran Journal—R
$-Messenger/Sacred Heart
$-Minnesota Christian—R
MovieGuide
$-National Catholic
$-New Wineskins—R
$-Our Sunday Visitor—R
Perspectives—R
Perspectives/Science
$-Prairie Messenger—R
PrayerWorks—R
Presbyterian Outlook
Priscilla Papers
Prison Living—R
Purpose Magazine—R
$-Science & Spirit
$-Social Justice—R
$-Spiritual Life
$-St. Anthony Messenger
$-Testimony—R
Trumpeter—R
$-U.S. Catholic
$-United Church Observer—R
Urban Kingdom—R
$-Way of St. Francis—R

CHRISTIAN EDUCATION/ LIBRARY
Jour. of Christianity—R

DAILY DEVOTIONALS
$-Brink Magazine—R
Penned from the Heart—R

MISSIONS
East-West Church
$-Glad Tidings (Canada)—R
Missiology

PASTORS/LEADERS
$-African American Pulpit
$-Catechumenate

$-Christian Century—R
$-Clergy Journal—R
Cross Currents
$-Diocesan Dialogue—R
$-Growth Points—R
Jour./Amer. Soc./Chur. Growth—R
Jour./Pastoral Care
Lutheran Forum
$-Lutheran Partners—R
$-Ministry & Liturgy—R
$-Parish Liturgy—R
$-Preaching Well—R
$-Proclaim—R
$-Reformed Worship—R
Rick Warren's Ministry—R
Sewanee Theo. Review
Sharing the Practice—R
$-This Rock
$-Today's Parish
$-Word & World
$-Worship Leader

TEEN/YOUNG ADULT
$-Boundless Webzine—R
$-Breakaway
$-Ignite Your Faith
$-InTeen—R
TeensForJC—R
$-Young Salvationist—R

WOMEN
$-Canticle
$-Esprit
$-Horizons (women)—R
Making Waves

THINK PIECES
ADULT/GENERAL
$-Alive Now—R
$-Annals of St. Anne
$-Associated Content—R
Baptist Standard
$-Catholic Forester—R
$-Catholic Peace Voice—R
$-CGA World—R
$-Christian Courier/Cdn.—R
$-Christian Journal—R
Christian Online
$-Christianity Today—R
$-ChristianWeek—R
$-Chronicle Christian/KS
$-City Light News—R
($)-Community Spirit—R
Desert Call—R
$-Dovetail—R
($)-E-Quality
$-Episcopal Life—R
$-Eureka Street
Evangelical Advocate—R
$-Faith Today
$-Gem—R
Good News Journal—R
$-Haruah—R

Heartlight—R
$-Home Times—R
$-In Touch
Island Catholic—R
$-Lifeglow—R
$-Light & Life
$-Lookout
$-Manna—R
Men of the Cross
$-MindFlights—R
$-Minnesota Christian—R
$-Montgomery's Journey
$-New Wineskins—R
$-Our Sunday Visitor—R
Pegasus Review—R
Penned from the Heart—R
Penwood Review
$-Positive Thinking—R
PrayerWorks—R
Presbyterian Outlook
Prison Living—R
Purpose Magazine—R
Reverent Submissions—R
$-Science & Spirit
$-Seek—R
$-St. Anthony Messenger
$-Stewardship—R
$-Testimony—R
$-Today's Christian—R
Trumpeter—R
$-U.S. Catholic
Urban Kingdom—R
$-Wittenburg Door—R
$-World & I—R

CHILDREN
$-Archaeology
Skipping Stones

CHRISTIAN EDUCATION/
LIBRARY
$-Children's Ministry

MISSIONS
$-Glad Tidings (Canada)—R

PASTORS/LEADERS
Alpha News
$-Catholic Servant
$-Enrichment—R
$-Ministry Today
Rick Warren's Ministry—R
$-Word & World

TEEN/YOUNG ADULT
$-Boundless Webzine—R
$-Breakaway
$-Brio—R
$-Real Faith in Life—R
$-TC Magazine
TeensForJC—R
$-Young Salvationist—R

WOMEN
CelebrateMoms—R
Crowned with Silver
Elegance—R
$-MomSense—R
$-Today's Christian Woman—R
Today's Leading Ladies—R
Women of the Cross

WRITERS
Areopagus
Money the Write Way—R
Opinari—R

TIME MANAGEMENT
ADULT/GENERAL
$-Associated Content—R
$-Bridal Guides—R
$-Catholic Forester—R
$-CBA Retailers
CBN.com—R
Christian Business
$-Christian Journal—R
Christian Online
$-ChristianWeek—R
$-Chronicle Christian/KS
$-City Light News—R
($)-Community Spirit—R
Disciple's Journal—R
Evangelical Advocate—R
Family Journal—R
$-Focus on the Family
$-Gem—R
Good News Journal—R
$-Home Times—R
$-Homeschooling Today—R
($)-HopeKeepers—R
$-In Touch
$-LarkNews.com
$-Lifeglow—R
$-Light & Life
$-Live—R
$-Living Light—R
$-Lookout
$-Majellan—R
Men of the Cross
MissionWares
$-Montgomery's Journey
($)-NRB Magazine—R
$-ParentLife
Penned from the Heart—R
$-Positive Thinking—R
Prison Living—R
Regent Global—R
$-St. Anthony Messenger
$-Stewardship—R
$-Testimony—R
$-Today's Christian—R
$-Together—R
Trumpeter—R
Urban Kingdom—R

$-Victory in Grace—R
$-World & I—R

CHILDREN
$-Archaeology

CHRISTIAN EDUCATION/
LIBRARY
Catholic Library
Christian Early Ed.—R
Christian Librarian—R
Christian School Ed.—R
$-Youth & CE Leadership

DAILY DEVOTIONALS
$-Brink Magazine—R
Penned from the Heart—R

PASTORS/LEADERS
Christian Management—R
$-Enrichment—R
$-Interpreter
Ministry in Motion—R
Rick Warren's Ministry—R
$-Willow—R
$-Your Church—R

TEEN/YOUNG ADULT
$-Boundless Webzine—R
$-Breakaway
$-Brio—R
TeensForJC—R
$-True Girl

WOMEN
CelebrateMoms—R
Christian Woman's Page—R
Elegance—R
$-Girlfriend 2 Girlfriend
Hearts at Home—R
Hope for Women
$-InspiredMoms—R
$-inSpirit—R
$-Journey
Just Between Us—R
Life Tools for Women
P31 Woman—R
Precious Times—R
Proverbs 31 Sisters
$-Today's Christian Woman—R
Today's Leading Ladies—R
Virtuous Woman—R
Woman of Worth—R
Women Today—R
WT Online—R

WRITERS
$-Adv. Christian Writer—R
$-Christian Communicator—R
$-Fellowscript—R
Money the Write Way—R
Opinari—R
Write Connection
$-Writer
$-Writers' Journal

TRAVEL

ADULT/GENERAL
$-Abilities
$-Angels on Earth
$-Arlington Catholic
$-Associated Content—R
$-Bridal Guides—R
$-Cappers
CBN.com—R
$-Chronicle Christian/KS
$-City Light News—R
$-Common Ground—R
($)-Community Spirit—R
Creation Care—R
$-Creative Nonfiction
Desert Voice—R
$-DisciplesWorld
Evangelical Advocate—R
$-Family Digest—R
Family Journal—R
$-Gem—R
Gold Country Families—R
Good News Journal—R
$-Grand
$-Home Times—R
($)-HopeKeepers—R
$-In His Presence—R
$-In Touch
Island Catholic—R
$-Lifeglow—R
$-Mature Living
$-Mature Years—R
MovieGuide
$-Over the Back Fence—R
$-Ozarks Senior Living—R
$-ParentLife
Sacred Journey—R
$-Seek—R
SingleAgain.com—R
$-Special Living—R
$-Testimony—R
$-Today's Christian—R
$-Upscale
Urban Kingdom—R
$-Way of St. Francis—R
Wisconsin Christian
$-World & I—R

CHILDREN
$-Archaeology
$-Faces
$-SHINEbrightly—R
Skipping Stones
$-Sparkle—R

MISSIONS
$-Glad Tidings (Canada)—R
$-PIME World—R

TEEN/YOUNG ADULT
$-Boundless Webzine—R
$-Brio—R

TeensForJC—R

WOMEN
$-Dabbling Mum—R
Hope for Women
$-InspiredMoms—R
Precious Times—R
$-Today's Christian Woman—R
Today's Leading Ladies—R

WRITERS
Money the Write Way—R

TRUE STORIES

ADULT/GENERAL
$-Advance
African Voices—R
$-Angels on Earth
Baptist Standard
Beacon
Behind the Hammer
$-Bible Advocate—R
Biblical Recorder
Breakthrough Intercessor—R
byFaith
$-Catholic Digest—R
CBN.com—R
$-Celebrate Life—R
Challenge Weekly
Charlotte World
$-Christian Journal—R
Christian Observer
Christian Online
Christian Ranchman
$-Chronicle Christian/KS
$-Citizen USA
$-City Light News—R
($)-Community Spirit—R
$-Creative Nonfiction
$-Culture Wars—R
$-Disaster News
$-Dovetail—R
E-Channels—R
($)-E-Quality
$-Enfoque a La Familia
Eternal Ink—R
Evangel/OR—R
Evangelical Advocate—R
Evangelical Times
$-Faith & Family
$-Focus on the Family
$-Gem—R
$-Gems of Truth—R
Gold Country Families—R
Good News Journal—R
Good News Today
$-Good News, Etc.—R
$-Guideposts—R
$-Haruah—R
Heartland Gatekeeper—R
Heartlight—R
Highway News—R

$-Home Times—R
($)-HopeKeepers—R
$-Horizons (adult)—R
$-In His Presence—R
$-In Touch
$-Indian Life—R
$-Lifeglow—R
$-Light & Life
$-Live—R
$-Lutheran Digest—R
$-Majellan—R
$-Mature Living
Men of the Cross
MESSAGE/Open Bible—R
Michiana Christian
$-Minnesota Christian—R
MissionWares
New Heart—R
$-New Wineskins—R
Nostalgia—R
$-Now What?—R
$-On Mission
$-ParentLife
Penned from the Heart—R
($)-Portrait of Achievement
$-Power for Living—R
PrayerWorks—R
$-Priority!—R
Prison Living—R
$-Pure Inspiration—R
Reverent Submissions—R
Sacred Journey—R
$-Science & Spirit
$-Seek—R
$-St. Anthony Messenger
$-Storyteller—R
$-Testimony—R
$-Today's Christian—R
$-Today's Pentecostal—R
Tri-State Voice
Trumpeter—R
Urban Kingdom—R
Victory Herald—R
$-Victory in Grace—R
$-Vista
$-War Cry—R
$-Way of St. Francis—R
$-Written

CHILDREN
$-Archaeology
$-Cadet Quest—R
$-Focus/Clubhouse Jr.
$-Guide—R
$-Nature Friend—R
$-New Moon—R
$-Our Little Friend—R
$-Partners—R
$-Pockets—R
$-Primary Treasure—R
$-SHINEbrightly—R

$-BGC World—R
Bread of Life—R
$-Catholic Forester—R
$-Catholic Peace Voice—R
$-CBA Retailers
CBN.com—R
$-Celebrate Life—R
$-CGA World—R
$-Chicken Soup Books—R
$-Christian Courier/Cdn.—R
$-Christian Examiner
$-Christian Journal—R
Christian News NW—R
Christian Online
Christian Ranchman
$-ChristianWeek—R
$-Chronicle Christian/KS
Church of England News
$-City Light News—R
$-Columbia—R
($)-Community Spirit—R
$-Creative Nonfiction
Desert Voice—R
Disciple's Journal—R
$-Dovetail—R
($)-E-Quality
$-EFCA Today—R
$-Episcopal Life—R
$-Evangel/IN—R
Evangel/OR—R
Evangelical Advocate—R
$-Faith & Family
$-Faith Today
Family Journal—R
$-Family Smart e-Tips—R
$-Gem—R
Godly Places
Good News Journal—R
$-Gospel Today—R
Heartlight—R
Holy House Ministries—R
$-Home Times—R
$-Homeschooling Today—R
($)-HopeKeepers—R
$-In His Presence—R
$-In Touch
$-Indian Life—R
Island Catholic—R
$-Light & Life
$-Liguorian
$-Live—R
$-Lookout
$-Majellan—R
$-Manna—R
$-Minnesota Christian—R
$-Montgomery's Journey
Mosaic—R
($)-Mutuality—R
$-National Catholic
$-New Wineskins—R
$-Our Sunday Visitor—R

Penned from the Heart—R
Perspectives—R
$-Prairie Messenger—R
PrayerWorks—R
Presbyterian Outlook
Priscilla Papers
Prison Living—R
$-Psychology for Living—R
$-Purpose—R
Purpose Magazine—R
Reverent Submissions—R
$-Seek—R
$-St. Anthony Messenger
$-Testimony—R
$-Today's Christian—R
$-Together—R
Trumpeter—R
$-U.S. Catholic
$-United Church Observer—R
Urban Kingdom—R
$-Vibrant Life—R
Victory Herald—R
$-War Cry—R
$-Wesleyan Life—R
West Wind Review
$-World & I—R
$-Written

CHILDREN
$-New Moon—R
Skipping Stones

CHRISTIAN EDUCATION/ LIBRARY
$-Teachers of Vision—R

DAILY DEVOTIONALS
Penned from the Heart—R

MISSIONS
$-Glad Tidings (Canada)—R
Women of the Harvest

PASTORS/LEADERS
$-African American Pulpit
$-Interpreter
Ministry in Motion—R
$-Word & World

TEEN/YOUNG ADULT
$-Boundless Webzine—R
$-Brio—R
TeensForJC—R
$-True Girl

WOMEN
$-At the Center—R
($)-Beyond the Bend—R
Breathe Again
$-Canticle
CelebrateMoms—R
Christian Woman's Page—R
Christian Women Today—R
$-Come to the Fire—R

Crowned with Silver
$-Dabbling Mum—R
Elegance—R
$-Esprit
First Lady
$-Fullfill
$-Girlfriend 2 Girlfriend
Handmaiden—R
Handmaidens
$-Heart & Soul
Hearts at Home—R
$-Herizons
Hope for Women
$-Horizons (women)—R
Inspired Women
$-inSpirit—R
$-Journey
Just Between Us—R
L.I.V.E.
Ladies First
Life Tools for Women
$-Link & Visitor—R
Lutheran Woman's Quar.
Making Waves
$-Melody of the Heart
$-MomSense—R
More to Life
P31 Woman—R
$-Pauses…
Precious Times—R
Proverbs 31 Sisters
Right to the Heart—R
Share
($)-Simply Blessed—R
$-SpiritLed Woman
$-Today's Christian Woman—R
Today's Leading Ladies—R
Together with God—R
Virtuous Woman—R
Woman of Worth—R
Women of the Cross
Women Today—R
Women's Ministry
WT Online—R

WORKPLACE ISSUES
ADULT/GENERAL
$-Associated Content—R
$-BGC World—R
byFaith
CBN.com—R
Christian Business
$-Christian Examiner
$-Christian Journal—R
Christian News NW—R
Christian Online
Christian Ranchman
$-Christian Retailing
$-ChristianWeek—R
$-Chronicle Christian/KS
$-City Light News—R

($)-Community Spirit—R
Desert Voice—R
$-Discipleship Journal—R
E-Channels—R
$-Eureka Street
$-Evangel/IN—R
Evangelical Advocate—R
$-Faith & Friends—R
$-Faith Today
Family Journal—R
Good News Today
$-Good News, Etc.—R
$-Good News/S. Florida
$-Gospel Today—R
Highway News—R
$-Home Times—R
($)-HopeKeepers—R
$-In His Presence—R
$-In Touch
Island Catholic—R
$-LarkNews.com
$-Light & Life
$-Live—R
$-Lookout
$-Majellan—R
$-Manna—R
$-Men of Integrity—R
$-Minnesota Christian—R
$-Montana Catholic
$-Montgomery's Journey
New Heart—R
$-Our Sunday Visitor—R
Penned from the Heart—R
Perspectives—R
$-Positive Thinking—R
Prison Living—R
$-Purpose—R
Purpose Magazine—R
Regent Global—R
Reverent Submissions—R
$-Seek—R
$-Testimony—R
$-Today's Christian—R
$-Together—R
$-U.S. Catholic
Urban Kingdom—R
Victory Herald—R
$-World & I—R

CHRISTIAN EDUCATION/ LIBRARY

Catholic Library
Christian Librarian—R
$-Group
Teach Kids Essentials—R
$-Teachers of Vision—R
$-Today's Catholic Teacher—R

MISSIONS

$-Glad Tidings (Canada)—R

PASTORS/LEADERS

Alpha News

$-Interpreter
$-Your Church—R

TEEN/YOUNG ADULT

$-Boundless Webzine—R

WOMEN

Elegance—R
$-Fullfill
$-Herizons
Hope for Women
Inspired Women
$-InspiredMoms—R
$-Journey
Life Tools for Women
Making Waves
More to Life
$-Today's Christian Woman—R
Today's Leading Ladies—R
Women Today—R
WT Online—R

WRITERS

$-Adv. Christian Writer—R

WORLD ISSUES
ADULT/GENERAL

($)-AGAIN—R
American Tract—R
$-Annals of St. Anne
$-Arlington Catholic
$-Associated Content—R
$-Aujourd'hui Credo—R
Baptist Standard
Beacon
Biblical Recorder
Breakthrough Intercessor—R
CanadianChristianity
$-Catholic Peace Voice—R
Catholic Register
CBN.com—R
$-CGA World—R
Challenge Weekly
Charlotte World
Christian C. L. RECORD—R
Christian Chronicle
$-Christian Examiner
Christian Observer
Christian Online
$-Christian Renewal—R
$-ChristianWeek—R
$-Chronicle Christian/KS
$-City Light News—R
($)-Community Spirit—R
$-Compass Direct
$-Creative Nonfiction
$-Culture Wars—R
Desert Christian
Desert Voice—R
$-Dovetail—R
($)-E-Quality
$-Eureka Street
$-Evangel/IN—R

Evangelical Advocate—R
Evangelical Times
$-Faith Today
Friends Journal—R
$-Gem—R
Good News Connection
Good News Journal—R
Good News Today
$-Good News, Etc.—R
$-Good News/S. Florida
Heartland Gatekeeper—R
Heartlight—R
$-Home Times—R
$-In Touch
$-Indian Life—R
Jerusalem Connection
$-Liberty
LifeSite News
$-Light & Life
$-Living Church
$-Lookout
$-Majellan—R
$-Minnesota Christian—R
MovieGuide
($)-Mutuality—R
$-New Wineskins—R
$-Our Sunday Visitor—R
Penned from the Heart—R
Perspectives—R
Presbyterian Outlook
$-Prism
Prison Living—R
$-Purpose—R
Purpose Magazine—R
Quaker Life—R
Sacred Journey—R
$-Salvo
$-Seek—R
$-Social Justice—R
$-St. Anthony Messenger
$-Testimony—R
$-Today's Christian—R
Tri-State Voice
Trumpeter—R
$-United Church Observer—R
Urban Kingdom—R
$-War Cry—R
$-Way of St. Francis—R
West Wind Review
$-World & I—R

CHILDREN

$-New Moon—R
Skipping Stones

CHRISTIAN EDUCATION/ LIBRARY

Catholic Library

DAILY DEVOTIONALS

$-Brink Magazine—R

MISSIONS
$-Glad Tidings (Canada)—R
Intl. Jour./Frontier—R
Lausanne World Pulse
$-Leaders for Today
Missiology
Mission Frontiers
$-New World Outlook
$-One
OpRev Equipper—R
$-PFI Global—R
$-PIME World—R

PASTORS/LEADERS
Alpha News
$-Christian Century—R
$-Ministry Today
$-Word & World

TEEN/YOUNG ADULT
$-Boundless Webzine—R
$-Brio—R
$-TC Magazine
TeensForJC—R
$-True Girl

WOMEN
$-Canticle
$-Esprit
Hope for Women
$-Horizons (women)—R
$-SpiritLed Woman
$-Today's Christian Woman—R
Today's Leading Ladies—R

WRITERS
Areopagus

WORSHIP
ADULT/GENERAL
$-Advance
($)-AGAIN—R
$-Angels on Earth
$-Annals of St. Anne
$-Arlington Catholic
$-Aujourd'hui Credo—R
$-BGC World—R
$-Bible Advocate—R
Bread of Life—R
Breakthrough Intercessor—R
$-Catholic Yearbook—R
CBN.com—R
$-CGA World—R
$-Christian Examiner
$-Christian Journal—R
Christian Online
Christian Ranchman
$-Christian Standard—R
$-Christianity Today—R
$-ChristianWeek—R
$-Chronicle Christian/KS
Church Herald & Holiness—R
$-City Light News—R

$-Columbia—R
($)-Community Spirit—R
Creation Care—R
$-Culture Wars—R
$-Discipleship Journal—R
$-Dovetail—R
E-Channels—R
Eternal Ink—R
$-Evangel/IN—R
Evangelical Advocate—R
$-Faith Today
$-Family Digest—R
($)-HopeKeepers—R
$-Imagine
$-In His Presence—R
$-Lifeglow—R
$-Light & Life
$-Liguorian
LiteraryTNT.com—R
$-Live—R
$-Living Church
$-Lookout
$-Lutheran Journal—R
$-Manna—R
$-Minnesota Christian—R
$-Montgomery's Journey
Mosaic—R
$-New Wineskins—R
Penned from the Heart—R
Perspectives—R
$-Power for Living—R
PrayerWorks—R
Presbyterian Outlook
$-Presbyterians Today—R
Priscilla Papers
Prison Living—R
Purpose Magazine—R
Reverent Submissions—R
$-Seek—R
Silver Wings—R
$-Spiritual Life
$-St. Anthony Messenger
$-Stewardship—R
Sword and Trumpet
Sword of the Lord—R
$-Testimony—R
Time of Singing—R
$-Today's Christian—R
Trumpeter—R
$-United Church Observer—R
Urban Kingdom—R
Victory Herald—R
$-War Cry—R
$-Way of St. Francis—R
$-Wesleyan Life—R
$-World & I—R

CHILDREN
$-Archaeology
$-BREAD/God's Children—R
$-Keys for Kids—R

$-Promise
$-Sparkle—R

CHRISTIAN EDUCATION/ LIBRARY
$-Group
$-RTJ—R
Teach Kids Essentials—R
$-Youth & CE Leadership

DAILY DEVOTIONALS
$-Brink Magazine—R
Penned from the Heart—R

MISSIONS
$-Glad Tidings (Canada)—R

MUSIC
Church Music
$-Creator—R

PASTORS/LEADERS
$-African American Pulpit
$-Barefoot—R
$-Clergy Journal—R
$-Enrichment—R
$-Growth Points—R
$-Interpreter
Jour./Amer. Soc./Chur. Growth—R
$-Leadership—R
$-Let's Worship
$-Lutheran Partners—R
$-Ministry & Liturgy—R
$-Ministry Today
$-Pray!—R
Preaching
Pulpit Helps—R
$-Reformed Worship—R
$-Rev. Magazine
$-RevWriter Resource
Rick Warren's Ministry—R
Sharing the Practice—R
Theological Digest—R
$-Today's Parish
$-Word & World
$-Worship Leader
$-Your Church—R

TEEN/YOUNG ADULT
$-Boundless Webzine—R
$-Brio—R
$-CLEAR Direction
$-CLEAR Horizon
$-Insight—R
$-TC Magazine
TeensForJC—R
$-True Girl

WOMEN
CelebrateMoms—R
Christian Woman's Page—R
Elegance—R
Hope for Women
$-Horizons (women)—R
$-Journey

$-Today's Christian Woman—R
Today's Leading Ladies—R
Virtuous Woman—R
Women Today—R
WT Online—R

WRITING HOW-TO

ADULT/GENERAL
$-Animal Trails—R
$-Associated Content—R
$-CBA Retailers
CBN.com—R
Christian Observer
Christian Online
($)-Community Spirit—R
Good News Journal—R
$-Haruah—R
$-Home Times—R
($)-HopeKeepers—R
LiteraryTNT.com—R
$-Live—R
Penwood Review
Reverent Submissions—R
SingleAgain.com—R
$-St. Anthony Messenger
Urban Kingdom—R
Victory Herald—R
$-Village Note Cards—R
$-World & I—R

CHILDREN
$-Archaeology
Skipping Stones

CHRISTIAN EDUCATION/ LIBRARY
Christian Librarian—R
$-Group

PASTORS/LEADERS
$-Newsletter Newsletter

TEEN/YOUNG ADULT
$-Boundless Webzine—R
TeensForJC—R
$-Young Christian—R

WOMEN
$-Dabbling Mum—R
Elegance—R
Hope for Women
Just Between Us—R
Precious Times—R
Right to the Heart—R
Today's Leading Ladies—R

WRITERS
$-Adv. Christian Writer—R
Areopagus
Author-Me
$-Best New Writing
$-ByLine
$-Christian Communicator—R
$-Cross & Quill—R

$-Fellowscript—R
$-Freelance Writer's Report—R
Money the Write Way—R
$-New Writer's Mag.
NW Christian Author—R
Once Upon a Time—R
Opinari—R
$-Poets & Writers
$-Shades of Romance—R
$-Spirit-Led Writer—R
$-Tickled by Thunder
$-WIN-Informer
Write Connection
$-Writer
$-Writer's Digest
Writers Manual
$-Writers' Journal
WriteToInspire
Writing Corner—R

YOUNG WRITER MARKETS
Note: These publications have indicated they will accept submissions from children or teens (C or T).

ADULT/GENERAL
African Voices
$-Ancient Paths (T)
$-Animal Trails
Anointed Pages
$-Aujourd'hui Credo (C or T)
Breakthrough Intercessor (C or T)
$-Bridal Guides (C or T)
$-Catholic Peace Voice (T)
$-Catholic Yearbook (C or T)
CBN.com (T)
$-Celebrate Life (C or T)
$-Christian Herald (T)
$-Christian Home & School (C or T)
$-Christian Journal (C or T)
Christian Online (C or T)
$-ChristianWeek (T)
Church Herald & Holiness (C or T)
$-Citizen USA (T)
$-City Light News (T)
$-Creative Nonfiction (T)
Desert Voice (T)
Diamond Dust (T)
$-Drama Ministry (T)
$-DreamSeeker (C or T)
E-Channels (T)
Eternal Ink (C or T)
Friends Voice
Gold Country Families (C or T)
$-Gospel Today
Haiku Hippodrome (C or T)
$-Haruah (T)
Holy House Ministries (C or T)
$-Home Times (T)
($)-HopeKeepers (T)
$-In His Presence (C or T)
$-Indian Life (C or T)

$-Interchange (C or T)
Island Catholic (C or T)
$-Leben (T)
LifeTimes Catholic (T)
$-Light & Life (C or T)
LiteraryTNT.com (C or T)
$-Lutheran Journal (C or T)
$-Majellan (C or T)
$-Manna (C or T)
$-Mature Living
Men of the Cross (T)
$-MindFlights (T)
MissionWares (T)
$-Montgomery's Journey (T)
Mosaic
$-New Wineskins (C or T)
Pegasus Review (T)
Penned from the Heart (C or T)
($)-Portrait of Achievement (C or T)
$-Priority! (C or T)
Prison Living (C or T)
$-Pure Inspiration (C or T)
Purpose Magazine (C or T)
Quaker Life (C or T)
Reverent Submissions (C or T)
Silver Wings (C or T)
$-Storyteller (C or T)
Urban Kingdom (T)
Victory Herald (C or T)
$-Vista (C or T)
$-Way of St. Francis (C or T)
Wisconsin Christian (C or T)

CHILDREN
$-American Girl
$-Archaeology (C or T)
$-Focus/Clubhouse (C)
$-Kids' Ark (C or T)
$-New Moon (C or T)
$-Pockets (C)

CHRISTIAN EDUCATION/ LIBRARY
Catholic Library
$-Children's Ministry (C or T)
Teach Kids Essentials (C or T)

DAILY DEVOTIONALS
Penned from the Heart (C or T)

MISSIONS
$-Glad Tidings (Canada) (T)
Koinonia
$-PIME World (T)

PASTORS/LEADERS
$-Cornerstone Youth (T)
$-Let's Worship
$-Reformed Worship (C or T)
$-RevWriter Resource (T)

TEEN/YOUNG ADULT
$-Boundless Webzine (T)
$-Breakaway (T)

$-CLEAR Direction (T)
$-CLEAR Horizon (T)
$-Credo (T)
$-Essential Connection
$-Ignite Your Faith (T)
$-Insight (T)
$-Listen
$-Steelroots (T)
$-Take Five Plus (T)
$-TC Magazine (T)
TeensForJC (T)
$-True Girl (T)
$-Young Christian (C or T)

WOMEN

CelebrateMoms (C or T)
$-Dabbling Mum (C or T)
Elegance (T)
($)-History's Women (T)
Precious Times (T)
Proverbs 31 Sisters
Today's Leading Ladies
Together with God (T)
Women of the Cross (T)
Women Today (T)

WRITERS

$-Canadian Writer's Jour. (T)
Esdras' Scroll (C or T)
$-Fellowscript (T)
Money the Write Way
NW Christian Author (T)
$-Spirit-Led Writer (T)
$-Tickled by Thunder (C or T)
Write Connection (T)
$-Writers' Journal (T)

YOUTH ISSUES
ADULT/GENERAL

American Tract—R
$-Annals of St. Anne
Anointed Pages
$-Arlington Catholic
$-Associated Content—R
$-Atlantic Catholic
$-Aujourd'hui Credo—R
$-BGC World—R
$-Bible Advocate—R
Bread of Life—R
$-Catholic Forester—R
$-Catholic Peace Voice—R
CBN.com—R
$-Chicken Soup Books—R
$-Christian Examiner
$-Christian Home & School
$-Christian Journal—R
Christian Motorsports
Christian News NW—R
Christian Online

Christian Ranchman
$-Christian Renewal—R
$-ChristianWeek—R
$-Chronicle Christian/KS
$-Citizen USA
$-City Light News—R
($)-Community Spirit—R
$-Culture Wars—R
Desert Voice—R
$-Dovetail—R
E-Channels—R
$-EFCA Today—R
$-Eureka Street
Evangelical Advocate—R
$-Faith & Family
$-Faith Today
Family Journal—R
$-Family Smart e-Tips—R
Godly Places
Good News Journal—R
$-Home Times—R
$-Homeschooling Today—R
$-In His Presence—R
$-In Touch
$-Indian Life—R
Island Catholic—R
Koinonia
LifeTimes Catholic
$-Light & Life
$-Living Church
$-Lookout
$-Majellan—R
$-Manna—R
MESSAGE/Open Bible—R
$-Montgomery's Journey
Mosaic—R
$-Our Sunday Visitor—R
Penned from the Heart—R
Presbyterian Outlook
Prison Living—R
$-Seek—R
SingleAgain.com—R
Spirituality for Today
$-St. Anthony Messenger
Sword of the Lord—R
$-Testimony—R
$-Today's Christian—R
Trumpeter—R
$-U.S. Catholic
Urban Kingdom—R
Victory Herald—R
$-Way of St. Francis—R
$-Wesleyan Life—R
$-World & I—R

CHILDREN

$-American Girl—R
$-Archaeology
$-BREAD/God's Children—R

$-Cadet Quest—R
$-Keys for Kids—R
$-New Moon—R
$-SHINEbrightly—R
Skipping Stones
$-Sparkle—R
$-Winner—R

CHRISTIAN EDUCATION/ LIBRARY

Catholic Library
$-Group
$-Journal/Adventist Ed.—R
$-Momentum
$-RTJ—R
$-Teachers of Vision—R
$-Youth & CE Leadership

PASTORS/LEADERS

$-Barefoot—R
$-Catholic Servant
$-Cornerstone Youth—R
$-InSite—R
$-Interpreter
$-Lutheran Partners—R
Plugged In
$-Word & World
$-Youthworker

TEEN/YOUNG ADULT

$-Boundless Webzine—R
$-Breakaway
$-Brio—R
Clarity Publishers
$-CLEAR Direction
$-CLEAR Horizon
Connected
$-Credo—R
Exodus Magazine
Focus/Dare 2 Dig Deeper
$-InsideOut—R
$-Insight—R
$-Listen—R
$-Risen
$-Sharing the VICTORY—R
$-Spirit
Student Life
$-TC Magazine
$-True Girl
$-Visions
$-Young Salvationist—R
$-YouthWalk

WOMEN

$-Esprit
Hearts at Home—R
Just Between Us—R
P31 Woman—R
Today's Leading Ladies—R
Together with God—R

ALPHABETICAL LISTINGS OF PERIODICALS AND E-ZINES

Following are the listings of periodicals. They are arranged alphabetically by type of periodical. (See table of contents for a list of types). Nonpaying markets are indicated in bold letters within those listings, e.g. **NO PAYMENT**. Paying markets are indicated with a $ in front of the listing.

If a listing is preceded by a (+) it is a new listing. It is important that freelance writers request writer's guidelines and a recent sample copy or visit a periodical's Website before submitting to any of these publications.

If you do not find the publication you are looking for, look in the General Index. See the introduction of that index for the codes used to identify the current status of each unlisted publication.

For a detailed explanation of how to understand and get the most out of these listings, as well as solid marketing tips, see the "How to Use This Book" section at the front of the book. Unfamiliar terms are explained in the "Glossary" on the CD.

+ —A plus sign means it is a new listing.
$ —A dollar sign before a listing indicates a paying market.
($) —A dollar sign in parentheses before a listing indicates they sometimes pay, or pay in books or other merchandise.

ADULT/GENERAL MARKETS

$ABILITIES MAGAZINE, 401—340 College St., Toronto ON M5T 3A9, Canada. (416)923-1885. Fax (416)923-9829. E-mail: ray@abilities.ca. Website: www.abilities.ca. Canadian Abilities Foundation; general. Raymond Cohen, ed-in-chief. Canada's foremost cross-disabilities lifestyle magazine. Open to freelance. Query; e-query preferred. Pays $50-250 Cdn. for 1st rts. Articles 750-2,000 wds. No simultaneous submissions. Requires disk. Kill fee 50%. Guidelines & theme list on Website. (Ads)
> **Tips:** "Ensure your query is strongly Canadian and includes strategies, news, or ideas on living with a disability. We don't publish material with an overtly religious tone. Articles must be disability-related with a positive tone and practical advice."

$ADVANCE, 1910 W. Sunset Blvd., Ste. 200, PO Box 26902, Los Angeles CA 90026-0176. Toll-free (888)635-4234. (213)989-4230. Fax (213)989-4590. E-mail: comm@foursquare .org, bshepson@foursquare.org, or through Website: www.foursquarechurch.org/advance. International Church of the Foursquare Gospel. Submit to Editorial Director. Quarterly mag. with bonus missions issue & online version; 32 pgs.; circ. 30,000. Subscription free. 100% assigned. Query (no complete mss); e-query OK. No full mss by e-mail. Payment negotiated individually. Pays on publication for all rts. Articles 2,000-3,000 wds.; book/music/video reviews 150 wds. Responds in 4 wks. No simultaneous submissions or reprints. Requires e-mail submissions (attached file). Kill fee negotiable. Regularly uses sidebars. Prefers NKJV. Guidelines (also by e-mail/Website); free copy on request. (No ads)
> **Tips:** "Query only via e-mail on relevant real-life topics."
> **2004 EPA Award of Excellence—Most Improved Publication; 2006, 2005 Award of Merit—Denominational.

+AFA JOURNAL, PO Drawer 2440, Tupelo MS 38803. (662)844-5036. Fax (662)842-7798. E-mail: randall@afa.net. Website: www.afajournal.org. American Family Assn. Randall Murphree, ed. To promote the biblical ethic of decency in American society with emphasis on moral issues that impact the family. Monthly mag. (11X); circ. 180,000. Subscription $25. Open to unsolicited freelance. Articles & reviews. Not in topical listings. (Ads)

AFRICAN VOICES, 270 W. 96th St., New York NY 10025. (212)865-2982. Fax (212)316-3335. E-mail: africanvoices@aol.com, or general@africanvoices.com. Website: www.africanvoices

.com. African Voices Communications Inc. Layding Kaliba, mng. ed.; Kim Horne, fiction ed.; Debbie Officer, book review ed. Publishes original fiction, nonfiction, and poetry by artists of color. Quarterly mag.; 48 pgs.; circ. 20,000. Subscription $12. 75% unsolicited freelance; 25% assigned. Query/clips; e-query OK. **PAYS IN COPIES** for 1st rts. Articles 500-2,500 wds. (25/yr.); fiction 500-2,000 wds. (20/yr.); book reviews 500-1,200 wds. Responds in 16 wks. Seasonal 4 mos. ahead. Accepts simultaneous submissions & reprints (tell when/where appeared). Requires accepted submissions by e-mail (copied into message). Uses some sidebars. Guidelines on Website; copy $5/9x12 SAE/$2.23 postage (mark "Media Mail"). (Ads)

Poetry: Layding Kaliba, poetry ed. Accepts 75-80/yr. Avant-garde, free verse, light verse, haiku, traditional; to 3 pgs. Submit max. 3 poems.

Fillers: Accepts 10/yr. Cartoons.

($)AGAIN MAGAZINE, 10090-A Hwy 9, PO Box 76, Ben Lomond CA 95005. Toll-free (800)967-7377. (831)336-5118. Fax (831)336-8882. E-mail: dsalibi@conciliarpress.com. Website: www.conciliarpress.com. Antiochian Orthodox Archdiocese of North America/Conciliar Press. Submit to Managing Editor. Historic Eastern Orthodox Christianity applied to our modern times. Quarterly mag.; 32 pgs.; circ. 5,000. Subscription $16. 1% unsolicited freelance; 99% assigned. Query; e-query OK. **USUALLY PAYS IN COPIES.** Articles 1,500-2,500 wds. (4/yr.); book reviews 800-1,000 wds. Responds in 6-8 wks. Seasonal 4-6 mos. ahead. Serials 2 parts. Accepts reprints (tell when/where appeared). Prefers requested ms on disk or by e-mail (copied into message). Uses some sidebars. Prefers NKJV. Guidelines on Website; copy for 9x12 SAE/4 stamps. (No ads)

Tips: "We are Orthodox in orientation, and interested in thoughtful, intelligent articles dealing with church history, Protestant/Orthodox dialog, relations between Protestants and Orthodox in foreign countries, also in modern ethical dilemmas—no fluff."

$ALIVE NOW, PO Box 340004, Nashville TN 37203-0004. (615)340-7218. Fax (615)340-7267. E-mail: alivenow@upperroom.org. Website: www.alivenow.org. The Upper Room. JoAnn Evans Miller, ed. Short, theme-based writings in attractive graphic setting for reflection and meditation. Bimonthly mag.; 64 pgs.; circ. 70,000. Subscription $14.95. 30% unsolicited freelance; 70% assigned. Complete ms/cover letter; e-query OK. Pays $35-150 on acceptance for newspaper, periodical, or electronic rts. Articles 250-500 wds. (25/yr.); fiction 250-500 wds. Responds 13 wks. before issue date. Seasonal 6-8 mos. ahead. Accepts simultaneous submissions & reprints (tell when/where appeared). Accepts e-mail submissions (copied into message). Uses some sidebars. Prefers NRSV. Guidelines/theme list (also on Website); copy for 6x9 SAE/4 stamps.

Poetry: Avant-garde, free verse, traditional; 10-45 lines; $25-100. Submit max. 5 poems. On issue's theme.

Tips: "Write for our theme list and make your submission relevant to the topic. Avoid the obvious and heavy-handed preachiness."

**This periodical was #46 on the 2008 Top 50 Christian Publishers list.

+THE AMBASSADOR, 712 Onstott Rd., Yuba City CA 95993. (530)933-1385. Fax (775)206-5914. E-mail: editor@TheAmbassadorofYS.com. Seth Halpern, ed./pub. To encourage the local Christian community. Monthly newspaper; circ. 5,000. Subscription $30. Open to unsolicited freelance. Query. Incomplete topical listings. (Ads)

$AMERICA, 106 W. 56th St., New York NY 10019-3893. (212)581-4640. Fax (212)399-3596. E-mail: articles@americamagazine.org. Website: www.americamagazine.org. Catholic. Submit to Editor-in-Chief. For thinking Catholics and those who want to know what Catholics are thinking. Weekly mag. & online version; 32+ pgs.; circ. 46,000. Subscription $48. 100% unsolicited freelance. Complete ms/cover letter; fax/e-query OK. Pays $100-200 on acceptance. Articles 1,500-2,000 wds. Responds in 6 wks. Seasonal 3 mos. ahead. Does not use sidebars. Guidelines (also on Website); copy for 9x12 SAE. (Ads) Incomplete topical listings.

Poetry: Buys avant-garde, free verse, light verse, traditional; 20-35 lines; $2-3/line.

AMERICAN TRACT SOCIETY, Box 462008, Garland TX 75046-2008. (972)276-9408. Fax (972)272-9642. E-mail: PBatzing@ATSTracts.org. Website: www.ATStracts.org. Peter Batzing, tract ed. Majority of tracts written to win unbelievers. New tract releases bimonthly; 40 new titles produced annually. 5% unsolicited freelance; 2% assigned. Complete ms/cover letter; e-query OK. **PAYS IN COPIES** on publication for exclusive tract rts. Tracts 600-1,200 wds. Responds in 6-8 wks. Seasonal 1 yr. ahead. Accepts simultaneous submissions & reprints (tell when/where appeared). Accepts requested ms on disk or by e-mail (attached or copied into message). Prefers NIV, KJV. Guidelines (also by e-mail)/free samples for #10 SAE/1 stamp. (No ads)

Special Needs: Youth issues, African American, cartoonists, critical issues.

Tips: "Read our current tracts; submit polished writing; relate to people's needs and experiences. Follow guidelines—almost no one does."

$ANCIENT PATHS, PO Box 7505, Fairfax Station VA 22039. E-mail: ssburris@cox.net. Website: www.editorskylar.com. Christian/nondenominational. Skylar Hamilton Burris, ed. For a literate Christian audience, or non-Christians open to and moved by traditional-themed poetry and fiction. Biennial literary mag.; 80+ pgs.; circ. 175. Subscription $12. 100% unsolicited freelance. Complete ms only; no queries. Pays $6 for prose & $6 for artwork on publication for one-time, reprint, & optional electronic rts. Not copyrighted. No articles. Fiction to 2,500 wds. (5/yr.). Responds in 5 wks. No seasonal. Accepts simultaneous submissions & reprints (tell when/where appeared). Accepts e-mail submissions only from outside U.S. No kill fee. Does not use sidebars. Prefers KJV. Also accepts submissions from teens (but must compete with adults). Guidelines (also by e-mail/Website); copy $10 (make check to Skylar Burris). (Ads—1/2 pg. $30)

Poetry: Buys 30-40/yr. Free verse, traditional; 4-60 lines; pays $2 & 1 copy. Submit max. 5 poems.

Tips: "Looking for shorter fiction (under 2,000 wds.). Visit the Website and read sample literature or order a copy. Read the great Christian writers—O'Connor, Lewis, Hopkins, Donne, Herbert, Tennyson, etc. Send your best work, even if it's been previously published (we're open to reprints). Stir your reader's emotions; make your reader think and feel without being too obvious."

ANGEL FACE, PO Box 102, Huffman TX 77336. E-mail: MaryAnka_50@msn.com. Website: www.maryanka.com. MaryAnka Press/Catholic. Mary Agnes Dalrymple, pub. Religious or general poetry based on the rosary, birth, rebirth, joy, light, sorrow, epiphany, hope, Jesus, Mary, the seasons of nature and the cycles of life, the search for God in everyday life, etc. (but open to all denominations). Annual literary mag.; 50 pgs.; circ. 100. Subscription $14. 10% unsolicited freelance. Complete ms/cover letter; no phone/fax/e-query. **PAYS 1 COPY FOR ONE-TIME RTS.** Poetry only. Responds in 1-6 mos. Accepts simultaneous submissions & reprints (tell when/where appeared). No submissions by e-mail or on disk. Guidelines (also on Website); copy $7.

Poetry: Accepts 35/yr. Free-verse, 60-65 lines. Submit max. 5 poems (typed).

Tips: "I am open to all viewpoints and have published poems by non-Christians as well as Catholic and protestant writers. Send your best work even if you are not sure it fits the rosary pattern. Info on the rosary and sample poems from past issues can be found on my Website."

Note: This publication is currently on hiatus and not accepting submissions.

$ANGELS ON EARTH, 16 E. 34th St., New York NY 10016. (212)251-8100. Fax (212)684-1311. E-mail: submissions@angelsonearth.com. Website: www.angelsonearth.com. Guideposts. Colleen Hughes, ed-in-chief; Meg Belviso, depts. ed. for features and fillers. Presents true stories about God's angels and humans who have played angelic roles on earth. Bimonthly mag.; 75 pgs.; circ. 550,000. Subscription $19.95. 90% unsolicited freelance. Complete ms/cover letter; no phone/fax/e-query. Pays $25-400 on publication for all rts. Articles 100-2,000 wds. (100/yr.); all stories must be true. Responds in 13 wks. Seasonal 6 mos. ahead. E-mail submissions from Website. Guidelines on Website (www.angelson earth.com/writers_Guidelines.asp); copy for 7x10 SAE/4 stamps.

Fillers: Buys many. Anecdotal shorts of similar nature (angelic); 50-250 wds.; $50-100.

Columns/Departments: Buys 50/yr. Messages (brief, mysterious happenings), $25. Earning Their Wings (good deeds), 150 wds., $50. Only Human? (human or angel?/ mystery), 350 wds.; $100. Complete ms.

Tips: "We are not limited to stories about heavenly angels. We also accept stories about human beings doing heavenly duties."

$ANGLICAN JOURNAL, 80 Hayden St., Toronto ON M4Y 2J6, Canada. (416)924-9199, ext. 307. Fax (416)921-4452. E-mail: editor@national.anglican.ca. Website: www.anglicanjournal .com. Anglican Church of Canada. Josie De Lucia, ed. asst. (jdelucia@national.anglican.ca). National newspaper of the Anglican Church of Canada; informs Canadian Anglicans about the church at home and overseas. Newspaper (10X/yr.) & online; 12-16 pgs.; circ. 200,000. Subscription $10 Cdn., $17 U.S. & foreign. 10% unsolicited freelance. Query only; fax/ e-query OK. Pays $50-250 or .23/wd. Cdn., on acceptance for 1st & electronic rts. Articles to 1,000 wds. (12-15/yr.); fiction for early teens, teens, and adults. Responds in 2 wks. Seasonal 2 mos. ahead. No reprints. Guidelines by e-mail/Website. (Ads)

Tips: "Select subject matter that would be of interest to a national audience."

$ANIMAL TRAILS, 2660 Peterborough St., Oak Hill VA 20171. E-mail: animaltrails@yahoo.com. Tellstar Publishing. Shannon Bridget Murphy, ed. Keeping animal memories alive through writing. Quarterly mag. 85% unsolicited freelance. Complete ms/cover letter; e-query OK. Pays .02-.05/wd. on acceptance for 1st, one-time, reprint, or simultaneous rts. Articles to 2,000 wds.; fiction to 2,000 wds. Responds in 2-8 wks. Seasonal 3 mos. ahead. Accepts simultaneous submissions & reprints (tell when/where appeared). Accepts disk or e-mail submissions (attached or copied into message.). No kill fee. Regularly uses sidebars. Prefers KJV. Guidelines by e-mail. (No ads)

Poetry: Buys variable number. Avant-garde, free verse, haiku, light verse, traditional; any length. Pays variable rates. Submit any number.

Fillers: Buys most types, to 1,000 wds.

Tips: "Most open to articles, stories, poetry and fillers that explain the value of animals and their relationship with God. The value of animals is the mission of *Animal Trails*. Include a Scripture reference."

$THE ANNALS OF SAINT ANNE DE BEAUPRE, 9795 St. Anne Blvd., St. Anne de Beaupre QC G0A 3C0, Canada. (418)827-4538. Fax (418)827-4530. E-mail: mag@revuesteannede beaupre.ca (for subscriptions only). Catholic/Redemptorist Fathers. Fr. Bernard Mercier, C.Ss.R., ed.; submit to Fr. R. Theberge, C.Ss.R., interim mng. ed. Promotes Catholic family values. Bimonthly mag.; 32 pgs.; circ. 25,000. Subscription $18.50 U.S. 80% unsolicited freelance. Complete ms/cover letter; no phone/fax/e-query. Pays $50 ($20 for fiction) on acceptance for 1st N.A. serial rts. only. Articles 1,500 wds. (350/yr.), & fiction 1,500 wds. (200/yr.). Responds in 4-5 wks. Seasonal 6 mos. ahead. No simultaneous submissions or reprints. No disk or e-mail submission. Does not use sidebars. Prefers NRSV. Guidelines; copy for #10 or 9x12 SAE. (No ads)

Tips: "Writing must be uplifting and inspirational, clearly written, not filled with long quotations. We tend to stay away from extreme controversy and focus on the family, good family values, devotion, and Christianity. Most open to Christian education, Christian living,

Christian growth, church life and testimonies. Write a well-researched, current story with 'across the board' appeal." Rights must be clearly stated. Typed manuscripts only.

ANOINTED PAGES MAGAZINE, 3900 W. Brown Deer Rd, Ste. A-149, Milwaukee WI 53209 (414)517-8876 or (414)759-4959. Website: info@anointedpages.com. Website: www .anointedpages.com. Interdenominational. Marvin Ivy, pub. (marvinivy@anointedpages .com); Jodine Ivy, editorial administrator (jodineive@anointedpages.com). To profile religious and community leaders and the lives that they are changing within their ministry and community, and to meet the needs of people with articles on the holistic lifestyle. Bimonthly mag. Subscription $19.99. Estab. 2007. Open to unsolicited freelance. Query. Articles. Also accepts submissions from teens.

ANSWERS MAGAZINE & ANSWERSMAGAZINE.COM, PO Box 510, Hebron KY 41048. (859) 727-2222. Fax (859)727-4888. E-mail: nationaleditor@answersmagazine.com. Website: www.answersmagazine.com. Answers in Genesis. Mike Matthews, exec. ed. Bible-affirming, creation-based. Quarterly mag. Articles to 300 wds. Responds in 30 days. Details on Website.

$THE APOCALYPSE CHRONICLES, Box 448, Jacksonville OR 97530. Phone/fax (541)899-8888. E-mail: James@ChristianMediaNetwork.com. Website: www.Christianmedia.tv. Christian Media. James Lloyd, ed./pub. Deals with the apocalypse exclusively. Quarterly & online newsletter; circ. 2,000-3,000. Query; prefers phone query. Payment negotiable for reprint rts. Articles. Responds in 3 wks. Requires KJV. No guidelines; copy for #10 SAE/2 stamps.
> **Tips:** "It's helpful if you understand your own prophetic position and are aware of its name, i.e., Futurist, Historicist, etc."

+ARIZONA FAMILY NEWS, 7070 E. 3rd Ave., Scottsdale AZ 85251. (480)481-2960. E-mail: jeff@arizonachristiannews.com Website: www.arizonachristiannews.com. Jeff Abramson, ed. To inform readers from a biblical perspective, raising the standard for family values, sourcing and networking within the Phoenix community. Monthly newspaper. Subscription free. Open to unsolicited freelance. Query. Incomplete topical listings. (Ads)

$ARKANSAS CATHOLIC, PO Box 7417, Little Rock AR 72217. (501)664-0125. Fax (501)664-6572. E-mail: mhargett@dolr.org. Website: www.arkansas-catholic.org. Catholic Diocese of Little Rock. Malea Hargett, ed.; Tara Little, assoc. ed. Statewide newspaper for the local diocese. Weekly tabloid; 16 pgs.; circ. 7,700. Subscription $18. 1% unsolicited freelance; 10% assigned. Query/clips; e-query OK. Pays $3/inch on publication for 1st rts. Articles 1,000 wds. Accepts simultaneous submissions & reprints. Accepts requested ms on disk or by e-mail. Uses some sidebars. Prefers Catholic Bible. Guidelines (also by e-mail); copy for 9x12 SAE/2 stamps. (Ads)
> **Columns/Departments:** Tara Little, ed. Buys 2/yr. Seeds of Faith (education). Complete ms. Pays $20.
> **Tips:** "All stories and columns must have an Arkansas and Catholic connection."

$ARLINGTON CATHOLIC HERALD, 200 N. Glebe Rd., Ste. 600, Arlington VA 22203. (703)841-2590. Fax (703)524-2782. E-mail: editorial@catholicherald.com. Website: www.catholic herald.com. Catholic Diocese of Arlington. Michael F. Flach, ed. Regional, for the local diocese. Weekly newspaper; 28 pgs.; circ. 53,000. Subscription $14. 10% unsolicited freelance. Query; phone/fax/e-query OK. Pays $50-150 on publication for one-time rts. Articles 500-1,500 wds. Responds in 2 wks. Seasonal 3 mos. ahead. Accepts simultaneous submissions. Prefers accepted ms on disk. Regular sidebars. Guidelines (also on Website); copy for 11x17 SAE. (Ads)
> **Columns/Departments:** Sports; School News; Local Entertainment; 500 wds.
> **Tips:** "All submissions must be Catholic related. Avoid controversial issues within the church."

$ASSOCIATED CONTENT, 88 Steele St., Ste. 400, Denver CO 80206-5715. (720)255-9185. E-mail: miguel@associatedcontent.com. Website: www.associatedcontent.com. Associated

Content. Miguel Chacon, submissions mngr. Weekly e-zine; 1000+ pgs. Free online. Estab. 2004. 100% unsolicited freelance. Query online. Pays $3-20 on acceptance for nonexclusive, electronic rts. Articles 400-5,000 wds. (1,000+/yr.); fiction 400-5,000 wds. (1,000+/yr.). Responds in 2 wks. Seasonal 1 mo. ahead. Accepts simultaneous submissions & reprints (tell when/where appeared). Accepts submissions online only. Guidelines on Website; copy online.

Poetry: Avant-garde, free verse, haiku, light verse, traditional.

Tips: "Look over Website and see what the other writers are doing. Sign up, fill out a profile, and submit your work."

**This periodical was #6 on the 2008 Top 50 Christian Publishers list (#6 in 2007, #7 in 2006).

$ATLANTIC CATHOLIC, 88 College St., Antigonish NS B2G 2L7, Canada. (902)863-4370. Fax (902)863-1943. E-mail: editor@thecasket.ca, or atlanticcatholic@thecasket.ca. The Casket Printing and Publishing Co. Ken Sims, pub.; Brian Lazzuri, mng. ed. Reports religious news that will inform, educate, and inspire Catholics. Biweekly tabloid; circ. 2,000. Subscription $28. Open to unsolicited freelance. Pays $25/story. Articles to 800 wds. Accepts e-mail submissions of mss up to 800 wds. (Ads)

Tips: "Most open to book and movie reviews, less than 700 words; also celebrity profiles, less than 700 words."

$AUJOURD'HUI CREDO, 1332 Victoria, Longueuil QC J4V 1L8, Canada. (450)466-7733. Fax (450)466-2664. E-mail: davidfines@egliseunie.org. Website: www.united-church.ca. United Church of Canada. David Fines, dir. The only French Reformed magazine in North America. Monthly mag.; 28 pgs.; circ. 250. Subscription $25 Cdn. 20% unsolicited freelance. Complete ms; fax/e-query OK. Pays $50 on publication for nonexclusive rts. Not copyrighted. Articles 1,500 wds. (10/yr.); fiction 800 wds. (6/yr.); reviews 100 wds. Responds in 4 wks. Seasonal 2 mos. ahead. Accepts simultaneous submissions & reprints (tell when/where appeared). Requires e-mail submissions (attached or copied into message). No kill fee. Uses some sidebars. Also accepts submissions from children/teens. Prefers TOB. Guidelines/theme list by e-mail; free copy. (Ads)

Poetry: Accepts free verse.

Tips: "Most likely to break in by being inclusive and intelligent. Contact director. Must write in French."

$AUSTRALIAN CATHOLICS, PO Box 553, Richmond Victoria 3121, Australia. Phone (61) (3)9421 9666. Fax (61)(3)9421 9600. E-mail: auscaths@jespub.jesuit.org.au, or through Website: www.australiancatholics.com.au. Jesuit Communications. Michael McVeigh, ed. Stories of faith and living for a contemporary Catholic audience. Mag. published 5X/yr.; 36 pgs.; circ. 200,000. Open to unsolicited freelance. Query or complete ms; e-query OK. Payment by negotiation on publication for 1st rts. Articles 800-1,200 wds. Seasonal 4 mos. ahead. Accepts reprints (tell when/where appeared). Uses some sidebars.

Tips: "We generally prefer articles on people, either as interviews or reflections on personal experiences. We generally don't consider an overseas submission, unless it can be made relevant for an Australian audience.

THE BAPTIST STANDARD, PO Box 660267, Dallas TX 75266-0267. (214)630-4571. Fax (214)638-8535. E-mail: marvknox@baptiststandard.com, or through Website: www.baptist standard.com/postnuke/index.php. Marv Knox, ed. The Texas Baptist News Journal. Biweekly newspaper. Subscription $20.50. Incomplete topical listings.

$B.C. CATHOLIC, 150 Robson St., Vancouver BC V6B 2A7, Canada. (604)683-0281. Fax (604) 683-8117. E-mail: bcc@rcav.bc.ca. Website: http://bcc.rcav.org. Roman Catholic Archdiocese of Vancouver. Paul Schratz, ed. News, education, and inspiration for Canadian Catholics. Weekly (48X) newspaper; 20 pgs.; circ. 20,000. Subscription $32. 20% unsolicited freelance.

Query; phone query OK. Pays .15/wd. on publication for 1st rts. Photos $30. Articles 300-3,000 wds. Responds in 6 wks. Seasonal 4 wks. ahead. Accepts simultaneous submissions & reprints (.05/wd.). Prefers e-mail submission (copied into message). Guidelines on Website; free copy. (Ads)

Tips: "Items of relevance to Catholics in British Columbia are preferred."

THE BEACON, PO Box 543, Calera AL 35040. (205)410-0656. E-mail: publisher@newsbeacon.com. Website: www.newsbeacon.com. Angela Carraway, mng. ed. (editor@newsbeacon.com; 205-369-2176). Weekly newspaper. Incomplete topical listings.

BEHIND THE HAMMER, 1018 Main St., Akron PA 17501. (717)859-2201. Fax (717)859-4910. E-mail: communications@mds.mennonite.net. Website: www.mds.mennonite.net. Mennonite Disaster Services. Scott Sundberg, ed. Quarterly & online mag. Subscription free. Open to freelance. Complete ms/cover letter. **NO PAYMENT.** Articles. Guidelines on Website; free copy. Not in topical listings.

Tips: "By sharing our stories we hope to encourage and motivate one another to continue expressing the love of God through MDS activity."

$BELIEVER'S BAY, PO Box 6362, Clearwater FL 33758. Toll-free (888)564-3534. E-mail: editor@BelieversBay.com. Website: www.BelieversBay.com. Tim Russ, pub. (tim@BelieversBay.com); Kevin Molloy, ed. To unite the body of Christ through communication, exhortation, and edification while focusing on ministries in the body of Christ. Monthly online mag. Mostly freelance. Complete ms by e-mail only (attached); e-query OK. **NO PAYMENT** for 1st & electronic rts. (keeps posted for 3 mos. & archives with permission). Articles 500-1,000 wds. Guidelines/monthly topical themes listed on Website submissions page.

Columns/Departments: Columns 300-500 wds. Looking for writers who focus on prophecy. Pays $15.

Special Needs: Focuses on prayer every month.

Tips: "We need all submissions via e-mail."

$BGC WORLD, 2002 S. Arlington Heights Rd., Arlington Heights IL 60005-4102. Toll-free (800)323-4215. (847)228-0200. Fax (847)228-5376. E-mail: bputman@baptistgeneral.org. Website: www.bgcworld.org. Baptist General Conference. Bob Putman, ed. Almost exclusively by, for, and about the people and ministries of the Converge Worldwide (Baptist General Conference). Bimonthly mag.; 16 pgs.; circ. 46,000. Subscription free. 5% unsolicited freelance; 95% assigned. Query/clips; e-query preferred. Pays $60-280 on publication for 1st, reprint, electronic rts. Articles 300-1,400 wds. (20-30/yr.). Responds in 5-9 wks. Seasonal 6 mos. ahead. Accepts simultaneous submissions & reprints (tell when/where appeared). Prefers accepted mss by e-mail (attached file). Kill fee 50%. Uses some sidebars. Prefers NIV. Guidelines/theme list (also by e-mail); free copy for #10 SAE. (Ads)

Columns/Departments: Buys 30/yr. Converge Connection (short news blurbs of happenings in Converge churches), 75-250 wds.; New Life (first-person or "as-told-to" story of Converge church member transformation or church transformation), 750-1,400 wds.; Outreach Ideas (from Converge churches), 250-400 wds.

Tips: "To break in, report on interesting happenings/ministry in converge (BGC) churches close to you for our Converge Connection or Outreach Ideas columns." Note: This publication will be changing their name; check Website.

**2007 EPA Award of Excellence—Denominational. This periodical was #47 on the 2008 Top 50 Christian Publishers list (#50 in 2007).

$BIBLE ADVOCATE, Box 33677, Denver CO 80233. (303)452-7973. Fax (303)452-0657. E-mail: bibleadvocate@cog7.org. Website: www.cog7.org/BA. Church of God (Seventh-day). Calvin Burrell, ed.; Sherri Langton, assoc. ed. Adult readers; 50% not members of the denomination. Monthly (8X) mag.; 32 pgs.; circ. 13,500. Subscription free. 25-35% unsolicited free-

lance. Complete ms/cover letter; no phone/fax/e-query. Pays $25-55 on publication for 1st, one-time, reprint, electronic, simultaneous rts. Articles 600-1,200 wds. (10-20/yr.). Responds in 4-8 wks. Seasonal 9 mos. ahead (no Christmas or Easter pieces). Accepts simultaneous submissions & reprints (tell when/where appeared). Accepts requested ms by e-mail (copied into message—preferred—or attached). Regularly uses sidebars. Prefers NIV, NKJV. Guidelines/theme list (also on Website); copy for 9x12 SAE/3 stamps. (No ads)
>   **Poetry:** Buys 6-10/yr. Free verse, traditional; 5-20 lines; $20. Submit max. 5 poems.
>   **Fillers:** Buys 5/yr. Prose; 100-400 wds.; $20.
>   **Special Needs:** Articles centering on upcoming themes (ask for theme list).
>   **Tips:** "If you write well, all areas are open to freelance, especially personal experiences that tie in with the monthly themes. Articles that run 650-700 words are more likely to get in. Also, fresh writing with keen insight is most readily accepted. Writers may submit sidebars that fit our theme for each issue."

BIBLICAL RECORDER, PO Box 18808, Raleigh NC 27619-8808. (919)847-2127. Fax (919) 847-6939. E-mail: editor@biblicalrecorder.org. Website: www.biblicalrecorder.org. Baptist. Tony W. Cartledge, ed. Newspaper. Subscription $15. Incomplete topical listings.

BOOKS & CULTURE, 465 Gundersen Dr., Carol Stream IL 60188. (630)260-6200. Fax (630)260-0114. E-mail: bceditor@booksandculture.com, or jwilson@christianitytoday .com. Website: www.booksandculture.com. Christianity Today Intl. John Wilson, ed. To edify, sharpen, and nurture the evangelical intellectual community by engaging the world in all its complexity from a distinctly Christian perspective. Bimonthly & online newsletter; circ. 12,000. Subscription $19.95. Open to freelance. Query. Articles & reviews. Incomplete topical listings. (Ads)
**2004 EPA Award of Merit—General.

THE BREAD OF LIFE, 35—5100 S. Service Rd., PO Box 127, Burlington ON L7R 3X5, Canada. (905)634-5433. E-mail: steeners@cyberus.ca. Website: www.thebreadoflife.ca. Catholic. Fr. Peter Coughlin, ed. Catholic Charismatic; to encourage spiritual growth in areas of renewal in the Catholic Church today. Bimonthly mag.; 32 pgs.; circ. 2,500. Subscription $30. 5% unsolicited freelance. Complete ms/cover letter; fax query OK. **NO PAYMENT.** Articles 750 wds.; book reviews 250 wds. Responds in 4-6 wks. Seasonal 6 mos. ahead. Accepts reprints (tell when/where appeared). No disk. Does not use sidebars. Prefers NAB, NJB. Guidelines; copy for 9x12 SAE/$2.23 postage (mark "Media Mail"). (Some ads)
>   **Poetry:** Accepts little.
>   **Fillers:** Accepts 10-12/yr. Facts, prose, quotes; to 250 wds.
>   **Tips:** "Most open to testimonies; contact managing editor. We do appreciate poetry submissions and 750 word testimonies of the power of Jesus/Holy Spirit active in your life. It is best if a writer includes a 2-3 line biography and photo for publication."

THE BREAKTHROUGH INTERCESSOR, PO Box 121, Lincoln VA 20160-0121. (540)338-5522. Fax (540)338-1934. E-mail: editor@intercessors.org. Website: www.intercessors.org. Nondenominational. Cherise Ryan, mng. ed. Preparing and equipping people who pray; encouraging in prayer and faith. Quarterly mag.; 36 pgs.; circ. 5,000. Subscription $18. 100% unsolicited freelance. Complete ms; fax/e-query OK. Accepts full mss by e-mail. **NO PAYMENT** for 1st, reprint rts. Articles 1,000 wds. (50/yr.); book reviews 300-600 wds.; music/video reviews 300 wds. Responds in 3 weeks. Seasonal 6 mos. ahead. Accepts simultaneous submissions. Accepts requested ms by e-mail (copied into message). Uses some sidebars. Also accepts submissions from children/teens. Any Bible version. Guidelines (also by e-mail/Website); copy for 6x9 SAE/3 stamps. (Ads)
>   **Poetry:** Accepts 4/yr. Free verse, traditional, 4-32 lines. Submit any number (as long as they're about prayer).

Fillers: Accepts 8/yr. Anecdotes, cartoons, facts, ideas, kid quotes, prayers, prose, quotes, short humor; to 300 wds.

Special Needs: International stories emphasizing how God is at work through prayer across the globe.

Contest: Pays $25 for article with most reader impact, plus one free subscription.

Tips: "Break in by submitting true articles/stories about prayer and its miraculous results, and articles that teach about an aspect of prayer using scripture to support each point." Manuscripts acknowledged but not returned.

BREAKTHROUGH MAGAZINE, (517)882-3595. E-mail: editor@breakthroughonlinemag.com. Website: www.breakthroughonlinemag.com. Baraka Miller, ed. "Every struggle endures a breakthrough, every breakthrough endures a struggle." Showcases those who have made their breakthrough in life and who are impacting their communities; sharing the joy of life, family, success, and above all Christ, the one who gives us strength to "Breakthrough." Webzine.

$BRIDAL GUIDES, 2660 Peterborough St., Oak Hill VA 20171. E-mail: bridalguides@ yahoo.com. Tellstar Publishing. Shannon Bridget Murphy, ed. Theme-based wedding/ reception ideas and planning for Christian wedding planners. Quarterly mag. 85% unsolicited freelance. Complete ms/cover letter; e-query OK. Pays .02-.05/wd. on acceptance for 1st, one-time, reprint, & simultaneous rts. Articles to 2,000 wds.; fiction to 2,000 wds. Responds in 2-8 wks. Seasonal 3 mos. ahead. Accepts simultaneous submissions & reprints (tell when/where appeared). Accepts disk or e-mail submissions (attached or copied into message.). No kill fee. Regularly uses sidebars. Also accepts submissions from children/ teens. Prefers KJV. Guidelines by e-mail. (No ads)

Poetry: Buys variable number. Avant-garde, free verse, haiku, light verse, traditional; any length. Pays variable rates. Submit any number.

Fillers: Buys most types, to 1,000 wds.; .02-.05/wd.

Special Needs: "Most open to wedding and planning articles that show readers how to successfully complete plans for their events. Illustrations and art either with or without manuscript packages. Romance fiction related to weddings, travel, and home."

BYFAITH (byFaith), 1700 N. Brown Rd., Ste. 105, Lawrenceville GA 30043. (678)825-1005. Fax (678)825-1001. E-mail: editor@byfaithonline.com (subject line: Editorial Submission). Website: www.byfaithonline.com. Presbyterian Church in America (PCA). Dick Doster, ed. (ddoster@byfaithonline.com). Provides news of the PCA; connects members, guests, and staff members to the denomination. Bimonthly mag.; 54 pgs. Subscription $19.95. Open to unsolicited freelance. Complete ms by e-mail ("Editorial Submission" in subject line). **NO MENTION OF PAYMENT.** Articles 500-3,000 wds. Guidelines on Website. Incomplete topical listings.

Tips: "We publish in 5 areas: stories that provoke thinking and creativity; very practical theology; articles that help readers understand the arts and culture; sensible, down-to-earth information; and PCA news."

**2008, 2006 EPA Award of Excellence—Denominational; 2007 EPA Award of Merit— Denominational.

$CANADA LUTHERAN, 302—393 Portage Ave., Winnipeg MB R3B 3H6, Canada. Toll-free (888)786-6707, ext. 172. (204)984-9172. Fax (204)984-9185. E-mail: editor@elcic.ca, or canaluth@elcic.ca. Website: www.elcic.ca/clweb. Evangelical Lutheran Church in Canada. Trina Gallop, ed. dir. (tgallop@elcic.ca); Lucia Carruthers, ed. Denominational. Monthly (8X) mag.; 42 pgs.; circ. 14,000. Subscription $22.60 Cdn.; $42 U.S. 40% unsolicited freelance; 60% assigned. Query or complete ms/cover letter; fax/e-query OK. Pays $40-110 (.10/wd.) Cdn. on publication for one-time rts. Articles 700-1,200 wds. (15/yr.);

fiction 850-1,200 wds. (4/yr.). Responds in 5 wks. Seasonal 10 mos. ahead. Accepts simultaneous submissions & reprints. Prefers e-mail submission (copied into message). Uses some sidebars. Prefers NRSV. Guidelines (also by e-mail). (Ads)

Tips: "Canadians/Lutherans receive priority here; others considered but rarely used. Want material that is clear, concise, and fresh. Articles that talk about real life experiences of faith receive our best reader response."

CANADIANCHRISTIANITY.COM, #200-20316—56 Ave., Langley BC V3A 3Y7, Canada. Toll-free (888)899-3777. E-mail: editor@canadianchristianity.com. Website: www.Canadian Christianity.com. A ministry of the Christian Info Society. Flyn Ritchie, ed. Online newspaper. Incomplete topical listings.

THE CANADIAN LUTHERAN, 3074 Portage Ave., Winnipeg MB R3K 0Y2, Canada. Toll-free (800)588-4226. (204)895-3433. Fax (204)897-4319. E-mail: communications@lutheran church.ca. Website: www.lutheranchurch.ca. Lutheran Church—Canada. Ian Adnams, ed. Monthly (10X) mag. Subscription $20. Open to unsolicited freelance. Not in topical listings. (Ads)

$CANADIAN MENNONITE, 490 Dutton Dr., Unit C5, Waterloo ON N2L 6H7, Canada. Toll-free (800)378-2524. (519)884-3810. Fax (519)884-3331. E-mail: submit@canadian mennonite.org. Website: www.canadianmennonite.org. Canadian Mennonite Publishing Service. Ross W. Muir, mng. ed. Seeks to promote covenantal relationships within the Mennonite Church Canada constituency (guided by Hebrews 10:23-25). Biweekly mag.; circ. 16,500. Subscription $32.50 Cdn.; $52.50 U.S. Open to unsolicited freelance. Pays .10/wd.; .05/wd. for reprints. Guidelines on Website. Not in topical listings. (Ads)

Tips: "We provide channels for sharing accurate and fair information, faith profiles, inspirational and educational materials, news, and analysis of issues facing the church."

$CAPPERS, 1503 S.W. 42nd St., Topeka KS 66609. (785)274-4300. Fax (785)274-4305. E-mail: cappers@cappers.com. Website: www.cappers.com. Ogden Publications. K. C. Compton, ed-in-chief. Timely news-oriented features with positive messages. Monthly mag.; 40-56 pgs.; circ. 150,000. Subscription $14.95. 40% unsolicited freelance. Complete ms/cover letter by mail only. Pays about $2.50/printed inch for nonfiction on publication, pays $100-400 for fiction on acceptance for one-time rts. Articles to 1,000 wds. (50/yr.); fiction to 2,000 wds., serials to 25,000 wds. (20/yr.). Responds in 2-6 mos. Seasonal 6 mos. ahead. No simultaneous submissions or reprints. Prefers requested ms by e-mail. Uses some sidebars. Guidelines (also on Website); copy $4/9x12 SASE/4 stamps. (Ads)

Poetry: Attn: Poetry Editor. Buys 50/yr. Free verse, light verse, traditional; 4-16 lines. Pays $10-15 on acceptance. Submit max. 5 poems.

Columns/Departments: Buys 12/yr. Garden Path (gardens/gardening), 500-1,000 wds. Payment varies. This column most open.

Tips: "Our publication is all original material either written by our readers/freelancers or occasionally by our staff. Every department, every article is open. Break in by reading at least 6 months of issues to know our special audience. Most open to nonfiction features and garden stories." Submissions are not acknowledged or status reports given.

$CATHEDRAL AGE, 3101 Wisconsin Ave. N.W., Washington DC 20016. (202)537-5681. Fax (202)364-6600. E-mail: Cathedral_Age@cathedral.org. Website: www.cathedralage.org. Protestant Episcopal Cathedral Foundation. Craig W. Stapert, pub. mngr. News from Washington National Cathedral and stories of interest to friends and supporters of WNC. Quarterly & online mag.; 36 pgs.; circ. 30,000. Subscription $15. 50% assigned freelance. Query; e-query OK. Pays to $750 on publication for all rts. Articles 1,200-1,500 wds. (10/yr.); book reviews 600 wds., ($250). Responds in 6 wks. Seasonal 6 mos. ahead. Requires requested ms on disk or by e-mail (attached file). Kill fee 50%. Uses some sidebars. Prefers NRSV. No guidelines; copy $5/9x12 SAE/5 stamps. (No ads)

Special Needs: Art, architecture, music.

Tips: "We assign all articles, so query with clips first. Always write from the viewpoint of an individual first, then move into a more general discussion of the topic. Human-interest angle important."

$CATHOLIC DIGEST, PO Box 6015, 1 Montauk Ave., Ste. 200, New London CT 06320-1789. (860)536-2611. Fax (860)536-5600. E-mail: cdsubmissions@bayard-inc.com. Website: www.CatholicDigest.com. Catholic/Bayard Publications. Dan Connors, ed-in-chief (dconnors@catholicdigest.com); submit to Articles Editor. Readers have a stake in being Catholic and a wide range of interests: religion, family, health, human relationships, good works, nostalgia, and more. Monthly & online mag.; 128 pgs.; circ. 400,000. Subscription $19.95. 15% unsolicited freelance; 20% assigned. Complete ms (for original material)/cover letter, tear sheets for reprints; no e-query. Pays $200-300 ($100 for reprints) on acceptance for 1st rts. Online-only articles receive $100, plus half of any traceable revenue. Articles 1,000-2,000 wds.; feature articles 1,200-1,700 wds. (60/yr.). Responds in 6-8 wks. Seasonal 5 mos. ahead. Accepts reprints (tell when/where appeared). Accepts requested ms on disk or by e-mail (copied into message). Regularly uses sidebars. Prefers NAB. Guidelines on Website; copy for 7x10 SAE/2 stamps. (Ads)

Fillers: Fillers Editor. Buys 200/yr. Anecdotes, cartoons, facts, jokes, quotes; 1 line to 300 wds.; $2/published line on publication. Submit to cdfillers@bayard-inc.com.

Columns/Departments: Buys 75/yr. Open Door (personal stories of conversion to Catholicism); 200-500 wds.; $2/published line. See guidelines for full list.

Special Needs: Family and career concerns of Baby Boomers who have a stake in being Catholic.

Contest: See Website for current contest, or send an SASE.

Tips: "We favor the anecdotal approach. Stories must be strongly focused on a definitive topic that is illustrated for the reader with a well-developed series of true-life, interconnected vignettes."

**This periodical was #31 on the 2008 Top 50 Christian Publishers list (#37 in 2007, #31 in 2006, #48 in 2005).

$CATHOLIC FORESTER, Box 3012, Naperville IL 60566-7012. Toll-free (800)552-0145. (630) 983-3381. Toll-free fax (800)811-2140. (630)983-3384. E-mail: magazine@catholic forester.com. Website: www.catholicforester.com. Catholic Order of Foresters. Mary Anne File, ed. For mixed audience, primarily parents and grandparents between the ages of 30 and 80+. Quarterly mag.; 40 pgs.; circ. 100,000. Free/membership. 20% unsolicited freelance. Complete ms/cover letter; no phone/fax/e-query. Pays .30/wd. on acceptance for 1st rts. Articles 1,000-1,500 wds. (12-16/yr.); fiction for all ages 500-1,500 wds. (12-16/yr.). Responds in 3 mos. Seasonal 6 mos. ahead. Accepts simultaneous submissions & reprints (tell when/where appeared). Accepts requested ms by e-mail. Uses some sidebars. Prefers Catholic Bible. Guidelines on Website; copy for 9x12 SAE/4 stamps. (No ads)

Poetry: Buys 3/yr. Light verse, traditional; to 15 lines. Pay .30/wd. Submit max. 5 poems.

Tips: "Looking for informational, inspirational articles on finances and health. Writing should be energetic with good style and rhythm. Most open to general interest and fiction."

**This periodical was #23 on the 2008 Top 50 Christian Publishers list (#26 in 2007, #19 in 2006, #36 in 2005, #37 in 2004).

$CATHOLIC INSIGHT, PO Box 625, Adelaide Sta., 31 Adelaide St. E., Toronto ON M5C 2J8, Canada. (416)204-9601. Fax (416)204-1027. E-mail: reach@catholicinsight.com. Website: www.catholicinsight.com. Life Ethics Information Center. Fr. Alphonse de Valk, ed./pub.

News, analysis, and commentary on social, ethical, political, and moral issues from a Catholic perspective. Monthly (11X) mag.; 44 pgs.; circ. 3,700. Subscription $35 Cdn., $55 U.S. 2% unsolicited freelance; 98% assigned. Query preferred; phone/fax/e-query OK. Pays $200 for 1,500 wds. ($250 for 2,000 wds.) on publication for 1st rts. Articles 750-1,500 wds. (20-30/yr.); book reviews 750 wds. ($85). Responds in 6-8 wks. Seasonal 2 mos. ahead. Accepts requested ms on disk. Uses some sidebars. Prefers RSV (Catholic). Guidelines (also by e-mail); copy $4 Cdn./9x12 SAE/$2 Cdn. postage or IRC. (Ads)

Tips: "We are interested in intelligent, well-researched, well-presented commentary on a political, religious, social, or cultural matter from the viewpoint of the Catholic Church."

$CATHOLIC NEW YORK, 1011—1st Ave., Rm. 1721, New York NY 10022. (212)688-2399. Fax (212)688-2642. E-mail: cny@cny.org. Website: www.cny.org. Catholic. John Woods, ed-in-chief. To inform New York Catholics. Biweekly newspaper; 40 pgs.; circ. 135,000. Subscription $24. 2% unsolicited freelance. Query or complete ms/cover letter. Pays $15-100 on publication for one-time rts. Articles 500-800 wds. Responds in 5 wks. Copy $3.

Tips: "Most open to columns about specific seasons of the Catholic Church, such as Advent, Christmas, Lent, and Easter."

$CATHOLIC PEACE VOICE, 532 W. 8th, Erie PA 16502-1343. (814)453-4955, ext. 235. Fax (814)452-4784. E-mail: info@paxchristiusa.org. Website: www.paxchristiusa.org. Dave Robinson, exec. dir. (Dave@paxchristiusa.org). For members of Pax Christi USA, the national Catholic Peace Movement. Bimonthly newsmag.; 16-20 pgs.; circ. 23,000. Subscription $20, free to members. 15-20% unsolicited freelance; 25-30% assigned. Complete ms; phone/fax/e-query OK. Pays $50-75 on publication for all & electronic rts. Articles 500-1,500 wds. (10-15/yr.); reviews 750 wds., $50. Responds in 1-2 wks. Accepts simultaneous submissions & reprints (tell when/where appeared). Accepted ms on disk or by e-mail (attached or copied into message). Uses some sidebars. Also accepts submissions from teens. Guidelines (also by e-mail); copy for 9x12 SAE/2 stamps. (Ads)

Poetry: Accepts 1-5/yr. Avant-garde, free verse, haiku, light verse, traditional. Submit max. 2 poems. No payment.

Tips: "Most open to features and news, as well as reviews and resources. E-mailing us and pitching a story is the best way to break into our publication. Emphasis is on non-violence. No sexist language."

THE CATHOLIC REGISTER, 1155 Yonge St., Ste. 401, Toronto ON M4T 1W2, Canada. (416)934-3410. Fax (416)934-3409. E-mail: editor@catholicregister.org, or news@catholic register.org, or through Website: www.catholicregister.org. Joe Sinasac, ed./pub.; Mickey Conlon, mng. ed. To provide reliable information about the world from a Catholic perspective. Weekly (47X) tabloid; circ. 33,000. Subscription $42.70. Open to unsolicited freelance. Not in topical listings. (Ads)

$CATHOLIC SENTINEL, 5536 N.E. Hassalo St., Portland OR 97213-3638. (503)281-1191. Fax (503)460-5496. E-mail: sentinel@ocp.org. Website: www.sentinel.org. Oregon Catholic Press. Bob Pfohman, ed. Weekly tabloid; 20 pgs.; circ. 16,000. Subscription $32. 2% unsolicited freelance; 0% assigned. Query/clips. Payment negotiable on publication for one-time rts. Articles 600-1,500 wds. Responds in 4 wks. Seasonal 2 mos. ahead. Accepts requested ms on disk or by e-mail (copied into message). Uses some sidebars. Prefers NAS. Incomplete topical listings. Guidelines on Website; copy for 9x12 SAE/3 stamps. (Ads)

Tips: "We're most open to local church news and feature articles."

$CATHOLIC TELEGRAPH, 100 E. 8th St., Cincinnati OH 45202. (513)421-3131. Fax (513)381-2242. E-mail: cteditorial@catholiccincinnati.org. Website: www.catholiccincinnati.org/tct/curfeat1.htm. Tricia Hempel, ed. Diocese newspaper for Cincinnati area (all articles must have a Cincinnati or Ohio connection). Weekly newspaper; 24-28 pgs.; circ. 100,000. Subscription $24. Limited unsolicited freelance; mostly assigned. Send résumé and writing samples for assignment. Pays varying rates on publication for all rts. Articles. Responds in 2-3 wks. Kill fee. No guidelines; copy $2/#10 SASE.

Fillers: Newsbreaks (local).

Special Needs: Personality features for "Everyday Evangelists" section. These are feature stories that offer a slice of life of a person who is making a difference as a Roman Catholic Christian in their community. Prefer to have a tie within the Archdiocese of Cincinnati; must be an Ohioan. Complete ms; 800 wds.; pays $40 (extra for photos of individual interviewed).

Tips: "Most likely to accept an article about a person, event, or ministry with an Ohio connection—Cincinnati-Dayton area."

$THE CATHOLIC YEARBOOK, 7010—6th St. N., Oakdale MN 55128. (651)702-0086. Fax (651)702-0074. E-mail: catholic2@msn.com. Apostolic Publishing Co. Inc. Roger Jensen, ed. Family magazine of articles and prayers, promoting the sharing of Christian fellowship among Catholics. Annual mag.; 68-72 pgs.; circ. 400,000. 60% unsolicited freelance; 40% assigned. Complete ms/cover letter. Pays $5-50 on publication for 1st rts. Articles 750-1,500 wds. (20/yr.). Response time varies. No simultaneous submissions; accepts reprints. Accepts articles on disk or by e-mail (attached file). No kill fee. Uses some sidebars. Prefers NIV. Also accepts submissions from children/teens. Guidelines. (Ads)

Poetry: Buys 10/yr. Light verse, traditional; 15-50 wds., up to 150 wds. Pays $8-30. Submit max. 3 poems.

Fillers: Buys 5-10/yr. Anecdotes, facts, games, prayers, quizzes, quotes, and word puzzles; 50-300 wds. Pays $5-30.

$CBA RETAILERS+RESOURCE, 9240 Explorer Dr., Colorado Springs CO 80920. Toll-free (800)252-1950. (719)272-3555. Fax (719)272-3510. E-mail: publications@cbaonline .org. Website: www.cbaonline.org. Christian Booksellers Assn. Submit queries to Kathleen Samuelson, publications mngr. (samuelson@cbaonline.org). To provide Christian retail store owners and managers with professional retail skills, product information, and industry news. Monthly trade journal (also in digital edition); 72-100 pgs.; circ. 8,000. Subscription $59.95 (for nonmembers). 10% unsolicited freelance; 80% assigned. Query/clips; fax/e-query OK. Pays .20-.30/wd. on publication for all rts. Articles 800-2,000 wds. (30/yr. assigned); book/music/video reviews, 150 wds., $30-35. Responds in 8 wks. Seasonal 4-5 mos. ahead. Prefers requested ms mailed in MS Word file. Regularly uses sidebars. Accepts any modern Bible version. (Ads/Advocase/972-304-1100)

Special Needs: Trends in retail, consumer buying habits, market profiles. By assignment only.

Tips: "Looking for writers who have been owners/managers/buyers/sales staff in Christian retail stores. Most of our articles are by assignment and focus on producing and selling Christian products or conducting retail business. We also assign reviews of books, music, videos, Spanish products, kids products, and software to our regular reviewers."

CBN.COM (CHRISTIAN BROADCASTING NETWORK), 977 Centerville Turnpike, Virginia Beach VA 23463. (757)226-3557. Fax (757)226-3575. E-mail: chris.carpenter@cbn.org, or through Website: www.CBN.com. Christian Broadcasting Network. Chris Carpenter, dir. of internal programming; Belinda Elliott, books ed. Online mag.; 1.6 million users/mo. Free online. Open to unsolicited freelance. E-mail submissions (attached as a Word document). Query/clips; e-query OK. **NO PAYMENT.** Devotions 500-700 wds.; Spiritual Life Teaching, 700-1,500 wds.; Living Features (Family, Entertainment, Health, Finance), 700-1,500 wds.; Movie/TV/Music Reviews, 500-1,000 wds.; Hard News, 300-700 wds.; News Features, 700-

1,500 wds.; News Interviews, 1,000-2,000 wds; fiction. Accepts reprints (tell when/where appeared). Also accepts submissions from teens. Prefers NLT/NASB/NKJV. Guidelines by e-mail; copy online. (No ads)

Special Needs: Adoption stories/references, world religions from Judeo/Christian perspective.

Tips: "In lieu of payment, we link to author's Website and provide a link for people to purchase the author's materials in our Web store."

$CELEBRATE LIFE, PO Box 1350, Stafford VA 22555. (540)659-4171. Fax (540)659-2586. E-mail: CLMag@all.org. Website: www.clmagazine.org. American Life League. Stephanie Hopping, ed. Covers all right-to-life matters according to Catholic teaching. Bimonthly mag.; 48 pgs.; circ. 70,000. Subscription $12.95. 50% unsolicited freelance; 50% assigned. E-query preferred. Pays on publication according to quality of article for 1st or reprint rts.; or work-for-hire assignments. Articles 400-1,600 wds. Seasonal 4 mos. ahead. Accepts few reprints. Prefers e-mail submissions or disk. No kill fee. Also accepts submissions from children/teens. Prefers Jerusalem Bible (Catholic). Guidelines/theme list on Website. (No ads)

Special Needs: Personal experience about abortion, post-abortion stress/healing, adoption, activism/young people's involvement, death/dying, euthanasia, eugenics, special needs children, personhood, chastity, large families, stem cell science, and other right-to-life topics.

Tips: "We are no-exceptions pro-life in keeping with the Catholic Church. Looking for interviews with pro-life leaders and nonfiction stories about people who live according to pro-life ethics despite diversity. Photos are preferred for personal stories. No fiction or poetry."

**This periodical was #43 on the 2007 Top 50 Christian Publishers list.

+CENTRAL FLORIDA EPISCOPALIAN, 1017 E. Robinson St., Orlando FL 32801. (407)341-6615. Fax (407)386-3236. E-mail: joethoma@aol.com. Website: www.cfdiocese.org. Episcopal Diocese of Central Florida. Joe Thoma, ed. To spread the Good Word of Jesus Christ to the people of Central Florida, the U.S., and the world. Monthly mag.; circ. 24,000. Subscription $10. Open to unsolicited freelance. Articles. Incomplete topical listings. (Ads)

$CGA WORLD, PO Box 249, Olyphant PA 18447. Toll-free (800)836-5699. (570)586-1091. Fax (570)586-7721. E-mail: cgaemail@aol.com. Website: www.catholicgoldenage.org. Catholic Golden Age. Barbara Pegula, mng. ed. For Catholics 50+. Quarterly newsletter. Subscription/membership $12. Uses little freelance. Query. Pays .10/wd. on publication for 1st, one-time, or reprint rts. Articles 600-1,000 wds.; fiction 600-1,000 wds. Responds in 6 wks. Seasonal 6 mos. ahead. Accepts reprints (tell when/where appeared). Accepts requested ms on disk. Guidelines; copy for 9x12 SAE/3 stamps. (Ads)

CHALLENGE WEEKLY, PO Box 68-800, Newton, Auckland, New Zealand 1032. Phone (64-9) 378 4052, or +64 027 271 2849. Fax (64-9)376-3855. E-mail: editor@challengeweekly .co.nz. Website: www.challengeweekly.co.nz. Challenge Publishing Society. Garth George, ed. New Zealand's Christian Newspaper. Proclaiming the good news that Jesus is the Christ. Weekly online newspaper. Subscription $68. Incomplete topical listings.

$CHALLENGING DESTINY—Currently on hiatus.

$CHARISMA & CHRISTIAN LIFE, 600 Rinehart Rd., Lake Mary FL 32746. (407)333-0600. Fax (407)333-7133. E-mail: charisma@strang.com. Website: www.charismamag.com. Strang Communications. J. Lee Grady, exec. ed.; Jimmy Stewart, mng. ed.; submit to Adrienne S. Gaines, assoc. ed. Primarily for the Pentecostal and Charismatic Christian community. Monthly & online mag.; 100+ pgs.; circ. 250,000. Subscription $19.97. 80% assigned freelance. Query only; no phone query, e-query OK. Pays up to $1,000 (for assigned) on publication for all rts. Articles 2,000-3,000 wds. (40/yr.); book/music reviews, 200 wds., $20-35. Responds in 8-12 wks. Seasonal 5 mos. ahead. Kill fee $50. Prefers accepted ms by e-mail. Regularly uses sidebars. Guidelines on Website; free copy. (Ads)

Tips: "Most open to news section, reviews, or features. Query (published clips help a lot)." **#1 Best-selling magazine in Christian retail stores.

THE CHARLOTTE WORLD, 201 S. College St., Ste. 2010, Charlotte NC 28244. (704)295-7906. Fax (704)295-7919. E-mail: warren.smith@thecharlotteworld.com. Website: www.the charlotteworld.com. World Newspaper Publishing. Warren Smith, ed. To report unreported, under-reported, or badly reported news, from a Christian perspective. Biweekly newspaper; circ. 20,000. Subscription $36. Open to unsolicited freelance. Query preferred. Articles; reviews. Incomplete topical listings. (Ads)

**2007 EPA Award of Merit—Newspaper; 2006 EPA Award of Excellence—Newspaper.

$CHICKEN SOUP FOR THE SOUL BOOK SERIES, PO Box 700, Cos Cob CT 06807. Fax (203)861-7194. E-mail: webmaster@chickensoupforthesoul.com. Website: www.chicken soup.com. Barbara LoMonaco, story acquisitions (blomonaco@chickensoupforthesoul .com). Inspirational anthologies to open your heart and rekindle your spirit; audience is open to all ages, races, etc. Quarterly trade paperback books; 385 pgs.; circ. 60 million. $14.95/book. 98% unsolicited freelance. Make submissions via Website. Pays $200 on publication for reprint, simultaneous, & electronic rts. Articles 1,200 wds. max. Seasonal anytime. Accepts simultaneous submissions & reprints (tell when/where appeared). Accepts e-mail submissions: stories@chickensoupforthesoul.com (attached file/Word). No kill fee. Guidelines/themes on Website; free sample. (No ads)

Fillers: Anecdotes, cartoons, facts, kid quotes, quotes, short humor; 10-200 wds. Pays.

Special Needs: See Website for a list of upcoming titles.

Contest: See Website for list of current contests.

Tips: "Visit our Website and be familiar with our book series. Send in stories via mail or e-mail, complete with contact information. Submit story typed, double spaced, max. 1,200 words, in a Word document."

CHOCOLATE PAGES ONLINE MAGAZINE, 33011 Tall Oaks St., Farmington Hills MI 48336-4551. (248)249-2300. Fax (248)471-2422. E-mail: pamperry@ministrymarketing solutions.com. Website: www.ministrymarketingsolutions.com. Ministry Marketing Solutions. Pam Perry, pub. About current books targeting the African American Christian market; goes to bookstores, book clubs, black media, Christian media, church reading groups, and writer's clubs. Books for review accepted via mail and press kits via e-mail.

CHRISTIAN BUSINESS DAILY.COM, c/o Selling Among Wolves LLC, 379 Interstate Blvd., Sarasota FL 34240. (941)377-9384. Fax (941)371-6211. E-mail: articles@christianbusiness daily.com. Website: www.christianbusinessdaily.com. Jeremy Harrison, online dir. Business news from a Christian world-view. E-zine. Open to freelance. Query. **NO PAYMENT.** Articles. Incomplete topical listings. (Ads)

THE CHRISTIAN CHRONICLE, PO Box 11000, Oklahoma City OK 73013. (405)425-5070. Fax (405)425-5076. E-mail: bailey.mcbride@oc.edu, or through Website: www.christian chronicle.org. Churches of Christ. Bobbie Ross Jr., ed.; Tamie Ross, online ed. An international newspaper for members of the Church of Christ. Monthly newspaper & online. Subscription $20 (one-time fee). Incomplete topical listings.

THE CHRISTIAN CIVIC LEAGUE OF MAINE RECORD, 70 Sewall St., Augusta ME 04330. (207)622-7634. Fax (207)621-0035. E-mail: email@cclmaine.org. Website: www.league record.com (online version of magazine). Michael Hein, administrator. Focuses on public policy, political action, some church and public service. Monthly newsletter; 4 pgs.; circ. 4,600. Subscription free. Some freelance. Query; phone/fax/e-query OK. **NO PAYMENT** for one-time rts. Articles 800-1,200 wds. (10-12/yr.). Responds in 4-8 wks. Accepts simultaneous query & reprints. Guidelines by e-mail/Website; free copy. (No ads)

Tips: "Most open to opinion pieces and news item commentary."

CHRISTIAN COMPUTING MAGAZINE, PO Box 319, Belton MO 64012. Toll-free phone/fax (800)456-1868. (816)331-8142. E-mail: steve@ccmag.com, or through Website: www.ccmag.com. Steve Hewitt, ed-in-chief. For Christian/church computer users. Monthly (11X) & online mag.; 2 pgs.; circ. 30,000. Subscription $14.95, or free digital version. 40% unsolicited freelance. Query/clips; fax/e-query OK. **NO PAYMENT** for all rts. Articles 1,000-1,800 wds. (12/yr.). Responds in 4 wks. Seasonal 2 mos. ahead. Accepts reprints. Requires requested ms on disk. Regularly uses sidebars. Guidelines; copy for 9x12 SAE.

Fillers: Accepts 6 cartoons/yr.

Columns/Departments: Accepts 12/yr. Telecommunications (computer), 1,500-1,800 wds.

Special Needs: Articles on Internet, DTP, computing.

$CHRISTIAN COURIER (Canada), 5 Joanna Dr., St. Catherines ON L2N 1V1, Canada. (U.S. address: Box 110, Lewiston NY 14092-0110). Toll-free (800)969-4838. (905)682-8311. Toll-free fax (800)969-4838. (905)682-8313. E-mail: editor@christiancourier.ca. Website: www.christiancourier.ca. Reformed Faith Witness. Harry Der Nederlanden, ed. To present Canadian and international news, both religious and general, from a Reformed Christian perspective. Biweekly tabloid; 24-28 pgs.; circ. 4,000. Subscription $40 Cdn.; $32, U.S. 20% unsolicited freelance; 80% assigned. Complete ms/cover letter; fax/e-query OK. Pays $75-120 U.S., up to .10/wd. for assigned ($50-100 for unsolicited); 30 days after publication for one-time, reprint, or simultaneous rts. Not copyrighted. Articles 700-1,200 wds. (40/yr.); fiction to 1,200-2,500 wds. (6/yr.); book reviews 800-1,200 wds. Responds in 1-3 wks. Seasonal 3 mos. ahead. Accepts simultaneous submissions & reprints (tell when/where appeared). Prefers accepted ms by e-mail (attached file). No kill fee. Uses some sidebars. Prefers NIV. Guidelines/deadlines on Website; no copy. (Ads)

Poetry: Buys 12/yr. Avant-garde, free verse, light verse, traditional; 10-30 lines; $20-30. Submit max. 5 poems.

Tips: "Suggest an aspect of the theme which you believe you could cover well, have insight into, could treat humorously, etc. Show that you think clearly, write clearly, and have something to say that we should want to read. Have a strong biblical world-view and avoid moralism and sentimentality." Responds only if material is accepted.

CHRISTIAN COURIER (WI), 1933 W. Wisconsin Ave., Milwaukee WI 53233. (414)345-3545. Fax (414)918-4503. E-mail: christiancourier@juno.com. Website: www.christiancourier newspaper.com. ProBuColls Assn. Dr. Dennis Hill, ed. To propagate the gospel of Jesus Christ in the Midwest. Monthly newspaper; circ. 10,000. 10% freelance. Query; phone/fax/ e-query OK. **PAYS IN COPIES,** for one-time rts. Not copyrighted. Articles 300-1,500 wds. (6/yr.). Responds in 4-8 wks. Seasonal 2 mos. ahead. Accepts reprints. Guidelines; free copy. (Ads)

Fillers: Anecdotes, facts, newsbreaks; 10-100 wds.

Tips: "We are always in need of seasonal feature/filler type of articles: Christmas, Easter, 4th of July, etc."

$CHRISTIAN EXAMINER, PO Box 2606, El Cajon CA 92021. (619)668-5100. Fax (619)668-1115. E-mail: info@christianexaminer.com. Website: www.christianexaminer.com. Keener Communications. Lori Arnold, ed. To report on current events from an evangelical Christian perspective, particularly traditional family values and church trends. Monthly & online newspaper; 24-36 pgs.; circ. 180,000. Subscription $19.95. 5% assigned. Query/clips. Pays .10/wd., on publication for 1st & electronic rts. Articles 600-900 wds. Responds in 4-5 wks. Seasonal 3 mos. ahead. No simultaneous submissions or reprints. Prefers e-mail submissions (copied into message). No kill fee. Uses some sidebars. Guidelines by e-mail; copy $1.50/9x12 SAE. (Ads)

Tips: "We prefer news stories."

**2007, 2006, 2005, 2004 EPA Award of Merit—Newspaper. Member of Fellowship of Christian Newspapers (FCN).

+CHRISTIAN HEALTH CARE NEWSLETTER, PO Box 3618, Peoria IL 61612-3618. (877)764-2426. Fax (309)382-3757. E-mail: smchcn@smchcn.org. Website: www.samaritan ministries.org. Samaritan Ministries Intl. Ray King, ed. Health issues. Monthly newsletter; circ. 12,000. Subscription $12. Open to unsolicited freelance. Articles & reviews. Incomplete topical listings. (Ads)

$THE CHRISTIAN HERALD, PO Box 68526, Brampton ON L6R 0J8, Canada. (905)874-1731. Fax (905)874-1781. E-mail: info@christianherald.ca. Website: www.christianherald.ca. Covenant Communications. Fazal Karim Jr., ed-in-chief. A Canadian-Christian tabloid with a focus on Christian arts and entertainment. Monthly tabloid; 24 pgs.; circ. 31,000. Subscription free, or $25 if mailed (Canadian residents add 5% sales tax). 5% unsolicited freelance; 95% assigned. Query; fax/e-query OK. Pays $20-100 or .10/wd. on publication for 1st rts. Articles 500-1,500 wds.; reviews 150-200 wds. (no payment). Responds in 4 wks. Seasonal 3 mos. ahead. Accepts simultaneous submissions & reprints (tell when/where appeared). Prefers e-mail submissions (attached file). No kill fee. Uses some sidebars. Also accepts submissions from teens. Prefers ESV, KJV, NLT. Guidelines (also by e-mail); copy for 9x12 SAE/$2 Canadian postage. (Ads)

Fillers: Accepts 10/yr. Cartoons, facts, games, jokes, prayers, quotes, and word puzzles; 20-100 wds. No payment.

Columns/Departments: Interviews (Christian newsmakers/personalities), 900 wds., $20-50.

Tips: "Most open to articles/columns with specific reference to Canadians, with Canadian quotes, relevance, etc."

$CHRISTIAN HISTORY & BIOGRAPHY, 465 Gundersen Dr., Carol Stream IL 60188. (630)260-0114. Fax (630)480-2004. E-mail: CHeditor@christianhistory.net. Website: www.christianhistory.net. Christianity Today Intl. David Neff, exec. ed.; Jennifer Trafton, mng. ed.; submit to Jennifer Golossanov, asst. ed. To teach Christian history to educated readers in an engaging manner. Quarterly mag. & newsletter; 52 pgs.; circ. 50,000. Subscription $19.95. 5% unsolicited freelance; 95% assigned. Query only. Pays .10-.25/wd. on publication for 1st rts. Articles 500-3,000 wds. (1/yr.). Responds in 2 mos. Accepts reprints (tell when/where appeared). Prefers accepted ms by e-mail (attached or copied into message). Kill fee 50%. Regularly uses sidebars. Prefers NIV. Guidelines/theme list (also by e-mail); copy for 9x12 SASE. (Ads)

Tips: "Let us know your particular areas of specialization and any books or articles you have published in the area of Christian history. Theme-related articles are usually assigned. Most open to nonthemed departments: Story Behind; People Worth Knowing; Turning Point. Please familiarize yourself with our magazine before querying."

**2008, 2005 EPA Award of Merit—General.

$CHRISTIAN HOME & SCHOOL, 3350 East Paris Ave. S.E., Grand Rapids MI 49512. (616)957-1070, ext. 239. Fax (616)957-5022. E-mail: mleon@CSIonline.org. Website: www.CSI online.org. Christian Schools Intl. Gordon L. Bordewyk, exec. ed. For parents of children of all ages; offering a biblical perspective on all areas of parenting. Triannual mag.; 36 pgs.; circ. 67,000. Subscription $13.95. 95% unsolicited; 5% assigned. Complete ms or query, prefers e-query. Pays $50-250 on publication for 1st rts. Articles 1,000-2,000 wds. (30/yr.); Christmas fiction 1,000-2,000 wds. (5/yr.); book reviews $25 (assigned). Responds in 4 wks. Seasonal 7 mos. ahead. Accepts simultaneous query. Accepts mss by e-mail (attached or copied into message). Regularly uses sidebars. Accepts submissions from children/teens. Prefers NIV. Guidelines/theme list (also on Website); copy for 7x10 SAE/4 stamps. (Ads). Check for changes at this publication.

Fillers: Parenting ideas; 100-250 wds.; $25-40.

Tips: "Writers can break in by having articles written about parenting (at all stages of life), geared from a Christian perspective and current with the times."

**2007 EPA Award of Merit—Organizational. This periodical was #36 on the 2008 Top 50 Christian Publishers list (#44 in 2007, #32 in 2006, #44 in 2005, #38 in 2004).

$CHRISTIANITY TODAY, 465 Gundersen Dr., Carol Stream IL 60188-2498. (630)260-6200. Fax (630)260-8428. E-mail: cteditor@christianitytoday.com. Website: www.christianity today.com/ctmag. Christianity Today Inc. David Neff, ed. For evangelical Christian thought leaders who seek to integrate their faith commitment with responsible action. Monthly & online mag.; 65-120 pgs.; circ. 155,000. Subscription $24.95. Not currently accepting freelance submissions; if you have written for them in the past, contact the editor you worked with or e-mail them to find out how to contact that editor. Pays .25-.35/wd. on publication for 1st rts. Articles 1,000-4,000 wds. (60/yr.); book reviews 800-1,000 wds. (pays per-page rate). Responds in 13 wks. Seasonal 8 mos. ahead. Accepts reprints (tell when/where appeared—payment 25% of regular rate). Kill fee 50%. Does not use sidebars. Prefers NIV. Guidelines on Website; copy for 9x12 SAE/3 stamps. (Ads)

Tips: "Read the magazine." Does not return unsolicited manuscripts.

**#8 Best-selling Magazine in Christian retail stores. 2008, 2006, 2005 EPA Award of Excellence—General. 2006, 2005, 2004 EPA Award of Merit—Online (for Christianity Today Online).

$CHRISTIANITY TODAY MOVIES, 465 Gundersen Dr., Carol Stream IL 60188. (630)260-6200. Fax (630)260-8428. E-mail: CTmovies@christianitytoday.com. Website: www .ChristianityTodayMovies.com. Christianity Today Intl. Mark Moring, ed. To inform and equip Christian moviegoers to make discerning choices about films, through timely coverage, insightful reviews and interviews, educated opinion, and relevant news, all from a Christian world-view. Weekly e-zine. Subscription free. 10% unsolicited freelance; 90% assigned. Query; fax/e-query OK. Accepts full mss by e-mail. Pays $75-125 on acceptance for 1st rts. Articles 500-2,000 wds. (150/yr.) & movie reviews 700-1,000 wds. ($100). Responds in 2 wks. No seasonal. Sometimes accepts simultaneous submissions and reprints (tell when/where appeared). Prefers e-mail submissions (attached file). Some kill fees 50%. Uses some sidebars. Prefers NIV. No guidelines; copy online. (Ads)

Tips: "Study our Website; know what we're doing. Always looking for commentaries and/or news pieces on trends in the industry, especially as they relate to a Christian audience.

**2007 EPA Award of Merit—Online. This periodical was #35 on the 2008 Top 50 Christian Publishers list.

$THE CHRISTIAN JOURNAL, 1032 W. Main, Medford OR 97501. (541)773-4004. Fax (541)773-9917. E-mail: info@thechristianjournal.org. Website: www.liftingthecross .com/journal-guidelines.php. Lifting the Cross Ministries. Chad McComas, ed. Dedicated to sharing encouragement with the body of Christ in Southern Oregon and Northern California. Monthly & online newspaper; 16-24 pgs.; circ. 15,000. Subscription $20; most copies distributed free. 50% unsolicited freelance; 50% assigned. Complete ms; phone/fax query OK. Pays .01/wd. on publication for one-time rts. Articles & fiction 600-700 wds.; reviews 300-500 wds.; children's stories 600 wds. Prefers articles by e-mail to info@the christianjournal.org (attached file). Also accepts submissions from children/teens. Guidelines/theme list (also by e-mail/Website); copy $1.20/9x12 SAE/3 stamps. (Ads)

Poetry: Accepts 12-20/yr. Free verse, haiku, light verse, traditional; 4-12 lines. Submit max. 2 poems.

Fillers: Accepts 50/yr. Anecdotes, cartoons, jokes, kid quotes, newsbreaks, prayers, quotes, short humor, or word puzzles; 100-300 wds.

Columns/Departments: Accepts 6/yr. Youth, 600-800 wds; Seniors, 600-800 wds.; Children's stories, 600 wds.

Tips: "Send articles on themes; each issue has a theme. Theme articles get first choice."

CHRISTIAN MEDIA, Box 448, Jacksonville OR 97530. (541)899-8888. E-mail: James@ChristianMediaNetwork.com. Website: www.ChristianMediaDaily.com, or www.Christian MediaNetwork.com. James Lloyd, ed./pub. Updates on world conditions, politics, economics, in the light of prophecy. Quarterly & online tabloid; 24 pgs.; circ. 25,000. Query; prefers phone query. **NO PAYMENT** for negotiable rts. Articles; book & music reviews, 3 paragraphs. Accepts simultaneous submissions & reprints. Prefers requested ms on disk. Requires KJV. Copy for 9x12 SAE/2 stamps.

Special Needs: Particularly interested in stories that expose dirty practices in the industry—royalty rip-offs, misleading ads, financial misconduct, etc. No flowery pieces on celebrities; wants well-documented articles on abuse in the media.

CHRISTIAN MOTORSPORTS ILLUSTRATED, PO Box 929, Bristow OK 74010-0929. (607) 742-3407. E-mail: articles@christianmotorsports.com, or through Website: www.christian motorsports.com. CPO Publishing. Roland Osborne, pub. Covers Christians involved in motorsports. Bimonthly mag.; 64 pgs.; circ. 40,000. Subscription $38/2 yrs. 50% unsolicited freelance. Complete ms; no phone/fax/e-query. **NO PAYMENT.** Articles 650-1,200 wds. (30/yr.). Seasonal 4 mos. ahead. Requires requested ms by e-mail (attached). Regularly uses sidebars. Guidelines on Website; free copy. (Ads)

Poetry: Accepts 10/yr. Any type. Submit max. 10 poems.

Fillers: Accepts 100/yr. Anecdotes, cartoons, facts, games, ideas, jokes, newsbreaks, prayers, prose, quizzes, quotes, short humor.

Columns/Departments: Accepts 10/yr.

Tips: "Most open to personal experiences of God's miraculous presence in lives: healing, salvation, deliverance from alcohol, drugs, pornography, etc., with some sort of motorsports as a background. Send a story on a Christian involved in motorsports: cars, tractors, motorcycles, airplanes, go-carts, lawnmowers, etc."

CHRISTIAN NEWS NORTHWEST, PO Box 974, Newberg OR 97132. Phone/fax (503)537-9220. E-mail: cnnw@cnnw.com. Website: www.cnnw.com. John Fortmeyer, ed./pub. News of ministry in the evangelical Christian community in western and central Oregon and southwest Washington; distributed primarily through evangelical churches. Monthly newspaper; 32-44 pgs.; circ. 33,000. Subscription $20. 10% unsolicited freelance; 5% assigned. Query; phone/fax/e-query OK. **NO PAYMENT.** Not copyrighted. Articles 300-400 wds. (100/yr.). Responds in 4 wks. Seasonal 3 mos. ahead. Accepts reprints (tell when/where appeared). Accepts e-mail submissions. Regularly uses sidebars. Guidelines (also by e-mail); copy $1.50. (Ads)

Tips: "Most open to ministry-oriented features. Our space is always tight, but stories on lesser-known, Northwest-based ministries are encouraged. Keep it very concise. Since we focus on the Pacific Northwest, it would probably be difficult for anyone outside the region to break into our publication."

**2006 EPA Award of Merit—Newspaper.

THE CHRISTIAN OBSERVER, 9400 Fairview Ave., Ste. 200, Manassas VA 22110. (703)335-2844. Fax (703)368-4817. E-mail: editor@christianobserver.org, or christianobserver@comcast.net. Website: www.ChristianObserver.org. Christian Observer Foundation; Presbyterian Reformed. Dr. Edwin P. Elliott, mng. ed. To encourage and edify God's people and families; print version of Presbyterians-Week. Monthly newspaper; 32 pgs.; circ. 2,000. Subscription $27. 10% unsolicited freelance; 90% assigned. Query; phone/e-query OK. **NO PAYMENT.** Accepts e-mail submissions. (Ads)

CHRISTIAN ONLINE MAGAZINE. E-mail: submissions@christianmagazine.org. Website: www .ChristianMagazine.org. Darlene Osborne, pub. Strictly founded on the Word of God, this magazine endeavors to bring you the best Christian information on the net. Monthly e-zine. Subscription free. 10% unsolicited freelance; 90% assigned. E-query. Articles 500-700 wds. Responds in 1 wk. Seasonal 2 mos. ahead. Prefers accepted ms by e-mail (attached file). **NO PAYMENT.** Regularly uses sidebars. Also accepts submissions from children/teens. Prefers KJV. Guidelines on Website. (Ads)

    Fillers: Accepts 50/yr. Prayers, prose, quizzes, short humor; 500 wds.

    Columns/Departments: Variety Column, 700-1,000 wds. Query.

    Tips: "Most open to solid Christian articles founded on the Word of God."

THE CHRISTIAN OUTLOOK, 492 Hob Moor Rd., Yardley, Birmingham B25 8UB, United Kingdom. Phone +44 (0)870 383 0197. Fax +44 (0)870 199 2302. E-mail through Website: www.thechristianoutlook.net. Nondenominational. Issues on life and living from a Christian perspective. Online newspaper. Free online. Open to unsolicited freelance. Submit through Website. Incomplete topical listings.

    Tips: "We also maintain forums for online interaction among Christians, and between Christians and non-Christians."

THE CHRISTIAN RANCHMAN/COWBOYS FOR CHRIST, 504 "D" F.M. 718, Newark TX 76071. (817)236-0023. Fax (817)236-0024. E-mail: cwb4christ@cowboysforchrist.net. Website: www.CowboysforChrist.net. Interdenominational. Ted Pressley, ed. Monthly tabloid; 20 pgs.; circ. 43,800. No subscription. 85% unsolicited freelance. Complete ms/cover letter. **NO PAYMENT** for all rts. Articles 350-1,000 wds.; book/video reviews (length open). Does not use sidebars. No guidelines; sample copy.

    Poetry: Accepts 40/yr. Free verse. Submit max. 3 poems.

    Fillers: Accepts all types.

    Tips: "We're most open to true-life Christian stories, Christian testimonies, and Christian or livestock news. Contact us with your ideas first."

$CHRISTIAN RENEWAL, Box 770, Lewiston NY 14092-0770, or PO Box 777, Jordan Sta., ON L0R 1S0, Canada. (905)562-5059. Fax (905)562-1368. E-mail: JVANDYK@aol.com. Website: www.crmag.com. Reformed (Conservative). John Van Dyk, ed. Church-related and world news for members of the Reformed community of churches in North America. Biweekly newspaper; 40-48 pgs.; circ. 4,000. Subscription $40 U.S./$43 Cdn. (christian renewal@hotmail.com). 5% unsolicited freelance; 20% assigned. Query/clips; e-query OK. Pays $25-100 for one-time rts. Articles 500-3,000 wds.; fiction 2,000 wds. (6/yr.); book reviews 50-200 wds. Seasonal 3 mos. ahead. Accepts simultaneous submissions & reprints. Prefers e-mail submission (copied into message). Uses some sidebars. Prefers NIV, ESV. No guidelines; copy $2. (Ads: christianrenewal@hotmail.com)

    Tips: "Most open to stories written from a reformed, biblical perspective."

$CHRISTIAN RESEARCH JOURNAL, PO Box 8500, Charlotte NC 28271-8500. (704)887-8200. Fax (704)887-8299. E-mail: submissions@equip.org. Website: www.equip.org. Christian Research Institute. Elliot Miller, ed-in-chief. Probing today's religious movements, promoting doctrinal discernment and critical thinking, and providing reasons for Christian faith and ethics. Quarterly mag.; 64 pgs.; circ. 30,000. Subscription $30. 75% freelance. Query or complete ms/cover letter; fax query OK; e-query & submissions OK. Pays .16/wd. on publication for 1st rts. Articles to 4,200 wds. (25/yr.); book reviews 1,100-2,500 wds. Responds in 4 mos. Accepts simultaneous submissions. Kill fee to 50%. Guidelines (also by e-mail— guidelines@equip.org); copy $6. (Ads)

Columns/Departments: Effective Evangelism, 1,700 wds.; Viewpoint, 875 wds.; News Watch, to 2,500 wds.

Special Needs: Viewpoint on Christian faith and ethics, 1,700 wds.; news pieces, 800-1,200 wds.

Tips: "Be familiar with the Journal in order to know what we are looking for. We accept freelance articles in all sections (features and departments). E-mail for writer's guidelines."

$THE CHRISTIAN RESPONSE, PO Box 125, Staples MN 56479-0125. (218)894-1165. E-mail: happyc@staplesnet.com. Website: www.brainerd.net/~hapco2. HAPCO Industries. Hap Corbett, ed./pub. Exposes anti-Christian bias in America and encourages readers to write letters against such bias. Bimonthly newsletter; 6 pgs. Subscription $13. 10% unsolicited freelance. Complete ms/cover letter; e-query OK. Accepts full mss by e-mail after acceptance. Pays $5-20 on acceptance for one-time rts. Articles 50-700 wds. (4-6/yr.). Responds in 2 wks. Seasonal 6 mos. ahead. Accepts simultaneous submissions & reprints. Does not use sidebars. Guidelines; copy for $1 or 3 stamps. (Ads—classified only)

Fillers: Buys 2-3/yr. Anecdotes, facts, quotes; up to 150 wds.; $5-10.

Special Needs: Articles on anti-Christian bias; tips on writing effective letters to the editor; pieces on outstanding accomplishments of Christians in the secular media.

Tips: "The best way to break in is to uncover an instance of a Christian being denied civil rights by any public unit or government agency because of being a Christian and writing a concise 500-700 word article about it."

$CHRISTIAN RETAILING, 600 Rinehart Rd., Lake Mary FL 32746. (407)333-0600. Fax (407)333-7133. E-mail: Christian.Retailing@strang.com. Website: www.christianretailing .com. Strang Communications. Andy Butcher, ed. (andy.butcher@strang.com). For Christian product industry manufacturers, distributors, retailers. Trade journal published 17X/yr.; circ. 10,500. Subscription $75. 75% assigned. Query/clips; no phone/fax/e-query. Pays .25/wd. on publication. Articles; book reviews. No simultaneous submissions. Accepts requested mss by e-mail (attached file). Kill fee. Uses some sidebars. Prefers NIV. Guidelines on Website. (Ads)

Tips: "Book reviews should focus on what the book contains and how it might help them in their walk with Christ." Also publishes 2 supplements: *The Church Bookstore* (8X/yr.) and *Inspirational Gift Trends* (4X/yr.).

$CHRISTIAN SINGLE and CHRISTIAN SINGLE ONLINE, One Lifeway Plaza, Nashville TN 37234. (615)251-2230. Fax (615)251-5008. E-mail: christiansingle@lifeway.com, or christiansingle@bssb.com. Website: www.christiansingle.com. Monthly mag. Print & online versions. No freelance.

$CHRISTIAN STANDARD, 8805 Governor's Hill Dr., Ste. 400, Cincinnati OH 45249. (513)931-4050. Fax (513)931-0950. E-mail: christianstd@standardpub.com. Website: www.christian standard.com. Standard Publishing/Christian Churches/Churches of Christ. Mark A. Taylor, ed. Devoted to the restoration of New Testament Christianity, its doctrines, its ordinances, and its fruits. Weekly & online mag.; 16 pgs.; circ. 48,000. Subscription $31.99. 40% unsolicited freelance; 60% assigned. Complete ms; no phone/fax/e-query. Pays $20-160 on publication for one-time, reprint, & electronic rts. Articles 800-1,600 wds. (200/yr.). Responds in 9 wks. Seasonal 8-12 mos. ahead. Accepts reprints (tell when/where appeared). Guidelines & copy on Website. (Ads)

Tips: "We would like to hear ministers and elders tell about the efforts made in their churches. Has the church grown? developed spiritually? overcome adversity? succeeded in missions?"

**2004 EPA Award of Merit—Most Improved Publication.

$CHRISTIANWEEK, Box 725, Winnipeg MB R3C 2K3, Canada. Toll-free (800)263-6695. (204)982-2060. Fax (204)947-5632. E-mail: editor@christianweek.org. Website: www .christianweek.org. Fellowship for Print Witness. Doug Koop, edit. dir.; Kelly Rempel, mng.

ed. Canada's leading Christian news source; telling the stories of God and His people in Canada. Biweekly tabloid newspaper (25X/yr.); 12-32 pgs.; circ. 32,000. Subscription $44.95 (Cdn.), $65.95 (U.S.). Query; phone/fax/e-query OK. Pays $30-100 on publication for 1st rts. News articles 300-600 wds. Responds in 1-3 wks. Seasonal 6 mos. ahead. Might accept simultaneous submissions or reprints (tell when/where appeared). Prefers accepted ms by e-mail (attached or copied into message). Uses some sidebars. Prefers NRSV. Also accepts submissions from teens. Guidelines/theme list (also by e-mail/Website). (Ads)

Tips: "Most open to general news, profiles, and features. Writers are encouraged to query first with ideas about people or news events in their own community (Canadian angles, please) or denomination that would be of interest to readers in other denominations or in other areas of the country."

**2004 EPA Award of Excellence—Newspaper.

+THE CHRONICLE—INDIANA EDITION, 18891 Stockton Dr., Noblesville IN 46060. (317)770-7670. E-mail: samgaw@indianachristiannews.com. Website: www.thechronicle online.net. Big Picture Media. Russ Jones, ed. Building up unity between churches and people in the community. Monthly newspaper; circ. 50,000. Subscription $25. Open to unsolicited freelance. Query. Articles & reviews. Incomplete topical listings. (Ads)

$THE CHRONICLE CHRISTIAN NEWSPAPER—KANSAS EDITION, PO Box 492, Newton KS 67114-0492. (316)283-8300. Fax (316)283-6090. E-mail: editor@thechronicleonline.net. Website: www.thechronicleonline.net. Big Picture Media Group Inc. Jackie Jones, ed. To inform the public of issues that affect our decision-making, to encourage and build up the body of Christ, to be a tool to bring others to a life-changing decision for Christ, and to give back to our community. Monthly tabloid & online newspaper; 32-36 pgs.; circ. 50,000. Subscription $31.50. 10% unsolicited freelance; 15% assigned. Query/clips or complete ms/cover letter; phone/fax/e-query OK. Accepts full mss by e-mail. Pays on publication for all rts. Responds in 2 wks. Seasonal 2-3 mos. ahead. Prefers e-mail submissions (attached file). Uses some sidebars. (Ads)

Fillers: Anecdotes, cartoons, facts, games, ideas, kid quotes, newsbreaks, party ideas, prayers, prose, quizzes, quotes, short humor, tips, and word puzzles.

Tips: "Always looking for great news (from a Christian perspective, of course)." See Website for editions from different cities.

CHURCH HERALD AND HOLINESS BANNER, 7407 Metcalf, Overland Park KS 66212. Fax (913)722-0351. E-mail: HBeditor@juno.com. Website: www.heraldandbanner.com. Church of God (Holiness)/Herald and Banner Press. Mark D. Avery, ed. Offers the conservative holiness movement a positive outlook on their church, doctrine, future ministry, and movement. Monthly mag.; 24 pgs.; circ. 1,100. Subscription $12.50. 5% unsolicited freelance; 5% assigned. Query; e-query OK. Accepts full mss by e-mail. **NO PAYMENT** for one-time, reprint, or simultaneous rts. Not copyrighted. Articles 600-1,200 wds. (3-5/yr.). Responds in 9 wks. Seasonal 6 mos. ahead. Accepts simultaneous submissions & reprints (tell when/where appeared). Accepts requested ms on disk or by e-mail (attached file). Uses some sidebars. Prefers KJV. Also accepts submissions from children/teens. Guidelines (also by e-mail); copy for 9x12 SAE/2 stamps. (No ads)

Fillers: Anecdotes, quizzes; 150-400 wds.

Tips: "Most open to short inspirational/devotional articles. Must be concise, well written, and get one main point across; 200-600 wds. Be well acquainted with the Wesleyan/Holiness doctrine and tradition. Articles which are well written and express this conviction are very likely to be used."

$+CHURCHMOUSE PUBLICATIONS LLC, PO Box 9, Hudson NH 03051. (603)578-1860. E-mail: submissions@churchmousepublications.com. Website: www.churchmousepublications .com. Clarice G. James & Susan W. Loud, eds. Guidelines by e-mail.

CHURCH OF ENGLAND NEWSPAPER, Religious Intelligence Ltd., 4th Fl., Central House, 142 Central St., London, England EC1V 8AR. Phone +44 20 7417 5800. Fax +44 20 7216 6410. E-mail: colin.blakely@churchnewspaper.com. Website: www.churchnewspaper.com. Religious Intelligence LTD. Colin Blakely, ed. Weekly newspaper; circ. 25,000. Subscription 60 pounds (UK); 85 pounds (U.S.). Query: phone/e-query OK. Accepts e-mail submissions (attached file). Uses some sidebars. Guidelines by e-mail. (Ads)

Tips: "Most open to news reports and general features."

$CITIZEN USA, 250 N. Cassel Rd., Dayton OH 45449. (937)233-6227. Fax (937)233-6231. E-mail: editor@ccn-usa.net. Website: www.citizenusa.us. Christian Media Group Inc. Pendra Lee Snyder, pub. Only Judeo-Christian newspaper in Ohio; news features, current events presented from Judeo-Christian world-view. Monthly newspaper; circ. 30,000. Subscription $52. 10% unsolicited freelance; 75% assigned. Query/clips; phone/ fax/e-query OK. Accepts full mss by e-mail. Pay $20-60 on publication for all (if assigned) or 1st rts. Articles 600-800 wds.; book reviews, 500-600 wds.; music reviews, 200-300 wds.; video reviews, 500 wds. (pays $20-25). Responds in 4 wks. Seasonal 2-3 mos. ahead. Prefers e-mail submissions (copied into message). No kill fee. Uses some sidebars. Also accepts submissions from teens. Prefers KJV. (Ads) Guidelines by e-mail/Website.

Fillers: Buys 4/yr. Cartoons, games, short humor, word puzzles. Pays $20-25.

Columns/Departments: Buys 4/yr. News features, under 800 wds., $20-50 or no payment. E-query.

Tips: "Most open to current news, feature articles, or social/political/current events. Some lifestyle; book or music reviews."

$CITY LIGHT NEWS, 9827E Horton Rd. S.W., Calgary AB T2V 2X5, Canada. (403)640-2011. Fax (403)640-2000. E-mail: editor@calgarychristian.com. Website: www.calgarychristian.com. CLN Productions. John Syratt, ed. A Christian newspaper serving the church audience in Central and Southern Alberta and Southeastern BC. Monthly newspaper; 20-32 pgs.; circ. 12,000. Subscription $24.95 Cdn. 10% unsolicited freelance; 60% assigned. Query; e-query OK. Pays $15-55 or .10/wd. Cdn., on publication for 1st rts.; $20/photo. Articles 150-550 wds. (12/yr.); reviews 150 wds. ($15). Responds in 2 wks. No simultaneous submissions; accepts reprints (tell when/where appeared). Prefers e-mail submissions (attached file). No kill fee. Uses some sidebars. Also accepts submissions from teens. Guidelines/theme list on Website; copy for 10x13 SAE/$3 postage. (Ads)

Fillers: Buys 12/yr. Anecdotes, cartoons, facts, jokes, kid quotes, newsbreaks, short humor; $30-50.

Tips: "Most open to articles of interest to general church audience; news or gripping stories—lighthearted or tragic; good news stories; celebrity testimony or story/photo; real-life humor."

$COLUMBIA, PO Box 1670 (06507-0981), 1 Columbus Plaza, New Haven CT 06510-3326. (203) 752-4398 or 4303. Fax (203)752-4109. E-mail: columbia@kofc.org, or through Website: www .kofc.org. Knights of Columbus. Tim S. Hickey, ed. Geared to a general Catholic family audience. Monthly & online mag.; 32 pgs.; circ. 1.6 million. Subscription $6; foreign $8. 25% unsolicited freelance; 75% assigned. Query; fax/e-query OK. Pays $250-600 on acceptance for 1st & electronic rts. Articles 500-1,500 wds. (12/yr.). Responds in 2 wks. Seasonal 3 mos. ahead. Occasional reprint (tell when/where appeared). Prefers e-mail submission (copied into message). Kill fee. Regularly uses sidebars. Free guidelines (also by e-mail)/copy. (No ads)

Special Needs: Essays on spirituality, personal conversion. Catholic preferred. Query first.

Tips: "We welcome contributions from freelancers in all subject areas. An interesting or different approach to a topic will get the writer at least a second look from an editor. Most open to feature writers who can handle church issues, social issues from an orthodox Roman Catholic perspective. Must be aggressive, fact-centered writers for these features."

**This periodical was #45 on the 2007 Top 50 Christian Publishers list (#45 in 2006, #49 in 2005).

$COMMON GROUND, #204—4381 Fraser St., Vancouver BC V6V 4G4, Canada. (604)733-2215. Fax (604)733-4415. E-mail: editor@commonground.ca. Website: www.common ground.ca. Common Ground Publishing. Joseph Roberts, sr. ed. Covers health, environment, spirit, creativity, and wellness. Monthly tabloid; circ. 70,000. Subscription $60 Cdn.; U.S. $50. 10% unsolicited freelance. Query by e-mail. Pays .10/wd. (Cdn.) on publication (although most articles are donated) for one-time or reprint rts. Articles 600-1,500 wds. (to 2,500 wds.), (12/yr.). Responds in 6-13 wks. (returns material only if clearly specified). Seasonal 3 mos. ahead. Accepts simultaneous submissions & reprints. Requires requested ms by e-mail. Guidelines on Website; copy $5. Incomplete topical listings. (Ads)

Tips: "Donated articles are given priority over paid articles. Once an article has been published, we will contact you with the final word count, after which you may submit an invoice."

$COMMONWEAL, 475 Riverside Dr., Rm. 405, New York NY 10115-0499. (212)662-4200. Fax (212)662-4183. E-mail: editors@commonwealmagazine.org. Website: www.commonweal magazine.org. Commonweal Foundation/Catholic. Paul Baumann, ed. A review of public affairs, religion, literature, and the arts, for an intellectually engaged readership. Biweekly jour.; 32 pgs.; circ. 20,000. Subscription $47. 20% unsolicited freelance. Query/clips; phone query OK. Pays $75-100 on publication for all rts. Articles 750-1,000 or 2,000-3,000 wds. (30/yr.). Responds in 3-4 wks. Seasonal 2 mos. ahead. Prefers requested ms by e-mail. Kill fee 2%. Uses some sidebars. Guidelines on Website; free copy. (Ads)

Poetry: Rosemary Deen, poetry ed. Buys 30/yr. Free verse, traditional; to 75 lines; .75/line. Submit max. 5 poems. Submit October-May, by mail only.

Columns/Departments: Upfronts (brief, newsy facts and information behind the headlines), 750-1,000 wds.; The Last Word (commentary based on insight from personal experience or reflection), 700 wds.

Tips: "Most open to meaningful articles on social, political, religious, and cultural topics; or columns."

($)COMMUNITY SPIRIT, KWHB TV-47 Office Bldg., 8835 S. Memorial, Tulsa OK 74133. (918) 307-2323. Fax (918)307-1221. E-mail: tom@mccloudmedia.com, or Tara@mccloudmedia .com. Website: www.communityspiritmagazine.com. McCloud Media. Tom McCloud, pub.; Tara Lynn Thompson, mng. ed. To glorify God by telling stories of individual Christians whose good works testify to God's active presence in Oklahoma. Monthly mag.; circ. 50,000. Subscription free. 40% unsolicited freelance; 60% assigned. Prefers e-query. Accepts full mss by e-mail. **PAYS FOR ASSIGNMENTS ONLY** on publication for all rts. Articles 800 wds. Accepts reprints (tell when/where appeared). Accepts requested mss by e-mail (attached file). Regularly uses sidebars. (Ads)

Fillers: Ideas.

$COMPANY: The World of Jesuits and Their Friends, PO Box 60790, Chicago IL 60660. (773)761-9432. Fax (773)761-9443. E-mail: editor@companymagazine.org. Website: www.companymagazine.org. Martin McHugh, ed.; Maureen Ryan, asst. ed. For people interested in or involved with Jesuit ministries. Quarterly & online mag.; 32 pgs.; circ. 120,000. Free subscription. 40% unsolicited freelance; 60% assigned. Complete ms/cover letter; e-query OK. Pays $250-450 on publication for one-time rts. Articles 1,500 wds. Responds in 6 wks. Seasonal 3 mos. ahead. Accepts simultaneous submissions & reprints (tell when/ where appeared). Prefers e-mail submission (attached file). Prefers NRSV, NAB, NJB. Guidelines (also by e-mail); copy for 9x12 SAE/4 stamps. (No ads)

Columns/Departments: Books with a Jesuit connection; Minims and Maxims (short items of interest to Jesuit world), 100-150 wds./photo; Letters to the Editor; Obituaries. No payment (usually).

Tips: "We welcome manuscripts as well as outlines of story ideas and indication of willingness to accept freelance assignments (please include résumé and writing samples with the latter two). Articles must be Jesuit-related, and writers usually have some prior association with and/or knowledge of the Jesuits. Looking for feature articles (Jesuit-related), historical, essays, or ministry-related articles."

$COMPASS DIRECT NEWS, PO Box 27250, Santa Ana CA 92799. (949)862-0304. Fax (949) 752-6536. E-mail: info@compassdirect.org. Website: www.compassdirect.org. Compass Direct. Jeff M. Sellers, mng. ed. To raise awareness of and encourage prayer for Christians worldwide who are persecuted for their faith. Online news source; circ. 730. E-mail subscription $25; for reprint rights $40. Uses little unsolicited freelance. Pays $125-175. Articles 800-1,200 wds.; no reviews. Query only. Guidelines by e-mail. (No ads)

Tips: "An international journalist could submit an article query on a current/specific instance of Christian persecution in a country with religious liberty restrictions. Be on the scene where persecution of Christians is taking place, and report it thoroughly and professionally."

CONNECTING POINT, PO Box 685, Cocoa FL 32923. (321)632-0130. Fax (321)632-5540. E-mail: lhoward@specialgatherings.com, or info@specialgatherings.com. Linda G. Howard, ed. For and by the mentally challenged (mentally retarded) community; primarily deals with spiritual and self-advocacy issues. Monthly mag.; 12 pgs.; circ. 1,000. Free. 75% unsolicited freelance. Complete ms; phone/fax/e-query OK. **NO PAYMENT** for 1st rts. Articles (24/yr.) & fiction (12/yr.), 250-300 wds. Responds in 3-6 wks. Seasonal 3 mos. ahead. Accepts simultaneous submissions & reprints. Guidelines (also by e-mail); copy for 9x12 SAE/$2.23 postage (mark "Media Mail").

Poetry: Accepts 4/yr. Any type; 4-30 lines. Submit max. 10 poems.

Fillers: Accepts 12/yr. Cartoons, games, word puzzles; 50-250 wds.

Columns/Departments: Accepts 24/yr. Devotion Page, 250 wds.; Bible Study, 250 wds. Query.

Special Needs: Self-advocacy, integration/normalization, justice system.

Tips: "All manuscripts need to be in primary vocabulary."

+CONNECTIONS LEADERSHIP/MOPS, 2370 S. Trenton Way, Denver CO 80231. (303)733-5353. Fax (303)733-5770. E-mail: Connections@MOPS.org. Website: www.MOPS.org. MOPS Intl. Carla Foote, ed. To provide leadership training and encouragement for leaders of chartered MOPS groups (Mothers of Preschoolers). Quarterly; circ. 25,000. Subscription $10. Open to unsolicited freelance. Query. Articles. Incomplete topical listings.

$THE COVENANT COMPANION, 5101 N. Francisco Ave., Chicago IL 60625. (773)907-3328. Fax (773)784-4366. E-mail: communication@covchurch.org. Website: www.covchurch .org. Evangelical Covenant Church. Jane Swanson-Nystrom, ed.; Cathy Norman Peterson, features ed. Informs, stimulates thought, and encourages dialog on issues that affect the denomination. Monthly mag.; 40 pgs.; circ. 12,000. Subscription $19.95. 10-15% unsolicited freelance; 75% assigned. Query or complete ms/cover letter; fax/e-query OK. Pays $35-100 after publication (within 3 wks.) for one-time or simultaneous rts. Articles 600-1,800 wds. (40/yr.). Prefers e-mail submission. Responds in 4 wks. Seasonal 4 mos. ahead. Accepts simultaneous submissions & reprints (tell when/where appeared). Some kill fees. Regularly uses sidebars. Prefers NRSV. Guidelines (also by e-mail); copy for 9x12 SAE/5 stamps or $2.50. (Ads)

CREATION, PO Box 4545, Eight Mile Plains QLD 4113, Australia. Phone 07 3840 9888. Fax 07 3840 9889. E-mail: mail@creation.info. Website: www.creationontheweb.com. Creation Ministries Intl. Carl Wieland, managing dir. A family, nature, science magazine focusing on creation/evolution issues. Quarterly mag.; 56 pgs.; circ. 55,000. Subscription $25. 30% unsolicited freelance. Query; phone/fax/e-query OK. **NO PAYMENT** for all rts. Articles to

1,500 wds. (20/yr.). Responds in 2-3 wks. Prefers requested ms on disk or by e-mail (attached file). Regularly uses sidebars. Guidelines (also by e-mail); copy $6.95. (No ads) **Tips:** "Get to know the basic content/style of the magazine and emulate. Send us a copy of your article, or contact us by phone."

CREATION CARE, 4485 Tench Rd., Ste. 850, Suwanee GA 30024. (678)541-0747 (office), or (404)414-7906 (direct). E-mail: een@creationcare.org. Website: www.creationcare .org/magazine. Evangelical Environmental Network. Rusty Prichard, PhD, ed. For Christians who care about stewardship of natural resources, environmental responsibility, sustainability, and simplicity. Quarterly mag.; 40 pgs.; circ. 6,000. Subscription $30 (free to supporters). 40% unsolicited freelance. Query; e-query OK. **NO PAYMENT.** Articles 750-2,100 wds. (20/yr.); book reviews 250 wds. Responds in 6-8 wks. Seasonal 4 mos. ahead. No simultaneous submissions. Accepts reprints (tell when/where appeared). Prefers accepted ms by e-mail. Regularly uses sidebars. Prefers NRSV, NIV. Guidelines by e-mail. (Ads)

Tips: "Significant redesign in fall 2007. Feature articles and reviews are often done by freelancers, also interviews/profiles, news features, essays. Writing is especially sought that conveys the concrete, real-life connections between care of creation, social justice, Christian ministry, personal discipleship, parenting, and community. Articles should focus on or appeal to evangelicals and other Christians with a vibrant, orthodox faith and a high view of Scripture."

$CREATION ILLUSTRATED, PO Box 7955, Auburn CA 95604. (530)269-1424. Fax (530)269-1428. E-mail: ci@creationillustrated.com. Website: www.creationillustrated.com. Tom Ish, ed./pub. An uplifting, Bible-based Christian nature magazine that glorifies God; for ages 9-99. Quarterly mag.; 68 pgs.; circ. 20,000. Subscription $19.95. 60% unsolicited freelance; 40% assigned. Query or query/clips; fax/e-query OK. Pays $75-125 within 30 days of publication for 1st rts. (holds rts. for 6 mos.). Articles 1,000-2,000 wds. (20/yr.). Responds in 2 mos. Seasonal 6 mos. ahead. Accepts simultaneous submissions & reprints (tell when/where appeared). Prefers e-mail submission (copied into message). Kill fee 25%. Some sidebars. Prefers NKJV. Guidelines/theme list (also on Website); copy $3/9x12 SAE/$2.23 postage (mark "Media Mail"). (Some ads)

Poetry: Buys 4/yr. Light verse, traditional; 10-20 lines; $15. Submit max. 4 poems.

Fillers: Games, 100-200 wds. Pays variable rates.

Tips: "Most open to an experience with nature/creation that brought you closer to God and will inspire the reader to do the same. Include spiritual lessons and supporting scriptures—at least 3 or 4 of each."

$CREATIVE NONFICTION, 5501 Walnut St., Ste. 202, Pittsburgh PA 15232. (412)688-0304. Fax (412)688-0262. E-mail: information@creativenonfiction.org. Website: www.creative nonfiction.org. Lee Gutkind, ed. Publishes compelling nonfiction stories with a strong narrative and research element. Triannual jour.; 150 pgs.; circ. 5,000. Subscription $29.95 for 4 issues. 80% unsolicited freelance; 20% assigned. Complete ms/cover letter; no phone/ fax/e-query. Pays $10/published page on publication for all rts. Articles to 5,000 wds. (30/yr.). Responds in 3-5 mos. Accepts simultaneous submissions; no reprints. No e-mail submissions. No kill fee. Does not use sidebars. Also accepts submissions from teens. Guidelines (also by e-mail/Website); copy $10/7x10 SAE/$2.23 postage (mark "Media Mail"). (Ads)

Contests: Sometimes sponsor contests; see Website for details.

$THE CRESSET: A Review of Arts, Literature & Public Affairs, Huegli Hall, Valpariso University, Valparaiso IN 46383. (219)464-6089. E-mail: cresset@valpo.edu. Website: www.valpo.edu/cresset. Valparaiso University/Lutheran. James Paul Old, ed. (tom .kennedy@valpo.edu). For college-educated, professors, pastors, laypeople; serious review essays on religious-cultural affairs. Mag. published 5X/yr.; 60 pgs.; circ. 4,500. Subscription

$20. 10% unsolicited freelance; 90% assigned. Query; e-query OK. Pays $100-500 on publication for all rts. Articles 2,000-4,500 wds. (2/yr.); book/music reviews, 1,000 wds. ($150). Responds in 15 wks. No simultaneous submissions or reprints. Prefers requested ms by e-mail (attached or copied into message). Regularly uses sidebars. Prefers NRSV. Guidelines on Website; copy $4. (No ads)

Poetry: John Ruff, poetry ed. Buys 20/yr. Avant-garde, free verse, light verse, traditional; to 40 lines; $15-25. Submit max. 4 poems.

Columns/Departments: Buys 20/yr. Books; Music; Science & Technology; World Views; all 1,000 wds., $100-250. Query.

CROSSHOME.COM: Your Christian Home on the Net! E-mail: webmaster@crosshome.com. Website: www.crosshome.com. Online mag. Open to solicited freelance. Complete ms by e-mail; e-query OK. **NO PAYMENT** for one-time rts. Articles 300-1,000 wds.; devotionals 300-1,000 wds. (prefers 350-650 wds.); book reviews 300-800 wds. Responds in 1-3 wks. (if accepted). Requires accepted ms by e-mail (attached file in Word). Prefers KJV, NKJV, NIV, NASB. Guidelines on Website (www.crosshome.com/guidelines.shtml); copy online. (Ads)

Poetry: Accepts free verse, traditional; 30-500 wds.

Columns/Departments: Open to submissions for regular columns, or ideas for new ones. (See guidelines.)

Special Needs: See Website/guidelines for list of channels where your writing might fit.

Tips: "We do archive all writing, but any submissions can be deleted by request of the author by e-mail."

$CULTURE WARS, 206 Marquette Ave., South Bend IN 46617-1111. (574)289-9786. Fax (574)289-1461. E-mail: jones@culturewars.com, or letters@culturewars.com, or fidelity press@sbcglobal.net. Website: www.culturewars.com. Ultramontagne Associates Inc. Dr. E. Michael Jones, ed. Issues relating to Catholic families and issues affecting America that affect all people. Monthly (11X) mag.; 48 pgs.; circ. 3,500. Subscription $39. 20% unsolicited freelance. Complete ms/cover letter; fax/e-query OK. Pays $100 & up on publication for all rts. Articles (25/yr.); book reviews $50. Responds in 12-24 wks. Query about reprints. Prefers requested ms on disk. Uses some sidebars. Developing guidelines; copy for 9x12 SAE/5 stamps.

Poetry: Buys 15/yr. Free verse, light verse, traditional; 10-50 lines; $25. Submit max. 2 poems.

Fillers: Buys 15/yr. Cartoons, quotes; 25 wds. & up; payment varies.

Columns/Departments: Buys 25/yr. Commentary, 2,500 wds.; Feature, 5,000 wds.; $100-250.

Tips: "All fairly open except cartoons. Single-spaced preferred; photocopies must be legible."

$DECISION/DECISION ONLINE, 1 Billy Graham Pkwy., Charlotte NC 28201-0001. (704)401-2432. Fax (704)401-3009. E-mail: submissions@bgea.org. Website: www.decisionmag.org. Billy Graham Evangelistic Assn. Bob Paulson, ed. Evangelism/Christian nurture; all articles must have connection to BGEA. Monthly (11X) & online mag.; 44 pgs.; circ. 400,000. Subscription $12. 5% unsolicited freelance; written mostly in-house. Query preferred; no phone/fax/e-query. Pays $200-400 on publication for 1st rts. Articles 400-1,000 wds. (8/yr.). Response time varies. Seasonal 3-5 mos. ahead. Accepts ms by e-mail (attached file). Kill fee 50%. Uses some sidebars. Prefers NIV. Guidelines (also by e-mail/Website); copy for 10x13 SAE/3 stamps. (No ads)

Poetry: Buys 6/yr. Free verse, light verse, traditional; 4-16 lines. Pays $1/wd. Submit max. 7 poems.

Columns/Departments: Buys 11/yr. Finding Jesus (people who have become Christians through Billy Graham ministries), 500-600 wds.; $200. Complete ms.

Special Needs: Personal experience articles telling how a Billy Graham ministry helped you live out your faith.

Tips: "Nearly all of our articles have some connection with a ministry of the Billy Graham Evangelistic Assn.—through the author's participation in the ministry or through the author's being touched by the ministry."

**2005 EPA Award of Merit—Organizational.

DESERT CALL: Contemplative Christianity and Vital Culture, Box 219, Crestone CO 81131. (719)256-4778. Fax (719)256-4719. E-mail: nada@fone.net. Website: www .spirituallifeinstitute.org. Spiritual Life Institute/Catholic. Suzie Ryan, ed. Practical spirituality and contemplative prayer; interfaith/interreligious dialog, the arts and culture, fiction. Quarterly mag.; 32 pgs.; circ. 2,000. Subscription $20. 15% unsolicited freelance; 10% assigned. Complete ms/cover letter; no phone/fax/e-query. **PAYS 3 COPIES** for 1st rts. Articles 1,000-2,500 wds. (4/yr.); some fiction. Responds in 15 wks. Seasonal 8 mos. ahead. Accepts reprints (tell when/where appeared). No disk or e-mail submissions. Uses some sidebars. No guidelines; copy $2.50/10x13 SAE. (No ads)

Poetry: Accepts 3/yr. Free verse, haiku, traditional; to 25 lines.

Fillers: Accepts 3/yr. Anecdotes, facts, prayers, prose, quotes; 50-250 wds.

DESERT CHRISTIAN NEWS, PO Box 4196, Palm Desert CA 92261. (760)772-2027. E-mail: smiller@desertchristiannews.org. Website: www.desertchristiannews.org. Susan Miller, ed. To encourage communication and unity amongst Christians in the Coachella Valley by sharing inspiring local news stories, feature articles, and information. Monthly newspaper; weekly TV/radio programs. Subscription $35. Open to freelance. Articles 500-750 wds. Query preferred. Articles; reviews. Guidelines on Website. (Ads) Incomplete topical listings.

THE DESERT VOICE, PO Box 567, Imperial CA 92251. (760)337-9200. Fax (760)355-0197. E-mail: editor@desertvoice.info. Website: www.desertvoice.info. Witness Publishing Inc. Alex Arroyave, ed. To reach the lost, and to provide family-friendly news not found elsewhere by bias or neglect, or simply because they don't feel it's important. Monthly newspaper; 20 pgs.; circ. 5,200. No subscriptions. Open to freelance. Complete ms/cover letter. **NO PAYMENT.** Articles & fiction 500-800 wds.; reviews 300 wds. Seasonal 2 mos. ahead. Accepts simultaneous submissions & reprints (tell when/where appeared). Prefers e-mail submissions (attached file). Uses some sidebars. Occasionally accepts submissions from teens. No guidelines or copy. (Ads)

Fillers: Jokes, kid quotes, quotes, word puzzles.

Special Needs: News.

DIAMOND DUST, E-mail: DiamondEditor@yahoo.com. Website: www.freewebs.com/diamond dustmagazine/writersguidelines.htm. Laura & Stephanie Rutlind, eds. To empower adults and teens in their Christian walk. Bimonthly Website and e-newsletter. Free online. Open to unsolicited freelance. Query or complete ms/cover letter. **NO PAYMENT** for one-time electronic rts. Articles 200-1,000 wds.; fiction to 1,200 wds.; devotionals 100-500 wds.; book/music reviews 150-500 wds. Responds in 4 wks. Seasonal 4 mos. ahead. Requires e-mail submissions (copied into message). Also accepts submissions from teens. Guidelines/theme list on Website; copy online.

Poetry: Accepts all types; under 30 lines. Submit max. 3 poems.

Fillers: Accepts facts, games, ideas, prayers, prose, quizzes, short humor, tips, and word puzzles; to 500 wds.

Special Needs: Fillers, seasonal mss, and general interest articles related to themes.

Tips: "We do not require submissions to be explicitly Christian, but we ask that they include good morals and clean content." Include a short bio (to 50 wds.) with your submission.

$DIRECTION, PO Box 436987, Chicago IL 60643. (708)868-7100, ext. 236. Fax (708)868-6759. E-mail: ecarey@urbanministries.com. Website: www.urbanministries.com. Urban

Ministries Inc. Submit to Evangeline Carey, developmental ed. An adult-level Sunday School quarterly publication consisting of student book and teacher's guide. Quarterly mag.; 64 pgs.; $18.45 (student) and $33.54 (teacher). 100% assigned. Query or query/clips; phone/fax/e-query OK. Accepts full manuscripts by e-mail. Pays to $200 ($300 for lessons) on acceptance, for all rts. Articles 1,500-3,500 wds. Responds in 4 wks. Seasonal 12 mos. ahead. No simultaneous submissions or reprints. Requires accepted ms on disk or by e-mail (attached or copied into message). Kill fee 50%. Does not use sidebars. Prefers KJV. Guidelines by e-mail; copy for SASE. (No ads)

Tips: "Send query with a writing sample, or attend our annual conference on the first weekend in November each year."

$DISASTER NEWS NETWORK, 9195C Red Branch Rd., Columbia MD 21045. Toll-free (888)384-3028. (410)884-7350. Fax (410)884-7353. E-mail: info@villagelife.org. Website: www.disasternews.net. Village Life Co. Submit to Editor. Online; an interactive daily news site on the World Wide Web. Query; phone/fax OK; e-query preferred. Pays $100-150 after publication for all rts. Articles 1,000 wds. (varies). Requires accepted ms by e-mail. Guidelines on Website. (Ads)

Tips: "Most open to 'people stories' related to faith-based disaster response and/or mitigation. Also, faith-based response to incidents of public violence. Authors are expected to have an e-mail submission address. Check our Website." Authors must be DNN pre-approved contractor writers.

$DISCIPLESHIP JOURNAL, Box 35004, Colorado Springs CO 80935. (719)548-9222. Fax (719)598-7128. E-mail: djwriters@navpress.com. Website: www.discipleshipjournal.com. NavPress/The Navigators. Sue Kline, sr. ed./pub.; Connie Willems, ed.; Dianne Bundt, DJ Plus ed. For motivated, maturing Christians desiring to grow spiritually and to help others grow; biblical and practical. Bimonthly mag.; 84+ pgs.; circ. 100,000. Subscription $23.97. 65% unsolicited freelance; 35% assigned. Query/clips; fax/e-query OK. Accepts full mss by e-mail, if requested. Pays .25/wd. (.05/wd. for reprints) on acceptance for 1st, plus 10% for electronic rts. Articles 1,200-2,800 wds. (60/yr.). Responds in 6-8 wks. Seasonal 9 mos. ahead. No simultaneous submissions; accepts reprints (tell when/where appeared). Prefers requested ms by e-mail (attached or copied into message). Kill fee 50%. Regularly uses sidebars. Prefers NIV. Guidelines (also on Website); copy for 9x12 SAE/$2.70 postage. (Ads)

Columns/Departments: Buys 60+/yr. DJ Plus (ministry how-to on missions, evangelism, serving, discipling, teaching, and small groups), under 400 wds. Complete manuscript. Pays .25/wd.

Special Needs: Small groups; discipling/one-on-one mentoring; biblical teaching.

Tips: "Most open to feature articles and DJ Plus. Our articles focus on biblical passages or topics. Articles should derive main principles from a thorough study of Scripture, should illustrate each principle, should show how to put each principle into practice, and should demonstrate with personal illustrations and vulnerability that the author has wrestled with the subject in his or her life. Target a specific kind of reader, include reader takeaway, and craft a fresh approach."

**The #4 Best-selling magazine in Christian retail stores. This periodical was #10 on the 2008 Top 50 Christian Publishers list (#2 in 2007, #4 in 2006, #3 in 2005, #3 in 2004). 2006, 2005 EPA Award of Merit—General. 2004 EPA Award of Excellence—General.

DISCIPLE'S JOURNAL, 10 Fiorenza Dr., Wilmington MA 01887-4421. Toll-free (800)696-2344. (978)657-7373. Fax (978)657-5411. E-mail: dddj@disciplesdirectory.com, or info@ disciplesdirectory.com. Website: www.disciplesdirectory.com. Kenneth A. Dorothy, ed. To strengthen, edify, inform, and unite the body of Christ. Monthly & online newspaper; 24-32 pgs.; circ. 8,000. Subscription $14.95. 5% unsolicited freelance. Query; fax/e-query OK. **NO**

PAYMENT for one-time rts. Articles 400 wds. (24/yr.); book/music/video reviews 200 wds. Responds in 2 wks. Seasonal 2 mos. ahead. Accepts simultaneous submissions & reprints (tell when/where appeared). Prefers requested ms on disk or by e-mail (attached file). Uses some sidebars. Prefers NIV. Guidelines/theme list (also by e-mail); copy for 9x12 SAE/$2.23 postage (mark "Media Mail"). (Ads)

Fillers: Accepts 12/yr. All types; 100-400 wds.

Columns/Departments: Financial; Singles; Men; Women; Business; Parenting; all 400 wds.

Tips: "Most open to men's, women's, or singles' issues; missions; or homeschooling. Send sample of articles for review."

$DISCIPLESWORLD, 6325 Guilford Ave., Ste. 213, Indianapolis IN 46220-1992. (317)375-8846. Fax (317)375-8849. E-mail: editor@disciplesworld.com. Website: www.disciples world.com. Christian Church (Disciples of Christ). Sherri Wood Emmons, mng. ed. The journal of news, opinion, and mission for this denomination in North America. Monthly (10X) mag.; 48 pgs.; circ. 14,000. Subscription $31. 30% unsolicited freelance; 70% assigned. Complete ms/cover letter or query with/without clips; e-query OK. Pays .16/wd. on publication for 1st rts. Articles 1,200-1,800 wds. (40/yr.); fiction 700-1,500 wds. (8-10/yr.); reviews 600 wds. (no payment). Responds in 1 mo. Seasonal 3 mos. ahead. Accepts simultaneous submissions; no reprints. Requires submissions by disk or e-mail (attached file). No kill fee. Uses some sidebars. Prefers NRSV. Guidelines/theme list on Website; copy for #10 SASE. (Ads)

Poetry: Buys 6-10/yr. Free verse, light verse; 12-30 lines. Pays $10-50. Submit max. 3 poems.

Columns/Departments: Buys 12-15/yr. Speak Out (opinion on an issue), 700 wds.; Disciples Go (travel to places relevant to Disciples), 700 wds., plus photos; $100. Quotable Quotes, 200 wds. (no pay).

Tips: "Our readers are mostly college-educated, active in their churches, proud of their Disciples heritage, and all over the board politically and theologically. We like things with a Disciples connection."

**This periodical was #48 on the 2008 Top 50 Christian Publishers list (#40 in 2007, #46 in 2006, #45 in 2005).

DIVINE ASCENT: A Journal of Orthodox Faith, PO Box 439, 21770 Ponderosa Way, Manton CA 96059. (530)474-5964. Fax (530)474-3564. E-mail: office@monasteryofstjohn.org. Website: www.monasteryofstjohn.org. Monastery of St. John of Shanghai & San Francisco/Orthodox Church in America. Fr. Jonah Paffhausen, Abbot & ed-in-chief. Focuses on contemporary Orthodox spirituality as seen in the lives and writings of saints, and holy men and women of our own time. Semi-annual & online jour.; 150 pgs. Subscription $25/2 yrs. 20% unsolicited freelance; 65% assigned. Query. **NO PAYMENT** for all rts. Articles (6/yr.); book reviews 500 wds. Responds in 4-8 wks. No reprints. Prefers disk or e-mail submissions (attached file). Does not use sidebars. Prefers RSV, KJV, NKJV. Guidelines by e-mail. (Ads, from Orthodox Christian businesses)

Tips: "Nothing Protestant."

$DOVETAIL: A Journal by and for Jewish/Christian Families, 775 Simon Greenwell Ln., Boston KY 40107. Toll-free (800)530-1596. (502)549-5499. Fax (549)549-3543. E-mail: di-ifr@bardstown.com. Website: www.dovetailinstitute.org. Dovetail Institute for Interfaith Family Resources. Mary Helene Rosenbaum, ed. Offers balanced, nonjudgmental articles for interfaith families and the professionals who serve them. Bimonthly mag.; 12-16 pgs.; circ. 1,000. Subscription/membership $39.95. 80% unsolicited freelance; 20% assigned. Query or complete ms; phone/fax/e-query OK. Pays $25 on publication for all rts. Articles 800-1,000 wds. (18-20/yr.); book reviews 500 wds., ($15). Responds in 2-6 wks. Seasonal 4 mos. ahead. Accepts simultaneous submissions & reprints (tell when/where appeared). Prefers requested ms on disk or by e-mail (copied into message). Uses some sidebars. Prefers RSV. Guidelines/theme list only by e-mail/Website; copy online PDF only. (Ads)

Poetry: Buys 1-2/yr. Traditional; $15. Submit max. 4 poems.

Columns/Departments: Buys 3-6/yr. Food & Family (Jewish & Christian), 500 wds.; Parent's Page, and Reviews; $15. Complete ms.

Special Needs: "We have expanded our scope to include other types of interfaith marriages, especially those involving a Muslim partner. Also soliciting stories for children and young adults for notebook publication. Author retains copyright. Stories must directly relate to interfaith family theme."

Tips: "Demonstrate real, concrete, practical knowledge of the challenges facing Jewish and Christian partners in a marriage. Do not send pieces of Christian interest only. No proselytizing." Show respect for the religious traditions of their Jewish staff and readers.

$DRAMA MINISTRY, PO Box 40387, Nashville TN 37204. Toll-free (866)859-7622. Fax (615)373-8502. E-mail: service@dramaministry.com, or through Website: www.drama ministry.com. Belden Street Music Company. Regi Stone, ed. Mag. published 8X/yr. & online; page count varies. Subscription $99.95. 50% unsolicited freelance; 50% assigned. Complete ms/cover letter for scripts; query for articles; e-query OK. Pays $100-150 for scripts on publication for one-time rts. Articles 500-700 wds. (10/yr.); scripts 2-10 minutes (80/yr.). Responds in 6-8 wks. Seasonal 6 mos. ahead. Accepts simultaneous submissions & reprints (tell when/where appeared). Requires submissions by e-mail (attached file). No kill fee. Does not use sidebars. Also accepts submissions from teens. Any Bible version. Guidelines/theme list on Website. (No ads)

Tips: "If your script is well written and you have a true understanding of what works within the church drama ministry, then you will break into our publication easily. Please adhere to and read writer's guidelines thoroughly (see Website). We do not respond unless we choose to publish your script."

$DREAMS & VISIONS: Spiritual Fiction, 35 Peter St. S., Orillia ON L3V 5A8, Canada. Phone/fax (705)329-1770. E-mail: skysong@bconnex.net. Website: www.bconnex .net/~skysong. Skysong Press. Steve Stanton, ed. An international showcase for short literary fiction written from a Christian perspective. Semiannual jour.; 56 pgs.; circ. 200. Subscription $12. 100% unsolicited freelance. Complete ms/cover letter; no phone/fax/e-query. Pays .01/wd. on publication for 1st rts. Fiction 2,000-6,000 wds. (12/yr.). Responds in 3-9 wks. No seasonal. Accepts simultaneous submissions & reprints (tell when/where appeared). Guidelines on Website; copy $5.95 (4 back issues to writers $12).

$DREAMSEEKER MAGAZINE, 126 Klingerman Rd., Telford PA 18969. (215)723-9125. E-mail: DSM@CascadiaPublishingHouse.com, or editor@CascadiaPublishingHouse.com. Website: www.CascadiaPublishingHouse.com. Cascadia Publishing House. Submit to The Editor. For readers committed to exploring from the heart, with passion, depth, and flair, their own visions and issues of the day. Quarterly print & online mag.; 52 pgs.; circ. 1,000 (including online). Subscription $14.95. 10% unsolicited freelance; 90% assigned. Query; e-query OK. Accepts full mss by e-mail. Pays $5 or .01/wd. on publication for 1st or one-time rts. Articles 750-1,500 wds. (10/yr.). Responds in 8 wks. No seasonal. No simultaneous submissions; rarely buys reprints (tell when/where appeared). Prefers submissions on disk or by e-mail (attached file). No kill fee. Does not use sidebars. Also accepts submissions from children/teens. Guidelines on Website; copy online. Incomplete topical listings.

+DUPAGE CHRISTIAN, 1616 E. Roosevelt Rd., Wheaton IL 60187. Toll-free (866)390-1353. Fax (630)929-8070. E-mail: marc@dupagechristian.com. Website: www.DupageChristian .com. Brownhardt Christian Media. Marc Browning, ed. Supporting Christian life in DuPage

County. Subscription $20. Open to unsolicited freelance. Complete ms. Articles. Incomplete topical listings. (Ads)

E-CHANNELS (formerly Channels), 3819 Bloor St. W., Toronto ON M9P 1K7, Canada. Phone/fax (519)651-2232. E-mail: cbbrown@rogers.com. Website: http://renewalfellowship .presbyterian.ca. The Renewal Fellowship/Presbyterian (P.C.C.). Calvin Brown, ed. For Presbyterians seeking spiritual renewal and biblical orthodoxy. Online mag.; 20 pgs.; circ. 2,000. Subscription $12. 10% unsolicited freelance; 90% assigned. Query; e-query OK. **PAYS IN COPIES** for one-time rts. Articles 1,000-1,500 wds. (15/yr.); book reviews 300 wds. Responds in 4 wks. Seasonal 4-6 mos. ahead. Accepts reprints (tell when/where appeared). Prefers mss by e-mail (attached file/RTF). Regularly uses sidebars. Also accepts submissions from teens. No guidelines; copy for #10 SAE/3 stamps. (Ads)

    Poetry: Accepts 3/yr. Free verse, haiku, light verse, traditional; 3 lines & up. Submit max. 6 poems.

    Fillers: Accepts 4/yr. Anecdotes, cartoons, prayers.; 6-100 wds.

$EFCA TODAY, 418 Fourth St. N.E., PO Box 315, Charlottesville VA 22902. (434)961-2500. Fax (434)961-2507. E-mail: Today@EFCA.org, or DianeMc@journeygroup.com. Website: www.efca.org/today. Evangelical Free Church of America/Journey Communications. Diane McDougall, ed. Denominational. Quarterly mag.; 32 pgs.; circ. 44,000. Subscription $10. 5% unsolicited freelance; 95% assigned. Query (preferred) or complete ms/cover letter; fax/e-query OK. Pays .23/wd. on acceptance for 1st and subsidiary (free use on EFCA Website or church bulletins) rts. Articles 300-500 wds. (4/yr.). Responds in 6 wks. Seasonal 6 mos. ahead. Accepts simultaneous submissions & reprints (tell when/where appeared). Prefers e-mail (attached file) or hard copy. Kill fee 50%. Regularly uses sidebars. Guidelines (also by e-mail/Website); copy $1/10x13 SAE/$2.23 postage (mark "Media Mail"). (Ads)

    Columns/Departments: Cover-Theme Section (variety of topics applicable to church leadership), 500-1,000 wds.; pays $46-250.

    Special Needs: Stories of EFCA churches in action.

    Tips: "Write about an EFCA church or leader and show how the topic is applicable to leaders in other EFCA churches. We are not a general-interest publication. 'Inspirational' pieces are not applicable."

    **2008, 2007, 2006 EPA Award of Merit—Denominational. 2005 EPA Award of Excellence—Denominational. This periodical was #41 on the 2007 Top 50 Christian Publishers list (#50 in 2006, #44 in 2004).

$EL HERALDO CRISTIANO (THE CHRISTIAN HERALD), PO Box 16040, Tampa FL 33687. (813)333-6999. Fax (813)333-9968. E-mail: info@elheraldocristiano.org. Website: www .elheraldocristiano.org. Pentecostal/published in Spanish. Joseph Diaz, ed./pub. Embracing the family for Christ. Estab. 2007; 36 pgs. Distributed in Tampa Bay area but nationwide eventually. Pays. Call or e-mail. Incomplete topical listings.

ENCOMPASS, 2296 Henderson Mills Rd. N.E., Ste. 406, Atlanta GA 30345-2739. Toll-free (800)914-2000. (770)414-1515. Fax (770)414-1518. E-mail: jabel@americananglican .org. Website: www.americananglican.org. The American Anglican Council. Jennifer Abel, ed. To provide news and information regarding the Episcopal Church and worldwide Anglican Communion; to provide inspirational articles for the spread of Christ's kingdom; to offer encouragement and challenge to the larger church. Monthly newsletter; 4-6 pgs.; circ. 45,000. Subscription free. Open to freelance. Query preferred; phone/e-query OK. **NO PAYMENT.** Articles 200-2,000 wds. Responds in 2 wks. Accepts articles by e-mail (attached file). Uses some sidebars. No guidelines; copy for 9x12 SAE/2 stamps.

    Tips: "Most open to features or aspects of important people in the Anglican scene in America; commentary on current events in the Anglican community from the orthodox point of view."

$ENFOQUE A LA FAMILIA, (formerly En Confianza), 8675 Explorer Dr., Colorado Springs CO 80920. Toll-free (800)434-2345. (719)548-4660. Fax (719)531-3383. E-mail: ardilama@ fotf.org. Website: www.enfoque.org. Focus on the Family. Marta Ardila, ed. To provide family-friendly material to our domestic Spanish constituents and inform the Hispanic community of culturally relevant issues that affect their families. Bimonthly mag.; circ. 30,000. Subscription free. Open to freelance. Complete ms/cover letter. Articles; no reviews. Incomplete topical listings. (No ads)

$EPISCOPAL LIFE and EPISCOPAL LIFE ONLINE, 815—2nd Ave., New York NY 10017. Toll-free (800)334-7626, ext. 6009. (212)716-6000. Fax (212)949-8059. E-mail: rwilliams@ episcopalchurch.org.; mdavies@episcopalchurch.org. Website: www.episcopal-life.org. Episcopal Church. Robert Williams, newspaper ed. (212)922-5385); Matthew Davies, online ed. Denominational. Monthly newspaper; 32 pgs.; circ. 280,000. Subscription $16.95. 10% assigned. Query/clips or complete ms/cover letter; phone query on breaking news only; e-query OK. Pays $50-300 on publication for 1st, one-time, or simultaneous rts. Articles 250-1,200 wds. (12/yr.); assigned book reviews 400 wds. ($35). Responds in 5 wks. Seasonal 4 mos. ahead. Accepts simultaneous submissions & reprints. Accepts e-mail submission. Kill fee 50%. Guidelines (by e-mail); free copy. (Ads)

> **Columns/Departments:** Nan Cobbey, column ed. (ncobbey@dfms.org). Buys 36/yr. Commentary on political/religious topics; 300-600 wds.; $35-75. Query.
>
> **Tips:** "All articles must have Episcopal Church slant or specifics. We need topical/issues, not devotional stuff. Most open to feature stories about Episcopalians—clergy, lay, churches, involvement in local efforts, movements, ministries."
>
> **This periodical was #50 on the 2008 Top 50 Christian Publishers list.

($)E-QUALITY, 122 W. Franklin Ave., Ste. 218, Minneapolis MN 55404. (612)872-6898. Fax (612)872-6891. E-mail: cbe@cbeinternational.org. Website: www.cbeinternational.org. Christians for Biblical Equality. Submit to E-Quality editor. Geared to serve those who are exploring biblical equality. Quarterly online jour.; circ. 8,000+. Subscription free. Open to freelance. Wants 1st, reprint, and electronic rts. Pays $0-40 in gift certificates, or membership (no cash). Feature articles 1,300-1,500 wds.; book reviews 500 wds. Responds in 4+ wks. Seasonal 4-6 mos. ahead. No simultaneous submissions. Guidelines/copy on Website. (Ads)

> **Tips:** "Most articles we publish fall into these three categories—all related to biblical equality: personal testimonies, teaching on relevant Bible passages, or reviews of books on biblical equality."

ETERNAL INK, 4706 Fantasy Ln., Alton IL 62002. E-mail: eternallyours8@yahoo.com. Website: www.eternal-ink.org. Nondenominational. E-mail publication with a Website; open to any serious effort or submission. Mary-Ellen Grisham, ed; Carl Phillips, features ed. (CarlPhil 10@aol.com); Pat Earl, devotions ed. Biweekly e-zine; 1 pg.; circ. 450. Subscription free. 25% unsolicited freelance; 75% assigned. Complete ms/cover letter; e-query OK. **NO PAYMENT** for one-time rts. Not copyrighted. Articles/devotions 300-500 wds. (26/yr.); reviews 300-500 wds. Responds in 6 wks. Seasonal 2 mos. ahead. Accepts simultaneous submissions & reprints. Accepts e-mail submissions (copied into message). No kill fee or sidebars. Prefers NIV. Occasionally accepts submissions from children/teens. Guidelines/copy by e-mail/Website. (No ads)

> **Poetry:** Elizabeth Pearson, poetry ed. (roybet@sbcglobal.net). Accepts 24-30/yr. Free verse, traditional, inspirational; to 30 lines. Submit max. 3 poems.
>
> **Fillers:** Ivie Bozeman, fillers ed. (ivie@rose.net). Accepts 24-30/yr. Anecdotes, jokes, kid quotes, prayers, prose, short humor; 150-250 wds.
>
> **Columns/Departments:** Accepts many/yr. See information on Website. Query.

Contest: Annual Prose/Poetry Contest in November-December, with 1st, 2nd, and 3rd place winners in each category. Book awards for first place winners. See Website.

Tips: "Please contact Mary-Ellen Grisham by e-mail with questions."

$EUREKA STREET: An Online Magazine of Public Affairs, the Arts and Theology, PO Box 553, Richmond VIC 3121, Australia. Phone 03 9421 9666. Fax 0 9421 9600. E-mail: eureka@eurekastreet.com.au. Website: www.eurekastreet.com.au. Jesuit Communications. Michael Mullins, ed.; submit to Tim Kroenert, asst. ed. An online magazine of public affairs, the arts, and theology. Daily e-zine; circ. 30,000. Subscription free. 35% unsolicited freelance; 35% assigned. Query; phone/e-query OK (complete ms for fiction). Accepts full mss by e-mail. Pays $200 on publication for one-time rts. Articles 600-800 wds.; fiction 700-1,000 wds.; reviews 400 wds. (pays $100). Responds in 1 wk. Seasonal 1 mo. ahead. No simultaneous submissions or reprints. Requires submissions by e-mail (attached). Uses some sidebars. Guidelines on Website (www.eurekastreet.com.au/ab_write.html).

Poetry: Philip Harvey (poetry@eurekastreet.com.au). Buys 50/yr. Avant-garde, free verse, haiku, light verse, traditional. Pays $50 for a set of 4 poems. Submit max. 3 poems.

Contest: Eureka Street/Reader's Feast Award for social justice/human rights writing; and Margaret Dooley Award for Young Writers. Website: www.crimeandjusticefestival.com/eureka.

$EVANGEL (IN), Box 535002, Indianapolis IN 46253-5002. (317)244-3660. E-mail: evangel editor@fmcna.org. Free Methodist/Light and Life Communications. Julie Innes, ed. For young to middle-aged adults; encourages spiritual growth. Weekly take-home paper (published quarterly); 8 pgs.; circ. 11,000. Subscription $9. 100% unsolicited freelance. Complete ms/cover letter; no e-query. Pays .04/wd. ($10 min.) on publication for one-time rts. Articles 1,200 wds. (100/yr.); fiction 1,200 wds. (100/yr.). Responds in 6-8 wks. Seasonal 12-15 mos. ahead. Accepts some simultaneous submissions & reprints (tell when/where appeared). Accepts requested mss by e-mail. Some sidebars. Prefers NIV. Guidelines (also by e-mail); copy for #10 SAE/1 stamp. (No ads)

Poetry: Buys 40+/yr. Free verse, light verse, traditional; 3-16 lines; $10. Submit max. 5 poems. Rhyming poetry not usually taken seriously.

Fillers: Buys 20/yr. Cartoons, crypto-word puzzles; to 100 wds; $10.

Tips: "Bring fresh insight to a topic. Submit material appropriate for the market and audience. Although we will cover a specific issue of concern to men or to women, we prefer that the problem be addressed universally. Don't ramble; stick to one thesis. A returned manuscript isn't always because of poor writing. Can also use short devotional material, 600 words or less."

EVANGEL (OR), 19532 N.E. Glisan St., Portland OR 97230. (503)492-4216. Fax (503)492-8965. E-mail: office@pnmc.org. Website: www.pnmc.org. Mennonite Church USA. Susan M. Palmer, ed. Official publication of the Pacific Northwest Mennonite Conference, featuring news and features about the churches, organizations, and people of the Mennonite Church USA in WA, OR, ID, AK, and W. MT. Quarterly mag.; 8 pgs.; circ. 3,000. Subscription free. 10% unsolicited freelance; 10% assigned. Query; phone/e-query OK. Accepts full mss by e-mail. PAYS IN COPIES for one-time rts. Not copyrighted. Articles 500-1,000 wds. (4/yr.). Responds in 2-4 wks. Seasonal 4 mos. ahead. No simultaneous submissions; accepts reprints (tell when/where appeared). Accepts requested mss on disk or by e-mail (attached file). Uses some sidebars. Guidelines (also by e-mail); copy for 9x12 SAE/.80 postage. (No ads)

Fillers: Accepts 2-4/yr. Newsbreaks, prose, 50-150 wds.

Special Needs: Features on local congregational activities.

Tips: "Become familiar with the views, beliefs of Mennonite Church USA. Visiting www.mennoniteusa.org is a good place to start. Please address issues from a Mennonite perspective. Check our Website."

THE EVANGELICAL ADVOCATE, Box 30, 1426 Lancaster Pike, Circleville OH 43113. (740) 474-8856. Fax (740)477-7766. E-mail: directordoc@cccuhq.org, or info@cccuhq.org. Website: www.cccuhq.org. Churches of Christ in Christian Union. Ralph Hux, dir. of communications. Provides news, information, and features which emphasize current events and world-view, appealing to the needs of our constituency, emphasizing fundamental evangelical holiness. Bimonthly mag.; 32-36 pgs.; circ. 4,000. Subscription $12. 15% unsolicited freelance; 15% assigned. Query (preferred) or complete ms/cover letter; fax/e-query OK. NO PAYMENT. Articles 500-1,000 wds. (15-20/yr.). Seasonal 2-3 mos. ahead. Accepts simultaneous submissions & reprints (tell when/where appeared). Prefers e-mail submissions (attached file). Regularly uses sidebars. Prefers KJV, NIV, NRSV. Theme list/guidelines by e-mail; copy for 9x12 SAE. (no ads)

Poetry: Accepts 6-12/yr. Traditional.

Tips: "Best way to break in is to submit material for review by e-mail."

EVANGELICAL TIMES, Faverdale North Industrial Estate, Darlington DL3 0PH, United Kingdom. Phone +44 1325 380232. E-mail: theeditors@evangelical-times.org. Website: www .evangelical-times.org. Edgar Andrews & Roger Fay, eds. For churches who hold a biblical, Christ-centered theology and the doctrines of grace; circulated worldwide. Monthly tabloid newspaper; 32 pgs.; circ. 40,000. Subscription $18 (surface), $28 (airmail). Incomplete topical listings.

Tips: "Our paper offers UK and world news, Christian comment, and a wide variety of articles (biblical, devotional, practical, topical, doctrinal, and historical), with a strong missionary dimension."

$FAITH & FAMILY: The Magazine of Catholic Living, 432 Washington Ave., North Haven CT 06473. (203)230-3800. Fax (203)230-3838. E-mail: editor@faithandfamilymag.com. Website: www.faithandfamilymag.com. Catholic/Circle Media Inc. Tom & April Hoopes, eds.; submit to Robyn Lee, asst. ed. Features writing for Catholics and/or Christian families of all ages. Bimonthly mag.; 100 pgs.; circ. 32,000. Subscription $17.95. 10% unsolicited freelance; 90% assigned. Query/clips; e-query preferred; no phone query. Pays .33/wd. on publication for 1st rts. Articles 700-3,000 wds. (35/yr.); brief reviews. Responds in 6-8 wks. Seasonal 6-9 mos. ahead. No reprints. Prefers e-mail submission (attached file). Kill fee. Regularly uses sidebars. Accepts illustrations from children. Prefers NAB. Guidelines (also on Website); copy $4.50/10x13 SAE. (Ads)

Fillers: Buys 10/yr. Anecdotes, cartoons, prose (brief).

Columns/Departments: Buys 75/yr. The Home Front (news); The Insider; Flair; The Season; Life Lessons; Faith & Folklore; Celebrations; Entertainment; The Where & How Guide; Spiritual Directions; and Back Porch; 600-1,200 wds. Query.

Tips: "Most open to well-written feature articles employing good quotations, anecdotes, and transitions about an interesting aspect of family life; departments; news items. To break in, submit ideas for The Home Front." Only wants Catholic theme-related material. **This periodical was #22 on the 2008 Top 50 Christian Publishers list (#33 in 2007, #21 in 2005, #5 in 2004).

$FAITH & FRIENDS, 2 Overlea Blvd., Toronto ON M4H 1P4, Canada. (416)422-6226. Fax (416)422-6120. E-mail: faithandfriends@can.salvationarmy.org. Website: www.faithand friends.ca. The Salvation Army. Lt. Colonel Ray Moulton, ed-in-chief; Geoffrey Moulton, mng. ed. Monthly mag.; 32 pgs.; circ. 50,000. Subscription $16.50 Cdn. 90% assigned. Query/clips; e-query OK. Pays up to $200 Cdn. on publication for one-time rts. Articles 500-1,000 wds. Responds in 2 wks. Seasonal 6 mos. ahead. Accepts simultaneous submissions & reprints (tell when/where appeared). Prefers accepted ms by e-mail (attached file). Uses some sidebars. Prefers TNIV. Guidelines (also on Website); free copy. (No ads)

Fillers: Buys 10/yr. Cartoons, games, jokes, quizzes, quotes, word puzzles; 50 wds.; $25.

Columns/Departments: God in My Life (how Christians in the workplace find faith relevant), 600 wds.; Words to Live By (simple Bible studies/discussions of faith), 600 wds.; Faith Builders (Movie & TV reviews from a spiritual and faith perspective), 750-1,000 wds.; Between the Lines (book reviews), 500 wds.; Someone Cares.

$FAITH TODAY: To Connect, Equip and Inform Evangelical Christians in Canada, M.I.P. Box 3745, Markham ON L3R 0Y4, Canada. (905)479-5885. Fax (905)479-4742. E-mail: fteditor@efc-canada.com. Website: www.faithtoday.ca. Evangelical Fellowship of Canada. Gail Reid, mng. ed.; Bill Fledderus, sr. ed.; Karen Stiller, assoc. ed. A general-interest publication for Christians in Canada; almost exclusively about Canadians, including Canadians abroad. Bimonthly mag.; 56 pgs.; circ. 18,000. U.S. subscription $30.15 Cdn. 20% unsolicited freelance; 80% assigned. Query only; fax/e-query preferred. Pays $80-500 (.20-.25 Cdn./wd.) on publication for 1st & electronic rts.; reprints .15/wd. Features 800-1,700 wds; cover stories 2,000 wds.; essays 650-1,200 wds.; profiles 900 wds; reviews 300 wds. (75-100/yr.) Responds in 6 wks. Prefers e-mail submission. Kill fee 30-50%. Regularly uses sidebars. Any Bible version. Guidelines on Website; copy for 9x12 SAE/$2.05 in Canadian funds. (Ads)

   Tips: "Most open to short, colorful items, statistics, stories, profiles for Kingdom Matters department. Content (not author) must be Canadian." Unsolicited manuscripts will not be returned.

   **This periodical was #42 on the 2006 Top 50 Christian Publishers list (#37 in 2005).

FAITHWEBBIN, PO Box 8732, Columbia SC 29202. Fax (775)908-9660. E-mail: editor@ faithwebbin.net. Website: www.faithwebbin.net. Tywebbin Creations. Mrs. Tyora Moody, ed. For Christian families. Monthly online mag. 100% unsolicited freelance. Complete ms by e-mail only; e-query OK. **NO PAYMENT.** Any Bible version. Articles 800-1,000 wds. (15-20/yr.). Responds in 1-2 wks. Seasonal 2 mos. ahead. Accepts reprints (tell when/where appeared). Requires e-mail submission (attached file). Regularly uses sidebars. Guidelines/theme list on Website. (No ads)

   Columns/Departments: Accepts 12/yr. Seek (original Bible study lessons and devotions), 1,000-1,200 wds.; Grow (Christian living: family, finance, marriage, etc.), 800-1,000 wds.

   Tips: "The two areas exclusively open to freelancers are Seek and Grow. Articles are normally accepted if they meet the length requirement and are not similar to what is already included on the site. Looking for fresh articles; love testimonial type devotions or articles that encourage and motivate the reader."

$THE FAMILY DIGEST, PO Box 40137, Fort Wayne IN 46804. Catholic. Corine B. Erlandson, manuscript ed. Dedicated to the joy and fulfillment of Catholic family life and its relationship to the Catholic parish. Bimonthly mag.; 48 pgs.; circ. 150,000. Distributed through parishes. 95% unsolicited freelance. Complete ms/cover letter; no phone/fax/e-query. Pays $45-60, 4-9 wks. after acceptance, for 1st rts. Articles 700-1,200 wds. (60/yr.). Responds in 4-9 wks. Seasonal 7 mos. ahead. Occasionally buys reprints (tell when/where appeared). No disk. Uses some sidebars. Prefers NAB. Guidelines; copy for 6x9 SAE/2 stamps. (Ads)

   Fillers: Buys 18/yr. Anecdotes drawn from experience, prayers, short humor; 25-100 wds.; pays $25.

   Tips: "Prospective freelance writers should be familiar with the types of articles we accept and publish. We are looking for upbeat articles which affirm the simple ways in which the Catholic faith is expressed in daily life. Articles on family life, parish life, seasonal articles, how-to pieces, inspirational, prayer, spiritual life, and church traditions will be gladly reviewed for possible acceptance and publication."

THE FAMILY JOURNAL MAGAZINE, PO Box 1005, Springfield OH 45501. (937)399-9612. E-mail: editor@familyjournalmagazine.org. Website: www.familyjournalmagazine.org. The

Nuz News. Carolyn Hayes, ed./pub. Christ-centered publication, sponsor-supported and free to readers; provides help for the young Christian and may also serve to introduce readers to Jesus Christ. Bimonthly mag./e-zine; circ. 4,500. Subscription $10. Open to unsolicited freelance. **Pays 6 copies** for one-time or reprint rts. Not copyrighted. Articles 500 wds.; query for fiction. Responds in 1 wk. Uses some sidebars. Prefers NIV. Guidelines by e-mail. (Ads)

$FAMILY SMART E-TIPS, PO Box 1125, Murrieta CA 92564-1125. (858)513-7150. Fax (951) 461-3526. E-mail: plewis@smartfamilies.com, or info@smqrtfamilies.com. Website: www .smartfamilies.com. Smart Families Inc. Paul Lewis, ed./pub. Christian parenting, with strong crossover to general families. E-newsletter. 20% unsolicited freelance. Complete ms preferred; fax/e-query OK. Pays $50-250 on publication for 1st rts. Articles 200-1,000 wds. Responds in 1-3 wks. Seasonal 4 mos. ahead. Accepts simultaneous submissions & reprints. Prefers e-mail submission (attached file). Uses some sidebars. Prefers NIV. No guidelines or copy. (No ads)

    Fillers: Games, ideas, quotes.

    Tips: "We are not a typical 'magazine' and have tight length requirements. Because of crossover audience, we do not regularly print Scripture references or use traditional God-word language."

FELLOWSHIP MAGAZINE, PO Box 412, 1109 Garner Ave., Fenwick ON L0S 1C0, Canada. Toll-free (800)678-2607. E-mail: minister@pelhamcommunitychurch.com. Website: www .fellowshipmagazine.org. Fellowship Publications/United Church of Canada/general lay audience. Rev. Dr. Diane Walker, ed. To provide a positive voice for orthodoxy and uphold the historic Christian faith within the denomination. Quarterly mag.; circ. 9,000. Subscription free for donation. Open to unsolicited freelance. **NO PAYMENT.** Not in topical listings. (Ads)

+FGBC WORLD, PO Box 576, Winona Lake IN 46590. (574)268-1122. Fax (574)268-5384. E-mail: lcgates@bmhbooks.com. Website: www.fgbcworld.com. Brethren Missionary Herald Co. Terry White, ed. Connecting people and churches of the Fellowship of Grace Brethren Churches. Bimonthly mag.; circ. 16,000. Open to unsolicited freelance. Query. Incomplete topical listings. (No ads)

+FLORIDA BAPTIST WITNESS, 1230 Hendricks Ave., Jacksonville FL 32207. (904)596-3165. Fax (904)346-0696. E-mail: jhannigan@floridabapristwitness.com. Website: www.florida baptistwitness.com. Florida Baptist Witness Inc. Joni B. Hannigan, ed. Publishes Good News about God's work that edifies, exhorts, and empowers Florida Baptists to exalt God and extend His kingdom. Weekly newspaper; circ. 46,000. Subscription $17.95. Open to unsolicited freelance. Complete ms. Articles. Incomplete topical listings. (Ads)

$FOCUS ON THE FAMILY MAGAZINE, 8605 Explorer Dr., Colorado Springs CO 80920. (719)531-3400. Fax (719)531-3499. Website: www.family.org. Focus on the Family. Andrea Vinley Jewell, mng. ed.; Linda Arnold, ed. asst. To help families use Christian principles to strengthen marriages, improve child rearing, purposefully embrace midlife, hold a biblical world view, and deal with the problems of everyday life. Monthly mag.; 32 pgs., 4 customized versions (young couples, parents, midlife, and single parents); circ. 800,000. Free subscription. 5% unsolicited freelance; 80% assigned; 15% staff written. Query; no phone/fax/e-query. No full mss by e-mail. Pays .30-.35 cents/wd. on acceptance for 1st & electronic rts. Articles 375-1,100 wds. Responds in 6 wks. Seasonal 7 mos. ahead. Accepts simultaneous submissions; no reprints. Accepts purchased or assigned articles by e-mail (attached file in text or Word). Uses some sidebars. Prefers NIV. Guidelines (also by e-mail); copy for 9x12 SAE/2 stamps. (No ads)

    Tips: "This magazine is 90% generated from within our ministry. It's very hard to break in. Midlife and single-parent areas most open to freelance. We look for unique angles and personal stories on common family-life topics. Writing must be concise, compelling, and accurate."

    **2005 EPA Award of Merit—Most Improved Publication.

$FOCUS ON YOUR CHILD NEWSLETTERS, (Early Stages, Discovery Years, Tween Ages, Teen Phases), 8605 Explorer Dr., Colorado Springs CO 80920. (719)531-3400. Fax (719)531-3499. E-mail: foycnewsletters@family.org. Website: www.focusonyourchild.com. Focus on the Family. Sheila Seifert, mng. ed. Four-color, segmented Christian parenting newsletters: *Early Stages* for parents of 0- to 3-year-olds; *Discovery Years* for parents of 4- to 7-year-olds; *Tween Ages* for parents of 8- to 12-year-olds; and *Teen Phases* for parents of 13- to 18-year-olds. Newsletter published 8X/yr.; 12 pages ea.; circ. 25,000. Subscription $2/mo. 5-10% unsolicited freelance; 80% assigned. Complete ms/cover letter. Accepts full mss by e-mail. Pays .25-.30/wd. on acceptance for nonexclusive rts. Articles 350-600 wds. (over 500/yr.); no reviews. Responds in 8 wks. Seasonal 7 mos. ahead. Accepts simultaneous submissions; no reprints. Accepts e-mail submissions (copied into message). No kill fees. Uses some sidebars. Prefers NIV. Guidelines by e-mail; copies online. (No ads—but those interested could contact Derek Hanson regarding the possibility.)

Fillers: Short parenting humor, 20-350 wds. Pays .25-.30/wd.

Special Needs: Dramatic narratives of true stories, or humor in regard to parenting.

Tips: "The editors are always interested in reviewing humorous personal experience, parenting ideas that focus on children—how a child was parented and NOT the parent's journey or a memory about a parent's childhood. The humorous, true story should contain at least one hands-on, parenting insight about how to raise children, and be focused on an individual child. Do not preach, moralize, or explain your point. The story should lend itself to your point."

**This periodical was #33 on the 2008 Top 50 Christian Publishers list.

THE FOUNDERS JOURNAL, PO Box 150931, Cape Coral FL 33915. (239)772-1400. Fax (239)772-1140. E-mail from Website: www.founders.org. Founders Ministries/Southern Baptist. Thomas K. Ascol, ed. Consistent with the doctrines of grace that speak from a historic Southern Baptist perspective. Quarterly jour. Subscription $20. Complete ms/cover letter and completed author information form from Website. Articles & book reviews. Responds in 4 mos. or you may contact them. Guidelines on Website. Incomplete topical listings.

FRIENDS JOURNAL, Quaker Thought and Life Today, 1216 Arch St., #2A, Philadelphia PA 19107-2835. (215)563-8629. Fax (215)568-1377. E-mail: info@friendsjournal.org. Website: www.friendsjournal.org. Quaker. Robert Dockhorn, sr. ed. Reflects Quaker life with commentary on social issues, spiritual reflection, Quaker history, and world affairs. Monthly mag.; circ. 8,000. Subscription $39. 70% freelance. Complete ms by e-mail preferred; e-query OK. **NO PAYMENT.** Articles to 2,500 wds.; news items 50-200 wds.; reports of Quaker events 450 wds. Responds in 3-16 wks. Accepts simultaneous submissions or reprints, if notified. Also accepts disk. Guidelines on Website; free copy. Incomplete topical listings.

Poetry: To 25 lines.

Fillers: Games, short humor, newsbreaks, and word puzzles.

THE FRIENDS VOICE, 2748 E. Pikes Peak Ave., Colorado Springs CO 80909. (719)632-5721. E-mail: thevoice@evangelicalfriends.org. Website: www.evangelicalfriends.org. Evangelical Friends International/North America. Becky Towne, sr. ed. Denominational newsletter intended for EFI-NA households. Triannual newsletter; 12 pgs.; circ. 21,000. Subscription $10. 25% unsolicited freelance from EFI-NA households. Query. **NO PAYMENT** for exclusive rts. Articles 450-900 wds. Accepted mss by e-mail (attached file). Uses some sidebars. Guidelines/theme list by e-mail; catalog. (No ads) Not included in topical listings.

Tips: "You must attend an EFI-NA church or meeting."

$THE GEM, 700 E. Melrose Ave., Box 926, Findlay OH 45839-0926. (419)424-1961. Fax (419)424-3433. E-mail: communications@cggc.org, or through Website: www.cggc.org. Churches of God, General Conference. Rachel L. Foreman, ed. To encourage and motivate people in their Christian walk. Monthly (13X) take-home paper for adults; 8 pgs.; circ. 6,000. Subscription $14. 80% unsolicited freelance; 20% assigned. Complete ms/cover letter; phone/fax/e-query OK. Pays $15 after publication for one-time rts. Articles 300-1,600 wds. (125/yr.); fiction 2,000 wds. (125/yr.); book/music reviews, 750 wds., $10. Responds in 12 wks. Seasonal 3 mos. ahead. Accepts simultaneous submissions & reprints (tell when/where appeared). Accepts requested ms on disk or by e-mail. Uses some sidebars. Prefers NIV. Guidelines on Website; copy for #10 SAE/2 stamps. (No ads)

Poetry: Buys 100/yr. Any type, 3-40 lines; $5-15. Submit max. 3 poems.

Fillers: Buys 100/yr. All types, except party ideas; 25-100 wds; $5-10.

Special Needs: Missions and true stories. Be sure that fiction has a clearly religious/Christian theme.

Tips: "Most open to real-life experiences where you have clearly been led by God. Make the story interesting and Christian."

**This periodical was #7 on the 2008 Top 50 Christian Publishers list (#9 in 2007, #37 in 2006, #24 in 2005, #30 in 2004).

$GEMS OF TRUTH, PO Box 4060, Overland Park KS 66204. (913)432-0331. Fax (913)722-0351. E-mail: sseditor1@juno.com. Website: www.heraldandbanner.com. Church of God (Holiness)/Herald & Banner Press. Arlene McGehee, Sunday school ed. Denominational. Weekly adult take-home paper; 8 pgs.; circ. 14,000. Subscription $2.45. Complete ms/cover letter; phone/fax/e-query OK (prefers mail or e-mail). Pays .005/wd. on publication for 1st rts. Fiction 1,000-2,000 wds. Seasonal 6-8 mos. ahead. Accepts simultaneous submissions & reprints (tell when/where appeared). Prefers KJV. Guidelines/theme list; copy. Not in topical listings. (No ads)

$GOD ALLOWS U-TURNS BOOK SERIES, c/o God Allows U-Turns, 100 W. Southlake Blvd., Ste. 142-600, Southlake TX 76092. (817)442-0721. E-mail: Allison@AllisonBottke.com. Website: www.AllisonBottke.com. Blog: www.godallowsuturns.blogspot.com. Series on hold for this year.

GODLY PLACES.COM, 4010 Cherryhill Ct., Arlington TX 76016. E-mail: admin@godlyplaces.com. Website: www.GodlyPlaces.com. Brian Howard, founder. Focuses on various types of ministry. Online publication. Go to Website, click on "Contact Us/Author Application," fill out application, and then submit directly to site.

Special Needs: Men's ministry, women's ministry, couple's ministry, family ministry, singles' ministry, teens' ministry, kids' ministry, online ministry, prophetic ministry, international missions, miscellaneous ministries, etc.

GOLD COUNTRY FAMILIES E-MAGAZINE, PO Box 580, Meadow Vista CA 95722. (530)878-4410. E-mail: editor@goldcountryfamilies.com; send queries to: writer-queries@goldcountryfamilies.com. Website: www.goldcountryfamilies.com. Patrick Witz, ed./pub. A free, online family-friendly monthly travel, dining, entertainment, and leisure magazine. Monthly e-magazine; averages 7,000 page views monthly. Free online. 100% unsolicited freelance (60/yr.). Query; e-query OK. Accepts full mss by e-mail. **NO PAYMENT** for 1st rts. & 30 days of electronic rts. (After 30 days rights revert to author but material stays online for at least 12 months.) Articles 500-2,000 wds. (60/yr.). Accepts simultaneous submissions & reprints (tell when/where appeared). Accepts e-mail submissions (copied into message or attached file). Uses some sidebars. Also accepts submissions from children/teens. Guidelines on Website; copy online. (Ads)

Tips: "Read magazine for style and content. We want to encourage and support new freelancers, as well as giving them published clips to advance their writing careers." Quality photos complimenting articles are highly recommended.

$GOOD NEWS, PO Box 150, Wilmore KY 40390. (859)858-4661. Fax (859)858-4972. E-mail: steve@goodnewsmag.org, or info@goodnewsmag.org. Website: www.goodnewsmag.org.

United Methodist/Forum for Scriptural Christianity Inc. Steve Beard, ed. Focus is evangelical renewal within the denomination. Bimonthly mag.; 44 pgs.; circ. 100,000. Subscription $20. 20% unsolicited freelance. Query first; no phone/fax/e-query. Pays $100-150 on publication for one-time rts. Articles 1,500-1,850 wds. (25/yr.). Responds in 24 wks. Seasonal 4-6 mos. ahead. Accepts simultaneous submissions & reprints (tell when/where appeared). Accepts requested ms on disk. Kill fee. Regularly uses sidebars. Prefers NIV. Guidelines (also on Website); copy $2.75/9x12 SAE. (Ads)

Tips: "Most open to features."

GOOD NEWS! 440 W. Nyack Rd., West Nyack NY 10994. (845)620-7438, ext. 20438. Fax (845)620-7723. E-mail: warren_maye@use.salvationarmy.org. Website: www.SAgoodnews.org. The Salvation Army. Warren Maye, ed. Monthly & online newspaper; 16 pgs.; circ. 30,000. 5% unsolicited freelance; 20% assigned.

GOOD NEWS CONNECTION, 105 Harris Ave., Portland ME 04103. Toll-free (800)357-0203. (207)797-4915. E-mail: Info@goodnewsconnction.com. Website: www.goodnews connection.com. Jim Duran, pub. Enriching thousands of families, in Maine and New Hampshire, through churches, bookstores, numerous retail outlets, and on the Web. Bimonthly & online newspaper; circ. 6,000. Subscription $16.95. Query preferred. Articles; no reviews. Incomplete topical listings.

$GOOD NEWS, ETC., PO Box 2660, Vista CA 92085. (760)724-3075. E-mail: rmonroe@ goodnewsetc.com. Website: www.goodnewsetc.com. Good News Publishers Inc. of California. Rick Monroe, ed. Feature stories and local news of interest to Christians in San Diego County. Monthly tabloid; 24-32 pgs.; circ. 42,000. Subscription $30. 5% unsolicited freelance; 5% assigned. Query; e-query OK. Pays $40-150 on publication for all, 1st, one-time, or reprint rts. Articles 500-900 wds. (15/yr.). Responds in 2 wks. Seasonal 2 mos. ahead. Accepts simultaneous submissions & reprints (tell when/where appeared). Prefers accepted ms on disk. Regularly uses sidebars. Prefers NIV. No guidelines; copy for 9x12 SAE/4 stamps. (Ads)

Tips: "Most open to local (San Diego), personality-type articles. A San Diego connection is needed."

**2005 EPA Award of Merit—Newspaper.

$GOOD NEWS IN SOUTH FLORIDA, PO Box 935148, Margate FL 33093. (954)564-5378. Fax (866)587-2911. E-mail: grif@goodnewsfl.org. Website: www.goodnewsfl.org. Blackstone Media Group. Grif Blackstone, ed. To report truth, provoke thought, and honor Jesus Christ. Monthly & online newspaper; circ. 80,000. Subscription $19.95. Open to freelance. Query preferred. Paying market. Articles; reviews. Incomplete topical listings. (Ads)

**2008, 2007 EPA Award of Merit—Newspaper.

GOOD NEWS JOURNAL, 9701 Copper Creek Dr., Austin TX 78729-3543. (512)249-6535. Fax (512)249-0018. E-mail: goodnews98@aol.com. Website: www.thegoodsnewsjournal.net. Evelyn W. Davison, pub. Christian paper for national circulation by subscription, and Central Texas by free distribution. Monthly newspaper; 24 pgs.; circ. 60,000. Subscription $29.95. 40% unsolicited freelance; 60% assigned. Query; fax/e-query OK. **NO PAYMENT** for one-time rts. Articles 200-600 wds. Accepts reprints. Prefers accepted ms by e-mail. Guidelines (also by e-mail/Website); copy for 9x12 SAE/2 stamps. (Ads)

Poetry: Accepts 4-6/yr. Traditional.

Fillers: Accepts many. All types; 10-50 wds.

Tips: "Most open to short helps, funnies, inspirations, and current issues."

THE GOOD NEWS TODAY, PO Box 2558, Providence RI 02906. Phone/fax (401)619-0418. E-mail: larry@goodnewsinri.org, or larry@thegoodnewstoday.org. Website: www.thegood newstoday.org. Good News Outreach. Lawrence L. Lepore, mng. ed. To evangelize the lost and unite the body of Christ in Rhode Island and S.E. Massachusetts. Monthly newspaper;

circ. 16,000. Subscription $20. Open to unsolicited freelance. Complete ms. Articles; book & movie reviews. Starting a new Boston edition. Incomplete topical listings. (Ads)

$GOSPEL TODAY MAGAZINE, 115 Scarlett Oak Way, PO Box 800 (30213), Fairburn GA 30213-3448. (770)719-4825. Fax (770)716-2660. E-mail: Gospeltodaymag@aol.com. Website: www.gospeltoday.com. Horizon Concepts Inc. Teresa Hairston, pub. (drhairstongt@aol.com). Ministry/Christian lifestyle directed toward urban marketplace. Bimonthly (8X) mag.; 64-80 pgs.; circ. 200,000. Subscription $14.97. 5% unsolicited freelance; 90% assigned. Query; e-query OK. Pays $75-250 on publication for all rts. Articles 1,000-3,500 wds. (4/yr.). Responds in 2 wks. Seasonal 3 mos. ahead. Accepts simultaneous submissions & reprints (tell when/where appeared). Prefers accepted ms by e-mail (attached file). Kill fee 15%. Uses some sidebars. Prefers NKJV. Guidelines on Website; copy $3.50. (Ads)

Fillers: Accepts 2-3/yr. Cartoons, word puzzles. No payment.

Columns/Departments: Precious Memories (historic overview of renowned personality), 1,500-2,000 wds.; From the Pulpit (issue-oriented observation from clergy), 2,500-3,000 wds.; Life & Style (travel, health, beauty, fashion tip, etc.), 1,500-2,500 wds.; Broken Chains (deliverance testimony), 1,200 wds. Query. Pays $50-75.

Tips: "Looking for great stories of great people doing great things to inspire others."

$GRAND, 4791 Baywood Point Dr., St. Petersburg FL 33711. Toll-free (800)810-0260. E-mail: wrcrisp@grandmagazine.com. Website: www.grandmagazine.com. General. Wendy Reid Crisp, ed-in-chief. Celebrates the vital spirit and active lifestyle of today's grandparents (ages 40-65); religious point of view must be love based and non-faith-specific. Bimonthly mag. Subscription $9.95. Open to unsolicited freelance. Query/clips; e-query only. Pays $100-500, 30 days after acceptance, for 1st rts. (include Webzine and e-zine permission). Features about 1,500 wds. Kill fee at editor's discretion. Guidelines on Website (www.grandmagazine online.com/template_WritersGuidelines.html). Incomplete topical listings. (Ads)

Columns/Departments: Departments, 650 wds., $100-200. Also buys shorter pieces for up-front section, "For Starters."

Special Needs: Topics of interest to grandparents only.

Tips: "Pay close attention to ethnic and socioeconomic balance."

$GUIDEPOSTS, 16 E. 34th St., 21st Fl., New York NY 10016-4397. (212)251-8100. Website: www.guideposts.com. Interfaith. Submit to Articles Ed. Personal faith stories showing how faith in God helps each person cope with life in some particular way. Monthly mag.; 52 pgs.; circ. 3 million. Subscription $13.94. 40% unsolicited freelance; 20% assigned. Complete ms/cover letter, by mail only; no electronic submissions. Pays $100-500 on publication for all rts. Articles 750-1,500 wds. (40-60/yr.), shorter pieces 250-750 wds ($100-250.). Responds only to mss accepted for publication in 2 mos. Seasonal 6 mos. ahead. Accepts simultaneous submissions & reprints. Kill fee 20%. Uses some sidebars. Free guidelines on Website/copy. (Ads)

Columns/Departments: Christopher Davis, column ed. Buys 24/yr. His Mysterious Ways (divine intervention), 250 wds.; What Prayer Can Do, 250 wds.; Angels Among Us, 400 wds.; Divine Touch (tangible evidence of God's help), 400 wds. ("This is our most open area. Write in 3rd person."); $100.

Contest: Writers Workshop Contest held on even years with a late June deadline. Winners attend a week-long seminar in New York (all expenses paid) on how to write for *Guideposts*. Also Young Writers Contest; $36,000 in college scholarships; best stories to 1,200 wds.; deadline November 29.

Tips: "Be able to tell a good story, with drama, suspense, description, and dialog. The point of the story should be some practical spiritual help that subjects learned through their experience. Use unique spiritual insights, strong and unusual dramatic details." First person only.

HAIKU HIPPODROME, PO Box 2340, Clovis CA 93613-2340. (559)347-0194. E-mail: clovis wings@aol.com. Poetry on Wings. Jackson Wilcox, ed. Bimonthly mag. & e-zine; 8 pgs.; circ. 100. Subscription by donation. 100% unsolicited freelance. Complete ms/cover letter; phone query OK; some e-queries. No full mss by e-mail. **PAYS 1 COPY & SUBSCRIPTION** on publication for 1st rts. Haiku 3 lines. Responds in 4 wks. Seasonal 3+ mos. ahead. No simultaneous submissions or reprints. Also accepts submissions from children/teens. Prefers KJV. Guidelines by mail; copy for #10 SAE/1 stamp. (Ads)

> **Poetry:** Accepts 225/yr. Haiku; 3 lines. Submit max. 3 poems.

> **Contest:** Every issue includes a Hippodrome Tanka: 3 lines (5-7-5), which are given. The contestant then provides 2 lines of 7 syllables each. Prize for best 3 is publication in next issue.

> **Tips:** "We accept a broad range of what many call English Haiku: (3 lines—often 5-7-5 syllables). However we encourage the style of the early haiku poets—seizing the actuality of the moment in nature and expressing it in the purity of a word or phrase."

HALO MAGAZINE, PO Box 1402, Sterling VA 20167. (540)877-3568. Fax (540)877-3535. E-mail: halomag@aol.com. Website: www.halomag.com. Marian Newman Braxton, ed. Designed to minister to the unsaved and encourage the Christian; reaches a wide audience, including churches, hospitals, and prison ministries across many states. Magazine. Subscription $20. Open to unsolicited freelance. Complete ms by mail or e-mail. **NO PAYMENT FOR NOW.** Articles 600-1,500 wds. Guidelines on Website. Incomplete topical listings.

> **Poetry:** Accepts original poems.

$HARUAH: Breath of Heaven, 9618 Misty Brook Grove, Memphis TN 38016. (901)213-3878. E-mail: editor@haruah.com. Website: www.haruah.com. Double-Edge Publishing. Steve Forstner, ed. A magazine dedicated to the art of writing; wanting to inspire and encourage our readers to think in new ways. Monthly e-zine & literary mag.; circ. 9,000. Subscription free online. Estab. 2006. 75% unsolicited freelance; 25% assigned. Complete ms/cover letter; no phone/fax query; e-query OK. No full mss by e-mail; use online submission form on Website. Pay $5 for one-time & electronic rts. No length limitations on articles (20+/yr.) or fiction (60+/yr.); reviews 500 wds. Responds in 4-6 wks. Seasonal several mos. ahead. No simultaneous submissions; some reprints (tell when/where appeared). Submit through their online submissions system. Does not use sidebars. Also accepts submissions from teens (students). Any Bible version. Guidelines on Website; copy online. (No ads)

> **Poetry:** Rochita Loenen-Ruiz, poetry ed. Accepts 24+/yr. Free verse, light verse, traditional, literary; any number of lines. Pays $2. Submit max. 3 poems.

> **Tips:** "Your story doesn't have to mention God, but we would prefer it to point to Him in one way or another. We have a family atmosphere and love to help emerging writers. But be aware that we keep our expectations for our publication high, and do not settle just to fill space. If you are thinking of submitting and aren't sure if your submission fits our guidelines, always feel free to e-mail a query. We have wonderful forums to mingle with the staff. Take advantage of those and get to know us."

HEARTBEAT/CMA, PO Box 9, Hatfield AR 71945. (870)389-6196. Fax (870)389-6199. E-mail: wendy@cmausa.org, or through Website: www.cmausa.org. Christian Motorcyclists Assn. Wendy McDaniel, ed. To encourage members and give them a tool when they are witnessing in the general world. Monthly; circ. 18,000. Subscription $12. Open to freelance. Complete ms/cover letter. Articles; no reviews. Incomplete topical listings. (Ads)

THE HEARTLAND GATEKEEPER, PO Box 241956, Omaha NE 68124. (402)926-2633. Fax (402)391-8744. E-mail: publisher@heartlandgatekeeper.org, or through Website: www .heartlandgatekeeper.org. Faith Missions Intl./nondenominational. Irene Jensen, ed./pub. To promote unity in the body of Christ, to encourage spiritual growth, to testify to the goodness of God through reporting from a Christian perspective, to reach those who have yet to know Jesus; for Omaha/Council Bluffs region. Monthly newspaper; circ. 10,000. Subscription $24. Open to freelance. Prefers query; e-query OK; use online submission form. **NO PAYMENT** for one-time or reprint rts. Articles 150-300 wds., 300-700 wds., or feature articles 500-1,000 wds. Accepts reprints (tell when/where appeared). E-mail submissions only. Guidelines on Website. Incomplete topical listings. (Ads)

HEARTLIGHT INTERNET MAGAZINE, PO Box 7044, Abilene TX 79608. E-mail: phil@heart light.org. Website: www.heartlight.org. Westover Hills Church of Christ. Phil Ware, ed. Offers positive Christian resources for living in today's world. Weekly online mag.; 20+ pgs.; circ. 70,000+. Subscription free. 20% unsolicited freelance. E-query. **NO PAYMENT** for electronic rts. Articles 300-450 wds. (25-35/yr.); fiction 500-700 wds. (12-15/yr.). Responds in 3 wks. Seasonal 2 mos. ahead. Accepts simultaneous submissions & reprints (tell when/where appeared). Prefers e-mail submission. Regularly uses sidebars. Prefers NIV. Copy available on the Internet.

> **Fillers:** Accepts 12/yr. Anecdotes, cartoons, games, ideas, jokes, newsbreaks, prayers, prose, quotes, short humor, word puzzles; to 350 wds.
>
> **Tips:** "Most open to feature articles, Just for Men or Just for Women, or Heartlight for Children."

HIGHWAY NEWS AND GOOD NEWS, 1525 River Rd., Marietta PA 17547. (717)426-9977. Fax (717)426-9980. E-mail: tfcio@transportforchrist.org. Website: www.transportforchrist.org. Transport for Christ. Jennifer Landis, ed. For truck drivers and their families; evangelistic, with articles for Christian growth. Monthly mag.; 16 pgs.; circ. 35,000. Subscription $30 or donation. 60% unsolicited freelance. Complete ms/cover letter; fax query OK; e-query preferred. **PAYS IN COPIES** for rights offered. Articles 600 or 1,500 wds. Seasonal 4 mos. ahead. Accepts simultaneous submissions & reprints (tell when/where appeared). Prefers requested ms by e-mail (attached or copied into message). Uses some sidebars. Prefers NIV. Guidelines/theme list; free copy for 9x12 SAE. (No ads)

> **Poetry:** Accepts 2/yr.; any type; 3-20 lines. Submit max. 5 poems.
>
> **Fillers:** Accepts 12/yr. Anecdotes, cartoons, facts, ideas, prayers, prose, short humor, tips; to 100 wds.
>
> **Tips:** "Looking for items affecting the trucking industry. Need pieces (any length) on health, marriage, and fatherhood. Most open to features and true stories about truckers. Send pictures."

HOLY HOUSE MINISTRIES NEWSLETTER, 9641 Tujunga Canyon Blvd., Tujunga CA 91042. (818)249-3477. Fax (818)249-3432. E-mail: HolyHouse9@aol.com. Website: http://holy houseministries.tripod.com. Rev. Kimberlie Zakarian, pres. Ministers to the unity of families by writing to individual members. Bimonthly newsletter; 6 pgs. Subscription free. 20% unsolicited freelance; 80% assigned. Query; e-query OK. Prefers accepted ms by e-mail. **PAYS 5 COPIES** for one-time rts. Articles 300 wds. (50/yr.). Responds in 2 wks. Seasonal 3 mos. ahead. Accepts reprints (tell when/where appeared). Uses some sidebars. Also accepts submissions from children/teens. No guidelines; copy for $1.25. Incomplete topical listings.

> **Tips:** "Most open to women's issues and prayer tips."

HOMECOMING. Contact by e-mail from their Website: www.gaithernet.com/home.php. Click on "Magazine." Bill & Gloria Gaither, pubs.; Joy MacKenzie, ed-at-large; Roberta Croteau, ed-in-chief. Open to submissions to several columns.

$HOMESCHOOLING TODAY, PO Box 244, Abingdon VA 24212. (276)628-7730. Fax (208)692-5505. E-mail: editor@homeschooltoday.com. Website: www.homeschooling today.com. Nehemiah Four LLC. Jim Bob Howard, ed-in-chief. Practical articles, encouragement, news, and lessons for homeschoolers. Bimonthly mag.; 72 pgs.; circ. 12,000. Subscription $21.99. 40% unsolicited freelance; 60% assigned. Complete ms by e-mail (attached file) or disk; fax/e-query OK. Pays .08/published wd. on publication for 1st rts.

Feature articles 2,000-2,200 wds.; articles 700-1,100 wds. (30/yr.); book reviews 500 wds. Responds in 5-9 wks. Seasonal 1 yr. ahead. Accepts simultaneous submissions; occasional reprints. Requires requested ms by e-mail (attached file). Kill fee 25%. Uses some sidebars, 200-400 wds. KJV, NKJV, ESV, or 1599 Geneva. Guidelines/theme list on Website; free copy. (Ads)

Columns/Departments: Buys 20-24/yr. Abacus (teaching math), 700-950 wds.; Living Literature (unit study with Living Books), 1,100-1,350 wds.; Thinking (biblical worldview), 850-1,000 wds.; Hearth and Homeschool (encouraging words for moms), 1,200-1,5,00 wds. Pays .08/wd. (See guidelines for additional departments.) Monthly e-newsletter: Homeschooling Helper (1 article, 1,000 wds. max.; .06/wd.). Semimonthly e-newsletter: Father-Led Home Education (1 article, 850 wds. max; display banner advertising in lieu of payment). Query.

$HOME TIMES FAMILY NEWSPAPER, PO Box 22547, West Palm Beach FL 33416-2547. Toll-free (888)439-3509. Fax (561)249-4932. E-mail: hometimes@aol.com. Website: www .hometimes.org. Neighbor News Inc. Dennis Lombard, ed./pub. Conservative, pro-Christian community newspaper. Monthly tabloid; 24-28 pgs.; circ. 8,000. Subscription $24. 15% unsolicited freelance; 25% assigned. Complete ms only/cover letter; no phone/fax/e-query. Pays $5-50 on acceptance for one-time rts. Articles 100-1,000 wds. (15/yr.); fiction 300-1,500 wds. (3/yr.). Responds in 2-3 wks. Seasonal 2 mos. ahead. Accepts simultaneous submissions & reprints (tell when/where appeared). Accepts requested ms by e-mail. No kill fee. Regularly uses sidebars. Also accepts submissions from teens. Any Bible version. Guidelines; 3 issues $3. (Ads)

Poetry: Buys 3-4/yr. Free verse, traditional; 2-16 lines; $5-10. Submit max. 3 poems.

Fillers: Uses 20-30/yr. Anecdotes, cartoons, facts, ideas, jokes, kid quotes, newsbreaks, prayers, prose, quizzes, quotes, short humor, tips, word puzzles; to 100 wds.; pays 3-6 copies, if requested.

Columns/Departments: Buys 30/yr. See guidelines for departments, to 600 wds.; $5-15.

Special Needs: Good short stories (creative nonfiction, or fiction). More faith, miracles, personal experiences, and people stories.

Tips: "Most open to personal stories or home/family pieces. Very open to new writers, but study guidelines and sample first; we are different. Published by Christians, but not religious. Looking for more positive articles and stories. Now seeking stringers in multiple viable markets to write local people features with photos. Journalism experience is preferred. E-mail query for more info with your name, brief background, and your address to hometimes2@aol.com."

($)HOPEKEEPERS MAGAZINE, PO Box 502928, San Diego CA 92150. Toll-free (888)751-7378. (858)486-4685. Toll-free fax (800)933-1078. E-mail: rest@restministries.org. Website: www .hopekeepersmagazine.com. Rest Ministries Inc. Lisa Copen, ed. For people who live with chronic illness or pain; offers encouragement, support, and hope dealing with everyday issues. Quarterly mag.; 64 pgs. Subscription $17.97. Estab. 2004. 40% unsolicited freelance; 60% assigned. Query; fax/e-query OK. **PAYS IN COPIES**; or to be determined for articles with extensive research; on publication. Articles 375-1,500 wds.; book reviews 300 wds. Responds in 6-8 wks. Seasonal 6 mos. ahead. Accepts simultaneous submissions & reprints. Prefers e-mail submissions (attached or copied into message). Regularly uses sidebars. Also accepts submissions from teens. Guidelines (also by e-mail/Website); free copy (call or see Website). (Ads)

Fillers: Accepts 25/yr. Facts, newsbreaks, tips; 40-90 wds.

Columns/Departments: Accepts 4/yr. Refreshments (devotional-style/journal writing), 350 wds.

Tips: "Topics should be 'attention grabbers' about specific emotions (Is it okay to be mad at God?), or experiences (parenting with a chronic illness), or helpful (5 things you should know about illness on the job). Most open to upbeat topical articles that give reader motivation to change/reflect; should be balanced with personal experience, others' experiences, facts, and scripture. Devotionals or 'my illness story' not accepted. Please read guidelines; 90% of submissions ignore guidelines. Content also accepted for online publications. Fiction is considered, but not used frequently."

$HORIZONS, 1300 N. Meacham Rd., Schaumburg IL 60173-4888. (847)843-1600. Fax (847)843-3757. E-mail: takehomepapers@garbc.org. Website: www.RegularBaptist Press.org. General Assn. of Regular Baptist Churches/Regular Baptist Press. Joan E. Alexander, ed. For adults associated with fundamental Baptist Churches. Weekly take-home paper that supports the adult curriculum by assisting adults in being grounded and growing Christians; 4 pgs. weekly. Open to freelance. Complete ms/cover letter including personal testimony; no phone/fax/e-query. Pays .05/wd. and up, on acceptance (usually) for 1st rts. Articles 800-1,000 wds. (if over 600 wds., use subheads); fiction 1,000-1,200 wds. Responds in 8-12 wks. Seasonal 1 yr. ahead. No simultaneous submissions; some reprints. Some sidebars. Prefers KJV. Guidelines/theme list on Website. Incomplete topical listings. (No ads)

Fillers: Buys 10-15/yr. Word puzzles.

Tips: "We are especially happy to meet competent writers who are using RBP materials in church, or are well acquainted with churches in which our materials are used. We recommend that prospective contributors purchase and study a full quarter of issues before submitting. We look for personal experience stories (both first person and as-told-to), articles with a story element to them, and well-written fiction that helps readers know more of God's character and ways. Check Website quarterly for updates concerning needs, themes, etc.; we're planning one year in advance. Also buy a copy of *Blueprint for Spiritual Maturity* on Website. It articulates our educational philosophy and identifies a broad list of areas where we want to help people grow spiritually. We look for articles that address those areas."

$IDEALS MAGAZINE, 2636 Elm Hill Pike, Ste. 120, Nashville TN 37214. (615)333-0478, ext. 433. Website: www.idealsbooks.com. Ideals Publications, a Guideposts Co. Melinda Rathjen, ed. Seasonal, inspirational, nostalgic magazine for mature men and women of traditional values. Soft-cover book/4X/yr.; 64 pgs. 40% unsolicited freelance. Complete ms/cover letter by mail only; no phone/fax/e-query. Pays .10/wd. on publication for one-time rts. Articles 600-800 wds. (20/yr.). Responds in 8-12 wks. Seasonal 8-10 mos. ahead. Accepts simultaneous submissions & reprints (tell when/where appeared). No disk. Does not use sidebars. Prefers KJV. Guidelines; copy $4.

Poetry: Buys 200+/yr. Free verse, light verse, traditional; 12-50 lines; $10. Submit max. 15 poems.

Tips: "Most open to holiday/seasonal poetry or essays appropriate for current features or holidays. Each issue has a particular theme: Easter, Mother's Day, Thanksgiving, and Christmas. Check current issue for themes."

$IMAGE, 3307 Third Ave. W., Seattle WA 98119. (206)281-2988. Fax (206)281-2335. E-mail: image@imagejournal.org. Website: www.imagejournal.org. Gregory Wolfe, pub./ed.; Mary Kenagy, mng. ed. Publishes the best literary fiction, poetry, nonfiction, and visual arts that engages the Judeo-Christian tradition. Quarterly jour.; 128 pgs.; circ. 5,200. Subscription $39.95. 50% unsolicited freelance; 50% assigned. Queries preferred; phone/fax/e-query OK. Pays $10/pg. ($200 max.) on acceptance for 1st rts. Articles/essays 4,000-6,000 wds. (10/yr.); fiction 4,000-6,000 wds. (8/yr.); book reviews 2,000 wds. Responds in 1-2 mos. No seasonal. Accepts simultaneous submissions; no reprints. No kill fees. Does not use sidebars. Any Bible version. Guidelines (also on Website); copy $16 (postpaid). (Ads)

Poetry: Buys 24/yr. Good poetry. Pays $2/line (up to $150). Submit max. 5 poems.

Tips: "Read the journal to understand what we publish. We're always thrilled to see high quality literary work in the unsolicited freelance pile, but we really can't typify what we're looking for other than good writing that's honest about faith and the life of faith. No genre fiction."

$IMAGINE: Arts Ministry Magazine for IMAGO DEI, 730 Armstrong Ave., Kansas City KS 66101-2702. (913)549-0043. Fax (913)385-7775. E-mail: lori@churcharts.org. Website: www.churcharts.org. IMAGO DEI: Friends of Christianity and the Arts. Terry Hoyland, sr. ed. For Christians interested in a broad view of the arts. Annual mag.; 100 pgs. 100% unsolicited freelance. Complete ms/cover letter; no phone/fax/e-query. No full mss by e-mail. Pays $15-25 on publication for one-time rts. Articles/fiction/reviews 1,000-2,500 wds. Responds in 6 wks. Accepts simultaneous submissions; no reprints. Prefers disk. No kill fee. Does not use sidebars. Any Bible version. Guidelines (also on Website); copy $9.95/9x12 SAE/$2 postage. (Ads)

> **Poetry:** Marie Asner, poetry ed. Buys 20-25/yr. Avant-garde, free verse, light verse, traditional; to 40 lines. Pays $15-25. Submit max. 3 poems.
>
> **Special Needs:** Arts ministry; drama ministry; visual arts; dance ministry.
>
> **Tips:** "Entire magazine is freelance written; open to any art form."

($)IMPACT MAGAZINE, 301 Geylang Rd., #03-04 Geylang Centre, Singapore 389344. Phone 65 6748 1244. Fax 65 748 3744. E-mail: editor@impact.com.sg. Website: www.impact.com.sg. Impact Christian Comm. Ltd. Andrew Goh, ed.; Loy Chin Fen, copy ed. To help young working adults apply Christian principles to contemporary issues. Bimonthly & online mag.; 56 pgs.; circ. 6,000. Subscription $20. 10% unsolicited freelance. Query or complete ms/cover letter; phone/fax/e-query OK. Accepts full ms by e-mail. Ranges from **NO PAYMENT** up to $40/pg., for all rts. Articles 1,200-1,500 wds. (12/yr.) & fiction (6/yr.); 1,000-2,000 wds. Seasonal 2 mos. ahead. Accepts reprints. Prefers e-mail submission (attached file). Uses some sidebars. Prefers NIV. Guidelines (also by e-mail); copy for $4/$3 postage (surface mail). (Ads)

> **Poetry:** Accepts 2-3 poems/yr. Free verse, 20-40 lines. Submit max. 3 poems.
>
> **Fillers:** Accepts 6/yr. Anecdotes, cartoons, jokes, quizzes, short humor, and word puzzles.
>
> **Columns/Departments:** Closing Thoughts (current social issues), 600-800 wds.; Testimony (personal experience), 1,500-2,000 wds.; Parenting (Asian context), 1,000-1,500 wds.; Faith Seeks Understanding (answers to tough questions of faith/Scripture), 80-1,000 wds.
>
> **Tips:** "We're most open to fillers and testimonies."

$INDIAN LIFE, PO Box 3765, Redwood Post Office, Winnipeg MB R2W 3R6, Canada. U.S. address: PO Box 32, Pembina ND 58271. (204)661-9333. Fax (204)661-3982. E-mail: ilm@indianlife.org. Website: www.indianlife.org. Indian Life Ministries/nondenominational. Jim Uttley, ed. An evangelistic publication for English-speaking aboriginal people in North America. Bimonthly tabloid newspaper; 16 pgs.; circ. 16,000. Subscription $15. 5% unsolicited freelance; 5% assigned. Query (query or complete ms for fiction); phone/fax/e-query OK. Pays .15/wd (to $200) on publication for 1st rts. Articles 150-2,500 wds. (20/yr.); fiction 500-2,000 wds. (8/yr.); reviews, 250 wds. ($40). Responds in 6 wks. Seasonal 4 mos. ahead. Accepts simultaneous submissions & reprints (tell when/where appeared). Accepts requested ms by e-mail (copied into message preferred). Some kill fees 50%. Uses some sidebars. Accepts submissions from children/teens. Prefers New Life Version, NIV. Guidelines (also by e-mail/Website); copy for 9x12 SAE/$2 postage (check or money order). (Ads)

> **Poetry:** Buys 4 poems/yr.; free verse, light verse, traditional, 10-100 wds.; pays $40. Submit max. 5 poems.
>
> **Fillers:** Kid quotes, quotes, short humor, 50-200 wds.; $10-25.
>
> **Special Needs:** Celebrity pieces must be aboriginal only. Looking for legends.

Tips: "Most open to testimonies from Native Americans/Canadians—either first person or third person—news features, or historical fiction with strong and accurate portrayal of Native American life from the Indian perspective. A writer should have understanding of some Native American history and culture. We suggest reading some Native American authors. Native authors preferred, but some others are published. Aim at a 10th-grade reading level; short paragraphs; avoid multisyllable words and long sentences."

INFUZE MAGAZINE: Art, Entertainment and Faith, 607 Ladford Ln., High Point NC 27265. (336)687-0157. E-mail through Website: www.infuzemag.com. Mr. Robin Parrish, ed./pub. Online mag. Open to unsolicited freelance. **NO PAYMENT**; nonprofit organization. Fiction 2,000 wds. & up. Guidelines on Website.

> **Poetry:** Accepts poetry. "We prefer poetry about people and what they feel, think, or experience." No length requirements.
>
> **Special Needs:** Original artwork short films and comic books. See guidelines.
>
> **Tips:** "No preachy fiction—a thought-provoking moral to the story is enough for us. This publication is unique. Be sure to download guidelines before submitting."

$+IN HIS PRESENCE, PO Box 14451, Knoxville TN 37914. (865)335-0072. Fax (865)524-5277. E-mail: ihp@samaritanpress.com. Website: www.samaritanpress.com. Samaritan Press. R. Michael Henegar, pres. Offers on-going serial-form stories and new articles and interviews to interest Christian communities. Monthly tabloid; 36+ pgs; circ. 25,000. Subscription $25. 80% unsolicited freelance; 20% assigned. Query; e-query OK. Pay negotiable on publication. Articles 600-1,200 wds.; fiction 2,000+ wds. Responds in 4-6 wks. Seasonal 3 mos. ahead. Accepts simultaneous submissions & reprints (tell when/where appeared). Wants accepted mss by e-mail. Sometimes pays kill fee. Also accepts submissions from children/teens. Prefers NKJV. Guidelines (also by e-mail/Website); copy for 9x12 SAE/$2 postage. (Ads)

> **Poetry:** Buys 10-15/yr. Light verse, traditional; 12-36 lines. Pay negotiable . Submit max. 2 poems.
>
> **Fillers:** Buys 12-15/yr. Anecdotes, cartoons, jokes, short humor; 60-600 wds. Pay negotiable.
>
> **Tips:** "All sections and departments are open to new writers and freelancers. Just let us see your work and have confidence in yourself and your ability."

$INTERCHANGE, 412 Sycamore St., Cincinnati OH 45202-4179. (513)421-0311. Fax (513) 421-0315. E-mail: richelle_thompson@episcopal-dso.org, or through Website: www .episcopal-dso.org. Episcopal Diocese of Southern Ohio. Richelle Thompson, dir. of communications. Regional paper for the Episcopal and Anglican Church in southern Ohio. Monthly (11X) newspaper; 16 pgs.; circ. 12,000. Free. 20% unsolicited freelance. Query or complete ms/cover letter. Pays $50-150 on acceptance for all rts. Articles 500-2,000 wds. (8-10/yr.). Responds in 4 wks. Accepts simultaneous submissions. Prefers requested ms on disk/CD. Regularly uses sidebars. Also accepts submissions from children/teens. Copy for 9x12 SASE.

> **Fillers:** Cartoons, facts, jokes.
>
> **Tips:** "Most open to features, especially with a local angle."

$THE INTERIM, 104 Bond St., Third Fl., Toronto ON M5B 1X9, Canada. (416)204-1687. Fax (416)204-1027. E-mail: interim@lifesite.net, or lsn@lifesitenews.com. Website: www.life site.net. The Interim Publishing Co. Paul Tuns, ed. Abortion, euthanasia, pornography, feminism, and religion from a pro-life perspective; Catholic and evangelical Protestant audience. Monthly & online newspaper; 24 pgs.; circ. 20,000. Subscription $35 Cdn. or U.S. 60% unsolicited freelance. Query; phone/e-query OK. Pays $50-150 Cdn., on publication. Articles 400-750 wds.; book, music, video reviews, 500 wds. ($50-75 Cdn.). Responds in 2 wks. Seasonal 2 mos. ahead. Accepts simultaneous submissions & reprints (tell when/where appeared). Prefers e-mail submission (copied into message). Kill fee. Uses some sidebars. Prefers RSV & others. No guidelines; catalog. (Ads)

Fillers: Cartoons.

Tips: "We are most open to news on life, family, and moral issues; informative commentary."

$IN TOUCH, 3836 DeKalb Technology Pkwy., Atlanta GA 30340. (770)451-1001. E-mail: writers@ intouch.org. Website: www.intouch.org. In Touch Ministries. Tonya Stoneman, ed. Publishing arm of Dr. Charles Stanley's international ministry. Monthly mag.; 48 pgs.; circ. 1 million. Subscription free. 25% unsolicited freelance; 25% assigned. Query, e-query OK. No full mss by e-mail. Pays varying rates on acceptance for 1st, electronic, nonexclusive rts. Articles 800-2,000 wds. (60/yr.). Responds in 6-8 wks. Seasonal 6 mos. ahead. No simultaneous submissions or reprints. Prefers e-mail submissions (attached or copied into message). Kill fee 50%. Uses some sidebars. Prefers NASB. Guidelines by e-mail/Website; copy for 6x9 SAE. (No ads)

Columns/Departments: Mighty in Spirit (exegetical), 1,200 wds.; Family Room (family topics), 800-1,200 wds.; By Faith (profiles), 800-1,200 wds.; Solving Problems (life issues), 800-1,200 wds. Payment varies.

**2007 EPA Award of Merit—Devotional.

+IPHC EXPERIENCE, PO Box 12609, Oklahoma City OK 73157. (405)787-7110. Fax (405) 789-3957. E-mail: sspencer@iphc.org. Website: www.iphcexperience.com. Intl. Pentecostal Holiness Church. Shirley G. Spencer, ed. To inform and inspire members of the denomination. Monthly mag.; circ. 20,000. Subscription $11.95. Open to queries only. Incomplete topical listings. (No ads)

ISLAND CATHOLIC NEWS, PO Box 5424 LCD9, Victoria BC V8R 6S4, Canada. (250)727-9429. Fax (250)727-3647. E-mail: lbeinhau@telus.net (editorial); icn@islandnet.com (administration). Website: www.islandnet.com/~icn. Island Catholic News Society. Patrick Jamieson, mng. ed. Dissenting, but concerned Catholics critical of the institution of the Catholic Church. Monthly tabloid; 12-16 pgs.; circ. 2,000. Subscription $35 Cdn./U.S. 90% unsolicited freelance; 10% assigned. Query; phone/fax/e-query OK. Accepts full mss by e-mail. **PAYS IN COPIES OR AD SPACE.** on publication acceptance for 1st, one-time or reprint rts. Articles 250/350/500 wds. (2-4/yr.); fiction 1,500 wds. (1-2/yr.); reviews 250-750 wds. Responds in 4 wks. Seasonal 2 mos. ahead. Accepts simultaneous submissions & reprints (tell when/where appeared). Accepts e-mail submissions. Regularly uses sidebars. Prefers Jerusalem Bible. Also accepts submissions from children/teens. Guidelines; copy for #10 SAE/3 stamps. (Ads)

Poetry: Accepts 10-20/yr. Avant-garde, free verse, haiku; 5-20 lines. Submit max. 4 poems.

Fillers: Prayers, prose, quotes.

Tips: "Call to chat."

+THE JERUSALEM CONNECTION, PO Box 20295, Washington DC 20041. (703)707-0014. Fax (703)707-9514. E-mail: jmh@tjci.org. Website: www.tjci.org. The Jerusalem Connection Intl. James M. Hutchens, ed. To inform, educate, and activate support for Israel and Jewish people; advocates for Christian Zionism. Bimonthly mag.; circ. 3,500. Subscription $30. Open to unsolicited freelance. Query. Articles. Incomplete topical listings. (Ads)

JOURNAL OF CHURCH AND STATE, Baylor University, One Bear Pl., #97308, Waco TX 76798-7308. (254)710-1510. Fax (254)710-1571. E-mail: Pat_Cornett@Baylor.edu. Website: www.baylor.edu/~church_state. J. M. Dawson Institute of Church-State Studies/Baylor University. Christopher Marsh, ed. Provides a forum for the critical examination of the interaction of religion and government worldwide. Quarterly jour.; 225 pgs.; circ. 1,700. Subscription $25 (indiv.); $39 (institution). 75% unsolicited freelance; 25% assigned. Complete ms (3 copies)/cover letter (also by e-mail); phone/fax query OK; no e-query. **NO PAYMENT** for all rights. Articles 25-30 pgs./footnotes (24/yr.). Responds in 9-18 wks. Prefers requested ms on disk, e-mail submission OK. Does not use sidebars. Prefers KJV. Guidelines (also by e-mail/Website); copy $8/$2.93 postage (mark "Media Mail"). (Ads)

Special Needs: Church-state issues, philosophy, religion.

Tips: "Open to feature articles only. Send three copies of essay and cover letter. Follow writers' guidelines."

KEYS TO LIVING, 105 Steffens Rd., Danville PA 17821. (570)437-2891. E-mail: owcam@verizon.net. Website: www.keystoliving.homestead.com. Connie Mertz, ed./pub. Educates, encourages, and challenges readers through devotional and inspirational writings; also nature articles, focusing primarily on wildlife in eastern U.S. Quarterly newsletter; 12 pgs. Subscription $10. 20% unsolicited freelance (needs freelance). Complete ms/cover letter; prefers e-mail submissions; no phone query. **PAYS 2 COPIES** for one-time or reprint rts. Articles 350-500 wds. Responds in 4 wks. Accepts reprints. No disk; e-mail submission OK (copied into message). Prefers NIV. Guidelines/theme list on Website; copy for 7x10 SAE/2 stamps. (No ads)

Poetry: Accepts if geared to family, nature, personal living, or current theme. Traditional with an obvious message.

Special Needs: More freelance submissions on themes only.

Tips: "We are a Christ-centered family publication. Seldom is freelance material used unless it pertains to a current theme. No holiday material accepted. Stay within word count." Celebrating 15 years of ministry.

$KINDRED SPIRIT, 3909 Swiss Ave., Dallas TX 75204. (214)841-3556. Fax (972)222-1544. E-mail: sglahn@dts.edu. Website: www.dts.edu/ks. Dallas Theological Seminary. Sandra Glahn, ed-in-chief. Publication of Dallas Theological Seminary. Quarterly mag.; 16-20 pgs.; circ. 30,000. Subscription free. 75% unsolicited freelance. Query/clips; fax/e-query OK. Pays $350 flat fee on publication for 1st & electronic rts. Articles 1,100 wds.; biblical fiction. Responds in 6 wks. Seasonal 8 mos. ahead. No simultaneous submissions; accepts reprints. Requires accepted mss by e-mail (attached or copied into message). Regularly uses sidebars. Prefers NIV. Guidelines on Website; copy. (No ads)

Special Needs: Profiles/interviews of DTS grads and faculty are open to anyone.

Tips: "Any news or profiles or expositions of Scripture with a link to DTS will receive top consideration; all topics other than interviews need to come from DTS graduates."

KOINONIA (formerly Glad Tidings), 102 Westwood Ln., Springdale AR 72762. (479)756-5074. E-mail: koinonia@mail.com. Website: www.holycatholicanglican.org. Holy Catholic Church—Anglican Rite. Holly Michael, ed. Seeks a variety of articles pertaining to the orthodox Christian faith. Quarterly online newsletter; 12-16 pgs. Subscription $10. Complete ms/cover letter; e-query OK. **PAYS IN COPIES** for one-time rts. Articles/short stories to 2,000 wds. Guidelines by e-mail; copy online. (Ads)

Tips: "All sections open."

$LARK NEWS.COM, E-mail: editor@larknews.com. Website: www.larknews.com. Flatiron Community Church. Joel Kilpatrick, pub.; Karen Hopkins, story ed. To publish cutting edge news on topics of interest to Christians. Online newsletter; circ. 45,000. Free online. Open to unsolicited freelance ideas. Submission form on Website. Pays $35 for ideas; no finished articles. Responds in 90 days, if interested. Guidelines on Website. Incomplete topical listings.

$THE LAYMAN, 136 Tremont Park Dr. N.E., PO Box 2210, Lenoir NC 28645. (828)758-8716. Fax (828)758-0920. E-mail: laymanletters@layman.org. Website: www.layman.org. Presbyterian Lay Committee. Charles F. Burge, exec. dir.; Parker T. Williamson, ed. emeritus; Debby Hill, mngr. of publications. For evangelical Christians interested in the Presbyterian and reformed denominations. Bimonthly & online newspaper; 24 pgs.; circ. 100,000. No subscriptions. 10% unsolicited freelance. Query. Pays negotiable rates on publication for 1st rts. Articles 800-1,200 wds. (12/yr.). Responds in 2 wks. Seasonal 2 mos. ahead. Prefers requested ms on disk. Regularly uses sidebars. Copy for 9x12 SAE/3 stamps. (No ads)

LEAVES, PO Box 87, Dearborn MI 48121-0087. (313)561-2330. Fax (313)561-9486. E-mail: leaves-mag@juno.com. Website: www.rc.net/detroit/mariannhill/leaves.htm. Catholic/ Mariannhill Fathers of Michigan. Jacquelyn M. Lindsey, ed. For all Catholics; promotes devotion to God and His saints and publishes readers' spiritual experiences, petitions, and thanksgivings. Bimonthly mag.; 24 pgs.; circ. 50,000. Subscription free. 50% unsolicited freelance. Complete ms/cover letter; phone/fax/e-query OK. **NO PAYMENT** for 1st or reprint rts. Not copyrighted. Articles 500 wds. (6-12/yr.). Responds in 4 wks. Seasonal 4 mos. ahead. Accepts reprints. Accepts e-mail submissions (copied into message). Does not use sidebars. Prefers NAB, RSV (Catholic edition). No guidelines or copy. (No ads)

Poetry: Accepts 6-12/yr. Traditional; 8-20 lines. Submit max. 4 poems.

Special Needs: Testimonies of conversion or reversion to Catholicism.

Tips: "Besides being interestingly and attractively written, an article should be confidently and reverently grounded in traditional Catholic doctrine and spirituality. The purpose of our magazine is to edify our readers."

$LEBEN, 2150 River Plaza Dr., Ste. 150, Sacramento CA 95833. (916)473-8866, ext. 4. E-mail: editor@Leben.us. Website: www.Leben.us. City Seminary Press. Wayne Johnson, ed. Focuses on Protestant Christian history and biography. Quarterly & online mag.; 24 pgs.; circ. 5,000. Subscription $9.95. 20% unsolicited freelance; 80% assigned. Complete ms; e-query OK. Accepts full mss by e-mail. Pays $175 or .05/wd. (copies & subscription) on acceptance for 1st & electronic rts. Articles 500-3,000 wds. (4/yr.). Responds in 2 wks. Accepts simultaneous submissions & reprints (tell when/where appeared). Prefers e-mail submissions (attached file). Uses some sidebars. Also accepts submissions from teens. Prefers KJV. Guidelines on Website; copy for 9x12 SASE/$2 postage. (Ads)

Fillers: Buys 4-6/yr. Short humor. Pays $5-10.

Special Needs: Reprints from old publications; historical, humor, etc.

Tips: "We feature stories that are biographical, historically accurate, and interesting— about Protestant martyrs, patriots, missionaries, etc., with a 'Reformed' slant."

$LIBERTY, Dept. of Public Affairs and Religious Liberty, 12501 Old Columbia Pike, Silver Springs MD 20904-1608. (301)680-6690. Fax (301)680-6695. E-mail: steeli@nad.adventist.org. Website: www.libertymagazine.org. Seventh-day Adventist. Lincoln Steed, ed. (lincoln .steed@nad.adventist.org). Deals with religious liberty issues for government officials, civic leaders, and laymen. Bimonthly mag.; 32 pgs.; circ. 200,000. Subscription $6.95. 95% unsolicited freelance. Query/clips; phone/fax/e-query OK. Pays $250 & up on acceptance for 1st rts. Articles & essays 1,000-2,500 wds. Responds in 5-13 wks. Requires requested ms on disk or by e-mail. Guidelines; copy.

$LIFEGLOW, Box 6097, Lincoln NE 68506-0097. (402)448-0981. Fax (402)488-7582. E-mail: info@christianrecord.org. Website: www.christianrecord.org. Christian Record Services Inc. Gaylena Gibson, ed. For sight-impaired adults over 25; interdenominational Christian audience; inspirational/devotional articles. Bimonthly mag.; 65 pgs. (lg. print); circ. 34,000. Free to sight-impaired. 95% unsolicited freelance. Complete ms; no phone/e-query. Pays .04-.05/wd. on acceptance for one-time rts. Articles & true stories 750-1,400 wds. Responds in 52 wks. Seasonal anytime. Accepts simultaneous submissions & reprints. Accepts requested ms on disk. Does not use sidebars. Guidelines; copy for 7x10 SAE/5 stamps. (No ads)

LIFESITE NEWS.COM, Canadian address: 104 Bond St. E., Third Fl., Toronto ON M5B 1X9, Canada. U.S. address: LPO Box 1008, Niagara Falls NY 14304-1008. Toll-free (866)787-9947. E-mail: editor@lifesitenews.com, or lsn@lifesitenews.com. Website: www.lifesite news.com. An originally written online daily news service covering life, faith, family, and freedom. John-Henry Westen, ed. 20 million page views/yr. Free subscription at www.life site.net/ldn/subscribe. Incomplete topical listings.

Tips: "Highly regarded as a leader in the field of pro-life and pro-family news."

LIFETIMES CATHOLIC eZINE. (810)743-2051. E-mail: bjubar@parishwebmaster.com (see guidelines for e-mail address for each department). Website: www.ParishWebmaster.com. Catholic. Brandon Jubar, ed. Designed to spread the Good News and minister to people online. Weekly online publication. Open to submissions. Query first. **NO PAYMENT.** Articles 300-600 wds. (300/yr.). Also accepts submissions from teens. Guidelines on Website.

   Columns: Weekly Reflection; Catholic Catechism; Faith & Spirituality; Family; Self-Improvement; Teen Issues; Teen 2 Teen.

$LIGHT & LIFE, Box 535002, Indianapolis IN 46253-5002. (317)244-3660. Fax (317)244-1247. E-mail: LLMeditor@fmcna.org. Website: www.freemethodistchurch.org/Magazine. Free Methodist Church of North America. Doug Newton, ed.; Cynthia Schnereger, mng. ed.; submit to Margie Newton, ms manager. Interactive magazine for maturing Christians; contemporary-issues oriented, thought-provoking; emphasizes spiritual growth, discipline, holiness as a lifestyle. Bimonthly mag.; 32 pgs. (plus pull-outs); circ. 13,000. Subscription $16. 95% unsolicited freelance. Query first; e-query OK. Pays .15/wd. on acceptance for 1st rts. Articles 500-1,700 wds. (24/yr.). Responds in 8-12 wks. Seasonal 12 mos. ahead. No simultaneous submissions. Prefers e-mail submission (attached file) after acceptance. No kill fee. Uses some sidebars. Prefers NIV. Also accepts submissions from children/teens. Guidelines on Website; copy $4. (Ads)

   Tips: "Best to write a query letter. We are emphasizing contemporary issues articles, well researched. Ask the question, 'What topics are not receiving adequate coverage in the church and Christian periodicals?' Seeking unique angles on everyday topics."

LIGHT OF THE WORLD NEWSPAPER, 177-34 Troutville Rd., Jamaica NY 11434. (718)938-7966. Fax (718)504-3814. E-mail: Christislight@aol.com. Julius Ogunnaya, ed. Monthly newspaper; 28 pgs.; circ. 20,000. Open to unsolicited freelance. E-query. **NO PAYMENT.** Articles 2 pgs. max. Guidelines by e-mail. Incomplete topical listings.(Ads)

   Poetry: Accepts poetry.

   Fillers: Cartoons, jokes, quizzes, and word puzzles.

   Contest: Youth Annual Essay Competition.

$LIGUORIAN, One Liguori Dr., Liguori MO 63057-9999. Toll-free (800)464-2555. (636)464-2500. Toll-free fax (800)325-9526. (636)464-8449. E-mail: liguorianeditor@liguori.org. Website: www.liguorian.org. Catholic/Liguori Publications. Rick Potts, C.Ss.R., ed-in-chief; Cheryl Plass, mng. ed. To help Catholics of all ages better understand the gospel and church teachings and to show how these teachings apply to life and the problems confronting them as members of families, the church, and society. Monthly (10X) mag.; 40 pgs.; circ. 120,000. Subscription $20. 30-40% unsolicited freelance; 60% assigned. Query, query/clips, or complete ms; phone/fax/e-query OK. Pays .12-.15/wd. on acceptance for 1st rts. Articles 1,200-2,200 wds. (30-50/yr.); fiction 1,800-2,000 wds. (10/yr.); book reviews 250 wds. No simultaneous submissions or reprints. Responds in 8-12 wks. Seasonal 6-8 mos. ahead. Prefers requested ms by e-mail (attached file). Sometimes pays kill fee. Uses some sidebars. Prefers NRSV. Guidelines (also by e-mail/Website); copy for 9x12 SAE/3 stamps. (Ads)

   Fillers: Buys 10/yr. Cartoons, jokes.

   Tips: "Most open to 1,000 word meditations; 1,800 word fiction; or 1,500 word personal testimonies. Send complete manuscript for fiction. Polish your own manuscript."

   **This periodical was #13 on the 2008 Top 50 Christian Publishers list (#16 in 2007, #22 in 2006, #6 in 2005, #42 in 2004).

+LITERARY TNT.COM, 1320 E. 30th, Apt. A, Texarkana AR 71854. Phone/fax (870)216-2243. E-mail: Tonja@LiteraryTNT.com. Website: www.kairosprofessional.com. Kairos Professional. Tonja Taylor, ed. Prefers Spirit-filled, Charismatic writers. Weekly e-zine (daily when they get enough material); 5 Web pgs. Subscription free online. 40% unsolicited freelance;

20% assigned. Query/clips or complete ms/cover letter; e-query OK. **NO PAYMENT FOR NOW** for one-time or nonexclusive rts. Articles 800-2,000 wds.; reviews 100 wds. Responds in 2 wks. Seasonal 3 mos. ahead. Accepts simultaneous submissions & reprints (tell when/where appeared). Prefers e-mail submissions (copied into message). Regularly uses sidebars. Also accepts submissions from children/teens (with parental permission). Prefers AMP, NIV, NASB. Guidelines (also by e-mail/Website); copy online. (Ads)

Poetry: Accepts 24/yr. Any type; 4-24 lines. Submit max. 5 poems.

Fillers: Accepts 36/yr. Anecdotes, facts, games, ideas, jokes, kid quotes, party ideas, prayers, prose, quizzes, short humor, and word puzzles; 50-300 wds.

Columns/Departments: SciLights (God in nature/science), to 1,000 wds.; Living Light (humor), to 2,000 wds.; Daily Light (devotions/essays), to 2,500 wds.; TNTimes (prophecy, prayer, spiritual warfare), to 2,000 wds.; Better Business (brag column for Christian businesses). Query for columns.

Special Needs: Games for kids. Christian ethics in business.

Contest: Planning contests for Easter, July 4th, and Christmas (perhaps others).

Tips: "All sections open. Send a cover letter or e-mail to introduce yourself and tell why you want to write for LiteraryTNT.com."

$LIVE, 1445 N. Boonville Ave., Springfield MO 65802-1894. (417)862-2781. Fax (417)862-6059. E-mail: rl-live@gph.org. Website: www.gospelpubling.com. Assemblies of God/Gospel Publishing House. Richard Bennett, adult ed. Inspiration and encouragement for adults. Weekly take-home paper; 8 pgs.; circ. 46,000. Subscription $14.80. 100% unsolicited freelance. Complete ms/cover letter; no phone/fax query; e-query OK. Pays .10/wd. (.07/wd. for reprints) on acceptance for one-time, or reprint rts. Articles 400-1,100 wds. (80-90/yr.); fiction 400-1,100 wds. (20/yr.). Responds in 4-6 wks. Seasonal 18 mos. ahead. Accepts simultaneous submissions & reprints (tell when/where appeared). Accepts e-mail submissions (attached file). No kill fees. Few sidebars. Prefers NIV, KJV. Guidelines (also by e-mail); copy for #10 SAE/1 stamp. (No ads)

Poetry: Buys 12-18/yr. Free verse, light verse, traditional; 8-25 lines; $60 ($35 for reprints) when scheduled. Submit max. 3 poems.

Tips: "We are often in need of good shorter stories (400-600 wds.), especially true stories or based on true stories. Often need holiday stories that are not 'how-to' stories, particularly for patriotic or nonreligious holidays. All areas open to freelance—human interest, inspirational, and difficulties overcome with God's help. Fiction must be especially good with biblical application. Follow our guidelines. Most open to well-written personal experience with biblical application. Send no more than two articles in the same envelope and send an SASE."

**This periodical was #5 on the 2008 Top 50 Christian Publishers list (#1 in 2007, #8 in 2006, #19 in 2005, #6 in 2004).

$LIVING, 1251 Virginia Ave., Harrisonburg VA 22802. Toll-free (888)833-3333. (540)433-5351. Fax (540)434-0247. E-mail: Tgether@aol.com. Website: www.churchoutreach.com. Shalom Foundation Inc. Melodie M. Davis, ed. A positive, practical, and uplifting publication for the whole family; mass distribution. Quarterly tabloid; 32-36 pgs.; circ. 50,000. Subscription free. 95% unsolicited freelance. Query or complete ms/cover letter; e-query OK. Pays $50 after publication for one-time rts. Articles 1,000-1,200 wds. (40-50/yr.). Responds in 13-18 wks. Seasonal 4 mos. ahead. Accepts simultaneous submissions & reprints (tell when/where appeared). Accepts requested ms by e-mail (copied into message; include e-mail address in message). Uses some sidebars. Prefers NIV. Guidelines (also by e-mail); copy for 9x12 SAE/4 stamps. (Ads)

Fillers: Buys 4-8/yr. Anecdotes, short humor; 100-200 wds.; $20-25.

Tips: "We are directed toward the general public, many of whom have no Christian interests, and we're trying to publish high-quality writing on family issues/concerns from a Christian perspective. That means religious language must be low key. Too much of what we receive is directed toward a Christian reader. We get far more than we can use, so something really has to stand out. Please carefully consider before sending. Need more articles of interest to men. Our articles need to have a family slant or fit the descriptor 'encouragement for families.'" When submitting by e-mail, put title of magazine and title of your piece in subject line. Also include your e-mail address in body of message.

$LIVING LIGHT NEWS, #200, 5306—89th St., Edmonton AB T6E 5P9, Canada. (780)468-6397. Fax (780)468-6872. E-mail: shine@livinglightnews.org. Website: www.livinglight news.org. Living Light Ministries. Jeff Caporale, ed. To motivate and encourage Christians; witnessing tool to the lost. Bimonthly tabloid; 36 pgs.; circ. 75,000. Subscription $24.95 U.S. 40% unsolicited freelance; 60% assigned. Query; e-query OK. Pays $20-125 (.05-.10/wd. Cdn. or .08/wd. U.S.) on publication for all, 1st, one-time, simultaneous, or reprint rts. Articles 350-700 wds. (75/yr.). Responds in 4 wks. Seasonal 3-4 mos. ahead. Accepts simultaneous submissions & reprints (tell when/where appeared). Guidelines by e-mail/Website; copy for 9x12 SAE/$2.50 Cdn. postage or IRCs (no U.S. postage). (Ads)

   Columns/Departments: Buys 20/yr., 450-600 wds., $10-30 Cdn. Parenting; relationships. Query.

   Special Needs: Celebrity interviews/testimonials of well-known personalities. Fun or informative articles (250-700 wds.) for Christian education supplement.

   Tips: "Most open to a timely article about someone who is well known in North America, in sports or entertainment, and has a strong Christian walk."

   **This periodical was #34 on the 2007 Top 50 Christian Publishers list (#38 in 2006, #34 in 2005, #25 in 2004).

LIVING STONES NEWS, 2031 E. First St., Duluth MN 55812. Phone/fax (218)728-4945. E-mail: corinne@livingstonesnews.com, editor@livingstonesnews.com, or through Website: www .livingstonesnews.com. Corinne E. Scott, pub. To glorify God, to reach out to the unsaved, and to bring hope, encouragement, peace, and the unconditional love of Jesus Christ to our readers. Monthly newspaper; circ. 7,000. Subscription free. Open to freelance. Query preferred. Articles. (Ads) Not included in topical listings.

$THE LOOKOUT, 8805 Governor's Hill Dr., Ste. 400, Cincinnati OH 45249. (513)931-4050. Fax (513)931-0950. E-mail: lookout@standardpub.com. Website: www.lookoutmag.com. Standard Publishing. Shawn McMullen, ed. For adults who are interested in learning more about applying the gospel to their lives. Weekly & online mag.; 16 pgs.; circ. 62,000. Subscription $26.99, plus $5 postage. 30% unsolicited freelance; 70% assigned. Query for theme articles; complete ms for others; e-query OK. Pays .11-.17/wd. on acceptance. Articles 500-1,600 wds. (200/yr.). Responds in 10 wks. Seasonal 6 mos. ahead. Accepts simultaneous submissions; no reprints. No disks or e-mail submissions. Kill fee 50%. Regularly uses sidebars. Prefers NIV. Guidelines/theme list (also by e-mail/Website: www.lookoutmag.com/write/default.asp); copy for #10 SAE/$1.

   Columns/Departments: Buys 24/yr. Outlook (personal opinion); Salt & Light (innovative ways to reach out into the community); Faith Around the World; all 800 wds.; .11/wd. Query.

   Tips: "Most open to feature articles according to our theme list. Get a copy of our theme list and query about a theme-related article at least six months in advance. Request sample copies of our magazine to familiarize yourself with our publishing needs (also available online). Send samples of published material."

   **This periodical was #17 on the 2008 Top 50 Christian Publishers list (#10 in 2007, #30 in 2006, #4 in 2005, #2 in 2004).

+**LOUISIANA BAPTIST MESSAGE,** PO Box 311, Alexandria LA 71309. (318)442-7728. Fax (318)445-8328. E-mail: editor@baptistmessage.com. Website: www.baptistmessage.com. Louisiana Southern Baptists. Kelly Boggs, ed. To report the news of what God is doing through Southern Baptists in Louisiana. Weekly newspaper; circ. 30,000. Subscription $14. Open to unsolicited freelance. Complete ms. Articles & reviews. Incomplete topical listings. (Ads)

$**THE LUTHERAN DIGEST,** Box 4250, Hopkins MN 55343. (952)933-2820. Fax (952)933-5708. E-mail: tldi@lutherandigest.com. Website: www.lutherandigest.com. The Lutheran Digest Inc. David L. Tank, ed. Blend of general and light theological material used to win nonbelievers to the Lutheran faith. Quarterly literary mag.; 64 pgs.; circ. 70,000. Subscription $16. 100% unsolicited freelance. Query or complete ms/cover letter; phone/fax/e-query OK. Pays $35-100+ ($25-50 for reprints) on acceptance for one-time & reprint rts. Articles to 1,000 wds., or no more than 7,000 characters—3,000 preferred (25-30/yr.). Accepts full mss by e-mail. Responds in 4-9 wks. Seasonal 6-9 mos. ahead. Accepts simultaneous submissions & reprints (tell when/where appeared). Accepts e-mail submissions (attached). No kill fee. Uses some sidebars. Rarely accepts submissions from children/teens. Guidelines (also on Website); copy $3.50/6x9 SAE. (Ads)

Poetry: Accepts 40+/yr. Light verse, traditional; short/varies; no payment. Submit max. 3 poems/mo.

Fillers: Anecdotes, cartoons, facts, short humor, tips; length varies; no payment.

Tips: "We prefer real-life stories over theoretical essays. We need well-thought-out, well-written, professional articles. More nature pieces. Compose well-written, short pieces that would be of interest to middle-aged and senior Christians—and also acceptable to Lutheran church pastors. (The word 'hope' is frequently associated with our publication.) Most open to thought-out, well-written, professional submissions. Too much inappropriate and irrelevant material received. Research our needs and submit only that that applies—not just what you've got."

$**THE LUTHERAN JOURNAL,** 7010—6th St. N., PO Box 28158, Oakdale MN 55128. (651)702-0086. Fax (651)702-0074. E-mail: christianad2@msn.com. Vance Lichty, pub.; submit to Editorial Assistant. Family magazine for, by, and about Lutherans, and God at work in the Lutheran world. Semiannual mag.; 40-48 pgs.; circ. 200,000. Subscription $6. 60% unsolicited freelance; 40% assigned. Complete ms/cover letter; fax query OK. Pays .01-.04/wd. on publication for all or 1st rts. Articles 750-1,500 wds. (25-30/yr.); fiction 1,000-1,500 wds. Response time varies. Seasonal 4-5 mos. ahead. Accepts reprints. Uses some sidebars. Prefers NIV, NAS, KJV. Accepts requested ms on disk. Also accepts submissions from children/teens. Guidelines; copy for 9x12 SAE/2 stamps. (Ads)

Poetry: Buys 14-6/yr. Light verse, traditional; 50-150 wds.; $10-30. Submit max. 3 poems.

Fillers: Buys 5-10/yr. Anecdotes, facts, games, prayers, quizzes, quotes; 50-300 wds.; $5-30.

Columns/Departments: Buys 40/yr. Apron Strings (short recipes); About Books (reviews), 50-150 wds.; $5-25.

Tips: "Most open to Lutheran lifestyles or Lutherans in action."

+**THE LUTHERAN WITNESS,** 1333 S. Kirkwood Rd., St. Louis MO 63122-7295. (314)996-1202. Fax (314)996-1126. E-mail: david.strand@lcms.org. The Lutheran Church—Missouri Synod. David L. Strand, ed. Official periodical of the denomination, for lay members of its congregations; to encourage responsible Christian action in church and society. Monthly mag.; circ. 200,000. Subscription $18. Open to unsolicited freelance. Complete ms. Articles. Incomplete topical listings. (Ads)

$+**THE MAJELLAN,** PO Box 43, Brighton, VIC 3186, Australia. Phone (61)3 95922777. Fax (61)3 95931337. E-mail: editor@majellan.org.au. Website: www.majallen.org.au. Catholic/Redemptorist. Margie Ulbrick, assoc. ed. For Catholic families/couples; emphasis on parenting and youth. Quarterly mag.; 48 pgs; circ. 23,000. 30% unsolicited freelance; 60%

assigned. Complete ms; e-query OK. Accepts full mss by e-mail. Pays $50-80 on acceptance for all rts. Articles 600-1,500 wds. (10/yr.). Responds in 2 wks. Accepts reprints (tell when/where appeared). Prefers e-mail submissions (attached). No kill fee. No sidebars. Also accepts submissions from children/teens. Guidelines by e-mail; copy. (No ads)

Special Needs: Family life.

Tips: "We prefer articles that are in a simple, easy-to-read style."

$+THE MANNA, PO Box 130, Princess Anne MD 21853. Phone/fax (410)543-9652. E-mail: manna@mylifeline.net. Website: www.wolc.org. Maranatha Inc. Randy Walter, ed. A free monthly tabloid featuring evangelical articles, and distributed in the marketplace in Delaware, Maryland, and Virginia. Monthly & online tabloid; 32-40 pgs; circ. 42,000. Subscription free. 10-15% unsolicited freelance; 15% assigned. Query/clips; e-query OK. No full mss by e-mail. Pays $30-50 on publication for 1st, one-time, or reprint rts. Articles 1,000-1,200 wds. Responds in 1-2 wks. Seasonal 3-4 mos. ahead. No simultaneous submissions. Accepts reprints (tell when/where appeared). Accepted articles on disk or by e-mail (copied into message). Uses some sidebars. Also accepts submissions from children/teens. No guidelines; copy for 9x12 SAE/2 stamps. (Ads)

Fillers: Anecdotes, ideas, party ideas, short humor, and tips. No payment.

Columns/Departments: Accepts up to 12/yr. Finances (business or personal); Counseling (Q & A); Personal Integrity (scriptural); all 800 wds. No payment.

Special Needs: Themes: marital fidelity, conquering fear, hypocrites, heaven, showing compassion, and What is Your Hope? Most open to these theme pieces.

Tips: "E-mail your query."

$MARIAN HELPER, Marian Helpers Center, Eden Hill, Stockbridge MA 01263. (413)298-3691. Fax (413)298-3583. E-mail: came@marian.org. Website: www.marian.org. Catholic/ Marians of the Immaculate Conception. Dave Came, exec. ed.; Steve LaChance, review ed. Quarterly & online mag.; circ. 500,000. Rarely uses unsolicited; 25% assigned freelance. Query/clips or complete ms/cover letter. Pays $250 for 1,000-1,200 wds. (2-page feature), for 1st rts. Articles 500-900 wds. Responds in 6 wks. Seasonal 6 mos. ahead. Kill fee 30%. Guidelines/copy for #10 SAE. (No ads)

Tips: "Write about God's mercy touching people's everyday lives, or about devotion to the Blessed Virgin Mary in a practical, inspirational, or fresh way."

MARKETPLACE, 12900 Preston Rd., Ste. 1215, Dallas TX 75230-1328. Toll-free (800)775-7657. (972)385-7657. Fax (972)385-7307. E-mail: art.stricklin@marketplaceministries .com. Website: www.marketplaceministries.com. Marketplace Ministries. Art Stricklin, ed. Focus is on working in the corporate workplace. Triannual mag.; 12 pgs.; circ. 16,000. Subscription free. 10% assigned. Query or complete ms; e-query OK. **NO PAYMENT** for all rts. Articles. Prefers e-mail submission. No copy. Incomplete topical listings. (No ads)

Tips: "We are attempting to cut back on freelance and use only assigned stories."

$MATURE LIVING, One Lifeway Plaza, MSN 175, Nashville TN 37234-0175. (615)251-5677. E-mail: rene.holt@lifeway.com (to request guidelines only); submit to matureliving@ lifeway.com. Website: www.lifeway.com. LifeWay Christian Resources/Southern Baptist. Woody Parker, ed-in-chief; submit to Rene Holt, ed. Christian leisure reading for senior adults (50+) characterized by human interest and Christian warmth. Monthly mag.; 52 pgs.; circ. 318,000. Subscription $21.95. 90% unsolicited freelance; 10% assigned. Complete ms/cover letter; no phone/fax/e-query. Accepts full mss by e-mail. Pays $75-105 for feature articles on acceptance for all rts. Articles 600-1,200 wds. (85/yr.); senior adult fiction 600-1,200 wds. (12/yr.). Responds in 8-10 wks. Seasonal 8 mos. ahead. No simultaneous submissions or reprints. No kill fee. Uses some sidebars. Prefers KJV, HCSB. Guidelines (also by e-mail); copy for 9x12 SAE/4 stamps. (Ads)

Poetry: Buys 24/yr. Traditional; 8-16 lines; $25. Submit max. 3 poems.

Columns/Departments: Buys 300+/yr. Cracker Barrel, 4-line verse, $15; Grandparent's Brag Board, 50-100 wds., $15; Over the Garden Fence (gardening), 300-350 wds.; Communing with God (devotional), 125-200 wds.; Fun 'n Games (wordsearch/crossword puzzles), 300-350 wds.; Crafts; Recipes; $15-50. Complete ms. See guidelines for full list.

Tips: "Almost all areas open to freelancers, except medical and financial matters. Study the magazine for its style. Write for our readers' pleasure and inspiration. Fiction for senior adults needs to underscore a biblical truth."

**This periodical was #44 on the 2008 Top 50 Christian Publishers list (#13 in 2007, #10 in 2006, #47 in 2004).

$MATURE YEARS, Box 801, Nashville TN 37202. (615)749-6292. Fax (615)749-6512. E-mail: matureyears@umpublishing.org. United Methodist. Marvin W. Cropsey, ed. To help persons in and nearing retirement years understand and appropriate the resources of the Christian faith in dealing with specific problems and opportunities related to aging. Quarterly mag.; 112 pgs.; circ. 55,000. Subscription $21. 60% unsolicited freelance; 40% assigned. Complete ms/cover letter; fax/e-query OK. Pays .05/wd. on acceptance for one-time rts. Articles 900-2,000 wds. (60/yr.); fiction 1,200-2,000 wds. (4/yr.). Responds in 9 wks. Seasonal 14 mos. ahead. Accepts reprints. Prefers accepted ms by e-mail (copied into message). Regularly uses sidebars. Prefers NRSV, NIV. Guidelines (also by e-mail); copy $5. (No ads)

Poetry: Buys 24/yr. Free verse, haiku, light verse, traditional; 4-16 lines; .50-1.00/line. Submit max. 6 poems.

Fillers: Buys 20/yr. Anecdotes (to 300 wds.), cartoons, jokes, prayers, word puzzles (religious only); to 30 wds.; $5-25.

Columns/Departments: Buys 20/yr. Health Hints, 900-1,200 wds.; Modern Revelations (inspirational), 900-1,100 wds.; Fragments of Life (true-life inspirational), 250-600 wds.; Going Places (travel), 1,000-1,500 wds.; Money Matters, 1,200-1,800 wds.

Special Needs: Articles on crafts and pets. Fiction on older adult situations. All areas open except Bible studies.

**This periodical was #30 on the 2007 Top 50 Christian Publishers list (#35 in 2006, #31 in 2005, #35 in 2004).

$MEN.AG.ORG (formerly HonorBound), 1445 N. Boonville Ave., Springfield MO 65802. (417)862-2781. Fax (417)832-0574. E-mail: men@ag.org. Website: www.men.ag.org. Assemblies of God. Darian Amsler, field & commun. coord. Targeting men, ages 25-60; Christian/Pentecostal distinctive. Weekly E-zine. 10% unsolicited freelance; 90% assigned. Prefers e-query. Pays $30 for 1st rts. Articles 350-1,000 wds. Responds in 1 wk. Seasonal 5 mos. ahead. Accepts simultaneous submissions & reprints (tell when/where appeared). Prefers e-mail submissions (attached file). Prefers NIV. Guidelines by e-mail/Website; copy online. (Ads)

Tips: "In being familiar with Website, submit articles (by e-mail) relevant to the faith, life, and culture."

($)MENNONITE HISTORIAN, 600 Shaftesbury Blvd., Winnipeg MB R3P 0M4, Canada. (204) 888-6781. E-mail: aredekopp@mennonitechurch.ca. Website: www.mennonitechurch.ca/programs. Mennonite Church Canada/Canadian Conference of Mennonite Brethren Churches. Alf Redekopp, ed. Gathers and shares historical material related to Mennonites; focus on North America, but also beyond. Quarterly newsletter; 8 pgs.; circ. 2,600. Subscription $12. 40% unsolicited freelance; 20% assigned. Complete ms/cover letter; phone/e-query OK. **NO PAYMENT EXCEPT BY SPECIAL ARRANGEMENT** for 1st rts. Articles 250-1,000 wds. (6/yr.). Responds in 3 wks. Seasonal 3 mos. ahead. Accepts simultaneous submissions & reprints (tell when/where appeared). Prefers e-mail submission (attached file). Does not use sidebars. Guidelines (also by e-mail); copy $1/9x12 SAE. (Ads)

Tips: "Must be Mennonite related (i.e., related to the life and history of the denomination, its people, organizations, and activities). Most open to lead articles. Write us with your ideas. Also genealogical articles."

$MEN OF INTEGRITY, 465 Gundersen Dr., Carol Stream IL 60188. (630)260-6200. Fax (630) 260-0114. E-mail: mail@menofintegrity.net. Website: www.MenofIntegrity.net. Christianity Today Intl. Harry Genet, mng. ed. Uses narrative to apply biblical truth to specific gritty issues men face. Bimonthly pocket-size mag.; 64 pgs.; circ. 70,000. Subscription $19.95. 10% unsolicited freelance. Complete ms. Pays $50 on acceptance for one-time & electronic rts. Articles 225 wds. (15/yr.). Responds in 6 wks. Accepts simultaneous submissions & reprints (tell when/where appeared). Accepts requested ms on disk or e-mail (attached file or copied into message). Does not use sidebars. Prefers NLT. Guidelines/theme list (also by e-mail); copy $4/#10 SAE. (Ads)

**2006 EPA Award of Merit—Devotional

MEN OF THE CROSS, 920 Sweetgum Creek, Plano TX 75023. (972)517-8553. E-mail: info@ menofthecross.com. Website: www.menofthecross.com. Greg Paskal, content mngr. (greg@ gregpaskal.com). Encouraging men in their walk with the Lord; strong emphasis on discipleship and relationship. Online community. 50% unsolicited freelance. Query by e-mail. **NO PAYMENT.** Not copyrighted. Articles 500-1,500 wds. (10/yr.). Responds in 2-4 wks. Seasonal 3 mos. ahead. Accepts simultaneous submissions; no reprints. Prefers e-mail submissions (attached or copied into message). Uses some sidebars. Prefers NIV, NKJV, NASB. Also accepts submissions from teens. Guidelines by e-mail; copy online. (No ads)

Poetry: Accepts 1/yr. Avant-garde, free verse; 50-250 lines. Submit max. 1 poem.

Special Needs: Christian living in the workplace.

Tips: "Appropriate topic could be a real, first-hand account of how God worked in the author's life. We are looking for humble honesty in hopes it will minister to those in similar circumstances. View online forums for specific topics."

MENSAJERO ALA BLANCA, PO Box 2910, Cleveland TN 37320-2910. (423)559-5223. Fax (423)449-5231. Website: www.mensajeroalablanca.com (in Spanish). Church of God of Prophecy. Diana M. Garcia, ed. To provide up-to-date and relevant material in the Spanish language in order to equip, educate, and edify the saints in the kingdom. Bimonthly mag.; circ. 4,000. Subscription $10. Open to freelance. Query preferred. Articles & reviews. (No ads) Incomplete topical listings.

$MESSAGE, Review and Herald Pub. Assn., 55 W. Oak Ridge Dr., Hagerstown MD 21740. (301)393-4100. Fax (301)393-4103. E-mail: message@RHPA.org. Website: www.message magazine.org. Review & Herald/Seventh-day Adventist. Washington Johnson II, ed. (wjohn son@rhpa.org). Pat Harris, asst. ed. (pharris@rhpa.org). For African Americans and all people seeking practical Christian guidance on current events and a better lifestyle. Bimonthly mag.; 32 pgs.; circ. 125,000. Subscription $14.95. 10-20% freelance written. Query or complete ms/cover letter; fax/e-query OK. Pays $50-250 on acceptance for 1st rts. Articles 700-1,200 wds.; fiction for children (ages 5-8), 500 wds. Responds in 6-10 wks. Seasonal 6 mos. ahead. Prefers requested ms by e-mail. Regularly uses sidebars. Prefers KJV. Guidelines on Website; copy for 9x12 SAE/2 stamps. (Ads)

Columns/Departments: Buys for each issue. Healthspan (health issues), 700 wds.; MESSAGE Jr. (biblical stories or stories with clear-cut moral for ages 5-8), 500 wds.; $50-300.

Tips: "As with any publication, writers should have a working knowledge of *Message*. They should have some knowledge of our style and our readers."

MESSAGE OF THE OPEN BIBLE, 2020 Bell Ave., Des Moines IA 50315-1096. (515)288-6761. Fax (515)288-2510. E-mail: message@openbible.org. Website: www.openbible.org. Open Bible Standard Churches. Andrea Johnson, ed. To inspire, inform, and educate the Open

Bible family. Bimonthly mag.; 16 pgs.; circ. 3,000. Subscription $9.95. 3% unsolicited freelance; 3% assigned. Query or complete ms/cover letter; e-query OK. **PAYS 5 COPIES.** Not copyrighted. Articles 750 wds. (2/yr.). Responds in 4 wks. Seasonal 4 mos. ahead. Accepts simultaneous submissions & reprints (tell when/where appeared). Accepts requested ms on disk or by e-mail. Regularly uses sidebars. Prefers NIV. Guidelines/theme list (also by e-mail); copy for 9x12 SAE/2 stamps. (No ads)

   Fillers: Accepts 6/yr. Facts, quotes, short humor; 50 wds.

   Tips: "A writer can best break in by giving us material for an upcoming theme, or something inspiring, specifically as it would relate to an Open Bible lay person."

$THE MESSENGER, 440 Main St., Steinbach MB R5G 1Z5, Canada. (204)326-6401. Fax (204)326-1613. E-mail: emcmessenger@mts.net, or through Website: www.emconf.ca/Messenger. Evangelical Mennonite Conference. Terry M. Smith, ed. Serves Evangelical Mennonite Conference members and general readers. Mag. published 22X/yr.; 16-24 pgs. Subscription $12. Uses little freelance, but open. Query preferred; phone/fax/e-query OK. Accepts full mss by e-mail. Pays $30-100 on publication for 1st rts. only. Articles. Not included in topical listings.

$THE MESSENGER OF SAINT ANTHONY, Via Orto Botanico 11, 35123 Padova, Italy (U.S. address: Anthonian Assn., 101 Saint Anthony Dr., Mt. Saint Francis IN 47146). (812)923-6356 or 049 8229924. Fax (812)923-3200 or 049 8225651. E-mail: m.conte@santantonio.org (editor); messenger@santantonio.org (ed. sec.); or info@santantonio.org. Website: www.saintanthonyofpadua.net. Catholic/Provincia Padovana F.M.C. Fr. Mario Conte OFM, ed.; Corrado Roeper, ed. sec. For middle-aged and older Catholics in English-speaking world; articles that address current issues. Monthly & online mag.; 50 pgs.; circ. 45,000. Subscription $25 U.S. 10% unsolicited freelance; 90% assigned. Query (complete ms for fiction); phone/fax/e-query OK. Pays $40/pg. (600 wds./pg.) for one-time rts. Articles 600-2,400 wds. (40/yr.); fiction 900-1,200 wds. (11/yr.). Responds in 8-10 wks. Seasonal 3 mos. ahead. Prefers e-mail submission (attached file or copied into message). Regularly uses sidebars. Prefers NEB (Oxford Study Edition). Guidelines (also by e-mail); free copy. (No ads)

   Columns/Departments: Buys 50-60/yr. Documentary (issues), 600-2,000 wds.; Spirituality, 600-2,000 wds.; Church Life, 600-2,000 wds.; Saint Anthony (devotional), 600-1,400 wds.; Living Today (family life), 600-1,400 wds.; $55-200. Complete ms.

   Special Needs: Short story of a moral or religious nature; St. Anthony.

   Tips: "Most open to short stories; Saint Anthony, and devotional articles on parishes named after Saint Anthony, local feasts/shrines in Saint Anthony's honour. All writers should bring a uniquely Catholic perspective to their articles."

$MESSENGER OF THE SACRED HEART, 661 Greenwood Ave., Toronto ON M4J 4B3, Canada. (416)466-1195. Catholic/Apostleship of Prayer. Rev. F. J. Power, S.J., ed. Help for daily living on a spiritual level. Monthly mag.; 32 pgs.; circ. 11,000. Subscription $14. 20% freelance. Complete ms; no phone query. Pays .10/wd. on acceptance for 1st rts. Articles 700-1,500 wds. (30/yr.); fiction 700-1,500 wds. (12/yr.). Responds in 5 wks. Seasonal 5 mos. ahead. No disk. Does not use sidebars. Guidelines; no copy. (No ads)

   Tips: "Most open to inspirational stories and articles."

$MESSIAH MAGAZINE, PO Box 649, Marshfield MO 65706-0649. (417)468-2741. Fax (417)468-2745. E-mail: amber@ffoz.org, or through Website: www.ffoz.org. First Fruits of Zion. Boaz Michael, ed. Dedicated to the study, exploration, and celebration of our righteous and sinless Torah-observant King—Yeshua of Nazareth. Mag. published 5X/yr.; 34 pgs.; circ. 10,000. Subscription for donation. Open to freelance. Query; fax query OK. Pays on acceptance for all rts. Articles (15-20/yr.). Responds in 3 wks. Seasonal 6 mos. ahead. Accepts simultaneous submissions; no reprints. Requires e-mail submissions (attached file). Does not use sidebars. Prefers NASB. Copy for $4/9x12 SAE/5 stamps. Incomplete topical listings. (No ads)

Tips: "F.F.O.Z. is a nonprofit ministry devoted to strengthening the love and appreciation of the Body of the Messiah for the land, people, and scriptures of Israel. Since our focus is unique, please be very familiar with our magazine before submitting your query. Our Torah Testimony column is always open, as are some of the others. Looking for something on Hebrew roots."

+MESSIANIC PERSPECTIVES, 611 Broadway, San Antonio TX 78215. (210)226-0421, ext. 130. E-mail: tommym@cjfm.org. Website: www.cjfm.org. CJF Ministries. Tommy Manning, ed. To provide for our constituency ministry-related news along with Bible teaching from a messianic perspective. Monthly mag.; circ. 30,000. Subscription $10. Open to unsolicited freelance. Complete ms. Articles & reviews. Incomplete topical listings. (No ads)

THE MESSIANIC TIMES, PO Box 2190, Niagara Falls NY 14302. Toll-free (866)612-7770. (905)685-4072. Fax (905)685-7371. E-mail: mteditor@bellsouth.net, or through Website: www.messianictimes.com. Times of the Messiah Ministries. Paul Liberman, pub. To unify the Messianic Jewish community around the world, to serve as an evangelistic tool to the Jewish community, and to educate Christians about the Jewish roots of their faith. Bimonthly newspaper; circ. 35,000. Subscription $19.99. Accepts freelance. Query preferred. Articles & reviews. Not in topical listings. (Ads)

METHODIST HISTORY, PO Box 127, Madison NJ 07940. (973)408-3189. Fax (973)408-3909. E-mail: RWilliams@gcah.org. Website: www.gcah.org. United Methodist. Robert J. Williams, ed. History of the United Methodism and Methodist/Wesleyan churches. Quarterly jour.; 64 pgs.; circ. 800. Subscription $20. 100% unsolicited freelance. Query; phone/fax/e-query OK. **PAYS 3 COPIES** for all rts. Historical articles to 5,000 wds. (15/yr.); book reviews 500 wds. Responds in 8 wks. Requires requested ms on disk. Does not use sidebars. Guidelines (also on Website); no copy. (Ads)

Special Needs: United Methodist church history.

+MICHIANA CHRISTIAN NEWS, PO Box 502, Niles MI 49120. (574)298-2737. Fax (269)687-2797. E-mail: mcooper@mcnews.org. Website: www.mcnews.org. CCDS, LLC. Mary Cooper, ed. To build up the Kingdom of God in the Lower Michigan and Northern Indiana communities. Monthly newspaper; circ. 10,000. Subscription $25. Open to unsolicited freelance. Query. Articles & reviews. Incomplete topical listings. (Ads)

MIDNIGHT CALL MAGAZINE, PO Box 280008, Columbia SC 29228. Toll-free (800)845-2420. (803)755-0733. Fax (803)755-6002. E-mail: info@midnightcall.com. Website: www.midnightcall.com. Arno Froese, ed. The world's only international voice of prophecy regarding end-time events. Subscription $22.50.

$+MINDFLIGHTS, 9618 Misty Brook Cove, Cordova TN 38016. E-mail: editor@mindflights.com. Website: http://mindflights.com/index.html. Double-Edged Publishing, Inc. Submit to Editorial Staff. Publishes speculative (sci-fi/fantasy) short fiction and poetry with a Christian or Christian-friendly slant. Monthly online & quarterly print mag. Estab. 2008. 100% unsolicited freelance. Complete ms/cover letter submitted via online form (no e-mail submissions). Pays $5-25 or .005/wd. on acceptance for 1st, reprint, and electronic rts. Articles under 2,000 wds. (1/yr.); fiction under 5,000 wds. (80/yr.). Responds in 3-4 wks. Seasonal 3 mos. ahead. No simultaneous submissions; reprints rarely (tell when/where appeared). No kill fee. No sidebars. Also accepts submissions from teens. Guidelines on Website; copy of print edition. (Ads)

Poetry: Buys 60-80/yr. Any type. Pays $5-25. Submit max. 3 poems.

Special Needs: Book and music reviews must be sci-fi/fantasy related.

Contest: Planning a poetry contest. All contests announced on Website.

Tips: "We like work that is original, interesting, and successfully melds the speculative and the spiritual without being preachy." Updates are posted online 2-3 times a week.

$MINNESOTA CHRISTIAN CHRONICLE, 623 N. Lilac Dr., Ste. A, Golden Valley MN 55422. (763)746-2468, ext. 213. Fax (763)746-2469. E-mail: editor@mcchronicle.com, or info@ mcchronicle.com. Website: www.mcchronicle.com. Keener Communications Group. Bryan Malley, ed. Local news and features of interest to the Christian community. Monthly newsletter; 24-40 pgs.; circ. 35,000. Subscription $19.95. 20% unsolicited freelance; 80% assigned. Query; phone/fax/e-query OK. Prefers e-mail submissions (attached file). Pays $20-200 one month after publication for all rts. Articles 250-1,000 wds. (50-100/yr.); reviews 400 wds. Responds in 5 wks. Seasonal 2 mos. ahead. Rarely accepts simultaneous submissions or reprints (tell when/where appeared). No kill fee. Regularly uses sidebars. Guidelines by e-mail; copy $2. (Ads)

> **Tips:** "Looking for church trend stories. We most often use freelancers in our local news and feature article sections. Stories with a strong Minnesota hook will be accepted. Unique ministries, events, and/or people interest our readers the most. We also encourage participation in communities."
> **2008, 2006, 2005 EPA Award of Merit-Newspaper; 2007 EPA Award of Excellence—Newspaper.

$+MIRACLES, HEALINGS, & THE UNEXPLAINED, 13527 N.E. Rose Pkwy, Portland OR 97230. (503)793-3026. Fax (503)256-0584. E-mail: solidgoldpub@comcast.net. Website: www.miracles-magazine.com. Sue Wade, ed./pub. Showing through the overwhelming evidence of miracles that Jesus is healing and revealing himself to people every day. Estab. 2007. Submit complete ms by e-mail (no attachments) or through Website. Pays $10-25 on publication. Guidelines & sample copy on Website. Incomplete topical listings.

$THE MIRACULOUS MEDAL, 475 E. Chelten Ave., Philadelphia PA 19144-5785. Toll-free (800)523-3674. (215)848-1010. Fax (215)848-1014. E-mail through Website: www .cammonline.org. Catholic. Rev. James O. Kiernan, C.M., ed. Fiction and poetry for Catholic adults, mostly women. Quarterly mag.; 36 pgs.; circ. 200,000. Subscription free to members. 40% unsolicited freelance. Query by mail only. Pays .03/wd. and up, on acceptance, for 1st rts. Religious fiction 1,000-2,000 wds.; some 1,000-1,500 wds. (6/yr.). Responds in 13 wks. Seasonal anytime. Accepts simultaneous submissions. Guidelines (also by e-mail); copy for 6x9 SAE/2 stamps. (No ads) Incomplete topical listings.

> **Poetry:** Buys 6/yr. Free verse, traditional; to 20 lines; $1 & up/line. Send any number. "Must have religious theme, preferably about the Blessed Virgin Mary."
> **Tips:** "Most open to good short stories, 1,500-2,500 wds., or poetry, with light religious theme."

MISSIONWARES.COM, 920 Sweetgum Creek, Plano TX 75023. (972)517-8553. E-mail: info@ missionwares.com. Website: www.missionwares.com. Greg Paskal, owner. Website targeted toward Christian technologists. E-zine. 50% unsolicited freelance. Complete ms; e-query OK. Accepts full mss by e-mail. **NO PAYMENT** for one-time rts. Not copyrighted. Articles 1,500-5,000 wds. (3-5/yr.). Responds in 3-4 wks. No seasonal. No simultaneous submissions or reprints. Accepts e-mail submissions (attached file in Word or PDF). Does not use sidebars. Also accepts submissions from teens. Prefers NIV, NKJV, NLT. Guidelines by e-mail; copy online. (No ads)

> **Special Needs:** Technical White Papers. Best practices in technology as outlined by biblical precedence.
> **Tips:** "We are looking for real world technologists who are willing to share real world examples of living their walk out in corporate America."

$THE MONTANA CATHOLIC, PO Box 1729, Helena MT 59624. (406)442-5820. Fax (406)442-5191. E-mail: rstmartin@diocesehelena.org. Website: www.diocesehelena.org. Catholic Diocese of Helena. Renee St. Martin Wizeman, ed. Publishes news and features from a Catholic perspective, particularly as they pertain to the church in western Montana. Monthly tabloid; 20 pgs.; circ. 9,000. Subscription $12-16. 5% freelance. Query or complete ms; e-query OK. Pays .05-.10/wd. on acceptance for 1st, one-time or simultaneous rts. Articles 400-1,200 wds. (5/yr.). Responds in 5 wks. Accepts simultaneous submissions. Kill fee 25%. Guidelines on Website. Incomplete topical listings. (Ads)

Tips: "Most open to seasonal pieces or articles with a tie to western Montana. Must have a Catholic angle."

$MONTGOMERY'S JOURNEY, 555 Farmington Rd., Montgomery AL 36109-4609. (334)213-7940. Fax (334)213-7990. E-mail: reachout@montgomerysjourney.com. Website: www .watsonmedia.com. Keep Sharing LLC. DeAnne Watson, pub. For protestant Christians and Christian families. Monthly mag.; 60-72 pgs.; circ. 18,000. Open to freelance. Complete ms by e-mail. Pays $25-50 on publication for one-time or reprint rts. Articles 900-1,500 wds. Seasonal 3 mos. ahead. Accepts requested ms on disk or by e-mail (attached file). No kill fee. Regularly uses sidebars. Also accepts submissions from teens. Guidelines by e-mail; no copy. (Ads)

Tips: "Most open to feature articles, instructional in nature, with subheads and sidebars."

MOSAIC, 4315 Village Centre Ct., Mississauga ON L4Z 1S2, Canada. (905)848-2600. Fax (905)848-2603. E-mail: mosaic@fmc-canada.org. Website: www.fmc-canada.org. Free Methodist Church in Canada. Lisa Howden, mng. ed. Reflecting the diversity of ministry expression within the Free Methodist family. Bimonthly tabloid; 8 pgs.; circ. 4,000. Open to unsolicited freelance. Query; phone/e-query OK. **NO PAYMENT.** Articles 800-1,200 wds. Responds in 2 wks. Seasonal 4 mos. ahead. Accepts reprints (tell when/where appeared). Accepts e-mail submissions (attached file). Guidelines/theme list by e-mail/Website; no sample copy. (Ads)

Tips: "Most open to inspirational pieces."

MOVIEGUIDE, 1151 Avenida Acaso, Camarillo CA 93012. Toll-free (800)577-6684. (770)825-0084. Fax (805)383-4089. E-mail through Website: www.movieguide.org. Good News Communications/Christian Film & Television Commission. Dr. Theodore Baehr, pub. Family guide to media entertainment from a biblical perspective. Monthly mag.; 48 pgs.; circ. 2,500. Subscription $40. 40% unsolicited freelance. Query/clips. **PAYS IN COPIES** for all rts. Articles 1,000 wds. (100/yr.); book/music/video/movie reviews, 750-1,000 wds. Responds in 6 wks. Seasonal 6 mos. ahead. Accepts requested ms on disk. Regularly uses sidebars. Guidelines/ theme list; copy for SAE/4 stamps. (Ads)

Fillers: Accepts 1,000/yr.; all types; 20-150 wds.

Columns/Departments: Movieguide; Travelguide; Videoguide; CDguide, etc.; 1,200 wds.

Contest: Scriptwriting contest for movies with positive Christian content. go to: www .kairosprize.com.

Tips: "Most open to articles on movies and entertainment, especially trends, media literacy, historical, and hot topics."

($)MUTUALITY, 122 W. Franklin Ave., Ste. 218, Minneapolis MN 55404-2451. (612)872-6898. Fax (612)872-6891. E-mail: mgreulich@cbeinternational.org, or cbe@cbeinternational .org. Website: www.cbeinternational.org. Christians for Biblical Equality. Megan Greulich, ed. Seeks to provide inspiration, encouragement, and information about equality within the Christian church around the world. Quarterly mag.; 32 pgs.; circ. 2,000. Subscription $40/ free to members. 80% assigned freelance. Query/clips; fax/e-query OK. **PAYS A GIFT CERTIFICATE TO THEIR BOOKSTORE** on publication for 1st or electronic rts. Articles 1,000-2,000 wds. (12/yr.); book reviews 500-800 wds. Responds in 6 wks. Accepts reprints (tell when/where appeared). Accepts requested ms on disk or by e-mail (attached file). Regularly uses sidebars. Prefers NRSV, TNIV. Guidelines (also on Website); copy for 9x12 SAE/3 stamps. (Ads)

$NATIONAL CATHOLIC REPORTER, 115 E. Armour Blvd., Kansas City MO 64111-1203. (816) 531-0538. Fax (816)968-2268. E-mail: pschaeffer@ncronline.org, or through Website: www .ncronline.org. Catholic. Pam Schaeffer, exec. ed.; Margot Patterson, opinion ed. (mpatterson@ ncronline.org). Independent. Weekly (44X) & online newspaper; 44-48 pgs.; circ. 120,000. Subscription $43.95 print; $34.95 online. Query/clips. Pays .20/wd. on publication, or varying rates by agreement. Articles & short stories, varying lengths. Responds in up to 6 wks. Accepts simultaneous submissions. Guidelines (also by e-mail/Website); copy on Website.

Columns/Departments: Query with ideas for columns.

NETWORK, PO Box 131165, Birmingham AL 35213-6165. (205)328-7112. E-mail: dolores@ networknewspaper.org. Website: www.networknewspaper.org. Interdenominational. Dolores Milazzo-Hicks, ed./pub. (dolores@networknewspaper.org). To encourage and nurture dialog, understanding, and unity in Christian communities. Monthly tabloid; 12-16 pgs.; circ. 10,000. Subscription $17.50. 50% unsolicited freelance. Phone/fax/e-query OK. **NO PAYMENT.** Not copyrighted. Articles to 500 wds. Accepts simultaneous submissions. Articles and news.

Tips: "Most open to feature stories that express the unity of the body of Christ and articles that encourage and uplift our readers. We also cover state, local, national, and international news."

NEW FRONTIER, 180 E. Ocean Blvd., 4th Fl., Long Beach CA 90802. (562)491-8331. Fax (562)491-8791. E-mail: New_frontier@usw.salvationarmy.org. Website: www.salvationarmy .usawest.org/newfrontier. Salvation Army Western Territory. Robert L. Docter, ed. To share the good news of the gospel and the work of the Salvation Army in the western territory with salvationists and friends. Biweekly newspaper; circ. 25,500. Subscription $12. Open to freelance. Prefers query. Articles & reviews. Not in topical listings. (Ads)

A NEW HEART, PO Box 4004, San Clemente CA 92674-4004. (949)496-7655. Fax (949)496-8465. E-mail: HCFUSA@juno.com. Website: www.HCFUSA.com. Aubrey Beauchamp, ed. For Christian healthcare givers; information regarding medical/Christian issues. Quarterly mag.; 16 pgs.; circ. 5,000. Subscription $25. 20% unsolicited freelance; 10% assigned. Complete ms/cover letter; phone/fax/e-query OK. **PAYS 2 COPIES** for one-time rts. Not copyrighted. Articles 600-1,800 wds. (20-25/yr.). Responds in 2-3 wks. Accepts simultaneous submissions & reprints. Accepts e-mail submission. Does not use sidebars. Guidelines (also by fax); copy for 9x12 SAE/3 stamps. (Ads)

Poetry: Accepts 1-2/yr. Submit max. 1-3 poems.

Fillers: Accepts 3-4/yr. Anecdotes, cartoons, facts, jokes, short humor; 100-120 wds.

Columns/Departments: Accepts 20-25/yr. Chaplain's Corner, 200-250 wds.; Physician's Corner, 200-250 wds.

Tips: "Most open to real-life situations which may benefit and encourage healthcare givers and patients. True stories with medical and evangelical emphasis."

$NEW WINESKINS, PO Box 41028, Nashville TN 37204-1028. (615)292-2940. Fax (615)292-2931. E-mail: info@wineskins.org. Website: www.wineskins.org. The ZOE Group Inc. Greg Taylor, mng. ed. Combines biblical and cultural scholarly focus with popular-level articles and art for a powerful journal/magazine hybrid. Bimonthly e-zine; 15-20 articles/mo. 50% unsolicited freelance; 50% assigned. Query; e-query preferred. Pays $50 for online articles by year end, for one-time and electronic rts. Articles 800-2,500 wds. (100/yr.); fiction 1,000-2,500 wds. (10/yr.); book reviews 800-1,200 wds. ($50). Responds in 1-2 mos. Seasonal 6 mos. ahead. Accepts simultaneous submissions & reprints (tell when/where appeared). Prefers e-mail submissions (attached or copied into message). No kill fee. Sometimes uses sidebars. Also accept submissions from children/teens. Prefers NIV or NRSV. Guidelines by e-mail/Website; copy on Website. (Ads)

Poetry: Buys 4-5/yr. Avant-garde, free verse, light verse; 100-2,000 wds. Pays $50. Submit max. 1 poem.

Tips: "Best way to break in is by reviewing books, specifically ones we request. Also by writing well-shaped and well-researched pieces that are more than just opinions."

NOSTALGIA, 1703 N. Normandie St., Spokane WA 99205. (509)323-2086. Fax (509)323-2096. E-mail: editor@NostalgiaMagazine.net, or info@nostalgiamagazine.net. Website: www .nostalgiamagazine.net. King's Publishing Group Inc. Mark Carter, ed. We provide a forum for baby boomers and before to share photos and stories of yesterday that enrich life today; we use exclusively dated images/photos. Bimonthly mag.; 48 pgs. Subscription $22.95. Estab. 2004. 90% unsolicited freelance; 10% assigned. Complete ms/cover letter; e-query OK. **PAYS COPIES** on publication for 1st, one-time, reprint, simultaneous, or electronic rts. Articles 400-1,500 wds. (150/yr.). Responds in up to 1 yr. Seasonal 4 mos. ahead. Accepts simultaneous submissions & reprints (tell when/where appeared). Prefers e-mail submissions (attached or copied into message). No kill fee. Regularly uses sidebars. Guidelines (also by e-mail); query for themes/topics; copy $5/9x12 SAE. (Ads)

    Special Needs: Photos and family memories from 1940s, 1950s, and 1960s.

    Tips: "Looking for personal family memories with interesting photos: traveling, camping, working together. Specific episodes are better than generalities (400-2,000 wds., 1 photo/400 wds.). Dig out a great fun photo showing people engaged in life, write a caption, submit. No genealogies. Send us a first-person account showing everyday life from the years 1950-1968, with great photos."

$NOW WHAT? Box 33677, Denver CO 80233. (303)452-7973. Fax (303)452-0657. E-mail: bibleadvocate@cog7.org. Website: http://nowwhat.cog7.org. Church of God (Seventh-day). Sherri Langton, assoc. ed. Articles on salvation, Jesus, social issues, life problems that are seeker sensitive. Monthly online mag.; available only online. 100% unsolicited freelance. Complete ms/cover letter; no query. Pays $25-55 on publication for first, one-time, electronic, simultaneous, or reprint rts. Articles 1,000-1,500 wds. (20/yr.). Responds in 4-8 wks. Accepts simultaneous submissions & reprints (tell when/where appeared). Accepts requested ms by e-mail (copied into message—preferred—or attached). Regularly uses sidebars. Prefers NIV. Guidelines (also on Website); copy of online article for #10 SAE/1 stamp. (No ads)

    Fillers: Buys 5-10/yr. Anecdotes, facts, prose, quotes; 50-100 wds.; $20.

    Special Needs: "Personal experiences must show a person's struggle that either brought him/her to Christ or deepened faith in God. The entire *Now What?* site is built around a personal experience each month."

    Tips: "The whole e-zine is open to freelance. Think how you can explain your faith, or how you overcame a problem, to a non-Christian. It's a real plus for writers submitting a personal experience to also submit an objective article related to their story. Or they can contact Sherri Langton for upcoming personal experiences that need related articles."

($)NRB MAGAZINE, 9510 Technology Dr., Manassas VA 20110-4167. (703)330-7000. Fax (703)330-7100. E-mail: vfraedrich@nrb.org, or info@nrb.org. Website: www.nrb.org. National Religious Broadcasters. Valerie D. Fraedrich, ed. Topics relate to Christian radio, television, satellite, church media, Internet, and all forms of communication; promoting access and excellence in Christian communications. Monthly (9X) & online mag.; 52 pgs.; circ. 9,300. Subscription $24; Canadians add $6 U.S.; foreign add $24 U.S. 70% unsolicited freelance. Complete ms/cover letter; fax/e-query OK. **PAYS 6 COPIES** ($100-200 for assigned) on publication for 1st or reprint rts. Articles 1,000-2,000 wds. (30/yr.). Responds in 6 wks. Seasonal 6 mos. ahead. Accepts simultaneous submissions & reprints (tell when/where appeared). Prefers accepted ms by e-mail. Regularly uses sidebars. Prefers NAS. Guidelines/theme list (also by e-mail); free copy. (Ads)

Columns/Departments: Valerie Fraedrich, asst. ed. Accepts 9/yr. Trade Talk (summary paragraphs of news items/events in Christian broadcasting), 50 wds.; Opinion (social issues), 750 wds. Columns coordinated in-house, 500 wds.

Special Needs: Electronic media; education. All articles must relate in some way to broadcasting: radio, TV, programs on radio/TV, or Internet.

Tips: "Most open to feature articles relevant to Christian communicators. Become acquainted with broadcasters in your area and note their struggles, concerns, and victories. Find out what they would like to know, research the topic, then write about it." Contact assistant editor for guidelines, reprint permission, classified ads, additional copies, etc.

$ON MISSION, 4200 North Point Pkwy., Alpharetta GA 30022-4176. (770)410-6382. Fax (770)410-6105. E-mail: onmission@namb.net. Website: www.onmission.com. North American Mission Board, Southern Baptist. Carol Pipes, ed. Helping readers share Christ in the real world. Quarterly & online mag.; 32 pgs.; circ. 200,000. Subscription free. 1-5% unsolicited freelance; 50-60% assigned. Query (complete ms for fiction); no phone/fax query; e-query OK. Accepts full mss by e-mail. Pays .25/wd. on acceptance for 1st rts. Articles 500-1,000 wds. (20/yr.). Responds in 8 wks. Seasonal 8 mos. ahead. No simultaneous submissions or reprints. Accepts e-mail submissions (attached or copied into message). Kill fee. Regularly uses sidebars. Prefers HCSB. Guidelines (also by e-mail/Website); copy for 9x12 SAE/$2.02 postage. (Ads)

Columns/Departments: Buys 4-8/yr. The Pulse (outreach/missions ideas); 500 wds. Query.

Special Needs: Needs articles on these topics: sharing your faith, interviews/profiles of missionaries, starting churches, volunteering in missions, sending missionaries.

Tips: "We are primarily a Southern Baptist publication reaching out to Southern Baptist pastors and lay people, equipping them to share Christ, start churches, volunteer in missions, and impact the culture. Write a solid, 750-word, how-to article geared to 20- to 40-year-old men and women who want fresh ideas and insight into sharing Christ in the real world in which they live, work, and play. Send a résumé, along with your best writing samples. We are an on-assignment magazine, but occasionally a well-written manuscript gets published."

**2007, 2006 EPA Award of Merit—Missionary; 2005 EPA Award of Merit—Most Improved Publication.

$OUR SUNDAY VISITOR, 200 Noll Plaza, Huntington IN 46750. Toll-free (800)348-2440. (260)356-8400. Fax (260)359-9117. E-mail: oursunvis@osv.com. Website: www.osv.com. Catholic. John Norton, ed.; Sarah Hayes, article ed. Vital news analysis, perspective, spirituality for today's Catholic. Weekly newspaper; 24 pgs.; circ. 68,000. 10% unsolicited freelance; 90% assigned. Query or complete ms; fax/e-query OK. Pays $100-800 within 4 wks. of acceptance for 1st & electronic rts. Articles 500-3,500 wds. (25/yr.). Responds in 4-6 wks. Seasonal 2 mos. ahead. No simultaneous submissions; rarely accepts reprints (tell when/where appeared). Kill fee. Regularly uses sidebars. Prefers RSV. Guidelines (also by e-mail/Website); copy for $2/10x13 SASE/$1.00 postage. (Ads)

Columns/Departments: Faith; Family; Trends; Profile; Heritage; Media; Q & A. See guidelines for details.

Tips: "Our mission is to examine the news, culture, and trends of the day from a faithful and sound Catholic perspective—to see the world through the eyes of faith. Especially interested in writers able to do news analysis (with a minimum of 3 sources), or newsier features."

**This periodical was #48 on the 2006 Top 50 Christian Publishers list (#14 in 2005).

$OVER THE BACK FENCE, PO Box 756, Chillicothe OH 45601. Toll free (800)718-5727. Fax (330)220-3083. E-mail: SarahW@longpointmedia.com Website: www.backfencemagazine .com. Long Point Media. Sarah Williamson, ed. Positive news about Southern Ohio.

Bimonthly mag.; 74 pgs.; circ. 15,000. Subscription $13.95. 60% unsolicited freelance. Query/clips; fax/e-query OK. Pays .10-.20/wd. on publication for one-time rts. Articles 750-1,000 wds. (9-12/yr.); fiction 300-850 wds. (8/yr.). Responds in 12 wks. Seasonal 1 yr. ahead. Accepts simultaneous submissions & reprints (tell when/where appeared). Requires requested ms on disk or by e-mail (copied into message). Regularly uses sidebars. Guidelines (also on Website); copy $4/9x12 SAE, or on Website. (Ads)

Columns/Departments: Buys 8/yr. Profiles from the Past (interesting history that never made the headlines), 800-1,000 wds.; Heartstrings (touching essays), 800 wds.; Shorts (humorous essays), 800 wds. Complete ms. Pays $80-120.

Special Needs: Think upbeat and positive. Articles on nature, history, travel, nostalgia, and family.

Tips: "We need material for our columns most often—Humorous Shorts, Profiles from the Past, and Heartstrings. It is best for writers to send things with appeal for Midwest readers and be generally positive. We do not publish articles that criticize or create a negative feeling about a geographical area or people."

+THE OZARKS CHRISTIAN NEWS, 149 Grand Ave., Branson MO 65616. (417)336-3636. Fax (417)336-0911. E-mail: lila@ozarkschristiannews.com. Website: www.OzarksChristian News.com. John Sacoulas, ed. Celebrating the common ground in the body of Christ. Monthly newspaper; circ. 20,000. Subscription $28. Open to unsolicited freelance. Complete ms. Articles & reviews. Incomplete topical listings. (Ads)

$OZARKS SENIOR LIVING NEWSPAPER, 2010 S. Steward, Springfield MO 65804. (417)862-0852. Fax (417)862-9079. E-mail: elefantwalk@msn.com. Website: www.slnewspaper.net. Metropolitan Radio Group Inc. Joyce Yonker O'Neal, mng. ed. Positive, upbeat paper for people 55+; includes religious articles. Monthly newspaper; 40 pgs.; circ. 40,000. 25-50% unsolicited freelance. Query or complete ms/cover letter; no phone/fax/e-query. Pays $20-35 for assigned; $5-35 for unsolicited; 30 days after publication for 1st, reprint, electronic rts. Articles 600 wds. (65/yr.). Responds in 2-5 wks. Seasonal 4 mos. ahead. Guidelines; copy for 9x12 SAE/5 stamps.

$PARENTLIFE, One Lifeway Plaza, Nashville TN 37234-0172. (615)251-2196. Fax (615)277-8142. E-mail: parentlife@lifeway.com. Website: www.lifeway.com/parentlife. LifeWay Christian Resources. Jodi Skulley, ed. (jodi.skulley@lifeway.com). A child-centered magazine for parents of children 12 and under. Monthly mag.; 52 pgs.; circ. 72,000. Subscription $29.65. 5% unsolicited freelance; 95% assigned. Query; e-query OK. Accepts full mss by e-mail. Pays $150-500 on acceptance for nonexclusive rts. Articles 500-1,500 wds. (60/yr.) Responds in 6 mos. Seasonal 1 yr. ahead. Accepts simultaneous submissions; no reprints. Prefers e-mail submissions (attached file). No kill fee. Regularly uses sidebars. Prefers HCSB. Guidelines/theme list (also by e-mail/Website); copy for 10x13 SASE. (Ads)

Columns/Departments: Buys 60/yr. A Healthy Life (parent health issues), to 500 wds.; On the Way (expectant parent topics), to 500 wds.; The Funny Life (funny family stories), 100 wds.; Single Parent Life, to 500 wds.; Working Life, to 500 wds. Pays $20-150. Query.

Tips: "Most open to feature articles. Writers can apply to write for *ParentLife* (www .lifeway.com/people)."

THE PEGASUS REVIEW, PO Box 88, Henderson MD 21640-0088. (410)482-6736. E-mail: editor@pegasusreview.com. Art Bounds, ed. Theme-oriented poetry, short fiction, and essays; not necessarily religious; in calligraphy format. Quarterly mag.; 12-14 pgs.; circ. 150. Subscription $12. 100% unsolicited freelance. Query or complete ms/cover letter (include background); e-query OK. No complete mss by e-mail. **PAYS 2 COPIES** for one-time rts. Fiction 2.5 pgs. is ideal, single-spaced (6-10/yr.); also one-page essays. Responds in 4 wks. Accepts simultaneous submissions & reprints (tell when/where appeared). No disk or e-mail submissions. Does not use sidebars. Also accepts submissions from teens. Prefers KJV. Guidelines/theme list by e-mail; copy $2.50. (No ads)

Poetry: Accepts 40-50/yr. Any type; 4-24 lines (shorter the better; pay attention to line length). Theme oriented. Submit max. 3 poems.

Fillers: Accepts 20/yr. Cartoons, prose, quotes; 100-150 wds.

Special Needs: 2008 themes: Jan—Courage; Apr—Family; July—Genius & Talent; October—Memories.

Tips: "Continue to persevere. No one ever said it would be easy, but the end result is worth the wait."

PENTECOSTAL MESSENGER, PO Box 850, Joplin MO 64802. Toll-free (800)444-4674. (417)624-7050. Toll-free fax (800)982-5687. (417)624-7102. E-mail: johnm@pcg.org. Website: www.messengerpublishing.com. Pentecostal Church of God. John Mallinak, ed. Denominational publication; ministry resource. Monthly (11X) mag.; circ. 5,000. Subscription $12. Accepts freelance. Prefers query. Complete ms. Articles. Copy $1.50. Not in topical listings. (Ads)

THE PENWOOD REVIEW, PO Box 862, Los Alamitos CA 90720-0862. E-mail: submissions@penwoodreview.com. Website: www.penwoodreview.com. Lori Cameron, ed. Poetry, plus thought-provoking essays on poetry, literature, and the role of spirituality and religion in the literary arts. Biannual jour.; 40+ pgs.; circ. 80-100. Subscription $12. 100% unsolicited freelance. Complete ms; no e-query. **NO PAYMENT** ($2 off subscription & 1 free copy), for one-time and electronic rts. Articles 1 pg. (single-spaced). Responds in 9-12 wks. Accepts requested ms by e-mail (copied into message). Guidelines (also by e-mail/Website); copy $6.

Poetry: Accepts 120-160/yr. Any type, including formalist; to 2 pgs. Submit max. 5 poems.

Special Needs: Faith and the literary arts; religion and literature. Needs essays (up to 2 pgs., single spaced).

Tips: "We publish poetry almost exclusively and are looking for well-crafted, disciplined poetry, not doggerel or greeting-card-style poetry. Poets should study poetry, read it extensively, and send us their best, most original work. Visit our Website or buy a copy for an idea of what we publish."

PERSPECTIVES: A Journal of Reformed Thought, 517 Peterson St., Alta IA 51002. E-mail: perspectives@rca.org. Website: www.perspectivesjournal.org. Reformed Church Press. Dr. Scott Hoezee & Dr. James Bratt, eds. To express the Reformed faith theologically; to engage issues that Reformed Christians meet in personal, ecclesiastical, and societal life; and thus to contribute to the mission of the church of Jesus Christ. Monthly (10X) & online mag.; 24 pgs.; circ. 3,000. Subscription $30. 75% unsolicited freelance; 25% assigned. Complete ms/cover letter or query; fax/e-query OK. **PAYS 6 COPIES** for 1st rts. Articles (10/yr.) and fiction (3/yr.), 2,500-3,000 wds.; reviews 1,000 wds. Responds in 20 wks. Seasonal 10 mos. ahead. Accepts reprints (tell when/where appeared). Prefers requested ms by e-mail (attached file). Uses some sidebars. Prefers NRSV. Guidelines on Website; no copy. (Ads)

Poetry: Rhoda Janzen, poetry ed. (Perspectives, Dept. of English, Hope College, Holland MI 49422-9000). Accepts 2-3/yr. Traditional. Submit max. 3 poems. Hard copy only.

Columns/Departments: Accepts 12/yr. As We See It (editorial/opinion), 750-1,000 wds.; Inside Out (biblical exegesis), 750 wds. Complete ms.

Tips: "Most open to feature-length articles. Must be theologically informed, whatever the topic. Avoid party-line thinking and culture-war approaches. I would say that a reading of past issues and a desire to join in a contemporary conversation on the Christian faith would help you break in here."

PERSPECTIVES ON SCIENCE & CHRISTIAN FAITH, PO Box 668, Ipswich MA 01938. (978)356-5656. Fax (978)356-4375. E-mail: asa@asa3.org. Website: www.asa3.org. American Scientific Affiliation. Submit to Arie Leegwater, ed. (1726 Knollcrest Cir. S.E., Grand Rapids MI 49546; leeg@calvin.edu). Quarterly journal; 72 pgs.; circ. 2,000+. Subscription $40/yr. 75% unsolicited freelance; 25% assigned. E-query. Accepts full mss by e-mail. **NO PAYMENT.** Articles 6,000 wds. (20/yr.). Responds in 2 wks. Seasonal 4 mos. ahead. No simultaneous submissions or reprints. Accepts submissions by disk or e-mail (attached file). Regularly uses sidebars. Guidelines on Website.

Special Needs: Science and faith; bioethics.

Tips: "Freelancer must have credentials to write about their subject, i.e., advanced degree in science or theology. Article must be well-researched and will be peer-reviewed."

$POETRY SCOUT - CENTRE MINISTRY, 6512 Arbor Lane, #614, Fort Worth TX 76132. E-mail: director@poetryscout-centreministry.com. Website: www.poetryscout-centreministry.com. Poetry Scout - Centre Ministry. Thomas L. Means, dir. Seeking Christian inspirational poetry writers to cost share in a partnership book publishing contract. Poetry only. (Ads only as Website links)

Poetry: Accepts 10 pages per poet per publishing contract; ten pages of theme-oriented poetry, quotes, and elaborating thoughts. Free verse or traditional (theme oriented); up to 32 lines/poem. Payment is based on contractual agreement with affiliated publisher, and within a partnership cost-share plan. Prescreen required of a 10-line inspirational poem reflecting the Trinity of God. Mail complete ms; send e-mail; or submit through Website.

PORTRAIT OF ACHIEVEMENT, PO Box 938711, Margate FL 33093. (954)485-0062. Website: www.poamagazine.org. Sharon Blackwood, pub. To deliver inspiring, provocative, and informative stories about our children's greatest achievements. Magazine. Subscription $15.99. Open to unsolicited freelance. Query or complete ms. **NO PAYMENT.** Articles. Also accepts submissions from children/teens. Guidelines on Website. Not in topical listings. (Ads)

Special Needs: Articles related to the health or welfare of children.

Tips: "Provide encouragement for children and parents."

$POSITIVE THINKING: Finding Joy & Fulfillment Every Day, 66 E. Main St., Pauling NY 12564. (212)251-8100. Fax (845)855-1036. E-mail: awong@guideposts.org. Website: www.guideposts.org. Guideposts. Amy Wong, ed. Spiritually oriented, based on positive thinking and faith. Bimonthly mag.; 36 pgs.; circ. 400,000. Subscription $15. 30% unsolicited freelance. Query preferred; phone/fax/e-query OK. Pays $75/pg. on publication for one-time rts. Articles 500-2,300 wds. (8/yr.). Responds in 3-4 wks. Seasonal 6 mos. ahead. Accepts reprints. Accepts submissions by e-mail. Does not use sidebars. Guidelines; copy for #10 SAE/1 stamp.

Special Needs: Contemporary heroes; overcoming (addiction, etc.) through faith. (1) Life-changing experiences that bring about faith in Jesus Christ. (2) Ways to improve prayer and spiritual life. (3) How positive thinking and faith provide answers to life's problems.

Tips: "Most open to true stories of finding faith through difficult circumstances. Avoid preachiness. How-tos (if applicable), stories (nonfiction only) that touch the heart and soul. Have a deep, living knowledge of Christianity. Our audience is 65-70% female, average age is 55."

$POWER FOR LIVING, MS #205—Manuscript Submission, 4050 Lee Vance View, Colorado Springs CO 80918. Toll-free (800)708-5550. (719)536-0100. Fax (719)535-2928. Website: www.cookministries.org. Cook Communications/Scripture Press Publications. Don Alban Jr., ed. To expressly demonstrate the relevance of specific biblical teachings to everyday life via reader-captivating profiles of exceptional Christians. Weekly take-home paper; 8 pgs.; circ. 250,000. Subscription $12. 15% unsolicited freelance; 85% assigned. Complete ms; no phone/fax/e-query. Pays up to .15/wd. (reprints up to .10/wd.) on acceptance for one-time rts. Profiles 700-1,500 wds. (20/yr.). Responds in 10 wks. Seasonal 1 yr. ahead. Accepts simultaneous submissions & reprints (tell when/where appeared). Accepts requested ms on disk. Kill fee. Requires KJV. Guidelines/copy for #10 SAE/1 stamp (Use address above, but change to MS #205—Sample Request). (No ads)

Special Needs: Third-person profiles of truly out-of-the-ordinary Christians who express their faith uniquely. We use very little of anything else.

Tips: "Most open to vignettes, 450-1,500 wds., of prominent Christians with solid testimonies or profiles from church history. Focus on the unusual. Signed releases required."

($)+P.O.W.E.R. MAGAZINE, 3030 E. 35th St., Indianapolis IN 46218. Toll-free (888)415-2224. E-mail: info@powermagazine.org. Website: www.powermagazine.org. Kimberly Stewart, ed. Compelling people to come to Christ. Online mag. Subscription $6. Open to unsolicited freelance. Pays sometimes. Articles. Guidelines by e-mail or through Website. Incomplete topical listings. (Ads)

$PRAIRIE MESSENGER: Catholic Journal, PO Box 190, Muenster SK S0K 2Y0, Canada. (306)682-1772. Fax (306)682-5285. E-mail: pm.canadian@stpeterspress.ca. Website: www.prairiemessenger.ca. Catholic/Benedictine Monks of St. Peter's Abbey. Peter Novecosky, OSB, ed.; Maureen Weber, assoc. ed. For Catholics in Saskatchewan and Manitoba, and Christians in other faith communities. Weekly tabloid (46X); 20 pgs.; circ. 6,900. Subscription $32 Cdn. 10% unsolicited freelance; 90% assigned. Complete ms/cover letter; phone/fax/e-query OK. Pays $55 ($2.75/column inch for news items) on publication for 1st, one-time, simultaneous, and reprint rts. Not copyrighted. Articles 800-900 (15/yr.). Responds in 9 wks. Seasonal 3 mos. ahead. Accepts simultaneous submissions & reprints. Regularly uses sidebars. Guidelines by e-mail/Website; copy for 9x12 SAE/$1 Cdn./$1.34 U.S. postage. (Ads)

Poetry: Accepts 35/yr. Avant-garde, free verse, haiku, light verse; 3-30 lines. Pays $20 Cdn.

Columns/Departments: Accepts 5/yr. Pays $55 Cdn.

Special Needs: Ecumenism; social justice; native concerns.

Tips: "Comment/feature section is most open; send good reflection column of about 800 words; topic of concern or interest to Prairie readership. It's difficult to break into our publication. Piety not welcome."

THE PRAYER CLOSET, PO Box 278, Hickory, MS 39332. (601)646-2295. E-mail: prayer@prayerclosetministries.org. Website: www.prayerclosetministries.org. Dr. Kevin Meador, ed. Challenges and equips believers in the area of prayer, fasting, spiritual warfare, journaling, and healing. Monthly newsletter; circ. 3,000. Free subscription online. **PAYS IN COPIES.** Prefers NKJV. Guidelines.

Tips: "We are looking for sound, biblically based articles concerning the above-listed topics."

PRAYERWORKS, PO Box 301363, Portland OR 97294. (503)761-2072. E-mail: VannM1@aol.com. Website: www.prayerworksnw.org. The Master's Work. V. Ann Mandeville, ed. For prayer warriors in retirement centers; focuses on prayer. Weekly newspaper and online (soon); 4 pgs.; circ. 1,500. Subscription free. 100% unsolicited freelance. Complete ms. **PAYS IN COPIES/SUBSCRIPTION** for one-time rts. Not copyrighted. Articles (30-40/yr.) & fiction (30/yr.); 350-500 wds. Responds in 3 wks. Seasonal 2 mos. ahead. Accepts simultaneous submissions & reprints. Does not use sidebars. Guidelines; copy for #10 SAE/1 stamp. (No ads)

Poetry: Accepts 20-30/yr. Free verse, haiku, light verse, traditional. Submit max. 10 poems.

Fillers: Accepts up to 50/yr. Facts, jokes, prayers, quotes, short humor; to 50 wds.
Tips: "Write tight and well. Half our audience is over 70, but 30% is young families. Subject matter isn't important as long as it is scriptural and designed to help people pray. Have a strong, catchy takeaway."

$PRECEPTS FOR LIVING, Annual Sunday School Commentary, PO Box 436987, Chicago IL 60643. E-mail: ecarey@urbanministries.com. Website: www.urbanministries.com. Urban Ministries Inc. Dr. Vincent Bacote, ed; submit to Evangeline Carey, developmental ed. *Precepts for Living* is a verse-by-verse Sunday School commentary geared toward an African American adult audience. Word studies are presented in the original Greek and Hebrew languages to further illuminate understanding of the text. KJV Scriptures. 500 pgs. Strict adherence to guidelines. Query/writing samples & clips; e-query OK. Lessons are assigned. Pays $200 per Bible Study lesson and $300 for More Light on the Text, a verse-by-verse commentary which includes Greek and Hebrew word studies, 120 days after acceptance, for all rts. Requires accepted ms by e-mail (attached).
Tips: "Should be astute in biblical education and how to correctly exegete scripture."

THE PRESBYTERIAN OUTLOOK, Box 85623, Richmond VA 23285-5623. Toll-free (800)446-6008. (804)359-8442. Fax (804)353-6369. E-mail: editor@pres-outlook.org. Website: www.pres-outlook.com. Presbyterian Church (USA)/Independent. Jack Haberer, ed.; Randy Harris, book review ed. For ministers, members, and staff of the denomination. Weekly (43X) mag.; 16-40 pgs.; circ. 10,000. Subscription $42.95. 5% unsolicited freelance; 95% assigned. Query; phone/fax/e-query OK. **NO PAYMENT** for all rts. Not copyrighted. Articles/fiction to 1,000 wds.; book reviews 1 pg. Responds in 1-2 wks. Seasonal 2 mos. ahead. Accepts e-mail submissions. Uses some sidebars. Prefers NRSV. Guidelines (also by e-mail); free copy. (Ads)
Tips: "Correspond (mail or e-mail) with editor regarding current needs; most open to features. Most material is commissioned; anything submitted should be of interest to Presbyterian church leaders."

$PRESBYTERIANS TODAY, 100 Witherspoon St., Louisville KY 40202-1396. Toll-free (888)728-7228, ext. 5637. (502)569-5637. Fax (502)569-8632. E-mail: today@pcusa .org. Website: www.pcusa.org/today. Presbyterian Church (USA). Eva Stimson, ed.; John Sniffen, assoc. ed. Denominational; not as conservative or evangelical as some. Monthly (10X) mag.; 48 pgs.; circ. 58,000. Subscription $19.95. 25% freelance. Query or complete ms/cover letter; phone/fax/e-query OK. Pays $75-300 on acceptance for 1st rts. Articles 800-2,000 wds. (prefers 1,000-1,500). (20/yr.). Also uses short features 250-600 wds. Responds in 2-5 wks. Seasonal 3 mos. ahead. Few reprints. Accepts requested ms on disk or by e-mail. Kill fee 50%. Prefers NRSV. Guidelines on Website: www.pcusa.org/today/guidelines/guidelines.htm); free copy. (Ads)
Fillers: Cartoons, $25; and short humor to 150 wds., no payment.
Tips: "Most open to feature articles about Presbyterians—individuals, churches with special outreach, creative programs, or mission work. Do not often use inspirational or testimony-type articles."
**This periodical was #40 on the 2006 Top 50 Christian Publishers list (#32 in 2005, #32 in 2004).

$PRIORITY! 440 W. Nyack Rd., West Nyack NY 10994. (845)620-7450. Fax (845)620-7723. E-mail: linda_johnson@use.salvationarmy.org. Website: www.prioritypeople.org. The Salvation Army. Linda D. Johnson, ed.; Robert Mitchell, assoc. ed. Quarterly & online mag.; 48-56 pgs.; circ. 28,000. Subscription $8.95. 50% assigned. Query/clips; e-query OK. Pays $200-800 on acceptance for 1st rts. Articles 400-1,700 wds. (8-10/yr.). All articles assigned. Responds in 2 wks. Occasionally buys reprints (tell when/where appeared). Prefers accepted ms by e-mail (in Word or copied into message). Kill fee 50%. Regularly uses sidebars. Prefers NIV. Occasionally buys submissions from children/teens. Guidelines/theme list by e-mail; copy $1/9x12 SAE. (Ads from nonprofits only)

Columns/Departments: Buys 5-10/yr. Prayer Power (stories about answered prayer, or harnessing prayer power); Who's News (calling attention to specific accomplishments or missions); Q & A (answers to current questions); My Take (unpublished writer's view); all 400-700 wds.; $200-400. Query.

Special Needs: All articles must have a connection to The Salvation Army. Can be from any part of the U.S. Looking especially for freelancers with Salvation Army connections; Christmas recollections (by August 1); people/program features.

Tips: "Most open to features on people. Every article, whether about people or programs, tells a story and must feature the Salvation Army. Stories focus on evangelism, holiness, prayer. The more a writer knows about The Salvation Army, the better. We are interested in finding a group of freelancers we can assign to specific features."

PRISCILLA PAPERS, 122 W. Franklin Ave., Ste. 218, Minneapolis MN 55404-2451. Send submissions to editor at: 130 Essex St., Gordon-Conwell Theological Seminary, S. Hamilton MA 01982. (612)872-6898. Fax (612)872-6891. E-mail: debbeattymel@aol.com. Website: www.cbeinternational.org. Christians for Biblical Equality. William David Spencer, ed.; Deb Beatty Mel, assoc. ed. Addresses biblical interpretation and its relationship to women and men ministering together, other race/ethnicity, economic class, and age issues in the society, the Christian community, and the family—from an Evangelical Egalitarian perspective. Quarterly jour.; 32 pgs.; circ. 2,000. Subscription $40 (includes subscription to *Mutuality*). 85% unsolicited freelance; 15% assigned. Query preferred; fax/e-query OK. **PAYS 3 COPIES, PLUS A FREE BOOK** for 1st & electronic rts. Articles 600-5,000 wds. (1/yr.); book review 600 wds. (free book). Slow and careful response. No reprints. Seasonal 12 mos. ahead. Prefers proposed ms on disk or by e-mail (attached file) with hard copy. No kill fee. Uses some sidebars. Prefers NIV, TNIV, NRSV. Guidelines on Website; copy for 9x12 SAE/$2.02 postage. (Ads)

Poetry: Accepts 1/yr. Avant-garde, free verse, traditional (on biblical gender equality themes); pays a free book.

Tips: "P.P. is the academic voice of CBE. Our target is the informed lay reader. All sections are open to freelancers. Any well-written, single-theme article (no potpourri) presenting a solid exegetical and hermeneutical approach to biblical equality from a high view of scripture will be considered for publication." Seeks original cover art work.

$PRISM: America's Alternative Evangelical Voice, 6 E. Lancaster Ave., Wynnewood PA 19096-3495. (484)384-2990. Fax (610)649-8090. E-mail: kristyn@esa-online.org. Website: www.esa-online.org/prism. Evangelicals for Social Action. Kristyn Komarnicki, ed. For Christians who are interested in the social and political dimensions of the gospel. Bimonthly mag.; 40 pgs.; circ. 5,000. Subscription $35. 50% unsolicited freelance. Complete ms/cover letter; e-query OK. Accepts full mss by e-mail. Pays $75-450 on publication for 1st & electronic rts. Articles 1,500-3,000 wds. (10-12/yr.); no fiction; book reviews, 500 wds., $75. Responds within 12 wks. Seasonal 9 mos. ahead. No reprints. Regularly uses sidebars. Prefers NRSV. Guidelines by e-mail; copy $3. (Ads)

Tips: "Looking for analysis on religious right; social justice. Understand progressive evangelicals and E.S.A. Read Tony Campolo, Ron Sider, and Richard Foster. Most open to features. We don't assign work to writers we haven't published before, so send a full manuscript."

**2008 Award of Merit—Organizational.

+PRISON LIVING MAGAZINE, 10645 N. Tatum Blvd., Ste. 200-661, Phoenix AZ 85028. Toll-free (800)419-2891. Fax (602)424-1776. E-mail: info@plmag.org. Website: www.pl mag.org. Total Life Ministry. Sandy Almendarez, content ed. For prisoners and their families and victims; inspirational articles related to prison issues. Quarterly mag.; 52 pgs; circ. 60,000. Subscription $16. Open to freelance. Complete ms; phone/fax/e-query OK. Accepts full mss by e-mail. **PAYS IN COPIES** for one-time rts. Articles 1,000 wds. (35/yr.); fiction 2,000 wds. (1/yr.); book reviews 300 wds. Responds in 3 wks. Seasonal 2 mos. ahead. Accepts simultaneous submissions & reprints (tell when/where appeared). Uses some sidebars. Guidelines by e-mail; copy for 9x12 SAE/$2 postage. (Ads)

Poetry: Accepts 12/yr. from prisoners/ex-felons only.

Fillers: Anecdotes, cartoons, facts, games, jokes, kid quotes, prayers, quotes, tips, word puzzles; to 300 wds.

Columns/Departments: Accepts 50/yr. Prisoner Profile (how prisoner lives best life in prison; Last Words (how death-row inmate lives best life in prison); Praiseworthy Acts (person/group doing good things for prisoners); Sports (anything sports related); The Bridge (company/group/person who helps ex-felons reintegrate into society after prison); Victims (how crime affected a person or family); plus several more; all 1,000 wds. Query or complete ms.

Tips: "Always need Sports, The Bridge, and Victims; those departments have little competition."

$PSYCHOLOGY FOR LIVING, 250 W. Colorado Blvd., Ste. 200, Arcadia CA 91007. (626)821-8400. Fax (626)821-8409. E-mail: editor@ncfliving.org. Website: www.ncfliving.org. Narramore Christian Foundation. Robert & Melanie Whitcomb, eds. Addresses issues of everyday life from a Christian and psychological viewpoint. Quarterly mag.; 8 pgs. (one issue 24 pgs.); circ. 7,000. Subscription for $20 donation. Open to freelance. Complete ms/cover letter; fax OK, e-query preferred. Pays $75-200, plus a subscription, on publication for 1st, one-time, or reprint rts. Articles 1,000-1,700 wds. Responds in 2-4 wks. Seasonal 4 mos. ahead. Accepts reprints (tell when/where appeared). Prefers accepted ms by e-mail (attached file). Uses some sidebars. Prefers NIV. Guidelines (also by e-mail); free copy. (No ads)

Tips: "Tell a story or illustration that shows how a psychological/emotional problem was dealt with in a biblical and psychologically sound manner. Not preachy."

$PURE INSPIRATION, 7 Waterloo Rd., Stanhope NJ 07874. (973)347-6900. Fax (973)347-6909. E-mail: marnold@lightstreampublishing.com. Website: www.pureinspiration mag.com. Lightstream Publishing LLC. Robert Becker, ed.; Marie Arnold, mng. ed. Inspires people to live positive, healthier lives—spiritually and emotionally—emphasizing our similarities, not our differences; readership is 75% women. Quarterly mag.; 100 pgs.; circ. 25,000. Subscription $19.97. Estab. 2006. 50% unsolicited freelance; 25% assigned. Query, query/clips, or complete ms/cover letter; fax/e-query OK. Pays $100-125/pg. on publication for 1st rts. Articles 1,500-2,000 wds. (25-30/yr.). Responds in 2-3 wks. Seasonal 6 mos. ahead. No simultaneous submissions; reprints negotiable (tell when/where appeared). Prefers e-mail submissions (attached file). Some kill fees. Some sidebars. Also accepts submissions from children/teens. Guidelines on Website); copy for 9x12 SAE/$2 postage. (Ads)

Poetry: Only inspirational poems.

Columns/Departments: Buys 10-12/yr. Share Your Story (true personal stories of inspiration), 1,000-1,500 wds., $100.

Tips: "Most open to any topic which is helpful to our readers, such as those that will help to improve their lives spiritually and inspire them."

$PURPOSE, 616 Walnut Ave., Scottdale PA 15683-1999. (724)887-3111. E-mail: Horsch@ mpn.org. Website: www.mpn.org. Mennonite Publishing Network. James E. Horsch, ed. Denominational, for older youth & adults. Monthly take-home paper; 32 pgs.; circ. 8,900. Subscription $22.65; $23.68 Cdn. 85% unsolicited freelance; 15% assigned. Complete ms (only)/cover letter; e-mail submissions preferred. Pays up to .07/wd. on acceptance for one-time rts. Articles & fiction, to 600 wds. (60/yr.). Responds in 6 mos. Seasonal 1 yr.

ahead. Accepts simultaneous submissions & reprints (tell when/where appeared). Regularly uses sidebars. Guidelines (also by e-mail); copy $2/6x9 SAE/2 stamps. (No ads)

Poetry: Buys 70/yr. Free verse, light verse, traditional; 3-12 lines; up to $2/line ($7.50-20). Submit max. 5 poems.

Fillers: Buys 100/yr. Anecdotes, cartoons, short stories; 300-600 wds.; up to .07/wd.

Tips: "All areas are open. Articles must carry a strong story line. First person is preferred. Don't exceed maximum word length, send no more than 3 works at a time."

**This periodical was #19 on the 2008 Top 50 Christian Publishers list (#38 in 2007, #43 in 2006, #50 in 2005, #28 in 2004).

PURPOSE MAGAZINE, PO Box 906, Temple Hills MD 20757. (614)418-1785. Fax (614)253-2283. E-mail: purposeforlife@gmail.com. Website: www.purposemagazine.com. Ellavation Enterprises Inc. Ella Coleman, pub./ed-in-chief. Christian magazine for a predominately African American audience; personal and family empowerment to inspire, motivate, and educate readers to live their God-given purpose. Bimonthly mag.; 32-40 pgs.; circ. 5,000. Subscription $25. 25% unsolicited freelance; 75% assigned. Query/clips; e-query OK. **PAYS A SUBSCRIPTION & PROMOTION.** Articles. Accepts reprints (tell when/where appeared). Prefers e-mail submissions (attached file in Word). Regularly uses sidebars. Also accepts submissions from children/teens. Prefers NKJV. Guidelines on Website; copy for 9x12 SASE. (Ads)

Poetry: Accepts very few; 30-40 lines. Submit max. 20 poems.

Fillers: Most types; 200-500 wds.

Columns/Departments: Financial wisdom. Complete ms.

Contests: Occasionally sponsors a contest.

QUAKER LIFE, 101 Quaker Hill Dr., Richmond IN 47374. (765)962-7573. Fax (765)962-1293. E-mail: quakerlife@fum.org. Website: www.fum.org. Friends United Meeting. Katie Terrell, ed. For Christian Quakers, focusing on news around the world, peace and justice, simplicity, and inspiration. Bimonthly mag.; 44 pgs.; circ. 4,000. Subscription $24. 50% unsolicited freelance; 50% assigned. Query; fax/e-query OK. Accepts full ms by e-mail. **PAYS 3 COPIES** on publication for 1st rts. Articles to 1,500 wds. (40/yr.); book reviews 300 wds.; music/video reviews, 200 wds. Responds in 4 wks. Seasonal 4 mos. ahead. Accepts some reprints (tell when/where appeared). Accepts e-mail submissions (attached in Word or copied into message). No kill fee. Uses some sidebars. Prefers RSV. Also accepts submissions from children/teens. Guidelines/theme list by e-mail/Website; copy for 9x12 SAE. (Ads)

Poetry: Accepts 2/yr.

Columns/Departments: Peace Notes (peace and justice news and ideas); Inspirations (1st person personal experience); Scripture for Living (applying biblical teachings); Perspectives (opinion); each 750 wds. Query or complete ms.

Special Needs: Leadership, church growth, personal experience.

Tips: "Write on current issues or a personal spiritual experience from a Christian perspective. Be more practical than academic. For general readers who are Christian Quakers."

RADIX MAGAZINE, PO Box 4307, Berkeley CA 94704. (510)548-5329. E-mail: RadixMag@aol.com. Website: www.RadixMagazine.com. Sharon Gallagher, ed.; Luci Shaw, poetry ed. Features in-depth articles for thoughtful Christians who are interested in engaging the culture. Quarterly mag.; 32 pgs. Subscription $15. 10% unsolicited freelance; 90% assigned. E-queries only. **PAYS IN COPIES** for 1st rts. Meditations, 300-500 wds. (2/yr.); book reviews 700 wds. Responds in 6 wks. to e-mail only. Seasonal 6 mos. ahead. No simultaneous submissions or reprints. Accepted submissions by e-mail only (attached file). Uses some sidebars. Prefers NRSV. Guidelines by e-mail; copy $5. (Ads)

Poetry: Accepts 12/yr. Avant-garde, free verse, haiku, traditional; 4-30 lines. Submit max. 1 poem.

Tips: "Most open to poetry, book reviews, meditations. Familiarity with the magazine is key."

REGENT GLOBAL BUSINESS REVIEW, 1000 Regent University Dr., Virginia Beach VA 23464. (757)226-4074. E-mail: rgbr@regent.edu. Website: www.regent.edu/rgbr. Regent University—School of Global Leadership & Entrepreneurship. Julianne R. Cenac, exec. ed. (Jcenac@regent.edu). For Christian leaders and managers who take their faith seriously and who give genuine thought to how to live out that faith in the workplace and everywhere else. Bimonthly e-zine; 30 pgs.; circ. 10,000. Free online. 25% unsolicited freelance; 75% assigned. Query/clips by e-mail only. **NO PAYMENT** for electronic rts. Feature articles 1,200-2,500 wds.; case studies 2,500-4,000 wds. (not including any data appendices); Tool Kit/Executive Summaries 250-500 wds. Responds in 2 wks. Seasonal 6 mos. ahead. No simultaneous submissions; accepts reprints. Requires accepted mss by e-mail (attached file). Regularly uses sidebars. Prefers NIV. Guidelines on Website.

Columns/Departments: Tool Kit (tips and resources) 250-500 wds.; Research Translations, 1,000-1,500 wds.

Tips: "If you are interested in contributing to the exploration and advancement of global business, we are interested in hearing from you. We seek articles from contributors who are recognized experts in their field or who have requisite experience and credentials to be qualified to speak authoritatively on the subject matter."

$RELEVANT & RELEVANTMAGAZINE.COM, 1220 Alden Rd., Orlando FL 32803-2546. Toll-free (877)538-4417. (407)660-1411. Fax (407)401-9100. E-mail: corene@relevantmedia group.com. Website: www.RelevantMagazine.com. Relevant Media Group. Corene Israel, print ed. Elizabeth Sloan, online ed. Targets culture-savvy twentysomethings who are looking for purpose, depth, and spiritual truth. Bimonthly & online mag.; 100 pgs. Subscription $12. 80% freelance. Send a one-paragraph query/clips; prefers e-mail; no phone/fax query. Pays $100-400 within 45 days of publication for 1st rts. & all electronic rts. for 6 mos.; nonexclusive rts. thereafter. Features 600-1,000 wds.; reviews 400-600 wds. Prefers submissions as Word attachments. Guidelines on Website (www.relevantmagazine.com/editorial); copy $2.98.

($)RELIEF JOURNAL, 60 W. Terra Cotta, Ste. B, Unit 156, Crystal Lake IL 60014-3548. E-mail: editor@reliefjournal.com. Website: www.reliefjournal.com. Kimberly Culbertson, ed-in-chief. Open to unsolicited freelance. Use online submissions system only; no mail or e-mail submissions. Complete ms. **NO REGULAR PAYMENT; CASH PRIZES FOR BEST IN EACH GENRE.** Creative nonfiction to 8,000 wds.; fiction to 10,000 wds. Accepts simultaneous submissions. Guidelines on Website. Incomplete topical listings.

Poetry: Accepts poetry that is well-written and makes sense; to 1,000 wds. Submit max. 5 poems.

REVERENT SUBMISSIONS JOURNAL, #2835, 1420 N.W. Gilman Blvd., Ste. 2, Issaquah WA 98027. (425)255-8825. E-mail: reverentsubmissions@comcast.net. Bev Fowler, pub. A theme-based journal for Christians of all faiths, seeking to provide experience, exposure, and credibility for Christian writers while encouraging others in their daily life and spiritual walk. Quarterly newsletter; 12 pgs.; circ. 125. Subscription $12. 100% unsolicited freelance. Query; e-query OK. Accepts full mss by e-mail. **PAYS 2 COPIES** for 1st, one-time, reprint rts. Not copyrighted. Articles & fiction to 800 wds. (up to 48/yr. for ea.); book reviews to 600 wds. Responds in 12 wks. Seasonal 3 mos. ahead. Accepts simultaneous submissions and reprints (tell when/where appeared). Prefers e-mail submissions (attached file). Does not use sidebars. Also accepts submissions from children/teens. Prefers NIV. Guidelines/theme list (also by e-mail); copy for 9x12 SAE/2 stamps. (No ads)

Poetry: Accepts 12-15/yr. Free verse, haiku, light verse, traditional; up to 400 wds. Format conducive to column format.

Fillers: Buys as needed. Anecdotes, ideas, jokes, kid quotes, prayer, prose, quotes, short humor, tips; up to 100 wds.

Tips: "Christian-focused articles/fiction/poetry on the theme of each issue, with bio, contact information, and correct word count. Order upcoming theme list. Manuscripts will not be returned."

RHUBARB, 606—100 Arthur St., Winnipeg MB R3B 1H3, Canada. E-mail: submit@rhubarb mag.com. Website: www.rhubarbmag.com. Mennonite Literary Society. Submit to The Editor. Designed to provide an outlet for the (loosely defined) Mennonite voice, reflecting the changing face of the Mennonite community, promoting dialog, and encouraging the Anabaptist tradition of reformation and protest. Quarterly mag. Subscription $25 Cdn., $20 U.S. Open to unsolicited freelance. Query for nonfiction; e-query OK. **NO REFERENCE TO PAYMENT.** Articles & fiction to 2,500 wds. Guidelines/theme list on Website.

> **Poetry:** To 30 lines.

ROCK & SLING: A Journal of Literature, Art and Faith, PO Box 30865, Spokane WA 99223. Fax (509)276-7833. E-mail: editors@rockandsling.org. Website: www.rockandsling.org. Susan Cowger, Kris Christensen, Laurie Klein, eds. Ardent, edgy, vibrant explorations of faith and experience. Semiannual jour.; 140 pgs. Subscription $18. 70% unsolicited freelance; 30% assigned. Complete ms/cover letter; no phone/fax/e-query. **PAYS 2 COPIES** for 1st rts. Essays & fiction to 5,000 wds.; book reviews assigned based on clips. Responds in 6 wks. (or up to 4 mos. if held for consideration). Accepts simultaneous submissions (if indicated); no reprints. Reads year round. Any Bible version. Guidelines (also by e-mail/Website); copy $10. Incomplete topical listings.

> **Poetry:** Accepts 75/yr; to 60 lines (longer if exceptional). Avant-garde, free verse. Submit max. 5 poems. Pays 2 copies.
>
> **Photos:** Accepts color for cover; B & W for journal. See guidelines.
>
> **Tips:** "Read widely. First read R & S to understand the kind of essays, memoirs, and reviews we publish. Then read the great essayists and poets, both historical and contemporary. We look for work that explores faith's tensions as well as joys, work rich with complexity of thought and emotion. Send your best. We do not publish genre writing, didacticism, devotionals, or testimonies."

$THE ROSE & THORN: A Literary E-zine. E-mail: BAQuinn@aol.com. Website: www.therose andthornezine.com. General. B. A. Quinn, ed. Showcases short fiction, poetry, essays, and anything of a literary nature; no children's or juvenile stories. Quarterly online literary mag. Open to freelance. Complete ms. Pays $5 and will provide a link to your Website. One-time nonexclusive rts. Articles/fiction to 2,000 wds. Requires submissions by e-mail (copied into message). Guidelines on Website.

> **Poetry:** Now accepting poetry. Submit max. 3 poems; prefers shorter poems. E-mail to poetryeditor@hotmail.com. Pays $5.
>
> **Special Needs:** Fiction, vignettes, and flash fiction; creative essays, perspective, humor.
>
> **Tips:** "We have eclectic tastes, so go ahead and give us a shot."

RUMINATE, Faith in Literature and Art, 140 N. Roosevelt Ave., Fort Collins CO 80521. (970)449-2726. E-mail: editor@ruminatemagazine.com. Website: www.ruminatemagazine.com. Brianna Van Dyke, ed.; submit to submissions@ruminatemagazine.com. An intimate and hip publication of faith literature and art; publishes work with both subtle and overt associations to the Christian faith as well as work that has no direct association. Quarterly mag.; 70 pgs.; circ. 1,500. Subscription $28. Estab. 2006. 100% unsolicited freelance. Complete ms/cover letter by e-mail only. **PAYS 3 COPIES OR SUBSCRIPTION** for 1st rts. Articles to 5,000 wds. (4-8/yr.); fiction to 5,000 wds. (8-12/yr.). Responds in 16 wks. Accepts simultaneous submissions; no reprints. Requires disk or e-mail submissions (attached file). Does not use sidebars. Guidelines/theme list on Website; order a copy on Website/$9. (Ads)

> **Poetry:** Lacee Perrin, poetry ed. (poetry@ruminatemagazine.com). Accepts 50/yr. Avant-garde, free verse, traditional; to 40 lines. Submit max. 4 poems.

Contest: Annual poetry contest deadline is May 15. Annual fiction contest deadline is November 15. Entry fee: $15. Prizes: $300 1st prize; $150 to runner-up. Details on Website. **Tips:** "We are looking for writers and artists who are interested in the process of creating quality work that reveals the nature of Christ."

SACRED JOURNEY: The Journal of Fellowship in Prayer, 291 Witherspoon St., Princeton NJ 08542. (609)924-6863. Fax (609)924-6910. E-mail: submissions@sacredjourney.org. Website: www.sacredjourney.org. Fellowship in Prayer Inc. Linda Baumann, ed. (lbaumann@sacredjourney.org). Multifaith spirituality. Bimonthly jour. & e-zine; 48 pgs.; circ. 4,500. Subscription $18. 75% unsolicited freelance; 25% assigned. Complete ms/cover letter; phone/fax/e-query OK. **PAYS 5 COPIES & SUBSCRIPTION** for one-time rts. Articles 750-1,500 wds. (30/yr.); reviews 500 wds. Responds in 2 mos. Seasonal 4 mos. ahead. Accepts simultaneous submissions & reprints (tell when/where appeared). Requires requested ms on disk or by e-mail. Does not use sidebars. Guidelines (also by e-mail/Website); copy $1.70/6x9 SAE. (No ads)

> **Poetry:** Accepts 6-8/yr. Free verse, haiku, light verse, traditional; 10-35 lines. Submit max. 3 poems.
>
> **Columns/Departments:** Accepts 30/yr. A Transforming Experience (personal experience of spiritual significance); Pilgrimage (journey taken for spiritual growth or service); Spirituality and the Family; Spirituality and Aging; to 1,500 wds.
>
> **Special Needs:** Meditation and service to others.
>
> **Tips:** "Write about your own spiritual experience and we'll consider it. Most open to a transforming experience feature."

$SALVO MAGAZINE, PO Box 410788, Chicago IL 60641. (773)481-1090. Fax (773)481-1095. E-mail: editor@salvomag.com. Website: www.salvomag.com. Fellowship of St. James. Bobby Maddex, ed. Geared toward young adults, 25-45, who want to free themselves from the false world-views emanating from Hollywood, the media, and the Academy. Quarterly mag.; 96 pgs.; circ. 2,800. Subscription $25.99. Estab. 2006. 25% unsolicited freelance; 75% assigned. Query/clips; no phone/fax query, e-query OK. Accepts full mss by e-mail. Pays .20/wd. on publication for 1st rts. Articles 600-2,500 wds. (16/yr.). Responds in 4 wks. No seasonal. No simultaneous submissions or reprints. Prefers e-mail submissions (attached file). Kill fee $100. Regularly uses sidebars. No Bible references. Guidelines/theme list on Website; copy $6.99. (Ads)

> **Columns/Departments:** Buys 12/yr. Dispatches (features) 2,000 wds.; The Trenches (tales of academic bias) 1,200 wds.; Random Flak (mini-features) 1,200 wds.; .20/wd.
>
> **Tips:** "We are most open for features on science, sex, and society—anything that deconstructs false ideology and world-views, using reason and logic alone."

+SAVED MAGAZINE, PO Box 22-2302, Hollywood FL 33022-3100. Toll-free (877)34SAVED. (954)921-4700. Fax (954)921-4724. E-mail: editorial@savedmagazine.com. Website: www.savedmagazine.com. Christian. Teri Tavernier, pub. (teri@savedmagazine.com). Targets diverse Christian population by infusing area businesses, neighborhoods, and ministries across economic and ethnic lines. Bimonthly mag. Subscription $15. Open to unsolicited freelance. No mention of payment. Articles. Editorial schedule on Website. Incomplete topical listings. (Ads)

$SCIENCE & SPIRIT MAGAZINE, 1319 Eighteenth St. N.W., Washington DC 20036-1802. (202)296-6267. E-mail: ss.heldref.org. Website: www.science-spirit.org. Science & Spirit Resources Inc./Heldref Publications. Submit to Editor. Well-researched and reported articles on the intersection of science and religion in health, environment, human relationships, technology, and ethics. Bimonthly mag.; 66 pgs.; circ. 7,500. Subscription $23.95. 20% freelance. Query by e-mail. Pays .20-.75/wd. for assigned, .20-.50/wd. for unsolicited for articles on acceptance for all rts. Makes work-for-hire assignments. No reprints. Articles

1,200-2,500 wds. (40/yr.) Responds in 1 mo. Seasonal 6 mos. ahead. Guidelines on Website; copy on Website.

Columns/Departments: Interlude (social/science environmental topic), 1,200-1,600 wds.; Critical Mass (news briefs covering all areas of science—physics, gender, space, psychology, etc.); pays $200-300. See Website for samples of departments.

Tips: "Common mistakes include shallow reporting, lack of in-depth writing, lack of diversity in religious perspectives. We're looking for well-researched articles that include interviews with scientists, theologians, and everyday people. The best articles include citations for recent research and current books. Thoughtful leads, transitions, and conclusions based on the writer's research and insight are a must."

+SCP JOURNAL, PO Box 4308, Berkeley CA 94704. (510)540-0300. Fax (510)540-1107. E-mail: scp@scp-inc.org. Website: www.scp-inc.org. Spiritual counterfeits Project Inc. Tal Brooks, ed. Deals with topics from apologetics to New Age, new religions, cults, occult, and cultural trends. Quarterly jour.; circ. 15,000. Subscription $25. Open to queries only. Articles. Incomplete topical listings. (No ads)

SEEDS OF HOPE: Hope for the Healing of Hunger and Poverty, 602 James Ave., Waco TX 76706-1476. (254)755-7745. Fax (254)753-1909. E-mail: Seedseditor@clearwire.net. Website: www.seedspublishers.org. Seeds of Hope Publishers. Katie Cook, ed. Committed to the healing of hunger and poverty in our world. Quarterly worship packet; 20 pgs. of camera-ready resources. Subscription $120. Individual packet $50. Back issues less expensive. Also quarterly newsletter, *Hunger News & Hope,* published through denominational offices of national churches. E-query OK. **NO PAYMENT.**

$SEEK, 8805 Governor's Hill Dr., Ste. 400, Cincinnati OH 45249. E-mail: seek@standard pub.com. Website: www.Standardpub.com. Standard Publishing. Margaret K. Williams, ed. Light, inspirational, take-home reading for young and middle-aged adults. Weekly take-home paper; 8 pgs.; circ. 29,000. Subscriptions $14.69 (sold only in sets of 5). 75% unsolicited freelance; 25% assigned. Complete ms; no phone/fax/e-query. Pays .07/wd. on acceptance for 1st rts., .05/wd. for reprints. Articles 500-1,200 wds. (150-200/yr.); fiction 500-1,200 wds. Responds in 18 wks. Seasonal 1 yr. ahead. Accepts reprints (tell when/where appeared). Prefers submissions by e-mail (attached file). Uses some sidebars. Guidelines/theme list (also on Website); copy for 6x9 SAE/2 stamps. (No ads)

Fillers: Buys 50/yr. Ideas, short humor; $15.

Tips: "We now work with a theme list. Only articles tied to these themes will be considered for publication. Check Website for theme list and revised guidelines."

**This periodical was #11 on the 2008 Top 50 Christian Publishers list (#7 in 2007, #26 in 2006, #27 in 2005, #20 in 2004).

SEEK (BIC), 431 Grantham Rd., PO Box A, Grantham PA 17027. (717)697-2634. Fax (717) 697-7714. E-mail: biccomm@bic-church.org. Website: www.BIC-church.org/seek. Denominational/Brethren in Christ Church. Rebekah Basinger, ed. Highlights the spiritual journeys and writings of our members. Quarterly magazine. Subscription free to members. Open to unsolicited freelance. Query preferred. **NO PAYMENT.** Articles & reviews. Not in topical listings.

SENIOR CONNECTION, PO Box 38, Dundee IL 60118. (847)428-0205. E-mail: churchpb@ flash.net. Website: www.seniorconnectionnewspaper.com. Churchill Publications/Catholic. Peter Rubino, ed. For Catholics ages 50 and up with ties to the Chicago area. Monthly newspaper; circ. 190,000. Subscription $18.95. Open to unsolicited freelance. Articles. Incomplete topical listings.

SHARING: A Journal of Christian Healing, 6807 Forest Haven, San Antonio TX 78240. (210)681-5146. Fax (210)681-5146. E-mail: Marjorie.George@dwtx.org. Website: www .orderofstluke.org. Order of St. Luke the Physician. Marjorie George, ed. For Christians interested in spiritual and physical healing. Monthly (10X) jour.; 16 pgs.; circ. 9,000. Subscription $20. 100% unsolicited freelance. Complete ms/cover letter. **NO PAYMENT** for one-time or reprint rts. Articles 750-900 wds. (50/yr.). Responds in 3 wks. Seasonal 2 mos. ahead. Accepts simultaneous submissions & reprints (tell when/where appeared). Prefers ms by e-mail. Some sidebars. Prefers RSV. Guidelines; copy for 8x10 SAE/2 stamps.

Poetry: Accepts 10-12/yr. Free verse, traditional; 6-14 lines.

Tips: "We're looking for crisp, clear, well-written articles on the theology of healing and personal witness of healing. We are totally open; best to send manuscript. We do not return manuscripts or poems, nor do we reply to inquiries regarding manuscript status."

$SIGNIFICANT LIVING: Maximizing Life After 50, 2800 Vision Ct., Aurora IL 60506. (630)801-3838. Fax (630)801-3839. E-mail: pshort@TLN.com. Website: www.significant living.org. Peg Short, ed-in-chief. Dedicated to serving adults in the second half of life (boomers to seniors), empowering them to live with Christ-like vitality, and inspiring them to serve others, so that our nation may be strengthened and God may be honored. Bimonthly mag.; 40 pgs.; circ. 25,000. Subscription by membership only $19.95. Estab. 2007. 5-10% unsolicited freelance; 90-95% assigned. Query; e-query OK. Accepts full mss by e-mail. Pays .20-.30/wd. on acceptance for all rts. Articles 1,000-1,200 wds. Responds in up to 2-3 wks. Seasonal 6 mos. ahead. Accepts simultaneous submissions & reprints (tell when/where appeared). Prefers e-mail submissions (attached file). Kill fee $25. Uses some sidebars. Guidelines by e-mail/Website; free copy. (Ads)

Fillers: For boomers & seniors. Anecdotes, cartoons, facts, jokes, short humor, word puzzles.

Tips: "Most open to features—role model stories that reflect issues for boomers and seniors. Open to celebrity and athlete stories, and features that are issue-oriented to boomers and seniors. Human interest and role-model stories of middle and senior adult issues."

SILVER WINGS, PO Box 2340, Clovis CA 93613-2340. (559)347-0194. E-mail: cloviswings@ aol.com. Poetry on Wings/Evangelical. Jackson Wilcox, ed. Christian understanding and uplift through poetry. Bimonthly mag.; 16 pgs.; circ. 300. Subscription free with donation. 100% unsolicited freelance. Query or complete ms; phone query OK. **PAYS ONE COPY** for articles for 1st rts.; book reviews 200 wds. Not copyrighted. Poetry only. Responds in 3 wks. Seasonal 3-12 mos. ahead. Sometimes accepts simultaneous submissions & reprints (tell when/where appeared). No disk or e-mail submissions. Does not use sidebars. Prefers KJV. Also accepts submissions from children/teens. Guidelines; copy for 6x9 SAE/2 stamps. (No ads)

Poetry: Accepts 175/yr. Free verse, haiku, light verse, traditional; 3-20 lines. Submit max. 3 poems. No payment. "Any poetry that conforms to Christian conduct, teaching, and morality. No profanity or mention of alcoholic beverages."

Fillers: Original sayings. No payment.

Contest: Annual poetry contest on a theme (December 31 deadline); send SASE for details. Winners published in March. $325 in prizes. $3 entry fee.

Tips: "We like poems with clear Christian message, observation, or description. Poetry should be easy to read and understand. Short poems get best attention. We are open to topics and material making a point that agrees with Christian teaching. We will even consider views that vary within the Christian community."

SINGLE AGAIN.COM WEBZINE & MAGAZINE, 1237 Crescendo Dr., Roseville CA 95678-5165. (916)773-1111. Fax (916)773-2999. E-mail: editor@singleagain.com. Website: www .singleagain.com. Messenger Publishing Group. Rev. Paul Scholl, pub. Caters to people trying to put their lives back together after divorce, separation, or death of a significant other. Quarterly & online newsletter; 8-10 pgs. Subscription $12. Open to freelance. Complete ms/cover letter by mail or e-mail (preferred). **NO PAYMENT** for simultaneous rts. Articles

500 wds. and up (50-75/yr.). Responds in 6 wks. Accepts simultaneous submissions & reprints (tell when/where appeared). Accepts requested mss by e-mail (attached file in Word only). Does not use sidebars. Guidelines on Website. Incomplete topical listings. (Ads)

Poetry: Accepts 6-12/yr. Any type to 24 lines. Submit max. 6 poems.

Fillers: Accepts 15-12/yr. Anecdotes, facts, ideas, jokes, kid quotes, prayers, prose, short humor, tips.

Tips: "Write from your heart first. Don't worry about your article being perfect. We will help you with any final editing."

$SOCIAL JUSTICE REVIEW, 3835 Westminster Pl., St. Louis MO 63108-3472. (314)371-1653. Fax (314)371-0889. E-mail: centbur@sbcglobal.net. Website: www.socialjusticereview.org. Central Bureau of the Catholic Central Verein. Rev. Edward Krause, C.S.C., ed. For those interested in the social teaching of the Catholic Church. Bimonthly mag.; 32 pgs.; circ. 5,000. Subscription $20. 90% unsolicited freelance. Query or complete ms/cover letter; no phone/fax/e-query. Pays .02/wd. on publication for one-time rts. Not copyrighted. Articles 1,500-3,000 wds. (80/yr.); book reviews 500 wds. (no payment). Responds in 1 wk. Seasonal 3 mos. ahead. Accepts reprints (tell when/where appeared). Prefers submissions on disk. No kill fee. Does not use sidebars. No guidelines; copy for 9x12 SAE/3 stamps. (No ads)

Columns/Departments: Virtue; Economic Justice (Catholic views); variable length. Query or complete ms. Pays .02/wd.

Tips: "Articles and reviews open to freelancers. Fidelity to papal teaching and clarity and simplicity of style; thoughtful and thought-provoking writing."

SOCIETY FOR PREVENTION OF CRUELTY TO HUMANS (SPCH), 12900 S.E. Nixon, Portland OR 97222. (503)659-2974. E-mail: scbaldwin@preventcrueltytohumans.com. Website: www.preventcrueltytohumans.com. Stan Baldwin, pub. To encourage personal acts of decency and kindness; to challenge and change the prevailing culture of cruelty. Mostly online publication. Open to unsolicited freelance. Submit by e-mail. **NO PAYMENT; CREDIT LINE & COPIES** for nonexclusive rts. Articles of variable length. Guidelines/copy on Website. (No ads)

Columns/Departments: Divisions of the Society include: Children, Seniors, the Workplace, Schools, Politics, Religion, Public Life (including media), Health Care, and others.

Tips: "Articles will be well-researched and offer hard data related to the damaging effects of meanness and cruelty. The writer will cite credible sources such as studies that have been done, professionals who have spoken, reliable statistics that have been compiled. Put a human face on the data with compelling anecdotes and examples."

$SOUND BODY, Box 448, Jacksonville OR 97530. Phone/fax (541)899-8888. E-mail: Susan@ChristianMediaNetwork.com. Websites: www.SoundBody.tv. Christian Media. James Lloyd, ed./pub. A health newsletter with an alternative slant. Quarterly & online newsletter. Query; prefers phone query. Payment negotiable for reprint rts. Articles. Responds in 3 wks. Requires KJV. No guidelines; copy for #10 SAE/2 stamps.

SOUTHWEST KANSAS FAITH AND FAMILY, PO Box 1454, Dodge City KS 67801. (620)225-4677. Fax (620)225-4625. E-mail: info@swkfaithandfamily.org. Website: www.swkfaithandfamily.org. Independent. Stan Wilson, pub. Dedicated to sharing the Word of God and news and information that honors Christian beliefs, family traditions, and values that are the cornerstone of our nation. Monthly newspaper; circ. 5,000. Subscription $18. Accepts freelance. Prefers e-query; complete ms OK. Articles; no reviews. Guidelines on Website. Incomplete topical listings. (Ads)

$SPECIAL LIVING, PO Box 1000, Bloomington IL 61702. (309)661-9277. E-mail: gareeb@aol.com. Website: www.specialiving.com. Betty Garee, pub./ed. For and about physically disabled adults, mobility impaired individuals. Quarterly mag.; 88 pgs.; circ. 12,000. Subscription $12. 90% unsolicited freelance; 5% assigned. Query; phone/fax/e-query OK. Pays .10/wd. on publication for 1st rts. Articles 300-800 wds. (50/yr.). Responds in 3 wks. Seasonal

6 mos. ahead. Accepts simultaneous submissions & reprints (tell when/where appeared). Prefers requested ms on disk. No kill fee. Uses some sidebars. No guidelines; copy $2. (Ads) **Fillers:** Buys 20/yr. Cartoons, tips.

Tips: "Query with a specific idea. Have good photos to accompany your article. Most open to mobility impaired concerns and successes."

SPIRITUALITY FOR TODAY, PO Box 7466, Greenwich CT 06836. (203)316-9394. Fax (203) 316-9396. E-mail: Clemons10@aol.com. Website: www.spirituality.org. Clemons Productions Inc. Dorothy Riera, asst. ed. Adults' spiritual renewal with articles that challenge reflection. Monthly mag.; 13-15 pgs.; circ. 495,000. Subscription free. Open to freelance. E-query OK. **NO PAYMENT.** Articles & short stories 1,000 wds. Guidelines by e-mail. (Ads) **Fillers:** Accepts anecdotes, prayers, quotes.

Tips: "Most open to human interest pertaining to the church (2 pages); and human values. Just submit an e-mail with article attached. We always respond to our e-mails." Spanish page included.

$SPIRITUAL LIFE, 2131 Lincoln Rd. N.E., Washington DC 20002-1199. Toll-free (888)616-1713. (202)832-5505. Fax (202)832-8967. E-mail: edodonnell@aol.com. Website: www .Spiritual-Life.org. Catholic. Edward O'Donnell, O.C.D., ed. Essays on Christian spirituality with a pastoral application to everyday life. Quarterly jour.; 64 pgs.; circ. 12,000. Subscription $22. 80% unsolicited freelance. Complete ms/cover letter; phone/fax/e-query OK. Pays $50-250 ($50/pg.) on acceptance for 1st rts. Articles/essays 3,000-5,000 wds. (20/yr.); book reviews 1,500 wds. ($15). Responds in 9 wks. Seasonal 9 mos. ahead. Accepts simultaneous submissions. Requires requested ms on disk. Does not use sidebars. Prefers NAB. Guidelines; copy for 7x10 SAE/5 stamps.

Tips: "No stories of personal healing, conversion, miracles, etc."

$SPORTS SPECTRUM, 105 Corporate Blvd., Ste. 2, Indian Trail NC 28105. (704)821-2971. Fax (704)821-2669. E-mail: editor@sportsspectrum.com. Website: www.sportsspectrum.com. Sports Spectrum Publishing. Brett Honeycutt, mng. ed. Designed to feature sports people and issues as a way of introducing the gospel to non-Christian sports fans and encouraging Christian sports fans. Quarterly mag.; 72 pgs.; circ. 11,000. Subscription $27.52. 80% assigned. Query/clips; e-query OK. Pays .21/wd. on acceptance for all rts. Not copyrighted. Articles 1,200-2,000 wds. (40/yr.). Responds in 3-4 wks. Requires accepted ms by e-mail (attached file). Kill fee 30-50%. Regularly uses sidebars. Prefers NIV. Guidelines (also by e-mail/Website); no sample copy. (Ads)

Tips: "The best thing a writer can do is to be aware of the special niche *Sports Spectrum* has developed in sports ministry. Then find athletes who fit that niche and who haven't been covered in the magazine."

**2007, 2006, 2005, 2004 EPA Award of Merit—General.

$STANDARD, 2923 Troost Ave., Kansas City MO 64109. (816)931-1900. Fax (816)412-8306. E-mail: clyourdon@wordaction.com. Website: www.wordaction.com. Nazarene. Charlie Yourdon, ed. Examples of Christianity in everyday life for adults, college-age through retirement. Weekly take-home paper; 8 pgs.; circ. 150,000. 100% unsolicited freelance. Complete ms. Pays .035/wd. (.02/wd. for reprints) on acceptance for one-time rts. Articles (20/yr.) or fiction (200/yr.) 700-1,500 wds. Responds in 12 wks. Seasonal 6-9 mos. ahead. Accepts simultaneous submissions & reprints (tell when/where appeared). No disk; accepts e-mail submissions (attached). Does not use sidebars. Prefers NIV. Guidelines by e-mail; copy for #10 SAE/2 stamps. (No ads)

Poetry: Buys 30/yr. Free verse, haiku, traditional; to 30 lines; .25/line. Submit max. 5 poems.

Fillers: Buys 50/yr. Word puzzles; $20.

Tips: "Fiction or true-experience stories must demonstrate Christianity in action. Show us, don't tell us. Action in stories must conform to Wesleyan-Arminian theology and practices." Themes follow the Christian year, not celebrating national holidays.

**This periodical was #29 on the 2008 Top 50 Christian Publishers list (#24 in 2007, #27 in 2006).

$ST. ANTHONY MESSENGER, 28 W. Liberty St., Cincinnati OH 45202-6498. (513)241-5615. Fax (513)241-0399. E-mail: StAnthony@AmericanCatholic.org. Website: www.American Catholic.org. Fr. Pat McCloskey, O.F.M., ed. For Catholic adults & families. Monthly & online mag.; 64 pgs.; circ. 305,000. Subscription $28. 55% unsolicited freelance. Query/clips (complete ms for fiction); e-query OK. Pays .20/wd. on acceptance for 1st, reprint (right to reprint), and electronic rts. Articles 1,500-3,000 wds., prefers 1,500-2,500 (35-50/yr.); fiction 1,500-2,500 wds. (12/yr.); book reviews 500 wds., $50. Responds in 3-9 wks. Seasonal 6 mos. ahead. Kill fee. Uses some sidebars. Prefers NAB. Guidelines on Website; copy for 9x12 SAE/4 stamps. (Ads)

Poetry: Christopher Heffron, poetry ed. Buys 20/yr. Free verse, haiku, traditional; 3-25 lines; $2/line ($20 min.) Submit max. 2 poems.

Fillers: Cartoons.

Tips: "Many submissions suggest that the writer has not read our guidelines or sample articles. Most open to articles, fiction, profiles, interviews of Catholic personalities, personal experiences, and prayer. Writing must be professional; use Catholic terminology and vocabulary. Writing must be faithful to Catholic belief and teaching, life, and experience. Our online writers' guidelines indicate the seven categories of articles. Texts of articles reflecting each category are linked to the online writers' guidelines for nonfiction articles."

**This periodical was #25 on the 2008 Top 50 Christian Publishers list (#22 in 2007, #33 in 2006, #40 in 2005, #40 in 2004).

$STEPS: A Magazine of Hope and Healing for Christians in Recovery, PO Box 215, Brea CA 92822-0215. (714)529-6227. Fax (714)529-1120. E-mail: barbaram@christian recovery.com. Website: www.nacronline.com. National Assn. for Christian Recovery. Barbara Milligan, assoc. ed. Serves a broad audience of individuals, families, couples, ministry leaders, pastors, support-group leaders, and mental-health professionals. Quarterly mag. Subscription with $30 membership. Open to freelance. E-query only (see guidelines first on Website); no complete mss. Pays a small honorarium, plus a 1-year subscription. Articles to 1,000 wds. Uses some sidebars.

Fillers: Anecdotes, cartoons, newsbreaks, short humor; to 350 wds. All on a recovery theme.

Special Needs: The recovery church (news items from recovery churches in the U.S. and around the world); Twelve Step practice for Christians (practical, hands-on articles, as well as articles relating Twelve Step practice to Christian history and teaching); Twelve Step history and the history of drug and alcohol treatment, global perspectives (profiles of people in recovery around the world); theology of recovery (thoughtful reflections on the theological meaning of Twelve Step principles or on themes in Christian theology as they relate to Christians in recovery).

Tips: "Read back issues to get an idea of our tone and style. You'll find some articles on our Website by going to the NACR Library. If you'd like to tell someone's story of recovery (not yours), interview them and write a profile. Focus on specific ways that person's relationship with God has affected their recovery; be specific about their ongoing struggles." Accepts no poetry.

$STEWARDSHIP, PO Box 1561, New Canaan CT 06840. Toll-free (888)320-5576. (203)966-6470. Fax (203)966-4654. E-mail: guy@parishpublishing.org, or info@parishpublishing .org. Website: www.parishpublishing.org. Parish Publishing LLC. Guy Brossy, principal.

Inspires parishioners to give to their church—abilities, time, and monies. Monthly newsletter; 4 pgs.; circ. 1 million. 50% unsolicited freelance; 50% assigned. Fax/e-query with cover letter. Pays $50 on acceptance for all & reprint rts. Articles 150, 200, or 300 wds. (50/yr.) Responds in 2 wks. Seasonal 3 mos. ahead. Accepts simultaneous submissions & reprints. Accepts e-mail submissions (attached or copied into message). Regularly uses sidebars. Free guidelines/copy. (No ads)

Tips: "Write articles that zero in on stewardship—general, time, talent, or treasure—as it relates to the local church."

$THE STORYTELLER, 2441 Washington Rd., Maynard AR 72444. (870)647-2137. Fax (870)847-2454. E-mail: storyteller1@hightowercom.com. Website: www.thestoryteller magazine.com. Fossil Creek Publishing. Regina Cook Williams, ed./pub.; Ruthan Riney, review ed. Family audience. Quarterly jour.; 72 pgs.; circ. 600. Subscription $20. 100% unsolicited freelance. Complete ms/cover letter; phone/e-query OK. Pays .0025/wd. on publication for 1st rts. Articles 2,500 wds. (60/yr.); fiction 2,500 wds. (100-125/yr.). Responds in 1 wk. Seasonal 3 mos. ahead. Accepts simultaneous submissions & reprints (tell when/where appeared). Responds in 1-2 wks. No disk or e-mail submissions. Does not use sidebars. Also accepts submissions from children/teens. Guidelines (also on Website); copy $6/9x12 SAE/5 stamps. (Ads)

Poetry: Accepts 100/yr. Free verse, haiku, light verse, traditional; 3-40 lines. Submit max. 3 poems. Pays $1/poem.

Fillers: Accepts 10-20/yr. Cartoons, quotes, tips; 25-50 wds. Writing-related only.

Special Needs: Original artwork. Funny or serious stories about growing up as a pastor's child or being a pastor's wife. Also westerns and mysteries.

Contest: Offers 1 or 2 paying contests per year, along with People's Choice Awards, and Pushcart Prize nominations. Go to www.thestorytellermagazine.com, for announcements of all forthcoming contests for the year.

Tips: "All sections of the magazine are open except how-to articles. Study the craft of writing. Learn all you can before you send anything out. Pay attention to detail, make sure manuscripts are as free of mistakes as possible. Follow the guidelines—they aren't hard."

**This periodical was #42 on the 2007 Top 50 Christian Publishers list.

STUDIO: A Journal of Christians Writing, 727 Peel St., Albury NSW 2640, Australia. Phone/fax +61 2 6021 1135. E-mail: studio00@bigpond.net.au. Submit to Studio Editor. Quarterly jour.; 36 pgs.; circ. 300. Subscription $60 AUS. 90% unsolicited freelance; 10% assigned. Query. **PAYS IN COPIES** for one-time rts. Articles 3,000 wds. (15/yr.); fiction 3,000 wds. (50/yr.); book reviews 300 wds. Responds in 3 wks. Accepts simultaneous submissions & reprints (tell when/where appeared). No disks; e-mail submissions OK. Does not use sidebars. Guidelines (send IRC); copy for $10 AUS. (Ads)

Poetry: Accepts 200/yr. Any type; 4-100 lines. Submit max. 3 poems.

Contest: See copy of journal for details.

Tips: "We accept all types of fiction and literary article themes."

THE SWORD AND TRUMPET, PO Box 575, Harrisonburg VA 22803-0575. Phone/fax (540) 867-9419. E-mail: swandtrump@verizon.net. Website: www.swordandtrumpet.org. Mennonite. Paul Emerson, ed. Primarily for conservative Bible believers. Monthly mag.; 37 pgs.; circ. 3,300. Subscription $15. **NO PAYMENT.** Articles. Prefers KJV. (No ads)

SWORD OF THE LORD NEWSPAPER, PO Box 1099, Murfreesboro TN 37133-1099. Toll-free (800)247-9673. (615)893-6700. Fax (615)895-7447. E-mail: guyking@swordofthe lord.com, or through Website: www.swordofthelord.com. Independent Baptists and other fundamentalists. Dr. Shelton Smith, pres./ed.; submit to Guy King. Revival and soul-winning. Biweekly newspaper; 24 pgs.; circ. 70,000. Subscription $15. Open to freelance. Query;

phone/fax/e-query OK. **NO PAYMENT.** Articles 500-1,000 wds.; fiction for 4-7 & 8-12 yrs. and teenagers. Responds in 13 wks. Seasonal 3 mos. ahead. Accepts simultaneous submissions & reprints (tell when/where appeared). Accepts disk or e-mail submissions (attached file). No kill fee. Does not use sidebars. Requires KJV. Guidelines (also by e-mail); no copy. (Ads)

Poetry: Accepts variable number. Free verse, light verse, traditional; any length.

Fillers: Accepts variable number. Facts, newsbreaks, prose.

Columns/Departments: Accepts variable number. Kid's Korner (children's stories); Teen Talk (teen issues); both 500-700 wds.

Tips: "Most open to Bible study, soul-winning material, Christian growth, and youth character building that does not stress graphic portrayals of 'what's really going on out there.' Only works from a fundamentalist viewpoint and using the KJV are considered." Does not reprint articles from Mennonite, Lutheran, or Catholic publications.

$TESTIMONY, 2450 Milltower Ct., Mississauga ON L5N 5Z6, Canada. (905)542-7400. Fax (905)542-7313. E-mail: testimony@paoc.org. Website: www.paoc.org/testimony. The Pentecostal Assemblies of Canada. Steve Kennedy, ed. To encourage a Christian response to a wide range of issues and topics, including those that are peculiar to Pentecostals. Monthly & online mag.; 24 pgs.; circ. 14,000. Subscription $24 U.S./$19.05 Cdn. (includes GST). 10% unsolicited freelance; 90% assigned. Query; fax/e-query OK. Pays $20-75 on publication for 1st rts. (no pay for reprint rts.). Articles 700-900 wds. Responds in 6-8 wks. Seasonal 4 mos. ahead. Accepts reprints (tell when/where appeared). Prefers e-mail submission (copied into message). Regularly uses sidebars. Prefers NIV. Guidelines/theme list (also by e-mail/Website); copy $2/9x12 SAE. (Ads)

Tips: "View theme list on our Website and query us about a potential article regarding one of our themes. Our readership is 98% Canadian. We prefer Canadian writers or at least writers who understand that Canadians are not Americans in long underwear. We also give preference to members of this denomination, since this is related to issues concerning our fellowship."

$THIS I BELIEVE ESSAYS, Website: www.npr.org/thisibelieve/guide.html. National Public Radio (NPR). Write and submit your own story of personal belief; those accepted will be recorded and read on the air. Guidelines & contract included on the Website. Complete ms. submitted through Website. Pays $200, 30 days after your essay is recorded. Personal essay 350-500 wds. Details on Website.

+3V MAGAZINE, PO Box 143, McKeesport PA 15132. Toll-free (877)279-5212. E-mail: jamar@jamarsubet.com. Website: www.3VMagazine.com. National Christian Men's publication. Jamar Subert, pub. A comprehensive resource directly related to the daily spiritual walk of Christian men and offers key insight concerning today's issues. Bimonthly mag. Subscription $10. Open to unsolicited freelance. Submit up to 100-word query through Website. No mention of payment. Articles. Incomplete topical listings.

TIFERET: A Journal of Spiritual Literature, 211 Dryden Rd., Bernardsville NJ 07924-1108. (908)432-2149. E-mail: editors@tireretjournal.com. Website: www.tiferetjournal.com. Donna Baier Stein, pub./ed-in-chief. Publishes writings from authors of many faiths. Quarterly literary mag.; 176 pgs. Open to unsolicited freelance. Only accepts electronic submissions via Website. **NO PAYMENT** for 1st rts. Articles; fiction. Responds in 4 mos. Accepts simultaneous submissions & rarely reprints. Prefers e-mail submissions (attached file). Guidelines on Website.

Poetry: Renee Ashley, poetry ed. Submit max. 6 poems.

Special Needs: Accepts artwork, black & white for interior; color for cover.

TIME OF SINGING: A Magazine of Christian Poetry, PO Box 149, Conneaut Lake PA 16316. E-mail: timesing@zoominternet.net. Website: www.timeofsinging.bizland.com. Lora Zill, ed. We try to appeal to all poets and lovers of poetry. Quarterly booklet; 44 pgs.; circ. 250.

Subscription $17. 95% unsolicited freelance; 5% assigned. Complete ms; e-query OK. **PAYS IN COPIES** for 1st, one-time, or reprint rts. Poetry only (some book reviews by assignment). Responds in 12 wks. Seasonal 6 mos. ahead. Accepts simultaneous submissions & reprints (tell when/where appeared). Accepts e-mail submission (attached file). Guidelines (also by e-mail/Website); copy $4 ea. or 2/$6.

Poetry: Accepts 150-200/yr. Free verse, haiku, light verse, traditional; 3-60 lines. Submit max. 5 poems. Always need form poems (sonnets, villanelles, triolets, etc.) with Christian themes. Fresh rhyme. "Cover letter not needed; your work speaks for itself."

Contest: Sponsors 1-2 annual poetry contests on specific themes or forms ($2 entry fee/poem) with cash prizes (send SASE for rules).

Tips: "Study poetry, read widely—both Christian and non-Christian. Work at the craft. Be open to suggestions and critique. If I have taken time to comment on your work, it is close to publication. If you don't agree, submit elsewhere. I appreciate poets who take chances, who write outside the box. *Time of Singing* is a literary poetry magazine, so I'm not looking for greeting card verse or sermons that rhyme."

$TODAY'S CHRISTIAN, 465 Gundersen Dr., Carol Stream IL 60188-2498. (630)260-6200. Fax (630)480-2004. E-mail: tceditor@christianitytoday.com. Website: www.todays-christian .com. Christianity Today Intl. Mark Moring, interim ed. A Christian *Reader's Digest* that uses both reprints and original material. Bimonthly & online mag.; 64 pgs.; circ. 75,000. Subscription $17.95. 35% unsolicited freelance; 20% assigned. Complete ms/cover letter; phone/fax/e-query OK. Pays .10/wd. on acceptance for 1st, reprint & electronic rts. Articles 500-1,500 wds. (50/yr.). Responds in 6-8 wks. Seasonal 9 mos. ahead. Accepts reprints ($50-100, tell when/where appeared). Accepts e-mail submissions (copied into message). Kill fee. Sidebars, 150-300 wds. Prefers NIV. Guidelines/theme list (also by e-mail/Website); copy for 6x9 SAE/4 stamps. (Ads)

Columns/Departments: Cynthia Thomas, columns ed. Buys 150/yr. Kids of the Kingdom (kids say and do funny things); all to 250 wds.; $35.

**This periodical was #15 on the 2008 Top 50 Christian Publishers list (# 17 in 2007, #16 in 2006, #18 in 2005, #16 in 2004).

$TODAY'S PENTECOSTAL EVANGEL, 1445 N. Boonville, Springfield MO 65802-1894. (417)862-2781. Fax (417)862-0416. E-mail: tpe@ag.org. Website: www.tpe.ag.org. Assemblies of God. Hal Donaldson, ed-in-chief; Ken Horn, ed.; submit to Scott Harrup, sr. assoc. ed. Denominational; Pentecostal. Weekly & online mag.; 32 pgs.; circ. 200,000. Subscription $28.99. 5% unsolicited freelance; 95% assigned. Complete ms/cover letter; no phone/fax/e-query. Accepts full mss by e-mail. Pays .06/wd. (.04/wd. for reprints) on acceptance for 1st & electronic rts. Articles 500-1,200 wds. (10-15/yr.); testimonies 200-300 wds. Responds in 6-8 wks. Seasonal 6-8 mos. ahead. No simultaneous submissions; accepts reprints (tell when/where appeared). Kill fee 100%. Prefers e-mail submissions (attached file). Uses some sidebars. Prefers NIV, KJV. Guidelines (also by e-mail/Website); copy for 9x12 SAE/$1.34 postage. (No ads)

Fillers: Anecdotes, facts, personal experience, testimonies; 250-500 wds. Practical, how-to pieces on family life, devotions, evangelism, seasonal, current issues, Christian living; 250 wds.; pays about $25.

Tips: "True, first-person inspirational material is the best bet for a first-time contributor. We reserve any controversial subjects for writers we're familiar with. Positive family-life articles work well near Father's Day, Mother's Day, and holidays."

$TOGETHER, 1251 Virginia Ave., Harrisonburg VA 22802. Toll-free (888)833-3333. (540)433-5351. Fax (540)434-0247. E-mail: Tgether@aol.com. Website: www.churchoutreach.com. Media for Living. Melodie Davis, ed. An outreach magazine distributed by churches to attract the general public to Christian faith and life. Quarterly tabloid; 8 pgs.; circ. 50,000. Free.

90% unsolicited freelance. Complete ms/cover letter or query; e-query OK. Pays $35-60 after publication for 1st & electronic rts. Articles 500-1,200 wds. (16/yr.). Responds in 9-17 wks. Seasonal 6 mos. ahead. Accepts simultaneous submissions & reprints. Accepts requested ms on disk or by e-mail (copied into message). Uses some sidebars. Prefers NIV. Guidelines/theme list (also by e-mail/Website); copy on Website. (No ads)

Tips: "Deal with contemporary themes with fresh style. We need a variety of salvation testimonies from all racial/ethnic groups, with excellent photos available (don't submit photos until requested)." When submitting by e-mail, put title of magazine and title of your piece in subject line. Also include your e-mail address in body of message.

TO GOD BE THE GLORY! PUBLICATIONS, PO Box 171, Bangor MI 49013-0171. Website: www.TheLordSavedMe.com. M. J. Reynolds, owner/CEO. This publication is undergoing some changes. Still offers poetry contests and other literary features. Write or visit Website for current information. An SASE is required for mail inquiries.

Contest: Holds a few poetry contests throughout the year.

TOUCHED BY THE HAND OF GOD. Website: www.touchedbythehandofgod.com. Barrett Batson, ed. People share stories of how God has opened doors, hearts, or minds for them in remarkable ways and at just the right time. Website. Free online. Open to unsolicited freelance. Complete ms. Use submission form on Website. **NO PAYMENT** for one-time or reprint rts. Personal stories to 600 wds. Guidelines on Website.

TRI-STATE VOICE, PO Box 110282, Nutley NJ 07110. (973)235-0776. Fax (973)235-1688. E-mail: tristatevoice@aol.com. Website: www.tristatevoice.com. Tom Campisi, ed. To be a voice to the Christian community in Greater NYC. Monthly newspaper; circ. 22,000. Subscription $24. Open to freelance. Query preferred. Articles; no reviews. Incomplete topical listings. (Ads)

THE TRUMPETER, 7757 S.W. 86th St., Ste. C-109, Miami FL 33143. (305)274-4880. Fax (302) 370-1485. E-mail: martiele@thetrumpeter.com. Website: www.thetrumpeter.com. Swanko Communications. Martiele Swanko, ed-in-chief. Unites all South Florida Christian denominations, ethnic groups, and cultures. Bimonthly & online mag.; 80+ pgs.; circ. 20,000. Subscription $19.95. 90% unsolicited freelance. Query; fax/e-query OK. **NO PAYMENT** for one-time rts. Features & sports, 900-1,000 wds.; articles 500-1,200 wds.; book/music/video reviews, 100 wds. Responds in 4 wks. Accepts reprints (tell when/where appeared). Requires requested ms on disk or by e-mail. Regularly uses sidebars. Prefers KJV. Guidelines/theme list (also by e-mail/Website). (Ads)

Fillers: Cartoons.

Columns/Departments: Accepts 100/yr. Around Town (local talk), 100-125 wds.; Arts & Entertainment, 400 wds.; Legal, 450 wds.; Political/Viewpoint, 100-125 wds.

Tips: "Call us for a special feature assignment. Be a good writer. Know how to effectively write a paragraph by the rules and use active verbs instead of adjectives."

$THE UNITED CHURCH OBSERVER, 478 Huron St., Toronto ON M5R 2R3, Canada. (416) 960-8500. Fax (416)960-8477. E-mail through Website: www.ucobserver.org. United Church of Canada. David Wilson, ed./pub. To voice hope for individual Christians, for the United Church, for God's world. Monthly (11X) mag.; circ. 70,000. Subscription $23 Cdn.; $30 U.S. 20% freelance written; uses a limited amount of material from non-United Church freelancers. Pays variable rates for 1st rts. (sometimes all rts.). Articles to 1,200 wds. Accepts reprints (tell when/where appeared). (Ads)

$UPSCALE MAGAZINE: Exposure to the World's Finest, 600 Bronner Brothers Way S.W., Atlanta GA 30310. (404)758-7467. Fax (404)755-9892. E-mail: features@upscalemag.com (department editors listed on Website). Website: www.upscalemagazine.com. Upscale Communications Inc. Joyce E. Davis, sr. ed. To inspire, inform, and entertain African Americans. Monthly mag.; circ. 250,000. Subscription $20. 75-80% unsolicited freelance. Query;

fax/e-query OK. Pays $100 & up on publication for 1st rts. Articles (135/yr.); novel excerpts. Seasonal 6 mos. ahead. Accepts simultaneous submissions. Responds in 5-9 wks. Kill fee 25%. Guidelines on Website; copy online.

Columns/Departments: Buys 6-10/yr. News & Business (factual, current); Lifestyle (travel, home, wellness, etc.); Beauty & Fashion (tips, trends, upscale fashion, hair); Arts & Entertainment. Query. Payment varies. These columns most open to freelance.

Tips: "We are open to queries for exciting and informative nonfiction." Uses inspirational and religious articles.

URBAN KINGDOM MAGAZINE.COM. Toll-free (800)346-5589. E-mail: info@urbankingdom magazine.com. Website: www.urbankingdommagazine.com. Urban Kingdom Media Group LLC. Vashti Dominique, pub. & ed-in-chief. Characterizes the contemporary lifestyle of Christian young men and young women; a media source of realism and truth, encouragement, and entertainment. Webzine; circ. 3,000. Open to freelance. Query/2 clips by e-mail to: writers@urbankingdommagazine.com; phone/e-query OK. **NO PAYMENT.** Articles to 1,000 wds.; fiction length varies; book reviews 500 wds. Responds in 3 wks. Seasonal 3 mos. ahead. Accepts simultaneous submissions & reprints (tell when/where appeared). Requires e-mail submissions (attached file). Uses some sidebars. Also accepts submissions from teens. Guidelines/theme list by e-mail/Website; copy online. (Ads)

Poetry: Uses regularly. All types; any length.

Fillers: Uses regularly. Anecdotes, cartoons, facts, ideas, newsbreaks, party ideas, prayers, prose, quizzes, quotes, sermon illustrations, short humor, tips; 200-300 wds. or 350-500 wds.

Columns: Has a number of columns in these areas: Music, Urban Mode, Arts & Entertainment, Health, Beauty & Grooming, Community, News & Political Commentary/Current Event, Sports, Business/Finance/Technology, Lifestyle, Testimony, Book Reviews.

Special Needs: Music; style; arts & entertainment; community; business, finance & technology; health, beauty & grooming; home & living; travel. "We would like to give a more balanced focus to men's issues and interest in fashion, sports, etc."

Tips: "Writer must be a good writer and spiritually active. We appeal to a very contemporary, nontraditional Christian market. Most open to Music; Arts & Entertainment; Book Review; Fashion; Boy's Lounge."

$U.S. CATHOLIC, 205 W. Monroe St., Chicago IL 60606. (312)236-7782. Fax (312)236-8207. E-mail: editors@claretians.org. Website: www.uscatholic.org. The Claretians. Meinrad Schrer-Emunds, exec. ed. (emundsm@claretians.org); Heidi Schlumpf, mng. ed.; Rev. John Molyneau C.M.F., ed. Devoted to starting and continuing a dialog with Catholics of diverse lifestyles and opinions about the way they live their faith. Monthly & online mag.; 52 pgs.; circ. 40,000. Subscription $22. 95% unsolicited freelance. Complete ms/cover letter; phone/fax/e-query OK. Pays $250-600 (fiction $300-400) on acceptance for all rts. Articles 2,500-4,000 wds.; fiction 2,500-3,500 wds. Responds in 5 wks. Seasonal 6 mos. ahead. Accepts requested ms on disk or by e-mail. Regularly uses sidebars. Guidelines; copy for 10x13 SASE. (Ads: Tom Toussaint, 312-236-7782, ext. 854)

Poetry: Submit poetry (and fiction) to literaryeditor@uscatholic.org. All types except light verse, to 50 lines; $75.

Columns/Departments: (See guidelines first.) Sounding Board, 1,100-1,300 wds., $250; Practicing Catholic, 750 wds., $150.

Tips: "Most open to features and essays. All manuscripts (except for fiction or poetry) should have an explicit religious dimension that enables readers to see the interaction between their faith and the issue at hand. Fiction should be well written, creative, with solid character development."

**This periodical was #20 on the 2008 Top 50 Christian Publishers list (#23 in 2007, #23 in 2006, #22 in 2005).

$VIBRANT LIFE, 55 W. Oak Ridge Dr., Hagerstown MD 21740-7390. (301)393-4019. Fax (301)393-4055. E-mail: vibrantlife@rhpa.org. Website: www.vibrantlife.com. Seventh-day Adventist/Review & Herald. Charles Mills, ed. Total health publication (physical, mental, and spiritual); plus articles on family and marriage improvement; ages 30-50. Bimonthly mag.; 32 pgs.; circ. 30,000. Subscription $20. 50% unsolicited freelance; 30% assigned. Query/clips; fax/e-query OK. Pays $100-300 on acceptance for 1st, one-time, reprint, or electronic rts. Articles 450-650 wds.; feature articles to 1,000 wds. (50-60/yr.). Responds in 5 wks. Seasonal 9 mos. ahead. Accepts simultaneous submissions & reprints (tell when/where appeared). Accepts e-mail submissions (attached file). Kill fee 50%. Regularly uses sidebars. Prefers NIV. Guidelines/themes on Website; copy $1/9x12 SAE. (Ads)

Tips: "Articles need to be very helpful, practical, and well documented. Don't be preachy. Sidebars are a real plus." Not accepting submissions until end of year; see Website.

**This periodical was #26 on the 2007 Top 50 Christian Publishers list (#7 in 2005, #7 in 2004).

VICTORY HERALD, Box 190, Tipton OK 73570. Phone/fax (580)667-4178. E-mail: dsmith@ pldi.net. Website: www.victoryherald.com. To promote and encourage writers to submit works of inspirational content and purpose that will reach out and touch the hearts of readers. Donna Smith, ed. Monthly e-zine. 70% unsolicited freelance; 30% assigned. Complete ms; e-query OK. Accepts full mss by e-mail. **NO PAYMENT** for one-time rts. Articles 500-750 wds.; fiction 750-1,200 wds. Responds in 2 wks. Seasonal 2 mos. ahead. Accepts simultaneous submissions & reprints (tell when/where appeared). Prefers submissions by e-mail (attached file or copied into message). Uses some sidebars. Also accepts submissions from children/teens. Guidelines on Website; copy online. (No ads)

Poetry: Accepts 24-36/yr. Free verse, haiku, light verse, traditional; 40-45 lines max. Submit max. 3 poems.

Fillers: Accepts 24-36/yr. Anecdotes, games, kid quotes, party ideas, prayers, prose, short humor, tips; 50-150 wds.

Columns/Departments: Complete ms; no payment.

Tips: "More open to inspirational works. Goal is to encourage writers to reach out to encourage others—to inspire others."

$VICTORY IN GRACE, 60 Quentin Rd., Lake Zurich IL 60047. (847)438-4494. Fax (847)438-4232. E-mail: cameron@victoryingrace.org, or julie@victoryingrace.org. Website: www .victoryingrace.org. Teaching and print ministry of Dr. James Scudder. Cameron Edwards, mng. ed. Serves to help and inspire viewers and listeners of *Victory in Grace* with Dr. James Scudder. Monthly mag.; 38 pgs.; circ. 15,000. Subscription $20. 5% unsolicited freelance; 95% assigned/in-house. E-query only. Pays .15/wd. on publication for 1st rts. Not copyrighted. Articles 1,200-1,500 wds. (20/yr.). Responds in 4-6 wks. Seasonal 6 mos. ahead. Accepts simultaneous submissions & reprints (tell when/where appeared). Prefers e-mail submissions (attached file). Sometimes pays kill fee. Regularly uses sidebars. Prefers KJV. Guidelines (also by e-mail); copy for 6x9 SAE (sign up on Website for 3 free issues).

Special Needs: True stories of how someone's life has changed through the ministry of *Victory in Grace.*

Tips: "Most open to a strong story about how God helps His people to cope with or overcome obstacles."

$VILLAGE NOTE CARDS, 742 Elmhurst Cir., Claremont CA 91711. (909)437-0808. Fax (206) 339-3765. E-mail: cards@villagenotecards.com. Website: www.villagenotecards.com. Diane Cooley, owner. A fine-art note card publisher seeking how-to-write articles for their Website. Estab. 2007. 100% unsolicited freelance. Complete ms; e-query OK. Accepts full mss by e-mail. Pays $5-25 on publication for electronic, nonexclusive rts. Articles 500-1,500 wds.

Responds in 4-6 wks. Accepts simultaneous submissions & reprints. Wants accepted mss on disk or by e-mail (attached or copied into message). Guidelines on Website.

Special Needs: Needs all kinds of "how-to-write" articles to assist card customers who have difficulty phrasing personal sympathy notes, apologies, thank-you notes, notes of encouragement, get well, etc.—any topic for which one might send a card.

Tips: "We are open to new writers. Articles should appeal to a broad audience."

$THE VISION, 8855 Dunn Rd., Hazelwood MO 63042-2299. (314)837-7300. Fax (314)837-1803. E-mail: WAP@upci.org. Website: www.upci.org/wap. United Pentecostal Church. Richard M. Davis, ed.; submit to Karen Myers, administrative aide. Denominational. Weekly take-home paper; 4 pgs.; circ. 6,000. Subscription $1.85/quarter. 95% unsolicited freelance. Complete ms/cover letter; no e-query. Pays $8-25 on publication for 1st rts. Articles 500-1,600 wds. (to 120/yr.); fiction 1,200-1,600 wds. (to 120/yr.); devotionals 350-400 wds. Seasonal 9 months ahead. Accepts simultaneous submissions & reprints. Guidelines (also by e-mail/Website); free copy/#10 SASE. (No ads)

Poetry: Buys 30/yr.; $3-12.

Tips: "Most open to fiction short stories, real-life experiences, and short poems. Whether fiction or nonfiction, we are looking for stories depicting everyday life situations and how Christian principles are used to solve problems, resolve issues, or enhance one's spiritual growth. Be sure manuscript has a pertinent, spiritual application. Best way to break into our publication is to send a well-written article that meets our specifications."

$VISTA, PO Box 50434, Indianapolis IN 46250-0434. (317)774-7900. E-mail: submissions@wesleyan.org, or wphsubmissions@yahoo.com. Website: www.wesleyan.org/wph. Wesleyan Publishing House. Jim Watkins, ed. Weekly take-home paper; 8 pgs. 62% unsolicited freelance; 38% assigned. Complete ms; e-query OK. Accepts full mss by e-mail. Pays $25-35 on publication for one-time and reprint rts. Articles 500-550 wds.; fiction 500-550 wds.; humor 250 wds. Seasonal 9 mos. ahead. No simultaneous submissions or reprints. Prefers e-mail submission (attached). No kill fee. Regularly uses sidebars. Also accepts submissions from children/teens. Prefers NIV. Guidelines (also by e-mail); copy $2.50. (No ads)

Poetry: Buys many/yr. Avant-garde, free verse, haiku, light verse, traditional. Pays $10-20. Submit max. 5 poems.

Fillers: Buys many/yr. Anecdotes, cartoons, facts, games, ideas, jokes, newsbreaks, prayers, prose, quotes, short humor, tips, and word puzzles, 60-175 wds.

Special Needs: Book excerpts from WPH products.

Tips: "Great market for beginning writers. Any subject related to Christian growth."

$WAR CRY, 615 Slaters Ln., Alexandria VA 22314. (703)684-5500. Fax (703)684-5539. E-mail: War_cry@USN.salvationarmy.org. Website: www.salvationarmypublications.org. The Salvation Army. Maj. Ed Forster, ed-in-chief; Jeff McDonald, mng. ed. Pluralistic readership reaching all socioeconomic strata and including distribution in institutions. Biweekly mag.; 24 pgs.; circ. 250,000. Subscription $10. 5% unsolicited freelance. Complete ms/brief cover letter; no phone/fax query; e-query OK. Accepts full mss by e-mail. Pays .15/wd. on acceptance for 1st, one-time, reprint rts. Articles 500-1,000 wds. (10/yr.); no fiction or poetry. Responds in 4-6 wks. Seasonal 1 yr. ahead. Accepts simultaneous submissions and reprints (tell when/where appeared). Prefers accepted ms by e-mail (attached or copied into message). No kill fee. Uses some sidebars. Prefers NIV. Guidelines (also by e-mail); copy for 9x12 SASE. (No ads)

Fillers: Buys 10/yr. Anecdotes (inspirational), 200-500 wds.; .15/wd.

**This periodical was #40 on the 2008 Top 50 Christian Publishers list (#17 in 2006, #33 in 2005, #21 in 2004).

$THE WAY OF ST. FRANCIS, 1112 26th St., Sacramento CA 95816-5610. (916)443-5717. Fax (916)443-2019. E-mail: ofmcaway@att.net. Website: www.sbfranciscans.org. Franciscan

Friars of California/Catholic. Sharon E. Melberg, mng. ed. For those interested in the message of St. Francis of Assisi as lived out by contemporary people. Bimonthly mag.; 49 pgs.; circ. 5,000. Subscription $15; $17 foreign. 60% unsolicited freelance; 40% assigned. Complete ms/cover letter; phone/fax/e-query OK. Accepts full mss by e-mail. Pays $50 (or up to 10 copies & 2 subscriptions) on publication for 1st rts. Articles 900-1,800 wds. (25/yr.); fiction 500-2,000 wds. (12/yr.); reviews 250 wds. Responds in 2 wks. Seasonal 6 mos. ahead. No simultaneous submissions; reprints accepted (tell when/where appeared). Prefers requested ms on disk or by e-mail (attached file). No kill fee. Uses some sidebars. Prefers NAB. Also accepts submissions from children/teens. Guidelines/theme list (also by e-mail/Website); copy for 6x9 SAE/$2.53 postage (mark "Media Mail"). (No ads)

Poetry: Accepts 4-6 poems/yr.; any type; 4-50 lines; pays $50.

Tips: "Write a piece that explores an aspect of Franciscan spirituality that is fresh and provocative. All fiction must have a Franciscan tie-in."

$WEAVINGS, 1908 Grand Ave., PO Box 340004, Nashville TN 37203-0004. (615)340-7200. E-mail: weavings@upperroom.org. Website: www.upperroom.org. The UpperRoom. Submit to The Editor. For clergy, lay leaders, and all thoughtful seekers who want to deepen their understanding of, and response to, how God's life and human lives are being woven together. Bimonthly mag. Subscription $28. Open to freelance. Complete ms. Pays .12/wd. & up on acceptance. Articles 1,250-2,500 wds.; sermons & meditations 500-2,500 wds.; stories (short vignettes or longer narratives) to 2,500 wds.; book reviews 750 wds. Responds within 13 wks. Accepts reprints. Accepts requested ms on disk or by e-mail. Guidelines/theme list on Website; copy for 7.5 x 10.5 SAE/5 stamps. Incomplete topical listings.

Poetry: Pays $75 & up.

Tips: "All contributions should reflect simplicity, authenticity, and inclusiveness."

$WESLEYAN LIFE, Box 50434, Indianapolis IN 46250-0434. (317)774-7909. Fax (317)774-7913. E-mail: communications@wesleyan.org. Website: www.wesleyan.org. The Wesleyan Church Corp. Dr. Norman G. Wilson, gen. ed.; Jerry Brecheisen, mng. ed. Denominational. Quarterly mag.; 40 pgs.; circ. 50,000. Subscription controlled. 10% freelance. E-mail submissions only. Pays $50-80 for unsolicited on publication for 1st or simultaneous rts. Articles 400-500 wds. (50/yr.). Responds in 2 wks. Seasonal 6 mos. ahead. Accepts simultaneous submissions & reprints (tell when/where appeared). Guidelines (also by e-mail/Website); copy $2. (Ads—limited)

Tips: "Most open to 400-500 word articles. Must be submitted electronically. No poetry."

WEST WIND REVIEW, 1250 Siskiyou Blvd., Ashland OR 97520. (541)552-6518 or (541)552-6641. E-mail: cwright@sou.edu, or WestWind@sou.edu. Website: www.sou.edu/English/westwind. Southern Oregon University. Student editor changes each year; Craig Wright, advisor. Strives to bring well-written, insightful stories and poems to the public. Annual anthology; 100-200 pgs.; circ. 250-500. 100% unsolicited freelance. Complete ms/cover letter & bio; no phone/e-query. **PAYS 1 COPY OF ANTHOLOGY** for 1st rts. Not copyrighted. Fiction (8-15/yr.). Accepts mss from May 15 through December 1. Responds in 5-10 wks. No simultaneous submissions or reprints. Does not use sidebars. No e-mail submissions. Guidelines on Website; copy $3. (No ads)

Poetry: Any type; any length. Submit max. 5 poems. Pays one copy of the anthology.

Special Needs: Poetry or short stories that reflect moving, human interest—in a tasteful manner. Fiction should be thoughtful, literary, and contemporary.

Tips: "We accept all submissions for consideration, and observe no borders in order to encourage original creativity. We accept all forms of poetry, prose, short story, and black & white photos. No erotica, sci-fi/fantasy, or racial bias."

$THE WILDWOOD READER, PO Box 55-0898, Jacksonville FL 32255. (904)705-6806. Website: www.wildwoodreader.com. Timson Edwards Co. Alex Gonzalez, pub. Focus is on adult, literary short fiction that is uplifting and motivational for living life in wellness and spirit. Biweekly jour.; 16 pgs.; circ. 100. Subscription $12. Estab. 2006. 100% unsolicited freelance. Query in writing. Pays $10-75, 60 days after publication for one-time rts. Fiction 800-2,400 wds. (18/yr.). Responds in 6 wks. Seasonal 4 mos. ahead. Accepts simultaneous submissions & reprints (tell when/where appeared). Requires CD by mail. Guidelines; no copy. (Ads)

   Contest: Sponsors regular contests with winners being published. Readers pick the best of the year for an annual.

   Tips: "Most open to good, solid, ready-to-print short stories that follow the indications above. I prefer new and emerging writers; we are not a high end publication yet, but working our way there. Your work must be edited and ready to publish."

WISCONSIN CHRISTIAN NEWS, PO Box 756, 1007 W. Arlington St., Marshfield WI 54449. (715)486-8066. E-mail: christiannews@charter.net. Website: www.wisconsinchristian news.com. Rob E. Pue, ed. Regional Christian newspaper for all of Wisconsin; nondenominational/evangelical. Monthly newspaper; 48 pgs.; circ. 10,000. Subscription $25. Open to freelance. **NO PAYMENT.** Articles 500-1,500 wds. Responds in 1 wk. Seasonal 2 mos. ahead. Accepts e-mail submissions (copied into message). Uses some sidebars. Also accepts submissions from children/teens. No guidelines; copy $2. (Ads)

$THE WITTENBURG DOOR, 5620 Columbia Ave., Dallas TX 75214, or PO Box 1444, Waco TX 76703-1444. (214)827-2625. Fax (254)827-7938. E-mail (submissions): dooreditor@ earthlink.net. Website: www.wittenburgdoor.com. Trinity Foundation. Robert Darden, sr. ed.; submit to John Bloom (webeditor@wittenburgdoor.com). Satire of evangelical church, plus issue-oriented interviews. Bimonthly mag.; 50 pgs.; circ. 7,500. Subscription $29.95. 90% unsolicited freelance; 10% assigned. Complete ms; e-query OK. Pays $50-250 on publication for 1st rts. Articles to 750 wds., prefers 500-750 wds. (45-50/yr.). Responds in 13 wks. Accepts simultaneous submissions & reprints (if from noncompeting markets; tell when/where appeared). Guidelines (also by e-mail); copy $5.95. (Ads)

   Tips: "We look for biting satire/humor—*National Lampoon* not *Reader's Digest.* Write something funny and insightful about the state of the modern church. Read more than one issue to understand our 'wavelength.' We see religious humor and satire as a redemptive tool, not a weapon. We desperately need genuinely funny articles with a smart, satiric bent. Write funny stuff about religion. Interview interesting people with something to say about faith and/or religion."

WORD & WAY, 3236 Emerald Ln., Ste. 400, Jefferson City MO 65109-3700. (573)635-5939, ext. 206. Fax (573)635-1774. E-mail: wordandway@wordandway.org. Website: www.wordand way.org. Baptist. Bill Webb, ed. (bwebb@wordandway.org/ext. 206). Biweekly. Subscription $16. To glorify God.

$THE WORLD & I ONLINE: The Magazine for Lifelong Learners, 3600 New York Ave. N.E., Washington DC 20002-1947. (202)635-4054. Fax (202)832-5780. E-mail: editors@ worldandi.com. Website: www.worldandi.com. Washington Times Corp. Charles Kim, pub. Scholarly and encyclopedic. Monthly & online journal.; 350 pgs.; print circ. 30,000. Subscription rates on Website. 5-8% unsolicited freelance; 85% assigned. Query/clips; e-query OK. Pays $400-800 on publication for all rts. Articles 1,000-5,000 wds. (1,200/yr.); book reviews 2,000-2,500 wds. ($400-500). Responds in 6-10 wks. Seasonal 5 mos. ahead. Accepts reprints (tell when/where appeared). Prefers requested ms on disk. Kill fee 20%. Uses some sidebars. Guidelines on Website; copy $5/9x12 SAE/$2.23 postage (mark "Media Mail"). (Ads)

   Poetry: Buys 4-6/yr. Haiku (Asian translation); $30-75. Submit max. 5 poems.

   Columns/Departments: Buys 60/yr., plus 12 photo essays. Seven different columns, various lengths. See sample copy.

Tips: "Life and Culture areas most open to freelancers. Offer a great/original idea (with established background as a writer), and writing samples. We especially appreciate scholarly contributions."
****This periodical was #34 on the 2008 Top 50 Christian Publishers list (#32 in 2007, #41 in 2006, #49 in 2004).

+WORSHIPPING WARRIORS, PO Box 20634, Indianapolis IN 46220. Website: www .worshippingwarriorsmagazine.org. PJ Productions LLC. Christian. Paula Jeaneen, pub. For everyday people experiencing God and living a lifestyle of worship everyday. Magazine. Incomplete topical listings. (Ads)
Tips: "I have a passion to reclaim the ministry of the arts in the Body of Christ."

$+WRITTEN, PO Box 250504, Atlanta GA 30325. (404)753-8315. E-mail: editor@written mag.com. Website: www.writtenmag.com. Zipporah Publications LLC. Michelle Gipson, pub. Celebrates the word and the reader; nationally syndicated insert to African American newspapers across the country. Bimonthly tabloid; 12-16 pgs; circ. 130,000. Subscription $8. Estab. 2006. 20% unsolicited freelance; 80% assigned. Query/clips; e-query OK. Pays $10-75 or .10/wd. on publication for one-time rts. Articles 500-750 wds. (6-8/yr.); reviews 250 wds. ($75). Responds in 3 wks. Seasonal 3 mos. ahead. Accepts simultaneous submissions; no reprints. Requires e-mail submissions (attached file in Word). No kill fee. Regularly uses sidebars. Also accepts submissions from teens. Guidelines (also on Website); copy for 9x12 SAE/$1 postage. (Ads—media kit available on Website)
Fillers: Accepts 1-3/yr. Facts, quotes, tips.
Contest: Next New Writer Contest.
Tips: "Our column for freelancers is 'First Person Singular.' We look for heartfelt stories from writers who have something to share with readers. We look for moving stories that 'bleed on the page.'"

XAVIER REVIEW, 1 Drexel Dr., Box 110C, New Orleans LA 70125. (504)520-7549 or (504) 520-7303. Fax (504)520-7944. Website: www.xula.edu. Xavier University of Louisiana. Nicole Pepinster Greene, ed. Publishes nondogmatic, thought-provoking, and sometimes humorous and even irreverent work on religious subject matters. Semiannual literary jour; 75 pgs.; circ. 300. Subscription $10 (individuals), $15(institutions). 90% unsolicited freelance; 10% assigned. Complete ms/cover letter; e-query OK. **PAYS IN COPIES** for 1st rts. Articles 250-5,000 wds. (3/yr.); fiction 250-5,000 wds. (6/yr.); book reviews 250-750 wds. Responds in 4 wks. Accepts simultaneous submissions; no reprints. Prefers accepted mss by e-mail (attached). No kill fee. Does not use sidebars. Guidelines on Website; copy for $2/7x10 SAE/3 stamps. (No ads)
Poetry: Accepts 20/yr. Avant-garde, free verse, traditional; 5-60 lines. Submit max. 5 poems.

CHILDREN'S MARKETS

$ADVENTURES, 2923 Troost Ave., Kansas City MO 64109-1538. (816)931-1900. Fax (816) 412-8306. E-mail: jns@wordaction.com, or through Website: www.wordaction.com. Julie Smith, ed. For 6- to 8-yr.-olds (1st & 2nd graders); emphasis on principles, character building. Weekly take-home paper; 4 pgs.; circ. 40,000. Subscription $11.96 ($2.99/ child/quarter). 25% unsolicited freelance. Query; e-query OK. Pays $15 on acceptance for multiple-use rts. Articles 200 wds. Responds in 4-6 wks. Accepts simultaneous submissions; no reprints. Accepts requested ms by e-mail (attached file). Prefers NIV. Guidelines/theme list (by e-mail); copy for #10 SAE/1 stamp. (No ads)
Special Needs: Recipes and crafts; activities.
Tips: "Looking for creative activities that 1st and 2nd graders can do on their own at home; crafts, recipes, simple science projects that can be connected to the theme."

$AMERICAN GIRL, PO Box 620497, Middleton WI 53562-0497. Toll-free (800)360-1861. (608)836-4848. Fax (608)831-7089. E-mail: im_agmag_editor@pleasantco.com. Website: www.americangirl.com. Pleasant Company Publications. Kristi Thom, ed.; Barbara E. Stretchberry, mng. ed. General market; for girls ages 8-12 to recognize and celebrate girls' achievements yesterday and today, inspire their creativity, and nurture their hopes and dreams. Bimonthly & online mag.; 50 pgs.; circ. 700,000. Subscription $22.95. 5% unsolicited freelance; 10% assigned. Query (complete ms for fiction); no e-query. Pays $1/wd. ($300 minimum) on acceptance for 1st or all rts. Articles 150-1,000 wds. (10/yr.); fiction to 2,300 wds. (6/yr.; $500 min.). Responds in 13 wks. Seasonal 6 mos. ahead. Accepts simultaneous submissions & reprints. Kill fee 50%. Uses some sidebars. Guidelines on Website; copy $3.95 (check)/9x12 SAE/$2.23 postage (mark "Media Mail"). (No ads)

Poetry: All poetry is by children.

Fillers: Cartoons, puzzles, word games; $50.

Columns/Departments: Buys 10/yr. Girls Express (short profiles on girls), to 150 wds. (query); Giggle Gang (visual puzzles, mazes, word games, math puzzles, seasonal games/puzzles), send complete ms. Pays $50-200.

Contest: Contests vary from issue to issue.

Tips: "Girls Express offers the most opportunities for freelancers. We're looking for short profiles of girls who are doing great and interesting things. Key: a girl must be the 'star' and the story written from her point of view. Be sure to include the ages of the girls you are pitching to us. Write for 8- to 12-year-olds—not teenagers."

$+ARCHAEOLOGY, 2660 Petersborough St., Oak Hill VA 20171. E-mail: youngchristian magazine@yahoo.com. Shannon Bridget Murphy, ed./pub. Biblical archaeology for children and teens. Quarterly mag./e-zine. New. Open to unsolicited freelance. Complete ms/cover letter; e-query OK. Pays .02-.05/wd. on acceptance for 1st, one-time rts. Articles 500-2,000 wds.; fiction 500-2,000 wds. Responds in 2-4 wks. Seasonal 6-8 mos. ahead. Accepts simultaneous submissions & reprints (tell when/where appeared). No kill fee. Regularly uses sidebars. Also accepts submissions from children/teens. Prefers KJV. Guidelines by e-mail.

Poetry: Open to any type of poetry from children and teens.

Fillers: Anecdotes, cartoons, facts, games, ideas, kid quotes, newsbreaks, party ideas, prayers, prose, quizzes, quotes, sermon illustrations, short humor, tips, and word puzzles.

$BEGINNER'S FRIEND, PO Box 4060, Overland Park KS 66204. (913)432-0331. Fax (913) 722-0351. E-mail: sseditor1@juno.com. Website: www.heraldandbanner.com. Church of God (Holiness)/Herald and Banner Press. Arlene McGehee, Sunday school ed. Denominational; for young children. Weekly take-home paper; 4 pgs.; circ. 2,700. Subscription $1.50. Complete ms/cover letter; phone/fax/e-query OK (prefers mail or e-mail). Pays .005/wd. on publication for 1st rts. Fiction 500-800 wds. Seasonal 6-8 mos. ahead. Accepts simultaneous submissions & reprints (tell when/where appeared). Prefers KJV. Guidelines/theme list; copy. Not in topical listings.

$BREAD FOR GOD'S CHILDREN, Box 1017, Arcadia FL 34265-1017. (863)494-6214. Fax (863)993-0154. E-mail: Bread@breadministries.org. Website: www.breadministries.org. Bread Ministries Inc. Judith M. Gibbs, ed. A family magazine for serious Christians who are concerned about their children or grandchildren. Bimonthly mag.; 32 pgs.; circ. 5,000. Subscription free. 20-25% unsolicited freelance. Complete ms; no e-query. Pays $10-25 ($30-50 for fiction) on publication for 1st rts. Not copyrighted. Articles 500-800 wds. (6/yr.); fiction & true stories 500-1,200 wds. for 4-10 yrs., 900-1,500 wds. for teens 14 and up (6/yr.). Responds in 8-12 wks. (may hold longer). Uses some simultaneous submissions & reprints (tell when/where appeared). Some sidebars. Prefers KJV. Guidelines (also by e-mail); 3 magazine copies for 9x12 SAE/5 stamps; 1 copy 3 stamps. (No ads)

Columns/Departments: Buys 5-8/yr. Let's Chat (discussion issues facing children),

500-800 wds.; Teen Page (teen issues), 600-900 wds.; and Idea Page (object lessons or crafts for children), 300-800 wds.; $10-30.

Tips: "Our child and youth fiction can always use a well-written piece about living out godly principles. We need good stories for the younger children—ages 4-10 years. Most open to fiction or real-life stories of overcoming through faith in Jesus Christ. No tag endings or adult solutions coming from children. Create realistic characters and situations. No 'sudden inspiration' solutions. Open to any areas of family life related from a godly perspective."

$CADET QUEST, PO Box 7259, Grand Rapids MI 49510. (616)241-5616. Fax (616)241-5558. E-mail: submissions@CalvinistCadets.org. Website: www.CalvinistCadets.org. Calvinist Cadet Corps. G. Richard Broene, ed. To show boys ages 9-14 how God is at work in their lives and in the world around them. Mag. published 7X/yr.; 24 pgs.; circ. 8,000. 35% unsolicited freelance. Complete ms/cover letter. Pays .04-.06/wd. on acceptance for 1st, one-time, or reprint rts. Articles 800-1,500 wds. (7/yr.); fiction 1,000-1,300 wds. (14/yr.). Responds in 4-6 wks. Accepts simultaneous submissions & reprints (tell when/where appeared). Accepts ms by e-mail (copied into message). Uses some sidebars. Prefers NIV. Guidelines, theme list (also on Website); copy for 9x12 SAE/3 stamps. (Ads—limited)

Fillers: Buys several/yr. Quizzes, tips, puzzles; 20-200 wds.; $5 & up.

Tips: "Most open to fiction or fillers tied to themes; request new theme list in January of each year (best to submit between February and May each year). Also looking for simple projects/crafts, and puzzles (word, logic)."

$CELEBRATE, 2923 Troost Ave., Kansas City MO 64109. (816)931-1900. Fax (816)412-8312. E-mail through Website: www.wordaction.com. Word-Action Publishing Co./Church of the Nazarene. Abigail Takala, ed. Weekly activity/story paper connects Sunday school learning to life for preschoolers (3 & 4), kindergartners (5 & 6), and their families. Weekly take-home paper; 4 pgs.; circ. 40,000. Subscription $10. 50% unsolicited freelance. Query or complete ms/cover letter; e-query OK. Pays $15 or .25/line on acceptance for multiple-use rts. Articles 200 wds. Responds in 4-6 wks. No seasonal. Accepts simultaneous submissions; no reprints. Accepts e-mail submissions (attached file). Prefers NIV. Guidelines by e-mail; theme list/copy for #10 SAE/1 stamp. (No ads)

Special Needs: Activities, recipes, poems, piggyback songs, and crafts for 3- to 6-year-olds.

Tips: "Activities should be something a preschooler or kindergartener can do mostly on their own at home. Supplies should be things commonly found around the house or easily obtained at craft stores."

$FACES, 30 Grove St., Ste. C, Peterborough NH 03458. Toll-free (800)821-0115. (603)924-7209. Fax (603)924-7380. E-mail: facesmag@yahoo.com. Website: www.cobblestone pub.com. Cobblestone Publishing/general. Elizabeth Crooker, ed. Introduces young readers (ages 9-14) to different world cultures, religion, geography, government, and art. Monthly mag.; 52 pgs.; circ. 15,000. Subscription $29.95. 90-100% freelance. Query only; e-query OK. Pays .20-.25/wd. on publication for all rts. Articles 300-800 wds. (45-50/yr.); fiction to 800 wds. (retold folktales, legends, plays; related to theme). Responds in 4 wks. to 4 mos. Accepts simultaneous submissions. Prefers disk or hard copy. Kill fee 50%. Guidelines/themes (also on Website); copy $4.95/9x12 SAE/$2.02 postage; also online.

Poetry: Any type to 100 wds.

Fillers: Activities, 100-600 wds.; .20-.25/wd.

$+FAITH DETECTIVES, 1300 N. Meacham Rd., Schaumburg IL 60173-4888. (847)843-1600. Fax (847)843-3757. E-mail: takehomepapers@garbc.org. Website: www.RegularBaptist Press.org. General Assn. of Regular Baptist Churches/Regular Baptist Press. Joan E. Alexander, ed. New Publication for juniors (grades 5 & 6). Guidelines still under development.

$FOCUS ON THE FAMILY CLUBHOUSE, 8605 Explorer Dr., Colorado Springs CO 80920. (719)531-3400. Website: www.clubhousemagazine.com. Focus on the Family. Jesse Florea, ed.; Joanna Lutz, asst. ed.; submit to Jamie Dangers, ed. asst. For children 8-12 years who desire to know more about God and the Bible. Monthly & online mag.; 24 pgs.; circ. 90,000. Subscription $18. 15% unsolicited freelance; 25% assigned. Complete ms/cover letter; no phone/fax/e-query. Pays .15-.25/wd. for articles, up to $300 for fiction on acceptance for nonexclusive license. Articles to 800 wds. (5/yr.); fiction 500-1,800 wds. (30/yr.). Responds in 8 wks. Seasonal 6 mos. ahead. Accepts simultaneous submissions; no reprints. No disk or e-mail submissions. Kill fee. Uses some sidebars. Prefers NIV. Also accepts submissions from children once a year. Guidelines; copy (call 1-800-232-6459). (No ads)

Fillers: Buys 6-8/yr. Quizzes, word puzzles, recipes; 200-800 wds.; .15-.25/wd.

Tips: "Most open to fiction, personality stories, quizzes, and how-to pieces with a theme. Avoid stories dealing with boy-girl relationships, poetry, and contemporary, middle-class family settings (current authors meet this need). We look for fiction in exciting settings with ethnic characters. Creatively retold Bible stories and historical fiction are easy ways to break in. Send manuscripts with list of credentials. Read past issues."

**2008, 2007, 2006, 2005, 2004 EPA Award of Merit—Youth.

$FOCUS ON THE FAMILY CLUBHOUSE JR., 8605 Explorer Dr., Colorado Springs CO 80920. (719)531-3400. Fax (719)531-3499. E-mail: joanna.lutz@fotf.org. Website: www.club housemagazine.com. Focus on the Family. Suzanne Hadley, ed.; Joanna Lutz, asst. ed.; submit to Jamie Dangers, ed. asst. For 4- to 8-year-olds growing up in a Christian family. Monthly & online mag.; 24 pgs.; circ. 65,000. Subscription $18. 25% unsolicited freelance; 50% assigned. Complete ms/cover letter; no phone/fax/e-query. Pays $25-200 ($50-100 for fiction) on acceptance for nonexclusive rts. Articles 100-500 wds. (1-2/yr.); fiction 250-1,000 wds. (10/yr.); Bible stories 250-800 wds.; one-page rebus stories to 200 wds. Responds in 8 wks. Seasonal 6-9 mos. ahead. Kill fee 25%. Uses some sidebars. Guidelines; copy (call 1-800-232-6459). (No ads)

Poetry: Buys 4-8/yr. Traditional; 10-25 lines (to 250 wds.); $50-100.

Fillers: Buys 4-8/yr. Recipes/crafts; 100-500 wds.; $50-100.

Special Needs: Bible stories, rebus, fiction, and crafts.

Tips: "Most open to short, nonpreachy fiction, beginning reader stories, and read-to-me. Be knowledgeable of our style and try it out on kids first. Looking for stories set in exotic places; nonwhite, middle-class characters; historical pieces; humorous quizzes; and craft and recipe features are most readily accepted."

**2007 EPA Award of Merit—Youth; 2004 EPA Award of Excellence—Youth.

GIRLS CONNECTION, 1445 N. Boonville Ave., Springfield MO 65802-1894. Website: http://mgc .ag.org/connection. Missionettes Girls Clubs/Assemblies of God. A program for winning girls to Jesus Christ through love and acceptance. Webzine.

$+GOD'S EXPLORERS, 1300 N. Meacham Rd., Schaumburg IL 60173-4888. (847)843-1600. Fax (847)843-3757. E-mail: takehomepapers@garbc.org. Website: www.RegularBaptist Press.org. General Assn. of Regular Baptist Churches/Regular Baptist Press. Joan E. Alexander, ed. New Publication for primaries (grades 1 & 2). Guidelines still under development.

$GOOD NEWS, 2621 Dryden Rd., Moraine OH 45439. (937)293-1415. Fax (937)293-1310. E-mail: service@pflaum.com. Website: www.pflaum.com. Catholic. Joan Mitchell CSJ, ed. For children in grades 2 and 3. Weekly (32X) take-home paper. Not in topical listings.

$GUIDE, 55 W. Oak Ridge Dr., Hagerstown MD 21740. (301)393-4037. Fax (301)393-4055. E-mail: Guide@rhpa.org. Website: www.guidemagazine.org. Seventh-day Adventist/Review and Herald Publishing. Randy Fishell, ed.; Rachel Whitaker, assoc. ed. A Christian journal for 10- to 14-yr.-olds, presenting true stories relevant to their needs. Weekly mag.; 32 pgs.; circ. 27,000. Subscription $49.95/yr. 90% unsolicited freelance; 10% assigned. Complete ms/cover letter; fax/e-query OK. Pays .06-.12/wd. ($25-140) on acceptance for 1st rts., reprint rts. True stories 750-1,500 wds. (300/yr.). Responds in 5 wks. Seasonal 8 mos.

ahead. Accepts reprints (tell when/where appeared; pays 50% of standard rate). Prefers requested ms by e-mail (attached file). Uses some sidebars. Prefers NIV. Guidelines on Website; copy for 6x9 SAE/2 stamps. (No ads)

Fillers: Buys 50/yr. Games, quizzes, word puzzles on a spiritual theme; 20-50 wds.; $25-40. Accepting very few games, only the most unusual concepts.

Special Needs: "Most open to true action/adventure, Christian humor, and true stories showing God at work in a 10- to 14-year-old's life. Stories must have energy and a high level of intrinsic interest to kids. Put it together with dialog and a spiritual slant, and you're on the 'write' track for our readers. School life."

Tips: "We use only true stories, including school situations, humorous circumstances, adventure, short historical and biographical stories, and almost any situation relevant to 10- to 14-year-olds. Stories must have a spiritual point or implication. We publish multipart true stories regularly; 3-12 chapters, 1,200 words each."

**This periodical was #24 on the 2008 Top 50 Christian Publishers list (#27 in 2007, #44 in 2006, #25 in 2005, #34 in 2004).

$JUNIOR COMPANION, PO Box 4060, Overland Park KS 66204. (913)432-0331. Fax (913) 722-0351. E-mail: sseditor1@juno.com. Website: www.heraldandbanner.com. Church of God (holiness)/Herald and Banner Press. Arlene McGehee, Sunday school ed. Denominational; for 4th-6th graders. Weekly take-home paper; 4 pgs.; circ. 3,500. Subscription $1.50. Complete ms/cover letter; phone/fax/e-query OK (prefers mail or e-mail). Pays .005/wd. on publication for 1st rts. Fiction 500-1,200 wds. Seasonal 6-8 mos. ahead. Accepts simultaneous submissions & reprints (tell when/where appeared). Prefers KJV. Guidelines/theme list; copy. Not in topical listings.

$JUNIORWAY, PO Box 436987, Chicago IL 60643. Website: www.urbanministries.com. Urban Ministries Inc. K. Steward, ed. (ksteward@urbanministries.com). Sunday school magazine with accompanying teacher's guide and activity booklet for 4th to 6th graders. Open to freelance queries; 100% assigned. Query and/or e-query with writing sample and/or clips; no phone queries. Pays $150 for curriculum 120 days after acceptance for all rts. Articles 1,200 wds. (4/yr); pays $80; poems (8/yr.), 200-400 wds; $40. Responds in 4 wks. No simultaneous submissions. Requires requested material by e-mail (attached file). Guidelines/copy for 10x13 SASE. (No ads)

Tips: "*Juniorway* principally serves an African American audience; editorial content addresses broad Christian issues. Looking for those with educational or Sunday school teaching experience who can accurately explain scriptures in an insightful and engaging way and apply those scriptures to the lives of children 9-11 years old."

$KEYS FOR KIDS, PO Box 1001, Grand Rapids MI 49501-1001. (616)647-4971. Fax (616) 647-4950. E-mail: Hazel@cbhministries.org, or geri@cbhministries.org. Website: www.cbhministries.org. CBH Ministries. Hazel Marett, ed.; Geri Walcott, ed. A daily devotional booklet for children (8-14) or for family devotions. Bimonthly booklet & online version; 80 pgs.; circ. 100,000. Subscription free. 100% unsolicited freelance. Complete ms; e-query OK. Accepts full mss by e-mail. Pays $25 on acceptance for 1st, reprint, or simultaneous rts. Devotionals (includes short fiction story) 375-425 wds. (60-70/yr.). Responds in 4-8 wks. Seasonal 4-5 mos. ahead. Accepts simultaneous submissions & reprints. Prefers NKJV. Guidelines (also by e-mail); copy for $1.34 postage. (No ads)

Tips: "We want children's devotions. If you are rejected, go back to the sample and study it some more. We use only devotionals, but they include a short fiction story. Any appropriate topic is fine."

$THE KIDS' ARK, PO Box 3160, Victoria TX 77903. Toll-free (800)455-1770. (361)485-1770. E-mail: editor@thekidsark.com. Website: http://thekidsark.com. Interdenominational. Joy Mygrants, sr. ed. To give kids, 6-10, a biblical foundation on which to base their choices in life. Quarterly mag. (soon to be online); 24 pgs.; circ. 8,000. 100% unsolicited freelance. Complete ms; e-query OK. Accepts full ms by e-mail. Pays $100 max. on publication for 1st, reprint ($25), electronic, worldwide rts. Fiction 600 wds. (12/yr.); no articles. Responds in 3-4 wks. No reprints. Prefers accepted submissions by e-mail (attached file). Kill fee 15%. Uses some sidebars. Also accepts submissions from children/teens. Prefers NIV. Guidelines/theme list on Website; copy for $1 postage. (Ads-limited)

Tips: "Open to fiction only. Think outside the box! Must catch children's attention and hold it; be biblically based and related to theme. We want to teach God's principles in an exciting format. Every issue contains the Ten Commandments and the plan of salvation."

$KID ZONE (formerly Discoveries), 2923 Troost Ave., Kansas City MO 64109. (816)931-1900. Fax (816)412-8306. E-mail: vlfolsom@wordaction.com, or kdadams@wordaction.com. Website: www.wordaction.com. Nazarene/Word Action Publishing. Virginia Folsom, ed.; submit to Kimberly Adams, asst. ed. For 8- to 10-yr.-olds, emphasizing Christian values and holy living; follows theme of Sunday school curriculum. Weekly take-home paper; 4 pgs.; circ. 30,000. 80% unsolicited freelance; 20% assigned. Query; phone/fax/e-query OK. Accepts full mss by e-mail. Pays $25. Articles & fiction 450 wds. Guidelines/theme list (also by e-mail); copy for #10 SAE/1 stamp.

Fillers: Puzzles & trivia; 250 wds.; $15.

Tips: "Request our theme list and samples. Send a sample of your material that you think would be appropriate for our publication. Break in by writing exciting, relevant, realistic stories and trivia pieces about info pertinent to kids."

$NATURE FRIEND, Helping Children Explore the Wonders of God's Creation, 4253 Woodcock Ln., Dayton VA 22821. (540)867-0764. Fax (540)867-9516. E-mail: editor@nature friendmagazine.com. Website: www.naturefriendmagazine.com. Dogwood Ridge Outdoors. Kevin Shank, ed. For ages 6-16. Monthly mag.; 24 pgs.; circ. 13,000. Subscription $34. 50-80% freelance written. Complete ms/cover letter; no phone/fax/e-query. Pays .05/wd. on publication for 1st rts. Articles 250-900 wds. (50/yr.); or fiction 500-750 wds. (40/yr.). Responds in 12-13 wks. Seasonal 4 mos. ahead. Accepts simultaneous submissions & reprints. Submit accepted articles on disk (Word format) or by e-mail. Uses some sidebars. KJV only. Guidelines $5 (www.dogwoodridgeoutdoors.com/v.php?pg=15); copy $5/9x12 SAE/$2 postage. (No ads)

Fillers: Buys 12/yr. Quizzes, word puzzles; 100-500 wds.; $10-15.

Columns/Departments: "Month" Nature Trails (seasonal, nature activity for each month); 100-450 wds. Write up as something you do each year, such as mushroom hunting, wildflower walk, snowshoeing, Christmas bird count, viewing a specific meteor shower, etc.

Tips: "We want to bring joy and knowledge to children by opening the world of God's creation to them. We endeavor to create a sense of awe about nature's Creator and a respect for His creation. I'd like to see more submissions of hands-on things to do with a nature theme (not collecting rocks or leaves—real stuff). The best way to learn about the content we use is to be a current, active subscriber."

$NEW MOON: The Magazine for Girls and Their Dreams, 2 W. First St., #101, Duluth MN 55802. Toll-free (800)381-4743. (218)728-5507. Fax (218)728-0314. E-mail: New moon@newmoongirlmedia.com. Website: www.newmoon.org. New Moon Publishing. Submit to Editorial Dept. A feminist publication for girls 8-14 years of age; we value diversity and take girls seriously. Bimonthly mag.; 48 pgs.; circ. 30,000. Subscription $34.95. 40% unsolicited freelance; 50% assigned. Query or complete ms/cover letter; e-query OK. Accepts full mss by e-mail. Pays .06/wd. on publication for all rts. Articles 600-1,200 wds. (12/yr.); fiction 1,200-1,500 wds. (6/yr.); book reviews 300 wds. Responds in 24 wks. No seasonal/holiday. Accepts simultaneous submissions & reprints (tell when/where appeared). Prefers accepted articles by e-mail (copied into message). No kill fee. Regularly uses sidebars. Also accepts submissions from girls and teens. Guidelines & theme list on Website; copy $7/9x12 SAE. (No ads)

Poetry: Buys 12/yr. Poetry from girls 8-14 only. Pays $10. Submit any number/any length.
Columns/Departments: Buys 18/yr. Herstory (women from history), 600 wds.; Women's Work (women in careers), 600 wds.; Body Language (health & puberty issues for girls), 600 wds.; pays .06/wd.
Tips: "We accept work from girls and women only. Girls can submit to any department. Adults must limit their submissions to fiction and the columns listed above."

$OUR LITTLE FRIEND, Box 5353, Nampa ID 83653-5353. (208)465-2580. Fax (208)465-2531. E-mail: ailsox@pacificpress.com. Website: www.pacificpress.com. Seventh-day Adventist. Aileen Andres Sox, ed. To help children understand their infinite value to their Creator and Redeemer; learn how to respond to God; show love to their family and friends; serve others in their world; find fulfillment participating in the Seventh-day Adventist Church. Weekly take-home paper for 0- to 5-yr.-olds; 8 pgs. 25% unsolicited freelance (or reprints); 50% assigned. Complete ms by e-mail. Pays $25-40 on acceptance for one-time or reprint rts. True stories 450-550 wds. (52/yr.); no articles. Responds in 26 wks. Seasonal 7 mos. ahead. Accepts simultaneous submissions & reprints; no serials. Prefers e-mail submissions (attached file). Guidelines (also on Website); copy for 9x12 SAE/2 stamps. (No ads)

$PARTNERS, Christian Light Publications Inc., Box 1212, Harrisonburg VA 22803-1212. (540)434-0768. Fax (540)433-8896. E-mail: partners@clp.org. Website: www.clp.org. Mennonite. Etta Martin, ed. Helping 9- to 14-yr.-olds to build strong Christian character. Weekly take-home paper; 4 pgs.; circ. 6,707. Subscription $10.90. 99% unsolicited freelance; 1% assigned. Complete ms; e-query OK. Pays .05/wd. on acceptance for 1st, multi-use, or reprint rts. Articles 200-800 wds. (100/yr.); fiction & true stories 400-1,600 wds. (200/yr.); serial stories up to 1,600 wds./installment; short-short stories to 400 wds. Responds in 6 wks. Seasonal 6 mos. ahead. Accepts reprints only 5 yrs. or more after last publication (tell when/where appeared); serials 2 parts. Prefers e-mail submissions (attached or copied into message). No kill fee. Requires KJV. Guidelines/theme list (also by e-mail); copy for 9x12 SAE/3 stamps. (No ads)

Poetry: Buys 250/yr. Traditional, story poems; 4-24 lines; .65-.75/line. Submit max. 6 poems.
Fillers: Buys 275/yr. Prose, quizzes, quotes, word puzzles (Bible-related); 200-800 wds.; .03-.05/wd.
Columns/Departments: Character Corner; Cultures & Customs; Historical Highlights; Maker's Masterpiece; Missionary Mail; Torches of Truth; or Nature Nook; all 200-800 wds.
Tips: "Most open to character-building articles and stories that teach a spiritual lesson. Please ask for our guidelines before submitting manuscripts. Someone who has experienced a genuine spiritual 'rebirth' has a much better chance of receiving an acceptance. Write in a lively way (showing, not telling) and on a child's level of understanding (ages 9-14). We do not require that you be Mennonite, but we do send a questionnaire for you to fill out if you desire to write for us."
**This periodical was #3 on the 2008 Top 50 Christian Publishers list (#14 in 2007, #15 in 2006, #15 in 2005, #12 in 2004).

$PASSPORT, 2923 Troost Ave., Kansas City MO 64109. (816)931-1900. Fax (816)412-8306. E-mail: rrpettit@wordaction.com, or kdadams@wordaction.com. Website: www.word action.com. Word Action/Nazarene Publishing House. Ryan Pettit, ed.; submit to Kimberly Adams, asst. ed. For preteens, 10- to 12-year-olds; supports the Sunday school lesson and provides an exciting way to learn about God and life. Weekly take-home paper; 4 pgs.; circ.

18,000. 30% unsolicited freelance. Pays $25. Articles 500 wds.; no fiction. Accepts reprints. Guidelines/theme list (also by e-mail); copy for #10 SAE/1 stamp.

Fillers: Cartoons & word puzzles; $15.

Tips: "Most open to creative, true-to-life stories, or creative puzzles and cartoons."

$POCKETS, PO Box 340004, Nashville TN 37203-0004. (615)340-7333. Fax (615)340-7267. E-mail: pockets@upperroom.org. Website: www.pockets.org. United Methodist/The Upper Room. Submit to Lynn W. Gilliam, ed. Devotional magazine for children (6-11 yrs.). Monthly (11X) mag.; 48 pgs.; circ. 67,000. Subscription $21.95. 75% unsolicited freelance. Complete ms/brief cover letter; no phone/fax/e-query. Pays .14/wd. on acceptance for one-time rts. Articles 400-800 wds. (10/yr.) & fiction 600-1,400 wds. (40/yr.). Responds in 8 wks. Seasonal 1 yr. ahead. Accepts simultaneous submissions & reprints (tell when/where appeared). No mss by e-mail. Uses some sidebars. Prefers NRSV. Also accepts submissions from children through age 12. Guidelines/theme list (also by e-mail/Website); copy for 9x12 SAE/4 stamps. (No ads)

Poetry: Buys 25/yr. Free verse, haiku, light verse, traditional; to 25 lines; $25-48. Submit max. 7 poems.

Fillers: Buys 50/yr. Games, word puzzles; $25-50.

Columns/Departments: Buys 20/yr. Complete ms. Kids Cook; Pocketsful of Love (ways to show love in your family), 200-300 wds.; Peacemakers at Work (children involved in environmental, community, and peace/justice issues; include action photos and name of photographer), to 600 wds.; Pocketsful of Prayer, 400-600 wds.; Someone You'd Like to Know (preferably a child whose lifestyle demonstrates a strong faith perspective), 600 wds. Pays .14/wd.

Special Needs: Two-page stories for ages 5-7, 600 words max. Need role model stories, retold Biblical stories, Someone You'd Like to Know, and Peacemakers at Work.

Contest: Fiction-writing contest; submit between 3/1 & 8/15 every year. Prize $1,000 and publication in *Pockets*. Length 1,000-1,600 wds. Must be unpublished and not historical fiction. Previous winners not eligible. Send to Pockets Fiction Contest at above address, and include an SASE for return of manuscript and response. Write "Fiction Contest" on envelope and on title/first page of manuscript.

Tips: "Well-written fiction that fits our themes is always needed. Make stories relevant to the lives of today's children and show faith as a natural part of everyday life. All areas open to freelance. Nonfiction probably easiest to sell for columns (we get fewer submissions for those). Read, read, read, and study. Be attentive to guidelines, themes, and study past issues."

**This periodical was #8 on the 2008 Top 50 Christian Publishers list (#11 in 2007, #12 in 2006, #10 in 2005, #4 in 2004).

$PRESCHOOL PLAYHOUSE, PO Box436987, Chicago IL 60643. Website: www.urban ministries.com. Urban Ministries Inc. Dr. R. Sailes, dir. of children's curriculum (rsailes@ urbanministries.com). Quarterly Sunday school curriculum for 2- to 5-year-olds with accompanying teacher's guide and curriculum resource materials. Open to freelance; 100% assigned. Query/clips and/or writing sample; no phone query. Pays $150 for curriculum 120 days after acceptance for all rts. Articles accepted only on assignment. No simultaneous submissions or reprints. Requires accepted ms by e-mail only (attached file). No kill fee. Will accept sidebars on assigned educational topics; pay varies. Requires NIV. Guidelines for #10 SASE. (No ads)

Tips: "*Preschool Playhouse* principally serves an African American audience; editorial content addresses broad Christian issues. Looking for those with educational or Sunday school teaching experience who can accurately explain scriptures in an insightful and engaging way and apply those scriptures to the lives of preschool children."

$PRIMARY PAL (KS), PO Box 4060, Overland Park KS 66204. (913)432-0331. Fax (913)722-0351. E-mail: sseditor1@juno.com. Website: www.heraldandbanner.com. Church of God (holiness)/Herald and Banner Press. Arlene McGehee, Sunday school ed. Denominational; for 1st-3rd graders. Weekly take-home paper; 4 pgs.; circ. 2,900. Subscription $1.50. Complete ms/cover letter; phone/fax/e-query OK (prefers mail or e-mail). Pays .005/wd. on publication for 1st rts. Fiction 500-1,000 wds. Seasonal 6-8 mos. ahead. Accepts simultaneous submissions & reprints (tell when/where appeared). Prefers KJV. Guidelines/theme list; copy. Not in topical listings.

$PRIMARY STREET, PO Box436987, Chicago IL 60643. Website: www.urbanministries.com. Urban Ministries Inc. Dr. R. Sailes, dir. of children's curriculum (rsailes@urbanministries.com). Quarterly Sunday school curriculum including teacher's guide and teaching resources primarily for children, ages 6-8. Open to freelance queries; 100% assigned. Pays $150 for curriculum 120 days from assignment date for all rts. Assignments only. No simultaneous submissions or reprints. Requires requested material by e-mail (attached file). No kill fee. Will accept sidebars on assigned educational topic: pay varies. Requires NIV. Guidelines for #10 SASE. (No ads)

> **Tips:** "Primary Street principally serves an African American audience; editorial content addresses broad Christian issues. Looking for those with educational or Sunday school teaching experience who can accurately explain scriptures in an insightful and engaging way and apply those scriptures to the lives of children 6-8 years old."

$PRIMARY TREASURE, Box 5353, Nampa ID 83653-5353. (208)465-2500. Fax (208)465-2531. E-mail: ailsox@pacificpress.com. Website: www.pacificpress.com. Seventh-day Adventist. Aileen Andres Sox, ed. To help children understand their infinite value to their Creator and Redeemer; learn how to respond to God; show love to their family and friends; serve others in their world; find fulfillment participating in the Seventh-day Adventist Church. Weekly take-home paper for 6- to 9-yr.-olds (1st-4th grades); 16 pgs. 50% freelance (assigned), 25% reprints or unsolicited. Complete ms by e-mail preferred. Pays $25-50 on acceptance for one-time or reprint rts. True stories 900-1,000 wds. (52/yr.); articles used rarely (query). Responds in 13 wks. Seasonal 7 mos. ahead. For simultaneous submissions & reprints see guidelines; serials to 10 parts (query). E-mail submission preferred (attached file). Guidelines (also on Website); copy for 9x12 SAE/2 stamps. (No ads)

> **Tips:** "We need true adventure stories with a spiritual slant; positive, lively stories about children facing modern problems and making good choices. We always need strong stories about boys and stories featuring dads. We need a spiritual element that frequently is missing from submissions."

$PROMISE, 2621 Dryden Rd., Moraine OH 45439. Toll-free (800)543-4383. (937)293-1415. Fax (937)293-1310. E-mail: service@pflaum.com. Website: www.pflaum.com. Catholic. Joan Mitchell CSJ, ed. For kindergarten and grade 1; encourages them to participate in parish worship. Weekly (32X) take-home paper. Not in topical listings.

$SEEDS, 2621 Dryden Rd., Moraine OH 45439. (937)293-1415. Fax (937)293-1310. E-mail: service@pflaum.com. Website: www.pflaum.com. Catholic. Joan Mitchell CSJ, ed. Prepares children to learn about God; for preschoolers. Weekly (32X) take-home paper; 4 pgs. Not in topical listings.

$SHINE BRIGHTLY, Box 7259, Grand Rapids MI 49510. (616)241-5616, ext. 3034. Fax (616)241-5558. E-mail: servicecenter@gemsgc.org. Website: www.gemsgc.org. GEMS Girls Clubs. Sara Hilton, ed. (sara@gemsgc.org). To show girls ages 9-14 that God is at work in their lives and in the world around them. Monthly (9X) mag.; 24 pgs.; circ. 13,000. Subscription $13.25. 80% unsolicited freelance; 20% assigned. Complete ms; no e-query. Pays .03-.05/wd. on publication for 1st or reprint rts. Articles 100-400 wds. (35/yr.); fiction 400-900 wds. (30/yr.). Responds in 4-6 wks. Seasonal 10 mos. ahead. Accepts simultaneous submissions & reprints. Accepts requested ms on disk. Regularly uses sidebars. Prefers NIV. Guidelines/theme list on Website; copy $1/9x12 SAE/3 stamps. (No ads)

Fillers: Buys 10/yr. Cartoons, games, party ideas, prayers, quizzes, short humor, word puzzles; 50-200 wds.; $5-10.

Special Needs: Craft ideas that can be used to help others. Articles on how words can help build others up or tear people down.

Tips: "Be realistic—we get a lot of fluffy stories with Pollyanna endings. We are looking for real-life-type stories that girls relate to. We mostly publish short stories but are open to short reflective articles. Know what girls face today and how they cope in their daily lives. We need angles from home life and friendships, peer pressure, and the normal growing-up challenges girls deal with."

SKIPPING STONES: A Multicultural Magazine, PO Box 3939, Eugene OR 97403. (541)342-4956. E-mail: editor@skippingstones.org. Website: www.skippingstones.org. Interfaith/multicultural. Arun N. Toké, exec. ed.; Nina Forsberg, asst. ed. A multicultural awareness and nature appreciation magazine for young people 7-17, worldwide. Bimonthly (5X) mag.; 36 pgs.; circ. 2,500. Subscription $25. 85% unsolicited freelance; 15% assigned. Query or complete ms/cover letter; no phone query; e-query/submissions OK. **PAYS IN COPIES** for 1st, electronic, and nonexclusive reprint rts. Articles (15-25/yr.) 750-1,000 wds.; fiction for teens, 750-1,000 wds. Responds in 9-13 wks. Seasonal 2-4 mos. ahead. Accepts simultaneous submissions. Accepts ms on disk or by e-mail. Regularly uses sidebars. Guidelines/theme list (also by e-mail/Website); copy $5/4 stamps. (No ads)

Poetry: Only from kids under 18. Accepts 100/yr. Any type; 3-30 lines. Submit max. 4-5 poems.

Fillers: Accepts 10-20/yr. Anecdotes, cartoons, games, quizzes, short humor, word puzzles; to 250 wds.

Columns/Departments: Accepts 10/yr. Noteworthy News (multicultural/nature/international/social, appropriate for youth), 200 wds.

Special Needs: Stories and articles on your community and country, peace, nonviolent communication, compassion, kindness, spirituality, tolerance, and giving.

Contest: Annual Book Awards for published books and authors (deadline February 1); Annual Youth Honor Awards for students 7-17 (deadline June 25). Send SASE for guidelines.

Tips: "Most of the magazine is open to freelance. We're seeking submissions by minority, multicultural, international, and/or youth writers. Do not be judgmental or preachy; be open or receptive to diverse opinions."

$SPARKLE, PO Box 7259, Grand Rapids MI 49510. (616)241-5616. Fax (616)241-5558. E-mail: amy@gemsgc.org, or servicecenter@gemsgc.org. Website: www.gemsgc.org. GEMS Girls' Clubs (nondenominational). Sara Hilton, ed. (sara@gemsgc.org). To prepare girls, grades 1-3, to live out their faith and become world changers; to help girls make a difference in the world. Published 6X/yr. (October-March). Subscription $10.25. 80% unsolicited freelance; 20% assigned. Complete ms; no e-query. Pays .03/wd. on publication for 1st, reprint, or simultaneous rts. Articles 200-400 wds. (10/yr.); fiction 200-400 wds (6/yr.). Responds in 6 wks. Seasonal 10 mos. ahead. Accepts simultaneous submissions & reprints. Accepts requested ms on disk. Regularly uses sidebars. Prefers NIV. Guidelines/theme list (also by e-mail/Website); copy $1/9x12 SAE/3 stamps. (No ads)

Fillers: Buys 10/yr. Games, party ideas, prayers, quizzes, short humor; 50-200 wds.; $5-15.

Tips: "Send in pieces that teach girls how to be world-changers for Christ, or that fit our annual theme. We also are always looking for games, crafts, and recipes. Keep the writing simple. Keep activities short. Engage a 3rd grader, while being easy enough for a first-grader to understand."

$STORY MATES, Box 1212, Harrisonburg VA 22803-1212. (540)434-0750. Fax (540)433-8896. E-mail: StoryMates@clp.org. Website: www.clp.org. Mennonite/Christian Light Publications Inc. Crystal Shank, ed. For 4- to 8-yr.-olds. Weekly take-home paper; 4 pgs.; circ. 6,385. Subscription $11.45. 90% unsolicited freelance. Complete ms. Pays up to .05/wd. on acceptance for 1st rts. (.06/wd. for 1st rts., plus reprint rts.). Realistic or true stories, 800-900 wds. (50-75/yr.); picture stories 120-150 wds. Responds in 6 wks. Seasonal 6 mos. ahead. Accepts simultaneous submissions & reprints (tell when/where appeared). No disk. Requires KJV. Guidelines/theme list (also by e-mail); copy for 9x12 SAE/3 stamps. Will send questionnaire to fill out. (No ads)

Poetry: Buys 25/yr. Traditional, any length. Few story poems. Pays up to .65/line.

Fillers: Quizzes, word puzzles, craft ideas. "Need fillers that correlate with theme list; Bible related." Pays about $10.

Special Needs: True or true-to-life stories the children can relate to.

Tips: "Carefully read our guidelines and understand our conservative Mennonite applications of Bible principles." Very conservative.

**This periodical was #49 on the 2007 Top 50 Christian Publishers list.

$+TRUTH TRAVELERS, 1300 N. Meacham Rd., Schaumburg IL 60173-4888. (847)843-1600. Fax (847)843-3757. E-mail: takehomepapers@garbc.org. Website: www.RegularBaptist Press.org. General Assn. of Regular Baptist Churches/Regular Baptist Press. Joan E. Alexander, ed. New Publication for middlers (grades 3 & 4). Guidelines still under development.

$VENTURE, 2621 Dryden Rd., Moraine OH 45439. (937)293-1415. Fax (937)293-1310. E-mail: service@pflaum.com. Website: www.pflaum.com. Catholic. Joan Mitchell CSJ, ed. For grades 4-6. Weekly (32X) take-home paper. Not in topical listings.

$WINNER MAGAZINE, 55 W. Oak Ridge Dr., Hagerstown MD 21740. (301)393-4017. Fax (301)393-4055. E-mail: jschleifer@rhpa.org. Website: www.winnermagazine.org. The Health Connection. Jan Schleifer, ed. For elementary school children, grades 4-6; Saying No to Drugs, and Yes to Life. Monthly (during school year) mag.; 16 pgs.; circ. 5,000. Subscription $19.25. 20% unsolicited freelance; 80% assigned. Complete ms. Accepts full mss by e-mail. Pays $80 on acceptance for 1st rts. Articles 600-650 wds. (25-30/yr.); fiction 600-650 wds. (18/yr.) Responds in 4-13 wks. Seasonal 6-8 mos. ahead. Accepts simultaneous submissions & reprints (tell when/where appeared). Prefers e-mail submission (attached file). Kill fee 50%. Guidelines (also by e-mail/Website); copy $2/9x12 SAE/3 stamps. (No ads)

Tips: "Winner is a positive lifestyle magazine. Most open to self-help stories, factuals on tobacco, alcohol, and other drugs—in story format (include sources), with a catchy ending. Each article needs at least three questions relating to the story and a puzzle/activity. We use celebrity pieces about drug-free young people who would be good role models. Need health articles on nutrition and exercise (have enough on sleep and drinking water). Articles on the dangers of using alcohol, tobacco, and drugs." Do not use Bible verses because magazine used in public schools.

CHRISTIAN EDUCATION/LIBRARY MARKETS

$CATECHIST, 2621 Dryden Rd., 3rd Fl., Dayton OH 45439. (937)847-5900. Fax (314)638-6812. E-mail: kdotterweich@peterli.com. Website: www.catechist.com. Catholic; Peter Li Education Group. Kass Dotterweich, ed. For Catholic school teachers and parish volunteer catechists. Mag. published 7X/yr.; 52 pgs.; circ. 52,000. Subscription $26.95. 30% unsolicited freelance; 70% assigned. Query (preferred) or complete ms. Pays $25-150 on publication. Articles 1,200 wds. Responds in 9-18 wks. Guidelines (also on Website); copy $3.

Tips: "Most open to short features, how-to lesson plans, and crafts."

CATHOLIC LIBRARY WORLD, Alumnae Library, Elms College, 291 Springfield St., Chicopee MA 01013-2839. (413)265-2354. Fax (413)594-7418. E-mail: gallagherm@elms.edu. Website: www.cathla.org. Catholic Library Assn. Sr. Mary E. Gallagher SSJ, gen. ed. For libraries at all levels—preschool to postsecondary to academic, parish, public, and private. Quarterly jour.; 80 pgs.; circ. 1,000. Subscription $60/$85 foreign. 90% unsolicited freelance; 10% assigned. Query or complete ms; phone/fax/e-query OK. **PAYS 1 COPY.** Articles; book/video reviews, 300-500 wds. Accepts requested ms on disk. Uses some sidebars. No guidelines; copy for 9x12 SAE. (Ads)

> **Special Needs:** Topics of interest to academic libraries, high school and children's libraries, parish and community libraries, archives, and library education. Reviewers cover areas such as theology, spirituality, pastoral, professional, juvenile books and material, and media.

> **Tips:** "Review section considers taking on new reviewers who are experts in field of librarianship, theology, and professional studies. No payment except a free copy of the book or materials reviewed. Query us by mail or e-mail."

$CHILDREN'S MINISTRY MAGAZINE, 1515 Cascade Ave., Loveland CO 80539. Toll-free (800)447-1070. Fax (970)292-4373. E-mail: jhooks@cmmag.com. Website: www.childrensministry.com. Group Publishing/nondenominational. Christine Yount Jones, exec. ed.; submit to Jennifer Hooks, mng. ed. (jhooks@cmmag.com). The leading resource for adults who work with children (ages 0-12) in the church. Bimonthly mag.; 140 pgs.; circ. 60,000. Subscription $29.95. 40% unsolicited freelance; 60% assigned. Complete ms/cover letter; e-query OK. Pays $25-400 on acceptance for all & electronic rts. Articles 50-1,800 wds. (250-300/yr.). Responds in 8-10 wks. Seasonal 6-9 mos. ahead. No simultaneous submissions or reprints. Accepts requested ms by e-mail (attached or copied into message). Regularly uses sidebars. Also accepts submissions from children/teens. Sometimes pays kill fee. Prefers NLT. Guidelines (also by e-mail/Website); copy $2/9x12 SAE/$2.23 postage (mark Media Mail). (Ads)

> **Fillers:** Buys 25-50/yr. Cartoons, kid quotes; 25-50 wds.; $25-60.

> **Columns/Departments:** Submit to Carmen Kamrath (ckamrath@cmmag.com). Buys 200+/yr. Age-level insights (age-appropriate ideas); Family Ministry (family ideas); Reaching Out (outreach ideas); 150-250 wds. Teacher Telegram (ideas for teachers); For Parents Only (parenting ideas); 150-300 wds.; $40-150. Complete ms.

> **Special Needs:** Seasonal ideas, outreach ideas, volunteer management, and family ministry. Always looking for new ideas, crafts, games, and activities.

> **Tips:** "All areas open to freelancers. Start small—ideas, activities, and personal essays. Or go big—wow us with a profoundly inspiring article that fits the magazine's makeup. We're looking for stand-out ideas and the very latest in this important ministry area. If you're in the trenches, we want to hear from you. We seek features from experts in practice or in theory. No poetry or fiction."

> **This periodical was #4 on the 2008 Top 50 Christian Publishers list (#8 in 2007, #5 in 2006, #1 in 2005, #14 in 2004).

CHRISTIAN EARLY EDUCATION, PO Box 65130, Colorado Springs CO 80962-5130. (719)528-6906. Fax (719)531-0631. E-mail: earlyeducation@acsi.org. Website: www.acsi.org. Assn. of Christian Schools Intl. D'Arcy Maher, sr. ed. Equips individuals serving children ages 0-5 from a biblical perspective. Quarterly mag.; 40 pgs.; circ. 5,500. Subscription $14. 10% unsolicited freelance; 90% assigned. Query; phone/fax/e-query OK. **PAYS IN COPIES.** Not copyrighted. Articles 600-1,800 wds. (12-15/yr.). Responds in 4 wks. Seasonal 10 mos. ahead. Accepts reprints (tell when/where appeared). Prefers e-mail submissions (attached file). Does not use sidebars. Prefers NIV. Guidelines/theme list (also by e-mail); copy $1.50/9x12 SAE. (Ads)

Columns/Departments: Accepts up to 10/yr. Staff Training (training for teachers of young children, to use in staff meeting), 400 wds.; Parents' Place (material suitable for parents of young children), 400 wds. Complete ms.

Tips: "Most open to these columns: Unique Perspectives, Footprints in Development, Professional Edge, Resource Review, Heart 2 Heart, and Field Trip."

$CHRISTIAN EDUCATORS JOURNAL, 73 Highland Ave., St. Catherines ON L2R 4H9, Canada. Phone/fax (905)684-3991. E-mail: bert.witvoet@sympatico.ca. Website: www.CEJonline .com. Christian Educators Journal Assn. Bert Witvoet, mng. ed. For educators in Christian day schools at the elementary, secondary, and college levels. Quarterly jour.; 36 pgs.; circ. 4,200. Subscription $7.50 (c/o James Rauwerda, 2045 Boston St. S.E., Grand Rapids MI 49506, 616-243-2112). 50% unsolicited freelance; 50% assigned. Query; phone/e-query OK. Pays $30 on publication for one-time rts. Articles 750-1,500 wds. (20/yr.); fiction 750-1,500 wds. Responds in 5 wks. Seasonal 4 mos. ahead. Accepts simultaneous submissions & reprints. Guidelines/theme list; copy $1.50 or 9x12 SAE/4 stamps. (Limited ads)

Poetry: Buys 6/yr. On teaching day school; 4-30 lines; $10. Submit max. 5 poems.

Tips: "No articles on Sunday school, only Christian day school. Most open to theme topics and features."

THE CHRISTIAN LIBRARIAN, Ryan Library, PLNU, 3600 Lomaland Dr., San Diego CA 92106. (619)849-2208. Fax (619)849-7024. E-mail: apowell@pointloma.edu. Website: www.acl .org. Assn. of Christian Librarians. Anne-Elizabeth Powell, ed-in-chief. Geared toward academic librarians of the Christian faith. Triannual jour.; 40 pgs.; circ. 800. Subscription $30. 50% unsolicited freelance; 50% assigned. E-mail; fax/e-query OK. **NO PAYMENT** for one-time rts. Not copyrighted. Articles 1,000-3,500 wds.; research articles to 5,000 wds. (6/yr.); reviews 150-300 wds. Responds in 5 wks. Accepts simultaneous submissions & reprints (tell when/where appeared). Prefers accepted ms by e-mail (attached file). Uses some sidebars. Guidelines (also by e-mail/Website); copy $5. (No ads)

Fillers: Anecdotes, ideas, short humor; 25-300 wds.

Special Needs: Articles dealing with the intersection of faith and professional duties in libraries. Interviews with library leaders, profiles of Christian academic libraries, international librarianship. Deal with all topics as they can be applied to librarianship.

Tips: "Reviews are a good way to gain publication. Write a tight, well-researched article about a current 'hot topic' in librarianship as it is defined in a Christian setting; or ethics of librarianship. Articles on 'how we did it right' are good entry publications."

CHRISTIAN SCHOOL EDUCATION, PO Box 65130, Colorado Springs CO 80962-5130. (719)528-6906. Fax (719)531-0631. E-mail: cse@acsi.org. Website: www.acsi.org. Association of Christian Schools Intl. Steven C. Babbitt, ed. To provide accurate information as well as provoke thought and reflection about the ministry of Christian school education worldwide. Quarterly mag.; 56 pgs.; circ. 70,000. Subscription $16. 2% unsolicited freelance; 98% assigned. Query preferred; phone query OK. **NO PAYMENT.** Asks for photocopy permission for member schools. Articles 650-2,600 wds.; book reviews 600 wds. Responds in 12 wks. No seasonal material. Accepts simultaneous submissions & reprints (tell when/where appeared). Requires submissions by disk or e-mail (attached file). Regularly uses sidebars. Prefers NIV, NKJV. Guidelines (also by e-mail). (Ads)

Tips: "Most articles for publication are solicited, therefore freelancers 'breaking into publication' is highly unlikely."

$CHURCH LIBRARIES, 9118 W. Elmwood Dr., #1G, Niles IL 60714-5820. (847)296-3964. Fax (847)296-0754. E-mail: linjohnson@ECLAlibraries.org. Website: www.ECLAlibraries.org. Evangelical Church Library Assn. Lin Johnson, mng ed. To assist church librarians in setting up, maintaining, and promoting church libraries and media centers. Quarterly mag.; 32-36 pgs.; circ. 450. Subscription $35. 25% unsolicited freelance. Complete ms or queries by e-mail only. Pays .05/wd. on acceptance for 1st or reprint rts. Articles 500-1,000 wds. (24-30/yr.); book/music/DVD reviews by assignment, 75-150 wds., free product. Responds in 4-6 wks. Seasonal 6 mos. ahead. Accepts reprints (tell when/where appeared). Requires e-mail submission. Regularly uses sidebars. Prefers NIV. Guidelines (also by e-mail/ Website); copy for 9x12 SAE/4 stamps. (Ads)

Tips: "Talk to church librarians or get involved in library or reading programs. Most open to articles and promotional ideas; profiles of church libraries; roundups on best books in a category (query on topic first). Book reviews assigned; need for reviewers fluctuates; if interested e-mail for availability."

CONGREGATIONAL LIBRARIES TODAY, 2920 S.W. Dolph Ct., Portland OR 97219-4055. (503)244-6919. Fax (503)977-3734. E-mail: csla@worldaccessnet.com. Website: www .cslainfo.org. Church and Synagogue Library Assn. Judith Janzen, exec. dir. To help librarians run congregational libraries. Bimonthly; 24 pgs.; circ. 3,000. Subscription $35, $40 Cdn., $45 foreign. Query; no e-query. NO PAYMENT. Requires accepted ms on disk. Articles. Book & video reviews 1-2 paragraphs. Guidelines; copy available. (Ads)

Fillers: Ideas.

$GROUP MAGAZINE, Box 481, Loveland CO 80539. (970)669-3836. Fax (970)292-4373. E-mail: rlawrence@grouppublishing.com, or croberts@grouppublishing.com, or info@ group.com. Website: www.grouppublishing.com, or www.groupmag.com. Rick Lawrence, ed.; Chris Roberts, asst. ed. For leaders of Christian youth groups; to supply ideas, practical help, inspiration, and training for youth leaders. Bimonthly mag.; 85 pgs.; circ. 55,000. Subscription $29.95. 50% unsolicited freelance; 50% assigned. Query; fax/e-query OK. Pays $150-350 on acceptance for all rts. Articles 175-2,000 wds. (100/yr.). Responds in 6-9 wks. Seasonal 5 mos. ahead. No simultaneous submissions or reprints. Accepts e-mail submissions (copied into message). No kill fee. Uses some sidebars. Any Bible version. Guidelines on Website; copy $2/9x12 SAE/3 stamps. (Ads)

Fillers: Buys 5-10/yr. Cartoons, games, ideas; $40.

Columns/Departments: Buys 30-40/yr. Try This One (youth group activities), to 300 wds.; Hands-on-Help (tips for leaders), to 175 wds.; Strange But True (profiles remarkable youth ministry experience), 500 wds. Pays $50. Complete ms.

Special Needs: Articles geared toward working with teens; programming ideas; youth ministry issues.

Tips: "We're always looking for effective youth ministry ideas, especially those tested by youth leaders in the field. Most open to Hands-On-Help column (use real-life examples, personal experiences, practical tips, scripture, and self-quizzes or checklists). We buy the idea, not the verbatim submission."

**This periodical was #36 on the 2007 Top 50 Christian Publishers list.

IDEAS UNLIMITED FOR EFFECTIVE CHILDREN'S MINISTRY, PO Box 12624, Roanoke VA 24027. (540)342-7511. E-mail: ccmbbr@juno.com. Website: www.CreativeChristian Ministries.com. Betty Robertson, ed. For anyone ministering to children. Monthly e-zine; circ. 4,200. Subscription free. 25% unsolicited freelance; 75% assigned. E-query or e-submissions only. NO PAYMENT for 1st, one-time, or simultaneous rts. Not copyrighted. Articles 100-600 wds. Responds in 3 wks. Seasonal 6 mos. ahead. Accepts simultaneous submissions & reprints. Guidelines by e-mail.

$THE JOURNAL OF ADVENTIST EDUCATION, 12501 Old Columbia Pike, Silver Spring MD 20904-6600. (301)680-5075. Fax (301)622-9627. E-mail: rumbleb@gc.adventist.org. Website: http://education.gc.adventist.org/jae. General Conference of Seventh-day Adventists. Beverly J. Robinson-Rumble, ed. For Seventh-day teachers teaching in the church's school system, kindergarten to university. Bimonthly (5X) jour.; 48 pgs.; circ. 10,800. Selected articles are translated into French, Spanish, and Portuguese for a twice-yearly

International Edition. Subscription $17.25 (add $1 outside U.S.). Percentage of freelance varies. Query or complete ms; phone/fax/e-query OK. Pays $25-300 on publication for 1st North American and translation rts., and permission to post on Website. Articles 1,000-2,000 wds. (2-20/yr.). Responds in 6-17 wks. Seasonal 6 mos. ahead. Accepts reprints (tell when/where appeared). Accepts requested ms on disk. Regularly uses sidebars. Guidelines on Website; copy for 10x12 SAE/5 stamps.

Fillers: Cartoons only, no payment.

Special Needs: "All articles in the context of parochial schools (not Sunday school tips); professional enrichment and teaching tips for Christian teachers. Need feature articles."

JOURNAL OF CHRISTIAN EDUCATION, PO Box 602, Epping NSW 1710, Australia. Phone/fax 61 2 9868 6644. E-mail: business@acfe.org.au; submit to editor@acfe.org.au. Website: http://jce.acfe.org.au. Australian Christian Forum on Education Inc. Dr. Grant Maple & Dr. Ian Lambert, eds. To consider the implications of the Christian faith for the entire field of education. Triannual jour.; 80 pgs.; circ. 400. Subscription $50 AUS, $45 U.S. for individuals; $64 AUS, $60 U.S. for institutions. 40% unsolicited freelance; 60% assigned. Complete ms/cover letter; phone/fax/e-query OK. **NO PAYMENT** for one-time rts. Articles 3,000-5,000 wds. (6/yr.); book reviews 400-600 wds. Responds in 4 wks. Seasonal 6 mos. ahead. Accepts requested ms on disk or by e-mail (attached file). Does not use sidebars. Guidelines by e-mail/Website); free copy. (No ads)

Tips: "Send for a sample copy, study guidelines, and submit manuscript. Most open to articles or book reviews. Open to any educational issue from a Christian perspective."

JOURNAL OF CHRISTIANITY AND FOREIGN LANGUAGES, Dept. of Germanic and Asian Languages, Calvin College, 3201 Burton St. S.E., Grand Rapids MI 49546. (616)957-8609. Fax (616)526-8583. E-mail: dsmith@calvin.edu. Website: www.spu.edu/orgs/NACFLA. North American Christian Foreign Language Assn. Dr. David Smith, ed. Scholarly articles dealing with the relationship between Christian belief and the teaching of foreign languages and literatures; mainly for college faculty. Annual jour.; 100 pgs.; circ. 100. Subscription $16 (indiv.), $27 (library). Open to freelance. Complete ms/cover letter; phone/fax/e-query OK. **PAYS IN COPIES/OFFPRINTS** for one-time rts. Articles 2,000-4,000 wds. (6/yr.); book/video reviews, 750 wds. Responds in 12-16 wks. No reprints. Requires requested ms on disk or by e-mail (attached file). Does not use sidebars. Guidelines on Website; no copy. (Ads)

Columns/Departments: Accepts 1-3/yr. Forum (position papers, pedagogical suggestions), 1,000-1,500 wds.

Tips: "Most open to Forum column; see www.spu.edu/orgs/nacfla for guidelines. Also see Website for abstracts and samples. Book reviews and opinion pieces must be related to Christianity and education in foreign languages and literature."

JOURNAL OF EDUCATION & CHRISTIAN BELIEF, Dept. of Germanic Languages, Calvin College, 3201 Burton St. S.E., Grand Rapids MI 49546. (616)957-8609. Fax (616)526-8583. E-mail: jecb@stapleford-centre.org. Website: www.jecb.org. Association of Christian Teachers. Editors: Dr. David Smith (use above address) & Dr. John Shortt, 1 Kiteleys Green, Leighton Buzzard, Beds LU7 3LD, United Kingdom. Phone +44 0 1525 379709. Semiannual jour.; 80 pgs.; circ. 400. Subscription $41.40. 80% unsolicited freelance; 20% assigned. Complete ms/cover letter; e-query OK. **NO PAYMENT** for 1st rts. Articles 5,000 wds. (12/yr.). Responds in 4-8 wks. Accepts reprints (tell when/where appeared). Prefers requested ms on disk or by e-mail (attached file). Does not use sidebars. Guidelines by e-mail; no copy. (No ads)

Tips: "Most open to reviews of books related to education and Christian belief; should be expert reviews addressed to an academic audience. Must address Christian education in competent, scholarly manner."

JOURNAL OF RESEARCH ON CHRISTIAN EDUCATION, Andrews University, Information Services Bldg., Ste. 101, Berrien Springs MI 49104. (269)471-6080. Fax (269)471-6274. E-mail: jrce@andrews.edu. Website: www.andrews.edu/jrce. Andrews University. Larry D. Burton, ed.; Linda Caviness, book rev. ed. Research related to Christian schooling (all levels) within the Protestant tradition. Triennial jour.; 100+ pgs.; circ. 400. Subscription $60. 100% unsolicited freelance. Complete ms/cover letter; phone/fax/e-query OK. **NO PAYMENT.** Articles 13-26, double-spaced pgs. (12-18/yr.); book reviews, 2-5 pgs. Responds in 1 wk.; decision within 6 mos. (goes through review board). No simultaneous submissions. Requires e-mail submissions. Does not use sidebars. Guidelines (also by e-mail). (No ads)
> **Tips:** "This is a research journal. All manuscripts should conform to standards of scholarly inquiry. Manuscripts are submitted to a panel of 3 experts for their review. Publication decision is based on recommendation of reviewers. Authors should submit manuscripts written in scholarly style and focused on Christian schooling. Submit an electronic copy along with a 100-word abstract and 30-word bio-sketch indicating institutional affiliation."

$KIDS' MINISTRY IDEAS, 55 W. Oak Ridge Dr., Hagerstown MD 21740. (301)393-4082. Fax (301)393-3209. E-mail: KidsMin@rhpa.org. Website: www.kidsministryideas.org. Seventh-day Adventist. Candy DeVore, ed. For adults leading children (birth-8th grade) to Christ. Quarterly mag.; 32 pgs.; circ. 2,500. Complete ms/cover letter; e-query OK. Accepts full ms by e-mail. Guidelines on request.

$MOMENTUM, 1077—30th St. N.W., Ste. 100, Washington DC 20007-3852. Toll-free (800) 711-6232. (202)337-6232. Fax (202)333-6706. E-mail: momentum@ncea.org, or through Website: www.ncea.org/news/momentum/WritingforMomentum.asp. National Catholic Educational Assn. Brian Gray, ed. Features outstanding programs, issues, and research in Catholic education. Quarterly jour.; 96 pgs.; circ. 23,000. Subscription $20 (free to members). 50% unsolicited freelance; 30% assigned. Query or complete ms; phone/e-query OK. Pays $50-100 on publication for 1st rts. Articles 500-1,500 wds. (25-30/yr.); research articles 3,500-5,000 wds.; book reviews 500-750 wds. ($50). No simultaneous submissions. Accepts full mss by e-mail. Regularly uses sidebars. Guidelines/theme list (also by e-mail/Website); copy $5/9x12 SAE/$2.23 postage (mark "Media Mail"). (Ads)
> **Columns/Departments:** From the Field (success ideas that can be used by other Catholic schools); DRE Directions (guidance for directors of religious education programs); both 700 wds.
> **Special Needs:** Religious education; teaching methods; Catholic school administration.
> **Tips:** "Always interested in parish-based religious education programs, especially for adolescents or whole-family catecheses. Good opportunity for freelancers because they are close to the sources."

$PRESCHOOL PLAYHOUSE, PO Box 436987, Chicago IL 60643. (708)868-7100. Fax (708) 868-7105. Website: www.urbanministries.com. Urban Ministries Inc. K. Steward, ed. Sunday school magazine with activities for 2- to 5-year-olds with accompanying teacher's manual. Quarterly mag. for teachers; take-home paper for students; 96 pgs. Subscription $4.99 (teacher/64 pgs.) and $2.85 (student). 80% assigned. Query/clips; fax/e-query OK. Pays $150, 120 days after acceptance, for all rts. Articles 6,000 characters for teacher, 2,900 characters for student (4/yr.). Responds in 4 wks. Seasonal 6 mos. ahead. Accepts simultaneous submissions. Requires requested ms on disk. Prefers NIV. Guidelines; copy $2.25/#10 SASE. (No ads)

$RTJ: The Magazine for Catechist Formation, PO Box 6015, New London CT 06320. Toll-free (800)321-0411, ext. 188. Fax (860)437-6246. E-mail: nwagner@twentythird publications.com. Website: www.twentythirdpublications.com. Catholic Publishers/Bayard. Nick Wagner, ed. For volunteer religion teachers who need practical, hands-on information as well as spiritual and theological background for teaching religion to kindergarten through high school. 7X/yr. mag.; 40 pgs.; circ. 32,000. Subscription $23.95. 40% unsolicited freelance; 60% assigned. Complete ms/cover letter; fax/e-query OK. Pays $50-125 on acceptance for 1st rts. Articles to 1,300 wds. (40/yr.); plays. Responds in 2-4 wks. Seasonal 6 mos. ahead. Accepts simultaneous submissions & rarely accepts reprints (tell when/where appeared). Prefers requested ms on disk or by e-mail (attached file). No kill fee. Regularly uses sidebars. Prefers NRSV (Catholic edition). Guidelines/theme list (also by e-mail); copy for 9x12 SAE/3 first class stamps. (Ads)

Fillers: Buys 20-30/yr. Anecdotes (about teaching), games, ideas, quizzes, crafts, successful class activities (especially seasonal); 50-300 wds.; $20-50.

Special Needs: Partnering with families; teaching the sacraments; prayer and prayer services; celebrating the seasons; spiritual formation for religion teachers/catechists; successful faith formation programs.

Tips: "Most open to articles on teaching skills; successful activity ideas/lessons; involving parents in religious education, especially in sacrament preparation; celebrating Advent and Lent; spiritual formation. Looking for clear, concise articles written from experience, for catechists and religion teachers (K-12). Articles should help readers move from theory/doctrine to concrete application." Unsolicited manuscripts not returned without an SASE.

**This periodical was #46 on the 2007 Top 50 Christian Publishers list (#49 in 2006, #43 in 2005, #43 in 2004).

$TEACHERS OF VISION MAGAZINE, 227 N. Magnolia Ave., Ste. 2, Anaheim CA 92801. (714) 761-1476. E-mail: tov@ceai.org. Website: www.ceai.org. Christian Educators Assn., Intl. Judy Turpen, contributing ed.; F. L. Turpen, editorial dir.; Denise Trippett, mng. ed. To encourage, equip, and empower Christian educators serving in public and private schools. Quarterly mag.; circ. 10,000. Subscription $20. 50% unsolicited freelance; 50% assigned. Query; prefers e-query (judy@ceai.org). Pays $20-40 ($30 for reprints) on publication for 1st or reprint rts. Articles 600-2,500 wds. (15-20/yr.); mini-features 400-750 wds., $25; very few book reviews 50 wds., (pays copies). Responds in 4-12 wks. Seasonal 4 mos. ahead. Accepts simultaneous submissions & reprints (tell when/where appeared). Accepts requested ms on disk or by e-mail (attached or copied into message). Regularly uses sidebars. Any Bible version. Guidelines/theme list on Website (www.ceai.org/fbenefits/teachers_of_vision/tov_index_ed.htm); copy for 9x12 SAE/4 stamps. (Ads)

Poetry: Accepts 2-3/yr. Free verse, haiku, light verse, traditional; 4-16 lines. Submit max. 3 poems.

Fillers: Educational only.

Special Needs: Legal and other issues in public education. Interviews; classroom resource reviews; living out your faith in your work.

Tips: "Know public education; write from a positive perspective as our readers are involved in public education by calling and choice. Most open to tips for teachers for living out their faith in the classroom in legally appropriate ways. No preachy articles."

TEACH KIDS ESSENTIALS (formerly Teach Kids!), PO Box 348, Warrenton MO 63383-0348. (636)456-4321. Fax (636)456-9935. E-mail: Yolanda.Derstine@cefonline.com ("TK Submission" in subject line). Website: www.teachkidsforum.com. Child Evangelism Fellowship. Yolanda Derstine, sr. ed. To equip Christians to lead the world's children (ages 4-11) to Christ and disciple them in the Word of God. Monthly newsletter; 8 pgs.; circ. 10,000. Subscription $36. Estab. 2008. 95% unsolicited freelance; 5% assigned. Complete ms; no phone/fax query; e-query preferred. Accepts full mss by e-mail. **PAYS A SUBSCRIPTION** on publication for nonexclusive rts. Articles 250-300 wds. (200+/yr.). Responds on acceptance. Seasonal 3 mos. ahead. Accepts simultaneous submissions & reprints (tell when/where appeared). E-mail submission OK (attached or copied into message). Prefers NIV. Also accepts submissions from children/teens. No guidelines; copy .50. (Ads—contact Kim.Pennell@cefonline.com)

Fillers: Anecdotes, facts, games, ideas, kid quotes, party ideas, tips—all related to kid's ministry.

Special Needs: "I have limited opportunity for lesson writers for our curriculum club (pays $500). the writer must be familiar with CEF party Club lessons, Christian hero lessons, and Bible lessons. This will be a hard place to break in. Writing for *Teach Kids Essentials* will help open that door. If interested, send a sample lesson, but I won't reply unless interested."

Tips: "Writers must show they have active involvement in children's ministry. Writing must be pertinent to children's ministry, concise, and well-written. Short, short, short."

$TODAY'S CATHOLIC TEACHER, 2621 Dryden Rd., Dayton OH 45439. (937)293-1415. Fax (937)293-1310. E-mail: mnoschang@peterli.com. Website: www.catholicteacher.com. Catholic; Peter Li Education Group. Mary C. Noschang, ed. Directed to personal and professional concerns of teachers and administrators in K-12 Catholic schools. Monthly mag. (6X during school yr.); 60 pgs.; circ. 45,000. Subscription $14.95. 30% unsolicited freelance; 30% assigned. Query; phone/fax/e-query OK. Pays $150-250 on publication for 1st rts. Articles 600-800, 1,000-1,200, or 1,500-2,500 wds. (40-50/yr.). Responds in 18 wks. Seasonal 3 mos. ahead. Accepts simultaneous submissions & reprints (tell when/where appeared). Prefers requested ms by e-mail (attached file). Regularly uses sidebars. Guidelines/theme list on Website; copy $3/9x12 SAE. (Ads)

Special Needs: Activity pages teachers can copy and pass out to students to work on. Try to provide classroom-ready material teachers can use to supplement curriculum.

Tips: "Looking for material teachers in grades 3-9 can use to supplement curriculum material. Most open to articles related to school curriculum and other areas, or lesson plans."

**This periodical was #35 on the 2007 Top 50 Christian Publishers list.

$YOUTH AND CHRISTIAN EDUCATION LEADERSHIP, 1080 Montgomery Ave., Cleveland TN 37311. Toll-free (800)553-8506. (423)478-7597. Fax (423)478-7616. E-mail: wanda_griffith@pathwaypress.org. Website: www.pathwaypress.org. Church of God/Pathway Press. Wanda Griffith, ed. To inform, equip, and inspire Christian education teachers and leaders. Quarterly mag.; 32 pgs.; circ. 10,000. Subscription $8. 10% unsolicited freelance; 90% assigned. Complete ms/cover letter; phone/e-query OK. Accepts full mss by e-mail. Pays $25-50 on publication for 1st or one-time rts. Articles 500-1,000 wds. (20/yr.). Responds in 2 wks. Seasonal 4 mos. ahead. Accepts simultaneous submissions; no reprints. Accepts requested ms on disk or by e-mail (attached file). No kill fee. Uses some sidebars. Prefers NIV. Guidelines on Website; copy $1/9x12 SAE. (No ads)

Fillers: Buys 4/yr. Cartoons, ideas, party ideas, tips, word puzzles; 250-300 wds. Pays $35.

Special Needs: Most open to how-to articles relating to Christian education. Local church ministry stories; articles on youth ministry, children's ministry, Christian education, and Sunday school.

**2004 EPA Award of Excellence—Denominational.

DAILY DEVOTIONAL MARKETS

Due to the nature of the daily devotional market, the following market listings give a limited amount of information. Because most of these markets assign all material, they do not wish to be listed in the usual way.

If you are interested in writing daily devotionals, send to the following markets for guidelines and sample copies, write up sample devotionals to fit each one's particular format, and send to the editor with a request for an assignment. **DO NOT** submit any other type of material to these markets unless indicated.

ANCHOR DEVOTIONAL, PO Box 79997, Riverside CA 92513-1997. Toll-free (800)65HAVEN. Fax (951)710-1115. E-mail: ministry@haventoday.org. Website: www.haventoday.org/anchor.php. Haven Ministries. Joyce Gibson, ed. Monthly devotional mag. Devotions 200 wds. Assigns one month of devotions on a theme (author picks theme). Query first for theme.

$+THE BRINK MAGAZINE, 114 Bush Rd., Nashville TN 37217. Toll free (800)877-7030. (615)361-1221. Fax (615)367-0535. E-mail: thebrink@randallhouse.com. Website: www.randallhouse.com. Randall House. Jacob Riggs, ed. Devotional magazine for young adults; focusing on Bible studies, life situations, discernment of culture, and relevant feature articles. Quarterly daily devotional mag.; 60 pgs.; circ. 10,000+. Estab. 2008. 20% unsolicited freelance; 80% assigned. Prefers e-query. Pays $50-150 on acceptance for all rts. Articles 500-2,000 wds. (10/yr.). Responds in 1-2 wks. Seasonal 6 mos. ahead. Accepts reprints (tell when/where appeared). Requires accepted articles by e-mail (attached file). No kill fee. Uses some sidebars. Guidelines by e-mail.

   Fillers: Buys 5-10/yr. Facts, ideas, newsbreaks, quizzes, quotes, tips; 50-200 wds. Pays $25-75.

   Tips: "Our feature articles (most open to freelancers) focus on culture from a biblical perspective. Culture includes but is not limited to: music, movies, TV, Internet, other media, holidays, politics, other religions, other events, hot topics, etc. We usually pick possible topics, then search for someone with experience in that area."

CLEAR LIVING, 114 Bush Rd., Nashville TN 37217. (615)361-1221. Fax (615)367-0535. E-mail: dianne.sargent@randallhouse.com, or through Website: www.randallhouse.com. Randall House. Dianne Sargent, ed. For adults 35-55 that encourages application of Scripture through devotions and experience, instructional, and inspirational articles. Quarterly mag.; circ. 28,000. Subscription $20. Open to freelance. Query with samples or complete devotionals by e-mail.

DAILY DEVOTIONS FOR THE DEAF, 21199 Greenview Rd., Council Bluffs IA 51503-4190. (712)322-5493. Fax (712)322-7792. E-mail: JoKrueger@deafmissions.com. Website: www.deafmissions.com. Jo Krueger, ed. Quarterly. Circ. 26,000. Prefers to see completed devotionals; 225-250 wds. **NO PAYMENT.** E-mail submissions OK.

$DEVOTIONS, 8805 Governor's Hill Dr., Ste. 400, Cincinnati OH 45249-3319. (513)931-4050. Fax (513)931-0904. E-mail: gwilde1@cfl.rr.com. Website: www.standardpub.com. Gary Allen, ed. Assigned by work-for-hire contract to previously published writers only. Query by e-mail only. Pays $20/devotion. Send list of credits rather than a sample.

$FORWARD DAY BY DAY, 300 W. Fourth St., Cincinnati OH 45202-2665. Toll-free (800)543-1813. (513)721-6659. Fax (513)721-0729. E-mail: rschmidt@forwarddaybyday.com. Website: www.forwardmovement.org. Richard H. Schmidt, ed./dir. Also online version. Send a couple of samples and request an assignment. Likes author to complete an entire month's worth of devotions. Subscription $6. No e-mail submissions. Length: 215 wds. Pays $300 for a month of devotions. Accepts reprints. (No ads)

FRUIT OF THE VINE, Barclay Press, 211 N. Meridian St., #101, Newberg OR 97132. (503)538-9775. Fax (503)554-8597. E-mail: info@barclaypress.com. E-mail submissions accepted at phampton@barclaypress.com. Website: www.barclaypress.com. Editorial team: Paula Hampton & Judy Woolsey. Send samples and request assignment. Subscription $18. Prefers 250 wds. **PAYS FREE SUBSCRIPTION & 6 COPIES.** Guidelines.

$LIGHT FROM THE WORD, PO Box 50434, Indianapolis IN 46250-0434. (317)774-7900. E-mail: submissions@wesleyan.org. Website: www.wesleyan.org/wph. Wesleyan. Lawrence W. Wilson, ed. dir. Devotions 220-230 wds. Pays $100 for seven devotions. Electronic submissions only. Send a couple of sample devotions to fit their format and request an assignment. No reprints.

MUSTARD SEED MINISTRIES DEVOTIONAL, 4854 W. 350S, Berne IN 46711. (260)334-5552. Fax (260)334-5993. E-mail: devotionals@mustardseedministries.org. Website: www .mustardseedministries.org. MustardSeed Ministries Inc. Wayne Steffen, ed. (Wayne@ mustardseedministries.org). Devotional mag. 100% unsolicited freelance. Complete ms; e-mail submissions preferred. **PAYS A UNIQUE, ATTRACTIVE PLAQUE.** Devotions 225-275 wds. Guidelines on Website.

> **Tips:** "We do not return any submissions and prefer that they are e-mailed to us. We are looking for submissions that are biblically based. Sincerity is as important as your writing skills. Most of us have a story to tell about how Christ touched our life in some situation that others in this world would benefit from; please send this to us." Also looking for articles for their newsletter. Guidelines on Website.

$MY DAILY VISITOR, 200 Noll Plaza, Huntington IN 46750. (260)356-8400. Fax (260)356-8472. E-mail: mdvisitor@osv.com. Website: www.osv.com. Catholic. Submit to The Editor. Scripture meditations based on the day's Catholic Mass readings. Bimonthly devotional booklet. Open to freelance. Pays $500 for a month's devotions (28-31 days), plus 5 copies, on acceptance for one-time rts. Not copyrighted. Devotions 125-135 wds. ea. (assigns a full month at a time). Guidelines on Website.

OUR DAILY JOURNEY, (formerly Our Journey), 3000 Kraft Ave. S.E., Grand Rapids MI 49512. (616)974-2663. Fax (616)957-5741. E-mail: tfelten@rbc.org. Website: www.rbc.org. RBC Ministries. Tom Felton, ed. Devotionals for today's young adult; features meditations on God's leading through life and community participation. Monthly devotional; 64 pgs. Subscription $5 or for donation. Open to unsolicited freelance. Complete ms (as a Word attachment). **PAYS 10 COPIES.** Articles/devotions 325-350 wds. Guidelines on Website. (No ads)

> **Special Needs:** Art and photographs. See guidelines.
>
> **Tips:** "Submit one article at a time, once a month."

PENNED FROM THE HEART, 304 Stow Neck Rd., Salem NJ 08079-3431. (856)339-9422. E-mail: ed4penned@gmail.com. Website: www.gloriaclover.com. Son-Rise Publications (toll-free 800-358-0777). Jana Carman, ed. Annual daily devotional book; about 240 pgs.; 5,000 copies/yr. 100% unsolicited freelance. Complete ms/cover letter; phone/e-query OK. **PAYS ONE COPY OF THE BOOK + A DISCOUNT TO RESELL BOOKS.** One-time rts. Devotions up to 250 wds. (365/yr.). Responds in 9-13 wks. Considers simultaneous submissions; accepts reprints (tell when/where appeared). Prefers mss by e-mail (attached). Also accepts submissions from children/teens. Guidelines (www.gloriaclover.com/ guidelines.html) & examples on Website. (No ads)

> **Poetry:** To 24 lines. Pays one copy.
>
> **Tips:** "Devotions must be biblically based, and something with an unexpected 'punch' is preferred. Build faith, encourage, and glorify God. No New Age material. Follow guidelines, specifically 250 words or less."

$THE QUIET HOUR, 4050 Lee Vance View, Colorado Springs CO 80919. (719)536-0100. Fax (407)359-2850. E-mail: schmidtd@cookministries.com. Website: www.cookministries.com. Cook Communications Ministries. Gary Wilde, ed; Doug Schmidt, mng. ed. Subscription $3.49/quarter. 100% freelance (makes 13 assignments/yr.). Pays $15-35/devotional on acceptance. Send list of credits only, rather than a sample. Accepts e-mailed sample devotional. Responds in 3 mos.

$+REJOICE! 600 Shaftesbury Blvd., Winnipeg MB R3P 0M4, Canada. (204)888-6781. Fax (204)831-5675. E-mail: ByronRB@mph.org. Website: www.mpn.net/rejoice. Mennonite Church/Mennonite Brethren Church. Byron Rempel-Burkholder, ed. Daily devotional magazine grounded in Anabaptist theology. Quarterly mag.; 112 pgs.; circ. 12,000. Subscription $29.60. 5% unsolicited freelance; 95% assigned. Pays $100-125 for 7-day assigned meditations, 250-300 wds. each; on publication for 1st rts. Also accepts testimonies 500-600 wds. (8/yr.) Prefers that you send a couple of sample devotions and inquire about assignment procedures; fax/e-query OK. Accepts assigned mss by e-mail (attached). Responds in 4 wks. Seasonal 8 mos. ahead. No simultaneous submissions or reprints. Some kill fees 50%. Uses some sidebars. Prefers NRSV. Guidelines by e-mail.

Poetry: Buys 8/yr. Free verse, light verse; 60 characters. Pays $25. Submit max. 3 poems.

Tips: "Don't apply for assignment unless you are familiar with the publication and Anabaptist theology."

$THE SECRET PLACE, Box 851, Valley Forge PA 19482-0851. (610)768-2434. Fax (610)768-2441. E-mail: thesecretplace@abc-usa.org. Website: www.judsonpress.com. Kathleen Hayes, sr. ed. Prefers to see completed devotionals, 200 wds. (use unfamiliar Scripture passages). 64 pgs. Circ. 150,000. 100% freelance. Pays $15 for 1st rts. Accepts poetry. Prefers e-mail submissions. No reprints. Guidelines.

$THESE DAYS, 100 Witherspoon St., Louisville KY 40202-1396. (502)569-5102. Fax (502)569-5113. E-mail: vpatton@presbypub.com. Website: www.ppcpub.com. Presbyterian Publishing Corp. Vince Patton, ed. Quarterly booklet; circ. 200,000. Subscription $6.95. Query/samples. 95% unsolicited freelance. Pays $14.25/devotion on acceptance for 1st and nonexclusive reprint rts. (makes work-for-hire assignments); 200 wds. (including key verse and short prayer). Wants short, contemporary poetry ($15) on church holidays and seasons of the year—overtly religious (15 lines, 33-character/line maximum). Query for their two feature segments (short articles): "These Moments" and "These Times." Guidelines; copy for 6x9 SAE/3 stamps.

$THE UPPER ROOM, PO Box 340004, Nashville TN 37203-0004. (615)340-7252. Fax (615) 340-7267. E-mail: TheUpperRoomMagazine@upperroom.org. Website: www.upperroom .org. Mary Lou Redding, ed. dir. 95% unsolicited freelance. Pays $25/devotional on publication. 72 pgs. This publication wants freelance submissions and does not make assignments. Phone/fax/e-query OK. Send devotionals up to 250 wds. Buys explicitly religious art, in various media, for use on covers only (transparencies/slides requested); buys one-time, worldwide publishing rts. Accepts e-mail submissions (copied into message). Guidelines (also on Website); copy for 5x7 SAE/2 stamps. (No ads)

Tips: "We do not return submissions. Accepted submissions will be notified in 6-9 wks. Follow guidelines. Need meditations from men." Always include postal address with e-mail submissions.

THE WORD AMONG US, 9639 Doctor Perry Rd., #126, Ijamsville MD 21754. Toll-free (800) 775-9673. (301)831-1262. Fax (301)831-1188. E-mail: lrz@wau.org. Website: www.wau .org. Catholic. Leo Zanchettin, ed. Daily meditations based on the Mass readings; inspirational essays; and stories of the saints and other heroes of the faith.

$THE WORD IN SEASON, PO Box 1209, Minneapolis MN 55440-1209. Fax (612)330-3215. E-mail: rochelle@rightnowcoach.com. Website: www.augsburgfortress.org. Augsburg Fortress. Rev. Rochelle Y. Melander, ed./mngr. 96 pgs. Devotions to 200 wds. Pays $20/devotion; $75 for prayers. Accepts e-mail submissions (copied into message) after reading guidelines. Guidelines at www.augsburgfortress.org, type "The Word in Season" in search box.

Tips: "We prefer that you write for guidelines. We will send instructions for preparing sample devotions. We accept new writers based on the sample devotions we request and make assignments after acceptance."

MISSIONS MARKETS

ACTION MAGAZINE: Men for Missions Intl., 941 Fry Rd., Greenwood IN 46142. (317)881-6752. Fax (317)865-1076. E-mail: mfmi@omsinternational.org. Website: www.mfmi.org. Gene Bertolet, ed. Informs the public of ministry opportunities, as well as reporting on the various OMS mission teams. Quarterly mag. Open to unsolicited freelance. Complete ms. Articles.

EAST-WEST CHURCH & MINISTRY REPORT, Southern Wesleyan University, Box 1020, Central SC 29630. (864)644-5221. Fax (864)644-5902. E-mail: melliott@swu.edu. Website: www.eastwestreport.org. Dr. Mark R. Elliott, ed. Encourages Western Christian ministry in Central and Eastern Europe and the former Soviet Union that is effective, culturally sensitive, and cooperative. Quarterly literary magazine; 16 pgs.; circ. 430. Print subscription $49.45; e-mail subscription $22.95. 25% unsolicited freelance; 75% assigned. Query; phone/fax/e-query OK. **PAYS IN COPIES** for all rts. Articles 1,400-2,000 wds. (4/yr.); book reviews, 400 wds. Responds in 4 wks. Prefers requested ms on disk or by e-mail. Regularly uses sidebars. Any Bible version. Guidelines on Website; copy $11.95. (No ads)

> **Tips:** "All submissions must relate to Central and Eastern Europe or the former Soviet Union."

$EVANGELICAL MISSIONS QUARTERLY, PO Box 794, Wheaton IL 60189. (630)752-7158. Fax (630)752-7155. E-mail: emq@wheaton.edu. Website: www.emqonline.com. Evangelism and Missions Information Service (EMIS). A. Scott Moreau, ed.; Laurie Fortunak, mng. ed.; Dave Broucek, book review ed. For missionaries and others interested in missions trends, strategies, issues, problems, and resources. Quarterly jour.; 136 pgs.; circ. 7,000. Subscription $24.95. 67% unsolicited; 33% assigned. Query; phone/fax/e-query OK. Pays $100 on publication for all & electronic rts. Articles 3,000-3,500 wds. (30/yr.); book reviews 400 wds. (query/pays $25). Responds in 2 wks. Accepts few reprints (tell when/where appeared). Prefers requested ms on disk or by e-mail (copied into message). Uses some sidebars. Kill fee negotiable. Prefers NIV. Guidelines on Website; free copy. (Ads)

> **Columns/Departments:** Buys 8/yr. In the Workshop (tips to increase missionary effectiveness), 800-2,000 wds.; Perspectives (opinion), 800 wds. Pays $50-100.
> **Tips:** "We consider all submissions. It is best to check our Website for examples and guidelines. Present an article idea and why you are qualified to write it. All articles must target evangelical, cross-cultural missionaries. 'In the Workshop' is most open to freelancers. Most authors have a credible connection to and experience in missions."

$GLAD TIDINGS, 50 Wynford Dr., Toronto ON M3C 1J7, Canada. Toll-free (800)619-7301. (416)441-1111. Fax (416)441-2825. E-mail: cwood@presbyterian.ca. Website: www.presbyterian.ca/wms. Women's Missionary Society/Presbyterian Church in Canada. Colleen Wood, ed. Challenges concerned Christians to reflect on their faith through articles and reports related to mission and social justice issues, locally, nationally, and internationally. Bimonthly mag.; 48 pgs.; circ. 4,500. Subscription $13 Cdn. 20% unsolicited freelance; 80% assigned. Query; e-query OK. Accepts full mss by e-mail. Pays $15-50 on publication for one-time or reprint rts. Articles 800-1.600 wds. (2-4/yr.); fiction 400-1,200 wds. (6/yr.); reviews 200 wds. (no payment). Responds in 3 wks. Seasonal 3-4 mos. ahead. Accepts simultaneous submissions & reprints (tell when/where appeared). Prefers e-mail submissions (attached or copied into message). No kill fee. Uses some sidebars. Also accepts submissions from teens. Prefers NRSV. Guidelines by e-mail; no copy. (Ads-limited)

> **Poetry:** Buys 6/yr. Avant-garde, free verse, haiku, light verse, traditional; 5-100 wds. Pays $10-20. Submit max. 5 poems.
> **Fillers:** Buys 4-6/yr. cartoons, games, kid quotes, prayers, short humor, word puzzles; $10-20.

Tips: "Writers can best break in with submissions of poetry, puzzles, or fiction. It is best to query as we often use themes."

INTERNATIONAL JOURNAL OF FRONTIER MISSIOLOGY, 1539 E. Howard St., Pasadena CA 91104. (626)398-2119. Fax (626)398-2101. E-mail: ijfm@wciu.edu. Website: www.ijfm .org. William Carey Intl. University. Rory Clark, mng. ed. Dedicated to frontiers in missions. Quarterly jour.; 48 pgs.; circ. 500. Subscription $18. 75% unsolicited freelance. Complete ms/cover letter; phone/fax/e-query OK. **NO PAYMENT** for one-time rts. Articles 2,000-8,500 wds. Seasonal 3 mos. ahead. Accepts simultaneous submissions & reprints. Accepts e-mail submissions. Does not use sidebars. Guidelines/theme list by e-mail/Website; no copy. (Ads)

Special Needs: Contextualization, church in missions, training for missions, mission trends and paradigms, de-westernization of the gospel and missions from the Western world, biblical world-view development, mission theology, Animism, Islam, Buddhism, Hinduism, nonliterate peoples, tent making, mission member care, reaching nomadic peoples, mission history, new religious movements and missions, science and missions, etc.

Tips: "Writers on specific issues we cover are always welcome. Although the circulation is small, the print run is 2,000 and used for promotional purposes. Highly recommended for mission schools, libraries, and mission executives."

+LAUSANNE WORLD PULSE, PO Box 794, Wheaton IL 60189. (630)752-7158. Fax (630)752-7155. E-mail: info@lausanneworldpulse.com. Website: www.lausanneworldpulse.com. Lausanne Committee for World Evangelism/Wheaton College. Naomi Frizzell, ed. News and information on evangelism and missions from around the world. Monthly online publication. Subscription free online. Open to unsolicited freelance. Query. Articles. Incomplete topical listings. (No ads)

$LEADERS FOR TODAY, Box 13, Atlanta GA 30370. (770)449-8869. Fax (770)449-8457. E-mail: rolandm@haggai-institute.com. Website: www.haggai-institute.com. Haggai Institute. Roland G. Moody, exec. production. Primarily for donors to ministry; focus is alumni success stories. Quarterly mag.; 16 pgs.; circ. 7,500. Subscription free. 100% assigned to date. Query; fax query OK. Pays .10-.25/wd. on acceptance for all rts. Articles 1,000-2,000 wds. Responds in 2-3 wks. Requires requested ms on disk or by e-mail (attached file). Kill fee 100%. Regularly uses sidebars. Prefers NIV. Guidelines/theme list; copy for 9x12 SAE/4 stamps. (No ads)

Tips: "If traveling to a developing country, check well in advance regarding the possibility of doing an alumni story. All articles are preassigned; query first."

**2005 EPA Award of Merit—Missionary.

MISSIOLOGY: An International Review, 204 N. Lexington Ave., Wilmore KY 40390. (859) 858-2216. Fax (859)858-2375. E-mail: missiology@asburyseminary.edu. Website: www .asmweb.org. American Society of Missiology/Asbury Theological Seminary. J. Nelson Jennings, ed. A scholarly journal for those who study and practice missions worldwide. Quarterly jour.; 128-136 pgs.; circ. 1,500. Subscription $26. 60% unsolicited freelance; 40% assigned. Complete ms/cover letter. **PAYS 20 COPIES** for 1st rts. Articles 3,000-4,000 wds. (20/yr.); book reviews 400 wds. Responds in 12 wks. No seasonal. No simultaneous submissions or reprints. Prefers requested ms by e-mail (attached file) or on disk. Uses some sidebars. Any Bible version. Guidelines (also by e-mail); copy for 6x9 SAE/$2.87 postage ($6 foreign). (Ads)

+MISSION CONNECTION, 6401 The Paseo, Kansas City MO 64131-1213. (816)333-7000, ext. 2350. Fax (816)822-8296. E-mail: nmi@nazarene.org. Website: www.nazarenemissions .org. Nazarene Missions Intl. Gail L. Sawrie, ed. A meeting place for equipping NMI leaders through interaction and resource exchange. Quarterly mag.; circ. 14,400. Open to unsolicited freelance. Complete ms. Articles. Incomplete topical listings. (No ads)

MISSION FRONTIERS, 1605 Elizabeth St., Pasadena CA 91104. (626)797-1111. Fax (626)398-2263. E-mail: mission.frontiers@uscwm.org. Website: www.missionfrontiers.org. U.S. Center for World Mission. Dr. Ralph Winter, ed.; Rick Wood, mng. ed. To stimulate a movement to establish indigenous churches where still needed around the world. Bimonthly & online mag.; 24 pgs.; circ. 100,000. Subscription free for donation. No unsolicited freelance; 100% assigned. Query. **NO PAYMENT.** Articles & reviews. Rarely responds. Accepts requested ms on disk or by e-mail (copied into message). Regularly uses sidebars. No guidelines; free copy. Incomplete topical listings. (Ads)

> **Fillers:** Cartoons.
>
> **Tips:** "Be a published missionary or former missionary. Be on the cutting edge of a strategic breakthrough or methods of reaching an unreached ethnic group." Looking for true-life, short sidebars of Muslims accepting Jesus, or impact of prayer in missions.

+MISSIONSMAGIZINET, PO Box 17, Uppsala, S-751 03, Sweden. +46(18)489-8000, or +46(18)489 8182. E-mail: karin.nytomt@livetsord.se. Website: www.livetsord.se. Livets Ord/Word of Life Church. Karin Nytomt, ed. To provide Bible teaching and to inform of our missions work through reports and feature stories. Published 7X/yr.; circ. 64,000. Open to unsolicited freelance. Query. Articles. Incomplete topical listings. (Ads)

$NEW WORLD OUTLOOK, 475 Riverside Dr., Rm. 1476, New York NY 10115-0122. (212)870-3765. Fax (212)870-3940. E-mail: nwo@gbgm-umc.org. Website: http://gbgm-umc.org/nwo. United Methodist. Christie R. House, ed. Denominational missions. Bimonthly mag.; 48 pgs.; circ. 24,000. Subscription $15. 20% unsolicited freelance. Query; fax/e-query OK. Pays $50-300 on publication for all & electronic rts. Articles 500-2,000 wds. (24/yr.); book reviews 200-500 wds. (assigned). No guaranteed response time. Seasonal 4 mos. ahead. Kill fee 50% or $100. Prefers e-mail submission (Word Perfect 6.1 or 8.1 in attached file). Regularly uses sidebars. Prefers NRSV. Guidelines; copy $3. (Ads)

> **Tips:** "Ask for a list of United Methodist mission workers and projects in your area. Investigate them, propose a story, and consult with the editors before writing. Most open to articles and/or color photos of U.S. or foreign mission sites visited as a stringer, after consultation with the editor."

$ONE, 1011 First Ave., New York NY 10022-4195. Toll-free (800)442-6392. (212)826-1480. Fax (212)826-8979. E-mail: cnewa@cnewa.org, or through Website: www.cnewa.org. Catholic Near East Welfare Assn. Michael La Civita, exec. ed. Interest in cultural, religious, and human rights development in Middle East, N.E. Africa, India, or Eastern Europe. Bimonthly mag.; 40 pgs.; circ. 100,000. Subscription $20. 50% unsolicited freelance; 50% assigned. Query/clips; fax query OK. Pays .20/edited wd. ($200) on publication for all rts. Articles 1,200-1,800 wds. (15/yr.). Responds in 9 wks. Accepts requested ms on disk. Kill fee $200. Prefers NAS. Guidelines (also by e-mail); copy for 8 x 11 SAE/2 stamps.

> **Tips:** "We strive to educate our readers about the culture, faith, history, issues, and people who form the Eastern Christian churches. Anything on people in Palestine/Israel, Eastern Europe, or India. Material should not be academic. Include detailed photographs with story or article."

OPREV EQUIPPER, PO Box 3488, Monument CO 80132-3488. (719)572-5908. Fax (775)248-8147. E-mail: bside@oprev.org. Website: www.oprev.org. Mission To Unreached Peoples. Bruce T. Sidebotham, dir. Provides information to equip U.S. military Christians for cross-cultural ministry. Quarterly & online newsletter; 8 pgs.; circ. 1,500. Subscription free. 40% unsolicited freelance; 60% assigned. Query; phone/e-query OK. **PAYS IN COPIES** for one-time rts. Not copyrighted. Articles 250-1,000 wds. (4/yr.). Responds in 4 wks. Seasonal 4 mos. ahead. Accepts simultaneous submissions & reprints (tell when/where appeared). Accepts requested ms on disk. Regularly uses sidebars. Prefers NIV. No guidelines; copy .50/9x12 SAE/4 stamps. (No ads)

Fillers: Accepts 4/yr. Newsbreaks, to 150 wds.

Columns/Departments: Accepts 4/yr. Agency Profile (describes a mission agency's history and work), 200-300 wds.; Area Profile (describes spiritual landscape of a military theater of operations), 300-750 wds., Resource Review (describes a cross-cultural ministry tool), 100-200 wds. Query.

Special Needs: Ministry in Afghanistan and Iraq. World news and analysis; cross-cultural communication; area profiles and people profiles on military theaters of operation.

Tips: "We need insights for military personnel on understanding and relating the gospel to Muslims."

$PFI GLOBAL LINK JOURNAL, (formerly PFI World Report), Box 17434, Washington DC 20041. (703)481-0000. Fax (703)481-0003. E-mail: communications@pfi.org. Website: www.pfi .org. Prison Fellowship Intl. Seldom uses freelance articles, but would consider articles with a direct connection to a Prison Fellowship organization outside of the United States.

$PIME WORLD, 17330 Quincy St., Detroit MI 48221-2765. (313)342-4066. Fax (313)342-6816. E-mail: pimeworld@pimeusa.org. Website: www.pimeusa.org. Pontifical Inst. for Foreign Missions/Catholic. Rick Schulte, ed. For those interested in and supportive of foreign missions. Published 5X/yr., plus newsletter supplement; 24 pgs.; circ. 16,000. Subscription $15. 10% unsolicited freelance. Complete ms; e-query OK. Pays $15-25 on publication for one-time rts. Photos $10. Articles 500-1,000 wds. Responds in 2 wks. Seasonal 4 mos. ahead. Accepts reprints (tell when/where appeared). Prefers e-mail submission (attached file). Uses some sidebars. Prefers NAB. Also accepts submissions from teens. Guidelines/theme list; copy for 6x9 SAE/2 stamps. (No ads)

Tips: "Features are open to freelancers. Needs missionary profiles; articles on PIME missionaries; interfaith dialog/experiences; and missions in Africa, especially Ivory Coast, Guinea Bissau, and Cameroon. Also issues like hunger, human rights, women's rights, peace, and justice as they are dealt with in developing countries by missionaries and locals alike."

THE RAILROAD EVANGELIST, PO Box 5026, Vancouver WA 98668-5026. (360)699-7208. E-mail: rrjoe@comcast.net. Website: www.railroadevangelist.com. Railroad Evangelistic Assn. Joe Spooner, ed. For railroad and transportation employees and their families. Tri-annual mag.; 16 pgs.; circ. 2,500. Subscription $8. 100% unsolicited freelance. Complete ms/no cover letter; phone query OK. **NO PAYMENT.** Articles 100-700 wds. (10-15/yr.); railroad-related fiction only, for children 5-12 yrs. Seasonal 4 mos. ahead. Accepts simultaneous submissions & reprints. Accepts e-mail submissions. Does not use sidebars. Guidelines (also by e-mail); copy for 9x12 SAE/2 stamps. (No ads)

Poetry: Accepts 4-8/yr. Traditional, any length. Send any number.

Fillers: Accepts many. Anecdotes, cartoons, quotes; to 100 wds.

Tips: "We need 400- to 700-word railroad-related salvation testimonies; or railroad-related human-interest stories; or model railroads. Since we publish only three times a year, we are focusing on railroad-related articles only. Just write and tell us or send us what you have. We'll let you know if we can use it or not."

WOMEN OF THE HARVEST, PO Box 151297, Lakewood CO 80215-9297. Toll-free (877) 789-7778. (303)985-2148. Fax (303)989-4239. E-mail: editor@womenoftheharvest.com. Website: www.womenoftheharvest.com. Women of the Harvest Ministries Intl. Inc. Cindy Blomquist, ed. To support and encourage women serving in cross-cultural missions. Bimonthly e-zine; 35 pgs.; circ. 8,000. Free online. 90% unsolicited freelance; 10% assigned. Complete ms; e-query OK. Accepts full ms by e-mail. **NO PAYMENT** for one-time & electronic rts. Articles 300-1,200 wds. Responds in 2 wks. Seasonal 3 mos. ahead. No simultaneous submissions or reprints. Prefers requested ms by e-mail (copied into message or attached file). Uses some sidebars. Guidelines/theme list on Website; copy online. (No ads)

Tips: "This is a magazine designed especially for women serving cross-culturally. We need articles, humor, and anecdotes related to this topic. Best way to break in is by having a cross-cultural missions experience or to be heading to the mission field."
**2008 EPA Award of Excellence—Online; 2006 EPA Award of Merit—Online. 2004 EPA Award of Merit—Christian Ministries.

MUSIC MARKETS

$CHRISTIAN MUSIC TODAY, 465 Gundersen Dr., Carol Stream IL 60188. (630)620-6200. Fax (630)260-8428. E-mail: music@christianitytoday.com. Website: www.ChristianMusicToday.com. Christianity Today Intl. Russ Breimeier, mng. ed. To inspire and inform readers about today's Christian music, artists, and industry trends through timely coverage, relevant news, insightful reviews and interviews, and educated opinion, all from a Christian world-view. Weekly e-zine. 5% unsolicited freelance; 95% assigned. Query; fax/e-query OK. Accepts full mss by e-mail. Pays $50-200 on acceptance for 1st rts. Articles 400-2,000 wds (200/yr.); music reviews, 300-700 wds., payment varies. Responds in 2 wks. Occasionally accepts simultaneous submissions & reprints (tell when/where appeared). Prefers e-mail submissions (attached file). Sometimes pays kill fee 50%. Uses some sidebars. Prefers NIV. No guidelines; copy online. (Ads)

  Columns/Departments: Buys 6-8/yr. Query. Glimpses of God (spiritual leanings in secular music), 1,000 wds. pays $75-100.

  Special Needs: Reviews of music videos.

  Tips: "Most open to Glimpses of God, news/trends, interviews, and commentaries."
  **This periodical was #27 on the 2008 Top 50 Christian Publishers list.

CHRISTIAN MUSIC WEEKLY, 7057 Bluffwood Ct., Brownsburg IN 46112-8650. (317)892-5031. Fax (317)892-5034. Canadian address: 775 Pam Cres, Newmarket ON L3Y 5B7, Canada. E-mail through Website: www.ChristianMusicWeekly.com. Joyful Sounds. Rob Green, ed. Trade paper for Worship, Inspirational, Adult Contemporary, and Southern Gospel Music radio formats. Weekly trade paper; 12 pgs.; circ. 300-1,200. Subscription $104 (paper) or $52 (PDF via e-mail). 25% unsolicited freelance; 75% assigned. Query by e-mail only. **PAYS IN COPIES** (will publish photo of writer and tiny bio). Articles 600-2,000 wds.; music reviews, 100-300 wds. Responds in 2 wks. Seasonal 2 mos. ahead. Accepts reprints. Requires requested ms on disk (DOS-ASCII), prefers e-mail submission. Guidelines by e-mail; copy for 9x12 SAE/2 stamps. (Ads)

  Fillers: Cartoons, short humor (particularly radio or music related).

  Columns/Departments: Insider (artist interview); Programming 101 (radio technique); retail, inspirational, especially for musicians and radio people; 600-2,000 wds.

  Special Needs: Songwriting and performance.

  Tips: "Most open to artist interviews. Must be familiar with appropriate music formats."

+CHURCH MUSIC QUARTERLY, 19 The Close, Salisbury, Wiltshire, SP1 2EB, United Kingdom. Phone +44 1722 424848. Fax +44 1722 424849. E-mail: cmq@rscm.com. Website: www.rscm.com. Royal School of Church Music. Julian Elloway, ed. Advice and inspiration for church musicians around the world. Quarterly mag.; 60 pgs; circ. 12,000. Subscription free with RSCM membership. 5% unsolicited freelance; 95% assigned. Query/clips; phone/fax/e-query OK. Accepts full mss by e-mail. Pays on publication. Articles. Incomplete topical listings. (Ads)

$CREATOR MAGAZINE, PO Box 3538, Pismo Beach CA 93448. Toll-free (800)777-6713. (707)837-9071. E-mail: creator@creatormagazine.com. Website: www.creatormagazine.com. Rod Ellis, ed. For interdenominational music ministry; promoting quality, diverse music programs in the church. Bimonthly & online mag.; 48-56 pgs.; circ. 6,000. Subscription $32.95. 35% unsolicited freelance. Query or complete ms/cover letter; fax/e-query OK. Pays $30-75 for assigned, $30-60 for unsolicited, on publication for 1st, one-time, reprint rts. Articles 1,000-10,000 wds. (20/yr.); book reviews ($20). Responds in 4-12 wks. Seasonal 4 mos. ahead. Accepts simultaneous submissions & reprints (tell when/where appeared). Prefers requested ms on disk. Regularly uses sidebars. Prefers NRSV. Guidelines/theme list; copy for 9x12 SAE/5 stamps. (Ads)

Fillers: Buys 20/yr. Anecdotes, cartoons, ideas, jokes, party ideas, short humor; 10-75 wds.; $5-25.

Special Needs: Articles on worship; staff relationships.

GOSPEL SYNERGY MAGAZINE: For The Good News—God's Word and Gospel Music, PO Box 286261, Chicago IL 60628. (708)272-6640. E-mail: alcarter@gospelsynergy.com, or through Website: www.gospelsynergy.com. Andre Carter, pub. To provide information such as promotions, advertising, and record deals to help grow gospel music ministries and the independent gospel artists. Monthly magazine. (Ads)

Tips: "There is a wealth of information that many ministries and artists are not taking advantage of. My assignment is to provide that information with articles, entertainment, and more."

THE HYMN: A Journal of Congregational Song, School of Theology, Boston University, 745 Commonwealth Ave., Boston MA 02215-1401. Toll-free (800)THE-HYMN. Fax (617)353-7322. E-mail: hymneditor@aol.com. Website: www.bu.edu/sth/hymn, or www.hymnsociety.org. Hymn Society in the U.S. & Canada. Beverly A. Howard, ed. (5423 Via Alberca, Riverside CA 92507-6477). For church musicians, hymnologists, scholars; articles related to the congregational song. Quarterly jour.; 60 pgs.; circ. 3,000. Subscription $75. 85% unsolicited freelance; 15% assigned. Query; phone/e-query OK. **NO PAYMENT** for all rts. Articles any length (12/yr.); book and music reviews any length. Responds in 6 wks. Seasonal 4 mos. ahead. Prefers requested ms on disk or by e-mail. Regularly uses sidebars. Any Bible version. Guidelines on Website; free copy. (Ads)

Special Needs: Articles on history of hymns or practical ways to teach or use hymns. Controversial issues as related to hymns and songs. Contact editor.

Contest: Hymn text and tune contests for special occasions or themes.

Tips: "Focus all articles on congregational song. No devotional material."

I AM MAGAZINE, 13055 Riverdale Dr. N.W., Ste. 500-222, Coon Rapids MN 55448. (651)248-9671, or (763)221-7119. E-mail: jerrvals2003@yahoo.com. Website: www.myspace.com/iammagazine. Jerrvals Records. Jerry Griffis, pub.; Val Griffis, ed. To reach gospel music listeners in the urban communities through genres such as gospel, traditional, contemporary, rap, and gospel hip-hop; as well as giving independent and national gospel artists and record companies an opportunity to gain exposure. Quarterly mag. Subscription $12. Open to unsolicited freelance. Query or complete ms. Articles. Guidelines on Website. Not in topical listings. (Ads)

TRADITION MAGAZINE, Phone/fax (712)762-4363. E-mail: bobeverhart@yahoo.com. National Traditional Country Music Assn. Inc. Bob Everhart, pres./ed. Bimonthly mag.; 56 pgs.; circ. 3,500. Subscription $25. 30% unsolicited freelance; 70% assigned. Query. **PAYS IN COPIES** for one-time rts. Articles 1,000-2,000 wds. (4/yr.). Responds in 6-8 wks. Uses some sidebars. Prefers KJV. Guidelines; copy for 9x12 SAE/2 stamps. (Ads)

Fillers: Cartoons.

Columns/Departments: Accepts 4-6/yr. Query.

Tips: "Most articles need to deal with traditional or old-time music."

Note: Also see "Resources: Songwriting" in the Resources section on the CD.

PASTOR/LEADERSHIP MARKETS

$THE AFRICAN AMERICAN PULPIT, PO Box 381587, Germantown TN 38183. Toll-free (800)509-8227. Phone/fax (412)364-1688. E-mail: mcgoeyeditor@comcast.net, Info@the africanamericanpulpit.com, or through Website: www.TheAfricanAmericanPulpit.com. Hope for Life Intl. Inc. Martha Simmons, pub.; Eugene L. Gibson Jr., co-ed. The only journal focused exclusively on the art of black preaching. Quarterly jour.; 96 pgs.; circ. 4,000. Subscription $40 ($59 to libraries). 50% unsolicited freelance; 50% assigned. Complete ms/cover letter; phone/e-query OK. Pays $50 (flat fee) on publication for all rts. Articles 1,500 wds., sermons 2,500 wds. Responds in 13-26 wks. Seasonal 6-9 mos. ahead. Requires requested ms on disk or by e-mail. Does not use sidebars. Any Bible version. Guidelines (also by e-mail/Website); copy. (Ads)

Special Needs: Any type of sermon by African American preachers, and related articles or essays.

Contest: Sponsors contest occasionally; advertised in the magazine.

Tips: "The entire journal is open to freelancers. We strongly encourage freelancers to submit to us (as many pieces as you can), and freelancers can call anytime with questions. We are always looking for how-to articles, sermon helps, homiletic-method essays, seminarian pieces, and practical pieces."

ALPHA NEWS, 2275 Half Day Rd., Ste. 185, Bannockburn IL 60015. Toll-free (888)949-2574. (212)406-5269. Fax (212)406-7521. E-mail: info@alphausa.org. Website: www.Alphausa .org. Alpha North America. Claudia Roux, ed. To keep church leaders informed about the Alpha course. Newspaper & online; circ. 195,000. Subscription free. Open to unsolicited freelance. Query preferred. Not in topical listings. (Ads)

$BAREFOOT, 2923 Troost Ave., Kansas City MO 64109-1593. Toll-free (866)355-9933. (816)931-1900. Fax (816)412-8306. E-mail: bfeditor@barefootministries.com, or through Website: www.barefootministries.com. Stephanie Wilson, ed. Dedicated to resourcing and equipping youth workers. 10% unsolicited freelance; 90% assigned. E-query preferred; fax query OK. Pays $50-100 on publication for all rts. Articles for youth workers 1,000-2,000 wds. (20-25/yr.); reviews 500 wds. ($25). Responds in 8 wks. Seasonal 6 mos. ahead. Accepts reprints (tell when/where appeared). Accepts e-mail submissions (attached or copied into message). Some kill fees. Does not use sidebars. Prefers NIV. Guidelines by e-mail; copy online. (No ads)

Fillers: Buys 20-40/yr. Anecdotes, cartoons, games, ideas, party ideas, short humor, and tips, 100-200 wds.; $20-40.

Special Needs: Youthworker and youth issues.

Tips: "We are most open to freelancers in the areas of product, music, and entertainment reviews. Where youth ministry articles and curricular pieces are concerned, we usually assign those to established youth ministry professionals."

$CATECHUMENATE: A Journal of Christian Initiation, 1800 N. Hermitage Ave., Chicago IL 60622-1101. Toll-free (800)933-1800. (773)486-8970. E-mail: editors@ltp.org. Website: www.LTP.org. Catholic. Mary Fox, ed. For clergy and laity who work with those who are planning to become Catholic. Bimonthly mag.; 48 pgs.; circ. 5,600. Subscription $20. 60% unsolicited freelance; 40% assigned. Query; phone/fax/e-query OK. Accepts full ms by e-mail. Pays $100-300 on publication for all rts. Articles 2,000-3,000 wds. (10/yr.); book reviews 800 wds. Responds in 2 wks. Seasonal 6 mos. ahead. No simultaneous submissions or reprints. Requires requested ms by e-mail (attached). No kill fee. Use some sidebars. Guidelines by e-mail; copy for 6x9 SAE/4 stamps. (No ads)

Poetry: Buys 6/yr. Any type; 5-20 lines; $75. Submit max. 5 poems. One-time rts.

Columns/Departments: Buys 26/yr. Sunday Word (Scripture reflection on Sunday readings, aimed at catechumen); 450 wds.; $200-250. Query for assignment.

Special Needs: Christian initiation; reconciliation.

Tips: "Writers should have worked at parishes or dioceses or taught in universities about Christian initiation."

$THE CATHOLIC SERVANT, 3204 E. 43rd St., Minneapolis MN 55406. (612)729-7321. Cell (612)275-0431. Fax (612)724-8695. E-mail: JohnSondag@sainthelena.us. Website: www.CatholicServant.org. Catholic. John Sondag, ed./pub. For Catholic evangelization, catechesis, and apologetics. Monthly tabloid; 12 pgs.; circ. 41,000 during school yr.; 33,000 summer. Query/clips; fax query OK. Pays $60 on publication. Articles 750-1,000 wds. (12/yr.). Responds in 4 wks. Seasonal 3 mos. ahead. Requested mss by e-mail only. Uses some sidebars. (Ads)

Fillers: Cartoons & short humor.

Columns/Departments: Opinion column, 500-750 wds.

Tips: "We buy features or column only." Be sure to indicate "Ms for Catholic Servant" in subject line of e-mail.

$THE CHRISTIAN CENTURY, 104 S. Michigan Ave., Ste. 700, Chicago IL 60603. (312)263-7510. Fax (312)263-7540. E-mail: main@christiancentury.org. Website: www.christian century.org. Christian Century Foundation. Submit to: Attention Manuscripts. For ministers, educators, and church leaders interested in events and theological issues of concern to the ecumenical church. Biweekly mag.; 48 pgs.; circ. 30,000. Subscription $49. 20% unsolicited freelance; 80% assigned. Query (complete ms for fiction); phone/fax query OK. Pays $125 on publication for all or one-time rts. Articles 1,500-3,000 wds. (150/yr.); fiction 1,000-3,000 wds. (3/yr.); book reviews, 800-1,500 wds.; music or video reviews 1,000 wds.; pays $0-75. Responds in 1-9 wks. Seasonal 4 mos. ahead. No simultaneous submissions. Accepts reprints (tell when/where appeared). No kill fee. Regularly uses sidebars. Prefers NRSV. Guidelines/theme list (also by e-mail/Website); copy $5. (Ads)

Poetry: Poetry Editor. Buys 50/yr. Any type (religious but not sentimental); to 20 lines; $50. Submit max. 10 poems.

Special Needs: Film, popular culture commentary; news topics and analysis.

Tips: "Keep in mind our audience of sophisticated readers, eager for analysis and critical perspective that goes beyond the obvious. We are open to all topics if written with appropriate style for our readers."

CHRISTIAN EDUCATION JOURNAL (CA), 13800 Biola Ave., LaMirada CA 90639. (562)903-6000, ext. 5528. Fax (562)906-4502. E-mail: editor.cej@biola.edu. Website: www.biola.edu/cej. Talbot School of Theology, Biola University. Kevin E. Lawson, ed. Academic journal on the practice of Christian education; for students, professors, and thoughtful ministry leaders in Christian education. Semiannual jour.; 200-250 pgs.; circ. 750. Subscription $28. Open to freelance. Query; e-query OK. Accepts full mss by e-mail. **NO PAYMENT** for 1st rts. Articles 3,000-6,000 wds. (20/yr.); book reviews 2-5 pgs. Responds in 4-6 wks. No seasonal. Might accept simultaneous submissions & reprints (tell when/where appeared). Requires e-mail submissions (attached file in Word format). Does not use sidebars. Any Bible version. Guidelines on Website; no copy. (Ads)

Tips: "Focus on foundations and/or research with implications for the conception and practice of Christian education." Book reviews must be preassigned and approved by the editor; guidelines on Website.

CHRISTIAN MANAGEMENT REPORT, PO Box 4090, San Clemente CA 92674-4090. Toll-free (800)727-4CMA. (877)487-0900. Fax (877)595-7649. E-mail: cma@cmaonline.org. Website: www.CMAonline.org. Christian Management Assn. DeWayne Herbrandson, exec. ed.

Management resources and leadership training for Christian nonprofit organizations and growing churches. Bimonthly jour.; 56-72 pgs.; circ. 3,500+. Subscription $39.95. 100% assigned. Complete ms; e-query encouraged. **PAYS 10 COPIES** for all, 1st, one-time, reprint, or electronic rts. Articles 770-1,500 wds./bio; book reviews 100-200 wds. Responds in 4 wks. Seasonal 6 mos. ahead. No simultaneous submissions; limited reprints. CMA members first choice. Prefers accepted ms by e-mail (attached file). Regularly uses sidebars. Prefers NIV, NLT. Guidelines (also by e-mail); free copy. (Ads)

Fillers: Cartoons.

Columns/Departments: Accepts 6/yr. General leadership issues, CEOs & senior team issues, general management issues, board governance, church leadership, church financial management, information technology, tax & legal trends; all 250-2,000 wds.

Special Needs: Evangelical Calendar of Events.

Tips: "All areas open. Submit a synopsis of article idea dealing with leadership and management issues relevant to megachurches or parachurch organizations. Send by e-mail (attached file)."

CHURCHLIFE INSPIRATION & HUMOR, 12372 W. 107th Terr., Overland Park KS 66210. Toll-free (888)638-7439. (719)302-3777. Fax (719)623-0251. Website: www.churchlifenews letter.com. Logos Media Network. Submit to The Editor. Humor and inspiration for pastors and church leaders. E-newsletter; circ. 65,000. Incomplete topical listings.

Fillers: Jokes, sermon illustrations, short humor.

$THE CLERGY JOURNAL, 6160 Carmen Ave. E., Inver Grove Heights MN 55076-4422. (651)451-9945. Fax (651)457-4617. E-mail: sfirle@logosstaff.com. Website: www.logos productions.com. Logos Productions Inc. Sharon Firle, mng. ed. Directed mainly to clergy—a practical guide to church leadership and personal growth. Monthly (9X) mag.; 56 pgs.; circ. 6,000. Subscription $46.95. 5% unsolicited freelance; 95% assigned. Complete ms/cover letter; fax/e-query OK. Pays $75-150 on publication for 1st rts. Articles 1,000-1,500 wds. (25/yr.). Responds in 4 wks. Seasonal 8 mos. ahead. Accepts simultaneous submissions & reprints (tell when/where appeared). Prefers requested ms by e-mail (attached file). No kill fee. Uses some sidebars. Prefers NRSV. Guidelines/theme list (also by e-mail/Website); copy for 9x12 SAE/4 stamps. (Ads—struran@logosstaff.com)

Columns/Departments: Ministry Issues; Preaching & Worship; Personal Issues; $75-150.

Special Needs: Church technology issues.

Tips: "Our greatest need is sermon writers who can write on assigned texts. Instructions sent on request. Our readers are mainline Protestant. We are interested in meeting the personal and professional needs of clergy in areas like worship planning, church and personal finances, and self-care—spiritual, physical, and emotional."

+COOK INTERNATIONAL, 4050 Lee Vance View, Colorado Springs CO 80918. (719)536-0100. Fax (719)536-3266. E-mail: kim.pettit@cookinternational.org. Cook International. Kim Pettit, ed. Seeks to encourage self-sufficient, effective indigenous Christian publishing worldwide to spread the life-giving message of the gospel. Monthly online publication; circ. 2,000. Subscription free. Open to unsolicited freelance. Query. Articles & reviews. Incomplete topical listings. (No ads)

$CORNERSTONE YOUTH RESOURCE, 55 W. Oak Ridge Dr., Hagerstown MD 21740. E-mail: iyr_editor@yahoo.com. Seventh-day Adventist. Patricia Humphrey, ed. For Christian youth leaders; a practical resource filled with ideas for creative youth ministry and programming. Quarterly mag.; 48 pgs.; circ. 2,200. 5% unsolicited freelance; 95% assigned. Query/clips; fax query OK; best to e-mail, as editor lives in Texas. Pays $25-350 on acceptance for 1st rts. Articles 700-900 wds. (16/yr.). Responds in 8-12 wks. Seasonal 12 mos. ahead. Accepts reprints (tell when/where appeared). Accepts e-mail submissions (attached file in Microsoft

Word). No kill fee. Regularly uses sidebars. Prefers KJV, NKJV, NIV. Also accepts submissions from teens. Guidelines (also by e-mail); copy for 9x12 SAE/$2.23 postage (mark "Media Mail"). (Ads)

Columns/Departments: Outreach Ideas (service activity ideas for teens), 800-1,000 wds.; Super Social Suggestions (social activities and games for teen groups), 800-1,000 wds.; Program Ideas (creative youth programming ideas), variable lengths.

Special Needs: Articles dealing with understanding and teaching youth. Innovative concepts in youth ministry.

Tips: "Areas most open to freelancers are the Super Social and Outreach Ideas. We are always looking for creative activity ideas that teen leaders can do with youth, ages 14-18. The activities should be fun to do and well written with clear, easy-to-follow instructions. Ideas that are tested and have worked well with your own youth group are preferred."

CROSS CURRENTS, 475 Riverside Dr., Ste. 1945, New York NY 10015. (212)870-2544. Fax (212) 870-2539. E-mail: editors@crosscurrents.org. Website: www.crosscurrents.org. Association for Religion and Intellectual Life. Charles P. Henderson, exec. dir.; submit to Managing Editor. For thoughtful activists for social justice and church reform. Quarterly mag.; 144 pgs.; circ. 5,000. Subscription $30. 25% unsolicited freelance; 75% assigned. Mostly written by academics. Complete ms/cover letter; e-query OK. **PAYS IN COPIES** for all rts. Articles 3,000-5,000 wds.; fiction 3,000 wds.; book reviews 1,000 wds. Responds in 4-8 wks. Seasonal 6 mos. ahead. No simultaneous submissions or reprints. Prefers requested ms on disk or by e-mail (attached file). Does not use sidebars. Guidelines on Website; no copy. (Ads)

Poetry: Accepts 12/yr. Any type or length; no payment. Submit max. 5 poems.

Tips: "Looking for focused, well-researched articles; creative fiction and poetry. Send two double-spaced copies; SASE; use *Chicago Manual of Style* and nonsexist language."

$DIOCESAN DIALOGUE, 16565 S. State St., South Holland IL 60473. (708)331-5485. Fax (708)331-5484. E-mail: acp@acpress.org. Website: www.americancatholicpress.org. American Catholic Press. Father Michael Gilligan, editorial dir. Targets Latin-Rite dioceses in the U.S. that sponsor a Mass broadcast on TV or radio. Annual newsletter; 8 pgs.; circ. 750. Free. 20% unsolicited freelance. Complete ms/cover letter; no phone/fax/e-query. Articles 200-1,000 wds. Pays variable rates on publication for all rts. Responds in 10 wks. Accepts simultaneous submissions & reprints. Uses some sidebars. Prefers NAB (Confraternity). No guidelines; copy $3/9x12 SAE/2 stamps. (No ads)

Fillers: Cartoons, 2/yr.

Tips: "Writers should be familiar with TV production of the Mass and/or the needs of senior citizens, especially shut-ins."

$EMMANUEL, 5384 Wilson Mills Rd., Cleveland OH 44143. (440)449-2103. Fax (440) 449-3862. E-mail: emmanuel@blessedsacrament.com. Website: www.blessedsacrament .com. Catholic. Rev. Paul Bernier SSS, ed. (pbernier@earthlink.net); Patrick Riley, book review ed. Eucharistic spirituality for priests and others in church ministry. Bimonthly mag.; 96 pgs.; circ. 3,000. Subscription $31; $36 foreign. 30% unsolicited freelance. Query or complete ms/cover letter; e-query OK. Pays $75-150 for articles, $50 for meditations, on publication for all rts. Articles 2,000-2,750 wds.; meditations 1,000-1,250 wds.; book reviews 500-750 wds. Responds in 2 wks. Seasonal 4 mos. ahead. Accepts manuscripts on disk or as e-mail attachments. Guidelines (also by e-mail)/theme list. (Ads)

Poetry: Buys 15/yr. Free verse, light verse, traditional; 8 lines & up; $35. Submit max. 3 poems.

Tips: "Most open to articles, meditations, poetry oriented toward Eucharistic spirituality, prayer, and ministry."

$ENRICHMENT: A Journal for Pentecostal Ministry, 1445 N. Boonville Ave., Springfield MO 65802. (417)862-2781, ext. 4095. Fax (417)862-0416. E-mail: enrichmentjournal@ag.org.

Website: www.enrichmentjournal.ag.org. Assemblies of God. Gary R. Allen, exec. ed.; Rick Knoth, mng. ed. (rknoth@ag.org). Enriching and encouraging Pentecostal ministers to equip and empower Spirit-filled believers for effective ministry. Quarterly jour.; 144-160 pgs.; circ. 33,000. Subscription $24; foreign add $30. 15% unsolicited freelance. Complete ms/cover letter. Pays up to .15/wd. ($75-350) on acceptance for 1st rts. Articles 1,000-2,800 wds. (25/yr.); book reviews, 250 wds. ($25). Responds in 8-12 wks. Seasonal 1 yr. ahead. Accepts simultaneous submissions & reprints (tell when/where appeared). Requires requested ms on disk or by e-mail (copied into message or attached). Kill fee up to 50%. Regularly uses sidebars. Prefers NIV. Guidelines/theme list on Website; copy for $7/10x13 SAE. (Ads)

>Fillers: Buys over 100/yr. Anecdotes, cartoon, facts, short humor, tips; $25-40, or .10-.20/wd.

>Columns/Departments: Buys 40/yr. For Women in Ministry (leadership ideas), Associate Ministers (related issues), Managing Your Ministry (how-to), Financial Concepts (church stewardship issues), Family Life (minister's family), When Pews Are Few (ministry in smaller congregation); Worship in the Church, Leader's Edge, Preaching That Connects, Ministry & Medical Ethics, History is His Story; all 1,200-2,500 wds.; $75-275. Query or complete ms.

>Tips: "Most open to EShorts: short, 150-250 word, think pieces covering a wide range of topics related to ministry and church life, such as culture, worship, generational issues, church/community, trends, evangelism, surveys, time management, and humor." **2008, 2007 EPA Award of Excellence—Christian Ministry. This periodical was #43 on the 2008 Top 50 Christian Publishers list (#47 in 2006).

$THE EVANGELICAL BAPTIST, PO Box 457, Guelph, ON N1H 6K9, Canada. (519)821-4830, ext. 229. Fax (519)821-9829. E-mail: eb@fellowship.ca. Website: www.fellowship.ca. Fellowship of Evangelical Baptist Churches in Canada. Jennifer Bugg, mng. ed. To enhance the life and ministry of pastors and leaders in local churches. Quarterly mag. Subscription $12. Query preferred. Pays .05/wd. on publication for one-time rts. Articles 800-2,400 wds.; book reviews 200-500 wds. Guidelines on Website.

$GROWTH POINTS, PO Box 892589, Temecula CA 92589-2589. Phone/fax (951)506-3086. E-mail: cgnet@earthlink.net. Website: www.churchgrowthnetwork.com. Dr. Gary L. McIntosh, ed. For pastors and church leaders interested in church growth. Monthly newsletter; 2 pgs.; circ. 8,000. Subscription $16. 10% unsolicited freelance; 90% assigned. Query; fax/e-query OK. Pays $25 for one-time rts. Not copyrighted. Articles 1,000-2,000 wds. (2/yr.). Responds in 4 wks. Accepts simultaneous submissions & reprints. Accepts requested ms on disk. Does not use sidebars. Guidelines; copy for #10 SAE/1 stamp. (No ads)

>Tips: "Write articles that are short (1,200 words), crisp, clear, with very practical ideas that church leaders can put to use immediately. All articles must have a pro church-growth slant, be very practical, have how-to material, and be very tightly written with bullets, etc."

$INSITE, PO Box 62189, Colorado Springs CO 80962-2189. (719)260-9400. Fax (719)260-6398. E-mail: editor@ccca.org, or info@ccca.org. Website: www.ccca.org. Christian Camp and Conference Assn. Alison Phillips, ed. To inform and inspire professionals serving in the Christian camp and conference community. Bimonthly mag.; 40 pgs.; circ. 8,750. Subscription $29.95. 15% unsolicited freelance; 85% assigned. Query; e-query OK. Pays .16/wd. on publication for 1st and electronic rts. Cover articles 1,500-2,000 wds. (12/yr.); features 1,200-1,500 wds. (30/yr.); sidebars 250-500 wds. (15-20/yr.) Responds in 4 wks. Seasonal 6 mos. ahead. Accepts simultaneous submissions & reprints (tell when/where appeared). Prefers e-mail submission (attached file). Kill fee. Regularly uses sidebars. Prefers NIV. Guidelines (also by e-mail); copy $4.95/10x13 SAE/$1.68 postage. (Ads)

Special Needs: Outdoor setting; purpose and objectives; administration and organization; personnel development; camper/guest needs; programming; health and safety; food service; site/facilities maintenance; business/operations; marketing and PR; relevant spiritual issues; and fund-raising.

Tips: "Most open to profiles and how-to pieces; get guidelines, then query first. Don't send general camping-related articles. We print stories specifically related to Christian camp and conference facilities; innovative programs or policies; how a Christian camp or conference experience affected a present-day leader. Review several issues so you know what we're looking for."

**2008, 2006, 2005, 2004 EPA Award of Merit—Christian Ministries; 2007 EPA Award of Excellence—Christian Ministries; 2006 EPA Award of Merit—Most Improved Publication.

$INTERPRETER and INTERPRETER ONLINE, PO Box 320, Nashville TN 37202-0320. (615)742-5407. Fax (615)742-5460. E-mail: knoble@umcom.org, or through Website: www.InterpreterMagazine.org. United Methodist Church. Kathy Noble, ed. For lay leaders and pastors of the United Methodist Church; focus on ministry ideas and resources, spiritual growth issues, with a practical slant. Bimonthly & online mag.; 44+ pgs.; circ. 225,000. Subscription $12. Some assigned freelance; very little unsolicited material. Query/clips. Pays on acceptance for all rts. Articles 500-1,000 wds. (6 print/yr.; some Web exclusive). Seasonal 6 mos. ahead. No simultaneous submissions or reprints. Use submission form on Website or submit via e-mail. No kill fee. Uses some sidebars. Prefers NRSV. Guidelines on Website; copy for 9x12 SAE/4 stamps. (Ads)

Columns/Departments: Buys 10/yr. Living Out Your Faith in the Real World (practical discipleship); Lighter Fare (healthy recipes for church occasions; limited/occasional humor); Leadership Link (leadership theory & practice); IdeaMart (resources to support local church ministry); The World is My Parish (stories of United Methodists around the world); all 200-250 wds.; payment varies.

Tips: "All articles must have a specific and prominent United Methodist connection. Very difficult for unsolicited freelancers to break in, as we have an excellent pool and depend on them for referrals. No stories about organizations, ministries, missions with an official United Methodist equivalent. All writers must have an understanding of United Methodist organization."

**This periodical was #19 on the 2005 Top 50 Christian Publishers list (#31 in 2004). Received awards from the Associated Church Press in 2008 and United Methodist Assn. of Communicators in 2007.

THE JOURNAL OF PASTORAL CARE & COUNSELING, 1549 Clairmont Rd., Ste. 103, Decatur GA 30033-4635. (404)320-0195. Fax (404)320-0849. E-mail: MngEd@jpcp.org. Website: www.jpcp.org. Dr. Orlo Strunk Jr., mng. ed. For chaplains/pastors/professionals involved with pastoral care and counseling in other than a church setting. Quarterly jour.; 116 pgs.; circ. 10,000. Subscription $35. 95% unsolicited freelance; 5% assigned. Query; phone/fax/e-query OK. **PAYS 10 COPIES** for 1st rts. Articles 5,000 wds. or 20 pgs. (30/yr.); book reviews 5 pgs. Responds in 8 wks. Accepts requested ms on disk. Does not use sidebars. Guidelines on Website; no copy. (Ads)

Poetry: Accepts 16/yr. Free verse; 5-16 lines. Submit max. 3 poems.

Special Needs: "We publish brief (500-600 wds.) 'Personal Reflections,' but they need to deal with clinical experiences that have led the writer to reflect on the religious and/or theological meaning generated."

Tips: "Most open to poems and personal reflections. Readers are highly trained clinically, holding professional degrees in religion/theology. Writers need to be professionals on topics covered."

JOURNAL OF THE AMERICAN SOCIETY FOR CHURCH GROWTH, c/o Dr. Gary L. McIntosh, ed., Talbot School of Theology, 13800 Biola Ave., LaMirada CA 90639. (562)944-0351. Fax (562)906-4502. E-mail: gary.mcintosh@biola.edu. Website: www.ascg.org. American Society for Church Growth. Dr. Gary L. McIntosh, ed. Targets professors, pastors, denominational executives, and seminary students interested in church growth and evangelism. Biannual jour. (winter & summer); 150 pgs.; circ. 400. Subscription $24. 66% unsolicited freelance; 33% assigned. Complete ms/cover letter; phone/fax/e-query OK. **PAYS IN COPIES** for one-time rts. Not copyrighted. Articles 15 pgs. or 4,000-5,000 wds. (10/yr.); book reviews 750-2,000 wds. Responds in 8-12 wks. Accepts simultaneous submissions & reprints (tell when/where appeared). Prefers requested ms on disk or by e-mail. Does not use sidebars. Any Bible version. Guidelines (also in journal)/theme list; copy $10. (Ads)

> **Tips:** "Provide well-researched and tightly written articles related to some aspect of church growth. Articles should be academic in nature, rather than popular in style. We're open to new writers at this time."

$LEADERSHIP, 465 Gundersen Dr., Carol Stream IL 60188. (630)260-6200. Fax (630)480-2004. E-mail: LJEditor@LeadershipJournal.net. Website: www.leadershipjournal.net. Christianity Today Intl. Marshall Shelley, ed-in-chief. Practical help for pastors/church leaders, covering the spectrum of subjects from personal needs to professional skills. Quarterly & online jour.; 124 pgs.; circ. 52,000. Subscription $24.95. 20% unsolicited freelance; 80% assigned. Query or complete ms/cover letter; fax/e-query OK. Accepts full mss by e-mail. Pays .15-20/wd. on acceptance for 1st & electronic rts. Articles 500-3,000 wds. (10/yr.).; book reviews 100 wds. (pays $25). Responds in 6 wks. Seasonal 6 mos. ahead. Accepts reprints (tell when/where appeared). Accepts requested ms by e-mail (copied into message). Kill fee 30%. Regularly uses sidebars. Prefers NIV. Guidelines on Website; copy for 9x12 SAE/$2 postage. (Ads)

> **Fillers:** Buys 80/yr. Cartoons, short humor; to 150 wds.; $25-50.

> **Columns/Departments:** Skye Jetuani, mng. ed. Buys 25/yr. Tool Kit (Practical stories or resources for preaching, worship, outreach, pastoral care, spiritual formation, and administration); 100-700 wds. Complete ms. Pays $50-250.

> **Tips:** "Leadership is a practical journal for pastors. Tell real-life stories of church life—defining moments—dramatic events. What was learned the hard way—by experience. We look for articles that provide practical help for problems church leaders face, not essays expounding on a topic, editorials arguing a position, or homilies explaining biblical principles. We want 'how-to' articles based on first-person accounts of real-life experiences in ministry in the local church."

> **2008 Award of Merit—General; 2006 Award of Excellence—Christian Ministries; 2007, 2004 EPA Award of Merit—Christian Ministries. This periodical was #18 on the 2008 Top 50 Christian Publishers list (#15 in 2007, #14 in 2006, #8 in 2005, #8 in 2004).

$LEAD MAGAZINE (formerly Sabbath School Leadership), 55 W. Oak Ridge Dr., Hagerstown MD 21740. (301)393-4095. Fax (301)393-4055. E-mail: fcrumbly@rhpa.org, or mchambers@rhpa.org. Website: www.myleadmagazine.org. Seventh-day Adventist/Review & Herald. Faith Crumbly, ed. Nurtures, educates, and supports adult Bible study and program leaders by providing training in leadership and interpersonal skills, plus programs. Monthly mag.; 32 pgs.; circ. 8,100. Subscription $34.95 (add $6 for addresses outside U.S., Canada, and Bermuda). 10% unsolicited freelance; 90% assigned. Complete ms. Pays $25-100 on acceptance for 1st rts. Articles 600-1,200 wds. (120-150/yr.). Responds in 1-2 wks. Seasonal 6-8 mos. ahead. Accepts reprints (tell when/where appeared). Prefers accepted ms by e-mail (attached file). Uses some sidebars. Guidelines/theme list on Website; copy for $2.36 in postage. (For ads, contact: Genia Blumenberg at gblumenberg@rhpa.org.)

Columns/Departments: Buys 5/yr. Tool Kit (interpersonal skills, organization, mentoring, training), 600-800 wds. Query. Pays $70-100.

$LET'S WORSHIP, One Lifeway Plaza, MSN 175, Nashville TN 37234-0170. (615)251-3775. Fax (615)251-2795. E-mail: craig.adams@lifeway.com. Website: www.lifeway.com. Southern Baptist/LifeWay Christian Resources. Craig Adams, ed-in-chief. Resources for pastors and worship leaders; countering the norm with contagious ideas. Quarterly mag.; 96 pgs.; circ. 5,500. Subscription $14.95. 10% unsolicited freelance; 90% assigned. Complete ms by e-mail only. Pays .105/wd. on acceptance for all, 1st, or one-time rts. Articles 1,500 wds. (50/yr.); book reviews 300 wds. ($50). Responds in 10 wks. Seasonal 10 mos. ahead. Accepts simultaneous submissions. Requires ms by e-mail (attached file or copied into message). Regularly uses sidebars. Prefers HCSB. No guidelines/copy. (No ads)

Columns/Departments: Wednesday Words (4-week Bible study with listening sheets); Bible study, 625 wds.; church choir; instrumental music; worship media; student worship; children's worship; listening sheet, 200 wds.; Drama (original scripts), 900 wds.

Special Needs: New worship songs, staff communication tools and tips, fresh hymn arrangements, children's worship ideas, media techniques and tools, drama scripts, puppet scripts, singing techniques and exercises, etc.

Tips: "This periodical exists to bring the entire church staff to the same page with regards to worship culture in the church community."

$THE LIVING CHURCH, PO Box 514036, Milwaukee WI 53203-3436. Toll-free (800)211-2771. (414)276-5420. Fax (414)276-7483. E-mail: tlc@livingchurch.org. Website: www.livingchurch.org. Episcopal/The Living Church Foundation Inc. John Schuessler, mng. ed. Independent news coverage of the Episcopal Church for clergy and lay leaders. Weekly mag.; 24+ pgs.; circ. 9,000. Subscription $42.50. Open to freelance. Query; phone/fax/e-query OK. Pays $25-100 (for solicited articles, nothing for unsolicited) for one-time rts. Articles 1,000 wds. (10/yr.). Responds in 2-4 wks. Seasonal 2 mos. ahead. Prefers requested ms by e-mail (attached or copied into message). Uses some sidebars. Guidelines (by e-mail); free copy. (Ads)

Columns/Departments: Accepts 5/yr. Benediction (devotional/inspirational), 200 wds. Complete ms. No payment.

Tips: "Most open to features, as long as they have something to do with the Episcopal Church."

LUTHERAN FORUM, PO Box 327, Delhi NY 13753-0327. (607)746-7511. E-mail: dkralpb@aol.com. Website: www.lutheranforum.org. American Lutheran Publicity Bureau. Sarah Hinlicky Wilson, ed. (editor@lutheranforum.org). For church leadership—clerical and laity. Quarterly mag.; 64 pgs.; circ. 3,200. Subscription $26.95. 20% unsolicited freelance; 80% assigned. E-query only. **PAYS 2 COPIES** for one-time rts. Articles 2,000-3,000 wds. (48/yr.) Responds in 26-32 wks. No simultaneous submissions or reprints. Accepts full mss by e-mail only (attached file). No sidebars. Prefers ESV. Guidelines/theme list on Website; copy for 9x12 SAE/$8. (Ads)

Poetry: Accepts 2-8/yr. Avant-garde, free verse, traditional. Submit max. 5 poems.

Special Needs: Hymns written by Lutheran composers only. Submit to Sally Messner, messner@lutheranforum.org.

Tips: "Review the departments on our Website and read back issues. 95% of material is by Lutheran writers. Clarity of expression and sophistication of theological analysis are essential. No devotions or personal essays."

$LUTHERAN PARTNERS, 8765 W. Higgins Rd., Chicago IL 60631-4101. Toll-free (800)638-3522, ext. 2884. (773)380-2884. Fax (773)380-2829. E-mail: Lutheran.partners@elca.org. Website: www.elca.org/lutheranpartners. Evangelical Lutheran Church in America. Submit to Editor; (review editors listed on Website). To encourage and challenge rostered leaders in the ELCA, including pastors and lay ministers. Bimonthly & online mag.; 40 pgs.; circ. 20,000. Subscription $13 (free to leaders), $19.50 outside North America. 10-15% unsolicited freelance; 85-90% assigned. Query; phone/fax/e-query OK. Pays $125-170 on publication for one-time rts. Articles 750-1,500 wds. (12-15/yr.). Responds in 16 wks. Seasonal 6-12 mos. ahead. Accepts simultaneous submissions & reprints (tell when/where appeared). Kill fee (rare). Prefers requested ms on disk or by e-mail (attached file). Regularly uses sidebars. Prefers NRSV. Guidelines/theme list (also by e-mail/Website); copy $2/9x12 SAE/5 stamps. (Ads)

Poetry: Buys 6/yr. Free verse, traditional; $50-75. Keep concise. Submit max. 6 poems.

Fillers: Buys 4-5/yr. Cartoons; ideas for parish ministry; to 500 wds.; $25.

Special Needs: Book reviews. Query the editor. Uses books predominately from mainline denominational and some evangelical publishers. Payment is copy of book. Youth and family issues, rural and urban ministry issues, men's issues. More articles from women and ethnic authors (especially if ordained or are in official lay-ministry leadership roles).

Tips: "Query me with ideas which show you know our audience, can feel their heartbeats, and walk in their shoes. First, we are a leadership publication. Our audience includes pastors and lay church staff. Your articles must answer concerns that leadership has. Secondly, understand Lutheran Church theology and ELCA congregational life. Pertinent topics include preaching, Christian education, youth and family issues, Lutheran identity, worship, Scripture and theology, and social issues."

**This periodical was #28 on the 2008 Top 50 Christian Publishers list (#48 in 2007).

$MINISTRY & LITURGY, 160 E. Virginia St., #290, San Jose CA 95112. Toll-free (888)273-7782. (408)286-8505. Fax (408)287-8748. E-mail: editor@rpinet.com. Website: www.rpinet.com/ml. Resource Publications Inc. Donna M. Cole, ed. dir. To help liturgists and ministers make the imaginative connection between liturgy and life. Monthly (10X) mag.; 50 pgs.; circ. 20,000. Subscription $50. 5% unsolicited freelance; 5% assigned. Query only; fax/e-query OK. Pays a stipend on publication for 1st rts. Articles & fiction 1,500 wds. (30/yr.). Responds in 4 wks. Seasonal 6 mos. ahead. Accepts reprints (tell when/where appeared). Requires requested ms on disk. Regularly uses sidebars. Guidelines/theme list; copy $4/11x14 SAE/2 stamps. (Ads)

Special Needs: The practice of ministry: music ministry, youth ministry, pastoral ministry, and liturgical ministry.

Contest: Visual Arts Awards.

Tips: "Writers need to be able to help our reader do his or her job better. Be familiar enough with contemporary issues in ministry to provide perceivable value to the reader. Provide new insight or valuable insight into issues of concern to members of a ministry team. Credibility (training and experience in ministry) is important."

MINISTRY IN MOTION E-ZINE, 11335 Rosewood Ave., Athens OH 45701. (740)797-4023. E-mail: customerservice@ministryinmotion.net. Website: www.ministryinmotion.net. Nondenominational. Thomas Hanover, ed. We seek to equip lay and clergy leaders for ministry in the 21st century through the resources of publications, coaching, consulting, and other Website tools. Bimonthly e-zine; circulation 700+. Subscription free online. 25% unsolicited freelance; 75% assigned. Query/published clips; e-query OK. Accepts full mss by e-mail. **NO PAYMENT** for one-time & electronic rts. Articles 700-1,000 wds. (25/yr.); book reviews 250 wds. Responds in 4 wks. Seasonal 2 mos. ahead. Accepts simultaneous submissions & reprints (tell when/where appeared). Prefers submissions by e-mail (attached file). Uses some sidebars. Prefers NIV or NRSV. Guidelines by e-mail/Website; copy online or e-mailed. (Ads)

Fillers: Short humor.

Columns/Departments: Ministry Employment (how to find employment in ministry field); Women's Ministries (how to lead effective women's ministries); 700-1,000 wds. Complete ms.

Tips: "Share leadership tips and insights. The more practical and how-to, the better. No theology or heavily scholastic articles; we are for the everyday church worker. Avoid church culture terms and lingo related to your own denomination. If no experience, send us some samples. We'll work with you."

$MINISTRY MAGAZINE: International Journal for Pastors, 12501 Old Columbia Pike, Silver Spring MD 20904. (301)680-6510. Fax (301)680-6502. E-mail: MinistryMagazine@ gc.adventist.org. Website: www.ministrymagazine.org. Seventh-day Adventist. Nikolaus Satelmajer, ed.; Willie E. Hucks II, assoc. ed. For pastors. Monthly jour.; 32 pgs.; circ. 19,000. Subscription $30.50. 90% unsolicited freelance. Query; fax/e-query OK. Pays $50-300 on acceptance for all rts. Articles 1,000-1,500 wds.; book reviews 100-150 wds. ($25). Responds within 13 wks. Prefers requested ms by e-mail. Uses some sidebars. Guidelines (also on Website)/theme list; copy for 9x12 SAE/5 stamps. (Ads)

$MINISTRY TODAY, 600 Rinehart Rd., Lake Mary FL 32746. (407)333-0600. Fax (407)333-7133. E-mail: ministrytoday@strang.com. Website: www.ministrytodaymag.com. Strang Communications. Submit to The Editor. Helps for pastors and church leaders, primarily in Pentecostal/charismatic churches. Bimonthly mag.; 70 pgs.; circ. 30,000. Subscription $24.95. 60-80% freelance. Query; fax/e-query preferred. Pays $50 or $500-800 on publication for all rts. Articles 1,800-2,500 wds. (25/yr.); book/music/video reviews, 300 wds., $25. Responds in 4 wks. Prefers accepted ms by e-mail. Kill fee. Regularly uses sidebars. Prefers NIV. Guidelines; copy $6/9x12 SAE. (Ads)

Tips: "Most open to columns. Write for guidelines and study the magazine. Please correspond with editor before sending an article proposal."

$NET RESULTS, PO Box 3930, Lubbock TX 79452-3930. (806)726-8094, ext. 198. Fax (806) 762-8873. E-mail: netresults@netresults.org. Website: www.netresults.org. Net Results Inc. Bill Tenny-Brittian, sr. ed. Offers Christian church leaders practical, ministry vitalization ideas and methods. Bimonthly & online mag.; 32 pgs.; circ. 12,000. Subscription $29.95. 20% unsolicited freelance; 80% assigned. Query; fax/e-query OK. Accepts full ms through e-mail. Now pays a small amount on publication for one-time rts. Articles 1,000-2,000 wds. (20/yr.). Response time varies. Seasonal 6 mos. ahead. No simultaneous submissions or reprints. Requires accepted ms by e-mail (attached file). No kill fee. Regularly uses sidebars. Prefers NRSV. Copy for 9x12 SAE. (Limited ads)

Tips: "We prefer practical, how-to articles on ideas that have worked in a local church setting."

$THE NEWSLETTER NEWSLETTER, PO Box 36269, Canton OH 44735. Toll-free (800)992-2144. E-mail: jburns@comresources.com, or through Website: www.newsletternewsletter .com. Communication Resources. John Burns, ed. To help church secretaries and church newsletter editors prepare their newsletter. Monthly & online newsletter; 14 pgs. Subscription $49.95. 100% assigned. Complete ms; e-query OK. Pays $50-150 on acceptance for all rts. Articles 800-1,000 wds. (12/yr.). Responds in 4 wks. Seasonal 4 mos. ahead. Accepts simultaneous submissions. Requires requested ms by e-mail. Kill fee. Guidelines (also by e-mail).

Tips: "Most open to how-to articles on various aspects of newsletter production—writing, graphics, layout and design, postal, printing, etc."

$OUTREACH MAGAZINE, 2230 Oak Ridge Way, Vista CA 92081-8341.(760)940-0600. Fax (760)597-2314. E-mail: llowry@outreach.com. Website: www.outreachmagazine.com. Lindy Lowry, ed. Tells the ideas, insights, and stories of today's outreach-focused churches and is designed to inspire, challenge, and equip churches to connect with their communities and show the love of God to people both locally and globally. Bimonthly mag.; 130 pgs.; circ. 35,000. Subscription $29.95. 20% unsolicited freelance; 80% assigned. Query/clips; e-query OK. Pays $400 for articles; $700-1,000 for feature articles; on publication for 1st rts. Articles 1,200-2,500 wds. Responds in 6-8 wks. Seasonal 6 mos. ahead. No simultaneous submissions; rarely accepts reprints (tell when/where appeared). Prefers submissions by e-mail (attached file). Sometimes pays kill fee. Regularly uses sidebars. Guidelines on Website; free copy. (Ads)

Columns/Departments: Accepts fewer than 10/yr. Pulse (tight and bright stories about churches finding unique ways to outreach), 50-250 wds.; From the Frontline (profile of one church and the unique way it's reaching its community), 800 wds.; SoulFires (as-told-to pieces from interview with someone doing outreach), 950 wds.; .30/wd. or flat fee. Query.

Special Needs: Interviews with non-Christians.

Tips: "Most open to interviews/profiles (SoulFires, Frames, The Outreach Interview); church stories (Pulse, Idea Bank, From the Front Line); outreach ideas from churches (Idea Bank, Connections, Big Idea).

$PARISH LITURGY, 16565 S. State St., South Holland IL 60473. (708)331-5485. Fax (708)331-5484. E-mail: acp@acpress.org. Website: www.americancatholicpress.org. American Catholic Press. Father Michael Gilligan, ed. dir. A planning tool for Sunday and holy day liturgy. Quarterly mag.; 40 pgs.; circ. 1,200. Subscription $24. 5% unsolicited freelance. Query; no phone/e-query. Pays variable rates for all rts. Articles 400 wds. Responds in 4 wks. Seasonal 4 mos. ahead. Accepts simultaneous submissions & reprints (tell when/where appeared). Uses some sidebars. Prefers NAB. No guidelines; copy available. (No ads)

Tips: "We only use articles on the liturgy—period. Send us well-informed articles on the liturgy."

+PLUGGED IN, 8605 Explorer Dr., Colorado Springs CO 80920. (719)531-3400. Fax (719) 548-5823. E-mail: waliszrs@fotf.org, or pluggedin@family.org. Website: www.pluggedin online.com. Focus on the Family. Bob Smithhouser, ed. To assist parents and youth leaders in better understanding popular youth culture, and equip them to impart principles of discernment in young people. Monthly newsletter; circ. 43,000. Subscription $24. Open to queries only. Articles. Incomplete topical listings. (No ads)

$PRAY! PO Box 35004, Colorado Springs CO 80935-3504. (719)531-3585. Fax (719)598-7128. E-mail: pray.mag@navpress.com. Website: www.navpress.com/magazines/Pray! The Navigators. Cynthia Bezek, ed. A magazine entirely about prayer for believers who want to grow in their relationship with Christ through prayer and intercession—whether new to prayer, seasoned prayer warriors, or prayer leaders. Bimonthly mag.; 56-64 pgs.; circ. 41,000. Subscription $21.97. 70% unsolicited freelance; 30% assigned. Complete ms or query; e-query OK. Accepts full mss by e-mail. Pays .20/wd. (.05/wd. for reprints), plus a subscription, on acceptance for 1st, one-time, reprint, or electronic rts. Articles 800-1,500 wds. (30/yr.). Responds in 8-12 wks. No seasonal. Accepts simultaneous submissions & reprints (tell when/where appeared). Prefers e-mail submission (attached file). Kill fee 50%. Regularly uses sidebars. Prefers NIV. Guidelines on Website; copy for 9x12 SAE/$2.70 postage. (Ads)

Fillers: Buys 25/yr. Ideas on prayer (no prayers or poetry); 100-500 wds.; $60.

Columns/Departments: Buys 8/yr. Prayer Journeys (tells a personal story of a breakthrough, milestone, epiphany, or even setback you experienced in your prayer journey, which can teach others and draw them closer to Jesus through prayer); 800 wds. Prayer Ideas (short, practical articles that offer fresh and helpful ideas for readers to try in either personal or corporate prayer), 150-500 wds. Prayer News (using journalistic style, tells of a prayer event, preferably interdenominational and city- or region-wide, to encourage or inspire others), 200-400 wds.; complete ms; .20/wd.

Special Needs: Especially needs articles that move readers beyond praying for personal needs and toward praying for neighborhoods, churches, cities, and the nation.

Tips: "Please note that any topics indicated in the topical listings must be closely related to prayer (no general articles on those topics). Most open to prayer journeys, prayer ideas, nontheme features. Make sure you move people toward prayer as a relationship with Jesus and not just into more religious forms and structures. Be personal, vulnerable, biblical, and passionate. Keep in mind that our readers already pray, are highly motivated to pray. Be fresh and practical in your approach."

**#9 Best-Selling Magazine in Christian Retail Stores. This periodical was #1 on the 2008 Top 50 Christian Publishers list (#4 in 2007, #11 in 2006, #42 in 2005, #36 in 2004).

PREACHING, PREACHING ONLINE & PREACHING NOW, 104 Woodmont Blvd., Ste. 300, Nashville TN 37205. (615)386-3011. Fax (615)312-4277. E-mail: editor@preaching.com. Website: www.preaching.com. Salem Communications. Dr. Michael Duduit, ed. Bimonthly; circ. 9,000. Subscription $24.95/2 yrs. 50% unsolicited freelance; 50% assigned. Query; fax/e-query OK. **PAYS A SUBSCRIPTION** for one-time & electronic rts. Responds in 4-8 wks. Seasonal 10-12 mos. ahead. Reprints from books only. Prefers requested ms by e-mail (attached file). Uses some sidebars. Guidelines on Website; copy online. (Ads.) Preaching Online is a professional resource for pastors that supplements *Preaching* magazine. Includes all content from magazine, plus additional articles and sermons. Articles $10-50. Sermons 1,500-2,000 wds. (pays $35). *Preaching Now* is a weekly e-mail/e-zine; circ. 19,000. No freelance submissions; accepts books for review. Guidelines on Website; copy $8. (Ads)

$PREACHINGTODAY.COM, 465 Gundersen Dr., Carol Stream IL 60188-2498. Toll-free (877)247-4787. (630)260-6200. Fax (630)260-0451. E-mail: blarson@christianity today.com. Website: www.preachingtoday.com. Christianity Today Intl. Brian Larson, ed. Open to fresh sermon illustrations from various sources for preachers (no recycled illustrations from other illustration sources). E-mail submissions only; use online submission form. Articles 250-500 wds. Responds in 1 mo. Guidelines on Website. Sermon illustrations only.

$PREACHING WELL, PO Box 3102, Margate NJ 08402. Toll-free (800)827-9401. (609)822-9401. Fax (609)822-1638. E-mail: techsupport@voicings.com. Website: www.voicings .com. Voicings Publications. James Colaianni Jr., pub. Sermon illustration resource for professional clergy. Monthly newsletter, 8 pgs. Subscription $47. 5% unsolicited freelance. Complete ms; e-query OK. Pays .10/wd. on publication for any rts. Illustrations/anecdotes 50-250 wds. Responds in 6 wks. Seasonal 4 mos. ahead. Accepts reprints. Prefers requested ms on disk or by e-mail. Guidelines/topical index (also by e-mail); copy for 9x12 SAE. (Ads)

Poetry: Light verse, traditional; 50-250 lines; .10/wd. Submit max. 3 poems.

Fillers: Various; sermon illustrations; 50-250 wds.; .10/wd.

Tips: "All sections open."

$THE PRIEST, 200 Noll Plaza, Huntington IN 46750-4304. Toll-free (800)348-2440.(260)356-8400. Fax (260)356-8472. E-mail: tpriest@osv.com. Website: www.osv.com. Catholic/Our Sunday Visitor Inc. Msgr. Owen F. Campion, ed.; submit to Murray Hubley, assoc. ed. For Catholic priests, deacons, and seminarians; to help in all aspects of ministry. Monthly jour.; 48 pgs.; circ. 6,500. Subscription $39.95. 40% unsolicited freelance. Query (preferred) or complete ms/cover letter; phone/fax/e-query OK. Pays $50-250 on acceptance for 1st rts. Articles 1,500-5,000 wds. (96/yr.); some 2-parts. Responds in 5-13 wks. Seasonal 4 mos. ahead. Uses some sidebars. Prefers disk or e-mail submissions (attached file). Prefers NAB. Free guidelines/copy. (Ads)

Fillers: Murray Hubley, fillers ed. Cartoons; $35.

Columns/Departments: Buys 36/yr. Viewpoint, to 1,000 wds.; $75.

Tips: "Write to the point, with interest. Most open to nuts-and-bolts issues for priests, or features. Keep the audience in mind; need articles or topics important to priests and parish life. Include Social Security number."

$PROCLAIM, PO Box 1561, New Canaan CT 06840. Toll-free (888)320-5576. Fax (203)966-4654. E-mail: meg@parishpublishing.org, or info@parishpublishing.org. Website: www.parishpublishing.org. Parish Publishing LLC. Meg Brossy, ed. The leading inspirational preaching resource for church leaders. Weekly newsletter; 4 pgs. Subscription $69.95. Also available digitally at www.proclaimsermons.com, which includes archives of sermons. 20% unsolicited freelance; 80% assigned. Query/clips. Pays to $100 on publication or acceptance for reprint rts. Articles or fiction. Responds in 2 wks. Seasonal 3 mos. ahead. Prefers accepted mss by e-mail (attached file). (No ads)

Tips: "Proclaim follows the *Catholic Lectionary* and the *Revised Common Lectionary* (RCL). Writers are usually priests and ministers, or in seminary."

PULPIT HELPS, 6815 Shallowford Rd., Chattanooga TN 37421. Toll-free (800)251-7206. (423)894-6060. Fax (423)894-1055. E-mail: publisher@pulpithelps.com. Website: www.pulpithelps.com. AMG International. Justin Lonas, pub. Primarily reaches Bible-believing Christian pastors and functions as their primary source for information for sermon preparation and news from the Christian world. Monthly & online; 40 pgs; circ. 12,000. Subscription $25. 10% unsolicited freelance; 70% assigned. Complete ms/cover letter; e-query OK. Accepts full mss by e-mail. **NO PAYMENT.** Articles 800-1,000 wds. (50-75/yr.); book reviews 250 wds. Responds in 2-4 wks. Seasonal 2-3 mos. ahead. Accepts simultaneous submissions & reprints (tell when/where appeared). Requires e-mail submission (attached file). Uses some sidebars. Prefers NAS (others accepted). Guidelines (also by e-mail); copy for 9x12 SAE/2 stamps. (Ads)

Fillers: Accepts 50-100/yr. Anecdotes, cartoons, jokes, quotes, sermon illustrations, short humor, word puzzles; 25-150 wds.

Columns/Departments: Ted Kyle, mng. ed. (editor@pulpithelps.com) Accepts 2-4/yr. Missions Spotlight (innovative approaches to reaching the lost for Christ around the world); 800-1,200 wds.

Tips: "Most open to Sermon Starters—sermon outlines designed to give a busy pastor a leg up; any good missions-focused pieces; any good essays reflecting thoughtful Christian scholarship."

$REFORMED WORSHIP, 2850 Kalamazoo S.E., Grand Rapids MI 49560-0001. Toll-free (800) 777-7270. (616)224-0763. Toll-free fax (888)642-8606. (616)224-0803. E-mail: info@reformedworship.org. Website: www.reformedworship.org. Faith Alive Christian Resources. Rev. Joyce Borger, ed. To provide worship leaders and committees with practical assistance in planning, structuring, and conducting congregational worship in the Reformed tradition. Quarterly & online mag.; 48 pgs.; circ. 4,600. Subscription $25.95. 30% unsolicited freelance; 70% assigned. Query; e-query OK. Accepts full mss by e-mail. Pays .05/wd. on publication for 1st & electronic rts. Articles 1,400 wds.; book reviews 200 wds. Responds in 4 wks. Seasonal 6 mos. ahead. Rarely accepts reprints (tell when/where appeared). Prefers e-mail submission (attached file). Uses some sidebars. Also accepts submissions from children/teens. Prefers TNIV. Guidelines on Website; copy for 9x12 SAE/$2.23 postage (mark "Media Mail"). (No ads)

Columns/Departments: Songs for the Season (music and background notes, usually 3 songs), 2,000 wds.; Worship Technology (intersection of worship and technology), 900 wds. Query.

Tips: "You need to understand and focus on the Reformed tradition of worship."

**2004 EPA Award of Merit—General.

RELEVANT LEADER & RELEVANT NETWORK.COM, 1220 Alden Rd., Orlando FL 32803. Toll-free (866)512-1108. (407)660-1411. Fax (407)401-9100. E-mail: adam@relevantmedia group.com. Website: www.RelevantNetwork.com. Relevant Media Group. Adam Smith, mng. ed. Targets culture-savvy, relevant-minded ministers and leaders of 18- to 34-year-olds. Bimonthly & online mag.; 36 pgs. 80% freelance. Send a one-paragraph query/clips; prefers e-mail; no phone/fax query. **NO PAYMENT** for print or online contributions for 1st rts. & all electronic rts. Print features 1,500 wds.; Website features 800-1,200 wds; reviews 400-600 wds. Responds in 4-6 wks. Prefers submissions as Word attachments. Guidelines on Website. Incomplete topical listings.

$REVIEW FOR RELIGIOUS, 3601 Lindell Blvd., St. Louis MO 63108-3393. (314)633-4610. Fax (314)633-4611. E-mail: review@slu.edu. Website: www.reviewforreligious.org. Catholic/Jesuits of Missouri Province. Rev. David L. Fleming, S.J., ed. A forum for shared reflection on the lives and experience of all who find that the church's rich heritages of spirituality support their personal and apostolic Christian lives. Quarterly mag.; 112 pgs.; circ. 5,000. Subscription $30. 100% unsolicited freelance. Complete ms/cover letter; no phone/fax/e-query. Accepts full ms by e-mail. Pays $6/printed pg. on publication for 1st rts. Articles/fiction 1,500-5,000 wds. (50/yr.). Responds in 9 wks. Seasonal 8 mos. ahead. Accepts requested ms on disk. Does not use sidebars. Prefers RSV, NAB. Guidelines on Website; copy for 10x13 SAE/5 stamps. (No ads)

> **Poetry:** Buys 10/yr. Light verse, traditional; 3-12 lines; $6. Submit max. 4 poems.
>
> **Tips:** "Read the journal. Do not submit an article without reading at least one issue. Submit an article based on our guidelines."

$REV. MAGAZINE, PO Box 481, Loveland CO 80539-0481. Toll-free (800)447-1070.(970)669-3836. Fax (970)679-4392. E-mail: lsparks@group.com, or info@group.com. Website: www.revmagazine.com. Group Publishing Inc. Lee Sparks, ed. For pastors; partnering with pastors. Bimonthly & online mag.; 104 pgs.; circ. 45,000. Subscription $29.95. 25% unsolicited freelance; 75% assigned. Complete ms/cover letter; e-query OK. Pays $300-400 on acceptance for all rts.; makes work-for-hire assignments. Articles 1,000-3,000 wds. (18-24/yr.) Responds in 9 wks. Seasonal 8 mos. ahead. Prefers requested ms on disk or by e-mail (attached file). Regularly uses sidebars. Guidelines on Website; copy $2/9x12 SAE/5 stamps. (Ads)

> **Fillers:** Buys 3/yr. Cartoons, ideas, sermon illustrations; $50.
>
> **Columns/Departments:** Ministry (preaching, worship, discipleship, outreach, family); Life (personal growth, health beat, home front); Leadership (church business, team work, leadership); Insight (today's trends, current culture, in the know); all 200-400 wds; $35-50.
>
> **Tips:** "We are most open to short (250 word) practical articles for our departments. Write articles that deal with personal and professional topics for pastors."

$THE REVWRITER RESOURCE, PO Box 81, Perkasie PA 18944. (215)453-5066. Fax (215) 453-8128. E-mail: editor@revwriter.com. Website: www.revwriter.com. Nondenominational/RevWriter Resources LLC. Rev. Susan M. Lang, ed. An electronic newsletter for busy lay and clergy congregational leaders. Monthly e-zine.; circ. 500. Subscription free. 90% unsolicited freelance; 10% assigned. Query; e-query preferred. Pays $20 on publication for 1st electronic rts. & one-year archival rts.; $10 for devotions. Articles 1,500 wds.; questions or exercises for group use, 250-500 wds. No simultaneous submissions or reprints. Also accepts submissions from teens. Guidelines by e-mail/Website; copy online. (Ads)

> **Fillers:** Buys 10/yr. Ministry ideas; Ministry Resources List to accompany article; 250-400 wds. These are usually written by the feature-article writer. Also Practical Wisdom section.

Contest: Read current issues of the magazine to learn about new contests they are running. There are often drawings for free books.

Tips: "I'm always looking for articles for the Practical Wisdom section which focuses on program or ministry ideas that worked for you. This is an easy area to break into. They are short pieces, usually 250-400 words. Articles should be practical how-tos for busy church leaders—materials they can use in their ministry settings. Be sure to read archived issues for previous formats and ministry resources already covered. Looking for a new approach to stewardship. Most open to devotion writing in Lent and Advent, and the monthly articles and discussion questions. Send me an e-query detailing the article you'd like to write and include your expertise in this area. The material must be practical and applicable to life as a busy congregational leader. They want information they can use."

SEWANEE THEOLOGICAL REVIEW, School of Theology, Box 46-W, Sewanee TN 37383-0001. (931)598-1475. E-mail: STR@sewanee.edu. Website: www.sewanee.edu/theology/str/strhome.html. Anglican/Episcopal. Jim D. Jones, mng. ed. For Anglican/Episcopal clergy and interested laity. Quarterly jour.; 120 pgs. Subscription $24. Open to freelance. Complete ms/cover letter; no e-query. **NO PAYMENT** for all rts. Articles (24/yr.). Responds in 9-26 wks. Seasonal 24 mos. ahead. No simultaneous submissions or reprints. Prefers requested ms on disk or by e-mail (attached file). Prefers NRSV. No guidelines; copy $8. Incomplete topical listings. (Ads)

Special Needs: Anglican and Episcopal theology, religion, history, doctrine, ethics, homiletics, liturgies, hermeneutics, biography, prayer, practice.

SHARING THE PRACTICE, c/o Central Woodward Christian Church, 3955 W. Big Beaver Rd., Troy MI 48084-2610. (248)644-0512. Website: www.apclergy.org. Academy of Parish Clergy/Ecumenical/Interfaith. Rev. Dr. Robert Cornwall, ed-in-chief (drbobcornwall@msn.com); Dr. Forrest V. Fitzhugh, book rev. ed. (s.spade@att.net). Growth toward excellence through sharing the practice of parish ministry. Quarterly international jour.; 40 pgs.; circ. 250 (includes 80 seminary libraries & publishers). Subscription $30/yr. (send to APC, 2249 Florinda St., Sarasota FL 34231-1414). 100% unsolicited freelance. Complete ms/cover letter; e-query OK; query/clips for fiction. **NO PAYMENT** for 1st, reprint, simultaneous, or electronic rts. Articles 500-2,500 wds. (25/yr.); reviews 500-1,000 wds. Responds in 2 wks. Seasonal 6 mos. ahead. Accepts simultaneous submissions & reprints (tell when/where appeared). Prefers e-mail submissions (copied into message). Uses some sidebars. Prefers NRSV. Guidelines/theme list (Word or WordPerfect attachment). Prefers NRSV. Guidelines/theme list (also by email); free copy. (No ads)

Poetry: Accepts 12/yr. Any type; 25-35 lines. Submit max. 2 poems.

Fillers: Accepts 6/yr. Anecdotes, cartoons, jokes, short humor; 50-100 wds.

Columns/Departments: Academy News; President's.

Contest: Book of the Year Award ($100+), Top Ten Books of the Year list, Parish Pastor of the Year Award ($200+). Inquire by e-mail to DIELPADRE@aol.com.

Tips: "We desire articles and poetry by practicing clergy of all kinds who wish to share their practice of ministry. Join the Academy."

$SMALL GROUPS.COM (formerly Small Group Dynamics), 465 Gundersen Dr., Carol Steam IL 60188. (630)260-6200. Fax (630)260-0114. E-mail: soneal@christianitytoday.com. Website: www.smallgroups.com. Christianity Today Intl. Sam O'Neal, ed. How-to for small groups. Monthly e-zine/newsletter. Query; e-query OK. Pays $20-60 for all rts. Articles 500-1,500 wds. Seasonal 2-3 mos. ahead. Prefers requested ms by e-mail (attached file). Accepts reprints. Guidelines/theme list on Website.

Fillers: Small group cartoons.

Special Needs: Brief testimonies of how God has worked in your group; humor in groups; icebreaker ideas, etc.

Tips: "Follow our themes. We use mostly practical, how-to oriented articles."

$SUNDAY SERMONS, PO Box 3102, Margate NJ 08402. Toll-free (800)827-9401. (609)822-9401. Fax (609)822-1638. E-mail: techsupport@voicings.com. Website: www.voicings.com. Voicings Publications. James Colaianni Jr., pub. Full-text sermon resource serving professional clergy since 1970. Bimonthly booklet; 60 pgs. Subscription $62 or $89. 5% unsolicited freelance. Complete ms; e-query OK. Pays .10/wd. on publication for any rts. Complete sermon manuscripts 1,200-1,500 wds.; illustrations/anecdotes 50-250 wds. Responds in 6 wks. Seasonal 4 mos. ahead. Accepts reprints. Prefers requested ms on disk or by e-mail. Guidelines/topical index (also by e-mail); copy for 9x12 SAE. Incomplete topical listings.

Fillers: Various; sermon illustrations; 50-250 wds.; .10/wd.

Tips: "Submit complete sermon, 1,200-1,500 words. Read sample sermons on our Website."

TECHNOLOGIES FOR WORSHIP, 3891 Holborn Rd., Queensville ON L0G 1R0, Canada. (905) 473-9822. Fax (905)473-9928. E-mail: krc@tfwm.com. Website: www.tfwm.com. ITC Inc. Kevin Rogers Cobus, ed. Bimonthly & online mag.; 92+ pgs.; circ. 35,000. Subscription $14.95. 100% unsolicited freelance. Query; phone/fax/e-query OK. **NO PAYMENT** for one-time rts. Articles 700-1,200 wds. Responds in 2 wks. Seasonal 2 mos. ahead. Accepts simultaneous submissions & reprints (tell when/where appeared). Prefers accepted ms by e-mail (attached or copied into message). Uses some sidebars. Free guidelines/theme list (also on Website)/copy. (Ads)

Special Needs: Website streaming resources for churches and ministries; technologies: audio, video, music, computers, broadcast, lighting, and drama; 750-2,500 wds.

Tips: "Call/fax/e-mail the editor to discuss idea for article or column. The publication is open to technical, educational articles that can benefit the church, providing hints, tips, guidelines, examples, studies, tutorials, etc. on new technology and new uses for it in the church."

THEOLOGICAL DIGEST & OUTLOOK, 415 Linwell Rd., St. Catherines ON L2M 2P3, Canada. (905)935-5369. Fax (905)935-7134. E-mail: p-d@niagara.com, or paul@first grantham.org. Website: www.ITCanada.com/~theology. United Church of Canada. Rev. Paul Miller, ed. For clergy and informed laity; evangelical/orthodox slant within denomination. Semiannual mag.; 32 pgs.; circ. 400. Subscription $15 Cdn., $19 U.S. 100% unsolicited freelance. Complete ms; phone/fax/e-query OK. **NO PAYMENT.** Articles 1,500-5,000 wds. (6-8/yr.). Responds in 2 wks. Accepts reprints (tell when/where appeared). Prefers disk or e-mail submissions. Does not use sidebars. Any Bible version. No guidelines. (No ads)

Tips: "Just submit."

$THIS ROCK, 2020 Gillespie Way, El Cajon CA 92020. (619)387-7200. Fax (619)387-0042. cpeacock@catholic.com. Website: www.catholic.com/magazines.asp. Catholic Answers. Cherie Peacock, ed. Deals with doctrine, evangelization, and apologetics. Monthly (10X) mag.; 48 pgs. Subscription $39.95. 10% unsolicited freelance; 90% assigned. Complete ms/cover letter; e-query OK. Pays $200-500 on acceptance for 1st & electronic rts. Articles 1,500-3,000 wds. (80/yr.). Responds in 4 wks. Seasonal 9 mos. ahead. Prefers RSV (Catholic version). No simultaneous submissions or reprints. Prefers e-mail submissions (attached file). Kill fee sometimes. Regularly uses sidebars. Guidelines (also by e-mail/Website); copy for 9x12 SAE/$2.23 postage (mark "Media Mail"). (No ads)

Columns/Departments: Buys 10/yr. Damascus Road (personal conversion story), 1,800-3,000 wds. Complete ms. Pays $200.

Tips: "Most open to Damascus Road—stories of conversion to Catholic Church."

$TODAY'S PARISH, 1 Montauk Ave., Ste. 200, New London CT 06320. Toll-free (800)321-0411, ext. 188 (editor). (860)536-2611. Fax (860)536-5674. E-mail: NWagner@twentythird publications.com. Websites: www.todaysparish.com, or www.twentythirdpublications.com. Catholic/Twenty-Third Publications. Nick Wagner, ed. Practical ideas and issues relating to parish life, management, and ministry. Mag. published 7X/yr.; 40 pgs.; circ. 14,800. Subscription $24.95. Very little unsolicited freelance. Query or complete ms. Pays $75-100 on publication for 1st rts. Articles 800-1,800 wds. (15/yr.). Responds 13 wks. Seasonal 6 mos. ahead. Guidelines; copy for 9x12 SASE.

$TORCH LEGACY LEADER, PO Box 165046, Irving TX 75016. Toll-free (877)867-2457. (404) 348-4478. Fax (817)887-3089. E-mail: info@torchlegacy.com. Website: www.torch legacy.com. Torch Ministries Intl. Daniel Whyte III, pres./ed. A biblically based journal for black church leaders and community leaders. Online jour. 60% unsolicited freelance; 40% assigned. Complete ms/cover letter; e-query OK. Pays $50 (flat fee) on publication for 1st rts. Best Black Sermon of the quarter receives $100 on publication. Articles 1,500 wds. Responds in 12 wks. Seasonal 6 mos. ahead. Requires requested ms on disk. Uses some sidebars. Prefers KJV. Guidelines (also by e-mail/Website). Incomplete topical listings.

Special Needs: Sermons; articles; essays on the spiritual, social, and moral crisis facing the black community in America, with biblically based solutions.

Tips: "We are looking for sound, biblically based material that can be used by God to help lift up black America to where it needs to be in every area of life."

RICK WARREN'S MINISTRY TOOLBOX, 1 Saddleback Pkwy., Lake Forest CA 92630-2244. Toll-free (877)727-8677. (949)609-8703. E-mail: Tobinp@saddleback.net, or info@ pastors.com. Website: www.pastors.com (archive: www.pastors.com/Legacy/RWMT/ MTAchive.asp). Tobin Perry, ed. dir. To mentor pastors worldwide. Weekly e-zine; circ. 177,000. Free e-mail newsletter. 10% unsolicited freelance; 90% assigned. Query; e-query OK. **NO PAYMENT** for one-time, reprint, simultaneous, & electronic rts. Will link readers to your site or book on Amazon in exchange for article. Articles 800-1,000 wds. (250/yr.). Responds in 6-8 wks. Seasonal 4 mos. ahead. Accepts simultaneous submissions & reprints (tell when/where appeared). Prefers accepted ms by e-mail (attached file). Uses some sidebars. Guidelines & copy by e-mail. (No ads)

Special Needs: Issues facing pastors and other ministry leaders. Time management, conflict resolution, facilitating change, communication and preaching, stewardship, worship, lay ministry, temptation, spiritual vitality, family matters, finances, creative ideas for ministry, vision, power, authority, encouragement, ministry and missions mobilization, small group leadership, facilitating spiritual growth, missions (specifically battling spiritual lostness, egocentric leadership, poverty, disease, and illiteracy locally and globally). Uses a lot of church leadership and pastoral book excerpts and articles adapted from books. The key is that the submission relates to church leaders, specifically pastors.

Tips: "We're very open to freelance contributions. Although we are unable to pay, this is a worldwide ministry to pastors."

$WILLOW, PO Box 3188, Barrington IL 60011-3188. (847)765-0070. Fax (847)765-5046. E-mail: Paulb@willowcreek.org, or csc@willowcreek.com. Website: www.willowcreek.com. Willow Creek Assn. Paul Braoudakis, mng. ed. To educate, inform, and inspire pioneering, innovative church leaders with ministry breakthroughs from churches all around the world. Quarterly & online newsletter; 40 pgs.; circ. 10,000. Subscription $39. 10% unsolicited; 25-30% assigned. Query/clips or complete ms; phone/fax/e-query OK. Pays .25/wd. on publication for all rts. Articles 500-1,000 wds.; book/music reviews 500 wds., video reviews 300 wds. Responds in 2 wks. Seasonal 2 mos. ahead. Accepts simultaneous submissions & reprints (tell when/where appeared). Requires requested ms on disk or by e-mail (attached file). Some sidebars. Prefers NIV, NLT. Free copy. (No ads)

Columns/Departments: News From the Frontlines (creative ministries within the church), 50-100 wds.; Strategic Trends (trends from growing churches), 200-250 wds.; .25/wd. Complete ms.

Tips: "Submit articles that will help other churches do what they do better. Any articles that pertain to doing a seeker-sensitive type of ministry will be considered. Also leadership issues in the church, outreach ideas, and effective evangelism."

**2008 Award of Merit—Organizational; 2007 EPA Award of Excellence—General; 2006 EPA Award of Merit—Most Improved Publication.

$WORD & WORLD: Theology for Christian Ministry, 2481 Como Ave., St. Paul MN 55108. (651)641-3210. Fax (651)641-3354. Website: www.luthersem.edu/word&world. E.L.C.A./ Luther Theological Seminary. Frederick J. Gaiser, ed. (fgaiser@luthersem.edu); Mark Thronveit, book rev. ed. (mthrontv@luthersem.edu). Addresses ecclesiastical and general issues from a theological perspective and addresses pastors and church leaders with the best fruits of theological research. Quarterly jour.; 104 pgs.; circ. 2,500. Subscription $24. 10% unsolicited freelance. Complete ms/cover letter; phone query OK. Pays $50 on publication for all rts. Articles 3,500 wds. Responds in 2-8 wks. Guidelines/theme list on Website; copy $7.

Tips: "Most open to general articles. We look for serious theology addressed clearly and interestingly to people in the practice of ministry. Creativity and usefulness in ministry are highly valued."

$WORSHIP LEADER, 32234 Paseo Adelanto, Ste. A, San Juan Capistrano CA 92675-3622. Toll-free (888)881-5861. (949)240-9339. Fax (949)240-0038. E-mail: editor@wlmag.com. Website: www.worshipleader.com. The Worship Leader Partnership. Julie Reid, exec. ed. A resource for current trends, theological insights, and planning programs for all those involved in church worship. Bimonthly (8X) mag.; 64-72 pgs.; circ. 50,000. Subscription $19.95. 20% unsolicited freelance; 80% assigned. Query/clips or complete ms by fax/e-mail OK. Pays $200-800 for assigned, $200-500 for unsolicited, on publication for all or 1st rts. Articles 1,200-2,000 wds. (15-30/yr.); reviews 300 wds. Responds in 6-13 wks. Seasonal 6 mos. ahead. Accepts e-mail submissions (attached file—MS Word). Kill fee 50%. Uses some sidebars. Prefers NIV. Guidelines/theme list on Website; copy $5. (Ads)

Tips: "Read our magazine. Become familiar with our themes. Submit a detailed and well-thought-out idea that fits our vision."

$YOUR CHURCH, 465 Gundersen Dr., Carol Stream IL 60188. (630)260-6200. Fax (630)260-0114. E-mail: YCEditor@yourchurch.net. Website: www.yourchurch.net. Christianity Today Intl. Submit to Mike Schreiter, mng. ed. We give pastors and church leaders practical information to help them in managing the business side of the church. Bimonthly trade journal; 68+ pgs.; circ. 75,000. Subscription free to church administrators. 10% unsolicited freelance; 90% assigned. Query/clips; phone/fax/e-query OK. Accepts full mss by e-mail. Pays .20/wd. on acceptance for 1st & electronic rts. Articles 1,000-2,000 wds. (10/yr.). Responds in 2 wks. Seasonal 6 mos. ahead. Accepts simultaneous submissions & reprints (tell when/where appeared). Prefers e-mail submission (attached file). Accepts full manuscripts by e-mail. Kill fee 50%. Regularly uses sidebars. Prefers NIV. Guidelines/theme list by e-mail; copy for 9x12 SASE. (Ads: 630-260-6202)

Fillers: Buys 18/yr. Cartoons, $125.

Columns/Departments: Query. Church Makeover (recent remodeling project), 500-700 wds, plus several high-resolution photos, before/after project; Ask the Experts (Q & A), 100-300 wds.; $50-200.

Special Needs: Church management articles; audio/visual equipment; books/ curriculum resources; music equipment; church products; furnishings; office equipment; computers/software; transportation (bus, van); video projectors; church architecture/construction.

Tips: "Write and ask to be considered for an assignment; tell of your background, experience, strengths, and writing history. All areas are open to freelancers—articles on every topic we cover. Writers who can research a topic, interview experts, and present clear, concise writing should persistently and consistently ask for assignments. It might take several months to get an assignment."

**This periodical was #16 on the 2008 Top 50 Christian Publishers list (#12 in 2007, #13 in 2006, #16 in 2005, #46 in 2004).

$YOUTHWORKER JOURNAL, 104 Woodmont Blvd., Ste. 300, Nashville TN 37205. (615)312-4250. Fax (615)385-4112. E-mail: proposals@youthworker.com. Website: www.Youth worker.com. Salem Communications. Steve & Lois Rabey, eds. For youth workers/church and parachurch. Bimonthly & online jour.; 72 pgs.; circ. 20,000. Subscription $39.95. 100% unsolicited freelance. Query or complete ms (only if already written); e-query preferred. Pays $50-300 on publication for 1st/perpetual rts. Articles 250-3,000 wds. (30/yr.); length may vary. Responds in 26 wks. Seasonal 6 mos. ahead. No reprints. Kill fee $50. Guidelines/theme list on Website: www.youthworker.com/editorial_guidelines.php; copy $5/10x13 SAE. (Ads)

Columns/Departments: Buys 10/yr. International Youth Ministry, and Technology in Youth Ministry.

Tips: "Read Youthworker; imbibe its tone (professional, though not academic; conversational, though not chatty). Query me with specific, focused ideas that conform to our editorial style. It helps if the writer is a youth minister, but it's not required. Check Website for additional info, upcoming themes, etc."

TEEN/YOUNG ADULT MARKETS

$BOUNDLESS WEBZINE, 8605 Explorer Dr., Colorado Springs CO 80920. (719)531-5181. Fax (719)531-3349. E-mail: editor@boundless.org. Website: www.boundless.org. Focus on the Family. Ted Slater, ed. For Christian singles up to their mid-30s. Weekly e-zine; 200,000 visitors/mo.; 130 page views/mo. on blog. Free online. 5% unsolicited freelance; 95% assigned. Query/clips; e-query OK. Accepts full ms by e-mail. Pays .30/wd. on acceptance for nonexclusive rts. Articles 1,200-1,800 wds. (140/yr.). Responds in 4 wks. Seasonal 4 mos. ahead. Accepts simultaneous submissions & reprints (tell when/where appeared). Requires e-mail submission (attached—preferred—or copied into message). No kill fee. Does not use sidebars. Also accepts submissions from teens. Prefers ESV, NIV. Guidelines (on Website); copy online. (No ads)

Tips: "See author guidelines on our Website. Most open to conversational, winsome, descriptive, and biblical."

**This periodical was #12 on the 2008 Top 50 Christian Publishers list (#25 in 2007, #24 in 2006, #23 in 2005, #22 in 2004).

$BREAKAWAY, 8605 Explorer Dr., Colorado Springs CO 80921. (719)548-5838. Fax (719)531-3499. E-mail: erin.prater@fotf.org. Website: www.breakawaymag.com. Focus on the Family. Michael Ross, ed.; submit to Erin Prater, ed. asst. The 15-year-old Christian teen (boy) is our target; boys 12-17 yrs. Monthly mag.; 32 pgs.; circ. 96,000. Subscription $18. 25% unsolicited freelance; 75% assigned. Query or complete ms/cover letter; no phone/fax/e-query. Pays .12-.15/wd. (.15-.20/wd. for fiction) on acceptance for 1st, one-time, or electronic rts. Articles 400-1,800 wds. (6/yr.); fiction to 2,000 wds. (3-4/yr.). Responds in 8-10 wks. Seasonal 6 mos. ahead. No simultaneous submissions or reprints. Kill fee $25. Uses some sidebars. Also accepts submissions from teens. Prefers NIV. Guidelines (also by e-mail/Website); copy for $1.50/9x12 SAE/3 stamps. (No ads)

Columns/Departments: Buys 2-3/yr. Epic Truth (devotional); 800 wds.

Tips: "Most open to nontypical, historical, and biblical fiction. Need strong lead. Brevity and levity a must. Have a teen guy or two read it. Make sure the language is up to date, but not overly hip." Needs drama-in-life stories involving boys.
**2008, 2005, 2004 EPA Award of Merit—Youth; 2007 EPA Award of Excellence—Youth.

$BRIO/BRIO & BEYOND, 8605 Explorer Dr., Colorado Springs CO 80920. (719)531-3400, ext. 1768. Fax (719)531-3499. E-mail: freelance@fotf.org. Website: www.briomag.com. Focus on the Family. Susie Shellenberger, ed.; submit to Ashley Mays, ed. asst. *Brio* is for teen girls, 12-16 yrs.; *Brio & Beyond* for young women, 16-19 years. Monthly mag.; 40 pgs.; circ. 185,000. Subscription $22. 20-50% unsolicited freelance; 50-75% assigned. Complete ms/cover letter; e-query OK. Accepts full mss by e-mail. Pays .15-.35/wd. on acceptance for 1st rts. Articles 800-1,000 wds. (10/yr.); fiction 1,200-2,000 wds. (10/yr.). Accepts requested ms by e-mail or disk. Responds in 6-8 wks. Seasonal 8 mos. ahead. Accepts simultaneous submissions & reprints (tell when/where appeared). Rare kill fee $100. Regularly uses sidebars. Prefers NIV. Guidelines/theme list (also by e-mail); copy $2. (No ads)
Special Needs: All topics of interest to female teens are welcome: boys, makeup, dating, weight, ordinary girls who have extraordinary experiences, female adjustments to puberty, etc. Also teen-related female fiction.
Special Needs: "We love quizzes! Anything a teen girl is interested in: music, sports, fashion, make-up, relationships, crafts, recipes, fiction, etc."
Tips: "Be familiar with the magazines by studying at least 3 issues. Choose *Brio* or *Brio & Beyond* to write for. We are looking for a fresh and conversational style. Most open to quizzes, sport articles, and fiction."
**The #5 best-selling magazine in Christian retail stores. 2007 EPA Award of Merit—Youth (*Brio & Beyond*); 2006 EPA Award of Merit—Youth (*Brio*). This periodical was #21 on the 2008 Top 50 Christian Publishers list (#50 in 2004).

+CLARITY PUBLISHERS, PO Box 361726, Birmingham AL 35236. Toll-free (888)811-9934. Fax (205)503-5460. E-mail: paulk@studentlife.net. Website: www.studentlife.net. Randy Hall, ed. Bible study curriculum intended to take junior and senior high students through the Bible in 6 years. Weekly online. Free subscription. Open to unsolicited freelance. Complete ms. Incomplete topical listings.

$CLEAR DIRECTION, PO Box 17306, Nashville TN 37217. (615)361-1221. Fax (615)367-0535. E-mail: clearmag@randallhouse.com. Website: www.randallhouse.com. Randall House. Jonathan Yandell, ed.; submit to Derek Lewis, ed. asst. Bringing junior high students to a closer relationship with Christ through devotionals, relevant articles, and pertinent topics. Quarterly mag.; 52 pgs.; circ. 5,300. Estab. 2004. Open to freelance. Complete ms/cover letter; query for fiction. Accepts full mss by e-mail. Pays $35-125 on publication for 1st rts. Articles 600-1,500 wds. (35/yr.); book reviews 600-800 wds. ($35). Responds in 6 wks. Seasonal 9 mos. ahead. Accepts simultaneous submissions; no reprints. Prefers e-mail submissions (attached file). No kill fee. Regularly uses sidebars. Also accepts submissions from teens. Prefers KJV. Guidelines by e-mail/Website; copy for 9x12 SAE. (No ads)
Columns/Departments: Buys 10/yr. Changing Lanes (describe how God is changing you), 600-800 wds.; Between the Lines (review of book selected by Randall House), 600-800 wds.; $35-50.
Tips: "We are open to freelancers by way of articles and submissions to 'Changing Lanes' (600-800 wds.) and for feature articles (1,200-1,500 wds.) All articles should be about an aspect of the Christian life or contain a spiritual element, as the purpose of this magazine is to bring junior high students closer to Christ."

$CLEAR HORIZON, PO Box 17306, Nashville TN 37217. (615)361-1221. Fax (615)367-0535. E-mail: clearmag@randallhouse.com. Website: www.randallhouse.com. Randall House. Jonathan Yandell, ed.; submit to Derek Lewis, ed. asst. Bringing high school students to a closer relationship with Christ through devotionals, relevant articles, and pertinent topics. Quarterly mag.; 52 pgs. Estab. 2004. Open to freelance. Complete ms/cover letter; query for fiction. Accepts full mss by e-mail. Pays $35-125 on publication for 1st rts. Articles 600-1,500 wds. (35/yr.); book reviews 600-800 wds. ($35). Responds in 6 wks. Seasonal 9 mos. ahead. Accepts simultaneous submissions; no reprints. Prefers e-mail submissions (attached file). No kill fee. Regularly uses sidebars. Also accepts submissions from teens. Prefers KJV. Guidelines by e-mail/Website; copy for 9x12 SAE. (No ads)

Columns/Departments: Buys 10/yr. Changing Lanes (describe how God is changing you), 600-800 wds.; Between the Lines (review of book selected by Randall House), 600-800 wds.; $35-50.

Tips: "We are open to freelancers by way of articles and submissions to 'Changing Lanes' (600-800 wds.) All articles should be about an aspect of the Christian life or contain a spiritual element, as the purpose of this magazine is to bring high school students closer to Christ."

CONNECTED, Box 6097, Lincoln NE 68506-0097. (402)488-0981. Fax (402)488-7582E-mail: editor@christianrecord.org. Website: http://connected.christianrecord.org. Christian Record Services Inc. Bert Williams, ed.; Jenann Elias, asst. ed. For sight-impaired young adults, 12-25 yrs.; for interdenominational Christian audience. E-zine. Not included in topical listings.

$CREDO MAGAZINE, PO Box 419527, Kansas City MO 64141. (816)931-1900. Fax (816)412-8312. E-mail: credomag@barefootministries.com. Website: www.credomagazine.com. Barefoot Ministries/Nazarene Publishing House. Stefanie Hendrickson, ed. A cutting-edge devotional magazine that also challenges teens in their spiritual walk with relevant articles dealing with the issues they are facing. Monthly mag.; 48 pgs.; circ. 15,000. Subscription $23.40. 20-30% unsolicited freelance; 70-80% assigned. Query. Pays $30-60 for articles; $60 for fiction; on acceptance for all rts. Articles 500-800 wds. (20-30/yr.); fiction 700-800 wds. (10-15/yr.); reviews 500 wds. ($25). Responds in 4-6 wks. Seasonal 4-6 mos. ahead. No simultaneous submissions; accepts reprints (tell when/where appeared). Requires e-mail submission (attached or copied into message). Kill fee. Uses some sidebars. Prefers NIV. Encourages submissions from teens. Guidelines/theme list (also by e-mail/Website); copy for 6x9 SAE/$1 postage (additional copies $1.95 ea.). (No ads)

Poetry: Accepts 10-15/yr. Any type. Will be used in the magazine or on the Web. No payment. Submit any number.

Columns/Departments: Buys 30-40/yr. Real Deal (life issues/relationships), 700-850 wds.; Kung Pao (features student's creative work—poetry, lyrics, short stories, essays, art, photos. etc.), 100-500 wds.; Unreal (fiction piece—looking for 4-6 part series with each part able to stand on its own), 800 wds.; Tune-Up (interviews/profiles/news on Christian artists and bands), 800-850 wds.; Life Zone (articles about youth God is using in cool ways), 800 wds.; $40-60.

Special Needs: All topics must be geared to teens.

Tips: "We are most open to freelancers in the areas of Kung Pao, Tune-Up, Life Zone, Unreal (fiction), and seasonal/fun articles written for teens. Also to music and entertainment reviews."

**This periodical was #42 on the 2008 Top 50 Christian Publishers list (#18 in 2007, #9 in 2006).

$DEVO'ZINE, PO Box 340004, Nashville TN 37203-0004. (615)340-7247. Fax (615)340-1783. E-mail: devozine@upperroom.org, or smiller@upperroom.org. Websites: www.devozine.org, and www.devozine.info. Upper Room Ministries. Sandy Miller, ed. Devotional; to help teens (12-18) develop and maintain their connection with God and other Christians. Bimonthly mag.; 80 pgs.; circ. 90,000. Subscription $21.95. 85% unsolicited freelance;

15% assigned. Query; phone/fax/e-query OK. Pays $25 for meditations, $100 for feature articles (assigned) on acceptance for these one-time rts.: newspaper, periodical, electronic, and software-driven rts., and the right to use in future anthologies. Meditations 150-250 wds. (350/yr.); articles 650-700 wds.; book/music/video reviews 650-700 wds., $100. Responds in 16 wks. Seasonal 6-8 mos. ahead. Accepts occasional reprints (tell when/where appeared). Accepts requested ms by e-mail or online submission. Regular sidebars. Prefers NRSV, NIV, CEV. Guidelines/theme list on Website; copy/7x10 SASE. (No ads)

> **Poetry:** Buys 25-30/yr. Free verse, light verse, haiku, traditional; to 150 wds. or 10-20 lines; $25. Submit max. 1 poem/theme, 9 themes/issue.

> **Tips:** "E-mail with ideas for weekend features related to specific themes."

> **This periodicals was #2 on the 2008 Top 50 Christian Publishers list (#3 in 2007, #1 in 2006, #2 in 2005, #1 in 2004).

$ESSENTIAL CONNECTION (EC), One Lifeway Plaza, Nashville TN 37234-0174. (615)251-2008. Fax (615)277-8271. E-mail: ec@lifeway.com. Website: www.lifeway.com. LifeWay Christian Resources of the Southern Baptist Convention. Mandy Crow, ed. Christian leisure reading and devotional guide for 7th-12th graders. Monthly mag.; 60 pgs.; circ. 120,000. Subscription $24.95. 10% unsolicited freelance; 90% assigned. Query; e-query OK. Pays $80-120 on acceptance for all rts. Articles 800-1,200 wds. (12/yr.); fiction 1,200 wds. (12/yr.). Responds in 10 wks. Seasonal 9 mos. ahead. No simultaneous submissions or reprints. Prefers e-mail submission (attached file or copied into message). No kill fee. Uses some sidebars. Prefers NIV. Guidelines (also by e-mail); free copy. (No ads)

> **Poetry:** Accepts 36/yr. All types. From teens only.

> **Special Needs:** Always in search of Christian humor; sports profiles. Most open to fiction (send complete ms).

> **Tips:** "We generally prefer writers to complete the writer process at www.lifeway.com/people."

+EXODUS MAGAZINE, 1108 SW Tennessee Ave., Lawton OK 73501. E-mail: submissions@exodusmag.com. Website: www.exodusmag.com. Rochelle Moyd, pub. For an urban youth/young adult audience, ages 15-25, moderately to highly computer literate, and most likely a minority. Mag. Open to unsolicited freelance. Submit by mail or e-mail. **NO PAYMENT** for one-time rts. Articles 1,000-2,000 wds. Guidelines on Website.

> **Columns/Departments:** Accepts many/yr., all 1,000-2,000 wds. Da Message (how to grow as Christians); Da Movement (profiles of youth groups or organizations); Story-2-Tell (testimonies); Young & Successful (young entrepreneurs); Shout! (submissions from youth); On the Grind (up and coming gospel artists); Hot or Not (ratings of new albums); Fashion & Faith (glorifying God through clothing).

$FOCUS ON THE FAMILY DARE 2 DIG DEEPER SERIES, Youth Culture Dept., 8605 Explorer Dr., Colorado Springs CO 80920-1051. (719)531-3400. Fax (719)531-3448. Website: www.family.org. Submit to Acquisitions Editor. A series of small booklets that deal with hard topics that teens (ages 12-18) are struggling with. Pays. Query editor with your ideas to be sure they haven't already covered the topic.

+G4T INK, 419 Mason St., Ste. 108, Vacaville CA 95688. (707)446-4463. Phone/fax (707) 4463. E-mail: info@generations4truth.org. Website: www.generations4truth.org. Generations 4 Truth. Jennifer Maul, public. mngr./ed. Ministry written for and by girls; also by adults who address teen issues. Quarterly mag.; 40-50 pgs; circ. 1,500. Estab. 2007. 70% unsolicited freelance; 30% assigned. Query/clips; e-query OK. **NO PAYMENT** for nonexclusive rts. Not copyrighted. Articles 200-400 wds. Responds in 4-6 wks. Accepts simultaneous submissions & reprints (tell when/where appeared). Accepts e-mail submissions (attached file in word.doc). Uses some sidebars. Prefers NIV. Accepts submissions from teens. Guidelines on Website; copy for 9x12 SAE. (No ads yet)

Poetry: Accepts 4-8/yr.

Fillers: Accepts cartoons, jokes, prayers, quizzes, short humor, and word puzzles.

$IGNITE YOUR FAITH, 465 Gundersen Dr., Carol Stream IL 60188. (630)260-6200. Fax (630)480-2004. E-mail: Iyf@igniteyourfaith.com. Website: www.IgniteYourFaith.com. Christianity Today Intl. Christopher Lutes, ed. Dedicated to creatively engaging and empowering teens to become fully devoted followers of Jesus Christ. Bimonthly (plus 4 special Christian-college issues) mag.; 68-94 pgs.; circ. 100,000. Subscription $19.95. 20% assigned. Query or query/ clips; fax/e-query OK. Pays .15-.20/wd. on acceptance for one-time & electronic rts. Articles 1,200-2,500 wds. (5-10/yr.); fiction 1,000-1,500 wds. (1-5/yr.). Responds in 3-6 wks. Seasonal 6 mos. ahead. Accepts simultaneous submissions; no reprints. Kill fee 50%. Uses some sidebars. Also accepts queries from teens. Guidelines on Website; copy $3/9x12 SAE. (Ads)

Poetry: Buys 1-5/yr. Free verse; 5-20 lines; $25-50. Submit max. 2 poems. Rarely purchase.

Tips: "Most open to as-told-to stories. Interview students and get their stories."

**2008, 2006 EPA Award of Excellence—Youth; 2007 EPA Award of Merit—Youth.

$INSIDEOUT, 8855 Dunn Rd., Hazelwood MO 63042-2299. (314)837-7300. Fax (314)837-4503. E-mail: youth@upci.org. Website: www.generalyouthdivision.org. United Pentecostal Church Intl. Daryle Williams, ed.; submit to Tamra Schultz (tschultz@upci.org). Addresses the spiritual concerns of youth 12-21 years. Bimonthly mag.; 20 pgs.; circ. 6,000. 30% freelance. Complete ms by e-mail only (attached file). Pays .065/wd. on publication for one-time rts. Articles 250-1,250 wds. (18/yr.); fiction 250-1,250 wds. Responds in 9 wks. Seasonal 4 mos. ahead. Accepts simultaneous submissions & reprints. Guidelines/themes on Website; copy for 9x12 SAE/3 stamps. (Ads)

Poetry: Buys 2-4/yr. Traditional; $15. Submit max. 5 poems.

Fillers: Buys 4/yr. Anecdotes, cartoons, short humor; 100 wds.; $15.

Columns/Departments: Buys 6-10/yr. Complete ms.

Tips: "Our primary objective is inspiration—to portray happy, victorious living through faith in God."

$INSIGHT, 55 W. Oak Ridge Dr., Hagerstown MD 21740-7301. (301)393-4038. Fax (301)393-4055. E-mail: insight@rhpa.org. Website: www.insightmagazine.org. Review and Herald Publishing Assn./Seventh-day Adventist. Dwain Esmond, ed. A magazine of positive Christian living for Seventh-day Adventist high school students, ages 13-19. Weekly take-home mag.; 16 pgs.; circ. 20,000. Subscription $49.95. 80% unsolicited freelance. Complete ms/cover letter; fax/e-query OK. Pays $50-85, on publication for 1st rts. Not copyrighted. Articles 1,200-1,700 wds. (120/yr.). Seasonal 6 mos. ahead. Accepts reprints (tell when/where appeared). Prefers e-mail submission (attached file). Kill fee. Regularly uses sidebars. Prefers NIV. Also accepts submissions from teens. Guidelines (also on Website); copy $2/#10 SASE. (No ads)

Poetry: Buys to 36/yr. All types; to 1 pg.; $10. By high school and college students only.

Columns/Departments: Buys 50/yr. On the Edge (drama in real life), 800-1,500 wds., $50-100; It Happened To Me (personal experience in first person), 600-900 wds., $50-75; Big Deal (big topics, such as prayer, premarital sex, knowing God's will, etc.) with sidebar, 1,200-1,700 wds., $75 + $25 for sidebar; So I Said (first-person opinion), 300-500 wds., $25-125. Complete ms.

Contest: Sponsors a nonfiction and poetry contest; includes a category for students under 21. Prizes to $250. June deadline (varies). Send SASE for rules.

Tips: "We look for teen-written or stories written from a teen perspective that are first-person accounts of experiencing God in everyday life. Also need stories by male authors, particularly some humor. Also profiles of Seventh-day Adventist teenagers who are making a notable difference."

**This periodical was #28 on the 2006 Top 50 Christian Publishers list (#28 in 2005, #19 in 2004).

$INTEEN, PO Box 436987, Chicago IL 60643. Website: www.inteen.net. Urban Ministries Inc. Submit to LaTonya Taylor (ltaylor@urbanministries.com). Christian education magazine used in Sunday school classes for teens ages 15-17; used with corresponding Teacher's Guide. Geared primarily toward African American teens. Open to freelance (few unsolicited accepted); 75% assigned. Query; prefers e-query. Pays $75-150 within 120 days of acceptance for all rts. Responds in 4 wks. Seasonal 1 yr. ahead. Accepts requested ms by e-mail (attached). Prefers NIV. Free guidelines/theme list/sample sheet for 10x13 SAE. (No ads)

Poetry: Buys up to 8/yr. Free verse; variable length; $25-60. Complete ms.

Special Needs: Feature articles of interest to youth workers for the Teacher's Guide.

Tips: "If you are interested in writing lessons, provide information about your background in Christian education, along with a writing sample. When querying regarding feature articles, include a published clip. We prefer to make assignments. Most open to Bible study guides applicable and interesting for teens. Writers must be able to accurately explain scriptures to teens."

$J.A.M.: JESUS AND ME, PO Box 436987, Chicago IL 60643. (708)868-7100, ext. 362. Fax (708)868-6759. E-mail: tlee@urbanministries.com. Website: www.urbanministries.com. Urban Ministries Inc. Timothy Lee, ed. Quarterly Sunday school magazine for 12- to 14-year-olds. Open to freelance. Query/clips; fax/e-query OK. Pays up to $150 for curriculum 120 days after acceptance for all rts. Articles 200-400 wds. Responds in 4 wks. Seasonal 6 mos. ahead. No simultaneous submissions or reprints. Requires accepted ms by e-mail. Prefers NIV. Guidelines; copy for #10 SASE. (No ads)

Tips: "J.A.M. principally serves an African American audience; editorial content addresses broad Christian issues. Looking for those with educational or Sunday school teaching experience who can accurately explain scriptures in an insightful and engaging way and apply those scriptures to the lives of children 12-14 years old."

$LISTEN MAGAZINE, 55 W. Oak Ridge Dr., Hagerstown MD 21740. (301)393-4019. E-mail: editor@listenmagazine.org. Website: www.listenmagazine.org. The Health Connection. Celeste Perrino-Walker, ed. Positive lifestyle magazine for teens/young adults; emphasizes values in a general tone. Monthly mag. (September-May); 32 pgs.; circ. 20,000/exposure 100,000. Subscription $26.95. 50% unsolicited freelance; 50% assigned. Query or complete ms; e-query OK. Pays .06-.10/wd. ($50-150) on acceptance for 1st or reprint rts. Articles 800 wds. (30-50/yr.); true stories 800 wds. (15/yr.). Responds in 2 wks. to 3 mos. Seasonal 1 yr. ahead. Accepts simultaneous submissions & reprints (tell when/where appeared). Accepts requested ms on CD or by e-mail (attached file). Uses some sidebars. Guidelines/theme list on Website; copy $2/9x12 SAE/2 stamps. (No ads)

Fillers: Uses 500-word quizzes based on topic in our theme list.

Special Needs: Anti-drug, tobacco, alcohol; positive role models. For true stories, needs stories dealing with everyday problems: peer pressure, decision making, friendship, family conflict, self-discipline, divorce, abuse, anorexia/bulimia, and making positive choices.

Tips: "Need good true stories and celebrity features. We've stopped using fiction. While it isn't always possible, we like to feature stories about individuals who overcome the temptation to experiment with drugs and alcohol, and/or who find a creative way to deal with a bad situation. We have a narrow focus. By offering us cutting edge articles on our subjects, you'll have a greater chance of breaking in."

**This periodical was #39 on the 2008 Top 50 Christian Publishers list (#29 in 2007, #20 in 2006, #13 in 2005, #11 in 2004).

$LIVING MY FAITH, 1300 N. Meacham Rd., Schaumburg IL 60173-4888. (847)843-1600. Fax (847)843-3757. E-mail: livingmyfaith@garbc.org, or realfaith@garbc.org. Website:

www.rbpstudentministries.org. Regular Baptist Press. Submit to Editor. For junior high youth (12-14); conservative/fundamental. Weekly devotional booklet; 12 pgs. Complete ms; no e-query. Pays .05/wd. and up, on acceptance. True & fiction stories to 1,000 wds. Responds in 4-8 wks. Requires KJV. Guidelines on Website.

$REAL FAITH IN LIFE, 1300 N. Meacham Rd., Schaumburg IL 60173-4888. (847)843-1600. Fax (847)843-3757. E-mail: realfaith@garbc.org. Website: www.rbpstudentministries.org. Regular Baptist Press. For senior high youth (14-17); conservative/fundamental. Quarterly devotional book; 112 pgs. Complete ms; no e-query. Pays .05/wd. and up, on acceptance for first (preferred) or one-time rts. Articles 400-1,200 wds. (if more than 600 wds., include subheads). Responds in 4-8 wks. Using mostly assignment writers who are using the RBP student ministries materials or are familiar with churches who do. Some reprints. Guidelines (also on Website: www.rbpstudentministries.org/contribute); copy.

Tips: "Check Website quarterly for updates concerning needs, themes, etc. Written chiefly by assignment."

$RISEN MAGAZINE: The Art & Soul of Pop Culture, 5677 Oberlin Dr., Ste. 202, San Diego CA 92121. (858)481-5650. Fax (858)481-5660. E-mail: michaels@risenmagazine.com, or info@risenmagazine.com. Website: www.risenmagazine.com (online version of the magazine). Risen Media LLC. Steve Beard, ed-in-chief; Regina Goodman, mng. ed. Audience is 18- to 35-year-old seekers and new believers; original photos and one-on-one interviews cut to the heart of today's cultural icons. Estab. 2004. Bimonthly mag.; 34 pgs.; circ. 45,000+. Subscription $19.95. Open to freelance. Query; phone/e-query OK. Pays $150-700. Articles. (Ads)

$SHARING THE VICTORY, 8701 Leeds Rd., Kansas City MO 64129-1680. Toll-free (800)289-0909. (816)921-0909. Fax (816)921-8755. E-mail: stv@fca.org. Website: www.Sharing TheVictory.com (online version of the magazine). Fellowship of Christian Athletes (Protestant and Catholic). Jill Ewert, ed. Equipping and encouraging athletes and coaches to take their faith seriously, in and out of competition. Monthly (9X—double issues in Jan., Jun. & Aug.) mag.; 40 pgs.; circ. 80,000. Subscription $19.95. 10% unsolicited freelance; 40% assigned. Query only/clips; e-query OK. Pays $50-350 on publication for 1st rts. Articles 1,000 wds. (5-20/yr.). Responds in 13 wks. Seasonal 6 mos. ahead. Accepts reprints, pays 50% (tell when/where appeared). Accepts requested ms on disk or by e-mail (attached or copied into message). Kill fee .05%. Uses some sidebars. Prefers HCSB. Guidelines on Website; copy $1/9x12 SAE/3 stamps. (Ads)

Special Needs: Articles on FCA camp experiences. All articles must have an athletic angle. Need stories featuring Christian female professional athletes with a FCA connection.

Tips: "FCA angle important; pro and college athletes and coaches giving solid Christian testimony; we run stories according to athletic season. Need articles on Christian pro athletes—all sports. It is suggested that writer actually look at the magazine for general style and presentation."

$SPIRIT, 1884 Randolph Ave., St. Paul MN 55105-1700. (651)690-7010. Fax (651)690-7039. E-mail: jmcsj9@aol.com. Catholic/Good Ground Press. Joan Mitchell, CSJ, ed. Religious education for Catholic high schoolers. Weekly newsletter; circ. 20,000. 50% freelance written. Complete ms/cover letter or query; fax/e-query OK. Pays $250-300 on publication for all rts. Articles 1,000-1,200 wds. (4/yr.); fiction 1,000-1,200 wds. (10/yr.; $125-300). Responds in 5 wks. Seasonal 6 mos. ahead. Accepts simultaneous submissions. Free guidelines/copy.

Tips: "No born-again pieces. Articles about teens must be written from their point of view."

$STEELROOTS MAGAZINE, 3000 World Reach Dr., Indian Land SC 29707. (803)578-1062. Fax (803)578-1710. E-mail: info@steelroots.com. Website: www.steelroots.com. Inspiration Network. Carter J. Theis, mng. ed. Provides a look into the lives of professional skaters, snowboarders, and surfers through articles written about and by athletes; intended for Christian and general audience. Quarterly mag.; 152 pgs.; circ. 30,000. Query/clips; phone/e-query OK. Accepts full ms by e-mail. Pays .15-.25/wd. for all rts. Articles 500-4,000 wds.; book/music reviews, 50 wds. Also accepts submissions from teens. Copy $5. Incomplete topical listings. (Ads)

Columns/Departments: Buys 12/yr. Evangelism Feature (explaining Jesus to those who don't know him), 2,000 wds.; Discipleship Feature (hitting a topic that's different, but important in Christianity), 2,000 wds.; Final Feature (lies that kids have bought into about Jesus/Bible), 1,000 wds.

Tips: "Send a sample—have some street credibility." Distributed through Christian bookstores, specialty shops, and at youth events.

STUDENT LIFE PUBLISHING, PO Box 36040, Birmingham AL 35236. Toll-free (800)718-2267. Fax (205)403-3969. E-mail: slpublishing@studentlife.net. Website: www.studentlife .net. Andy Blanks, exec. ed. Bible study curriculum intended to take jr. high and sr. high school students through the Bible in 6 years. Ty Gullick, exec. ed. for new Bible study curriculum for adult learners. Weekly online. Subscriptions on a sliding scale. Open to freelance. Complete ms/cover letter. (No ads)

$TAKE FIVE PLUS YOUTH DEVOTIONAL GUIDE, 1445 N. Boonville Ave., Springfield MO 65802-1894. (417)862-2781, ext. 4359. Fax (417)862-6059. E-mail: rl-take5plus@gph .org. Assemblies of God. Glen Ellard, sr. ed. Devotional for teens. By assignment only. Query. Accepts e-mail submissions. Pays $25/devotion or $120 for a set of 6. Devotions exactly 210-235 wds. (not over that). Guidelines on Website.

Poetry: Accepts poetry from teens; no more than 25 lines.

Tips: "The sample devotions need to be based on a scripture reference available by query. You will not be paid for the sample devotions." Also accepts digital photos.

$TC MAGAZINE, 915 E. Market, Ste. 10750, Searcy AR 72149. (501)279-4660. Fax (501)279-4931. E-mail: editor@tcmagazine.org. Website: www.tcmagazine.org. Institute for Church & Family. Laura Kaiser, ed. To help teenagers (13-19) discover style in faith and love. Quarterly mag.; 52 pgs.; circ. 8,000. Subscription $12.95. Estab. 2006. 10% unsolicited freelance; 40% assigned. Complete ms; fax or e-query OK. Accepts full mss by e-mail. Pays variable rates on publication for all rts. Articles 500-1,200 wds. (10/yr.); no fiction. Responds only if chosen for publication. Seasonal 6 mos. ahead. No simultaneous submissions or reprints. No kill fee. Uses some sidebars. Also accepts submissions from teens. Guidelines on Website; copy $3.95/9x12 SAE. (Ads—e-mail to request rate book & media kit)

Columns/Departments: Buys 5/yr. Complete ms. College (college prep for high schoolers), 800-1,000 wds.; Humor (funny article in first person), 800 wds.

Tips: "We really look for teen writers. First-person articles about personal experience are desired. No fiction at this time."

TEENS FOR JC.COM, 2855 Lawrenceville-Suwanee Rd., Ste. 760-355, Suwanee GA 30024. Phone/fax (770)831-8622. E-mail: uvaldes@aol.com, or info@teensforjc.com. Website: www.teensforjc.com, or www.plgkmedia.com. PLGK Communications Inc. Quentin Plair, pres./CEO. Salutes the fun and exhilaration of being a Christian teen. Monthly e-zine. 90% unsolicited freelance; 10% assigned. Complete ms/cover letter; no phone/fax/e-query. Accepts requested ms on disk or by e-mail (attached file). **NO PAYMENT** for one-time rts. Not copyrighted. Articles 100-5,000 wds. (15/yr.) & fiction 100-5,000 wds. (12/yr.); reviews 200 wds. Responds in 12 weeks. Seasonal 4 mos. ahead. Accepts simultaneous submissions & reprints (tell when/where appeared). No kill fee. Uses some sidebars. Also accepts submissions from teens. Guidelines (also on Website). (Ads)

Poetry: Accepts many; any type; 1-200 lines.

Fillers: Accepts many; cartoons, facts, games, jokes, party ideas, prayers, prose, quizzes, short humor, tips, word puzzles; 10-750 wds.

Columns/Departments: Accepts 36/yr. School Tips (teen tips for scholarly excellence); Scoop (current info); Music (music reviews/stories); Speak Out (opinion articles by teens); all 100-500 wds.

Tips: "Provide information teens need to lay a foundation for a successful life. Looking for great stories."

$TRUE GIRL, The Magazine for Catholic Teens. (219)324-2780. E-mail: editor@true girlonline.com. Website: www.truegirlonline.com. Catholic. Brandi Lee, ed-in-chief. For Catholic teenage girls; covers faith, life, and fashion. Bimonthly mag.; 32 pgs.; circ. 3,500. Subscription $18.95. Open to freelance. E-query preferred; no phone/fax query. Accepts full mss by e-mail. Pays .15-.20/wd. for 1st & electronic rts. Articles 800-1,200 wds.; no fiction; reviews 50-100 wds. ($25). Responds in 4-6 wks. Seasonal 12 mos. ahead. No simultaneous submissions or reprints. Some kill fees. Regularly uses sidebars. Also accepts submissions from teens (no pay). Prefers NAB or NRSV (Catholic editions only). Guidelines (also by e-mail); copy $4.99/7x10 SAE. (Ads)

Fillers: Buys Unlimited number. Facts, prayers, quizzes, quotes, word puzzles.

Columns/Departments: Social Justice; Health/Hygiene/Beauty; Teen Issues; Life Plan; Entertainment; Make-It-Your-Own; True Girl Saint. Pays by the word.

Tips: "Our feature articles are most open to freelancers. Reading back issues is imperative to understanding our mission, style, tone, and audience. A firm grasp of our reader's needs for educational, spiritual, and entertainment resources will help guide submissions."

$VISIONS, 2621 Dryden Rd., Moraine OH 45439. (937)293-1415. Fax (937)293-1310. E-mail: service@pflaum.com. Website: www.pflaum.com. Catholic. Joan Mitchell CSJ, ed. For grades 7 & 8. Weekly (32X) take-home paper. Not in topical listings.

$YOUNG ADULT TODAY, PO Box 436987, Chicago IL 60643. Website: www.youngadult today.net. Urban Ministries Inc. Submit to LaTonya Taylor (ltaylor@urbanministries.com). Christian education magazine used in Sunday school classes for 18- to 24-year-olds; used with corresponding leader's guide. Geared primarily toward African American young adults; editorial content also focuses on broadly Christian/discipleship issues. Open to freelance (few unsolicited accepted); 75% assigned. Query; prefers e-query. Pays $75-150 within 120 days of acceptance for all rts. Responds in 4 wks. Seasonal 1 yr. ahead. Reprint friendly (tell when/where appeared). Accepts requested ms by e-mail (attached). Prefers NIV. Free guidelines/theme list/sample sheet for 10x13 SAE. (No ads)

Poetry: Buys up to 8/yr. Free verse; variable length; $25-60. Complete ms.

Special Needs: Feature articles of interest to young adult leaders for the Teacher's Guide.

Tips: "If you are interested in writing lessons, provide information about your background in Christian education, along with a writing sample. When querying regarding feature articles, include a published clip. We prefer to make assignments. Please be knowledgeable about and sensitive to the concerns of this age group."

$YOUNG CHRISTIAN, 2660 Petersborough St., Oak Hill VA 20171. E-mail: youngchristian magazine@yahoo.com. Website: http://groups.yahoo.com/group/youngchristianmagazine. Tellstar Publishing. Shannon Bridget Murphy, ed. Christian writing with the Lord's message for children and teens. Quarterly mag. 85% unsolicited freelance. Complete ms/cover letter; e-query OK. Pays .02-.05/wd. on acceptance for 1st or one-time rts. Articles 500-2,000 wds.; fiction 500-2,000 wds.; book/tape reviews. Responds in 2-8 wks. Seasonal 3-6 mos. ahead. Accepts simultaneous submissions & reprints (tell when/where appeared). Accepts disk; prefers e-mail submissions (attached or copied into message). No kill fee. Regularly uses sidebars. Prefers KJV. Guidelines by e-mail. (No ads)

Poetry: Buys variable number. Avant-garde, free verse, haiku, light verse, traditional; any length; variable rates. Submit any number.

Fillers: Buys anecdotes, cartoons, facts, ideas, kid quotes, party ideas, prayers, prose, quizzes, quotes, short humor, tips, and word puzzles; to 1,000 wds.

Tips: "Most open to nonfiction, fiction, poetry, and fillers written by children and teens. Include a scripture reference. *Young Christian* will provide information to teachers and educational employees on request. Accepts books, CDs, or tapes to be reviewed, but no written reviews."

$YOUNG SALVATIONIST, PO Box 269, Alexandria VA 22313-0269. (703)684-5500. Fax (703)684-5539. E-mail: ys@usn.salvationarmy.org. Website: http://publications.salvation armyusa.org. The Salvation Army. Curtiss A. Hartley, ed. For teens and young adults in the Salvation Army. Monthly (10X) & online mag.; 24 pgs.; circ. 48,000. Subscription $4.50. 80% unsolicited freelance; 20% assigned. Complete ms preferred; e-query OK. Pays .15/wd. (.10/wd. for reprints) on acceptance for 1st, one-time, or reprint rts. Articles (60/yr.) & fiction (10/yr.), 600-1,200 wds.; short evangelistic pieces, 350-600 wds. Responds in 9 wks. Seasonal 6 mos. ahead. Accepts reprints (tell when/where appeared). Accepts requested ms on disk or by e-mail. Uses some sidebars. Prefers NIV. Guidelines/theme list (also on Website); copy for 9x12 SAE/3 stamps. (No ads)

Contest: Sponsors a contest for fiction, nonfiction, poetry, original art, and photography. Send SASE for details.

Tips: "Our greatest need is for nonfiction pieces that are relevant to the readers and offer clear application to daily life. We are most interested in topical pieces on contemporary issues that affect a teen's daily life, and pieces that work with the day-to-day challenges of faith. Although we use fiction and poetry, they are a small percentage of the total content of each issue."

**This periodical was #9 on the 2008 Top 50 Christian Publishers list (#5 in 2007, #3 in 2006, #12 in 2005, #9 in 2004).

$YOUTH COMPASS, PO Box 4060, Overland Park KS 66204. (913)432-0331. Fax (913)722-0351. E-mail: sseditor1@juno.com. Church of God (holiness)/Herald and Banner Press. Arlene McGehee, Sunday school ed. Denominational; for teens. Weekly take-home paper; 4 pgs.; circ. 4,800. Subscription $1.50. Complete ms/cover letter; phone/fax/e-query OK (prefers mail or e-mail). Pays .005/wd. on publication for 1st rts. Fiction 800-1,500 wds. Seasonal 6-8 mos. ahead. Accepts simultaneous submissions & reprints (tell when/where appeared). Prefers KJV. Guidelines/theme list; copy. Not in topical listings.

$YOUTHWALK, 4201 N. Peachtree Rd., Atlanta GA 30341. (770)451-9300. Fax (770)454-9313. E-mail: yw@ywspace.org. Website: www.ywspace.org. Walk Thru the Bible Ministries. Laurin Makohon, ed. (laurin@ywspace.org). To help students navigate their Bibles, connect with God, and their own faith. Monthly devotional mag.; circ. 30,000. Subscription $18. 5% unsolicited freelance; 25% assigned. Complete ms. Pays $50-250. Articles 600-1,500 wds.; no reviews. Requires NIV. (No ads)

Tips: "We accept freelance for feature articles only; no devotionals. Submit a complete manuscript of a real-life teen story."

**2008, 2007 EPA Award of Excellence—Devotional; 2006 EPA Award of Merit—Devotional.

WOMEN'S MARKETS

$AT THE CENTER, PO Box 100, Morgantown PA 19543. Toll-free phone/fax (800)588-7744. E-mail: publications@rightideas.us, or elaine@rightideas.us. Website: www.atcmag.com. Right Ideas Inc. Jerry Thacker, ed.; submit to Elaine Williams, asst. ed. Designed to help staff, volunteers, and board members of Crisis Pregnancy Centers/Pregnancy Care Centers with relevant information and encouragement. Quarterly online mag. Subscription free. 20% unsolicited freelance; 80% assigned. Complete ms; phone/fax query OK; e-query preferred. Pays $150 on publication for 1st, reprint, or simultaneous rts. Articles 1,000-1,200 wds. (15/yr.). Responds in 8-10 wks. Seasonal 6-8 mos. ahead. Accepts simultaneous submissions & reprints. Accepts e-mail submissions (attached or copied into message). No kill fee. Uses some sidebars. Prefers NKJV, ESV. Guidelines/idea list (also by e-mail); copy online. (Ads: elaine@rightideas.us)

> **Special Needs:** Articles that give ideas for other centers in the areas of recruiting and retaining volunteers, ways to reach abortion-minded clients, and creative fund-raising ideas.
>
> **Tips:** "Looking for practical articles of help and encouragement for those involved in the work of CPC/PCC ministry—center directors, staff, and volunteers. If someone has been involved in crisis pregnancy work, their insight into many areas of the ministry can be helpful to staff and board. Need good techniques for counseling abortion-minded clients."

($)BEYOND THE BEND, 22 Williams St., Batavia NY 14020. (585)343-2810. Fax (585)343-3245. E-mail: submissions@beyondthebend.com. Website: www.beyondthebend.com. PC Publications. Patti Chadwick, ed. (Patti@beyondthebend.com). For women in midlife. Estab. 2006. Monthly e-zine. Subscription free online. 50% unsolicited freelance; 50% assigned. Complete ms/cover letter or query; e-query OK. **PAYS IN FREE BOOKS** for one-time and reprint rts. Articles 500-1,000 wds. (25/yr.); reviews 500 wds. Responds in 1 wk. Seasonal 6 mos. ahead. Accepts simultaneous submissions & reprints (tell when/where appeared). Prefers e-mail submissions (attached or copied into message). Uses some sidebars. Guidelines on Website; copy online. (Ads)

> **Fillers:** Accepts 20/yr. Anecdotes, facts, ideas, quotes, sermon illustrations, short humor, and tips; 25-50 wds.
>
> **Tips:** "Just e-mail me with a good story."

BREATHE AGAIN MAGAZINE, 222 W. 21st St., Ste. F126, Norfolk VA 23517. (757)404-1582. Fax (757)626-1669. E-mail: info@breatheagain.org. Website: www.breatheagainmagazine .com. Nicole Cleveland, ed./pub. (editor@breatheagain.org). Stirring stories about overcoming adversity and living triumphant, successful lives encourage and motivate women not only to endure but to overcome life's most challenging moments. Monthly online mag. Open to stories of overcoming.

$CANTICLE, 325 Scarlet Blvd., Oldsmar FL 34677. Toll-free (800)558-5452. (734)429-2952. E-mail: editor@canticlemagazine.com. Website: www.canticlemagazine.com. Women of Grace/Catholic. Heidi Saxton, ed. Dedicated solely to the woman's vocation within the church. Bimonthly jour.; 32 pgs.; circ. 4,000. Subscription $29.95. 75% unsolicited freelance; 25% assigned. Query or complete ms; e-query OK. Pays $50-150 on publication for 1st rts. Articles 600 or 1,200 wds. Responds in 4-6 wks. Seasonal 4 mos. ahead. Requires e-mail submissions in attached file after acceptance. No kill fee. Regularly uses sidebars. Prefers NAB or RSV (Catholic version). Guidelines/theme list on Website; copy online. (Ads)

> **Columns/Departments:** Buys 6/yr. Send complete ms. Solitary Genius (singles, widows; religious perspective), 600 wds.; pays $50-75. List of columns in guidelines; 500-750 wds.; $75 for assigned, less for unsolicited.
>
> **Contest:** Check "Silent Canticle" blog for details (see below).
>
> **Tips:** "Read guidelines and theme list, and read regularly our Catholic Writers' blog, the 'Silent Canticle' at http://heidihesssaxton.blogspot.com."

CELEBRATEMOMS.ORG, PO Box 570, Theodore AL 36590-0570. Toll-free (866)324-2893. E-mail: mhowell@celebratemoms.org. Website: www.celebratemoms.org. Nondenominational. Melissa Howell, co-founder/ed. Online conference and retreat center for moms.

Interactive Website; continually updated. Estab. 2006. 20% unsolicited freelance; 80% assigned. Query/published clips; e-query OK. Accepts full mss by e-mail. **NO PAYMENT; BYLINE & LINK TO WEBSITE** for one-time & electronic rts. Articles. Responds in 6 wks. Seasonal 3 mos. ahead. Accepts simultaneous submissions & reprints (tell when/where appeared). Requires e-mail submission (attached file). Uses some sidebars. Also accepts submissions from children/teens. Any Bible version. Guidelines by e-mail; copy online. (No ads)

Fillers: Accepts several/yr. Anecdotes, facts, games, ideas, kid quotes, party ideas, prayers, prose, quizzes, quotes, short humor, tips, word puzzles.

Tips: "All areas open to freelancers. Read submission guidelines carefully and follow them. Be patient waiting for replies."

CHRISTIAN WOMAN'S PAGE. E-mail: editor@christianwomanspage.org. Website: www .christianwomanspage.org. Nondenominational. Janel Messenger, ed./pub. Strives to provide women with the whys and hows to live Christianity lovingly and practically in day-to-day life. Monthly e-zine & weekly blog. Carries 12-16 articles/issue; 90,000 unique visitors/yr. 98% unsolicited freelance; 2% assigned. Complete ms/cover letter by e-mail only. **NO PAYMENT** for 1st, one-time, reprint, simultaneous, nonexclusive rts. Articles 1,200-1,700 wds.; devotions no less than 700 wds.; larger articles can be broken into parts; reviews 500-700 wds.; fiction 1,800 wds. Responds in 3-5 wks. Seasonal 2 mos. ahead. Accepts simultaneous submissions & reprints (tell when/where appeared). Requires e-mail submissions (copied into message). No sidebars. Prefers NIV. Guidelines/needs list on Website; copy online. (No ads)

Poetry: Accepts 3-5/yr. Light verse, traditional. Submit max. 3 poems.

Fillers: Accepts several/yr. Anecdotes, facts, ideas, short humor, and tips.

Columns/Departments: No columns, but open to them.

Tips: "We are an excellent new writer's market. We will use almost every well-written article submitted if it fits with our mission—encouraging women to live with passion and love for Jesus Christ."

CHRISTIAN WOMEN TODAY, Box 300, Sta. A, Vancouver BC V6C 2X3, Canada. (604)514-2000. Fax (604)514-2124. E-mail: editor@christianwomentoday.com. Website: www.christian womentoday.com. French Website: www.chretiennes.com. Campus Crusade for Christ, Canada. Karen Schenk, pub.; Stacy Wiebe, ed. For Christian women, 20-60 yrs. Monthly online mag.; 2 million hits/mo. 30% unsolicited freelance. Query first; e-query preferred. **NO PAYMENT.** Lifestyle articles 200-500 wds.; features 500-1,000 wds.; life stories 500 wds. Seasonal 4 mos. ahead. Accepts simultaneous submissions & reprints (tell when/where appeared). Prefers e-mail submission (attached file). Guidelines/theme list on Website (www.christianwomentoday.com/volunteer/submissions.html). (Ads)

Tips: "The writer needs to have a global perspective, have a heart to build women in their faith, and help develop them to win others to Christ. Text should be written for online viewing with subheads and bullets in the body of the article."

CHURCHWOMAN, 475 Riverside Dr., Ste. 1626A, New York NY 10115. Toll-free (800)298-5551. (212)870-2347. Fax (212)870-2338. E-mail: cwu@churchwomen.org. Website: www.churchwomen.org. Church Women United. Julie Drews, ed. Shares stories of women acting on their faith and engaging in the work for peace and justice around the world. Quarterly mag.; 28 pgs.; circ. 3,000. Subscription $10. 1% unsolicited freelance. Query. **PAYS IN COPIES.** Articles to 3 pgs. Prefers accepted ms by e-mail (copied into message). Guidelines; copy $1.

$COME TO THE FIRE MAGAZINE (formerly Women Alive!), PO Box 480052, Kansas City MO 64148. (816)268-8928. E-mail: pamenderby@gmail.com. Website: www.cometothe fire.org. Pam Enderby, mng. ed. To encourage women to live holy lives by applying Scripture to their daily lives. Bimonthly & online mag.; 21 pgs.; circ. 4,000. Subscription $13.95.

50% unsolicited freelance; 2% assigned. Complete ms/no cover letter, or query; no phone/fax query; e-query OK. Accepts full mss by e-mail. Pays $25-50 on publication for one-time, simultaneous, or reprint rts. Articles 500-1,200 wds. (30/yr.). Responds in 4-6 wks. Seasonal 6 mos. ahead. Accepts simultaneous submissions & reprints (tell when/where appeared). Uses some sidebars. Prefers e-mail submissions (attached file). Prefers NIV. Guidelines/theme list by e-mail/website; copy for $3/9x12 SAE/3 stamps. (No ads)

Special Needs: Looking for keys to building healthy relationships between mothers/ daughters and mothers/sons with a spiritual emphasis; caring for elderly parents; and loving your husband God's way.

Tips: "We look for articles that draw women into a deeper spiritual life—articles on surrender, prayer, parenting—yet written with personal illustrations."

COMFORT CAFÉ. E-mail: info@comfortcafe.net. Website: www.comfortcafe.net. Ruth Wood, ed. Women's publication. Online mag. Open to freelance. Complete ms/cover letter; e-query OK. **NO PAYMENT** for one-time electronic rts. Articles 500-1,200 wds.; life stories, 800-1,200 wds., devotions 300-500 wds. Responds in 4-6 wks. Guidelines & copy on Website.

Tips: "We minister to women facing difficult life challenges. Your submission should offer hope, help, and healing, allowing readers to see and experience the reality of God's love and provision in our lives. Write in first-person narrative."

CROWNED WITH SILVER, PO Box 10, Masonville CO 80541. E-mail: crownedwithsilver@ yahoo.com. Website: www.crownedwithsilver.com. Submit to The Editor. Return to biblical femininity; Christian homemaking encouragement regarding home schooling, etiquette, marriage, womanhood, and nostalgic wisdom from the past. Quarterly mag. Subscription $14. Articles & fiction.

Tips: "Send your article via e-mail and follow the topics indicated. Write 500 words— no longer—not shorter."

$THE DABBLING MUM, 508 W. Main St., Beresford SD 57004. (605)763-2549. E-mail: dm@ thedabblingmum.com. Website: www.thedabblingmum.com. Nondenominational. Alyice Edrich, ed. Balance your life while you glean from successful entrepreneurs, parents, and Christians—just like you. Weekly e-zine; circ. 40,000. Subscription free online. 90% unsolicited freelance; 10% assigned. Complete ms submitted online; e-query OK. Accepts full mss by e-mail. Pays $20-40 (reprints $5-10) on acceptance for 1st, reprint, electronic & nonexclusive archival rts. Articles 500-1,500 wds. (96/yr.). Responds in 4-8 wks. Seasonal 1 mo. ahead. No simultaneous submissions; accepts reprints (tell when/where appeared). Accepts e-mail submissions (copied into message). No kill fee or sidebars. Also accepts submissions from children/teens, if it fits the topic. Prefers KJV or NAS. Guidelines/editorial calendar/copy on Website. (Ads)

Tips: "We have a 'most wanted' section in our writers' guidelines to update writers on our current needs. It's imperative you study the style of the publication. We need business ideas, marketing, advertising, direct sales, hosting a writing event, niche writing, and fiction-writing articles."

**This periodical was #49 on the 2008 Top 50 Christian Publishers list (#39 in 2007).

+ELEGANCE, PO Box 2084, Waldorf MD 20604. (240)412-1819. E-mail: sisterinchrist2@ yahoo.com. Website: www.YouAreRoyalty.org. Royalty Inc. Brenda Douglas, pub. For women and teen girls. Quarterly e-zine. Subscription free online. 90% unsolicited freelance. Query; e-query OK. Accepts full mss by e-mail. **NO PAYMENT.** Articles. Seasonal 2 mos. ahead. Accepts simultaneous submissions & reprints (tell when/where appeared). Accepts articles by e-mail (attached in Word). Uses some sidebars. Guidelines by e-mail; copy online.

Fillers: Cartoons, facts, ideas, jokes, quotes, short humor, tips, and word puzzles.

Columns/Departments: Seeking His Face (spiritual growth); In His Image (character development); Focus on the Family (family life); Health & Fitness (diet & exercise); Majestic Teens (teen interests); Women in Leadership; Appreciation for Diversity; all 1,000-1,500 wds.

Tips: "All sections open to freelancers."

$ESPRIT, Evangelical Lutheran Women, 302-393 Portage Ave., Winnipeg MB R3B 3H6, Canada. (204)984-9160. Fax (204)984-9162. E-mail: esprit@elcic.ca. Website: www.elw.ca. Catherine Pate, ed. For Christian women. Quarterly mag.; 36 pgs.; circ. 5,000. Subscription $18 Cdn., $27 U.S. 65% unsolicited freelance; 35% assigned. Complete ms/cover letter; phone/e-query OK. Pays $18/500 wd. pg. Cdn. on publication for 1st or one-time rts. Articles & fiction 350-1,300 wds. Responds in 2-4 wks. Seasonal 4 mos. ahead. Accepts simultaneous submissions. Prefers accepted mss by e-mail (attached). Uses some sidebars. Requires NRSV. Guidelines (also on Website); copy for #10 SAE/$3.50 Cdn. postage or $6 U.S. (Limited ads)

Poetry: Light verse, traditional; 8-100 lines; $18. Submit max. 3 poems.

Columns/Departments: Buys 4/yr. Family Matters, 1,300 wds.

Tips: "Most open to social justice, world issues, and women's issues (justice, violence). We are currently focusing on topical, well-researched articles with a particular eye on world events. Any submissions should emphasize this research-based approach."

**This periodical was #32 on the 2008 Top 50 Christian Publishers list (#20 in 2007, #34 in 2006, #30 in 2005, #18 in 2004).

FIRST LADY, PO Box 1233, Mableton GA 30126. E-mail: mail@firstladymagazine.com. Website: www.firstladymagazine.com, or www.FLMezine.com. Tracey L. Smith, pub. To educate, encourage, and inspire women about many aspects of life from a Christian viewpoint. Quarterly mag.; circ. 20,000. Subscription $10. Articles.

$FULLFILL, 2370 S. Trenton Way, Denver CO 80231-3822. E-mail: info@fullfill.org. Website: www.fullfill.org. MOPS Intl. Submit to FullFill Editor. Encourages women in all seasons of life to realize, utilize, and maximize their influence. Quarterly mag. & online community. Open to unsolicited freelance. Complete ms preferred; considers queries. Pays varying amounts on publication. Articles 1,000-1,500 wds. Requires e-mail submissions (attached or copied into message—write@fullfill.org). Guidelines/themes on Website (click on "About Us," then "Write"). Incomplete topical listings.

Columns/Departments: Coaching Corner (coaching on personal growth, life management, professional growth), 650 wds.

$GIRLFRIEND 2 GIRLFRIEND (formerly Simple Joy). E-mail: submission@simplejoy.org. Website: www.simplejoy.org. Jean Ann Duckworth, pub. (editor@simplejoy.org); submit to The Editor. For women (target age 30-55) interested in a simpler way of life; general. Monthly online mag. Open to freelance. Complete mss; e-query OK. Pays $10 honorarium on publication for articles to 1,000 wds. (72-120/yr.); within 60 days of publication; for one-time rts. Seasonal 4 mos. ahead. Prefers e-mail (attached file in Word format). Guidelines on Website. Incomplete topical listings.

Special Needs: Focuses on 4 specific areas: reducing stress, enhancing joy, simplifying life, and building/strengthening relationships.

Tips: "Read the current issue to better understand our mission and market. We like working with first-time authors."

THE HANDMAIDEN, PO Box 76, Ben Lomond CA 95005. Toll-free (800)967-7377. (831)336-5118. Fax (831)336-8882. E-mail: czell@conciliarpress.com. Website: www.conciliarpress .com/pages/handmaiden.html. Antiochian Orthodox Archdiocese of North America. Carla Zell, ed. For women serving God within the Eastern Orthodox tradition. Quarterly jour.; 64 pgs.; circ. 3,000. Subscription $16.50. 5% unsolicited freelance; 95% assigned. Query; e-query OK. **PAYS IN COPIES/SUBSCRIPTION.** Articles 1,000-2,000 wds. (8/yr.).

Responds in 6-8 wks. Seasonal 6 mos. ahead. Accepts reprints (tell when/where appeared). Prefers hard copy or e-mail submissions (copied into message). Uses some sidebars. Prefers NKJV. Guidelines (also by e-mail)/theme list; copy for 7x10 SAE/4 stamps. (No ads) **Poetry:** Catherine Grace Bond, poetry ed. Accepts 4-8/yr. Free verse, light verse, traditional. Submit max. 3 poems.

Columns/Departments: Heroines of the Faith (lives of women saints within Orthodox tradition), 1,000-2,000 wds.

Tips: "Most open to theme features, sidebars, and poetry."

HANDMAIDENS. E-mail: iona@handmaidens.org. Website: www.handmaidens.org. Iona Hoeppner, ed. For women of all (or no) denominations; consider the sensitivities of those whose theology may differ from your own. E-zine. Open to unsolicited freelance. Complete ms. **NO PAYMENT** for one-time rts. Articles; fiction. Requires e-mail submissions (copied into message). Guidelines on Website.

Poetry: Accepts poetry.

Tips: "We welcome your art, photos, poetry, essays, articles, short stories, devotional material, links, almost anything of interest to Christian women."

$HEART & SOUL, 2514 Maryland Ave., Baltimore MD 21218. Toll-free (800)834-8813, ext. 105. (410)576-9199. Fax (410)662-4596. E-mail: editor@heartandsoul.com. Website: www.heartandsoul.com. General. Submit to Editorial Dept. The African American woman's ultimate guide to total well-being (body, mind, and spirit). Bimonthly mag.; 88-96 pgs.; circ. 300,000. Subscription $18. Open to unsolicited freelance. Query preferred. Pays on acceptance. Articles 800-1,500 wds. Guidelines on Website. (Ads) Incomplete topical listings.

HEARTS AT HOME, 1509 N. Clinton Blvd., Bloomington IL 61701-1813. (309)828-MOMS. E-mail: mag@hearts-at-home.org. Website: www.hearts-at-home.org. Connected to annual conferences by the same name (held in Normal IL, Grand Rapids MI, and Rochester MN). Rachel Kitson, ed-in-chief. To encourage and educate mothers at home. Bimonthly mag.; 26 pgs.; circ. 1,500. Subscription $10. Open to unsolicited freelance. Complete ms by e-mail; e-query ok. **PAYS 5 COPIES FOR ONE-TIME RTS.** Articles 250-720 wds. (40-50/yr.); fiction to 720 wds.; devotionals to 720 wds. Accepts reprints (tell when/where appeared). Prefers e-mail submissions (attached Word file to mag@hearts-at-home.org). Uses some sidebars. Any Bible version. Guidelines/theme list (also by e-mail/Website); copy $2/6x9 SAE/2 stamps. (No ads)

Poetry: Light verse, traditional; 10-25 lines (to 250 wds.).

Fillers: Anecdotes, cartoons, facts, ideas, party ideas, short humor; 25-100 wds.

Columns/Departments: Motherhood; Parenting; Marriage; Personal Growth; Spiritual Growth; Family Management; to 720 wds.

Special Needs: Articles that challenge mothers in their growth as a parent; uplift spouses in relationship with each other and children; encourage spiritual growth; educate mothers on networking, finding time for themselves, or overcoming personal challenges; tips on saving time and money; and using personal experiences to better parent kids.

Tips: "Submit a well-written, balanced, positive article which will encourage, educate, and/or entertain our audience. Personal stories of the triumphs and trials of being a mom are preferred. This publication is designed to be by moms and for moms. Please include a short biography to go with your article."

$HERIZONS, PO Box 128, Winnipeg MB R3C 2G1, Canada. Toll-free (888)408-0028. (204) 774-6225. Fax (204)786-8038. E-mail: editor@herizons.ca, or through Website: www.herizons.ca. Herizons Magazine Inc. Submit to The Editor. Focuses on empowering women in their relationships, work, culture, health, social justice, spirituality, and family by incorporating current research and feminist theory in articles, essays, and interviews that inspire, inform, and engage readers. Quarterly mag. Subscription $25.94 Cdn.; $33.94 U.S. Open to unsolicited freelance. Query or complete ms; no e-query. Pays $200 Cdn. ($130 U.S.)/1,000 wds. on publication for nonexclusive 1st N.A. rts. Articles 1,000-3,000 wds.; news 500-800 wds.; reviews 400 wds. Responds in 12 wks. Prefers e-mail submissions (copied into message). Guidelines on Website (www.herizons.ca/writers.html). (Ads)

Tips: "With reviews, preference is given to Canadian authors, filmmakers, musicians. Articles in which the writer is engaged with the material she writes about work best; personal experiences, journalism-style articles, interviews, articles which bring in current research and a clear feminist perspective are all things we look for."

($)HISTORY'S WOMEN, 22 Williams St., Batavia NY 14020. (585)343-2810. Fax (585)343-3245. E-mail: submissions@historyswomen.com. Website: www.historyswomen.com. PC Publications. Patti Chadwick, ed. Online magazine highlighting the extraordinary achievements of women throughout history. Weekly e-zine; 20 pgs.; circ. 21,000. Subscription free online. 20% unsolicited freelance. E-query/e-submissions only. **PAYS IN COPIES & FREE E-BOOKS** (occasionally pays $10, if budget permits) for 1st, one-time, reprint, or electronic rts. Articles 400-1,200 wds. (20/yr.). Responds in 1-2 wks. Seasonal 3 mos. ahead. Accepts simultaneous submissions & reprints (tell when/where appeared). Prefers e-mail submission (copied into message). Does not use sidebars. Also accepts submissions from teens. Guidelines on Website; copy on site archive. (Ads)

Columns/Departments: Buys 10-20/yr. Women to Admire, in these columns: Women of Faith; First Women (pioneers in their field); Social Reformers; Amazing Moms; Women Who Ruled (women rulers); Early America; all 500-1,000 wds., $10. Query or complete ms.

HOPE FOR WOMEN MAGAZINE, PO Box 3241, Muncie IN 47307. Toll-free fax (800)936-2214. E-mail: Editor@hopeforwomenmag.com. Website: www.hopeforwomenmag.com. Virtuous Publications Inc. Submit to Editor. Quarterly mag.; 72 pgs.; circ. 10,000. Subscription $14.95. 95% unsolicited freelance; 5% assigned. Query/clips; e-query OK. Accepts full mss by e-mail. **NO PAYMENT** for 1st rts. Articles 500-2,000 wds.; reviews 300 wds. Responds in 4-6 wks. Seasonal 2-3 mos. ahead. No simultaneous submissions or reprints. Accepts e-mail submissions (attached file). Guidelines/theme list (also by e-mail); copy for #10 SASE. (Ads)

Fillers: Newsbreaks, party ideas, tips; .10/wd.

Columns/Departments: Relationships (nurturing and maintaining positive relationships), 800-1,200 wds.; Light (tough issues usually kept quiet in the church), 800-1,000 wds.; Journey (helps for a woman's life journey), 500-800 wds.; .10-.15/wd. Query. Additional columns listed on Website.

Tips: "Each issue features at least one interview with a woman of faith—often a celebrity—who has come through a difficult time and grown stronger in her faith because of it."

$HORIZONS, 100 Witherspoon St., Louisville KY 40202-1396. (502)569-5688. Fax (502)569-8085. E-mail: yvonne.hileman@pcusa.org, or sharon.gillies@pcusa.org. Website: www .pcusa.org/horizons. Presbyterian Church (USA)/Presbyterian Women. Yvonne Hileman, asst. ed. Justice issues and spiritual life for Presbyterian women. Bimonthly mag. & annual Bible study; 40 pgs.; circ. 25,000. Subscription $18. 10% unsolicited freelance; 90% assigned. Complete ms preferred; fax/e-query OK. Pays $50/600 wds. on publication for all rts. Articles 600-1,800 wds. (10/yr.) & fiction 800-1,200 wds. (5/yr.); book reviews 100 wds. ($25). Responds in 3 mos. Seasonal 6 mos. ahead. Accepts simultaneous submissions & reprints (tell when/where appeared). Accepts requested ms on disk or by e-mail (attached file or copied into message). Kill fee. Regularly uses sidebars. Prefers NRSV. Guidelines/theme list (also by e-mail/Website); copy $4/9x12 SAE. (No ads)

Poetry: Buys 5/yr. All types; $50-100. Submit max. 5 poems.

Fillers: Cartoons, church-related graphics; $50.

Tips: "Most open to devotionals, mission stories, justice and peace issues. Writer should be familiar with constituency of Presbyterian women and life in the Presbyterian Church (USA)."

**This periodical was #6 on the 2006 Top 50 Christian Publishers list (#11 in 2005, #10 in 2004).

$INSPIREDMOMS.COM, PO Box 293477, Lewisville TX 75077. (972)979-7438. E-mail: editor@ inspiredmoms.com. Website: www.inspiredmoms.com. Inspired Life Ministries Inc. Wendy Stewart-Hamilton, site ed. Bimonthly e-zine (3 mo. summer edition & 1 mo. Christmas edition). Majority of content provided by staff writers, guest writers, and podcast speakers by assignment. Open to unsolicited freelance. Complete ms/bio; e-query OK. Pays $10/published article or podcast. Articles to 1,200 wds.; podcasts in MP3 format up to 10 minutes in length. Accepts reprints. Responds in 2-3 wks. Guidelines/theme list on Website.

Tips: "Staff writers are selected yearly for the upcoming publication season. Send résumé and two sample articles for moms for future assignment consideration by August 1 of current year. We need authors who can write for work-at-home and homeschool moms."

+INSPIRED WOMEN MAGAZINE, E-mail: publisher@inspiredwomenmagazine.com. Website: www.inspiredwomenmagazine.com. Christian. Adriana Zamot, pub. Offers the women of the world information about the issues that affect us everyday. Monthly online mag. Open to unsolicited freelance. Query first; e-query preferred. **NO PAYMENT** for one-time rts. Articles. Guidelines & copy online. Incomplete topical listings.

$INSPIRIT MAGAZINE, 5101 N. Francisco Ave., Chicago IL 60625. (773)907-3332. Fax (773) 784-4366. E-mail: wmc@covchurch.org. Website: www.covchurch.org/women. Dept. of Women Ministries. Ruth Hill, ed-in-chief (ruth.hill@covchurch.org). To inform and inspire women across the Evangelical Covenant denomination. Quarterly mag.; 50 pgs.; circ. 2,500. Subscription $10. 40% unsolicited freelance; 60% assigned. Complete ms/cover letter; phone/fax/e-query OK. Must include e-mail contact address. Pays $25-35 on publication. Articles about 750 wds. (4/yr.); fiction 750-800 wds. (4/yr.). Seasonal 2.5 mos. ahead. Accepts simultaneous submissions & reprints (tell when/where appeared). Prefers e-mail submissions (attached file). Uses some sidebars. Prefers TNIV or NIV. Guidelines/theme list on Website; copy for 6x9 SAE/$2.50. (Ads)

Tips: "Follow themes printed in issues and guidelines posted on our Website."

$JOURNEY: A Woman's Guide to Intimacy with God, One Lifeway Plaza, Nashville TN 37234-0175. (615)251-5659. E-mail: journey@lifeway.com. Website: www.lifeway.com. LifeWay Christian Resources. Articles to: Manuscript Submissions at address above. Devotional submissions to: Susan Nelson, Walk Through the Bible, 4201 N. Peachtree Rd., Atlanta GA 30341. Pamela Nixon, lead ed.; Tammy Drolsum, ed. Devotional magazine for women 30-50 years old. Monthly mag.; 44 pgs.; circ. 215,000. Subscription $24.95. 15% unsolicited freelance; 85% staff or assigned. Subscription $22.05. Query/clips or complete ms/cover letter; no phone/fax/e-query or e-submissions. Pays $50-100 on acceptance for all rts. Articles 350-1,000 wds. (10-12/yr.). Responds in 8 wks. Seasonal 6-7 mos. ahead. Regularly uses sidebars. Prefers HCSB. Accepts requested ms on disk. Guidelines; copy for 6x9 SAE/2 stamps.

Special Needs: Strong feature articles, 750-1,000 words (including sidebars) on topics of interest to women 30-50 years old ranging from practical applications of faith to spiritual growth, as well as profiles of Christian women in leadership positions.

Tips: "Most open to feature articles that are well written with a thorough understanding of our magazine and target audience. Strong sample devotionals written in *Journey* style may be considered for assignment of a devotional."

JUST BETWEEN US, 777 S. Barker Rd., Brookfield WI 53045. Toll-free (800)260-3342. (262)786-6478. Fax (262)796-5752. E-mail: jbu@elmbrook.org. Website: www.just

betweenus.org. Elmbrook Church Inc. Shelly Esser, ed. Ideas, encouragement, and resources for wives of evangelical ministers and women in leadership. Quarterly mag.; 32 pgs.; circ. 8,000. Subscription $19.95. 85% unsolicited freelance; 15% assigned. Query; phone/fax/ e-query OK. **NO PAYMENT** for one-time rts. Articles 250-500 wds. or 1,200-1,500 wds. (50/yr.). Responds in 8 wks. Accepts simultaneous submissions & reprints. Regularly uses sidebars. Prefers NIV. Guidelines (also by e-mail/Website); copy $4/9x12 SAE. (Ads)

Fillers: Accepts 15/yr. Anecdotes, cartoons, ideas, prayers, quotes, short humor; 50-250 wds.

Columns/Departments: Accepts 12/yr. Hospitality; Keeping Your Kids Christian; Women's Ministry (program ideas); all 700-900 wds.

Tips: "Most open to feature articles addressing the unique needs of women in leadership (Bible-study leaders, women's ministry directors, pastor's wives, missionary wives, etc.). Some of these needs would include relationship with God, staff, leadership skills, ministry how-tos, balancing ministry and family, and marriage. The best way to break in is to contact the editor directly."

LADIES FIRST MAGAZINE, For Women Who Choose to Put God First, 4370 Hwy. 6 N., Ste. 211, Houston TX 77084. (281)440-2770. Fax (281)440-2772. E-mail: editor@ladiesfirst magazine.com, or info@ladiesfirstmagazine.com. Website: www.LadiesFirstMagazine.com. The Master Orchestrator Marketing firm. Connie Stewart, ed. (editor@ladiesfirstmagazine .com; www.myspace.com/pastorconniestewart). Articles and information tailored for women who are single, married, professionals, stay-at-home moms, pastors, First Ladies, students, or business owners. Quarterly mag. Subscription $25. Articles. Incomplete topical listings.

LIFE TOOLS FOR WOMEN: Online Women's Lifestyle Magazine, 40 MacEwan Park Rise, N.W., Calgary AB T3K 3Z9, Canada. (403)295-1932. Fax (403)291-2515. E-mail: editor@life toolsforwomen.com. Website: www.lifetoolsforwomen.com. Judy Rushfeldt, ed. Equipping women to reach their potential. Monthly online mag. Monthly page views: 45,000. Articles 500-1,200 wds. **NO PAYMENT.** Provides a byline and up to 50-word bio, including e-mail & Website link. Prefers e-query & e-submission (attached file). Guidelines on Website.

$THE LINK & VISITOR, 100-304 The East Mall, Etobicoke ON M9B 6E2, Canada. (416)622-8600, ext. 305. Fax (416)622-2308. E-mail: rjames@baptistwomen.com. Website: www .baptistwomen.com. Baptist Women of Ontario and Quebec. Renee James, ed. A positive, practical Baptist magazine for Canadian women who want to reach others for Christ. Bimonthly mag.; 24 pgs.; circ. 4,000. Subscription $17 Cdn., $17 U.S. 50% freelance. Complete ms; e-query OK. Pays .06-.10/wd. Cdn., on publication for one-time or simultaneous rts.; some work-for-hire. Articles 750-1,800 wds. (30-35/yr.). Responds in 16 wks. Seasonal 4 mos. ahead. Accepts simultaneous submissions & reprints (tell when/where appeared). Requires e-mail submission (copied into message). No kill fee. Uses some sidebars. Prefers NIV (inclusive language), NRSV, NLT. Guidelines/theme list on Website; copy for 9x12 SAE/2 Cdn. stamps. (Ads—limited/Canadian)

Poetry: Buys 3/yr. Free verse; 12-32 lines; pays $10-20. Submit max. 3 poems.

Tips: "Feature writers who know our magazine and our readers will know what topics and types of stories we are looking for. Canadian writers only, please."

+L.I.V.E. (LIVE IN VICTORY EVERYDAY), E-mail: editor@liveinvictory.org. Website: www.liveinvictory.org. Cheryl A. Griffin, ed-in-chief. A Christian publication targeting women and dedicated to excellence, enlightenment, and empowerment. Online mag. Free subscription. Open to freelance. Send complete ms by e-mail. E-mail for guidelines. Incomplete topical listings. (Ads—advertising@vlinternational.org)

Tips: "Our mission is to promote the application of the principles of the Word of God by using the magazine as a tool to empower people to live in victory in every area of their lives! The magazine is a ministry. We look to showcase, share and encourage people around the globe who are impacting the lives of others with the message of victory!"

LUTHERAN WOMAN'S QUARTERLY, PO Box 411993, St. Louis MO 63141-1993. Toll-free (800) 252-5965. Fax (314)268-1532. E-mail: editor@lwml.org. Website: www.lwml.org. Lutheran Women's Missionary League. Nancy Graf Peters, ed-in-chief. For women of the Lutheran Church—Missouri Synod. Quarterly mag.; 44 pgs.; circ. 200,000. Subscription $5.50. 25% unsolicited freelance; 75% assigned. Complete ms/cover letter. **NO PAYMENT.** Not copyrighted. Articles 750-1,200 wds. (4/yr.); fiction 750-1,200 wds. (4/yr.). Responds in 2 wks. Seasonal 5 mos. ahead. Regularly uses sidebars. Prefers NIV. Guidelines/theme list (also by e-mail); no copy.

> **Tips:** "Most open to articles. Must reflect the Missouri Synod teachings. Most of our writers are from the denomination. We set themes two years ahead. Contact us for themes and guidelines."

MAKING WAVES, 47 Queen's Park Cr. E., Toronto ON M5S 2C3, Canada. (416)929-5184. Fax (416)929-4064. E-mail: barfoot@wicc.org. Website: www.wicc.org. Women's Inter-Church Council of Canada. Gillian Barfoot, ed. A Christian feminist journal committed to addressing issues related to women, justice, and theology from an ecumenical faith perspective. Triannual mag.; circ. 1,400. Subscription for $35 donation. Open to unsolicited queries. Prefers e-mail submissions. Articles 500-800 wds., or 800-1,500 wds. Incomplete topical listings. Guidelines on Website. (No ads)

> **Tips:** "We are connected to a wider network of women and men working to free church and society from racism, ageism, and sexism, and from the teachings and practices that discriminate against women."

$+MARYLAND WOMEN OF WORSHIP, 3117 Ferndale Ave., Baltimore MD 21207. E-mail: mdwomenofworship@yahoo.com. Website: www.marylandwomenofworship.com. Wilhelmina Street, ed. Mag. & quarterly devotional guide. Open to unsolicited freelance. Complete ms by mail or e-mail. Pays $12. Articles 300 wds. Guidelines, themes, deadlines, & devotional format on Website.

> **Special Needs:** Study lessons (see Website).

$MELODY OF THE HEART: Reconciling Hearts; Offering Hope, 8409 S. Elder Ave., Broken Arrow, OK 74011-8286. (918)451-4017. E-mail inquiries: Use Online Contact Form (No mail submissions). E-mail from Website: http://epistleworks.com/HeartMelody. EpistleWorks Creations. JoAnn Reno Wray, ed./pub. Christian publication for women 30-65+ yrs.; heart-stirring, tight writing to bring practicality and joy to life. Bimonthly Webzine; 100,000+ hits monthly. Open to freelance. Query with online form. Pays on publication for reprint or 1st electronic rts: $40 for columnists (1st rights only. Columnists commit to one year/6 columns.); $20-25 for articles and short fiction. After initial publication, articles archived for 6 mos. Articles 750-900 wds; short fiction to 1,000 wds. Response only if work accepted. Guidelines on Website.

> **Poetry:** Buys up to 12/yr. Poetic Hearts Department. Poems must match themes; 4-24 lines; $8-12 /poem. Submit 2 poems max./issue, only at Online Form. "Avoid overused end-line rhymes. Try something other than iambic pentameter. Poetry should be a distillation of thought and emotion evoking a sense of time, place, and/or unchanging truth. Receive more poems than anything else. Make yours stand out with skillful word choice and innovative ideas that celebrate God's Word."

> **Fillers:** Buys 18-30/yr.; 50-150 wds. Short humor, kid comments, health news, anecdotes, marriage shorts, animal antics, household tips, scripture + insight (short), Did You Know facts, money saving ideas, more. Pays $5-10. Complete ms at Online Form. Sponsors periodic Essay Contests with cash prizes and publication, announced online at the site or in the Melody Mailer Email Newsletter to subscribers which can be signed up for at the site.

> **Columns/Departments:** Will review queries for new columns. Columns must be origi-

nal, never published elsewhere, on theme each issue, and writers must commit to one year/6 issues. Pays $40 on publication. Cook's Corner (recipes/stories behind them), 500-800 wds.; Heart-Stirring Reviews (products, books, music reviews) 500-750 wds.; Holiday Stories, 650-750 wds.; How Do I? (helping women with everyday problems), 500-750 wds.; Life Steps (illustrating work of God in your life or Personality Profiles of another individual), 500-750 wds.; Short Fiction (contemporary, romance, historical, biblical, mystery, for adult women), under 1000 wds.; Winning Hearts (reaching the world for Jesus), 750 wds.

Special Needs/Photos: Uses some freelance photos/illustrations.

Tips: "I often receive submissions by postal mail when guidelines clearly state these won't be reviewed. Don't skim, assuming you know what's needed. No matter where you submit, follow the three basic rules of submission: 1.) Study the guidelines. 2.) Study the guidelines. 3.) Study the guidelines. Don't forget to read the magazine's articles to determine style and content. Editors know when writers skip the process of full study and then fire off queries or submissions that miss the mark."

$MOMSENSE (MomSense), 2370 S. Trenton Way, Denver CO 80231. (303)733-5353. Fax (303)733-5770. E-mail: MomSense@mops.org. Website: www.MomSense.org, or www.MOPS.org. MOPS Intl. Inc. (Mothers of Preschoolers). Mary Darr, ed. Nurtures mothers of preschoolers from a Christian perspective with articles that both inform and inspire on issues relating to womanhood and motherhood. Bimonthly mag.; 32 pgs.; circ. 120,000. Subscription $23.95. 20% unsolicited freelance; 30% assigned. Complete ms/cover letter & bio; e-query OK. Accepts full mss by e-mail. Pays .15/wd. on publication for 1st & reprint rts. Articles 600 (15-20/yr.). Responds in 10-12 wks. Seasonal 6 mos. ahead. Accepts simultaneous submissions & reprints (tell when/where appeared). Prefers requested ms by e-mail (attached file or copied into message). Some kill fees 10%. Uses some sidebars. Prefers NIV. Guidelines/theme list (also by e-mail/Website—Mom Resources/Writers Guidelines); copy for 9x12 SAE/$1.34 postage. (Ads)

Poetry: Buys 6/yr. Any type to 400 wds. Pays .15/wd. Submit max. 6 poems.

Fillers: Accepts 10/yr. Tips. No payment.

Special Needs: "We always need practical articles to the woman as a woman, and to the woman as a mom."

Contest: Sponsors several contests per year for writing and photography. Check Website for details on current contests.

Tips: "Most open to theme-specific features. Writers are more seriously considered if they are a mother with some connection to MOPS (but not required). Looking for original content ideas that appeal to Christian and non-Christian readers."

**This periodical was #14 on the 2008 Top 50 Christian Publishers list (#21 in 2007).

MORE TO LIFE (MTL), 415 Second St., Indian Rocks Beach FL 33785. (727)596-7625. Fax (727)593-3523. E-mail: info@munce.com. Website: www.MTLMagazine.com. The Munce Group. Andrea Stock, ed. Lifestyle magazine for women who are discovering their spiritual core and true purpose. 8X/yr. mag.; 36-72 pgs.; circ. 250,000-2 million. Incomplete topical listings. (Ads)

Tips: "This magazine will draw attention to the quality, variety, and relevance of Christian products for everyday living and guide the readers back to Christian retail stores."

$+PAUSES...: An Oasis for Today's Catholic Woman, N1261Briarwood Ln., Merrill WI 54452. (715)536-2450. E-mail: sallie.2@netzero.com. Catholic. Sallie Bachar, ed. To inspire, encourage, and enable Catholic women to reach the fullness of their potential in and through the Catholic Church. Quarterly newsletter; 8 pgs. Subscription $10. 100% unsolicited freelance. Complete ms/cover letter; e-query OK. Pays $10 on publication for one-time rts. Articles 300-500 wds. (50/yr.); reviews 200 wds. Responds in 4 wks. Seasonal 3 mos. ahead.

Accepts simultaneous submissions; no reprints. Accepts submissions by e-mail (copied into message). No sidebars. Guidelines (also by e-mail); copy for 6x9 SAE/2 stamps. (Ads)

PRECIOUS TIMES, 3857 Birch St., Ste. 215, Newport Beach CA 92660. Toll-free (800)299-0696. (714)564-3949. E-mail: precioustimesmag@gmail.com or bookrevieweditor@precioustimesmag.com. Website: www.precioustimesmag.com. Independent. Marilyn White, pub/ed-in-chief. To help black women (ages 20-60) grow in their relationship with God, self, and others; biblical, but not preachy. Quarterly mag.; 76 pgs.; circ. 350,000. Subscription $18. 90% unsolicited freelance; 10% assigned. Complete ms; e-query OK. **PAYS 5 COPIES** for 1st rts. Personal testimonies, 1,800-2,000 wds.; everyday-life information, 1,200-2,400 wds.; health/fitness/beauty, 1,200 wds.; celebrity/personality interviews, 1,800-2,400 wds.; book reviews, 250-300 wds.; music reviews, 200-500 wds; fiction, 2,400-3,200. (20 articles/yr.; 4 fiction.) Responds in 12 wks. Seasonal 10 mos. ahead. Accepts simultaneous submissions & reprints (tell when/where appeared). Requires e-mail submissions (attached or copied into message in Word only). Uses some sidebars. Prefers NIV. Also accepts submissions from teens. Guidelines (also by e-mail/Website); copy $5/9x12 SAE. (Ads)

  Columns/Departments: Business, Health, Beauty, Finance; 600 wds.

  Tips: "Provide practical theology for contemporary issues. All articles should have a personal perspective, be relevant, and use real life anecdotes. We prefer a black woman's perspective on life issues."

PROVERBS 31 SISTERS—Has been combined with *A Virtuous Woman.*

P31 WOMAN, 616-G Matthews-Mint Hill Rd., Matthews NC 28105. (704)849-2270. Fax (704)849-7267. E-mail: editor@proverbs31.org. Website: www.proverbs31.org. Proverbs 31 Ministries. Glynnis Whitwer, ed.; submit to Janet Burke, asst. ed. (janet@proverbs31.org). Seeks to offer a godly woman's perspective on life. Monthly mag.; 16 pgs.; circ. 10,000. Subscription for donation. 50% unsolicited freelance; 50% assigned. Complete ms; e-query OK. **PAYS IN COPIES** for one-time rts. Not copyrighted. Articles 200-1,000 wds. (40/yr.). Responds in 4-6 wks. Seasonal 3 mos. ahead. Accepts simultaneous submissions & reprints (tell when/where appeared). Prefers accepted ms by e-mail (attached file or copied into message). Uses some sidebars. Prefers NIV. Guidelines/theme list (also on Website); copy on Website. (No ads)

  Fillers: Accepts 12/yr. Ideas, party ideas, prose; to 100 wds.

  Tips: "Looking for articles that encourage women and offer practical advice as well."

RIGHT TO THE HEART OF WOMEN E-ZINE, 2217 Lake Park Dr., Longmont CO 80503. (303)772-2035. Fax (303)678-0260. E-mail: rmontgomery@rebekahmontgomery.com. Website: www.righttotheheartofwomen.com. Rebekah Montgomery, ed. Encouragement and helps for women in ministry. Weekly online e-zine; 5 pgs.; circ. 15,000. Subscription free. 10% unsolicited freelance; 90% assigned. Query; e-query OK. **NO PAYMENT** for nonexclusive rts. Articles 100-800 wds. (20/yr.). Responds in 2 wks. Seasonal 2 mos. ahead. Accepts simultaneous submissions & reprints (tell when/where appeared). Requires accepted mss by e-mail (copied into message). Does not use sidebars. No guidelines; copy on Website. (Ads)

  Columns/Departments: Accepts 10/yr. Women Bible Teachers; Profiles of Women in Ministry; Women's Ministry Tips; Author's and Speaker's Tips; 100 wds. Query.

  Special Needs: Book reviews must be in first person, by the author. Looking for women's ministry event ideas.

  Tips: "For free subscription, subscribe at Website above; also view e-zine. We want to hear from those involved in women's ministry or leadership. Also accepts manuscripts from AWSAs (see www.awsawomen.com). Query with your ideas."

SHARE, 10 W. 71st St., New York NY 10023-4201. (212)877-3041. Fax (212)724-5923. E-mail: CDofANatl@aol.com. Website: www.catholicdaughters.org. Catholic Daughters of the Americas. Peggy O'Brien, exec. dir.; submit to Peggy Eastman, ed. For Catholic women. Quarterly mag.; circ. 95,000. Free with membership. Most articles come from membership, but is open. **NO PAYMENT.** Buys color photos & covers. Guidelines/copy. (Ads)

Tips: "We use very little freelance material unless it is written by Catholic Daughters."

SIMPLY BLESSED CHRISTIAN WOMEN'S MAGAZINE, PO Box 291205, Columbia SC 29229. (803)968-5196. Fax (803)234-4071. E-mail: jjpublisher@yahoo.com. Website: www .simplyblessedmag.com. J and J Publishing Co. Stephanie McKenny, ed./pub. For all women 25-55, focusing on encouraging and empowering them to perform in their roles at a greater capacity along with sharing information that will assist them in their day-to-day lifestyles. Bimonthly mag.; 40+ pgs. Subscription $18. Estab. 2007. 60% unsolicited freelance; 40% assigned. Query/clips; e-query OK. Accepts full mss by e-mail. **NO PAYMENT.** Not copyrighted. Articles 800-1,000 wds. (3/yr.); fiction 800-1,000 wds. (3/yr.); reviews 500 wds. Responds in 2 wks. Seasonal 3 mos. ahead. Accepts reprints (tell when/where appeared). Accepts e-mail submissions (attached file). Uses some sidebars. Prefers KJV or AMP. Guidelines (also by e-mail); copy for $2/9x12 SAE. (Ads)

Fillers: Accepts 6/yr. Cartoons, facts, prayers, tips; 200-300 wds.

Columns/Departments: Accepts 6-10/yr. Seasoned Sisters (women 50+); Pastor's Wives Corner (encouragement for pastor's wives); Health Awareness; Single & Satisfied; all 500-800 wds. Query.

Tips: "Most open to health, marriage, singles, wealth, and business."

$SPIRITLED WOMAN, 600 Rinehart Rd., Lake Mary FL 32746. (407)333-0600. Fax (407)333-7100. E-mail: spiritledwoman@strang.com. Website: www.spiritledwoman.com. Strang Communications. Brenda J. Davis, ed. To call women, ages 20-60, into intimate fellowship with God so He can empower them to fulfill His purpose for their lives. Bimonthly mag.; 100 pgs.; circ. 100,000. Subscription $17.95. 1% unsolicited freelance; 99% assigned. Query (limit to 500 wds.); e-query OK. Pays to $300 ($50 for humor, $75 for testimonies) on publication for 1st and all electronic rts. Articles 1,200-2,000 wds. Responds in 18-26 wks. No simultaneous submissions. Guidelines (also by e-mail); copy. (Ads)

Columns/Departments: Testimonies; Final Fun (funny stories or embarrassing moments, to 200 wds.); cartoons; $25-50.

Tips: "Most of our articles are commissioned. Mainly we want high-impact feature articles that depict a practical and spiritual application of scriptural teachings. Need brief testimonies of 350 words or less (open to all); profiles of women in ministry. Articles need to deal with the heart issues that hold a woman back. Also humorous anecdotes and book excerpts."

**2007 EPA Award of Merit—Most Improved Publication.

$TODAY'S CHRISTIAN WOMAN, 465 Gundersen Dr., Carol Stream IL 60188-2498. (630)260-6200. Fax (630)260-0114. E-mail: TCWedit@christianitytoday.com. Website: www.Todays ChristianWoman.com. Blog: http://blog.todayschristianwoman.com/editors. Christianity Today Intl. Ginger Kolbaba & Camerin Courtney, eds.; submit to Andrea Bianchi, asst. ed. To help Christian women (30-40 yrs.) grow in their relationship to God by providing practical, biblical perspectives on marriage, sex, parenting, work, health, friendship, single life, and self. Bimonthly mag.; 60+ pgs.; circ. 210,000. Subscription $17.95. 50% unsolicited freelance; 50% assigned. Query only; fax/e-query OK. Pays .20/published wd. on publication for 1st & electronic rts. Articles 800-1,500 wds. (30/yr.); no fiction. Responds in 12 wks. Seasonal 6 mos. ahead. Accepts reprints (tell when/where appeared); no simultaneous submissions. Accepts e-mail submission (attached). Uses some sidebars. Prefers NIV. Guidelines (also by e-mail/Website); copy $5. (Ads)

Columns/Departments: Camerin Courtney, ed. of What I'm Learning About... (personal account of a topic God is teaching you). Buys 6/yr. , 800 wds., $100. Complete ms. Columns will not be acknowledged or returned.

Special Needs: Articles slanted for mature Christians that deal with spiritual life topics; short humor pieces.

Tips: "Break in by submitting to column (see above)."

**The #3 best-selling magazine in Christian retail stores.

+**TODAY'S LEADING LADIES MAGAZINE,** P.O. Box 173968, Hialeah FL 33017. (954)559-6106. E-mail: tllmagazine@aol.com. Website: www.todaysleadingladiesministries.org. Today's Leading Ladies Intl. Ministries. Tracy R. Butler, ed.-in-chief. From CEOs to everyday women, ages 20-75, we are an empowering platform geared towards the amazing journeys and accomplishments of women worldwide. Quarterly & online mag.; 36-40 pgs; circ. 8,000. Subscription $18. 70% unsolicited freelance; 30% assigned. Complete ms/cover letter; e-query OK; query for fiction. Accepts full mss by e-mail. **NO PAYMENT** for all, one-time, or reprint rts. Articles 350 wds. (35/yr.); fiction (15/yr.); reviews 1/2 pg. Responds in 2-3wks. Seasonal 3 mos. ahead. Accepts simultaneous submissions & reprints (tell when/where appeared). Prefers submissions by e-mail (attached). Uses some sidebars. Prefers KJV/NIV. Guidelines/theme list by e-mail/Website. (Ads)

Poetry: Unlimited number. Free verse, light verse, traditional; 200-300 wds. Submit any number. Spiritual; empowerment for women.

Fillers: Unlimited number. Anecdotes, facts, ideas, party ideas, prayers, quotes, tips, 75-150 wds.

Special Needs: Sisterhood; mother-daughter relationships; beauty tips, fashion, entrepreneurship.

Tips: "Join our contributing writer's team, bringing fresh, new ideas, materials and interviews geared toward our platform. We especially need to fill our 'Empowered Living' and 'My Sister's Keeper' columns."

TOGETHER WITH GOD, PO Box 5002, Antioch TN 37011. Toll-free (877)767-7662. (615)731-6812. Fax (615)731-0771. E-mail: twg@wnac.org. Website: www.wnac.org. Women Nationally Active for Christ of National Assn. of Free Will Baptists. Sarah Fletcher, ed. A women's magazine with emphasis on fulfilling the Great Commission. Bimonthly mag.; 32 pgs.; circ. 7,500. Subscription $12. Estab. 2007. 25% unsolicited freelance; 75% assigned. Complete ms/cover letter. Accepts full ms by e-mail. **PAYS IN COPIES** for 1st rts. Articles 750-1,200 wds. (10/yr.). Responds in 8 wks. Seasonal 12 mos. ahead. No simultaneous submissions; accepts reprints (tell when/where appeared). Prefers e-mail submissions (attached file). Regularly uses sidebars. Also accepts submissions from teens. Prefers KJV. Guidelines/theme list by e-mail; copy for 10x13 SAE/$1. (No ads)

Columns/Departments: What Works (practical tips/lists about women's health, homes, fitness, fashion, or finances; My Mentor (women 13-40 write about older women's influence in life); 500-700 wds.

Special Needs: Christian life, family issues, creative outreach.

Contest: Annual Creative Arts Contest. March 1 deadline. Categories include Programs, Articles, Poetry, Plays/Skits, Devotionals, Art/Photography. Open to our subscribers, Women Active for Christ, or any woman active in the Free Will Baptist Church.

Tips: "Most open to articles. Bulk of material comes from Women Active for Christ or Free Will Baptist writers."

A VIRTUOUS WOMAN, 594 Ivy Hill, Harlan KY 40831. (606)573-6506. E-mail: submissions@ avirtuouswoman.org. Website: www.avirtuouswoman.org. Independent Seventh-day Adventist ministry. Melissa Ringstaff, dir./ed. Strives to provide practical articles for women ages 20-60 years; based on Proverbs 31. Monthly e-zine; circ. 20,000+ online. 80% unsolicited freelance; 20% assigned. Complete ms/cover letter; e-query OK. Accepts full mss by e-mail. **NO PAYMENT** for first, reprint, electronic, anthology rts. Articles 500-2,000 wds. (150+/yr.);

reviews 500-1,000 wds. Responds in 6-8 wks. Seasonal 6 mos. ahead. No simultaneous submissions; accepts reprints (tell when/where appeared). Accepts e-mail submissions (attached file in DOC or TXT or copied into message). Uses some sidebars. Prefers KJV, NIV, NLT. Guidelines/theme list on Website; copy for 9x12 SAE/$2.02 postage & $3.50. (Ads)

Poetry: Accepts 5/yr. Free verse, traditional. Submit max. 2 poems.

Fillers: Accepts 12/yr. Anecdotes, facts, ideas, jokes, party ideas, prayers, quizzes, and tips; to 200 wds.

Tips: "Write practical articles that appeal to the average woman—articles that women can identify with. Do not preach. Read our writer's helps for ideas." This magazine now combined with *Proverbs 31 Sisters.*

A WOMAN OF WORTH, 594 Ivy Hill, Harlan KY 40831. (606)573-6506. E-mail: submissions@ avirtuouswoman.org. Website: www.avirtuouswoman.org. A Virtuous Woman. Melissa Ringstaff, dir./ed. Strives to provide practical articles for women ages 20-60 years; based on Proverbs 31. Quarterly jour. & cookbook; 40-48 pgs.; circ. 20,000. Subscription $24.95. 90% unsolicited freelance. Complete ms/cover letter; e-query OK. Accepts full mss by e-mail. **PAYS 1 COPY** for first, reprint, electronic, & anthology rts. Articles 500-2,000 wds. (100/yr.); fiction 500-2,000 (1-2/yr.); reviews 500 wds. Responds in 6-8 wks. Seasonal 6 mos. ahead. No simultaneous submissions; accepts reprints (tell when/where appeared). Accepts submissions on disk or by e-mail (copied into message or attached in DOC or TXT). Regularly uses sidebars. Prefers KJV, NIV, NLT. Guidelines/theme list on Website; copy for 9x12 SAE/$6.75.

Poetry: Accepts 4-6/yr. Free verse, traditional; 20-30 lines. Submit max. 2 poems.

Fillers: Accepts 5-10/yr. Facts, short humor, and tips; 100-500 wds.

Columns/Departments: Accepts 100+/yr. Has a number of columns open to freelancers. See Website for list and length.

Contests: Occasionally runs contests for readers.

Tips: "Articles should be practical, giving reader useful ideas to apply to her own life. We like inspiring articles that offer encouragement and hope."

WOMEN OF THE CROSS, 920 Sweetgum Creek, Plano TX 75023. (972)517-8553. Greg Paskal, content mngr. (greg@gregpaskal.com). Encouraging women in their walk with the Lord; strong emphasis on discipleship and relationship. Online community. 50% unsolicited freelance. Complete ms by e-mail; e-query OK. **NO PAYMENT.** Articles 500-1,500 wds. (10/yr.). Responds in 2-4 wks. Seasonal 3 mos. ahead. Accepts simultaneous submissions; no reprints. Prefers e-mail submissions (attached or copied into message). Uses some sidebars. Prefers NIV, NKJV, NASB. Also accepts submissions from teens. Guidelines by e-mail. (No ads)

Poetry: Accepts 2/yr. Avant-garde, free verse, haiku, or light verse; 50-250 lines. Submit max. 1 poem.

Columns/Departments: Accepts 10/yr. Features (Christian living, encouragement); Article (to other women); all 500-1,500 wds.

Special Needs: Personal stories of growing in the Lord; faith-stretching stories about international adoption.

Tips: "Appropriate topics could be first-hand accounts of how God worked in the author's life through a personal or family experience. View online forum for specific topics."

WOMEN'S MINISTRY MAGAZINE, 4319 S. National Ave., #303, Springfield MO 65810-2607. (417)888-2067. Fax (417)888-2095. E-mail: publisher@womensministry.net. Website: www.womensministry.net, or www.jenniferrothschild.com. Jennifer and Philip Rothschild, pubs. Where more than 25,000 women's ministry leaders find news, events, and tips for women's ministry in the local church. Online newsletter. Subscription free. Open to freelance. Guidelines by e-mail.

Special Needs: Punchy, practical tips and ideas related to leading effective women's ministry.

WOMEN TODAY MAGAZINE, Box 300, Sta. A, Vancouver BC V6C 2X3, Canada. Toll-free (800) 563-1106, ext. 252. (604)514-2000 (no phone calls). Fax (604)514-2002. E-mail: editor@womentodaymagazine.com. Website: www.womentodaymagazine.com. Campus Crusade for Christ, Canada. Karen Schenk, pub.; Claire Colvin, sr. ed. For the professional, pre-seeking woman, 20-60 years; provides quality information that leads into a discussion of spiritual things and a presentation of the gospel. Monthly e-zine; 1.5 million hits/mo.; 100,000 unique visitors/mo. 60% unsolicited freelance; up to 10% assigned. Must use online submission system on Website; e-query OK. Accepts full ms by e-mail. **NO PAYMENT** for one-time or reprint rts. Articles 300-1,000 wds. (12-24/yr.). Responds in 8-12 wks. to accepted material only. Seasonal 4 mos. ahead. Accepts simultaneous submissions & reprints. Requires online submission. Does not use sidebars. Also accepts submissions from teens. Guidelines/theme list on Website. (Ads)

Columns/Departments: Columns tend toward how-to; 600-1,000 wds. Beauty & Fashion; Health & Fitness; Food & Cooking; Advice.

Tips: "Write on a topic from the theme list 4-5 months in advance. Beauty/fashion, relationships, and self-esteem are big draws on our site, and we can always use more great content. To break in, make your article approachable to an unchurched audience, avoid Christian jargon, and speak the truth plainly."

WT ONLINE, 1445 N. Boonville Ave., Springfield MO 65802-1894. (417)862-2781, ext. 4066. Fax (417)862-0503. E-mail: womanstouch@ag.org, or womens@ag.org. Website: www.wtonline.ag.org. Assemblies of God Women's Ministries Dept. Darla J. Knoth, mng. ed. Inspirational online magazine for women. Monthly Webzine. 20% unsolicited freelance. Query only; fax/e-query OK. **NO PAYMENT.** Articles 500-800 wds. (20/yr.). Responds in 13 wks. Seasonal 9-12 mos. ahead. Accepts simultaneous submissions & reprints (tell when/where appeared). Accepts e-mail submission. Kill fee. Regularly uses sidebars. Prefers NIV. Guidelines/theme list on Website; copy for 9x12 SAE/3 stamps. (Ads)

Columns/Departments: Buys 30/yr. The Single Woman (never married, widowed, divorced), 400 wds.; Family Matters (single or married moms); I Still Do! (marriage), 400 wds.

Tips: "Request guidelines and theme list for guidance on types of articles needed."
**2008, 2005 EPA Award of Merit—General.

WRITERS' MARKETS

$ADVANCED CHRISTIAN WRITER, 9118 W. Elmwood Dr., #1G, Niles IL 60714-5820. (847) 296-3964. Fax (847)296-0754. E-mail: ljohnson@wordprocommunications.com. Website: www.ACWriters.com. American Christian Writers/Reg Forder, Box 110390, Nashville TN 37222. Toll-free (800)21-WRITE. E-mail: ACWriters@aol.com (for samples, advertising, and subscriptions). Lin Johnson, mng. ed. A professional newsletter for published writers. Bimonthly newsletter; 8 pgs.; circ. 500. Subscription $19.95. 60% unsolicited freelance. Query, correspondence, & mss by e-mail only. Pays $20 on publication for 1st or reprint rts. Articles 500-1,000 wds. (18/yr.). Responds in 4-6 wks. Seasonal 6 mos. ahead. Accepts reprints (tell when/where appeared). Uses some sidebars. Requires e-mail submission. Prefers NIV. Guidelines (also by e-mail); copy for #10 SAE/1 stamp. (Ads)

Special Needs: Behind the scenes look at a publishing house (how it started, how editorial operates, current needs, submission procedures); how-to; opinion pieces; time management; workplace issues.

Tips: "We accept articles only from professional, well-published writers and from editors. We need manuscripts about all aspects of being a published freelance writer and how to increase sales and professionalism; on the advanced level; looking for depth beyond the basics."

AREOPAGUS MAGAZINE. E-mail for UK: editor@areopagus.org.uk. E-mail from U.S.: editor@ areopagus.org.uk. Website: www.areopagus.org.uk. Areopagus Publications. Julian Barritt, ed. For amateur Christian writers, producing both general and Christian writing. Quarterly mag.; 32 pgs.; circ. 100. Subscription $17 U.S. 100% unsolicited freelance. Complete ms/cover letter (if subscriber); e-query OK. **NO PAYMENT.** Articles 1,800 wds. (6/yr.); fiction 1,800 wds. (5/yr.); book reviews 300 wds. Responds in 1 mo. Seasonal 4 mos. ahead. Accepts e-mail submissions (attached or copied into message). Does not use sidebars. Any Bible version. Guidelines; copy on Website.

Poetry: Accepts 40/yr.; any type; to 60 lines. Submit max. 3 poems.

Fillers: Accepts 10/yr. Facts, ideas, newsbreaks, prose, short humor, to 200 wds.

Contest: Sponsors a quarterly, subscribers-only, writing competition (fiction, nonfiction, or poetry) with prizes of 28 pounds (UK only).

Tips: "Items are selected by merit from subscribers only. If not accepted, a recommendation for resubmission is given if there is potential."

AUTHOR-ME.COM. E-mail: Peachy2@prodigy.net. Website: www.Author-Me.com. Independent. Bruce L. Cook, pub.; Adam W. Smith, ed. dir. (awsmith@patriot.net); Winona Rasheed, mng. ed. (mzcoffeecake2001@yahoo.com). Endeavors to encourage and nurture new writers in their craft. Accepts freelance. Complete ms. **NO PAYMENT.** No submissions from writers under age 14. Edit manuscripts before submitting. Requires e-mail submissions from Website form. Guidelines on Website.

Poetry: Submit max. 4 poems.

$BEST NEW WRITING (formerly Writers' Notes), PO Box 11, Titusville NJ 08560. E-mail: editor@hopepubs.com. Website: www.bestnewwriting.com. In 2006, Writers' Notes Magazine was transformed in this annual anthology, which carries the results of the Eric Hoffer Award for Books and Prose. Submit books via mail; no queries. The prose category is for creative fiction and nonfiction less than 10,000 wds. Annual award for books features 14 categories. Pays $500 for winning prose; $1,500 for winning book. Guidelines at www .HofferAward.com.

$BYLINE, PO Box 111, Albion NY 14411-0111. E-mail: robbi@bylinemag.com. Website: www.BylineMag.com. General market. Robbi Hess, ed. Offers practical tips, motivation, and encouragement to freelance writers and poets. Bimonthly mag.; 48 pgs.; circ. 3,500+. Subscription $29. 90% unsolicited freelance. Query; e-query OK. Pays $10-75 for features; $25 for fiction; less for shorts, following publication for 1st rts. Articles 1,500-1,800 wds. (75/yr.); personal essays 500 wds.; fiction to 2,000 wds. (11/yr.). Responds in 3 mos. Seasonal 6 mos. ahead. Accepts simultaneous submissions. No full mss by e-mail. Encourages sidebars. Guidelines on Website; copy $5. (Ads)

Poetry: Donna Marbach, poetry ed. Buys 50-100/yr. Any type; to 30 lines; $10. Writing themes only. Submit max. 3 poems.

Fillers: Anecdotes, prose, short humor for humor page; 50-400 wds.; $10-15. Must pertain to writing.

Columns/Departments: Buys 50-60/yr. End Piece (personal essay on writing theme), 550 wds., $35; First Sale accounts, 300 wds., $10; Only When I Laugh (writing humor), short, $15-25. Complete ms.

Contests: Sponsors many year round; details included in magazine, on Website, or send SASE for flier.

Special Needs: Accepts articles only about writing and selling; likes mainstream fiction. **Tips:** "All areas except our regular columns are open to freelancers. We get much more fiction than nonfiction. Always looking for instructive, well-written articles." ****This periodical was #41 on the 2008 Top 50 Christian Publishers list.

$CANADIAN WRITER'S JOURNAL,** White Mountain Publications, Box 1178, New Liskeard ON P0J 1P0, Canada. Canada-wide toll-free (800)258-5451. (705)647-5424. Fax (705)647-8366. E-mail: cwj@cwj.ca. Website: www.cwj.ca. Deborah Ranchuk, ed./pub. How-to articles for writers. Bimonthly mag.; 64 pgs.; circ. 350. Subscription $35. 75% unsolicited freelance; 15% assigned. Complete ms/cover letter or query; phone/fax/e-query OK. Pays $7.50 Cdn./published pg. (about 450 wds.) on publication (2-9 mos. after acceptance) for onetime rts. Articles 400-2,000 wds. (200/yr.); fiction to 1,200 wds (see contest below); book/music/video reviews 250-500 wds. ($7.50). Responds in 9 wks. Seasonal 3 mos. ahead. Accepts simultaneous submissions & reprints (tell when/where appeared). Prefers e-mail submission (copied into message only). Some sidebars. Prefers KJV. Also accepts submissions from teens. Guidelines (also by e-mail/Website); copy $9. (Ads)

Poetry: Buys 40-60/yr. All types; to 40 lines; $2-5. Submit max. 10 poems.

Fillers: Buys 15-20/yr. Anecdotes, cartoons, ideas, quotes; 20-200 wds.; $3-5.

Contest: Sponsors semiannual short fiction contest (March 31 and September 30 deadlines); to 1,200 wds. Entry fee $5. Prizes $100, $50, $25. All fiction needs are filled by this contest. E-mail: cwc-calendar@cwj.ca.

Tips: "Send clear, complete, concise how-to-write articles with a sense of humor and usefulness. Read the guidelines and follow them, please."

****This periodical was #30 on the 2008 Top 50 Christian Publishers list (#19 in 2007).

$CHRISTIAN COMMUNICATOR,** 9118 W. Elmwood Dr., #1G, Niles, IL 60714-5820. (847)296-3964. Fax (847)296-0754. E-mail: ljohnson@wordprocommunications.com. Website: www.ACWriters.com. American Christian Writers/Reg Forder, Box 110390, Nashville TN 37222. Toll-free (800)21-WRITE. Fax (615)834-0450; ACWriters@aol.com (for samples, advertising or subscriptions). Lin Johnson, mng. ed.; Mona Hodgson, poetry ed. For Christian writers/speakers who want to improve their writing craft and speaking ability, stay informed about writing markets, and be encouraged in their ministries. Monthly (11X) mag.; 20 pgs.; circ. 3,000. Subscription $29.95. 70% unsolicited freelance. Complete ms/queries by e-mail only. Pays $5-10 on publication for 1st or reprint rts. Articles 650-1,000 wds. (22/yr.). Responds in 4-6 wks. Seasonal 6 mos. ahead. Accepts reprints (tell when/where appeared). Requires e-mail submission. Guidelines by e-mail; copy for 9x12 SAE/3 stamps to Nashville address. (Ads)

Poetry: Buys 22/yr. Free verse, haiku, light verse, traditional; to 20 lines. Poems on writing or speaking; $5. Send to Mona Hodgson: mona@monahodgson.com.

Columns/Departments: Buys 80/yr. A Funny Thing Happened on the Way to Becoming a Communicator (humor), 75-300 wds.; Interviews (published authors or editors), 650-1,000 wds.; Speaker's Corner (techniques for speakers), 650-1,000 wds.

Tips: "I need editor profiles and articles for speaker's column."

CHRISTIANWRITERS.COM. Website: www.christianwriters.com. A free online writers' resource community to provide a supportive, family atmosphere where writers may easily access the tools and resources to create, market, and publish their work. Accepts articles, short fiction, poetry, and devotionals. Submit through Website. Guidelines on Website.

$CROSS & QUILL, 1624 Jefferson Davis Rd., Clinton SC 29325-6401. (864)697-6035. E-mail: CQarticles@cwfi-online.org, or cwfi@cwfi-online.org. Website: www.cwfi-online.org. Christian Writers Fellowship Intl. Sandy Brooks, ed./pub. For Christian writers, editors, agents, conference directors. Bimonthly newsletter; 16 pgs.; circ. 1,000+. Subscription $25; CWFI membership $45. 75% unsolicited freelance; 25% assigned. Complete ms; query for electronic submissions. Pays $10-25 on publication for 1st or reprint rts. Articles 200-800 wds. (50/yr.); book reviews 100 wds. ($5). Responds in 2 mos. Seasonal 6 mos. ahead. Accepts reprints (tell when/where appeared). Uses some sidebars. Accepts e-mail submission (copied into message) to CQArticles@cwfi-online.org. Guidelines (also by e-mail/Website); copy $2/9x12 SAE/3 stamps. (Ads)

Poetry: Accepts 12/yr. Any type; to 12 lines. Submit max. 3 poems. Must pertain to writing/publishing.

Fillers: Accepts 12/yr. Anecdotes, cartoons, prayers; 25-100 wds. Pays in copies.

Columns/Departments: Accepts 36/yr. Writing Rainbows! (devotional), 500-600 wds.; Writers Helping Writers (how-to), 200-800 wds.; Editor's Roundtable (interview with editor), 200-800 wds.; Tots, Teens & In-Betweens (juvenile market), 200-800 wds.; BusinessWise (business side of writing), 200-800 wds.; Connecting Points (how-to on critique group), 200-800 wds.

Special Needs: Good "meaty" informational articles on children's writing; fiction market; studying the markets; program ideas for groups; etc.

Tips: "Most open to informational articles that explain how to improve writing skills, how to keep records, how to organize and run a writers' group. Keep in mind our audience is primarily writers and others associated with Christian publishing. Stick to informational, nuts and bolts type articles, and follow our guidelines."

ESDRAS' SCROLL (formerly Poetic Voices), PO Box 63, McDonaugh GA 30253. (770)507-3225. Fax (615)658-4078. E-mail: submissions@voicesofchrist.org. Website: www.voicesof christ.org. Voices of Christ Literary Ministries. Theresa H. Johnson, ed. We prefer poetry, and creative writing that is relevant to time/seasons in which we live. Seasonal e-zine/literary mag.; circ. 5,000. Subscription free. 100% unsolicited freelance. Call or query; e-query OK. Accepts full mss by e-mail. **NO PAYMENT** for one-time, reprint, electronic rts. Articles & fiction 500-1,500 wds.; book reviews 250 wds. Responds in 6 wks. Seasonal 2 mos. ahead. Accepts simultaneous submissions & reprints (tell when/where appeared). Prefers e-mail submissions (attached). Uses some sidebars. Also accepts submissions from children/teens. Prefers KJV. Guidelines on Website; copy online. (Ads)

Poetry: Accepts up to 100/yr. Any type; 3-30 lines. Submit max. 3-5 poems. "Poetry is our main focus, specifically poetry that addresses social issues."

Fillers: Accepts up to 20/yr. Cartoons, sermon illustrations, short humor; 250 wds.

Tips: "Submit creative work that is relevant to the times/seasons in which we live. In particular, writings that address social, government, educational, or even religious issues from a spiritual perspective. We readily review and accept poetry that addresses current social issues of concern to the church and society that uphold Christian principles. In addition, we actively seek poetry that deals with end-time ministry." Fiction for children and teens, 12 years and up.

$FELLOWSCRIPT, PO Box 26016, 650 Portland St., Dartmouth NS B2W 6P3, Canada. E-mail: submissions@inscribe.org. Website: www.inscribe.org. InScribe Christian Writers' Fellowship. Joanna Mallory, acq. ed. To provide encouragement, instruction, news, and helpful information for the membership of InScribe Christian Writers' Fellowship. Quarterly newsletter; 28-44 pgs.; circ. 150-200. Subscription $40 (includes membership). 45% unsolicited freelance; 55% assigned. Complete ms; e-query OK. Pays $5 or .025/wd. Cdn. on publication for 1st or one-time rts. or .015/wd. for reprint rts. Articles 600-1,200 wds. (70/yr.); book reviews (writing related), 300-500 wds. ($5). Responds in 4-6 wks. Seasonal 3-4 mos. ahead. Accepts simultaneous submissions & reprints (tell when/where appeared). Requires mss by e-mail (attached or copied into message). No kill fee. Uses some sidebars. Also accepts submissions from teens. Prefers NIV or NKJV. Guidelines on Website; copy for $3.50 in U.S. or Cdn. stamps or IRCs. (Ads if writing related)

Fillers: Accepts 4-8/yr. Anecdotes, cartoons, facts, tips (all writing-related); 300-600 wds. Pays $5.

Special Needs: Articles of practical help to writers, from beginners to advanced.

Contest: Fall contest in conjunction with InScribe's fall conference every year in September (August deadline). Categories include fiction, poetry, children's stories, essays, and nonfiction. Details on Website, or write and ask to be put on mailing list.

Tips: "We're a bit overstocked at present. The best submissions for us are practical articles on an aspect of writing, written in conversational style and with a good takeaway."

$FICTION FIX NEWSLETTER: The Nuts and Bolts of Crafting Better Fiction. E-mail: administration@coffeehouseforwriters.com. Website: www.coffeehouseforwriters.com/news.html. Carol Lindsay, ed. For writers and aspiring writers of short stories and novels. Monthly newsletter; circ. 5,000. To subscribe, send blank e-mail to FictionFix-subscribe@topica.com. E-query only. Responds in 2-3 wks. Pays to $20 ($30-50 for assigned) within 10 days of publication for 1st electronic rts. How-to articles 300-1,500 wds. Prefers submission by e-mail (copied into message only/see guidelines for specifics). Guidelines on Website.

Columns/Departments: This Writer's Opinion (reviews of writing books), 300-500 wds.; The Writing Life (personal writing stories). No payment.

Tips: "Articles must be received by the 10th of the previous month. Articles received after the 10th will be considered for a later publication."

$FREELANCE WRITER'S REPORT, 45 Main St., PO Box A, North Stratford NH 03590-0167. (603)922-8383. E-mail: editor@writers-editors.com. Website: www.writers-editors.com. General/CNW Publishing Inc. Dana K. Cassell, ed. Covers marketing and running a freelance writing business. Monthly newsletter; 8 pgs. 25% freelance. Complete ms via e-mail (attached or copied into message). Pays .10/wd. on publication for one-time rts. Articles to 900 wds. (50/yr.). Responds within 1 wk. Seasonal 2 mos. ahead. Accepts simultaneous submissions & reprints (tell when/where appeared). Does not use sidebars. Guidelines on Website; copy for 6x9 SAE/2 stamps (for back copy); $4 for current copy.

Fillers: Prose fillers to 400 wds.

Contest: Open to all writers. Deadline March 15, 2009. Nonfiction, fiction, children's, poetry. Prizes; $100, $75, $50. Details on Website.

Tips: "No articles on the basics of freelancing; our readers are established freelancers. Looking for marketing and business building for freelance writers/editors/book authors."

$MERLYN'S PEN: Fiction, Essays, and Poems by America's Teens, 11 S. Angell St., Ste. 301, Providence RI 02906. Toll-free (800)247-2027. (401)751-3766. Fax (401)274-1541. E-mail: merlyn@merlynspen.org. Website: www.merlynspen.com. General. R. James Stahl, ed. Magazine; circ. 5,000. Subscription $29.95. Query; no e-query. Pays $20-200 on publication for all rts. Articles 500-5,000 wds.; fiction to 8,500 wds. Responds in 10-12 wks.

Poetry: Free verse, metric verse; $20-50.

MONEY THE WRITE WAY, PO Box 488, Dobbins CA 95935. (530)788-8179. E-mail: carmel@moneythewriteway.com. Website: www.moneythewriteway.com. Write Spirit Publishing. Carmel Mooney, pub. Educates, inspires, and supports Christian writers, travel writers, authors, and e-publishing enthusiasts in making money as a writer of integrity. Monthly e-zine; 8-15 pgs.; circ. 4,000. Subscription free. 80% unsolicited freelance; 10% assigned. Query; e-query OK. **PAYS IN COPIES,** free advertising for writer, and occasionally up to $10; for one-time rts. Articles 300-800 wds. (36/yr.); book reviews 300-500 wds. Responds in 2-4 wks. Seasonal 2 mos. ahead. Accepts simultaneous submissions & reprints (tell when/where appeared). Accepts mss by e-mail (attached file). Does not use sidebars. Prefers NIV. Guidelines; copy for #10 SAE or by e-mail. (Ads)

Fillers: Accepts 6-12/yr. Anecdotes, facts, ideas, quotes, tips; 50-100 wds. No payment (usually), or up to $5.

Columns/Departments: Accepts 36+/yr. Marketing for Writers—Marketing with Integrity, 300-800 wds.; monthly guest article (how-to or personal experience essay), 300-800 wds.; Boast Post (short pieces on personal writing accomplishments), 50-100 wds.

Special Needs: Christian writing: tips, resources, how-to, reviewing, travel writing, success stories, and marketing. Propose a column for us.

Contest: Occasionally sponsors writing contests.

Tips: "Most open to Boast Post (column), or how-to-write/marketing/breaking-in articles. Send a concise, focused query that is an example of writer's tone and expertise."

$NEW WRITER'S MAGAZINE, PO Box 5976, Sarasota FL 34277-5976. (941)953-7903. E-mail: newriters@aol.com. General/Sarasota Bay Publishing. George S. Haborak, ed. Bimonthly mag.; circ. 5,000. 95% freelance. Query or complete ms by mail. Pays $10-50 ($20-40 for fiction) on publication for 1st rts. Articles 700-1,000 wds. (50/yr.); fiction 700-800 wds. (2-6/yr.). Responds in 5 wks. Guidelines; copy $3.

Poetry: Buys 10-20/yr. Free verse, light verse; 8-20 lines. Pays $5 min. Submit max. 3 poems.

Fillers: Buys 25-45/yr. Writing-related cartoons; buys 20-30/yr.; pays $10 max. Anecdotes, facts, newsbreaks, short humor; 20-100 wds.; buys 5-15/yr. Pays $5 max.

Tips: "We like interview articles with successful writers."

NORTHWEST CHRISTIAN AUTHOR, Attn.: NCWA, PO Box 428, Enumclaw WA 98022. Toll-free (800)731-6292. E-mail: acquisitions@nwchristianwriters.org. Website: www.nwchristian writers.org. Northwest Christian Writers Assn. Mike Owens, acq. ed. To encourage Christian authors to share the gospel through the written word and to promote excellence in writing. Bimonthly newsletter; 12 pgs.; circ. 200. Subscription $12; or $25 including membership. 40% unsolicited freelance; 60% assigned. Complete ms/cover letter; e-query OK. **PAYS 3 COPIES** for one-time or reprint rts. Not copyrighted. Articles 300-1,000 wds. (20/yr.); book reviews 100 wds. Responds in 2 wks. Accepts simultaneous submissions & reprints (tell when/where appeared). Prefers e-mail submission (attached file). Uses some sidebars. Also accepts submissions from teens. Guidelines on Website; no copy. (No ads)

Poetry: Accepts 3/yr. Free verse, light verse. Submit max. 3 poems.

Fillers: Anecdotes, tips; 50-250 wds.

Profiles: Every issue includes a profile (800-1,000 wds.) of a NWCW member and short sample of their work.

Special Needs: How-tos on nonfiction and fiction writing. Focus on genre techniques.

Tips: "Most open to articles on writing techniques, particularly for specific genres. Stay within word count. E-queries should have 'NW Christian Author' in subject line. Include 1-3 sentence author bio with article."

ONCE UPON A TIME, 553 Winston Ct., St. Paul MN 55118. (651)457-6223. E-mail: audrey ouat@comcast.net. Website: http://onceuponatimemag.com. Audrey B. Baird, ed./pub. Highly specialized magazine for children's writers and illustrators, offering help, instruction, encouragement in an over-the-fence-type friendly way. Quarterly mag.; 32 pgs.; circ. 1,000. Subscription $27. 50% unsolicited freelance. Complete ms/cover letter; no phone/fax/e-query. **PAYS IN COPIES** for one-time rts. Articles 100-900 wds. (80-100/yr.). Responds in 6 wks. Seasonal anytime. Accepts simultaneous submissions & reprints (tell when/where appeared—must be 1 yr. from last publication). Uses some sidebars. Guidelines (also on Website); copy $5. (Ads)

Poetry: Accepts 80-100/yr. Free verse, haiku, light verse, traditional; to 30 lines. Writing/illustrating related. Submit max. 6 poems. "About rhyming poetry: pay attention to rhythm—it's not enough to rhyme—rhyming poetry must have rhythm (and near rhyme is not enough). I'm willing to help and to edit and to suggest, but do your part first with revision until the piece is as good as you can get it."

Fillers: Accepts 20-30/yr. Anecdotes, cartoons, ideas, short humor, tips (all writing/illustrating related); to 100 wds.

Special Needs: How-to articles on writing and illustrating (by those qualified to write them) up to 800 wds.; short pieces on writing & illustrating, 100-400 wds.

Tips: "Send a good, tight article on the writing life—any aspect—that is either educational, informative, entertaining, humorous, or inspiring. We like a friendly, upbeat tone. Humor is always looked for. We get too many articles on rejection. I am open to them if you state what you learned from them or how you persevered in spite of them. Articles on good advice you've received that resulted in publication for you are always good. We like success stories and particularly look for how-to pieces. Perseverance is a strong theme for us. Read the writing books. Read the market guides. Attend conferences. Learn how to write before you attempt it."

OPINARI NEWSLETTER: For Christian Authors, Publishing Professionals and Booklovers: Hope. Dream. Believe., 5113 W. Running Brook Rd., Columbia MD 21044. (443) 745-1004. E-mail: info@opinebooks.com. Website: www.opinari.com. Jean Purcell, ed. Information, ideas, and opportunities for new and advanced Christian writers. Subscription free (sign up via "The Writer's Center" link on Website). 100% assigned freelance. To submit articles, ads, or book reviews, request guidelines by e-mail. **NO PAYMENT** for nonexclusive rts. Articles to 250 wds. Responds in 3 wks. Accepts reprints (tell when/where appeared). Accepts submissions by e-mail (attached file). Guidelines/theme list by e-mail; free copy. (No ads)

   Columns/Departments: My View (topics related to unique challenge of Christians who write for publication); 300-450 wds.

   Special Needs: All articles/essays/ideas should relate to writing or the writer's life.

   Tips: "*Opinari*'s reach is expanding."

$POETS & WRITERS MAGAZINE, 90 Broad St., Ste. 2100, New York NY 10004-2272. (212) 226-3586. Fax (212)226-3963. E-mail: editor@pw.org. Website: www.pw.org. General. Submit to The Editors. Professional trade journal for poetry, fiction, and nonfiction writers. Subscription $19.95. Bimonthly mag.; circ. 60,000. Query/clips by mail; e-query OK. Pays $150-500 on acceptance for 1st & nonexclusive rts. Articles 500-3,000 wds. (35/yr.). Responds in 4-6 wks. Seasonal 4 mos. ahead. Some kill fees 25%. Guidelines on Website; copy $4.95. (Ads)

   Tips: "Most open to News & Trends, The Literary Life, and The Practical Writer (columns)."

$SHADES OF ROMANCE MAGAZINE, 7127 Minnesota Ave., St. Louis MO 63111. E-mail: sormag@yahoo.com. Website: www.sormag.com. Blog: www.sormag.blogspot.com. LaShaunda Hoffman, ed. A guide for readers and writers of multicultural romance and fiction. E-zine. E-query only. Pays $20 for articles, $25 for fiction within 30 days of publication (through PayPal) for electronic rts. Articles 500-800 wds. (6/yr.); short stories 500-1,500 wds. (6/yr.); devotions 200-500 wds. Responds in 2-4 wks. Seasonal 2 mos. ahead. Accepts simultaneous submissions & reprints (tell when/where appeared; pays $10). Accepts e-mail submissions (attached file). Does not use sidebars. Guidelines/themes by e-mail/Website; copy online. (Ads)

$SPIRIT-LED WRITER. E-mail: query@spiritledwriter.com. Website: www.SpiritLedWriter.com. Lisa A. Crayton, pub./ed. Internet magazine for Christian beginning, intermediate, and advanced writers. Monthly e-zine. Query by e-mail (put "Query: [subject]" in subject line). Pays $10-20 on publication for one-time, reprint, and electronic rts. Articles to 1,200 wds. (70+/yr.); reviews to 500 wds. Responds in 8 wks. Accepts reprints. Submit accepted mss by e-mail (no attachments). Regularly uses sidebars. Also accepts submissions from teens. Guidelines by e-mail/Website; copy online. (Ads)

Columns/Departments: Buys several/yr. Musing Dept. (writing-related personal reflections), 700-900 wds.; God's Glory Dept. (writing success stories), 500-700 wds.; Business (articles on the business of writing), to 1,200 wds.; Children's Column (how-to on writing for youth), to 1,200 wds.; $10-20.

Special Needs: Writing-related devotionals; conference coverage (700-900 wds.); and book reviews of writing books, 250-500 wds. ($5-10, depending on whether they supply the book). Also articles on writing for youth or on advanced writing topics.

Tips: "Easiest to break in with a success story (God's glory), musing article, or devotional. We seek how-to and feature articles with a writing theme. We are not a general, Christian-living publication. We reject many manuscripts because they are general, not writing-related. Make it relevant to writing and writers."

$TICKLED BY THUNDER, 14076—86A Ave., Surrey BC V3W 0V9, Canada. (604)591-6095. E-mail: info@tickledbythunder.com. Website: www.tickledbythunder.com. Larry Lindner, ed. For writers wanting to better themselves. Quarterly chapbook (3-4X); 24 pgs.; circ. 1,000. Subscription $10 Cdn. or U.S. 90% unsolicited freelance; 10% assigned. Complete ms/cover letter; e-query OK from subscribers only (use online form). Pays $2-5 (in Cdn. or U.S. stamps) on publication for one-time rts. Articles 1,500 wds. (5/yr.); fiction 2,000 wds. (20/yr.); book/music/video reviews 1,000 wds. Responds in 16 wks. Seasonal 6 mos. ahead. Accepts simultaneous submissions. Prefers requested ms on disk, no e-mail submission. Uses some sidebars. Also accepts submissions from children/teens. Guidelines (also by e-mail/Website); copy $2.50/6x9 SAE. (Ads)

Poetry: Accepts 20-40/yr. Any type; to 40 lines. Submit max. 5-7 poems. "Try sending seasonal poetry well in advance."

Contest: For fiction (February 15 annual deadline) and poetry (February 15, May 15, August 15, and October 15 annual deadlines). Article contests for subscribers only (February 15, May 15, August 15, and October 15 deadlines). Send SASE for guidelines.

Tips: "Write a 300-word article describing how you feel about your successes/failures as a writer. Be specific, and focus—don't be at all general or vague; tell what works for you. Be original; say something classic in a new way. Use imagery. For fiction, surprise me. Write to put me on the edge of my seat—hold my attention—then wrap it up with something unexpected. Need book reviews of writing books."

$WIN-INFORMER, PO Box 11337, Bainbridge Island WA 98110. (206)842-9103. Fax (206) 842-0536. E-mail: writersinfonetwork@juno.com. Website: www.christianwritersinfo.net. Writers Information Network. Elaine Wright Colvin, ed. Send books to be announced or reviewed to 5359 Ruby Pl. N.E., Bainbridge Island WA 98110. CBA industry news and trends to keep professional writers, editors, agents, and speakers in touch with the changing marketplace. Bimonthly mag.; 24-32 pgs.; circ. 1,000. Subscription $49.95 ($60 Canada/foreign in U.S. funds). 33% unsolicited; 20% assigned. Complete ms submitted in body of e-mail only. Pays $20-50 (or subscription) on acceptance for 1st rts. Articles 50-500 wds. (30/yr.); book reviews, 100-300 wds. Accepts e-mail submissions only. Responds in 1 mo. Uses some sidebars. Guidelines on Website; copy $5/9x12 SAE/6 stamps. (No ads, but likes to announce news of members' successes)

Poetry: Any type; writing related.

Fillers: Anecdotes, facts, ideas, newsbreaks, quizzes, quotes, prayers, short humor; 50-300 wds.; $10-20.

Columns/Departments: Columns are continuously changing to meet the needs of an evolving industry. Check a recent copy for current column needs.

Special Needs: "Hot news of our growing, changing market whenever and wherever you hear it—at a writers conference, in a magazine news announcement, from your editor or agent, at your writers group—pass it on. If you make it into a round-up article of what many industry insiders are saying, we'll even pay you. Our readers want to be kept on the cutting edge of what is happening in the CBA industry."

Tips: "If it works for you, we want to hear about it. If you learn a hot tip, we'd love to share it. We are in a crowded marketplace and a tight book-publishing industry. We really do need each other! This industry is built on networking and relationships. We want tried and proven ideas—what's working for you and other professional writers and speakers. Give us articles on shopping your book proposal; keeping up with Web networking; balancing writing and blogging hours."

THE WRITE CONNECTION, 3706 N.E. Shady Lane Dr., Gladstone MO 64119. Phone/fax (816) 459-8016. E-mail: HACWN@earthlink.net. Website: www.hacwn.org. Heart of America Christian Writers' Network. Jeanette Littleton, exec. ed.; Pat Mitchell, ed. Monthly newsletter; 4 pgs.; circ. 150. Subscription free with HACWN membership $25. 50% unsolicited freelance; 50% assigned. Complete ms/cover letter; phone/e-query OK. **NO PAYMENT** for 1st or reprint rts. Articles 400 wds. (15/yr.); book reviews 200 wds. Responds in 8 wks. Accepts simultaneous submissions; no reprints. Accepts requested mss by e-mail. Uses some sidebars. Also accepts submissions from teens. (Ads)

Poetry: Accepts 5/yr. Free verse, light verse, traditional; to 12 lines. Submit max. 3 poems.

Fillers: Accepts 25/yr. Anecdotes, facts, ideas, jokes, prayers, prose, quotes, short humor, tips—solely dealing with writing.

$THE WRITER, 21027 Crossroads Cir., Waukesha WI 53186. (262)796-8776. Fax (262)798-6468. E-mail: queries@writermag.com. Website: www.writermag.com. General. Jeff Reich, ed. How-to for writers; lists religious markets on Website. Monthly mag.; 60-68 pgs.; circ. 30,000. Subscription $32.95. 80% unsolicited freelance. Query; no phone/fax query (prefers hard copy or e-query). Pays $300-500 for feature articles; book reviews ($40-80, varies); on acceptance for 1st rts. Features 600-3,500 wds. (60/yr.). Responds in 4-6 wks. Uses some sidebars. Guidelines (also on Website). (Ads)

Fillers: Prose; writer-related cartoons $50. Send cartoons to slange@writermag.com.

Columns/Departments: Buys 24+/yr. Freelance Success (shorter pieces on the business of writing); Off the Cuff (personal essays about writing; avoid writer's block stories). All 600-1,600 wds. Pays $100-300 for columns; $25-75 for Take Note. Query 4 months ahead. See guidelines for full list of columns.

Special Needs: How-to on the craft of writing only.

Contests: Occasionally sponsors a contest.

Tips: "Get familiar first with our general mission, approach, tone, and the types of articles we do and don't do. Then, if you feel you have an article that is fresh and well suited to our mission, send us a query. Personal essays must provide takeaway advice and benefits for writers; we shun the 'navel-gazing' type of essay. Include plenty of how-to, advice, and tips on techniques. Be specific. Query for features six months ahead. All topics indicated must relate to writing."

**This periodical was #45 on the 2008 Top 50 Christian Publishers list.

$WRITER'S CHRONICLE: The Magazine for Serious Writers, The Association of Writers & Writing Programs, George Mason University, MSN 1E3, 4400 University Dr., Fairfax VA 22030-4444. (703)993-4301. Fax (703)993-4302. E-mail: chronicle@awpwriter.org. Website: www.awpwriter.org. D. W. Fenza, ed-in-chief. Bimonthly mag. Subscription $20. Pays $11/100 wds. on publication for 1st rts. Articles to 7,000 wds. max. No simultaneous submissions. No kill fee. Guidelines on Website.

Special Needs: Author interviews, essays, trends, and literary controversies. No poetry or fiction.

$WRITER'S DIGEST, 4700 E. Galbraith Rd., Cincinnati OH 45236. (513)531-2690, ext. 1739. Fax (513)891-7153. E-mail: wdsubmissions@fwpubs.com. Website: www.writersdigest

.com. General/F & W Publications. Kara Gebhart Uhl, mng. ed. To inform, instruct, or inspire the freelancer and author. Monthly mag.; 76 pgs.; circ. 140,000. Subscription $27. 20% unsolicited; 60% assigned. Strongly prefers e-query (responds in 8 wks.). Pays .30-.50/wd. on acceptance for 1st & electronic (sometimes) rts. Articles 800-1,500 wds. (75/yr.). Responds to mail query in 2 mos. Seasonal 8 mos. ahead. Requires requested ms on disk or by e-mail (or copied into message). Kill fee 25%. Regularly uses sidebars. Guidelines/editorial calendar on Website; copy $5.25 (attn: Lyn Menke). (Ads)

Contests: Sponsors annual contest for articles, short stories, poetry, and scripts. Also The National Self-Publishing Book Awards. Send SASE for rules.

Tips: "We're looking for fiction technique pieces by published authors."

**This periodical was #38 on the 2008 Top 50 Christian Publishers list.

$WRITERS' JOURNAL, PO Box 394, Perham MN 56573-0394. (218)346-7921. Fax (218)346-7924. E-mail: editor@writersjournal.com. Website: www.writersjournal.com. Val-Tech Media/General. Leon Ogroske, ed. Advice, tools, and markets for writers, communicators, and poets. Bimonthly mag.; 68 pgs.; circ. 26,000. Subscription $19.97. 90% unsolicited freelance; 10% assigned. Complete ms/cover letter; phone/fax/e-query OK. Usually pays $30, plus subscription, on publication for one-time rts. Articles 1,200-2,200 wds. (30-40/yr.); fiction 2,000 wds. (contest entries only). Responds in 6-28 wks. Accepts simultaneous submissions; no reprints. Accepts requested ms by e-mail (copied into message). No kill fee. Uses some sidebars. Also accepts submissions from teens. Guidelines on Website; copy $5/SASE/$1.82 postage. (Ads)

Poetry: Esther M. Leiper, poetry ed. Buys 25/yr. All types; to 10 lines; $5/poem. Submit max. 4 poems. Guidelines at www.writersjournal.com/PoetryContest.htm.

Fillers: Buys 20/yr. Any type, 10-200 wds. Pays $1-10.

Contest: Runs several contests each year. Prizes up to $500. Categories are short story, horror/ghost, romance, travel writing, and fiction; 3 poetry; 2 photo. Guidelines on Website.

Tips: "Be concise; no wordiness. Avoid personal essays. Write to the reader. We are looking for a well-written article on freelance income; articles on how to write better and how to sell what authors write. Also looking for articles on obscure income markets for writers. General story construction and grammar tips."

WRITERS MANUAL, Ste. 402, 7231—120th St., Delta BC V4C 6P5, Canada. E-mail: editor@ writersmanual.com. Website: www.writersmanual.com (click on "Get Interviewed!"). Krista Barrett, ed-in-chief. Looking for author and/or freelance interviews. One-time rts.

WRITETOINSPIRE.COM. E-mail: editor@writetoinspire.com. Website: www.writetoinspire .com. Online publication. Provides good how-to information for Christian writers. **NO PAYMENT** for 1st or one-time rts. Articles 500-700 wds., written in an online style. Send submissions in body of e-mail (no attachments). Guidelines on Website.

WRITING CORNER. E-mail: deanna@biznessconcepts.com. Website: www.writingcorner.com. Deanna Lilly, ed. Online publication. Open to unsolicited freelance. Query or complete ms by e-mail (no attachments). **NO PAYMENT** for nonexclusive rts. Articles 600-900 wds.; fiction 600-900 wds. Responds in 2 wks. Accepts reprints. Guidelines on Website: www.writing corner.com/admin/sub-guidelines.htm.

MARKET ANALYSIS

PERIODICALS IN ORDER BY CIRCULATION

ADULT/GENERAL

Guideposts 3,000,000
Columbia 1,600,000
In Touch 1,000,000
Stewardship 1,000,000
Focus on the Family 800,000
Angels on Earth 550,000
Marion Helpers 500,000
Spirituality for Today 495,000
Catholic Digest 400,000
Catholic Yearbook 400,000
Decision 400,000
Positive Thinking 400,000
Mature Living 318,000
St. Anthony Messenger 305,000
Charisma 250,000
Power for Living 250,000
Upscale Magazine 250,000
War Cry 250,000
Anglican Journal 215,000
Australian Catholics 200,000
Gospel Today 200,000
Liberty 200,000
Lutheran Journal 200,000
Lutheran Witness 200,000
Miraculous Medal 200,000
On Mission 200,000
Today's Pentecostal Evangel 200,000
AFA Journal, 180,000
Christianity Today 155,000
Cappers 150,000
Family Digest 150,000
Standard 150,000
Written 130,000
MESSAGE 125,000
Company 120,000
Liguorian 120,000
Catholic Forester 100,000
CGA World 100,000
Discipleship Journal 100,000
Good News (KY) 100,000
Today's Christian 75,000
ParentLife 72,000
Heartlight Internet 70,000+
Alive Now 70,000
Celebrate Life 70,000
Common Ground 70,000
Lutheran Digest 70,000
Men of Integrity 70,000
United Church Observer 70,000
Christian Home & School 67,000
Lookout 62,000
Prison Living 60,000
Presbyterians Today 58,000
Creation 55,000

Mature Years 55,000
Arlington Catholic 53,000
Discovery Years 52,600
Christian History 50,000
Chronicle—IN Edition 50,000
Community Spirit 50,000
Faith & Friends 50,000
Leaves 50,000
Wesleyan Life 50,000
Christian Standard 48,000
America 46,000
BGC World 46,000
Florida Baptist Witness 46,000
Live 46,000
Encompass 45,000
LarkNews.com 45,000
Messenger of St. Anthony 45,000
EFCA Today 44,000
The Manna 42,000
Christian Motorsports 40,000
Senior Living 40,000
U.S. Catholic 40,000
Highway News 35,000
Minnesota Christian 35,000
Lifeglow 34,000
Christian News NW 33,000
Faith & Family 32,000
Advance 30,000
Cathedral Age 30,000
Christian Computing 30,000
Christian Research 30,000
Eureka Street 30,000
Homeschooling Today 30,000
Kindred Spirit 30,000
Louisiana Baptist Message 30,000
Messianic Perspectives 30,000
Vibrant Life 30,000
World & I 30,000
Seek 29,000
CLEAR Living 28,000
Priority! 28,000
Annals of St. Anne 25,000
Arizona Family News 25,000
Focus on Your Child 25,000
In His Presence 25,000
LifeLine Journal 25,000
Pure Inspiration 25,000
Significant Living 25,000
Central FL Episcopalian 24,000
Catholic Peace Voice 23,000
Majellan 23,000
Friends Voice 21,000
African Voices 20,000
Commonweal 20,000
Creation Illustrated 20,000
Interim 20,000

IPHC Experience 20,000
Ozarks Christian 20,000
Trumpeter 20,000
Faith Today 18,000
Heartbeat 18,000
Montgomery's Journey 18,000
Canadian Mennonite 16,500
Marketplace 16,000
Over the Back Fence 15,000
SCP Journal 15,000
Victory in Grace 15,000
Canada Lutheran 14,000
DisciplesWorld 14,000
Gems of Truth 14,000
Testimony 14,000
Bible Advocate 13,500
Light & Life 13,000
Books & Culture 12,000
Christian Health Care 12,000
Covenant Companion 12,000
Special Living 12,000
Spiritual Life 12,000
Evangel 11,000
Messenger/Sacred Heart 11,000
Sports Spectrum 11,000
Christian Retailing 10,500
Messiah Magazine 10,000
Michiana Christian 10,000
Presbyterian Outlook 10,000
Regent Global Bus. Review 10,000
Vision 10,000
NRB Magazine 9,300
Fellowship 9,000
Haruah 9,000
Living Church 9,000
Montana Catholic 9,000
Sharing 9,000
Purpose 8,900
E-Quality 8,000+
Aspiring Retail 8,000
Disciple's Journal 8,000
Friends Journal 8,000
Home Times 8,000
Arkansas Catholic 7,700
Science & Spirit 7,500
Wittenburg Door 7,500
Psychology for Living 7,000
Creation Care 6,000
Gem 6,000
Impact 6,000
Vision 6,000
Image 5,200
AGAIN 5,000
Ambassador 5,000
Breakthrough Intercessor 5,000

Creative Nonfiction 5,000
Cross Currents 5,000
Leben 5,000
New Heart 5,000
Pentecostal Messenger 5,000
Prism 5,000
Purpose Magazine 5,000
Review for Religious 5,000
Social Justice Review 5,000
Way of St. Francis 5,000
Christian Civic League/ME 4,600
Cresset 4,500
Family Journal 4,500
Evangelical Advocate 4,000
Mensajero Ala Blanca 4,000
Quaker Life 4,000
Wireless Age 4,000
Catholic Insight 3,700
Culture Wars 3,500
Evangel 3,500
Jerusalem Connection 3,500
Sword and Trumpet 3,300
Evangel (OR) 3,000
Message/Open Bible 3,000
Perspectives 3,000
Prayer Closet 3,000
UrbanKingdom 3,000
Salvo Magazine 2,800
Mennonite Historian 2,600
Bread of Life 2,500
MovieGuide 2,500
Railroad Evangelist 2,500
Apocalypse Chronicles 2,000-3,000
Perspectives/Science 2,000+
Atlantic Catholic 2,000
CCMI Partners 2,000
Channels 2,000
Desert Call 2,000
Mutuality 2,000
Priscilla Papers 2,000
Jour./Church & State 1,700
Ruminate 1,500
Church Herald/Holiness 1,100
Connecting Point 1,000
Dovetail 1,000
DreamSeeker 1,000
Methodist History 800
Compass Direct 730
Storyteller 600
Eternal Ink 450
Gold Country Families 450
Silver Wings 300
Studio 300
Xavier Review 300
West Wind Review 250-500
Aujourd'hui Credo 250
Time of Singing 250
Dreams & Visions 200
Ancient Paths 175
Pegasus Review 150
Reverent Submissions 125

Angel Face 100
Haiku Hippodrome 100
Wildwood Reader 100
Penwood Review 80-100

CHILDREN

American Girl 700,000
Keys for Kids 100,000
Focus/Clubhouse 90,000
Pockets 67,000
Focus/Clubhouse Jr. 65,000
Our Little Friend 45,000-50,000
Adventures 40,000
Celebrate 40,000
Primary Treasure 35,000
Kid Zone 30,000
New Moon 30,000
GUIDE 27,000
Primary Street 20,000
Passport 18,000
Faces 15,000
Nature Friend 13,000
SHINEbrightly 13,000
BREAD for God's Children 10,000
Cadet Quest 8,000
Kids' Ark 8,000
Partners 6,519
Story Mates 6,385
Winner 5,000
Junior Companion 3,500
Primary Pal (KS) 2,900
Beginner's Friend 2,700
Skipping Stones 2,500

CHRISTIAN EDUCATION/ LIBRARY

Christian School Education 70,000
Children's Ministry 60,000
Group 55,000
Catechist 52,000
Today's Catholic Teacher 45,000
RTJ 32,000
Momentum 23,000
Jour./Adventist Ed. 10,800
Teachers of Vision 10,000
Teach Kids Essentials 10,000
Youth & CE Leadership 10,000
Christian Early Education 5,500
Christian Educator's Journal 4,200
Ideas Unlimited 4,200
Church & Synagogue Libraries 3,000
Kids' Ministry Ideas 2,500
Catholic Library World 1,000
Christian Librarian 800
Church Libraries 450
Jour./Christian Education 400
Jour./Ed. & Christian Belief 400
Jour./Research on C. E. 400
Jour./Christianity/Foreign Lang. 100

DAILY DEVOTIONALS

These Days 200,000
Secret Place 150,000
Our Journey 80,000
CLEAR Living 28,000
Daily Devotions for the Deaf 26,000
Rejoice! 12,000
The Brink 10,000+
Penned from the Heart 5,000

MISSIONS

One 100,000
Mission Frontiers 75,000
MissionsMagazinet 64,000
New World Outlook 24,000
Montgomery's Journey 18,000
PIME World 16,000
Mission Connection 14,400
Women of the Harvest 8,000
Leaders for Today 7,500
Evangelical Missions 7,000
Glad Tidings 4,500
Railroad Evangelist 2,500
Missiology 1,500
OpRev Equipper 1,500
Intl. Jour./Frontier 500
East-West Church & Ministry 430

MUSIC

CCM Magazine 70,000
Senior Musician 32,000
I am Magazine 15,000
Church Music 12,000
Creator 6,000
Tradition 3,500
Hymn 3,000
Christian Radio 500
Christian Music 300-1,200

NEWSPAPERS

Layman 450,000
Episcopal Life 280,000
Anglican Journal 200,000
Alpha News 195,000
Christian Examiner 180,000
Catholic New York 135,000
Nat. Catholic Reporter 120,000
Catholic Telegraph 100,000
Living 90,000
Good News/S. Florida 80,000
Living Light News 75,000
Common Ground 70,000
Sword of the Lord 70,000
Our Sunday Visitor 68,000
Good News Journal 60,000
Arlington Catholic Herald 53,000
Chronicle/Kansas 50,000
Living 50,000
Together 50,000

Christian Ranchman 43,800
Good News, Etc. 42,000
Evangelical Times 40,000
Senior Living 40,000
Messianic Times 35,000
Minnesota Chr. Chronicle 35,000
Catholic Register 33,000
ChristianWeek 32,000
Christian Herald 31,000
Christian News NW 30,000
Citizen USA 30,000
Good News! 30,000
Interim 30,000
New Frontier 25,500
Christian Media 25,000
Life Gate 23,000
B.C. Catholic 20,000
Charlotte World 20,000
Light of the World 20,000
Heartbeat/CMA 18,000
Catholic Sentinel 16,000
Good News Today 16,000
Indian Life 16,000
Christian Journal 15,000
Christian Voice 15,000
City Light News 12,000
Interchange 12,000
Christian Courier (WI) 10,000
Heartland Gatekeeper 10,000
Network 10,000
Spiritual Voice News 10,000
Wisconsin Christian News 10,000
Star of Zion 9,200
Catholic New Times 8,500
Choice Newspaper 8,000
Disciple's Journal 8,000
Arkansas Catholic 7,700
Living Stones News 7,000
Prairie Messenger 6,900
Home Times 6,000
Desert Voice 5,200
SW KS Faith & Family 5,000
Christian Courier (Canada) 4,000
Christian Renewal 4,000
Atlantic Catholic 2,000
Christian Observer 2,000
Insight (for the blind) 2,000
Island Catholic News 2,000
PrayerWorks 1,500
B.C. Christian News 1,000
Hunted News 1,000
Anglican 300

PASTORS/LEADERS

Interpreter 225,000
Alpha News 195,000
Rick Warren's Ministry 177,000
Your Church 75,000
Church Life Inspiration 65,000
Leadership 52,000
Plugged In 50,000

Worship Leader 50,000
Rev. 45,000
Plugged In 43,000
Catholic Servant 41,000
Pray! 41,000
OUTreach 35,000
Technologies/Worship 35,000
Enrichment 33,000
Christian Century 30,000
Ministry Today 30,000
Torch Legacy Leader 22,000
Lutheran Partners 20,000
Ministry & Liturgy 20,000
Youthworker 20,000
Ministry 19,000
Preaching Now 19,000
This Rock 15,870
Today's Parish 14,800
Net Results 12,000
Pulpit Helps 12,000
Jour./Pastoral Care 10,000
Willow 10,000
Preaching 9,000
InSite 8,750
Sabbath School Leadership 8,100
Growth Points 8,000
Priest 6,500
Clergy Journal 6,000
Catechumenate 5,600
Let's Worship 5,500
Cross Currents 5,000
Review for Religious 5,000
Reformed Worship 4,600
African American Pulpit 4,000
Christian Management Report 3,500+
Lutheran Forum 3,200
Emmanuel 3,000
Single Adult Min. Jour. 3,000
Environment & Art 2,500
Word & World 2,500
Cornerstone Youth Resource 2,200
Church Worship 1,500
Parish Liturgy 1,200
Christian Ed. Jour. 750
Diocesan Dialogue 750
Ministry in Motion 700+
RevWriter Resource 500
Jour./Amer. Soc./Chur. Growth 400
Theological Digest 400
Sharing the Practice 250

TEEN/YOUNG ADULT

Brio 185,000
Essential Connection 120,000
Ignite Your Faith 100,000
Breakaway 96,000
Devo'Zine 90,000
Sharing the Victory 80,000
Young Salvationist 48,000
Risen Magazine 45,000+

Steelroots 30,000
YouthWalk 30,000
Young & Alive 25,000
Insight 20,000
InTeen 20,000
Listen 20,000
Spirit 20,000
Credo 15,000
Student Leadership 8,500
TC Magazine 8,000
InsideOut 6,000
CLEAR Direction 5,300
Youth Compass 4,800
True Girl 3,500
G4T Ink 1,500

WOMEN

Precious Times 350,000
Heart & Soul 300,000
More to Life 250,000-2,000,000
Journey 215,000
Today's Christian Woman 210,000
Lutheran Woman's Quarterly 200,000
Melody of the Heart 130,000
MOMSense 120,000
SpiritLed Woman 100,000
Share 95,000
Life Tools for Women 45,000
Dabbling Mum 40,000
Connections Leadership/MOPS 25,000
Horizons 25,000
Women's Ministry 25,000
History's Women 21,000
A Virtuous Woman 20,000+
First Lady 20,000
A Woman of Worth 20,000
Right to the Heart 15,000
Hope for Women 10,000
P31 Woman 10,000
Just Between Us 8,000
Today's Leading Ladies 8,000
Together with God 7,500
CoLaborer 7,300
Esprit 5,000
Link & Visitor 4,000
Women Alive! 4,000
ChurchWoman 3,000
Handmaiden 3,000
inSpirit 2,500
Hearts at Home 1,500
Making Waves 1,400

WRITERS

Writer's Digest 140,000
Poets & Writers 60,000
The Writer 30,000
Writers' Journal 26,000
Fiction Fix 5,000
New Writer's 5,000
Poetic Voices 5,000

Money the Write Way 4,000
Byline 3,500+
Christian Communicator 3,000
Beginnings 1,500
Cross & Quill 1,000+

Once Upon a Time 1,000
Tickled by Thunder 1,000
WIN-Informer 1,000
Advanced Christian Writer 500
Canadian Writer's Journal 385

NW Christian Author 200
FellowScript 150-200
Write Connection 150
Areopagus (UK) 100
The Write Touch 40

PERIODICAL TOPICS IN ORDER OF POPULARITY

NOTE: Following is a list of topics in order by popularity. To find the list of publishers interested in each of these topics, go to the Topical Listings for periodicals and find the topic you are interested in. The numbers indicate how many periodical editors said they were interested in seeing something of that type or on that topic. (*—new topic this year)

MISCELLANEOUS TALLIES

African American Markets 19
Canadian/Foreign Markets 72
Newspapers/Tabloids 86
Online Publications 183
Photographs 227
Take-home Papers 38
Young Writer Markets 121

TOPICS BY POPULARITY

1. Christian Living 275
2. Family Life 236
3. Current/Social Issues 215
4. Book Reviews 211
5. Inspirational 211
6. Interviews/Profiles 200
7. Faith 195
8. Prayer 195
9. Personal Experience 193
10. Poetry 176
11. Relationships 176
12. Holiday/Seasonal 172
13. Christian Education 171
14. Spirituality 170
15. Evangelism/Witnessing 165
16. Marriage 164
17. Women's Issues 164
18. Devotionals/Meditations 159
19. Humor 158
20. Controversial Issues 153
21. True Stories 150
22. Discipleship 145
23. Parenting 144
24. Personal Growth 143
25. Spiritual Life 142
26. Church Life 141
27. Church Outreach 140
28. Ethnic/Cultural Pieces 140
29. Worship 139
30. Miracles 136
31. Leadership 135
32. Encouragement 133

33. Youth Issues 130
34. Ethics 126
35. How-to 123
36. Health 122
37. World Issues 120
38. Death/Dying 117
39. Essays 116
40. News Features 114
41. Theological 114
42. Church Growth 113
43. Church History 112
44. Social Justice 112
45. Short Story: Adult/Religious 111
46. Fillers: Cartoons 107
47. Historical 103
48. Singles Issues 101
49. Religious Freedom 99
50. Bible Studies 97
51. Money Management 97
52. Stewardship 97
53. Spiritual Gifts 96
54. Time Management 95
55. Men's Issues 94
56. Short Story: Contemporary 93
57. Spiritual Renewal 93
58. Christian Business 91
59. Opinion Pieces 91
60. Fillers: Anecdotes 90
61. Celebrity Pieces 89
62. Church Traditions 89
63. Workplace Issues 89
64. Think Pieces 87
65. Fillers: Short Humor 85
66. Environmental Issues 83
67. Divorce 82
68. Spiritual Warfare 82
69. Inner Life 81
70. Music Reviews 81
71. Healing 80
72. Salvation Testimonies 79
73. Short Story: Biblical 78
74. Book Excerpts 77
75. Short Story: Humorous 77
76. Homeschooling 75

77. Church Management 71
78. Lifestyle Articles 71
79. Senior Adult Issues 71
80. Apologetics 70
81. Sports/Recreation 69
82. Doctrinal 67
83. Fillers: Facts 67
84. Political 67
85. Religious Tolerance 67
86. Short Story: Adventure 65
87. Fillers: Ideas 64
88. Short Story: Historical 63
89. Travel 62
90. Writing How-to 62
91. How-to Activities (juv.) 61
92. Fillers: Word Puzzles 60
93. Nature 60
94. Racism 59
95. Food/Recipes 58
96. Video Reviews 58
97. Fillers: Prayers 57
98. Fillers: Quotes 57
99. Feature Articles 56
100. Crafts 55
101. Self-help 54
102. Peace Issues 53
103. Economics 51
104. Liturgical 51
105. Fillers: Prose 50
106. Short Story: Parables 49
107. Holy Spirit 45
108. Movie Reviews 45
109. Fillers: Quizzes 44
110. Fillers: Tips 44
111. Short Story: Literary 44
112. Creation Science 43
113. Recovery 43
114. Short Story: Juvenile 43
115. Short Story: Teen/Young Adult 43
116. Fillers: Jokes 42
117. Science 42
118. Short Story: Allegory 41
119. Sociology 41
120. Photo Essays 40

121. Short Story: Mystery/Suspense 39
122. Fillers: Games 38
123. Exegesis 37
124. Fillers: Newsbreaks 36
125. Prophecy 35
126. Short Story: Ethnic 35
127. Grandparenting 34
128. Psychology 34
129. Cults/Occult 33
130. Website Reviews 33
131. Short Story: Fantasy 32
132. Missions 31
133. Revival 31

134. Short Story: Adult/General 31
135. Short Story: Science Fiction 31
136. Sermons 30
137. Short Story: Frontier 29
138. Homiletics 28
139. Nostalgia 28
140. Fillers: Party Ideas 27
141. Fillers: Kid Quotes 25
142. Short Story: Westerns 22
143. Short Story: Skits 20
144. Short Story: Romance 19
145. Short Story: Historical/ Romance 17

146. Short Story: Speculative 17
147. Small Group Helps 17
148. DVD Reviews 14
149. Short Story: Mystery/Romance 14
150. Short Story: Plays 14
151. Teacher Helps 14
152. Short Story: Frontier/Romance 12
153. Short Story: Senior Adult Fiction 11
154. Fillers: Sermon Illustrations 9
155. Puppet Plays 4

SUMMARY OF INFORMATION ON CHRISTIAN PERIODICAL PUBLISHERS FOUND IN THE ALPHABETICAL LISTINGS

NOTE: Following is some general information based on typical averages of the information supplied by the periodical publishers in this guide. This information will be valuable in determining what numbers or percentages are typical in the various categories.

WANTS QUERY OR COMPLETE MANUSCRIPT

Not all periodicals indicate a preference, but 45-50 percent prefer or accept a complete manuscript, 35-38 percent want or will accept a query, 3-5 percent require a query, and 12-15 percent will accept either.

ACCEPTS PHONE/FAX/E-MAIL QUERY

Every year fewer periodical publishers are accepting phone or fax queries, and at this point almost none do. The majority now prefer e-mail queries—either directly or through an online form available on their Website. It is suggested that you reserve phone queries for timely material that won't wait for the regular mailed query. If you phone in a query, be sure you have your idea well thought out and can present it succinctly and articulately. It is always important to use the form of communication they indicate in their listing.

SUBMISSIONS ON DISK

This question has almost become obsolete, as the majority of publishers that don't want a hard copy now want an e-mail submission. Individual listings will indicate which ones still want or accept a disk.

SUBMISSIONS BY E-MAIL

This area continues to show some significant changes in editors' perceptions of e-mail submissions. When asked if they would accept submissions by e-mail, now more than half say yes. Of those, 40 percent wanted the article copied into the message, 42 percent wanted them sent as an attached file, and the last 18 percent would accept them either way. Generally speaking, those who prefer the article copied into the message fear viruses, while those who prefer an attached copy don't like losing the coding when you copy it into the message.

PAYS ON ACCEPTANCE OR PUBLICATION

Of the publishers that indicated, 40 percent of the publishers pay on acceptance, while 60 percent pay on publication.

PERCENTAGE OF FREELANCE

Many of the publishers responded to the question about how much freelance material they use. Based on the figures we have, for the average publisher, 40 percent of the material purchased is unsolicited freelance and 60 percent is assigned.

CIRCULATION

In dividing the list of periodicals into three groups, according to size of circulation, the list comes out as follows: Publications with a circulation of 100,000 or more (up to 3,000,000) make up 15 percent of periodicals; publications with a circulation between 50,000 and 100,000, 10 percent; the remaining 75 percent have a circulation of 50,000 or less. If we break that last group into three more groups by circulation, we come out with circulations of 33,000-50,000 making up 10 percent; 18 percent with circulations of 17,000-32,000; and the remaining 72 percent with less than 17,000. That means that 52 percent of all the periodicals that reported their circulation are at a circulation of 17,000 or less. Overall, circulations seem to be dropping.

RESPONSE TIME

The average response time is just over eight weeks, one week longer than reported three years ago. Those who are writing and submitting regularly will have no problem confirming that most publishers are taking longer to respond to submissions.

REPRINTS

Nearly 50 percent of the periodicals included in the market guide accept reprints. Although until the last few years it was not necessary to tell a publisher where a piece had been published previously, that has changed. Most Christian publishers now want a tear sheet of the original publication and a cover letter telling when and where it appeared originally. Be sure to check the individual listings to see if a publisher wants to know when and where a piece has appeared previously. Most are also paying less for reprints than for original material.

PREFERRED BIBLE VERSION

The most preferred Bible version is the New International Version, the preference of more than half the publishers. Other preferred versions are the King James Version, the New Revised Standard Version, the New American Bible, New American Standard, Revised Standard Version, and New King James. The NIV seems a good choice for those who didn't indicate a preference, although the more conservative groups seem to favor the KJV.

GREETING CARD/GIFT/SPECIALTY MARKETS

This listing contains both Christian/religious card publishers and secular publishers that have religious lines or produce some religious or inspirational cards. Keep in mind that the secular companies may produce other lines of cards that are not consistent with your beliefs, and that for a secular company, inspirational cards usually do not include religious imagery. All of these are paying markets. Support group for greeting card writers can be found at http://groups.yahoo.com/group/GreetingCardWriters.

(+) Indicates new listing
NOTE: See the end of this listing for specialty product lists.

CARD PUBLISHERS

AFRICAN AMERICAN EXPRESSIONS, 10266 Rockingham Dr., Sacramento CA 95827-2515. Toll-free (800)684-1555. (916)424-5000. Fax (916)424-5053. E-mail: gperkins@black-gifts.com, or info@black-gifts.com. Website: www.black-gifts.com. Greg Perkins, pres. Christian card publishers and specialty products. Open to freelance; buys 5-10 ideas/yr. Prefers outright submissions. Pays $35 on acceptance. No royalty. Responds in 2 wks. Uses rhymed, unrhymed, traditional, and light verse. Produces invitations and conventional, humorous, informal, inspirational, juvenile, novelty, and religious cards. Needs anniversary, birthday, Christmas, friendship, get well, graduation, keep in touch, love, miss you, Mother's Day, new baby, relatives (all occasions), sympathy, valentines, wedding, and pastor appreciation. Holiday/seasonal 9 mos. ahead. Open to ideas for new card lines, calendars/journals, novelty/gift items, magnets, and stationery. No guidelines; free catalog.

ALEGRIA COLLECTION, PO Box 835008, Miami FL 33283-5008. (305)253-4646. Fax (305) 253-4604. E-mail: ventas@alegriacollection.com. Website: www.alegriacollection.com. Spanish greeting cards.

AMERICAN GREETINGS, One American Rd., Cleveland OH 44144-2398. (216)252-7300. Fax (216) 252-6778. Website: www.americangreetings.com. Kathleen McKay, ed. No unsolicited material.

ARTFUL GREETINGS, PO Box 52428, Durham NC 27717. Toll-free (800)638-2733. (919)484-0100. Fax (919)484-3099. E-mail: myw@artfulgreetings.com. Website: www.artfulgreetings.com. Black art greeting cards and gifts.

BLUE MOUNTAIN ARTS INC., PO Box 4549, Boulder CO 80306. (303)449-0536. Fax (303) 447-0939. E-mail: editorial@sps.com. Website: www.sps.com. Submit to Editorial Department. General card publisher that does a few inspirational cards. Open to freelance; buys 50-100 ideas/yr. Prefers outright submissions. Pays $300 for all rts. for use on a greeting card, or $50 for one-time use in a book, on publication. No royalties. Responds in 12-16 wks. Uses unrhymed or traditional poetry; short or long, but no one-liners. Produces inspirational and sensitivity. Needs anniversary, birthday, Christmas, congratulations, Easter, Father's Day, friendship, get well, graduation, keep in touch, love, miss you, Mother's Day, new baby, please write, relatives, sympathy, thank you, valentines, wedding, reaching for dreams. Holiday/seasonal 3 mos. ahead. Open to ideas for new card lines. Send any number of ideas (1 per pg.). Open to ideas for gift books. Guidelines; no catalog.

> **Contest:** Sponsors a poetry card contest online. Details on Website.
> **Tips:** "We are interested in reviewing poetry and writings for greeting cards, and expanding our field of freelance poetry writers."

C4YOURSELF GREETING CARDS, 1406 Sycamore St., Cincinnati OH 45202. (513)608-1878. E-mail: info@c4yourself.biz. Website: www.c4yourself.biz. Angela Morrow, creator. Christmas cards & cards for all occasions. Also does desk calendars. E-mail with card ideas.

CHRISTIAN INSPIRATIONS, Quadriga Art Inc., 30 E. 33rd St., New York NY 10016. (212)685-0751. Fax (212)889-6868. E-mail through Website: www.quadrigaart.com. Suzanne Kruck, VP. Christian card publisher. No unsolicited submissions; request permission in writing to send submissions. Pays on acceptance; no royalty. Responds in 4-6 wks. All types of verse, 4-6 lines. All kinds of cards and greetings, except Halloween and St. Patrick's. Seasonal 12 mos. ahead. Not open to new card lines or specialty products. No guidelines; catalog.

CREATIVE CHRISTIAN GIFTS, PO Box 915441, Longwood FL 32791-5441. Toll-free (866)325-1857. (407)924-3347. E-mail: sales@creativechristiangifts.com. Website: www.creativechristiangifts.com. Greeting cards & note cards.

CURRENT INC., PO Box 2559, Colorado Springs CO 80901. (719)594-4100. Fax (719)534-6259. No freelance.

DAYSPRING CARDS INC., Box 1010, 21154 Hwy 16 East, Siloam Springs AR 72761. Fax (479) 524-9477. E-mail: info@dayspring.com (type "write" in message or subject line). Website: www.dayspring.com. Christian/religious card publisher. Please read guidelines before submitting. Prefers outright submission. Pays $60/idea on acceptance for all rts. No royalty. Responds in 4-8 wks. Uses unrhymed, traditional, light verse, conversational, contemporary; various lengths. Looking for inspirational cards for all occasions, including anniversary, birthday, relative birthday, congratulations, encouragement, friendship, get well, new baby, sympathy, thank you, wedding. Also needs seasonal cards for friends and family members for Christmas, Valentine Day, Easter, Mother's Day, Father's Day, Thanksgiving, graduation, and Clergy Appreciation Day. Include Scripture verse with each submission. Send 10 ideas or less. Guidelines by phone or e-mail; no catalog.

Tips: Prefers submissions on 8 x 11 inch sheets, not 3x5 cards (one idea per sheet).

DESIGN DESIGN INC., 19 La Grave S.E., Grand Rapids MI 49503. (616)771-2448. Fax (616) 774-2440. Website: www.designdesign.us. Rebecca Cooper, ed. A general card publisher that does a few inspirational and religious cards. Open to freelance submissions. Prefers outright submissions (but not of artwork). Rights purchased depend on product. Uses rhymed, unrhymed, traditional, and light verse. Produces anniversary, birthday, Christmas, congratulations, Easter, Father's Day, friendship, get well, graduation, Halloween, love, miss you, Mother's Day, new baby, relative (all occasions), St. Patrick's Day, sympathy, Thanksgiving, thank you, valentines, and wedding. Open to new card lines. Open to ideas for gift/novelty items, greeting books, magnets, and stationery. Guidelines on Website; no catalog.

DESIGNER GREETINGS, PO Box 140729, Staten Island NY 10314. Toll-free (800)654-6960. (718)981-7700. Fax (866)981-0151. E-mail: info@designergreetings.com, or through Website: www.designergreetings.com. Fern Gimbelman, art dir. 50% freelance. Holiday/seasonal 6 mos. ahead. Responds in 2 mos. Pays on acceptance for greeting card rts. Guidelines on Website. Uses rhymed or unrhymed verse. Produces announcements, conventional, humorous, informal, inspirational, invitations, juvenile, sensitivity, soft line, studio. Up to 50% freelance.

DICKSON'S LIFE PUBLISHING, 709 B Ave. East, Seymour IN 47274. (812)522-1308. Fax (812)522-1319. E-mail: rick@lawson-falle.com. Website: www.dicksonsgifts.com. Rick Tocquigny, pres. Christian/religious card publisher. Open to freelance; buys 25-50 ideas/yr. Prefers outright submissions. Pays $50 on acceptance for nonexclusive rts. Royalties 2-3%. Responds in 4 wks. Uses rhymed, unrhymed, traditional, light verse; under 75 wds. Produces all types of cards. Needs anniversary, birthday, Christmas, congratulations, Easter, Father's Day, friendship, get well, graduation, keep in touch, love, miss you, Mother's Day, new baby, please write, relative (all occasions), St. Patrick's Day, sympathy, Thanksgiving, thank you, valentines, wedding, adult baptism, mission trip blessings, confirmation, and first communion. Holiday/seasonal 18 mos. ahead. Open to ideas for new card lines; submit max. 3 ideas. Open to ideas for activity/coloring books, bookmarks, calendars/journals, gift/novelty items, magnets, mugs, plaques, stationery, t-shirts/apparel, and toys. No guidelines/catalog.

GIBSON GREETINGS, PO Box 371804, Cincinnati OH 45222-1804. E-mail: wcallah@gibson greetings.com. Website: www.gibsongreetings.com. No freelance.

HEAVENLY DESIGNS, 118 Burnell Pl. S.E., Leesburg VA 20175. Toll-free (866)707-0113. Phone/fax (703)737-0113. E-mails: cindyjames@birthverse.com, or bjames@birthverse .com. Website: www.birthverse.com. Bob & Cindy James, owners. Inspirational greeting cards.

HERMITAGE ART CO. INC., 5151 N. Ravenswood Ave., Chicago IL 60640. Toll-free (800)621-7992. (773)561-3773. Fax (773)561-4422. E-mail: Office@hermitageart.com. Website: www .hermitageart.com. Color bulletins, bookmarks, specialty items.

INSPIRATIONART & SCRIPTURE INC., PO Box 5550, Cedar Rapids IA 52406-5550. Toll-free (800)728-5550. (319)365-4350. Fax (319)861-2103. E-mail: Customerservice@inspiration art.com. Website: www.inspirationart.com. Publishes Christian posters. Charles Edwards, creative dir. Open to freelance. Buys 20-30 ideas/yr. Prefers e-mail contact. Pays $150-250, 30 days after publication, for right to publish as a poster; or royalties 5% of net. Responds in 4 wks. Seasonal 6 mos. ahead. Open to new ideas for posters, bookmarks, or puzzles. Submit up to 3 ideas. Artist's guidelines on Website; catalog on Website or for $3.

NORTHERN CARDS, Creative Department, 5694 Ambler Dr., Mississauga ON L4W 2K9, Canada. Toll-free (877)627-7444. (905)625-4944. Fax (905)625-5995. E-mail: artists@northern cards.com. Website: www.northerncards.com/docs/artists.shtml. Open to writers and artists. Greeting cards.

NOVO CARD PUBLISHERS INC., 3630 W. Pratt Ave., Lincolnwood IL 60712. Toll-free (800)624-2426. (847)763-0077. Fax (847)763-0020. E-mail: art@novocard.net. Website: www.novocard.net. Submit to Art Production. General card publisher that does a few inspirational and religious cards. Open to freelance; buys 10 ideas/yr. Prefers outright submissions. Pays $2/line on acceptance for all rts. No royalties. Responds in 5 wks. Uses traditional and light verse; 5-20 lines (nothing too brief). Produces baby announcements, conventional, humorous, inspirational, invitations, juvenile, religious, studio. Needs anniversary, birthday, Christmas, congratulations, Easter, Father's Day, friendship, get well, miss you, Mother's Day, new baby, relatives (all occasions), sympathy, Thanksgiving, thank you, valentines, wedding. Seasonal 6-8 mos. ahead. Open to ideas for new card lines. Submit enough ideas to show style. Guidelines/needs list; no catalog.

    Tips: "We don't want anything too brief or too lengthy. We like verse that holds everyone's hearts, especially the male gender."

OATMEAL STUDIOS, PO Box 138, Town Road 35, Rochester VT 05767. (802)767-3171. E-mail: Dawn@oatmealstudios.com. Website: www.oatmealstudios.com. Dawn Abraham, editor. Needs: birthday, relative birthday, birthday making fun of getting older. Also does Thank You cards. Submit ideas on 3x5 index cards with your name and address on each one. Writer's guidelines and artist's guidelines on Website. E-mail submissions OK.

PLESH CREATIVE GROUP INC., 38 A Park St., Medfield MA 02052. (508)359-6400. Fax (508)359-6448. E-mail: JMPlesh@yahoo.com. Website: www.PleshCreative.com. Submit to: Suzanne Comeau. General card publisher with a religious line. Open to freelance. Prefers outright submissions. Buys all rts. Pays $30-50 on acceptance. No royalties. Responds in several wks. Uses rhymed, unrhymed, traditional, and light verse; 8-10 lines or shorter. Produces conventional, humorous, inspirational, juvenile, religious.

P. S. GREETINGS/FANTUS PAPER PRODUCTS, 5730 N. Tripp Ave., Chicago IL 60646-6723. Toll-free (800)621-8823. (773)267-6150. Fax (773)267-6055. E-mail: artdirector@ps greetings.com. Website: www.psgreetings.com. General card publisher with a religious line. Submit to Design Director; Re: Freelance Writer. Open to freelance. Holiday/seasonal 6 mos. ahead. Responds in 1 mo. Pays flat fee on publication; no royalty. Responds in 3-4 wks.

Rhymed, unrhymed, traditional, light verse. Produces announcements, conventional, humorous, informal, inspirational, invitations, juvenile, novelty, religious, sensitivity, softline, studio. Not open to ideas for new card lines or specialty products. Guidelines/copy for #10 SASE (also on Website).

RED FARM STUDIO, 1135 Roosevelt Ave., Pawtucket RI 02861-0347. Toll-free (877)REDFARM. (401)728-9300. Toll-free fax (888)860-3276. E-mail: redfarm@quadrigaart.com. Website: www.redfarmstudio.com. Thomas Scott, pres.; Steven Scott, VP; submit to Production Coordinator. General card publisher with a religious line. 100% freelance; buys 100 ideas/yr. Outright submission. Pays variable rates (about $4/line) within 1 mo. of acceptance for exclusive rts. No royalties. Responds in 2 mos. Use traditional and light verse; 1-4 lines. Produces announcements, invitations, religious. Needs anniversary, birthday, Christmas, friendship, get well, new baby, sympathy, wedding. Holiday 6 mos. ahead. Not open to ideas for new card lines. Submit any number of ideas. Guidelines/needs list for SASE.

BOB SIEMON DESIGNS INC., 3501 W. Segerstrom Ave., Santa Ana CA 92704-6497. (714)549-0678. Fax (714)979-2627. Website: www.bobsiemon.com. No freelance.

SOLE SOURCE GREETINGS, Attn: Art Submissions or Attn: Copy Submissions, 1 Idea Way, Caldwell ID 83605-6902. Toll-free (800)346-5860 or (800)285-1657. Toll-free fax (800)455-0642. E-mail through Website: www.solesourcegreetings.com. Send artwork via e-mail as a JPG or PDF file (see Website for size details). Check Website for samples of greetings. Open to: thinking of you, birthday, thank you, sympathy, new baby, congratulations, anniversary, wedding, etc. Also business-specific cards. Pays up to $500 for artwork; pays $25/message. Royalties 5% on retail sales; 2.5% on wholesale catalog sales.

WARNER PRESS INC., 1201 E. 5th St., PO Box 2499, Anderson IN 46018-9988. (765)644-7721. Fax (765)640-8005. E-mail: rfogle@warnerpress.org. Website: www.warnerpress.org. Karen Rhodes, product mktg. ed.; Robin Fogle, ed. asst. Producer of church resources (greeting cards, bulletins, coloring books, puzzle books). 30% freelance; buys 30-50 ideas/yr. Query for guidelines. Pays $30-35 on acceptance (for bulletins); material for bulletins cannot be sold elsewhere for bulletin use, but may be sold in any other medium. No royalties. Responds in 6-8 wks. Uses rhymed, unrhymed, traditional verse, and devotionals for bulletins; 16-24 lines. Accepts 10 ideas/submission. Guidelines for bulletins; no catalog.

    Also Does: Also open to ideas for coloring books, church resource items.

WORLD LIBRARY PUBLICATIONS, 3708 River Rd., Ste. 400, Franklin Park IL 60131. Toll free (800)621-5197, ext. 2800. (847)233-2742. Fax (847)233-2762. E-mail: odegard@jspaluch.com. Website: www.wlpmusic.com. A division of J. S. Paluch Co. Jennifer Odegard, marketing dir. A music, liturgy, and art publisher with some greeting cards in their line. Open to freelance. Query. Pays on publication; pays some negotiable royalties. Traditional verse. Produces inspirational & religious cards; anniversary, birthday, Christmas, Easter, St. Patrick's Day, sympathy. Holiday/seasonal 10-12 mos. ahead. Not open to ideas for new card lines. Open to ideas for various specialty items; all religious themed. Also does books/CDs. Send any number of ideas. Guidelines; catalog for 9x12 SASE.

ADDITIONAL CARD PUBLISHERS

NOTE: Following is a list of card publishers who did not respond to our questionnaire. You may want to contact them on your own to see if they are open to freelance submissions.

BERG CHRISTIAN ENTERPRISES, 4525 S.E. 63rd Ave., Portland OR 97206. (503)777-4101.

BLACK FAMILY GREETING CARDS, 20 Cortlandt Ave., New Rochelle NY 10801. Bill Harte, pres.

BLACKSMITH CARDS & PRINTS, 37535 Festival Dr., Palm Desert CA 92211. Bob Smith, pres.

CD GREETING CARDS, PO Box 5084, Brentwood TN 37024-5084.

CRT CUSTOM PRODUCTS INC., 7532 Hickory Hills Ct., Whites Creek TN 37189.

DESIGNS FOR BETTER LIVING, 1716 N. Vista St., Los Angeles CA 90046.

$KRISTIN ELLIOTT INC., 6030 N. Orchard Rd., Tucson AZ 85704-5310.

GOOD NEWS IN SIGHT, 2610 Mirror Lake Dr., Fayetteville NC 28303-5212.

GRACE PUBLICATIONS, PO Box 9432, Wyoming MI 49509-0432.

GREENLEAF INC., 951 S. Pine St., #250, Spartanburg SC 29302-3370. Greenleaf Foundation Inc.

HIGHER HORIZONS, PO Box 78399, Los Angeles CA 90016-0399.

LUCY & ME GALLERY, 13232 Riviera Pl. N.E., Seattle WA 98125-4645. Diane Roger, card ed.

ALFRED MAINZER INC., 3933—29th St, Long Island City NY 11101-3707. Toll-free (800)22-cards. (718)392-4200. Fax (718)392-2681.

MORE THAN A CARD, 5010 Baltimore Ave., Bethesda MD 20816.

OAKSPRINGS IMPRESSIONS, PO Box 572, Woodacre CA 94973-0572. (415)488-9194. Fax (415)488-0194.

$FREDERICK SINGER & SONS INC., 520 S. Fulton Ave, Mount Vernon NY 10550-5011.

THESE THREE INC., 314 Washington Rd., #1001, South Hills PA 15216-1638. Jean P. Bridgers, card ed.

RANDALL WILCOX PUBLISHING, 826 Orange Ave., #544, Coronado CA 92118.

CAROL WILSON FINE ARTS, PO Box 17394, Portland OR 97217. Gary Spector, ed.

GAME MARKETS

NOTE: Some of the following markets for games, gift items, and videos have not indicated their interest in receiving freelance submissions. Contact these markets on your own for information on submission procedures before sending them anything.

BIBLE GAMES CO., 14389 Cassell Rd., PO Box 237, Fredericktown OH 43019. Toll-free (800)824-2637. (740)694-8042. Fax (740)694-8072. E-mail: info@biblegamescompany .com. Website: www.biblegamescompany.com. JoAnn Vozar, operations mngr. Produces Bible games. 10% freelance. Buys 1-2 ideas/yr. Query. Pays on publication for all rts. (negotiable). Royalties 8%. Responds in 6-8 wks. Open to new ideas. One game per submission. Guidelines & catalog online.

> **Tips:** "Send developed and tested game play, target market, and audience. Must be totally nonsectarian and fully biblical—no fictionalized scenarios." Board games, CD-ROMs, computer games, and video games.

CACTUS GAME DESIGN INC., 751 Tusquittee St., Hayesville NC 28904. (828)389-1536. Fax (828) 389-1534. E-mail: rob@cactusgamedesign.com. Website: www.cactusgamedesign.com. Rob Anderson, pres. Produces card games, board games, and computer games. Open to freelance submissions. Buys 2-4 ideas/yr. Query by e-mail. Pays variable amounts on acceptance for game rts. Pays 5-15% royalty for complete games only. Responds in 4 wks. Open to new ideas for games. Guidelines (www.cactusgamedesign.com/inventors.php); catalog for .75 postage.

GOODE GAMES INTERNATIONAL, Original Family Fun Games, PO Box 1099, Nicholasville KY 40356. Toll-free (800)257-7767. (859)881-4513. E-mail: info@goodegames.com. Website: www.goodegames.com. Contact: Mike Goode.

TALICOR, 901 Lincoln Pkwy., Plainwell MI 49080. (269)685-2345. Fax (269)685-6789. E-mail: webmaster@Talicor.com. Website: www.Talicor.com. Nicole Hancock, pres. Produces board games and puzzles. 100% freelance; buys 10 ideas/yr. Outright submissions. Pays variable rates on publication for all rts. Royalty 4-6%. Responds in 4 wks. Seasonal 6 mos. ahead. Open to new ideas for board games, novelty items, puzzles, or toys. Submit 1-4 ideas. No guidelines; catalog for 9x12 SAE/$2.23 postage (mark "Media Mail").

WISDOM TREE, PO Box 8682, Tucson AZ 85738-8682. Fax (520)825-5702. E-mail: Thuff 80691@aol.com. Website: www.wisdomtreegames.com. Brenda Huff, owner. Produces Bible-based computer games and does sales and marketing of Bible-based and family-friendly educational games. Responds in 1-6 wks. Seasonal 8 mos. ahead. Open to review of beta versions of computer games, computer software, or video games. Also networks with Christian Game Developers Group to put projects together. Catalog on request.
   Special Needs: "Storybook/puzzle game engine."

GIFT/SPECIALTY ITEM MARKETS

ANCHOR WALLACE PUBLISHERS, 1000 Hwy 4 S., PO Box 7000, Sleepy Eye MN 56085-0007. Toll-free (800)533-3570. Toll-free fax (800)582-2352. E-mail: contactus@anchorwallace .com. Website: www.anchorwallace.com. Worship bulletins, foil & 4-color elegant certificates.

ARTBEATS, 129 Glover Ave., Norwalk CT 06850-1311. (203)847-2000. Fax (203)846-2105. E-mail: Richard@nygs.com, or mail@nygs.com. Website: www.NYGS.com. New York Graphic Society. Richard Fleischmann, pub. Produces prints and posters. Open to free-lancers; purchases 100 ideas/yr. Outright submissions. Pays on publication. Royalties 10%. Responds in 3 wks. Does conventional, inspirational, juvenile, religious, and sensitivity prints and posters. Open to new ideas. Guidelines on Website; no catalog.

ART 2 INSPIRE INC., 140 E. 52nd St., Ste. 2C, New York NY 10022. Toll-free (888)999-4188. (212)486-7700. Fax (212)486-7077. E-mail: info@art-2-inspire.com. Website: www.Art-2-inspire.com. Catholic art posters.

+ASHLEIGH MANOR, PO Box 3851, Frederick MD 21705-3851. Toll free (800)327-4212. Fax (301)631-0108. E-mail: TLawton@ashleighmanor.com. Website: www.ashleighmanor.com. Produces specialty products: religious frames & giftware, bookmarks, gift/novelty items. Free catalog.

BE ONE CHRISTIAN SPORTSWEAR, 3208 Merrywood Dr., Sacramento CA 95825. (916)483-7630. E-mail: Blaine@beone.com. Website: www.BeOne.com. Christian clothing.

CARPENTREE INC., Carpentree Design, 2724 N. Sheridan, Tulsa OK 74115. Toll-free (800)736-2787. (918)582-3600. Fax (918)587-4329. E-mail through Website: www.carpentree.com. Submit to Design Dept. Produces framed art and verse. Buys several ideas/yr. Prefers out-right submission. Rights purchased are negotiable. Pays on publication; negotiable royalty. Responds in 12-15 wks. Uses rhymed, unrhymed, and traditional verse for framed art; 4-16 lines. Open to ideas for new specialty items. Submit max 3-10 ideas. Open to ideas for framed art, tabletop items, and gift/novelty items. Guidelines; catalog $5/10x13 SAE.

CHRISTIAN ART GIFTS, 1025 N. Lombard Rd., PO Box 1443, Lombard IL 60148. Toll-free (800)521-7807. (630)599-0240. Fax (630)599-0245. Website: www.christianartgifts.com. Friendship cards, greeting books, bookmarks, mugs.

DESTINY IMAGE GIFTS, PO Box 310, Shippensburg PA 17257. Toll-free (800)722-6774. (717)532-3040. Fax (717)532-9291. E-mail: dlm@destinyimage.com, or through Website: www.destinyimage.com. Don Milam, ed. mngr. No unsolicited e-mail submissions; use online submission form. Gift products. Guidelines on Website.

DEXSA: The Giving Company, PO Box 109, Hudson WI 54016. Toll-free (800)933-3972. (715)386-8701. Toll-free fax (888)559-1603. E-mail through Website: www.dexsa.com. John Larson, owner. Gifts.

DOT GIBSON PUBLICATIONS, PO Box 117, Waycross GA 31502. Toll-free (800)336-8095. (912)285-2848. Fax (912)285-0349. E-mail: info@dotgibson.com. Website: www.dot gibson.com. Dot Gibson, pub. (dot@dotgibson.com). Publishes inspirational gift books and children's books. Free catalog.

EAGLES WINGS, 2101 Old Hickory Tree Rd., St. Cloud FL 34772. (407)892-6358. Fax (407) 892-6759. E-mail: info@eagleswings.com. Website: www.eagleswings.com. Apparel.

GREENACRE WORKSHOP. Toll-free (800)851-7715. Toll-free fax (888)860-3276. (401) 728-0350. E-mail: info@greenacreworkshop.com, or redfarm@quadrigaart.com. Website: www.greenacreworkshop.com. Coloring/activity books; Paintables.

HERITAGE PUZZLE INC., PO Box 328, Pfafftown NC 27040-0328. Toll-free (888)348-3717. Toll-free fax (866)727-8209. E-mail: heritagepuzzle@triad.rr.com. Website: www.heritage puzzle.com. Religious jigsaw puzzles.

JODY HOUGHTON DESIGNS INC., 5434 River Rd. N. #135, Keizer OR 97303-4429. Toll-free (800)733-8253. E-mail: jody@jodyhoughton.com. Website: www.jodyhoughton.com.

KNOW HIM CHRISTIAN GEAR, 6200 S. Troy Cir., Ste. 140, Englewood CO 80111-6474. Toll-free (888)256-6944. (303)662-9512. Fax (303)662-9942. E-mail: Doug.Mckenna@ knowhim.com, or through Website: www.KnowHim.com. Doug McKenna, pres. Christian apparel.

JAMES LAWRENCE COMPANY, 1501 Livingstone Rd., PO Box 188, Hudson WI 54016. Toll-free (800)546-3699. (715)386-3082. Fax (715)386-3699. E-mail: brian@jameslawrence company.com. Website: www.jameslawrencecompany.com. Brian Johnson, gen. mngr. Producer of specialty products. Open to freelance. Buys variable number/yr. Prefers e-mail contact. Prefers exclusive rts. Pays $50-100/verse on acceptance. Negotiable royalties. Responds in 3-4 wks. Inspirational verse no shorter than 4 lines and no longer than 5 stanzas of 4 lines ea. Holiday 6-9 mos. ahead. Open to new ideas for gift/novelty items, magnets, mugs, plaques. Send any number of ideas. No guidelines or catalog. View Website before submitting.

LIGHTHOUSE CHRISTIAN PRODUCTS, 1050 Remington Rd., Schaumburg IL 60173. (847)519-1825. Fax (847)519-1844. E-mail: customerservice@lcpgifts.com. Website: www.lcpgifts.com. Christian gift products.

LIVING EPISTLES, 2232 S. Main St., #444, Ann Arbor MI 48103. Toll-free (800)294-8637. Fax (205)759-9889. E-mail: LivingEpistlesService@livingepistles.com, or through Website: www.livingepistles.com. Apparel.

LORENZ CORP., 501 E. Third St., Dayton OH 45401. Toll-free (800)444-1144, ext. 1. (937) 228-6118. Fax (937)223-2042. E-mail: info@lorenz.com. Website: www.lorenz.com. Gift products, stationery, book marks, buttons, postcards, posters, and more. Guidelines on Website.

MCBETH CORP, PO Box 400, Chambersburg PA 17201. Toll-free (800)876-5112. (717)263-5600. Fax (717)263-5909. E-mail: mcbethcorp@supernet.com. Website: www.wholesale central.com/mcbethcorp. Gifts, jewelry, calendars, Christmas items, activity books, greeting cards, and more.

NOT OF THIS WORLD CLOTHING CO., 169 Radio Rd. #8, Corona CA 92879. (951)354-9528. Fax (951)354-9529. E-mail: info@notw.com, or info@c28.com. Website: www.notw.com. Shirts, wallets, belts, belt buckles.

POWERMARK: Comics Worth Reading, E. Hwy. CC, Ste. E104, Nixa MO 65714. Toll-free (877)769-2669. Fax (417)724-0119. E-mail: webmaster@powermarkcomics.com. Website: www.powermarkcomics.com. Contact: Steve Benintendi. Christian comic books.

RED LETTER 9, 2910 Kerry Forest Pkwy, D4, Tallahassee FL 32309. Toll-free (866)804-4833. Toll-free fax (866)804-4832. E-mail: info@redletter9.com. Website: www.redletter9.com. Apparel and gift items.

SERENDIPITY PUZZLE CO., a division of The Marek Group, W228 N821 Westmound Dr., Waukesha WI 53186. (262)549-8930. Fax (262)549-8910. E-mail: diane.bucher@ serendipitypuzzles.com. Website: www.serendipitypuzzles.com. Diane Bucher-Gilboy, dir. of sales. Produces specialty products. Open to freelance. Purchases 50+ ideas/yr. Prefers outright submissions through e-mail. Payment & royalty (decided case-by-case) on acceptance. Responds in 2 wks. Seasonal 2 mos. ahead. Open to new ideas for specialty items. Submit 2 or more ideas at a time. Manufactures custom orders. Free catalog.

Tips: "The Marek Group is a nationally recognized, high quality commercial printing and manufacturing company, specializing in catalogs, publications, direct mail, variable data, Web-to-print applications, and the manufacturing of puzzles and board games."

SOLID LIGHT CO., 7787 Graphics Way, Lewis Center OH 43035. Toll-free (800)726-9606. (740)548-1200. Fax (740)548-1223. Website: www.solidlightco.com. Apparel.

SONTEEZ CHRISTIAN T-SHIRTS, PO Box 44106, Phoenix AZ 85064. Toll-free (800)874-4485. Website: www.sonteez.com. T-shirts.

VIDA ENTERTAINMENT, 201 East City Hall Ave., Norfolk VA 23451. Toll-free (877)YES-VIDA. (757)626-3102. E-mail: sales@vidaentertainment.com. Website: www.vidaentertainment .com. Books, DVDs, comics, & toys.

SOFTWARE DEVELOPERS

AMG SOFTWARE, 6815 Shallowford Rd. (37421), PO Box 22000, Chattanooga TN 37422. Toll-free (800)266-4977. (423)894-6060, ext. 275. Toll-free fax (800)265-6690. (423)894-9511. E-mail: danp@amginternational.org. Website: www.amgpublishers.org. AMG International. Dan Penwell, dir. of prod. dev./acq. Bible software.

BAKER SOFTWARE, Box 6287, Grand Rapids MI 49516-6287. (616)676-9185. Fax (616)676-9573. Website: www.BakerBooks.com. Baker Publishing Group.

B & H SOFTWARE, 127 Ninth Ave. N., Nashville TN 37234. (615)251-3638. Website: www.broad manholman.com.

BIBLESOFT, 22014—7th Ave. S., Seattle WA 98198-6235. (206)824-0547. Fax (206)824-1828. Website: www.biblesoft.com.

ELLIS ENTERPRISES INC., 5100 N. Brookline, #465, Oklahoma City OK 73112. (405)948-1766. Fax (405)917-2250. E-mail: mail@ellisenterprises.com. Website: www.ellisenterprises .com, or www.BibleLibrary.com. Contact: Dr. John Ellis. Produces the Micro Bible, Ultra Bible, Mega Bible, and Maxima Bible. Check out additional products on their Website.

LOGOS BIBLE SOFTWARE (formerly Logos Research Systems), 1313 Commercial St., Bellingham WA 98225-4307. (360)527-1707. Fax (360)527-1707. E-mail: info@logos.com, or suggest@logos.com. Website: www.logos.com. Contact: Dan Pritchett (Dan@logos.com). Publishes the Logos Bible Software Series X Scholar's Library, Leader's Library, Bible Study Library, and more. Over 8,000 titles from more than 100 publishers now compatible with the system.

NAVPRESS SOFTWARE, 16002 Pool Canyon Rd., Austin TX 78734.

OLIVE TREE BIBLE SOFTWARE, PO Box 48271, Spokane WA 99228-1271. (509)465-0302. Fax (509)467-4976. E-mail: drew@olivetree.com, or support@olivetree.com. Website: www.OliveTree.com. Drew Hunter, pres. Bible software.

RIVER DEEP. Appears to now be a part of Broderbund. E-mail: cust_serv@broderbund.com. Website: www.broderbund.com. Software developer.

ZONDERVAN NEW MEDIA, 5300 Patterson St. S.E., Grand Rapids MI 49530. Toll-free (800) 226-1122. (616)698-6900. Fax (616)698-3483. Website: www.zondervan.com. Contact: Britt Dennison. Software.

VIDEO/CD/DVD MARKETS

ALPHA OMEGA PUBLICATIONS, 804 N. 2nd Ave. E., Rock Rapids IA 51246. Toll-free (800) 622-3070. Website: www.AOP.com. Videos & DVDs.

AMG PUBLISHERS/CD/CD-ROMS, 6815 Shallowford Rd. (37421), PO Box 22000, Chattanooga TN 37422. Toll-free (800)266-4977. (423)894-6060, ext. 275. Toll-free fax (800)265-6690 or (423)894-9511. E-mail: danp@amginternational.org. Website: www.amgpublishers.org. AMG International. Dan Penwell, dir. of prod. dev./acq. Bible CD-ROMs.

BIG IDEA INC., 230 Franklin Rd., Bldg. 2A, Franklin TN 37064. Toll-free (800)295-0557. (615)224-2200. E-mail: customerservice@bigidea.com. Website: www.bigidea.com. Query; no unsolicited ideas. Movies, videos, music, books, and games.

CANDLELIGHT MEDIA GROUP, 3323 State Hwy. 276, Emory TX 75440. Toll-free (800)747-2696. E-mail: info@candlelightmedia.com. Website: www.candlelightmedia.com. Videos, DVDs.

CLOUD TEN PICTURES, PO Box 1440, Niagara Falls NY 14302. (905)684-5561. Fax (905)684-7946. Website: www.cloudtenpictures.com. Film production and acquisition, video distribution, and marketing. Cloud Ten Pictures (maker of the Left Behind movies) is committed to making quality, Christian-themed films. For all inquiries, contact C.E.O.: Andre van Heerden; andrev@cloudtenpictures.com.

CROWN VIDEO/CROWN COMEDY, 15397—117 Ave., Edmonton AB T5M 3X4, Canada. Toll-free (800)661-9467. (780)471-1417. Fax (780)474-0418. E-mail: info@crownvideo.com. Website: www.crownvideo.com; www.christiandvd.com; www.garysmalleyvideos.com. Precision Media Group. Distributor of Christian Films, stand-up comedy, and music.

DALLAS CHRISTIAN VIDEO. Toll-free (877)516-2900. Fax (972)644-5926. E-mail: DCV6681@aol.com. Website: www.dallaschristianvideo.com. Contact: Bob Hill. Videos.

RUSS DOUGHTEN FILMS INC., 5907 Meredith Dr., Des Moines IA 50322. Toll-free (800)247-3456. (515)278-4737. Fax (515)278-4738. E-mail: rdoughten@rdfilms.com, or evangelism@rdfilms.com. Website: www.rdfilms.com. Russell S. Doughton Jr., pres. Submit to Production Dept. Produces and distributes feature-length Christian movies. Open to ideas. Guidelines; free catalog.

GOSPEL COMMUNICATIONS, PO Box 455, Muskegon MI 49443-0455. Toll-free (800)467-7353. (231)773-3361. Fax (231)777-1847. E-mail: marilyn@gospelcommunications.org. Website: www.GospelDirect.com. Contact: Marilyn Bush. Videos, DVDs, books, Bibles, and music.

TOMMY NELSON VIDEOS, PO Box 141000, Nashville TN 37214. Website: www.tommynelson.com. Contact: Bill Reeves, entertainment dir. Video producer.

PROPHECY PUBLICATIONS, PO Box 7000, Oklahoma City OK 73153. Toll-free (800)475-1111. Fax (405)636-1054. E-mail: Krissie@prophecyinthenews.com. Website: www.prophecyinthenews.com. Contact: J. R. Church. Religious education videos; fiction videos.

TYNDALE FAMILY VIDEO, 351 Executive Dr., Carol Stream IL 60188. (630)668-8300. Website: www.tyndale.com. Videos.

VISION VIDEO/GATEWAY FILMS, PO Box 540, Worcester PA 19490-0540. Toll-free (800)523-0226. (610)584-3500. Fax (610)584-6643. E-mail: info@VisionVideo.com. Website: www.VisionVideo.com. Contact: Karen Rutt.

WACKY WORLD STUDIOS, 148 E. Douglas Rd., Oldsmar FL 34677-2939. (813)818-8277. Fax (813)818-8396. E-mail: info@wackyworld.tv, or through Website: www.wackyworld.tv. Full service custom art and design studio. Videos, DVDs.

ZONDERVAN NEW MEDIA, 5300 Patterson St. S.E., Grand Rapids MI 49530. Toll-free (800) 226-1122. (616)698-6900. Fax (616)698-3483. Website: www.zondervan.com. Videos.

SPECIALTY PRODUCTS TOPICAL LISTINGS

NOTE: Most of the following publishers are greeting card/specialty market publishers, but some will also be found in the book publisher listings.

ACTIVITY/COLORING BOOKS

Cook, David C.
Dickson's Life Pub.
Greenacre Workshop
Knight George Pub.
McBeth Corp.
Rainbow Publishers
Serendipity Puzzle
Warner Press
World Library Pub.

AUDIOTAPES

AMG Publishers
AMG Software
Bible Games
Eldridge Plays
Fair Havens
McRuffy Press
Tyndale House
W Publishing
Zondervan New Media

BANNERS

Serendipity Puzzle
World Library Pub.

BOARD GAMES/ GAMES

Bethel Publishing
Bible Games
Big Idea
Cactus Game
Carson-Dellosa
Cook, David C.
Goode Games
Knight George Pub.
Master Books
Mission City Press
Morris, William
Review and Herald
Salt Works
Serendipity Puzzle
Standard Publishing
Talicor
Tyndale House
WinePress

BOOKMARKS

Ashleigh Manor
Blue Mountain Arts
Christian Art Gifts
Christian Inspirations
Dickson's Life Pub.

Hermitage Art
InspirationArt
Lorenz
Serendipity Puzzle
Warner Press
World Library Pub.

CALENDARS/ DAILY JOURNALS

Abingdon Press
African Amer. Expressions
American Tract
Barbour
Blue Mountain Arts
C4Yourself Greetings
Christian Inspirations
Dickson's Life Pub.
Group Publishing
McBeth Corp.
Neibauer Press
Serendipity Puzzle
Tyndale House
Women of the Promise
World Library Pub.

CD-ROMs

AMG Publishers
AMG Video/CD
Bible Games
Cactus Game
Cook, David C.
Fair Havens
Georgetown Univ. Press
Group Publishing
Our Sunday Visitor
World Library Pub.

CHARTS

Rose Publishing
Serendipity Puzzle

COMIC BOOKS

Cactus Game
Infuze
Kaleidoscope Press
Lighthouse Publishing
Nelson, Thomas
PowerMark
Serendipity Puzzle
Vida Entertainment
ZonderKidz

COMPUTER GAMES

Bible Games
Big Idea

Cactus Game
Cook, David C.
Dean Press, Robbie
Grupo Nelson
Knight George Pub.
WinePress
Wisdom Tree
Wood Lake Books

COMPUTER SOFTWARE

AMG Publishers
AMG Software
Baker Software
B & H Software
BibleSoft
Ellis Enterprises
Libros Liguori
Logos Bible Software
NavPress Software
Olive Tree/Software
Regal
Resource Public.
River Deep
Wisdom Tree
World Library Pub.
Zondervan New Media

DVDs

Anglicans United
Big Idea
Candlelight Media
Crown Video
Gospel Communications
Vida Entertainment
Wacky World
WinePress
World Library Pub.

GIFT BOOKS

ACTA Publications
Adams Media
Ambassador Books
American Binding
Baker Books
Ballantine
B & H Publishing
Barbour
Big Idea
Black Forest/Tennessee
Blue Mountain Arts
Booklocker.com
Book Publishers
Brown Books
Christian Inspirations
Christian Writer's Ebook

Contemporary Drama
Cook, David C.
Countryman, J.
Creation House
DCTS Publishing
Dean Press, Robbie
Dimensions for Living
Editorial Portavoz
Eerdmans Pub., Wm. B.
Elderberry Press
Essence
Evergreen Press
Fairway Press
Faith Communications
Gibson Public., Dot
Gollehon Press
Green Key Books
GRQ
Guardian Angel
HarperOne
Hay House
Hidden Brook Press
Holy Fire Publishing
Howard Books
Illumination Arts
IMD Press
Kaleidoscope Press
Lift Every Voice
Lighthouse Publishing
Monarch Books
Mt. Olive College Press
New Leaf
New Seeds
One World
Our Sunday Visitor
Pleasant Word
Providence Pub.
Ravenhawk Books
Regal
Review and Herald
Rose Publishing
Salt Works
Serendipity Puzzle
Tate Publishing
Trafford Publishing
Vida Entertainment
VMI Publishers
White Stone Books
WinePress
Woodland Gospel
Word Alive
World Library Pub.

GIFT/NOVELTY ITEMS

Abingdon Press
African Amer. Expressions
Artful Greetings
Ashleigh Manor
Blue Mountain Arts
Carpentree
Carson-Dellosa

Christian Art Gifts
Christian Inspirations
Cook, David C.
Design Design
Destiny Image
Dexsa
Dickson's Life Pub.
Hermitage Art
Houghton Designs, Jody
Lawrence Co., James
Lighthouse Christian
Lorenz
McBeth Corp.
Red Letter 9
Salt Works
Serendipity Puzzle
Talicor

GREETING BOOKS

Blue Mountain Arts
Christian Art Gifts
Christian Inspirations
Design Design
Houghton Designs, Jody
Serendipity Puzzle

MAGNETS

African Amer. Expressions
Blue Mountain Arts
Christian Inspirations
Design Design
Dickson's Life Pub.
Houghton Designs, Jody
Lawrence Co., James
World Library Pub.

MUGS

Christian Art Gifts
Christian Inspirations
Dickson's Life Pub.
Lawrence Co., James

MUSIC

Gospel Communications

NOTECARDS

Creative Christian Gifts

PLAQUES

Christian Inspirations
Dickson's Life Pub.
Houghton Designs, Jody
Lawrence Co., James

POSTCARDS

Abingdon Press
Houghton Designs, Jody
Lorenz
Serendipity Puzzle
Warner Press
World Library Pub.

POSTERS

ArtBeats
Art 2 Inspire
InspirationArt
Life Cycle Books
Lorenz
Serendipity Puzzle
World Library Pub.

PUZZLES

Bible Games
Christian Inspirations
Heritage Puzzle
InspirationArt
Rainbow Publishers
Serendipity Puzzle
Talicor

STATIONERY

African Amer. Expressions
Christian Inspirations
Design Design
Dickson's Life Pub.
Lorenz
Serendipity Puzzle

SUNDAY BULLETINS

Anchor Wallace
Christian Inspirations
Hermitage Art
Serendipity Puzzle
Warner Press
World Library Pub.

T-SHIRTS/APPAREL

Be One Christian
Christian Inspirations
Dickson's Life Pub.
Eagles Wings
Know Him
Living Epistles
Not of This World
Red Letter 9
Solid Light
SonTeez
World Library Pub.

TOYS

Dickson's Life Pub.
Lighthouse Christian
Mission City Press
Standard Publishing
Talicor
Vida Entertainment

VIDEOS/VIDEO GAMES

Abingdon Press
Alpha Omega
AMG Video/CD
Anglicans United

Bible Games
Big Idea
Cactus Game
Candlelight Media
Cloud Ten
Cook, David C.
Crown Video
Dallas Christian Video
Destiny Image
Doughten Films, Russ

Editorial Unilit
Fair Havens
Focus on the Family
Gospel Communications
Group Publishing
Howard Books
Master Books
Nelson Videos, Tommy
Pauline Books
Prophecy Publications

Regal
Tyndale Family Video
Tyndale House
Vision Video
Wacky World
Wisdom Tree
W Publishing
Zondervan New Media

CHRISTIAN WRITERS' CONFERENCES AND WORKSHOPS

Visit the following Websites for information on these and other conferences available across the country: www.freelancewriting.com/conferences, or www.screenwriter.com/insider/Writers Calendar.html. Link to these conference Websites at www.stuartmarket.com.

(+) Indicates a new listing

ALABAMA

SOUTHERN CHRISTIAN WRITERS CONFERENCE. Tuscaloosa/First Baptist Church; June 2009. Contact: Joanne Sloan, SCWC, PO Box 1106, Northport AL 35473. (205)333-8603. Fax (205)339-4528. E-mail: SCWCworkshop@bellsouth.net. Website: http://web.mac.com/wmdsloan/iweb/SCWC. Editors & agents in attendance. Attendance: 200+.

ARIZONA

AMERICAN CHRISTIAN WRITERS PHOENIX CONFERENCE. Grace Inn; October 30-31, 2009; October 29-30, 2010. Contact: Reg A. Forder, Box 110390, Nashville TN 37222. Toll-free (800)21-WRITE. E-mail: ACWriters@aol.com. Website: www.ACWriters.com. Attendance: 40-80.

CATHOLIC SCREENWRITERS WORKSHOP. Tucson; February 2009. Contact: Fr. Tom Santa, CssR, 7101 W. Picture Rocks Rd., Tucson AZ 85743-9645. Toll-free (866)737-5751. (520) 744-3400. Fax (520)744-8021. E-mail: office@desertrenewal.org. Website: www.desert renewal.org. See Website for additional writers' events.

ARKANSAS

ANNUAL ARKANSAS WRITERS CONFERENCE. Little Rock; June 5-6, 2009 (always 1st Friday & Saturday of June). Website: www.geocities.com/penwomen. Attendance: 150-175. Sponsors 30 contests; one entry fee covers all contests.

CALIFORNIA

ACT ONE: WRITING PROGRAM. Hollywood; summer of 2009. Contact: Chris Riley, 2690 N. Beachwood Dr., Hollywood CA 90068. (323)464-0815. Fax (323)468-0315. E-mail: info@ actoneprogram.com. Website: www.ActOneProgram.com. These are intensive training sessions for screenwriters, taught by professionals working in Hollywood. Offers track for television writers. No editors or agents in attendance. Limited to 30 students (by application).

AMERICAN CHRISTIAN WRITERS ANAHEIM CONFERENCE. October 23-24, 2009; October 22-23, 2010. Contact: Reg A. Forder, Box 110390, Nashville TN 37222. Toll-free (800)21-WRITE. E-mail: ACWriters@aol.com. Website: www.ACWriters.com. Attendance: 40-80.

ANTELOPE VALLEY CHRISTIAN WRITER'S CONFERENCE. Lancaster; May 1-2, 2009. Sponsored by the High Desert Christian Writer's Guild and Quartz Hill School of Theology. Theme: Streams in the Desert. Contact: Don Patterson, 6223 Almond Valley Way, Quartz Hill CA 93536. (661)722-0891. Fax (661)943-3484. E-mail: don@theology.edu. Website: www.av writers.com.

BIOLA MEDIA CONFERENCE. La Mirada; May 2009. Contact: Craig Detweiler, Biola University, 13800 Biola Ave., La Mirada CA 90639. Toll-free (866)334-2266. Website: www.biola media.com.

CASTRO VALLEY CHRISTIAN WRITERS SEMINAR. Castro Valley; February 2009. Contact: Pastor Jon Drury, 19300 Redwood Rd., Castro Valley CA 94546-3465. (510)886-6300. Fax (510)581-5022. E-mail: jond@redwoodchapel.org. Website: www.christianwriter.org. Doesn't usually have editors; no agents in attendance. Attendance: 200.

+MOUNT HERMON CHRISTIAN SONGWRITERS CONFERENCE. Near Santa Cruz; August 2009. Call (888)MH-CAMPS or visit Website: www.mounthermon.org/songwriters.

MOUNT HERMON CHRISTIAN WRITERS CONFERENCE. Mount Hermon (near Santa Cruz); April 3-7, 2009; also Head-Start Clinic (mentoring) April 1-2, 2009. Also offers a Career Track for professional writers (details on Website); and a teen track. Contact: David R. Talbott, Box 413, Mount Hermon CA 95041-0413. (831)430-1238. Fax (831)335-9218. E-mail: rachelw@mhcamps.org. Website: www.mounthermon.org/writers (no brochure; all details on Website December 1). Speaker for 2009: Bill Butterworth. Many editors and agents in attendance. Offers partial scholarships. Cash awards. Attendance: 425.

MOUNT HERMON HEAD-START MENTORING CLINIC. Mount Hermon, CA. This fall mentoring track has been replaced by a mentoring session the two days prior to the regular spring conference; April 1-2, 2009. See the listing for Mount Hermon Christian Writers' Conference for details.

ORANGE COUNTY CHRISTIAN WRITERS FELLOWSHIP SPRING WRITERS DAY. Mariners Church/Irvine; April 2009 (tentative). Contact: John DeSimone, dir.; Peg Matthew Rose, ed., PO Box 982, Lake Forest CA 92630. (714)538-7070. Fax (949)458-1807. E-mail: editor@occwf.org. Website: www.occwf.org. Editors and possibly agents in attendance. Offers full and partial scholarships. See Website for list of faculty and conference date. Attendance: 100-150+.

SAN DIEGO CHRISTIAN WRITERS GUILD FALL CONFERENCE. San Diego; September 2009. Contact: Jennie Gillespie, PO Box 270403, San Diego CA 92198. (760)294-3269. E-mail: info@sandiegocwg.org. Website: www.sandiegocwg.org. Editors and agents in attendance. Attendance: 180.

SANTA BARBARA CHRISTIAN WRITERS CONFERENCE. Westmont College; October 2009. Contact: Opal Mae Dailey, PO Box 40860, Santa Barbara CA 93140. Phone/fax (805)682-0316 (call first for fax). E-mail: opalmaedailey@aol.com. Attendance: 50.

SOCIETY OF CHILDREN'S BOOK WRITERS & ILLUSTRATORS CONFERENCE IN CHILDREN'S LITERATURE. New York City, January 30-February 1, 2009; Los Angeles, August 7-10, 2009. Society of Children's Book Writers & Illustrators. Contact: Lin Oliver, 8271 Beverly Blvd., Los Angeles CA 90048. (323)782-1010. Fax (323)782-1892. E-mail: scbwi@scbwi.org. Website: www.scbwi.org. Includes a track for professionals. Editors and agents in attendance. Attendance: 900.

WRITERS SYMPOSIUM BY THE SEA. San Diego/Point Loma Nazarene University; February 2-6, 2009. Contact: Dean Nelson, Professor, Journalism Dept., PLNU, 3900 Lomaland Dr., San Diego CA 92106. (619)849-2592. Fax (619)849-2566. E-mail: deannelson@pointloma .edu. Website: www.pointloma.edu/writers. Speakers include Brian McLaren. No editors/ agents in attendance. No scholarships. Attendance: 500.

+WRITE TO PUBLISH WORKSHOP. Corona; March 2009. Contact: Carol Duhart, Advantageous Events, Inc., 3190 Castelar Ct., Ste. 103, Corona CA 92888. (714)953-7141. E-mail: info@advantageousevents.com. Website: www.advantageousevents.com.

COLORADO

AD LIB CHRISTIAN ARTS RETREAT. Franciscan Retreat Center; Colorado Springs; September 26-28, 2009. Contact: Prof. Richard Terrell, 6905 Forest Lake Blvd., Lincoln NE 68516. (402)486-4198. Cell (402)440-8851. E-mail: richard.terrell@doane.edu. Website:

www.adlibchristianarts.org. Gather for Sabbath, fellowship, display/discuss art/writing projects, and work on what we love to do. Guest artists are the editors of *Ruminate*, CO-based arts journal. No working editors or agents. Attendance: limited to 20.

COLORADO CHRISTIAN WRITERS CONFERENCE. Estes Park; May 13-16, 2009 at the YMCA of the Rockies. Director: Marlene Bagnull, LittD, 316 Blanchard Rd., Drexel Hill, PA 19026-3507. Phone/fax (610)626-6833. E-mail: mbagnull@aol.com. Website: www.writehis answer.com/Colorado. Conferees choose 6 hour-long workshops from 42 offered or a Fiction or Nonfiction Clinic (by application) plus one 6.5 hour continuing session from 7 offered. One-on-one appointments, paid critiques, editors panels, and general sessions. Thursday evening concert. Teens Write Saturday afternoon, plus teens are welcome to attend the entire conference at 60% off. Contest (registered conferees only) awards four $100 discounts off May 2010 conference. Faculty of 60 authors, editors, and agents. Attendance: 260.

GLEN EYRIE FICTION WRITER'S CONFERENCE. Colorado Springs; January 2009. Contact: Craig Dunham, 3820 N. 30th, Colorado Springs CO 80904. Toll-free (800)944-4536. (719) 634-0808. Fax (719)272-7448. Website: www.gleneyriegroup.org. Some editors/agents in attendance. Attendance: 100. Check Website for conferences and dates.

GMA MUSIC IN THE ROCKIES CONFERENCE. Estes Park; July 26-31, 2009. Contact: John W. Styll, dir., 1205 Division St., Nashville TN 37203. Toll-free (800)GMA-3211. (615)242-0303. Fax (615)254-9755. Website: www.gospelmusic.org. Offers advanced track and teen track; critiques, talent, competition, and seminars. A & R and industry reps on site; teaching and judging. Attendance: 1,200.

JERRY B. JENKINS CHRISTIAN WRITERS GUILD WRITING FOR THE SOUL CONFERENCE. Colorado Springs; February 19-22, 2009; February 17-20, 2010. Sponsored by the Jerry B. Jenkins Christian Writers Guild. Held at the luxurious 5-star, 5-diamond Broadmoor Hotel in 2009; moving to Denver for 2010. Host: Jerry B. Jenkins. Speakers for 2009 include: Gary Chapman, Jerry B. Jenkins, Karen Kingsbury, Dennis Hensley, and McNair Wilson. More than 30 editor and agents in attendance. Payment plans available. Special meal rates offered for nonparticipating spouses or parents of teens. Offers multiple general sessions with national keynote speakers and in-depth workshops on 6 tracks; plus appointments with publisher's reps. Contact: Paul Finch, 5525 N. Union Blvd., Ste. 200, Colorado Springs CO 80918. Toll-free (866)495-5177. (719)495-5177. Fax (719)495-5181. E-mail: paul@christianwritersguild.com. Website: www.christianwritersguild.com. Offers partial scholarships. Attendance: 450.

CONNECTICUT

WESLEYAN WRITERS CONFERENCE. Wesleyan University/Middletown; June 2009 (tentative, see Website). Contact: Anne Greene, Director, Wesleyan Writers Conference, 294 High St., Rm. 207, Middletown CT 06459. (860)685-3604. Fax (860)685-2441. E-mail: agreene@ wesleyan.edu. Website: www.wesleyan.edu/writers. Includes an advanced track. Editors and agents in attendance. Offers fellowship and scholarship awards. Attendance: 100.

DELAWARE

DELAWARE CHRISTIAN WRITERS CONFERENCE. Word of Life Christian Center, Newark; April 24-25, 2009. E-mail: johnriddle@sprintmail.com. Website: www.DelawareChristian WritersConference.com. Director: John Riddle, 6 Basset Pl., Bear DE 19701. (302)834-4910. Editors, agents, advanced track, young writers program, writing contests, editorial appointments, and evaluations.

FLORIDA

AMERICAN CHRISTIAN WRITERS ORLANDO CONFERENCE. November 21, 2009; November 20, 2010. Contact: Reg A. Forder, Box 110390, Nashville TN 37222. Toll-free (800)21-WRITE. E-mail: ACWriters@aol.com. Website: www.ACWriters.com. Attendance: 40-80.

+CHRISTIAN CRUISERS CLUB 1ST ANNUAL WRITING CRUISE. Leaving from Miami; March 29-April 5, 2009. Contact: Emily Hightower, PO Box 2014, Elkton KY 42220. (270)265-7003. Fax (270)265-7004. E-mail: cruisersclub@bellsouth.net. Website: www.christian writingcruise.com. Offers track for those who write for teens. Speakers: Tama Westman and Terry Burns. Editors & agents in attendance. Offers partial scholarships.

CHRISTIANS IN THEATRE ARTS (CITA) ANNUAL NETWORKING CONFERENCE. Orlando FL; June 15-21, 2009. Contact: Bryanne Barker, PO Box 26471, Greenville SC 29616. (864)679-1898. Fax (864)679-1899. E-mail: admin@cita.org. Website: www.cita.org. Usually offers an advanced track. Sponsors a play contest (rules on Website). Attendance: 350.

FLORIDA CHRISTIAN WRITERS CONFERENCE. Lake Yale Conference Center; Leesburg FL; February 25-March 1, 2009; March 4-7, 2010. Contact: Billie Wilson, 2344 Armour Ct., Titusville FL 32780. (321)269-5831. Fax (321)747-0246. E-mail: billiewilson@cfl.rr.com. Website: www.flwriters.org. Offers advanced track (15 hours of class time—by application only) & teen track. Speakers for 2009: Cecil Murphey & T. Davis Bunn. Editors and agents in attendance. Offers full & partial scholarships. Offers awards in 11 categories. Awards open to registrants; mss submitted to conference for review are considered for an award. Attendance: 350.

INTERNATIONAL CHRISTIAN RETAIL SHOW. (Held in a different location each year.) July 12-16, 2009 in Denver CO. Contact: Scott Graham, Box 62000, Colorado Springs CO 80962-2000. Toll-free (800)252-1950. (719)265-9895. Fax (719)272-3510. E-mail: sgraham@cbaonline.org. Website: www.christianretailshow.com. Entrance badges available through book publishers or Christian bookstores. Attendance: 8,000.

WORD WEAVERS ANNUAL RETREAT. Lake Yale; February 6-8, 2009. Contact: Larry J. Leech II, 911 Alameda Dr., Longwood FL 32750. (407)925-6411. E-mail: leech@cfl.rr.com. Website: www.wordweaversFL.com. Sponsors a contest. No editors/agents in attendance. Offers 2 full scholarships. Attendance 35-40.

GEORGIA

AMERICAN CHRISTIAN WRITERS ATLANTA CONFERENCE. May 1-2, 2009; May 21-22, 2010. Contact: Reg Forder, Box 110390, Nashville TN 37222. Toll-free (800)21-WRITE. E-mail: ACWriters@aol.com. Website: www.ACWriters.com. Attendance: 40-80.

CATCH THE WAVE WRITERS CONFERENCE. Woodstock; September 2009. Contact: Pam Barnes, PO Box 2673, Woodstock GA 30188. E-mail: Cynthiasimmons@christian authorsguild.org. Website: www.christianauthorsguild.org. Sponsors a short story contest and an article contest. Editors and agents in attendance. No scholarships. Attendance: 60.

+EAST METRO ATLANTA CHRISTIAN WRITERS CONFERENCE. Covington; August 8-9, 2009. Contact: Colleen Jackson, PO Box 2896, Covington GA 30015. (404)444-7514. E-mail: cjac401992@aol.com. Website: www.emacw.org. Speaker: Elizabeth Sherrill. Check Website for location and details.

GEORGIA CHRISTIAN WRITERS' SPRING FESTIVAL. Atlanta area; May 2, 2009 (first Saturday in May each year). Contact: Lloyd Blackwell, 3049 Scott Rd. N.E., Marietta GA 30066. (770)421-1203. E-mail: lloydblackwell@worldnet.att.net.

SOUTHEASTERN WRITERS ASSN. ANNUAL WORKSHOP. St. Simons Island; June 14-18, 2009. Contact: Sheila Hudson, registrar, 161 Woodstone Dr., Athens GA 30605. E-mail: sheilahudson@charter.net. Website: www.southeasternwriters.com. Attendance: limited to 100. Occasionally offers an advanced track. Sponsors a contest on the Website. Agents & editors in attendance.

ILLINOIS

KARITOS CHRISTIAN ARTS CONFERENCE. Bolingbrook; August 2009. Contact: Bob Hay, 24 N. Belmont Ave., #B, Arlington Heights IL 60004-6174. (847)749-1284. E-mail: bob@karitos.com, or literaryarts@karitos.com. Website: www.karitos.com. Features workshops in all areas of the arts, including writing. Also general sessions and evening celebrations. Attendance: 300-400.

WRITE-TO-PUBLISH CONFERENCE. Wheaton (Chicago area); June 3-6, 2009. Contact: Lin Johnson, 9118 W. Elmwood Dr., #1G, Niles IL 60714-5820. (847)296-3964. Fax (847)296-0754. E-mail: lin@WriteToPublish.com. Website: www.WriteToPublish.com. Offers advanced track (prerequisite: 1 published book). Majority of faculty are editors; also has agents. Attendance: 250.

INDIANA

AMERICAN CHRISTIAN WRITERS FORT WAYNE CONFERENCE. Clarion Downtown; March 27-28, 2009; March 26-27, 2010. Contact: Reg A. Forder, Box 110390, Nashville TN 37222. Toll-free (800)21-WRITE. E-mail: ACWriters@aol.com. Website: www.ACWriters.com. Attendance: 40-80.

AMERICAN CHRISTIAN WRITERS INDIANAPOLIS CONFERENCE. June 6, 2009; July 24, 2010. Contact: Reg A. Forder, Box 110390, Nashville TN 37222. Toll-free (800)21-WRITE. E-mail: ACWriters@aol.com. Website: www.ACWriters.com. Attendance: 40-80.

BETHEL COLLEGE CHRISTIAN WRITERS' WORKSHOP. Bethel College/Mishawaka; spring 2009. Contact: English Dept. Chair, 1001 W. McKinley Ave., Mishawaka IN 46544. (574)257-3427. Website: www.BethelCollege.edu/writersworkshop. Editors sometimes in attendance; no agents. Sometimes offers full or partial scholarships. Attendance: 130.

EARLHAM SCHOOL OF RELIGION: THE MINISTRY OF WRITING COLLOQUIUM. Richmond; late October 2009. Editors in attendance. Contact: '09 Writing Colloquium, Susan Yanos, Earlham School of Religion, 228 College Ave., Richmond IN 47374-4095. Toll-free (800)432-1377. (765)983-1423. Fax (765)983-1688. E-mail: yanossu@earlham.edu. Website: www.esr.earlham.edu. Attendance: 200.

MIDWEST WRITERS WORKSHOP. Muncie/Ball State University Alumni Center; late July 23-25, 2009 (always the last Thursday, Friday, and Saturday of July). Contact: Dept. of Journalism, Ball State University, Muncie IN 47306-0484. Director: Jama Kehoe Bigger. (765)282-1055. E-mail: midwestwriters@yahoo.com. Website: www.midwestwriters.org. Sponsors a contest. Editors and agents in attendance. Offers full scholarships. Attendance: 150.

IOWA

CEDAR FALLS CHRISTIAN WRITERS' WORKSHOP. Riverview Conference Center/Cedar Falls; June 10-13, 2009; June 9-12, 2010. Contact: Jean Vaux, 1703 Sunnyside Dr., Cedar Falls IA 50613-4644. (318)277-1721. Fax (319)277-1721. E-mail: vauxcom@cfu.net. Website: www.shellybeachonline.com. Speakers: Dennis Hensley, Traci Groot, Shelly Beach. No editors/agents in attendance: Offers partial scholarships. Attendance: 35.

IOWA SUMMER WRITING FESTIVAL. University of Iowa/Iowa City; June & July 2009. This is a general writer's conference that comes highly recommended for good, solid instruction. Contact: Amy Margolis, Iowa Summer Writing Festival, C215 Seashore Hall, University of Iowa, Iowa City IA 52242-5000. (319)335-4160. Fax (319)335-4743. E-mail: iswfestival@ uiowa.edu. Website: www.uiowa.edu/~iswfest. For two months, June and July, you can sign up for either one-week workshops or weekend workshops on a wide variety of topics. Write for a catalog of offerings (available in February).

OKOBOJI CHRISTIAN WRITERS RETREAT. Okoboji; not being held in 2009; September 2010. Contact: Denise Triggs, PO Box 281, Okoboji IA 51355. (712)332-7191. E-mail: waterfalls42@hotmail.com. Website: www.waterfallsretreats.com. No editors or agents in attendance. No scholarships. Attendance: 20-30.

QUAD-CITIES CHRISTIAN WRITERS' CONFERENCE. Eldridge; March 27-28, 2009; April 9-10, 2010. Contact: Twila Belk, 4350 Tanglewood Rd., Bettendorf IA 52722. (563)332-1622. E-mail: Twila@gottatellsomebody.com. Website: www.qccwc.com. Speakers include: Cecil Murphey, Susan May Warren, Kim Peterson, Cynthia Ruchi, Frank Ball, Michelle Rayburn. No editors or agents in attendance. Offers full scholarships. Attendance 100+.

KANSAS

CALLED TO WRITE. Greenbush Educational Center/Girard; April 3-4, 2009. Contact: Deborah Vogts, 17300 Ness Rd., Erie KS 66733. E-mail: debvogts@gmail.com. Website: www.christian writersfellowship.blogspot.com. Speakers include: Kim Vogel Sawyer and John Riddle. Attendance: 50-60.

KENTUCKY

KENTUCKY CHRISTIAN WRITERS' CONFERENCE. Elizabethtown; June 19-20, 2009. Contact: Judy Sliger, registrar, PMB 235, 803 N. Dixie Ave., Elizabethtown KY 42701. E-mail: registrar@kychristianwriters.com. Website: www.kychristianwriters.com. Editors in attendance. Workshops and appointments with editors. Attendance: 100.

MARYLAND

AMERICAN CHRISTIAN WRITERS BALTIMORE CONFERENCE. March 21, 2009. Contact: Reg Forder, Box 110390, Nashville TN 37222. Toll-free (800)21-WRITE. E-mail: AC Writers@aol.com. Website: www.ACWriters.com. Attendance: 40-80.

SANDY COVE CHRISTIAN COMMUNICATORS' EXPERIENCE. Sandy Cove/North East; September-October 2009. Offers Beginner, Advanced & Teen Tracks—screenwriting, online, music, fiction, nonfiction, manuscript evaluations, 1-on-1 mentoring. Contact: Sharon Noris Elliott, Writers' Conference Director, Sandy Cove Ministries, 60 Sandy Cove Rd., North East MD 21901. Toll-free (800)234-2683. E-mail: info@sandycove.org. Website: www.sandycove.org/writers. Editors and agents in attendance. Attendance: 150.

MASSACHUSETTS

CAPE COD ANNUAL SUMMER WRITERS' CONFERENCE and YOUNG WRITERS' WORK-SHOP (ages 12-16). Craigville Conference Center; August 16-21, 2009. Contact: Jacqueline M. Loring, exec. dir., PO Box 408, Osterville MA 02655-0408. (508)420-0200. Fax (508)420-0212. E-mail: writers@capecodwriterscenter.org. Website: www.capecodwriters center.org. Offers an advanced track. Editors and agents in attendance. Week-long workshops are $125; personal conferences $50; and manuscript evaluations $125 (also open to writers not attending the conference). Deadline for submissions is July 15. Attendance: 200. Young Writers Workshop runs concurrent with conference.

MICHIGAN

ACW DETROIT CONFERENCE. Detroit; fall 2009. Contact: Pam Perry, pres., 33011 Tall Oaks, Farmington MI 48336. (248)426-2300. Fax (248)471-2422. E-mail: PamPerry@ministrymarketingsolutions.com. Offers class/track for advanced writers. Attendance: 300. Editors/agents in attendance.

AMERICAN CHRISTIAN WRITERS GRAND RAPIDS CONFERENCE. June 26-27, 2009; June 11-29, 2010. Contact: Reg Forder, Box 110390, Nashville TN 37222. Toll-free (800)21-WRITE. E-mail: ACWriters@aol.com. Website: www.ACWriters.com. Attendance: 40-80.

+BREAKING THROUGH WORKSHOP. Canton; January 2009. Contact: Sabrina Adams, PO Box 871066, Canton MI 48187. (877)841-3400. Website: www.zoelifepub.com.

+CATHOLIC WRITER'S CONFERENCE. Plymouth; May 2009. Contact: Karina Fabian, dir. Website: www.rbtecwc.blogspot.com. Free.

+FESTIVAL OF FAITH & WRITING. Calvin College, Grand Rapids; April 15-17, 2010 (held every other year). Contact: Shelly LeMahieu Dunn, Calvin College, 1795 Knollcrest Cir. S.E., Grand Rapids MI 49546. Toll free (800)688-0122. (616)526-6770. E-mail: ffw@calvin.edu. Website: www.calvin.edu/festival. Editors and sometimes agents in attendance.

MARANATHA CHRISTIAN WRITERS SEMINAR. Maranatha Bible & Missionary Conference/Muskegon; September 2009. Contact: Maranatha, 4759 Lake Harbor Rd., Muskegon MI 49441-5299. (231)798-2161. E-mail: info@maranatha-bmc.org. Website: www.WriteWithPurpose.org. Editors in attendance. Attendance: 50.

ORIGINAL & ADVANCED SPEAK UP WITH CONFIDENCE SEMINARS. Cornerstone University, Grand Rapids MI, June 2009. For details & to register, go to: www.carolkent.org, click on "Speak Up Seminars." Contact: Carol Kent, 3141 Winged Foot Dr., Lakeland FL 33803-5437. Toll-free in U.S. (888)870-7719; outside U.S. (810)982-0898. Fax (810)987-4163. E-mail: Speakupinc@aol.com. Website: www.SpeakUpSpeakerServices.com. Speaking seminars. Offers advanced training and opportunities to be coached in small groups. Also offers a workshop on writing for speakers who write for publication. Upcoming conferences listed on Website. Attendance: 100.

MINNESOTA

AMERICAN CHRISTIAN WRITERS MINNEAPOLIS CONFERENCE. August 7-8, 2009; August 6-7, 2010. Contact: Reg Forder, Box 110390, Nashville TN 37222. Toll-free (800)21-WRITE. Website: www.ACWriters.com. Attendance: 40-80.

MINNESOTA CHRISTIAN WRITERS SPRING & FALL SEMINARS. Minneapolis/St. Paul; spring seminar, April 25, 2009; fall seminar, October or November 2009. Contact: Mrs. Pat Van der Merwe, 19820 Olde Sturbridge Rd., Corcoran MN 55340. (763)478-6145. E-mail: pdvdm@comcast.net. Website: www.mnchristianwriters.org. No editors or agents in attendance; no scholarships. Attendance: 40.

THE WRITING ACADEMY SEMINAR. Mount Olivet Retreat Center outside Minneapolis; July 29-August 3, 2009. Sponsors year-round correspondence writing program and annual seminar. Contact: Mar Korman, 1128 Mule Lake Dr. N.E., Outing MN 56662. (218)792-5144. E-mail: info@wams.org. Website: www.wams.org. Attendance: 30. Sponsors a writing contest open to members (rules are posted on Website).

WRITING SEMINARS/NORTH HENNEPIN COMMUNITY COLLEGE. Minneapolis; new classes every Monday and Thursday, year round. Instructor: Louise B. Wyly. Topics include Fiction I, II, III; children and teen writing; personal experiences; Beginning & Advanced; The Artist's Way; and memoirs. Now offers a Creative Writing Certificate for 6 classes and an Advanced Creative Certificate for 6 classes. Attendance: 24 (2 classes each quarter). Contact: Louise Wyly, 6315—55th Ave. N., Apt. 219, Minneapolis MN 55428-3581. (763)533-6207. E-mail: Lsnowbunny@aol.com. Website: www.nhcc.edu (click on "Training and Development"); watch NHCC Bulletin for details, or call (612)424-0880 to inquire. Also sponsors a writers' Alaskan cruise; details available.

MISSOURI

AMERICAN CHRISTIAN WRITERS SPRINGFIELD CONFERENCE. August 15, 2009; August 14, 2010. Contact: Reg A. Forder, Box 110390, Nashville TN 37222. Toll-free (800)21-WRITE. E-mail: ACWriters@aol.com. Website: www.ACWriters.com. Attendance: 40-80.

HEART OF AMERICA CHRISTIAN WRITERS' NETWORK CONFERENCES. Kansas City; November 2009, check Website for dates of additional events. Contact: Jeanette Littleton, 3706 N.E. Shady Lane Dr., Gladstone MO 64119. Phone/fax (816)459-8016. E-mail: jeanette dl@earthlink.net. Website: www.HACWN.org. Offers classes for new and advanced writers. Has editors and agents in attendance. Offers partial scholarships. Contest details on brochure. Attendance: 125.

+WRITER'S BREAKTHOUGH WORKSHOP. Kansas City; May 2009. Contact: Dr. Grace LaJoy Henderson, PO Box 181, Raymore MO 64083. E-mail: poetry@gracelajoy.com. Website: www.writersbreakthrough.com. Churches, groups, community organizations, libraries, etc., can request a mini Writer's Breakthrough Workshop to be held at their facility at anytime during the year. Attendance: 100.

NEBRASKA

MY THOUGHTS EXACTLY WRITERS RETREAT. Fremont; October 2009. Contact: Cheryl Paden, PO Box 1073, Fremont NE 68026-1073. (402)727-6508. Geared toward the beginning writer. No editors or agents in attendance. Attendance: 10.

NEW HAMPSHIRE

WRITERS WORKSHOPS BY MARY EMMA ALLEN. Taught as requested by writer's groups, conferences, schools, and libraries. Topics include: Workshops for Young Writers (for schools and home-parenting groups); Writing Family History Workshop; Blogging for Fun, Profit, & Promotion. Contact: Mary Emma Allen (instructor), 55 Binks Hill Rd., Plymouth NH 03264. (603)536-2641. E-mail: me.allen@juno.com. Websites: http://maryemmallen .blogspot.com, www.onebooktwobook.com.

NEW MEXICO

THE GLEN WORKSHOP. St. John's College/Santa Fe; July 26-August 7, 2009 (tentative). Includes fiction, poetry, nonfiction, memoir, on-site landscape painting, figure drawing, collage and mixed media, and several master classes. Contact: Julie Mullins, St. John's College, 1160 Camino Cruz Blanca, Santa Fe NM 87505-4599. (206)281-2988 (*Image*). Fax (206)281-2335 (*Image*). E-mail: image@imagejournal.org. Website: www.imagejournal

.org/page/events/the-glen-workshop. Offers an advanced track. Two *Image* editors; no agents in attendance. Offers full and partial scholarships. Attendance: 200.

GLORIETA CHRISTIAN WRITERS' CONFERENCE. Glorieta (18 mile N. of Santa Fe); October 14-18, 2009; October 13-17, 2010. Editors and agents in attendance. Contact: Marita Littauer, 2201 San Pedro Dr. N.E., Bldg 1, Ste. 225, Albuquerque, NM 87176. Toll-free (800)433-6633. (505) 899-4283. Fax (505)899-9282. E-mail: classrvcs@aol.com. Website: www.glorietachristian writersconference.com. Editors and agents in attendance. Partial scholarships. Attendance: 400.

SOUTHWEST WRITERS MINI WORKSHOPS. Albuquerque; various times during the year (check Website for dates). Contact: Wendy Bickel, 3721 Morris St. N.E., Ste. A, Albuquerque NM 87111-3611. (505)265-9485. E-mail: swwriters@juno.com. Website: www.south westwriters.com. General conference. Sponsors the Southwest Writers Contests annually and monthly (see Website). Agents and editors in attendance. Attendance: 50.

NEW YORK

ANNUAL INTERNATIONAL CONFERENCE ON HUMOR, HOPE AND HEALING. Saratoga Springs; June 2009. General. Contact: The HUMOR Project Inc., 480 Broadway, Ste. 210, Saratoga Springs NY 12866. (518)587-8770. Toll-free fax (800)600-4242. E-mail: info@ humorproject.com. Website: www.humorproject.com.

NORTH CAROLINA

AMERICAN CHRISTIAN WRITERS GREENSBORO CONFERENCE. Holiday Inn; March 21, 2009. Contact: Reg Forder, Box 110390, Nashville TN 37222. Toll-free (800)21-WRITE. E-mail: ACWriters@aol.com. Website: www.ACWriters.com. Attendance: 40-80.

AMERICAN CHRISTIAN WRITERS GREENSBORO CONFERENCE. March 14, 2009. Contact: Reg A. Forder, Box 110390, Nashville TN 37222. Toll-free (800)21-WRITE. E-mail: AC Writers@aol.com. Website: www.ACWriters.com. Attendance: 40-80.

BLUE RIDGE MOUNTAIN CHRISTIAN WRITERS CONFERENCE. LifeWay Ridgecrest Conference Center; May 17-21, 2009. Contact: Alton Gansky, 9983 Rose Dr., Oak Hills CA 92344-0220. (760)949-8075. E-mail: alton@altongansky.com, or Yvonne Lehman, PO Box 188, Black Mountain NC 28770. Website: www.brmcwc.com. Offers track for advanced writers. Editors and agents in attendance. Sponsors a contest. Full & partial scholarships. Attendance: 350-400.

SHE SPEAKS CONFERENCE. Concord; June 26-28, 2009 (usually 3rd weekend). Contact: LeAnn Rice, Proverbs 31 Ministries, 616-G Matthews-Mint Hill Rd., Matthews NC 28105. (704)849-2270. Fax (704)849-7267. E-mail: office@Proverbs31.org. Website: www.She SpeaksConference.com. Offers a track for teens. Speakers include: Lysa TerKeurst, Renee Swope, and acquisitions editors from major publishing houses. Editors & agents in attendance. Attendance: 550.

OHIO

AMERICAN CHRISTIAN WRITERS COLUMBUS CONFERENCE. June 12-13, 2009; June 4-5, 2010. Hosted by Columbus Christian Writers Assn./Pat Zell, (937)593-9207. Contact: Reg Forder, Box 110390, Nashville TN 37222. Toll-free (800)21-WRITE. E-mail: ACWriters@ aol.com. Website: www.ACWriters.com. Attendance: 40-80.

AMERICAN CHRISTIAN WRITERS DAYTON CONFERENCE. August 8, 2009. Contact: Reg A. Forder, Box 110390, Nashville TN 37222. Toll-free (800)21-WRITE. E-mail: ACWriters@ aol.com. Website: www.ACWriters.com. Attendance: 40-80.

DAYTON CHRISTIAN WRITERS GUILD CONFERENCE. Dayton; June 2009. Contact: Tina V. Toles, PO Box 251, Englewood OH 45322-2227. Phone/fax (937)836-6600. Cell: (937)371-6083. E-mail: daytonwriters@ureach.com. Website: www.daytonchristianwriters .com. Attendance 30-80.

NORTHWEST OHIO CHRISTIAN WRITERS ONE-DAY SEMINAR. Toledo; September 2009 (3rd or 4th Saturday). Contact: Kathy Douglas. E-mail: mlka@toast.net. Attendance: 50.

+NORTHWEST OHIO CHRISTIAN WRITERS SPRING TWO-DAY RETREAT. Lial Retreat Center/Whitehouse; May 1-2, 2009. Contact: Kathy Douglas. E-mail: mlka@toast.net. Advance registration required. Attendance: limited to 20.

PEN TO PAPER LITERARY SYMPOSIUM. Dayton; October 2-3, 2009; October 1-2, 2010. Contact: Valerie L. Coleman, Pen of the Writer, PMB 175—5523 Salem Ave., Dayton OH 45426. (937)307-0760. Fax (515)474-3643. E-mail: info@penofthewriter.com. Website: www .penofthewriter.com/pentopaper. Editors and agents in attendance. For Power Awards contest details, go to: www.penofthewriter.com/awards.

WRITE ON! WORKSHOP. Dayton; March 28, 2009; March 27, 2010. Contact: Valerie Coleman, Pen of the Writer, PMB 175—5523 Salem Ave., Dayton OH 45426. (937)307-0760. Fax (515)474-3643. E-mail: info@penofthewriter.com. Website: www.penofthewriter.com/ WriteOn. Speakers: Valerie Coleman & Wendy Beckman. Editors in attendance. Full and partial scholarships. Attendance: 50.

OKLAHOMA

AMERICAN CHRISTIAN WRITERS OKLAHOMA CITY CONFERENCE. La Quinta Hotel; February 20-21, 2009; March 19-20, 2010. Contact: Reg Forder, Box 110390, Nashville TN 37222. Toll-free (800)21-WRITE. E-mail: ACWriters@aol.com. Website: www.ACWriters .com. Attendance: 40-80.

OREGON

HEART TALK. A workshop for people beginning to speak or write for publication. Portland/Western Seminary; March 14, 2009 (writing). Speaker: Robin Jones Gunn. Contact: Women's Center for Ministry, Western Seminary, 5511 S.E. Hawthorne Blvd., Portland OR 97215-3367. (503)517-1931. Fax (503)517-1889. E-mail: wcm@westernseminary.edu. Website: www.westernseminary.edu/women. Beverly Hislop, exec. dir. of Women's Center for Ministry. Attendance: 125. Offers partial scholarships based on need. Conference alternates between writing one year and speaking the next. Workshops and editors/publicists available for consultation. Check Website for details.

OREGON CHRISTIAN WRITERS COACHING CONFERENCE. Portland/Salem area; July 27-30, 2009. Website: www.OregonChristianWriters.org. Includes about 7 hours of training under a specific coach/topic. Offers advanced track. Editors and agents in attendance. Attendance: 250.

PENNSYLVANIA

GREATER PHILADELPHIA CHRISTIAN WRITERS' CONFERENCE. Philadelphia Biblical University, Langhorne; August 6-8, 2009 (tentative). Founder and director: Marlene Bagnull, LittD, 316 Blanchard Rd., Drexel Hill, PA 19026-3507. Phone/fax (610)626-6833. E-mail: mbagnull@aol.com. Website: www.writehisanswer.com/Philadelphia. Conferees choose six hour-long workshops from 42 offered or a Fiction or Nonfiction Clinic (by application) plus one 6.5-hour continuing session from 7 offered. One-on-one appointments, paid critiques, editors panels, and general sessions. Contest (registered conferees only) awards four $100 discounts off 2010 conference. Especially encourages African American writers. Faculty of 50-60 authors, editors, and agents. Attendance: 250.

HIGHLIGHTS FOUNDATION FOUNDERS WORKSHOPS. Honesdale; February-December 2009. Contact: Kent Brown, Highlights Foundation, 814 Court St., Honesdale PA 18431. (570)253-1192. Fax (570)253-0179. E-mail: contact@highlightsfoundation.org. Website: www.HighlightsFoundation.org. Editors and agents in attendance. Modest grants may be available. For children's writers. Targeted workshops that allow you to select a topic that fits your writing needs—from sports to nature, from magazine to books, from fiction to nonfiction, and from picture books to young adult novels. Offers a track for advanced writers. General.

HIGHLIGHTS FOUNDATION WRITERS WORKSHOP AT CHAUTAUQUA. July 11-18, 2009. Contact: Kent Brown, Highlights Foundation, 814 Court St., Honesdale PA 18431. (570)253-1192. Fax (570)253-0179. E-mail: contact@highlightsfoundation.org. Website: www.highlightsfoundation.org. For children's writers and illustrators. Week-long conference. Offers an advanced track. Offers full and partial scholarships (applications received through January 2009). Editors and agents in attendance. General.

MERCER COUNTY ANNUAL ONE-DAY WRITERS' WORKSHOP (sponsored by St. Davids Writers' Conference); Stoneboro; April 25, 2009. Contact: Evelyn Minshull, 724 Airport Rd., Mercer PA 16137, (724)475-3239, eminshull@hotmail.com; or Gloria Clover, 26 Everbreeze Dr., Hadley PA 16130, (724)253-2635; gloworm@certainty.net. Websites: www.gloriaclover.com; www.stdavidswriters.com. Occasionally has editors or agents in attendance. Sponsors a contest. No scholarships. Attendance: 120.

MONTROSE CHRISTIAN WRITERS CONFERENCE. Montrose; July 25-31, 2009; July 25-30, 2010. Contact: Patti Souder, c/o Montrose Bible Conference, 5 Locust St., Montrose PA 18801-1112. Toll-free (800)598-5030. (570)278-1001. Fax (570)278-3061. E-mail: mbc@montrosebible.org. Website: www.montrosebible.org. Tracks for advanced writers and teens. Editors & agents in attendance. Attendance: 100. Provides a few partial scholarships.

ST. DAVIDS CHRISTIAN WRITERS' CONFERENCE. Grove City College, Grove City; June 22-27, 2009. Offers writer's retreat. Contest in 10 categories for attendees only. Lora Zill, director. Contact: Audrey Stallsmith, registrar, 87 Pines Rd. E., Hadley PA 16130-1019. (724)253-2738. Fax (724)946-3689. E-mail: registrar@stdavidswriters.com. Website: www.stdavids writers.com. Attendance: 70.

SUSQUEHANNA VALLEY WRITERS WORKSHOP. Lewisburg; October 2-3, 2009. Contact: Marsha Hubler. (570)837-0002. E-mail: ckwriter@evenlink.com. Website: www.marsha hubler.com. Editors/agents in attendance.

WEST BRANCH CHRISTIAN WRITERS MINI-CONFERENCE. Montoursville; October 2009. Contact: Roberta Updegraff, 332 S. Pine Run Rd., Linden PA 17744. (570)584-2280. E-mail: bobbiup@suscom.net. Editors in attendance. Classes geared for beginners, but includes classes for more experienced. Also sponsors a contest (personal essay, poetry, nonfiction, devotional). Attendance: 90.

TENNESSEE

AMERICAN CHRISTIAN WRITERS MEMPHIS CONFERENCE. First Baptist Church; May 15-16, 2009; April 30-May 1, 2010. Contact: Reg A. Forder, Box 110390, Nashville TN 37222. Toll-free (800)21-WRITE. E-mail: ACWriters@aol.com. Website: www.ACWriters.com. Attendance: 40-80.

AMERICAN CHRISTIAN WRITERS NASHVILLE MENTORING RETREAT. Radisson Opryland Hotel; April 17-18, 2009; April 9-10, 2010. Contact: Reg Forder, Box 110390, Nashville TN 37222. Toll-free (800)21-WRITE. E-mail: ACWriters@aol.com. Website: www.ACWriters.com. Attendance: 40-80.

COLLEGIATE JOURNALISM CONFERENCE. Nashville; October 2009 (usually 1st or 2nd weekend). Contact: Kimberly Allen, (615)782-8664. E-mail: Kallen@sbc.net. Website: www.bp news.net/journalism. Attendance: 120-150.

TEXAS

AMERICAN CHRISTIAN WRITERS DALLAS CONFERENCE. La Quinta Arlington; February 27-28, 2009; March 12-13, 2010. Contact: Reg Forder, Box 110390, Nashville TN 37222. Toll-free (800)21-WRITE. E-mail: ACWriters@aol.com. Website: www.ACWriters.com. Attendance: 40-80.

AMERICAN CHRISTIAN WRITERS HOUSTON CONFERENCE. February 14, 2009. Contact: Reg Forder, Box 110390, Nashville TN 37222. Toll-free (800)21-WRITE. E-mail: ACWriters@ aol.com. Website: www.ACWriters.com. Attendance: 40-80.

EAST TEXAS CHRISTIAN WRITERS CONFERENCE. Marshall; June 5-6, 2009; June 4-5, 2010 (1st Friday & Saturday of June annually). Contact: Dr. Jerry Hopkins, East Texas Baptist University, 1209 N. Grove St., Marshall TX 75670. (903)923-2083. Fax (903)923-2077. E-mail: Jhopkins@ETBU.edu. Website: www.ETBU.edu/news/CWC/default.htm. Speaker 2009: Cecil Murphey. Offers an advanced track; contest. Editors & agents in attendance. Partial scholarships for students only. Attendance: 200.

ECPA CHRISTIAN BOOK EXPO DALLAS 2009. Dallas; March 20-22, 2009. This event, a first for the Evangelical Christian Publishers Association, will bring together publishers, authors, and consumers. ECPA is inviting publishers, ministries, authors, and booksellers to exhibit in this open-to-the-public event. For more information, contact Mark Kuyper, (480)966-3998.

INSPIRATIONAL WRITERS ALIVE!/AMARILLO SEMINAR. April 18, 2009 (tentative/usually the first Saturday after Easter). Contact: Jerry McClenagan, 6808 Cloud Crest, Amarillo TX 79124. (806)355-7117. E-mail: jerrydalemc@sbcglobal.net (preferred contact). Attendance: 50. Sponsors an annual contest.

NORTH TEXAS CHRISTIAN WRITERS' CONFERENCE. Keller; September 11-12, 2009; September 10-11, 2010 (second Friday & Saturday after Labor Day). Contact: Frank Ball, NTCW Conference, Cross Timbers Community Church Keller Campus, 2525 Florence Rd., Keller TX 76262. (817)915-2597. E-mail: info@ntchristianwriters.com. Website: www.ntchristian writers.com. No editors or agents in attendance. Offers partial scholarships. Sponsors a contest for conference registrants only. Attendance: 250.

TEXAS CHRISTIAN WRITERS CONFERENCE. Houston; August 1, 2009; August 7, 2010. Contact: Martha Rogers, 6038 Greenmont, Houston TX 77092-2332. (713)686-7209. E-mail: marthalrogers@sbcglobal.net. Website: www.martharogers.com. Editors & agents in attendance. Sponsors a contest: Inspirational Writers Alive! Open competition; May 15 deadline. Attendance: 70. If you want to start another group in Texas, contact Martha Rogers.

YWAM HANDS-ON SCHOOL OF WRITING AND WRITERS TRAINING WORKSHOPS. Lindale; September-December 2009. Contact: Carol Scott, 15186 CR 440, Lindale TX 75771. (903)882-9663. Fax (903)882-1161. E-mail: contactus@ywamwoodcrest.com, or through Website: www.ywamwoodcrest.com. List of workshops on Website or for SASE. Attendance: 10-20.

UTAH

AMERICAN CHRISTIAN WRITERS SALT LAKE CITY CONFERENCE. September 19, 2009. Contact: Reg Forder, Box 110390, Nashville TN 37222. Toll-free (800)21-WRITE. E-mail: ACWriters@aol.com. Website: www.ACWriters.com. Attendance: 40-80.

+UTAH CHRISTIAN WRITERS' CONFERENCE. Bluffdale; fall 2009. Contact: Julie Scott, PO Box 3, Bountiful UT 84011-0003. (801)294-5485. E-mail: julie.compelled2Tell@mac.com. Website: www.utahchristianwriters.com. Speaker: Virginia Smith. ACW Chapter.

VIRGINIA

+NATIONAL CHRISTIAN WRITERS CONFERENCE. Norfolk; February 2009. Contact: Antonio L. Crawford, PO Box 415, Highland Springs VA 23075. (804)998-8014. Fax (804)594-3668. E-mail: ncwcbe@yahoo.com. Website: www.nationalchristianwritersconference.com.

+PENINSULA CHRISTIAN WRITERS ANNUAL WORKSHOP. Yorktown; spring (no date set). Contact: Yvonne Ortega, PO Box 955, Yorktown VA 23692. E-mail: yvonne@yvonne ortega.com.

+RICHMOND CHRISTIANS WHO WRITE CONFERENCE. Contact: Rev. Thomas C. Lacy, 12114 Walnut Hill Dr., Rockville VA 23146-1854. (804)749-4050. Fax (804)749-4939. E-mail: RichmondCWW@aol.com. Blog: http://rcww.blogspot.com. October 16-17, 2009. Speaker: Karen Whiting.

WASHINGTON

AMERICAN CHRISTIAN WRITERS SPOKANE CONFERENCE. September 25-26, 2009; September 24-25, 2010. Contact: Reg Forder, Box 110390, Nashville TN 37222. Toll-free (800)21-WRITE. E-mail: ACWriters@aol.com. Website: www.ACWriters.com. Attendance: 40-80.

IMAGE FESTIVAL OF LITERATURE AND THE ARTS. No conference scheduled for 2009. Contact: Julie Mullins, Program Director, Image, 3307 Third Ave. W., Seattle WA 98119. (206)281-2988. Fax (206)281-2335. E-mail: Image@imagejournal.org. Website: www.imagejournal.org.

NORTHWEST CHRISTIAN WRITERS RENEWAL. Bothell; May 1-2, 2009. Contact: Judy Bodmer, 11108 NE 141 Pl., Kirkland WA 98034. (425)488-2900. E-mail: jbodmer@msn.com. Website: www.nwchristianwriters.org. Speaker: Dennis Hensley. Editors and agents in attendance. Offers full scholarships. Attendance: 165.

WRITER'S WEEKEND AT THE BEACH. Ocean Park; February 2009. Contact: Birdie Etchison/Pat Rushford, PO Box 877, Ocean Park WA 98640-0877. (360)665-6576. E-mail: etchi son@reachone.com or prushford@comcast.net. Website: www.patriciarushford.com. (Registration form on Website.) Critiques and one-on-one time. Offers discounts for students. Attendance: 40-50.

WISCONSIN

GREEN LAKE CHRISTIAN WRITER'S CONFERENCE. Green Lake; August 23-28, 2009; August 22-27, 2010. Contact: Jan White or Sharon Young, Green Lake Conference Center, W2511 State Rd. 23, Green Lake WI 54941-9599. Toll-free (800)558-8898. (920)294-7327. Fax (920)294-3848. E-mail for information: janwhite@glcc.org. Website: www.glcc.org. Has editors in attendance. Offers partial scholarships. Sponsors a contest for conference attendees only. Attendance: 40-80.

LIGHTHOUSE CHRISTIAN WRITERS FALL SEMINAR. Oconto; no conference planned for now. Contact: Lois Wiederhoeft, 901 Aubin, PO Box 42, Peshtigo WI 54157. (715)582-1024. E-mail: 2loisann@myway.com. Website: www.mychristiansite.com/ministries/lhchristian writers/fall.html.

CANADA/FOREIGN

AMERICAN CHRISTIAN WRITERS CARIBBEAN CRUISE. November 28-December 5, 2009; November 29-November 5, 2010. Contact: Reg A. Forder, Box 110390, Nashville TN 37222. Toll-free (800)21-WRITE. E-mail: ACWriters@aol.com. Website: www.ACWriters.com. Attendance: 15-30.

ASSOCIATION OF CHRISTIAN WRITERS (UK) MEMBERS CONFERENCE. Hoddesdon, Herts UK. Contact: Brian Vincent, dir., 23 Moor End Ln., Thame Oxon, OX9 3BQ, United Kingdom. Phone 01823-442 372. E-mail through Website: www.christianwriters.org.uk. Membership (900) open. Sponsors an occasional writers' weekend for members only. Next one in June 2009. Editors in attendance; no agents. No scholarships.

COMIX35 CHRISTIAN COMICS TRAINING SEMINAR. Various international locations & dates. Contact: Nate Butler, PO Box 4458, Albuquerque NM 87196-4458. E-mail: comix35@comix35.org. Website: www.comix35.org. Speakers: Nate Butler & others. Sometimes has editors/agents in attendance. Attendance: 15-20. Sponsors a contest (details on Website).

CRUISIN' FOR CHRIST. Caribbean cruise; 2010. Contact: Kendra Norman-Bellamy (blessed_to_write@yahoo.com) E-mail: Cruisin_For_Christ@yahoo.com. Writing workshops on board.

INSCRIBE CHRISTIAN WRITERS' FELLOWSHIP FALL CONFERENCE. Edmonton AB, Canada; September 2009. Contact: Eunice Matchett, 4304—45th St., Drayton Valley AB T7A 1G7, Canada. (780)542-7950. Fax (780)514-3702. E-mail: query@inscribe.org. Website: www.inscribe.org (click on "Events"). Some editors in attendance, no agents. Sponsors a fall contest open to nonmembers; details on Website. Attendance: 50+.

+ISRAEL TOUR FOR CHRISTIAN WRITERS. February 8-17, 2010. American Christian Writers. Contact: Reg A. Forder, Box 110390, Nashville TN 37222. Toll-free (800)21-WRITE. E-mail: ACWriters@aol.com. Website: www.ACWriters.com. Attendance: 15-30.

LITTWORLD 2009 CONFERENCE. Nairobi, Kenya; November 1-6, 2009. Contact: John D. Maust, director, 351 S. Main Pl., Ste. 230, Carol Stream IL 60188-2455. (630)260-9063. Fax (630)260-9265. E-mail: MaiLittWorld@sbcglobal.net. Website: www.littworld.org. Sponsors a contest. Editors in attendance. Offers partial scholarships. Attendance: 200 from 40 countries.

WRITE! CANADA. Guelph, Ontario; June 18-20, 2009. Contact: N.J. Lindquist, The Word Guild, 698A Highpoint Ave., Waterloo ON N2V 1G9, Canada. (519)886-4196. E-mail: info@ thewordguild.com. Website: www.thewordguild.com. Hosted by The Word Guild, an association of Canadian writers and editors who are Christian. Offers an advanced track. Editors and agents in attendance. Contests for attendees. Offers full & partial scholarships. Attendance: 250. Also sponsors one-day conferences in various Canadian cities.

CONFERENCES THAT CHANGE LOCATIONS

ACFW NATIONAL CONFERENCE. Location varies; September 2009 (usually third week). Contact: ACFW Conference Committee, PO Box 101066, Palm Bay FL 32910-1066. (574)370-0988. E-mail: pr@acfw.com. Website: www.acfw.com. Offers advanced track. Contest. Editors & agents in attendance. Attendance: 400.

ACT ONE: SCREENWRITING WEEKENDS. Two-day workshops; see Website for dates and locations. Contact: Conference Coordinator, 2690 Beachwood Dr., Lower Fl., Hollywood CA 90068. (323)464-0815. Fax (323)468-0315. E-mail: info@ActOneProgram.com. Website: www.ActOneprogram.com. Open to anyone who is interested in learning more about the craft of screenwriting. Speakers vary: Sheryl Anderson, Thom Parham, Dean Batali, Chris & Kathy Riley. No editors or agents in attendance. Attendance: 75.

AMERICAN CHRISTIAN FICTION WRITERS CONFERENCE. Rotates cities; Denver, September (3rd weekend) 2009. Contact: Robin Miller, pres., PO Box 101066, Palm Bay FL 32910-1066. E-mail: pr@acfw.com. Website: www.ACFW.com. Offers a track for published writers. Editors and agents in attendance. Sponsors 2 contests (details on Website). Offers scholarships each year to ACFW members only.

AMERICAN CHRISTIAN WRITERS CONFERENCES. Various dates and locations (see individual states where held). Also sponsors an annual Caribbean cruise in November/December. Contact: Reg A. Forder, Box 110390, Nashville TN 37222. Toll-free (800)21-WRITE. E-mail: ACWriters@aol.com. Website: www.ACWriters.com. Attendance 30-40.

AUTHORIZEME. Various locations and dates. Contact: Sharon Norris Elliott, PO Box 1519, Inglewood CA 90308-1519. (310)508-9860. Fax (323)567-8557. E-mail: Authorize Me@sbcglobal.net. Website: www.AuthorizeMe.net. AuthorizeMe is a 12-hour, hands-on seminar that teaches you how to get your book idea out of your head, down onto paper, and into a professional book proposal. Seminars offered nationwide. For a list of scheduled seminars, or to sponsor a seminar in your area, check Website. Offers full & partial scholarships. Attendance: 5-50.

CATHOLIC MEDIA CONVENTION. Anaheim, CA; May 27-29, 2009. Contact: Thomas Conway, exec. dir., 205 W. Monroe St., Chicago IL 60606-5013. (312)380-6789. Fax (312)361-0256. E-mail: TConway@catholicpress.com. Website: www.catholicmediaconvention.org. For media professionals. Editors/agents in attendance. Partial scholarships. Annual book awards. Attendance: 550.

CHILDREN'S AUTHORS' BOOTCAMPS. Held in several locations each year; various dates. General. Contact: Bootcamp c/o Linda Arms White, PO Box 231, Allenspark CO 80510. Phone/fax (303)747-1014. E-mail: CABootcamp@msn.com. Website: www.WeMakeWriters.com. Upcoming dates and details on Website.

CHRISTIAN LEADERS AND SPEAKERS SEMINARS (The CLASSeminar). Sponsors several seminars across the country each year. Check Website for CLASSeminar dates and locations. For anyone who wants to improve their communication skills for either the spoken or written word, for professional or personal reasons. Speakers: Florence Littauer and Marita Littauer. Contact: Marita Littauer, 2201 San Pedro Dr. N.E., Bldg. 1, Ste. 225, Albuquerque, NM 87110-4133. (505)899-4283. Fax (505)899-9282. E-mail: info@classervices.com. Website: www.classervices.com. Attendance: 75-100.

EVANGELICAL PRESS ASSOCIATION CONVENTION. (Held in a different location each year); Indianapolis IN, May 6-8, 2009. Contact: Doug Trouten, dir., PO Box 28129, Crystal MN 55428. (763)535-4793. Fax (763)535-4794. E-mail: director@epassoc.org. Website: www.epassoc.org. Attendance: 300-400. Annual convention for editors of evangelical periodicals; freelance communicators welcome. This will be a joint meeting with the Associated Church Press for the first time in 20 years.

THE EXPERTIZING WORKSHOP. Held in Boston, New York, and San Francisco; every 3 mos. (October, January, April, July). Contact: Alyza Harris, Expertizing.com, PO Box 590239, Newton MA 02459. (617)630-0945. E-mail: alyza@PublishingGame.com. Website: www.Expertizing.com, or www.Expertizing.com/forum.htm. Learn how to get more media attention for your book and business. Speaker: Fern Reiss. Attendance: Limited to 6.

FAITHWRITERS CONFERENCE. Contact: Scott Lindsay. Website: www.faithwriters.com/conference.php. This conference was cancelled in 2008, so check Website for future conference plans.

INTERNATIONAL CHRISTIAN RETAIL SHOW. Denver CO (held in a different location each year); July 12-16, 2009. Contact: CBA, Box 62000, Colorado Springs CO 80962-2000. Toll-free (800)252-1950. (719)265-9895. Website: www.cbaonline.org. Entrance badges available through book publishers or Christian bookstores. Attendance: 8,000.

JERRY B. JENKINS CHRISTIAN WRITERS GUILD. PO Box 88196, Black Forest CO 80908. Toll-free (866)495-5177. Fax (719)495-5181. E-mail: contactus@christianwriters guild.com. Website: www.christianwritersguild.com. Owned by Jerry B. Jenkins, author of the Left Behind series. Students enrolled in correspondence courses are personally mentored by seasoned professional writers or editors. The Guild also offers annual memberships, a critique service, associated benefits (advocacy, supplemental insurance, etc.), conferences, and contests. Call for a Free Starter Kit.

+MUSE ONLINE WRITERS CONFERENCE. Website: www.freewebs.com/themuseonlinewriters conference. Contact: Lea Schizas. E-mail: museitupeditor@yahoo.ca. This is a free online conference. Check Website for upcoming conferences.

+NEW ENGLAND CHRISTIAN WRITERS CONFERENCE. Location to be announced; fall 2009. Contact: Lauren Yarger, exec. dir./producer, Masterworks Productions, Inc., 2 Long Lott Rd., West Granby CT 06090. (860)658-7733. E-mail: masterworkproductions@yahoo.com. Website: www.masterworkproductions.org.

+ONE-DAY INTENSIVES WITH CECIL MURPHEY. Various dates & locations. Contact: Cecil Murphey, 4297 Tucker North Ct., Tucker GA 30084-3632. (678)694-1111. E-mail: cec_ haraka@msn.com. Participants must have a manuscript in process and a laptop computer with a USB port. Limited to 5 students.

THE PUBLISHING GAME WORKSHOP. Various cities throughout the year (check Website for dates and locations). Workshops held every 3 mos. (September, December, March, and June). Contact: Alyza Harris, Peanut Butter and Jelly Press, PO Box 590239, Newton MA 02459. Phone/fax (617)630-0945. E-mail: info@PublishingGame.com, or Alyza@ publishinggame.com. Website: www.PublishingGame.com (dates, locations, and registration forms on Website). Speaker: Fern Reiss. Editors and agents in attendance. Attendance: limited to 18.

+SPAN'S SMALL PUBLISHERS MARKETING CONFERENCE. Sponsored by the Small Publishers Assn. of North America. A marketing-specific, information-packed conference for authors, self-publishers, and independent presses. Contact: Scott Flora, 1618 W. Colorado Ave., Colorado Springs CO 80904-4029. (719)475-1726. Fax (719)471-2182. E-mail: scott@spannet.org. Website: www.SPANnet.org/conference.htm. Check Website to see if being held during 2009.

"WRITE HIS ANSWER" SEMINARS & RETREATS. Various locations around U.S.; dates throughout the year; a choice of focus on periodicals or books (includes self-publishing or mastering the craft). Contact: Marlene Bagnull, LittD, 316 Blanchard Rd., Drexel Hill PA 19026-3507. Phone/fax (610)626-6833. E-mail: mbagnull@aol.com. Website: www.write hisanswer.com/Writing_Seminars.htm. Attendance: 20-60. One- and two-day seminars by the author of *Write His Answer: A Bible Study for Christian Writers.*

+WRITER'S NUDGE WORKSHOPS. Various locations & dates. Contact: Mary Busha, 1370-B Deerfield Rd., Lebanon OH 45036. (513)228-1205. E-mail: marybusha@writersnudge .com. Website: www.writersnudge.com.

AREA CHRISTIAN WRITERS' CLUBS, FELLOWSHIP GROUPS, AND CRITIQUE GROUPS

(*) An asterisk before a listing means the information was not verified or updated by the group leader.
(+) A plus sign before a listing indicates a new listing.

ALABAMA

CHRISTIAN FREELANCERS. Tuscaloosa. Contact: Joanne Sloan, 4195 Waldort Dr., Northport AL 35473. (205)333-8603. E-mail: cjosloan@bellsouth.net. Membership (25) open.

ARIZONA

EAST VALLEY CHRISTIAN WRITERS. Mesa. Contact: Brenda Jackson, 519 E. 8th Ave., Mesa AZ 85204. E-mail: BrendaAtTheRanch@yahoo.com. Membership (5) open.
FOUNTAIN HILLS CHRISTIAN WRITERS GROUP. Contact: Jewell Johnson, 14223 N. Westminster Pl., Fountain Hills AZ 85268. (480)836-8968. E-mail: tykeJ@juno.com. Membership (7-16) open. ACW Chapter.

ARKANSAS

LITTLE ROCK ACW CHAPTER. Contact: Carole Geckle, 5800 Ranch Dr., Little Rock AR 72223. (501)228-2477. Fax (501)224-2529. E-mail: cgeckle@familylife.com. Membership (25) open. Sponsors a contest open to nonmembers if they have attended before.
SILOAM SPRINGS WRITERS. Contact: Margaret Weathers, 716 W. University St., Siloam Springs AR 72761. (479)524-6598. E-mail: Rosie1st2000@yahoo.com. Membership (28) open. Periodically sponsors a contest open to nonmembers, and a seminar in September.

CALIFORNIA

BAY AREA WRITERS CRITIQUE GROUP. Fremont. Contact: Carol Hall, 35665 Gleason Ln., Fremont CA 94536. (510)791-790-0318. E-mail: cahall@rocketmail.com. Membership (5-6) open to experienced writers only.
CASTRO VALLEY CHRISTIAN WRITERS GROUP. Contact: Pastor Jon Drury, 19300 Redwood Rd., Castro Valley CA 94546-3465. (510)886-6300. E-mail: jdrury@redwoodchapel.org. Website: www.christianwriter.org. Membership (10) open. Sponsoring a Christian Writers Seminar, February 2009.
CHINO VALLEY CHRISTIAN WRITERS CRITIQUE GROUP. Chino Hills. Contact: Nancy I. Sanders, 6361 Prescott Ct., Chino CA 91710-7105. (909)590-0226. E-mail: jeffandnancys@gmail.com. Website: www.nancyisanders.com. Membership (15) open.
CHRISTIAN WRITERS GUILD OF SANTA BARBARA. Contact: Opal Mae Dailey, (805)682-0316/(805)252-9822. E-mail: opalmaedailey@aol.com, or cwfsb@sbcglobal.net. Meets monthly. Membership open.
CHRISTIAN WRITERS NETWORK. Paradise (near Chico). Contact Director: Cornelia O'Kirwan (530)872-8259/connie6656@att.net; or Co-director: Barbara Larsen (530)872-5119/RLarsen307@comcast.net. Membership open.
HIGH DESERT CHRISTIAN WRITERS GUILD. Quartz Hill. Contact: Don Patterson, 6223 Almond Valley Way, Quartz Hill CA 93536. (661)722-5695. E-mail: don@theology.edu. Website: www.theology.edu/writers. Membership (30) open. Presents the Sable Quill-Pacesetter

Award each year to the writer in the group who has shown the most progress or professional achievement. Cosponsors the Antelope Valley Christian Writers Conference, May 2009.

NOVEL IDEA CHRISTIAN WRITERS SWARM. Norwalk/Cerritos. Contact: Derrell B. Thomas, 11239½ Ferina St., Norwalk CA 90650-5507. (562)292-9997. E-mail: derrell.writer@gmail .com. Membership (15) open.

ORANGE COUNTY CHRISTIAN WRITERS FELLOWSHIP. Various groups meeting throughout the county. Contact: Peggy Matthews Rose (editor@occwf.org) or write OCCWF, PO Box 982, Lake Forest CA 92630. Membership (190) open. Annual membership includes a bimonthly newsletter, information on local critique groups, advance notice of writing opportunities through an e-mail list, and reduced fees for annual Spring Writer's Day (usually on a Saturday in April; see Website for details). Conference includes keynote speakers, workshops, and consultations. See Website for details: www.occwf.org.

PEGGY LESLIE'S CRITIQUE GROUP/SAN DIEGO CHRISTIAN WRITERS GUILD. El Cajon. Contact: Peggy Leslie, 329 Quail Run, El Cajon CA 92019. (619)447-6258. E-mail: gnp leslie@cox.net. Website: www.sandiegocwg.org. Membership (6) open.

SACRAMENTO CHRISTIAN WRITERS. Citrus Heights. Contact: Beth Miller Self, 2012 Rushing River Ct., Elverta CA 95626-9756. (916)992-8709. E-mail: cwbself@msn.com. Website: www.scwriters.org. Membership (25) open. Sponsors a contest for members. Sponsors a seminar every 5 years; the next one, in 2010, will be their 30th anniversary as a group.

SAN DIEGO COUNTY CHRISTIAN WRITERS' GUILD. Contact: Jennie & Bob Gillespie, PO Box 270403, San Diego CA 92198. (760)294-3269. E-mail: info@sandiegocwg.org. Website: www.sandiegocwg.org. Membership (200) open. To join their Internet newsgroup, e-mail your name and address to: info@sandiegocwg.com. Sponsors 10 critique groups, fall seminar (September 2009), and spring awards banquet.

SANTA CLARA VALLEY CHRISTIAN WRITER'S GROUP. Cupertino. Contact: Richard M. Hinz, 550 S. 4th St., Apt. E, San Jose CA 95112, (408)297-3336, Rickhinz@yahoo.com. Or, Bob Schaetzle, (408)739-9516, heb_6@hotmail.com. Membership (14) open.

S.C.U.M. San Leandro. Contact: John B. Olson, 1261 Estrudillo Ave., San Leandro CA 94577. (510)357-4441. E-mail: johno@litany.com. Membership (12) open. Fiction writers only.

SECRET GARDEN WRITERS GROUP. Castro Valley CA. Contact: Susy Flory. (510)828-5360. E-mail: irishbreakfast@comcast.net. Membership (8) open.

SOUTH VALLEY CHRISTIAN WRITERS/ACW CHAPTER. Group connects by e-mail only. Contact: Mary E. Kirk, 4446 Rockcrest Dr., Fairfax VA 22032-1822. E-mail: mkirk81@sbcglobal.net.

TEMECULA CHRISTIAN WRITERS CRITIQUE GROUP. Contact: Rebecca Farnbach, 41403 Bitter Creek Ct., Temecula CA 92591-1545. (951)699-5148. Fax (951)699-4208. E-mail: sunbrook@hotmail.com. Membership (12) open. Part of San Diego Christian Writers Guild.

WORDSMITHS (Professional Christian writers). Montclair. Contact: Nancy I. Sanders, 6361 Prescott Ct., Chino CA 91710-7105. (909)590-0226. E-mail: jeffandnancys@gmail.com. Website: www.wordsmiths8.wordpress.com. Membership (8) not open (contact for membership information).

THE WRITE BUNCH. Stockton. Contact: Shirley Cook, 3123 Sheridan Way, Stockton CA 95219-3724. (209)477-8375. E-mail: shirleymcp@sbcglobal.net. Membership (7) not currently open.

COLORADO

WORDS FOR THE JOURNEY CHRISTIAN WRITERS GUILD/ROCKY MOUNTAIN REGION. Parker. Contact: Michele Cushatt. E-mail: michelle@MicheleCushatt.com. Website: www .wordsforthejourney.org, and www.wftj.blogspot.com. Membership (100+) open. See separate listing for Texas region.

DELAWARE

DELMARVA CHRISTIAN WRITERS' FELLOWSHIP. Georgetown. Contact: Candy Abbott, PO Box 777, Georgetown DE 19947-0777. (302)856-6649. Fax (302)856-7742. E-mail: candy .abbott@verizon.net. Website: www.delmarvawriters.com. Membership (20+) open.

FLORIDA

ADVENTURES IN CHRISTIAN WRITING. Orlando. Contact: Joanna Adicks Wallace, 1107 E. Amelia St., Orlando FL 32803-5327. Phone/fax (407)841-2157. E-mail: joannaw14@bell south.net. Membership (20) open.

BRANDON CHRISTIAN WRITERS/ACW CHAPTER. Contact: Ruth C. Ellinger, (813)685-7387. E-mail: Writer@Ruthellinger.com. Membership (15) open.

+FIRST COAST CHRISTIAN WRITERS/ACW CHAPTER. Jacksonville. Contact: Loraine Haataia, PhD, PO Box 600956, Jacksonville FL 32260-0956. E-mail: president@First CoastChristianWriters.org. Website: www.FirstCoastChristianWriters.com. Blog: http://First CoastChristianWriters.blogspot.com. Membership (10+) open.

HOBE SOUND WRITERS GROUP/ACW CHAPTER. Hobe Sound. Contact: Faith Tofte, 9342 Bethel Way, Hobe Sound FL 33455. (772)545-4023. E-mail: faithtofte@bellsouth.net. Membership (5) open.

MIAMI-DADE ACW CHAPTER. Miami/Ft. Lauderdale. Contact: Lynne Cooper Sitton, 8441 N.W. 78th Ct., Tamarac FL 33321. E-mail: LynneCSitton@cs.com. Chapter of ACW South Florida. Membership (8-10) open. Meetings alternate locations with Broward Chapter. Website: http://groups.yahoo.com/group/ACWSouthFlorida.

MID-FLORIDA CHRISTIAN WRITERS. Winter Garden. Contact: Joy Shelton, 1040 Glensprings Ave., Winter Garden FL 34787. (407)654-9076. Fax (407)654-9079. E-mail: JoySprinkles@ aol.com. Membership (10) open.

PALM BEACH CHRISTIAN WRITERS ASSN. West Palm Beach. Contact: Natalie Ferrone, 964 Imperial Lake Rd., West Palm Beach FL 33413. (561)574-0201. E-mail: nataliekim71@msn .com. Membership (10) open. ACW chapter.

SUNCOAST CHRISTIAN WRITERS. Clearwater. Contact: Elaine Creasman, 13014—106th Ave. N., Largo FL 33774-5602. Phone/fax (727)595-8963. E-mail: emcreasman@aol.com. Membership (10) open.

WORD WEAVERS. Longwood. Contact: Larry J. Leech II, 911 Alameda Dr., Longwood FL 32750. (407)925-6411. E-mail: lleech@cfl.rr.com. Website: www.WordWeaversFL.com. Membership (90+) open. Planning a conference for February 6-8, 2009 in Lake Yale.

GEORGIA

ATLANTA CHRISTIAN WRITERS/ACW CHAPTER. Contact: Susan Schreer Davis, 3750 Apple Way, Marietta GA 30066. (770)971-2381. E-mail: sschreer@bellsouth.net. Membership (15) open.

CHRISTIAN AUTHORS GUILD. Woodstock. Contact: Mike Anderson, PO Box 2673, Woodstock GA 30188. (770)928-2588. Fax (770)924-6935. E-mail: info@christianauthorsguild.org. Website: www.christianauthorsguild.org. Membership (66) open. Sponsors a contest and an annual fall conference in September.

EAST METRO ATLANTA CHRISTIAN WRITERS/ACW CHAPTER. Covington. Contact: Colleen Jackson, PO Box 2896, Covington GA 30015. (404)444-7514. E-mail: cjac401992@aol .com. Website: www.emacw.org. Membership (40) open. Sponsoring a seminar; date and location to be decided. Check Website for monthly meeting and seminar dates and location.

GEORGIA WRITERS ASSN./CHRISTIAN WRITERS POD. Woodstock/Marietta. Contact: Lloyd Blackwell, 3049 Scott Rd. N.E., Marietta GA 30066. (770)421-1203. E-mail: lloydblack well@worldnet.att.net. Membership (73) open. Meets twice monthly. Sponsors a contest, an annual cooperative published book, and a seminar in September.

NORTHEAST GEORGIA WRITERS. Gainesville. Ruthanna Bass, pres. (wrbass@bellsouth.net), or contact: Elouise Whitten, 660 Crestview Ter., Gainesville GA 30501-3110. (770)532-3007. Membership (42) open. Sponsors contest open to members. Conference pending.

+SUBURBAN ATLANTA CHAPTER/ACW. Atlanta. Contact: Rev. Diana R. Williams, 2130 Dillard Crossing, Tucker GA 30084-5878. (770)496-0711. E-mail: Dianarwilliams@aol.com. Membership (11) open. Sponsors a Writer's Brunch in July.

IDAHO

ACW SANDPOINT. Contact: Anita Aurit, 403 Louis Ln., Sandpoint ID 83864. (208)610-0626. E-mail: AnitaAurit@gmail.com. Website: www.heroes.com/ACW.htm. Group blog: http://acw sandpoint.blogspot.com. Membership open.

IDAHOPE WRITERS (IDAhope). Boise. Contact: Angela Meuser, c/o Rediscover Bookshop, 7079 Overland Rd., Boise ID 83709. (208)327-7679. E-mail: ameuser@cableone.net. Membership (20) open.

IOWA

APPLES OF GOLD WRITERS OF IOWA. Marion. Contact: Kimn Swenson Gollnick, 550 Edinburgh Ave., Marion IA 52302-5614. (319)373-2302. E-mail: kimn.gollnick@gmail.com. Website: www.KIMN.net. Membership (10-12) open.

CEDAR RAPIDS CHRISTIAN WRITER'S GROUP. Contact: Susan Fletcher, 513 Knollwood Dr. S.E., Cedar Rapids IA 52403. (319)365-9844. E-mail: skmcfate@msn.com. Membership (4) open.

+FELLOWSHIP OF CHRISTIAN WRITERS/ORANGE CITY IA. Contact: Judith Vander Wege, 304 Frankfort Ave. S.E., Orange City IA 51041. Phone/fax (712)707-9313. E-mail: judith vanderwege@orangecitycomm.net. Website: http://Spokesman-Ink.org. Membership open (new group). For critique, teaching, motivation, and fellowship. sponsors a fall poetry contest: entry fee $5.

KANSAS

CHRISTIAN WRITERS FELLOWSHIP. Girard. Contact: Deborah Vogts, 17300 Ness Rd., Erie KS 66733. (620)244-5619. E-mail: debvogts@gmail.com. Website: www.ChristianWriters Fellowship.blogspot.com. Membership (35) open. Sponsors a contest and a seminar April 3-4, 2009 (see separate listing).

CREATIVE WRITERS FELLOWSHIP. North Newton, Hesston, Moundridge, Halstead. Contact: Esther Groves, secretary, 405 West Bluestem, Apt. H4, North Newton KS 67117-8069. (316) 283-7224. Membership (20) open.

KENTUCKY

JACKSON CHRISTIAN WRITERS CLUB. Vancleave. Contact: Donna Woodring, PO Box 10, Vancleve KY 41385-0010. (606)693-5000, ext. 174. E-mail: donnaw@kmbc.edu. Membership (5) not currently open. Meets occasionally.

LOUISVILLE CHRISTIAN WRITERS/ACW CHAPTER. Contact: Lana Jackson, pres., 7804 Foxlair Way, Louisville KY 40220-3283. (502)968-3602. E-mail: info@lcwriters.com, or LanaHJackson@insightbb.com. Website: www.LCWriters.com. Meeting details on Website. Membership (22) open.

LOUISIANA

SOUTHERN CHRISTIAN WRITERS GUILD. Mandeville. Contact: Grace Booth or Marlaine Peachey, 806 Harmony Ln., Mandeville LA 70471. (985)626-4282. Fax (985)624-3108. E-mail: peachlane@bellsouth.net. Website under construction. Has monthly speakers. Membership (30) open.

MAINE

*****MAINE FELLOWSHIP OF CHRISTIAN WRITERS.** China. Contact: Beth Rogers, 720 Essex St., Bangor ME 04401. (207)942-1616. E-mail: BethR58@aol.com. Membership (15) open.

MARYLAND

ANNAPOLIS FELLOWSHIP OF CHRISTIAN WRITERS. Annapolis. Contact: Jeri Sweany, 3107 Ervin Ct., Annapolis MD 21403-4620. (410)267-0924. Membership (12-15) open.
BALTIMORE AREA CHRISTIAN WRITERS/ACW CHAPTER. Owings Mills. Contact: Theresa V. Wilson, PO Box 47182, Windsor Mill MD 21244-3571. (443)804-3435. E-mail: acwriters group@aol.com. Website: www.writersinthemarketplace.org. Membership (27) open.
MCC WRITERS' GROUP. Joppa. Contact: Virginia Colclasure or Dawn Sexton, c/o Mountain Christian Church, 1824 Mountain Rd., Joppa MD 21085. (410)877-1824 (church). E-mail: Vcolclasure@clearviewcatv.net, or mccwriters@clearviewcatv.net. Spring & fall writing workdays. Sponsors breakaway critique groups. Membership (12) open.
THIRD SATURDAY CHRISTIAN WRITERS GROUP. Howard County. Contact: Claire K. DeBakey. (443)413-6790. E-mail: c.debakey@att.net. Membership (12+) open.

MASSACHUSETTS

CENTRAL MASSACHUSETTS CHRISTIAN WRITERS FELLOWSHIP. Sturbridge. Contact: Barbara Shaffer, 168 Warren Rd., Brimfield MA 01010-9615. (413)245-9620. E-mail: history find2@aol.com. Membership (10) open.

MICHIGAN

AMERICAN CHRISTIAN WRITERS DETROIT. Contact: Pamela Perry, 33011 Tall Oaks St., Farmington MI 48336-4551. (248)426-2300. Fax (248)471-2422. E-mail: PamPerry@ ministrymarketingsolutions.com. Website: www.ministrymarketingsolutions.com. Membership (175) open. Sponsors a fall seminar in Detroit.
THE CALLED AND READY WRITERS. Detroit. Contact: Wanda Burnside, 20700 Civic Center Dr., Ste. 170, Southfield MI 48076. (313)792-2801. Fax (313)861-7578. E-mail: mwwginc@aol.com. Website: www.thecalledandreadywriters.org. Sponsoring a spring poetry workshop April 2009. Fall writers' conference, and special book signing events. Poetry critique available. Membership (70) open (over 25 published book authors).

MINNESOTA

MINNESOTA CHRISTIAN WRITERS GUILD. Minneapolis/St. Paul. Contact: Mary Fran Heitzman, pres., 10417 Colorado Rd., Bloomington MN 55438. (952)831-7790. Fax: (952)253-0712. E-mail: maryfheitxman@comcast.net. Website: www.mnchristianwriters.org. Membership (125) open. Sponsors a spring contest for members only and annual spring (March) and fall (October) seminars in Minneapolis/St. Paul. Monthly meetings (Sept.-May); monthly newsletter. Sponsors critique circles throughout Minnesota.

MISSISSIPPI

BYHALIA CHRISTIAN WRITERS/ACW CHAPTER. Contact: Marylane Wade Koch, Byhalia MS. (901)351-0870. E-mail: bcwriters@gmail.com. Has an online yahoo group. Membership (40) open. Works with ACW on an annual seminar in Memphis area; May 15-16, 2009.

MISSOURI

CHRISTIAN WRITERS WORKSHOP OF ST. LOUIS/ACW CHAPTER. Brentwood area. Contact: Ruth Houser, 3148 Arnold-Tenbrook Rd., Arnold MO 63010-4732. (636)464-1187. E-mail: Houser RA@juno.com. Also contact: Ruth McDaniel (636)464-1187. Membership (10-12) open.

HEART OF AMERICA CHRISTIAN WRITERS' NETWORK. Overland Park KS. Contact: Mark and Jeanette Littleton, 3706 N.E. Shady Lane Dr., Gladstone MO 64119. Phone/fax (816)459-8016. E-mail: HACWN@earthlink.net. Website: www.HACWN.org. Membership (150) open. Sponsors monthly meetings, weekly critique groups, professional writer's fellowships, a contest (open to nonmembers), a newsletter, marketing e-mails, and a conference in November.

OZARKS CHAPTER OF AMERICAN CHRISTIAN WRITERS. Springfield. Meets monthly. Contact: Jeanetta Chrystie, pres., OCACW, 5042 E. Cherry Hills Blvd., Springfield MO 65809-3301. (417)832-8409. E-mail: DrChrystie@mchsi.com. Susan Willingham, newsletter ed.; OzarksACW@yahoo.com. Guidelines on Website: www.ClearGlassView.org/OzarksACW/index.htm. Will sponsor a poetry contest (open to nonmembers) between March 1 and June 30, 2009. See Website for other events. Membership (35) open.

MONTANA

WRITERS IN THE BIG SKY. Helena. Contact: Lenore Puhek, 1215 Hudson St., Helena MT 59601-1848. (406)443-2552. E-mail: lpuhek@mt.net. Membership (9) open.

NEBRASKA

CENTRAL NEBRASKA FELLOWSHIP OF CHRISTIAN WRITERS, ARTISTS, AND MUSICIANS (C-WAM). Kearney. Contact: Carolyn R. Scheidies, 415 E. 15th, Kearney NE 68847-6959. (308)234-3849. E-mail: crscheidies@mail2faith.com (put C-WAM in subject line). Membership (10) open; more on Internet Loop.

***MY THOUGHTS EXACTLY WRITERS GROUP.** Fremont. Contact: Cheryl A. Paden, PO Box 1073, Fremont NE 68025. (402)727-6508. Membership (6-8) open. Periodically sponsors a writers' retreat; October 2008.

WORDSOWERS CHRISTIAN WRITER'S GROUP/ACW CHAPTER. Bellevue. Contact: Kelly Haack, 16268 Orchard Cir., Omaha NE 68135-1336. (402)593-7936. E-mail: haackkj@cox.net. Website: www.wordsowers.com. Membership (20) open.

NEW JERSEY

NORTH JERSEY CHRISTIAN WRITER'S GROUP. Ringwood. Contact: Louise Bergmann DuMont, PO Box 36, Ringwood NJ 07456. (973)962-9267. E-mail: LouiseDumont@gmail.com. Writers blog: www.njcwg.blogspot.com. Membership (30) open. E-mail for information.

NEW MEXICO

SOUTHWEST WRITERS. Albuquerque. Contact: Rob Spiegel, pres., 3721 Morris St. N.E., Ste. A, Albuquerque NM 87111-3611. (505)265-9485. E-mail: swwriters@juno.com. Website: www.southwestwriters.com. Membership (700) open. Sponsors an annual and a monthly contest (open to nonmembers), a series of mini-conferences in Albuquerque (see Website for dates) and afternoon workshops in the months without mini-conferences. Semimonthly e-lert notices are open to nonmembers. General.

NEW YORK

*BROOKLYN WRITER'S CLUB. Contact: Ann Dellarocco, PO Box 184, Bath Beach Sta., Brooklyn NY 11214-0184. (718)680-4084. Membership (10-20) open.
NEW YORK CHRISTIAN WRITERS GROUP. Manhattan. Contact: Marilyn Driscoll, 350—1st Ave., New York, NY 10010 (Manhattan). (212)529-6087. E-mail: madrisc@rcn.com. Membership (8) open.
THE SCRIBBLERS/ACW CHAPTER. Riverhead. Contact: Bill Batcher, pres., c/o First Congregational Church, 103 First St., Riverhead NY 11901. E-mail: bbatcher@optonline.net. Membership (12) open. Meets monthly and sponsors annual writing retreat.
SOUTHERN TIER CHRISTIAN WRITERS' FELLOWSHIP. Johnson City. Contact: Jean Jenkins, 3 Snow Ave., Binghamton NY 13905-3810. (607)797-5852. E-mail: jdjenkins2@verizon.net. Membership (8) open.

NORTH CAROLINA

COVENANT WRITERS. Lincolnton. Contact: Robert Redding, 3392 Hwy. 274, Cherryville NC 28021-9634. (704)445-4962. E-mail: minwriter@yahoo.com. Membership (10) open.
SEVEN SERIOUS SCRIBES. Cary. Contact: Katherine W. Parrish, 103 Chimney Rise Dr., Cary NC 27511-7214. (919)467-1924. E-mail: servantsong@aol.com. Critique group. Membership (7) not currently open, but encourages others to start similar groups in the area.

OHIO

COLUMBUS CHRISTIAN WRITERS ASSN. Contact: Barbara Taylor Sanders, (614)306-3637. E-mail: BTSanders@columbus.rr.com. Website: www.cwacolumbus.com. Membership (25) open.
CREATIVE FORCE—ACW NORTHGATE. Sunbury. Contact: Lark Lamontagne, 450 Township Rd. 208, Marengo OH 43334-5301. (740)625-6032. Fax (740)625-6572. E-mail: llamontagne@att.net. Membership (15) not currently open.
DAYTON CHRISTIAN SCRIBES. Kettering. Contact: Cynthia Hinkle, 28 Stanton Dr., Springboro OH 45066. (937)886-9037. E-mail: cynthia.hinkle@sbcglobal.net. Membership (35) open.
DAYTON CHRISTIAN WRITERS' GUILD. Englewood. Contact: Tina Toles, PO Box 251, Englewood OH 45322. (937)836-6600. E-mail: daytonwriters@ureach.com. Website: www.daytonwriters.com. Membership (25) open. Sponsoring a conference in June 2009.

FAITH WRITERS. Milford. Contact: Sharon Siepel or Shaunna Howat, 5910 Price Rd., Milford OH 45150. (513)831-3770, ext. 112. E-mail: ssiepel@faithchurch.net. Website: www.faith church.net. Membership (20) open.

LEBANON AREA WRITERS. Contact: Mary Busha, 1370 Deerfield Road, #B, Lebanon, OH 45036. (513)228-1205. Email: joyofwriting45@yahoo.com. Membership (15+) open. Secular; several Christians attend.

MIDDLETOWN AREA CHRISTIAN WRITERS. Franklin. Contact: Donna J. Shepherd. (513)423-1627. E-mail: donnashepherd@cinci.rr.com. Website: www.middletownwriters .blogspot.com. Membership (15) open.

NORTHWEST OHIO CHRISTIAN WRITERS/ACW CHAPTER. Bowling Green. Contact: Katherine Douglas, pres., 5702 Angola Rd, Lot 139, Toledo OH 43615. (419)867-0805. E-mail: mlka@toast.net. Meets the 4th Fridays of January, March, May, July, and October. Membership (50) open. Sponsors a spring writers' retreat (May 1-2, 2009) and a Saturday seminar in September.

OKLAHOMA

FELLOWSHIP OF CHRISTIAN WRITERS (FCW), PO Box 471031, Tulsa, OK 74147. (918) 256-2138. E-mail: lavonlewis@sbcglobal.net. Website: http://fellowshipofchristianwriters .org. Founded as Tulsa Christian Writers, FCW has helped to encourage, equip, launch, and inspire hundreds of writers for over 26 years. Membership (60) open; includes local and at-large group membership. Local group meets monthly in Tulsa. FCW membership benefits include a monthly 8-10 page newsletter, eligibility to members-only contests, book and tape discounts, free access to online critique groups, and a link on FCW Website to your Website. FCW also conducts a Free List Serve with over 750 members at Yahoo Groups—http:// groups.yahoo.com/group/FCW—or send an email to FCW-subscribe@yahoogroups.com. Local membership $35/yr. At-large membership $25/yr. Contact: Lavon Lewis at the PO Box or via e-mail: Lavon@fellowshipofchristianwriters.org.

+SONRISE CHRISTIAN WRITERS. Oklahoma City. Contact: Marlys Norris, 6209 N.W. 82nd St., Oklahoma City OK 73132. E-mail: marlysj@sbcglobal.net. Starting a new group; membership open.

WORDWRIGHTS, OKLAHOMA CITY CHRISTIAN WRITERS. Contact: Milton Smith, 6457 Sterling Dr., Oklahoma City OK 73132-6804. (405)721-5026. E-mail: HisWordMatters@ yahoo.com. Website: www.shadetreecreations.com. Membership (20) open. Occasional contests for members only. Cosponsors an annual writers' conference with American Christian Writers, February 27-28, 2009, in Oklahoma City; send an SASE for information.

OREGON

GOD'S WORDSMITHS—ADVANCED. King City/Beaverton/Highlands. Contact: Crystal Ortmann, 11625 S.W. King George Dr., King City OR 97224-2624. Phone/fax (503)372-0529. E-mail: cjortmann@comcast.net. Membership (3) not currently open. Serious, published writers only; prefer those who have published books.

OREGON CHRISTIAN WRITERS. Contact: Mary Hake, pres. E-mail: president@oregon christianwriters.org. Website: www.oregonchristianwriters.org. Meets for 3, all-day Saturday conferences annually: February, in Salem; May, in Eugene; and October, in Portland. Newsletter published one month before each one-day conference. Annual 4-day Coaching Conference July 27-30, 2009, in Portland/Salem metro area. Membership (400) open.

PORTLAND CHRISTIAN WRITERS GROUP. Contact: Stan Baldwin, (503)659-2974. Serious group; must write regularly. Waiting list available.

ROYAL PEN-DANTS. Salem/Portland area. Primarily for those writing for children. Contact: Carole Farmen. (503)362-2148. E-mail: cfarmen@msn.com. Membership (6) open only to committed, producing writers.

WORDSMITHS. Gresham. Contact: Susan Thogerson Maas, 27526 S.E. Carl St., Gresham OR 97080-8215. (503)663-7834. E-mail: susan.maas@verizon.net. Group is temporarily suspended, but open to new members. Christian and general writers.

WRITER'S DOZEN CRITIQUE GROUP. Springfield. Contact: Denise Nash, 42892 Leaburg Dr., Leaburg OR 97489-9619. (541)896-3816. E-mail: dcarlson@efn.org. Membership (12) not currently open.

PENNSYLVANIA

ARTISTS' JUNCTION WRITER'S GATHERING. Lancaster. Contact: Deb or Jan, PO Box 282, Lancaster PA 17608. (717)295-2533. E-mail: aji@artistsjunction.org. Website: www.artistsjunction.org. Membership open.

THE FIRST WORD. Sewickley (15143). Contact: Shirley S. Stevens, 712 Ridge Ave., Pittsburgh PA 15202-2223. (412)761-2618. E-mail: poetcat@comcast.net. Membership (10) open. Affiliated with the St. Davids Christian Writers' Conference.

GREATER PHILADELPHIA CHRISTIAN WRITERS' FELLOWSHIP. Newton Square. Contact: Marlene Bagnull, 316 Blanchard Rd., Drexel Hill, PA 19026. Phone/fax (610)626-6833. E-mail: Mbagnull@aol.com. Website: www.writehisanswer.com. Membership (25) open. Meets one Thursday morning a month, September-June. Sponsors annual writers' conference (August 6-8, 2009, tentative) and contest (open to registered conferees only).

INDIAN VALLEY CHRISTIAN WRITERS FELLOWSHIP/ACW CHAPTER. Telford (Bucks County). Contact: Cheryl Wallace, 952 Route 113, Sellersville PA 18960-2962. (215)453-0415. E-mail: wallacewriter@verizon.net. Membership (24) open.

INSPIRATIONAL WRITERS' FELLOWSHIP. Brookville. Contact: Jan R. Sady, 2026 Langville Rd., Mayport PA 16240-5610. (814)856-2560. E-mail: janfran@windstream.net. Membership (15) open. Sometimes sponsors a conference.

JOHNSTOWN CHRISTIAN WRITERS' GUILD. Contact: Betty Rosian, 108 Deerfield Ln., Johnstown PA 15905-5703. (814)255-4351. E-mail: wordsforall@atlanticbb.net. Membership (15) open.

+LANCASTER CHRISTIAN WRITERS/ACW. Lititz. Contact: Jeanette Windle, 121 E. Woods Dr., Litiz PA 17543. (717)626-8752. E-mail: jeanette@jeanettewindle.com. Website: pending. Membership (100+) open. Sponsors a one-day spring conference.

WEST BRANCH CHRISTIAN WRITERS. Williamsport. Contact: Cindy Emmet Smith, 31 Lower Market St., Milton PA 17847. (570)742-0789. E-mail: cswriter@yahoo.com. Membership (15) open. Frequently sponsors a one-day conference in the fall.

SOUTH CAROLINA

COLUMBIA CHRISTIAN WRITERS. Contact: Kim Andrysczyk, 201 Sutton Way, Irmo SC 29063. (803)781-3510. E-mail: kimbocraig@juno.com. Meets monthly. Membership (6) open.

GREENVILLE CHRISTIAN WRITERS GROUP. Contact: Nancy Parker, 3 Ben St., Greenville SC 29601. (864)232-1705. E-mail: Nancy@jjparker.com. Membership (20) open.

+UPSTATE SOUTH CAROLINA ACW CHAPTER. Anderson. Contact: Elva Martin, 104 Oak Knoll Ter., Anderson SC 29625-2507. Phone/fax (864)226-7024. E-mail: elvamartinministries@charter.net. Membership (18) open. Sponsors a conference; October 2009 in Anderson.

WRITING 4 HIM. Spartanburg. Contact: Linda Gilden, PO Box 2928, Spartanburg SC 29304. E-mail: RoseWriter@aol.com. Membership (20) open.

TEXAS

CENTEX CHAPTER—AMERICAN CHRISTIAN FICTION WRITERS (ACFW) (formerly Austin Christian Writers Guild; merged with this group), serving Central TX region. Contact: Lin Harris, 129 Fox Hollow Cv., Cedar Creek TX 78612-4844. (512)601-2216. E-mail: linharris@ austin.rr.com. Website: http://home.austin.rr.com/linharris/centex.html. Membership (50) open. Meetings, critique groups, workshops, and conferences announced on Website.

CHRISTIAN WRITERS GROUP OF GREATER SAN ANTONIO. Universal City/San Antonio area. Contact: Brenda Blanchard, 2827 Olive Ave., Schertz TX 78154-3719. (210)945-4163. E-mail: brendablanchard1@aol.com. Has quarterly guest speakers. Membership (25) open.

DALLAS CHRISTIAN WRITERS GUILD. Plano. Contact: Jan Winebrenner, 2709 Winding Hollow, Plano TX 75093. E-mail: janwrite@earthlink.net. Website: www.dallaschristianwriters .com. Membership (30) open.

+DALLAS-FORT WORTH READY WRITERS/ACFW BRANCH. Colleyville. Contact: Dawn Morton Samaniego (Dawn Michelle Michals). E-mail: dawn@dawnmichellemichals.com. Website: www.dfwreadywriters.blogspot.com. Meeting info on Website. Membership open.

DENTON CHRISTIAN WRITERS GUILD. Denton. E-mail: info@dentonchristianwriters.com. Website: www.dentonchristianwriters.com. Membership (4) open.

INSPIRATIONAL WRITERS ALIVE! Groups meet in Houston, Pasadena, Jacksonville, Amarillo, Humble, and Port Neches. Contact: Martha Rogers, 6038 Greenmont, Houston TX 77092-2332. (713)686-7209. E-mail: marthalrogers@sbcglogal.net. Membership (130 statewide) open. Sponsors summer seminar, August 2009, monthly newsletter, and annual contest (January 1-May 15) open to nonmembers.

INSPIRATIONAL WRITERS ALIVE!/AMARILLO CHAPTER. Contact: Helen Luecke, 2921 S. Dallas, Amarillo TX 79103. (806)376-9671. Sponsors a seminar, March 2009.

INSPIRATIONAL WRITERS ALIVE!/EAST TEXAS CHAPTER. Jacksonville. Contact: Maxine Holder, director & founding member, 4785 FM 1248 S., Rusk TX 75785-5254. (903)795-3986. E-mail: mholder787@aol.com. Membership (14) open. Sponsors a contest through First Baptist chapter/Houston. Starting a new chapter in Tyler TX. Call Maxine Holder or Lynda Garrison (903)581-0348.

NORTH TEXAS CHRISTIAN WRITERS/ACW CHAPTERS. Meetings held in Argyle, Arlington, Dallas, Fort Worth, Keller, Lewisville. Contact: Frank Ball, PO Box 820802, Fort Worth TX 76182-0802. (817)715-2697. E-mail: info@ntchristianwriters.com. Website: www.nt christianwriters.com. Membership (100+) open. Sponsors an annual seminar after Labor Day; September 2009.

ROCKWALL CHRISTIAN WRITERS' GROUP. Lake Pointe Church/Rockwall. Contact: Leslie Wilson, 535 Cullins Rd., Rockwall TX 75032-6017. (972)772-3442. Cell (214)505-5336. E-mail: LesliePWilson@aol.com. Website: http://rcwg.blogspot.com. Membership (20) open.

WORDS FOR THE JOURNEY CHRISTIAN WRITERS GUILD/SOUTHEAST TEXAS REGION. Contact: Linda Kozar, 7 S. Chandler Creek Cir., The Woodlands TX 77381. (281)362-1791. Prefers cell (832)797-7522. E-mail: zarcom1@aol.com. Website: www.wordsforthejourney .org. Membership (75) open. See separate listing for Rocky Mountain CO Region.

UTAH

UTAH CHRISTIAN WRITERS FELLOWSHIP/ACW CHAPTER. Salt Lake City area. Contact: Julie Scott, PO Box 3, Bountiful UT 84011-0003. (801)294-5485. E-mail: julie.compelled2Tell@ mac.com. Website: www.utahchristianwriters.com. Sponsoring a writers' conference in fall 2009 in Bluffdale UT. Membership (20) open.

VIRGINIA

CAPITAL CHRISTIAN WRITERS. Fairfax. Leader: Betsy Dill, PO Box 873, Centreville VA 20122-0873. Phone/fax (703)803-9447. E-mail: ccwriters@gmail.com. Website: www.ccwriters .org. Sponsors Saturday workshops 1-2 times a year. Membership (45) open.

NEW COVENANT WRITER'S GROUP. Newport News. Contact: Mary Tatem, 451 Summer Dr., Newport News VA 23606-2515. (757)930-1700. E-mail: rwtatem@juno.com. Membership (8) open.

PENINSULA CHRISTIAN WRITERS/ACW CHAPTER. Yorktown. Contact: Yvonne Ortega, PO Box 955, Yorktown VA 23692. E-mail: yvonne@yvonneortega.com. Membership (5) open. Sponsors Annual Writers Workshop, likely in the spring.

RICHMOND CHRISTIANS WHO WRITE/ACW CHAPTER. Contact: Rev. Thomas C. Lacy, 12114 Walnut Hill Dr., Rockville VA 23146-1854. (804)749-4050. Fax (804)749-4939. E-mail: RichmondCWW@aol.com. Blog: http://rcww.blogspot.com. Sponsoring a conference October 16-17, 2009. Membership (50) open.

TIDEWATER CHRISTIAN WRITERS FORUM/ACW CHAPTER. Norfolk. Contact: Peter D. Mallett, 1270 Pall Mall St., #A, Norfolk VA 23513. (757)889-9917. E-mail: F18Pete@aol.com. Website: http://groups.yahoo.com/group/TidewaterChristianWF. Membership (8) open. ACW Chapter 3055 (www.acwriters.com).

WASHINGTON

NORTHWEST CHRISTIAN WRITERS ASSN. Bothell WA. Contact: Lorie Reichel-Howe, PO Box 428, Enumclaw WA 98022-0428. Toll-free (800)731-6292. Fax (360)802-9992. E-mail: president@nwchristianwriters.org. Website: www.nwchristianwriters.org. Speakers Clearinghouse available on Website. Membership (175) open. Meets monthly. bimonthly newsletter. Sponsors a contest and Northwest Christian Writers Renewal in May (see separate listing).

SPOKANE CHRISTIAN WRITERS. Contact: Ruth McHaney Danner, PO Box 18425, Spokane WA 99228-0425. (509)328-3359. E-mail: ruth@ruthdanner.com. Membership (20) open.

+WALLA WALLA CHRISTIAN WRITERS. Walla Walla. Contact: Helen Heavirland, PO Box 146, College Place WA 99324. Phone/fax (541)938-3838. E-mail: hlh@bmi.net. Membership open.

WALLA WALLA VALLEY CHRISTIAN SCRIBES. College Place. Contact: Helen Heavirland, PO Box 146, College Place WA 99324-0146. Phone/fax (541)938-3838. E-mail: hlh@bmi.net. Membership (8) open.

WRITERS IN THE ROUGH/ACW CHAPTER. Arlington. Contact: Rick Bell, 9111 96th St. N.E., Arlington WA 98223-8865. (360)653-7420. E-mail: bellvista@verizon.net. Membership (12) open.

WISCONSIN

+CHRISTIAN WRITERS GROUP. Manitowoc. Contact: Becky McLafferty. (920)758-9196. New group. Membership open.

LIGHTHOUSE CHRISTIAN WRITERS. Klondike. Contact: Lois Wiederhoeft, 901 Aubin, Lot 115, Peshtigo WI 54157. (715)582-1024. E-mail: 2loisann@myway.com. Or, Mary Jansen, PO Box 187, Mountain WI 54149; (715)276-1706. Website: www.mychristiansite.com/ministries/lhchristianwriters. Membership (9) open.

THE LIVING WORD/ACW CHAPTER. Superior. Contact: Amy Trees, pres., 1421 E. 5th St., Superior WI 54880. (715)398-7244. E-mail: TheLivingWordSuperior@yahoogroups.com. Website: http://LivingWordWriters.bravehost.com. Membership (30) open.

WORD AND PEN CHRISTIAN WRITERS CLUB/ACW CHAPTER. Menasha. Contact: Chris Stratton, Appleton WI. (920)739-0752. E-mail: wordandpen@mychristiansite.com. Website: www.mychristiansite.com/ministries/wordandpen. Membership (14) open.

*WORDSMITHS (W.R.W.A.). Marinette/Menominee. Wisconsin Regional Writers Assn. (general group that includes Christians). Contact: Mildred Utke, 2709 Northland Cir. Dr., Marinette WI 54143-4277. (715)735-0127. Membership (4) open.

WRITER'S CRITIQUE GROUPS. Fort Atkinson & Watertown. Contact: James B. Robar, N2963 Buena Vista Rd., Fort Atkinson WI 53538. (920)568-1677. E-mail: jim@jamesbrobar.com. Membership (4) open.

CANADIAN/FOREIGN

ASSOCIATION OF CHRISTIAN WRITERS. 23 Moorend Ln., Thame, Oxon, OX9 3BQ, UK. Contact: Brian Vincent, dir., 31 Newlands Rd., Ruishton, Taunton, SOM., TA3 5J2, United Kingdom. Phone 01823-442 372. E-mail from Website: www.christianwriters.org.uk. Membership (900) open. Sponsors an occasional writers' weekend for members only. Next one in 2009.

FRASER VALLEY CHRISTIAN WRITERS GROUP. Abbotsford BC. Contact: Helmut Fandrich, 2461 Sunnyside Pl., Abbotsford BC V2T 4C4, Canada. Phone/fax (604)850-0666. E-mail: helmut8@coneharvesters.com. Membership (20) open.

INSCRIBE CHRISTIAN WRITERS' FELLOWSHIP. Edmonton (various locations across Canada). Contact: Eunice Matchett, 4304—45 St., Drayton Valley AB T7A 1G7, Canada. (780)542-7950. E-mail: scrappi@telusplanet.net. Website: www.inscribe.org. Membership (250) open. Sponsors a newsletter and 2 contests, details on Website (one open to nonmembers). Also sponsors annual conference in September.

NEW ZEALAND CHRISTIAN WRITERS GUILD. Contact: Janet Fleming, Box 115, Kaeo 0448, New Zealand. (MJflamingos@xtra.co.nz), or Janet Pointon (Pointon@clear.net.nz). Website: www.freewebs.com/nzchristianwritersguild. Membership (150) open. Workshops, biannual weekend retreat, local groups, home study courses, and bimonthly magazine.

SWAN VALLEY CHRISTIAN WRITERS GUILD. Swan River, MB. Contact: Addy Oberlin, Box 132, Swan River MB R0L 1Z0, Canada. Phone/fax (204)734-4269. E-mail: waltadio@mts.net. Membership (10) open. Sponsors a contest open to nonmembers.

+THE WORD GUILD. Meets in various cities. Contact: Jeanette Duncan, 698A Highpoint Ave., Waterloo ON N2V 1G9, Canada. (519)886-4196. E-mail: info@thewordguild.com. Website: www.thewordguild.com. Membership (320) open. Sponsors contests open to nonmembers (see contest listings). Sponsoring an annual conference in Guelph ON, June 11-13, 2009.

NATIONAL/INTERNATIONAL GROUPS (no state location)

AMERICAN CHRISTIAN FICTION WRITERS. Robin Miller, pres.; PO Box 101066, Palm Bay FL 32910. Phone/fax (321)984-4018. E-mail: pr@acfw.com. Website: www.ACFW.com. E-mail loop, online courses, critique groups, and e-newsletter for members. Send membership inquiries to address above. Membership (1,500) open. Sponsors contests for published and unpublished members. Sponsors annual seminar in September.

AMERICAN CHRISTIAN WRITERS SEMINARS. Sponsors conferences in various locations around the country (see individual states for dates and places). Call or write to be placed on mailing list for any conference. Events are Friday and Saturday unless otherwise noted. Brochures usually mailed three months prior to event. Contact: Reg Forder, Box 110390, Nashville TN 37222. Toll-free (800)21-WRITE. Website: www.ACWriters.com.

CHRISTIAN WRITERS FELLOWSHIP INTL. (CWFI). Contact: Sandy Brooks, 1624 Jefferson Davis Rd., Clinton SC 29325-6401. (864)697-6035. E-mail: cwfi@cwfi-online.org. Website: www.cwfi-online.org. To contact Sandy Brooks personally: sandybrooks@cwfi-online.org. No meetings, but offers market consultations, critique service, writers books, and conference workshop tapes. Connects writers living in the same area, and helps start writers' groups. Membership (1,000+) open.

CHRISTIAN WRITERS' GROUP INTL. (CWGI). Website: http://christianwritersgroup.org. An international organization of born-again Christians who write. Purpose: to assist Christians as they fulfill their calling to write by offering resources, information, education, support, networking, and interaction with Christian writers, editors, and publishers. Includes critique and prayer subgroups for members only. Periodically offers CWGI members scholarships to writing conferences. Editors and publishers are welcome. To join, send a blank e-mail to CWG-subscribe@yahoogroups.com, or sign up at http://groups.yahoo.com/group/CWGI. Executive director: Brandy Brow. Membership (700+) open.

FAITH, HOPE & LOVE is the inspirational chapter of Romance Writers of America. Charges yearly dues (see Website), but you must also be a member of RWA to join (see their Website for annual dues). Chapter offers these services: online list service for members, a Web page, 20-pg. bimonthly newsletter, annual contest, monthly online guest chats with multi-published authors and industry professionals, connects critique partners by mail or e-mail, and latest romance-market information. To join, contact RWA National Office, 16000 Stuebner Airline Rd., Ste. 140, Spring TX 77379. (832)717-5200. Fax (832)717-5201. E-mail: info@rwanational.org. Website: www.rwanational.org. Or go to FHL Website: www.faithhopelove-rwa.org. Inspirational Readers Choice Contest by subgenre categories for published works; deadline April 1; cash prizes. Send SASE for guidelines. Membership (150+) open.

JERRY B. JENKINS CHRISTIAN WRITERS GUILD. Contact: Kerma Murray, 5525 N. Union Blvd., Ste. 200, Colorado Springs, CO 80918. Toll-free (866)495-5177. Fax (719)495-5187. E-mail: ContactUs@ChristianWritersGuild.com. Website: www.ChristianWritersGuild.com. This international organization of 1,800 members offers annual memberships, mentor-guided correspondence courses for adults (two-year Apprentice; advanced one-year Journeyman; and Craftsman) and youth (Pages: ages 9-12, and Squires: 13 and up), writing contests, conferences, critique service, writers resource books, monthly newsletter, and more. Critique service accepts prose samples of 1-15 pages. Professional writing assessment covers proper language usage, pacing, presentation, purpose, and persuasiveness. Call for pricing structure. Members receive 10% off.

NATIONAL ASSN. OF WOMEN WRITERS. General. Contact: Sheri McConnell, 24165 IH-10 W., Ste. 217-637, San Antonio TX 78257. Toll-free phone/fax (866)821-5829. E-mail: info@naww.org. Website: www.naww.org. Over 40 chapters across the U.S. (see Website for list of locations). Membership (3,000+) open. Sponsors regional events across the U.S. and national TeleSummits.

PEN-SOULS (prayer and support group, not a critique group). Conducted entirely by e-mail. Contact: Janet Ann Collins, 632 Pelton Way, Grass Valley CA 95945. (530)272-4905. E-mail: jan@janetanncollins.com. Membership (13) open.

THE WRITING ACADEMY. Contact: Inez Schneider, new member coordinator, 4010 Singleton Rd., Rockford IL 61114. (815)877-9675. Website: www.wams.org. Membership (75) open. Sponsors year-round correspondence writing program and annual seminar in August held in Minneapolis.

EDITORIAL SERVICES

It is often wise to have a professional editor critique your manuscript before submitting it to an agent or publisher—some agents even require a written evaluation. The following people offer this kind of service. I cannot personally guarantee the work of any of these editors, so you will want to ask for references or samples of their work.

The following abbreviations indicate what kinds of work they are qualified to do:

B—brochures
BCE—book contract
    evaluation
CA—coauthoring

GE—general editing/
    manuscript evaluation
GH—ghostwriting
LC—line editing or copyediting

NL—newsletters
PP—PowerPoint
SP—special projects
WS—Website

The following abbreviations indicate the types of material they evaluate:

A—articles
BP—book proposals
BS—Bible studies
D—devotionals
E—essays
F—fillers

GB—gift books
JN—juvenile novels
N—novels
NB—nonfiction books
P—poetry
PB—picture books

QL—query letter
S—scripts
SS—short stories
TM—technical material
YA—young adults

(+) Indicates new listing

ALABAMA

+TRACY RUCKMAN CRITIQUES, 198 Lake Berry Ln., Lowndesboro AL 36752. E-mail: tracy edits@yahoo.com. Website: www.tracyruckman.com. E-mail/mail. B/GE/GH/LC/NL/SP/WS. Edits A/BP/D/E/F/GB/N/NB/QL/SS/Web content/freelance photography. Graphic design and layout for print or e-mail newsletters, brochures, one-sheets, display advertising. Charges by hour, project or flat rate. Rate sheet on Website.

ARIZONA

CARLA'S MANUSCRIPT SERVICE/CARLA BRUCE, 10229 W. Andover Ave., Sun City AZ 85351-4509. Phone/fax (623)876-4648. E-mail: Carlaabruce@cox.net. Call/e-mail/write with deposit of $100. GE/GH/LC/typesetting/PDF files for publishers. Edits A/BP/BS/D/E/F/GB/N/NB/P/QL/SS/TM. Charges $25/hr. or gives a project estimate after evaluation. Does ghostwriting for pastors and teachers; professional typesetting. Twenty-three years ghostwriting/editing; 12 years typesetting.

+KATHY WILLIAMSON MINISTRIES/KATHY WILLIAMSON, PO Box 11660, Prescott AZ 86304. (928)925-5410. E-mail: kathy@wisdomforliving.org. Website: www.kathy williamson.org. Christian copywriter; provides services for Christian authors to help get their books finished. Also advises on how to promote on the Internet.

ARKANSAS

+KAIROS PROFESSIONAL/TONJA TAYLOR, 1302 E. 30th Ave., Apt. A, Texarkana AR 71854. (870)216-2243. Fax (870)216-2243. E-mail: tonja@kairosprofessional.com. Website:

www.KairosProfessional.com. E-mail contact. CA/GE/GH/LC/NL/PP/SP/WS/writing coach. Edits: A/BP/BS/D/E/F/GB/N/NB/P/QL/SS/TM. 20+ years' experience in writing, editing, and publishing. If you mention you saw her listing in this guide, charges $1.25/pg. for copy/line editing; $1/pg. for typing/word processing; $25/hr. with $25 min. and half up front for coaching/consulting (includes marketing advice and promotion), critiques, Websites, special projects, newsletters.

CALIFORNIA

CHRISTIAN COMMUNICATOR MANUSCRIPT CRITIQUE SERVICE/SUSAN TITUS OSBORN, 3133 Puente St., Fullerton CA 92835-1952. Toll-free (877)428-7992. (714)990-1532. Fax (714)990-0310. E-mail: Susanosb@aol.com. Website: www.christiancommunicator.com. Call/e-mail/write. For book, send material with $160 deposit. Staff of 18 editors. BCE/CA/GE/GH/LC/SP. Edits A/BP/BS/D/E/F/GB/JN/N/NB/P/PB/QL/S/SS/TM. $100 for short pieces/picture books. Three-chapter book proposal $160 (up to 40 pgs.). Additional editing $40/hr. Over thirty years' experience.

CITY BOY EDITORIAL SERVICE/STEVEN HUTSON, 5022 Avenue N, Ste. 102-128, Palmdale CA 93551. (661)722-4896. Toll-free fax (866)501-4280. E-mail: steve@hutsonbooks.com. Website: www.hutsonbooks.com/editorial. Call/e-mail. CA/GE/LC/SP/WS. Edits A/BS/D/E/GB/JN/N/NB/SS. Published author; assistant director of Antelope Valley Christian Writers Conference. Proofreading $1/pg.; copyediting $1.95/pg.; 3-chapter critique $95 (up to 100 pgs.). Other projects at $30/hr., or upon discussion with client.

EDITORIAL, BOOK DESIGN, AND PRODUCTION SERVICES/DESTA GARRETT, dg-ink Book Design, PO Box 1182, Daly City CA 94017-1182. (650)994-2662. Fax (650)991-3050. E-mail: dg@dg-ink.net. Website: www.dg-ink.net, includes work samples. Write/call/e-mail. B/GE/LC/NL/SP. Complete editing and production for author, including for self-publishing using Adobe InDesign Creative Suite. Edits A/BS/D/E/NB/SS/TM/educational material. Has 20 years' experience doing all aspects of editing, production, and publishing of all types of material for nonprofit Christian foundation, up to large illustrated, indexed research books. Charges $50/hr.; $40/hr. for Christian authors with Christian material.

+ENCORE COMMUNICATIONS/ERICA MONGE, PO Box 727, Orange CA 92856. (602)350-7504. Fax (866)520-3072. E-mail: ericar@mongewriter.com. Website: www.mongewriter .com. E-mail contact; send material with $100 deposit. B/GE/LC/NL/PP/SP/WS/press releases/writing coach. Edits: A/BP/BS/D/E/F/GB/JN/N/NB/P/PB/QL/S/SS/TM. Fifteen years' experience as published writer/editor. Exec. editor of a Christian publication. Specializes as a writing coach, helping writers get their work published and get paid. Has a B.A. and M.A.; credentialed minister. Send manuscript or sample writings and $100 deposit. Will return a written proposal, and $100 will be applied to final invoice. Projects typically estimate at $75/hr.

GET PUBLISHED IN AMERICA.COM/B. K. NELSON, 1565 Paseo Vida, Palm Springs CA 92264. Toll-free (800)371-0076. (760)778-8800. Fax (760)778-0034. E-mail: bknelson4@cs.com. Website: www.bknelson.com. E-mail/write. BCE/CA/GE/LC/SP. Edits A/BP/BS/D/E/F/GB/JN/N/NB/P/PB/QL/S/SS/TM. Twenty-two years as a literary agent. Contact for rates.

VICKI HESTERMAN, PhD/EDITING & WRITING SERVICES, PO Box 6788, San Diego CA 92166. E-mail: vhes@mac.com (cc it to backup address: vhesterman@hotmail.com; indicate "editorial/photo work" in subject line). E-mail or mail only; will follow up within 1-2 days with phone call if requested. CA/GE/GH/LC/SP. Edits A/BP/BS/D/E/F/GB/JN/N/NB/PB/QL/SS/TM/photo books, memoirs. Cost competitive, depends on scope and condition of project. Send or e-mail letter explaining project, with several sample pages, for quote of cost. Edits/develops nonfiction material, including editorials; works with book and article writers and publishers as coauthor, line editor, or in editorial development. Book editor, book author, university writing professor, newspaper reporter, writing curriculum development, documentary photography.

DARLENE HOFFA, 512 Juniper St., Brea CA 92821. (714)990-5980. E-mail: jack.darlene .hoffa@roadrunner.com. E-mail contact. GE. Edits A/BP/D/F/NB. Twenty years' experience; author of 11 books. Charges $20/hr. or $1.50/ms pg.

KATHY IDE/EDITORIAL SERVICES, 203 Panorama Ct., Brea CA 92821. (714)529-1212. Fax (714)529-5267. E-mail: Kathy@kathyide.com. Website: www.KathyIde.com. E-mail contact. B/CA/GE/GH/LC/NL/SP/WS, writing coach. Edits A/BP/BS/D/F/GB/JN/N/NB/QL/S/SS. Charges by the hour (mention this listing and get a $5/hr. discount). Freelance author, editor (full-time since 1998), and speaker. Has done proofreading and editing for Moody, Thomas Nelson, Barbour/Heartsong, and WinePress.

LIGHTHOUSE EDITING/DR. LON ACKELSON, 13326 Community Rd., #11, Poway CA 92064-4754. (858)748-9258. Fax (858)748-7431. E-mail: Isaiah68LA@sbcglobal.net. Website: www.lighthouseedit.com. E-mail/write. B/BCE/CA/GE/GH/LC/NL. Edits A/BP/BS/D/E/N/NB/QL/SS. Charges $35 for article/short story critique; $60 for 3-chapter book proposal. Send SASE for full list of fees. Editor since 1981; senior editor 1984-2002.

KAREN O'CONNOR COMMUNICATIONS/KAREN O'CONNOR, 10 Pajaro Vista Ct., Watsonville CA 95076. E-mail: karen@karenoconnor.com. Website: www.karenoconnor.com. E-mail. GE/LC. Book proposal commentary/editing. Edits A/BP/D/F/NB/QL. One-hour free evaluation; $90/hr. or flat fee depending on project. Has 32 years of writing/editing; 25+ years teaching writing; 55 published books and hundreds of magazine articles.

SHIRL'S EDITING SERVICE/SHIRL THOMAS, 9379 Tanager Ave., Fountain Valley CA 92708-6557. (714)968-5726. E-mail: Shirlth@verizon.net. E-mail (preferred)/write, and send material with $100 deposit. GE/GH/LC/SP/rewriting/analysis. Edits A/BP/D/F/GB/N/P/QL/SS/greeting cards/synopses. Consultation, $75/hr.; evaluation/critique, $75/hr.; mechanical editing $65/hr.; content editing/rewriting $75/hr.

LAURAINE SNELLING/KMB COMMUNICATIONS INC., 19872 Highline Rd., Tehachapi CA 93561-7796. (661)823-0669. Fax (661)823-9427. E-mail: TLsnelling@yahoo.com. Website: www.LauraineSnelling.net. E-mail contact. GE. Edits JN/N/SS. Charges $50/hr. with $100 deposit, or by the project after discussion with client. Award-winning author of 60 books (YA and adult fiction, 2 nonfiction); teacher at writing conferences.

THE STRONG WORD COMMUNICATION SERVICES/ANITA K. PALMER, 5800 Lake Murray Blvd., Unit 14, La Mesa CA 91942-2500. (619)208-7202. Fax (619)697-1823 (call ahead). E-mail: anita@thestrongword.com. Website: www.thestrongword.com. E-mail contact. B/CA/GE/GH/LC/NL/SP/WS. Edits A/BP/D/E/N/NB/SS/memoirs. Published author. Former newspaper and magazine editor with 25 years' experience; experienced in media relations and marketing. Have freelanced for most of the major Christian publishing houses and some general houses. Quick, trustworthy, and reliable. Competitive rates; happy to negotiate: per project, per hour, or per page.

TINA DEE COMMUNICATIONS, PO Box 246, Poway CA 92074. (858)775-3580. E-mail: Editing AtTinaDeeBooks@gmail.com. Website: www.TinaDeeBooks.com. E-mail contact. CA/GE/LC, proofreading, mentoring new writers. Edits JN/N/S/SS. Editorial levels with competitive rates and endorsements listed on Website. Offers 5-page sample edit. Freelance author/editor. Contributing member of The Christian PEN (Proofreaders/Editors Network). Instructor of mentoring clinics for beginning writers.

THE WORD WORKS/SONJA L. STRUTHERS, 40960 California Oaks Rd., Ste. 369, Murrieta CA 92562-4615. Phone/fax (951)696-5631. E-mail: info@mywriter.net. Website: www.my writer.net. Call/e-mail. B/GE/GH/LC/NL/SP/WS/writing coach. Edits: A/BP/E/F/NB/QL/SS/TM. Graduate of Irvine College Writing Program; award-winning editor & publisher for Inland Empire Mensa. Offers quote upon review of project only.

COLORADO

ALPHA TRANSCRIPTION/CHERYL A. COLCHIN, 1832 S. Lee St., Unit G, Lakewood CO 80232-6255. (303)978-0880. Fax (303)989-9595. E-mail: alphatranscription@juno.com. Call/e-mail/write. Typing for authors, preferably from cassette tapes, but will consider legible longhand material. Rate determined after discussion with client. Has worked with Dr. Larry Crabb, David Wilkerson, literary agents, and authors since 1988.

+EDIT EXPRESS/BRAD LEWIS & OTHER EDITORS, Colorado Springs CO. (719)649-4478. Fax (866)542-5165. E-mail: projectmanager@editexpress.net. Website: www.editexpress .net. Submit through Website (preferred) or by e-mail. Line editing/substantive editing for nonfiction books or individual chapters (in preparation for submitting to editors). A place where authors and publishers' representatives can submit manuscripts online and know the charges will be based on the length of the manuscript and the speed with which they need the substantive editing completed.

EDIT RESOURCE/ERIC & ELISA STANFORD, 3578-E Hartsel Dr. PMB 387, Colorado Springs CO 80920. (719)599-7808. E-mail: info@editresource.com. Websites: www.editresource .com, www.inspirationalghostwriting.com, www.bookproposals.net. E-mail contact. CA/GE/GH/LC/NL/SP/copywriting/proposal development. Edits A/BP/BS/D/E/F/GB/N/NB/QL/book doctoring. Rates determined after discussion with client. Combined 35 years of professional editing experience.

+SUSAN MARTINS MILLER WRITING & EDITORIAL, INC., 3042 Montebello Dr. W., Colorado Springs, CO 80918. (719)659-2426. E-mail: susan@susanmartinsmiller.com. Website: www .susanmartinsmiller.com. E-mail contact. CA/GE/GH/LC/SP. Edits A/BS/D/JN/N/NB/book rewrites. Rates determined after discussion with client. 20+ years' editing experience.

OMEGA EDITING/MICHAEL P. COLCHIN, 1832 S. Lee St., Unit G, Lakewood CO 80232-6255. (303)978-0880. Fax (303)989-9596. E-mail: omegaediting@juno.com. Write/call/e-mail. B/CA/GE/GH/LC/NL/SP. Edits A/BP/BS/D/NB/QL/SS/TM. Charges $45 & up, or by the project after discussion with client. Works in partnership with authors and publishers as ghostwriter, coauthor, editor, or in editorial development. Published book and article author; 13 years' experience as freelance editor.

THE PERFECT PAPER/PATRICIA UNGER, 16695 Von Neuman Dr., Monument CO 80132. Phone/fax (719)481-4688. E-mail: dpunger@comcast.net. Websites: www.theperfect paper.biz, www.aperfectsolutionva.com. Call/e-mail/send with $25 deposit. B/BCE/GE/GH/LC/NL/SP/PP/transcription. Edits A/BP/D/E/F/JN/N/NB/P/QL/S/SS. Charges $2.50-3.50/page for smaller projects (up to 30 pgs.); $60/hr. for projects over 30 pgs. Twenty years' experience transcribing, proofreading and copyediting.

SCRIBBLE COMMUNICATIONS/BRAD LEWIS, Colorado Springs CO. (719)649-4478. Fax (866)542-5165. E-mail: brad.lewis@scribblecommunications.com. Website: www.scribble communications.com. E-mail contact. GE/GH/LC/substantive editing/developmental editing. Edits A/BP/BS/D/NB/QL/Website content. Edited nearly 100 nonfiction books; senior editor of the *New Men's Devotional Bible* (Zondervan); content editor for *New Living Translation Study Bible* (Tyndale). Charges by project, mutually agreed upon with publisher, and stated in editor's/author's agreement.

+SHEVET WRITING SERVICES/MARJORIE VAWTER, 3605 W. 94th Ave., Westminster CO 80031-3156. Phone/fax (720)540-9516 (call ahead for fax). E-mail: shevetwriter@ pcisys.net. Website: www.shevetwritingservices.com. E-mail contact. GE/LC. Edits: N/NB. Has been editing/proofreading for last 8 years (last 3 full time); edits manuscripts for an agent. Testimonials and endorsements on Website.

A WAY WITH WORDS/RENEE GRAY-WILBURN, 1820 Smoke Ridge Dr., Colorado Springs CO 80919. (719)265-6626. E-mail: waywords@earthlink.net. Call/e-mail. B/CA/GE/GH/LC/

NL/SP. Edits A/BS/D/E/F/GB/JN/N/NB/PB/QL/SS/TM. Line editing/copyediting: $15-25/hr. & up. Project prices negotiable. Has had a writing company for over 12 years. Provides editorial services for independent authors, Christian publishers, ministries, and small businesses (proofed nearly 100 books). Open to coauthoring opportunities.

FLORIDA

EDITORIAL SERVICES/SHARON LEE ROBERTS, 240 San Marco Dr., Venice FL 34285. (941)484-0773. Fax (941)488-0847. E-mail: prose-and-poetry@peoplepc.com Call/e-mail/fax/write. GE/LC. Edits A/D/F/P/PB/SS. Charges $25/hr. for critique/evaluation/line editing/copyediting ($25 minimum) or $2.50/pg., or negotiable fee for project. Published author of 3 children's storybooks and hundreds of articles, short stories, and poems for children and adults. Former editorial assistant for *Living Streams*, a Christian writer's magazine.

EDITORIAL SERVICES/DIANE E. ROBERTSON, PO Box 364, Venice FL 34284-0364. (941) 928-5302. E-mail: pswriter1@netzero.net. E-mail contact. GE/GH/LC/SP. Edits A/N/NB/SS. Published novelist; published 200+ articles, short stories, children's stories; previously served as associate editor of two magazines; presently teaches Short Story, Novel-Writing, and Magazine Writing creative writing classes at a community college. E-mail a brief description of project to get an estimate or copy of rate sheet. Charges $20/hr.

EDITORIAL SERVICES/LESLIE SANTAMARIA, Winter Springs FL. E-mail: santamaria@mpinet.net. E-mail first. GE/LC. Edits A/BP/D/E/JN/N/NB/PB/QL/S/SS. Critiques: $65 for short pieces/picture books; $100 for 3-chapter book proposals. Editing services: by the page based on $35/hr. Published author and book reviewer with extensive book and magazine editing experience and a BA in English. Specializes in children's, poetry, and devotions.

LIGHTPOST COMMUNICATIONS/SEAN FOWLDS, 305 Pinecrest Rd., Mount Dora FL 32757-5929. (352)383-2485. E-mail: sfowlds@earthlink.net. Website: www.seanfowlds.com. E-mail contact. B/GE/LC/NL/SP/copy for Websites. Edits A/BP/BS/D/E/F/GB/NB/P/PB/QL/S/SS/TM. Offers coaching, writing, and editing services. Negotiated sliding scale starting at $35/hr. Former editor of a national publication.

GEORGIA

EDITORIAL SERVICES/GLORIA SPENCER, 1455 Johnson Rd., Conyers GA 30094. (770)294-8599. E-mail: gfespencer@aol.com. E-mail contact. GE/GH/LC. Edits A/BP/BS/D/N/NB/SS. Over 15 years' experience editing fiction/nonfiction books, articles, and book proposals. Charges $15/hr. or by the project after initial free consultation.

+FAITHWORKS EDITORIAL & WRITING, INC./NANETTE THORSEN-SNIPES, PO Box 1596, Buford GA 30515. Phone/fax (770)945-3093. E-mail: nsnipes@bellsouth.net. Website: www.nanettesnipes.com. E-mail contact. Freelance editor, book doctor, copyeditor/line editor, proofreader, work-for-hire projects with publishers. Edits juvenile fiction/short stories; juvenile or adult nonfiction/articles/business/humor. Author of over 500 articles/stories; has stories in over 45 compilation books.

BONNIE C. HARVEY, PhD, 5579B Chamblee Dunwoody Rd., Ste. 357, Atlanta GA 30038. (404)299-6149. Cell (404)580-9431. Fax (404)297-6651. E-mail: BoncaH@aol.com. Website: www.bookimprove.com. Call/e-mail/write to discuss terms & payment. CA/GE/GH/LC/SP/theology. Edits A/BS/D/GBE/JN/P/N/NB/QL/S/SS/theological and academic articles. Does critiquing, editing, book consulting, book proposals, and rewriting. Charges $20/hr. for reading/critiquing; $20/hr. for proofreading; $25/hr. for editing, $45-75/hr. for rewriting. Has PhD in English; 14 years teaching college-level English; teaches English and writing classes at Kennesaw University; over 27 years' experience as editor; has ghostwritten books and authored 22 books. Does agenting; see separate listing.

ON-TIME EDITORIAL SERVICES/LEIGH DELOZIER, 73 Price Quarters Rd., Ste. 124, McDonough GA 30253. (770)851-6263. Fax (866)321-9914. E-mail: leighdelozier@ bellsouth.net. Website: www.leighdelozier.com, or www.leighdelozier.net. Call/e-mail. B/GE/LC/NL/SP/Sunday school curriculum. Edits A/BP/D/GB/JN/QL. Also helps create press releases, media kits, and other promotional materials. BS in Journalism; 20 years' experience in publishing and public relations; multipublished author in Christian and corporate markets. Fees by the hour, page, or project, depending on the work. Basic proofreading $25/hr.; editing/rewriting $35-60/hr.

+WRITE AVENUE/JILL COX-CORDOVA, 1310 Shiloh Trail East N.W., Kennesaw GA 30144. (678)521-0899. E-mail: jcoxwritemind@aol.com. Website: www.writeavenue.com. E-mail contact. GE/LC/media résumés/writing coach. Edits A/BP/BS/E/GB/N/NB/QL/SS. Offers a variety of other services. CNN.com Live sr. producer; journalist for 18 yrs in both print and broadcast; media studies professor for 3 yrs. See Website for list of services and charges.

+WRITTEN BY A PRO/SHARLA TAYLOR, 3745 Hwy 17, Ste. 500, PMB 178, Richmond Hill GA 31324. (912)656-6857. E-mail: writtenbyapro@msn.com. Website: www.writtenbya pro.com. E-mail contact. CA/GE/GH/LC/SP/author assistance for ms preparation/SAT help for college-bound/writing coach. Edits: A/BP/BS/D/E/GB/JN/N/NB/QL/SS/TM. Operates an online writing/editing service for authors & job seekers; tutors college-bound students, and teaches writing to middle school and high school students. E-mail or see Website for rates.

IDAHO

+WRITE WORDS EDITING/SUSAN LOHRER, PO Box 702, Porthill ID 83853-0702. E-mail: susan@inspirationaleditor.com. Website: www.InspirationalEditor.com. E-mail contact. GE/LC/writing coach. Edits: A/BP/N/QL/SS. Specializes in editing women's fiction and romance. Member of Christian Editor Network, Christian Proofreaders and Editors Network, and Romance Writers of America. E-mail for rates.

ILLINOIS

ALICE 'N INK/ALICE PEPPLER, 1285 Luther Ln., Apt. 173B, Arlington Hts. IL 60004-8176. (773)878-5943. E-mail: apeppler@aol.com. Website: www.apeppler.com. Call/e-mail/ write. B/GE/LC/NL. Edits A/BP/BS/D/E/F/GB/JN/N/NB/P/PB/QL/SS ($25/hr.). Three-chapter book proposal, including market analysis $103; additional editing $30/hr. Publishing experience of 25 years. Published author of Christian books, articles, poetry, monographs. Quality work; quick turnaround.

AMY BADOWSKI'S EDITING SERVICE, 649 Frances Ave., Loves Park IL 61111-5910. E-mail: Amy.Badowski@gmail.com. GE/LC. Edits A/BP/D/E/JN/N/NB/SS. BA English Studies, magna cum laude. Pursuing MA. Teaching. Charges $40-100 for articles; $250-750 for books.

+EDITORIAL SERVICES/MELISSA JUVINALL, 206 Ambrose Way, Normal IL 61761. (309) 452-8917. E-mail: kangaj1@hotmail.com. Website: www.bearla.com. E-mail contact. GE/LC. Edits BS/GB/JN/N/NB/PB/TM. Has a B.A. & M.A. in English; specializes in children's lit; 7 years' editing experience; judge for Christy Awards. Charges by the page for proofreading and copyediting; by the hour for critiquing.

THE WRITER'S EDGE, PO Box 1266, Wheaton IL 60187. E-mail: info@writersedgeservice.com. Website: www.WritersEdgeService.com. No phone calls. A manuscript screening service for 90 cooperating Christian publishers. Charges $95 to evaluate a book proposal and if publishable, they will send a synopsis of it to 90 publishers who might be interested. If not publishable they will tell how to improve it. If interested, send an SASE for guidelines and a Book Information Form; request a form via e-mail or copy from Website. The Writer's Edge now handles previously published books, including self-published books or those that are out of print and available for reprint. Requires a different form, but cost is the same. Reviews novels, nonfiction books, juvenile novels, Bible studies, devotionals, biography, and theology, but no poetry. See Website for details.

INDIANA

DENEHEN INC./DR. DENNIS E. HENSLEY, 6824 Kanata Ct., Fort Wayne IN 46815-6388. Phone/fax (260)485-9891. E-mail: dnhensley@hotmail.com. E-mail/write. GE/GH/LC. Edits A/BP/BS/D/E/F/JN/N/NB/P/QL/SS/comedy/academic articles/editorials/Op-Ed pieces/columns/speeches/interviews. Rate sheet for SASE. Author of 51 books & 3,000 articles and short stories; PhD in English; University English professor; columnist for *Writer's Journal* and *Advanced Christian Writer.*

+EDITORIAL SERVICES/AMANDA SEVERNS, 3162 E. 300 South, Rochester IN 46975. (574) 223-6519. E-mail: severnsa@yahoo.com. E-mail contact. B/CA/GE/GH/LC/NL/PP/SP. Edits: A/BP/BS/D/E/F/GB/JN/N/NB/P/PB/QL/SS. B.A. in English with a minor in business; magazine editor; published author. Negotiable rates.

EDITORIAL SERVICES/APRIL STIER, 7768 N. 100 E., Ossian IN 46777-9360. (260)402-1883. E-mail: april_lynn@mac.com. E-mail/write. CA/GE/LC. Edits A/BP/BS/D/E/F/GB/N/NB/QL/SS. Charges $20/hr. for proofreading/copyediting; $27/hr. for line editing, and $250 and up for manuscript evaluation. Send SASE or e-mail for rate sheet. BA in English, AA in writing, BA in Biblical Studies; published writer.

+MENTOR'S PEN EDITORIAL SERVICES/CHRISTINA MILLER, 7084 S. 585 W., Huntingburg IN 47542. (812)536-3549. E-mail: Christina@mentorspen.com. Website: www.mentorspen.com. E-mail contact. BCE/GE/LC/writing coach. Edits: BP/N/NB/QL. Published writer, five years' experience editing and critiquing, fiction contest judge. Offers free 5-page sample edit.

TYPING/EDITORIAL SERVICES/BARBARA BUIS, 4978 S. County Rd. 75 West, Greencastle IN 46135. (765)653-4497. E-mail: truk4jsuschrst@yahoo.com. Call/e-mail. LC/Transcription from tapes. Edits A/BS/D/N/SS/(anything). Has typed 4 books and helped edit 3 books. Charges $1.50/pg.

XARISCOM/JAMES WATKINS, 318 N. Lenfesty Ave., Marion IN 46952. (765)618-7913. E-mail: jim@jameswatkins.com. Website: www.jameswatkins.com. E-mail contact. GE/GH/LC/WS. Edits A/BP/BS/D/NB/QL/S. Award-winning author of 14 books & 2,000+ articles & an editor; winner of four editing and 2 book awards. 20+ years' experience. Charge $50 for 2,000 words of critique, editing, market suggestions; $5/pg. for content editing; $15/pg. for rewriting/ghosting; $50/hr. for Website evaluation/consulting.

KANSAS

AFFORDABLE NOVEL CRITIQUE SERVICE/SALLY BRADLEY, 239 N. 4th Ter., Louisburg KS 66053-4179. E-mail: sally@sallysbradley. Website: www.sallybradley.com. E-mail contact. B/GE/LC/SP. Edits BP/N/QL/SS. BA in English, former editor for Christian publishers, contest judge, member of Christian PEN (Proofreaders and Editors Network) and the Christian Editor Network. Services, prices, and client referrals on Website. Will tailor services to fit your needs.

KENTUCKY

EDITORIAL SERVICES/MARILYN A. ANDERSON, 127 Sycamore Dr., Louisville KY 40223-2956. (502)244-0751. Fax (502)452-9260. E-mail: shelle12@aol.com. Call/e-mail. GE/LC. Edits A/BS/D/E/F/NB/TM. Charges $15-20/hr. for proofreading; $25/hr. for extensive editing; or negotiable by the job or project. Holds an MA and BA in English; former high school English teacher; freelance consultant since 1993. References available. Contributing member of The Christian PEN.

EDITORIAL SERVICES/BETTY L. WHITWORTH, 11740 S. Hwy 259, Leitchfield KY 42754. (270)257-2461. E-mail: Blwhit@bbtel.com. Call/e-mail. GE. Edits A/D/JN/N/NB/SS. Typing fees based on project (reasonable). Editing for novels and nonfiction books: $50 deposit with first 100 pgs., fee based on amount of work. Send entire manuscript for everything else. Retired English teacher, newspaper columnist for 18 yrs., published over 1,000 stories/articles; author of 4 books; has worked with over 60 writers.

MARYLAND

+OPINE'S CONSULTING WITH AUTHORS, a Consulting Service outgrowth of Opine Publishing, 5113 W. Running Brook Rd., Columbia MD 21044-1522. (443)745-1004. E-mail: info@opinebooks.com. Website: www.opinebooks.com. E-mail contact with project summary and 2 chapters as attachment; or send with $45 deposit. GE/LC/NL/SP/WS/writing coach. Edits A/BP/D/NB/QL/SS (e-mail with project idea to determine if I can help you). Editor of 7 published books; author of articles & book; founded and directed publishing company; Website developer; newsletter development; BA in English. Charges reasonable fee in agreement with client, with deposit and payment schedule.

OWEN-SMITH & ASSOCIATES, INC./RHONDA OWEN-SMITH, 2916 Old Court Rd., Pikesville MD 21208. (410)602-8970. Fax (410)602-1056. E-mail: mapress@aol.com. E-mail/write. Does marketing, PR, media, publicity, direct response. Twenty-five years of relevant experience; published author; master's degree. Résumé & references available. Charges $25/hr. with 4 hr. minimum. All work based on contractual terms.

MASSACHUSETTS

WORD PRO/BARBARA A. ROBIDOUX, 127 Gelinas Dr., Chicopee MA 01020-4813. (413)592-4386. Fax (413)594-8375. E-mail: Ebwordpro@aol.com. Call/e-mail. GE/LC/writing coach. Edits A/BP/D/E/F/NB/QL/SS/TM. Fee quoted upon request. BA in English; 18 years as freelancer; book reviewer; on staff of TCC Manuscript critique service.

MICHIGAN

CALLED AND READY WRITERS CONSULTATION SERVICE/MARY EDWARDS/WANDA J. BURNSIDE, PO Box 211018, Detroit MI 48221. (313)491-3504. Fax (313)861-7578. E-mail: wtvision@hotmail.com. Website: www.thecalledandreadywriters.org. E-mail/$50 deposit. B/BCE/CA/GE/GH/LC/NL/PP/SP/WS/writing coach. Edits A/BP/BS/D/E/F/GB/JN/N/NB/P/PB/QL/S/SS/gospel tracts. Forty years' experience in editing. Has member and nonmember rates. Charges by the page or type of project.

+EDITORIAL SERVICES/ADAM BLUMER, 719 East H St., Iron Mountain MI 49801. (906)774-9576. E-mail: adam@blumer.org. Website: www.blumer.org/adam. E-mail contact. BCE/GE/GH/LC. Edits A/BP/BS/D/F/GB/JN/N/NB/PB/QL/SS. More than 15 years' experience in writing, editing, proofreading, and Website updating. Employed as full-time editor for 14 years; B.A. in print journalism.

WALLIS EDITORIAL SERVICES/DIANA WALLIS, 547 Cherry St. S.E., #6C, Grand Rapids MI 49503-4755. (616)459-8836. E-mail: WallisEdit@sirus.com. Call/e-mail. GE/LC/SP/WS/ proofreading. Edits A/BS/D/JN/N/NB/TM/advertising and promotional copy, Website content, educational materials for students and parents/teachers, catalog copy. Rates per project rather than per hour. Calvin College graduate, 15 years freelancing for publishers, corporations, and ad agencies; details on request.

THE WRITE SPOT/ARLENE KNICKERBOCKER, Where Quality and Economy Unite, PO Box 424, Davison MI 48423-9318. (810)793-0316. E-mail: writer@thewritespot.org. Website: www.thewritespot.org. E-mail/write. B/CA/GE/GH/LC/NL/classes and speaking/writing coach. Edits: A/BP/BS/D/NB/P/QL/SS. Twelve years of published credits; references available. Prices on Website.

WRITING CAREER COACH.COM/TIFFANY COLTER, Michigan. E-mail: Tiffany@WritingCareer Coach.com. Website: www.writingcareercoach.com. E-mail contact. GE/GH/SP/writing coach/writing career coaching business planning. Edits BP/N/NB/QL. BA; Daphne Award-Winning Writer; multiple articles published; regular contributor to *Toledo Business Journal;* feature writer/columnist. Charges $20/hr. for content editing and career coaching. See Website for other services.

MINNESOTA

+NOBLE CREATIVE, LLC/SCOTT NOBLE, PO Box 131402, St. Paul MN 55113. (651)494-4169. E-mail: snoble@noblecreative.com. Website: www.noblecreative.com. E-mail contact. B/GE/GH/LC/NL/SP/WS. Edits A/BP/BS/D/E/F/GB/N/NB/QL/SS/TM. More than two decades' experience, including several years as asst. ed. at *Decision Magazine*. Masters degree in Theological Studies. Charges by the hour or the project.

NORTH COUNTRY TRANSCRIPTION (Psalm 96:12): Writing, Editing and Secretarial Services/CONNIE PETTERSEN. (218)927-6176. E-mail: cardinals4connie@gmail.com. Call/e-mail. Manuscript typing; edits for punctuation/spelling/grammar, etc. Published author of short fiction; journalist with over 300 articles published in *NewsHopper;* 30 years' secretarial/transcription experience. Types novels/nonfiction mss, résumés, etc. Transcription by digital voice or tape. Fees: base $14/hr. or by a 65-character, computer-counted line, plus postage. Free estimates. Confidentiality guaranteed. References.

MISSOURI

BLUE MOUNTAIN EDITORIAL SERVICE/BARBARA WARREN, 4721 Farm Road 2165, Exeter MO 65647. (417)835-3235. E-mail: barbarawarren@mo-net.com. Website: www.barbara warrenbluemountainedit.com. E-mail contact. GE/LC/content editor/writing coach. Edits N/NB. Charges $20/hr. Twenty years' experience.

EDITORIAL SERVICES/JUDI LUDWIG, 6040 Sutherland Ave., St. Louis MO 63109-2246. (314)457-0026. E-mail: tludwig4@sbcglobal.net. E-mail contact. GE/LC. Edits A/BP/BS/D/ E/GB/JN/N/NB/QL/S/SS/TM. Charges $1.50/12 pt., double-spaced page, plus postage. Has M.A. in Media Communications; editor for Christian book publisher; book author.

THERE'S AN ANGEL IN YOUR INKWELL/CAROL NEWMAN, PO Box 480835, Kansas City MO 64148-0835. (913)681-1168. Fax (913)681-1173. E-mail: carol@angelinyourinkwell .com. Website: www.angelinyourinkwell.com. E-mail contact. GE/GH. Edits A/BP/D/E/F/ NB/P/QL/SS. Variable rates according to project; average $40/hr.; 1/2 hr. free consultation. Twenty years national inspirational writer, teacher, and writing coach.

MONTANA

+THE WRITE EDITOR/ERIN K. BROWN, Corvallis MT. E-mail: thewriteeditor@gmail.com. Website: www.writeeditor.net. E-mail contact. GE/LC/NL. Edits A/BP/BS/D/E/F/JN/N/NB/QL/SS. Has a certificate in Editorial Practices: Graduate School, USDA, Washington DC; Christy Award judge 2006-2008; member of Editorial Freelancers Assn.; The Christian PEN.

NEBRASKA

+REDEEMING WORDS/LAURA EVANS, PO Box 252, Wisner NE 68791-0252. E-mail: Laura@redeemingwords.com. Website: www.redeemingwords.com. E-mail contact. Focus is solely on editing, critiquing, and mentoring beginning and intermediate poets. Well-published poet; taught poetry for adult education; BS in English Literature. Charges $10 for up to 30 lines. See Website for sample critique.

NEVADA

+EDITORIAL SERVICES/JEANETTE HANSCOME, 3201 Heights Dr., Reno NV 89503. (925) 487-7550. E-mail: jeanettehanscome@sbcglobal.net. Website: www.jeanettehanscome.com. E-mail contact. B/CA/GE/SP/writing coach. Edits A/D/E/F/JN/N/NB/QL/S/SS/YA novels & nonfiction. Author of 3 teen books with Focus on the Family; editor for 3 years; has led a critique group; teaches at writers' conferences.

NEW HAMPSHIRE

AMGD ENTERPRISES/SALLY WILKINS, PO Box 273, Amherst NH 03031-0273. (603)673-9331. E-mail: SEDWilkins@aol.com. E-mail contact. B/GE/LC/NL. Edits A/BP/F/NB/QL. Published nonfiction adult and juvenile books and articles; edited 2 successful book proposals; experienced critiquer. Rate sheet for SASE.

NEW JERSEY

+TOPNOTCH WRITING SOLUTIONS/MARYANN DIORIO, PhD, 1216 Forest Dr., Millville NJ 08332-2597. (856)327-1231. Fax (856)327-0291. E-mail: DrMaryAnn@TopNotchWriting Solutions.com. Website: www.TopNotchWritingSolutions.com. E-mail contact. GE/NL/SP/WS/writing coach (www.TopNotchLifeandCareerCoaching.com). Edits A/BP/F/P/QL/SS. 25+ years' experience; award winner; 4 published bks.; hundreds of published articles, short stories, and poems. Charges $55/hr. or by the project. Rate sheet available on request.

+WRITER'S RELIEF, INC./RONNIE L. SMITH, 409 S. River St., Hackensack NJ 07601. (866) 405-3003. Fax (201)641-1253. E-mail: Ronnie@wrelief.com. Website: www.writersrelief .com. Call or e-mail. LC/NL. Edits A/BP/BS/F/GB/JN/N/NB/P/PB/QL/SS. Fourteen years' experience as an Author's Submission Service. Free monthly newsletter for writers contains dated list of markets. Contact for rates.

NEW MEXICO

EDITORIAL SERVICES/JEANNE SHANNON, 1217 Espejo St. N.E., Albuquerque NM 87112-5215. (505)296-0691. E-mail: jspoetry@aol.com. Website: www.thewildflowerpress.com. E-mail contact. GE/LC. Edits A/BP/BS/E/F/JN/N/NB/P/QL/SS/TM. Published author; several years' experience as a technical writer/editor; MA in English; currently a small press publisher. Charges $1.25/pg. for copyediting/line editing; $25/hr. for more comprehensive editing.

NEW YORK

EDITORIAL SERVICES/STERLING DIMMICK, 311 Chemung St., Apt. 5, Waverly NY 14892-1463. (607)565-4247. E-mail: sterlingdimmick@hotmail.com. Call. CA/GE/GH/LC/SP. Edits A/BP/BS/D/E/F/GB/JN/N/NB/P/PB/QL/S/SS/TM. Has an AAS in Journalism; BA in Communication Studies. Charges $20/hr. or by the project.

EDITORIAL SERVICES/LAURIE GRAZIANO, 658 E. 34th St., Brooklyn NY 11203-6102. E-mail: grazianolau@yahoo.com. E-mail/write. Research/market columns/interviews/instructional. Will write A/D/F/P greeting card copy. Experienced writer, contributing editor, staff writer, regular columnist. Charges $15-75/hr., or by the project.

+EDITORIAL SERVICES/DENISE SYED, 7681 Whispers Ln., Ontario NY 14519. (585)747-1923. Fax (315)524-8848. E-mail: Denise@aheartcreative.com. Website: www.aheart creative.com. E-mail contact. B/BCE/CA/GE/GH/LC/NL/PP/SP/WS. Edits A/BP/BS/D/E/F/GB/JN/NB/PB/SS/TM/legal writing. Retired lawyer with experience in legal writing, technical writing, and writing pertaining to the arts. Loves nonfiction. Encourages writers to be thorough in theology and application, and literary in tone.

NORTH CAROLINA

+EDITORIAL SERVICES/MIKE & JASMIN MORRELL, Raleigh NC. (770)313-1718. E-mail: jasminis@gmail.com. E-mail contact. B/GE/LC/NL/SP/WS. Edits: A/BP/BS/D/E/F/GB/JN/N/NB/PB/QL/SS. Has edited for Christian publishers and mainstream curriculum publishers. Developmental editing: $8/pg.; copyediting $6/pg. Requires 50% of fee upfront. Requested revisions are included in original fee.

ANNA W. FISHEL, 3416 Hunting Creek Dr., Pfafftown NC 27040. (336)924-5880. E-mail: awfishel@triad.rr.com. Call/write/e-mail. CA/GE/SP. Edits A/D/E/JN/N/NB/P/SS. Charges by the hour. Estimates offered. Two decades of professional editing experience; editor with major Christian publishing house for over 10 years; published author of 6 children's books.

PREP PUBLISHING/PATTY SLEEM, 1110 1/2 Hay St., Fayetteville NC 28305. (910)483-6611. Fax (910)483-2439. E-mail: preppub@aol.com. Website: www.prep-pub.com. Write. GE/LC/SP. Edits N/NB. Project price based on written query and initial free telephone consultation. BA in English, MBA from Harvard, author of more than 25 books.

OHIO

+IZZY'S OFFICE/DIANE STORTZ, PO Box 31239, Cincinnati OH 45231. (513)602-6720. E-mail: diane@izzysoffice.com. Website: www.izzysoffice.com. E-mail contact. CA/GE/GH/LC. Edits: A/BP/BS/D/E/GB/JN/NB/PB. Former editorial director for a Christian publisher (10 yrs.); published author, experience as children's editor and magazine copyeditor. See Website for client list and list of projects. Copyediting or substantive editing by the hour or per-project basis; book proposal package $750; evaluation and 2-chapter critique $350. One-half payment amount due before work begins.

+PROOF PERFECT/KAREN HAWLEY, PO Box 53394, Cincinnati OH 45253-0394. (513)619-1841. Fax (513)598-6909. Cell (513)257-7007. E-mail: proofperfectbykhawley@yahoo .com. Freelance writer/editor/proofreader.

WRITER'S NUDGE/MARY BUSHA, 1370-B Deerfield Rd., Lebanon, OH 45036. (513)228-1205. E-mail: marybusha@writersnudge.com. Website: www.writersnudge.com. E-mail contact. BCE/CA/GE/LC/writing coach. Edits A/BP/BS/D/E/GB/JN/N/NB/PB/QL/SS. Offers workshops/seminars. Over 30 years of editorial and writing experience. Evaluates your project and bids on the project.

OKLAHOMA

+EDITORIAL SERVICES/RICHARD W. RUNDELL, PO Box 983, Haskell OK 74436-0983. (918)482-5066. E-mail: rwrundell@windstream.net. E-mail contact. GE/LC. Edits: A/D/NB. Over 20 years' editing experience; author of books, articles, booklets, devotionals, and book reviews. Rates negotiable.

EPISTLEWORKS CREATIONS/JOANN RENO WRAY, Helping Writers Reach Their High Call, 8409 S. Elder Ave., Broken Arrow, OK 74011-8286. (918)451-4017 or Cell (918)695-4528. E-Mail: epedit@epistleworks.com. Website: http://epistleworks.com. Call/write/e-mail (prefer). B/CA/GE/GH/LC/NL/SP/research. Edits A/BP/D/F/N/NB/P/SS. Creates graphic art such as covers and logos; Website design and content. PR materials such as fliers, brochures, booklets, and Web ads, including animated. Uses signed contracts with clients. Experienced writer, editor, and artist since 1974. Has been a columnist, an editor for a Tulsa monthly Christian newspaper, published an online magazine, edited books for pastors and ministers, has spoken and taught at national Christian Writers' conferences. Over 3,000 articles published. Charges start at $30/hr. with a required $45 nonrefundable consulting fee (deducted from total bill). Discounts for churches and ministries. Accepts checks, money orders, or PayPal. See Website for detail on services. Gives binding estimates. Gives detailed time clock report. Mentoring services and email writing classes available. Speaker and teacher.

TWEEN WATERS EDITORIAL SERVICES/TERRI KALFAS, PO Box 1233, Broken Arrow OK 74013-1233. (918)346-7960. Fax (918)455-0794. E-mail: tlkalfas@cox.net. E-mail contact. B/BCE/CA/GE/GH/LC/SP. Edits A/BP/BS/D/N/NB/QL/TM/project management/book doctoring. Multiple editorial and freelance writing services. Twenty years' experience as reporter, writer, editor, editorial development director, and director of publishing. Equally skilled in copywriting for catalogs, direct marketing, and fund-raising. Former tech school writing instructor. Award-winning fiction writer. Available as conference speaker and workshop teacher. Charges $3 per pg./$25/hr./negotiable on special projects.

WINGS UNLIMITED/CRISTINE BOLLEY, 712 N. Sweetgum Ave., Broken Arrow OK 74012-2156. (918)250-9239. Fax (918)250-9597. E-mail: WingsUnlimited@aol.com. Website: www .wingsunlimited.com. E-mail contact. CA/GE/GH/LC/SP. Edits BP/D/NB. All fees negotiated in advance: developmental edits (format/house-style/clarity) range from $1,500-$3,000; 100-250 pgs.; substantive rewrite averages $5,000/250 pgs. Specializes in turning sermon series into books for classic libraries. Author/coauthor/ghostwriter of 30+ titles. Over 25 years' experience in development of best-selling titles for major Christian publishing houses.

OREGON

EDITING GALLERY LLC/CAROL L. CRAIG, 2622 Willona Dr., Eugene OR 97408. (541)342-7300. E-mail: carollcraig@comcast.net. Website: www.editinggallery.com. Call/e-mail. GE/LC/synopses/writing coach. Edits Fiction BP/N/QL/memoirs. English major; 15+ years' experience. Charges $75/hr.

EDITORIAL SERVICES/FLORENCE C. BLAKE, 4865 Hwy. 234, #176, White City OR 97503. E-mail: florblake@ccountry.net (put "Edit Service" in subject line). E-mail contact. B/GE/LC/NL/SP. Edits A/D/E/F/NB/SS Christian tracts. Freelance writers since 1999 with over 200 sales, community college writing teacher, senior contributing editor for general publication. Charges $2/double-spaced page.

+HONEST EDITING, Bill Carmichael, David Sanford & editing team. E-mails: bill@booksand manuscripts.com, or dsanford@sanfordci.com. Website: www.honestediting.com. E-mail contact. GE/LC/SP. Edits: BP/JN/N/NB. Check Website for full list of services and instructions.

PICKY, PICKY INK/SUE MIHOLER, 1075 Willow Lake Road N., Keizer OR 97303-5790. (503)393-3356. E-mail: smiholer@hotmail.com. E-mail contact. LC. Edits A/BP/BS/D/ NB/QL. Charges $30 an hour or $50 for first 10 pages of a longer work; writer will receive a firm completed-job quote based on the 1st 10 pages. Freelance editor for several book publishers since 1998. Will help you get your manuscript ready to submit.

+SANFORD COMMUNICATIONS EDITORIAL SERVICE, 16778 S.E. Cohiba Ct., Damascus OR 97089. (503)890-0456. E-mail: info@sanfordci.com. Website: www.sanfordci.com. Eight people on staff. Works with publishers, corporations, and individual authors. See Website for details.

SALLY STUART, 1647 S.W. Pheasant Dr., Aloha OR 97006. (503)642-9844. Fax (503)848-3658. E-mail: stuartcwmg@aol.com. Website: www.stuartmarket.com. Blog: www.stuartmarket .blogspot.com. Call/e-mail. BCE/GE/agent contracts. Edits A/BP/E/GB/JN/N/NB/SS. No poetry or picture books. Charges $40/hr. for critique; $45/hr. for phone/personal consultations. Contact for availability (not available March-June). For books, send a copy of your book proposal: cover letter, chapter-by-chapter synopsis for nonfiction (5-page overall synopsis for fiction), and the first three chapters, double spaced. Comprehensive publishing contract evaluation $80-150. Author of 36 books and 40+ years' experience as a writer, teacher, marketing expert.

PENNSYLVANIA

ANGAH CREATIVE SERVICES/DANIELLE CAMPBELL-ANGAH, 961 Taylor Dr., Folcroft PA 19032. (610)457-8300. E-mail: dcangah@angahcreative.com. Website: www.angahcreative .com. Ten years' writing experience; 5 years' editing experience.

REBECCA CARANFA, 502 Idaho Ave., Verona PA 15147-2910. Phone/fax (412)795-7711. E-mail: BlessingsofGod77@comcast.net. B/GE/NL/SP. Edits A/D/E/GB/JN/N/NB/P/SS/TM. Charges $25/hr. or estimate after evaluation of material. 20 years' experience. Teaching background.

MICHELE T. HUEY EDITORIAL SERVICES, 121 Homestead Ln., Glen Campbell PA 15742-8404. (814)845-7683. Fax (call first). E-mail: writeon4writers@yahoo.com. Website: www .writeon4writers.com. E-mail contact. GE/LC. Edits A/D/N/NB/QL/SS. English/composition/ journalism teacher for 20 yrs.; newspaper reporter, feature writer, editor, columnist for 10 yrs.; writing mentor for The Christian Writers Guild and The Writing Academy. Charges $.0125/wd. (estimates given). Provide the total number of words and a sample page or two of your manuscript. Follows rates suggested at www.writersmarket.com/content/ howmuch3.asp.

STRONG TOWER PUBLISHING/HEIDI NIGRO, PO Box 973, Milesburg PA 16853-0973. E-mail: strongtowerpubs@aol.com. Website: www.strongtowerpublishing.com. E-mail contact. GE/LC/ NL/PP/WS/rewriting/developmental editing/writing coach. Edits A/BS/D/E/F/GB/N/NB/ P/SS/TM. Specializes in general theological and eschatological mss. Twenty years' experience in editing in book and magazine publishing. Manuscript evaluation, $59-109; proofing, $2 per 250-word-page; copyediting, $4/250-word-page; developmental editing and book development $40 per hour or by project. Other projects negotiable. Provides free 5-page sample edit. Theological manuscripts must be consistent with basic statement of faith.

WORDS FOR ALL REASONS/ELIZABETH ROSIAN, 108 Deerfield Ln., Johnstown PA 15905-5703. (814)255-4351. E-mail: wordsforallreasons@atlanticbb.net. Website: www.101steps .zoomshare.com. E-mail contact. CA/GE/GH/LC. Edits A/BP/BS/D/E/F/GB/N/NB/P/QL/SS. Over 35 years' experience writing, teaching, and editing; over 1,000 published works, plus inspirational novel, how-to book, and 6 chapbooks. Rate sheet on Website.

WRITE HIS ANSWER MINISTRIES/MARLENE BAGNULL, LittD, 316 Blanchard Rd., Drexel Hill PA 19026-3507. Phone/fax: (610)626-6833. E-mail: mbagnull@aol.com. Website: www .writehisanswer.com. Call/write. GE/LC/typesetting. Edits A/BP/BS/D/JN/N/NB/SS. Charges $35/hr.; estimates given. Call or write for information on At-Home Writing Workshops, a correspondence study program. Author of 5 books; compiler/editor of 3 books; over 1,000 sales to Christian periodicals.

WRITE NOW SERVICES/KAREN APPOLD, 2012 Foxmeadow Cir., Royersford PA 19468. (610) 948-1961. Fax (610)672-9960. E-mail: KarenAppold@comcast.net. Website: www.Write NowServices.com. Call/e-mail. Does B/GE/GH/LC/NL/SP/WS. Edits A/E/F/QL/SS. Professional editor, writer, consultant since 1993 for magazines, journals, newsletters, and newspapers. Hundreds of published articles and extensive magazine and newspaper editing. Rates determined after free evaluation of project.

SOUTH CAROLINA

+EDITORIAL SERVICES/LINDA J. LEE, 106 Quail Creek Dr., West Columbia SC 29169-3434. (803)939-9713. E-mail: ljlee@bellsouth.net. E-mail contact. B/CA/GE/LC/NL/SP. Edits A/BP/BS/D/E/F/GB/JN/N/NB/P/PB/QL/S/SS/TM.

TENNESSEE

CHRISTIAN WRITERS INSTITUTE MANUSCRIPT CRITIQUE SERVICE, PO Box 110390, Nashville TN 37222. Toll-free (800)21-WRITE. E-mail: ACWriters@aol.com. Website: www .ACWriters.com. Call/write. BCE/CA/GE/GH/LC/SP. Edits A/BP/BS/D/E/F/JN/N/NB/P/PB/S/ SS/TM. Send SASE for rate sheet and submission slip.

EDIT PLUS/CHARLES STROHMER, PO Box 4325, Sevierville TN 37876. (865)453-7120. Fax (865)428-0029. E-mail: wiselife@esper.com. Call/e-mail. CA/GE/LC/NL/SP. Edits A/BP/BS/ D/E/NB/QL/TM. Twenty years' experience as author and editor for major Christian publishers. Call/e-mail to discuss project and rates. Rates vary according to the type of work, e.g., ms evaluation, line editing, rewriting, or book proposal.

+WRITING COACH/LINDA WINN, 138 Bluff Dr., Winchester TN 37398. (931)962-8801. E-mail: lhwinn@comcast.net. Writing coach.

TEXAS

ASSURANCE EDITING SERVICES/MAUREEN B. MCCLAIN, PO Box 1051, Sanger TX 76266-1051. (940)458-3814. E-mail: Assuranceedit@juno.com. E-mail/write. LC. Edits A/BP/BS/D/E/F/GB/JN/N/NB/P/QL/SS. Published book and devotional writer; freelancer for 10+ years. E-mail for prices.

+EDITORIAL SERVICES/KELLEY MATHEWS, Th.M., 216 Birdbrook Dr., Anna TX 75409. (214)769-1829. E-mail: kmathews@newdoor.info. Website: www.newdoors.info. E-mail contact. CA/GE/LC/NL/SP. Edits: A/BP/BS/D/GB/NB/PB/TM. Has 12 years' experience in editing/proofreading; coauthored 4 books; authored numerous articles. Charges $30/hr. for proofreading; $50/hr. for copyediting; negotiable flat fee for large book projects. Specializes in theological and women's issues.

EDITORIAL SERVICES/DAYLE SHOCKLEY, 25510 Foxbriar, Spring TX 77373. (281)350-2902. E-mail: dayle@dayleshockley.com. Write/e-mail. GE/GH/NL/PP/SP. Edits A/BP/D/E/ GB/NB/SS. Freelancer since 1987; special contributor to the *Dallas Morning News* since 1999; author of 3 books and dozens of articles. Contact for rates.

FACETS BUSINESS COMMUNICATIONS/GEM SMITH, PO Box 79216, Houston TX 77279. (713) 780-4676. E-mail: gem@facetscom.com. Website: www.facetscom.com. Call/e-mail. B/GE/NL/ SP/WS/content development. Edits A/BP/BS/D/E/GB/N/NB/QL/S/SS/TM. Published freelance writer/editor/speaker for 30 years. Has worked with technical/scientific/theological material and authors with English as a second language; also newsletters, manual, and training scripts. Works by the hour with deposit, after discussing project with client. Average is $35-50/hr.

PWC EDITING/PAUL W. CONANT, 527 Bayshore Pl., Dallas TX 75217-7755. (972)913-9123. Fax (972)557-7558. E-mail: pwcediting@gmail.com. Website: www.pwc-editing.com. E-mail contact. LC/NL/SP. Edits A/BS/D/E/N/NB/S/TM/dissertations/textbooks/Web pages. Writer, editor; proofreader for book publishers and magazines. Dissertations, $18/hr.; short works, $25/hr.; negotiable terms for long works. Charges publishers up to $25/hr. Prefers to work up a page rate based on a minimum 10-page sample, giving new clients between 1 and 2 hours of free editing.

+SPREAD THE WORD COMMERCIAL WRITING/KATHERINE SWARTS, Houston TX. (832) 573-9501. E-mail: katherine@spreadthewordcommercialwriting.com. Website: www .spreadthewrdcommercialwriting.com. Blog: http://newsongsfromtheheart.blogspot.com. E-mail contact only. Charges up to $80/hr. B/CA/GE/GH/LC/NL/SP/WS. Edits: BP/BS/D/ GB/NB/PB/QL. No personal-experience books. Send at least a second draft. Editor will preview author's work before acceptance. MA in written communication from Wheaton College; over 100 published articles, poems, short stories, and textbooks.

THE WRITE WAY EDITORIAL SERVICES/JANET K. CREWS/B. KAY COULTER, 806 Hopi Trl., Temple TX 76504-5008. (254)778-6490 or (254)939-1770. E-mails: janetcrews@ sbcglobal.net or bkcoulter@sbcglobal.net. Website: www.writewayeditorial.com. Call/e-mail. B/CA/GE/GH/LC/NL/SP/scan to Word document/voice to Word document/graphics. Edits A/BP/BS/D/GB/JN/N/NB/QL/SS. Published author of 3 books; contributor to 2 books; 4 years with this editorial service; certified copyeditor. Free estimate; 50% of estimate as a deposit; $30/hr. Contact for additional details.

UTAH

RIVERWRITERS.COM/KATHLEEN WRIGHT. Sandy UT. Phone/fax (801)572-5227. E-mail: kathleen@riverwriters.com. Website: www.riverwriters.com. E-mail contact. GE/fiction coaching. Edits N/QL/fiction synopsis. Also a writing coach. Charges by the hour; e-mail for current rate. BA in journalism, 20+ years' editing/writing experience. Clients include beginning writers through multipublished award winners.

VIRGINIA

EDITOR FOR YOU/MELANIE RIGNEY, 4201 Wilson Blvd., #110328, Arlington VA 22203-1859. (703)863-3940. E-mail: editor@editorforyou.com. Website: www.editorforyou.com. E-mail contact. GE/LC/writing coach. Edits BP/D/E/N/NB/QL/SS. Charges $65/hr. for content editing & coaching (provides a binding ceiling on number of hours); fees vary for ms evaluation. Editor of *Writer's Digest* magazine for 5 years; book editor/manager of Writer's Digest Books for 3 years; 30 years of editing experience; frequent conference speaker/contest judge.

EDITORIAL SERVICES/SKYLAR HAMILTON BURRIS, PO Box 7505, Fairfax Station VA 22039. (703)944-1530. E-mail: SSburris@cox.net. Website: www.editorskylar.com. E-mail contact. LC/NL/WS. Edits A/BS/D/E/F/GB/JN/P/N/NB/S/SS/TM. Charges authors $2/double-spaced pg. for editing. Charges businesses $35/hr. (for newsletter editing, writing, design);

or $2/double-spaced page. Specializes in working with self-publishing and POD authors. BA and MA in English. Eight years as a magazine editor; 10+ years of newsletter editing and design. Free sample edit of 2 pages.

SCRIVEN COMMUNICATIONS/KATHIE NEE SCRIVEN, 1902 Stevens Rd., #1406, Woodbridge VA 22191-2748. Phone/fax (703)492-6442. Cell (703)408-1184. Call or write. B/GE/GH/LC/NL/SP/WS. Edits A/BP/BS/D/E/F/GB/JN/N/NB/P/PB/QL/S/SS/bio sketches & résumés. Charges $20-22/hr (rates vary depending on amount of rewriting needed, type of project, and turnaround time; more if a lot of rewriting is required). Free half-hour consultation and estimate given. Discount for ministries. Brochure available for SASE. Has a BS in mass communication/journalism; 20 years' experience in print media; has edited 46 books plus over 50 smaller projects; worked as an editor for several publications, plus several years' marketing experience. Specializes in Christian living books for adults. Does consulting for authors planning to self-publish. Brochure available on request.

WASHINGTON

BY BRENDA: WRITER & DESIGNER/BRENDA WILBEE, 7463 Leeside Dr., Blaine WA 98230. (360)746-0308. E-mail: BeeWilbee@gmail.com. Website: www.BrendaWilbee.com. E-mail contact. Offers design services for brochures, newsletters, Websites, and PowerPoint. Has MA in Professional Writing; AA in Graphic Design; author of 9 CBA books and over 100 articles; long-time contributor to *Daily Guideposts*; and has freelanced as both a writer and designer. Charges are available on Website and can be discussed via e-mail.

DOCUMENT DRIVEN/JANICE HUSSEIN, 16420 S.E. McGillivray, #103-103, Vancouver WA 98683. (503)789-6245. E-mail: Janice@documentdriven.com. Website: www.document driven.com. Call/e-mail. GE/LC. Edits N/QL/synopsis; submission & manuscript critiques. MS in Writing/Publishing; MBA. Fee scale on Website; charges by project.

EDITORIAL SERVICES/MARION DUCKWORTH, 15917 N.E. 41st St., Vancouver WA 98682-7473. (360)896-8599. E-mail: mjduck@comcast.net. Website: www.MarionDuckworth Ministries.com. E-mail/write. GE/Writing coach. Edits A/BP/BS/NB/QL; also does consultations. Charges $25/hr. for critique or consultation. Negotiates on longer projects. Author (for over 25 years) of 17 books and 300 articles; writing teacher for over 25 years; extensive experience in general editing and manuscript evaluation.

+FICTION FIX-IT SHOP/MEREDITH EFKEN, 93 S. Jackson St. #77543, Seattle WA 98104-2818. (402)445-2529. E-mail: editor@fictionfixitshop.com. Website: www.fictionfixitshop .com. E-mail contact. GE/LC/writing coach. Edits BP/N/YA novels. All editors and coaches (except copyeditors) are published novelists. FFS is a member of the Christian PEN and Editorial Freelancers Assn. Rates listed on Website. Editing is hourly; coaching rated by package on a monthly basis.

LOGOS WORD DESIGNS INC./LINDA L. NATHAN, PO Box 735, Maple Falls WA 98266-0735. (360)599-3429. Fax (360)392-0216. E-mail: linda@logosword.com. Website: www.logos word.com. Call/e-mail. B/CA/GE/GH/LC/NL/SP/résumés, consultations, writing assistance, manuscript submission services. Edits A/BP/BS/D/E/F/JN/N/NB/PB/QL/S/SS/TM/academic, legal, apologetics, conservative political. Over 30 years' experience in wide variety of areas, including publicity, postdoctoral; BA Psychology; some MA work. Quote per project. See Website for rates.

+SUNCATCHER PUBLICATIONS/HEIDI THOMAS, Vernon WA. (360)336-5803. E-mail: suncat@ aceweb.com. E-mail contact. GE/LC. Edits: A/E/JN/N/NB/QL/SS. Journalism degree from U. of Montana and 2-year certificate in fiction writing from U. of Washington. Has 30+ years of writing experience; teaches writing; is member of the Christian PEN and Northwest Independent Editors Guild.

WISCONSIN

MARGARET HOUK: EDITING SERVICES, West 2355 Valleywood Ln., Appleton WI 54915-8712. (920)687-0559. Fax (920)687-0259. E-mail: marghouk@juno.com. Call/write. GE/LC. Edits A/BP/D/E/F/NB/QL (all for teens or adults). Author of 5 books and 700 articles; has taught writing and manuscript marketing for many years. Will quote fee based on free phone interview and writing sample.

CANADIAN/FOREIGN

AOTEAROA EDITORIAL SERVICES/VENNESSA NG, PO Box 228, Oamaru 9444, New Zealand. Phone +64273033738. (A U.S. based number is available to clients.) E-mail: editor@ aotearoaeditorial.com. Website: www.aotearoaeditorial.com. E-mail contact. GE/LC. Edits BP/N/SS. Page rates vary depending on project: start from $1.50/critique, $1/basic proofread, and $3.00/copyedit. (Rates are in U.S. dollars and can be paid by PayPal.) Six years' critiquing experience.

DORSCH EDITORIAL/AUDREY DORSCH, 1275 Markham Rd., #305, Toronto ON M1H 3A2, Canada. (416)439-4320. Fax (416)439-5089. E-mail: audrey@dorschedit.ca. Website: www.dorschedit.ca. Audrey Dorsch, ed. Editorial services: substantive editing, copyediting, indexing, proofreading, layout.

BERYL HENNE, 1028—77 University Cres., Winnipeg MB R3T 3N8, Canada. (204)9275-1799. E-mail: bhenne@mts.net. Write or e-mail. GE/LC/SP. Edits A/D/E/NB. Charges $25/hr. for copyediting; $32/hr. for content editing; will negotiate on larger projects. Has 5 years book and magazine editing, plus 20 years freelancing. Has worked with many self-publishing authors.

+WENDY M. MCNEICE, PO Box 656, Capalaba QLD 4157, Australia. Phone 042 787 0330. Fax 07 32072263 (call first, Eastern Standard Time). E-mail: scribe@scribeofspirit.com. Website: www.scribeofspirit.com. E-mail contact. CA/GH/writing coach. Multiple award-winning writer, columnist in international magazine; B.A.

WENDY SARGEANT, PO Box 5617, Alexandra Hills QLD 4161, Australia. Phone 0427 870 330. Fax 07 3822 3054 (call first, Eastern Standard Time). E-mail: Wendysargeant@ bigpond.com. Website: www.editorsqld.com/freelance/Wendy_Sargeant.htm. E-mail contact. B/CA/GE/GH/LC/NL/SP/WS (writing & evaluation) /PP/instructional design/writing coach. Edits A/BP/BS/D/E/F/GB/JN/N/NB/PB/QL/S/SS/TM copywriting. Special interests: technical material, business humor, children's books, educational books (primary, secondary, tertiary, and above), fiction, history, legal. Manuscript assessor and instructional designer with The Writing School. Award-winning author published in major newspapers and magazines. Editing educational manuals. Project officer and instructional designer for Global Education Project, United Nationals Assoc. Information specialist for Australian National University. See Wendy's writing under scribeofspirit.com. Charges $45/hr for articles/short stories; .02/wd. for copywriting; $300-400+ for book assessment.

CHRISTIAN LITERARY AGENTS

The references in these listings to "published authors" refer to those who have had one or more books published by royalty publishers, or who have been published regularly in periodicals. If a listing indicates that the agent is "recognized in the industry," it means he or she has worked with the Christian publishers long enough to be recognized by editors as credible agents.

Do not assume that because an agent is listed below, I can personally vouch for him or her. I am not able to check out each one as thoroughly as you need to. Asking editors and other writers at writers' conferences is a great way to find a good, reliable agent. You might also want to visit www.agentresearch.com and www.sfwa.org/beware/agents.html for tips on finding an agent. For a database of over 500 agencies, go to: www.literaryagent.com.

Finally, at the site for the Association of Authors' Representatives, www.aar-online.org, you will find a list of agents who don't charge fees, except for office expenses. Their Website will also provide information on how to receive a list of approved agents. Some of the listings below indicate which agents belong to the Association of Authors' Representatives, Inc. Those members have subscribed to a set code of ethics. Lack of such a designation, however, does not indicate the agent is unethical; most Christian agents are not members. If they do happen to be members, it should give you an extra measure of confidence. For a full list of member agents, go to: www.publishersweekly.com/aar.

(+) Indicates new listing

AGENT RESEARCH & EVALUATION INC., 425 N. 20th St., Philadelphia PA 19130. (215)563-1867. Fax (215)563-6797. E-mail: info@agentresearch.com. Website: www.agentresearch .info. This is not an agency but a service that tracks the public record of literary agents and helps authors use the data to obtain effective literary representation. Charges fees for this service. Offers a free "agent verification" service at the site. (Answers the question of whether or not the agent has created a public record of sales.) Also offers a newsletter, Talking Agents E-zine, free if you send your e-mail address. See Jerry Jenkins's comments on this service on their Website, in the "Story So Far" section.

ALIVE COMMUNICATIONS, 7680 Goddard St., Ste. 200, Colorado Springs CO 80920. (719)260-7080. Fax (719)260-8223. E-mail: submissions@alivecom.com. Website: www.alive com.com. Agents: Rick Christian, president; Lee Hough, Beth Jusino, Joel Kneedler. Well known in the industry. Estab. 1989. Represents 100+ clients. New clients on referral only. Handles adult and teen novels and nonfiction, gift books, crossover and general market books. Deals in both Christian (70%) and general market (30%). Member Author's Guild & AAR.

> **Contact:** E-mail to: submissions@alivecom.com. Responds in 6 wks. to referrals; may not respond to unsolicited submissions.
> **Commission:** 15%
> **Fees:** Only extraordinary costs with client's preapproval; no review/reading fee.
> **Tips:** If you have a referral, send material by mail and be sure to mark envelope "Requested Material." Unable to return unsolicited materials.

AMBASSADOR AGENCY, PO Box 50358, Nashville TN 37205. (615)370-4700, ext. 230. Fax (615)661-4344. E-mail: Wes@AmbassadorAgency.com. Website: www.AmbassadorAgency .com. Agent: Wes Yoder. Estab. 1973. Recognized in the industry. Represents 20 clients. Open to unpublished authors and new clients. Handles adult nonfiction, crossover books. Also has a Speakers Bureau.

> **Contact:** E-mail.

THE ANDERSON LITERARY AGENCY INC., 435 Convent Ave., Ste. 5, New York NY 10031. (212)234-0692. E-mail: gilescanderson@gmail.com. Agent: Giles Anderson. Open to unpublished authors and new clients. General agent. Handles adult religious nonfiction.

AUTHORCOACHING.COM: An Agent/Coaching Service for Inspirational Authors, PO Box 428, Newburg PA 17240. (717)423-6621. Fax (717)423-6944. E-mail: keith@author coaching.com. Website: www.AuthorCoaching.com. Coach: Keith Carroll. Estab. 2000. Works with all inspirational authors.

    Contact: By letter, fax, phone, e-mail.

    Fees: Visit Website for detailed description of fees.

BENREY LITERARY, PO Box 12721, New Bern NC 28561. (252)638-5787. E-mail: janet@ benreyliterary.com. Website: www.BenreyLiterary.com. Agent: Janet Benrey. Estab. 2006. Recognized in the industry. Represents 30+ clients. Prefers referrals from current clients, or to meet writers at writer's conferences. Handles adult religious/inspirational novels (romance, contemporary women's, mystery, true crime); nonfiction (Christian living); general (thriller or cozy).

    Contact: Requires e-queries.

    Commission: 15%; foreign 20%.

MEREDITH BERNSTEIN LITERARY AGENCY, 2095 Broadway, Ste. 505, New York NY 10023. (212)799-1007. Fax (212)799-1145. Agents: Meredith Bernstein. Estab. 1981. Represents 85 clients. Open to unpublished authors and new clients. Handles nonfiction & fiction on spirituality. Member AAR.

    Contact: Query with SASE. Considers simultaneous queries.

    Commission: 15%; foreign 20%.

    Fees: Charges $75/yr. disbursement fee.

    Tips: "We obtain most of our new clients through conferences and referrals from others."

BOOKS & SUCH/JANET KOBOBEL GRANT, 52 Mission Circle, Ste. 122, PMB 170, Santa Rosa CA 95409-5370. (707)538-4184. E-mail: representation@booksandsuch.biz. Website: www.booksandsuch.biz. Agents: Janet Kobobel Grant, Wendy Lawton, Etta Wilson, Rachel Zurakowski. Well recognized in industry. Estab. 1997. Represents 150 clients. Open to new or unpublished authors (with recommendation only). Handles fiction and nonfiction for all ages, picture books, gift books, crossover, and general books.

    Contact: E-mail query (no attachments); no phone query. Accepts simultaneous submissions. Responds in 6-8 wks.

    Commission: 15%.

    Fees: No fees.

    Tips: "Especially looking for nonfiction. Also historical fiction for adults."

CURTIS BROWN LTD., 10 Astor Pl., New York NY 10003-6935. (212)473-5400. Agents: Maureen Walters, Laura Blake Peterson, and Ginger Knowlton. Member AAR. General agent; handles religious/inspirational novels for all ages, adult nonfiction, and crossover books.

    Contact: Query with SASE; no fax/e-query. Submit outline or sample chapters. Responds in 4 wks. to query; 8 wks. to ms.

    Fees: Charges for photocopying & some postage.

BROWNE & MILLER LITERARY ASSOCIATES, 410 S. Michigan Ave., Ste. 460, Chicago IL 60605. (312)922-3063. Fax (312)922-1905. E-mail: mail@browneandmiller.com. Website: www.browneandmiller.com. Agent: Danielle Egan-Miller. Estab. 1971. Recognized in the industry. Represents 75+ clients, mostly general, but also select Christian fiction writers. Open to new clients and talented unpublished authors, but most interested in experienced novelists looking for highly professional, full-service representation including rights management. Handles teen and adult fiction, adult nonfiction, and gift books for the general market; adult Christian fiction only. Member AAR, RWA, MWA, and The Author's Guild.

Contact: E-query to mail@browneandmiller.com, or mailed query letter/SASE.

Commission: 15%, foreign 20%.

PEMA BROWNE LTD., 11 Tena Pl., Valley Cottage NY 10989-2215. (845)268-0029. E-mail: ppb ltd@optonline.net. Website: www.pemabrowneltd.com. Agent: Pema Browne. Recognized in industry. Estab. 1966. Represents 20 clients (2 religious). Open to unpublished authors; very few new clients at this time. Handles novels and nonfiction for all ages; picture books/novelty books, gift books, crossover books. Only accepts mss not previously sent to publishers; no simultaneous submissions. Responds in 6-8 wks.

Contact: Letter query with credentials; no phone, fax or e-query. Must include SASE. No simultaneous submissions. No attachments.

Commission: 20% U.S. & foreign; illustrators 30%.

Fees: None.

Tips: "Check at the library in reference section, in Books in Print, for books similar to yours. Have good literary skills, neat presentation. Know what has been published and research the genre that interests you."

SHEREE BYKOFSKY ASSOCIATES INC., 74930 Country Club Dr., Ste. 540, PMB 52, Palm Desert CA 92260. (760)485-4808. E-mail: deirdreheather@yahoo.com. Website: www .shereebee.com. Agents: Deidre Quinn, Heather McCue. Estab. 1984. Represents 24 clients. Open to unpublished authors and new clients. Handles adult Christian fiction & nonfiction; children's novels & nonfiction; picture books. Member AAR.

Contact: Query by e-mail. Accepts simultaneous submissions, if notified. Responds in 6 wks. (asks for a 6-week exclusive).

Commission: 15%; foreign 20%.

Fees: No fees.

Tips: "We are starting a west coast branch that will be working with Christian and children's authors. Our associate, Janet Rosen, has sold to Christian publishers in the past."

CASTIGLIA LITERARY AGENCY, 1155 Camino del Mar, Ste. 510, Del Mar CA 92014. (858)755-8761. Fax (858)755-7063. E-mail: JacLAgency@aol.com. Website: www.castiglialiterary agency.com. Agents: Julie Castiglia and Sally Van Haitsma. Estab. 1993. Recognized in the industry. Represents 50 clients. Open to unpublished authors (with credentials) and selected new clients by referrals from editors, clients or published professionals. Handles adult religious/inspirational nonfiction, Christian fiction, and general crossover books. Member AAR.

Contact: Letter only/SASE. No phone/fax/e-query.

Commission: 15%; 25% foreign.

Fees: For excessive postage and copying, FedEx or messenger service.

Tips: "I do not look at unsolicited manuscripts."

DONNA COFFEN, LITERARY AGENT/PUBLICIST, PO Box 822, Huntsville TX 77342. (936)291-2220. E-mail: admin@literaryagentpublicist.com. Website: www.literaryagent publicist.com. Agent: Donna Coffen. Estab. 2006. Represents 3 clients. Open to unpublished authors and new clients (in Texas only). Handles novels & nonfiction for all ages, picture books, poetry books, articles, short stories, poetry.

Contact: By letter, phone, or e-mail. Accepts simultaneous submissions. Responds in 4 wks.

Commission: 15%; foreign 20%.

Fees: Charges a $35 reading fee.

Note: Currently only accepting Texas-based authors.

THE BLYTHE DANIEL AGENCY INC., 4044 Cherry Plum Dr., Colorado Springs CO 80920. (719)213-3427. E-mail: blythe@theblythedanielagency.com. Website: www.theblythedanielagency .com. Agent: Blythe Daniel. Recognized in the industry. Estab. 2005. Represents 20 clients.

Open to unpublished authors with a platform and previously published authors. Handles adult religious/inspirational novels, adult nonfiction, limited children's books, and crossover books.
Contact: By e-mail or mail. Accepts simultaneous submissions. Responds in 3 weeks.
Commission: 15%; foreign 20%.
Fees: Agreed-upon expenses.
Tips: "Preferences are authors who have a solid proposal on the topic of their book, including research on their audience, comparison to competitor's books, why they want to write on the topic, and what the author uniquely brings to the topic. Authors need to have a marketing plan to promote their book and the ability to promote their own book."

DANIEL LITERARY GROUP, 1701 Kingsbury Dr., Ste. 100, Nashville TN 37215. (615)730-8207. E-mail: greg@danielliterarygroup.com. Website: www.danielliterarygroup.com. Agent: Greg Daniel. Estab. 2007. Recognized in the Industry. Represents 23 clients. Open to unpublished authors and new clients. Handles adult religious/inspirational novels & nonfiction, crossover & secular books.
Contact: E-mail only. Accepts simultaneous submissions. Responds in 3 wks.
Commission: 15%; foreign 20%.
Fees: None.

+JAN DENNIS LITERARY SERVICES, 19350 Glen Hollow Cir., Monument CO 80132. (719)559-1711. E-mail: jpdennislit@msn.com. Agent: Jan Dennis. Estab. 1995. Represents 20 clients. Open to unpublished authors and new clients. Handles teen/YA & adult religious/inspirational novels, adult nonfiction, crossover, and general books.

DYSTEL & GODERICH LITERARY MANAGEMENT INC., 1 Union Square W., Ste. 904, New York NY 10003. (212)627-9100. Fax (212)627-9313. E-mail: Miriam@dystel.com. Website: www.dystel.com. Agents: Jane Dystel, Miriam Goderich, Stacey Glick, Michael Bourret, Jim McCarthy, and Lauren Abramo. Estab. 1994. Recognized in the industry. Represents 5-10 religious book clients. Open to unpublished authors and new clients. Handles fiction and nonfiction for adults, gift books, general books, crossover books. Member AAR.
Contact: Query letter with bio. Brief e-query; no simultaneous queries. Responds to queries in 3-5 wks.; submissions in 2 mos.
Commission: 15%; foreign 19%.
Fees: Photocopying is author's responsibility.
Tips: "Send a professional, well-written query to a specific agent."

EAMES LITERARY SERVICES, 4117 Hillsboro Rd., Ste. 251, Nashville TN 37215. (615)403-4550. Fax (615)463-9361. E-mail: info@eamesliterary.com. Website: www.eamesliterary.com. Agents: John Eames (John@eamesliterary.com) and Ahna Phillips (Ahna@eamesliterary.com). Open to unpublished authors and new clients. Handles adult religious/inspirational novels & nonfiction. Guidelines on Website.

EPIC LITERARY AGENCY. 7107 S. Yale Ave., #327, Tulsa OK 74136. (918)267-3248. E-mail: KevinD@EpicLiterary.com, or info@EpicLiterary.com. Website: www.EpicLiterary.com. Agent: Kevin D. Decker. Estab. 1996. Represents up to 12 clients. Not currently open to unpublished authors; possibly open to new clients. Handles children's novels & nonfiction, picture books, screenplays, TV/movie scripts, gift books, crossover books.
Commission: 15%; foreign 20%.
Fees: Charges only for special travel or out-of-ordinary expenses.
Tips: "Please query first; we do not accept unsolicited manuscripts."

FARRIS LITERARY AGENCY INC., PO Box 570069, Dallas TX 75357-0069. (972)203-8804. Fax (972)226-1799. E-mail: farris1@airmail.net, or agent@farrisliterary.com. Website: www.farrisliterary.com. Agents: Mike Farris and Susan Morgan Farris. Accepting new clients only by referral or through writers' conferences. Handles Christian adult and teen fiction, spiritual or inspirational nonfiction, screenplays, general books, crossover books.

Contact: Mail or e-mail query (no attachments).
Commission: 15%; foreign 20%.
Fees: Expense for copies and postage only.
Tips: "Please keep your query to one page and allow 2 weeks for a response to queries and 4-6 weeks for response to submissions."

FINE PRINT LITERARY MANAGEMENT (merger of the Peter Rubie Literary Agency and the Imprint Agency), 240 W. 35th St., Ste. 500, New York NY 10001. (212)279-1776. Fax (212) 279-0927. E-mail: peter@fineprintlit.com. Website: www.fineprintlit.com. Agent: Peter Rubie and 7 other agents. Open to unpublished authors and new clients. General agent. Handles adult religion/spirituality nonfiction for teens and adults.
Contact: Query/SASE; accepts e-query. Responds in 2-3 mos.
Commission: 15%; foreign 20%.

SARA A. FORTENBERRY LITERARY AGENCY, 1001 Halcyon Ave., Nashville TN 37204. (615) 385-9074. Recognized in the industry. Estab. 1995. Represents 30 clients. Open to unpublished authors or new clients only by referral. Handles adult nonfiction and novels, picture books, gift books, and general books, crossover books.
Contact: Unpublished authors query by mail; published authors by phone or mail. Query letters should be accompanied by referral, book proposal, and SASE.
Commission: 15%; foreign 10%, plus subagent commission.
Fees: Standard expenses directly related to specific projects (copies, messenger, overnight shipping, and postage).
Tips: "For my purposes, a published author is one who has had a book published by a commercial (royalty) publisher."

SAMUEL FRENCH INC., 45 W. 25th St., New York NY 10010-2751. (212)206-8990. Fax (212) 206-1429. E-mail: publications@samuelfrench.com. Website: www.samuelfrench.com, www.bakersplays.com. Agent: Roxane Heinze-Bradshaw. Estab. 1830. Open to new clients. Handles rights to some religious/inspirational stage plays. Owns a subsidiary company that also publishes religious plays.
Contact: Query or send complete manuscript by mail. Accepts simultaneous submissions; responds in 10 wks.
Commission: Varies.
Fees: None.

SANFORD J. GREENBURGER ASSOCIATES INC., 55 Fifth Ave., New York NY 10003. (212) 206-5600. Fax (212)463-8718. Website: www.greenburger.com. Agents: Heide Lange, Faith Hamlin, Dan Mandel, Matthew Bialer, Jeremy Katz, Tricia Davey. Estab. 1945. Represents 500 clients. Open to unpublished authors and new clients. General agent; handles adult religious/inspirational nonfiction. Member of AAR.
Contact: Query/proposal/3 sample chapters to Heide Lange by mail with SASE, or by fax; no e-query. Accepts simultaneous queries. Responds in 6-8 wks. to query; 2 mos. to ms.
Commission: 15%; foreign 20%.
Fees: Charges for photocopying and foreign submissions.

GROSVENOR LITERARY AGENCY, 1425 K St. N.W., Ste. 1100, Washington DC 20005. Home office: (301)564-6231; DC office: (202)626-6401. E-mail: dcg@fr.com. Website: www.gliterary.com. Agent: Deborah Grosvenor. Estab. 1996. Represents 30 clients. Open to few unpublished authors and new clients. General agent; handles adult religious/inspirational nonfiction.
Contact: Letter. Responds in 1-2 mos.
Commission: 15%; foreign 20%.
Fees: None.

JOY HARRIS LITERARY AGENCY, 156 Fifth Ave., Ste. 617, New York NY 10010. (212)924-6269. Fax (212)924-6609. Agent: Joy Harris. Represents 100 clients. Handles religious/inspirational fiction. Member of AAR.

Contact: Proposal/outline or sample chapters. Responds in 2 mos.

Commission: 15%; foreign 20%.

Fees: Charges some office expenses.

HARTLINE LITERARY AGENCY, 123 Queenston Dr., Pittsburgh PA 15235. (412)829-2483. Fax (888)279-6007. E-mail: joyce@hartlineliterary.com. Website: www.hartlineliterary.com. Agents: Joyce A. Hart, adult novels (romance, mystery/suspense, women's fiction) and nonfiction; Tamela Hancock Murray, adult fiction (romance, mystery/suspense, women's) and nonfiction, tamela@hartlineliterary.com; Terry Burns, adult fiction & nonfiction, YA, terry@hartliterary.com; Diana Flegal (adult novels & nonfiction), diana@hartlineliterary.com; Erik Scmidgal (adult novels & nonfiction), erikws@hartlineliterary.com. Recognized in industry. Estab. 1992. Represents 150 clients. Open to published authors (or selected unpublished). Handles novels and nonfiction, gift books, general market books, crossover books. No poetry.

Contact: E-mail preferred. Accepts simultaneous submissions; responds in 12 wks.

Commission: 15%; foreign 20%; films 20% & 25%.

Fees: Office expenses (very few); no reading fee.

Tips: "Please look at our Website before submitting. Guidelines are listed, along with detailed information about each agent. Be sure to include your biography and publishing history with your proposal. The author/agent relationship is a team effort. Working together we can make sure your manuscript gets the exposure and attention it deserves."

THE HARVEY LITERARY AGENCY, LLC., 5579-B Chamblee Dunwoody Rd., Ste. 357, Dunwoody GA 30338. (404)299-6149. Cell: (404)580-9431. Fax (404)297-6651. E-mail: BoncaH@aol.com. Website: www.bookimprove.com. Agent: Dr. Bonnie C. Harvey. Represents 25+ clients. Recognized in the industry. Open to unpublished authors and new clients. Handles adult novels & nonfiction, juvenile & children's books.

Contact: By e-mail, letter, or phone.

Commission: 15%; foreign negotiable.

Fees: Office expenses. May require a paid edit before representation.

JEFF HERMAN AGENCY, PO Box 1522, Stockbridge MA 01262. (413)298-0077. Fax (413)298-8188. E-mail: Jeff@jeffherman.com. Website: www.jeffherman.com. Agents: Jeff Herman and Deborah Herman. Estab. 1987. Recognized in the industry. Represents 100+ clients with religious books. Open to unpublished authors and new clients. Handles adult nonfiction (recovery/healing, spirituality), gift books, general books, crossover.

Contact: Query by mail/SASE; or by e-mail. Accepts simultaneous submissions & e-queries.

Commission: 15%; foreign 10%.

Fees: No reading or management fees; just copying and shipping.

Tips: "I love a good book from the heart. Have faith that you will accomplish what has been appointed to you."

HIDDEN VALUE GROUP, 1240 E. Ontario Ave., Ste. 102-148, Corona CA 92881. Phone/fax (951)549-8891. E-mail: bookquery@hiddenvaluegroup.com. Website: www.HiddenValue Group.com. Agents: Jeff Jernigan & Nancy Jernigan. Estab. 2001. Recognized in the industry. Represents 17+ clients with religious books. Open to previously published authors only. Handles adult novels and nonfiction, gift books, and crossover books. No poetry, articles, or short stories.

Contact: Prefers letter; e-mail OK. Accepts simultaneous submissions. Responds in 3-4 wks.

Commission: 15%; foreign 15%.

Fees: None.

Tips: "Women's nonfiction is of great interest. Make sure the proposal includes author bio, 2 sample chapters, and manuscript summary."

HORNFISCHER LITERARY MANAGEMENT, PO Box 50544, Austin TX 78763. E-mail: queries@hornfischerlit.com, or jim@hornfischerlit.com. Website: www.hornfischerlit.com. Agent: James D. Hornfischer. Estab. 2001. Represents 45 clients. Open to unpublished authors and new clients (with referrals from clients). Considers simultaneous submissions. Responds in 1 mo. General agent; handles adult religious/inspirational nonfiction.

    Contact: E-query only for fiction; query or proposal for nonfiction (proposal package, outline, and 2 sample chapters). Considers simultaneous queries. Responds to queries in 6-8 wks.

    Commission: 15%; foreign 25%.

ANDREA HURST LITERARY MANAGEMENT, 5050 Laguna Blvd., Ste. 112-330, Elk Grove CA 95758. (916)686-1995. E-mail: judy@andreahurst.com. Website: www.andreahurst.com. Agent: Judy Mikalonis. Handles adult nonfiction (Christian and mainstream), YA fiction (Christian & Mainstream), adult fiction (Christian & contemporary only). No end times, romance, historical, science fiction, or demon/vampire-centered fiction.

    Contact: E-mail queries only.

    Commission: 15%.

    Tips: "Fiction authors must be previously published in the traditional market to be considered. Nonfiction authors must have a strong platform."

WILLIAM K. JENSEN LITERARY AGENCY, 119 Bampton Ct., Eugene OR 97404. Phone/fax (541)688-1612. E-mail: Bill@wkjagency.com. Website: www.wkjagency.com. Agent: William K. Jensen. Estab. 2005. Recognized in the industry. Represents 38 clients. Open to unpublished authors and new clients. Handles adult fiction (no science fiction or fantasy), nonfiction for all ages, picture books, gift books, crossover books.

    Contact: E-mail only. Accepts simultaneous submissions. Responds in 12 wks.

    Commission: 15%.

    Fees: No fees.

NATASHA KERN LITERARY AGENCY INC., PO Box 1069, White Salmon WA 98672. Website: www.natashakern.com. Agent: Natasha Kern. Recognized in the industry. Estab. 1987. Represents 40 clients, 14 religious. Open to unpublished authors and new clients. Handles adult religious/inspirational fiction & nonfiction, and crossover books.

    Contact: Accepts e-queries at: queries@natashakern.com only; 3 pg. synopsis & 3 sample pgs.; no SASE required. Responds in 2-4 wks. to queries.

    Commission: 15%; 20% foreign (includes foreign-agent commission).

    Fees: No reading fee.

    Tips: "We represent a wide range of inspirational fiction and nonfiction; adult only." See submission guidelines on Website.

K J LITERARY SERVICES, LLC, 1540 Margaret Ave., Grand Rapids MI 49507. (616)551-9797. E-mail: kim@kjliteraryservices.com. Website: www.kjliteraryservices.com. Agent: Kim Zeilstra.

    Contact: E-query preferred; phone query OK.

    Commission: 15%.

    Tips: "Taking new authors by referral only."

THE STEVE LAUBE AGENCY, 5025 N. Central Ave., #635, Phoenix AZ 85012-1502. (602)336-8910. E-mail: info@stevelaube.com. Website: www.stevelaube.com. Agent: Steve Laube. Estab. 2004. Well recognized in the industry. Represents 60+ clients. Open to new and unpublished authors. Handles adult Christian fiction and nonfiction, history, theology, how-to, health, Christian living. No YA, children's books, or poetry. Accepts simultaneous submissions. Responds in 6-8 wks.

Contact: Letter with proposal and sample chapters by mail is preferred; use guidelines on Website. No e-queries.
Commission: 15%; foreign 20%.
Fees: No fees.
Tips: "Looking for fresh and innovative ideas. Make sure your proposal contains an excellent presentation."

LEVINE GREENBERG LITERARY AGENCY INC., 307—7th Ave., Ste. 2407, New York NY 10001. (212)337-0934. Fax (212)337-0948. Website: www.levinegreenberg.com. Agent: James Levine. West Coast Office: 112 Auburn St., San Rafael CA 94901. (415)785-1582. Fax (415) 785-1583. Agent: Arielle Eckstut. Estab. 1989. Represents 250 clients. Open to unpublished authors and new clients. General agent; handles adult religious/inspirational nonfiction. Member AAR.
Contact: See guidelines/submission form on Website; prefers e-query.
Commission: 15%; foreign 20%.
Fees: Office expenses.
Tips: "Our specialties include spirituality and religion."

LITERARY AND CREATIVE ARTISTS INC., 3543 Albemarle St. N.W., Washington DC 20008. (202)362-4688. Fax (202)362-8875. E-mail: lca9643@lcadc.com, or muriel@lcadc.com. Website: www.lcadc.com. Agent: Muriel Nellis. AAR member. Open to established authors only at this time. General agent. Handles adult religious nonfiction. Submission guidelines on Website. Responds in 3 wks. E-query.

THE LITERARY GROUP INTL., The Stanford Bldg., 51 E. 25th St., Ste., 401, New York NY 10010. (212)274-1616. Fax (212)274-9876. E-mail: js@theliterarygroup.com. Website: www.theliterarygroup.com. Agent: Frank Weimann. Recognized in the industry. Estab. 1986. Represents 300 clients (120 for religious books). Open to new clients and unpublished authors. Handles fiction and nonfiction for all ages, picture books, general, and crossover.
Contact: Letter.
Commission: 15%; foreign 20%.
Fees: No fees.
Tips: "Looking for fresh, original spiritual fiction and nonfiction. We offer a written contract which may be canceled after 30 days."

LITERARY MANAGEMENT GROUP INC., PO Box 40965, Nashville TN 37204. (615)812-4445. E-mail: brucebarbour@literarymanagementgroup.com. Website: www.literarymanagement group.com. Agents: Bruce R. Barbour & Margaret Langstaff. Estab. 1995. Well recognized in the industry. Represents 100+ clients. Open to published authors who have a platform and a compelling story or idea. Handles nonfiction only. Other services offered: book packaging and consulting.
Contact: E-mail preferred. Will review proposals, no unsolicited mss.
Commission: 15%; foreign 20%.
Fees: No fees or expenses on agented books.
Tips: "Follow guidelines, proposal outline, and submissions format on Website. Use Microsoft Word. Study the market and know where your book will fit in."

STERLING LORD LITERISTIC INC., 65 Bleecker St., New York NY 10012. (213)780-6050. Fax (212)780-6095. E-mail: claudia@sll.com, or info@sll.com. Website: www.sll.com. Agent: Claudia Cross. Recognized in the industry. Represents 10 clients with religious books. Open to unpublished clients with referrals and to new clients. Handles adult and teen Christian fiction, spiritual adult nonfiction, gift books, crossover books, general books.
Contact: Letter, fax or (e-query with referral only). Accepts simultaneous submissions, if informed. Responds in 4-6 wks.

Commission: 15%; foreign 20%.

Fees: "We charge for photocopy costs for mss or costs above and beyond the usual cost of doing business."

MACGREGOR LITERARY, 2373 N.W. 185th Ave., Ste. 165, Hillsboro OR 97124. Website: www.MacGregorLiterary.com. Agents: Chip MacGregor & Sandra Bishop. Estab. 2006. Recognized in the industry. Represents 60 clients. Open to unpublished authors, if writing is great, and new clients with referral. Handles adult religious/inspirational novels, nonfiction, & crossover books.

> **Contact:** E-mail query to: submissions@macgregorliterary.com. Accepts simultaneous submissions. Responds in 4 wks.
>
> **Commission:** 15%; foreign 20%.
>
> **Fees:** No fees or expenses except in special situations.
>
> **Tips:** "Authors are paid directly by the publisher. We use an at-will agreement (not a term agreement). We've represented award winners and bestsellers. With the addition of another agent in 2008, MacGregor Literary looks forward to expanding our list and furthering our commitment to representing books that make a difference. We have secured more than 1,000 book deals for authors with all the major publishers in both CBA and ABA."

MANUS & ASSOCIATES LITERARY AGENCY, 425 Sherman Ave., Ste. 200, Palo Alto CA 94306. (650)470-5151. Fax (650)470-5159. E-mail: manuslit@manuslit.com. Website: www.manuslit.com. Agents: Jillian Manus, Penny Nelson, Dena Fischer, and Jandy Nelson. Members AAR. Estab. 1994. Open to unpublished authors and new clients. Handles adult religious/inspirational novels & nonfiction.

> **Contact:** Query by mail/fax/e-query (no attachments). For fiction, send first 30 pages, bio, and SASE. For nonfiction, send proposal/sample chapters. Responds in 8 weeks.
>
> **Commission:** 15%.

MCHUGH LITERARY AGENCY, 1033 Lyon Rd., Moscow ID 83843-9167. (208)882-0107. E-mail: elisabet@moscow.com. Agent: Elisabet McHugh. Estab. 1995. Represents 49 clients. Recognized in the industry. Open to unpublished authors and new clients. General agent; handles adult and teen religious/inspirational nonfiction, crossover books, general books.

> **Contact:** E-mail first.
>
> **Commission:** 15%; foreign 20%.
>
> **Fees:** None, but clients provide copies of manuscripts.
>
> **Comments:** "Be professional!"

WILLIAM MORRIS LITERARY AGENCY, 1325 Avenue of the Americas, New York NY 10019. (212)586-5100. Fax (212)246-3583. E-mail: vs@wma.com. Website: www.wma.com. Agent: Valerie Summers. Recognized in the industry. Estab. 1898. Hundreds of clients with religious books. Not open to unpublished authors or new clients. Handles all types of material. Member AAR.

> **Contact:** Send query/synopsis, publication history by mail/SASE. No fax/e-query. No unsolicited mss.
>
> **Commission:** 15%; foreign 20%.
>
> **Fees:** None.

+MORTIMER LITERARY AGENCY, 52645 Paui Rd., Aguanga CA 92536. (951)763-2600. Fax (951)763-0060. E-mail: kmortimer@mortimerliterary.com. Website: www.mortimerliterary.com. Agent: Kelly L. Mortimer. Estab. 2006. Recognized in the industry. Represents 7 clients. Only signs unpublished authors; open to limited number of new clients. Handles teen & adult religious/inspirational novels & nonfiction, crossover, and general books.

> **Contact:** Query by e-mail; accepts simultaneous submissions; responds in 2 days on queries, 4 wks. on partials, and 2-3 mos. on full mss.
>
> **Commission:** 15%; foreign 20%.

Fees: Postage only (comes out of advance or is paid at end of year if no sale).

Special Needs: In Christian mss, looking for contemporary (stand alone & series), romance, historical, nonfiction. In general mss: contemporary, historical, romance, paranormal, and nonfiction.

Tips: "Romance Writers of America Recognized Agent; degree in contract law."

NAPPALAND LITERARY AGENCY, PO Box 1674, Loveland CO 80539. (970)635-0641. Fax (970)635-9869. E-mail: literary@nappaland.com. Website: www.nappaland.com. Nappaland Communications Inc. Agent: Mike Nappa. Estab. 1995. Recognized in the industry. Represents 10 clients. Not open to unpublished authors; open to new clients only by referral from a current Nappaland author. Handles literary nonfiction, cultural concerns, Christian living, women's issues, suspense fiction, and women's fiction.

Contact: By e-mail. Accepts simultaneous submissions; responds in 8-10 wks. Unsolicited queries are automatically rejected.

Commission: 15%.

Fees: None.

Tips: "Cold queries just don't work—so don't send them. The only way we will consider a new author is if that person is somehow associated with—and recommended by—a current Nappaland author."

NUNN COMMUNICATIONS INC., 1612 Ginger Dr., Carrollton TX 75007. (972)394-NUNN. E-mail: info@nunncommunications.com. Website: www.nunncommunications.com. Agent: Leslie Nunn Reed. Estab. 1995. Represents 20 clients. Recognized in the industry. Not open to unpublished authors. Handles adult nonfiction, gift books, crossover books, and general books.

Contact: By e-mail. Responds in 4-6 wks.

Commission: 15%.

Fees: Charges office expenses if over $100.

ALLEN O'SHEA LITERARY AGENCY, LLC., 615 Westover Rd., Stamford CT 06902. (203)359-9965. E-mail: MA615@aol.com. Website: www.publishersmarketplace.com/members/AllenOShea. Agents: Marilyn Allen and Coleen O'Shea. Estab. 2003. Represents 4 clients with religious books. Recognized in the industry. Open to unpublished authors (with credentials & platform) and new clients. Handles teen novels and adult nonfiction.

Contact: Query by mail or e-mail. No simultaneous submissions. Responds in 4 wks.

Commission: 15%; foreign 15-25%.

Fees: For photography and overseas mailing.

Tips: "We specifically like practical nonfiction."

KATHI J. PATON LITERARY AGENCY, PO Box 2240, New York NY 10101-2240. (212)265-6586. E-mail: KJPLitBiz@optonline.net. Website: www.PublishersMarketplace.com/members/KJPLitBiz. Agent: Kathi Paton. Estab. 1987. Handles adult nonfiction: Christian life and issues.

Contact: Prefers e-mail query.

Commission: 15%; foreign 20%.

Fees: For photocopying.

PATRICK-MEDBERRY ASSOCIATES, 25379 Wayne Mills Pl., #155, Valencia CA 91355. (661)251-4428. E-mail: patrickmedberry@sbcglobal.net. Agents: Peggy Patrick & C. J. Medberry. Estab. 2005. Management & production company specializing in Christian writers, directors, and producers, as well as religious and inspirational novels, screenplays, TV/movie scripts, crossover books, general books, and screenplays. Open to unpublished authors and new clients.

Contact: Query by letter, fax, or e-mail; no calls.

Commission: 10%.

Fees: None.

QUICKSILVER BOOKS, LITERARY AGENTS, 508 Central Park Ave., #5101, Scarsdale NY 10583. Phone/fax (914)722-4664. E-mail: quickbooks@optonline.net. Website: www.quicksilverbooks.com. Agent: Bob Silverstein. Estab. 1973. Not yet recognized in the industry. Represents 10 clients with religious books. Open to unpublished authors and new clients. General agent; handles adult religious/inspirational nonfiction and fiction.

    Contact: Query by e-mail, or letter with SASE. Considers simultaneous submissions. Responds in 2-5 wks.

    Commission: 15%; foreign 20%.

    Fees: Charges only for foreign mailings.

RLR ASSOCIATES, LTD., Literary Dept., 7 W. 51st St., New York NY 10019. (212)541-8641. Fax (212)541-6052. Also has a California office. E-mail: sgould@rlrassociates.net. Website: www.rlrliterary.net. Scott Gould, literary assoc. Estab. 1972. Represents 50+ clients. Open to unpublished authors and new clients. General agency; handles adult religious/ inspirational nonfiction.

    Contact: Query with SASE. Considers simultaneous submissions. Responds in 5 wks.

    Commission: 15%; foreign 20%.

ROSENBAUM & ASSOCIATES LITERARY AGENCY, PO Box 277, Brentwood TN 37024-0277. (615)834-8564. Fax (615)834-8560. E-mail: bucky@rosenbaumagency.com. Website: www.rosenbaumagency.com. Agent: Bucky Rosenbaum. Estab. 2006. Well recognized in the industry. Represents 30-40 clients. Open to a limited number of new clients and unpublished authors by referral only. Handles mostly adult nonfiction, and some general books, crossover books.

    Contact: Unpublished query by mail/SASE; published authors by phone or e-mail. No simultaneous submissions.

    Commission: 15%; foreign 20%.

    Fees: Only extraordinary costs with client's permission; no reading fees.

    Tips: "Request a product proposal template by e-mail."

RITA ROSENKRANZ LITERARY AGENCY, 440 West End Ave., Ste. 15D, New York NY 10024-5358. (212)873-6333. Agent: Rita Rosenkranz. Estab. 1990. Represents 30 clients. Open to unpublished authors and new clients. General agent; handles adult religious/inspirational nonfiction. Member AAR.

    Contact: Proposal package (outline and sample chapter); no fax/e-query. Accepts simultaneous submissions. Responds in 2 wks. to query.

    Commission: 15%; foreign 20%.

    Tips: "A strong cover letter is very important. Be sure to identify competition to your book, and be sure it's a valid project."

GAIL ROSS LITERARY AGENCY, 1666 Connecticut Ave. N.W., #500, Washington DC 20009. (202)328-3282. Fax (202)328-9162. E-mail: jennifer@gailross.com. Website: www.gail ross.com. Contact: Jennifer Manguera. Estab. 1988. Represents 200 clients. Open to unpublished authors and new clients (mostly through referrals). General agent; handles adult religious/inspirational nonfiction, history, health, and business books.

    Contact: Query with outline, sample pages, résumé/SASE; no e-query. Accepts simultaneous queries.

    Commission: 15%; foreign 25%.

    Fees: Office expenses.

+CAROL SUSAN ROTH LITERARY & CREATIVE, PO Box 620337, Woodside CA 94062. (650)323-3795. E-mail: carol@authorsbest.com. Website: www.AuthorsBest.com. Agent: Carol Susan Roth. Recognized in the industry. Estab. 1996. Represents 40 clients. Open to unpublished authors and new clients. Handles adult religious/inspirational nonfiction, gift books, crossover, general, health, science & spirit (no fiction or memoirs).

Contact: Query with your pitch, author bio, and platform.
Commission: 15%.
Fees: None. "I do make referrals out to ghostwriters and publicists upon request."
Tips: "We are interested in working with experts who are interested in developing many books."

DAMARIS ROWLAND AGENCY, 5 Peter Cooper Rd., #13H, New York NY 10010. (212)387-9988. Cell (646)712-0577. Fax (212)358-9411. Agent: Damaris Rowland. Estab. 1994. Represents 40 clients. Open to unpublished authors and new clients. No New Age material. Very selective.
Contact: Query letter.
Commission: 15%; foreign 20%.
Fees: Some office expenses.

+SANFORD COMMUNICATIONS INC., 16778 S.E. Cohiba Ct., Damascus OR 97089. (503)890-0456. E-mail: info@sanfordci.com. Website: www.sanfordci.com. Eight people on staff. Recognized in the industry. See Website for details.

SCHIAVONE LITERARY AGENCY INC., 236 Trails End, West Palm Beach FL 33413-2135. Phone/fax (561)966-9294. E-mail: profschia@aol.com. Website: www.publishersmarket place.com/members/profschia. Agent: James Schiavone, EdD. Recognized in the industry. Estab. 1997. Represents 6 clients. Open to unpublished and new clients. Handles adult, teen, and children's fiction and nonfiction; celebrity biography; general books; crossover books.
Contact: Query letter/SASE; one-page e-mail query (no attachments).
Commission: 15%, foreign 20%.
Fees: No reading fees; authors pay postage only.
Tips: Works primarily with published authors; will consider first-time authors with excellent material. Actively seeking books on spirituality, major religions, and alternative health. Very selective on first novels.

SUSAN SCHULMAN LITERARY AGENCY, 454 W. 44th St., New York NY 10036. (212)713-1633. Fax (212)581-8830. E-mail: schulman@aol.com. Website: www.schulman agency.com. Agent: Susan Schulman; Rights & Permissions: Eleanora Tevis; Submissions Editor: Linda Migalti Kiss. Estab. 1980. Building recognition in the Christian marketplace; well-established in general publishing. Represents 12 clients with religious books. Open to unpublished authors and new clients. Handles books for, by, and about women and women's issues and interests, including spiritual studies, historically based fiction and nonfiction, contemporary women's fiction, parenting, relationships, social trends, inspirational collections, especially if on one topic, as well as children's books, including early readers, picture books, young adult fiction and limited nonfiction. Member AAR.
Contact: Prefers mail contact; e-query OK. Responds only if interested. Accepts simultaneous submissions. Responds in 2-3 wks.
Commission: 15%; foreign 20% (shared 50/50 with foreign co-agent).
Fees: Only agreed-upon office expenses. No fees.
Tips: "We are interested in sophisticated religious and spiritual material, especially nonfiction or historically based fiction or nonfiction, as well as personal memoirs, all appropriate for a well-educated audience."

SCOVIL, CHICHAK, GALEN LITERARY AGENCY, 276 Fifth Ave., Ste. 708, New York NY 10001. (212)679-8686. Fax (212)679-6710. E-mail: annaghosh@scglit.com, or info@scglit.com. Website: www.scglit.com. Agent: Anna Ghosh. Open to unpublished authors and new clients. General agent. Handles adult religious/spirituality nonfiction. Submission guidelines on Website.

SCRIBBLERS HOUSE, LLC, PO Box 1007, Cooper Station, New York NY 10276-1007. E-mail: query@scribblershouse.net, or from Website: www.scribblershouse.net. Agents: Stedman

Mays & Garrett Gambino. Estab. 2003. Not recognized in the industry. Some clients with spiritual books. Open to unpublished and new clients, but very selective. Handles adult nonfiction. **Contact:** Prefers e-query; go to Website for instruction. Accepts simultaneous submissions. Responds in 8-12 wks.
Fees: Office expenses; no reading or other fees.
Tips: "See Website for most up-to-date information."

SERENDIPITY LITERARY AGENCY, LLC, 305 Gates Ave., Brooklyn NY 11216. (718)230-7689. Fax (718)230-7829. E-mail: rbrooks@serendipitylit.com. Website: www.serendipitylit.com. Agent: Regina Brooks. Member AAR. Estab. 2000. Represents 50 clients; 3 with religious books. Recognized in the industry. Open to unpublished authors and new clients. General agent; handles fiction & nonfiction for all ages, picture books, gift books, crossover books, general books. No science fiction.
Contact: By e-mail or letter; no faxes. Accepts simultaneous submissions. Responds in 8-12 wks.
Commission: 15%; foreign 20%.
Fees: None.

THE SEYMOUR AGENCY, 475 Miner Street Rd., Canton NY 13617. (315)386-1831. E-mail: marysue@slic.com. Website: www.theseymouragency.com. Agent: Mary Sue Seymour. Estab. 1992. Member of AAR. Ellen Feig (efeig@hotmail.com) handles film rts. Recognized in the industry. Represents 25 religious clients. Open to unpublished authors and new clients (prefers published authors). Handles romance novels, Christian chick lit, Christian historical romance, and nonfiction for all ages, general books, crossover books.
Contact: Query letter or e-mail with first 50 pages of ms; no fax query. For nonfiction, send proposal with chapter one. Simultaneous query OK. Responds in 1 mo. for queries and 2-3 mos. for mss.
Commission: 15% for unpublished authors; 12.5% for published authors; foreign 20%.
Fees: None.
Tips: "E-mails loglines for scripts to Ellen Feig, an attorney, who will also review contracts."

THE SHEPARD AGENCY, 73 Kingswood Dr., Bethel CT 06801. (203)790-4230. Fax (203)798-2924. E-mail: shepardagcy@mindspring.com. Website: http://home.mindspring.com/~shepardagcy. Agent: Jean Shepard. Recognized in the industry. Estab. 1987. Represents 11 clients. Open to unpublished authors; no new clients at this time. Handles fiction and nonfiction for all ages; no picture books; especially business, reference, professional, self-help, cooking, and crafts. Books only.
Contact: By e-mail.
Commission: 15%; foreign variable.
Fees: None except long-distance calls and copying.

KEN SHERMAN & ASSOCIATES, 9507 Santa Monica Blvd., Beverly Hills CA 90210. (310)273-3840. Fax (310)271-2875. E-mail: ken@kenshermanassociates.com. Agent: Ken Sherman. Estab. 1989. Represents 50 clients. Open to unpublished authors and new clients. Handles adult religious/inspirational novels, nonfiction, screenplays and TV/movie scripts.
Contact: By referral only. Responds in 1 mo.
Commission: 15%; foreign 20%; dramatic rts. 15%.
Fees: Charges office expenses and other negotiable expenses.

WENDY SHERMAN ASSOCIATES, 450 Seventh Ave., Ste. 2307, New York NY 10123. (212)279-9027. Fax (212)279-8863. Website: www.wsherman.com. Agents: Wendy Sherman, Michelle Brower, Emmanuelle Alspaugh. Open to unpublished authors and new clients. General agents. Handle adult religious nonfiction.
Contact: Query by mail/SASE or send proposal/1 chapter. No phone/fax/e-query. Guidelines on Website.
Commission: 15%; foreign 20%.

JACQUELINE SIMENAUER LITERARY AGENCY, PO Box A.G., Mantoloking NJ 08738-0390. (732)262-0783. Open to unpublished authors. Handles spiritual fiction & nonfiction. **Contact:** For fiction, query with first 3 chapters, synopsis, bio, and SASE. For nonfiction, send query with SASE. Simultaneous & e-query OK. **Commission:** 15%; foreign 20%.

MICHAEL SNELL LITERARY AGENCY, PO Box 1206, Truro MA 02666-1206. (508)349-3718. Agent: Michael Snell. Estab. 1978. Represents 200 clients. Open to unpublished authors and new clients. General agent: handles adult religious/inspirational nonfiction. **Contact:** Query with SASE. No simultaneous submissions. Responds in 1-2 wks. **Commission:** 15%; foreign 15%.

SPENCERHILL ASSOCIATES, LTD./KAREN SOLEM, PO Box 374, Chatham NY 12037. (518) 392-9293. Fax (518)392-9554. E-mail: ksolem@klsbooks.com. Agent: Karen Solem. Member of AAR. Recognized in the industry. Estab. 2001. Represents 15 clients. Not currently open to unpublished authors or new clients. Handles adult novels and nonfiction, general books, crossover books. **Contact:** No accepting clients at this time. **Commission:** 15%; foreign 20%. **Fees:** Photocopying and Express Mail charges only.

STEELE-PERKINS LITERARY AGENCY, 26 Island Ln., Canandaigua NY 14424. (585)396-9290. Fax (585)396-3579. E-mail: pattiesp@aol.com. Agent: Pattie Steele-Perkins. Member AAR. Handles inspirational romance novels. **Contact:** Proposal/3 chapters. Considers simultaneous submissions. Responds in 6 weeks. E-mail instead of calling. **Commission:** 15%.

LESLIE H. STOBBE, 300 Doubleday Rd., Tryon NC 28782. (828)808-7127. Fax (978)945-0517. E-mail: lstobbe@alltel.net. Well recognized in the industry. Estab. 1993. Represents 75 clients. Open to new clients. Handles adult fiction and nonfiction. **Contact:** By e-mail. **Commission:** 15% **Fees:** None. **Tips:** "I will not accept clients whose theological positions in their book differ significantly from mine."

STONE MANNERS AGENCY, 6500 Wilshire Blvd., Ste. 550, Los Angeles CA 90048. (323)655-1313. Fax (323)655-7676. Handles religious/inspirational TV/film screenplays as well as general screenplays. **Contact:** Queries only.

SUITE A MANAGEMENT TALENT & LITERARY AGENCY, 120 El Camino Dr., Ste. 202, Beverly Hills CA 90212. (310)278-0801. Fax (310)278-0807. E-mail: suite-A@juno.com. Agent: Lloyd D. Robinson. Recognized in the industry. Estab. 2001. Several clients. Open to new and unpublished clients (if published in other media). Specializes in screenplays and novels for adaptation to TV movies. **Contact:** By mail or fax only. For consideration of representation, send current bio, and for each screenplay, your WGA registration number, log line, and 2 paragraph synopsis only. Complete scripts or e-mail submissions are not read; attachments are deleted. Responds only if interested. **Commission:** 10% **Comments:** Representation limited to adaptation of novels and true-life stories for film and television development. Work must have been published for consideration.

MARK SWEENEY & ASSOCIATES, 28540 Altessa Way, Ste. 201, Bonita Springs FL 34135. (239)594-1957. Fax (239)594-1935. E-mail: sweeney2@comcast.net. Agent: Mark Sweeney.

Recognized in the industry. Estab. 2003. Open to unpublished authors and new clients on a restricted basis. Handles adult religious/inspirational novels & nonfiction, crossover books, general books.

Contact: E-mail.

Commission: 15%; foreign 15%.

Fees: None.

TALCOTT NOTCH LITERARY SERVICES, 276 Forest Rd., Milford CT 06461. (203)877-1146. Fax (203)876-9517. E-mail: gpanettieri@talcottnotch.net. Website: www.talcottnotch.net. Agent: Gina Panettieri. Not yet recognized in the industry; building a Christian presence. Estab. 2003. Represents 25 clients (3 with religious books). Open to unpublished authors and new clients. Handles nonfiction & fiction, crossover & general market books for all ages.

Contact: By e-mail. Accepts simultaneous submissions; responds in 8 wks.

Commission: 15%; foreign or with co-agent 20%.

Fees: None.

Tips: "While Christian and religious books are not our main focus, we are open to unique and thought-provoking works from all writers. We specifically seek nonfiction in areas of parenting, health, women's issues, arts & crafts, self-help, and current events. We are open to academic/scholarly work as well as commercial projects."

3 SEAS LITERARY AGENCY, PO Box 8571, Madison WI 53708. (608)221-4306. E-mail: three seaslit@aol.com. Website: www.threeseaslit.com. Agent: Michelle Grajkowski. Estab. 2000. Represents 40 clients. Open to unpublished authors and new clients. General agent; handles adult religious/inspirational novels & nonfiction.

Contact: E-query only with synopsis & 1 chapter (queries@threeseaslit.com). Considers simultaneous submissions. Responds in 2-3 mos.

Commission: 15%; foreign 20%.

TRIDENT MEDIA GROUP, LLC., 41 Madison Ave., 36th Fl., New York NY 10010. (212)262-4810. Fax (212)262-4849. E-mail: pfedorko@tridentmediagroup.com. Website: www .tridentmediagroup.com. Agent: Paul Fedorko. Open to unpublished authors and new clients. General agent. Handles adult religious nonfiction.

Contact: No unsolicited mss. Query/SASE first; send outline and sample chapters on request. Responds to queries in 3 wks.; mss in 6 wks.

VAN DIEST LITERARY AGENCY, PO Box 1482, Sisters OR 97759. (541)549-0477. Fax (541) 549-1213. Website: www.ChristianLiteraryAgency.com. Agents: David & Sarah Van Diest. Estab. 2004. Represents 20 clients. Open to unpublished authors and new clients. Recognized in the industry. Handles teen & adult novels, nonfiction for all ages, crossover books.

Contact: By e-mail. Responds in 4 wks.

Commission: 15%; 25% for first-time authors.

+VERITAS LITERARY AGENCY, 510 Sand Hill Cir., Menlo Park CA 94025. E-mail: agent@ veritasliterary.com. Website: www.veritasliterary.com. Agent: Katherine Boyle. Member AAR. Handles serious religious nonfiction (no New Age).

Contact: Query with SASE; e-query OK (no attachments); no fax queries.

WATERSIDE PRODUCTIONS INC., 2055 Oxford Ave., Cardiff-by-the-Sea CA 92007. (760)632-9190. Fax (760)632-9295. E-mail: webrown@waterside.com. Website: www.waterside .com. Agent: William E. Brown. Christian agent in a highly regarded general agency. Interested in handling Christian books, or books which otherwise challenge and engage readers from a Judeo-Christian perspective. Prefers nonfiction, but will look at fiction (the bar is very high). In addition to spiritually oriented books, devotions, theology, chick lit and mom lit, list includes business books: leadership, marketing, sales, business development.

Contact: Query via online form (see Website). Considers simultaneous submissions.

Commission: 15%; foreign 25%.

WHALIN LITERARY AGENCY, 23623 N. Scottsdale Rd., Ste. D-3 #481, Scottsdale AZ 85255. (480)575-8622. E-mail: query@whalinagency.com. Website: www.whalinagency.com. Agent: W. Terry Whalin. Estab. 2007. Open to unpublished authors and new clients. Handles adult religious/inspirational novels & nonfiction. No YA, children's books or poetry.
  Contact: Letter/proposal & sample chapters by mail (preferred); use guidelines on Website. No e-query unless requested. Accepts simultaneous submissions; responds in 6-8 wks.
  Commission: 15%; foreign 20%.
  Fees: None
  Tips: "Follow the submission guidelines on agency Website. Actively looking for fresh and creative ideas from writers who want to reach the Christian and general marketplace. Best tip is to get a copy of *Book Proposals That Sell* (Whalin; Write Now Publications) and study it in depth before submitting."

WOLGEMUTH & ASSOCIATES INC., 8600 Crestgate Cir., Orlando FL 32819. (407)909-9445. Fax (407)909-9446. E-mail: rwolgemuth@cfl.rr.com. Agent: Robert D. Wolgemuth; Andrew D. Wolgemuth (awolgemuth@cfl.rr.com); Erik S. Wolgemuth (ewolgemuth@cfl.rr.com). Member AAR. Well recognized in the industry. Estab. 1992. Represents 55 clients. No new clients or unpublished authors. Handles mostly adult nonfiction; most other types of books handled only for current clients.
  Contact: By letter.
  Commission: 15%.
  Fees: None.
  Tips: "We work with authors who are either best-selling authors or potentially best-selling authors. Consequently, we want to represent clients with broad-market appeal."

WOMACK PUBLISHING AGENCY, PO Box 2163, Merced CA 95344. (209)658-2226. E-mail: WomackAgency@aol.com. Agent: David A. Womack. Estab. 1998. Recognized in the industry. Slogan: *Representing Good Authors to Good Publishers.* Adheres to the Canon of Ethics of the Assn. of Authors' Representatives. Represents 25 clients. Open to unpublished authors and new clients. Handles Christian fiction & nonfiction for adults, some general books; no children's or juvenile books.
  Contact: Query by e-mail. No simultaneous queries.
  Commission: 15%; foreign 20%.
  Fees: No up-front fees.

WORDSERVE LITERARY GROUP, 10152 S. Knoll Cir., Highlands Ranch CO 80130. (303)471-6675. Website: www.wordserveliterary.com. Agents: Greg Johnson and Rachelle Gardner. Estab. 2003. Represents 60 clients. Recognized in the industry. Open to new clients. Handles novels & nonfiction for all ages, gift books, crossover books, general books.
  Contact: Visit Website for submission guidelines. Responds in 4 wks.
  Commission: 15%; foreign 10-15%.
  Fees: None.
  Tips: "Nonfiction: First impressions count. Make sure your proposal answers all the questions on competition, outline, audience, felt need, etc. Fiction: Make sure your novel is completed before you submit a proposal (synopsis, plus 5 chapters)."

THE WRITER'S EDGE. See listing under Editorial Services—Illinois.

WRITERS HOUSE, 21 W. 26th St., New York NY 10010. (212)685-2400. Fax (212)685-1781. E-mail: azuckerman@writerhouse.com. Website: www.writershouse.com. Agent: Albert Zuckerman. Estab. 1974. Represents 440 clients. General agency; handles adult religious/inspirational fiction. Member of AAR.
  Contact: One-page query by mail/SASE. No e-mail/fax queries. Responds in 1 mo. to query.
  Commission: 15%; foreign 20%.
  Fees: No fees.

Tips: "See Website for details. Write a compelling query so we'll ask to see your manuscript."

YATES & YATES, 1100 W. Town and Country Rd., Ste. 1300, Orange CA 92868-4654. (714)480-4000. Fax (714)480-4001. E-mail: email@yates2.com. Website: www.yates2.com. Estab. 1989. Recognized in the industry. Represents 50+ clients. Not currently open to unpublished authors or new clients. Handles adult novels, nonfiction for adults and teens, TV/Movie scripts, general books, crossover books.

> **Contact:** E-mail.
> **Commission:** Negotiable
> **Fees:** Negotiable.

ZACHARY SHUSTER HARMSWORTH LITERARY AND ENTERTAINMENT AGENCY, 1776 Broadway, Ste. 1405 (212)765-6900. Fax (212)765-6490; and 535 Boylston St., Ste. 1103, Boston MA 02116. (617)262-2400. Fax (617)262-2468. E-mail: mchappell@zshliterary .com. Website: www.zshliterary.com. Agent: Mary Beth Chappell (Boston office). Recognized in the industry. Represents 15-30 religious clients. Open to unpublished authors and new clients. Handles adult religious/inspirational novels & adult nonfiction, crossover books, general books.

> **Contact:** E-mail query letter. Accepts simultaneous submissions. Responds in 2 wks. or queries, 8 wks. on full mss. Commission: 15%; foreign & film 20%.
> **Fees:** Office expenses only.
> **Tips:** "We are looking for inspirational fiction, Christian nonfiction, especially that which focuses on the emerging/emergent church or that which would appeal to readers in their 20s and 30s, and teen/YA series."

ADDITIONAL AGENTS

Note: The following agents did not return a questionnaire, but most have been identified as secular agents who handle religious/inspirational manuscripts. Be sure to send queries first if you wish to submit to them. Always check out an agent thoroughly before committing to work with him or her. Ask for references and a list of books represented, check with the Better Business Bureau, and ask your writing friends.

DAVID BLACK LITERARY AGENCY, 156 Fifth Ave., Ste. 608, New York NY 10010. Agent: David Black. Handles religious nonfiction.

> **Contact:** Query by mail. No e-query. Not currently accepting unsolicited queries.

DUNOW, CARLSON & LERNER, 27 W. 20th St., Ste. 1003, New York NY 10011. Agent: Betsy Lerner. Open to unpublished authors and new clients. General agent. Handles adult religious nonfiction.

DENISE MARCIL LITERARY AGENCY, 156—5th Ave, Ste. 625, New York NY 10011. Agent: Denise Marcil. General agent. Handles religious nonfiction. Member of AAR.

THE AMY RENNERT AGENCY, 98 Main St., #302, Tiburon CA 94920. E-mail: arennert@ pacbell.net. Agent: Amy Rennert. Open to unpublished authors and new clients. General agent. Handles adult religious nonfiction.

> **Contact:** Query with SASE; no e-query.

SOBEL WEBER ASSOCIATES, 146 E. 19th St., New York NY 10003. Agent: Nat Sobel. Open to unpublished authors and new clients. General agent. Handles adult religious nonfiction.

STEPHANIE VON HIRSCHBERG LITERARY AGENCY, 1385 Baptist Church Rd., Yorktown Heights NY 10598. (914)243-9250.

WILSON MEDIA, PO Box 613, Hastings-on-Hudson NY 10706. E-mail: wilsonmedia@ verizon.net. Agent: Robert Wilson. Open to unpublished authors and new clients. General agent. Handles adult religious nonfiction.

CONTESTS

Below is a listing of all the contests mentioned throughout this guide, plus additional contests that will be of interest. Some are sponsored by book publishers or magazines, some by conferences or writers' groups. The contests are arranged by genre or type of material they are looking for such as poetry, fiction, nonfiction, etc. Send an SASE to each one you are interested in to obtain a copy of their complete contest rules and guidelines, or check out their Website. (This is particularly important because many contests had not set deadlines and final details for the next year's contests when this guide was written and so some details may change.) A listing here does not guarantee the legitimacy of a contest. For guidelines on evaluating contests and to determine if a contest is legitimate, go to: www.sfwa.org/beware/contests.html.

(+) Indicates a new listing

CHILDREN/YOUNG ADULT CONTESTS, WRITING FOR

+THE CHILDREN'S WRITER CONTESTS. Offers a number of contests for children's writers. Website: www.childrenswriter.com.

DELACORTE DELL YEARLING CONTEST FOR FIRST MIDDLE-GRADE NOVEL, Random House Inc., 1745 Broadway, 9th Fl., New York NY 10019. Website: www.randomhouse.com/ kids/writingcontests/index.html#middlegrade. Contemporary and historical fiction manuscripts, 96-160 pgs., for ages 9-12. Submit between April 1 and June 30. Prizes: $1,500, book contract, and $7,500 advance.

DELACORTE DELL YEARLING CONTEST FOR FIRST YOUNG ADULT NOVEL, Random House Inc., 1745 Broadway, 9th Fl., New York NY 10019. Website: www.randomhouse .com/kids/writingcontests/index.html#youngadult. Contemporary and historical fiction manuscripts, 100-224 pgs., for ages 12-18. Submit between October 1 and December 31. Prizes: $1,500, book contract, and $7,500 advance.

HIGHLIGHTS FOR CHILDREN FICTION CONTEST, 803 Church St., Honesdale PA 18431. (570)253-1080. Website: www.highlights.com. Offers 3 prizes of $1,000 each for stories up to 800 words for children; for beginning readers to 500 words. See Website for guidelines and current topic. No crime, violence, or derogatory humor. No entry fee or form required. Entries must be postmarked between January 1 and January 31.

CORETTA SCOTT KING BOOK AWARD, Coretta Scott King Task Force, American Library Assn., 50 E. Huron St., Chicago IL 60611. Toll-free (800)545-2433. E-mail: feedback@ala.org. Website: www.ala.org. Annual award for children's books by African American authors and/or illustrators published the previous year. Books must fit one of these categories: preschool to grade 4; grades 5-8; grades 9-12. Deadline: December 1 each year. Guidelines on Website. Prizes: a plaque, a set of encyclopedias, and $1,000 cash. Recipients are authors and illustrators of African descent whose distinguished books promote an understanding and appreciation of the "American Dream."

LEE & LOW BOOKS NEW VOICES AWARD, 95 Madison Ave., New York NY 10016. E-mail: info@leeandlow.com. Website: www.leeandlow.com. Annual award for a children's fiction or nonfiction picture book story by a writer of color; to 1,500 wds. Deadline: between May 1 and October 31. Prizes: $1,000 plus publication contract; & $500 for Honor Award Winner. Guidelines on Website.

MILKWEED PRIZE FOR CHILDREN'S LITERATURE, Milkweed Editions, 1011 Washington Ave. S., Ste. 300, Minneapolis MN 55415. (612)332-3192. E-mail: editor@milkweed.org. Website: www.milkweed.org. Annual prize for unpublished novel intended for readers 8-13; 90-200 pgs. Prize: $10,000 advance against royalties and publication. Guidelines on Website.

POCKETS WRITING CONTEST, PO Box 340004, Nashville TN 37203-0004. (615)340-7333. Fax (615)340-7267. E-mail: pockets@upperroom.org. Website: www.pockets.org. United Methodist. Lynn W. Gilliam, ed. Devotional magazine for children (6-11 yrs.). Fiction-writing contest; submit between 3/1 and 8/15 every yr. Prize: $1,000 and publication in Pockets. Length: 1,000-1,600 wds. Must be unpublished and not historical fiction. Previous winners not eligible. Send to Pockets Fiction Contest at above address, designating "Fiction Contest" on outside of envelope. Send SASE for return and response.

SKIPPING STONES YOUTH HONOR AWARDS, PO Box 3939, Eugene OR 97403. (541)342-4956. E-mail: editor@skippingstones.org. Website: www.skippingstones.org. Interfaith/multicultural. Arun N. Toké, exec. ed.; Nina Forsberg, asst. ed. A multicultural awareness and nature appreciation magazine for young people 7-17, worldwide. Annual Book Awards for published books and authors. Deadline: February 1. Annual Youth Honor Awards for students 7-17. Deadline June 25. Send SASE for guidelines.

+SOCIETY OF CHILDREN'S BOOK WRITERS & ILLUSTRATORS GOLDEN KITE AWARDS. Offers $2,500 in cash awards. Website: www.scbwi.org.

FICTION CONTESTS

+AIM MAGAZINE SHORT STORY CONTEST. For best short story that promotes brotherhood among people and cultures. No entry fee. Deadline: August 15. Prize: $100. E-mail: apiladoone@aol.com. Website: www.aimmagazine.org.

+AMAZON BREAKTHROUGH NOVEL AWARD. In cooperation with Penguin and Hewlett-Packard. Penguin will publish winning novel with a $25,000 advance. Details: www.publishersweekly.com/article/CA6485525.html?nid=2286&source=title&rid=154587 6347.

AMERICAN CHRISTIAN FICTION WRITERS CONTESTS, President; PO Box 101066, Palm Bay FL 32910-1066. Phone/fax (321)984-4018. E-mail: genesis@ACFW.com. Website: www .ACFW.com. Sponsors a fiction contest and others. See Website for current contests and rules.

BAAL HAMON SHORT STORY CONTEST, 28 Akinniranye St., PO Box 2338, Akure, Ondo State, Nigeria. Phone: +234 (0)34 216 339. E-mail: info@baalhamon.com. Website: www.baal hamon.com. Short Story Contest. Guidelines by e-mail (info@baalhamon.com).

+BARD FICTION PRIZE. Awarded annually to a promising, emerging young writer of fiction. Entries must be previously published. Deadline: July 15. No entry fee. Prizes: $30,000 and appointment as writer in residence for one semester at Bard College, Annandale-on-Hudson NY. E-mail: bfp@bard.edu. Website: www.bard.edu/bfp.

BOSTON REVIEW SHORT STORY CONTEST, Boston Review, 35 Medford St., Ste. 302, Somerville MA 02143. Website: www.bostonreview.net. Prize: $1,500 (plus publication) for an unpublished short story to 4,000 words. Entry fee: $20. Deadline: October 1. Details on Website.

BULWER-LYTTON FICTION CONTEST. For the worst opening line to a novel. Deadline: April 15. Website: www.bulwer-lytton.com. Rules on Website.

CANADIAN WRITER'S JOURNAL SHORT FICTION CONTEST, White Mountain Publications, Box 1178, New Liskeard ON P0J 1P0, Canada. (705)647-5424. Canada-wide toll-free (800)258-5451. Website: www.cwj.ca. Sponsors semiannual short fiction contests. Deadline: March 31 and September 30. Length: to 1,200 wds. Entry fee: $5. Prizes: $100, $50, $25. All fiction needs for CWJ are filled by this contest. E-mail: cwc-calendar@cwj.ca.

ALEXANDER PATTERSON CAPON PRIZE FOR FICTION, New Letters, UMKC, University House, 5101 Rockhill Rd., Kansas City MO 64110. (816)235-1168. E-mail: newletters@ umkc.edu. Website: www.newletters.org. Deadline: May 18. Entry fee: $15. Prize: $1,500.

CHARACTERS ANNUAL SHORT STORY CONTEST, PO Box 708, Newport NH 03773-0708. (603)863-5896. E-mail: hotdog@nhvt.net. Website: www.cdavisnh.com. Annual Short Story Contest. Deadline: August 30. Prizes: Six prizes in 2 categories: adult authors and children authors (to age 16). All genres to 1,500 words. Entry fee: $3 per story. First prize: $50 (others to be announced). Details on Website.

THE CHRISTY AWARDS, 1571 Glastonbury Rd., Ann Arbor MI 48103. Phone/fax (734)663-7931. E-mail: CA2000DK@aol.com. Website: www.christyawards.com. Awards in 9 fiction genres for excellence in Christian fiction. Nominations made by publishers, not authors. For submission guidelines and other information, see Website. Awards are presented at an Annual Christy Awards Banquet held Friday prior to the annual ICRS convention in July.

GLIMMER TRAIN PRESS FICTION CONTESTS. Sponsors 3 fiction contests during the year: Fiction Open, Very Short Fiction Award, and Short-Story Award for New Writers. General. Lengths and deadlines vary. Entry fee: $15. Prizes: $1,200 and publication, $500 and $300. Open to all writers, all themes. Submit original, unpublished stories. Glimmer Train Press, 1211 N.W. Glisan St., #207, Portland OR 97209. (503)221-0836. Website: www.glimmertrain.com.

SERENA MCDONALD KENNEDY AWARD, Snake Nation Press. Website: www.snakenationpress .org. Novellas to 50,000 words, or short story collection to 200 pgs. (published or unpublished). Deadline: check Website. Entry fee: $25. Prize: $1,000 and publication. Guidelines on Website.

C. S. LEWIS CONTESTS. Check Website for current contests: www.cslewisclassics.com.

+THE MARY MCCARTHY PRIZE IN SHORT FICTION, PO Box 4456, Louisville KY 40204. (502)458-4028. E-mail: sarabandeb@aol.com. Website: www.sarabandebooks.org. Prize: $2,000 and publication of a collection of short stories, novellas, or a short novel (150-250 pgs.), plus a standard royalty contract. Deadline: between January 1 and February 15. Entry fee: $25.

NATIONAL WRITERS ASSOCIATION NOVEL WRITING CONTEST, The National Writers Assn., 3140 S. Peoria #295, Aurora CO 80014. (303)841-0246. Website: www.nationalwriters .com. Details and entry form on Website.

NATIONAL WRITERS ASSOCIATION SHORT STORY CONTEST, The National Writers Assn., 10940 S. Parker Rd., #508, Parker CO 80134. (303)841-0246. Website: www.national writers.com. Guidelines on Website.

THE FLANNERY O'CONNOR AWARD FOR SHORT FICTION, University of Georgia Press, 330 Research Dr., Athens GA 30602. Website: www.ugapress.uga.edu. For collections of short fiction, 50,000-75,000 wds. Prize: $1,000, plus publication under royalty book contract. Entry fee: $25. Deadline: between April 1 and May 31 (postmark). Guidelines on Website.

OPERATION FIRST NOVEL. Sponsored by the Jerry B. Jenkins Christian Writers Guild, 5525 N. Union Blvd., Ste. 200, Colorado Springs CO 80918. For unpublished novelists who are students or annual members of the Christian Writers Guild. Winner receives a book contract with a major CBA publisher. Length: 75,000-100,000 wds. Deadline: October 2009 (check Website for exact date). No entry fee. For contest rules, go to www.ChristianWritersGuild .com/contest.

KATHERINE ANNE PORTER PRIZE FOR FICTION, Literary Contest/Fiction, Nimrod Journal, University of Tulsa, 800 S. Tucker Dr., Tulsa OK 74104. (618)631-3080. E-mail: nimrod@ utulsa.edu. Website: www.utulsa.edu/nimrod/awards.html. Quality prose and fiction by emerging writers of contemporary literature, unpublished. Deadline: between January 1 and April 30. Entry fee: $20. Prizes: $2,000 and publication; $1,000 and publication.

TAMARAK AWARD, Website: www.minnesotamonthly.com. Short fiction to 4,000 wds. Prize: $10,000. Winning story to be published in the fall issue of *Minnesota Monthly*. For residents of Minnesota, North Dakota, South Dakota, Iowa, Wisconsin, and Michigan only. Spring deadline. Details on Website.

PETER TAYLOR PRIZE FOR THE NOVEL, Knoxville Writers' Guild, PO Box 2565, Knoxville TN 37901-2565. Website: www.knoxvillewritersguild.org/guide.htm. For unpublished novels, 40,000 words or more. Deadline: between February 1 and April 30. Entry fee: $25. Prizes: $1,000 and publication. Guidelines on Website.

TOBIAS WOLFF AWARD IN FICTION, Western Washington University, Bellingham WA. E-mail: bhreview@cc.wwu.edu. Website: www.wwu.edu/~bhreview. Short story or novel excerpt to 8,000 wds. Deadline: postmarked between December 1 and March 15. Entry fee: $15 for first story/chapter; $10 each additional. Prize: $1,000, plus publication. Details on Website.

WORD SMITTEN'S TENTEN FICTION COMPETITION, Word Smitten LLP, PO Box 5067, St. Petersburg FL 33737. E-mail: award@wordsmitten.com. Website: www.wordsmitten.com. Annual contest for a short story of exactly 1,010 words. Deadline: July 1. Entry fee: $18. Prize: $1,010, plus publication.

WRITER'S JOURNAL ANNUAL FICTION CONTEST, Val-Tech Media, PO Box 394, Perham MN 56573. E-mail: writersjournal@writersjournal.com. Website: www.writersjournal.com. Deadline: January 30. Entry fee: $15. Maximum 5,000 wds. Prizes: $500, $200, $100, plus publication. Sponsors several contests; see Website.

NONFICTION CONTESTS

AMY WRITING AWARDS. A call to present spiritual truth reinforced with biblical references in general, nonreligious publications. First prize is $10,000 with a total of $34,000 given annually. To be eligible, submitted articles must be published in a general, nonreligious publication and must be reinforced with at least one passage of Scripture. Deadline is January 31 of following year. For details and a copy of last year's winning entries, contact: The Amy Foundation, PO Box 16091, Lansing MI 48901-6091. (517)323-6233. E-mail: amyfoundtn@aol.com. Website: www.amyfound.org.

AWP CREATIVE NONFICTION PRIZE, Assoc. of Writers and Writing programs, George Mason University, Fairfax. E-mail: awp@awpwriter.org. Website: www.awpwriter.org. For authors of book-length manuscripts; submit only 150-300 pgs. Prize: $2,000. Guidelines on Website.

THE BECHTEL PRIZE, Teachers and Writers Magazine Contest. E-mail: info@twc.org. Website: www.twc.org/publications/bechtel_prize. Contemporary writing articles (unpublished) to 5,000 words. Deadline: May or June (varies). Prize: $2,500, plus publication.

ERMA BOMBECK WRITING COMPETITION. Website: www.wcpl.lib.oh.us/adults/erma.html. Entry fee: none. Prizes: $100 prize in each category and free registration in writer's conference. Personal essay (humor or human interest), 450 wds. Deadline: January (varies). Use online entry form.

THE BROSE PRIZE, The Brose Foundation, Lake Forest College, 555 N. Sheridan, Lake Forest IL 60045. (847)735-5175. Fax (847)735-6192. E-mail: rmiller@lfc.edu. Offered only every 10 years for unpublished work; next contest 2010. Deadline: September 1, 2010. Prizes: $4,000-$15,000. Entries become the property of the college. Open to a book or treatise on the relationship between any discipline or topic and the Christian religion. Send SASE for guidelines.

DOROTHY CHURCHILL CAPON PRIZE FOR ESSAY, New Letters, UMKC, University House, 5101 Rockhill Rd., Kansas City MO 64110. (816)235-1168. E-mail: newletters@umkc.edu. Website: www.newletters.org. Deadline: May 18. Entry fee: $15. Prize: $1,500.

THE DABBLING MUM.COM CONTESTS, E-mail: dm@thedabblingmum.com. Website: www.thedabblingmum.com. Alyice Edrich, ed. Balance your life while you glean from successful entrepreneurs, parents, and Christians—just like you. Every 2-3 months they have an essay contest (http://thedabblingmum.com/contests/index.htm).

ANNIE DILLARD AWARD IN CREATIVE NONFICTION. Essays on any subject to 8,000 wds. Deadline: between December 1 and March 15. Entry fee: $15 for first; $10 each additional. First prize: $1,000. Unpublished works only, to 8,000 wds. Manuscripts to: Bellingham Review, Mail Stop 9053, Western Washington University, Bellingham WA 98225. (360)650-4863. E-mail: bhreview@cc.wwu.edu. Website: www.wwu.edu/~bhreview. Details on Website.

+MARGARET DOOLEY AWARD FOR YOUNG WRITERS, PO Box 553, Richmond VIC 3121, Australia. +613 9421 9600. Fax +613 9421 9600. E-mail: dooleyaward@eurekastreet .com.au. Website: www.crimeandjusticefestival.com.au/eureka. For writers under 35. Deadline: Mid-June. E-mail submissions only. Prizes: $1.500, $350, $150. Details on Website.

+EUREKA STREET/READER'S FEAST AWARD, PO Box 553, Richmond VIC 3121, Australia. +613 9421 9600. Fax +613 9421 9600. E-mail: eureka@eureksstreet.com.au. Website: www.crimeandjusticefestival.com/eureka. For unpublished essays on social justice and human rights. $5,000 award to an Australian writer. Deadline: Mid June. E-mail submissions only. Details on Website.

EVENT CREATIVE NONFICTION CONTEST, The Douglas College Review, PO Box 2503, New Westminster BC V3L 5B2, Canada. (604)527-5293. E-mail: event@douglas.bc.ca. Website: http://event.douglas.bc.ca. Previously unpublished creative nonfiction to 5,000 wds. Deadline: mid-April. Entry fee; $29.95. Prizes: Three $500 prizes and publication in Event.

GRAYWOLF PRESS NONFICTION PRIZE, 2402 University Ave., Ste. 203, St. Paul MN 55114. (651)641-0036. Website: www.graywolfpress.org/Company_Info/Submission_Guidelines/ Graywolf_Press_Nonfiction_Prize_Submission_Guidelines. For the best literary nonfiction book by a writer not yet established in the genre. Deadline: between September 1 and 30. Entry fee: none. Prize: $12,000 advance and publication.

GUIDEPOSTS CONTEST, 16 E. 34th St., New York NY 10016. (212)251-8100. Website: www .guideposts.org. Interfaith. Writers Workshop Contest held on even years with a late June deadline. True, first-person stories (yours or someone else's), 1,500 wds. Needs one spiritual message, with scenes, drama, and characters. Winners attend a week-long seminar (all expenses paid) on how to write for *Guideposts.*

JEBAIRE YOUTH ESSAY CONTEST, Stand Up and Be Counted. Website: www.jebairepublishing .com. Shannon Clark, contest coordinator (SClark@jebairepublishing.com). Sponsors an annual contest for youth, ages 9-16. Essays 700-1,200 words on specific topics. Deadline: between April 1 and June 15. Guidelines available on Website or by e-mail. Submissions must be mailed to above address. Twenty winners will have their work published in a nonfiction anthology and receive a copy of the book.

CORETTA SCOTT KING AWARDS, American Library Assn. Toll-free (800)545-2433, ext. 4294. E-mail: olos@ala.org. Website: www.ala.org. Offered annually to an African American author and illustrator to promote understanding and appreciation of culture and the contributions of all people. Prize: $1,000, plus a set of encyclopedias. Guidelines on Website.

+LIFT EVERY VOICE ESSAY CONTEST, 820 N. LaSalle Blvd., Chicago IL 60610. (312)329-2140. Fax (312)329-4157. E-mail: lifteveryvoice@moody.edu. Website: www.lifteveryvoice books.com. African American imprint of Moody Publishers. Submit to Nora Darby, asst. coord. To advance the cause of Christ through publishing African American Christians who educate, edify, and disciple Christians. Essay contest; August 31 deadline. See Website for details.

+LIGHT OF THE WORLD ANNUAL YOUTH ESSAY COMPETITION, 177-34 Troutville Rd., Jamaica NY 11434. (718)504-3814. E-mail: Christislight@aol.com. Julius Ogunnaya, ed. Details by mail or e-mail.

RICHARD J. MARGOLIS AWARD of Blue Mountain Center, c/o Margolis & Assocs., 533 Boyston St., 8th Fl., Boston MA 02116. E-mail: hwsm@margolis.com. Website: www.margolis .com/award. Given annually to a promising young journalist or essayist whose work combines warmth, humor, wisdom, and concern with social justice. Deadline: July 1. Prize: $5,000. Guidelines on Website.

NATIONAL WRITERS ASSOCIATION NONFICTION CONTEST, Website: www.nationalwriters .com. Annual nonfiction contest. Deadline: December 31. Entry fee: $18. Prizes: $50, $100, $200. Guidelines on Website.

OPERATION FIRST BOOK (nonfiction). Sponsored by the Jerry B. Jenkins Christian Writers Guild, 5525 N. Union Blvd., Ste. 200, Colorado Springs CO 80918. For unpublished authors who are students or annual members of the Christian Writers Guild. Winner receives $10,000 and their proposal is considered by a major Christian publisher. Length: 75,000-100,000 wds. Deadline: September 2009 (check Website for exact date). Entry fee: none. For contest rules, go to www.ChristianWritersGuild.com and click on "Contests."

+REVIVAL NATION SPIRIT WORD WRITING CONTEST, PO Box 30001, Sarnia ON N7T 0A7, Canada. (519)330-6346. E-mail: publishing@revivalnation.com. Website: www.revival nation.com. Nonfiction book on specific topics. October 31 deadline. Entry fee: $25. Prize: Publication with a $1,000 advance. Details on Website.

LAMAR YORK PRIZE FOR NONFICTION, The Chatahoochi Review, George Perimeter College, 2101 Womack Rd., Dunwoody GA 30338. Website: www.gpc.edu/~gpccr. Essays up to 5,000 wds. Deadline: between October 1 and January 31. Entry fee: $12. Prize: $1,000 and publication in The Chatahoochi Review. Guidelines on Website.

PLAY/SCRIPTWRITING/SCREENWRITING CONTESTS

+AMBASSADOR SCREENWRITING AWARDS, (formerly Faith and Values Screenwriting Competition). E-mail: info@ambassadorcommunication.biz. Website: www.ambassador communications.biz/faithandvalues.html. Honors the best in faith-based TV series pilots and feature-length screenplays. Claire Hutchinson, contest coordinator. Monetary prizes. Check Website for details and current status of this contest.

ANNUAL SCRIPTAPALOOZA SCREENPLAY COMPETITION. (323)654-5809. E-mail: info@scriptapalooza.com. Website: www.scriptapalooza.com. Deadline: April 13. Prize: $10,000. Details on Website.

AUSTIN FILM FESTIVAL SCREENWRITERS COMPETITION, 1145 W. 5th St., Ste. 210, Austin TX 78703. (512)478-4795. E-mail: info@austinfilmfestival.com. Website: www.austinfilm festival.com. Offers two first prizes for unpublished screenplays in the Adult/Family and Comedy categories. Deadline: March 27- May 15 (postmark). Entry fee: $40. Prizes: $5,000, plus travel expenses and admission to the festival. See current details on Website.

BAKER'S PLAYS HIGH SCHOOL PLAYWRITING COMPETITION. Plays may be about any subject and any length as long as the play can be reasonably produced by high school students on a high school stage. Deadline: January 30 (may vary). Guidelines on Website: www .bakersplays.com.

CITA PLAY DEVELOPMENT COMPETITION, PO Box 26471, Greenville SC 29616. E-mail: admin@cita.org. Website: www.CITA.org. (click on "Playwriting"). To encourage Christian playwrights, the writing of new plays and musicals that are informed by a biblical world-view in influencing our culture and furthering the Kingdom of God. Info on upcoming competitions will be listed on Website as available.

CITA THEATRICAL SKETCH WRITING CONTEST. E-mail: information@cita.org. Website: www.CITA.org. Click in "Playwrighting." Details will be listed on Website when competitions are available.

KAIROS PRIZE FOR SPIRITUALLY UPLIFTING SCREENPLAYS. John Templeton Foundation. E-mail: contact@kairosprize.com. Website: www.kairosprize.com. Biannual. For first-time screenwriters with a religious message. Prizes: $25,000, $15,000, $10,000. Guidelines on Website.

MOONDANCE INTERNATIONAL FILM FESTIVAL COMPETITION, 970—9th St., Boulder CO 80302. E-mail: director@moondancefilmfestival.com. Website: www.moondancefilm festival.com. Open to films, screenplays, and features. Deadline: May 15 (may vary). Entry fee: $25-75. Prize: winning entries screened at festival. Details on Website.

NATIONAL CHILDREN'S THEATRE FESTIVAL, Actor's Playhouse at the Miracle Theatre, Coral Gables FL. E-mail: maulding@actorsplayhouse.org. Website: www.actorsplayhouse.org. Annual playwriting prize offering $500 and full production of winning musical, and author's transportation and lodging at the festival. Deadline: April 1. Entry fee: $10 (entry form on Website). Earl Maulding, festival dir. Details on Website.

NICHOLL FELLOWSHIPS IN SCREENWRITING, 1313 N. Vine St, Hollywood CA 90028-8107. (310)247-3010. E-mail: nicholl@oscars.org. Website: www.oscars.org/nicholl/index .html. International contest held annually, open to any writer who has not optioned or sold a treatment, teleplay, or screenplay for more than $5,000. Up to five $30,000 fellow-ships offered each year to promising authors. Guidelines/required application form on Website.

MILDRED & ALBERT PANOWSKI PLAYWRITING AWARD, Award Coordinator, Forest Roberts Theatre, Northern Michigan University, Marquette MI 49855-5364. Website: www.nmu .edu/theatre. Unpublished, unproduced, full-length plays. Deadline: October 31 (varies). Prizes: $2,000, a summer workshop, a fully mounted production, and transportation to Marquette. Send SASE for guidelines and application.

THE WRITERS NETWORK ANNUAL SCREENPLAY & FICTION COMPETITION, *Fade In* mag-azine, 287 S. Robertson Blvd., #467, Beverly Hills CA 90211. (310)275-0287. E-mail: writers net@aol.com. Website: www.fadeinonline.com. Deadline: May 31. Must submit online. Over $10,000 in cash prizes. Guidelines on Website.

POETRY CONTESTS

ANHINGA PRIZE FOR POETRY, E-mail: info@anhinga.org. Website: www.anhinga.org. A $2,000 prize for original poetry book in English. Winning manuscript published by Anhinga Press. For poets trying to publish a first or second book of poetry. Submissions: 48-80 pages. Number pages and include $25 reading fee. Deadline: between February 15 and May 1 each year. Details on Website.

ANNUAL CAVE CANEM POETRY PRIZE. Supports the work of African American poets with excellent manuscripts who have not found a publisher for their first book. Deadline: May 16 (varies). Prize: $500, publication by a national press, and 50 copies of the book. Details on Website: www.cavecanempoets.org. E-mail: ccpoets@verizon.net.

MURIEL CRAFT BAILEY MEMORIAL POETRY AWARD, CWG Poetry Contest 2008, 4956 St. John Dr., Syracuse NY 13215. E-mail: poetry@comstockreview.org. Awarded annually. Deadline: July 1. Prizes: $100 to $1,000. Finalists published in the Comstock Review. Unpublished poems to 40 lines. Entry fee: $4 for each poem (no limit on number of sub-missions). Details on Website: www.comstockreview.org.

+BALTIMORE REVIEW POETRY CONTEST. All styles and forms of poetry. April 1-July 1. Entry fee: $10. Prizes: $300 & publication; $150; $50. Details on Website: www.baltimorereview .org/contest.html.

BLUE MOUNTAIN ARTS/SPS STUDIOS POETRY CARD CONTEST, PO Box 1007, Boulder CO 80306. (303)449-0536. E-mail: poetrycontest@sps.com. Website: www.sps.com. Biannual contest (even years). Deadline: June 30. Rhymed or unrhymed original poetry (unrhymed preferred). Poems also considered for greeting cards or anthologies. Prizes: $300, $150, $50. Details on Website.

BOSTON REVIEW ANNUAL POETRY CONTEST. Deadline: June 1. First prize: $1,500, plus publication. Submit up to 5 unpublished poems. Entry fee: $20 (includes a subscription to Boston Review). Submit manuscripts in duplicate with cover note. Send manuscript and fee to: Poetry Contest, *Boston Review*, 35 Medford St., Ste. 302, Somerville MA 02143. Website: www.bostonreview.net. Details on Website.

VIRGINIA BRENDEMUEHL PRIZE FOR POETRY, *Rock & Sling: A Journal of Literature, Art and Faith*, PO Box 30865, Spokane WA 99223. Fax (509)276-2971. E-mail: editors@rock andsling.org. Website: www.rockandsling.org. Prize: $1,000, plus publication in *Rock & Sling*. Check Website for details and current status of this contest.

CHRISTIAN NEWS TODAY FREE POETRY CONTEST. E-mail: publisher@christiannews today.com. Website: www.christiannewstoday.com. Any length or type; need to be poems of faith. Deadline: may vary. Prize: a surprise gift bag, plus having their poem featured on the main page of Website for 30 days. E-mail submissions. Check Website for details and current status of this contest.

DREAM HORSE PRESS NATIONAL POETRY CHAPBOOK PRIZE, PO Box 2080, Aptos CA 95001-2080. E-mail: dreamhorsepress@yahoo.com. Send 16-24 pages of poetry (paginated). Entry fee: $15. Deadline: May 31. Prize: $500 and 25 copies of chapbook. See Website for details: www.dreamhorsepress.com. Electronic submissions OK, with electronic fee payment.

DREAM HORSE PRESS ORPHIC PRIZE FOR POETRY (book prize), PO Box 2080, Aptos CA 95001-2080. E-mail: dreamhorsepress@yahoo.com. Send 48-80 pages of poetry (paginated). Entry fee: $25. Deadline: December 1 (may vary). Prize: $1,000 and 20 copies of chapbook. See Website for details: www.dreamhorsepress.com. Electronic submissions OK, with electronic fee payment.

49TH PARALLEL POETRY AWARD, Mail Stop 9053, Western Washington University, Bellingham WA 98225. (360)650-4863. E-mail: bhreview@cc.wwu.edu. Website: www.wwu.edu/~bhreview. Contact: Brenda Miller. Poems in any style or on any subject. Deadline: between December 1 and March 15. Entry fee: $18 for first entry; $10 for each additional entry. First prize: $1,000 and publication. Detail on Website.

GRIFFIN POETRY PRIZE. Contact: Ruth Smith, mngr., The Griffin Trust for Excellence in Poetry, 6610 Edwards Blvd., Mississauga ON L5T 2V6, Canada. (905)565-5993. E-mail: info@ griffinpoetryprize.com. Website: www.griffinpoetryprize.com. Prizes: two $50,000 awards (one to a Canadian and one to a poet from anywhere in the world) for a collection of poetry published in English during the preceding year. All submissions must come from publishers. Deadline: December 31. Details on Website.

SARA HENDERSON HAY PRIZE, *The Pittsburgh Quarterly*, 6336 Crombie St., Pittsburgh PA 15217. Enter up to 3 poems, no more than 100 lines each. Deadline: July 1. Prize: $600. Entry fee: $10. Details: www.city-net.com/~tpq.

TOM HOWARD/JOHN H. REID POETRY CONTEST, 351 Pleasant St., PMB 222, Northampton MA 01060. Website: www.winningwriters.com/tompoetry.htm. Deadline: between December 15 and September 30. Poetry in any style or genre. Published poetry accepted. Entry fee: $6 for every 25 lines. Prizes: $2,000 first prize; total of $5,250 in cash prizes. Details on Website.

BARBARA MANDIGO KELLY PEACE POETRY AWARDS, Nuclear Age Peace Foundation, PMB 121, 1187 Coast Village Rd., Ste. 1, Santa Barbara CA 93108-2794. (805)965-3443. E-mail: communications@napf.org. Website: www.wagingpeace.org. Annual series of awards to encourage poets to explore and illuminate positive visions of peace and the human spirit. Deadline: July 1. Prizes: $1,000 for Adult; $200 for Youth 13-18 years; and $200 for Youth ages 12 and under. Adult entry fee: $15 for up to 3 poems (no youth fee).

THOMAS MERTON POETRY OF THE SACRED CONTEST. Poetry that expresses, directly or indirectly, a sense of the holy or that, by mode of expression, evokes the sacred. The tone may be religious, prophetic, or contemplative. Deadline: December 31. First prize: $500; three Honorable Mentions, $100 each. Submit 1 poem. Entry fee: none. Submit to: The Thomas Merton Prize, The Thomas Merton Foundation, 2117 Payne St., Louisville KY 40206-2011, or e-mail to: hgraffy@mertonfoundation.org. Details: call (502)899-1991 or visit Website: www.mertonfoundation.org.

+MINDFLIGHTS POETRY CONTEST, 9618 Misty Brook Cove, Cordova TN 38016. E-mail: editor@mindflights.com. Website: http://mindflights.com/index.html. Double-Edged Publishing, Inc. Submit to Editorial Staff. Publishes speculative (sci-fi/fantasy) short fiction and poetry with a Christian or Christian-friendly slant. Monthly online & quarterly print mag. Planning a poetry contest. All contests announced on Website.

KATHRYN A. MORTON PRIZE IN POETRY, Sarabande Books, PO Box 4456, Louisville KY 40204. (502)458-4028. E-mail: info@sarabandebooks.org. Website: www.sarabandebooks .org. Prize: $2,000, plus publication of a book of poetry. Submit: minimum of 48 pages of poetry. Entry fee: $25. Deadline: January 1 through February 15 (postmark).

NATIONAL WRITERS ASSOCIATION POETRY CONTEST, The National Writers Assn., 3140 S. Peoria, #295, Aurora CO 80014. Website: www.nationalwriters.com. Annual poetry contest. Entry fee: $10. Prizes: $25, $50, $100. Details and entry form on Website.

NEW LETTERS PRIZE FOR POETRY, New Letters, UMKC, University House, 5101 Rockhill Rd., Kansas City MO 64110. (816)235-1168. E-mail: newletters@umkc.edu. Website: www.new letters.org. Deadline: May 18. Entry fee: $15. Prize: $1,500 for best group of 3 to 6 poems.

+JESSE BRYCE NILES CHAPBOOK CONTEST. Submit 25-34 pages of poetry. August 1-September 30. Entry fee: $15. Prizes: $1,000. Details on Website: www.comstockreview.org.

+OZARKS CHAPTER ACW POETRY CONTEST. Contact: Jeanetta Chrystie, pres., OCACW, 5042 E. Cherry Hills Blvd., Springfield MO 65809-3301. (417)832-8409. E-mail: DrChristie@ mchsi.com. Susan Willingham, newsletter ed.; OzarksACW@yahoo.com. Website: www.ClearGlassView.org/OzarksACW/index.htm. Will sponsor a poetry contest (open to non-members); between March 1 and June 30, 2009. See Website for details.

+PARSON PLACE PRESS POETRY CONTEST. Guidelines on Website: www.parsonplace press.com.

POETRY SOCIETY OF VIRGINIA POETRY CONTESTS, PO Box 35685, Richmond VA 23235. Website: www.poetrysocietyofvirginia.org. Sponsors a number of poetry contests. Categories for adults and students. Prizes: $10-100. Entry fee per poem for nonmembers: $3. List of contests on Website.

SILVER WINGS CONTEST, PO Box 2340, Clovis CA 93613-2340. (559)347-0194. E-mail: cloviswings@aol.com. Jackson Wilcox, ed. Annual poetry contest on a theme. Deadline: December 31. Send SASE for details. Winners published in March issue. $325 in prizes. Entry fee: $3 entry fee.

SLIPSTREAM ANNUAL POETRY CHAPBOOK COMPETITION, Dept. W-1, Box 2071, Niagara Falls NY 14301. Website: www.slipstreampress.org/contest.html. Prize: $1,000, plus 50 copies of chapbook. Deadline: December 1. Send up to 40 pages of poetry. Reading fee: $20.

SOUL-MAKING LITERARY COMPETITION, National League of American Pen Women, Nob Hill, San Francisco Branch, 1544 Sweetwood Dr., Colma CA 94015-2029. E-mail: pennobhill@ aol.com. Website: www.soulmakingcontest.us. One-page poems only (single- or double-spaced). Up to 3 poems/entry. Deadline: November 30. Entry fee: $5. Prizes $25, $50, $100.

HOLLIS SUMMERS POETRY PRIZE, Ohio University Press, 19 Circle Dr., The Ridges, Athens OH 45701. (740)593-1155. E-mail: oupress@ohio.edu. For unpublished collection of original poems, 60-95 pgs. Entry fee: $20. Deadline: October 31. Prize: $1,000, plus publication in book form. Details on Website: www.ohiou.edu/oupress/poetryprize.htm.

THE MAY SWENSON POETRY AWARD, Utah State University Press, 7800 Old Main Hill, Logan UT 84322-7800. (435)797-1362. Website: www.usu.edu/usupress. Collections of original poetry, 50-100 pgs. Deadline: September 30. Prize: $1,000, publication, and royalties. Reading fee: $25. Details on Website.

TIME OF SINGING POETRY CONTESTS, PO Box 149, Conneaut Lake PA 16316. E-mail: timesing@zoominternet.net. Website: www.timeofsinging.bizland.com. Lora Zill, ed. Sponsors 1-2 annual poetry contests on specific themes or forms. Entry fee: $2/poem. Cash prizes. Details on Website.

KATE TUFTS DISCOVERY AWARD, Claremont Graduate University, 150 E. 10th St., Harper East B7, Claremont CA 91711-6165. (909)621-8974. E-mail: tufts@cgu.edu. Presented annually for a first or very early work by a poet of genuine promise. Prize: $10,000. Work submitted must be a book published between September 15, 2008, and September 15, 2009. Deadline: September 15. Details and entry form on Website: www.cgu.edu/tufts.

UTMOST NOVICE CHRISTIAN POETRY CONTEST, Utmost Christian Writers Foundation, 121 Morin Maze, Edmonton AB T6K 1V1, Canada. E-mail: nnharms@telusplanet.net. Website: www.utmostchristianwriters.com/poetry-contest/poetry-contest-rules.php. Nathan Harms. Entry fee: $10/poem (10 poems max.). Prizes: $500, $300, $100; 15 honorable mentions $50 ea.; Best Rhyming Poem $250. Deadline: August 31 (may vary). Details and entry form on Website.

WAR POETRY CONTEST, 351 Pleasant St., PMB 222, Northhampton MA 01060. E-mail: war contest@winningwriters.com. Website: www.winningwriters.com/annualcontest.htm. Sponsored by Winning Writers. Submit 1-3 unpublished poems on the theme of war, up to 500 lines total. Prizes: $1,500 first prize; $5,000 in total prizes. Deadline: between November 15 and May 31. Entry fee: $15.

+WINNING WRITERS. Variety of poetry contests. Website: www.winningwriter.com.

YALE SERIES OF YOUNGER POETS COMPETITION, PO Box 209040, New Haven CT 06520. (203)432-0960. Fax (203)432-0948. E-mail: robert.flynn@yale.edu. Website: www.yale .edu/yup. Robert Flynn, ed./religion. Yale Series of Younger Poets competition. Open to poets under 40 who have not had a book of poetry published. Submit manuscripts of 48-64 pgs. Deadline: between October 1 and November 15. Entry fee: $15. Publishes one book each year. Details: on Website. Send complete manuscript.

MULTIPLE-GENRE CONTESTS

AMERICAN LITERARY REVIEW CONTESTS, PO Box 311307, University of North Texas, Denton TX 76203. E-mail: americanliteraryreview@yahoo.com. Website: www.engl.unt.edu/alr. Now sponsors three contests: short fiction, creative nonfiction, and poetry. Prize: $1,000 and publication in fall issue of the magazine. Entry fee: $15. Deadline: between June 1 and September 1. Details on Website.

BAKELESS LITERARY PUBLICATION PRIZES, Bread Loaf Writers Conference, Middlebury College, Middlebury VT 05753. E-mail: bakeless@middlebury.edu. Website: www .bakelessprize.org. Book series competition for new authors of literary works of poetry, fiction, and nonfiction. Entry fee: $10. Deadline: between September 15 and November 1. Details on Website.

BEST NEW CANADIAN CHRISTIAN AUTHOR CONTEST, The Word Guild, Box 34, Port Perry ON L9L 1A2, Canada. E-mail: admin@thewordguild.com. Website: www.thewordguild.com. Encourages first-time authors to write fiction and nonfiction books expressing Christian faith in a clear, original, and inspiring way (for authors who have never had a royalty-paying book published before). Deadline: End of November. Entry fees: $50 Cdn. (without a critique); $125 (with a critique). Prize: Cash or book publishing contract. Details on Website.

+BEST NEW WRITING (formerly Writers' Notes), PO Box 11, Titusville NJ 08560. E-mail: editor@ hopepubs.com. Website: www.bestnewwriting.com. In 2006, *Writers' Notes* magazine was transformed in this annual anthology, which carries the results of the Eric Hoffer Award for Books and Prose. Submit books via mail; no queries. The prose category is for creative fiction and nonfiction less than 10,000 wds. Annual award for books features 14 categories. Pays $500 for winning prose; $1,500 for winning book. Guidelines at www.HofferAward.com.

BYLINE CONTESTS, PO Box 111, Albion NY 14411-0111. (585)355-8172. E-mail: Robbi@ bylinemag.com. Website: www.BylineMag.com. General market. Robbi Hess, ed. Sponsors many contests year round; details included in magazine, on Website, or send SASE for flier.

CANTICLE WRITING CONTEST. Blog: http://heidihesssaxton.blogspot.com. Heidi Saxton, ed. Check blog for details on current contest. Winners published in *Canticle* magazine.

CHICKEN SOUP FOR THE SOUL CONTESTS. Website: www.chickensoup.com. See Website for list of current contests.

CHRISTIAN SMALL PUBLISHER BOOK OF THE YEAR. Website: www.christianpublishers.net. Honors books produced by small publishers each year for outstanding contributions to Christian life. Categories: nonfiction, fiction, children's. Books need to have been published this year or last. Deadline: November 15. Eligible small publisher must have annual revenues of $350,000 or less. Details and nomination form on Website.

COLUMBIA FICTION/POETRY CONTEST, 415 Dodge Hall, 2960 Broadway, New York NY 10027. Website: www.columbiajournal.org/contests.htm. Length: 20 double-spaced pages or up to 5 poems. Prize: $500 in each category, plus publication. Deadline: January 15 (varies). Details on Website.

CRAZY HORSE FICTION PRIZE & LYNDA HULL MEMORIAL POETRY PRIZE, *Crazy Horse*, Dept. of English, College of Charleston, 66 George St., Charleston SC 29424. E-mail: crazy horse@cofc.edu. Website: http://crazyhorse.cofc.edu. Deadline: between September 1 and December 16. Reading fee: $15. Prizes: $2,000 in each category. Winners published in *Crazy Horse.* Guidelines on Website.

ECPA CHRISTIAN BOOK AWARD, 9633 S. 48th St., Ste. 140, Phoenix AZ 85044. (480)966-3998. E-mail: info@ecpa.org. Website: www.ECPA.org. Presented annually to the best books in Christian publishing. Awards recognize books in 6 different categories: Bibles, Fiction, Children & Youth, Inspiration & Gift, Bible Reference & Study, and Christian Life. Only ECPA members in good standing can nominate products. Deadline: January each year. Awards are presented annually at the International Christian Retail Show.

E.F.S. RELIGIOUS FICTION & NONFICTION WRITING COMPETITION, E.F.S. Enterprises Inc., 2844 Eighth Ave., Ste. 6E, New York NY 10039. (212)283-8899. E-mail: info@efs-enter prises.com. Website: www.efs-enterprises.com. Inspirational/religious fiction or nonfiction. Deadline: September 30. Entry fee: $25. Prizes: Publishing contract for grand prize winner; $50 for 1st place. Details & entry form on Website.

EVANGELICAL PRESS ASSOCIATION ANNUAL CONTEST, PO Box 28129, Crystal MN 55428. (763)535-4793. E-mail: director@epassoc.org. Website: www.epassoc.org. Sponsors annual contest for member publications.

FAULKNER-WISDOM CREATIVE WRITING COMPETITION, Faulkner House, 624 Pirate's Alley, New Orleans LA 70116. (504)586-1609. E-mail: Faulkhouse@aol.com. Website: www.wordsandmusic.org. Unpublished novels, novellas, short stories, essays, and poetry. Deadline: between January 15 and May 22 (postmark). Entry fees: $10-35. Prizes: $750-7,500. Guidelines on Website.

FREELANCE WRITER'S REPORT CONTEST, 45 Main St., PO Box A, North Stratford NH 03590-0167. (603)922-8383. E-mail: editor@writers-editors.com. Website: www.writers-editors .com. Dana K. Cassell, ed. Open to all writers. Deadline: March 15. Nonfiction, fiction, children's, poetry. Prizes: $100, $75, $50. Details on Website.

+GOD USES INK NOVICE CONTEST, The Word Guild, 698A Highpoint Ave., Waterloo ON N2V 1G9, Canada. (519)886-4196. E-mail: info@thewordguild.com. Website: www.theword guild.com. Prizes: Free registration to the next Write! Canada Writers' Conference (a nearly $400 value), plus other cash prizes. Open to everyone who has never been paid for their writing. Three age categories: 14-19; 20-29; and 30 plus. Deadline: Second week in April.

+INSCRIBE CHRISTIAN WRITERS' CONTEST. Edmonton AB, Canada. Contact: Eunice Matchett, 4304-45th St., Drayton Valley AB T7A 1G7, Canada. (780)542-7950. Fax (780)514-3702. E-mail: query@inscribe.org. Website: www.inscribe.org. Sponsors a fall contest open to nonmembers; details on Website.

INSIGHT WRITING CONTEST, 55 W. Oak Ridge Dr., Hagerstown MD 21740-7301. (301)393-4038. Fax (301)393-4055. E-mail: insight@rhpa.org. Website: www.insightmagazine.org. Review and Herald/Seventh-day Adventist. Dwain N. Esmond, ed. A magazine of positive Christian living for Seventh-day Adventist high schoolers. Sponsors short story and poetry contests; includes a category for students 22 or under. Prizes: $50-$250. Deadline: June 1. Submit by e-mail. Details on Website.

+INSPIRATIONAL WRITERS ALIVE! OPEN COMPETITION 2009, c/o Winonna Peveto, PO Box 55363, Houston TX 77255-5363. E-mail: marthalrogers@sbcglobal.net. Categories: adult short story, juvenile short story, articles, poetry, book proposals (child & adult), drama. Entry fees: $10 nonmembers, $5 members for all categories except proposals; proposals $15/$7. Deadline May 15. Prizes: $30, $20, $15. E-mail for complete guidelines.

INTERNATIONAL LIBRARY OF PHOTOGRAPHY FREE PHOTO CONTEST, 3600 Crondall Ln., Ste. 101, Owings Mills MD 21117. Website: www.picture.com/contest/enter.asp. Ongoing contest. Prize: $100,000 in prizes to amateur photographers. Submit photos electronically on Website. Details on Website.

MINISTRY & LITURGY VISUAL ARTS AWARDS, 160 E. Virginia St., #290, San Jose CA 95112. (408)286-8505. Fax (408)287-8748. E-mail: mleditor@rpinet.com. Website: www.rpinet .com/vaaentry.pdf. Visual Arts Awards held in 5 categories through the year. Best in each category wins $100. Entry fee: $30. Different deadline for each category (see Website).

MISSISSIPPI REVIEW PRIZE, 118 College Dr., #5144, Hattiesburg MS 39406-0001. (601)266-4321. E-mail: rief@mississippireview.com. Website: www.mississippireview .com/contest.html. Fiction & Poetry. Prize: $1,000 in each category. Deadline: April 1 to October 1. Entry fee: $15.

MOM'S CHOICE AWARDS. The Just For Mom Foundation. Website: www.momschoiceawards .org. Various award categories. Details on Website.

NEW MILLENNIUM AWARDS. Website: www.newmillenniumwritings.com/awards.html. Prizes: $1,000 award for each category. Best Poem, Best Fiction, Best Nonfiction, Best Short-Short Fiction (fiction and nonfiction 6,000 wds.; short-short fiction to 1,000 wds.; 3 poems to 5 pgs. total). Entry fee: $17 each. Deadline: June 17. Guidelines on Website. Enter online or off.

+ONCE WRITTEN CONTESTS. Fiction and poetry contests. Website: www.oncewritten.com.

+POWER AWARDS. E-mail: info@penofthewriter.com. Website: www.penofthewriter.com/ awards. Established to assist self-published authors obtain industry recognition. Online voting in 5 genres: fiction, nonfiction, anthology, poetry, and children's. Winners receive stickers for books, framed certificates, online promotion, and one-year posting on Pen of the Writer Website.

RUMINATE POETRY AND FICTION CONTEST, 140 N. Roosevelt Ave., Fort Collins CO 80521. (970)449-2726. E-mail: editor@ruminatemagazine.com. Website: www.ruminatemagazine .com. Brianna Van Dyke, ed. An intimate and hip publication of faith literature and art. Annual poetry contest deadline May 15; annual fiction contest deadline November 15. Entry fee: $15. Prizes: $300 1st prize; $150 to runner-up. Details on Website.

MONA SCHREIBER PRIZE FOR HUMOROUS FICTION AND NONFICTION, 15442 Vista Haven Pl., Sherman Oaks CA 91403. E-mail: brashcyber@pcmagic.net. Website: www.brash cyber.com. Humorous fiction and nonfiction to 750 wds. Prizes: $500, $250, and $100. Entry fee: $5. Deadline: December 1.

SHARING THE PRACTICE AWARDS, c/o Central Woodward Christian Church, 3955 W. Big Beaver Rd., Troy MI 48084-2610. (248)644-0512. E-mail: drobcornwall@msn.com. Website: www.apclergy.org. Academy of Parish Clergy/Ecumenical/Interfaith. Growth toward excellence through sharing the practice of parish ministry. Book of the Year Award ($100+), Top Ten Books of the Year list, Parish Pastor of the Year award ($200+). Inquire by e-mail to DIELPADRE@aol.com.

SOUL-MAKING LITERARY COMPETITION, Webhallow House, 1544 Sweetwood Dr., Colma CA 94015-2029. E-mail: PenNobHill@aol.com. Website: www.SoulMakingContest.us/page3 .html. Lists various competitions: prose and poetry. Prizes: up to $100. Entry fee: $5. Guidelines on Website.

THE STORYTELLER CONTESTS, 2441 Washington Rd., Maynard AR 72444. (870)647-2137. Fax (870)647-2454. E-mail: storyteller1@hightowercom.com. Contest Website: www.the storytellermagazine.com. Fossil Creek Publishing. Regina Cook Williams, ed./pub. Family audience. Offers 1 or 2 paying contests per year, along with People's Choice Awards, and Pushcart Prize nominations.

TICKLED BY THUNDER CONTESTS, 14076—86A Ave., Surrey BC V3W 0V9, Canada. (604) 591-6095. E-mail: info@tickledbythunder.com. Website: www.tickledbythunder.com. Larry Lindner, ed. Sponsors 9 writing contests each year in various genres. Entry fee $10 for non-subscribers. Prizes: $5-150 Cdn. Details on Website or by mail.

+WORD GUILD CANADIAN CHRISTIAN WRITING AWARDS, The Word Guild, 698A Highpoint Ave., Waterloo ON N2V 1G9, Canada. (519)886-4196. E-mail: info@theword guild.com. Website: www.thewordguild.com. The following may be entered by author, writer, or publisher: fiction and nonfiction books, articles, columns, reviews, poems, song lyrics, scripts/screenplays published in the last year. Prizes: Cash and recognition. Deadline: Round One October; Round Two January.

THE WRITER CONTESTS, 21027 Crossroads Cir., Waukesha WI 53189. (262)796-8776. E-mail: editor@writermag.com. Website: www.writermag.com. General. How-to for writers. Occasionally sponsors a contest. Check Website.

WRITER'S DIGEST, 4700 E. Galbraith Rd., Cincinnati OH 45207. (513)531-2690, ext. 1483. Fax (513)531-1843. E-mail: wdsubmissions@fwpubs.com. Website: www.writersdigest .com. Sponsors annual contests for articles, short stories, poetry, children's fiction, self-published books, and scripts (categories vary). Deadlines: vary according to contest. Prizes: $25,000 or more for each contest. See Website for list of current contests and rules.

WRITERS' JOURNAL CONTESTS, PO Box 394, Perham MN 56573-0394. (218)346-7921. Fax (218)346-7924. E-mail: writersjournal@writersjournal.com. Website: www.writersjournal .com. Leon Ogroske, ed. Runs several contests each year. Prizes: $10 to $500. Variety of categories. Different starter lines and deadlines for each category. Details on Website, or send SASE.

WRITERS' UNION OF CANADA AWARDS & COMPETITIONS, 90 Richmond St. E., Ste. 200, Toronto ON M5C 1P1, Canada. (416)703-8982. Fax (416)504-9090. E-mail: info@writers union.ca. Website: www.writersunion.ca. Various competitions. Prizes: $500-10,000. Details on Website.

+WRITTEN/NEXT NEW WRITER CONTEST, PO Box 250504, Atlanta GA 30325. (404)753-8315. E-mail: editor@writtenmag.com. Website: www.writtenmag.com. Zipporah Publications, LLC. Michelle Gipson, pub. Celebrates the word and the reader; nationally syndicated insert to African American newspapers across the country. Details on Website.

YOUNG SALVATIONIST CONTEST, PO Box 269, Alexandria VA 22313-0269. (703)684-5500. Fax (703)684-5539. E-mail: ys@usn.salvationarmy.org. Website: http://publications .salvationarmyusa.org. Sponsors a contest for fiction, nonfiction, poetry, original art, and photography. Send SASE for details.

SPONSORED BY WRITERS' CONFERENCES/GROUPS

(This list includes only those contests that are open to nonmembers of the groups or nonattendees at the conferences.)

ANNUAL GREEN LAKE WRITERS CONTEST, Green Lake Conference Center, Attn: Program, W2511 State Rd. 23, Green Lake WI 54941. Poetry, fiction, nonfiction, and general inspiration. Deadline: June 4. Prizes: $50, $25, and $15 in each category. You do not have to be present or attend conference to enter. Entry fee: $5 (for poetry) or $10 (other genres) for each entry.

+CATCH THE WAVE SHORT STORY/ARTICLE CONTESTS. Contact: Pam Barnes, PO Box 2673, Woodstock GA 30188. E-mail: Cynthiasimmons@christianauthorsguild.org. Website: www.christianauthorsguild.org. Sponsors a short story contest and an article contest.

+FELLOWSCRIPT FALL CONTEST, PO Box 26016, 650 Portland St., Dartmouth NS B2W 6P3, Canada. E-mail: submissions@inscribe.org. Website: www.inscribe.org. Inscribe Christian Writers' Fellowship. Joanna Mallory, acq. ed. To provide encouragement, instruction, news, and helpful information for the membership of InScribe Christian Writers' Fellowship. Fall contest in conjunction with Inscribe's Fall Conference every year in September (August deadline). Categories include fiction, poetry, children's stories, essays, and nonfiction. Details on Website, or write and ask to be put on mailing list.

OZARK CREATIVE WRITERS CONTESTS. Contact: Sheila P. Smith, 223 Sycamore Dr., Bluff City TN 37618. E-mail submissions only: ozarkcreativewriters@earthlink.net. Website: www .ozarkcreativewriters.org. Contest details on Website.

SOUTHWEST WRITERS ANNUAL CONTEST, 3721 Morris NE, Ste. A, Albuquerque NM 87111-3611. (505)265-9485. E-mail: swriters@juno.com. Website: www.southwestwriters.org. Novels, short stories, short nonfiction, and others. Includes inspirational/spiritual novels. Deadline: May 1; late deadline May 15 (Include a $5 extra fee). Prizes: Cash prizes in each category of $150, $100, $50; plus a $1,000 Storyteller Award selected from the first-place winners. Guidelines on Website or by mail.

RESOURCES FOR CONTESTS

ADDITIONAL CONTESTS. You will find some additional contests sponsored by local groups and conferences that are open to nonmembers. See individual listings in those sections.

BYLINE MAGAZINE CONTEST LISTINGS. Website: www.bylinemag.com/contests.asp.

CHECK FOR LITERARY SCAMS. For help in determining if a contest is legitimate or not, go to: www.windpub.com/literary.scams.

FREELANCE WRITING: WEBSITE FOR TODAY'S WORKING WRITER. Website: www.free lancewriting.com/writingcontests.php.

KIMN SWENSON GOLLNICK'S WEBSITE. Contest listings. Website: www.KIMN.net/contests.htm.

MAJOR LITERARY AWARDS

AUDIES: www.audiopub.org
CALDECOTT MEDAL: www.ala.org

EDGAR: www.mysterywriters.org
HEMINGWAY FOUNDATION/PEN AWARD: www.pen-ne.org
HUGO: http://worldcon.org/hugos.html
NATIONAL BOOK AWARD: www.nationalbook.org
NATIONAL BOOK CRITICS CIRCLE AWARD: www.bookcritics.org
NEBULA: http://dpsinfo.com/awardweb/nebulas
NEWBERY: www.ala.org
NOBEL PRIZE FOR LITERATURE: www.nobelprize.org
PEN/FAULKNER AWARD: www.penfaulkner.org
+PINNACLE AWARD/ECPA. Website: www.ECPA.org.
PULITZER PRIZE: www.pulitzer.org
RITA: www.rwanational.org/cs/contests_and_awards

DENOMINATIONAL LISTING OF BOOK PUBLISHERS AND PERIODICALS

An attempt has been made to divide publishers into appropriate denominational groups. However, due to the extensive number of denominations included, and sometimes incomplete denominational information, some publishers inadvertently may have been included in the wrong list. Additions and corrections are welcome.

ANTIOCHIAN ORTHODOX
Book Publishers:
Conciliar Press
Periodicals:
AGAIN
The Handmaiden

ASSEMBLIES OF GOD
Book Publishers:
Gospel Publishing House
Periodicals:
Enrichment
Live
Men.ag.org
Testimony
Today's Pentecostal Evangel
WT Online

BAPTIST, FREE WILL
Book Publishers:
Randall House
Randall House Digital
Periodicals:
Heartbeat
Together with God

BAPTIST, SOUTHERN
Book Publishers:
B & H Publishing
Baylor Univ. Press
Founders Press
New Hope Publishers
Southern Baptist Press
Periodicals:
Founders Journal
Journey
Let's Worship
Louisiana Baptist Messenger
Mature Living
On Mission
ParentLife

BAPTIST (other)
Book Publishers:
Earthen Vessel (Reformed)
Judson Press (American)
Mercer Univ. Press
Periodicals:
African American Pulpit (American)
BGC World (Converge Worldwide)

Faith Detectives (Regular)
Florida Baptist Witness
Friends Journal
God's Explorers (Regular)
Heartbeat (Free Will)
Link & Visitor
Living My Faith (Regular)
Real Faith in Life (Regular)
Secret Place (American)
Sword of the Lord (Independent)
Truth Travelers (Regular)

CATHOLIC
Book Publishers:
ACTA Publications
Alba House
American Catholic Press
Canticle Books
Catholic Book Publishing
Catholic Univ./America Press
Cistercian Publications
HarperOne (Cath. bks.)
Libros Liguori
Liguori Publications
Liturgical Press
Loyola Press
Oregon Catholic Press
Our Sunday Visitor
Pauline Books
Pauline Kids
Paulist Press
Pflaum Publishing
Regnery Publishing
St. Anthony Messenger
St. Catherine of Siena Press
Tau-Publishing
Periodicals:
America
Angel Face
Annals of St. Anne
Arkansas Catholic
Arlington Catholic Herald
Atlantic Catholic
Australian Catholics
Bread of Life
Canticle
Catechist
Catechumenate
Catholic Digest
Catholic Forester
Catholic Insight

Catholic Library World
Catholic New York
Catholic Peace Voice
Catholic Register
Catholic Sentinel
Catholic Servant
Catholic Telegraph
Catholic Yearbook
CGA World
Columbia
Commonweal
Culture Wars
Desert Call
Diocesan Dialogue
Emmanuel
Faith & Family
Family Digest
Interim
Island Catholic News
Koinonia
Leaves
Liguorian
Marian Helper
Messenger/Sacred Heart
Messenger/St. Anthony
Miraculous Medal
Montana Catholic
National Catholic Reporter
One
Our Sunday Visitor
Parish Liturgy
Prairie Messenger
Priest
Promise
Review for Religious
RTJ
Seeds
Share
Social Justice Review
Spirit
Spiritual Life
St. Anthony Messenger
St. Joseph's Messenger
This Rock
Today's Catholic Teacher
Today's Parish
True Girl
U.S. Catholic
Venture
Visions
Way of St. Francis

CHRISTIAN CHURCH/ CHURCH OF CHRIST

Book Publishers:
Chalice Press (Disciples of Christ)
College Press (Church of Christ)
Star Bible
Periodicals:
DisciplesWorld (Disciples of Christ)

CHURCH OF GOD (Anderson, IN)

Book Publishers:
Warner Press

CHURCH OF GOD (Cleveland, TN)

Book Publisher:
Pathway Press
Periodical:
Youth and CE Leadership

CHURCH OF GOD (holiness)

Periodicals:
Beginner's Friend
Church Herald and Holiness Banner
Gems of Truth
Junior Companion
Primary Pal (KS)
Youth Compass

CHURCH OF GOD (other)

Periodicals:
Bible Advocate (Seventh-day)
Gem
Now What? (Seventh-day)

CHURCH OF THE NAZARENE

Book Publishers:
Beacon Hill Press
Lillenas (music)
Periodicals:
Adventures
Celebrate
Credo Magazine
Kid Zone
Mission Connection
Passport

EPISCOPAL/ANGLICAN

Book Publishers:
Forward Movement
Latimer Press
Morehouse Publishing
Periodicals:
Central Florida Episcopalian
Episcopal Life
Interchange

Living Church
Sewanee Theological Review

LUTHERAN

Book Publishers:
Augsburg Fortress
Augsburg/Worship & Music
Concordia
Concordia Academic
Congregational Life & Learning
Langmarc Publishing
Lutheran University Press
Lutheran Voices
Northwestern Publishing
Periodicals:
Canada Lutheran (ELCC)
Canadian Lutheran
Cresset
Esprit (ELCC)
Lutheran Digest
Lutheran Forum
Lutheran Journal
Lutheran Partners (ELCA)
Lutheran Witness
Lutheran Woman's Quarterly
　(MO Synod)
Word & World (ELCA)

MENNONITE

Book Publisher:
Kindred Books
Periodicals:
Canadian Mennonite
Evangel (OR)
Mennonite Historian
Messenger, The
Partners
Purpose
Rejoice!
Story Mates

METHODIST, FREE

Periodicals:
Evangel
Light and Life

METHODIST, UNITED

Book Publishers:
Abingdon Press
Dimensions for Living
United Methodist Publishing House
Periodicals:
Alive Now
Good News/KY
Interpreter
Mature Years
Methodist History
New World Outlook
Pockets
Upper Room

PENTECOSTAL, UNITED

Periodicals:
InsideOut
Vision (adult)

PRESBYTERIAN

Book Publishers:
P & R Publishing
Presbyterian Publishing
Periodicals:
Channels (PCC)
Glad Tidings
Horizons/women (USA)
Layman (USA)
Presbyterian Outlook (USA)
Presbyterians Today

QUAKER/FRIENDS

Book Publishers:
Barclay Press
Friends United Press
Periodicals:
Fruit of the Vine
Quaker Life

REFORMED CHURCHES

Periodicals:
Perspectives
Reformed Worship
Vision (MI)

SEVENTH-DAY ADVENTIST

Book Publishers:
Pacific Press
Review and Herald
Periodicals:
Connected
Cornerstone Youth Resources
Guide Magazine
Insight (MD)
Journal/Adventist Ed
Kids' Ministry Ideas
Liberty
Message
Our Little Friend
Primary Treasure
Sabbath School Leadership
Vibrant Life

WESLEYAN CHURCH

Book Publisher:
Wesleyan Publishing House
Periodicals:
Light from the Word
Vista
Wesleyan Life

MISCELLANEOUS DENOMINATIONS

Evangelical Covenant Church
Covenant Companion
inSpirit Magazine
Evangelical Free Church
EFCA Today
Foursquare Gospel Church
Advance

Grace Brethren Churches
BMH Books
Open Bible Standard Churches
MESSAGE of the Open Bible
Orthodox Church in America
Divine Ascent
Pentecostal Holiness Church
IPHC Experience
Plymouth Brethren
Chapter Two (books)

United Church of Canada
Aujourd'hui Credo
Fellowship Magazine
Theological Digest & Outlook
United Church Observer
United Church of Christ
Pilgrim Press
United Church Press

LIST OF BOOK PUBLISHERS AND PERIODICALS BY CORPORATE GROUP

Following is a listing of book publishers, followed by a list of periodicals, that belong to the same group or family of publications.

BARBOUR PUBLISHING
Barbour Publishing
Heartsong Presents
Heartsong Presents Mysteries

CHRISTIANITY TODAY, INTL.
Books & Culture
Christian History & Biography
Christianity Today
Christianity Today Movies
Christian Music Today
Ignite Your Faith
Leadership
Men of Integrity
PreachingToday.com
SmallGroups.com
Today's Christian
Today's Christian Woman
Your Church

CHRISTIAN MEDIA
Apocalypse Chronicles
Christian Media
Sound Body

DAVID C. COOK
Lion Publishing (books)
Scripture Press
Victor Books
Power for Living
Quiet Hour
The Rock

FOCUS ON THE FAMILY
Focus on the Family (books)
Boundless Webzine
Breakaway
Brio
Brio and Beyond
Clubhouse
Clubhouse Jr.
Focus on the Family
Focus on Your Child
Plugged In
Teen Phases
Tween Ages

BILLY GRAHAM EVANG. ASSN.
Decision
Decision Online

GROUP PUBLICATIONS INC.
Group Publishing
Children's Ministry
Group Magazine
Rev. Magazine

GUIDEPOSTS
GuidepostsBooks
Ideals Children's Books
Ideals Press
Angels on Earth
Guideposts
Ideals Magazine
Positive Thinking

HARPERCOLLINS
Avon Inspire
HarperOne
ZonderKidz
Zondervan

THE NAVIGATORS
NavPress
NavPress Student Resources
Pray!

THOMAS NELSON PUBLISHERS
J. Countryman
Editorial Betania
Editorial Caribe
Editorial Catolica
Editorial Diez Puntos
Grupo Nelson
Leader Latino
Nelson, Fiction, Thomas
Tommy Nelson
W Publishing Group

RANDALL HOUSE
CLEAR Direction
CLEAR Horizon
CLEAR Living

RANDOM HOUSE
Multnomah Books
WaterBrook Press

THE SALVATION ARMY
Faith & Friends
Good News!
New Frontier
Priority!
War Cry
Young Salvationist

STANDARD PUBLISHING
Standard Publishing (books)
Christian Standard
Devotions
The Lookout
Seek

STRANG COMMUNICATIONS
Charisma
Charisma House (books)
CharismaKids (books)
Creation House (co-publishing)
FrontLine (books)
Publicaciones Casa (books)
Realms (books)
Siloam (books)
Christian Retailing
Ministry Today
SpiritLed Woman

THE UPPER ROOM
Upper Room Books
Alive Now
Devo'Zine
The Upper Room
Weavings

URBAN MINISTRIES
Direction
InTeen
J.A.M.: Jesus and Me
Juniorway
Precepts for Living
Preschool Playhouse
Primary Street
Young Adult Today

GENERAL INDEX

This index includes periodicals, books, greeting cards/specialty markets, and agents, as well as some of the organizations/resources and specialty lists or areas you may need to find quickly. Conferences, groups, and editorial services are listed alphabetically by state in those sections (not in the index). Check the table of contents for the location of supplementary listings.

Note: Due to the many changes in the market, and to help you determine the current status of any publisher, all markets (past and present) are listed in this index. If they are not viable markets, their current status will be indicated here. The following codes are used: (ABD) asked to be deleted, (BA) bad address or contact information, (ED) editorial decision, (NF) no freelance, (NR) no recent response, (OB) out of business, (UTC) unable to contact. These changes will be noted in this listing for five years before being dropped altogether. Information that appears only on the CD is indicated by this symbol: ⊙.